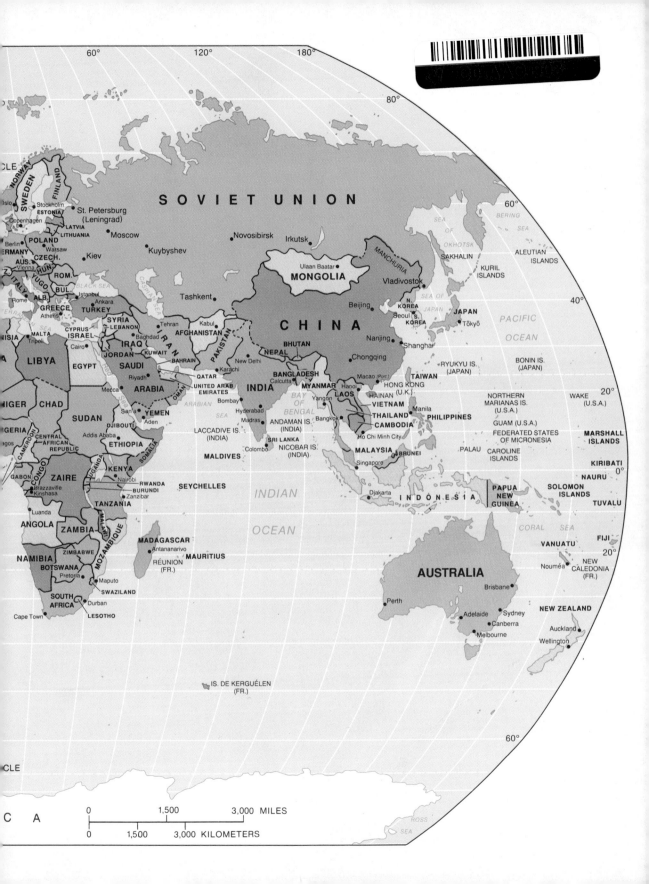

60°   120°   180°

80°

SWEDEN
NORWAY
FINLAND
Oslo
Stockholm
St. Petersburg
(Leningrad)
ESTONIA
Copenhagen
LATVIA
LITHUANIA
Moscow
Novosibirsk
Irkutsk
60°
BERING
SEA

SEA
OF
OKHOTSK

ALEUTIAN
ISLANDS

Berlin
POLAND
Warsaw
Kiev
Kuybyshev
MANCHURIA
SAKHALIN
KURIL
ISLANDS

GERMANY
AUS.
CZECH.
Vienna
HUN.
ROM.

S O V I E T   U N I O N

Ulaan Baatar
MONGOLIA
Vladivostok

ITALY
YUGO.
BUL.
Rome
ALB.
Istanbul
BLACK SEA
CASPIAN SEA
Tashkent
Beijing
N.
KOREA
Seoul
S.
KOREA
SEA OF
JAPAN
JAPAN
Tōkyō
PACIFIC

GREECE
Athens
TURKEY
Ankara
40°

OCEAN

TERR.
CYPRUS
SYRIA
LEBANON
ISRAEL
Tehran
IRAN
Kabul
AFGHANISTAN
PAKISTAN
C H I N A
Nanjing
Shanghai

NISIA
MALTA
Tripoli
Baghdad
IRAQ
JORDAN
KUWAIT
Cairo
BAHRAIN
New Delhi
NEPAL
BHUTAN
Chongqing
RYUKYU IS.
(JAPAN)
BONIN IS.
(JAPAN)

LIBYA
EGYPT
SAUDI
Riyadh
QATAR
UNITED ARAB
EMIRATES
Karachi
BANGLADESH
Calcutta
MYANMAR
Macao (Port.)
HONG KONG
(U.K.)
TAIWAN
20°
WAKE
(U.S.A.)

NIGER
CHAD
Mecca
ARABIA
OMAN
I N D I A
Bombay
Yangon
Hanoi
LAOS
HAINAN
VIETNAM
Manila
NORTHERN
MARIANAS IS.
(U.S.A.)

ARABIAN
SEA
San'a
YEMEN
Aden
Hyderabad
BAY
OF
BENGAL
Bangkok
THAILAND
CAMBODIA
PHILIPPINES
GUAM (U.S.A.)

NIGERIA
Lagos
SUDAN
DJIBOUTI
Addis Ababa
ETHIOPIA
Madras
ANDAMAN IS.
(INDIA)
Ho Chi Minh City
FEDERATED STATES
OF MICRONESIA
MARSHALL
ISLANDS

CENTRAL
AFRICAN
REPUBLIC
LACCADIVE IS.
(INDIA)
SRI LANKA
Colombo
NICOBAR IS.
(INDIA)
MALAYSIA
BRUNEI
PALAU
CAROLINE
ISLANDS
KIRIBATI

GABON
CONGO
ZAIRE
UGANDA
KENYA
Nairobi
MALDIVES
Singapore
NAURU
0°

Brazzaville
Kinshasa
RWANDA
BURUNDI
Zanzibar
SEYCHELLES
SOLOMON
ISLANDS
TUVALU

CAMEROON
TANZANIA
MALAWI
I N D I A N
Djakarta
I N D O N E S I A
PAPUA
NEW
GUINEA

Luanda
ANGOLA
ZAMBIA
MADAGASCAR
Antananarivo
O C E A N
CORAL   SEA
FIJI
VANUATU
20°

ZIMBABWE
MOZAMBIQUE
RÉUNION
(FR.)
MAURITIUS
Nouméa
NEW
CALEDONIA
(FR.)

NAMIBIA
BOTSWANA
Pretoria
Maputo
A U S T R A L I A
Brisbane

SOUTH
AFRICA
Durban
SWAZILAND
LESOTHO
Perth
Adelaide
Sydney
Canberra
NEW ZEALAND
Auckland
Wellington

Cape Town
Melbourne

IS. DE KERGUÉLEN
(FR.)

60°

CLE

C A

0   1,500   3,000 MILES

0   1,500   3,000 KILOMETERS

ROSS
SEA

Dara Khambata
AMERICAN UNIVERSITY

Riad Ajami
OHIO STATE UNIVERSITY

INTERNATIONAL BUSINESS

THEORY AND PRACTICE

MACMILLAN PUBLISHING COMPANY
NEW YORK

Maxwell Macmillan Canada
TORONTO

Maxwell Macmillan International
NEW YORK   OXFORD   SINGAPORE   SYDNEY

Editor: Charles E. Stewart, Jr.
Production Supervisor: Publication Services
Production Manager: Aliza Greenblatt
Text Designer: Robert Freese
Cover Designer: Robert Freese

This book was set in Goudy Oldstyle by Publication Services.
and was printed and bound by R. R. Donnelley & Sons.
The cover was printed by Lehigh Press.

Macmillan Publishing Company
866 Third Avenue, New York, New York 10022

Macmillan Publishing Company is part
of the Maxwell Communication Group of Companies.

Maxwell Macmillan Canada, Inc.
1200 Eglinton Avenue East
Suite 200
Don Mills, Ontario M3C 3N1

Library of Congress Cataloging-in-Publication Data
   International business : theory and practice / Dara Khambata, Riad
Ajami
     p.   cm.
   Includes bibliographical references and index.
   ISBN 0-02-363531-2
   1. International trade.   I. Ajami, Riad A.   II. Title.
   HF1379.K43   1992
   658'.049–dc20   91-17263
                                                              CIP

Printing: 1 2 3 4 5 6 7   Year: 2 3 4 5 6 7 8

Dedicated to

FARIDA KHAMBATA
ALI R. C. AJAMI
AND
OUR STUDENTS

Preface

International business has grown significantly in the past three decades, and this rapid and continuous growth has contributed to the importance of this subject as an academic course. Furthermore, the American Assembly of the Collegiate Schools of Business (AACSB) has mandated the internationalization of business curricula. Many business schools have chosen to offer a comprehensive course that will expose students to all aspects of international business. The objective of this text is to inform the reader about the major and minor issues in international business. It should satisfy the demands for the first course in international business at both the undergraduate and graduate levels. It is assumed that the reader has basic knowledge in the functional areas of business, such as finance, marketing, accounting, and management.

The text is divided into seven parts. Part One deals with the size and scope of international business and the role of multinational corporations in the field of international business. Part Two presents the institutional framework and economic theories. It includes the monetary, trade, and regulatory aspects of international business and an analysis of foreign exchange markets. Part Three evaluates the environmental constraints in international business. In particular, its focus is on analyzing national economies and the impact of sociocultural factors and legal issues on the operations of multinational corporations.

Part Four emphasizes regional issues in international business, specifically, the impact of the harmonization of the European Economic Community and the momentous changes in Eastern Europe. This part also looks at the motives and incentives for foreign direct investment and the related problems. Part Five covers the operational management of a multinational firm with a particular focus on international marketing, finance, accounting, taxation, and staffing and labor relations.

Part Six covers strategic issues in international business, such as planning, control, management information systems, and production and technology management for multinationals. Part Seven looks at ethical issues, such as multinationals and the environment and future changes or developments that will influence the modus operandi of firms involved in international business.

The distinctive features of this book are the chapters on regional, environmental, social, and ethical issues and an in-depth look at functional activities. Many case studies are provided to explain and support theory.

Many colleagues have given the authors invaluable assistance in the preparation of this book. The authors would like to express their deep appreciation to the following reviewers whose criticism and suggestions helped improve the text: Jeffrey A. Fadiman, San Jose State University; Phillip D. Grub, George Washington University; M. Yasar Geyikdagi, State University of New York at Old Westbury; James Goode, Ohio State University; and Kamel Abdallah, Otterbein College.

The authors are also grateful to the following international business doctoral candidates at Ohio State University who pretested the book and provided invaluable feedback: C. Bulent Aybar, Marca M. Bear, Michael Blaine, Janine Bowen, Veronica Horton, Claudio Milman, Stephen Preece, Brenda Richey, John Stansbury, and Tracy Thoman.

The authors are also indebted to Brigid Holleran, Charles Bachman, Tom Brockmeier, and particularly Arun Sharma—who drafted the end-of-chapter cases and some chapters—

for their unstinting help and effort. Their good will and good humor were essential in the preparation of the manuscript.

Finally, the authors hold themselves totally responsible for any errors and misinterpretations.

Dara Khambata

Riad Ajami

Brief Contents

Contents

CHAPTER SIX Supranational Organizations and International Institutions   154

CHAPTER EIGHT **International Law**   225

CHAPTER NINE **Sociocultural Factors**   248

CHAPTER TEN **Comparative Management**   266

PART FOUR Regional Issues in International Business and the Nation-State   281

CHAPTER ELEVEN Foreign Investment: Researching Risk   283

CHAPTER TWELVE Doing Business with the Pacific Rim   301

PART FIVE Functional Operations in International Business 373

CHAPTER FIFTEEN International Marketing 375

CHAPTER SIXTEEN **International Finance**   414

CHAPTER SEVENTEEN **International Accounting**   436

CHAPTER EIGHTEEN International Taxation   457

CHAPTER TWENTY-ONE **Managing Production and Technology**   539

PART SEVEN **Social and Ethical Issues and the Future of International Business**   563

CHAPTER TWENTY-TWO **Ethical Questions: Multinationals and Earth's Environment** 565

Case Studies   609

PART ONE

SCOPE OF INTERNATIONAL BUSINESS AND THE MULTINATIONAL CORPORATION

CHAPTER 1

An Introduction to International Business and Multinational Corporations

CHAPTER OBJECTIVES

This chapter will:

- Present the historical context of international business and establish the role of multinational corporations in the current business environment.
- Describe the various operating advantages and disadvantages facing the multinational corporation.
- Show how increases in world trade patterns are increasing competition and the complexity of conducting business.
- Define the field of international business and its various forms of study.

Current Scope and Historical Antecedents

In the world of business in the early 1990s, there is evidence of vast business interrelationships that span the globe. Far more than ever before, products, capital, and personnel are becoming intertwined, as business entities increasingly consider their market areas as being global rather than simply domestic or even foreign. More and more companies, some of which have annual sales levels larger than the gross national product of some countries, consider every corner of the globe a feasible source of raw materials and labor or as a new market possibility.

As business has expanded across national borders, it has been followed by banks and financial institutions to meet its need for capital for investment and operations around the world. Financial markets have also become intricately linked, and movements and changes in the U.S. stock market have a direct impact on equity markets in other parts of the world.

Today, only a naive business person would believe that an enterprise can grow and prosper entirely within the confines of its domestic market borders. Domestic business must at least be aware of international sources of competition, because they are an ever-present and growing threat as international business relationships become increasingly intricate and complex. The source of these changes in the dynamics of world markets and economies is international business activity being pursued around the globe.

What Is International Business?

In its purest definition, international business is described as any business activity that crosses national boundaries. The entities involved in business can be private, governmental, or a mixture of the two. International business can be broken down into four types: foreign trade, trade in services, portfolio investments, and direct investments.

In *foreign trade* visible physical goods or commodities move between countries as exports or imports. Exports consist of merchandise that leaves a country. Imports are those items brought across national borders into a country. Exporting and importing comprise the most fundamental, and usually the largest, international business activity in most countries.

In addition to tangible goods, countries also *trade in services,* such as insurance, banking, hotels, consulting, and travel and transportation. The international firm is paid for services it renders in another country. The earnings can be in the form of fees or royalties. Fees are generated through the satisfaction of specific performance and can be earned through long- or short-term contractual agreements, such as management or consulting contracts. Royalties accrue from the use of one company's process, name, trademark or patent by someone else.

One example of a fee situation is the turnkey operation, in which a foreign government or enterprise hires the expertise appropriate to starting a new concern, plant, or operation. The turnkey managers come into a foreign environment and get an operation up and running by designing the

plant, setting up equipment, and training personnel to take over. The foreign firm can then merely take over the reins of management and continue operating the facility. Alternatively, a firm can earn royalties from abroad by licensing the use of its technology, processes, or information to another firm or by selling its franchise in overseas markets.

Portfolio investments are financial investments made in foreign countries. The investor purchases debt or equity in the expectation of nothing more than a financial return on the investment. Resources such as equipment, time, or personnel are not contributed to the overseas venture. *Direct investments* are differentiated by much greater levels of control over the project or enterprise by the investor. The level of control can vary from full control, when a firm owns a foreign subsidiary entirely, to partial control, as in arrangements such as joint ventures with other domestic or foreign firms or a foreign government. The methods of conducting international business will be discussed more thoroughly in subsequent chapters.

History of International Business

International business is not new, having been practiced around the world for thousands of years, although its forms, methods, and importance are constantly evolving. In ancient times, the Phoenicians, Mesopotamians, and Greeks traded along routes established in the Mediterranean. Commerce continued to grow throughout history as sophisticated business techniques emerged, facilitating the flow of goods, resources, and funds between countries. Some of these business methods included the establishment of credit for exchange, banking, and pooling of resources in joint stock ventures. This growth was further stimulated by colonization activities, which provided the maritime nations with rich resources of raw materials as well as enormous potential markets, in the new worlds.

The Industrial Revolution further encouraged the growth of international business by providing methods of production for mass markets and more efficient methods of utilizing raw materials. As industrialization increased, greater and greater demand was created for supplies, raw materials, labor, and transportation. The flow and mobility of capital also increased as higher production provided surplus income, which was, in turn, reinvested in further production domestically or in the colonies. The technological developments and inventions resulting from the Industrial Revolution accelerated and smoothed the flow of goods, services, and capital between countries.

By the 1880s the Industrial Revolution was in full swing in Europe and the United States, and production grew to unprecedented levels, abetted by scientific inventions, the development of new sources of energy, efficiencies achieved in production, and transportation, such as domestic and international railroad systems. Growth continued in an upward spiral as mass production met and surpassed domestic demand, pushing manufacturers to seek enlarged, foreign markets for their products. It led ultimately to the emergence of the multinational corporation (MNC) as a new organizational entity in the international business world.

The Multinational Corporation

During its early stages, international business was conducted in the form of enterprises that were owned singly or in partnerships. As the size of organizations grew with industrialization and need for capital by companies increased, corporations began to displace privately held firms. These corporations had the distinct advantage of being entities with a separate legal identity, consequently limiting the liability of the principals or owners. At the same time, by issuing shares of stock, the corporation could tap an enormous pool of excess funds held by potential individual investors.

With the emergence of the multinational enterprise in the late 1800s and early part of the twentieth century, the corporation underwent yet another modification.[1] Some early multinational enterprises were those who sought resources and supplies abroad, such as oil in Mexico (Standard Oil), precious minerals (Amalgamated Copper, International Nickel, Kennecot), fruit in the Caribbean (United Fruit), or rubber in Sumatra (U.S. Rubber). Other firms entered foreign markets in a search for markets to absorb their excess domestic production or to obtain economies of scale in production. Some of these early market seekers from the United States were Singer, National Cash Register Company, International Harvester (now Navistar), and Remington, who sought to use their advantages of superior metal production skills against European producers.

These early entrants were quickly followed by companies with other areas of expertise, such as Cable Telephone, Eastman Kodak, and Westinghouse. All of these early U.S. multinational firms marketed their products primarily in the neighboring countries of Canada and Mexico and in European markets.

Definition of a Multinational Corporation

There is no formal definition of a multinational corporation, although various definitions of an MNC have been proposed using different criteria. Some believe that a multinational firm is one that is structured so that business is conducted or ownership is held across a number of countries or one that is organized into global product divisions. Others look to specific ratios of foreign business activities or assets to total firm activities or assets. Under these criteria, a multinational firm is one in which a certain percentage of the earnings, assets, sales or personnel of a firm come from or are deployed in foreign locations. A third definition is based on the perspective of the corporation, that is, its behavior and its thinking. This definition holds that if the management of a corporation holds the perception and the attitude that the parameters of its sphere of operations and markets is

---

[1] Wilkins 1970.

multinational, then the firm is indeed a multinational corporation.

In his study of the topic, Howard V. Perlmutter[2] looks at this attitude held by the decision-makers of an organization and differentiates between ethnocentric, polycentric, and geocentric organizational types. Ethnocentric organizations are those that are focused in a home or domestic environment and therefore exclude MNCs. Polycentric organizations have investments, operations, or markets in several countries, but do not integrate the management of these international functions. Geocentric organizations, on the other hand, are integrated and have a world perspective regarding the breadth and reach of possible organizational operations. Some students of international business (and sticklers for linguistic accuracy) dispute the use of the terms "global" or "world" corporation in reference to MNCs. They argue that a truly global corporation or enterprise looks to every market in the world as a potential market and allocates resources without regard for the location of its home country. Under this definition, for example, an international corporation with subsidiaries and markets in Europe and South America would not be considered a global enterprise.

The existence of different definitions for multinational corporations is not surprising. There are many different types of multinational corporations and most definitions characterize only a particular type. Because there are so many possible ways in which a corporation can be organized and transact business across national borders, it is indeed very difficult for any one definition to adequately describe all forms of multinational corporations.

FROM DOMESTIC TO MULTINATIONAL CORPORATION

Another problem in standardizing the definition of a multinational corporation is the gradual evolution of purely domestic companies to multinational status. In this process, the point cannot be clearly demarcated where a company becomes a multinational. Such demarcations, if at all possible, also cannot explain or describe adequately the wide differences that corporations may have in the extent to which they have gone international.

The United Nations does not use the terms "multinational corporations" or "multinational enterprises." Instead, it calls them "transnational corporations," but this term is not used widely. This text will use the terms "multinational corporation" (MNC) and "multinational enterprise" (MNE) interchangeably to identify a firm that conducts international business from a multitude of locations in different countries.

Multinational Corporations Come of Age

The multinational corporation began to flourish in the decade following World War II, primarily in the United States. It was spurred by reconstruction efforts in Europe and an inflow of U.S. dollars geared to take advantage of new opportunities, as countries of the ravaged continent attempted to rebuild their economies. U.S. corporations, having prospered through wartime demand, channeled investments into other countries, notably in Europe and Canada. During the period from 1950 to 1970, the book value of U.S. direct foreign investments skyrocketed from $11.8 billion to $78.1 billion.[3]

As the European economy strengthened during this period, the motives of U.S. companies doing business there switched from an aggressive market- and profit-seeking stance to a defensive position of protecting European market share and domestic/U.S. markets from encroachments by increasingly strong European competitors. In the 1960s, U.S. firms also began to take advantage of the availability of new capital and debt markets—the Eurodollar and Eurobond markets emerging in that part of the world. During this period, the orientation of U.S. MNCs also began to change, from

---

[2] Perlmutter 1969.

[3] U.S. Department of Commerce Bureau of International Commerce 1975.

seeking raw materials and being involved in the extractive industries to focusing more on overseas manufacturing industries.

By the 1970s the United States had lost its nearly complete dominance of multinational industry, partially because of the reemergence of strong European concerns, but more emphatically because of the entry of serious contenders from Japan, the emerging giant in the East. In 1989 twenty of the top fifty firms in the world, ranked according to market value by *Business Week* (see Table 1–1), were Japanese. These firms were primarily in the areas of banking, oil, electronics, and telecommunications. Of the top ten firms, only three were U.S., with IBM in second place with a market value of $68.89 billion, General Electric fifth with a market value of $62.54 billion, and Exxon sixth with a value of $60.00 billion. The top international firm in the world was Nippon Telegraph and Telephone with a market value of $118.79 billion—almost twice the size of IBM, its closest rival.

Indeed, in the 1990s this trend of increasing Japanese clout in the world economy is likely to continue to grow as Japanese firms, banks, and investment houses use this strength and leverage to increase their share of markets around the world by continuing their emphasis on reinvestment to spur continued growth. For example, by mid-1989 Japanese automakers had captured as much as 24 percent of the U.S. market. If ranked according to sales, in 1989 only three of the top ten world firms were of U.S. origin and these were the oil company Exxon (seventh) and automakers General Motors (fifth) and Ford (ninth). In contrast, six of the top ten were Japanese-based multinational trading and automobile firms. Only one was from another region—the energy firm Royal Dutch Shell, which was ranked eighth in sales.

Similarly, in a 1990 identification by *Forbes* magazine of the top twenty-five largest public companies outside of the United States, Japanese holdings were the top seventeen and European firms held the other eight slots. At the very top was Sumitomo Corporation with revenues of $158.221 billion (see Table 1–2).

A Look at Present-Day Multinationals

In order to understand the complexities of operations pursued by multinational firms, it is helpful to look at the structure and operations of three multinational business organizations. In this way, the student of international business can envision the enormity and complexity of operations for a global bank, a multinational manufacturing company, and an international conglomerate—Citicorp, Sony and Nestlé.

CITICORP (USA)

Citicorp is a prime example of a truly global corporation. Indeed, the company calls itself a global financial services company and attempts to provide a full range of banking services in all parts of the world. With a market value of nearly $8 billion, Citicorp was ranked thirty-fourth among the world's largest banks in 1987.[4] More recently, with revenue levels of $37.97 billion in 1989 the bank was sixth in the *Forbes* annual listing of the 100 largest U.S. multinational corporations.[5] By year-end of 1988, Citicorp held total assets of $207.7 billion, employed 90,000 people, of whom nearly half (42,000) worked overseas in 1,938 branch, representative, affiliate, and subsidiary offices. In the United States alone, Citicorp has 1,118 offices in forty states and the District of Columbia.[6]

The company's operations are organized into three bank divisions—Individual Bank, Institutional Bank, and Investment Bank. Individual bank customer service is provided through bank branch activities, credit card services, and mortgage services. Citicorp has expanded its product line for individuals by developing multiple products, such as Citi-One, a multiretail product account that integrates a customer's bank and credit card statement, and CitiFunds, a multicurrency deposit and investment account that gives cus-

[4] Lee 1988.
[5] "U.S. Firms with the Biggest Foreign Revenue," *Forbes* 1990.
[6] Information on the scope and activities of Citicorp is from their 1988 Annual Report.

TABLE 1-1
The Global 1000—The Leaders

Rank 1990	Rank 1989	Company	Country	Market Value (billions of U.S. dollars)
1	1	Nippon Telegraph & Telephone	Japan	118.79
2	6	International Business Machines	U.S.	68.89
3	2	Industrial Bank of Japan	Japan	67.61
4	10	Royal Dutch/Shell Group	Neth./Britain	67.14
5	12	General Electric	U.S.	62.54
6	8	Exxon	U.S.	60.00
7	3	Sumitomo Bank	Japan	55.81
8	4	Fuji Bank	Japan	53.17
9	11	Toyota Motor	Japan	50.44
10	24	Mitsui Taiyo Kobe Bank	Japan	49.80
11	5	Dai-Ichi Kangyo Bank	Japan	49.57
12	7	Mitsubishi Bank	Japan	47.17
13	16	American Telephone & Telegraph	U.S.	46.96
14	13	Sanwa Bank	Japan	45.60
15	9	Tokyo Electric Power	Japan	41.68
16	19	Philip Morris	U.S.	39.11
17	17	Hitachi Ltd.	Japan	33.04
18	25	Merck	U.S.	32.72
19	14	Nomura Securities	Japan	32.54
20	22	Long-Term Credit Bank of Japan	Japan	32.44
21	85	Bristol-Myers Squibb	U.S.	32.13
22	40	Wal-Mart Stores	U.S.	31.89
23	39	Coca-Cola	U.S.	30.42
24	18	Mastushita Electric Industrial	Japan	29.63
25	33	British Petroleum	Britain	29.55
26	29	General Motors	U.S.	29.45
27	31	British Telecommunications	Britain	29.15
28	15	Nippon Steel	Japan	28.17
29	28	Du Pont	U.S.	27.98
30	35	Amoco	U.S.	27.34
31	32	Bellsouth	U.S.	27.10
32	60	Procter & Gamble	U.S.	26.78
33	47	Atlantic Richfield	U.S.	26.05
34	43	Mobil	U.S.	25.67
35	101	Allianz	West Germany	24.98
36	52	Chevron	U.S.	24.94
37	21	Kansai Electric Power	Japan	24.80
38	23	Tokai Bank	Japan	23.52
39	27	Mitsubishi Heavy Industries	Japan	23.49
40	20	Toshiba	Japan	22.91
41	96	Nestlé	Switzerland	22.81
42	86	Daimler-Benz	West Germany	22.58
43	34	Ford Motor	U.S.	22.48
44	66	Unilever	Neth/Britain	22.15
45	79	Eli Lilly	U.S.	21.82
46	95	Siemens	West Germany	21.29
47	68	Johnson & Johnson	U.S.	21.28
48	61	GTE	U.S.	21.13
49	48	Bell Atlantic	U.S.	20.56
50	48	NEC	Japan	20.45

Rank 1990	Rank 1989	Company	Country	Market Value (billions of U.S. dollars)
51	26	Nissan Motor	Japan	19.93
52	54	Japan Air Lines	Japan	19.91
53	74	Glaxo Holdings	Britain	19.68
54	87	Pepsico	U.S.	19.48
55	115	Hanson Trust	Britain	19.24
56	57	Nippon Credit Bank	Japan	19.19
57	36	Bank of Tokyo	Japan	19.12
58	64	Pacific Telesis	U.S.	19.09
59	114	Boeing	U.S.	19.05
60	143	Deutsche Bank	West Germany	19.03
61	78	Sony	Japan	18.78
62	82	Assicurazioni Generali	Italy	18.71
63	120	Waste Management	U.S.	18.63
64	30	Mitsubishi Trust & Banking	Japan	18.54
65	70	Minnesota Mining & Mfg.	U.S.	18.39
66	92	B.A.T. Industries	Britain	17.99
67	37	Chubu Electric Power	Japan	17.92
68	99	Fiat Group	Italy	17.89
69	77	Southwestern Bell	U.S.	17.55
70	38	Sumitomo Trust & Banking	Japan	17.55
71	51	Fujitsu	Japan	17.39
72	72	Nynex	U.S.	17.27
73	73	Ameritech	U.S.	17.24
74	112	Walt Disney	U.S.	17.20
75	63	Dow Chemical	U.S.	16.76
76	67	Mitsubishi Corp.	Japan	16.71
77	97	American International Group	U.S.	16.61
78	98	Abbott Laboratories	U.S.	16.57
79	89	American Home Products	U.S.	16.53
80	46	NKK	Japan	16.19
81	45	Tokio Marine & Fire	Japan	15.92
82	110	Texaco	U.S.	15.70
83	76	Seibu Railway	Japan	15.64
84	121	British Gas	Britain	15.56
85	58	All Nippon Airways	Japan	15.42
86	44	Tokyo Gas	Japan	15.14
87	50	Asahi Glass	Japan	15.14
88	49	Daiwa Securities	Japan	14.95
89	313	Nintendo	Japan	14.47
90	69	Daiwa Bank	Japan	14.23
91	193	ASEA ABB Brown Boveri	Sweden/Switz.	14.16
92	105	Tokyu Corp.	Japan	14.12
93	94	Imperial Chemical Industries	Britain	14.02
94	174	Roche Holding	Switzerland	13.99
95	55	Mitsubishi Electric	Japan	13.95
96	41	Mitsubishi Estate	Japan	13.91
97	111	US West	U.S.	13.90
98	150	Schlumberger	U.S.	13.87
99	179	Elf Aquitaine	France	13.75
100	53	Nikko Securities	Japan	13.37

SOURCE: *Business Week*, July 16, 1990

TABLE 1–2
The 25 Largest Public Companies Outside the U.S.

Company/business	Country	Sales (millions)	Employees (thousands)
Sumitomo Corp./trading	Japan	$158,221	13.0
C Itoh & Co. Ltd/trading	Japan	147,016	10.0
Mitsui & Co. Ltd/trading	Japan	136,578	10.8
Marubeni Corp./trading	Japan	131,419	7.3*
Mitsubishi Corp./trading	Japan	129,689	32.0
Nissho Iwai Corp./trading	Japan	108,118	7.2
Royal Dutch/Shell/oil & gas	Holland	85,536	135.0
Toyota Motor Corp./automotive	Japan	61,052	91.8
Hitachi Ltd/multicompany	Japan	49,557	274.5
British Petroleum Co./oil & gas	UK	48,602	119.9
Toyo Menka Kaisha/trading	Japan	45,055	3.3
Nichimen Corp./trading	Japan	42,989	2.8*
Nippon Tel & Tel/comminications	Japan	42,166	283.3
Matsushita El Ind/consumer electronics	Japan	42,030	198.3
Daimler-Benz Group/automotive	Germany	40,633	368.2
Nissan Motor Co. Ltd/automotive	Japan	39,525	129.5
Kanematsu Corp./trading	Japan	39,219	2.7*
Fiat Group/automotive	Italy	38,044	289.3
Volkswagen Group/automotive	Germany	34,760	250.6
Siemens Group/electrical equipment	Germany	32,676	365.0
Unilever/food processing	Holland	31,256	300.0
Toshiba Corp./multicompany	Japan	29,757	125.0
Dai-Ichi Kangyo Bank/banking	Japan	29,628	18.5*
Nestlé/food processing	Switz.	29,341	196.9
Tokyo Electric Power Co./utility	Japan	28,636	39.6

*Not consolidated.
SOURCE: *Forbes*, July 23, 1990, page 318

tomers an opportunity to move their money into investments of different currency denominations.

The Institutional Bank supplies such financial services as credit and transaction processing to corporations and governments around the world. The Investment Bank is involved in intermediating international capital flows, which it does by managing the financial positions taken by its insti-

tutional customers, using, among other methods, currency swaps and trading in world currencies. The three banks work together in providing larger institutional clients with a full range of products and services worldwide.

In addition to these banking services, Citicorp is also in the business of providing information services to its global customer base. These services gather, analyze, package, and distribute financial information worldwide and integrate banking, electronic publishing, and telecommunication services around the world.

Citicorp's orientation is global in that its objective is to bring financial services to the consumer marketplace around the world, which includes the super multinational corporate and investment entities, as well as smaller local businesses in far-flung markets and individuals around the world.

The company's advertising campaign centers on the theme of America retaining its preeminence in world markets through a reliance on their strengths, abilities, and entrepreneurship. This is clear in a recent campaign theme "Citicorp. Because Americans want to succeed, not just survive."

Sony Corporation (Japan)

Sony Corporation, based in Tokyo, Japan, is a major world manufacturer of televisions, videotape recorders, cassette tape recorders, radios, and audio equipment. While Sony's reach is not as wide as Citicorp's in terms of international scope, product line, or diversity, the company's success since its incorporation in 1946 is still remarkable. Since the 1940s, Sony has constantly continued its growth and development in the electronics and telecommunications fields, producing in Japan in 1950 the first tape recorder and magnetic tape. This accomplishment was followed by the production of transistors in 1954, the technology of which was applied to radios, televisions, and tape recorders. This period was followed by one of growth in the 1960s, culminating with the production of the Trinitron color television tube in 1968. Advances followed in video equipment that led to the introduction of the Betamax in 1975 and the subsequent introduction of the Walkman personal cassette tape player and radio.

Sony's enormous growth was evidenced in a quintupling of sales in the decade from 1972 to 1981. By 1985 Sony's sales had reached nearly $5 billion,[7] produced through the efforts of some 14,400 employees. In the United States, Sony has operations in six states—California, Florida, Maryland, Pennsylvania, Alabama, and Washington—which include a color television manufacturing plant in San Diego that employs 1,600 workers, and a cassette component manufacturing facility in Alabama that employs 1500 workers.

Sony's success lies in its enormous research and development strengths, its international production base, which also includes manufacturing facilities in Europe, Latin America, South Korea, and Singapore, and its continuously strong financial position. The company's prospects remain excellent. In 1987, continuing an association in a joint (50/50) record-producing venture with CBS, the company went a step further and acquired CBS Records in the United States for $2 billion. The CBS label has such artists as Bob Dylan and Michael Jackson under contract.

The company also announced in 1988 that it would unveil a line of VHS videocassette recorders and, thus, provide a full product line of entertainment and recording equipment, ranging from televisions to VCRs to camcorders. The new product line allows consumers a choice regarding the type of format they prefer—high-quality Betamax, the more popular VHS, or the newly-launched 8 mm video technology. This move may be a tacit acknowledgement that the company cannot continue to rely on growth by the introduction of innovative products, such as the Walkman, and has to achieve sales growth through the supply of a wide range of popular electronic equipment.

Sony does continue to emphasize its engineering capacity, keeping it close to home and near to research facilities. Some 90 percent of the company's engineers remain in Japan, as does production of all of the company's Walkmans,[8] despite the fact that overseas sales constitute 70 percent of Sony's total sales revenue. The company has overall overseas production of about 25 percent and would like to raise that percentage by 5 to 10 percent in the next few years.[9]

---

[7] *Ward's Business Directory of Major International Companies* 1985.

[8] *The Economist* 1988.
[9] Ibid.

NESTLÉ SA (SWITZERLAND)

Nestlé is the world's leading food processor and, like Citicorp, is a truly global corporation. Based in Vevey, Switzerland, the company has interests, markets, and manufacturing plants around the world and employs more than 140,000 persons.

Nestlé's originated in Switzerland with the founding by chemist Henri Nestlé of a condensed milk factory in the mid-1800s and a factory to manufacture a milk-based baby food product. In the early part of the 1900s, these two factories merged and rapidly expanded their operations and manufacturing facilities to all of Europe, the United States, and Latin America.

In the 1930s the firm's fortunes were abetted by its move into the instant drink market with one of its major products, Nescafé instant coffee, which was introduced in 1938. Since then, the company has continued to grow because of its strategies of diversification, market expansion, and product development. At present, Nestlé's product line includes instant drinks; dairy products; culinary products, such as bouillon, soups, spices, and dehydrated sauces; chocolate and candy; frozen foods and ice cream; infant and dietetic products; and liquid drinks. In addition, the company manufactures pharmaceutical products, such as instruments and medicines, owns and runs restaurants and hotels in the United States and Europe, and has a minority share in L'Oréal, a producer of cosmetics, perfumes, and beauty products[10] (see Perspective 1–1).

The bulk of the company's sales remain in the top three product areas of drinks, dairy products, and culinary and sundry products. Nestlé operates and manufactures in all of its major markets, although manufacturing operations predominate in Europe, the United States, and Latin America. The company has major marketing subsidiaries in forty-four countries, including Third World countries, where foodstuffs are primarily sold.

Nestlé's revenues gave it a ranking of twenty-fourth in *Forbes* magazine's 1990 listing of the twenty-five largest companies outside of the

United States (see Table 1–2). *Business Week* ranked it forty-first in 1990, according to its market value of $22.81 billion (see Table 1–1). This success has been partially attributed to the leadership provided by Nestlé's president, Helmut Maucher, who took over the reins of the company in 1981. By 1986 the company had nearly doubled its earnings to $1.2 billion. Maucher cut the bureaucracy by 10 percent and pared down reporting requirements. His motto is, "Let's have more pepper and less paper." He attributes Nestlé's success to its stable food products. He says, "People rave about high tech and ignore food because it's stable, not cyclical. But food is a growth industry."[11]

Americans will be surprised to learn the extent of Nestlé's holdings in the United States. In 1989 *Forbes* ranked Nestlé ninth in their annual listing of the 100 largest investments in the United States, with its ownership of 100 percent of Nestlé Enterprises, Carnation, and Alcon Laboratories. These U.S. subsidiaries yield sales revenue estimated at $7.8 billion.[12]

In the United States, Nestlé or its subsidiaries have manufacturing facilities in twelve states—New York, Maryland, Oklahoma, Illinois, Indiana, Minnesota, Ohio, Wisconsin, New Jersey, Texas, Nebraska, and South Carolina. These plants produce such familiar products as Ovaltine, Nescafé, Stouffer frozen foods, Deer Park spring water, Libby vegetables and other canned foods, Beech-nut baby food, and Taster's Choice coffee. In addition, the company produces dairy products, such as cheeses, chocolates, candies, cookies, and their own cans for fruit and vegetable packing.

Operating Advantages and Disadvantages of Multinationals

MNC's have certain unique advantages and disadvantages in their operations that make them quite different from purely domestically oriented com-

[10] Stopford 1984.

[11] Tully 1987.

[12] "The 100 Largest Foreign Investments in the U.S.," *Forbes* 1990.

PERSPECTIVE 1–1   Switzerland's Nestlé Fights to Stay on Top

VEVEY, Switzerland—A pretty woman looks indignantly out of the television screen: Her boyfriend has just run off with her mother. "That's hard to swallow," she says. "Not like these little things"—a handful of Nestlé's Chocolait Chips.

Another commercial shows a man clad in his underwear shivering on a window ledge. From inside, a woman sneaks him a steaming cup of Nestlé's Maggi soup, then turns to greet her unsuspecting spouse.

Is this Nestlé S.A., that citadel of Swiss conservatism? Ever since Henri Nestlé sold the world's first can of baby formula in this town on the shores of Lake Geneva in 1867, Nestlé has been better known for pablum than prurience, and what that bearded inventor would think of his offspring now is anyone's guess.

CHANGES COOKING

But racy advertising isn't the only sign of the changes cooking at the world's biggest food company, with expected sales of 40 billion Swiss francs ($27 billion) this year. The wave of mega-mergers sweeping the food industry, with about a dozen in the past three years of more than $1 billion each, is threatening Nestlé's premier position. Philip Morris Cos.' takeover of Kraft Inc., for instance, will create a $20 billion U.S. food behemoth. The Anglo-Dutch giant Unilever PLC, No. 1 in consumer products, is rapidly expanding its food interests. And as rivals gain ground, Nestlé has resolved anew to stay on top, even if it means the end of the subdued Nestlé style.

"My concern is how to make Nestlé bigger," says Helmut Maucher, the Swiss company's affable West German chief executive. "Big is not negative in itself. The others are getting bigger, too."

Big was behind Nestlé's first-ever hostile takeover, the $4.4 billion raid on British confectioner Rowntree PLC this year. The pursuit of growth is changing Nestlé's time-honored methods of doing business, realigning its geographic strategy and propelling its forays into non-food sectors.

All that doesn't mean Nestlé doesn't sometimes act like a clumsy giant. By industry standards, many of its practices are ultraconservative and the company's profit growth has lagged. And what seems bold in sedate Switzerland often looks cautious in places like the U.S.

Nestlé seems to go in cycles. After a lull to digest its $3 billion U.S. acquisition of Carnation Co. in 1985, the Swiss superpower is stirring again. With more ready cash and a bigger research budget than any other food company, it is in an enviable position to take part in the food industry's world-wide consolidation.

NOT-SO-LUMBERING GIANT

"They're aggressive," says Frederic Binggeli, an analyst at the Geneva private banker Lombard Odier & Cie. "But you don't always get that impression, because they're so big. The impact is diluted. They can take an interest in something that might be important in 10 years."

This year, Nestlé has spent more than $6 billion on acquisitions, including $1.2 billion for the assets of Italy's Buitoni S.p.A., $325 million for the Cooper Surgical unit of Cooper Cos. of the U.S., and Rowntree. That adds to an empire that spans five continents, with more than 400 factories and 169,000 workers.

The purchases illustrate Nestlé's intention to be a market leader. With Rowntree and the Buitoni interests, for example, it will come close to top-

SOURCE: Margaret Studer and Diana Federman, *Wall Street Journal*, November 11, 1988.

Nestlé's Dominance The major food manufacturers' 1987 sales in billions of Swiss francs*

Rank	Company	Total Sales	% Food	Food Sales
1	Nestle	35.2	96%	33.8
2	Unilever (Neth./U.K.)	40.8	49	20.0
3	Philip Morris (U.S.)	41.5	47	19.6
4	Kraft (U.S.)	14.8	100	14.8
5	RJR Nabisco (U.S.)	23.6	60	14.1
6	Taiyo Fishery (Japan)	11.8	100	11.8
7	IBP (U.S.)	11.5	100	11.5
8	ConAgra (U.S.)	13.5	82	11.1
9	Mars (U.S.)	11.0	99	10.9
10	Sara Lee (U.S.)	13.7	72	9.9

*Currencies translated at average 1987 rates.
SOURCE: Bank Vontobel

pling Mars Inc., as the world's biggest candy company.

The acquisitions also highlight other goals. With Kit-Kat, the world's second-biggest selling candy bar, and other Rowntree prizes, Nestlé can better cater to the cross-border melding of consumer tastes. Buitoni not only brings a powerful European brand into the Nestlé fold, it gives Nestlé a strong footing in Italy. With the European Community's advance toward a planned single market by 1992, Nestlé is taking a second look at countries like Italy, Spain, Portugal and even Turkey. Europe will account for 50% of total Nestlé sales in 1989, up from 43% now.

At the same time, as the quantity of food consumed levels off in industrial countries, Nestlé is shifting from old-fashioned items, like canned vegetables, to more expensive convenience foods.

New Openings

Even in developing countries, Nestlé foresees huge potential for extending its brand names and highly processed products. The company is opening seven factories in Asia this year and next. It thinks Asian sales, now 13% of the company total, could reach 20% in the 1990s.

The acquisition of Cooper Surgical reinforces Nestlés lead in eye-care products, a sector it entered in 1977. Nestlé also indirectly owns a sizable stake in L'oréal S.A., the world' biggest cosmetic maker, and is likely someday to seek control of the French company, analysts say. They predict Nestlé eventually will muscle into pharmaceuticals, perhaps even tackling one of the Swiss drug giants.

When Mr. Maucher became Nestlé chief executive in 1981, profits had been eroded by a surge in the Swiss franc and heavy reliance on the Third World, where Nestlé's marketing of infant formula had provoked a damaging consumer boycott. But he cut bureaucracy, scrapped losing businesses and negotiated the boycott's end. With Carnation, he achieved the long-term target of boosting sales in North America from 19% of group sales in 1982 to 29% last year.

He doesn't win universal praise. Nestlé was stung by criticism from Zurich's business daily, the Neue Zuercher Zeitung, for borrowing to buy Carnation and for taking the company into pet food. Likewise, Nestlé's battle for Rowntree was deemed unseemly in some quarters, especially for the attention it attracted to Switzerland's restrictions on hostile takeovers.

Nestlé's current dividend payout represents about 28% of profits, the norm for Switzerland but far below the food-industry average of 37%. While safety-minded Swiss shareholders may accept this, it isn't clear how long such a level can be reconciled with Nestlé's global ambitions. Mr. Maucher doesn't rule out going to European capital markets should an acquisition prospect prove irresistible.

NOT WITHOUT WORRIES

In his seven-year reign, sales have risen 45%, while earnings were up 79% in the period to a projected 1.97 billion francs this year. But Nestlé isn't without its worries. Some lines have been losing market share as competition mounts. The marketing of two infant-formula products in the U.S., Nestlé's first big push into that U.S. product-market, has been controversial. And the boycott over Nestlé's Third World activities recently resurfaced, despite its conciliatory measures.

Yet analysts are enthusiastic about Nestlé's prospects. "It's a good investment," says Michael Clark, a Swiss-companies analyst at Morgan Grenfell Group in London. "Earnings growth in 1989 looks better than it has in years," he says, with forecasts ranging up to 18%.

Adds Joelle Ben Hamida, an analyst at Geneva private bankers Pictet & Cie.: "In the course of the '80s, Nestlé has taken on a whole new industrial dimension. [It] has been stunningly successful."

panies. The international success of the MNCs is primarily because of their ability to overcome the disadvantages and capitalize on their advantages. These advantages, as well as the disadvantages, depend to a large extent upon the nature of individual corporations themselves and on each of their types of business. Studies of MNCs, however, show that a pattern of common characteristics exists across the broad spectrum of different corporations operating around the globe (see Perspective 1–2).

ADVANTAGES GAINED BY MNCS
Superior Technical Know-how   Perhaps the most important advantage that MNCs enjoy is patented technical know-how, which enables them to compete internationally. Most large MNCs have access to higher or advanced levels of technology which was either developed or acquired by the corporation. Such technology is patented and held quite closely. It can be in the areas of production, management, services, or processes. Widespread application of such technology gives the MNC a strong competitive advantage in the international market, because it results in the production of efficient, hi-tech, and low-priced products and services that command a large international market following. The communications and funds transfer technology developed by Citibank is an example of how an MNC can obtain a competitive advantage by developing and patenting and then exploiting advanced technology.[13] IBM, Control Data Corporation in computers, Boeing, McDonnel Douglas in aviation, Dupont and Davis in chemicals are further examples.

Large Size and Economies of Scale   Most MNCs tend to be large. Some of them, such as IBM or Exxon, have sales that are larger than the gross national products of many countries. The large size confers significant advantages of economies of scale to MNCs. The high volume of production lowers per-unit fixed costs for the company's products, which is reflected in lower final costs. Competitors who produce smaller volumes of goods must price them higher in order to

---

[13] Some texts use the term "proprietary technology" for technology that has been patented by a firm.

PERSPECTIVE 1–2   Come Back Multinationals

The flow of foreign direct investment by multinational companies was five times greater, at $50 billion, in 1986 than it was 15 years earlier. In the early 1970s any prediction of such growth would have provoked fresh demands for a United Nations "code of conduct" to control the behaviour of what were then widely labelled as exploitative giants.

No longer. The UN still wants such a code, but its most recent report on the activities of what it calls "transnational corporations" stresses the good that such companies do. Third-world governments are coming to appreciate the employment, skills, exports and import-substitutes that they deliver.

The developing world's resentment of the direct investment of multinationals once stemmed from these companies' very rationale for setting up factories abroad. One of their reasons was to gain better access to foreign markets: this was construed as a threat to crowd-out local firms. Their second reason was the quest for lower manufacturing costs: this was exploitation. The fact that a search for fickle comparative advantage led such companies to invest abroad was taken to imply a lack of commitment to the society and employment of the host country.

The UN report debunks many of these bogeyman assumptions. One old bogey was *size*—the idea that multinationals are always big, powerful and liable to abuse their power. Although giant corporations certainly account for a large share of the world economy, smaller companies are nowadays just as likely as big ones to invest abroad.

The 600 biggest companies in the world—the "billion dollar club" because their annual sales exceed $1 billion—still create a fifth of the world's total value-added in manufacturing and agriculture. But half of all the world's companies that have operations abroad are small or medium-sized. Japan and Britain were two of the world's largest exporters of capital in the first half of the 1980s: 23% of Japanese "multinationals" employed fewer than 300 people in 1984; and in 1981 78% of the British firms with direct investments overseas employed fewer than 500. The smallest company in the billion-dollar club (America's Pennwalt Corporation) has, in contrast, nearly 10,000 employees.

Multinationals increase employment in their host countries. The UN's conservative estimate of direct employment by multinationals is 65m, or 3% of the world's labour force. Add indirect employment, such as jobs created by suppliers and by the general lift to an economy that multinationals can provide—and such companies may generate 6% of world employment. American multinationals employed almost $6\frac{1}{2}$m people abroad in 1984, 32% of these in developing countries, 42% in Europe, 5% in Japan and 14% in Canada.

Foreign investors increase a host country's *output* and *exports*. This is especially important for developing, or newly industrialising, countries which need fast growth and foreign exchange to service bank debt. Foreign-owned companies accounted for 55% of Singapore's employment in manufacturing industry in 1982, 63% of its manufacturing output and 90% of its exports of manufactured goods. They produced 70% of Zimbabwe's industrial output. In 1983 nearly 30% of Argentina's manufacturing output and exports came from multinationals. It is often easier for a multinational to export than for an indigenous firm to do so. It has better distribution and marketing networks overseas, and can sometimes circumvent protectionism in other countries more effectively.

Such truths are hitting home; but there is still some third-world resistance to multinationals in the service industries. This is a pity, because the UN report shows that services are taking an increasing share of multinationals' foreign direct

SOURCE: *The Economist*, November 26, 1988.

Multinationals' foreign direct investment, (billions of $)
Stocks held abroad by companies from:

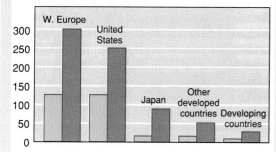

Stocks held by foreign companies in:

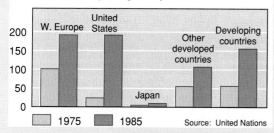

1975   1985   Source: United Nations

services by a foreign company thus appears to offer the prospect of outflows of profit, not accompanied by an increase in exports or inflows of high-tech skills. The UN also reports a "widespread impression that service industries consist largely of technologically stagnant, small-scale personal services based on unskilled labour working with little capital in ways that have not changed for many years."

The impression is wrong. The UN says that service multinationals bring with them what it calls "soft technology"—the skills required to run an efficient business. They train much of the skilled labour that they need locally, rather than import it. They often give these workers more of the sorts of skills that can usefully be hired by indigenous rival companies. By contrast, skills taught in manufacturing are sometimes appropriate only to a sophisticated multinational. The local subsidiaries of service multinationals are, the UN finds, more "complete and free-standing" than those in manufacturing, precisely because they add their value *in situ*.

The report shows how often exporting industries can be hobbled by inefficient services. A study of 17 developing countries found that, while the average price of a range of labour-intensive services was only 60% that in America, the prices of high-technology services (such as electricity, air transport and telecommunications) were often over twice the American level, despite subsidies. This handicaps industry. While these countries had an average GDP per head that was 20% of the American level, their spending per head on telecoms was only 1% of America's.

Slowly the message is registering: the best multinational code for the third world may well be the one that you can dial, and that gets you through.

investment—particularly, but not only, within the rich countries. Services' share of America's outward investment rose from 24% in 1975 to 34% in 1985; from 29% to 35% of Britain's; and from 36% to 52% of Japan's. They accounted for 19% of Mexico's inward foreign investment in 1971, then 23% in 1981; for 20% of foreign investment in Nigeria in 1975, then 37% in 1982.

EXPORTABLE SERVICES

Why the sensitivity? Despite huge foreign earnings from hotels, services often seem less exportable than goods. Although services like insurance can be exported, meals in restaurants, health care and local transport networks cannot. Investment in

recover higher fixed costs. This situation is especially true in such capital-intensive industries as steel, petrochemicals, and automobiles, in which the fixed costs form a substantial proportion of total costs. Thus, an MNC such as Nippon Steel of Japan can sell its products at much cheaper prices than those of companies with smaller plants.

Lower Input Costs

Large Size The large production levels of multinationals necessitates the purchase of inputs in commensurately large volumes. Bulk purchases of inputs enable MNCs to bargain for lower input costs, and they are able to obtain substantial volume discounts. The lowered input costs imply less expensive and, therefore, more competitive finished products. Nestlé, which buys huge quantities of coffee on the market, can command much lower prices than smaller buyers.

Ability to Access Raw Materials Overseas Many MNCs lower input and production costs by accessing raw materials in foreign countries. In many of these cases, MNCs supply the technology to extract and/or refine the raw materials. In addition to lowering costs, such access can give them monopolistic control over the raw materials because they often supply technology only in exchange for such monopolistic control. This control gives them the opportunity of manipulating the supply of the raw materials, or even denying access, to the competitors for this raw material.

Ability to Shift Production Overseas The ability to shift production overseas is another advantage enjoyed by MNCs. In order to increase their international competitiveness, MNCs relocate their production facilities overseas to take advantage of lower costs for labor, raw materials, and other inputs, and, often, incentives offered by host countries. The reduced costs achieved at these locations are exploited by exporting lower-cost goods to foreign markets. Several major MNCs have set up factories in such low-cost locations as Taiwan, South Korea, the Philippines, and Mexico, to name only a few. This advantage is unique to MNCs, and it gives them a distinct edge over purely domestic corporations.[14]

Scale Economies in Shipment, Distribution, and Promotion
Scale economies allow MNCs to achieve lower costs in shipment expenses. The large volumes of freight they ship across nations permits them to negotiate lower rates with the shippers. Some of the very large corporations, especially the oil giants, have operations that are large enough to justify the purchase of their own ships, which is an even more effective way to reduce costs.

Distribution and promotion costs are also lowered for MNCs because of their high volumes of production. The distributors in different countries charge lower commissions to move the products because they are able to make substantial profits on their high volumes. A similar lowering of costs accrues with promotional expenses. MNCs have large advertising budgets and are valuable clients for advertising agencies and the media. Consequently, they are able to obtain cheaper rates. More importantly, MNCs are often able to standardize a promotional message and use it in different countries (for example, the Marlboro cigarette advertisements or several Coca-Cola promotions that have been released in different countries using standardized messages).

Brand Image and Good Will Advantages
Many of the MNCs possess product lines that have established a good reputation for quality, performance, value, and service. This reputation spreads abroad through exports and promotion, which adds to the arsenal of potent weapons of the MNC in the form of brand image or good will, which it is able to use to differentiate its own products from others in its genre. The MNC is able to leverage this good will or brand image by standardizing its product line in different countries and achieving economies of scale. For example, Sony Walkmans do not have any special modifications for different countries (except for voltage) and the home-based plant churns out standardized products for the world market. Similarly, Levi Strauss & Company is able to market its standard denim jeans around the globe even though clothing fashions vary widely within different cultures. Moreover, good will and brand names allow the company to charge premium prices for its products (e.g. Sony), because the customers are convinced that the products are good values even at premium prices.

Access to Low-cost Financing
As a result of their size, MNCs require large amounts of financing, generally, they are excellent credit risks. Therefore, they are the favored customers of the financial institutions that lend to them at their best rates. The lower costs of financing for the

---

[14] For further details, see Hout et al., 1982.

MNCs adds to their competitive strength. MNCs also have the additional advantage of access to different financial markets, which allows them to borrow from the source offering the best deal; the funds are then transferred internally to required locations. This access enables MNCs to avoid credit rationing in some countries and to obtain financing at costs lower than those available to their domestic-oriented competitors.

Financial Flexibility

MNCs also have an advantage in being able to manipulate their profits and shift them to lower tax locations. This greater financial leverage can be used to artificially lower prices to enter new markets or increase market shares in existing ones. The manipulations of profits to save taxes is generally accomplished through transfer pricing, where the overseas subsidiaries are charged artificially higher prices for products supplied to them by the parent company. There are also several financial mechanisms with the objectives of shifting profits and manipulating taxes.

Information Advantages

Multinationals have a global market view and are able to collect, process, analyze, and exploit their in-depth knowledge of worldwide markets. They use this knowledge to create new openings for their existing products or create new products for potential market slots. Their special knowledge is used to diversify and expand the market coverage of their products and to design strategies to counter the marketing efforts of their competitors. Moreover, excess production can be sold off, as the company can quickly find new markets through its global search and marketing mechanism.

Information-gathering abilities of an MNC are an advantage not only in marketing, but in all other aspects of its operation. The MNC is able to gather commercial intelligence, forecast government controls, and assess political and other risks through its information network. The network also provides valuable information about changing market and economic conditions, demographics, social and cultural changes, and many other variables that affect the business of MNEs in different countries. Access to this information provides the MNE with the opportunity to position itself appropriately to respond to any contingencies or to exploit any opportunities.

Managerial Experience and Expertise

Because MNCs function simultaneously in a large number of very different countries, they are able to assimilate a bank of valuable managerial experience. This experience provides insights into dealing with different business situations and problems around the globe. The MNC also acquires expertise in different ways of approaching business problems and can effectively apply this knowledge to its other locations. For example, a multinational located in Japan can acquire in-depth knowledge of Japanese management methods and apply them successfully elsewhere. MNCs also develop expertise in multicountry operations management as their executives gather experience working in different countries on their way to senior management positions.

Diversification of Risks

The simultaneous presence of MNCs in different countries allows them to more effectively bear the risk of cyclic economic declines. Generally these cycles have an incongruous pattern among different countries. Thus, if operations in one country suffer losses, these losses can be offset by gains in other countries. Simultaneous operations also impart considerable flexibility to MNC operations, which enables them to diversify the political, economic, and other risks that they face in different countries. Thus, if a MNC is not able to keep up production levels in one country, it can still retain its market share by serving the market with products from a factory located in a different country. In another instance, if raw material supply is stopped from one source, the global presence of the MNC assures supplies from alternative sources.

DISADVANTAGES FACED BY MNCs

Business Risks

MNCs have to bear several serious risks that are not borne by companies whose operations are purely domestic in nature.

Since MNCs do business outside the borders of their own countries, they deal with the currencies of other countries, which renders them vulnerable to fluctuations in exchange rates. Violent movements in exchange rates can wipe out the entire profit of a particular business activity. MNCs often have to live with this risk because it is extremely difficult to eliminate it.

Host-country Regulations   Operating in different countries subjects MNCs to a myriad of host-country regulations that vary from country to country and, in most cases, are quite different from those of the home country. The MNC has the difficult task of familiarizing itself with these regulations and modifying its operations to ensure that it does not overstep them. Regulations are often changed, and such changes can have adverse implications for MNCs. For example, a country may ban the import of a certain raw material or restrict the availability of bank credit. Such constraints can have serious effects on production levels. In many developing countries national controls are quite pervasive and almost every facet of private business activity is subject to government approval. The MNCs of developed countries are not used to such controls, and their methods of doing business are not geared to work in this type of environment.

Different Legal Systems   MNCs must operate under the different legal systems of different countries. In some countries the legislative and judicial processes are extremely cumbersome and contain many nuances that are not easily understood by outsiders. Some legislation can also prohibit the type of business activity the MNC would regard as normal in its home country.

Political Risks   Host countries are sovereign entities and their actions normally do not admit any appeals. There is little that an MNC can do if a host country is determined to take actions that are inimical to its interest. This political risk, as it is known, increases in countries whose governments are unstable and tend to change frequently.

Operational Difficulties   Multinationals work in a wide variety of business environments, which creates substantial operational difficulties. There are often unwritten business practices and market conventions that prevail in host countries. MNCs that lack familiarity with such conventions will find it difficult to conduct business in accordance with them. Often the normal methods of operation of an MNC can be quite contrary to a country's business practices. A typical example is informal credit. In many countries retailers agree to stock goods of a manufacturing company only if they are offered a market-determined period of credit that is not covered by a written document. The accounting and sales policies of an MNC may not permit such arrangements. On the other hand, doing business in that country may not be at all possible without such arrangements. The multinational must therefore adjust its business practices or lose business entirely.

Cultural Differences   Cultural differences often lead to major problems for MNCs. Many find that their expatriate executives are not able to turn in optimal performance because they are not able to adjust to the local culture, both personally as well as professionally. On the other hand, local managers of MNCs often have difficulties in dealing with the home office of an MNC because of culturally based mutual communication and understanding problems. Inability to understand and respond appropriately to local cultures has often led MNC products to fail. Misunderstanding of local cultures, work ethics, and social norms often leads to problems between MNCs and their local customers, business associates, government officials, and even their own employees.

Many of the problems and challenges of doing international business center around overcoming disadvantages and capitalizing on advantages that arise when corporations go international. These problems and challenges will be discussed in detail in subsequent chapters.

Recent Trends in World Trade
Expanding Volume

The sheer volume of trade between nations has grown enormously since World War II. In 1948 world trade was only $51 billion. It rose to $331.72 billion in 1970 and to $2.627 trillion in 1988 (see Figure 1–1). The international trade arena continues to be dominated by the industrialized countries, who account for as much as 73.5 percent of world trade. Major changes have occurred in trading patterns, however, within the industrialized countries. For example, Japan increased its share of world exports from 6.1 percent in 1970 to 10.1 percent in 1988. On the other hand, the U.S. share of world exports declined from 13.7 percent in 1970 to 12.0 percent in 1988. These trends have very important implications for international business. It is clear that the world trading environment is now truly international, in the sense that it is no longer dominated by any one country. There has, in fact, been a reversal of roles for some countries, most significantly, the United States, which incurred huge trade deficits in the 1980s and has moved from being the world's largest creditor to being the world's largest debtor. There are many reasons for this dramatic change.

U.S. faces intense competition in its home market as well as in foreign markets from several countries, especially Germany, Japan, Sweden, France, Italy, etc. Apart from these, new competition has surfaced in the form of the newly industrializing economies of the Pacific rim, popularly known as the Four Tigers. These countries, Hong Kong, Republic of Korea, Taiwan, and Singapore have been rapidly increasing their share of the world trade.

Increased Competition

Competition on the international trade front is likely to intensify. The emergence of a commercially unified Europe in 1992, the further strengthening of Asian exporting capabilities, and the continuing increase in Japanese exports are likely to put further pressures on the United States. To respond to these pressures, the United States will have to take a more active and positive approach to international business (see Table 1–3). The realization that we live in a globalized world must become more deeply rooted. Increased attention to international business is therefore not only likely, but necessary.

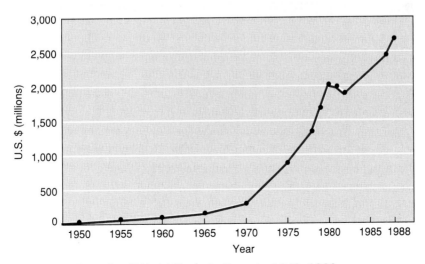

FIGURE 1–1   Growth of World Trade in Exports, 1948–1988.
SOURCE: International Monetary Fund.

TABLE 1–3
The Superpower Contenders Compared The data presented here—with a few exceptions—are for 1987, the latest year for which comparable data are available for all countries.

	United States	Soviet Union	Japan	European Community	China
Population (in millions)	243.8	284.0	122.0	323.6	1,074.0
Gross National Product (in billions of 1987 U.S. dollars*)	$4,436.1	$2,375.0	$1,607.7	$3,782.0	$293.5
Per capital GNP (1987 U.S. dollars*)	$18,200	$8,360	$13,180	$11,690	$270
GNP Growth Rate					
1966–70 (annual average)	2.8%	5.1%	11.0%	4.6%	N.A.
1971–75 (annual average)	2.3%	3.1%	4.3%	3.0%	5.5%
1976–80 (annual average)	3.3%	2.2%	5.0%	3.0%	6.1%
1981–85 (annual average)	3.0%	1.8%	3.9%	1.5%	9.2%
1987	2.9%	0.5%	4.2%	2.9%	9.4%
Inflation (change in consumer prices)	3.7%	-0.9%	0.1%	3.1%	9.2%
Total Labor Force (in millions)	121.6	154.8	60.3	143.0	512.8
Agricultural	3.4	33.9	4.6	11.9	313.1
Nonagricultural	118.2	120.9	55.7	131.1	199.7
Unemployment Rate	6.1%	N.A.	2.8%	11.0%	N.A.
Foreign Trade					
Exports (in millions of U.S. dollars)	$250.4	$107.7	$231.2	$953.5**	$44.9
Imports (in millions of U.S. dollars)	$424.1	$96.0	$150.8	$955.1**	$40.2
Balance (in millions of U.S. dollars)	-$173.7	$11.7	$80.4	-$1.6	$4.7

	United States	Soviet Union	Japan	European Community	China
Energy					
Consumption (in bbl. of oil equiv. per capita)	55.6	37.3	22.7	24.4	4.8
Oil Reserves (in billions of barrels)	33.4	59.0	0.1	7.6	18.4
Oil Production (in millions of bbl. a day)	9.9	12.7	Negligible	3.1	2.7
Natural Gas Reserves (in trillions of cubic feet)	186.7	1,450.0	1.0	112.9	30.7
Coal Reserves (in billions of metric tons)	263.8	244.7	1.0	90.5	170.0
Agriculture					
Grain Production (in kilograms per capita)	1,150	740	130	480	402
Meat Production (in kilograms per capita)	109	65	31	82	18
Military					
Active Armed Forces	2,163,200	5,096,000	245,000	2,483,400	3,200,000
Ready Reserves	1,637,900	6,217,000	46,000	4,565,800	1,200,000
Defense Expenditures Share of GNP	6.5%	15–25%	1.6%	3.3%	4–5%
Living Standard					
Life Expectancy (years)	75	69	78	76	68
Automobiles (registrations per thousand)	570	42	235	347	Negligible

*Data were converted at U.S. purchasing power equivalents
**Data include trade between E.C. members
SOURCE: *Wall Street Journal*, January 2, 1989

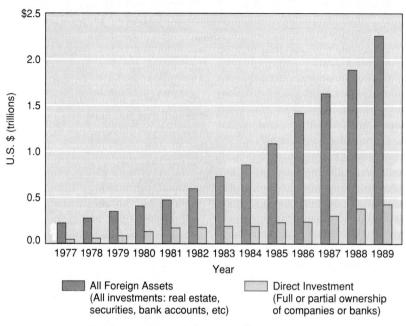

FIGURE 1–2   Foreign investment in the United States, 1977–1989.
SOURCE: Department of Commerce, *Survey of Current Business*, 1990

Increasing Complexity

The nature of international business also continues to grow more complex. As more and more nations industrialize, they offer both opportunities as well as threats in the field of international business. Many developing countries, such as Mexico, the Philippines, Hong Kong, and South Korea, have large corporations that are now competing for export markets as well as foreign direct investment opportunities in other countries. Many of the ex-socialistic bloc countries are opening, selectively, their economies for trade with the rest of the world. There is also increasing emphasis on boosting the trade participation of the heavily indebted countries of Latin America and sub-Saharan Africa, as that is seen to be an important solution for the their current debt crises. Many developing countries, disappointed by the performance of commodities trade, which had been their mainstay, are shifting their emphasis to the production and export of manufactured goods. This shift opens new opportunities

for relocating production facilities, thereby establishing manufacturing and trading arrangements. As these economies mature, they are better able to offer infrastructural facilities that provide electricity, transportation, communications, and labor and that can support large-scale manufacturing facilities. Low labor costs and government incentives are attracting overseas investments on a large scale to such countries. Consequently, foreign direct investment (FDI) continues to grow rapidly worldwide. In fact the rate of growth of FDI exceeds the rates of overall growth of the world economy.[15] For example, during the 1980s, FDI in the United States increased from $83 billion to more than $400 billion, an annual rate of more than 19 percent, while the U.S. economy grew only 3 to 4 percent per year. Figure 1–2 illustrates the growth of assets and FDI in the United States from 1977 to 1989. Increasing FDI also implies a stimulus to international trade as

[15] World Bank 1990.

PERSPECTIVE 1–3 **On Global Leadership**

The trade deficit has been a way of sharing our expansion with other countries; they've been going out to lunch on our trade deficit.

—*George Schultz*
Former secretary of state

We have been enjoying a free lunch on borrowed money.

—*Fred Bergsten*
Director of the Institute
for International Economics

Information technology changes everything, and here Japan leads.

—*Makoto Kuroda*
Former chief trade negotiator for Japan

America is the most vital nation in the West and will remain so.

—*Helmut Schmidt*
Former chancellor of
West Germany

If we continue selling American enterprises, we will become a nation of workers, not capitalists.

—*Lester Thurow*
Dean of Sloan School of
Management at MIT

Japan is like a thin bottom pan on a hot fire—very vulnerable to external forces.

—*Chung Hoon Mok*
President of Hyundai
Construction

Economic perestroika will fail. It cannot work.

—*Valery Giscard d'Estaing*
Former president of France

Europe will be a bigger and more attractive market in 1992 and will seek reciprocity.

—*Gianni de Michaelis*
Deputy prime minister of
Italy

No nation can be a power in a nuclear world without nuclear weapons, and Japan and West Germany won't be allowed by others to have such weapons.

—*Richard Nixon*
Former president of the
United States

The Japanese will find out that money isn't everything, just as we found out armaments aren't everything.

—*Anatoll Adamishin*
Soviet Deputy
Foreign Minister

We have to get all over the world and be good corporate citizens. You can't go over with skates to play basketball.

—*John Welch*
Chairman of
General Electric

SOURCE: *Wall Street Journal*, June 30, 1989.

cross-border investments involve the substantial flow of merchandise.

Trade in Services

Trade in services is also growing rapidly. The revolution in communications ushered in by the use of computer satellite-based networks has enabled almost instantaneous transmission of information from any part of the world. This development has resulted in an enormous expansion of the services industry—banking, travel and tourism, and consulting—all of which have expanded rapidly across the world, integrating trade in services more than ever into a global business framework.

The Field of International Business Studies

The large volumes of trade, the existence of huge multinational business entities, and the rapidly changing international business environment merely emphasize the fundamental interrelationships of business firms, governments, economies, and markets in the world today. Thus, the study of international business and the knowledge of the forces operating in the world have direct implications for everyone in the modern world—from consumers who are presented with an increasing array of foreign product choices, to political leaders who find more and more that political concerns are directly tied to economic and international trade concerns, and, naturally, to the business manager who faces increasing competition not only from domestic but also from foreign producers of goods and services, who, despite many disadvantages, have many factors working in their favor (see Perspective 1–3).

The study of international business also provides the modern business manager with a greater awareness of wider business opportunities than those within local borders, which, in strategic management terms, means that the parameters of the manager's external environment, as well as the possible configuration of that external environment, have expanded for the modern and progressive firm.

The study of international business, however, does not merely expand the parameters of the external environment of the modern business firm. It stimulates a more basic, attitudinal change in doing business in this widened environment. The business manager is exposed to the problems that inward-looking attitudes—ethnocentrism and parochialism—can and do create for international business. The business manager is encouraged to become aware of these constraints and to overcome them by seeking practical solutions in the real world. Promotion of the awareness that people and cultures do differ around the globe and that these differences are sometimes crucial to the conduct of international business, is very important. It is the starting point for developing attitudinal changes that move business managers to flexibility and adaptability in dealing with the varied situations that arise in the conduct of international business.

These developments in the past fifty years provide a fascinating area of study for the student of international business because it was a time of unparalleled growth and activity. The trend is likely to continue upward, with increases in the flow of goods, capital, investments, and labor across national borders, plus the growth of truly global industries and corporations.

Discussion Questions

1. Why has international business become so important in today's environment?
2. What are some of the reasons why corporations choose to develop international operations?
3. What differentiates the modern multinational corporation from the import-export firm?
4. What factors makes international business more complex than conducting domestic businesses?
5. Obtain the annual report of a large multinational corporation and identify the scope of its international operations and the countries in which it currently operates.
6. What are some of the conflicts that may occur between a multinational corporation and the local government hosting the multinational?
7. How can increases in world trade affect the small businessperson in your hometown?
8. How can studying international business increase your understanding of the world around you?

Bibliography

1988. "Michael Jackson Signs Under a Japanese Label." *Euromoney* (March): 25–35.
1988. "Walkman Factories Don't Walk." *The Economist* (March 12): 66–67.

1990. "The 100 Largest Foreign Investments in the U.S." *Forbes* (July 23): 358.

1990. "U.S. Firms with the Biggest Foreign Revenue." *Ibid,* 362.

CITICORP. 1988. *1987 Annual Report.*

GAFFNEY, CHARLES, and TED HOLDEN. 1990. "The Global 1000—The Leaders: Who's Sitting on Top of the World." *Business Week* (July 18): 111–114.

HOUT, THOMAS, MICHAEL E. PORTER, and EILEEN RUDDEN. 1982. "How Global Companies Win Out." *Harvard Business Review* (September/October): 74-75.

LEE, PETER. 1988. "More Power to the Japanese." *Euromoney* (February): 76–77.

PERLMUTTER, HOWARD, 1969. "The Tortuous Evolution of the MNC." *Columbia Journal of World Business* (January/February): 9–18.

STOPFORD, JOHN M. 1984. *The World Directory of Multinational Enterprises, 1982–83.* Detroit: Gale Research Company.

TULLY, SHAWN. 1987. "The World's 50 Biggest Industrial CEO's: Stirring the Coffee Pot." *Fortune* (August 3): 43–45.

U.S. DEPARTMENT OF COMMERCE. *Survey of Current Business* (published quarterly). Washington, DC: Government Printing Office.

U.S. DEPARTMENT OF COMMERCE BUREAU OF INTERNATIONAL COMMERCE. *Trends in Direct Investment Abroad by U.S. Multinational Corporations* (published quarterly). Washington, DC: Government Printing Office.

Ward's Business Directory of Major International Companies. 1985. Belmont, CA: Information Access Company.

WHITESIDE, DAVID E., OTIS PORT, and LARRY ARMSTRONG. 1988. "Sony Isn't Mourning the 'Death' of Betamax." *Business Week* (January 25): 37.

WILKINS, MIRA. 1970. *The Emergence of the Multinational Enterprise: American Business Abroad from the Colonial Era to 1914.* Cambridge, MA: Harvard University Press.

WORLD BANK. 1990. *The World Development Report, 1990.* Washington, DC: Oxford University Press.

Chapter Case Study _____

Transworld Minerals, Inc.

John Wright reclined fully his first-class seat and pulled a sleeping mask over his eyes—he wanted to relax, he told the air hostess, and would not have dinner for the next two or three hours. Wright was, however, anything but relaxed. A senior vice president in charge of international investment planning with Transworld Minerals, Inc., a large multinational corporation based in Dallas, Texas, he was returning from a business trip to Salaysia, a small mineral-rich country in Asia. His company was considering a major investment there in a new coal mining project, using Transworld's recently developed advanced technology that highly automated all operations. Wright had just finished a preliminary evaluation of the prospects.

On the face of it, it looked like a great investment that would generate substantial revenues in the long run. Salaysia had enormous deposits of coal in the northeastern parts of the country, located principally in the Nebong Province. Most of these deposits had been recently discovered, as a result of a sustained geological exploration undertaken by Salaysia with the help of a large exploration firm from Australia. Most of the deposits were of high-quality anthracite coal, which was in considerable demand in steel manufacturing plants in Japan and other, newly industrializing economies of Southeast Asia.

The government seemed encouraging, primarily because it did not have the technology to exploit these reserves and was badly in need of additional export revenues to meet the deficits in its balance of payments, which meant, however, that much of the project would have to be financed by Transworld.

Transworld had substantial financial resources. Its net working capital had been expanding steadily over the past five years, and it had been on schedule in repayment of all its loans from leading international banks in four countries—the United States, United Kingdom, Japan, and Hong Kong. It had an excellent credit standing, and two years ago, it had floated a successful bond issue in the U.K. market that raised £150 million to finance a major project in Zambia. It had good working relationship with banks in Singapore and Hong Kong, two leading financial centers in the region. Wright also had had discussions with the local branches of three multinational banks in Salaysia, and they appeared to be interested, at least on a preliminary consideration basis.

Transworld was the world leader in advanced coal mining technology—its latest processes resulted in high-speed extraction, that is, the stacking and loading of coal from depths that had not been accessible to most of the existing mining techniques. Because the technology was highly automated, there were substantial economies because of saved labor costs. Most of the operations would be optimized by Transworld by using its sophisticated, computer-based optimization models that would generate the best possible sequencing, timing, and coordination of different operations, which would be at least 20 percent more efficient than the technology currently in use in Salaysia.

The company had substantial marketing strength. It ran coal mining operations in several countries in Asia and Africa and had other mineral extraction operations in Latin America. Most of the products were sold to industrial consumers in Japan, Italy, and France. Transworld had strong business relationships with major shipping lines and considerable strength at the bargaining table while negotiating pricing for shipping its products.

The world market for coal was expected to remain strong, and Transworld could reasonably expect to make at least an average level of profit on the exports of Salaysian coal.

There were a few problems. Salaysia's local coal mining company was exerting substantial pressure on the home government to allow it to run the new project. It argued that it could access a similar level of technology by entering into a joint venture with Intermetals, an Australian mining company from which it could obtain the technical know-how, while the local implementation of the entire project would be in its hands. This venture would mean that Salaysia would only be buying the technical know-how from Australia, and the entire mining, extraction, processing, shipping, and marketing operations would be carried out by the Salaysian Coal Mining Company. The company had access to relatively dated machinery and extraction processes, but it had considerable financial strength and good relations with the labor force. Although it was relatively unknown abroad, the company was a major force in Salaysia's domestic mining industry. The management of the Salaysian Coal Mining Company also had good relations with the current minister of industries and was attempting to convince him that placing the entire project into the hands of the multinational Transworld would be detrimental to the national interest and that it could lead to foreign domination of the domestic coal mining industry.

The Industries Ministry was weighing the two alternatives and had called for additional details before the proposals could be submitted to the Industrial Approvals Board of the Salaysian government for a final decision.

Questions

1. What additional incentives should Wright suggest to improve the attractiveness of Transworld's proposal to the Industries Ministry?
2. What strategy should Transworld adopt to offset the political advantage enjoyed by the Salaysian Coal Mining Corporation?

CHAPTER 2

The Nature of International Business

CHAPTER OBJECTIVES

This chapter will:

- Explain the difference between the domestic and international contexts of business.
- Introduce the various entry methods a corporation may use to establish international business.
- Relate the changes in world trade patterns in terms of countries, products, and direct investment.
- Discuss the role of central governments in establishing trade policy and providing environments which support or restrict international trade.

Domestic versus International Business

The student of business is certainly familiar with the nature of doing business in a domestic market economy. A firm needs to identify its potential market, locate adequate and available sources of supplies of raw materials and labor, raise initial amounts of capital, hire personnel, develop a marketing plan, establish channels of distribution, and identify retail outlets. As an overlay upon this comprehensive system, the firm must also establish management controls and feedback systems— accounting, finance, and personnel functions.

Not only must the neophyte international businessperson contend with establishing an international component to add to domestic operations, he must also contend with the fact that international business activities are conducted in environments and arenas that differ from his own in all aspects—in economies, cultures, government, and political systems. The differences range along a continuum. For example, economies can range from being market-oriented to centrally planned, and political systems from democracies to autocracies. Countries are widely divergent in cultural parameters—ethnic varieties, religious beliefs, social habits, and customs. The problems and difficulties these differences generate are exacerbated by problems of distance, which complicate the firm's ability to communicate clearly, transmit data and documents, and even find compatible business hours, because of the time zones around the world. A U.S. firm with a subsidiary operation in the Far East faces a fifteen-hour time difference. Consequently, U.S. standard hours of 9 A.M. to 5 P.M. would be the equivalent of midnight to 8 A.M. overseas.

Business activities require vast investments of time, energy, and personnel on the domestic level. Adding an international component merely intensifies the number of steps necessary and the length and breadth of the firm's reach of effort and activity. Imagine establishing international components for all business functions as separate and discrete units. The prospective commitment is staggering and is generally avoided by many domestic businesses.

It is more likely that domestic firms enter foreign markets in a progressive way, beginning with exporting, which involves the least amount of resources and risk, before moving to a full-scale commitment in the form of establishing wholly owned overseas subsidiaries. A concern must take many factors into consideration before deciding whether or not to move overseas. It must evaluate its own resources—personnel, assets, experience in overseas markets, and the suitability of its products or organization for transplantation overseas. It is also crucial that a firm decide on the minimum and optimum levels of return it wishes to receive, as well as the amount of risk it is willing to bear. A firm must also evaluate the level of control necessary to manage the overseas operation. These factors must be critiqued in light of competition expected in markets abroad and the potential business opportunities that are to be created by the international operation.

All of these factors must be weighted in terms of the overall short-term and long-term strategic goals and objectives of the firm. For example, a firm may have a long-term goal to build a production facility abroad to serve a foreign market within ten years. Consequently, it would be unwise to enter into a short-term licensing agreement that would hold up their use of their rights for a long period of time.

Methods of Going International

Exporting

Exporting requires the least amount of involvement by a firm in terms of resources required and allocated to serving an overseas market. Basically, the company uses existing domestic capacity for production, distribution, and administration and designates a certain portion of its home production to a market abroad. It makes the goods locally and sends them by air, ship, rail, truck, or even pipeline across its nation's borders into another country's market.

Entrance into an export market frequently begins casually, with the placement of an order by a customer overseas. At other times, an enterprise sees a market opportunity and actively decides to take its products or services abroad. A firm can be either a direct or indirect exporter. As a direct exporter, it sees to all phases of the sale and transmittal of the merchandise. In indirect exporting, the exporter hires the expertise of someone else to facilitate the exchange. This intermediary is, of course, happy to oblige for a fee. There are several types of intermediaries: manufacturers' export agents who sell the company's product overseas; manufacturers' representatives who sell the products of a number of exporting firms in overseas markets; export commission agents who act as buyers for overseas markets; export commission agents who act as buyers for overseas customers; and export merchants who buy and sell on their own for a variety of markets.

Sales contacts within the foreign market are made through personal meetings, letters, cables, telephone calls, or international trade fairs. Some of these trade expositions take unusual forms. For example, in an attempt to promote the sale of U.S. products in Japanese markets, the Japanese government established a traveling trade show on a train. In the initial stages, the objective of the exporter is to develop an awareness of outstanding features of the firm's products, such as competitiveness against local products, innovation, durability, or reasonable prices.

The mechanics of exporting require obtaining appropriate permission from domestic governments (for example, for food products, and some technology and products considered crucial for national security); securing of reliable transportation and transit insurance; and fulfillment of requirements imposed by the importing nation, such as payment of appropriate duties, declarations, and inspections. Prior to the completion of the transaction, terms must be worked out for payment. The parties must establish the terms of the sale and whether the buyer will be extended credit, must open a letter of credit, pay in advance, or pay cash on delivery. In addition, the participants in the sale must also determine which currency will be used in the exchange. The currency used is especially crucial in light of fluctuations in exchange rates between countries.

ADVANTAGES OF EXPORTING

The prime advantage of exporting is that it involves very little risk and low allocation of resources for the exporter, who is able to use domestic production toward foreign markets and thus increase sales and reduce inventories. The exporter is not involved in the problems inherent in the foreign operating environment; the most that could be lost is the value of the exported products or an opportunity if the venture fails to establish the identity or characteristics of the product.

Exporting also provides an easy way to identify market potential and establish recognition of a name brand. If the enterprise proves unprofitable, the company can merely stop the practice with no diminution of operations in other spheres and no long-term losses of capital investments.

DISADVANTAGES OF EXPORTING

Exporting can be more expensive than other methods of overseas involvement on a per-unit basis because of mistakes (see Perspective 2–1) and the costs of fees, or commissions, export duties, taxes, and transportation. In addition, exporting could lead to less than optimal market penetration because of improper packaging or promotion. Exported goods could also be lacking features appropriate to specific overseas market. Relying on exporting alone, a firm may have trouble maintaining market share and contacts over long distances. Additional market share could be lost if local competition copies the products or services offered by the exporter. The exporting firm also could face restrictions against its products from the host country.

PERSPECTIVE 2–1   The Twelve Most Common Mistakes of Potential Exporters

1. **Failure to obtain qualified export counseling and to develop a master international marketing plan before starting an export business.** To be successful, a firm must first clearly define goals, objectives, and the problems encountered. Secondly, it must develop a definitive plan to accomplish an objective despite the problems involved. Unless the firm is fortunate enough to possess a staff with considerable export expertise, it may not be able to take this crucial first step without qualified outside guidance.

SOURCE: U.S. Department of Commerce. *A Basic Guide to Exporting*, pages 85–86.

2. **Insufficient commitment by top management to overcome the initial difficulties and financial requirements of exporting.**

   It may take more time and effort to establish a firm in a foreign market than in domestic ones. Although the early delays and costs involved in exporting may seem difficult to justify when compared to established domestic trade, the exporter should take a long-range view of this process and carefully monitor international marketing efforts through these early difficulties. If a good foundation is laid for export business, the benefits derived should eventually outweigh the investment.

3. **Insufficient care in selecting overseas distributors.**

   The selection of each foreign distributor is crucial. The complications involved in overseas communications and transportation require international distributors to act with greater independence than their domestic counterparts. Also, since a new exporter's history, trademarks, and reputation are usually unknown in the foreign market, foreign customers may buy on the strength of a distributor's reputation. A firm should therefore conduct a personal evaluation of the personnel handling its account, the distributor's facilities, and the management methods employed.

4. **Chasing orders from around the world instead of establishing a basis for profitable operations and orderly growth.**

   If exporters expect distributors to actively promote their accounts, the distributors must be trained, assisted, and their performance must be continually monitored. This requires a company marketing executive permanently located in the distributor's geographical region. New exporters should concentrate their efforts in one or two geographical areas until there is sufficient business to support a company representative. Then, while this initial core area is expanded, the exporter can move into the next selected geographical area.

5. **Neglecting export business when the U.S. market booms.**

   Too many companies turn to exporting when business falls off in the United States. When domestic business starts to boom again, they neglect their export trade or relegate it to a secondary place. Such neglect can seriously harm the business and motivation of their overseas representatives, strangle the U.S. company's own export trade and leave the firm without recourse when domestic business falls off once more. Even if domestic business remains strong, the company may eventually realize that they have only succeeded in shutting off a valuable source of additional profits.

6. **Failure to treat international distributors on an equal basis with domestic counterparts.**

   Often, companies carry out institutional advertising campaigns, special discount offers, sales incentive programs, special credit term programs, warranty offers, etc., in the U.S. market but fail to make similar assistance available to their international distributors. This is a mistake that can destroy the vitality of overseas marketing efforts.

7. **Assuming that a given market technique and product will automatically be successful in all countries.**

   What works in one market may not work in others. Each market has to be treated separately to insure maximum success.

8. **Unwillingness to modify products to meet regulations or cultural preferences of other countries.**

   Local safety and security codes, as well as import restrictions, cannot be ignored by foreign distributors. If necessary modifications are not made at the factory, the distributor must do them—usually at greater cost and, perhaps, not as well. It should also be noted that the resulting smaller profit margin makes the account less attractive.

9. **Failure to print service, sale, and warranty messages in locally understood languages.**

Although a distributor's top management may speak English, it is unlikely that all sales personnel (let alone service personnel) have this capability. Without a clear understanding of sales messages or service instructions, these persons may be less effective in performing their functions.

10. **Failure to consider use of an export management company.**
    If a firm decides it cannot afford its own export department (or has tried one unsuccessfully), it should consider the possibility of appointing an appropriate export management company (EMC).

11. **Failure to consider licensing or joint-venture agreements.**
    Import restrictions in some countries, insufficient personnel/financial resources, or a too limited product line cause many companies to dismiss international marketing as unfeasible. Yet, many products that can compete on a national basis in the United States can be successfully marketed in most markets of the world. A licensing or joint venture arrangement may be the simple, profitable answer to any reservations. In general, all that is needed for success is flexibility in using the proper combination of marketing techniques.

12. **Failure to provide readily available servicing for the product.**
    A product without the necessary service support can acquire a bad reputation in a short period, potentially preventing further sales.

While some of these problems can be addressed by establishing direct exporting capability through the establishment of a sales company within the foreign market to handle the technical aspects of export trading and keep abreast of market developments, demand, and competition, many firms choose instead to expand their operations in foreign spheres to include other forms of investments.

Licensing

Through licensing, a firm (licensor) grants a foreign entity (licensee) some type of intangible rights, which could be the rights to a process, a patent, a program, a trademark, a copyright, or expertise. In essence, the licensee is buying the assets of another firm in the form of know-how or research and development. The licensor can grant these rights exclusively to one licensee or nonexclusively to several licensees.

ADVANTAGES OF LICENSING

Licensing provides advantages to both parties. The licensor receives profits in addition to those generated from operations in domestic markets. These profits may be additional revenues from a single process or method used at home that the manufacturer is unable to utilize abroad. The method or process could have the beneficial effect of extending the life cycle of the firm's product beyond that which it would experience in local markets.

Additional revenues could also represent a return on a product or process that is ancillary to the strategic core of the firm in its domestic market, that is, the firm could have developed a method of production that is marketable as a separate product under a licensing agreement. In addition, by licensing the firm often realizes increased sales by providing replacement parts abroad. In addition, it protects itself against piracy by having an agent in the licensed user who watches for copyright or patent infringement.

The licensee benefits from acquiring the rights to a process and acquires state-of-the-art technology while avoiding the research and development costs.

DISADVANTAGES OF LICENSING

The prime disadvantage of licensing to the licensor is that it limits future profit opportunities associated with the property by tying up their rights for an extended period of time. Additionally, by licensing these rights to another, the firm loses control over the quality of its products and processes, the use or misuse of the assets, and even the protection of its corporate reputation.

To protect against such problems, the licensing agreement should clearly delineate the appropriate uses of the process, method, or name, as well as the allowable market and reexport parameters for the licensee. The contract should also stipulate contingencies and recourse, should the licensor fail to comply with its terms.

Franchising

Franchising is similar to licensing, except that in addition to granting the franchisee permission to use a name, process, method, or trademark, the firm assists the franchisee with the operations of the franchise and/or supplies raw materials. The franchiser generally also has a larger degree of control over the quality of the product than under licensing. Payment is similar to licensing in that the franchiser pays an initial fee and a proportion of its sales or revenues to the franchising firm.

The prime examples of U.S. franchising companies are service industries and restaurants, particularly fast-food concerns, soft-drink bottlers, home and auto maintenance companies (for example, McDonald's, Kentucky Fried Chicken, Tastee Freeze, Holiday Inn, Hilton, and Disney in Japan).[1]

ADVANTAGES AND DISADVANTAGES OF FRANCHISING

The advantages accruing to the franchiser are increased revenues and expansion of its name brand identification and market reach. The greatest disadvantage, as with licensing, is coping with the problems of assuring quality control and operating standards. Franchise contracts should be written carefully and provide recourse for the franchising firm, should the franchiser not comply with the terms of the agreement. Other difficulties with franchises come with their need to make slight adjustments or adaptations in the standardized product or service. For example, some ingredients in restaurant franchises may need to be adapted to suit the tastes of local clientele, which may differ from those of the original customers.

Management Contracts

Management contracts are those in which a firm basically rents its expertise or know-how to a government or company in the form of personnel who come into the foreign environment and run the concern. This method of involvement in foreign markets is often used with a new facility, after expropriation of a concern by a national government, or when an operation is in trouble.

Management contracts are frequently used in concert with turnkey operations. Under these agreements, firms provide the service of overseeing all details in the start-up of facilities, including design, construction, and operation. These are usually large-scale projects, such as production plants or utility constructions. The problem faced in turnkey operations is often the time length of the contract, which yields long payout schedules and carries greater risk in currency markets. Other problems can arise in the form of an increase in potential competition in the future as overseas capacity is increased by the new facilities. Turnkey operations also face all the problems of operating in remote locations.

Contract Manufacturing

Contract manufacturing is another method for firms to enter the foreign arena. Here the MNE contracts with a local firm to provide manufacturing services. This arrangement is akin to vertical integration, except that instead of establishing its own production locations, the MNE subcontracts the production, which it does in two ways. In one case it enters into a full production contract with the local plant producing goods to be sold under the name of the original manufacturer. The other way is to enter into contracts with another firm

---

[1] D.A. Ball, 1986. *Business America.*

to provide partial manufacturing services, such as assembly work or parts production.

Contract manufacturing has the advantage of expanding the supply or production expertise of the contracting firm at minimum cost. It is as if it can diversify vertically without a full-scale commitment of resources and personnel. By the same token, the firm also forgoes some degree of control over the production supply timetable when it contracts with a local firm to provide specific services. These problems are, however, no more substantial than operating normal raw material supplier contracts.

Direct Investment

When a company invests directly within foreign shores, it is making a very real commitment of its capital, personnel, and assets beyond domestic borders. While this commitment of resources increases the profit potential of a MNC dramatically by providing greater control over costs and operations of the foreign firm, it is also accompanied by an increase in the risks involved in operating in a foreign country and environment (see Perspective 2–2).

PERSPECTIVE 2–2   The Myth of Economic Sovereignty

Every industrial country, including Japan, has more of its economy under the control of foreign firms than a decade ago. As the pace of economic integration has quickened, the complaints have grown louder. Businesses that spend their profits overseas are attacked (at home) for not investing in their own country and (abroad) for scheming to undermine their host economy.

Assessing the impact of foreign direct investment (FDI) is difficult, because every country defines it in its own way. In America owning 10% or more of a company constitutes "control" and thus counts as a direct investment. In West Germany the ratio is 25%, in Britain and France 20%. Foreign ownership is different again. This covers (a) the stock of direct investment that secured control and (b) acquisitions financed in the host country (these are not counted in direct investment).

Luckily Ms. DeAnne Julius, the chief economist at Royal Dutch-Shell, an oil company, has, in a recent book,* done a remarkable job of wading through the national accounts. Unsurprisingly,

she finds that the extent of foreign ownership varies tremendously across the big five economies. Only 1% of Japan's assets were owned by foreign-controlled firms in 1986, and just 0.4% of its workers were employed by them. In America, by contrast, foreign-controlled firms owned 9% of the assets, employed 4% of the workers, and accounted for one-tenth of all sales.

Even so, compared with Europe, America looks almost autarkic. In Britain foreign-controlled firms owned 14% of the assets, employed one in seven workers and accounted for one-fifth of all sales. In West Germany the foreign-owned companies owned 17% of assets and accounted for 19% of sales. In France, the dominance of foreigners was greater still.

Foreigners may own only a small share of American business, but in absolute terms America has been the biggest recipient of new foreign investment. Between 1980 and 1988 the flow of foreign investment into America totalled $252 billion at 1980 prices (see chart). By 1988 direct investment was flowing in at the rate of $41 billion a year. America's direct investment overseas proceeded at a much slower pace. Measured at book value (an unrealistic assumption), America's as-

* Julius, DeAnne. 1989. *Global Companies and Public Policy.* RIIA/Pinter.

SOURCE: *The Economist,* June 23, 1990, page 67.

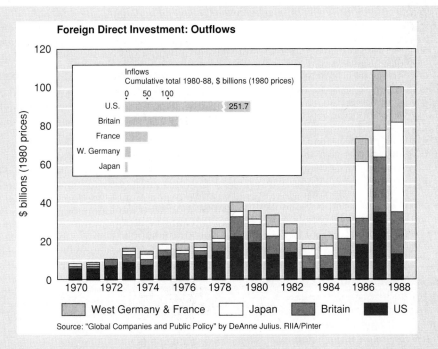

Foreign Direct Investment: Outflows

Inflows
Cumulative total 1980-88, $ billions (1980 prices)

U.S. — 251.7

Legend: West Germany & France | Japan | Britain | US

Source: "Global Companies and Public Policy" by DeAnne Julius. RIIA/Pinter

sets abroad are now worth less than foreigners' assets in America.

Letting foreigners bid for domestic assets should ensure that they will be used in the most efficient way. Domestic consumers will benefit from lower prices and/or better goods. Like free trade in goods, free trade in capital lets companies exploit their comparative advantage in superior management, better technology, what have you. Investors and recipients alike should gain from FDI.

Usually, anyway. In principle, direct investment might sometimes harm the recipient country. A company's spending on R&D, for example, may benefit the economy by more than the cost to the business: it may, in other words, carry an external benefit. If so, and if foreign firms spent less on R&D than domestic firms, then purchases of domestic firms by foreign ones could harm the country's economy. By a similar argument, if there are economies of scale in producing something, then letting a foreign firm into the domestic market might enable it to drive out domestic producers and make monopoly profits.

The most authoritative analysis of these and other economic objections to foreign invest-

ment is a study[**] by Mssrs Edward Graham of Duke University and Paul Krugman of the Massachusetts Institute of Technology. In America, they found, foreign companies spend more per worker on R & D than their domestic counterparts, and pay their workers as much. So even if foreign companies merely displace domestic firms, the spin-offs are unlikely to be smaller than from domestic ones. In fact, some foreign investment will supplement rather than replace domestic investment. Some advocates of "industrial policy," such as Mr. Robert Reich of Harvard University, therefore argue that foreign investment should be subsidised.

LET GOVERNMENTS COMPETE

Perhaps the most profound change that flows of foreign investment cause is this: a country's trade balance, so often a focus of attention, no longer reflects how well a country's businesses are doing.

[**] *Foreign Direct Investment in the United States.* Edward Graham and Paul Krugman. 1989. Institute for International Economics.

When Texas Instruments sells a silicon chip from its plant in Singapore to its parent in America this counts as an American import. If trade balances were defined in terms of ownership, rather than geography, it would not. In many ways it would indeed make more sense to measure trade balances that way.

Putting America's trade balance on to an ownership basis would make pleasant reading for Americans worried about their role in the world economy. Ms Julius estimates that in 1986 a third of America's exports were bought by American-owned companies abroad. About a fifth of America's imports were bought from American-owned companies abroad, and another third were bought by foreign-owned companies in America receiving goods from their own countries.

Worldwide, sales by American-owned companies to non-American-owned ones exceeded America's conventionally measured exports by a factor of five. Purchases from foreign companies were three times greater than America's imports. On an ownership basis, America's trade deficit of $144 billion in 1986 becomes a surplus of $57 billion.

Foreign direct investment has already reduced the freedom of governments to determine their own economic policy. If a government tries to push tax rates up, for example, it is increasingly easy for businesses to shift production overseas. Equally, if governments fail to invest in roads, education and so on, domestic entrepreneurs are likely to migrate. In short, foreign investment is forcing governments, as well as companies, to compete.

As with other forms of international activity, direct investment runs a continuum from joint ventures where risk is shared (but so are returns), to wholly owned subsidiaries where MNEs have the opportunity to reap the rewards but must also shoulder the lion's share of risk. Multinationals decide to make direct investments for two main reasons. The first is to gain access to enlarged markets. The second reason is to take advantage of cost differentials in overseas markets that arise from closer production resources, available economies of scale, and prospects for developing operating efficiences. Both reasons lead to the enjoyment of enhanced profitability. Alternatively, a firm enters a foreign market for defensive reasons to counter strategic moves by its competitors or to follow a market leader into new markets.

Joint Ventures

Joint ventures are business arrangements in which two or more firms or entities join together to establish some sort of operation (see examples in Perspective 2–3). Joint ventures may be formed by two MNEs, an MNE and a government, or an MNE and local businesspersons. If there are more than two participants in the deal, it is also called a consortium operation.

PERSPECTIVE 2–3   Cross-Border Alliances Become Favorite Way To Crack New Markets

NEW YORK—American Telephone & Telegraph Co. has big ambitions in the semiconductor industry. It wants to sell a broad range of chips head to head with some of the world's largest chip makers. There is just one problem: AT&T has nowhere near enough products to vault it into

SOURCE: Bernard Wysocki, Jr. with Philip Revzin. *Wall Street Journal*, March 26, 1990.

the big leagues. In fact, as a niche player, it constantly risks getting outflanked—if not crushed—by competitors who have a full line of chips and services.

So a few weeks ago, AT&T struck a deal, the sort of deal that will probably be a hallmark of business in the 1990s. The company reached out to NEC Corp., the big chip maker in Tokyo, and proffered a trade: some of AT&T's computer-aided design technology for some of NEC's advanced logic chips, a product AT&T doesn't make but very much wants to sell.

"These days it's just too expensive to go it alone," says Rock Pennella, AT&T Microelectronics' vice president of marketing.

TYING THE KNOT

This sort of cross-border marriage has been around for 30 years. But in the last few years—and especially in the last few weeks—the number of international joint ventures has rocketed. It has become clear that new alliances of this sort are now often crucial for dealing with increasingly global markets for a variety of products. Just last week, Texas Instruments Inc. and Kobe Steel Ltd. announced plans to make logic semiconductors in Japan. They join a growing list of similar ventures: Corning and Ciba-Geigy (medical equipment); Volvo and Renault (autos); Motorola and Toshiba; Texas Instruments and Hitachi (semiconductors). All have found that forming a partnership is sometimes the fastest, cheapest and least risky way to stay in, or get in, the global game.

But probably the most striking example of late is the decision by giants Mitsubishi of Japan and Daimler-Benz AG of West Germany to talk about an array of possible joint projects spanning everything from autos to aircraft. Both want to get into new markets and new products, and see each other as the means to that end.

"It's a world-wide trend," says Arthur Mitchell, a New York lawyer who has negotiated a number of U.S.-Japanese joint ventures. "Above all, it's a way to get into markets."

VOULEZ-VOUS UN PARTNER?

The European market is driving many of the alliances these days. The post-1992 European Community, as planned, will be an integrated economy of 320 million consumers. Upheaval in the East bloc has only increased the potential size of this new market. Japanese companies, traditionally weak in Europe, are desperate to be players. Hence, Mitsubishi's interest in teaming up with a powerful European "insider." (It is conceivable, for instance, that Daimler-Benz could distribute Mitsubishi's small cars in Easter Europe.)

The sizzling pace of developments in Europe doesn't fully explain the rash of partnerships announced in recent months, however. In the past few weeks alone, IBM and Siemens announced joint research in advanced semiconductor chips; the chairman of British Aerospace said he was looking for a "strategic alliance" with U.S. companies; and, AT&T formed another joint venture: It agreed to make and market Mitsubishi Electric's memory chips in exchange for access to the technology that goes into designing the chip, and the right to sell the semiconductor.

KEEP SEPARATE CHECKING ACCOUNTS

Alliances—different from simply buying a stake in another company—can get complicated fast, and the successful ventures tend to carefully follow a couple of rules of thumb: The partners know exactly what the common objective is, and they make contingency plans in case the marriage doesn't work out. "It's a bit like prenuptial agreements," says Martyn Roetter, a director of the consulting firm Arthur D. Little. "You don't want to think about divorce in the throes of love. But the name of the game in alliances is to be specific and realistic about what all the partners are trying to get out of it."

Compared with their Asian partners and rivals, U.S. companies sometimes appear naive in this regard. They fail to understand that collaboration is another form of competition. "In an alliance you have to learn skills of the partner, rather than just see it as a way to get a product to sell while avoiding a big investment," says C.K. Prahalad, professor of business at the University of Michigan and an expert on global alliances.

Toyota Motor Corp., for example, has certainly benefited from its five years of joint venture with General Motors Corp. in operating an auto plant in Fremont, Calif. But did GM?

Kunio Shimazu, a senior Toyota executive and one of the planners of the California venture, called New United Motor Manufacturing Inc., can tick off the objectives Toyota achieved: "We learned about U.S. supply and transportation. And we got the confidence to manage U.S. workers." And all that knowledge, he says, was quickly transferred to Georgetown, Ky., where Toyota opened a plant of its own in 1988.

General Motors, on the other hand, had a product, the Chevrolet Nova, which the plant produced. But some of the GM managers assigned to the joint venture complain that their new knowledge was never put to good use inside GM. They say they should have been kept together as a team to educate GM's engineers and workers about the Japanese system. Instead, they were dispersed—to Canada, to Europe, to the truck division, to GM's Electronic Systems subsidiary.

"In GM, a one-man crusade doesn't get you anywhere, unless you want to be a sacrificial lamb," says Stephen Bera, who left the joint venture to become a consultant for Arthur Young & Co. "Did Toyota learn more than General Motors? Absolutely."

Says a GM spokesman: "Who learned more, Toyota or GM? I don't know. I learned a lot, we experienced the Toyota system and we adapted a lot." He admits that some of the joint venture's "graduates" were clustered together as a team at GM, and others, although dispersed, nonetheless transferred useful skills form the venture.

Part of Japan's advantage is that it often does view the ventures as largely another form of competition. You shake hands with your right hand, while making a fist with your left. You learn everything you can from your Western partner while keeping as many of your own secrets to yourself. Then you strike out on your own, sometimes in the very market once controlled by your partner. The American European company has historically gone into deals as teacher rather than student.

YANKS, TO THE BLACKBOARD

"There's a lot of cultural arrogance in American and European firms—the not-invented-here syndrome," says Prof. Prahalad. "But the value in these partnerships is learning what the other guy knows. That is why Japanese and Korean companies seem to get most of the benefits."

The good news here is that American and European attitudes are changing. Probably nowhere has this sea change been more profound than in the semiconductor industry. Ten years ago, the leading edge of the industry was firmly in the U.S. All throughout the 1980s, however, that leadership has moved toward Japan, especially in state-of-the-art memory chips.

When the West German electronics giant Siemens tried to get back into the semiconductor business a few years ago, it played student to Toshiba, because it had little choice. "We couldn't afford the 'not-invented-here' syndrome," says Karl Zaininger, president of Siemens's U.S. research and development operation. He points out that Siemens learned to produce the one-megabit memory chip with Toshiba, then produced the next generation on its own. And that gave Siemens the credibility to join up with IBM on even more advanced chip projects. For its part, Toshiba says it got an improved sales network in Europe and a second source for its chips.

While Americans may lack experience in learning from Asian rivals, they have plenty of experience in European markets. More experience than Japanese companies, certainly. IBM, Hewlett-Packard, Digital Equipment, Ford and others have been in Europe for decades. Perhaps more important, the U.S. firms have tended to regard Europe as a whole, more so than even some indigenous companies. That philosophy will be a big plus come the 1992 integration.

HAPPY TOGETHER

Take, for instance, General Electric's jet engine partnership with Snecma, a French government-controlled aerospace concern. It was formed in 1974, mostly as a way for GE to penetrate the market for engines for the Airbus that, until then, had been dominated by Airbus Industrie, the highly politicized and protected European aircraft consortium. What came out of the GE-French partnership was the most successful commercial-jet engine in history, a midsized engine for the Airbus 320, the Boeing 737 and other planes. Last year alone, the joint venture landed orders or commitments for engines valued at more than $11 billion.

Throughout the 1970s and 1980s, the GE venture steadily took business away from its rivals, principally United Technologies' Pratt & Whitney unit. In so doing, GE had to overcome cultural, linguistic, logistical and foreign-exchange problems that remain vexing, says Brian Rowe, senior vice president in charge of GE's engine group. The French side, for example, likes to bring in senior executives from outside the industry, such as from the air force, who then have to spend valuable time getting up to speed. GE is more inclined to bring in experienced GE executives. Then there is the matter of problem solving. "The French want more data," Mr. Rowe says, "the Americans are more intuitive."

Yet the venture works, observers say, because it is structured well. Investment and revenue are split 50-50. Both GE and Snecma delegate broad responsibility to their senior engine executives. GE handles system design and much of the highest-tech work, while the French company works on fans, boosters, low-pressure turbines and the like. Until recently, GE handled most of the marketing, but Snecma is taking a bigger role in that, since the number of customers has steadily expanded to 125 from six.

IRRECONCILABLE DIFFERENCES

No amount of cross-cultural harmony can fix a venture with deep conceptual flaws, though. One of the most talked up alliances of the 1980s, the partnership between AT&T and Ing. C. Olivetti & Co., the Italian office equipment maker, failed because it was simply a bad idea—at least according to Carlo De Benedetti, chairman of Olivetti.

The deal called for AT&T to sell Olivetti's personal computers in the U.S. In return, Olivetti would sell AT&T's computers and telephone-switching machines in Europe. But the logic of the deal was based on the assumption that the two industries—computers and telecommunications—were converging. To this day, there is debate whether a convergence is actually happening. Olivetti is now convinced it isn't.

"What's the result today of putting together computers and telecommunications? A total failure, which everybody now realized," says Mr. De Benedetti. "It wasn't the fault of AT&T or Olivetti. The idea wasn't right."

That is easy to say in hindsight. But it wasn't so clear when the deal started unraveling a couple of years ago. Tensions between the two companies were high. Olivetti thought AT&T wasn't marketing Olivetti computers hard enough in the U.S. AT&T complained that Olivetti wasn't selling enough of AT&T's computers and telecommunications products in Europe.

One top AT&T executive believes that most of the problems in the venture stemmed from cultural differences. "I don't think we or Olivetti spent enough time understanding behavior patterns," says Robert Kavner, AT&T group executive. "We knew the culture was different but we never really penetrated. We would get angry, and they would get upset."

Mr. Kavner says AT&T's attempts to fix the problems, such as delays in deliveries, were transmitted in curt memos that offended Olivetti officials. "They would get an attitude, 'Who are you to tell us what to do,' " he says. Or the Olivetti side would explain its own problems, Mr. Kavner says, and AT&T managers would simply respond, "Don't tell me about your problems. Solve them."

What the AT&T executives did develop, however, was a close working relationship with some Olivetti executives, friendships that Mr. Kavner says continue to this day. "The irony is," he says, "we probably have the foundation in place today" for a successful AT&T-Olivetti joint venture.

Not to say that Olivetti and AT&T don't still disagree. Ask them about the prospects for the Mitsubishi-Daimler alliance, and you get a reminder not only of the challenges of putting a venture together, but of how partners can see the world in very different—and potentially divisive—ways.

"I don't think global alliances like this [Mitsubishi-Daimler] will be a major factor in the future," contends the chastened Mr. De Benedetti of Olivetti. "I'm incapable of seeing the practical, common, immediate results of these sort of mythical alliances."

Notes Mr. Kavner of AT&T: "I think it could be wonderfully successful—if people go to work on the specifics. But people won't get suntans putting this together. It's hard work."

Each party to these ventures contributes capital, equity, or assets. Ownership of the joint venture need not be a 50–50 arrangement and, indeed, it ranges according to the proportionate amounts contributed by each party to the enterprise. Some countries stipulate the relative amount of ownership allowable to foreign firms in joint ventures. In India, for example, strict limits are placed on the level of ownership foreign firms can have in joint ventures. These limits run against the philosophies of some corporations. IBM, for example, will not operate as a minority shareholder in foreign markets, and consequently does not operate in India.

In some countries these strictures upon joint ownership are slowly changing. PepsiCo announced in September 1988 that it had gained approval from the government of India to enter into a joint venture with the Indian companies Tata Industries and Punjab Agro-Industries. The contract of $15.4 million signals a change in government policy from 1978 when Coca-Cola exited India when faced with Indian laws requiring local majority ownership and product formula disclosures.[2]

ADVANTAGES OF JOINT VENTURES
Joint ventures provide many advantages for both local and international participants. By entering a local market with a local partner, the MNE finds an opportunity to increase its growth and access to new markets while avoiding excessive tariffs and taxes associated with the entry of products. At the same time, joining forces with local businesses often neutralizes local existing and potential competition and protects the firm against the risk of expropriation because local nationals have a stake in the success of the operations of the firm. It is also frequently easier to raise capital in local markets when host-country nationals are involved in the operation. In some cases, host governments provide tax benefits as incentives to increase the participation of foreign firms in joint enterprises with local businesspersons.

DISADVANTAGES OF JOINT VENTURES
The involvement of local ownership can also lead to major disadvantages for overseas partners in joint ventures. Some of the problems that can be experienced by the MNE partners are limits on profit repatriation to the parent office; successful operations becoming an inviting target for nationalization or expropriation by the host government; and problems of control and decision-making. For example, different partners might have different objectives for the joint ventures. An MNE might have a goal of achieving profitability on a shorter timetable than its local partner, who might be more concerned about long-term profitability and maintaining local employment levels. It is a key

[2] *Washington Post*, September 20, 1988, page E1.

necessity, therefore, that firms establish guidelines regarding the objectives, control, and decision-making structures of joint ventures before entering into agreements.

Joint ventures tend to be relatively lower risk operations because the risks are shared by individual partners. Nevertheless, not having full control of the operation remains a predominant problem for the overseas participants in these ventures. A firm can achieve full control over operations, decision-making, and profits only when it establishes its own wholly owned subsidiary on foreign soil.

Wholly Owned Subsidiaries

By establishing its own foreign arm, a firm retains total control over marketing, pricing, and production decisions and maintains greater security over its technological assets. In return, it is entitled to 100 percent of the profits generated by the enterprise. Although it faces no problems with minority shareholders, the firm bears the entire risk involved in operating the facility. These risks are the same as those customarily encountered in domestic operations, but with an additional layer of special risks associated with international operations, such as expropriation, limits on profits being repatriated, and local operating laws and regulations, including the requirement to employ local labor and management personnel. In these cases, the MNCs do not have the benefit of local shareholders to run interference for them with local governments.

In establishing a subsidiary, a firm must choose either of two routes—acquire an ongoing operation or start from scratch and build its own plant. Buying a firm has the advantage of avoiding start-up costs of capital and a time lag. It is a faster process that is often easier to capitalize at local levels and generally cheaper than building. Buying also has the advantages of not adding to a country's existing capacity levels and of improving good will with host-country nationals.

A company may decide to build a new plant if no suitable facilities exist for acquisition or if it has special requirements for design or equipment. Although building a plant may avoid acquiring the problems of an existing physical plant, the firm may face difficulties in obtaining adequate financing from local capital markets and may generate ill-will among local citizenry.[3]

Globalized Operations

Some theorists believe that consumers around the world are becoming increasingly alike in their goals and requirements for products and product attributes.[4] As a result, the world is moving toward becoming a global market in which products would be standardized across all cultures, which would enable corporations to manufacture and sell low-cost reliable products around the world. Such firms would be characterized by globalized operations, as distinct from multinational operations. A firm that has globalized operations would be able to take advantage of business opportunities occurring anywhere in the world and would not be constrained to specific sectors. Indeed, some firms have been able to achieve substantial globalization of operations as their products cross national borders, without being adapted to individual country preferences. Prime examples include Levi-Strauss & Company, PepsiCo, and Coca-Cola and several other companies ranging from consumer goods to fast food.

Portfolio Investments

Portfolio investments do not require the physical presence of a firm's personnel or products on foreign shores. These investments can be made in the form of marketable securities in foreign markets, such as notes, bonds, commercial paper, certificates of deposit, and noncontrolling shares of stock. They can also be investments in foreign bank accounts or as foreign loans. Investors make decisions to acquire securities or invest money abroad for several reasons, primarily to diversify

---

[3] Kitching 1974.

[4] Levitt 1983.

their portfolios among markets and locations, to achieve higher rates of return, to avoid political risks by taking their investments out of the country, or to speculate in foreign exchange markets.

Portfolio investments can either be made by individuals or through special investment funds. These investment funds pool local resources for investment in overseas stock and financial markets. Some governments, such as South Korea, Brazil, India, and Taiwan allow foreign investors to access their stock markets only through these funds.[5] Most developed countries allow free access to their stock markets to overseas investors. Some developing countries that also allow free access are Malaysia, Kenya, the Philippines, and Jordan.[6]

There are several factors that determine the degree to which a particular country will be able to attract portfolio investments. Political stability and economic growth are the most basic factors. The size, liquidity, and stability of stock markets, the level of government taxes, and the nature of government regulation are also important determinants. The degree of restrictions on repatriation of income and capital invested are other major variables that affect the attractiveness of a country to overseas portfolio investors. Most of international portfolio investment is concentrated in the industrialized countries, and the United States, Japan, France, the United Kingdom, Switzerland, the Netherlands, and Canada receive substantial amounts of portfolio investments in their markets. Some emerging stock markets, such as Malaysia, South Korea, Taiwan, Greece, and Portugal, also have been able to attract significant amounts of foreign portfolio investment.

Recent Trade Patterns and Changes in Global Trade

As the world has become more and more industrialized and as markets have become global entities, trade has increased proportionately and grown tremendously both in volume and dollar terms. Concomitantly, patterns in trade have also changed, as new nations enter the world trading arena. In 1948 world trade totaled $51.4 billion. This figure rose to $331.0 billion in 1970 and reached $2.627 trillion in 1986.[7]

Most of the world's trade is carried out between the industrialized countries. This group of countries, comprising Western Europe, North America, and Japan, currently accounts for 77 percent of exports sent to other countries and receives 77.2 percent of all imports.[8] In comparison, developing countries account for only 23 percent of exports and take 22.8 percent of imports. These figures include the volumes attributed to OPEC members, which account for 6.2 percent of world exports and 5.97 percent of imports. OPEC's participation in world trade declined in the second half of the 1980s because prices and demand for oil have fallen since the early 1970s. OPEC nevertheless retains a major proportion of the share of developing countries in world trade. Without the contribution of OPEC, the share of the remaining developing countries in world trade is only 16.8 percent.

This pattern of trade is changing, however, as the fortunes of nations change in different trading regions. While high-income developed countries continue to hold the lion's share of world trade, greater portions of activity are being taken over by new entrants into the world market. The most notable, of course, is Japan, which has completely reversed its fortunes, prospects, and future since its reconstruction and growth after World War II. In 1950 Japan had merchandise exports of $820 million and imports of $974 million; by 1970 this level had risen to exports of $19.318 billion and imports of $8.881 billion. By 1988 Japan was exporting $264.772 billion worth of products in world markets and importing products and commodities valued at $183.252 billion.[9] (Table 2–1 lists the leading exporters of the world in 1988.)

[5] International Finance Corporation 1988.
[6] Ibid.
[7] World Bank 1990.
[8] Ibid.
[9] Ibid.

TABLE 2–1
World's Leading Exporters (1988)

Countries		Exports (billions of U.S. dollars)
1.	West Germany	322.555
2.	United States	315.313
3.	Japan	264.772
4.	France	161.702
5.	United Kingdom	145.076
6.	Italy	128.534
7.	Canada	111.364
8.	Netherlands	103.206
9.	Belgium-Luxembourg	88.953
10.	Hong Kong	63.161
11.	South Korea	60.696
12.	Taiwan	60.382
13.	Singapore	39.205
14.	Brazil	33.689
15.	Saudi Arabia	26.475[a]

SOURCE: International Monetary Fund, *International Financial Statistics*, 1988
[a] 1987 data

Japan is being joined by other countries that are nipping at the heels of the wealthy, industrialized nations and rapidly increasing their levels of industrialization, production, and exports. They include the so-called "four tigers" or newly industrialized countries (NICs)—South Korea, Taiwan, Singapore, and Hong Kong. Trade activity by these nations is slowly moving the focus of international trade patterns away from traditional routes of north-north activity between developed countries, to those of increased trade between north and south, that is between developed and developing nations. Similarly, the growth in trade by less-developed countries is increasing, as economic development and increases in standards of living provide citizens of those nations with higher incomes and surplus resources to spend on goods other than basic necessities.

These trends in the trade patterns of the twentieth century indicate a reduction of U.S. and European dominance in the world trade arena. On the other hand, the Asian and Middle Eastern countries are increasing their participation in world trade, because of their rapid industrialization and the importance of petroleum and petroleum products. U.S. trade with these countries has also been increasing significantly, marking a departure from its traditional trading pattern that relied to a very large extent on trade with European trading partners. Furthermore, changes in the international political climate, especially the thawing of relations with centrally-planned-economy countries, as they move toward market economies, has led to marked increases of U.S. trade with the Soviet Union and the People's Republic of China. Rapid and far-reaching technological developments have also affected trade patterns because raw material monopolies have been shattered by hi-tech substitutes, such as synthetic products. Countries that were major exporters of such raw materials have had to look for other products to export, and export market shares have shifted dramatically in these commodities, for example, rubber and metals.

Product Groups

In world trade the major product categories of goods are exports of manufactured goods, machinery, and fuels, which account for three-quarters of all world commodity trade. The remaining one-quarter of commodity types are crude commodities, agricultural products, and chemicals. Until 1972 manufactured goods continued to increase in relative importance in world trade. After that, they began to decline in importance because of the increase in oil prices and the worldwide recession that followed. The developed countries account for the largest proportion of goods traded in world markets. In 1988, among the industrialized countries, the United States provided 12 percent of world exports and received 16.8 percent of world imports. Canada provided 4.2 percent and took 4.1 percent of the goods, while Japan provided 10.1 percent and took 6.7 percent. West Germany emerged as the world's leading exporter and provided 12.3 percent of commodities traded while taking 9.1 percent.

Lesser-developed countries have increased their relative shares of world trade. Non-middle Eastern Asian countries increased their exports from 7.1 percent in 1980 to 9.3 percent in 1987, as compared to an overall decline in total Middle East exports from 10 percent in 1980 to 3.94 percent in 1987. The regions of Africa and Central and South America provided 2.3 percent and 4.2 percent, respectively, of world commodity exports in 1986. The USSR has increased its share since 1980 from 3.8 percent of exports to 4.6 percent in 1986 and increased its imports from 3.1 percent to 4.2 percent in the same period.[10]

Patterns of Direct Investment

As trading patterns in merchandise continue to change, so do the patterns of countries investing in resources abroad. Many believe that direct investment activity is a natural adjunct to trading activities in different locations—that is, investment funds follow trade activity. Direct investment can be measured according to the source country of funds or ownership. Generally, foreign direct investment of capital is differentiated from portfolio investments according to levels of managerial involvement and control by owners. Some countries distinguish effective control according to a level of percentage ownership. The United States, for example, uses a level of 10 percent as a criteria.

World foreign direct investment levels have been estimated at $800 billion by the end of 1989.[11] These figures are misleading, however, because they reflect the book value of the investments, which is the value at which they were acquired and are historical figures that do not account for appreciation in value over time or for inflation. Moreover, the data does not include the value of investments in some centrally planned economies, such as the USSR and the former Soviet bloc nations of Eastern Europe, because no figures are available.

[10] United Nations 1986.

[11] U.S. Department of Commerce 1989.

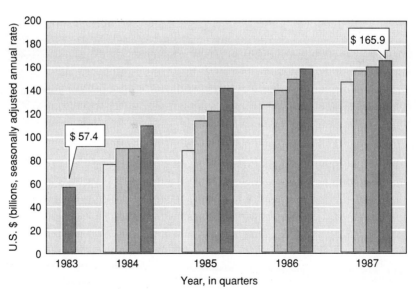

FIGURE 2–1   Net Foreign Investments in the United States, 1983–1987.
SOURCE: U.S. Department of Commerce

According to recent studies, the bulk of world direct investment is within the industrialized countries of the world. The United States (see Figure 2–1) and United Kingdom alone account for about 40 percent of the world total foreign direct investment. Fewer than twenty countries hold more than 95 percent of direct overseas investments. Foreign direct investments are generally made according to two patterns—geographically between countries that are in close proximity to each other, and along such traditional lines as those based on the strength of historical or political alliances or those made by countries in their former colonies.

Investments, in general, are made by very large firms and have seen the highest growth in the areas of manufacturing, petroleum, and industries that require high levels of capital assets. The investments are made primarily in industrial countries with the lowest level of risk and the largest possible markets.

Government Involvement in Trade Restrictions and Incentives

All governments attempt to restrict or support international trade or transfers of resources. This intervention can take the form of controlling the flow of trade and transfer of goods, controlling the transfer of capital flows, or controlling the movement of personnel and technology. Rationales for intervention vary but fall into several patterns, all of which are based on the notion that the governmental actions will promote the best interests of the nation.

Governments may be motivated by economic goals, such as increasing revenues or the supply of hard currency in the country. They also may have economic or monetary considerations in equalizing balances of trade or keeping inflation to a minimum. They may cite country objectives, such as maintaining self-sufficiency, economic independence, and national security. There may be specific concerns in the country regarding the welfare of the populace, such as health and safety considerations or full employment goals. Political objectives also play a major role in establishing trade policy by governments.

Protectionism

Protectionism refers to government intervention in trade markets to protect specific industries in its economy. Impetus for protecting industries comes from special-interest groups within different sectors of the economy who plead their case for protecting domestic capacity and production facilities. Many believe that calls for protectionism should be interpreted as a need for the country to make structural changes in its industrial base, in order to increase its competitiveness in foreign markets, rather than have government intervention hold up inefficient industries.

One rationale promulgated for protecting industry is to ensure full employment. This argument holds that the substitution of imports for domestic products causes jobs to be lost at home and that protecting industries is necessary for a strong domestic employment base.

A second rationale is that of protecting infant industries, which is especially true in less-developed and developing countries. The infant-industry justification holds that newly established industries cannot compete effectively at first against established giants from industrialized nations. Consequently, the industry is protected (theoretically) until such time as it can grow to achieve economies of scale and operational efficiencies matching those of its major competitors. Under this scenario, difficulties occur when the time comes to withdraw such protection, which by then has become institutionalized and is vociferously defended by industry participants.

A third rationale for protecting specific industries is that the industrialization objectives of a country justify a promotion of specific sectors of the economy in order to diversify the economic structure. Thus, protection and incentives are given to those industries that are expected to grow quickly, bring in investment dollars, and yield higher marginal returns. For this reason, many developing countries attempt to promote the growth of industries that provide high value–added materials and emphasize the use of agricultural or locally available primary raw materials.

The ultimate rationale for protectionism is more accurately based in emotionalism than in sound economic arguments, and its cost is high. Protectionism leads to higher prices for consumers for imported products and components. It may lead to retaliation by importing countries, which may

reduce the home country's exports abroad and employment in local markets. Protectionism also may increase opportunity costs by allocating the resources of a country inappropriately and at the expense of other sectors of the industrial base of economy.

The methods of governmental intervention in markets takes several different forms (see Perspective 2–4). The primary and most direct method is through the application of tariffs to exports or imports. A less direct method is the application of nontariff barriers.

PERSPECTIVE 2–4   The Peril of Protectionism: Why 'Managed Trade' Is a Sham

Few industries receive more protection from imports than textiles and apparel. Quotas limit imports. Tariffs are still high, averaging about 22 percent on apparel. In 1986, this protection raised clothing expenses for a typical American family about $240. For every extra job saved in the United States, consumers pay about $50,000. So what do these industries want? Yes: more protection.

Congress is complying, and it's hard to say anything kind about the result. Legislation passed by both the House and Senate would limit growth of textile and apparel imports to a mere 1 percent annually. Consumer clothing costs would rise further. Poor families would be hurt most, because they spend a larger share of their income on clothes. All this legislation shows is that trade protection is addictive.

Guiding the legislation through the Senate is Ernest Hollings of South Carolina. Back in 1960, when Hollings was his state's governor, he success-

fully urged presidential candidate John Kennedy to support action to restrict textile imports. In 1961, the Kennedy administration began negotiating quotas on cotton products. Since then, restrictions have been progressively toughened and extended to more products.

The time has long passed when protection might be justified as a way of saving jobs. Consider South Carolina. Its unemployment rate (4.7 percent in July) is below the national average. True, textile employment dropped about 30,000 (22 percent) between 1980 and 1987. But the state's total employment jumped 206,000 in the same period. Textile jobs now account for only one in 10 of nonfarm jobs; in 1950, the share was one in three. The decline mostly reflects the growth of other jobs.

Listening to Hollings' rhetoric, you'd think that imports had obliterated the textile and apparel industries. Not so. Imports are highest in apparel, where they had 34 percent of domestic consump-

SOURCE: Robert J. Samuelson: *Washington Post*, September 21, 1988.

tion in 1987. In textiles—the yarns and fabrics used for clothes, curtains and other products—import penetration was much lower. It was 5 percent for yarns and 14 percent for the industrial and household textiles that go into sheets and towels.

It's important to distinguish between the textile and apparel industries. Textiles is highly automated, and the drop in its work force (down 123,000 since 1980 to 725,000) mostly reflects the adoption of faster, more efficient machinery. Production has been rising slowly. By contrast, apparel has always been labor intensive. The image of women at sewing machines is not far from the truth. Lots of workers are always losing their jobs, because small companies constantly go in and out of busines. In 1982, 45 percent of apparel establishments had fewer than 20 workers.

The wonder is that Congress is considering this dreary legislation at all. It flagrantly violates the United States' foreign trade obligations and would surely provoke retaliation by other countries against U.S. exports. Any gains made by U.S. textile and apparel workers would probably be offset by losses in other industries. The timing is particularly bad, because U.S. exports are expanding rapidly. It makes no sense to give countries a pretext to impose their own limits.

For years, protectionists have sought to make their cause respectable. "Managed trade" is one idea they've tried to peddle. "Free trade" may be economically efficient, the argument goes, but it's socially undesirable. Import surges cause too much unemployment too quickly. It's better to negotiate import restrictions. Everyone ultimately benefits. Exporting countries can predict their markets. Industries in importing countries can adapt to new competition or contract gradually.

It sounds reasonable. But in practice, "managed trade" is a sham. Textiles and apparel are no exception. Once industries get protection, they simply want more. The United States has had quotas on sugar imports since 1934. Imports have been cut so severely in the 1980s that they're now a

third of what they were in 1982. U.S. sugar prices are about double the world level.

Or take steel. In 1983, the Reagan administration negotiated import quotas on steel that expire in 1989. Because the U.S. industry has improved its competitiveness, any need for protection has diminished. Between 1982 and 1987, the cost of producing a ton of steel dropped from about $700 to $480. Still, the industry wants the quotas renewed and tightened. Protection is being used to raise prices. The victims are major steel users, such as Deer & Co., which makes tractors and farm equipment.

This isn't "managed" trade; it's permanent protection. The point of trade is to raise living standards of all countries. Inevitably, that means specialization. Countries' export industries are those where relative efficiency is highest. Of course, there's some disruption. All economic changes—from new technologies, for example—risk disruption. But are Americans better off because they export computers and import clothes and shoes? The answer is yes.

Sen. Hollings and other supporters of the textile bill seem oblivious to this logic. The logic works especially well in clothing. Developing countries with large numbers of low-skilled workers can make clothes inexpensively. Export earnings then enable them to buy more advanced consumer products and machinery from developed countries. What Hollings proposes is a policy to depress the living standards of Americans and the Third World.

But why should he care? The great beneficiaries of the drive for more trade restrictions are political middlemen. These are legislators, lawyers, lobbyists, publicists and consultants. The more power is centralized in Washington, the more important they become. So Hollings' policy is as self-interested as it is undesirable. President Reagan has promised to veto the textile bill. It doesn't appear that Hollings and friends have enough votes to override the veto. Good: the sooner this legislation is killed, the better.

Tariffs

Tariffs or duties are a basic method of intervention and may be used either to protect industries by raising the price of imports, to bring import prices even with domestic prices, or to generate revenues. Tariffs may be placed on goods leaving the country as export duties or on goods entering the country as import duties. They are the most typical controls on imports. Tariffs are assessed in three different ways:

1. Ad valorem duties are assessed on the value of the goods and are levied as a percentage of that value.
2. Specific duties are assessed according to a physical unit of measurement, such as on a per ton, per bushel, or per meter rate, and are stipulated at a specific monetary value.
3. Compound tariffs are a combination of ad valorem and specific duties.

DETERMINING TARIFFS

Tariffs have an advantage as a tool for government intervention in international markets because they can be varied and applied on a selective basis according to commodity or country of origin. Some countries can be assessed higher duties on their imports than others. These duties are prescribed according to tariff schedules. Single-column schedules are those in which the duties on products and commodities are the same for everyone. Multicolumn schedules list tariffs rates for different products and different countries accorded to trade agreements between the two countries.

Some countries that are treated separately are those who have most-favored-nation (MFN) status accorded to them. These countries have entered into agreements under which all the signatories are accorded the same preferential tariff status. Countries enter into these agreements to facilitate entry of their own exports and for political and other economic reasons. There are many groups of trading partners in the world, the largest and most important of which is the General Agreement on Tariffs and Trade (GATT), which was

established soon after World War II with an original membership of nineteen countries.

General Agreement on Tariffs and Trade

The purpose of GATT is to establish an umbrella under which its signatory members can meet to establish reciprocal reductions in tariffs and the liberalization of trade in a mutual and nondiscriminatory manner. A major objective of the body is to extend tariff accords and most-favored-nation status to all members. Under GATT, methods and rules of trade liberalization are established with provisions for monitoring trade activity, enforcement, and the settling of disputes. GATT rules allow for certain exceptions to reduce trade barriers, such as allowing countries to continue to provide support for domestic agriculture and for developing countries to protect infant industries.

Reductions in trade barriers are achieved through the meeting of the signatories in negotiating sessions, or trade rounds. These meetings are held periodically to discuss the further lowering of barriers to trade. In recent rounds, GATT members have attempted to deal with nontariff problems and other current issues, such as trade in agriculture and services, technology transfer, and nonmonetary barriers put up by countries to discourage free trade. (For a more detailed discussion of GATT, see Chapter 6.)

Regional Trade Groups

Trade groups organized along regional or political lines are less pervasive and influential. Two major regional trading groups are the European Economic Community (EEC), composed of twelve European countries, and the Latin American Free Trade Area (LAFTA), which has eleven trading partners.

Trade groups are also organized according to specific commodity types and enter into agreements to monitor and/or control the supply of

The Nature of International Business 51

those commodities. Ten such basic commodities have been identified by the United Nations—coffee, cocoa, tea, sugar, cotton, rubber, jute, sisal, copper, and tin. Some of these commodities are traded on open and free markets and find that their prices fluctuate to a great degree. Sales of other commodities, such as sugar, rubber, tin, cocoa, and coffee, come under the aegis of international commodity agreements that promote use of import and export quotas and a system of buffer stocks.

Generally, under these agreements prices are allowed to move up and down within a certain range, but if the price moves above or below that range, an outside collective agency is authorized to buy or sell the commodity to support its price. Similarly, a commodity agreement may provide for quotas on exports from individual supply countries to limit supplies of the commodities on world markets, thus shoring up prices.

Cartels

Another form of a commodity agreement group is the cartel, in which a group of commodity-producing countries join forces to bargain as a single entity in world markets. A cartel can be formed only when there is a relatively small group of producers who hold an oligopoly position, that is, they control the bulk of the commodity supply. The most notable cartel in recent years has been the Organization of Petroleum Exporting Countries (OPEC), which is composed primarily of Middle East countries, such as Saudi Arabia, Qatar, Iraq, Libya, Algeria, Kuwait, the United Arab Emirates, and Iran, as well as other oil-producing countries in the world, such as Venezuela, Ecuador, Nigeria, and Gabon.

In the early 1970s, OPEC was able to raise the price of crude oil fourfold, from $3.64 per barrel to $11.65 per barrel, within a single year. It was able to do so because it had a great deal of leverage in the world marketplace—its members controlled more than half of the world production of oil in 1973. World demand for oil was very high and the top oil-consuming countries were not able to

meet the demand with domestic supplies.[12] There were few suitable energy substitutes being utilized around the world. The cartel was also successful because its members adhered to their production and pricing agreements.

Frequently, cartels fail because members violate their agreements by dropping prices or raising production and forcing the other members back into a competitive position. Although this did not occur with OPEC, the cartel's hold on world markets began to slip in the mid-1970s as a worldwide recession, conservation, and the use of energy substitutes reduced the demand for oil. In addition, non-OPEC producers increased their production to take advantage of price escalations in world markets. Consequently, OPEC's grip on the world crude oil market loosened decidedly by the mid-1980s.

Nontariff Barriers to Merchandise Trade

Non tariff barriers have become a controversial topic in trade activity over the past decade. They are a matter of concern because they are not traditional methods of discouraging imports through the application of duties. Instead, they work to slow the flow of goods into a country by increasing the physical and administrative difficulties involved in importing.

Nontariff barriers can take a number of forms that provide effective restraints on trade.

Government discrimination against foreign suppliers in its bidding procedures. The Japanese government announced international competitive bidding for the supply and installation of electronic equipment (such as air traffic control systems) at the new airport at Osaka, but it stipulated that all bidders must have at least five years experience of work done in Japan. The catch was that foreign suppliers were not

[12] Daniels, John and Lee Radebaugh, 1972. "The Middle East Squeeze on Oil Grants." *Business Week* (July 29): 56.

permitted to work in Japan, and there was no way they could have accumulated the required five years experience. As a result, despite opening up bidding to foreign suppliers, the Japanese government effectively excluded them.

- Highly involved and rigorous customs and country-entry procedures. France was recently brought to task by GATT because of its treatment of Japanese videocassette recorders (VCRs), which were only allowed to enter the country through one port of entry with very limited inspection resources. This bottleneck was effective in slowing the flood of Japanese VCRs to France to a trickle.
- Excessively severe inspection and standards requirements that could involve jettisoning an entire shipment of a product even if only one sample has failed to meet the standard. Another way of erecting this type of nontariff barrier is to require that foreign goods be tested for safety in a country's own laboratories and taking great amounts of time to certify that the goods are safe for domestic consumption.
- Stipulations that goods are required to contain a certain percentage of domestic content material.
- Some countries have restrictions on services, such as those that prohibit transportation carriers from serving specific destinations or those that only allow advertising featuring models of that country's nationality.

Quotas

The most widely used method of restricting quantity, volume, or value-based imports is the imposition of quotas upon imports into a country. These quotas may be unilateral according to commodity and stipulate that only a certain aggregate amount of the import from any source may enter a country. Alternatively, they can be selective on a country or regional basis. A type of quota is an embargo, which prohibits all trade between countries. Another type, encountered only in recent

trade history, is the voluntary entry restriction, in which foreign countries agree to restrict their exports to a country, but are actually forced into compliance, through the use of direct or subtle political pressure by major trading partners.

While the imposition of quotas may impede the flow of imports into a country, it does little to help that country find a level of readjustment, that is, it does nothing in the way of leading to lowered domestic prices. It often leads to higher import prices, as in the case of Japanese automobiles in the United States. The restriction of Japanese cars in U.S. markets merely led to increased prices for those autos coming into the country because demand continued to be high and supply was limited. Since then, the nature of Japanese automobiles entering the United States has changed as well, moving from the durable low-end automobiles to the higher value-added luxury automobiles.

Nontariff Price Barriers

Nontariff and competitive barriers can also be implemented as adjustments in prices. For example, some countries use subsidies to enhance the competitiveness of their exports in international markets. Some subsidized services, such as export promotion, are permissible according to trade conventions. Others, such as special tax incentives or government provisions of fundamental research, are being contested by trading nations as being against free trade.

The imposition of quotas also causes serious administrative problems for the authorities of both the importing and exporting countries. Once quotas are imposed, the amount of goods to be sent from the exporting country is not determined by market demand but by an arbitrary ceiling. The quantity of goods allowed to be exported under the quota ceilings are often much lower than the normal export levels, which implies that all exporters of the affected country cannot export at their previous levels. The new levels have to be determined by the authorities, which for large and spread-out export industries is an expensive and cumbersome process. The problems arise for the importing country because the imported quantities under the quota rules are not adequate to meet market demand, and the government has to take over the role of the market in allocating the available goods imported under quota rules. Apart from the expense and delays of the administrative process that is required to accomplish nonmarket distribution of imported goods, there is also the danger of creating inequities, because it is often difficult to verify genuine needs and claims.

Some countries raise the effective costs of exporting by assessing special fees for importing, requiring customs deposits, or establishing minimum sales prices in foreign markets, thereby making it less profitable for exporters to send goods to their markets. Similarly, the manipulation of exchange rates can affect the position of a country's goods in overseas markets because undervaluing one's currency exchange rate will make that country's goods more competitive abroad.

Another type of nontariff price barrier is erected by valuing imports at customs under the ad valorem method of assessing tariffs. Countries can vary their valuation criteria and value goods at their own country's retail prices rather than at the wholesale/invoice prices being paid by the importer.

In determining the appropriate pricing levels for tariffs in the event of disputes, one would first use the invoice price, then the price of identical goods, then similar goods. A particular problem arises when goods are entering a market-based economy from a centrally planned or nonmarket economy where there is no established pricing structure or valuation procedure. A landmark case in this area was the Polish Golf Cart Case, in which U.S. customs authorities alleged that Polish manufacturers purposely underpriced their golf carts to compete in U.S. markets. A similar case occurred when nonmarket economies tried to bring chemical fertilizers into the United States at below market prices, which was achieved by undervaluing the costs of crucial inputs such as natural gas.

Government Restriction of Exports

In addition to controlling or taxing national imports, governments often have laws and regulations that limit certain types of exports generally or to specific countries. Governments apply these limits to maintain domestic supply and price levels of goods, to keep world prices high, or to meet national defense, political, or environmental goals. In the United States, under the Export Administration Act of 1969 and its amendments of 1979, U.S. export licenses can be limited because of foreign policy objectives, for the protection of the economy from a drain of limited or scarce resources, or for military use by the recipient nations. Licenses are required for the export of items on the U.S. controlled commodity list and for the export of any product to communist countries. The administration of these licenses is overseen by the U.S. Department of Commerce in tandem with the departments of State and Defense.

Summary

International business requires the same basic functional and operational activities as domestic business activities. As international business crosses borders, however, it encounters different economies, cultures, legal systems, governments, and languages, which must be integrated into business policies and practices. Entry into international business varies along a continuum, beginning with the simplest form, exporting, through other entry methods, which include, licensing, franchising, contract manufacturing, direct investment, joint ventures, wholly owned subsidiaries, globalized operations, and portfolio investments.

Recent changes in global trade patterns reveal a reduction in the dominance of the United States and Europe, while Asian (especially Japan and the four tigers) and Middle East countries are increasing their levels of output. Direct investment, 40 percent of which is held by the United States and the United Kingdom, is generally located in the industrialized countries, where risks are lowest and potential returns are high.

The governments of host countries play an important role in either restricting or supporting international trade. Often, international trade policies are determined to achieve economic or monetary goals, maintain national security, improve health, safety and employment levels, or support specific political objectives. Protectionism, tariffs, nontariff barriers, and government restrictions on exports are direct and indirect methods of restricting international trade.

Discussion Questions

1. Which factors should a firm consider before it decides to conduct business internationally?
2. Which method of going international would you use if you were:
   - an automobile manufacturer?
   - a software developer?
   - an oil exploration/production company?
   - an electrical company generation power plant builder?
   - a farmer with large surplus of wheat?
   - a restaurant operator with a new barbecue rib recipe?

   Discuss the reasons that you used for making your decision.
3. When might a corporation "go international" using a joint venture approach rather than a wholly owned subsidiary approach? Give an example.
4. What type of business transaction generally uses a turnkey operation approach?
5. Identify the ten leading exporting countries as of 1988.
6. Who are the "four tigers"?

7. Which country has increased its exports from $820 million in 1950 to $284 billion by 1988? How does this compare to the United States?
8. Give a recent example where Japan has invested directly in the United States.
9. How might multinational direct investment help or hurt the country receiving the investment?
10. Discuss the methods governments use to protect their domestic business environments.

Bibliography

BARTHOLOMEW, DOUGLAS. 1989. "Mexico Opens the Door." *Euromoney*, (September): 233, 236.

BELASSA, BELA, ed. 1978. *Changing Patterns in Foreign Trade and Payments*, 3rd ed. New York: Norton.

CZINKOTA, MICHAEL R. 1986. "International Trade and Business in the Late 1980s: An Integrated U.S. Perspective." *Journal of International Business Studies* (Spring): 127–134.

INTERNATIONAL FINANCE CORPORATION. 1990. *Emerging Stock Markets Fact Book*. Washington DC: International Finance Corporation.

KITCHING, JOHN. 1974. "Winning and Losing with European Acquisition." *Harvard Business Review*, (March/April): p. 81

LEVITT, THEODORE. 1983. "Globalization of Markets." *Harvard Business Review* (May/June): 92–102.

MIRUS, ROLF, and B. YEUNG. 1986. "Economic Incentives for Countertrade." *Journal of International Business Studies* (Fall): 27–39.

SCHOENING, NILES C. 1988. "A Slow Leak: Effects of the U.S. Shifts in International Investment." *Survey of Business* (Spring): 21–26.

SUZUKI, KATSHIKO. 1989. "Choice Between International Capital and Labor Mobility of Diversified Economies." *Journal of International Economics* (November):347–361.

UNITED NATIONS. 1986. *Statistical Yearbook*. New York: United Nations.

U.S. DEPARTMENT OF COMMERCE. 1989. *Survey of Current Business*. Washington DC: Government Printing Office.

WORLD BANK. 1990. *World Development Report, 1990*. New York: Oxford University Press.

Chapter Case Study

Electronics International Ltd.

Electronics International Ltd. is a large consumer electronics manufacturer based in Southampton, England. Its product line consists of transistor radios, tape recorders, audio components and systems, personal stereos, and so on. Annual sales in 1989 were $186 million, 44 percent of which came from overseas sales. Most of the company's exports went to developing countries in Asia and Africa, with a small percentage of its products going to Turkey and Greece. Its most important export market is Zempa, a relatively prosperous developing country in the western part of Africa. Exports to Zempa total nearly 26 percent of all export revenues and have been showing an upward trend for the past six years.

Total sales to Zempa in 1989 were $120 million, up from $40 million in 1982 and $110 million in 1988. The company controlled approximately 20 percent of the audio products market in Zempa, with the rest being taken up by other competitors, all of whom were overseas corporations. Zempa has no audio products manufacturing industry, and all domestic requirements are met through imports. Electronics International was the third biggest player in the Zempa market, with the top two slots being occupied by a German company and a Japanese company, respectively. Electronics International's products were well-established and enjoyed considerable customer loyalty.

Recently, some problems have emerged. The government of Zempa has become increasingly concerned about the relatively backward state of its manufacturing industry and wants to rapidly industrialize the economy by attracting overseas investment in key sectors. One of the important priorities for the Zempa government in this connection is the consumer electronics industry. As a part of its policy to develop the lo-cal economy by stimulating domestic manufacturing activity, the Zempa government sounded out the major exporters of consumer electronics products about setting up domestic production facilities in Zempa. The managing director of Electronics International received a letter from the Zempa government, inviting the company to set up a manufacturing facility in Zempa and promising considerable official assistance should the company decide to do so.

Electronics International was asked to evaluate this offer and to reply within three months. The government also said that other leading suppliers were also considering setting up local manufacturing establishments in Zempa.

The idea of setting up a manufacturing operation in Zempa did not appeal initially to the managing director. The company was doing well as an exporter and sales had been increasing each year. There had been no difficulties in shipping its products, and most of the goods were transported by sea and costs were acceptable. True, there were some problems with the local customs authorities, but they were not insurmountable. The distributors were good, reliable people who were pushing sales hard and were meeting their contractual obligations to the company without any major problems. The government's regulations regarding remittance of payments for imports/exports were tedious and at times a little frustrating, but with the help of the company's local agents, most of the issues regarding repatriation of exchange proceeds were resolved in reasonable time. Therefore, why should the company think of setting up manufacturing operations in Zempa? The infrastructure for industry in Zempa was relatively undeveloped. The electricity supply was especially unreliable. There was little trained manpower and the production of electronic products requires workers who are adept at carrying out the delicate assembling tasks. The managing director was about to dictate a letter thanking the government for the invitation to set up a factory and conveying the company's decision to stay on only as an exporter, when he decided to consult Bill McLowan, the company's strategic planning director at Electronics International. A couple of days later, McLowan presented a seven-page executive memo that differed from the thoughts of the managing director. There were five main points raised in the memo.

1. Zempa is a valuable market for Electronics International and as the economy of the country develops, the market size is likely to continue to grow rapidly. What is therefore needed is an increase not only in sales volume, but also an increase in market share. The memo pointed out that although the sales of Electronics International's products had risen steadily over the past six years, its market share had stagnated while those of its main competitors have increased.

2. The Zempa government had not only invited Electronics International to set up manufacturing facilities, but also had solicited investments from its two major competitors. If both competitors accepted the invitation and set up local manufacturing operations, they could outprice Electronics International from the Zempa market because costs of local production were bound to be lower, given the lower wage rates and other input costs.

3. Zempa was under increasing domestic and external economic pressure. There was considerable inflation, primarily because of a substantial federal budget deficit (the government had not been able to raise required levels of revenues). Although the external balance position had been comfortable in the past five years because of firm commodity prices (commodities were the main exports of Zempa, generating 95 percent of export revenues), indicators of a weakening were already there. In the event of a balance-of-payments crisis, the government was likely to limit imports, and one of the first items to be put on the banned list would be consumer electronics, because they would be deemed nonessential in the face of competing demands from such imports as defense equipment.

4. Although there were some impediments to the establishment of manufacturing operations, at this stage the government had assured the company of all assistance. If the company went in now and the other competitors did not, it would gain considerable leverage with the home government, which could be used to attack the dominance of the competition.

5. There were certain risks—the local currency might depreciate and the lack of training of local workers and the state of local infrastructural facilities might impair the efficiency of the plant. There may be other constraints imposed later on the manufacturing operation. Given the emerging scenario, however, these risks were worth taking, and the company should at least in principle accept the invitation from the government of Zempa and prepare for further negotiations.

McLowan's memo seemed to open new lines of thought, but it did not convince the managing director. He asked his secretary to organize a meeting of the international investment committee to discuss the issues of exporting and direct investment in Zempa.

Questions

1. What strategy should Electronics International adopt in this situation? Continue exporting or make direct investment?

2. Are there any other alternatives open for Electronics International?

PART TWO

INSTITUTIONAL FRAMEWORK AND ECONOMIC THEORIES

CHAPTER 3

Theories of Trade and Economic Development

CHAPTER OBJECTIVES

This chapter will:

- Present the major trade and economic theories that attempt to explain international trade.
- Describe the continuum of political economic development within the global community of nations and identify the First, Second and Third worlds.
- Define the problems facing lesser-developed countries and address the North dialogue.
- Briefly discuss the recent dynamic changes occurring in the global economy.

An Introduction to International Trade Theories

Theories of international trade attempt to provide explanations of trade motives, underlying trade patterns, and the ultimate benefits that come from trade. An understanding of these basic factors enables individuals, private interests, and governments to better determine how to act for their own benefit within the trading systems. The ma-

jor questions to be answered through such an examination of trade are:

Why does trade occur? Is it because of price differentials, supply differentials, or differences in individual tastes? What is traded and what are the prices or terms agreed upon in these trading actions? Do trade flows relate to specific economic and social characteristics of a country? What are the gains from trade and who realizes these gains? What are the effects of restrictions put on trading activity? The theories discussed in this chapter answer some of these questions. Although no theory by itself offers all the answers, the different theories do contribute significantly to our understanding.

Trade Theories

Theories of trade have evolved over time, beginning with the emergence of strong nation-states and the organization of systematic exchanges of goods between these nations. The theories are associated with discrete time periods, and the earliest of these periods was that of mercantilism.

Mercantilism

Mercantilism became popular in the late seventeenth and early eighteenth centuries in Western Europe and was based on the notion that governments (not individuals, who were deemed untrustworthy) should become involved in the transfer of goods between nations in order to increase the wealth of each national entity. Wealth was defined, however, as an accumulation of precious metals, especially gold.

Consequently, the aims of the governments were to facilitate and support all exports while limiting imports, which was accomplished through the conduct of trade by government monopolies and intervention in the market through the subsidization of domestic exporting industries and the allocation of trading rights. Additionally, nations imposed duties or quotas upon imports to limit their volume. During this period colonies were acquired to provide sources of raw materials or precious metals. Trade opportunities with the colonies were exploited, and local manufacturing was repressed in those offshore locations. The colonials were often required to buy their goods from their mother countries.

The concept of mercantilism incorporates two fallacies. The first was the incorrect belief that gold or precious metals have intrinsic value, when actually they cannot be used for either production or consumption. Thus, nations subscribing to the mercantilism notion exchanged the prod-

ucts of their manufacturing or agricultural capacity for this nonproductive wealth. The second fallacy is that the theory of mercantilism ignores the concept of production efficiency through specialization. Instead of emphasizing cost-effective production of goods, mercantilism emphasizes sheer volumes of exports and imports and equates the amassing of wealth with acquisition of power.

Neomercantilism corrected the first fallacy by looking at the overall favorable or unfavorable balance of trade in all commodities, that is, nations attempted to have a positive balance of trade in all goods produced so that all exports exceeded imports. The term "balance of trade" continues in popular use today as nations attempt to correct their trade deficit positions by increasing exports or reducing imports so that outflow of goods balances the inflow.

The second fallacy, a disregard for the concept of efficient production, was addressed in subsequent theories, notably the classical theory of trade, which rests on the doctrine of comparative advantage.

Classical Theory

What is now called classical theory of trade superseded the theory of mercantilism at the beginning of the nineteenth century and coincided with three economic and political revolutions—the Industrial Revolution, the American Revolution, and the French Revolution. This theory was based in the economic theory of free trade and enterprise that was evolving at the time. In 1776, in *The Wealth of Nations*,[1] Adam Smith rejected as foolish the concept of gold being synonymous with wealth. Instead, Smith insisted that nations benefited the most when they acquired through trade those goods they could not produce efficiently and produced only those goods that they could manufacture with maximum efficiency. The crux of the

---

[1] This book has been reprinted by various publishers. For the specific references in this chapter, the edition used was the Modern Library edition.

argument was that costs of production should dictate what should be produced by each nation or trading partner.

Under this concept of absolute advantage, a nation would only produce those goods that made the best use of its available natural and acquired resources and its climatic advantages. Some examples of acquired resources are available pools of appropriately trained and skilled labor, capital resources, technological advances, or even a tradition of entrepreneurship.

The use of such absolute advantage is the simplest explanation of trading behavior. For example, take two trading nations, Greece and Sweden, which both have the capacity to produce olives and martini glasses. In Greece 500 crates of green olives require 100 units of resources to produce, from cultivation and harvesting to processing and packaging. Because of the lack of manufacturing facilities and machinery in that country, however, 100 crates of martini glasses (an equivalent value to 500 crates of olives) take 500 resource units to produce because each glass must be hand-blown. This contrasts with the situation in Sweden, where the production of 100 crates of martini glasses can be easily mechanized and uses only 300 resource units. Because of Sweden's northern climate, however, olives can only be grown in greenhouses under man-made environmental conditions, a very expensive process requiring 600 units to produce 500 crates. Comparison of these figures leads to a clear conclusion as to how trade should be conducted to provide the citizens of Greece and Sweden with the perfect cocktail. Olives should be grown in Greece and traded for glasses produced in Swedish glass factories, because of the number of resource units required for each country to produce olives and glasses:

Country	Olives (500 crates)	Martini Glasses (100 crates)
Greece	100 units	500 units
Sweden	600 units	300 units

If Sweden concentrates on the production of martini glasses and Greece on the production of olives, production costs are minimized for both products at 100 resource units/500 crates of olives and 300 resource units/100 crates of martini glasses, for a total of 400 resource units.

The conclusion reached, of course, was that each country should produce the good that it could manufacture at minimum cost. What if, however, a country could produce both or several goods or commodities at costs lower than the other country? Do both nations still have impetus to trade?

Comparative Advantage

This question was considered by David Ricardo,[2] who developed the important concept of comparative advantage in considering a nation's relative production efficiencies as they apply to international trade. In Ricardo's view, the exporting country should look at the relative efficiencies of production for both commodities and make only those goods it could produce most efficiently.

Suppose for example, in our illustration that Greece developed an efficient manufacturing capacity so that martini glasses could be produced by machine rather than being hand-blown. In fact, since the development of the productive capacity and capital plants were newer than those in Sweden, Greece could produce 100 crates of martini glasses using only 200 resource units as opposed to the 300 units required by Sweden. Thus, Greece's comparative costs would fall below that of Sweden for both products and its comparative advantage vis-à-vis those products would be higher. Therefore, the resource units required to produce olives and glasses would now be:

Country	Olives (500 crates)	Martini Glasses (100 crates)
Greece	100 units	200 units
Sweden	600 units	300 units

Logically, Greece should be the producer of both olives and martini glasses, and Sweden's capital and labor used in making these happy-hour sup-

[2] Ricardo 1948.

plies should be directed to Greece, so that maximum production efficiencies are achieved. Neither capital nor labor is entirely mobile, however, so each country should specialize—Greece in olives at 100 resource units per 500 crates and Sweden in glass production at 300 resource units per 100 crates. Greece is still better off at maximizing its efficiencies in olive production. By doing so, it produces twice as many goods for export with the same amount of resources than if it allocated production to glassmaking, even at the new, more efficient production level.

While Sweden's production costs for glasses are still higher than those of Greece at 300 units, the resources of Sweden are better allocated to this production than to expensive olive-growing. In this way, Sweden minimizes its inefficiencies and Greece maximizes its efficiencies. The point is not that a country should produce all the goods it can more cheaply, but only those it can make cheapest. Such trading activity leads to maximum resource efficiency.

The concepts of absolute advantage and comparative advantage were used in a subsequent theory development by John Stuart Mill,[3] who looked at the question of determining the value of export goods and developed the concept of terms of trade. Under this concept, export value is determined according to how much of a domestic commodity each country must exchange to obtain an equivalent amount of an imported commodity. Thus, the value of the product to be obtained in the exchange was stated in terms of the amount of products produced domestically that would be given up in exchange. For example, Sweden's terms with Greece would be exporting of 100 crates of glasses for an equivalent 500 crates of olives.

Weaknesses of Early Theories

While the work of Smith, Ricardo, and Mill went far in describing the flow of trade between nations, classical theory was not without its flaws. For the example, the theory incorrectly assumed

[3] Mill 1884.

- the existence of perfect knowledge regarding international markets and opportunities.
- full mobility of labor and production factors throughout each country.
- full labor employment within each country.

The theory also assumed that each country had, as its objective, full production efficiency. It neglected such other motives as traditional employment and production history, self-sufficiency, or political objectives.

In addition, the theory is overly simplistic in that it deals only with two commodities and two countries. In reality, given the full range of production by many countries and interplay of many motives and factors, the trade situation is actually an ongoing dynamic process in which there is interplay of forces and products.

The largest area of weakness in classical theory is that while we considered all resource units used in production, the only costs considered by classical economists were those associated with labor. The theorists did not account for other resources used in the production of commodities or manufactured goods for export, such as transportation costs, the use of land, and capital. This failing was addressed by subsequent trade theorists, who, in modern theory, include all factors of production in looking at theories of comparative advantage.

More Recent Theories
Factor Endowment Theory

The Eli Heckscher and Bertil Ohlin theory of factor endowment addressed the question of the basis of cost differentials in the production of trading nations. They posited that each country allocates its production according to the relative proportions of all its production factor endowments—land, labor, and capital on a basic level, and, on a more complex level, such factors as management and technological skills, specialized production facilities, and established distribution networks.

Thus, the range of products made or grown for export would depend on the relative availability of different factors in each country. For example, agricultural production or cattle grazing would be emphasized in such countries as Canada and Australia, which are generously endowed with land. Conversely, in small-land-mass countries with high populations, export products would center on labor-intensive articles. Similarly, rich nations might center their export base on capital-intensive production.

In this way, countries would be expected to produce goods that require large amounts of the factors they hold in relative abundance. Because of the availability and low costs of these factors, each country should also be able to sell its products on foreign markets at less than international price levels. Although this theory holds in general, it does not explain export production that arises from taste differences rather than factor differentials. Some of these situations can be seen in sales of luxury imported goods, such as Italian leather products, deluxe automobiles, and French wine, which are valued for their quality, prestige, or panache. Like classical theory, the Heckscher-Olin theory does not account for transportation costs in its computation, nor does it account for differences among nations in the availability of technology.

Economist Paul Samuelson extended the factor endowment theory to look at the effect of trade upon national welfare and the prices of production factors. Samuelson posited that the effect of free trade among nations would be to increase overall welfare by equalizing not only the prices of the goods exchanged in trade, but also of all involved factors. Thus, according to his theory, the returns generated by use of the factors would be the same in all countries.[4]

The Leontief Paradox

An exception to the Heckscher-Ohlin theory was examined by W. W. Leontief in the 1950s. Leontief found that U.S. exports were less capital-intensive than imports, although the presumption according to the Heckscher-Ohlin theory would have been that of capital rather than labor-intensive export goods, because the proportion of capital endowments at that time was higher than labor in the United States. The answer, as outlined by Leontief, was that these factor endowments are not homogeneous, and they differ along parameters other than relative abundance.[5] Labor pools, for example, can range from being unskilled to highly skilled. Similarly, production methods can be more technically sophisticated or advanced in different locations within a nation. Thus, it made sense at the time that U.S. exported products were made through the efforts of highly skilled labor and imported products were produced through the efforts of less-skilled workers in other countries.

Criticisms

Although these more recent theories seem to go far in explaining why nations trade, they have nonetheless come under criticism as being only partial explanations for the exchange of goods and services between nations. Some of these criticisms are that

- the theories assume that nations trade, when in reality trade between nations is initiated and conducted by individuals or individual firms within those nations.
- traditional theory also assumes perfect competition and perfect information among trading partners.
- they are limited in looking at either the transfer of goods or of direct investments. No theories explain the comprehensive dynamic flow of trade in goods, services, and financial flows.
- they do not recognize the importance of technology and expertise in the areas of marketing and management.

Consequently, some scholars have looked separately at the reasons why firms enter into trade or foreign investment. One of these theories is

[4] Samuelson 1948 and 1949.

[5] Leontief 1954.

the international product life cycle, which looks at the path a product takes as it departs domestic shores and enters foreign markets.

Modern Theories

International Product Life Cycle

The international product life cycle theory puts forth a different explanation for the fundamental motivations for trade between and among nations.[6] It relies primarily on the traditional marketing theory regarding the development, progress, and life span of products in markets. This theory looks at the potential export possibilities of a product in four discrete stages in its life cycle. In the first stage, innovation, a new product is manufactured in the domestic arena of the innovating country and sold primarily in that domestic market. Any overseas sales are generally achieved through exports to other markets, often those of industrial countries. In this stage, the company generally has little competition in its markets abroad.

In the second stage, the growth of the product, sales tend to increase. Unfortunately, so does competition as other firms enter the arena and the product becomes increasingly standardized. At this point, the firm begins some production abroad to maximize the service of foreign markets and to meet the activity of the competition.

As the product enters the third stage, maturity, exports from the home country decrease because of increased production in overseas locations. Foreign manufacturing facilities are put in place to counter increasing competition and to maximize profits from higher sales levels in foreign markets. At this point, price becomes a crucial determinant of competitiveness. Consequently, minimizing costs becomes an important objective of the manufacturing firm. Production also frequently

shifts from being within foreign industrial markets to less costly lesser-developed countries to take advantage of cheaper production factors, especially low labor costs. At this point the innovator country may even decide to discontinue all domestic production, produce only in third world countries, and reexport the product back to the home country and to other markets.

In the final stage of the product life cycle, the product enters a period of decline. This decline is often because new competitors have achieved levels of production high enough to effect scale economies in the production that are equivalent to those of the original manufacturing country.

The international product life cycle theory has been found to hold primarily for such products as consumer durables, synthetic fabrics, and electronic equipment,* that is, those products that have long lives in terms of the time span from innovation to eventual high consumer demand. The theory does not hold for products with a rapid time span of innovation, development, and obsolescence.

The theory holds less often these days because of the growth of multinational global enterprises that often introduce products simultaneously in several markets of the world. Similarly, multinational firms no longer necessarily first introduce a product at home. Instead, they might launch an innovation from a foreign source in the domestic markets to test production methods and the market itself, without incurring the high initial production costs of domestic environment.

Other Modern Investment Theories

Other theorists explain investing overseas by firms as a response to the availability of opportunities not shared by their competitors, that is, they take advantage of imperfections in markets and only enter foreign spheres of production when

---

[6] Vernon 1966.

their competitive advantages outweigh the costs of going overseas. These advantages may be production, brand awareness, product identification, economies of scale, or access to favorable capital markets. These firms may make horizontal investments, producing the same goods abroad as they do at home, or they may make vertical investments, in order to take advantage of sources of supplies or inputs.

Going a step further, some believe that firms within an oligopoly enter foreign markets merely as a competitive response to the actions of an industry leader and to equalize relative advantages. Oligopolies are those market situations in which there are few sellers of a product that is usually mass merchandized. Two examples are the automobile and steel industries. In these situations no firm can profit by cutting prices because competitors quickly respond in kind. Consequently, prices for oligopolistic products are practically identical and are set through industry agreement (either openly or tacitly).

Thus, firms within an oligopoly must be keenly aware of the actions, market reach, and activities of their competitors. Unless their response to the actions of competitors is follow the leader, they will yield precious competitive edges to their competitors. Therefore, it follows that when a market leader in an oligopoly establishes a foreign production facility abroad, its competitors rush to follow suit.

Thus, the impetus for a firm to go abroad may come from a wish to expand for internal reasons—to use existing competitive advantages in additional spheres of operations, to take advantage of technology, or to use raw materials available in other locations. Alternately, the motive might arise from external forces, such as competitive actions, customer requests, or government incentives. The final determinant however, is based in a cost-benefit analysis. The firm will move abroad if it can use its own particular advantages to provide benefits that outweigh the costs of exporting or production abroad and provide a profit.

Theories of Economic Development

Beyond merely examining what types of economic systems exist in the world, those involved in international business must place notions about methods of allocating resources within a country in a theoretical framework. How do basically agrarian national economies become producers of sophisticated manufactured goods? How does economic development come about?

Classical economic theory, put forth by economists Thomas Malthus, David Ricardo, John Stuart Mill, and Adam Smith in the late 1700s and early 1800s, held little hope for a nation to sustain its economic growth. This dismal forecast was because of the substantial weakness in the theory (as evidenced by subsequent historical events), which assumed that no developments would be achieved in technology or production methods. Instead, these economists, Malthus foremost among them, predicted that the finite availability of land would limit any nation's development and that the natural equilibrium in labor wages would hover at subsistence levels because of the interaction of labor supply, agricultural production, and wage systems. For example, they believed that if labor supplies were low, wages would rise and would motivate workers to increase their number. Increases in the size of the population and labor pool would then put stress on finite supplies of food, increase the costs of nourishment, and ultimately lead to decreases in wages because of increased competition for such employment.

In a nutshell, classical theory holds that expanding the labor pool leads to declines in the accumulation of capital per worker, lower worker productivity, and lower incomes per person, eventually causing stagnation or economic decline. Naturally, this theory was proven incorrect by numerous scientific and technological discoveries, which provided for greater efficiencies in production and greater returns on inputs of land, capital, and labor. It was also knocked awry by the growing acceptance of birth control as a means of limiting population size.

Rostow's Stages of Economic Growth

A more recent and applicable theory of economic development was provided in the 1960s by Walter W. Rostow, who attempted to outline the various stages of a nation's economic growth and based his theory on the notion that shifts in economic development coincided with abrupt changes within the nations themselves.[7] He identified five different economic stages for a country—traditional society, preconditions for takeoff, takeoff, the drive to maturity, and the age of high mass consumption.

STAGE 1: TRADITIONAL SOCIETY

Rostow saw traditional society as a static economy, which he likened to the pre-1700s attitudes and technology experienced by the world's current economically developed countries. He believed that the turning point for these countries came with the work of Sir Isaac Newton, when people began to believe that the world was subject to a set of physical laws but was malleable within these laws. In other words, people could effect change within the system of descriptive laws as developed by Newton.

STAGE 2: PRECONDITIONS FOR TAKEOFF

Rostow identified the preconditions for economic takeoff as growth or radical changes in three specific, nonindustrial sectors that provided the basis for economic development:

1. Increased investment in transportation, which enlarged prospective markets and increased product specialization capacity.
2. Agricultural developments providing for the feeding and nourishing of larger, primarily urban, populations.
3. An expansion of imports into the country.

[7] Rostow 1961.

These preconditioning changes were to be experienced in concert with an increasing national emphasis on education and entrepreneurship.

STAGE 3: TAKEOFF

The takeoff stage of growth occurs, according to Rostow, over a period of twenty to thirty years and is marked by major transformations that stimulate the economy. These transformations could include widespread technological developments, the effective functioning of an efficient distribution system, and even political revolutions. During this period barriers to growth are eliminated within the country and, indeed, the concept of economic growth as a national objective becomes the norm. To achieve the takeoff, however, Rostow believes that three conditions must be met:

1. Net investment as a percentage of net national product must increase sharply.
2. At least one substantial manufacturing sector must grow rapidly. This rapid growth and larger output trickles down as growth in ancillary and supplier industries.
3. A supportive framework for growth must emerge on political, social, and institutional fronts. For example, banks, capital markets, and tax systems should develop and entrepreneurship should be considered a norm.

STAGE 4: THE DRIVE TO MATURITY

Within Rostow's scheme, this stage is characterized as one where growth becomes self-sustaining and a widespread expectation within the country. During this period, Rostow believes that the labor pool becomes more skilled and more urban and that technology reaches heights of advancement.

STAGE 5: THE AGE OF MASS CONSUMPTION

The last stage of development, as Rostow sees it, is an age of mass consumption, when there is a shift to consumer durables in all sectors and when the populace achieves a high standard of living, as evidenced through the ownership of such sophisticated goods as automobiles, televisions, and appliances.

Since its introduction in the 1960s, Rostow's framework has been criticized as being overly ambitious in attempting to describe the economic paths of many nations. Also, history has not proved the framework to be true. For example, many lesser-developed countries exhibit dualism, that is, state-of-the-art technology is used in certain industries and primitive production methods are retained in others. Similarly, empirical data has shown that there is no twenty-to-thirty-year growth period. Such countries as the United Kingdom, Germany, Sweden, and Japan are more characterized by slow, steady growth patterns than by abrupt takeoff periods.

The Big Push: Balanced versus Unbalanced Growth

While Rostow was attempting to place economic development within a sequential framework, the debate during the 1950s and 1960s centered on whether development efforts should center on specific economic sectors within countries or should be made in all major sectors of the economy—manufacturing, agriculture, and service.

Economist Ragnar Nurske advocated that development efforts should consist of a synchronized use of capital to develop wide ranges of industries in nations. He believed that only a concerted overall effort would propel developing nations beyond the vicious circle of poverty's perpetuating itself because of the limited supply of capital caused by low savings rates.

The advocates of channeling capital to all sectors in a balanced approach also support the big push thesis and believe that these investments cannot be made gradually. They must be made all at once for the positive impetus to be sufficient to overcome significant barriers to development, such as the lack of an adequate infrastructure.

The theory of balanced development has been criticized because it ignores the economic notion of overall benefits accruing from specialization in development and production. It has also been criticized for being unrealistic, that is, if a country had enough resources to invest in all sectors of the economy at once, it would, in fact, not be undeveloped. The theory also assumes that all nations would be starting from the same zero point, when, in reality, their economies may have some historical strengths or investment capacity. The theory has been discredited, to a very significant extent, by the actual progress of less-developed countries in the 1960s and 1970s. These countries experienced a great deal of growth without any attempts to synchronize simultaneous investments in all sectors, as recommended by proponents of balanced growth theory, but most remain comparatively undeveloped (see Perspective 3–1).

PERSPECTIVE 3–1 **Third World Dead End?**

As the newly liberated countries of Eastern Europe seek to ignite their stagnant economies, they face a daunting reality: Outside of the industrial West, economic development has become an increasingly rare phenomenon.

Since the mid-1950s, when the idea of the "Third World" first surfaced, only four of its members have truly managed to escape it. Singapore, Hong Kong, South Korea, and Taiwan have, in two short decades, gone from helpless paupers dependent on foreign handouts to industrial dynamos envied even in the West. Today, Singapore has a higher per-capita income than Israel, and South Korea earns more from exports than Spain.

SOURCE: Michael Massing, *Washington Post*, December 23, 1990.

These "newly industrializing countries"—NICS, as they're called—are widely regarded as models for the rest of the Third World, and for the newly liberated countries of the crumbled Soviet bloc. Development experts regularly trek to East Asia, seeking to extract the essence of NIC success, doctoral candidates churn out monographs analyzing NIC policy debates, Third World leaders send fact-finding missions to the region. From Guyana to Ghana, government ministers talk about turning their countries into another Singapore or South Korea.

Outside of East Asia, however, the NIC magic has proved almost impossible to duplicate. The very concept of development now seems a quaint anachronism in much of the Third World. The number of "least developed countries" (LDCs)—11 in the mid-1960s—now surpasses 40. In the poor Southern Hemisphere, the 1980s are now widely regarded as a lost decade, a time of plummeting incomes, soaring unemployment and spreading hunger. Even such one-time powerhouses as Brazil, site of the 1970s "miracle," and Argentina, where the working class once supped on steak, have turned anemic. What has gone wrong?

The NICs' success can be summed up in one word: exports. Small in size, limited in population and poor in resources, these countries all had to look outward in order to grow. In doing so, they could draw on one great asset: disciplined labor forces willing to work for low wages. In the late 1960s, all four countries began luring foreign investors with special tax incentives and promises of cheap labor. Hundreds of manufacturers set up shop, and before long these nations were sending jeans, radios, and baseball gloves around the world. Double-digit growth rates became common. The East Asian "tigers," they were called.

Here, it seemed, was a surefire formula for success. In the late 1970s, development experts began championing the East Asian model. Especially enthusiastic were the International Monetary Fund and the World Bank, which pushed exports at every turn. But not just any exports. Traditional products like corn, rice and bananas were frowned upon as dull, unmarketable, passe. Governments were urged to produce more exotic goods—orchids and irises, macadamia nuts and kiwis, baseballs and brassieres—that could find favor with consumers in New York and Paris.

To help Third World nations complete in the world market, the IMF and World Bank developed a handy package of "structural adjustment" guidelines joining the wisdom of the Orient to the austerity measures beloved by the IMF. Governments—often as a condition for receiving loans—were urged to: freeze wages; cut public spending; pare the government payroll; adopt investment incentives; sell publicly owned companies; lift price controls; freeze the money supply; and eliminate red tape. Dozens of countries signed on—all hoping soon to become NICs.

It didn't work out that way. Few of the countries undertaking structural adjustment have turned into tigers. Most have become turkeys. Take the case of Jamaica. In the early 1980s, this Caribbean island seemed an ideal candidate for achieving NIC status. Wages were low, the workforce fairly well trained and the world's most prosperous market only a short plane ride away. Michael Manley, the socialist prime minister, whose misconceived policies had set Jamaica back a decade, was replaced by Edward Seaga, a free-market enthusiast with proven administrative skills.

Seaga was convinced the East Asian model could work at home. Working closely with the IMF and the World Bank, he zestfully slashed tariffs, cut the government payroll and put dozens of state-owned companies up for sale. A special trade agency promoted the production of honey, flowers and other non-traditional exports. Glossy brochures touted "Investing in the New Jamaica," and no investor was too small to obtain a special audience with the prime minister. Seaga traveled frequently to the United States, meeting with businessmen and trade groups, lining up allies. David Rockefeller, among others, agreed to help.

It was for naught. During Seaga's eight years in office, the Jamaican economy grew a puny 0.6 percent a year, industrial production remained stagnant and exports actually fell 4.5 percent a year. All in all, structural adjustment proved a grand flop, and in 1989 disgruntled Jamaicans voted Seaga out of office and Manley back in.

Seaga's failure points up the problems that most Third World countries face in following the NIC model. First, Seaga's exertions in search of foreign investment produced few dividends. Some Americans did set up shop, but the amount of capital involved—and the number of jobs generated—fell far short of expectations. Many investors—turned off by Jamaica's strong unions and volatile political climate—bypassed the island for more tranquil spots like the Dominican Republic and Thailand.

Clearly, in the drive for foreign investment, the NICs had a unique advantage in being first. In the late 1960s, East Asia had few competitors as a source of cheap labor, and foreign manufacturers flocked there by the hundreds. Today, virtually every country—even Cuba—wants foreign capital, and investors commonly circle the globe in search of the most lucrative deals. Now, with Eastern Europe coming on the market, competition for capital will grow even fiercer.

The same is true for exports. In the late 1960s, conditions were ideal for nations seeking foreign markets. The world economy was booming, global trade was expanding. Today, of course, *everyone* wants to export. The world economy has slowed, and trade barriers are going up everywhere. Finding new markets is proving difficult for the United States, much less for small nations with limited experience abroad.

In other respects, too, the East Asian model has caused mischief in the Third World. To hear the IMF and World Bank tell it, the NIC miracle was a simple matter of unleashing the marketplace. Certainly the private sector's role was pivotal in these countries. But the public sector played an important part as well. In Singapore, for instance, the government of Lee Kuan Yew intervened forcefully in the economy, setting production priorities, allocating capital and building infrastructure. Even

in a mature economy like Japan, the state actively assists the private sector.

The development experts prefer not to dwell on such fine distinctions. In their view, the state is inherently evil, the market inherently good. Overall, though, unbridled capitalism has fared little better than socialism in the Third World. In Asia, the Philippines, a welcome mat for Western capital, has not done much better than nearby Vietnam. In Africa, neither Zaire nor Liberia seems a good advertisement for Western-style economics. In this hemisphere, meanwhile, the sprawling shantytowns of Lima, Rio and Caracas bear squalid witness to the dark underside of capitalist development. Chile has done somewhat better than its neighbors, yet even its per-capita income barely exceeds $1,500 per year, and a large sector of the population has failed to share in the country's recent growth.

The truth is, nothing in the Third World— socialism or capitalism, centralization or deregulation, Marxism or the marketplace—seems to work. Still, development is possible in the Third World, but fostering it would require a radical change in attitude. Particularly essential is a new approach to the countryside.

In most Third World countries—capitalist and socialist alike—the rural sector invariably gets pushed aside. Compared to the glitter of new assembly plants and free trade zones, the countryside seems hopelessly backward. Yet it is here that most of the Third World's rapidly growing population resides. And it is here that the real potential for development lies.

The rice farmers, corn growers and chicken breeders of the Third World represent a vast labor force—most of it untapped. Throughout Asia, Africa and Latin America, land is being worked much as it was in the 17th century. Tools remain archaic and farm techniques prehistoric. Scarce credit has made even fertilizer a luxury, and bad roads keep all but the most determined farmers from getting to market. To aggravate matters, governments often keep crop prices artificially low to provide cheap food for the city.

Consequently, many Third World nations—even fertile ones—must import food at great cost. In Jamaica, for instance, 50 percent of the population lives in the countryside, yet agriculture contributes only 6 percent to GNP. In 1988, Jamaica imported more than 400,000 metric tons of grain—a sin for so lush an island.

The marketplace can play a role in rectifying this. If farmers can get a fair price for their crops, they will invariably produce more. But the private sector alone is not enough. Exploiting the potential of the countryside would require Third World governments—and the financial institutions that back them—to channel far more resources into agriculture. Roads must be built, technical assistance provided, credit expanded. And, where peasants lack land, the government must try to provide some.

By boosting rural incomes, such policies would help alleviate the terrible rural poverty that afflicts so many Third World societies. They would also help increase food production, enabling governments to save valuable foreign reserves now squandered on imports. Prosperity in the countryside would help create an expanded domestic market for local industries—putting them in a better position to exploit foreign markets.

This, in fact, is one of the lessons of the NIC experience. South Korea, for one, carried out extensive agrarian reform in the 1960s. Long before anyone began thinking about exports, the government redistributed land, raised crop prices and expanded rural credit. Farm production boomed, setting the stage for the country's subsequent takeoff.

Sadly, such realities are rarely mentioned in the NIC literature. Yet things may be changing. In July, the World Bank issued its first comprehensive report on world poverty in a decade. The document makes for grim reading. More than one billion people in the Third World live in absolute poverty, the report states, adding that "many developing countries have not merely failed to keep pace with the industrial countries; they have seen their incomes fall in absolute terms."

Of all the causes contributing to this deterioration, the bank asserts, none is more important than the abandonment of the countryside. "The expansion of agriculture is the driving force behind effective rural development, which in turn lays the foundation for broadly based, poverty-reducing growth," the study states.

What a welcome change from all the talk about NICs, exports and structural adjustment. The question is, will the bank follow up on its own analysis?

Hirschman's Strategy of Unbalance

Some theorists have advocated a strategy of selective investment as the engine of growth in developing countries. Albert O. Hirschman promulgated the idea of making unbalanced investments in economic sectors to complement the imbalances that already exist within the economy of a nation. Hirschman argued the less-developed countries do not have access to adequate resources to mount a balanced, big-push investment strategy. Investments should be made instead in strategically selected economic areas, in order to provide growth in other sectors through backward and forward linkages. Backward linkages spur new investments in input industries, while forward link-

ages do so in those sectors that buy the output of the selected industry. Thus, in Hirschman's scheme, careful analysis must be made in the situation of each country as to what investment constitutes the best means to reach an ultimate balance among all investment sectors.

The Global Continuum: Where Nations Fall Today

All trading nations of the world fall within the descriptive continuum of political structures, forms of economic organization, and levels of development. The existence of these three descriptive parameters provides for enormous variation in categorizing world trading nations.

The Political Continuum

Political systems constitute the methods in which societies organize in order to function smoothly and such orientation provides one such classification continuum. Certainly the student of international business is cognizant of the two extremes of political organization in the global political arena of the 1990s. At one extreme, there exists societies in which all members have significant power in the decision-making process surrounding the activities, policies, and objectives of their government. These systems are often pluralistic (incorporating a number of different views), use the concept of majority rule in deciding major issues, and often employ a system of representative democracy, where officials are elected to represent their regional constituencies. These nations generally afford all of their citizens some degree of liberty and equality.

At the other end of the political spectrum is the totalitarian state, which is identified by a singular lack of decision-making power among the country's individual citizens. In such a political system, decisions regarding policies, objectives, and the direction of the nation are controlled by a select few individuals who generally operate under the auspices of the government. In these states, the activities and liberties of citizens are often restricted.

All nations in the world fall somewhere along this continuum and take various forms within its parameters—from being highly democratized to being nearly entirely totalitarian. Until recently, most individuals would recognize that the two world powers, the United States and the Soviet Union, have represented the two extremes in the modern political world. Recent changes in the political structure of the Soviet Union, where the Soviet republics, such as Lithuania, Estonia, and Latvia, and even the Russian Republic, are seeking greater independence from the central government in Moscow, are resulting in the development of a new, hopefully more democratic political system.

The Economic Continuum

The political orientation of a country can also be placed within the scope of its economic structure, which, similarly, runs along a continuum. Economic orientations vary according to two separate dimensions—the degree of private versus public (state) ownership of property; and the level of governmental (versus individual) control over the resources of the nation.

At one extreme is capitalism, which relies on the forces of the marketplace in the allocation of resources. In this free-enterprise system, the market, in the form of consumer sovereignty, defines the relationship between prices for goods and services, quantities produced domestically, and overall supply and demand. For example, if supplies of a product are low and public demand is high, its price will rise as consumers compete to acquire this scarce resource. Similarly, if there is little or no demand for products, manufacturers will have no motivation to produce them.

In free-market economies, the creation of profit is generally considered to be the operational motive of business and profitability tends to be the test of success. Capitalist economies also promote the ownership of private property by individuals and theoretically attempt to limit public (state) ownership of property.

In modern free-market countries, however, governments still intervene at some level and own some property. They set legal and regulatory requirements to provide for the general safety and welfare of the populace and levy taxes in order to provide services, such as the national defense or a network of highways. They own resource reserves, land, national parks, and large amounts of capital assets. Indeed, governments often provide the largest single market for manufacturers in many capitalist countries.

The appropriate level of government involvement in the play of market forces continues to be the subject of much debate among economists, politicians, and political parties in many countries. This debate is perhaps best exemplified by the policies put in place by President Ronald Reagan and Prime Minister Margaret Thatcher of the United Kingdom, where significant efforts were made to reduce the role of the central government and promote deregulation of many industries.

At the other end of the economic spectrum are the centrally planned or nonmarket economies. Within this economic form, the government decides what is to be produced, when and where it will be made, and to whom it will be sold. The state controls the sources and means of production, raw materials, and the distribution systems. In addition, the state frequently owns many of the basic and integral industries of the country, which are run in the form of state monopolies and include large-scale power-generating facilities, manufacturing industries, and entire transportation systems. In addition to these production and manufacturing monopolies, all trade with the outside world is financed and conducted by a state trading monopoly.

This centrally planned type of economic structure is based on the belief that a single central agency can coordinate economic activity to provide harmony in the interrelationship of all sectors of the economy. Before 1989 the world's centrally planned or nonmarket economies were most strongly represented by the members of ex-COMECON, or ex-communist nations of the world, which included the USSR, Poland, Romania, Czechoslovakia, People's Republic of China, Cuba, Vietnam, and North Korea, among others. Since then, only China, Cuba, North Korea, and Vietnam are maintaining the economic form, as the other ex-COMECON members become more oriented toward a free-market system.

The nonmarket form of economic organization is not without its problems. The most significant of these are the difficulties arising from attempts to coordinate all factors of production. Frequently, governments attempt to reach their objective of harmonious economic activity by developing complex and extensive goals in the form of long-term (five-year or more) plans for the nation. They attempt to affect production and outcome by setting manufacturing quotas, but this can lead to high costs. For example, production may be geared toward reaching quota levels, not toward achieving efficiencies, which can result in high production costs.

In addition, nonmarket economies also experience problems further down the line, especially with the procurement of raw materials for production. There are either insufficient supplies of raw materials or mismatches of the timing of supply deliveries. Another problem is insufficient long-term planning, especially at the local production facility level. Manufacturing operators have incentives to reach only their production goals for the season or the year; future, long-term production capacity or technological developments are less relevant. Nonmarket economies also face the problem of determining appropriate prices for goods and services produced within their borders. These valuation problems stem from the absence of external criteria of worth, as supplied through consumer demand for products or prices paid for input resources and raw materials. Thus, in these economies prices are set primarily according to the amount of labor involved in their production and are often as much a product of politics and ideology as of actual production costs.

Between these two extremes are mixed economic systems, which combine features of both market and nonmarket systems. These nations combine public and private ownership in varying amounts. Their intention is to provide economic security for the country as a whole, by having some amount of public resource ownership and/or government involvement in decision-making. In these systems public involvement often takes the form of state ownership of utilities or energy sources. The welfare state and heavy involvement of government in the economic planning of the nation are also basic features of mixed economies. An example of this kind of system exists in modern-day France, which took a turn toward central planning as a social democracy with the election of François Mitterrand in 1981. After his election Mitterrand held true to his campaign promises and supported the nationalization of many firms within industries considered crucial to the strategic position of the nation, such as the high technology electronic industry.

To a lesser extent, Japan is also a mixed economy. While there is less government ownership of resources, the state, through its Ministry of International Trade and Industry and Ministry of Finance, is intimately involved in business decisions regarding investments, disinvestments, production, and markets. The government is also intricately involved in conducting basic research and development and deciding long-term and short-term future direction. The government does this by organizing major companies into research consortia, which join together to conduct applied research on new technology. When that research bears fruit, in the form of marketable applications, the consortium disbands and each company takes the technology back to its own labs to use in product development.

Integrating Both Continua

The two ranges of political and economic organization of nations can be put together in a general framework. Overall, democratic societies tend to be oriented toward a free-market, capitalist perspective. Supply and demand in production is determined to a degree by consumers in the marketplace; sources of supply and the means of production are owned by private interests or individuals. In contrast, totalitarian societies are characterized by the governments' allocation of resources by the government and state ownership of the means of production.

It appears, however, that as nations of the world become more and more interdependent, the boundaries begin to blur between political and economic descriptions. More and more governments are moving toward a mixture of both public and private ownership of property and allocation of resources. This convergence can perhaps be accounted for by the increasingly apparent knowledge that none of the existing systems provides equitably for all segments of society.

The place each country holds in both the economic and political continua is an important consideration for foreign firms, when considering whether or not to do business. The decision-maker must take into account, for example, whether the political structures of the home and host country are complementary, whether the tendency is toward private or public ownership of resource allocation and production, and to what degree the state controls the daily operations of business firms.

Patterns of World Development

Background: The Role of GNP

Traditionally, countries of the world have been divided into three separate categories known as the First, Second, and Third worlds. Their assigned categorizations are based on specific economic criteria, such as the gross national product (GNP) per capita. GNP per capita is a benchmark used in determining levels of development, because it represents a measure of production relative to population that can be compared across nations. GNP is determined by totaling the dollar value of the goods and services a country produced in, for example, one year and dividing that number by its population, thereby providing a measure of a country's economic activity level as a per person value. In addition to GNP per capita, development level determinations include assessments of annual export levels, relative growth over time, energy consumption per capita, and the relative percentage of agriculture in total production and employment.

In addition, development levels are ascertained according to social criteria, such as life expectancies, infant mortality levels, the availability of health and educational facilities, literacy rates, demographic and population trends, and standards of housing and nutrition.

The Developed Countries

The industrialized or developed countries are commonly referred to as the First World. These nations generally have economies that are based in industrial manufacturing and are the wealthiest in the world in terms of incomes and standards of living. The industrialized countries are largely in the Northern Hemisphere. They are the United States and Canada in North America and the nations of Western Europe. Beyond these two geographic areas, only New Zealand, Australia, Japan, and perhaps the Republic of South Africa represent the east, or the Southern Hemisphere in this group.

In the developed countries, the average gross national product per capita is $17,080 and ranks as follows for individual countries in descending order from the wealthiest nation (Norway) to the poorest (Spain):[8]

Country	GNP per Capita
Norway	$19,990
United States	19,840
Sweden	19,300
Finland	18,590
West Germany	18,480
Denmark	18,450
Canada	16,690
France	16,060
Austria	15,470
Netherlands	14,520
Belgium	14,490
Italy	13,330
United Kingdom	12,810
Australia	12,340
New Zealand	10,000
Ireland	7,750
Spain	7,740

In addition to high production capacity per person, each of these countries has levels of adult literacy reported in the 90th percentile, large values of exported products, low infant mortality figures, and low citizen per physician ratios. For example, the ratio of population per doctors in the United States is one doctor for every 470 citizens; in Japan, this figure is 1:660; and in the United Kingdom, 1:650.[9]

[8] The World Bank. 1990. *The World Development Report 1990*. New York: Oxford University Press.
[9] Ibid.

The Second World

The so-called Second World consists of the non-market, centrally planned economy countries of Eastern Europe and the USSR. Because these countries are generally closed to Western scrutiny, data is unavailable for compilation of gross national product per capita. Literacy rates for these nations are reported to be about 90%.

With the sweeping political and economic changes that are taking place within these countries, better data is likely to become available.

The Third World

The Third World is generally considered to include developing, less-developed, and underdeveloped countries. More recently, this enormous majority of countries has been recategorized according to income as Middle-Income Developing Countries and Low-Income Developing Countries. These categorizations, determined in 1981 by the World Bank, designate those countries with per capita GNP of less than $545 as low-income and those with GNP per capital greater than $545 but less than $5,999 as middle-income.[10]

Lesser-Developed Countries

The poorest nations of the world are generally found on the continents of Asia, Africa, and South America. Their poverty is evidenced by inadequate diets, primitive housing, limited schooling, and minimal medical facilities. The common features of most lesser-developed countries are low per capita GNP and the division into two very disparate classes—a very rich upper class and a very poor lower class. There is hardly any middle class to act as buffer between them. The richer elements have more access to, and are affected by, the westernization of ideas and values, whereas the lower classes, with less education and awareness to externalities, tend to cling to traditional values, which leads to inherent conflicts between the two.

[10] Ibid.

LDCs have widely varying political systems, which run the gamut from communist countries, such as the People's Republic of China, to democracies, such as India and Costa Rica, and autocratic regimes, such as Chile. They also have a number of problems in common, which essentially center on the difficulties of achieving greater industrialization in light of increasing levels of population growth and limited resources.

A major problem in LDCs is that their populations are growing rapidly, at a rate of 2.5 to 4.0 percent per year, as compared to approximately 1 percent per year in the industrialized countries (see Figures 3–1 and 3–2).[11] This growth forces LDCs to continue allocating scarce resources for

providing the basic necessities of food, clothing, and shelter for their populace. As a result, few resources remain within these countries for increasing development, income levels, education, and training (see Figure 3–3). Consequently, these nations are frequently faced with unemployment, underemployment, and a relatively unproductive labor force.

Similarly, most of the economies of LDCs are dependent on agriculture, which often suffers from low productivity but employs the major portion of the work force. This dependency is often coupled with limited or scarce natural resources, as well as severely limited capital bases to fund ongoing development efforts. Thus, exports are often limited to very few, basic, low valued-added products that are vulnerable to the violent fluctuations of world commodity prices.

[11] Ibid.

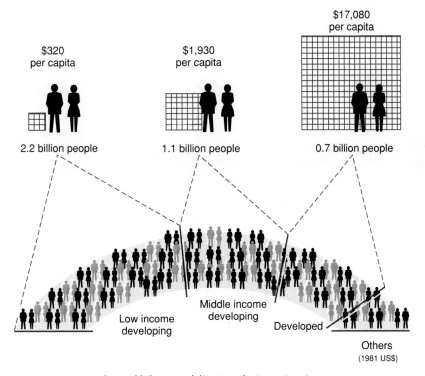

FIGURE 3–1   Nearly Half the World's Population Live in Low-Income Developing Countries, Where the Average GNP per Capita is $320. "Others" are Eastern Europe and OPEC Countries.
SOURCE: World Bank, *World Development Report, 1990.*

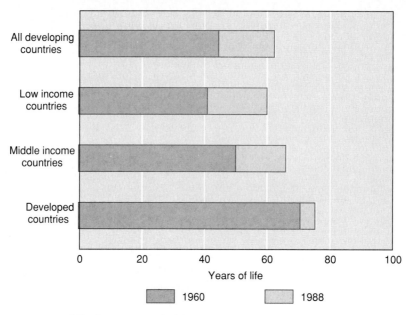

FIGURE 3–2   Life Expectancy in Years.
SOURCE: World Bank, *The Development Data Book, 1990.*

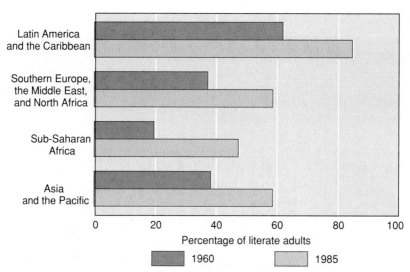

FIGURE 3–3   Growth in Adult Literacy Rates in Developing
Countries Since 1960.
SOURCE: World Bank, *The Development Data Book, 1990.*

Thus, the situation in LDCs is a continuous vicious cycle. As populations increase (see Figure 3–4), economic activity continues to focus on limited and low-profit agricultural and natural resource production. There is not enough capital available because of low savings. More improvements in the labor pool and diversification of the export base are extremely difficult. Added to these problems, LDCs frequently have undeveloped banking systems, high levels of bureaucratic graft, political instability, serious international debt problems, severe hard currency needs, and high levels of inflation.

The Fourth World: Black, Shadow, Second, and Submerged Economies

While the United Nations and the World Bank consistently use the identification of gross national product per person to evaluate the relative wealth of a nation vis-à-vis its neighbors and trading partners, this figure may not be fully representative of the actual production of a nation, because in many countries, even the United States, there exists an underground economy, in which transactions do not enter official records and are not, therefore, shown in the overall figures of the nation's GNP. Unofficial sales and purchases of goods and services are commonly known as black-market transactions, and they make the official GNP figure somewhat lower than it actually is.

Alternately, goods can be traded in barter systems, in which no money changes hands but an economic exchange has been made, or transfers are made in exchange rates between currencies that differ from officially cited rates. These systems also lead to a distortion of aggregate economic data and tax evasion by the participants. They are ubiquitous in Third World nations and are called shadow, second, or submerged economies, or black work, as the underground economy is called in France.

In India, for example, it has been estimated that the black economy accounts for anywhere from 6 percent to 48 percent of the gross national product and is fueled by high levels of taxation on one side and the complexities of navigating an intricate bureaucratic maze on the other, where paying bribes is often a matter of course in doing business.

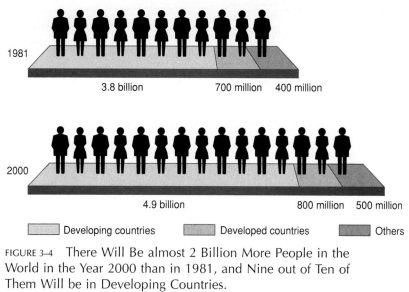

1981
3.8 billion   700 million   400 million

2000
4.9 billion   800 million   500 million

Developing countries   Developed countries   Others

FIGURE 3–4   There Will Be almost 2 Billion More People in the World in the Year 2000 than in 1981, and Nine out of Ten of Them Will be in Developing Countries.
SOURCE: World Bank, *The Development Data Book,* 1990.

Even though the government recently reduced its top tax rate from 97.75 percent to 50 percent, most Indian businesspersons still reportedly hide more income than they declare and make under-the-table deals through the use of a thriving black economy of money dealers and brokers who have developed a multitude of tax evasion methods (see Perspective 3–2).

PERSPECTIVE 3–2   India's Onerous Taxes and Red Tape Spawn a Huge Underground Economy

BOMBAY, India—The money-changers of Bombay change rupees into rupees.

More precisely, they convert ill-gotten "black" rupees into "white" rupees, or vice versa. They also lend money, with one interest rate for white, another for black.

India has an enormous underground, or black, economy built on the twin foundations of high taxes and the state's intricate system of economic regulations and controls, cemented together with a huge, underpaid, and therefore bribable, army of civil servants. It grows every time a businessman evades a tax, pays a bribe or edges around government regulations.

DRIVING THE ECONOMY

Indians who indulge in the black economy—those with incomes to hide or the means to bribe—probably account for less than 10% of the population. But those Indians make the entire economy work. Few business transactions in India are totally aboveboard.

Prime Minister Rajiv Gandhi's government, by slashing tax rates and loosening industrial controls, is hoping to dam this Ganges of black cash. But economists say the task is daunting.

This secret economy eludes measurement, though that hasn't stopped economists from estimating it to be anywhere from 6% to 48% of the gross national product, the total value of the goods and services India produces. A blunt study commissioned by the government in 1985 found the black economy to be "quite pervasive," growing rapidly and the equivalent of 21% of GNP. But even that study ignored major components of the black economy, including bribes, undeclared capital gains and money earned illegally.

Black money can be the undeclared fortune won on the stock market, and the interest that fortune earns in the bank. It can be the money that buys an apartment or a dinner at a fancy hotel. It's the soiled bills a bureaucrat collects in bribes, and the business an industrialist gets in return for his bribe.

AVOIDING TAXES

Tax cuts don't seem to have stemmed the flow. In 1986, Mr. Gandhi lowered the country's top income-tax rate to 50% from 97.75%. But a middle-class Indian still has to contend with real-estate tax, wealth tax and jewelry tax, not to mention the sales and excise taxes that bring New Delhi the bulk of its revenue. With a clever accountant or an envelope of cash, many taxes can be evaded.

The government admits that, in total, Indians hide more income than they declare. But on average, the authorities convict only 16 people a year-out of 4.5 million Indians eligible to pay income tax.

The black economy also feeds on the maze of government rules and restrictions. For example, India restricts the production of many goods, and manufacturers must be licensed to make them. If an industrialist wants a license, he can bribe a bureaucrat. When that same industrialist wants

SOURCE: Anthony Spaeth, Wall Street Journal, July 25, 1988.

to produce more goods than his license allows, he bribes an inspector. He records his black earnings in separate books and invests and spends them in black ways.

Another flood of black cash comes from government spending, which has multiplied 50 times in the past three decades and now accounts for almost a quarter of GNP. The government's black-money report found that "leakages" from government spending are one of the largest sources of black money. In many public works projects, 10% to 50% of the budgets disappear into the pockets of contractors and bureaucrats, the report said.

"Significant cuts and kickbacks to key decision-makers has become the rule rather than the exception," it said.

Whether money is made legally, by an upright doctor in his office or through a kickback scheme, it turns black the moment it is hidden from tax authorities.

Much conspicuous spending is done with black money, especially in glitzy Bombay, but it is more than matched by surreptitious investments in gold, dollars, the Indian stock market and real estate.

Black money has begotten black brokers, black investment managers, entire buildings of black apartments and even a class of government-issued bonds that only black investors buy. So much black money has poured into one village near Bombay that real-estate prices have soared to almost $100,000 a hectare. But the local record books say the land is still selling at 1950s prices: $2,500 to $3,700 a hectare.

This allows the seller to reap enormous undeclared profits and the local real-estate agents to underdeclare their commissions. And it allows the buyer from the city to park some black cash.

Even more dizzying are the procedures involved when a businessman converts white money to black, and vice versa. If an investor makes a killing on a stock and wants to hide it from the tax man, he simply asks his stockbroker to record a series of fictitious, money-losing trades. Payment is in cash, not a traceable check.

When a businessman has black money, but needs white for an aboveboard investment, the stockbroker does the reverse: He creates a portfolio of fictitious, money-winning transactions.

WILLING CLIENT

Or the businessman can go to another kind of broker, who matches him up with a willing corporate client. For a fee, the broker composes a portfolio of correspondence, sometimes going back years, that documents "commissions" paid the individual. The corporation issues checks to the businessmen equal to those commissions: the businessman repays the corporation in black cash. The corporation gets a small commission and reduces its tax liability. The individual, at a price, turns his black cash to white.

So ingrained is the black culture in Bombay that when people win a horse race or the lottery, they rarely redeem their ticket. They sell it, at a premium, to a black-money broker. The broker resells the ticket, at a higher premium, to a client who wants to launder black money. At day's end, it is the black-money businessman who has officially won the lottery—after losing 10% to 30% of his cash in fees.

By lowering tax rates and lessening its regulation of industry, done for separate reasons, the government has indirectly attacked the black-money problem. It also declares occasional tax amnesties.

And in 1979, the government tried to flush out black cash by demonetizing the 1,000-rupee note, worth $124 at the time and considered the staple of the black stash. But black-money holders sold their 1,000-rupee notes for as little as 330 rupees to people with nothing to hide when they converted the bills.

BLACK BONDS

The government even issues bonds to soak up black cash, promising that no one will ask where the money came from. Despite meager interest rates, $770 million of the bonds have sold since 1981.

But it is still debatable if the black economy is shrinking because of Mr. Gandhi's actions. "On the basis of anecdotes I've heard. I would conclude it is," says A.V.L. Narayana, a New Delhi economist who helped write the black-money report. "But there is no statistical proof."

In Bombay, it is still cheaper to borrow black money than white, because black money is in much greater supply.

Since the 1960s, the world has seen dramatic changes in the patterns of world trade and, indeed, in the relative importance of groups of trading nations and historical trade leaders. The past twenty years or more have seen a shift in trading patterns away from the industrialized countries and toward greater involvement of the less-developed countries and the rising stars in the world, the newly industrialized countries of Asia—South Korea, Hong Kong, Taiwan, and Singapore. Figure 3–5 is a representation of changing world market shares since the halcyon days of trading activities for the industrialized countries. In every category, except perhaps agriculture, where the benefits of the latest in technological development and the use of high-yield fertilizer products are being realized, the developed countries of the world have lost market share primarily to LDCs and to the newly industrialized countries (NICs). The Japanese market share is also remarkable in this scheme, as it shows increases in technology-intensive manufacturing and the transportation trade, while labor-intensive clothing and textile products and land-intensive agricultural production have decreased.[12]

Japan's economy has grown at an average annual rate of 4.3 percent since 1965. This compares to a rate of growth of 1.6 percent in the United States, 1.8 percent in the United Kingdom, 2.5 percent in France, and 2.7 percent in Canada. The four tigers—Hong Kong, South Korea, Singapore, and Taiwan—have also had very high growth rates in this period.[13] Hong Kong and South Korea have had annual growth rates of 6.3 percent and 6.8 percent, while Singapore and Taiwan grew at 7.2 percent and 3.6 percent, respectively.

The trend of increasing competition to the pre-eminence of the United States is likely to continue in the foreseeable future. Not only will competition increase from the NICs and Japan, but other contenders, such as Brazil and India, are seen as waiting in the wings. This shift of focus in world economic activity is also expected to be encouraged by the opening up of traditionally limited markets, such as the People's Republic of China, and the movement toward free-market economies in the Soviet Union and Eastern Europe.

Summary

International trade theories attempt to explain motives for trade, underlying trade patterns, and the ultimate benefits of trade. Beginning with the Western European notion of mercantilism, nations, not individuals, should be involved in the transfer of goods between countries in order to increase the wealth of home countries, specifically through the accumulation of gold. The classical theories of absolute and comparative advantage looked at cost efficiencies of production as motivators of trade. Weaknesses in their basic assumptions led to the development of the factor endowment theory, which explains trade among nations on the basis of factors, or inputs, used in production, such as land, labor, capital, technology, facilities, and distribution networks.

Recent theorists have found that individuals, rather than nations, initiate and conduct trade. Further, traditional theories ignore the importance of technology and marketing and management skills. The international life cycle theory offers different motivations for trade based on the four stages of a product—innovation, growth, maturity, and decline. Other modern theories

[12] United Nations, *Handbook of International Trade and Development Statistics*, 1988, Appendix A.
[13] World Bank, *The World Development Report, 1990.*

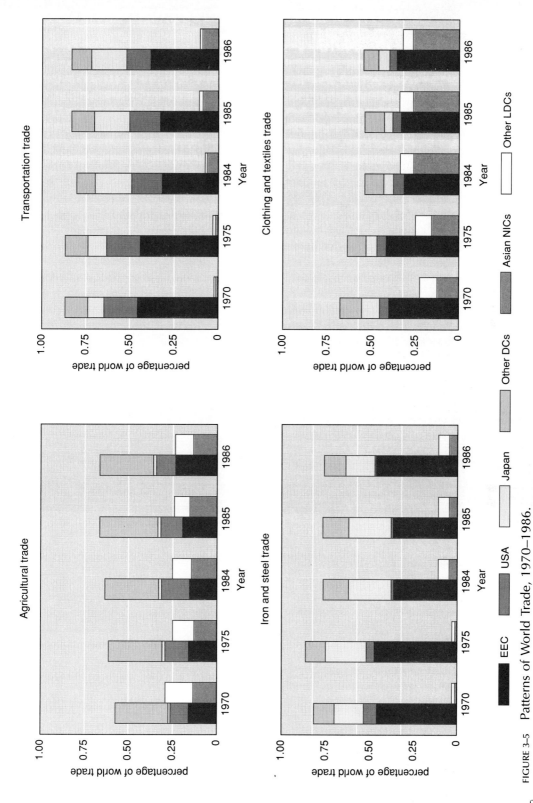

FIGURE 3-5 Patterns of World Trade, 1970–1986.
SOURCE: United Nations, *Handbook of International Trade and Development Statistics*, 1988.

explain foreign investment as natural competitive responses where firms seek to optimize market opportunities offering production advantages, economies of scale, and favorable capital markets, or firms are reacting to investment decisions of competitors by following the leader.

Economic development theories attempt to explain the transition from an undeveloped economy to a developed, manufacturing-oriented economy. The classical economic theory limited a nation's development and economic growth to its supply of land and labor and discounted any effects of technology improvements that might create greater efficiencies. Rostow's theory of economic growth attempts to relate economic development to changes within society and identified five stages—traditional society, preconditions for takeoff, takeoff, the drive to maturity, and the age of high mass consumption. The big push theories argued that only synchronized uses of capital to develop wide ranges of industries in combination with an overall popular effort would propel developing nations into more developed stages. Alternatively, Hirschman's strategy of unbalance advocated selective investment in developing countries to create backward and forward linkages.

Political and economic systems run along a continuum that has democratic free-market economies on one extreme and totalitarian centrally planned economies on the other.

Nations have been divided into three categories—the First, Second and Third worlds—based principally on gross national product per capita criteria. A fourth, or Shadow, world exists where many transactions are not included in official GNP figures, thereby significantly understating real national wealth. Other social criteria influence categorization, such as life expectancy, infant mortality levels, literacy rates, and health and education standards.

Trading patterns have shifted away from industrialized countries toward lesser developed and newly industrialized countries. Increasing competition from NICs, such as Brazil and India, are challenging the preeminence of the United States.

Discussion Questions

1. What were the fallacies of the theory of mercantilism?
2. Briefly describe the differences between the theories of absolute and comparative advantage. What were the shortcomings of these theories?
3. Discuss the various stages of the international product life cycle. Give an example of a product that was introduced to various countries under this theory.
4. Discuss the differences between a free-market economy and a centrally planned economy. What type of economy exists in Japan?
5. Select a country from the First World and the Third World and compare:
   - GNP per capita
   - Annual export levels
   - Life expectancy
   - Literacy rates
   - Energy consumption levels
   - GNP growth rates

   What do you find similar/different?
6. What problems or concerns may exist when GNP per capita is used as an indicator to evaluate national economies and potential business opportunities? What other factors could be used?

Bibliography

BERKER, G. S., and R. J. BARRO. 1988. "A Reformulation of the Economic Theory of Fertility." *Quarterly Journal of Economics* (February): 1–25.

FARDOUST, SHAHROUKH, and A. DHARESHWAR. 1990. *Long-Term Outlook for the World Economy Issues and Projections for the 1990s,* Edison, NJ: World Bank Publications.

GULTEKIN, M. N., N. B. GULTEKIN, and A. PENATI. 1989. "Capital Controls and International Capital Market Segmentation: The Evidence from the Japanese and American Stock Markets." *Journal of Finance* (September): 849–869.

HECKSCHER, E. 1919. "The Effects of Foreign Trade on Distribution of Income." *Economisc Tidskrift:* 497–512.

HELLER, H. ROBERT. 1973. *International Trade: Theory and Empirical Evidence,* 2nd ed. Englewood Cliffs, NJ: Prentice-Hall.

LEONTIEF, W. W. 1954. "Domestic Production and Foreign Trade: The American Capital Position Re-examined." *Economia Internationale* (February): 3–32.

McCARTHY, F. DESMOND. 1990. *Problems of Developing Countries in the 1990s.* Edison, NJ: World Bank Publications.

MILL, J. S. 1845. Principals of Political Economy. New York: D. Appleton & Co.

MUNDELL, ROBERT. 1957. "International Trade and Factor Mobility." *American Economic Review* (June): 321–335.

OFFICER, LAURENCE H., ed. 1987. *International Economics.* Boston: Kluwer Academic Publishers.

OHLIN, BERTIL. 1933. *Inter-regional and International Trade.* Cambridge, MA: Harvard University Press.

RICARDO, DAVID. 1948. *The Principals of Political Economy and Taxation.* New York: E.P. Dutton & Co.

ROSTOW, W. W. 1961. *The Stages of Economic Growth, A Non-Communist Manifesto.* New York: Cambridge University Press.

SAMUELSON, R. A. 1948. "International Trade and the Equalization of Factor Prices." *Economic Journal* (June): 186.

———. 1949. "International Factor Price Equalization, Once Again." *Economic Journal* (June): 74.

SMITH, ADAM. n.d. *The Wealth of Nations.* New York: Modern Library.

VERNON, R. 1966. "International Investment and International Trade in the Product Life Cycle." *Quarterly Journal of Economics* (May): 190–207.

WORLD BANK. 1990. *The Development Data Book.* Washington, DC: World Bank Publications.

———. 1990. *Trends in Developing Economies 1990.* Edison, NJ: World Bank Publications.

———. 1990. *World Development Report, 1990.* New York: Oxford University Press.

CHAPTER 4

International Monetary System and Balance of Payments

CHAPTER OBJECTIVES

This chapter will:

- Define the important terms and concepts of the international monetary system.
- Provide a brief history of the development of the monetary system, from the gold standard to the establishment of the International Monetary Fund.
- Introduce the objectives, roles, and structure of the International Monetary Fund.
- Describe the origins, uses, and valuation methodology of the special drawing right.
- Explain the problems affecting the Bretton Woods system that resulted in development of the managed, or dirty, float.
- Identify areas of reform facing the international monetary system.

International Monetary Terminology

In order to conduct international business or international trade, a well-organized and internationally accepted system must exist to settle the financial transactions that arise out of trade payments. Moreover, this system has to be in step with the nature of the financial transactions that occur in international business and trade and must be flexible enough to accommodate the constant changes in the patterns, directions, volumes, and nature of the financial flows. This mechanism is broadly termed the "international monetary system," or IMS. Although international trade dates back thousands of years, the use of money as a medium of settlement is relatively recent. Initially, barter was the primary trading mechanism. It was replaced by more formalized systems that relied on the use of gold as the basis for the settling of international transactions.

The settlement of transactions can be relatively easy when trade is carried on domestically, within the borders of individual countries, because the currency of the country is acceptable to all involved parties. Once more than one currency is involved, however, a need arises to develop an internationally acceptable basis to settle transactions.

Hard Currencies

The first requirement for setting up an IMS is to arrive at an international agreement establishing the basis upon which to settle transactions. Arriving at this basis is not easy, because it involves valuing the currency of one country against the currency of one or more other countries. Thus, if a currency forms the basis of the settlement, then it has to be accepted by everyone involved.

Currencies of certain countries have a fairly wide acceptance for the settlement of international obligations and are used as a medium in international transactions. These currencies are known as hard currencies. The U.S. dollar, British pound, Japanese yen, and deutsche mark are examples of hard currencies. Hard currencies can be used by two countries in settling their transactions even if that particular currency is not the home currency of either country. For example, trade transactions between Canada and Mexico can be settled in U.S. dollars, a currency acceptable to both countries even though it is not the home currency of either country. Another important feature of hard currencies is that there is usually a free and active market for them. In other words, if necessary, these currencies can be easily acquired and disposed of internationally in large quantities. There are also usually very few restrictions on the transfer of such currencies in and out of their home country. Hard currencies, therefore, are an important basis on which to construct an international monetary system.

Soft Currencies

Soft currencies, on the other hand, are not widely accepted as a medium for settling international financial transactions. Usually there is no free market or foreign exchange for them. Thus, they are not easy to acquire and disposal is even more difficult. Many soft currencies are subject to restrictions by the monetary/governmental authorities on their transfer in and out of their countries. Examples of soft currencies are the Russian ruble, Polish zloty, Chinese yuan, and the Brazilian cruzeiro.

Convertibility

Linked to the notion of hard and soft currencies is the concept of convertibility, whereby a currency can be freely converted into another currency. Some countries impose restrictions on currencies so that they cannot be freely converted into the currencies of other countries. These restrictions usually exist in countries that have centrally controlled economies and where transactions outside the country can be made only with official approval. Convertibility implies the availability of a free and active market for a currency. While currency may be unrestricted in terms of governmental regulations for conversion into other currencies, there may not be an adequate demand by persons outside the country. Such currencies are also said to be lacking in convertibility. Therefore, hard currencies possess the characteristic of convertibility, while soft currencies do not.

When full convertibility of a currency is restricted, a black market often arises that operates outside the control of the government. Essentially, the black market is a free market that parallels the official market and provides full conversion into the local currency, but at a substantial premium over the official rate. The black market in developing countries often operates around parks, international hotels, or transportations stations.

Exchange Rate

When a currency of any one country is used as a medium of settlement of an international transaction, its value has to be fixed vis-à-vis the currency of the other country, either directly or in terms of a third currency. This fixing of a price or value of one currency in terms of another currency is known as the determination of the exchange rate. The exchange rate essentially indicates how many units of one currency can be exchanged for one unit of the other currency or vice versa. Exchange rates are not usually fixed permanently. The values of a currency may change upward or downward, because of a variety of factors. The frequency with which the currency values change also depends upon the type of exchange rate arrangement of a currency. More fundamentally, however, it has to be understood that the movement of the value of a currency can be either up or down.

Appreciation

When the value of a currency is revised or changes upward, it is said to have appreciated.[1] Appreciation of a currency implies that it has become more expensive in terms of other currencies (that is, more units of other currencies will be needed to purchase the same amount of this currency, or fewer units of the appreciated currency will buy the same amount of the other currency). For example, the exchange rate of the U.S. dollar and the pound sterling is $1\delta = 2U.S.\$$. If, for example, the pound sterling appreciates by 50 percent, then one pound will be equal to three U.S. dollars. More U.S. dollars can be purchased by the same amount of currency (that is, one pound). Alternatively, in this example, before appreciation two U.S. dollars could buy one pound sterling. After appreciation, three U.S. dollars will be needed to buy the same amount of the foreign currencies, that is, one pound.

[1] If a currency is fixed against some other currency, any formal upward adjustment of its value against the reference currency is termed a revaluation. Correspondingly, any formal downward adjustment is termed a devaluation.

Depreciation

When the price of a currency is changed downward, it is said to have depreciated. A currency, upon depreciation, becomes less expensive in terms of another currency. Fewer units of the other currency can be purchased with the same amount of the currency after its devaluation. Alternatively, more units of the depreciated currency are needed to purchase the same amount of foreign currency.

For example, at the current exchange rate, one U.S. dollar buys three German marks. After depreciation, one U.S. dollar becomes equal to two German marks. In effect, one dollar now can buy only two units of German marks after depreciation. Alternatively, it would take one and a half dollars to buy three German marks instead of only one U.S. dollar, as was the case before depreciation.

A Brief History of the International Monetary System

The first form of an international monetary system, emerged toward the latter half of the nineteenth century. In 1865 four European countries founded the Latin Monetary Union. Its monetary system rested on the use of bimetallic currencies that had international acceptability within member countries of the union. Bimetallism (using gold and silver) was the basis upon which the values of the different currencies were determined.

The Gold Standard

The gold standard, which replaced the bimetallic standard as a system with wide international acceptance, lasted from its introduction in 1880 until the outbreak of World War I in 1914. The central feature of the gold standard was that exchange rates of different countries were fixed, and the parities or values were set in relation to gold.

Thus, gold served as the common basis for the determination of individual currency values. Each country adhering to the gold standard specified that one unit of its currency would be equal to a certain amount of gold. Thus, if country A's currency equaled two units of gold and country B's currency equaled four units of gold, the exchange rate of country A's currency against that of the currency of country B's would be one to two.

The Gold Specie Standard

The gold specie standard was a pure gold standard. The primary role of gold was as an internationally accepted means of settlement through an arrangement of corresponding debits and credits between the different nations. At the same time, gold was in the form of coins, the primary means of settling domestic transactions. Therefore, the gold specie standard required that gold should be available in unlimited quantities at fixed prices through the monetary authorities. There could be no restraints on the import or export of gold, and anyone could have coins struck at the mint if he possessed the requisite amount of gold. In effect, this system meant that the face value of gold coins was the same as their exact intrinsic value. The amount of coins, and therefore currency, that a country could issue would be limited to the amount of gold in the possession of a country or its citizens.

Gold Bullion Standard

Under the gold bullion standard, the direct link between gold and actual currency that a country could issue was eliminated. Currency could either be in the form of gold or paper, but the issuing authority of the currency would give a standing guarantee to redeem the currency it had issued in gold on demand at the announced price, which would be fixed. Gold was thus backing the issue, but the requirement to maintain exact proportions between the amount of gold in a country's possession and the amount of currency was eliminated, because the authority could reasonably expect that not all the paper currency that it had issued would

come up for redemption at the same time. There was, however, a clear need to maintain a link between the amount of a currency in use and the amount of gold available in the depository of the issuing authority, because a certain proportion of gold backup had to be maintained to honor the estimated requested redemption.

The gold bullion standard was widely adopted in the late nineteenth century. Under the gold bullion standard, international transactions could be settled fairly easily, because each country had defined the value of its currency in terms of gold. Thus, a person with U.S. dollars could trade in those dollars for gold with the U.S. authorities and, obtain British pounds in England with the gold.

On a country level, the gold standard proved an effective mechanism to settle overall international transactions. A country with a balance of payments deficit faced a situation where it had to lose some of its gold to pay its debts to the surplus country. This led to a reduction in money supply (that was partially backed by gold) and a reduction in prices, which increased the country's export competitiveness and made imports costly. As a result, the balance of payments tended to move away from the deficit toward an equilibrium position because of increasing exports and declining imports. The effect on the surplus country, on the other hand, was the opposite, which in turn moved away from its surplus position to a position of overall balance of payments equilibrium.

Exchange rates were fixed under the gold standards and could not fluctuate beyond upper and lower limits, known as the upper and lower gold points. This slight fluctuation was possible because of the costs involved in the physical movement of equilibrating gold flows from the deficit to the surplus country. If exchange rates went beyond the gold points, the physical transfer of gold would become more remunerative and push the price back within the gold points.

The gold standard worked fairly well during the period from 1880 to 1914. The supply of gold was reasonably steady and the world economy continued to grow steadily, free from any major international financial crisis. The British empire was at its zenith and London was the center of international trade and finance. The central role played by the United Kingdom in general and the Bank of England in particular inspired confidence in the system, which became widely accepted.

The outbreak of World War I, however, radically changed the scenario for the gold standard. Pressures on the U.K.'s finances because of war expenditures and the resultant gold outflows shook popular confidence in the system. During the war years, no universal system prevailed, most major currencies were in effect floating freely, and the war effort was financed by the creation of large amounts of money that was not backed by gold.

The Interwar Years (1918–1939)

At the end of World War I, the IMS was in a state of disarray. Most currencies had undergone wide fluctuations, and the economies of several European countries were severely damaged by the war. Several attempts were made, primarily motivated by Great Britain, to return to the gold standard in the years immediately following the end of World War I. For Great Britain, perhaps, this was an attempt to restore its preeminent prewar position in the international monetary arena. Great Britain therefore announced a prewar exchange parity linked to gold. This was not a realistic exchange rate, however, and it was actually grossly overvalued, given the external balance situation at that time. As a result, Great Britain was forced to redeem substantial amounts of its currency in gold, which led to further outflows of gold and increased pressure on the UK monetary situation.

While Great Britain tried to maintain a strong currency, redeemable in gold, several other countries, eager to improve their international competitive position, began a rush of currency devaluations without any formal agreement with other countries on what a desirable and internationally acceptable value of their currencies should be vis-à-vis other currencies. Apart from the fact

that most economies were damaged by war, different countries witnessed different rates of inflation, which upset their international competitive positions at their current level of exchange rates. In an effort to become more competitive, most countries ended up creating a devaluation race, with no formal boundaries or an agreed upon set of rules. The position was clearly one of a non-system, where the values of the currencies were determined by the arbitrary decisions of national authorities and the play of market forces.

The difficulties caused by the Great Depression, the problems Germany faced in financing its war reparations, the collapse of the Austrian banking system, and the introduction of exchange controls (restrictions on convertibility of currencies), were symptomatic of the chaos that afflicted the international monetary framework in the 1930s. The United States, having become the world's leading economic power as well as the major creditor, added to the general monetary difficulties by continuing to maintain a relatively undervalued exchange rate, despite having huge balance of payments surpluses. Moreover, by acquiring substantial quantities of gold, which it financed by its balance of payment surpluses, the United States exerted further pressure on the economically beleaguered nations of Europe. Some countries, such as Great Britain and France, established strict exchange controls to ensure the availability of foreign exchange to meet essential imports. Currency blocs were also formed (for example, the Dollar Area Bloc and the Sterling Area Bloc). In each currency bloc, there were several member countries who had no exchange controls, but all collectively exercised exchange controls with countries outside the bloc.

The Bretton Woods System (1944–1973)

During World War II there was a general and increasing recognition of the futility of the arbitrary and antagonistic exchange rate and the monetary policies that had been followed by the major industrialized countries during the 1920s and 1930s.

It was realized that these policies had been largely counterproductive and had resulted in lower trade and employment levels in most countries. It was also found that these nonformal arrangements had led to a worldwide misallocation of resources that had retarded the efficiency of their utilization.

As a result, in 1943 the United States and Great Britain took the initiative toward creating a stable and internationally acceptable monetary system. At the United Nations Monetary and Financial Conference at Bretton Woods, New Hampshire, in 1944, delegates of forty countries, after considerable negotiations, agreed to create a new international monetary arrangement.

The Bretton Woods Agreement adopted a gold exchange standard, primarily along the proposals made by the U.S. delegation, which was led by Haddy Dexter White. The gold exchange standard got its basic logic from the gold standard because it sought to bring gold back into a position of international monetary preeminance and, at the same time, to revive the system of fixed exchange rates. The new system recognized the difficulties inherent in completely rigid exchange rates and made some provisions for flexibility.

Under the Bretton Woods system participants agreed to stipulate a par value for their respective currencies, either directly in terms of gold or indirectly by linking its par value to the gold content of the U.S. dollar. The exchange rates could fluctuate to the extent of 1 percent of the par value on either side. The par values themselves could not be changed except with the concurrence of the International Monetary Fund, an institution set up by the Bretton Woods Agreement. Usually, the fund would not object to changes up to 10 percent in par values.

Thus, the U.S. dollar had a central role in the arrangement. The U.S. government guaranteed that it would be ready to buy or sell unlimited quantities of gold at U.S.$35 per ounce in redemptions of the dollar. To maintain its par value in terms of the U.S. dollar, each participant in the system agreed to buy or sell its currency in requisite amounts against the U.S. dollar.

The dollar's convertibility into gold gave it the primary position in the system because member countries could hold either dollars or gold as their reserves. Many preferred to hold U.S. dollars, which had the advantage of interest income accruing on the reserves, but was not true of reserves held in the form of gold. Moreover, many central banks used the dollar as their currency of intervention (that is, the currency they bought or sold to maintain the values of their own currencies within the par value limits prescribed by the arrangements). The dollar, being the reserve currency, also became the predominant currency for settlement of international trade and financial transactions.

The International Monetary Fund

Aims

The Bretton Woods Conference created the International Monetary Fund to administer the exchange rate arrangements and to secure orderly monetary conditions. More specifically, the five aims of the IMF, as laid out in its articles, are to achieve the following:

1. Promote international cooperation through consultation and collaboration by member countries on international monetary issues
2. Facilitate a balanced growth of international trade
3. Promote exchange rate stability and orderly exchange rate arrangements
4. Foster a multilateral system of international payments and seek elimination of exchange restrictions that hinder the growth of world trade
5. Try to reduce both the duration and magnitude of imbalances in international payments

The IMF was asked to deal with three of these goals as a first priority. It was to administer the exchange rate arrangements agreed upon by the member countries, to provide member countries with financial resources to correct temporary payments imbalances, and to provide a forum in which the members could consult and collaborate on international monetary issues of common concern.

Membership

Initially the IMF had forty member countries and now has more than 150. Growth in membership was particularly rapid in the 1960s, as newly independent nations of Asia and Africa became members. Prior to 1990 Eastern bloc countries, such as the USSR, Czechoslovakia, and East Germany, were not members of the IMF. Political and economic changes in Eastern Europe in 1989 and 1990, however, have resulted in these countries applying for and receiving IMF membership. (East Germany entered the IMF on a de facto basis upon reunification with West Germany.)

Membership in the fund is based on subscription to its resources in the form of a quota. A member's quota, being equal to its subscription to the fund, determines the voting power of the member, as well as, to a considerable extent, its access to the fund's resources. Quotas of members are periodically adjusted to reflect changes in the underlying criteria that were used to establish them initially (see Perspective 4–1). Size of quotas are determined by a set formula that takes into account several factors, such as national income, gold and dollar balances, average imports, variability of exports, and so on. The method of computation has undergone several refinements and changes since its inception. There is now a greater emphasis on trade and trade variability as criteria for determining a country's quotas rather than using such criteria as gross domestic product.

PERSPECTIVE 4–1   Increase in Fund Quotas Approved

A 50 percent increase in Fund quotas, or membership subscriptions, was approved by the Board of Governors of the IMF on June 28, 1990. As a result, total fund quotas will rise from about SDR 90.1 billion (roughly $120 billion) to SDR 135.2 billion ($180 billion). This action marked the completion of the Ninth General Review of Quotas. The previous general increase in fund quotas took place in 1983, when subscriptions were increased by 47.5 percent.

The new increase followed a recommendation by the Interim Committee, the IMF's advisory body, at its meeting in early May in Washington, DC, that the fund's Board of Governors should approve a 50 percent increase in the total of Fund quotas in accordance with understandings agreed by the fund's Executive Board and during the

course of the Interim Committee meeting. The 151 member countries signified their approval by the formal vote of the Board of Governors.

The size of a member's quota in the IMF determines its voting power in the institution; it also influences the amount a member can borrow from the fund when it encounters difficulties in its international finances, and determines the amount of its own currency that a member must provide in the form of subscriptions to the fund. When a member's currency is used by the fund, it receives a market-based rate of interest and an increase in its reserve position at the IMF. If a member should have a balance of payments need, it may use its reserve position at any time. The relative size of quotas also determines members' shares in any allocation of SDRs.

SOURCE: *Finance & Development*, September 1990, page 21.

Quotas are expressed in terms of special drawing rights (SDRs), the fund's accounting unit. (The SDR is a reserve asset that fund members agreed to create in 1969. Its value is calcualted daily, based on the market exchagne rates of the world's five major currencies. On July 16, 1990, SDR 1 = $1.33957.)

As the world economy grows, and with it international trade and payments as well as the magnitude of the potential financing needs of individual countries, the fund's resources must be enlarged to help maintain the fund's central position in the international monetary system. That is why at intervals of not more than five years, the fund's quota structure is reviewed and, if necessary, revised to better reflect changes in the world economy as well as changes in members' relative economic positions. The Tenth General Review of Quotas will be conducted not later than March 31, 1993, although it could be conducted earlier in case of a clear need to do so.

The distribution of the quota increase under the Ninth Review was guided by two main principles. First, all members should receive a meaningful increase in quotas and, second, the distribution should be based on methods that are applied uniformly to all members. In order to provide a meaningful increase in quotas and to help maintain a balance between different groups of countries, 60 percent of the overall increase in quotas will be distributed to all members in proportion to their present individual quotas. The remaining 40 percent will be distributed in proportion to members' shares in the total of the calculated quotas (i.e., the quotas that broadly reflect members' relative economic positions). The calculated quotas are derived from formulas that employ data on members' GDP, current account transactions, and official reserves.

As part of the Ninth Review, it was agreed also that there will be a realignment of the quota shares of the major industrial countries, which are among the biggest shareholders in the IMF. Under the new structure, the Unitd States will remain the largest shareholder, with 19.62 percent of total quotas. The Federal Republic of Germany and Japan will be the next largest, each with 6.1 percent, followed by the United Kingdom and France, each with 5.48 percent of total quotas. Currently, the United Kingdom is the second largest shareholder, followed by Germany, France, and Japan. It was also agreed that Italy will have a quota share of 3.4 percent (the sixth largest shareholder after Saudi Arabia) and Canada will have a quota share of 3.2 percent. In addition, there was a special adjustment of the quotas of the fund's smallest members (the 20 members with present quotas of less than SDR 10 million).

Two things must now happen for the increase to come into effect. First, the membership must approve an amendment to the IMF's Articles of Agreement, the international treaty that all members sign upon joining, to provide for the suspension of a member's voting and related rights if that member does not fulfill its obligations under the treaty. Second, individual members with 85 percent of total present quotas up to December 30, 1991, or 70 percent thereafter, must formally consent to the increase in their quotas, having taken the necessary steps under their laws to ratify the increase. These actions are expected to be completed by the end of 1991.

The quota increase will permit the fund to maintain in the near future its ability to extend financing, particularly under its enlarged access policy. At present, around 50 countries—almost one third of the membership—are using financing from the IMF as they implement economic policies to coutner their difficulties. Current borrowers from the IMF include a number of highly indebted countries like Mexico and Venezuela, which are attempting to restore strong growth to their economies; Eastern European members like Poland and Hungary that are moving their economies to a free-market basis; as well as many of the world's poorest countries like Ghana, Madagascar, Nepal, and Togo that are attempting to reverse many years of economic decline or stagnation.

Structure

The highest decision-making body of the IMF is the Board of Governors, which consists of one governor appointed by each member of the fund. Generally, they are the ministers of finance or governors of central banks of the member countries. Day-to-day operations are overseen by the Executive Board, which consists of executive directors appointed by the countries with the largest quotas as one group and groups of countries with smaller quotas jointly elect one executive director. In 1990 there were twenty-two executive directors, seven appointed by the largest quota holders and fifteen elected by the other members in groups of different countries.

The United States has the largest quota, 19.6 percent. Other large quota holders are Germany, France, Japan, the United Kingdom, and Saudi Arabia. Because major decisions require an 85 percent majority, the United States has an effective veto power over major decisions.

Operation of the fund is headed by a managing director, who is elected by the executive board for an initial term of five years. The managing director reports to the board of governors and participates in the deliberations of major committees of the fund. Traditionally, the managing director has been from one of the European member countries of the fund.

Forms of IMF Assistance

The IMF offers assistance to its member countries by making financial resources available to them through a wide range of sources. The basic facility, known as a credit tranche drawing, permits a member country to borrow from the fund, in four tranches or stages, funds equaling its total subscription to the fund or its quota. Each tranche constitutes 25 percent of the member country's quota. Borrowings under this facility are short-term and are repayable in eight quarterly installments, the last of which has to be within five years of the drawing. This was the most utilized facility during the initial years of the fund. Since 1980, borrowings through other special facilities have exceeded those made under the basic credit tranche facility.

Extended Fund Facility

The extended fund facility was established in 1974 to provide member countries with financial resources for periods long enough to allow them to take corrective measures with respect to their balance of payments difficulties. The basic rationale of this facility is to allow the countries time to correct structural and policy distortions in their economies without having to bear the shocks of too rapid a transition. Moreover, the resources provided under the facility help the member countries tide over temporary balance-of-payments deficits that may occur in the course of corrective action. Assistance is provided on the basis of specific corrective programs proposed by the borrowing countries. These programs are usually spread over a period of three years. Borrowing up to 140 percent of the quota is permitted under the facility, subject to the upper limit of 165 percent of the quota not being exceeded when the borrowers' outstanding in the credit tranche facility are also taken into account. Repayments are to be made on a longer schedule than the credit tranche facility, and the first installment begins after four and one-half years, and the last is made ten years after the borrowing.

Compensatory Financing Facility

The compensatory financing facility was established in 1963 to provide financial assistance primarily to less-developed countries that were faced with balance of payments difficulties because of temporary export shortfalls that occurred because of factors beyond their control. Later, coverage of the facility was broadened to provide assistance to member countries facing balance of payments difficulties because of an increase in the costs of cereal imports. Since the facility is designed to finance the imbalances arising out of shortfalls in exports or because of an increase in the cost of cereal imports, computation of allowable drawings under this facility is based on the estimated shortfall in exports or increased import costs as measured against a median export performance/cereal import costs of the country. Repayments are normally made within three to five years after the borrowings.

Supplementary Financing Facility and Enlarged Access Policy

The supplementary financing facility was created in 1979 to meet the needs of member countries whose imbalances in their balance of payments could not be financed from their normal quota allocations. Funds for this facility are raised by borrowings from surplus countries.

Under the enlarged access policy, the IMF was able to continue to finance payments imbalances of certain member countries, in excess of normal quota allocations. Access to the resources of the fund under the enlarged access policy was extended to a cumulative total of up to 300 percent of a member's quota, depending upon the difficulty of the balance of payments situation and the nature of efforts being made to remedy the situation by the borrower. In exceptional cases the IMF can allow borrowings even in excess of these limits. The repayment schedule is spread over a long period, with the last repayment installment due seven years after the borrowing date.

Structural Adjustment Facilities

Structural adjustment facilities and enhanced structural adjustment facilities are relatively new facilities established by the IMF and are designed to provide financial assistance to member countries that are undertaking specific programs of structural adjustment within their economies.

Structural adjustment programs are essentially a set of policy measures designed to improve the overall efficiency and productive capacity of the economy, as well as to remove existing distortions or other operational deficiencies. Repayments under the facilities are spread over a longer term than other facilities and the borrower has to agree to a specific policy-change program, which it must treat as its own and not as one imposed by the IMF. Several countries of Africa, Asia, and Latin America will benefit from these new facilities.

IMF Conditionality

Conditionality is the technical term used to denote the policies that member countries who receive financial assistance from the IMF are expected to follow within their own economies, in order to remedy their balance of payments problems. The basic rationale provided by the IMF for requiring conditionality to accompany its lending is the need to address the root causes of the problem and generate in the borrower the capacity to meet its own balance of payments shortfalls and to be able to repay the fund loans. Conditionality is, of course, different for different countries, because the reasons for balance of payments problems differ in varying situations.

There are, however, four conditions that are found in nearly all IMF lending programs:

1. The achievement of a realistic exchange rate that would improve the external competitiveness of the economy. This most often means a substantial devaluation of the currency for many countries.
2. The elimination of subsidies and controls within the domestic economy, in order to achieve a more efficient allocation of resources and to remove the impediments to enhancing the productivity of the economy.
3. Reductions of tariff, trade, and exchange restrictions, thereby creating a relatively more open external sector.

4. A reduction of public sector/government spending, which is intended to eliminate excess demand and its impact on the balance of payments.

As the balance of payments problems have become increasingly difficult both in terms of their magnitude and their complexity, the conditionality of the IMF has tended to allow a longer time-frame for borrower countries to make the necessary policy adjustments. Moreover, IMF conditionality has tended to change from focusing almost exclusively on demand side measures to policies that are aimed to stabilize the supply conditions in the economies of borrowers. Some of the policies that IMF conditionality requires in the area of supply side stabilization are raising real interest rates, economic pricing of public services, and tax reforms intended to expand manufacturing output and employment.

The IMF, while providing financial assistance to member countries, receives from the borrowers specific policy programs that are to be followed during the period the member country is in receipt of assistance. These programs include specific targets for certain economic benchmarks, such as bank credit, budgetary deficits, external borrowings, and so on. The programs also contain official commitments not to increase restrictions on exchange rates. The IMF uses these targets as well as assurances as basic criteria to assess the performance of borrower countries. The performance of the borrowers in terms of their criteria is taken into account by the IMF while releasing further tranches of assistance. This practice allows the IMF to monitor and to some extent influence the policies of the countries utilizing its resources. Detailed guidelines have been laid down by the Executive Board of the IMF, under which the performance criteria are used to phase and control the financial assistance of the IMF to member countries.

In some cases there has been considerable resentment against the imposition of conditionality, both on grounds of its not being appropriate for the conditions prevalent in several borrower countries and that it is an infringement of a country's sovereign right to determine its economic policy. In some countries IMF conditionality has been blamed for causing considerable problems for the poorest sections of society and for taking a heavy social toll by its economic prescriptions. Counter-arguments hold that the IMF is often a scapegoat for economic ills that originated well before its establishment. Moreover, some politicians in the borrowing countries have found it convenient to pass on to the IMF the blame and responsibility for tough economic measures.

IMF conditionality, although basically remaining the same, has thus tended to be modified to take into account the realities in the borrowing countries and now stresses the role of the borrower countries in taking the primary responsibility for carrying out adjustment programs as a part of their own official policy and not as an outside prescription.

Special Drawing Rights

Using an SDR

Special drawing rights (SDRs) were created as a reserve asset by the International Monetary Fund in 1970. SDRs are essentially book entries that represent the right of the country holding them to access resources of equivalent value. SDRs owe their origin to the crisis in the international monetary system that began to emerge during the 1960s, when the volume of trade expanded much faster than the production of gold. Under the Bretton Woods arrangements, countries could hold reserves either in the form of gold or U.S. dollars. Reserves of U.S. dollars with other countries meant that the United States would have to run ever-larger balance of payments deficits. It was feared that a serious liquidity crisis could result if the United States was not able to sustain and manage large deficits, or if the deficits themselves increased to a point where they threatened the stability of the external balance of the United States. SDRs were therefore created as an additional reserve asset to complement existing reserves of U.S. dollars and gold.

Apart from being an international reserve asset, SDRs are the unit of accounting for all transactions between the IMF and its member countries. In addition, SDRs are used to settle international transactions between central banks of member countries of the IMF. SDRs are not, however, a privately used or traded international currency for commercial or other purposes. Certain international organizations, such as the Asian Development Bank, the Arab Monetary Fund, and the World Bank, have been permitted to hold SDRs.

SDRs are allocated to member countries by the Board of Governors of the IMF. Allocations of SDRs are made on the same basis as ordinary quotas to the funds of member countries. Holdings of SDRs constitute a part of the countries' international reserves in addition to gold, foreign exchange, and reserve assets with the IMF. Holding an SDR gives the bearer the option to acquire foreign exchange from the monetary authorities of another member of the IMF. In fact, the IMF intends the SDR to become the principal reserve asset of the international monetary system.

Valuation of SDRs

Originally, the value of the SDR was fixed in terms of gold, with one SDR being equivalent to .888671 grams of fine gold or thirty-five SDRs being equal to one fine ounce of gold. In 1974 this basis of SDR valuation was replaced by a system that utilized a weighted average of sixteen currencies, called a basket. Under this arrangement, which lasted from 1974 to 1980, the value of the SDR was determined on a daily basis. The currencies in this basket were those of member countries of the IMF whose shares in world exports of goods and services exceeded 1 percent each during the years from 1967 to 1972. While this arrangement lasted, there were some changes made in the basket composition that were meant to reflect the changing proportions of world trade being handled by different countries whose currencies were in the basket and those whose share increased over time, even though their currencies were not in the basket.

Despite the changes made to reflect the changing position of the shares of different countries in the world's exports of goods and services, this arrangement continued to suffer from certain problems. For one, many of the currencies in the basket were not actively traded internationally, at least in the forward market, which made actual weighing extremely difficult. To remedy this situation and to simplify the calculation procedure, a new SDR basket was introduced in 1980 that comprised the currencies of five countries that had the largest share in world exports of goods and services. The currency composition of the new SDR basket was as follows:

U.S. dollar	42%
Deutsche mark	19%
Japanese yen	13%
French franc	13%
Pound sterling	13%

The value of the SDR is determined by the prevailing market value of the currencies adjusted according to their basket weights. Since the 1980 valuation, the basket weights of the deutsche mark and the Japanese yen have increased, while the weight of the U.S. dollar has decreased.

Although SDRs are meant as a reserve asset and only to be used to settle official transactions between the IMF and its members and between the members themselves, there have been commercial uses of SDRs. The commercial utility of SDRs derives from the relatively stable nature that comes from its basket composition, which evens out wide fluctuations that are the bane of all major international currencies. As a result, many international borrowers have denominated their bonds and other borrowing instruments in SDRs. SDRs have also been used to denominate trade invoicing, even though settlement is ultimately made in one of the traditional currencies. Other users of SDRs include International Air Transport Association for fixing international airfares and the Republic of Egypt for denominating tolls for transit through the Suez Canal.

A major controversy surrounding SDRs is their use as a mechanism to create aid financing to meet the requirements of lesser-developed countries. LDCs hold that SDRs should not be linked to quotas, but to the actual needs of IMF member countries. Several industrialized countries, however, including the United States, feel that this instrument is primarily meant for creating international reserves and liquidity, and its use as an aid-financing mechanism would distort the original intentions and result in excess liquidity in the international economy. It has also been argued that aid would be extremely difficult to monitor from the utilization point of view if it were channeled through the SDR mechanism.

Although it is intended to be a major reserve asset, the SDR comprises much less than 10 percent of the world's international resources. A greater role for the SDR, however, would be in the interest of both developed and developing countries.

Difficulties in the Bretton Woods System

Because the U.S. dollar was a key international reserve currency under the Bretton Woods system, the deficit in the U.S. balance of payments was essential, if the liquidity requirements of the international monetary system were to be fully met. If the U.S. dollar deficits grew larger and larger, however, the holders of dollars would tend to lose confidence in the currency as a reserve and in the capacity of the United States to honor its obligations.

Signs of a future crisis became apparent in the late 1950s, when the United States started running extremely large balance of payments deficits. U.S. expansion and investment overseas, aid under the Marshall plan, and a strong economic recovery by Europe were some of the factors that went into making the U.S. trade account into one of almost constant deficit. By the 1960s it was clear that many European and other countries were growing increasingly uncomfortable with their holdings of U.S. dollars as reserves, and many of them wanted to redeem them for gold at the officially announced price. Moreover, given

the central role of the dollar in the system, it could not to be devalued to improve the competitive position of the United States versus other countries.

The crisis of confidence was reflected in a run on gold, which pushed its market price well above the announced official price of U.S.$35 per fine ounce. The central banks of various countries did manage to stabilize the price of gold, at least at the official level, by forming a gold pool and undertaking open-market operations. As a result, however, the gold market was split in two—the official and the unofficial—with U.S. authorities ready to redeem U.S. dollars received only from official sources in gold. Moreover, the U.S. government exerted pressure on the European and other holders of dollar reserves not to press for redemptions into gold.

Another inherent defect in the system was that it passed on the effects of U.S. domestic monetary policies to other countries. If the United States followed expansionary policies, other countries were forced to follow a reverse policy to maintain exchange parity. Moreover, the U.S. rates of inflation continued to be higher than those of European countries. Further, the inability to neutralize the inflationary effects of U.S. dollar holdings irked many countries, who felt that they were losing control over their domestic monetary policies. Meanwhile the German mark and Dutch guilder had to be revalued, and in 1968 the pound was substantially devalued.

By 1970 U.S. gold reserves had fallen U.S.$11 billion, while short-term official holdings of U.S. dollars were more than double this amount. The crisis came to a head in 1970, with a decline in U.S. interest rates that sparked a massive outflow of capital from the United States to Europe. The pressure on the value of the U.S. dollar continued unabated despite central bank support from many European countries. As a result, in May 1971, Switzerland and Austria revalued their currencies, and Germany and the Netherlands allowed the prices of their currencies to be determined by the market. A continued flight from the U.S. dollar strengthened doubts about the ability of the U.S. dollar to maintain convertibility into gold.

These doubts were confirmed on August 15, 1971, when President Richard Nixon announced the suspension of the convertibility of the U.S. dollar into gold. With the abandonment of dollar convertibility into gold, the underlying basis of the fixed exchange rate arrangements of the Bretton Woods system collapsed, and many other countries stopped fixing their exchange rates according to official parities, allowing them to be determined instead by the market.

An attempt was made to return to fixed parities in 1971, through the Smithsonian Agreement, under which the U.S. raised the official price of gold to U.S.$38 per fine ounce, marking a 7.9 percent devaluation of the dollar. The bands within which currencies could fluctuate against each other were widened to a range of 2.25 percent on each side of the fixed rate, but the dollar was not made convertible into gold. Moreover, the movement of capital across countries continued to put pressure on exchange rate parities. Faced with either heavy outflows or inflows of foreign currencies, several countries were forced to abandon the freshly fixed parities and allow their currencies to float freely on the international markets. Despite raising the price of gold for a second time, to U.S.$42.2 per ounce, the United States was not able to stem the outflow of dollars, and it became extremely difficult for European countries to maintain the value of their currencies against the U.S. dollar. By the end of the first quarter of 1973, most of the European countries had withdrawn from their participation in the system of parities established under the Smithsonian Agreement.

The Floating Rate Era: 1973 to the Present

The transition to a system of floating exchange rates was not the result of any formal agreement, such as the one that had created the system of fixed exchange rates. It occurred primarily because the earlier system broke down and there was no agreed upon formal arrangement to replace it. In fact, at this stage there was no universal agreement on an appropriate exchange rate arrangement. Universal agreement continues to elude the international monetary community, and a variety of exchange rate arrangements are followed by different groups of countries, as shown in Table 4–1. The most important types of exchange arrangements are different types of floating rates, pegging, crawling pegs, basket of currencies, and fixed rates.

Pure Floating Rates

Under the pure floating rate arrangement the exchange rate of the currency of a country is determined entirely by such market considerations as demand and supply. The government or the monetary authorities make no efforts to either fix or manipulate the exchange rate. Although many industrialized countries officially state that they follow a policy of floating for their exchange rates, most of them do intervene to influence the direction of the movement of their exchange rates.

Managed or Dirty Floating Rates

An important feature of the managed float system is the necessity for the central bank or the monetary authorities to maintain a certain level of foreign exchange reserves. Foreign exchange reserves are needed because the authorities are required to buy or sell foreign currencies in the market to influence exchange rate movements. On the other hand, under a free floating rate arrangement, this is not necessary, because the exchange market is cleared by a free play of the forces of supply and demand, which fix a particular exchange rate that is the equilibrium rate at any given point of time. Thus, no foreign exchange reserves are needed by a country that follows a system of free floating exchange rates.

Pegging

Under a pegging arrangement, a country links the value of its currency to that of another currency,

TABLE 4–1
Exchange Rate Arrangements as of March 31, 1990

Pegged				
Single Currency			**Currency composite**	
U.S. dollar	French franc	Other	SDR	Other
Afghanistan	Benin	Bhutan (Indian	Burundi	Algeria
Angola	Burkina Faso	rupee)	Iran, Islamic	Austria
Antigua and Barbuda	Cameroon	Kiribati (Australian	Republic of	Bangladesh
Bahamas	Central African	dollar)	Libyan Arab	Botswana
Barbados	Republic	Lesotho (South	Jamahiriya	Cape Verde
	Chad	African rand)	Myanmar	
Belize		Swaziland (South	Rwanda	Cyprus
Djibouti	Comoros	African rand)		Fiji
Dominica	Congo	Tonga (Australian	Seychelles	Finland
Dominican Republic	Côte d'Ivoire	dollar)	Zambia	Hungary
Ethiopia	Equatorial Guinea			Iceland
	Gabon			
Grenada				Israel
Guyana	Mali			Jordan
Haiti	Niger			Kenya
Iraq	Senegal			Kuwait
Jamaica	Togo			Malawi
Liberia				Malaysia
Nicaragua				Malta
Oman				Mauritius
Panama				Mozambique
Peru				Nepal
St. Kitts and Nevis				Norway
St. Lucia				Papua New Guinea
St. Vincent and The				Poland
Grenadines				Romania
Sierra Leone				Sao Tome and
Sudan				Principe
Suriname				Solomon Islands
Syrian Arab Republic				Somalia
Trinidad and Tobago				Sweden
Yemen Arab Republic				Tanzania
Yemen, People's				Thailand
Democratic				
Republic of				Uganda
				Vanuatu
				Western Samoa
				Zimbabwe

TABLE 4-1 (*continued*)
Exchange Rate Arrangements as of March 31, 1990

Flexibility Limited vis-à-vis a Single Currency or Group of Currencies		More Flexible		
Single currency	Cooperative arrangements	Adjusted according to a set of indicators	Other managed floating	Independently floating
Bahrain	Belgium	Chile	China	Argentina
Qatar	Denmark	Colombia	Costa Rica	Australia
Saudi Arabia	France	Madagascar	Ecuador	Bolivia
United Arab Emirates	Germany, Federal Republic of	Portugal	Egypt	Brazil
	Ireland		El Salvador	Canada
	Italy		Greece	Gambia, The
	Luxembourg		Guinea	Ghana
	Netherlands		Guinea Bissau	Guatemala
	Spain		Honduras	Japan
			India	Lebanon
			Indonesia	Maldives
			Korea	New Zealand
			Lao People's Democratic Republic	Nigeria
				Paraguay
				Philippines
			Mauritania	
			Mexico	South Africa
				United Kingdom
			Morocco	United States
			Pakistan	Uruguay
			Singapore	Venezuela
			Sri Lanka	
			Tunisia	Zaïre
			Turkey	
			Viet Nam	
			Yugoslavia	

SOURCE: Internation Monetary Fund, *Annual Report 1990,* page 87.

usually that of its major trading partner. Pegging to a particular currency implies that the value of the pegged currency moves along with the currency to which it is pegged and does not really fluctuate. It does fluctuate, however, against all other currencies to the same extent as the currency to which it is pegged (for example, the currency of the Ivory Coast, the CFA franc, is pegged to the French franc).

Crawling Pegs

Under a crawling peg arrangement, a country makes small periodic changes in the value of its currency with an intent to move it to a particular value over a period of time. The system, however, can be taken advantage of by currency speculators, who can make substantial profits by buying or selling the currency just before its revaluation or devaluation. The advantage of this system is that it enables a country to spread its exchange rate adjustment over a longer period than pegging, thereby avoiding the shocks that can be caused to the economy by sudden and steep revaluations or devaluations.

Basket of Currencies

Many countries, particularly LDCs, are increasingly fixing the rates of their currencies in terms of a basket of currencies. The arrangement is similar to that used for valuation of SDRs. The basic advantage of the system is that it imparts a degree of stability to the currency of a country as the movements in currencies that comprise the basket even out. The selection of the currencies that are to be included in the basket is generally determined by their importance in financing the trade of a particular country. In most currency baskets, different currencies are assigned different weights, in accordance with their relative importance to the country. Thus, a basket of currencies for a country may comprise different currencies with different weights. The actual method of computation of the exchange rate from the basket is relatively similar but may have individual variations. Some coun-

tries, although fixing their exchange rate in terms of a basket of currencies, may choose to conduct most of their official transactions in one or two currencies, which are known as the intervention currencies.

Fixed Rates

Under a fixed rate arrangement, a country announces a specific exchange rate for its currency and maintains this rate by agreeing to buy or sell foreign exchange in unlimited quantities at this rate. At present, however, there are hardly any countries that still follow a completely rigid system of exchange rates. Some of the countries of the socialist bloc do have fixed exchange rates that are announced from time to time and that are used for all official transactions, particularly countries with which they have bilateral trade arrangements.

European Monetary System

Several European countries that are members of the European Economic Community (EEC), concerned by the collapse of the Bretton Woods arrangements, decided in 1979 to enter into an exchange rate arrangement that would regulate movements in their currencies with respect to each other. The currencies of these countries, with respect to the U.S. dollar, were to float jointly. Limits for variations of currencies within the member-country group were fixed at a 2.5 percent range, while as a group, the currencies would vary within a range of 4.5 percent against the U.S. dollar. These arrangements were also a part of the general scheme to achieve significant economic and monetary integration among the member countries of the EEC. One way of achieving greater monetary integration was to reduce the level of fluctuation from their parity values of currencies of different countries within the EEC. The lower range of 2.5 percent prescribed for intracommunity fluctuation was termed the "snake," while the broader range of 4.5 percent fluctuation as a group against the U.S. dollar was called the "tunnel."

International monetary cooperation was, however, not so easy to come by in practice, because different member countries were subject to their own individual constraints and found that keeping up with the limits imposed by the "snake" arrangements did not serve their best economic interests. As a result, France, Great Britain, and Italy withdrew their participation from this arrangement within two years of its inception.

Violent fluctuation in exchange rates in the international markets and renewed interest in achieving greater economic and monetary integration within the members of the EEC prompted efforts to reconsider the establishment of a system of fixed parities, with a limited amount of flexibility, for the exchange rates of member countries. In pursuit of these objectives, the European Monetary System (EMS) was established by nine member countries of the EEC in 1979. In some ways, it was a successor to the erstwhile "snake" arrangement and reflected the experience gained with that arrangement.

Under the EMS arrangements, the currencies of France, West Germany, Belgium, Netherlands, Luxembourg, Italy, Ireland, Denmark, Spain, and Great Britain (who did not join initially) are linked together and cross parities have been established for them with a specific range within which these currencies can fluctuate from their parity values with respect to each other. Following the decision of Great Britain to become a full member of the EMS on October 5, 1990, the only two EEC countries not members of the EMS are Portugal and Greece.

The EMS is designed around a new composite currency known as the European Currency Unit (ECU). The value of the ECU is derived in a manner similar to the SDR and has similar functions, although its private use is far more widespread. The computation of the value of the ECU is based on a weighted average of nine currency values of EMS member countries. The percentage weights of different currencies in the ECU basket are:

Deutsche mark	35.45%
French franc	17.39%
British pound	15.78%
Italian lira	8.09%
Dutch guilder	11.09%
Belgian franc	8.14%
Luxembourg franc	0.30%
Danish krone	2.63%
Irish pound	11.10%

These proportions reflect the shares of different countries in intra-European trade and the total size of their economies, as indicated by their gross national products. The value of the ECU against the currencies of nonmember countries varies with the fluctuation in the market values of individual currencies weighted by the computing formula. The values of member currencies with respect to the ECU are computed by multiplying the absolute amount of each currency in the ECU basket with its central rate against the currency whose value is being determined and then adding the result for all currencies.

The ECU is also used as the unit of account in settlement of official transactions between central banks of member countries. The degree of fluctuation that currencies undergo from their central parities with respect to each other are also determined in terms of ECUs. Private use of the ECU is growing, and the currency is being increasingly utilized to denominate Eurocurrency borrowings, trade invoicing, and even travelers' checks. In fact, on a global scale, more external borrowings are denominated in ECU than all other currencies with the exception of the U.S. dollar, the deutsche mark, and the Japanese yen.

Under the EMS exchange rate arrangements, currencies of member countries are fixed in terms of each other through their common link to the ECU. Fluctuations up to 2.25 percent from this parity is permitted (this range is 6 percent for the Italian lira and the British pound). Thus, the different currencies form a bilateral parity. Parities have to be maintained within the permitted range by central bank interventions, that is, purchases and sales of domestic/foreign currencies to influence price movements, which are to take place in currencies of EMS member countries. All member countries, regardless of their individual policies, are required to maintain these parities. To help member central banks undertake these intervention operations, the system provides an exchange of limited short-term loans between participating central banks. Settlement of these transactions is done through the European Fund for Monetary Cooperation (FECOM), into which the EMS central banks deposit 20 percent of their gold and dollar reserves and receive an equivalent credit in their account denominated in ECUs. Resources of the fund are used to square the credits and debits that arise out of the intervention operations carried out by member central banks to maintain EMS parities.

Although it has come under severe pressure because of the continued weakness of the Italian lira and the French and Belgian francs, the EMS has proved remarkably resilient. This achievement is all the more significant when one considers the context in which it operates—one of violently fluctuating exchange rates and widely differing economic performances and policies of its member countries. With the impending economic integration measures scheduled in 1992, the EMS should become all the more advantageous for member countries as a system of stable exchange rates that ties in with the coordination and convergence in economic policies that is expected to take place (see Perspective 4–2).

PERSPECTIVE 4–2   Europe's Emerging Economic and Monetary Union

After more than a decade of experience with the European Monetary System (EMS), the 12 member countries of the European Community are now engaged in important discussions and negotiations about the path to economic and monetary union (EMU). This perspective takes a look at key issues relating to the design and implementation of monetary policy in the emerging EMU, without endorsing or dismissing specific institutional proposals for transition to EMU. The emphasis is on the interrelationships among price stability, current account equilibrium, and exchange rate stability, as well as the questions of the degree of coordination and rules versus discretion. Also considered are the critical implications of fiscal policy for the conduct of monetary policy, along with alternative ways of encouraging fiscal discipline.

MONETARY POLICY GOALS

Progress toward EMU necessarily requires a consensus to be reached among participating countries on the goals of monetary policy. During the 1960s and the 1970s, monetary policies in the major industrial nations typically embraced a number of objectives, notably price stability, full employment, and sustainable economic growth (and for some, exchange rate stability and stability of the financial system). But in the last decade or so, governments have concentrated on the objective of controlling inflation, with price stability being regarded—appropriately in our view—as a necessary (albeit not sufficient) condition for achieving other economic goals, including sustainable economic growth.

Consistent with this tendency, there appears to be a broad agreement that a European system of central banks, or "EuroFed," should have an explicit mandate to pursue price stability (see "Europe: The Quest for Monetary Integration," by Horst Ungerer in *Finance & Development*, December 1990, for a discussion of the institutional aspects of EMU). To give "teeth" to this com-

SOURCE: Jacob A. Frenkel and Morris Goldstein, *Finance & Development*, March 1991, pages 2–5.

mitment, some have proposed giving the "Eu-roFed" substantial independence, while prohibiting it from granting credit to the public sector. What is less clear is how policy-making authorities should respond to developments in current accounts and frame their exchange rate objectives.

Historically, not all potential EMU members have placed the same emphasis on the current account balance relative to other goals. But the further liberalization of European capital markets might increase the importance of any differences among countries in the importance attached to current account objectives, by making it easier to finance intra-European external imbalances. There is also the matter of Europe's aggregate current account position, which could well influence a future ECU/U.S. dollar or ECU/yen exchange rate. (ECU stands for European Currency Unit, a composite basket of the EC currencies.)

What then should the authorities' attitude be on current account imbalances? Several analysts—ourselves included—believe that such imbalances are not inherently good or bad, but must be assessed on a case-by-case basis. For example, imbalances that arise from temporary differences among countries in the age distribution of the population—which in turn yield differences in private saving patterns—are likely to be benign, whereas an imbalance that reflects unsustainable borrowing abroad to finance a consumption spree should surely be placed in the malign category.

We see merit in a framework that would consider at least the following factors:

- Whether the fiscal position is appropriate (in terms of both the level and composition of government spending, as well as the structure of taxes and borrowing used to finance the budget).
- Whether increased investment associated with the external imbalance can be expected to provide a rate of return that exceeds the cost of borrowing (including externalities).
- Whether any increased consumption associated with the imbalance is temporary and desirable

for purposes of smoothing movements in consumption over time.

One needs to know the origin of an imbalance before one can decide both if the imbalance needs correcting and how that can best be accomplished.

As for the role of exchange rate objectives, several issues arise: the management of the union's exchange rate vis-á-vis non-EMU currencies; the loss of the nominal exchange rate as a policy instrument; and the choice between rapid and gradual approaches to EMU, with "hard" and "soft" exchange rate commitments, respectively.

Exchange Rate Management in a Tripolar System   In recent years, we have increasingly felt that a tri-polar exchange rate system, in which exchange rate commitments are "looser" and "quieter" across the poles than within regional currency areas, represents a feasible and desirable evolution of the international monetary system. By tri-polar, we mean a regime where many currencies are linked either to the US dollar, the Japanese yen, or a European currency (e.g., the deutsche mark or th ECU). "Loose" exchange rate commitments imply that exchange rate targets are altered more frequently and are subject to wider margins than with "tighter" commitments. "Quiet" and "loud" commitments are merely a shorthand for distinguishing between confidential and publicly announced exchange rate targets.

Several of the arguments for such a system are directly relevant to how an evolving EMU might react to exchange rate movements outside the union. First, an exchange rate system that has as its regional nominal anchors, three relatively independent central banks—each committed to price stability—is not conducive to policy "blueprints" that require monetary policy in the anchor countries to give first priority to keeping exchange rates within loud target zones. Second, real exchange rates across the three poles need some flexibility to be able to reflect changes in real economic conditions over time. Third, better disciplined monetary and fiscal policy within each of the currency areas would go a long way toward establishing more disciplined exchange markets across the poles. Fourth, intervention to manage exchange rates across the poles (i.e., $/ECU, $/yen, ECU/yen) should be saved for cases where there is strong evidence of bubbles or large misalignments in exchange rates.

This should not be interpreted as a call for return to "benign neglect" in the management of major currency exchange rates. Quite the contrary, as we regard a reasonable degree of exchange rate stability for key currencies as a public good for the system. Our argument instead is that the stabilizing effect of any official exchange rate commitment on expectations depends on its credibility. A looser commitment across the poles—wherein authorities 'keep their powder dry" for large, clear-call misalignments and do not claim that the primary assignment of monetary policy is for external balance—should be more credible than a (nominally) tighter and louder commitment. But the same logic also points to tight, loud exchange rate commitments *within* currency areas, one of which is an emerging EMU. Here, the incentives for stabilizing exchange rates are greater—because these economies are more open, because trade flows among union members account for a large share of members' total trade, because exchange rate stability is closely linked to larger, regional integration objectives, and because there are larger gains in anti-inflationary credibility to be had by "tying one's hands" on monetary policy via exchange rate fixity.

Nominal Exchange Rates within the Union

What about the pressing issue of managing exchange rates within, and on the way to, monetary union? One key issue relates to the consequences of losing the nominal exchange rate as a policy instrument. Economic theory suggests that the types of shocks hitting an economy (monetary or real) should be an important factor in the choice of an exchange rate regime. The potential problem of a monetary union is adjusting to

country-specific real shocks. Here, three questions need to be addressed:

1. Are the real economic shocks that typically hit European economies industry-specific rather than country-specific? If they are industry-specific and if potential EMU members have well-diversified industrial structures, then it is possible that these shocks largely cancel out at the country level; but if shocks are predominantly country-specific, potential difficulties are obviously greater.

2. Will the increased competition in goods and factors markets associated with 1992 increase the downward flexibility of money wages and prices in Europe? If so—and we do not discount this possibility—it will be less costly to achieve needed changes in real exchange rates via changes in internal wages and prices.

3. Is there in operation a federal fiscal authority that could automatically adjust a country's tax and transfer payments in the event of country-specific real shocks—and in a roughly budget-neutral fashion for the union as a whole? As is well known, this kind of tax and transfer system operates as a cushioning device in the United States.

The more confident one can be that the answers to these questions are "yes," the less concerned can monetary authorities afford to be in embracing greater (nominal) exchange rate fixity on the path to EMU.

The Exchange Rate Regime in the Transition to EMU

Assume, in keeping with the spirit of EMU, that a judgment has been made to make use of the nominal exchange rate as a policy instrument only in "exceptional" circumstances. This still leaves unanswered whether the transition should be rapid or gradual and whether exchange rate commitments should be absolute or conditional.

One option would be to move rapidly to EMU itself, that is, to a common currency (e.g., the

ECU) and to a central monetary authority (e.g., the EuroFed). This would carry a number of attractions. First, it gives maximum credibility to exchange rate stability by eliminating exchange rates within the union. A common currency is harder to "undo" than a commitment to "irrevocably fixed" exchange rates, and market participants presumably know it. Second, a common currency allows EMU participants to obtain more of the efficiency gains associated with moving closer to one money than do fixed exchange rates. Third, a central monetary authority can in principle avoid the negative externalities associated with beggar-thy-neighbor policies taken by competing national monetary authorities. Fourth, a central monetary authority may be able to implement monetary control more effectively than individual national central banks—because the demand for money in the wider area may be more stable under open capital markets and full financial liberalization than are individual-country money demands.

On the negative side, two concerns arise about a rapid move to EMU. One is that the participating countries will not be "ready" for a common currency or a common monetary policy, be it because of inadequate convergence of economic performance (particularly of inflation), inadequate consensus on the goals or framework for monetary policy, or inadequate experience with common institutions. To some observers, this lack of readiness calls either for a two-track approach—where the fast track is limited to a subset of potential members who already are ready in terms of convergence of economic performance—or for waiting together until a wider group of members is ready. A second objection is that an administrative, centralized approach to currency and monetary management will result in average—or even worse, collusive, below-average—performance; in contrast, a "competitive" approach—so the argument goes—would allow the market to converge on "the best in the Community."

Another option would be to pursue a slower transition to EMU, characterized by the coexistence of a federal monetary authority and national central banks, and by a looser commitment to fixed exchange rates. This option clearly provides more scope for learning by doing and for making monetary policy more accountable to national governments. But as critics point out, such a strategy cannot escape the constrain that only two of the following three objectives can be obtained simultaneously: open capital markets, fixed exchange rates, and independent monetary policy. With capital controls all but gone and with increased opportunities for diversification of currency portfolios, a commitment to truly fixed exchange rates will be credible only if monetary policy coordination—ex ante and ex post—is tighter than in the past. In fact, the very liberalization processes that give rise to increased currency substitution, along with any destabilizing speculation, may well call for more frequent recourse to coordinated interest rate adjustments; otherwise, national monetary control is apt to be rendered less effective.

A related challenge thrown up by the coexistence of central and national monetary authorities and by a desire to introduce more symmetry of adjustment into the system, is that the rules of the game may become more difficult to define than in the existing EMS. Not only does the assignment of responsibilities have to be clearly understood, but also that assignment has to respect the primacy of price stability as a goal of EMU.

CARRYING OUT MONETARY POLICY

During the transition to EMU, EC member governments will also have to come to terms with at least two important issues relating to the implementation of monetary policy: the degree of coordination and rules versus discretion.

We see the current process of financial liberalization, innovation, globalization, and securitization as strengthening the case for closer coordination of monetary policy on at least three counts:

1. The shift away from credit rationing and quantitative lending restrictions means that the transmission mechanism of monetary policy

falls more heavily on interest rates and exchange rates—the "competitive" variables most often the subject of beggar-thy-neighbor complaints. Coordination is a way of discouraging such practices. The degree of conflict that exists in the transition to EMU is not irrelevant for prospects of actually achieving EMU.

2. When there is a sudden, large increase in currency substitution, it may become more difficult to implement reliable monetary control at the national level without stronger coordination among monetary authorities.

3. The problem of systemic risk does not lend itself easily to an autonomous, competitive approach, and this is of particular relevance to the Europe of 1992 and beyond. In an environment where there are increasing competitive pressures in financial services, universal banking throughout the region, equity prices moving more closely across countries, and a desire on the part of monetary authorities to establish or maintain anti-inflationary credibility, it would not be surprising if some financial institutions experienced difficulties. A national monetary authority might act to contain such difficulties by providing emergency liquidity support or by activating official or private deposit insurance schemes. However, official safety nets, as with other types of insurance, raise moral hazard issues; in this case, the encouragement to undertake an unduly high share of risky activities, giving rise to unfavorable consequences for the public sector's liability.

This problem could be reduced if financial institutions maintained adequate capital requirements, or if access to deposit insurance went hand-in-hand with restrictions on institutions' activities. But in a world of financial liberalization, any single country's attempt to impose stiffer regulatory standards could result merely in firms fleeing to countries with more lax standards (resulting in a form of regulatory arbitrage). A coordinated approach

to regulation can accomplish what a competitive approach cannot. The recently concluded Basic Agreement on risk-weighted capital standards for commercial banks in the Group of Ten countries is a case in point.

This brings us to the familiar issue of rules versus discretion, which would need to be addressed whether a coordinated or competitive approach to monetary policy was selected. Those who favor policy rules make essentially three arguments. First, rules are a viable mechanism for imposing discipline on economic policymakers who might otherwise manipulate the instruments of policy for their own objectives and to the detriment of the public. Second, rules can reduce the cost of negotiations and burden-sharing conflicts. Third, rules are regarded as enhancing the predictability of policy actions, thereby improving the private sector's ability to make informed resource allocation decisions.

These arguments in favor of policy rules are powerful, but their immediate operational attractiveness is blunted by two considerations—both of which are relevant to an emerging EMU. One is that rules that do not adapt to major changes in the operating environment run the risk of worsening policy performance. The weakening in many countries of the link between narrow monetary aggregates and the ultimate goals of monetary policy in the face of large-scale financial innovation and institutional change is a leading case in point. In recognition of these changes in the operating environment, several prominent supporters of policy rules have incorporated trend changes in velocity into their money supply or national-income rules (what we might call "evolutionary" rules)— while several monetary authorities have indicated that they now employ a more eclectic approach to monetary policy (where the behavior of monetary aggregates is taken into account along with a set of other variables). A second consideration is that rules will impart greater discipline to policy only to the extent that penalties for breaking the rules are significant enough to ensure that the rules are followed. The sanctions available against sovereign nations for breach of economic policy commitments should not be exaggerated.

SEARCH FOR FISCAL DISCIPLINE

A striking lesson of the 1980s is that when fiscal policy is undisciplined and works in a direction opposite to that of monetary policy, efforts to promote price stability, effective external adjustment, and exchange market stability will be seriously handicapped. Basically, there are three potential mechanisms for encouraging greater fiscal discipline.

The Exchange Rate Regime Experience is not kind to the view that the exchange rate regime by itself can enforce discipline on fiscal policy. Thus after more than ten years of operation—and with a clear progression toward greater fixity of exchange rates—there is little evidence of fiscal policy convergence is the EMS. Monetary policy convergence, yes—but not fiscal policy convergence. In a similar vein, the North American experience with much greater exchange rate flexibility hardly suggests that this exchange rate regime can consistently rein in fiscal policies. It is not difficult to construct theoretical examples where the exchange rate regime sends either a false signal, or no signal at all, about the need for fiscal adjustment. Typically, this comes about because the higher interest rate associated with fiscal expansion induces a capital inflow that either prompts a loosening of monetary policy (to keep the exchange rate within its target), or simply makes the fiscal deficit easier to finance.

The Market What then about the discipline imposed by "the market?" Such market discipline is usually said to operate via two channels. The first is the higher cost of borrowing associated with consistent fiscal imprudence—as the markets exact an increasing risk premium to reflect lower expected repayment. At some point, markets could even impose their ultimate sanction, by refusing to lend altogether to the unrepentant borrower. The second is via pressures for tax harmonization. In short, a government that spends a lot will eventually have to tax a lot, but high taxes will, in turn, induce firms and individuals to move to jurisdictions with lower taxes. Declining tax revenues will then force tax harmonization, and finally, a halt to excessive spending.

For market discipline to work, the following conditions need to be satisfied.

- The market must have accurate and comprehensive information on the size and composition of the debtor's obligations, so that it can make a valid assessment of debt-servicing obligations relative to ability-to-pay. Credit-rating agencies can of course assist in this information processing task, but they need to be cautious since a rating change can become a self-fulfilling prophecy. In addition, debtors may not have incentives to reveal unfavorable information before mandated reporting dates.
- There must not be any implicit or explicit guarantee of a bail out. For if there is the expectation of a bail out, then the interest rate charged will reflect the creditworthiness of the guarantor—not that of the debtor. The market's perception of a bail out is sometimes cited as a reason why in the 1970s interest rate spreads on bank loans to developing countries were so slow to rise. It is of course possible for the overseeing fiscal authority to issue a no bail-out pledge. The problem is that it may be difficult to make this pledge credible if troubled debtors were in the past bailed out.
- The financial system must be strong enough for any given debtor not to be regarded as too large to fail; if other financial institutions are large holders of the troubled debtor's obligations, it will be harder to exercise discipline.
- The borrower's debt must not be monetized by central bank purchases—that is, be allowed to be translated into an expansion of the money supply. This is because the resulting erosion of

the real value of the debt will make it difficult for the market to price it accurately.

- There must be neither high costs of mobility nor the provision of public services that compensate for tax differentials (this condition applies specifically to tax harmonization). If mobility costs are high, individuals and firms are less likely to "vote with their feet" when taxes are raised. If better public services are offered in high tax districts, then high taxes do not provide an incentive to leave.

The empirical evidence on market discipline is quite limited. From the viewpoint of an emerging EMU, perhaps the most relevant work is that dealing with common currency areas that have federal fiscal systems (such as the United States and Canada), and where there is no explicit or implicit guarantee of a bail out for fiscal adventurism at the local level. A recent analysis of whether US states with higher debt burdens actually paid higher interest rates on their debt was undertaken by Professor Barry Eichengreen of the University of California at Berkeley. He found only a weak, positive relationship between debt burdens and the cost of borrowing, and no evidence that borrowing costs accelerate at very high debt levels. Moreover, even if stronger empirical evidence linking borrowing costs to fiscal irresponsibility were available, it would give us only half the picture. Still missing is evidence that higher borrowing costs actually induce governments to correct fiscal policy excesses; to our knowledge, no such tests are yet available.

Peer Group Surveillance   This would offer still another mean of encouraging fiscal discipline. One possibility would be a fiscal policy rule that put a ceiling on each participant's fiscal deficit. The main difficulty with rigid fiscal policy rules is that they may not take adequate account of relevant differences between countries—in private savings rates, outstanding debt stocks, the uses to which government expenditures are put, past credit histories, etc. In addition, there may be few sanctions that can be imposed on noncomplying members. For these reasons, peer group surveillance typically takes place in a voluntary, discretionary format. But this mode of operation faces its own obstacles: fiscal policy is inflexible (at least relative to monetary policy); it operates with long and variable lags that depend in good measure on the pace of legislative actions; and the effects of fiscal policy on macro-variables of interest hinge on what kind of fiscal action is taken (taxes versus expenditures, expenditures on tradables versus nontradables, taxes on saving versus investment, etc.). Then, too, surveillance exercises invariably employ multi-indicator methods, where the tendency of different indicators to point in different directions gives considerable scope for discretion in policy diagnosis and prescription.

The likelihood that no single mechanism can be relied upon to yield fiscal discipline means that a broad-based approach that leans both on markets and on surveillance will be called for. The transition to EMU will proceed a lot smoother if fiscal policy can be made to work with monetary policy in achieving EMU's basic economic goals.

Difficulties in the Floating Rate Era

Exchange rates in the floating rate era have been marked by violent fluctuations that have been prompted by a variety of factors. There were periodic crises in the international monetary system that were reflected in the violent fluctuations of exchange rates.

The first major crisis to affect the international monetary system after the breakdown of the Bretton Woods arrangements was the oil crisis that began in 1973, when the Organization of Petroleum Exporting Countries (OPEC) placed an embargo on their exports of oil and which by 1974 resulted in a fourfold increase in oil prices. For some nations, such as the United States and Japan, this meant a sudden and substantial increase in the volume of their import payments, which put pressure on their balance of payments. The industrialized countries were able to meet this crisis by adjusting their economies to a lower level of oil consumption and more aggressive export policies that increased foreign exchange earnings. The oil-exporting countries, on the other hand, accumulated substantial balance of payments surpluses, which were denominated in U.S. dollars. In 1974 the United States lifted capital controls on the international movements of dollars, making them freely transferable across the globe. As long as the dollar remained the primary currency for holding and recycling the dollars held by OPEC countries (also known as petrodollars), the value of the dollar continued to be strong, despite a virtually continuous trade deficit.

The continuous trade deficits, however, and policies that encouraged capital outflows, caused the confidence in the dollar to weaken, leading to a sharp fall in its price in 1978. Further, this decline of confidence in the dollar was exacerbated by the difficulties the United States faced in Iran because of its revolution, as well as the problems created by the second oil crisis of 1979, when the OPEC countries indulged in yet another round of dramatic prices increases. The attractiveness of the dollar was enhanced yet again, very quickly, as U.S. authorities decided on a monetary policy that would result in higher U.S. interest rates, which in turn would attract overseas demand for the dollar and raise the exchange rate.

The changed monetary policy also helped to maintain international confidence in the U.S. dollar in the face of the second oil shock as well as the unsettled conditions in Iran, especially in the light of the general freeze on Iranian assets held in the United States. A major factor in this new confidence was the expectation that inflation would remain at a lower level in the United States than in other countries. Therefore, investments made in the United States seemed attractive. To invest in the United States meant that the overseas investors had to acquire U.S. dollars, which increased the demand and strengthened the exchange rate of the currency. Although the United States ran huge balance of payments deficits from

1981 to 1985, the dollar's value continued to appreciate. Apart from the high interest rates and low inflation, U.S. investments were attractive because of the strong performance of the U.S. economy, which continued to enjoy a virtually uninterrupted expansion. Moreover, the United States seemed to be the safest haven for investors, as political crises affected many parts of the world and threatened to spread to many more. Other factors that strengthened the U.S. dollar in this period were the decline in the price of oil, the reinvestment of funds by major commercial banks in the U.S. market, and speculative actions of investors in the foreign exchange markets, who kept pushing the value of the dollar even higher by making speculative purchases and increasing demand.

Fluctuations in the U.S. Dollar: The Plaza and Louvre Accords

Continued appreciation of the dollar had by early 1985 caused enough economic problems for the United States to precipitate active government action to arrest this trend. The high price of the dollar had made U.S. exports expensive and imports cheap, which led to a decline in the former and a steep rise in the latter, creating a huge deficit in the U.S. trade account. Moreover, most of this deficit was financed not by internal resources but by external borrowings. As a result, the United States decided to follow policies that would reduce the attractiveness of overseas investments in dollar assets and improve the budgetary and trade deficit position. The most important of these policies were an attempt to reduce U.S. interest rates, a reduction of the budget deficit, and coordinated action to bring down the value of the dollar, an action to be taken by the monetary authorities of the major industrialized countries.

The third policy was initiated in September 1985, when finance ministers of the United States, Japan, France, West Germany, and United Kingdom, as well as their central bank governors, met at the Plaza Hotel in New York City and reached an agreement on coordinated action to be taken to bring down the value of the dollar. The agreement, known as the Plaza Accord, prompted a dramatic decline in the already depreciating dollar, which continued to fall steadily over the next year and a half. By the end of the first quarter of 1987, the value of the dollar had fallen so much that it was considered too weak. Therefore, in 1987 the group of seven industrialized countries (the United States, United Kingdom, West Germany, France, Canada, and Italy) agreed during their annual summit, held that year in Paris, to arrest the decline in the value of the dollar. The agreement, known as the Louvre Accord, did not have such a dramatic and immediate impact in achieving its objective as the Plaza Accord, because the dollar continued to decline for a while. By 1988, however, the dollar had recovered some of its strength.

The Plaza Accord was successful primarily because it was in a relatively better position to achieve its objectives, with the dollar already on a downward path. On the other hand, the Louvre Accord had a much more difficult agenda—to reverse the trend in the international foreign exchange markets. Moreover, the Louvre Accord required a relatively consistent and long-term policy coordination effort that was not so likely to come to pass, given the individual economic imperatives and policies of signatories.

Issues for Reform

The violent fluctuations in exchange rates ever since the inception of the floating era have raised serious questions on the efficiency and desirability of the present arrangements for settlement of international financial obligations. It is evident that the system has not proved to be perfect, and there have been several adverse effects, especially for the less-developed nations of the world. Some of the main issues that have to be addressed in this context are:

1. International exchange rate stability.
2. Enhancement of international liquidity.

3. A more equitable international monetary system from the point of view of the less-developed countries.

International Exchange Rate Stability

While there is general agreement that the current state of violent fluctuations in exchange rates is not desirable, there is no definite agreement on how this should be achieved, if it is at all possible.

Some proponents of the extreme view seek a return to the gold standard, citing the stabilizing role of gold and the near complete exchange stability the world enjoyed during the days of the gold standard. Conditions have since changed drastically, however, and it is hardly likely that there would be enough gold to back the enormous volume of international obligations now in circulation. Another proposal to restore international exchange rate stability is to return to fixed exchange rates. It is argued that a return to fixed rates would reduce international currency volatility, which would improve international trading efficiency and remove the costs involved in avoiding possible losses because of currency fluctuation. Fixed rates are also claimed to have a moderating influence on domestic monetary and fiscal policies and engender a conservative approach that fosters macroeconomic stability. Moreover, fixed rates would allow a consistent approach toward domestic resource allocations, and its patterns would not have to change to take into account major movements in exchange rate and competitive positions of different industries. Fixed exchange rates also do not permit speculation, which has caused serious disruption in the international markets and caused substantial losses to persons involved in international trade transactions.

Fixed exchange rates, however, do have their down side. First, they hold domestic policies "ransom" to external conditions as external conditions force changes in domestic policies if exchange rates have to be maintained at a predetermined level. Defending a particular exchange rate requires the maintenance of substantial foreign exchange reserves and incurring considerable losses on the foreign exchange markets during intervention operations. Large reserves tend to be a wasteful use of resources because they do not yield the highest possible rate of return, and return considerations are overshadowed by safety and liquidity requirements. Moreover, some countries, especially the less-developed ones, simply may not have the access to sufficient amounts of foreign currencies to maintain the needed levels of exchange reserves.

As of now it is not likely that the international monetary system will revert to a system of fixed exchange rates, at least in the foreseeable future, but it does remain as an option at the back of the minds of a large number of international economists.

TARGET ZONES

The target zone arrangement was perhaps the most actively and seriously discussed arrangement of the late 1980s, as an alternative to the present non-system. The target zone system envisions the establishment of relative wide bands around certain parities, within which currencies of countries participating in the system can fluctuate with reference to one other. Once a currency approaches the limit at the edge of a band, the central banks would intervene in the exchange market to bring it back into line. The major mechanism, however, would be the long-term coordination of national economic policies that would keep the values of participating currencies within the target zones and would not need frequent intervention by central banks. The target zone proposal has definite merit, in as much as it seeks to provide exchange rate stability while making necessary provisions for flexibility, which is essential, in the current international economic environment. Implementation of target zones, however, faces a number of hurdles. First, there must be agreement on what the range of permitted fluctuations should actually be and, even before that is determined, the basic parity of exchange rates around this range should be established. Second, mechanisms have to be es-

tablished to prevent speculation in the international foreign exchange markets taking advantage of the system. Third, if the system is to work, a serious commitment is needed from participating countries to coordinate their national economic policies. This commitment, even if given initially, is difficult to maintain, given the varied pressures that national governments face at home. Moreover, with changes in governments taking place periodically, there is no real guarantee that the policy commitments given by one government will be honored by the next.

International Liquidity

International liquidity depends upon the amounts of internationally acceptable monetary reserves available to different countries. The importance of international liquidity stems clearly from its role in financing the external transactions of all countries. Through the 1980s the liquidity position of the developing countries tended to worsen because of a number of factors—lower export earnings, higher export costs, reduced access to external commercial borrowings because of the debt crisis, large debt service requirements, and reductions in official development assistance in real terms—all of which have limited the capacity of these countries to continue to finance crucial imports needed for sustaining their ongoing developmental efforts and to give them the elbow room to make necessary adjustments in their economies.

As a result, many developing countries have been seeking an enhancement of international liquidity through greater access to IMF resources. This access is sought by an increase in the quota sizes allocated to different countries. The argument of the developing countries is that the quota sizes should not be determined by the existing criteria, but by assessing the financing requirements of individual countries. A link of SDR allocations to the aid requirements of developing countries has been strongly advocated for several years. This view is opposed by the developed countries who feel that there is no real need to increase the present level of liquidity in the international economy. They feel that the resources of the IMF are meant for specific purposes, and the present procedures are designed to ensure their optimal utilization. According to the opponents, developmental assistance is best routed through the World Bank, because it is accompanied by serious appraisal and follow-up procedures. Discretionary use of the resources of the IMF could lead to excessive borrowing, which could prove counterproductive and promote a lax attitude toward the tough decisions needed to be taken by the developing countries to improve the efficiency and productivity of their economies. Moreover, according to the industrialized countries, enough resources are available to countries who can prove their creditworthiness to receive them.

A More Equitable International Monetary System

Many developing countries have raised the issue that the international monetary system as it exists today is weighted heavily in favor of the industrialized countries. All key decisions of the IMF, for example, are subject to a veto by the United States, because an 85 percent majority is needed to make these decisions, and the United States holds 19.6 percent of the total votes. Moreover, although the developing countries comprise more than 70 percent of the world's population, their share of IMF votes is only 38 percent. One way for the LDCs to achieve a greater voice in the international monetary arena is an increase in their IMF votes to 50 percent. Little progress has been made in this direction so far. Another route that can be taken by developing countries is to reduce their reliance on the currencies and financial systems of industrial countries in settling transactions among themselves. As a result, several regional clearing arrangements have been established to promote the use of the currencies of developing countries. Most of them, however, have not been able to achieve any great success because of a number of different problems that have arisen since their in-

troduction. Regional clearing arrangements have not been abandoned, however, and efforts are underway to find ways to make these systems more effective and beneficial to the developing countries. One example of such an arrangement is the Asian Clearing Union.

Summary

The ability to properly value and exchange one currency for another is fundamental to conducting international business. Hard currencies, such as the U.S. dollar, deutsche mark, and the British pound are easily acquired and disposed of in a free and open market. Soft currencies are not easily exchanged because of government controls. The international monetary system serves as the basis for currency exchange by establishing the internationally accepted framework and methodologies of valuation.

The early forms of the IMS used gold as the basis for exchanging one currency for another. International events, such as World War I, large balance of payments deficits in the United Kingdom and Europe, and World War II, along with the emergence of the United States as the world's largest creditor, ultimately led to the development of the gold exchange standard at Bretton Woods. The International Monetary Fund was designed to administer and enforce the Bretton Woods agreements by providing financial assistance for balance of payments problems through its facilities operations. Gaining IMF assistance, however, required implementation of conditionalities, which aimed at stabilizing the economies of borrowers.

Special drawing rights, or paper gold, were created as reserve assets by the IMF when the United States began experiencing larger balance of payments deficits and gold production could not keep pace with the increasing volume of international trade. Initially fixed in terms of gold, valuation of the SDR in 1974 was changed to a basket of sixteen currencies and, in 1980, a basket of the G-5 currencies (i.e. $,£, DM, FF, YEN).

The U.S. dollar was the key component of the Bretton Woods Agreement and provided the liquidity required by the IMS. As U.S. deficits grew, however, confidence in the dollar as a reserve currency fell, requiring its devaluation. Two unsuccessful attempts in 1971 and 1974, along with the abandonment of rights to convert U.S. dollars into gold resulted in the development of the modern IMS, the floating rate era. A variety of methods have developed, including managed or dirty floats, crawling pegs, and fixed rates.

The floating rate era has been armed by extreme volatility caused by a variety of factors. These include the oil crises of the 1970s, the chronic fiscal and balance of payments deficits of the United States, and the appreciation of the U.S. dollar because of its relative political stability and position as a safe haven. In 1985 and 1987, the Plaza and Louvre agreements, respectively, implemented policies to bring down and then arrest the decline of the value of the U.S. dollar.

The current monetary system has clear shortcomings, particularly for developing countries. Monetary system reformists are suggesting that new policies be implemented to increase international exchange rate stability and enhance international liquidity.

Discussion Questions

1. What is the difference between a hard currency and a soft currency?
2. What was the importance of gold within the early international monetary system? What problems arose under this system?
3. Describe the Bretton Woods Agreement. What position did gold hold within this system?
4. Outline the structure of the International Monetary Fund. What are its aims? What is conditionality?
5. What is a special drawing right?
6. Discuss the difficulties that occurred in the late 1960s and early 1970s that required the United States to abandon the gold exchange system?
7. What is the difference between a pure floating rate and a managed, or dirty, floating rate? Provide an example of currencies that are managed.
8. Why are international exchange rate stability and liquidity important for conducting international business?

Bibliography

ALIBER, ROBERT Z. 1976. *The International Money Game*, 2nd ed. New York: Basic Books.

DEANE, MARJORIE. 1988. "At Quiet Bank-Fund Meetings: Thoughts of Monetary Reform." *Financier* (November): 13–16.

GLASCOCK, J. L., and D. J. MEYER. 1988. "Assessing the Regulatory Process in an International Context: Mixed Currency SDRs and U.S. Bank Equity Returns." *Atlantic Economic Journal* (March): 39–46.

HEINONEN, KERSTIN. 1990. "The Role and Future of the SDR." *Kansallis-Osake-Pankki Economic Review* (July): 567–577.

HOSEFIELD, J. K. 1969. *The International Monetary Fund, 1945–1965*. Washington DC: International Monetary Fund.

INTERNATIONAL MONETARY FUND. *Annual Report*. Washington DC: International Monetary Fund (annual).

———. *IMS Survey*, Washington DC: International Monetary Fund (bimonthly).

POZO, SUSAN. 1987. "The ECU as International Money." *Journal of International Money and Finance*. (June): 1988. 195–206.

SAXENA, R. B., and H. R. BAKSHI. 1988. "IMF Conditionality—A Third World Perspective." *Journal of World Trade* (October): 67–79.

SCAMMELL, W. M. 1987. *The Stability of the International Monetary System*. Totowa, NJ: Roman & Littlefield.

SUZUCKI, Y., J. MIYAKE, and M. OKABE, 1990. *The Evolution of the International Monetary System: How Can Efficiency and Stability Be Attained?*, Tokyo: University of Tokyo Press.

TEW, BRIAN. 1988. *The Evolution of the International Monetary System: 1945–1988*. London: Hutchinson Education.

TRIFFIN, R. 1968. *Our International Monetary System: Yesterday, Today and Tomorrow*, New Haven, CT: Yale University Press.

APPENDIX
Balance of Payments

The Balance of Payments (BOP) is an accounting system for the financial transactions of a country with the rest of the world. The BOP shows trade inflows and outflows for a country and draws a picture of how the nation has financed its international economic and commercial activities. It measures the value of all export and import goods and services, capital flows, and gold exchanges between a home country and its trading partners. This accounting of the flows of goods and capital between nations provides crucial information in determining a nation's economic health. Thus, it becomes critical information for policymakers and officials on the domestic front and within supranational organizations, as well as for all international business people, especially potential investors of resources across national borders.

Identifying just how a nation finances its activities and what claims other countries hold on its assets provides one measure of its economic strength. In what type of position is a country to meet claims against its assets? How able is the country to purchase goods or services from other countries? The measures provided by the BOP system are not entirely instructive on an annual basis; what is more important are the displays it shows over time in trading patterns and aggregate annual flows of goods, capital, and reserves between nations.

PRELIMINARY DEFINITIONS
In order to understand the balance of payments, it is important to comprehend some of the terminology used in the process. First of all, the balance of payments is a system based on the **double entry** accounting method. Thus, for each transaction, two entries are made—a debit and a credit. For example, if a country imports goods and services, the value of the payment made for such imports will be debited in one account that records transactions relating to trade and credited in other accounts that either record the increase of assets of the country held by foreigners or the decrease in short-term foreign assets held by residents. For example, if the United States imported $50,000 of wines from the United Kingdom, the payment would be recorded as a debit in the current account, which records the transactions in goods and services, and be recorded as a credit in the capital account, which records inflows and outflows of financial assets from the country. The entry in a particular subhead of the capital account will depend upon the manner in which payment is made for imports. If payment is made out of the foreign exchange reserves of the country, the sub accounthead head for the decrease in short-term foreign assets is credited to the account. On the other hand, if the payment is made in the local currency and the local currency continues to be held by the U.K. firm then the account subhead credited is the increase in short-term domestic assets held by foreigners.

Because each entry in the balance of payments is matched by an equal and opposite entry by definition, the account has to balance. The following chart illustrates the organization of information in a balance of payments. Table 4–1 is a complete balance of payments for the United States.

The trade flows are organized into four separate categories or accounts—the current account, the capital account, the official reserves account, and the net statistical discrepancy.

Information on the flow of goods in and out of a country is usually provided by customs information collected as merchandise crosses international borders. Information on service flows is generally estimated through the use of statistical sampling of actual expenditures. Information on payments made for exports and imports, as well as outflows and inflows because of credit and capital flows is provided by commercial banks. Financial institutions also provide information on capital and credit flows across the borders of a country. Finally,, the monetary authority or central bank of each country reports official borrowings, and each country maintains its own accounts. In the United States, the Department of Commerce maintains the records of national accounts. The figures for each country are then synthesized by two agencies—the United

Balance of Payments

	Debits	Credits
1. Current Account		
A. Merchandise imports and exports		
B. Services		
Net goods and services balance		
C. Unilateral transfers		
To abroad		
From abroad		
Net current account balance		
2. Capital Account		
A. Direct investment		
To abroad		
From abroad		
B. Porfolio investment		
To abroad		
From abroad		
C. Short-term capital		
To abroad		
From abroad		
Net capital account		
3. Offical reserves account		
A. Gold export or import (net)		
B. Increase or decrease in foreign exchange (net)		
C. Increase or decrease in liabilities to foreign central banks (net)		
4. Net statistical discrepancy		

Nations and the International Monetary Fund—into an aggregate global snapshot of flows between nations.

The position of a country in any of these accounts is in equilibrium when outflows equal inflows; it is in deficit when outflows of foreign exchange because of imports and other payments exceed inflows because of exports or other receipts. A country can be in surplus when total foreign exchange inflows exceed total outlows. The final balance is done in an attempt to capture a history of all flows between nations, whether they be because of reserves of gold, currencies, food stuffs, manufactured goods, investments of home country funds abroad, the provision of insurance, travel facilities, and hotel accommodations or other services.

CURRENT ACCOUNT

The current account takes note of three separate types of flows between nations, similar to the concept of revenues (credits) and expenses (debits) in business operations. The first type of transfers are visibles—financial inflows and outflows arising out of actual exchanges of merchandise between countries through exporting and importing. Exports add to the account and imports subtract from the balance of the account. The net position of this section of the BOP is the balance of trade (BOT).

Flows of imports and exports are not only evaluated according to volumes, but also according to the terms of trade of a nation. Terms of trade refer to the ratio of the export prices of a country

TABLE 4-2
U.S. Balance of Payments Aggregated Presentation: Transactions Data. 1982-1989 (in billions of SDRs)

	Code	1982	1983	1984	1985	1986	1987	1988	1989
A. Current Account, excl. Group F	A C A	**-6.58**	**-41.81**	**-101.97**	**-110.80**	**-113.23**	**-111.30**	**-94.38**	**-82.71**
Merchandise: exports f.o.b.	1 A A 4	191.12	188.84	214.64	212.97	190.43	193.31	237.58	282.40
Merchandise: imports f.o.b.	1 A B 4	224.33	251.88	324.54	-332.69	-313.88	-316.60	332.31	370.85
Trade balance	1 A C 4	33.21	63.05	109.90	-119.72	-123.45	123.28	94.73	88.45
Other goods, services, and income: credit	1 S A 4	127.64	126.90	147.55	152.72	143.84	151.22	156.75	186.29
Reinvested earnings	1 E 1 A 4	1.12	6.66	8.07	18.56	15.27	26.40	11.32	16.81
Other investment income . . .	1 N A X	74.57	64.67	75.75	68.63	60.41	54.32	68.82	80.59
Other	1 S A Y	51.96	54.57	63.73	65.52	68.17	70.51	76.61	88.90
Other foods, services, and income: debit	1 S B 4	92.69	96.48	127.38	128.67	-120.20	128.31	145.47	169.41
Reinvested earnings	1 E 1 B 4	2.17	.09	2.82	1.17	1.87	1.27	4.90	2.66
Other investment income . . .	1 N B X	51.88	48.97	63.04	-63.36	-59.04	62.50	73.74	93.92
Other	1 S B Y	42.97	47.42	-61.52	-66.48	-63.03	64.53	66.84	72.83
Total: goods, services, and income	1 T C 4	1.75	-32.63	89.73	-95.67	-99.80	100.37	83.45	71.56
Private unrequited transfers . . .	1 K C 4	1.29	1.20	1.73	-2.04	-1.59	1.43	1.33	1.24
Total, excl. official unrequited transfers	1 U C 4	.45	33.83	91.46	-97.71	-101.39	101.80	84.79	72.80
Official unrequited transfers . . .	1 H C A	7.03	7.97	10.52	-13.08	-11.83	9.50	9.59	9.91
Grants (excluding military) . . .	1 H 1 B K	-4.99	-5.91	-8.40	-10.99	-10.00	7.79	7.73	8.00
Other	1 H C Y	2.05	2.06	2.12	-2.09	-1.83	1.70	1.86	1.91
B. Direct Investment and Other Long-Term Capital, excl. Groups F through H	9 Z 1 X A	**-6.64**	**-1.73**	**38.20**	**71.53**	**62.72**	**25.99**	**68.59**	**59.44**
Direct investment	3 X A	14.78	10.79	21.91	1.42	5.87	2.14	30.43	22.40
In United States	3 Y X 4	12.57	11.20	24.73	18.88	28.71	36.17	43.50	47.67
Abroad	3 L X 4	2.22	.41	2.82	17.46	22.84	34.03	13.07	25.26
Portfolio investment	6 Z 1 X A	.94	4.38	28.56	62.42	61.28	24.51	30.04	35.04
Other long-term capital									
Resident official sector	4 Z 1 X A	6.04	4.36	-4.16	-1.02	-.41	-1.16	.33	1.73
Disbursements on loans extended	4 C 1 Y 4	-7.81	-7.64	-7.58	-5.84	-6.06	-3.75	-4.30	-3.02
Repayments on loans extended	4 C 1 W 4	3.45	4.29	3.97	4.23	4.81	5.54	7.40	4.76
Other	4 Z 1 X Y	1.68	1.01	-.56	.59	.84	-2.95	2.77	.01
Deposit money banks	5 Z 1 X A	-14.45	12.54	-8.11	8.72	-4.02	.50	7.80	.27
Other sectors	8 Z 1 X A	—	—	—	—	—	—	—	—
Total, Groups A plus B	B 1 X A	**-13.22**	**-43.54**	**-63.78**	**-39.26**	**-50.50**	**-85.30**	**-25.79**	**-23.27**

	Code								
C. Other Short-Term Capital, excl. Groups F through H	9 Z 2 2 X A	-16.54	31.20	40.74	29.29	11.99	40.57	6.16	9.75
Resident official sector	4 Z 2 2 X A	6.51	5.24	1.39	-1.37	-.32	-1.47	-.19	.81
Deposit money banks	5 Z 2 2 X A	-24.14	27.65	26.47	24.11	22.80	35.67	2.98	7.67
Other sectors	8 Z 2 2 X A	1.09	-1.69	12.88	6.56	-10.49	6.37	3.37	1.27
D. Net Errors and Omissions	A X 4	31.41	8.43	23.46	15.71	9.78	1.10	-7.14	27.59
Total, Groups A through D	D 1 X A	1.65	-3.91	.43	5.74	-28.73	-43.63	-26.77	14.06
E. Counterpart Items	2 C 4	-.13	-.43	-.59	1.24	1.46	.97	-.48	1.32
Monetization/demonetization of gold	2 A M 4	-.03	-.26	-.23	-.04	-.20	.12	-.17	.09
Allocation/cancellation of SDRs	2 B M 4	—	—	—	—	—	—	—	—
Valuation changes in reserves	2 F 4	-.11	-.17	-.36	1.28	1.66	.85	-.31	1.23
Total, Groups A through E	E 1 X A	1.52	-4.34	-.16	6.97	-27.27	-42.66	-27.27	15.39
F. Exceptional Financing	Y X B	—	—	—	—	—	—	—	—
Security issues in foreign currencies	6 Q 1 X B	—	—	—	—	—	—	—	—
Total, Groups A through F	F 1 X 4	1.52	-4.34	-.16	6.97	-27.27	-42.66	-27.25	15.39
G. Liabilities Constituting Foreign Authorities' Reserves	9 W X 4	2.87	5.02	2.64	-2.12	28.46	36.64	29.91	5.78
Total, Groups A through G	G 1 X 4	4.39	.68	2.48	4.85	1.19	-6.03	2.66	21.66
H. Total Change in Reserves	2 R 4	-4.39	-.68	-2.48	-4.85	-1.19	6.03	-2.66	-21.16
Monetary gold	2 A R 4	.03	.25	.23	.05	.21	.12	.17	.11
SDR's	2 B R 4	-1.24	-.04	-.95	-.88	-.22	-.39	.09	-.41
Reserve position in the Fund	2 C R 4	-2.32	-4.14	-.97	.90	1.29	1.59	.76	.36
Foreign exchange assets	2 D R 4	-.86	3.25	-.78	-4.91	-2.46	4.94	-3.68	-21.00
Other claims	2 E R 4	—	—	—	—	—	—	—	—
Credit from the Fund and Fund administered resources	2 Y R 4	—	—	—	—	—	—	—	—
Conversion rates: U.S. dollars per SDR	S B Z	1.1040	1.0690	1.0250	1.0153	1.1732	1.2931	1.3439	1.2818

SOURCE: International Monetary Fund, *Balance of Payments Yearbook*, 1988.

to its import prices. A rise in export prices in relation to import prices improves the balance of trade if the trade volumes remain constant. Generally, rising prices for exports will tend to eventually squeeze the volume of exports in relation to imports. Quantities of goods traded between nations tend to change slowly, thus, initially, a rise in the terms of trade will improve a country's trade balance in the short-term, with deleterious effects on the balance becoming apparent only in the long-term. In recent years, for example, both Japan and West Germany have seen rises in their terms of trade that led to a shrinking of their trade surpluses. The United States experienced a faster rise in its terms of trade in the early 1980s, but its terms have fallen since 1986.[1]

The second category of transfers within the current account are invisibles and services between nations, including such items as transportation of people or goods, tourist services provided by other countries, supplying insurance for foreign policy buyers, international consulting services, and such financial and banking services as loans or fees for establishing lines of credit or acting as brokers in foreign exchange transactions. This category also includes the transfer of investment income from international investments overseas back to home-country residents and the remittance of profits back to parent corporations. These transfers are considered to be income resulting from the employment of production factors abroad, such as investment capital. The actual movement of the factors of production, that is, capital in the form of dollars going into plant and equipment overseas, is differentiated as a capital movement because the factor itself is moved across borders.

The third category within the current account keeps track of unilateral or unrequited transfers by countries to other countries, which is the flow of funds or goods for which no quid pro quo is expected. These items include aid provided by a government or private interests to other countries,

which can be in the form of grants issued by the government, money sent home to their families by immigrants, and private funding and aid by foundations and international aid agencies, such as the Red Cross. Unrequited transfers can be private funding and aid by foundations and international aid agencies, such as the Red Cross that provide financial and physical assistance in the event of national disasters. Unrequited transfers are made to institutions and private individuals alike.

The current account is considered the most important of the four BOP accounts because it measures all income-producing activity generated through foreign trade and is considered the prime indicator of the trading health of a nation. A balance of trade deficit, however, is not in itself a negative condition in certain instances, and it could be considered normal for a country as long as other services, transfers, and capital accounts can finance the deficit within the merchandise sector. Some countries have chronic balance of trade deficits but are economically healthy, because of their strength in other sectors, such as Switzerland, whose forte is the financial services sector. Other countries exhibit continuing deficits in their balances of trade because they are in the process of development.

The balance of trade and the current account are not the only indicators of the position of a country. The history and level of development of a nation must also be considered in assessing its relative health. Another important indicator in weighing national economic strength in relation to other countries is the BOP capital account.

CAPITAL ACCOUNT

The capital account of a nation measures its net changes in financial assets and liabilities abroad. It also chronicles the flow of investment funds across national borders. The capital account notes an inflow when residents of a country receive funds from foreign investors. These funds may be invested in stocks (equity) or bonds (debt) or any other financial assets that foreign owners hold and for which resident borrowers are liable for

---

[1] "Terms of Trade," *The Economist*, September 24, 1988.

payment. The resident is then required to remit to the foreign financiers returns on the investment in the form of dividends or profits. Naturally, an outflow of funds occurs when a resident of the home country acquires assets abroad; the overseas counterpart then incurs an international liability.

The capital account is made up of three separate segments. The first is long-term capital movements, which can be in the form of either direct or portfolio investments. Direct investments are those made by individuals or multinational corporations in facilities or assets abroad where the investor has control over the use and disposition of the assets. For balance of payment purposes, effective control is determined as that time when foreign owners from one country hold more than 50 percent of voting stock or when a single resident or an organized group from one country owns more than 25 percent of voting stock in a foreign company.

Long-term portfolio investments are those in which investors contribute capital to a foreign concern and invest their funds in stocks or bonds but do not control the facility or the assets of the enterprise. These investments are considered long-term if they are held for more than a year. Portfolio investments that mature in less than a year are considered short-term capital flows, the third segment of the capital account. Some short-term movements are considered as being compensatory, in that they finance other activities, such as those in the current account. Others represent autonomous international financial movements undertaken for their own sake in order to speculate on fluctuations in exchange and interest rates. Many of these actions consist of trading and hedging activity undertaken in international financial forward, futures, options, and swaps markets.

These capital outflows can have the effect of increasing aggregate demand overseas or of displacing exports from the home country. By the same token, however, investment outflows may also provide for returns from abroad in the form of dividends, profits, or increased equity.

OFFICIAL RESERVES ACCOUNT

This balance of payments account exists for government use only, to account for the position of one government against other, that is, they reflect the actual holdings of a country and what might be the equivalent of cash or near-cash assets for a corporate entity. This account reflects holdings of gold and foreign exchange. It also takes into account loans between governments and decreases and increases in liabilities to foreign central banks and the country's balance in special drawing rights with the International Monetary Fund.

NET STATISTICAL DISCREPANCY

In theory, the balance of payments should balance perfectly within the account of one single country and among all countries of the world as trade flows progress in an orderly fashion and as all nations of the world report those flows consistently and accurately. In actuality, this scenario is far from the truth, because of differences in accounting practices, functions, mistakes, and unsanctioned transfers of funds between countries through smuggling, underground economic activity, and the sale of illegal items. Thus, the balance of payments includes a separate account that adjusts for these discrepancies, which can be sizable amounts. In 1986, for example, the net statistical discrepancy for the U.S. balance of payments reached $24 billion.[2]

PROBLEMS IN BALANCE OF PAYMENTS

Balance of payments problems occur when a country's external assets or liabilities increase beyond proportion, that is, either when the balance of payments shows either a surplus or deficit of external resources. Although surpluses and deficits in the balance of payments are a normal feature, they pose a problem when they are excessive and persistent to a point where they cannot be sustained. While surpluses also pose certain problems for a country, it is the deficits that present the real dif-

[2] U.S. Department of Commerce (March) 1988.

ficulties. Deficits generally occur when a country is not able to match the outflows of foreign exchange because of imports, debt service, or other payments with its export or other inflows. If the deficit remains persistent, a country is faced with several options. The country can

- borrow from other governments and multilateral institutions to fill the gap between the inflows and outflows.
- draw down its level of foreign exchange reserves to meet the shortfall.
- devalue its currency in order to make exports attractive and imports unattractive, so that the gap between inflows and outflows is corrected.
- make fundamental adjustments in its economy to reduce the outflows and increase the inflows of foreign exchange, which could include reducing the level of nonessential imports, controlling local inflation, improving domestic productivity and efficiency, and improving the allocative efficiency of the economy.

The issue of BOP problems has attracted considerable attention, especially after 1973, when the less-developed countries of the world faced huge increases in their oil bills, which increased their expenditures of foreign exchange and, by creating a recession in Western countries, reduced their foreign exchange earnings. BOP difficulties lead to problems in the domestic sector. When external creditors find that a country is not able to service its borrowings, they are reluctant to lend it additional money or tend to charge higher rates of interest for a perceived higher risk. The country facing the crisis loses access to external credit with which to finance essential imports for meeting developmental and consumer needs. Moreover, it is not easy to make fundamental economic adjustments. For one, many developing countries have large sections of population at or below poverty levels, and any economic adjustment measures calling for reduction in government subsidies or assistance for these sections of the population are not likely to be politically acceptable. Moreover, there are entrenched vested interests in different sectors of the economy that are eager to main-

tain the status quo and even resort to disruptive activities to prevent their privileges from being disturbed.

The intention of the adjustment measures, however, has a reasonably sound theoretical basis. Devaluing the currency to bring it closer to its actual market value boosts exports and discourages imports by making them more expensive. Controlling inflation also increases export competitiveness, as does the increase in productivity and efficiency of the domestic industries. Reducing the demand for imports automatically reduces the outflows of foreign exchange.

Although the BOP problems can be resolved through these actions, there is considerable cost involved. Devaluation can lead to an increase in domestic inflation because import prices will be higher. Moreover, the advantage of devaluation is lost if the export sector of a country is using a large proportion of imported inputs. The terms of trade of a country also worsen with devaluation, as it is forced to part with a greater quantity of exports for the same quantity of imports. Reduction in import demand leads to economic slowdowns, which exacerbate existing problems of stagnant growth and high unemployment.

The policymakers of a country, therefore, have to tread very carefully and balance these diverse and often conflicting considerations while attempting to correct imbalances in the position of their external payments. Creditors, trading partners, and multilateral institutions play a vital role in determining the success of the efforts of a country to resolve BOP problems. If they follow supportive policies, a country can overcome its fundamental constraints and recover its external balance. Its problems can be exacerbated, however, if the creditors and trading partners follow a "beggar my neighbor" policy, for example, by indulging in competitive devaluation or manipulating interest rates to attract foreign capital that might be needed by other countries in difficulty.

U.S. TRADE DEFICITS

The position of the United States in world trade in the 1980s illustrates, these problems.

Some form of balance of payments statistics have been maintained by the U.S. government since 1790, when America had a deficit of $1 million in goods and services.[3] In the twentieth century, the United States had a positive balance in goods and services for more than six decades. During that period, the largest surpluses were during the war years of 1943 and 1944, when surpluses were $11.038 billion and $12.452 billion, respectively, reflecting U.S. exports directed toward the war effort. In 1947 the balance in goods and services also reflected U.S. efforts toward wartorn countries, and the surplus was $11.617 billion.[4]

In the late 1960s the U.S. balance of payments began to come under pressure and in the 1970s the current account began to show substantial deficits. A number of factors contributed to the reversal of trends, including the huge increase in U.S. imports, the emergence of strong competition in world export markets from Europe and Japan and the quadrupling in the price of oil.

In the 1980s the situation continued to worsen. Imports rose from $333 billion in 1980 to nearly $500 billion in 1986. On the other hand, exports remained relatively stagnant, growing only marginally from $342 billion to $372 billion over this period. The large gap between inflows and outflows because of exports and imports was financed primarily by private capital transfers into the United States. The effect of the private capital flows into the United States nullified the effect of the huge trade deficit on the U.S. currency, which continued to appreciate between 1980 and 1985.

The strength of the dollar, however, further weakened U.S. competitiveness in international markets and enabled Europe, Japan, and some of the Pacific Rim countries to build substantial market shares not only in overseas markets, but also the U.S. domestic market. In fact, the years of an overvalued dollar had tended to make the deficit structural, or built in, in character, which occurred because overseas manufactures, taking ad-

vantage of the high dollar, were able to under-price their products and capture U.S. domestic market shares in such areas as consumer electronics and automobiles. Having achieved market penetration, the long period of dollar overvaluation gave overseas exporters opportunity to consolidate and secure their gains by building dealer networks, after sales service arrangements and consumer brand loyalty. Thus, even though the dollar depreciated substantially after 1985, there was no significant drop in either the market shares covered by the overseas exporters or the overall volume of imports.

Given the size of the economy, however, the trade deficits do not create a calamity. While there is cause for concern and reason for remedial action, there is no reason for panic, both because of the size of the deficit and its nature.

Some analysts, such as economist Robert B. Reich, believe that attention should be focused on the reasons behind these deficits. For example, the United States currently runs a deficit with the four tigers—Hong Kong, South Korea, Singapore, and Taiwan. Some Americans worry about this situation, but Reich asks the questions of exactly what are U.S. interests in world trade and who are "we"? He notes that while Americans are exporting less, they may not be selling fewer goods in world markets because "these days about half of the total exports of American multinational corporations come from their factories in other countries," compared to a one-third equivalent twenty years ago.[5] Thus, he maintains that nearly a third of our imbalance with the Pacific Rim countries, for example, results from the multinationalization of industry and U.S. subsidiaries making products there and selling them back to Americans on domestic soil. He also notes that some U.S. companies are key export players in other market arenas. For example, IBM, a U.S. company, is Japan's largest exporter of computers and has 18,000 employees and annual sales of $6 billion.[6]

---

[3] U.S. Department of Commerce 1976.
[4] Ibid.

[5] Reich 1988.
[6] Ibid.

QUESTIONS

1. What is the balance of payments?
2. What are the four basic accounts under the balance of payments?
3. Name a source for the U.S. balance of payments. What source(s) exist for international balance of payments?
4. Examine the U.S. balance of payments (Table 4–2). What do you observe about the current account over time? Are U.S. exports greater or less than U.S. imports. Do services improve the merchandise import and export balance?

APPENDIX BIBLIOGRAPHY

1988. "March of the Middleman." *The Economist* (September 24): 93–94.

1988. "Terms of Trade." *The Economist* (September 24): p. 92.

1988. "Walkman Factories Don't Walk." *The Economist* (March 12): 66.

ASHEGHIAN, PARVIS. 1985. "The Impact of Devaluation on the Balance of Payments of Less Developed Countries: A Monetary Approach." *Journal of Economic Development* (July): 143–151.

BUSINESS COUNCIL FOR INTERNATIONAL UNDERSTANDING. 1983. *Descriptive Brochure.* Washington DC.

CROOK, OLIVE 1988. "One Armed Policy Maker." *The Economist* (September): 51–57.

GRAY, H. P., and G. E. MAKINEN. 1967. "Balance of Payments Contributions of Multinational Corporations." *Journal of Business* (July): 339–343.

INTERNATIONAL MONETARY FUND *Balance of Payments Yearbook.* Washington DC: International Monetary Fund (Annual).

GLADWELL, MALCOLM. 1988. "Scientist Warns of U.S. Reliance on Foreigners." *Washington Post* (September 9): El.

McGRAW, THOMAS K. 1986. *America Versus Japan.* Boston: Harvard Business School Press.

NAKAMAL, TADASHI. 1984. "Growth Matters More than Surpluses." *Euromoney* (February): 101–103.

OBSTFELD, MAURICE. 1984. "Balance of Payments Crises and Devaluation." *Journal of Money, Banking and Credit* (May): 208–217.

REICH, ROBERT B. 1988. "The Trade Gap: Myths and Crocodile Tears." *New York Times* (February 2): 34.

SOLOP, J., and E. SPITALLER. 1980. "Why Does the Current Account Matter?" *International Monetary Fund Staff Papers,* (March): 101–134.

STRINER, HERBERT E. 1984. *Regaining The Lead: Polities for Economic Growth.* New York: Praeger.

———. 1988. *Survey of Current Business* (March, June, September, and December issues).

U.S. DEPARTMENT OF COMMERCE. 1976. *Historical Statistics of the United States: Colonial Times to 1970.*

WORLD BANK. 1990. *The World Development Report, 1990,* Washington, DC: Oxford University Press.

YODER, STEPHEN KREIDER. 1988. "All Eyes Are on MITI Research Wish List," *Wall Street Journal* (August 24): 10.

———. 1988. "If Japan Poses Threat in Superconductors, Shoji Tanaka Is Why." *Wall Street Journal* (April 29): 1, 24.

YOSHIHARA, NANCY. 1988. "Japan Absolutely, Positively Irks Federal Express." *Washington Post* (August 16): C3.

Chapter Case Study _____

Structural Adjustments in Masawa

Masawa is a small country located in southwestern Africa, with an area of approximately 240,000 square miles and a population of approximately 60 million. The northern and western parts of the country are hilly terrain, while the southern and eastern areas are plains. Masawa has substantial natural resources—mineral deposits of manganese, copper, and tin in the northern hill areas and large tropical forests in the southeastern parts of the country. The eastern part has most of the cultivated land, and agricultural production, especially cereal crops, is concentrated there. There are some cocoa plantations in the western part of the country and cocoa is an important commercial crop. The main exports of Masawa are copper, tin, and cocoa. Manganese deposits are too small to be commercially viable for export.

The country attained its independence from colonial rule in 1961 and since then has seen four political upheavals. Emorgue Watiza, a leader of the country's freedom movement, was the first president. He ruled Masawa for six years before being ousted by the military, which installed General Ramaza, who was assassinated in 1974 and replaced by another military ruler, Colonel Waniki. Colonel Waniki instituted a series of political reforms, and after eleven years of power, handed over the reins of government to Dr. Sabankwa, the winner of the country's first democratic election. Dr. Sabankwa brought excellent credentials to the presidency. He held a Ph.D. in political science and government from the University of Paris and had been active in the movement for restoration of democracy in Masawa. He belonged to the Waldesi tribe, which comprised 30 percent of the population and enjoyed almost total loyalty of his tribesmen. Waldesi, the largest single tribe in the ethnic composition of Masawa, includes three other major and sixteen minor tribes. The three other major tribes are the Mokoti (18 percent), Lemata (15 percent), and Simoki (11 percent). The remaining 27 percent of the population is made up of members of the smaller tribes, none of which individually constituted more than 5 percent of the population.

Dr. Sabankwa enjoyed considerable support from the Simoki and several minor tribes at the time of his election. After five years in office, however, that support has eroded, and rumblings of discontent have been heard, even from his own Waldesi tribesmen, especially those living in the urban areas. Much of the discontent is clearly the result of the economic difficulties the country is facing, which in turn has led to considerable difficulties for both the urban and rural populations. Reactions, however, tend to be more pronounced in the densely populated and politically conscious urban areas.

Most of the economic difficulties of Masawa began before the election of Dr. Sabankwa. The country had little in the way of industrial or technological development when it attained independence and the annual per capita GNP was $160. Much of the agriculture was conducted along primitive lines and was largely dependent on seasonal rainfall, which tended to be fairly erratic over the years. In the initial years of independence, Masawa's rulers sought to adopt a centralized planning approach to economic development, which assigned a key role to the government in nearly all aspects of economic activity. The public sector accounts for 90 percent of industrial production, and all key infrastructure projects are run by government agencies. Masawa has a large number of highly paid civil servants who administer the wide range of economic and other controls imposed by the government. Although private enterprise is officially permitted, there are a number of bureaucratic disincentives for entrepreneurship. A typical new venture in the private sector needs separate approvals from thirty-two different government agencies and departments.

As in many other countries of the developing world, the state-owned industrial enterprises of Masawa have had losses for a variety of reasons, including inefficient management, overstaffing, administered prices of products, and outmoded technology. The government has guaranteed most of the debt taken on by the enterprises and has had to resort to substantial deficit financing to make good on these obligations.

The government of Masawa has faced a major budget deficit every year for the past eleven years, and, for several reasons, the deficit had become a permanent feature of the government's finances. Government expenditures have been rising rapidly in four areas—defense, oil imports, administrative expenses of the government, and subsidies to industrial enterprises, and price subsidies for essential consumption items, especially food. On the other hand, revenues have been stagnant, principally because of the absence of strong measures to secure better tax compliance by the vast majority of taxpayers. The government has, therefore, resorted to large-scale deficit financing, which has pushed the inflation rate progressively higher every year. In 1989, Masawa experienced 93 percent inflation, and there were indications that this number would increase by another 40 percent in 1990.

Imports have been increasing steadily over the past seven years, while exports are stagnant, because the world market for the principal exports continue to be sluggish. The exchange rate of Masawa is overvalued by about 70 percent, and there is a large premium on the black market for foreign currencies. The country has suffered considerable flight of capital as wealthy industrialists lost faith in the political and economic stability of Masawa.

The external debt of Masawa, largely to official creditors, is well above the level considered dangerous for sustaining the debt service schedule. The country has no access to the international capital market, having defaulted on the amortization of earlier loans, taken primarily by state-owned corporations. Foreign exchange reserves are at a dangerously low level and are sufficient only to finance two weeks of imports.

Dr. Sabankwa called a meeting of his cabinet to discuss the issue of accepting an International Monetary Fund structural adjustment loan, in order to tide the country over the immediate problems on the balance of payments front and to improve the prospects in the future. Before a full meeting of the cabinet, the finance minister briefed Dr. Sabankwa on the pertinent issues, and, after long, late night conversation with the finance minister, Dr. Sabankwa realized he had a difficult situation to resolve.

The IMF is willing to extend a $3 billion loan to Masawa under its structural adjustment lending program, but its wants Masawa to draw up a set of concrete economic measures to restructure the economy. Although several measures have been recommended by the IMF, five are the most important:

1. The level of imports should be reduced.
2. Masawa should devalue the exchange rate by 40 percent.
3. The government should initiate a phased reduction of official subsidies on food.
4. The government should take steps toward privatizing state-owned enterprises.
5. Administrative expenses of the government should be reduced by cutting the government staff and their salaries.

While these measures seem sensible and useful, effective implementation of them would create many practical difficulties. First, cutting food subsidies would be an extremely unpopular measure and might spark civil disturbances, especially in the urban areas. Moreover, those most affected would be the urban poor, who are already under great economic hardship. Devaluing the exchange rate also has ominous implications. Politically, it might be viewed as a weakening of the economy and provide another reason for opposition groups to attack the government's handling of the economic situation. Further, the costs of imports would rise and contribute to an increase in the already high inflation rate. Privatization would also be difficult, since there are few people in Masawa with the managerial or technical expertise to take over the operations of these enterprises. Further, there was bound to be strong opposition from the trade unions to any move for privatization.

Reducing the level of imports would be a feasible option, but it would hurt the growth rate considerably, because imports of essential industrial equipment and machinery would have to be curtailed. Further, a very large cut in im-

ports might not even be possible because of the inelastic level of defense and oil imports.

As he mulled over these issues, Dr. Sabankwa wondered if a compromise solution could be found—would these steps, if implemented, not generate political unrest that would lead to the fall of his government?

Questions

1. What would be your position if you were a member of Dr. Sabankwa's cabinet?
2. Should Masawa accept the plan as it exists or should it insist on some modification? If modification is needed, what changes should be made? What arguments should be made to convince IMF officials to agree to these modifications in the structural adjustment plan?

CHAPTER 5

Foreign Exchange Markets

CHAPTER OBJECTIVES

This chapter will:

- Suggest the underlying need for foreign exchange markets.
- Introduce the terms and definitions used in the foreign exchange markets.
- Describe the structure and operations of the foreign exchange markets.
- Present the mathematical formulas used to compare currency movements in the foreign exchange markets.
- Discuss common techniques used to manage currency risk and exposure.
- Explain the need for and problems associated with forecasting foreign exchange rates.

Background

Nearly all international business activity requires the transfer of money from one country to another. Trade transactions must be settled in monetary terms—buyers in one country pay suppliers in another. Repatriation of dividends, profits, and royalties from overseas investments, contributions of equity, and other kinds of finance from such investments also involves the transfer of funds across national borders. The transfer of funds poses problems quite different from the transfer of goods and services across national borders. Buyers and sellers are willing to accept and use goods and services from other countries quite routinely. For example, U.S. consumers are content to drive Japanese cars, such as Toyotas and Hondas, while the Japanese are quite willing to use U.S. supercomputers or other hi-tech products.

This internationalization of product usage, however, is not found when it comes to accepting the currency of another country. While the U.S. importer is happy to receive Japanese products and the Japanese importer is glad to accept U.S. products, neither is normally in a position to accept the other's currency. A U.S. importer usually has to pay a Japanese exporter in Japanese yen, while a U.S. exporter will generally want to be paid in U.S. dollars. This is quite logical, since each country has its own currency, which is legal tender within its borders, and exporters are likely to prefer the currency that they can use at home for meeting costs and taking profits.

A U.S. importer who must pay a Japanese exporter has to acquire Japanese yen. To do so, he must exchange his own currency, dollars, into yen. Such an exchange of one currency for another is called a foreign exchange transaction.

For example, a German company invests in an electronics manufacturing facility in Australia. Therefore, it must convert its deutsche marks into Australian dollars to meet project costs in Australia. In another example, a U.S. multinational has a plant located in Great Britain. At the end of the financial year, it wants to repatriate its profits to the corporate headquarters in the United States. Therefore, it will convert British pounds sterling, profits earned by the plant in Great Britain, into U.S. dollars. As another example, suppose a Japanese investor has a large stock holding on Wall Street. After a rally in which his holdings appreciate substantially, he wants to repatriate his profits to Japan. To do so, he would convert his U.S. dollar profits into Japanese yen.

How do the German company, the U.S. multinational, and the Japanese investor convert the currency in their possession into the currency they desire? The answer is provided by the foreign exchange market.

The Structure of the Foreign Exchange Market

The demand for conversion of one currency into another gives rise to the demand for foreign exchange transactions. The foreign exchange markets of the world serve as the mechanism through which these numerous and complex transactions are completed efficiently and almost instantaneously.

The main intermediaries in the foreign exchange market are major banks worldwide that deal in foreign exchange. These banks are linked together by a very advanced and sophisticated telecommunications network that connects the banks with major clients and other banks around the world. There is no physical contact between the dealers of various banks in the foreign exchange market, unlike the stock exchanges or the futures markets, which have specific trading floors or pits.

Some of the larger and more active banks have installed computer terminals called dealing screens in their trading rooms. Through these terminals banks can execute trades and receive written confirmations on on-line printers. Telephone transactions are normally confirmed by an exchange of Telex messages or transaction notes.

Banks who are active in foreign exchange operations set up extremely sophisticated facilities for their foreign exchange traders, which are located in trading (or dealing) rooms, which are equipped with instantaneous telecommunication facilities.

A very important feature of modern trading rooms is their access to information about political, economic, and other current events as they unfold. A major source of this information is the British news agency Reuters, which furnishes subscribing banks with a dedicated communication system that provides on-screen information beamed from the central news room of the agency. There are also many services, including Reuters and Telerate, that provide up-to-the-second information on the prevailing exchange rates quoted by banks worldwide. Any changes in exchange rates anywhere in the world can be immediately brought to the notice of traders.

Exchange trading is an extremely specialized operation that puts enormous pressure on traders because rates change rapidly and there are chances to make huge profits or incur massive losses. Bank managements continually monitor the activity and progress of their dealing rooms, while setting very clear guidelines in order to limit the level of risk the traders can take while trading currencies on behalf of the bank.

To relieve traders from the task of booking orders, trading rooms are supported by backup accounting departments that record the transactions made by the traders and to do the necessary computations to track the trading activity. They also supply the traders with background data and analytical reports to optimize the strategy and performance of traders. Such information is fed into electronic trading boards that are clearly visible to traders. Generally, this information includes the risk exposure of the bank in each currency and the current rates for different currencies, as well as a host of other information.

Exchange trading at a bank usually begins everyday in the early morning with an in-house conference of traders and senior managers to discuss the currency expectations and the strategy for the day. Most trading is conducted during local business hours, but the ease of communication made possible by the latest technology enables banks to continue to trade with banks in other time zones after the local business day is over. Therefore, some major banks have a system of shifts, where traders come in to trade in the markets in different time zones. By using night trading desks, many major banks have been able to establish twenty-four-hour trading operations.

There are two levels in the foreign exchange market. One is the customer, or retail market, where individuals or institutions buy and sell foreign currencies to banks dealing in foreign exchange. For example, if IBM wishes to repatriate profits from its German subsidiary to the United States, it can approach a bank in Frankfurt with an offer to sell its deutsche marks in exchange for U.S. dollars. This type of transaction will occur in what is called the customer market.

Suppose the bank does not have a sufficient amount of U.S. dollars. In this situation the bank can approach other banks to acquire dollars in exchange for deutsche marks or some other currency. Such sales and purchases are termed interbank transactions and collectively constitute the interbank market. Interbank transactions are both local and international.

The interbank market is extremely active. Banks purchase and sell currencies from and to one another to meet shortages and reduce sur-

pluses that result from transactions with their customers. Transactions in the interbank markets are almost always in large sums. Amounts less than a quarter of a million U.S. dollars are not traded in interbank markets. Values of interbank transactions usually range from $1 million to $10 million per transaction, although deals above this range are also known to take place. A large proportion of the transactions in interbank markets arises from banks trading currencies to make profits from movements in exchange rates around the world.

It is important to note that in all this trading activity in foreign exchange markets, billions of dollars of international currency are exchanged without any physical transfer of money. How are the transactions settled? The answer lies in a system of mutual account maintenance. Banks in one country maintain accounts at banks in other countries. These accounts are generally denominated in the home currency of the bank with the account. In banking parlance these are called vostro accounts, which essentially means "your account with us," or nostro accounts, which means, literally, "our account with you." Thus, if Citibank New York has a deutsche mark account with Dresdner Bank in Frankfurt, it will term the Dresdner account its nostro account. For Dresdner, this will be a vostro account. Similarly, Dresdner Bank would have a U.S. dollar account with Citibank or another bank in the United States. For Dresdner this will be a nostro account, while for the U.S bank it will be a vostro account. Foreign exchange transactions are settled by debits or credits to nostro and vostro accounts.

Market Participants

The foreign exchange market has many different types of participants. These participants differ not only in the scale of their operations, but also in their objectives and methods of functioning.

INDIVIDUALS

Individuals may participate in foreign exchange markets for personal as well as business needs. A personal need would be sending a monetary gift to an overseas relative. To do that, the sender would utilize the market to obtain the currency of the relative's country. Individual business needs arise when a person is involved in international business. For example, individual importers use the foreign exchange market to obtain the currencies needed to pay their overseas suppliers. Exporters, on the other hand, use the markets to convert the currencies received from their foreign buyers into domestic or other currencies. Business or leisure travelers also participate in the foreign exchange market by buying and selling foreign and local currencies to meet expenses on their overseas trips.

INSTITUTIONS

Institutions are very important participants in the foreign exchange markets because of their large and different currency requirements. Multinational corporations typically are major participants in the foreign markets, continually transferring large sums of currencies across national borders, a process that usually requires the exchange of one currency for another. Financial institutions that have international investments are also important foreign exchange market participants. These institutions include pension funds, insurance companies, mutual funds, and investment banks. They need to switch their multicurrency investments quite often, generating substantial transaction volumes in the foreign exchange market.

Apart from meeting their basic transaction needs, both the individual and institutional participants use the foreign exchange markets to reduce the risks they incur because of adverse fluctuations in exchange rates.

BANKS

Banks are the largest and most active participants in the foreign exchange markets. Banks operate in the foreign exchange market through their traders. (British banks and many others use the term "exchange dealer" rather than "exchange trader." These terms can be used interchangeably.) Exchange traders at banks buy and sell currencies, acting upon the requests of their customers and on behalf of the bank itself.

Customer-requested transactions form a very small proportion of trading operations by banks in the foreign exchange markets. To a very large extent, banks treat foreign exchange market operations as an independent profit center. In fact, some major banks make substantial profits on the strength of their market expertise, information, trading skills, and ability to hold on to risky investments that would not be feasible for smaller participants. On occasion, banks can also incur substantial losses. As a result, foreign exchange operations are closely monitored at banks.

CENTRAL BANKS AND OTHER OFFICIAL PARTICIPANTS

Central banks enter the foreign exchange market for a variety of reasons. They can buy substantial amounts of foreign currencies to either build up their foreign exchange reserves or to bring down the value of their own currency, which in their opinion may be overvalued by the markets (see Figure 5–1). They can enter the markets to sell large amounts of foreign currencies to shore up their own currencies. In the latter part of the 1980s, central banks and treasurers of the United States, Japan, and West Germany intervened quite often to correct the imbalances between the values of the yen and deutsche mark versus the U.S. dollar.

The main objective of central banks is not to profit from their foreign exchange operations or avoid risks. It is to move the values of their own and other important currencies in line with the values they consider appropriate for the best economic interest of their country.

Central banks of countries that have an official exchange rate for their currency must continually participate in the foreign exchange markets to ensure that their currency is available at the announced rate.

SPECULATORS AND ARBITRAGERS

Participation by speculators and arbitragers in the foreign exchange market is driven by pure profit motive. They seek to profit from the wide fluctuations that occur in foreign exchange markets.

Having a Big Mac Attack?

Here's what a McDonald's Big Mac cost in different countries as of June 30, 1988. The U.S. equivalent prices indicate which currencies are overvalued and which are undervalued versus the dollar.

Country	Foreign Price	U.S. Equivalent	Over/under U.S. Valuation
Norway	28 kronen	$4.21	+92%
Finland	16.6 markkaa	3.84	+75
Switzerland	4.50 francs	2.99	+37
France	17.2 francs	2.81	+28
Japan	370 yen	2.78	+27
Italy	3500 lire	2.60	+19
Spain	280 pesetas	2.30	+ 5
W. Germany	4.05 marks	2.23	+ 2
U.S.*	2.19 dollars	2.19	—
England	1.04 pounds	1.78	−19
Australia	2.00 dollars	1.59	−27
Yugoslavia	2,300 dinars	1.47	−33
Singapore	2.80 dollars	1.37	−37
Hong Kong	7.60 dollars	0.97	−56
Turkey	1,300 liras	0.95	−57
Hungary	43 forints	0.74	−66

*New York City price

FIGURE 5–1   The price of a Big Mac around the globe.
Source: *Wall Street Journal,* September 23, 1988.

In other words, they do not have any underlying commercial or business transactions that they seek to cover in the foreign exchange market. Typically, speculators buy large amounts of a currency when they believe it is undervalued and sell it when the price rises, or vice versa.

Arbitragers are persons who try to exploit the differences in exchange rates between different markets. If the exchange rate for the pound is cheaper in London than in New York, they would buy pounds in London and sell them in New York, making a profit. Arbitrage opportunities are now increasingly rare, however, because instantaneous communications tend to equalize worldwide rates simultaneously.

A substantial part of the speculative and arbitrage transactions comes from exchange traders of commercial banks. Often this is a conscious effort to maximize profits with clearly defined profit objectives, loss limits, and risk-taking boundaries. In fact, the overwhelming proportion of foreign exchange market transactions today are driven by speculation.

Foreign Exchange Brokers

Foreign exchange brokers are intermediaries who bring together parties with opposite and matching requirements in the foreign exchange markets. They are in simultaneous contact with scores of banks through hot lines and attempt to match the buying requirements of some banks with the selling needs of others. They do not deal on their own account and are not a party to the actual transactions. For their services they charge an agreed-upon fee, which is often called brokerage.

By bringing together various market participants with complementary needs, foreign exchange brokers contribute significantly to the "perfectness of information," which makes the foreign exchange markets as efficient as they are. Apart from this, brokers also perform another important function. They preserve the confidentiality and anonymity of the participants. In a typical deal, the broker will not reveal the identity of the other party until the deal is sealed. This achieves a more uniform conduct of business as deals are decided purely on market considerations and are not influenced by other considerations that might be introduced if the identity of counterparties became known.

Location of Foreign Exchange Markets

The foreign exchange market is truly global, working around the clock and throughout the world. The very nature of foreign exchange trading, as well as the revolution in telecommunications, has resulted in a unified market where distances and even time zones have been compressed. Traditionally, London, and later New York, were the main centers of foreign trading. Other centers, however, such as Tokyo, Hong Kong, Singapore, and Frankfurt have become extremely active. Smaller but significant markets exist in many European and some Asian countries.

The individual foreign exchange trading centers are closely linked to form one global market. Trading spills over from one market to another and from one time zone to another. Price levels in one trading center immediately affect other centers. As the market closes in one time zone, others open in different time zones, taking cues from the activities of the earlier market in setting up trading and price trends. A continuous pattern is thus established, giving the impression of one unified market across the world.

Japan

Because of its position in the time zones, Japan can be considered the market where the world's trading day begins. The Japanese markets, led by Tokyo, are extremely active, with a very high daily turnover. Most of the deals are backed by customer-related requests to finance or settle international commercial transactions. Dollar-yen deals predominate in the market, because of the large share of U.S.-related business in the international transactions of Japan.

With the deregulation of Japanese foreign exchanges, the element of speculative activity has increased considerably, especially in the Tokyo market. The volume of trading in the market has also increased as the securities and equity markets of Japan have opened up to foreign investment and some foreign investment banks have been allowed to operate in Japan. Brokers are extensively used in the Japanese markets, especially in transactions between banks located within the country. The market, however, closes at a set time in the afternoon, thus putting a limit on the volume of transactions that can take place. This system has inhibited somewhat the development of the Tokyo market, which would otherwise be significantly larger.

Singapore and Hong Kong

Singapore and Hong Kong are the next markets to open, about one hour after Tokyo. These markets are much less regulated, and in pursuit of their aim to become major international financial centers, both markets offer liberal access to overseas banks and commercial establishments. At the same time, the authorities have attempted to create a friendly market environment to promote maximum trading activity. Market activity has increased considerably because several overseas banks, attracted by the incentives offered, have opened branches in both centers. Brokers are heavily involved in local transactions in Singapore, while international transactions are done primarily through direct deals between banks. The trading activity of Hong Kong is a mix of direct deals and broker-intermediated transactions. Singapore has an edge over Hong Kong with respect to market size. The Hong Kong market, being smaller, also tends to be more volatile.

Bahrain

This market in the Middle East emerged as an important center of foreign exchange trading in the 1970s, as oil-linked commercial transactions grew considerably. Located in the middle of overlapping time zones, Bahrain is often used by traders in other markets to serve as a link in their global cycle. Bahrain provides a link between the closing of the Far Eastern and opening of the European markets because it is open during the time lag.

European Markets

Europe, taken as a whole, is the largest foreign exchange market. Its main centers are London, Frankfurt, and Zurich. European banks have no set closing time for foreign exchange trading and are free to trade twenty-four hours a day, but they generally cease trading in the afternoon. Both direct and brokered deals are common in European trading. Some of Europe's markets, such as Paris, exhibit a unique feature—rate fixing. Once a day representatives of the larger banks and the central banks meet to fix the exchange rate of the U.S. dollar against local currencies and hence against one another. The fixed rate represents the balance of offers and bids and is close to what it would be internationally. There is, however, sometimes a small discrepancy, which offers an opportunity for arbitrage. This opportunity, of course, exists only for a very short time, as market pressures quickly equalize the prices. The fixed rate is important primarily because it is considered to be the legal official rate and is often specified in contracts.

U.S. Markets

The New York market opens next. It is one of the largest markets and the top foreign exchange trading firms are headquartered there. The volume of business in New York has increased tremendously since deregulation in the banking system and the increasing presence of overseas banks. Both brokered as well as direct dealing are common in the New York exchange market. The U.S. West Coast markets are essentially tied to New York and closely follow the trading patterns that are established there.

Market Volumes

Foreign exchange markets are clearly located in the largest financial markets in the world. Their turnover exceeds several times over that of securities, futures, options, and commodities markets. The actual turnover figures, however, are difficult to ascertain, because banks do not publish data on the volume of their transactions. Moreover, a single transaction can be rolled several times.

In 1979 one study estimated the daily turnover of the world foreign exchange market to be about

U.S.$200 billion.[1] A survey by the Federal Reserve Bank of New York put the daily turnover of U.S. banks at $50 billion.[2] The *Wall Street Journal* has estimated turnover to be as much as U.S.$250 billion per day on a global level. The currencies that predominate in foreign exchange trading activity on a worldwide basis are the U.S. dollar, deutsche mark, yen, Swiss franc, pound sterling, Canadian dollar, French franc, Italian lira, and the Australian dollar. Some other currencies of increasing importance in foreign exchange markets are the Swedish krona, Dutch guilders, and Belgian francs.

A daily turnover of $250 billion would amount to an annual figure of $91.25 trillion. The enormity of this figure, which estimates the annual volume of global foreign exchange trading, can be appreciated if one compares it with the U.S. gross national product, which is $4.5 trillion.

Uses of the Foreign Exchange Market

The foreign exchange market provides the means by which different categories of individuals and institutions acquire foreign exchange to meet different needs, but it is important to understand the economic functions performed by the foreign exchange markets and their role in international trade in goods and services. Two basic functions are the avoidance of risk and the financing of international trade.

International trade transactions, which must be settled monetarily, carry significant risks both to the buyer and the seller. If the transaction is invoiced in the currency of the seller, the seller stands to lose if the currency depreciates in the time lag between agreement on the price and the actual date of payment. Consider, for example, a British importer of U.S. computers. The importer agrees to buy the shipment of computers for $150,000, and the current exchange rate is 1.5 dollars to the pound. At this rate, the costs to the British importer is £100,000. Usually, in such instances payments are made after goods are shipped or received. In this example assume a lag of three months between the signing of the contract and the actual payment by the British importer. Suppose, in this period the value of the U.S. dollar appreciates and it becomes equal to one pound. In this event, the British importer will have to part with £150,000 to purchase the $150,000 needed to meet the contractual obligation. As a result, the importer stands to make a substantial loss of £50,000. Although this is an exaggerated example, the risks are indeed real and can often wipe out the entire profit from a transaction.

Foreign exchange markets provide mechanisms to reduce this risk and assure a certain minimum return.

Foreign exchange markets also provide the financing mechanism for international trade transactions. Financing is required to cover the costs of goods that are in transit. These costs are considerable if goods are sent by sea. At the same time, the risks are also high because the counterparties are in different countries, and, in the event of default, the recourse for the party defaulted against is limited. These problems are solved efficiently through the foreign exchange markets, specifically through the use of internationally accepted documentation procedures, the most important being letters of credit.

Types of Exposure in Foreign Exchange Markets

There are four major types of risks or exposure that a corporation faces in the course of its international business activity—transaction exposure, economic exposure, translation exposure, and tax exposure.

---

[1] Federal Reserve Bank of New York. 1986. *Summary Results of U.S. Foreign Exchange Markets Survey Conducted in March 1986*. New York: Federal Reserve Bank of New York.

[2] Ibid.

Transaction Exposure

Transaction exposure is the risk of future cash flows of a company being disturbed by fluctuations in exchange rates. A company that is expecting inflows of foreign currency will be faced with transaction exposure to the extent that the value of these inflows can be affected by a change in the rate of their currency against the preferred currency for conversion. Exchange rates are extremely volatile and a sharp movement can adversely affect the real value of cash flows in the desired currency. A corporation can have both inflows and outflows in a currency. Moreover, it can have different amounts of inflows and outflows in different currencies. In this situation, the company nets out its exposure in each currency by matching some currency inflows and outflows. The net exposure in each currency is aggregated for all currencies to arrive at a measurement of the total transaction exposure for the company. The period over which the cash flows are considered for arriving at the figure for transaction exposure will depend upon the individual methods and views of the company. Companies use a variety of methods to assess the degree to which their net exposed cash flows are at risk. These methods can center on the time lag between the initiation and completion of the transaction, the use of currency correlations, or statistical projections of exchange rate volatility. Sophisticated strategies for assessing transaction exposure often include some element of all of these considerations.

Economic Exposure

Economic exposure is a relatively broader conception of foreign exchange exposure. The prime feature of economic exposure is that it is essentially a long-term, multitransaction-oriented way of looking at the foreign exchange exposure of a firm involved in international business. The standard definition of economic exposure is the degree to which fluctuations in exchange rates will affect the net present value of the future cash flows of a company.

Economic exposure is a particularly serious problem for multinational corporations with operations in several different countries. Since currency fluctuations do not follow any set pattern, each operation is exposed to a different degree and nature of economic exposure. Measuring the degree of economic exposure is even more difficult than measuring translation exposure. Economic exposure involves operational variables, such as costs, prices, sales, and profits, and each of these is also subject to fluctuation in value, independent of the exchange rate movements. Many techniques are used to measure economic exposure. Most of these techniques rely on complex mathematical and statistical models that attempt to capture all the variables. Use of regression analysis and simulation of cash flow positions under different exchange rate scenarios are two examples of such techniques.

Managing economic exposure can involve extremely complex strategies and instruments, some of which are outside the foreign exchange market.

Translation Exposure

Translation exposure is the degree to which the consolidated financial statements and balance sheets of a company can be affected by exchange rate fluctuations. It is also known as **accounting exposure**.

Translation exposure arises when the accounts of a subsidiary are consolidated at the head office at an exchange rate that differs from the rate in effect at the time of the transaction.

Tax Exposure

Tax exposure is the effect that changes in the gains or losses of a company because of exchange rate fluctuations can have on its tax liability. An unexpected or large gain based solely on exchange rate fluctuations could upset the tax planning of a multinational by causing an increased tax liability. Gains and losses from translation exposure generally have an effect on the tax liability of a company at the time they are actually realized.

Types of Foreign Exchange Markets

There are two main types of foreign exchange transactions that are often characterized as different markets—spot and forward, transactions. Often dealers specialize in one of the three transaction categories.

The Spot Market

The spot market consists of transactions in foreign exchange that are ordinarily completed on the second working day. Within the spot market, there can be three types of spot transactions:

1. Cash, where the payment of one currency and delivery of the other currency are completed on the same business day.
2. Tom (short for tomorrow), where the transaction deliveries are completed on the next working day.
3. Spot, where the deliveries are completed within forty-eight hours of striking the deal.

PRICE QUOTATION IN EXCHANGE MARKETS

The prices of currencies in the spot market can be expressed as direct quotes or indirect quotes. When the price of one currency is expressed as a direct quote, it reflects the number of units of home currency that are required to buy the foreign currency. A direct quote on the New York market would be $.25 = FF1. An indirect quote is the reverse; the home currency is expressed as a unit and the price is shown by the number of units of foreign currency that are required to purchase one unit of the home currency. For example, in the New York market an indirect quote would be $1 = 1.475 DM (to purchase one unit of the home currency, the U.S. dollar, 1.475 deutsche marks are needed).

An important feature of foreign exchange price quotation is the number of decimals used. Since large amounts are traded, quotes are usually given at least up to the fourth decimal, especially for such major currencies as pound sterling and the U.S. dollar. Thus, a quote for pound sterling would be 1£ = $1.7643.

LONG AND SHORT POSITIONS

A bank can be in the spot market in three positions:

1. Long, when it buys more than what it sells of a currency.
2. Short, when it buys less than it sells of a currency.
3. Square, when it buys and sells the same amount of currency.

Whenever a bank is long or short in a currency, it is exposed to a certain amount of risk. The risk arises in a long position because the value of its excess currency could depreciate if that currency falls in price. Thus, the market value of the assets of a bank would be lower than the cost price. In a short position, the bank agreed to sell more currency than it had in its possession. If the price of the currency in which the bank is short rises, the bank will experience a loss. The bank will have to acquire and deliver the currency at a higher price than the agreed upon selling price. Both long and short positions can also result in profits, if the currency in question appreciates or depreciates. Since large losses are possible, banks must carefully evaluate the amount of exposure they can withstand. Specific limits are laid down for long and short positions in each currency, as well as aggregate limits for all major currencies.

There are usually two types of trading strategy followed by banks in the spot market. One strategy is to determine whether the currency is going to appreciate or depreciate and then assume a long or short position, allowing the trader to profit from the currency movement. This strategy is often called running a position, or positions trading. The other strategy is to assume and liquidate long and short positions very quickly (often within minutes), as exchange rates fluctuate during the business day. This strategy is known as in and out trading.

The Forward Market

The forward market consists of transactions that require delivery of currency at an agreed upon future date. The rate at which this forward transaction will be completed is determined at the time the parties agree on a contract to buy and sell. The time between the establishment of contracts and the actual exchange of currencies can range from two weeks to more than a year. The more common maturities for forward contracts are one, two, three, or six months. Some forward transactions are termed outright forwards, to distinguish them from swap transactions.

Forward transactions typically occur when exporters, importers, or others involved in the foreign exchange market must either pay or receive foreign currency amounts at a future date. In such situations there is an element of risk for the receiving party if the currency it is going to receive depreciates during the intervening period.

To fix a minimum value on the foreign exchange proceeds, these recipients can lock into a rate in advance by entering into a forward contract with their bank. Under such a contract, the bank is obligated to purchase the currency from the exporter at the agreed upon rate, regardless of the rate that prevails on the day when the foreign currency is actually delivered by the exporter. Banks in turn enter into contracts with other banks to offset these customer contracts, which gives rise to interbank transactions in the forward market.

The date on which the currencies are to be delivered under a forward contract is fixed in advance and is usually specific. In some customer contracts, however, the banks provide an option to the customers to deliver currencies within a certain time range that can be from the beginning of a month up to ten, twenty, or thirty days. The costs of such contracts are, naturally, higher than contracts with specific maturity dates, because banks have to incur additional costs and efforts to create offsetting contracts in the interbank market. Forward contracts are popular with customers who are not certain of the dates on which they will have to pay or receive foreign currency amounts and would therefore like some leeway in executing their contractual obligations.

Foreign Exchange Rates

A foreign exchange rate can be defined as the price of one currency expressed in units of another currency. The price of pound sterling expressed in terms of U.S. dollars could be 1.6840. Therefore, 1.16840 would be the foreign exchange rate of the pound. Many journals and newspapers report foreign exchange rates either daily or periodically. Figure 5–2 shows the foreign exchange quotations from the *Wall Street Journal*. Note that exchange rates are expressed both as indirect and direct quotes in the left- and right-hand columns of the table, respectively.

Since it is often confusing to decide whether a rate is an indirect or direct quote, a uniform standard of exchange rate quotation was adopted in 1978. Under this standard, the U.S. dollar was to be the unit currency and other currencies were expressed as variable amounts relative to the U.S. dollar. This method, where foreign currency prices are quoted as one U.S. dollar, is known as stating the price in European terms. The prices of some currencies, such as the U.K. pound and Australian dollar, however, are quoted in terms of variable units of U.S. dollars per unit of their currency. Such quotations are known as American terms.

Bid and Offer Rates

Rates in the foreign exchange market are quoted as bid and offer rates. A bid is the rate at which the bank is willing to buy a particular currency, and an offer is the rate at which it is willing to sell that currency. Banks in the market are generally required by convention and practice to quote their bid and offer prices for particular currencies simultaneously.

When quoting their bid and offer rates for a particularly currency, banks quote a price for buying the currency that is lower than the price they charge for selling it. The difference between the buying and selling price is called the bid-offer spread. In a typical spot market transaction a U.S. dollar–pound sterling quote would be 1.8410–1.8420. The rate on the left-hand side would be the bid rate at which the bank would be willing to sell 1.8410 dollars in exchange for a pound. The quote on the right-hand side would be the offer rate at which the bank would be willing to buy 1.8420 dollars for a pound. Notice that the selling rate is higher because the bank is prepared to sell fewer dollars for a pound (1.8410) than it is prepared to buy. The use of both American and European terms reverses the bid-offer order. Moreover, a bid quote for one currency is an offer quote for the other currency in the transaction. To avoid confusion, a useful rule of thumb is to remember that in its quote the bank will always part with smaller amounts of the currency it is selling than it will receive when it is buying. In the example, the bank is willing to part with 1.8410 U.S. dollars per unit of pound sterling when selling them, but it wants to receive 1.8420 dollars per unit of pound sterling when it is buying.

In practice, exchange traders quote only the last two decimals of the exchange rate, especially in the interbank market. The interbank quotations of bid-offer rates feature extremely fine spreads because transactions are in huge volumes and the competition is intense.

Cross Rates

Exchange rates are quoted prices of one currency in terms of another currency. In practice, however, prices of all currencies are not always quoted in terms of all other currencies, which is particularly true of currencies for which there is no active market. For example, rate quotations for Malaysian ringgits in terms of Swedish krona are not easily available, but both currencies are quoted against the U.S. dollar. Their rates with reference to the dollar can be compared and a rate can be determined between these two currencies.

Premiums and Discounts

The spot price and forward price of a currency are invariably different. When the forward price of the currency is higher than the spot price, the currency is said to be at a premium. The difference between the spot price and forward price in this case is called the forward premium. When the forward rate of a currency is lower than the spot rate, the currency is said to be at a discount. The difference between the spot and forward rate in this case is called the forward discount. Some illustrations of forward premiums and discounts are:

Spot rate for U.S. dollar/deutsche mark
$$= DM1.58$$
Forward rate for U.S. dollar/deutsche mark
$$= DM1.68$$

Notice that in the forward rate, it will require 1.68 deutsche marks to buy one U.S. dollar, while in the spot rate only 1.58 deutsche marks are required. The U.S. dollar is costlier in the forward quote than the spot quote and is therefore at a premium against the deutsche mark. The premium on forward quotes of the U.S. dollar is .10 deutsche mark.

Now, assume the following exchange rates between the U.S. dollar and deutsche mark:

Spot rate: 1.68 DM = U.S.$1
Forward rate: 1.48 DM = U.S.$1

In this case the spot rate for the U.S. dollar is more expensive, in terms of deutsche marks, than the forward rate. In other words, the U.S. dollar is cheaper in the forward market, because only 1.48 DM are needed to buy one U.S. dollar forward, whereas 1.68 DM are needed to buy one U.S. dollar in the spot market. Thus, the U.S. dollar is at a discount of .20 DM in the forward market.

It is very important to recognize the type of quotation when considering forward premiums and discounts. When the quotes are indirect, that is, where the home currency is expressed as a unit and

FIGURE 5-2
Exchange Rates Table from the *Wall Street Journal*, September 19, 1990.

EXCHANGE RATES
Tuesday, September, 18,1990

The New York foreign exchange selling rates below apply to trading among banks in amounts of $1 million and more, as quoted at 3 p.m. Eastern time by Bankers Trust Co. Retail transactions provide fewer units of foreign currency per dollar.

Country	U.S. $ equiv.		Currency per U.S.$	
	Tues.	Mon.	Tues.	Mon.
Argentina (Austral)	.0001709	.001473	5850.01	6790.25
Australia (Dollar)..	.8295	.8340	1.2055	1.1990
Austria (Schilling).	.09162	.09172	10.92	10.90
Bahrain (Dinar) ...	2.6522	2.6522	.3771	.3771
Belgiun (Franc)				
Commerical rate.	.03133	.03138	31.92	31.87
Brazil (Cruzeiro)...	.01367	.01369	73.13	73.03
Britain (Pound) ...	1.9130	1.9145	.5227	.5223
30-Day Forward..	1.9019	1.9041	.5258	.5252
90-Day Forward..	1.8824	1.8839	.5312	.5308
180-Day Forward.	1.8546	1.8560	.5392	.5388
Canada (Dollar)...	.8628	.8636	1.1590	1.1580
30-Day Forward..	.8595	.8603	1.1635	1.1624
90-Day Forward..	.8535	.8540	1.1717	1.1710
180-Day Forward.	.8470	.8469	1.1807	1.1808
Chile (Official rate)	.003300	.003374	303.00	296.38
China (Renmimbi).	.211752	.211752	4.7225	4.7225
Colombia (Peso)...	.001912	.001912	523.00	523.00
Denmark (Krone) .	.1686	.1694	5.9296	5.9037
Ecuador (Sucre)				
Floating rate	.001148	.001133	871.20	883.00
Finland (Markka)..	.27211	.27315	3.6750	3.6610
France (Franc)	.19231	.19231	5.2000	5.2000
30-Day Forward..	.19199	.19200	5.2087	5.2084
90-Day Forward..	.19124	19124	5.2290	5.2290
180-Day Forward.	.19010	.19010	5.260	5.2605
Germany (Mark) ..	.6433	.6462	1.5545	1.5475
30-Day Forward..	.6432	.6461	1.5547	1.5476
90-Day Forward..	.6429	.6457	1.5555	1.5486
180-Day Forward.	.6416	.6444	1.5586	1.5518
Greece (Drachma).	.006803	.006812	147.00	146.80
Hong Kong (Dollar)	.12889	.12885	7.7587	7.7610
India (Rupee).....	.05672	.05672	17.63	17.63
Indonesia (Rupiah)	.0005414	.0005371	1847.03	1862.02
Ireland (Punt)	1.7300	1.7350	.5780	.5764
Israel (Shekel)	.4932	.4886	2.0277	2.0467
Italy (Lira)	.0008606	.0008615	1162.01	1160.75

(*continued*)

EXCHANGE RATES
Tuesday, September, 18, 1990

The New York foreign exchange selling rates below apply to trading among banks in amounts of $1 million and more, as quoted at 3 p.m. Eastern time by Bankers Trust Co. Retail transactions provide fewer units of foreign currency per dollar.

Country	U.S. $ equiv.		Currency per U.S.$	
	Tues.	Mon.	Tues.	Mon.
Japan (Yen)	.007252	.007321	137.90	136.60
30-Day Forward	.007252	.007320	137.89	136.62
90-Day Forward	.007248	.007317	137.96	136.66
180-Day Forward . . .	.007240	.007308	138.13	136.83
Jordan (Dinar)	1.5221	1.5221	.6570	.6570
Kuwait (Dinar)	z	z	z	z
Lebanon (Pound)	.000851	.000844	1175.00	1185.00
Malaysia (Ringgit) . . .	.3709	.3709	2.6965	2.6960
Malta (Lira)	3.2669	3.3058	.3061	.3025
Mexico (Peso)				
Floating rate	.0003463	.0003460	2888.00	2890.01
Netherland (Guilder) .	.5720	.5726	1.7483	1.7465
New Zealand (Dollar)	.6265	.6255	1.5962	1.5987
Norway (Krone)	.1662	.1667	6.0180	5.9975
Pakistan (Rupee)	.0463	.0463	21.61	21.61
Peru (Inti)	.00000251	.00000233	399042.30	428632.66
Philippines (Peso)	.04141	.04141	24.15	24.15
Portugal (Escudo)	.007214	.007272	138.61	137.52
Saudi Arabia (Riyal) .	.26734	.26734	3.7406	3.7406
Singapore (Dollar) . . .	.5667	.5667	1.7645	1.7645
South Africa (Rand)				
Commerical rate . . .	.3915	.3902	2.5543	2.5628
Financial rate	.2584	.2571	3.8700	3.8900
South Korea (Won) . .	.0013976	.0013976	715.50	715.50
Spain (Peseta)	.010235	.010246	97.70	97.60
Sweden (Krona)	.1749	.1756	5.7160	5.6955
Switzerland (Franc) . .	.7740	.7828	1.2920	1.2775
30-Day Forward	.7742	.7831	1.2916	1.2770
90-Day Forward	.7741	.7830	1.2919	1.2772
180-Day Forward . . .	.7734	.7820	1.2930	1.2788
Taiwan (Dollar)	.037216	.037188	26.87	26.89
Thailand (Baht)	.03937	.03956	25.40	25.28
Turkey (Lira)	.0003733	.0003722	2679.03	2687.02
United Arab (Dirham)	.2731	.2731	3.6618	3.6618
Uruguay (New Peso)				
Financial	.000765	.000723	1307.00	1383.00
Venezuela (Bolivar) . .				
Floating rate	.02123	.02123	47.10	47.10
SDR	1.40142	1.40085	.71356	.71385
ECU	1.32739	1.32573	. . .	. . .

Special Drawing Rights (SDR) are based on exchange rates for the U.S., West German, British, French and Japanese currencies. Source: International Monetary Fund.

European Currency Unit (ECU) is based on a basket of community currencies. Source: European Community Commission.

Z-Not quoted.

the foreign currency as a variable, forward premiums are subtracted from the spot rate to arrive at the forward rate. Similarly, forward discounts are added to the spot rate to get the forward rate. For example:

Premium:
Spot rate: U.S.$1 = 1.784 DM
Forward premium on DM = .010 DM
Forward rate for U.S.$/DM = 1.774 DM
Discount:
Spot rate: U.S.$1 = 1.784 DM
Forward discount on DM = .020 DM
Forward rate for U.S.$/DM = 1.804

When the exchange rates are quoted as direct rates, that is, where the foreign currency is the unit, premiums are added to the spot rate to arrive at the forward rate while discounts are subtracted.

Consider a situation where pound sterling is at a premium:

Spot rate: 1£ = $1.78
Forward Premium of the Pound = .10
Forward rate = £1 = $1.88

Consider a situation where pound sterling is at a discount and direct quotations are used—the forward rates will be calculated as:

Spot: £1 = $1.864
Forward discount: $.020
Forward rate £1 = $1.844

Notice that the method of arriving at the forward rate is reversed when moving from direct to indirect rates and vice versa. Remember, however, that the basic rule applicable to all types of quotations is that a currency at a premium will buy more units of the other currency in the forward market than in the spot market, while the reverse will be the case when the currency is at a discount. Also, it is important to note that the premium and discount calculations will be applied at the variable currency, either in a direct or indirect quote. Thus, in one of the examples above, currencies that are at a premium/discount are the ones that are variable, that is, whose rates are not expressed as a unit.

Forward premiums and discounts arise when the exchange markets expect the future value of cur-

rencies to be either higher or lower. The amount of premium can and does vary quite often with the length of the forward quote, and banks often quote a series of exchange rates indicating the forward premium or discount over a range of forward deliveries. The following is a typical foreign exchange forward quotation:

Transaction	U.S.$/DM
Spot	1.6560
30-day forward	1.6550
60-day forward	1.6540
90-day forward	1.6530

In this quotation, the thirty-day forward quote shows DM at a premium of 10 points, while sixty-day and ninety-day premiums are at 20 and 30 points, respectively. Points here represent values in terms of the fourth decimal place of the exchange rate quotation.

Another important point to remember is that forward premiums and discounts are relative. When one currency is at a premium against another, the other currency is simultaneously at a discount against it. This is only natural, because the exchange rate is the value of one currency in terms of another currency. In one example, DM is at a 10-point premium against the U.S. dollar for thirty-day forward rates. Therefore, the U.S. dollar is at a 10-point discount against the DM for thirty-day forward rates.

FORWARD RATES IN PERCENTAGE TERMS

Another way of expressing forward premiums and discounts is by quoting them as annualized percentages. There are two ways these can be calculated, one for indirect rates and the other for direct rates. The formula for computing forward rates when direct rates are used is:

$$\text{Forward premium or discount} = \frac{\text{Forward rate} - \text{spot rate}}{\text{Spot rate}} \times \frac{12}{n^*} \times 100$$

*Duration of forward contract where n = number of months.

Consider a situation where the U.S.$/£Stg. rates are quoted as under:

A. Spot U.S.$/£Stg. = $1.6420
   30-day forward U.S.$/£Stg. = $1.6400
B. Spot U.S.$/£Stg. = $1.7435
   30-day forward U.S.$/£Stg. = $1.7455

Quotation A shows that the U.S. dollar is at a premium of 20 points for the thirty-day forward rate against the pound sterling. This premium can be expressed in percentage terms using the formula:

$$\frac{1.6400 - 1.6420}{1.6420} \times \frac{12}{1} \times 100 = -1.4616\%$$

Thus, the U.S. dollar is at a premium of 1.46 percent against the U.S. dollar.

Quotation B shows that the U.S. dollar is at 20-point discount against the pound in a thirty-day forward contract. This discount can be calculated as follows:

$$\frac{1.7455 - 1.7435}{1.7435} \times \frac{12}{1} \times 100 = +1.37\%$$

Thus, the U.S. dollar here is at a 1.37 percent discount against the pound.

FORWARD PREMIUMS AND DISCOUNTS USING INDIRECT QUOTES

The formula for calculating forward rates as annual percentages using indirect quotes is:

$$\text{Forward discount} = \frac{\text{spot rate} - \text{forward rate}}{\text{forward rate}}$$
$$\times \frac{12}{n} \times 100$$

or

premium as a forward rate percent per annum

Suppose the following quotes are available in the New York interbank market:

A. Spot U.S.$/DM = DM1.5670
   3-month forward U.S.$/DM = DM1.5570
B. Spot U.S.$/DM = DM1.5670
   6-month forward U.S.$/DM = DM1.5520

These rates can be expressed in percentage per annum terms, using the formula for indirect quotes.

Quote A shows that the U.S. dollar is at a 100-point discount against the deutsche mark for a three-month forward contract, expressing this as a percentage on an annual basis would work out as:

$$\frac{1.5670 - 1.5570}{1.5570} \times \frac{12}{3} \times 100 = 2.57\%$$

Thus, the U.S. dollar is at a 2.57 percentage per annum discount against the U.S. dollar.

Quote B shows that the U.S. dollar is at a discount of 150 points over the deutsche mark for a six-month forward contract. Expressed in percentage terms on an annual basis works out to be:

$$\frac{1.5670 - 1.5520}{1.5520} \times \frac{12}{6} \times 100 = +1.93\%$$

Thus, the $ is at a discount of 1.93 percent per annum against the deutsche mark for a six-month forward contract.

Devaluation and Revaluation of Exchange Rates

Exchange rates move up and down almost continuously in the exchange market. A downward movement is a devaluation, while an upward movement can be termed revaluation. Devaluation has a specific meaning in the context of exchange rate policy, where a country lowers the officially fixed value of its currency. We are using the term to mean a downward movement in the currency. Similarly, revaluation has a specific meaning, which is the reverse of devaluation, but in this section it is used to mean upward movements in currency prices. Both devaluation and revaluation are considered on a spot basis. It is important to measure these changes in exchange rates to compute the actual implications they have for foreign exchange transactions. The formulas for calculating the changes are different for direct and indirect quotes.

The formula for calculating the changes for direct quotes is:

Percent devaluation or revaluation
$$= \frac{\text{ending rate} - \text{beginning rate}}{\text{beginning rate}} \times 100$$

For example, suppose the following quotes for £Stg. are available on June 12, 1989, for spot transactions in the New York interbank market:

A. 10:00 A.M.   £Stg./U.S.$ = $1.6800
   12:00 A.M.   £Stg./U.S.$ = $1.6400
B. 12:30 P.M.   £Stg./U.S.$ = $1.6700
   2.30 P.M.   £Stg./U.S.$ = $1.6900

In example A the U.S. dollar has seen a revaluation of 400 points against the pound. This revaluation expressed in percentage terms is:

$$\frac{1.6400 - 1.6800}{1.6800} \times 100 = 2.38\%$$

Thus, the dollar rose 2.38 percent against the pound.

In example B, the pound has been revalued against the U.S. dollar by 200 points. Expressed in percentage terms, this revaluation is:

$$\frac{1.690 - 1.670}{1.670} \times 100 = 1.19\%$$

Thus, the Pound Sterling appreciated or was revalued by 1.1 percent against the U.S. dollar.

The formula for measuring changes in spot rates when indirect quotes are used is:

Percentage change in spot rate
$$= \frac{\text{Beginning rate} - \text{ending rate}}{\text{ending rate}} \times 100$$

For example, suppose the following quotations are available in the New York interbank market for spot rates on June 12, 1991 and June 14, 1991:

A. 10:00 A.M.   U.S.$/DM = DM1.6530
   12:00 P.M.   U.S.$/DM = DM1.6030
B. 10:00 A.M.   U.S.$/DM = DM1.6700
   12:00 P.M.   U.S.$/DM = DM1.6150

In example A, the U.S. dollar has suffered a devaluation against the deutsche mark of 500 points. This devaluation expressed in percentage terms is:

$$\frac{1.6530 - 1.6030}{1.6030} \times 100 = 3\%$$

Thus, the deutsche mark has fallen 3 percent against the U.S. dollar.

In example B, the U.S. dollar has seen a devaluation against the deutsche mark of 550 points. Expressed in percentage per annum terms:

$$\frac{1.6700 - 1.6150}{1.6150} \times 100 = 3.4\%$$

Thus, the U.S. dollar has been devalued 3.4 percent against the deutsche mark.

Triangular Arbitrage

Occasionally, prices of one currency can vary from one market to the other. A currency may be cheaper in New York and costlier in London. If such a situation arises, it provides an opportunity for market participants to buy the currency in New York and sell it in London. This activity is known as triangular arbitrage and as intermarket arbitrage (see Figure 5–3). Whether such arbitrage is possible is indicated by comparing actual quotations for a currency in one market and its price in another market from cross-rate quotations. There are several steps an arbitrager must take to profit from such an opportunity. For example, assume that the following exchange rates are quoted in the interbank market:

New York : $\dfrac{\text{U.S.\$/FF} = \text{FF5.2350}}{\text{U.S.\$/DM} = \text{DM1.7650}}$

Paris :   FF/DM = FF2.9200

The French franc and deutsche mark are each quoted against the U.S. dollar in New York and against each other in Paris, but we can also compute the exchange rate of francs against the

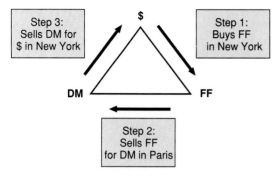

FIGURE 5-3   An example of triangular arbitrage.

deutsche mark in the New York market through the mechanism of cross rates:

$$\frac{FF5.2350}{DM1.7650} = FF2.9660$$

It is evident that the two rates for French franc in terms of the deutsche mark in New York and Paris are not the same. It would be profitable, therefore, to buy French francs in New York and sell them in Paris. Thus, a U.S. arbitrager can get 523,500 French francs in the New York market for $100,000, and then sell these in Paris for 179,281 deutsche marks. The deutsche marks can then be sold in the New York market and bring $101,575.54. The arbitrager can make a clean profit of $1,575.54 without incurring any risk.

Arbitrage opportunities exist for a very short time in the interbank markets, because market movements quickly bring the rates back into line. (Refer to the steps in Figure 5–3.)

If such an opportunity were indeed present in the interbank market, there would be an enormous number of arbitragers acting upon the same strategy. Thus, the first step in selling the U.S. dollars and acquiring French francs would push up the demand for French francs and decrease the demand for U.S. dollars. As a result, there would be upward pressure on the price of French francs in the New York market. The second step, the sale of French francs acquired in New York for deutsche marks in Paris, would lead to enormous

selling pressure on French francs and buying pressure on deutsche marks. This would push down the price of French francs and push up the price of deutsche marks in this market. Large quantities of deutsche marks would be unloaded in the New York market for U.S. dollars, again pushing down the price of deutsche marks and increasing the price of the U.S. dollar. The net effect of these pressures would be an increase in the price of French francs in New York, while the price of French francs in Paris would go down.

The converse movement would soon be enough to equalize prices in the two markets and eliminate the arbitrage opportunity. In fact, with modern information and computing technology arbitrage opportunities hardly ever exist. If they arise momentarily, they are almost instantaneously eliminated as exchange traders are able to spot them simultaneously and execute transactions that move the rates back into proper alignment i.e. the cross rates and quoted rates for currencies in different markets are the same.

Covered Interest Arbitrage

Covered interest arbitrage is a technique used to exploit the misalignment between the forward exchange rates of two currencies and their interest rates for the corresponding period. Usually, the differences in the interest rates of two countries for securities of similar risk and maturity should be equal but opposite in sign to the forward exchange premiums or discounts of their respective currencies, if transaction costs are ignored. This proposition is known as the theory of interest rate parity. For example, assume that the following are U.S. and German exchange and interest rates:

U.S.$/DM spot = U.S.$1/1.6750 DM
U.S.$ 3-month forward rate
= U.S.$1/1.6650 DM
3-month U.S. Treasury bill rate
= 8.44% per annum
3-month West German 3-month government
note rate = 6% per annum

A U.S. investor could invest $100,000 in three-month T-bills and earn 8.44 percent interest. At the end of three months, he would earn $2,110 and end up with a total cash balance of $102,110. If he chose to invest in three-month German government notes, he would first convert his $100,000 into deutsche marks at the prevailing rate of 1.6750 DM. He would receive 167,500 deutsche marks, which he would invest in the German government notes with a three-month interest rate of 6 percent. He would receive 170,013 deutsche marks at the end of three months as principal and interest. This sum would be convertible to U.S. dollars at a forward rate of 1.6650, which would yield $102,110. Thus, the investor would receive the same return regardless of the country in which he invests. The higher interest rate of the United States is compensated by the higher premium of the deutsche marks. Thus, there is no transnational flow of investment funds between the two countries.

When these conditions are not present, that is, if the interest rate parity does not hold, an opportunity arises for arbitrage. This type of arbitrage takes advantage of the disequilibrium between the interests rates and forward exchange premiums and discounts between two currencies. The basic strategy is to invest in another country and cover the exchange risk at favorable terms, so that the profits being made are completely riskless. Moreover, arbitragers need not even invest their own funds. They can borrow funds and return them after taking their profits at the maturity of the transactions.

For example, assume that the following are the interest rates and spot and forward exchange rates for US dollars and pound sterling:

U.S.$/£Stg spot = $1.7840 = £1
U.S.$/£Stg forward = $1.7720 = £1
U.S. 3-month prime rate = 12% per annum
U.K. 3-month prime rate = 16% per annum

The arbitrager makes six steps:

1. The arbitrager borrows $100,000 in the United States at a prime rate of 3 percent (12% ÷ 4).

2. He exchanges the dollars for pounds at the spot rate of 1£ = $1.7840, which yields 56,053.812 pounds.

3. The pounds are invested in three-month deposits in the United Kingdom at a rate of 4 (16% ÷ 4) percent, which yields £58,295.96 at the end of the three months.

4. The maturity proceeds of the U.K. deposit (interest and principal) are covered by a forward contract for reconversion into U.S. dollars at the prevailing fund rate of 1£ = $1.7720. The investor locks in 1.7720 × 58,295.96, or $103,300.44.

5. The arbitrager repays the U.S. loan taken at 3 percent, $103,000.

6. A profit of $300.44 is taken by the arbitrager.

Thus, the arbitrager has made a completely riskless profit of $300.44, without even investing any of his own funds. Again, such opportunities arise only rarely, and if they do, they are quickly eliminated by market movements. If the situation described arises, there will be huge borrowings in the U.S. dollar, conversions into pound sterling, investments in sterling deposits, and reconversion into U.S. dollars. This situation will tend to raise U.S. interest rates, appreciate the spot rate of pound sterling, depress U.K. interest rates, and reduce the forward premium that the U.S. dollar enjoys over the U.K. pound. All these changes will make it less profitable to borrow funds in the U.S. and convert them to pound sterling for deposit in the United Kingdom and then reconvert back into U.S. dollars. The arbitrage opportunity, therefore, is eliminated and the interest rate and forward premiums and discounts move back into line.

Currency Futures Markets

Currency futures are standard value forward contracts that obligate the parties to exchange a particular currency on a specific date at a predetermined exchange rate. Currency futures are traded at the International Money Market Division (IMM) of the Chicago Mercantile Exchange (CME). These futures were introduced in 1972 because in the new environment of floating exchange rates, it was believed that the interbank market would not be able to provide foreign exchange services to small investors or corporations that wanted to speculate in currency fluctuations through a daily trading strategy. Speculators are the main participants in the currency futures market, which has a daily turnover in excess of $40 billion. More recently, commercial banks have begun to deal in currency futures through arbitrage companies, which grew out of the IMM operations. The activity of the IMM adds liquidity to the interbank market.

Differences Between Futures and Forwards Markets

Although futures are similar to forward contracts, in that they allow market participants to fix their forward liability by locking into a future exchange rate, there are important differences between the two.

One of the most important differences is that while forward contracts can be of any size, futures contracts are of specific sizes (for example, Canadian $50,000 or 125,000 Swiss francs). Thus, if a company wishes to buy a Swiss francs currency future, it will have to enter into a contract for at least SF125000. Larger contracts will be in multiples of this amount. Forward contracts are available in a variety of currencies, including some that are not actively traded. Currency futures contracts are available only in specific currencies, usually the currencies of the industrialized countries.

Futures contracts have standardized maturity dates that are regulated by the exchange authorities, while forward contracts have a relatively wide range of maturities. The element of standardization also affects the future margin requirements. (Margins are deposits paid by persons entering into contracts as security for ensuring compliance with contractual obligations.) Futures contracts stipulate specific initial and maintenance margins, but forward contract margins are negotiable between banks and their clients. The futures markets are highly regulated and brokers can charge only fixed commissions. Regulation in forward markets is almost nonexistent and commissions can vary.

Futures markets are highly speculative in nature, and rate movements are more volatile than the forward market. In fact, this extreme volatility has resulted in the fixing of maximum price changes that are permissible on a particular trading day. Similarly, standards of minimum movements in rates have been fixed to affect a change in futures quotes. Operationally, perhaps the greatest difference between the two markets is the facility to exit or liquidate a position in the futures market, which is not available in the forward market. In the futures market, corporations or individuals can liquidate their existing position before settlement date by selling an equivalent futures contract. This facility makes it easier for the speculators and hedgers in the futures markets to cut their losses or take their profits without having to wait for the contract period to expire.

Foreign Currency Options

Foreign currency options are contracts that give the buyer the right but not the obligation to buy or sell a specified amount of foreign exchange at a set price for an agreed upon period.

For example, a U.S. corporation enters into an option contract to buy 100,000 Swiss francs within a two-month period at a rate of 3.6 Swiss francs per U.S. dollar. If the rate of the Swiss francs appreciates against the U.S. dollar to where each franc is equal to one dollar, the corporation can exercise the option and acquire the foreign currency at the previous rate and not the prevailing rate. On the other hand, if the Swiss franc depreciates to, say, four francs to the dollar, then it would not be economical for the corporation to utilize the contract at the fixed rate of 3.6 francs to the dollar. Thus, the corporation would choose to buy its Swiss francs off the market and let the option go unexercised.

There are two types of options. A call option allows the option purchaser to buy the underlying foreign currency. A put option allows the option buyer to sell the underlying currency.

Option Terminology

Options markets are characterized by their unique terminology, which describes essential features of the contracts. Eight of the important terms are:

1. Writer: A person who confers the right but not the obligation to another person to buy or sell the foreign currency.
2. Strike price or exercise price: The rate at which the option can be exercised, that is, the rate at which the writer of the option will buy or sell the underlying foreign currency to the purchaser in the event the latter exercises his option.
3. At the money option: An option whose exercise or strike price is the same as the prevailing spot exchange rate.
4. In the money option: An option whose exercise price is better, at the time of contract writing, than the spot price for the relative currency.
5. Out of the money option: A currency option whose exercise price is worse for the purchaser than the prevailing spot price.
6. American option: An option that can be exercised at any date between the initiation of the contract and maturity date.
7. European option: An option that can be exercised only on maturity date.
8. Option premium: The price paid by the purchaser of the option to its writer. Option premium is higher for in the money options and lower for out of the money options. Moreover, option premiums are higher than the prevailing forward premiums in the interbank markets for contracts of similar maturities.

Forecasting Foreign Exchange Rates

Forecasting exchange rates is often vital to the successful conduct of international business. Inaccurate foreign exchange forecasts or projections can eliminate entire profits from international transactions or result in enormous cost overruns that could threaten the viability of overseas operations. Exchange rates must be forecast for any decision that involves the transfer of funds from one currency to another over a period time. For example, when companies approach foreign markets to borrow or invest foreign currencies, they must project future exchange rates to compute even roughly their possible costs and returns. If a British company is borrowing Japanese yen, it will have to forecast the long-term pound-yen rate to compute what its repayment liabilities are going to be over the life of the loan and amortization period. Similarly, decisions involving both financial and nonfinancial investments overseas require foreign exchange forecasts to calculate the returns profile, because it depends considerably on the rate at which the foreign currency is going to be acquired for investment and the rate at which earnings will eventually be repatriated. Even when it is simply a question of hedging foreign exchange risks, currency forecasts are important. Only when a corporation has a clear view of what it believes the future direction of exchange rate movements will be can it make a proper hedging decision and decide which hedging strategy or instrument is best for its purposes.

Problems in Forecasting Foreign Exchange Rates

It is generally recognized that there is no perfect foreign exchange forecast nor even a perfect methodology to forecast foreign exchange rates. There is no accurate and precise explanation for the manner in which exchange rates move. Movements of exchange rates depend upon the simultaneous interaction of a variety of factors. How these factors influence each other and how they influence exchange rate movements is impossible to quantify or predict. Exchange rates have been known to react violently to single, unexpected events, which have thrown many forecasts and theories completely off balance for that period.

Participants in foreign exchange markets, especially corporate treasurers, grapple with uncertainty and use a variety of techniques to develop some sense of what exchange rates are going to do in the future.

Fundamental Forecasting

Fundamental forecasting is a technique that attempts to predict future exchange rates by examining the influence of major macroeconomic variables on the foreign exchange markets. The main macroeconomic variables that are used in this analysis are inflation rates, interest rates, the balance of payments situation, economic growth trends, unemployment trends, and industrial and other major economic activities. These variables are quantified through comprehensive models that build relationships between the different factors with various statistical techniques, especially regression analysis.

A major problem with fundamental forecasting is that the timing of the events that influence exchange rates, and the gap between the occurrence of these events and their impact on exchange rates, is very difficult to measure. The latest data to make precise quantitative estimates of the relevant macroeconomic variables are seldom readily available. Perhaps the greatest weakness of fundamental analysis in forecasting exchange rates is that it takes into account only some of the factors that influence the movement of rates in the foreign exchange markets. There are several other noneconomic, nontangible factors, such as market sentiment, investor fears, speculative intentions, and political events that have an enormous influence on exchange rates and can override, at least in the short run, other fundamental considerations and factors.

Technical Forecasting

Technical forecasting relies on past exchange rate data to develop quantitative models and charts that can be used to predict future exchange rates. Technical analysts try to see historical patterns in the previous exchange rate movements and attempt to build future patterns on that basis. This approach relies more on personal views and perceptions than on strong economic analysis. There are other technical models that use economic techniques to forecast exchange rates. These models try to capture as many variables as possible and incorporate them into complex models, ascribing to each variable a certain level of influence in the overall computation of the future exchange rate movements.

Technical models have been found to be of questionable use in practice. Studies conducted over the past few years have shown that technical models have not proved to be accurate predictors of future exchange rate movements, but their widespread adoption by many market participants has given them an unique influence as factors to exchange rate movements. Because a large number of market participants using similar models will tend to behave in a similar manner, moving the exchange rate in the direction indicated by their model is a sort of a self-fulfilling prophesy. Usually, technical models concentrate on the near term and are favored more by participants who have an interest in short-term trading and speculation in the exchange markets. Many companies, however, use technical models to provide a way of looking at foreign exchange possibilities, and if they are in agreement with the corporate view, they could serve to reinforce that view.

Assessing Market Sentiments

Another forecasting technique is the assessment of market sentiment, as reflected in the spot and forward rates of currencies. If the spot and forward rates of currencies are expected to appreciate, there would be buying pressure from speculators, which would push the exchange rate up to the expected level. Thus, the spot and forward rates that prevail can be seen as the realized expectations of future movements of currency. Some market participants base their forecasts on this logic, especially for future rates, and treat the forward rate as an unbiased estimator of the future spot rate.

Forecasting Strategy

As is evident, no one technique is truly adequate for forecasting future movements in the exchange rate. Usually, corporate participants base their expectations on a combination of techniques and their individual experience and expertise in the area. The importance given to each type of forecasting technique will depend upon the views of the individual firm. It is important that a comprehensive and broad-based view be taken when making foreign exchange rate projections. These projections should be constantly reviewed and updated.

Summary

The foreign exchange market acts as the intermediary through which complex transactions between different currencies are completed. Individuals and institutions, such as multinational corporations, pension funds, commercial banks, central banks, arbitragers, speculators, and foreign exchange brokers all participate in the market to varying degrees, with the large international banks being the most active. Located in major business centers around the world (London, New York, and Japan are the largest), the foreign exchange market has three basic functions—settlement of trade transactions, avoidance of risk because of currency fluctuations, and the financing of international trade.

The three major transactions in the foreign exchange market are the spot, forward, and swap transactions. Based on the prices of currencies and using various formulas, traders attempt to take advantage of momentary disequilibriums in the prices of currencies, or currency and interest dis-

parities, by trading in different locations or markets. They also try to minimize losses associated with unanticipated changes in currency values. Some of the techniques used are triangular arbitrage, covered interest arbitrage, and hedges.

Forward contracts, which are generally used by large international banks and MNCs, can be tailor-made for any contract size or currency, but they require execution of the transaction on the date of contract maturity. Futures contracts differ from forward contracts by offering standardized, regulated contracts of smaller sizes, which can be easily liquidated. Options are yet another form of currency contract, which, like futures contracts, are standardized and can be easily liquidated. Options offer the right, not the obligation, to buy or sell a foreign currency at a set price up to an agreed date.

Corporations face four major types of risk or exposure in their international activities—transaction exposure, economic exposure, translation exposure, and tax exposure. Forecasting foreign exchange rates is often vital to conducting international business, but generating accurate forecasts is extremely difficult. Fundamental forecasting examines macroeconomic variables, such as balance of payments, inflation rates, and unemployment trends to predict future exchange rates, while technical forecasting relies on historical exchange rate data to predict future currency exchange rates.

Discussion Questions

1. Why does international business need a foreign exchange market?
2. Who are the participants in foreign exchange transactions?
3. Where are foreign exchange markets located? Where are the main centers of foreign trading?
4. Discuss the four types of risk facing multinational corporations.
5. What is the difference between the spot and the forward markets?

6. You currently hold $1 million and are interested in exchanging U.S. dollars for deutsche marks. The current spot rate of $1 = 1.475 DM is a direct quote. True or false?
7. What is a long position? Short position? Square position?
8. What is the bid-offer spread for a U.S.$/£Stg quote of $1.8410–$1.8420?
9. What is covered interest arbitrage?
10. What is the difference between the futures and forward markets?
11. What is an option?
12. What is the difference between fundamental forecasting and technical forecasting?

Bibliography

ALIBER, ROBERT Z. 1976. *The International Money Game*, 2nd ed. New York: Basic Books.

BLACK, FISHER, and MARTIN SCHOLES. 1973. "The Pricing of Options and Corporate Liabilities." *Journal of Political Economy* (May/June): 637–659.

BUCKLEY, ADRIAN. 1987. "Multinational Finance: The Risks of FX." *Accountancy* (February): 80–82.

CHOI, J. J. 1989. "Diversification, Exchange Risk and Corporate Risk." *International Business Studies* (Spring): 145–155.

DORNBUSCH, R. 1983. "Equilibrium and Disequilibrium Exchange Rates." *Zeitschrift für Wirtschafts und Sozialwissenshaften* 102: 573–599.

DUFEY, G., and I. GIDDY. 1975. "Forecasting Exchange Rates in a Floating World." *Euromoney* (November): 28–35.

ENSIG, PAUL. 1937. *The Theory of Forward Exchange.* London: Macmillan.

GRIFFITHS, SUSAN H., and P. S. GREENFIELD. 1989. "Foreign Currency Management: Part I—Currency Hedging Strategies." *Journal of Cash Management* (July/August): 141.

KWOK, CHUCK. 1987. "Hedging Foreign Exchange Exposures: Independent versus Integrative Approaches." *Journal of International Business Studies* (Summer): 33–52.

MA, CHRISTOPHER K., and G. W. KAO. 1990. "On Exchange Rate Changes and Stock Price Reactions." *Journal of Business Finance and Accounting* (Summer): 441–449.

MADURA, JEFF. 1989. *International Financial Management,* 2nd ed., St Paul, MN: West Publishing.

MCKINNON, RONALD I. 1990. "Interest Rate Volatility and Exchange Risk: New Rates for a Common Monetary Standard." *Contemporary Policy Issues* (April): 1–17.

SOENEN, L. A., and R. AGGARWAL. 1987. "Corporate Foreign Exchange and Cash Management Practices." *Journal of Cash Management* (March/April): 62–64.

SWEENEY, R. J. 1986. "Beating the Foreign Exchange Market." *Journal of Finance* (March): 163–182.

TAYLOR, MARK P. 1989. "Covered Interest Arbitrage and Market Turbulence." *Economic Journal* (June): 376–391.

WALSH, CARL E. 1987. "Interest Rates and Exchange Rates." *FRBSF Weekly Letter* (June 5): 41.

WOO, WING THYE. 1987. "Some Evidence of Speculative Bubbles in the Foreign Exchange Market." *Journal of Money, Credit, and Banking* (November): 499–514.

Chapter Case Study 1

Global Bank Corporation

Global Bank Corporation is a major international bank headquartered in New York City, with branches in eleven other countries—Canada, West Germany, Brazil, Great Britain, Japan, France, Australia, Netherlands, Singapore, Hong Kong, and Dubai. Total assets in 1989 were $90 billion, and the bank was among the top 500 banks in the world. The bank is organized into three main divisions—retail banking, institutional banking, and investment banking. Global retail banking undertakes transactions with individual customers, for example, savings accounts, checking and money market accounts, issuance of certificates of deposit, operation of automated teller machines, loans to individual customers for different purchases, funds transfer facilities, and so on. The institutional banking division carries out business with the bank's institutional and corporate customers—the trusts of major companies and other large clients. Much of the work of the institutional banking division is concerned with devising comprehensive financing arrangements for its clients. The investment banking division of Global has three main functional areas:

1. The capital markets group, which provides a wide range of services to companies seeking to raise funds in the international financial markets.
2. The private banking group, which provides fund management and advisory services to large net worth clients.
3. Foreign exchange division, which carries out exchange trading and handles foreign exchange transactions and provides advisory services.

The foreign exchange trading function of the bank is decentralized to levels of operation for each country and further to each individual trading operation. Each level of decentralization, however, has to operate within established trading and exposure limits that are laid down by the corporate risk management committee of the bank, which meets every month at the headquarters in New York City. A typical trading operation at Global Bank Corporation is divided into two main areas—interbank exchange market trading and customer-based trading. The former is primarily a speculative operation aimed at generating substantial profits for the bank from interbank trading, while the latter operation is intended to serve customers by providing them with a wide range of foreign exchange services, ranging from risk management to a simple sale or purchase of different foreign currencies. The interbank trading division has been fairly successful in the past four years and has consistently made profits, although the level of profits has varied over the years. The main focus of the trading activity is the Tokyo, New York, and London markets. At other centers, the trading operations of the bank are more oriented toward meeting the foreign exchange needs of customers.

In the past five years, the Singapore and Hong Kong markets have become extremely active and a large number of international banks have set up trading operations to generate profits from the booming interbank market. The investment banking division is planning to set up new operations in this area. Both markets have an environment relatively free of regulation and excellent communication and other infrastructural facilities for establishing trading operations. Singapore seems to be a more stable alternative because the future of the Hong Kong market is generally perceived to be uncertain in the light of the 1997 deadline when the British colony will pass to the sovereign jurisdiction of the People's Republic of China. Although the Chinese authorities have given repeated assurances that the current free economy status of Hong Kong will not be changed for the next fifty years, a large number of professionals are leaving Hong Kong.

Despite the advantages, establishing new interbank trading center in Singapore has given rise to some doubts. The bank has not opened a new trading center for the past seven years and will have to hire a new team. Some senior investment banking division executives feel that while interbank trading is a good source of profit and helps to strengthen the company's bottom line, it is also risky. Having a fourth interbank trading operation will increase the overall exposure of the bank and will make controls more difficult to enforce. Other executives feel that because the exchange market is an around-the-clock operation, a presence in the Singapore market will allow the bank to have an active presence in all time zones and increase the effectiveness of overall global trading oper-

ations. At present, there is a time lag between the closing of the Tokyo market and the opening of the London market, when the bank has no presence. Further, the proponents of the Singapore trading location argue that once this trading location has stabilized, a fifth location can be opened somewhere in the Middle East, for example, in Bahrain. The profits from the Singapore trading center in the interbank market could be used for aggressive pricing of corporate foreign exchange products to later capture increased market share.

Questions

1. Should Global Bank Corporation set up a new foreign exchange operation at Singapore? If so, what should be given priority (such as interbank trading or customer Telex sources)?
2. What additional information would you consider relevant in evaluating a proposal to set up a new foreign exchange trading operation?

Chapter Case Study 2

Chemtech, Inc.

As he walked into his office in downtown Frankfurt one Tuesday morning, Jorge Muller, corporate treasurer of Chemtech, smiled at his secretary. "Good morning, Marita," he said. "Anything important happen while I was away?" he continued, referring to his short trip to Paris that had spilled over from the weekend to Monday. "Nothing much," replied Marita, "except there was a call from Mr. Carl Volten of Hamburg Bank. He wants you to call him as soon as possible." "Thanks," Muller replied as he sat down to begin work on what he knew would be a critical week.

Chemtech, Inc. is a leading pharmaceutical manufacturer in Germany and had total sales of more than $26 billion in 1989. The company had been founded just after World War II and had established a strong market presence in both the German domestic market and several international markets. The emphasis of the company has always been to push ahead in the export markets of the industrialized countries, because opportunities to sell its sophisticated and fairly high-priced products in markets of less-developed countries were limited. Total export sales come from the following countries:

U.S.	$6 billion
U.K.	2 billion
France	2 billion
Italy	1.50 billion
Canada	.75 billion
Sweden	.70 billion
Japan	1.20 billion
Total	$14.15 billion

While Chemtech has enjoyed great success in its export markets and sales have grown at an average of 11 percent over the past seven years, profits from exports have not grown at the same pace. International competition has intensified in most markets, U.S. and Swiss pharmaceutical manufacturers, and the firm has been forced to give greater discounts to retain market share. Although productivity has risen, it has not risen enough to offset increasing production costs, especially the higher labor costs that Chemtech encountered over the past three years, following a settlement with the labor unions. One of the most important problems, however, has been the continued appreciation of the deutsche mark against the U.S. dollar and pound sterling, which has reduced export profits considerably. The problem has been particularly acute in the past eight months, because a continuously weakening dollar has hurt export revenues and, therefore, profitability by as much as 9 percent.

Muller was asked by the director of finance of Chemtech to come up with a strategy to guard against foreign exchange fluctuation losses. He had called his friend and long-time adviser Karl Volten, vice-president of corporate foreign exchange services at Hamburg Bank, for suggestions.

Volten was a foreign exchange expert with many years of top-level experience in advising large corporations on managing their foreign exchange exposures. He had an MBA in finance from a major U.S. university and had worked as an exchange trader in the New York branch of the Hamburg Bank for six years. He had been assistant vice-president of corporate foreign exchange advisory services for three years and has held his current position for the past two and a half years.

Volten felt that Chemtech should buy U.S. $/DM call options on the IMM exchange through the New York branch office of the Hamburg Bank. By purchasing an option the company could lock in a minimum deutsche mark price for the dollar revenues it earns from U.S. operations, and if the deutsche mark weakens before maturity of the contract, the company could not exercise the option. As a matter of policy, Chemtech repatriated U.S. dollar profits every six months, and options could be bought for six months maturities. Options could also be sold off before the due date.

For example, the ruling $/DM rate today was U.S.$1 = 2.5 DM. It is expected that the deutsche mark will be strengthened further, although no one can predict by how much. Chemtech can lock in a particular level of exchange rate by buying a deutsche mark call option for the strike price of 2.3 deutsche marks per dollar. There would be an up-front cost for the option of .3 deutsche mark for every dollar of the contract amount. The company would therefore be locking into an effective rate of 2DM = $1.

The strategy has several advantages. For one, the company is covered against excess depreciation of the dollar. If the dollar appreciates beyond 2.3 deutsche marks, the company could simply forgo the option and buy deutsche marks in the open market. In fact, if the dollar goes beyond 2.6, the company can recover its entire hedging cost of .3 deutsche mark per dollar and actually profit from the option transaction. If, on the other hand, the dollar weakens beyond 2.3 deutsche marks, the company can ex-

ercise the option and buy the deutsche marks at this price. Hedging costs will be fully recovered if the dollar weakens to DM 2 = $1, and any further weakening of the dollar will mean additional profits for Chemtech.

The strategy appeared extremely attractive to Muller. "We win on both sides," he figured, "since we are saved from any excess strengthening of the deutsche mark and still have the opportunity of making substantial gains on any large weakening of the currency. It's a lot better than going for the plain old forward contract for 2.2 deutsche marks per dollar. True, we lock in our price at 2.2 and we are saved against any depreciation of the dollar beyond that, but if the dollar strengthens against the deutsche mark, we would be locked out of the opportunity to profit from it. I think I will prepare a report for the treasurer," he decided.

Questions

1. Is the suggested options strategy completely risk free?
2. If you were the treasurer, what would you think of this proposal? Are there any reasons for rejecting this strategy in favor of forward contracts?
3. Under what circumstances would a forward contract be a better alternative to achieve the objectives of the company?

CHAPTER 6

Supranational Organizations and International Institutions

CHAPTER OBJECTIVES

This chapter will:

- Identify major international trade organizations, such as GATT and UNCTAD, and the roles they play in shaping and molding the international business environment.
- Describe the major financial institutions, such as the IMF, World Bank, and the IFC, and the assistance they provide in channeling financial resources to developing countries.
- Review the growth of regional financial institutions and their important positions as providers of financial resources.

Background

Increasing economic, financial, and commercial interdependence among nations of the world after World War II worked to create a need to coordinate international action and policies to secure the smooth flow of trade. Apart from regular, periodic meetings of officials and businesspersons from different countries, a need was felt for the establishment of permanent organizations to provide stability and continuity to the process of international economic interchange. Some supranational bodies were set up in the period immediately following World War II, while more were established

in the following decades. Two major categories of international organizations can be identified— those having a global focus and those set up to meet the needs of particular regions.

Trade Organizations
General Agreement on Tariffs and Trade

The General Agreement on Tariffs and Trade (GATT) was established initially as a temporary measure to reduce trade barriers among its twenty-two founding members. Since its inception in

1947, GATT has evolved into a permanent body to include most industrial and developing countries, excluding those of the socialist block.

GATT was originally established to avoid the kind of competitive protectionism that had plagued international trade in the period between the two world wars, which was reflected in high tariff barriers and a major slump in trade volumes. The objectives of GATT—liberalization of the international trade restrictions and the lowering of tariff barriers—were to be achieved by multilateral negotiations and voluntarily agreed rules of conduct. As a permanent international body, GATT was to provide the forum for the conduct of these negotiations and the development of necessary ground rules for liberalizing the international trade environment. GATT was also intended to serve as an agency for mediation and settlement of trade disputes.

One of the main tenets of GATT regulations is the requirement for its members to comply with the most-favored-nation clause, which obligates all member countries to give the same tariff concessions to all GATT countries that they give to any one member country. For example, if Germany reduces import duty on Japanese TV sets from 40 percent to 10 percent, then it must level the same rate of duty to TV sets from other countries.

There are, however, important exceptions to the most-favored-nation clause, which recognize the need for preferential treatment to be given to the less-developed countries, which without special treatment are not able to compete on a one-to-one basis with the industrialized countries. The developing countries thus have preferential access to the markets of developed countries for some of their products under the generalized system of preferences.

The second major exception relates to the establishment of regional trading alliances—members of regional trade agreements can extend trade concessions to each other without extending these concessions to countries who are not members of the alliance. Regional trade agreements, such as the European Economic Commu-

nity (EEC) and the Association of South East Asian Nations (ASEAN), are two examples. To ease the problem of dealing with tariffs and duties on individual products, most negotiations center around making generalized reductions in tariff rates for a large number of products in certain categories.

In the eight rounds or negotiating sessions to date, GATT has made significant changes. The average tariffs on industrial products, levied by the developed countries, have come down significantly, and GATT countries have accounted for 85 percent of world trade since its inception.

There are still several problems, however, such as an increasing emphasis on protectionism, not only from the developing countries, but also from the industrialized world. The use of nontariff barriers to discriminate against imports from other countries has enabled many member countries to negate the intended effects of the tariff reductions agreed to under the GATT rules of conduct.

Further, GATT regulations have been imprecise, and many signatory states have found loopholes to evade the requirements, almost on a routine basis. Many trade issues arose in the 1970s and 1980s that had not been foreseen by earlier negotiations, and provisions for regulating them were not included in the agreements. There are also substantial difficulties between major trading partners, as relative economic and competitive strengths change and new arrangements and terms are sought by old trading partners.

Currently, GATT is negotiating a new set of comprehensive agreements and rules of conduct at the Uruguay round that began in 1986. The midterm review of the Uruguay round found a consensus on a substantial reduction of tariffs by all members. It was agreed to liberalize trade in natural resource-based products, such as forestry products, minerals, nonferrous metals, and fisheries products. Considerable differences, however, continue with respect to agriculture. Because of national sensitivity on this issue, it has remained excluded from the general GATT rules of conduct, and countries have followed independent policies to protect this sector. During the Uruguay round, the U.S. position on agriculture has been to continue support to farmers, but that support should not be based on the type or amount of commodity produced. Moreover, according to the U.S. view, there should be a gradual phasing out of all subsidiaries and import barriers, even in the agricultural sector. The EEC, the other major exporter of agricultural products, prefers an arrangement to reduce short-term agricultural subsidies while basic reform is negotiated over a longer term. It sees as politically unworkable the U.S. position of a quick elimination of agricultural subsidies and tariffs.

Important decisions have also been taken with respect to the import of tropical products from developing countries. Most industrialized countries offered concessional tariffs in importing such products from developing countries, although there were significant differences among the industrialized countries on the timetable for the actual implementation of these concessions.

Among the other issues that are under negotiation and review are provisions for temporary restrictions for imports where domestic producers are seriously affected; greater control and monitoring of the use of subsidiaries to promote exports; trade-related investment measures; the GATT rules and procedures for settlement of trade disputes, especially the establishment of time-bound programs for dispute resolution; surveillance by GATT of trade policies of member countries and the role of GATT in international economic policymaking.

Two new issues of importance emerged at the Uruguay round of GATT negotiations—trade in services and protection of intellectual property rights.

TRADE IN SERVICES

Trade in services is becoming an increasingly important factor in overall trade patterns, both for the developed and developing countries. Developing countries were initially opposed to the inclusion of trade in services as a part of GATT negotiations and although eventually they did agree to having services included in the negotiations, they did not commit themselves to agreeing to any

general rules of conduct to be framed by GATT on this issue. Current negotiations, however, are expected to establish a framework of ground rules for trade in services. The guiding principle of these rules is transparency, or nondiscrimination and treatment of foreign enterprises on the same basis as domestic enterprises. The industrialized countries are likely to press for progressive liberalization of trade in services, while the developing countries may demand greater shares in the international services market and greater mobility of their work forces to move to the developed countries as a part of the liberalization of rules regarding manpower services.

INTELLECTUAL PROPERTY RIGHTS

At the Uruguay round negotiations, the developed countries have argued that GATT rules of conduct should be framed to adequately protect intellectual property rights, particularly against international infringement. The developing countries are opposed to this viewpoint, reasoning that protecting intellectual property rights is the concern primarily of the World Intellectual Property Organization and not GATT, and that GATT should be concerned only with those aspects of intellectual property rights protection that are tantamount to trade distortion or trade restrictions. This issue is likely to continue to be controversial, as no agreement, even in principle, has been reached between the developed and developing countries.

OTHER PROBLEMS IN GATT NEGOTIATIONS

Apart from disagreements on the issues of agriculture and intellectual property rights, there has been considerable discussion on the regulation of trade in textiles and clothing, which has been pushed out of normal GATT rules for some time, and countries are free to impose their own restrictions and tariffs. This situation is against the interests of the developing countries, because textiles and clothing make up an area where they are able to compete with the industrialized countries and are frustrated by the imposition of protectionist measures against their exports by many developed countries. The industrialized countries do not want trade in clothing and textiles to be liberalized, fearing adverse effects on their domestic industries, while the developing countries are pressing hard for the reimposition of GATT rules that would give them freer access to the markets of developed countries.

Another important area that eludes consensus among GATT countries is the issue of allowing temporary restrictions on imports in the event that domestic producers in a country are adversely affected. While some countries favor nondiscriminatory provisions, others are for selective restrictive action against particular supplier nations in the event of a domestic production crisis. It is apparent that agreement on this issue is very difficult to achieve, and compliance is entirely voluntary. Moreover, there are numerous ways in which a country can evade the GATT stipulations in this area.

Judging by the progress made by the current round of negotiations, it is clear that major hurdles remain in the emergence of an international consensus on several important trade issues. The hands of negotiators are tied because of the self-interests of their own constituents, which differ widely and in many instances are in direct conflict with each other. Further, adherence to and compliance with GATT rules is purely voluntary, and there is little that the agency can do by way of enforcing its stipulations.

Significant progress has been made during the Uruguay round, however, and in many areas differences have either been resolved or at least considerably narrowed. The agreement on services, although limited in scope and tentative, has broken new ground for the expansion of the scope of GATT and for creating a liberal and orderly environment for international trade in this increasingly important sector. GATT is attempting to tackle the new issues raised by the ever-changing and increasing mechanisms of protectionism that are devised by member states to bypass GATT rules of conduct without technically violating them. The success of GATT as the prime body for coordinated action to liberalize and promote growth in world trade will clearly depend upon the degree of flexibility shown both by the industrial and developing countries in adjusting their positions to arrive at generally acceptable conclusions that are in the common interest (see Perspectives 6–1, 6–2, and 6–3).

PERSPECTIVE 6–1 GATT Brief: The American Connection

The Uruguay round of talks on trade liberalisation, the most complex and far-reaching ever undertaken, is due to end in December after four years of talking in the GATT, the world body dedicated to reducing trade barriers. Success would mean freer and fairer trade, with benefits for all. Failure could mean the fragmentation of the world trading system into warring trading blocks, with damaging, perhaps catastrophic consequences. Which way things go depends crucially on America, the dominant voice in GATT and the Uruguay round. Ominously, it is not setting a good example.

The GATT system, fashioned in 1947 chiefly by American and British officials, depends on three supports:

- A code of fair trade conduct—the general agreement itself, a treaty which enshrines the principle of non-discrimination in trade. Members

SOURCE: *The Economist*, April 21, 1990, pages 85–86.

must provide the best trade terms available, by treating all others as they treat the "most favoured nation".

- The progressive liberalisation of trade through successive, multilateral bargaining rounds.
- The settlement of disputes by reference to GATT rules.

GATT can claim a good deal of success. Seven completed trade rounds, all of them initiated by America, have slashed tariffs (the only form of protection permitted under GATT rules) from an industrial-country average of 40% in 1947 to less than 5% today. The volume of world trade in goods has grown ten-fold since GATT's creation, rising by 6% a year since 1983. GATT membership has risen from the 23 founders to 96 countries today, who together account for almost 90% of world trade.

Nevertheless, the general agreement is looking threadbare. By common consent the 43-year-old rules are no longer up to the job of regulating the world's trading system. As tariff walls have tumbled, other less visible forms of protection have taken their place, such as awkward quality and safety standards, discriminatory public purchasing or obstructive customs procedures. So too have "voluntary" restraints that circumvent GAT. Nearly 250 of these "voluntary" export restraints and market-sharing arrangements (essentially quotas) were in force last year. The United States and the European Community have the keenest appetite for such pacts, usually aimed at restraining Japanese and other Asian exporters.

America and the EC are also under fire for over-assertive use of anti-dumping and countervailing duties, levies which GATT allows to protect domestic industry from the predatory pricing or unfair government subsidies of foreign competitors. But many Asian exporters claim they are being harassed by an anti-dumping crusade that amounts to disguised protectionism. Both sides want new and clearer rules.

An increasing amount of trade, perhaps as much as a third, is conducted outside GATT rules.

The multi-fibre arrangement, which limits third-world exports of textiles and clothing to the West, is the only permitted bundle of trade restrictions under GATT. But GATT rules on agriculture are too fuzzy to be effective and in other areas, such as services, there are no rules at all. Yet services — banking, insurance, consultancy, telecommunications, transport and the like — now account for over $600 billion of international trade, compared with merchandise trade worth $3.1 trillion in 1989, and their share is growing rapidly. In the United States services account for 76% of all employment and over 90% of new jobs.

Free-trade areas and customs unions, which give better terms to members than to outsiders, have proliferated. GATT rules stipulate that trade blocks which demolish trade barriers internally must not raise them externally. But it has no proper enforcement mechanism to prevent the emergence of a "fortress Europe" if the EC's 1992 single-market programme veers that way, nor for that matter a "fortress North America" if Canada, the United States and Mexico were to arrange preferential terms for the trade they do with one another.

The pattern of world trade (and trade politics) has shifted dramatically. America is no longer the workshop, granary and intellectual powerhouse of the world rolled into one, though last year it regained its title as the world's biggest goods exporter, from West Germany, after three years as number two. Faced with tougher competition, especially from East Asia, industries in America and Europe have been quick to cry foul. Governments on both sides of the Atlantic have been tempted to opt for unilateral, national remedies to perceived grievances, because GATT's disputes procedures are slow and cumbersome.

OPENING THE WORLD

In September 1986 in Punta del Este, Uruguay, GATT members launched the Uruguay round of trade negotiations, the eighth in GATT's history, and by far the most ambitious. Its 15 negotiating groups are dealing not just with the traditional is-

Uruguay round negotiating goals

1 Tariffs: Overall cut of one-third
2 Non-tariff measures: Reduction and elimination
3 Natural resource-based products: Liberalisation of trade in fisheries, forestry, non-ferrous metals and minerals products
4 Textiles and clothing: Phase out the multi-fibre arrangement and bring textiles trade within normal GATT rules
5 Agriculture: Reduce farm subsidies and other forms of support tied to production and open up domestic markets
6 Tropical products: Tariff cuts and elimination of non-tariff barriers
7 GATT articles: Redrafting of some rules such as third-world exemption from the ban on import controls for balance-of-payments reasons
8 GATT codes: Strengthening GATT's voluntary codes such as those on anti-dumping and technical barriers to trade
9 Safeguards: New rules governing emergency protection against imports, including disciplines on (or elimination of) "grey area" measures such as voluntary export restraints
10 Subsidies and countervailing measures: Tightening disciplines on subsidies and measures taken to counteract them
11 Intellectual property: A comprehensive agreement covering standards and principles of protection for trade in ideas
12 Investment measures: Possible new disciplines to curb trade-restricting conditions on foreign investment
13 Disputes settlement: Measures to make the process speedier and more effective
14 Functioning of the GATT system: Trade-policy review of members already instituted, more frequent ministerial meetings, better co-operation with the International Monetary Fund and the World Bank
15 Services: A general agreement applying fair-trade rules to trade in services

sues of tariffs and non-tariff barriers, but with a major recasting of GATT rules (see box at left). The object is to extend fair-trade disciplines and to liberalise trade in virtually all goods and services, as well as to strengthen GATT's authority with better disputes procedures and regular surveillance of members' trade policies. The round, which has 105 participants (GATT members plus some developing countries planning to join), is due to end in December 1990 with a ministerial meeting in Brussels.

Once again America has been the country which has taken the initiative and largely set the agenda, insisting that the round tackle agriculture and new issues such as services trade, intellectual property and rules on foreign investment.

America's radical plan to abolish agricultural export subsidies within five years, and virtually all other farm supports within ten, is unlikely to be agreed. But it has succeeded in pushing the previously immovable EC to talk about reducing the $275 billion which rich countries spend each year on farm supports.

American's blueprint for a services-trade agreement to parallel the GATT rules on merchandise trade has served as the model for a draft agreement now under discussion. Other trailblazing American proposals include rules to limit restrictions on foreign investment such as minimum local-content requirements and to curb the piracy of intellectual property (patents, copyright, trademarks, microchip designs) which is reckoned to be costing America $60 billion a year. Countries are bound to argue over the details. But America's proposals, unveiled since last summer, have shoved the negotiations forward, pulling along even countries like India and Brazil which initially opposed inclusion of "new issues" in the Uruguay round.

CLOSING AMERICA

Yet trading partners are now questioning whether America's commitment to freer trade really extends beyond the limited horizons of Washington's lobbyists. Where American industry sees benefits in liberalisation and better rules, America has forced the pace. Where so-called "sensitive" industries are involved, the textiles and farm goods critical for developing countries, America has dragged its feet.

Trading partners also point to America's flouting of GATT rules, especially action under section 301 of the 1988 Trade Act, which can require American retaliation against countries deemed "unfair" traders who do not agree to mend their ways. Japan, Brazil and India were singled out last year by Mrs Carla Hills, America's trade representative. Decisions on Japanese and Indian "offences" are due in June, just as the Uruguay round is coming to a head.

Under GATT rules no country, however affronted, can retaliate unilaterally. If a trading partner is found by an independent panel under GATT's disputes procedure to have broken the rules, and refuses to put the matter right, the aggrieved country can ask other GATT members to authorise compensation. In practice this has been granted only once (and not used).

Ironically, Canada and the EC came close to securing the right to initiate reprisals against the United States for its failure to implement a ruling by a GATT panel against a discriminatory American oil levy. Congress eventually agreed to scrap the levy late last year, some 2½ years after the panel made its ruling. Another judgment in 1987, which called on America to change its system of charging fees on imports to pay for America's customs service, has still not been implemented. Contrast this with the mere 12 months' grace that America grants trading partners under its own trade laws before America retaliates when they lose a GATT ruling.

America has resorted to unilateral trade sanctions in rows with Brazil over pharmaceutical patents and with the EC over hormones in beef. Against all GATT rules, America has also refused to change its own patent-infringement procedures, which a GATT panel ruled discriminated unfairly against imports. Quite illegally, America says it will change its procedures only when the Uruguay round reaches an agreement for tougher protection of intellectual property.

Small wonder then that some GATT members are asking themselves why they should agree to America's plea for tougher GATT rules when America does not consider itself bound to respect the existing ones. And they argue that America's delaying tactics in accepting and implementing GATT rulings make a nonsense of the disputes settlement procedure, which America says it wants to beef up.

America's delay in changing its patent-infringement procedures has created a damaging precedent for other countries which dislike GATT judgments. Already the EC and Canada have followed suit by linking required action on soyabean subsidies and import restrictions for ice cream and yo-

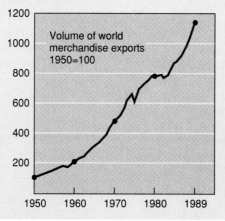

GATT Does It

Volume of world merchandise exports 1950=100

Leading merchandise exporters, 1989	
	billions
United States	$ 364.4
West Germany	341.4
Japan	275.2
France	177.0
Britain	152.7
Italy	140.6
Canada	120.1
Soviet Union	108.3
Holland	107.0
Belgium/Luxembourg	97.5

Source: GATT

ghurt (both American complaints) to the outcome of the agriculture negotiations.

America's trade officials are not apologetic. The Uruguay round, they claim, is the Bush administration's top trade priority. But until adequate international rules exist for the $1 trillion of trade that now goes undisciplined by GATT rules, they say, America will continue to use sanctions or the threat of sanctions to defend American interests, prise open markets (Mrs Hills's famous "crowbar") and further American objectives in the Uruguay round.

"We are totally committed to the maintenance of an open and fair trade policy," insists Mr Rufus Yerxa, America's ambassador to GATT, adding that the task of the Uruguay round is to create the conditions which would make resort to unilateral and bilateral solutions unnecessary. Mr Yerxa also claims that America is one of the most open economies in the world. It takes over 50% of the manufactured exports of developing countries, for example, compared with less than 30% for the EC and 8% for Japan.

What Mr Yerxa fails to point out is that while other countries are moving in the direction of liberalising trade, America is going into reverse. A report last December on American trade policy compiled by GATT economists noted that American barriers had increased over the past decade, despite presidential resistance to more extreme measures. On one estimate, the proportion of America's imports affected by significant barriers has doubled to nearly 25% since 1980.

On March 1, 1991 the administration's "fast track" negotiating authority for the Uruguay round—it allows the President to seek a simple yes or no from Congress—expired. Unless Mr Bush can present a satisfactory trade package before then to a Congress that is sceptical and suspicious of GATT, all the talking over the past four years will have been in vain. It would be sad, and bad for the world trading system, if the threat of a Congressional veto, rather than a positive belief in the virtues of free trade, were to be America's trump card between now and the end of the Uruguay round.

PERSPECTIVE 6–2   GATT Brief: A better deal for poor countries

Pronouncements from American academics that "GATT is dead" sit oddly with the institution's growing popularity. Twelve countries are queuing to join its ranks, now 96-strong. Taiwan and the Soviet Union may soon join the queue. All face stiffer entry terms than in the past. Whether former or still communist countries or developing ones, they will be expected to subscribe in full to GATT's market-based rules and to pay a substantial deposit by way of liberalising trade. Far from putting them off, such

demands have increased GATT's attraction to countries trying to join the club.

What does GATT have to offer to budding members as varied as Venezuela, Bulgaria and China? In recent years the most pressing reason has been the wish to take part in the Uruguay round of trade talks, launched in 1986 and due to finish this December. Under the rules of the round, participation is limited to GATT members and developing countries which applied for full membership before April 1987. If successful, the

SOURCE: *The Economist*, April 28, 1990, pages 80–81.

round will produce new trading rules, more open markets and deals covering for the first time foreign direct investment, intellectual property and services. Countries want to know what is being discussed, perhaps nudge the outcome in the direction of their interests, and reap the benefits when an agreement is made.

Even without being in on the Uruguay round, GATT membership has big advantages. Most valuable are:

- Non-discrimination, called "most-favoured nation" treatment. All GATT members must be given the most favourable trading terms available. The only exceptions relate to customs unions and other free-trade arrangements, and some preferential treatment for developing countries.

"Most-favoured nation" status can be critical for third-world countries now jettisoning dead-end policies of import substitution in favour of export-led development. For these countries, expanding exports is impossible without access to the large markets of the developed world. Former planned economies switching to market-based policies also need such treatment. Because they are outside GATT, they face higher barriers to their exports and are seldom in a strong position to negotiate better terms.

- The multilateral nature of GATT, including its disputes procedures, means that small countries with a grievance against large ones can appeal to accepted rules. Thus when America imposed a discriminatory levy on oil imports, a protest by Venezuela, a non-member, was ignored. Mexico, which joined GATT in 1986, took the case to GATT (together with Canada and the European Community) and won.

GATT membership also offers small countries some protection, however imperfect, against being bullied by big countries. Brazil has hauled America into GATT's dock for retaliating over alleged breaches by Brazilian companies of American pharmaceutical patents. Since unilateral retaliation (whatever the grievance) is contrary to GATT rules, Brazil has a strong legal case. The fact that intellectual property is not yet covered by GATT agreements does not exonerate America, which is still not supposed to act on its own.

- Joining GATT can also help cement economic reform in many developing countries. All GATT's recent members began to liberalise their trade policies and domestic economies before applying for membership. But writing the changes into a protocol of accession to GATT that has the status of international law makes backsliding much more difficult (which is a plus for foreign investors) and helps deflect domestic grumbling as barriers against imports are knocked away.

Mexico was the first to pay the higher GATT entry fee. It agreed to "bind" (ie, not raise again) most of its tariffs at a maximum 50%. Tariffs were later sliced to a maximum 20% and import-licensing was reduced drastically. Costa Rica, which has just completed membership formalities, is binding virtually all its tariffs with a maximum of 55% and is scrapping import quotas. Bolivia and Tunisia have agreed similar terms.

By contrast India, one of GATT's original members, imposes taxes on imports estimated to average 143%. None of its tariffs is bound. Nor has recent liberalisation made much of a dent in its extensive system of import controls. Because the Indians joined early, their high tariffs and import barriers are perfectly legal. But by insisting on their right to restrict imports, the Indians are hurting themselves more than others.

Stiffer entry terms have not proved to be damaging for most new members. Quite the contrary. There is plenty of evidence to suggest that countries almost always benefit from freer trade even if they open their markets unilaterally. The considerable gains from GATT membership are a further plus.

OF EAST . . .

Hence the new-found enthusiasm for GATT in Eastern Europe, following the political and economic upheavals of the past year. Four East European countries (Hungary, Poland, Czechoslovakia and Romania) have been nominal members for some time. But, as centrally planned economies, they could not take on normal GATT obligations (for instance, tariff cuts) when they joined, so they were never entitled to full GATT benefits, including most-favoured nation treatment. (America has only just granted permanent most-favoured nation status to Poland, Hungary, and Czechoslovakia.)

Now Poland has become the first country in GATT to renegotiate its membership terms to reflect its moves to a market economy. Others may follow suit. Bulgaria, which wants to join, will almost certainly have to accept standard GATT disciplines from the outset.

GATT does not require countries to adopt western-style capitalism. It does not care who owns the factories or how they are run. It does assume that businesses can decide how much to buy and sell abroad in response to price signals and that prices broadly reflect costs. Where prices are fixed by bureaucrats and goods are allocated by plan directives, GATT rules cannot operate sensibly. For instance, GATT permits members to levy extra duties if goods are being dumped on their markets at prices below production costs. But if no one knows what production costs are, how can dumping be proved or disproved?

The Eastern Europeans were allowed in to GATT on special terms to take account of their centrally planned economies, but failed to fulfil even these terms. GATT members are rightly leery of repeating those mistakes, especially when the economies concerned are potential trading giants, like China and the Soviet Union. America, for one, says it will accept them as GATT members only if economic reforms result in a "market-oriented" system.

In 1986 the big trading nations welcomed, mainly for political reasons, China's formal application to resume its GATT place vacated in 1950. (Russia's bid around the same time to become an observer at the Uruguay round was cold-shouldered.) Now, after the faltering of China's "open-door" reform programme and the brutal crushing of the country's pro-democracy movement in June 1989, the West has changed its tune. Membership talks are stalled.

This is unlikely to help Taiwan, which at the beginning of this year asked to join. Taiwan's government carefully avoided any claim to be the "true" China, requesting GATT accession as an "autonomous customs territory" (and the world's 13th-largest exporter). But China is outraged and western countries still seem reluctant to offend.

As for the Soviet Union, the West is encouraging but cautious. America and the EC say their decision late last year to back Russia's request for observer status does not mean they will necessarily support a future membership application.

The Russians have been told to wait until after the end of the Uruguay round. But in any event, the Soviet government is nowhere near being ready to submit an application for membership. Its economic and trade reforms are also well behind schedule. Subsequent negotiations on entry terms could take several years.

Until recently, GATT members argued about whether the organisation should adapt its rules to accommodate centrally planned economies in order to become a truly global trade policeman. With prospective members now expected to embrace free-market principles, and apparently willing (at least in theory) to do so, the question has become irrelevant. Western countries still worry that the admission of China, and even more so the Soviet Union, could upset the political equilibrium in GATT. But that lies far in the future.

...AND SOUTH

Meanwhile, GATT members are reappraising the special rules that exist for another group, the 70-plus developing countries. They can use import curbs, export subsidies and other trade barriers that are prohibited to others. Under rules added to the GATT in 1965, developing countries are entitled to "differential and more favourable treatment", which means they do not need to offer anything in return for trade benefits.

In practice, trade preferences have chiefly benefited the richer developing countries. At the same time, third-world nations generally have been put in the vulnerable position of supplicants for charity, while western countries got on with the more profitable business of bargaining among themselves. Past international trade rounds have been mostly rich-country affairs, dominated by America, the EC and Japan.

In the Uruguay round third-world countries are playing a significant role for the first time. The price has been agreement (in principle) that the more advanced among them would take on more GATT obligations by accepting much the same trade disciplines as industrial countries, and by liberalising their often heavily protected markets. As with GATT's new members, many developing countries themselves see advantages in adopting the "do as you would be done by" approach, offering and receiving more.

In negotiations on textiles, tropical products and tariffs, western concessions are explicitly contingent on market-opening measures by the big third-world exporters. In agriculture and the "new areas" (services, intellectual property and foreign investment), America wants to go even further,

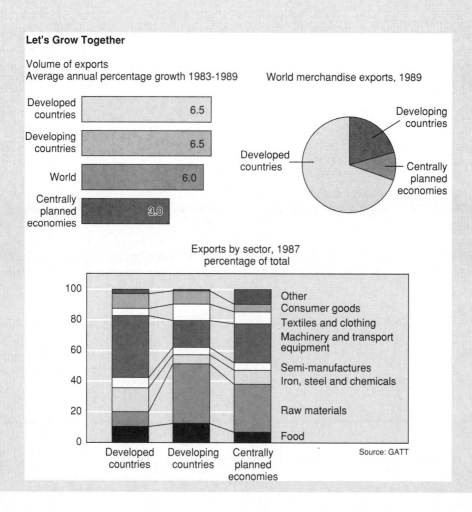

Let's Grow Together

Volume of exports
Average annual percentage growth 1983-1989

Developed countries 6.5
Developing countries 6.5
World 6.0
Centrally planned economies 3.0

World merchandise exports, 1989

Developing countries
Developed countries
Centrally planned economies

Exports by sector, 1987
percentage of total

Other
Consumer goods
Textiles and clothing
Machinery and transport equipment
Semi-manufactures
Iron, steel and chemicals
Raw materials
Food

Developed countries   Developing countries   Centrally planned economies

Source: GATT

arguing against any special treatment for developing countries. Rich and poor would sign on for the same set of rules, with the poor merely being given more time to implement them. But most other countries think there will have to be specific recognition of third-world concerns to persuade developing countries to sign the final deals.

The West also wants to tighten the rules that allow developing countries to maintain otherwise illegal import curbs because of balance-of-payments difficulties. Of the $1 trillion in trade not subject to multi-lateral rules, according to America, half relates to trade by developing countries protected under this clause, often long after their balance-of-payments problems have disappeared. South Korea, which has been running massive trade surpluses for several years, only recently agreed under pressure to "disinvoke" the clause, which will entail opening its market to farm imports.

These are difficult issues. But GATT has the advantage that it has never been a forum for north-south (or east-west) wrangles. Countries do not vote as blocks. Indeed they scarcely vote at all but take all big decisions by consensus. This has the obvious drawback of encouraging fudges and compromises. But most GATT members believe it helps prompt the search for solutions all can accept, given the diversity of interests that transcend crude divisions between rich and poor or market and planned economies.

Instead, countries have come together in a shifting set of ad-hoc alliances in the Uruguay round, with rich and poor discovering common interests. Thus the 14-strong Cairns group of agricultural "free traders", which is playing a central role in the farm talks, includes Australia, Canada, Brazil, Argentina, Thailand and Hungary.

Some countries are now calling for GATT to be promoted to the first league of international institutions, to reflect its graduation from rich traders' club to near-universal world trade organisation. Forty-three years after its creation, GATT remains a curious legal hybrid, its secretariat still formally servicing the interim committee of an International Trade Organisation that was never established because America's Congress objected to giving bureaucrats in Geneva decision-making powers on foreign trade, investment and competition policy.

The current suggestion is for something less ambitious: a World Trade Organisation that would administer and police the large number of separate agreements and codes—perhaps as many as two dozen—that will emerge from a successful trade round. The WTO would also be given strengthened powers to settle trade disputes.

Talk about a new, more powerful trade organisation is all well and good. But there is a danger that it could distract attention from the far more urgent task of securing effective trade liberalisation in the Uruguay round.

PERSPECTIVE 6–3   **GATT Brief: Centre Stage for Services?**

While squabbles over agriculture, textiles and high-tech exports have hogged the trade limelight during the Uruguay round, the series of trade talks due to end in December, negotiators are quietly

getting on with producing a general agreement on trade in services (known, inelegantly, as GATS). If successful, such an agreement could overshadow the much publicised disputes over farming and mi-

SOURCE: *The Economist*, May 5, 1990, pages 88–89.

crochips, becoming as significant as the creation 43 years ago of the general agreement on tariffs and trade (GATT), which covers trade in goods.

Any agreement on services would be designed to extend internationally agreed rules to the fast-growing cross-border trade in services, worth more than $600 billion a year. It would also promote moves to dismantle trade barriers and to open markets to foreign competition.

America and other rich countries are the main enthusiasts for a services deal. Their services—banking, insurance, telecommunications, transport, tourism, construction, consultancy and public services—account for well over half of their national output and employment. In America, the world's biggest exporter of services, nearly 70% of GDP comes from services, which employ three-quarters of American workers and represent 18% of America's total exports. But even in developing countries services often account for nearly half of GDP and considerably more in some of the newly industrialising nations.

Nevertheless freer trade in services will mean adjustment costs, as well as benefits. Governments may have to alter some regulations on services, including rules intended to protect consumers from shady finance companies or unqualified architects. The changes would be needed to conform to yet-to-be-decided international standards, if the existing rules inadvertently distort trade. Allowing more competition from foreign service companies may mean admitting foreign capital and workers, both touchy issues. Some sectors, such as shipping and civil aviation, may have to abandon restrictive practices.

Last December the services negotiating group produced the first draft of a framework agreement. Admittedly the 15 pages are laced with 167 square brackets where countries disagree. But trade officials do not seem downhearted. They are aiming, ambitiously, to have a basic text agreed in the second half of July, ready for the imprimatur of trade ministers when they meet to conclude the Uruguay round in Brussels in early December.

By July governments will have to indicate how far they are prepared to open up their markets as a first step, which services they want covered (or not), and what if any special arrangements should be made to accommodate the needs of third-world development. At any of these hurdles, the talks could stumble.

Negotiators acknowledge the problems but warn against over-pessimism. When the Uruguay round was launched in September 1986, many developing countries were strongly opposed even to having services on the agenda.

The talks began without any participant having much idea what a services deal might look like or what it might cover. And the report that went to the mid-term ministerial review of the round in Montreal in December 1988 was so peppered with square brackets that it was described by Mr Clayton Yeutter, then America's trade representative, as the "worst I've ever seen come to a ministerial meeting."

Though crucial details still have to be settled, most of the broad principles and general shape of the eventual agreement are clear, and accepted even by developing countries such as Brazil and India that initially opposed any services agreement.

The framework deal will apply to all types of services trade, whether supplied across frontiers, at home to foreign customers, or by foreign companies in foreign markets (normally involving cross-border movement of capital and labour). But countries will be able to put "reservations" on specific services which they want to keep out of the liberalisation pot first time around.

America and the EC have jointly proposed that signatories be allowed to continue to restrict the way services are delivered to their home markets. Thus poor countries would still be able legally to bar foreign banks from setting up subsidiaries; rich countries would be able to forbid foreign accountants or architects from practising unless they qualified locally or had qualifications recognised as equivalent. These barriers would then be lowered by negotiation in subsequent bargaining sessions.

For services covered by the agreement, certain principles, mostly borrowed and adapted from GATT, will apply:

- Non-discrimination between countries or, in the jargon, "most-favoured nation" treatment: every country subscribing to the services agreement must be given the most favourable trading terms available.
- Transparency: openness about rules, regulations and procedures affecting services trade.
- National treatment: equal treatment of foreign and domestic companies. (But signatories initially will be able to back out of this for named services.)
- Progressive lowering of remaining barriers, with "appropriate" flexibility for developing countries whose poverty might justify higher, but temporary, barriers.

Other rules would cover safeguards and exceptions, state aids, regional trading blocks, and the mechanics of bargaining and disputes-settlement. If established, the accord would probably have its own small secretariat in Geneva alongside GATT, and it would be open to all GATT members to become signatories.

AMERICAN ANXIETIES

So far, so good. From here on, the going gets tricky. First, America—to everyone else's irritation—is flirting with the idea of excluding sizeable industries from any services pact. Those excluded would be completely outside the scope of an agreement. Though countries could negotiate separate agreements for these sectors if they wished, they would not be otherwise subject to international rules nor to progressive liberalisation. American shipping and aviation lobbies are pushing hard for exclusion. America's Treasury (though not the country's banks) wants to keep banking out.

All three groups have different reasons for seeking exclusion of their industries. The shipping industry wants to retain America's Jones act, which reserves coastal traffic for American-built, American-registered, American-owned and American-crewed vessels.

For its part, the aviation industry says that the international system of bilateral landing rights under the 1944 Chicago Convention has worked well—so if it ain't broke, why fix it?

As for banking, America's Treasury officials say they are worried that prudential supervision might be compromised by the horse-trading which accompanies any trade deal. But the real reason for Treasury opposition to including banking is less edifying. Treasury officials do not want to cede territory to the president's trade representative, who speaks for the United States in all GATT matters and would presumably do the same in any GATT-style services agreement.

America is not the only country with powerful lobbies arguing for exclusion. Any concession to America could lead to irresistible pressure for yet more concessions to others, fatally weakening the attraction of any multilateral services agreement. That danger may help to ensure there are no exclusions at all.

EUROPEAN WORRIES

The EC says it will refuse to sign any agreement that does not include banking and other financial services. Given the EC's clout in services trade, that is an effective veto on America's proposals to leave financial services out of any services-trade agreement.

All agree, however, that tricky industries may need some special rules. For example, few countries quibble with the idea that the "most favoured nation" principle cannot be applied to aircraft-landing rights. Officials point out, however, that just because landing rights cannot be given to all-comers does not mean that cargo handling or ticketing systems cannot be opened up.

By early May countries must indicate which of the 100-plus service industries identified by GATT they would be prepared to liberalise first time around as their "entry fee" to a services agreement. The fee can be lower for poor countries. but, controversially, America and the EC want the framework deal to include a "non-application" clause. This would permit any signatory to refrain from extending the agreement's benefits to any other country which it believes has made too few market-opening commitments.

Critics complain that this would open the door to the very sort of bilateral arm-twisting that international rules are supposed to prevent. America and the EC could use the threat of "non-

application" to secure strict reciprocity in services trade, which would make a mockery of the "most-favoured nation" principle.

Thus the EC could decide not to open its markets to banks from a third country where "national treatment" did not result in comparable market opportunities. This was the issue on which the EC was forced by international pressure to back down in redrafting its second banking directive in 1989. The EC originally had in mind American laws that prevent interstate banking and the

At your service

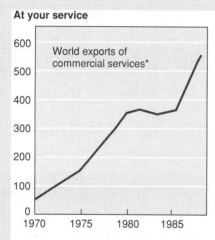

World exports of commercial services*

Leading exporters, 1987	(billions)
United States	$56
France	53
Britain	43
West Germany	41
Italy	33
Japan	28
Holland	23
Spain	22
Belgium/Luxembourg	19
Austria	15

By region as percentage of total, 1987

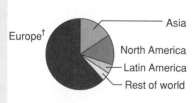

Europe†   Asia
North America
Latin America
Rest of world

As % of total exports, 1987	
Egypt	53
Greece	44
Kenya	40
Spain	39
Austria	36
Sudan	35
Philippines	32
Morocco	32
Israel	29
France	28

* Shipment, passenger, and port services, travel, tourism, and other private services.
† includes intra-E-C
Source: GATT

mixing of lending and securities operations, enshrined in the Glass-Steagall act, a separation also enforced in Japan.

The EC says it would use "non-application" solely to ensure that key countries agree to include banking within a multilateral services pact from the start. But no one believes that European governments are going to open their market of 360m consumers to American and Japanese banks for nothing. Tough talks lie ahead.

DEVELOPING PROBLEMS

The question of third-world development could prove even more difficult to resolve. Developing countries have overcome their initial fears that a services agreement would simply give aggressive western multinationals *carte blanche* to trample their fledgling service industries.

Many developing countries are big service producers and exporters in their own right. South Korea (shipping and construction), Singapore (travel and engineering services), Hongkong (financial services and shipping) and Mexico (tourism) rank among the world's top 20 services exporters. Because India and the Philippines have lots of highly educated workers but low wage rates, they boast flourishing businesses developing sophisticated computer software.

With services increasingly involved in the manufacture of goods, poor countries now see that there could be advantages for them in opening their markets to cheap, efficient services from abroad and to the know-how that comes with them. A recent OECD report estimated that requiring industry to buy local insurance doubled the transport and insurance costs for half of all third-world imports.

The American government (though not its services exporters) has taken the view that trade liberalisation alone is so beneficial that developing countries do not need any special rules, just more time to dismantle existing barriers. Others, rich and poor, disagree. They point out that since third-world countries can liberalise unilaterally if they wish, there has to be something extra to encourage them to sign an international deal. In Montreal ministers instructed negotiators to devise ways of encouraging the development of third-world service industries and of helping to promote third-world services exports.

So far, they have failed dismally. There have been ritual demands from developing countries such as India for the preferential treatment of their exports of services, while they continued to enjoy protection at home. Other third-world proposals would require foreign entrants to guarantee transfers of technology and to abide by special conditions including the use of local labour and materials.

None of these demands is acceptable to the industrial countries. But an earlier disagreement about the free movement of workers seems to have been laid to rest. Even third-world countries are reluctant to open their borders to armies of unskilled workers, while both rich and poor countries seem to agree on the regulated movement of professionals. On semi-skilled workers there is scope for compromise though they may differ on details.

A services agreement could survive without third-world support. Western negotiators think the draft under discussion could win the support of all the OECD's 24 countries and the more advanced poor ones. Together these account for the bulk of world services trade.

Some enthusiasts go further. They say a services deal would survive even the collapse of the Uruguay round. "Countries have no intention of letting four years of hard bargaining go to waste," says one GATT insider.

A free-standing services accord with some 30-40 signatories would be second-best to a Uruguay-round package deal including some 100 countries. But unless there are internationally agreed rules, the world's growing trade in services is likely to produce more and more trade friction. To reduce that friction and keep services trade growing, a limited deal would be better than no deal at all.

United Nations Conference on Trade and Development

UNCTAD was established in 1964 to address concerns of developing nations on issues of international trade that affected their economic development. The main concern of most developing countries was that under the old system unequal players were asked to play on a level playing field. The less-developed countries, which were extremely weak economically and industrially backward, had no way of competing with the industrialized nations in the world market on the same terms. Moreover, they argued, given the structure of the international economy, they were parting with more of their goods as exports than they were receiving as imports. In effect, the prices of their exports were not rising as did prices of their imports. This feature is conceptualized in economics as the terms of trade argument. Further, their exports suffered from low demand and price elasticities, which meant that they could not raise export prices by reducing supplies. On the other hand, their imports were critical for them and their supplies were controlled by large monopolistic entities that could charge extortionary prices.

UNCTAD was established to provide a forum for the developing countries to communicate their views on international trade issues to the industrialized countries and to seek trade concessions from them. After considerable and sustained pressure from the developing countries, the developed countries agreed to an across-the-board reduction of tariffs for developing countries under an arrangement known as the generalized system of preferences. The GSP tariff reductions, however, were for only limited amounts of imports from developing countries and did not create any significant niches for developing country exporters in the markets of industrialized countries. Moreover, since the liberalization in tariffs were only for manufactured goods, many developing countries with little industrial activity, cannot benefit from the reduced tariffs.

Seven UNCTAD conferences have been held, the last being held in Geneva in 1987. Membership of the UNCTAD rose from 119 in 1964 to nearly 170 countries in 1987. Although the deliberations and resolutions of UNCTAD have not solved the problems faced by developing countries in the international trade area, they have had important positive effects on the international trade environment in general. UNCTAD conferences have resulted in a better and more informed understanding of the respective positions on various issues of the developed and developing countries, which was reflected in the greater cordiality at the 1987 meeting of UNCTAD, where the traditional confrontational approach was less evident.

A number of permanent working committees have been formed, such as a committee on manufactures, a committee on invisibles and finance, and a committee on commodities. These committees continue to deal with major issues and analyze in depth complex problems, thereby contributing to an increase in the level of understanding of the problems by representatives and officials of different countries. Thus, UNCTAD has become a permanent international organization that focuses global attention on the trade development problems of LDCs and actively investigates issues in all their complexity and implications. UNCTAD also has emerged as an important source of suggestions for solving these problems, especially because of the broad knowledge base it has created over the years. At the time of its inception, UNCTAD was hailed as one of the most important events since the establishment of the United Nations. Although the concrete impact of the organization has been limited, it has kept alive the dialogue between the industrial and developing world and is likely to continue to promote better understanding between them.

Regional Trade Groupings

Regional trade groupings have emerged in the past two decades as major forces shaping the pattern of international trade. These arrangements have enabled countries located in different geographic locations to pool their resources and lower restrictions on trade between themselves, in order to achieve greater economic growth.

Regional groupings offer several advantages over global trade arrangements to their members. Because there are fewer countries involved, and their state of economic development is relatively homogenous, it is easier to find commonality of interest and arrive at a workable agreement on the basis of voluntary adherence by member countries.

Regional groupings offer the additional advantages of cultural, geographical, and historical homogeneity that provides an environment conducive to the spirit of mutual cooperation. Even with all the positive factors, however, regional groupings can still face severe internal dissension among member states, especially if the general economic situation is poor and countries follow restrictive, inward-looking policies. The experience of regional groupings in international trade has therefore varied considerably. While the EEC and ASEAN are notable successes, trade arrangements in Africa and Latin America have not achieved any significant benefits for their member countries.

THE EUROPEAN ECONOMIC COMMUNITY (EEC)

The European Economic Community is by far the most important and successful regional trade grouping in the world. After 1992, its role is likely to become even more important as the degree of integration among the members will become significantly higher. (See Chapter 13.)

ASSOCIATION OF SOUTH EAST ASIAN NATIONS

ASEAN was founded in 1967 by Singapore, Thailand, Malaysia, Indonesia, and the Philippines. Brunei joined the organization when it attained its independence in 1984.

Over the past twenty years, ASEAN has made significant progress. Preferential trading arrangements have been established under which special,

lower tariffs are levied on the import of goods from member states. Members have cooperated on the coordinated development of industry in the region through the industrial project scheme, whereby member states select a particular project for establishment in a country and in which every other member state holds equity. To counter the problem of food shortages in some parts of the region, member states have created the food security reserve scheme, under which a common stockpile of rice is maintained for supplementing the needs of any member country experiencing a shortfall.

Several other coordinated projects have proved that this regional arrangement has worked. An ASEAN finance corporation has been established to finance joint ventures, and agreements have been reached between central banks of member countries to reduce exchange rate fluctuations and exchange imbalances by using currency exchange arrangements between themselves. ASEAN has fostered regional cooperation in other areas, such as projects for education, population control, and cultural exchanges between member states.

ASEAN has enabled the member states to represent their region as a collective body and improve their bargaining position with nonmember states, especially the industrialized countries. The aura of political stability and regional amity engendered by the body has also been a major factor in attracting overseas investment in several member countries. In fact, after 1982 the region became the largest recipient of foreign direct investment of all the developing regions of the world, even surpassing Latin America.

Active cooperation between members is supported by a small secretariat located in Jakarta. Among the other notable achievements of ASEAN in the two decades of its existence are

- an emergency sharing scheme on crude oil and oil products.
- joint approaches to problems in international commodity trade.
- a program for cooperation on the development and utilization of mineral resources.
- a planning center for agricultural development.

- a center for development of forest tree seeds.
- a program for tourism cooperation.
- a plant quarantine training center.

ASEAN, however, has not been an unqualified success, and progress has been slow, particularly in coordinated industrial development, because of several constraints. The level of complementarity between the member states is low, and many of them have competitive economic structures, especially because industrial output in most countries tends to be quite similar. Unlike the EEC, ASEAN members are under significant financial stress, and large resources have to be mobilized to fund their ambitious development programs and government expenditures. Because import duties comprise a major source of revenue for the ASEAN countries, tariffs can only be reduced to the extent of being able to absorb the revenue loss. The lack of financial resources also constrains the development of joint industrial projects. The issues of equitable distribution of benefits from jointly owned or jointly run projects and of tariff preferences are difficult to resolve, given their complex implications.

On balance, however, ASEAN has been a significant success. If a continued political will on the part of member countries to sustain the progress of cooperation is forthcoming, there is no doubt that the arrangement will bring greater economic and political coordination to the region, which has already emerged as an important economic zone, even by global standards.

THE ANDEAN PACT

The Andean Pact was signed by five Latin American countries—Bolivia, Chile, Colombia, Ecuador, and Peru—in 1969 and in effect created a subregional trading arrangement. An important motivation for the creation of the Andean Pact was a growing dissatisfaction among several Latin American countries about restrictions on trade in goods and services.

The Andean Pact works through a secretariat that handles all administrative and executive matters. The decisions of the pact are made through a commission made up of a representative from each member country. Disputes between members on the interpretation of the pact's statutes are heard and settled by the Andean Court of Justice. Although progress has been relatively slow, some important steps towards regional integration have been taken by the Andean Pact countries.

Industry Sectoral Programs

Under the industry sectoral programs, a number of industry sectors are selected for the implementation of coordinated or rationalized development plans that aim to achieve the best utilization of competitive advantages available in different countries in the region. Thus, the country having a competitive advantage in a particular industrial product will concentrate on the production of that product, while other products related to that industry will be manufactured by other member countries. Countries exchange their allocated products among other member states on a tariff-free basis. At present, sectoral cooperation in industrial activity encompasses petrochemicals, automotive products, and metals.

Foreign Direct Investment

The Andean Pact countries have been able to establish coordinated policies to promote and control foreign direct investments. The idea is to achieve a certain similarity of restrictions in all member countries in order to develop leverage in negotiating investments permissions with overseas investors, and to prevent the possibility of the investors gaining unfair advantages by playing one country of the region against another, by creating intraregional competition to attract foreign investment flows. Chile, however wanted to attract greater levels of foreign direct investments and left the Andean Pact in 1976, because it could not hope to do so under the restrictive provisions of the Andean Pact.

The Andean Pact has made little progress in tariff reduction among its member countries. Further regional cooperation in Latin America has been limited because most countries have been beset by serious internal economic problems following the debt crises (see Perspective 6–4).

PERSPECTIVE 6–4   Five Latin Ministers Embrace Free Trade

Shortly before the Gulf crisis began dominating the headlines, President Bush announced that he was interested in establishing a free-trade zone covering the entire Western Hemisphere: from northern Canada to the southern tip of South America. His announcement followed on the heels of the first stage of talks leading to a Mexican-U.S.-Canadian free-trade agreement, which are moving much quicker than anyone imagined when they were first announced. All this represents a significant shift in Latin American thinking concerning economic development.

For decades, Latin American leaders were under the false impression that the best way to develop their economies was to protect local industry from foreign competition. This led to statist capitalism, which benefited a few well-placed industrialists but left the vast majority of citizens cut off from the rest of the world. The industrialists got lazy because they didn't have to compete with anyone—including their fellow countrymen—and the products they manufactured became inferior and over-priced. Uncompetitive islands of economic and political instability resulted.

It's a little early to say "all that has changed." But Latin leaders are now generally accepting the notion that if they integrate their economies with the rest of the world—this hemisphere in particular—they stand a much better chance of growing and of benefiting from foreign ideas and capital. Recently Wall Street Journal editors asked five Latin American economic ministers their views on a hemispheric trade zone. Their responses:

COLOMBIA: RUDOLF HOMMES, FINANCE MINISTER

President Bush's idea of creating a Western Hemisphere free-trade zone is of great importance. It is the first concrete proposal of the U.S. to promote the integration of the Americas based on trade, an important element of social and political cohesion.

However, in analyzing this initiative it is necessary to point out that since it is not entirely based on economic grounds—but is associated with the geopolitical relations of power—it can introduce new economic inefficiences. For example, the economic integration with Latin American and Caribbean countries could lead to a specialization of the productive basis of those countries that is determined by the competitive advantages that may exist with relation to the U.S. and Canadian economies, but could not necessarily exist with respect to the economies of the rest of the world.

The idea, in principle, is feasible, provided that the U.S. and its prospective Southern partners tame their protectionist instincts in order to make it work. This would seem plausible inasmuch as the international experience shows that human well-being benefits from the effective practice of free trade.

In this sense, it is clear that Latin American leaders and technocrats are finally aware that protectionism is outmoded and ruinous: The degree of protection given to local production is a measure of the inefficiency that a community is willing to tolerate in detriment to its own well-being, and the economic development of the past 50 years in the Latin American countries has been delayed by a social ideology that has made them accept an outrageous level of inefficiency for the sake of a vague but vehement nationalism.

As explained until now, the outline of the Bush initiative seems to miss one element that would enhance these positive expectations. While it would seek the free market of goods, services, capital and technology within the free-trade area in the medium term, it avoids referring to the conditions that would permit what is essential for the success of an integrated market: the free movement of people.

SOURCE: *Wall Street Journal*, September 13, 1990

Another important aspect of President Bush's proposal is the flexibility given to each country to choose between bilateral integration mechanisms and those that strengthen sub-regional blocks. The same could be said with respect to the freedom conferred to each country to choose their own time frame for developing an agreement. However, free access to the U.S. and Canadian markets is the common incentive that would move Latin American countries in either direction. This suggests that the bilateral option would be the most popular choice.

A key to the success of the integration process is the equal treatment of and the non-discrimination among participants, independent of the way in which they choose to join. It may be that the implementation of the initiative will not occur in the context of GATT-like negotiations but that a series of general principles will be clearly defined and will be compulsory for all participant members. Nevertheless, it is hoped that the principles established by the U.S. government will not be the same it is trying to advance in the Uruguay Round because our expectation is that this initiative would be more advantageous for Latin American trade.

Of course, this initiative will not comprehensively absorb all bilateral issues. Colombia, for example, will be looking beyond it or even beyond the Andean Initiative to advance its own bilateral agenda with the U.S.

MEXICO: JAIME SERRA-PUCHE, MINISTER OF TRADE AND INDUSTRY

President Bush's initiative concerning a hemispheric free trade zone has caught the imagination of Latin America. The initiative will provide the means to complement adequately national economies in order to facilitate a new era of trade and investment relations—as well as enhancing cooperation on scientific and technological issues. Free trade is crucial in today's increasingly interdependent world. The global economy requires active trade and investment flows

so domestic economies can prosper and grow. Of course, trade agreements between developed and developing nations need to recognize their differences so that every participant benefits fully from liberalized trade regimes.

Mexico's own structural change is based on a simple premise: Mexico has to insert itself in the global economy. Mexico's international competitiveness requires adequate domestic policies and proper external market access, so the country can benefit fully from international trade and investment flows.

On the one hand, domestic policies are consistent with the outward orientation of the economy: Foreign investment has been liberalized; non-tariff trade barriers have been dismantled; intellectual-property-rights legislation is under review to assure the necessary protection to patents, licenses, trademarks and industrial secrets; and unnecessary regulatory obstacles are being and will continue to be removed. Overall, these policies have substantially enhanced the competitiveness of Mexico's non-oil exports, which in the course of the past seven years have increased by a factor of four, surpassing the export performance of the most dynamic countries during this period.

On the other hand, trade negotiations to assure external market access are a crucial complement to domestic policy. With each region of the world, we are building stronger economic relations, based on the principles of free trade. With the U.S., in particular, we have initiated preparatory talks that will lead to the negotiation of a free-trade agreement.

One important consequence of the free-trade agreement between Mexico and the U.S. will be the increased competitiveness of the region vis-a-vis the rest of the world. In sum, a free-trade agreement will complement Mexico's internationalization strategy and it will substantially increase bilateral trade and investment flows. The benefits of such a pact will undoubtedly accrue to both countries, in terms of employment, efficiency, and international competitiveness.

BRAZIL: ZELIA CARDOSA DE MELLO, FINANCE MINISTER

The Brazilian government has been carrying out a tremendous effort to reform the structure of its economy. The new foreign trade and industrial policies, which encompass the gradual elimination of tariffs and trade barriers in general, have facilitated a greater integration of the Brazilian economy with the world economy.

In this context, international cooperation is more than welcomed. We feel that to the extent that this cooperation is renewed and expanded, Brazil will be able to react to it more swiftly and more effectively.

The guidelines of the new U.S. free-trade initiative are a positive sign to Latin America as whole. They represent a new approach of the U.S. government toward the region. We hope to be able to explore in more detail the proposals made and to examine ways and means to apply them for mutual benefit. They touch three points of fundamental importance: the debt question, the new investments in the region and the building up of an open trade market. By dealing with those three essential matters they follow a path that we consider to be potentially fruitful.

The feasibility of the proposals depends, at this stage, on the mechanisms of dialogue we may establish and, of course, on the political will to carry them out.

Brazil has discussed the initiative with the governments of Argentina, Chile and Uruguay and intends to follow up this discussion. The idea of sharing our views with those of neighbor countries had the implicit purpose of giving a response resulting from deep reflection and coordinated views. We are sure that the elements are given for the new steps we all intend to take in our relations with the U.S.

CHILE: ALEJANDRO FOXLEY, MINISTER OF FINANCE

There is a growing awareness throughout Latin America that having an open, trading economy is the surest path for pulling our economies out of the poverty trap. But an export drive can only succeed if it can secure export markets. Unfortunately, many countries of the world—including the U.S.—do not always reflect in their actions the free-trade gospel they preach. There is also the danger of having "trading blocks" develop, most notably in Europe and the Pacific. Latin America is not beyond reproach either, having allowed its regional trading arrangements to languish in the past 20 years. I welcome President Bush's proposal as a much-needed antidote to this dangerous world-wide tendency. It is now up to all countries in the hemisphere to move swiftly and begin taking concrete steps.

A free-trade agreement in the Americas would ultimately benefit every country in the hemisphere, rich or poor. For Latin America, greater openness would mean greater foreign competition. But it would also provide much-needed overseas customers. I believe many of us are ready to take up this challenge. At the same time, growing Latin American exports to the U.S. and Canada would have as a counterpart a more stable and prosperous set of economies south of the Rio Grande, among which Northern firms could also find promising trade and investment partners. There would be some temporary adjustment costs, but the long-run mutual benefits are clear. The proposal therefore seems feasible. What is now needed is the political will to move forward.

At this point it seems practical to proceed in stages. Those countries that are ready to open up their markets should start negotiations, whether bilaterally or in larger groups. Any concession made to the participants in the early stages could also be extended to other countries that may decide to join the process at a later date. Chile already has low and uniform tariffs and no non-tariff barriers whatsoever. We believe that is a helpful starting point for discussion with the U.S. or any other countries of the region.

ARGENTINA:
ANTONIO ERMAN GONZALEZ,
MINISTER OF ECONOMY

We are enthusiastic about President Bush's proposal. We believe that economic integration is the most important challenge that the American nations have in this decade, and the most effective method to compete in the world economy. Argentina wants to move forward toward this goal by pursuing the following steps:

1) Achieve an agreement with the U.S. that will homogenize the regulatory framework in both countries, allowing free movement of capital; and

2) Establish a free-trade zone with Brazil and other countries in the southern cone by 1994 so as to become a more meaningful trading partner to integrate with North America.

Financial Organizations

International Monetary Fund

The role of the IMF as a supranational organization is discussed in considerable detail in Chapter 4. It is, however, useful to recall that the role of the IMF as a supranational organization has been expanding in recent years with its efforts to coordinate the response of the financial world to the debt crisis and make its own efforts in this regard. The other important role of the IMF is making loans for structural adjustment in economies facing severe macroeconomic instability and distortions. There is an increasing emphasis on coordination of lending activities between the IMF and other supranational lenders, as well as on assessing the social impact of IMF programs for structural adjustment in developing countries.

The World Bank

The World Bank was created (along with the IMF) at the Bretton Woods Conference in New Hampshire in July 1944, and it officially came into existence on December 27, 1945. The initial objective of the World Bank was to make financial resources available to European countries to rebuild their war-shattered economies and later to provide critically needed external financing to developing countries at affordable rates of interest. The creation of the World Bank, together with the IMF, was also intended to strengthen the structure and encourage the development and efficiency of international financial markets.

The World Bank consists of four main agencies:

1. International Bank for Reconstruction and Development (IBRD, generally known as the World Bank).
2. The International Development Association (IDA).
3. The International Finance Corporation (IFC).
4. The Multilateral Investment Guarantee Agency (MIGA).

INTERNATIONAL BANK FOR RECONSTRUCTION AND DEVELOPMENT

The main objective of the World Bank today is to support social and economic progress in developing countries by promoting better productivity and utilization of resources so that their citizens may live a better and fuller life. The World Bank seeks to achieve its objectives by making available financial assistance to developing countries, especially for specific economically sound infrastructural projects, for example, in the areas of power and transport. The basic rationale for the emphasis on such projects is that a good infrastructure is necessary for the developing countries to carry out programs of social and economic development. In the 1970s World Bank loans were also given to promote the development of the social services sectors of borrowing countries—education, water supply and sanitation, urban housing, and so on. Loans were also provided for the development of indigenous energy resources, such as oil and natural gas. Since the early 1980s much World Bank lending has been policy-based, that is, it has aimed to support economic adjustment measures by borrowing countries, particularly those faced with heavy external debt service requirements. Policy-based lending, sector policy lending, and structural adjustment lending programs of the World Bank provide critically needed financial assistance to countries attempting to alter the current orientation of their economies to enhance productivity and efficiency in the allocation of resources, improving external competitiveness, reducing overburdening subsidies, and repairing other economic distortions that prevent a higher rate of growth and create macroeconomic instability.

Another important aspect of financial assistance provided by the World Bank is loan guarantees. The World Bank helps member developing countries to obtain increased access at better terms to international financial markets by guaranteeing repayment of loans. This form of assistance has been increasingly used to improve resource flows from private creditors to the highly indebted developing countries. The use of guarantees is also being considered by the World Bank in order to help member-country borrowers issue securities in the international financial markets.

World Bank Lending

There are five major categories of World Bank loans:

1. Specific investment loans are loans made for specific projects in the areas of agricultural and rural development, urban development, energy, and so on. They have a maturity ranging from five to ten years.
2. Sector operations loans comprise about a third of the World Bank lending and are aimed at financing development of particular sectors of a country's economy such as oil, energy or agriculture. Loans under this category are also provided to the borrower's financial institutions, which then lend the funds to actual users in a particular sector of the economy.

3. Structural adjustment and program loans are targeted at providing the financial support needed by member countries who are undertaking comprehensive institutional and policy reforms to remove imbalances in the external sector. These loans, therefore, support entire programs of structural adjustment and are not specific to any particular project or sector of the economy.
4. Technical assistance loans are provided to member countries who need to strengthen their technical capacity to plan their development strategies and design and implement specific projects.
5. Emergency reconstruction loans are provided to member countries whose economies, especially the infrastructure, have experienced sudden and severe damage because of natural disasters, such as earthquakes or floods. The emphasis of these loans, apart from restoring the disrupted infrastructural facilities, is also on strengthening the capacity of borrower countries to handle future events of this type.

Since 1982 World Bank loans are made at variable rates of interest that are adjusted twice a year and are based on a spread of 0.5 percent on the average cost of the outstanding borrowings of the bank. Apart from interest, World Bank borrowers have to pay a front-end fee and a commitment fee on their borrowings. Repayment terms, including grace periods and final maturity, are determined on the basis of the per capita income of the borrowing country. Final maturity can range up to twenty years for countries with the lowest per capita income.

Fund-Raising by the World Bank

The primary capital resources of the World Bank come from contributions made by its more than 150 member countries, but, nearly all loan funds are raised by borrowings in international financial markets. The bank enjoys a AAA credit rating in the world's financial markets, which enables it to obtain easy access to funds and excellent borrowings terms in its chosen markets. Borrowings by the bank had surpassed $100 billion by the end of the 1980s. Borrowings are made in the variety of major international currencies that also reflect the nature of the loan portfolio of the bank. Approximately twenty different currencies have been used by the bank to raise funds in the international markets. The World Bank borrows at variable interest rates which are adjusted twice a year.

The World Bank has played a pioneering role in the development of the currency swap market, whereby it improves its access and terms to preferred markets or adjusts its borrowing currency mix with the lending currency mix. The bank also uses interest-rate swaps to adjust mismatches in its borrowing and lending portfolios and improve the management of interest rate risk.

The bank has made significant profits on its operations over the years, even though it charges a relatively low spread to its borrowers. As a matter of policy, all profits are transferred to the general reserve, which is maintained as a safeguard against the contingencies of loan or other financial losses.

Organizational Structure

Each member country subscribes to a certain proportion of the total paid-in capital of the bank. The subscription of each country differs and depends generally upon its international economic importance. The member countries are, in effect, the shareholders of the bank and the ultimate guarantors of its financial obligations. The United States has the largest share of paid-in capital (20.6 percent) and is, therefore, the largest shareholder of the bank. Major industrialized countries, such as Japan, Germany, United Kingdom, and France, are among the other important shareholders.

The Board of Governors of the Bank is the highest policymaking body, and each member state appoints one representative to the board, usually either its finance minister or the governor of the central bank. Each country also appoints an alternate member to its representative on the Board of Governors. The Board of Governors makes only major policy decisions about the functioning of the bank, such as capital increases, major changes

in lending emphasis, and the creation of new affiliates, which are approved at its annual meetings.

Day-to-day administration of the bank's work is entrusted to the president of the bank, who is traditionally from the United States. The president is supported by a twenty-two-member board of executive directors who are appointed by member governments. The major industrial countries, Saudi Arabia, and China have their own executive directors, while other member states, with lesser shares, form regional groupings to appoint executive directors. The bank has four major administrative divisions:

1. The operations division, which is essentially responsible for World Bank lending.
2. Financial operations division, which is responsible for raising and managing the financial resources of the bank.
3. The policy, planning and research division, which is concerned with in-depth economic studies, analysis, and planning to support the objectives of the bank.
4. The administration and personnel division.

World Bank headquarters are in Washington, D.C., and there are regional representative offices in many developing countries. Its staff, which at the end of 1989 numbered 6,000, consists of personnel drawn from more than one hundred nationalities and represent a wide variety of professional skills.

THE INTERNATIONAL DEVELOPMENT ASSOCIATION

The International Development Association was established in 1960 to provide long-term funds at concessionary rates to the poorest member countries of the bank. The affiliate does not have a separate organizational structure, and its operations are conducted by the staff of the World Bank. The president of the World Bank is also the president of IDA. The basic objective of the association is to provide long-term financing to those members who cannot afford to borrow on normal World Bank terms. IDA funds are used to promote long-term, long-gestation development projects.

As member countries grow economically and their per capita income increases beyond a particular level, they graduate from IDA assistance and become eligible for World Bank loans under its various lending programs.

IDA loans have long maturities—fifty years with a ten-year grace period for the repayment of principal. Since 1982 a nominal service charge of .75 percent per annum is levied, and a commitment fee of .5 percent is charged on approved but undispersed credits. IDA funds are raised from member country subscriptions, repayments of outstanding credits, and allocations from the income of the bank. IDA funds are periodically replenished by member countries (eight to date).

As of June 30, 1990, IDA had approved $35.82 million in financial assistance to member countries. The five largest recipients of IDA credits are India, Pakistan, Bangladesh, Indonesia, and Egypt. Although in recent years IDA replenishments have led to a certain amount of debate on the amount of contributions to be made by the industrialized countries, there is no doubt that the role of the IDA is critical in providing sorely needed external assistance to many countries with large populations that are at the lowest rung of the global economic ladder.

INTERNATIONAL FINANCE CORPORATION

The IFC was established in 1956 with the objective of promoting the development of private enterprises in member countries. The IFC operates primarily through its own staff, but it is overseen by the bank's board of executive directors. The president of the World Bank is also the president of IFC.

The IFC makes equity investments and extends loans to private enterprises in developing countries. In accordance with its mandate, the IFC cannot accept government guarantees of its loans. The primary role of the IFC, however, is not providing financial assistance by itself. It serves as a catalyst to promote private capital flows to the private sector in developing countries. The IFC is never the sole financier in any particular transac-

tion, and its contribution is usually a minor proportion of the total mobilized amount. The corporation also does not accept management positions or seats on the boards of directors of the organizations to which it lends funds. In addition, the IFC provides financial, technical, and legal advice to its investee companies. Advisory services are also provided to companies who do not borrow directly from the IFC.

As a matter of policy, the IFC exits from investee companies as they develop and mature, usually selling its interests to local parties. The importance of the activities of the IFC has grown in recent years, with increasing emphasis on the development of the private sector by the industrialized countries and its growing acceptance by many developing countries, which are increasingly disillusioned by the lackluster performance of parastatal enterprises in their countries.

Apart from its traditional investment activities, the IFC has also played an important role in strengthening the financial infrastructure of developing countries through its capital markets department. The department provides needed technical and legal assistance to many developing countries to strengthen their financial markets. The IFC provides assistance in this area for such issues as framing legal statutes to regulate securities markets and the development of financial institutions, such as leasing companies, venture capital companies, commercial banks, credit rating agencies, and export-import financing institutions.

The IFC also plays an important catalyzing role in setting up depository institutions; establishing trading, disclosure, and market practice standards; and directing external flows toward developing countries by helping to establish and develop capital markets and financial institutions and by participating in and promoting international investment efforts through pooled investment vehicles, such as country funds.

Although in the past the IFC had funded its investments from its own capital and borrowings from the World Bank, it has also raised substantial amounts on its own by directly borrowing in the international capital markets. The IFC is rated a

AAA borrower by major U.S. credit rating agencies.

MULTILATERAL INVESTMENT GUARANTEE AGENCY

The MIGA was established in 1988, its main objective to promote overseas direct investment flows into developing countries by providing guarantees against noncommercial risks that investors face in most economies. Noncommercial risks are generally risks arising out of political actions by most governments, such as confiscation, expropriation, and nationalization of the assets of the overseas enterprise. Other noncommercial risks covered by MIGA include risks arising out of such unforeseen circumstances as wars and civil disturbances.

THE FUTURE ROLE OF THE WORLD BANK GROUP

The role of the World Bank group has constantly evolved ever since its inception. The next few decades pose several major challenges to the organization, as it pursues its fundamental objectives of improving the living standards of people in poor countries by catalyzing greater economic growth and sustainable development. In the past decade, the World Bank has had to deal with a whole set of new issues created by the international debt crisis and the flow of much-needed external capital to industrial countries instead of the developing world. Given the significant gaps in the demand and supply of external resources for the developing countries as a whole, the bank will have to make additional efforts to meet the enhanced requirements of its member countries. Further, it will be required to increasingly collaborate with other multilateral institutions, such as the IMF, on the important issue of providing economic and institutional resources to many developing countries with a view to improving their levels of productivity and efficiency. The bank may also increasingly adopt a regional approach to solving difficult problems that need a broader geographical approach than specific country operations.

Along with the main objective of fighting poverty in many countries across the world, the World Bank is likely to pay increasing attention to the question of the fragile environment and the global ecosystems and their interrelationships with the consequences of development, particularly in the context of the environmental impact of bank-financed projects. Another new direction for the World Bank is the increasing association with the work of nongovernmental voluntary organizations in developing countries.

Internally, there is likely to be an ever greater need for political and financial support to the bank from member governments, especially those of the industrialized countries.

The Inter-American Development Bank

The Inter-American Development Bank was established in 1959 with the primary objective of promoting social and economic development in Latin America. The bank, headquartered in Washington, DC, has forty-three member countries, including sixteen outside the Western Hemisphere, which are known as nonregional members.

The main operations of the IADB are focused on providing long-term public financing to member countries. The main areas for which loans are extended include agriculture and rural development, transport, communications, and mining. Since the onset of the debt crisis, the IADB has adopted special lending programs that aim to direct financing where it is most urgently needed. Loans are made on a project basis, with proposals being initiated by borrowing countries and examined and approved by the bank. The bank also provides technical assistance to the member countries for the preparation of project proposals and their implementation.

Unlike the World Bank, a significant portion of the funding of the IADB comes from member contributions to the paid-in capital of the bank. The United States has the largest contribution of paid-in capital (36 percent), followed by Canada and some other nonregional countries. Loans are, however, made only to Latin American countries, and only to governments. The announced policy of IADB is to stop lending to a country whose account falls in arrears. In recent years the IADB has borrowed substantial funds in the international financial markets to supplement its resources for financing development in member countries. It continues to be well-regarded in the international capital markets, despite the debt crisis faced by many of its member nations.

The role of the bank has been expanded to undertake financing of social projects, such as health, education, and rural development. Moreover, the smaller and economically weaker countries of Latin America have been given the highest priority in the extension of loans. Loans typically have a maturity period between thirty and forty years and carry an interest rate between 3 and 4 percent. In addition, IADB assists member states in mobilizing resources in their internal markets, especially through cofinancing arrangements.

The Asian Development Bank

The Asian Development Bank was founded in 1966 with the objective of promoting economic growth and cooperation in Asia and the Far East, including the South Pacific region. Although membership is primarily concentrated among countries of the region, major industrialized countries, such as Japan, the United States, Canada, and Germany, are also members in the capacity of donors.

The Asian Development Bank provides different types of financial and technical assistance to member countries in the region including guarantees, investment loans, and direct technical assistance. The important areas that receive ADB assistance are agriculture, industry, energy development, transport and communications, development of finance institutions, water supply, sanitation, and urban development.

Most ADB loans are long-term and maturities range from ten to thirty years. Loans carry a fixed rate of interest that varies according to the prevailing rates in the international financial markets at the time of the extension of the loan, although in recent years the ADB has also started to lend at

variable rates, like the World Bank. Repayment and grace periods vary, depending upon the per capita income of the borrowing country. Grace periods range from two to seven years.

The ADB has a soft loans facility known as the Asian Development Fund, in which concessional terms are granted to borrowing countries. This facility is funded by member country contributions. Loans from this facility are provided free of interest and a nominal service charge is levied of 1 percent per annum. Repayments are spread over a forty-year period, including a grace period of ten years.

The African Development Bank

The African Development Bank (AfDB) was established in 1963 with the primary objective of accelerating the development process and improving socioeconomic conditions in the newly independent countries of Africa. The bank is headquartered at Abidjan, Ivory Coast. An important characteristic of the AfDB is its strong emphasis on maintaining its fundamentally African character and orientation. In fact, until 1982 non-African countries were not permitted to become members of the bank. Non-African countries are now allowed to become members only with certain specific safeguards aimed at preserving the unique African orientation and identity of the bank. The bank is organized into three different affiliates, the largest entity being the bank itself, which lends to the more economically advanced member states and charges rates of interest at a spread over the cost of its own borrowed funds. The second affiliate is a soft loan window, known as the African Development Fund, which channels concessional assistance to poorer member countries. There is no interest on this assistance, only a nominal service charge of 0.75 percent per annum. The ADF receives its resources from the non-African countries, including several industrialized countries. The third affiliate is the Nigeria Trust Fund (NTF), which lends funds at rates and maturities that are between those charged by the AfDB and the ADF. The NTF, set up in 1976, is funded entirely by the Nigerian government. The bank raises its resources from paid-in capital by member countries, concessional loans from governments of industrialized countries, and, more recently, significant borrowings in the international financial markets that have been supported by the excellent credit ratings earned by the bank from major U.S. credit rating agencies.

The European Investment Bank

The European Investment Bank (EIB) was established in 1957 by the Treaty of Rome, in conjunction with the creation of the European Economic Community. Although the bank is a separate legal entity, it is intimately connected with EEC activities and pursues three objectives:

1. To contribute to the balanced development of the community by assisting the development of less-favored regions.
2. To promote the common interest of member states.
3. To contribute to the modernization of the industrial enterprises in the community, especially to improve their international competitiveness.

The EIB attempts to implement these objectives by promoting funds for investment in projects that serve these ends. EIB raises its resources both from paid-in subscriptions by member states and from borrowings in the international markets. Loans are made to finance projects in individual member countries and projects that serve the interest of the community as a whole, for example, projects to develop energy resources or infrastructural facilities that benefit all member states.

Germany, France, Italy, and the United Kingdom are the four largest shareholders of the EIB, having each subscribed 19.127 percent of the paid-in capital. Much of the EIB lending operations are for long-term loans at fixed rates of interest, with maturities varying from seven to twenty years. The bank is operated on a purely nonprofit basis, al-though it does generate income internally to meet its operating expenses and to build up a general reserve, which is prescribed as being equal to 10 percent of its subscribed capital.

Another important feature of the EIB is its policy to lend to developing countries that are not members of the EEC. Although such lending has fluctuated in recent years, significant amounts have been channeled to developing countries by the bank over the past two decades.

Support to developing countries is complemented by the operations of the European Development Fund (EDF), which is funded out of allocations made from the budgetary resources of the EEC.

Overseas Economic Cooperation Fund

The OECF is a development bank, established and funded by the government of Japan, with the objective of providing financial assistance to developing countries. Although OECF assistance is provided to developing countries across the world, the main recipients have been Asian countries. Most of the assistance is on concessional terms. Borrowers are usually required to bid for the assistance in terms of the interest rates they are willing to pay. As trade surpluses in Japan continue to grow, the activities of the OECF are expanding, and it is expected to play a major role in financing development efforts in Third World countries in the future.

European Bank for Reconstruction and Development

The EBRD was established in London in 1991 to promote development in Eastern Europe. Its funds have been raised by 41 countries/ members. They include the 12 EEC members, 20 other developed countries and 7 east and central European countries. The bank has been capitalized at 10 billion ECUs (i.e. $12.2 bn) and it will lend to all east and central European countries to assist in the transformation from command economies to free market based democracies.

Summary

As nations become increasingly interdependent, the need has increased to coordinate international actions and policies. Since World War II, permanent international institutions, or supranational organizations, have been formed to serve the vital role of providing economic stability and continuity in the world economy. Some institutions have a global focus, while others are designed to meet more specific regional needs.

The General Agreement on Tariffs and Trade (GATT), charged with liberalizing international trade restrictions, offers the most-favored-nation clause to member organizations. Eight rounds of GATT meetings have been held, resulting in significant reductions in tariffs on industrial products. The most recent round, the Uruguay round, has been negotiating a comprehensive agreement on agricultural trade, trade in services, and intellectual property rights protection. The GATT rounds highlight the differences in perspective that exist between developed and developing countries, as negotiators attempt to establish a coordinated, nonprotectionist global trade policy that serves the common interests of all parties.

In contrast to the GATT, the United Nations Conference on Trade and Development (UNCTAD) is a forum for developing countries to communicate their international trade perspectives as a group to the industrialized countries. Although limited in impact, UNCTAD has served to improve the dialogue between the developing and developed countries.

Groups such as the EEC, ASEAN, and the Andean Pact have been established to coordinate regional trade policy, with the EEC and ASEAN being the most successful. The Andean Pact has made little progress in coordinating trade policy, partly because of the economic disruption of member countries caused by the oil crises of the 1970s and the debt crisis of the 1980s.

The IMF and the World Bank are international lending institutions, each performing specialized roles in the international monetary system. While the IMF focuses primarily on lending for structural adjustments because of balance of payments problems, the World Bank, comprised of four main agencies (IBRD, IDA, IFC, and MIGA), provides external financing to developing countries at affordable rates of interest. IBRD's main objective is to support social and economic progress in developing countries and offers five major types of loans—specific investment loans, sector operations loans, structural adjustment and program loans, technical assistance loans, and emergency reconstruction loans. The IDA provides long-term funds (loans with maturities of fifty years with ten-year grace periods) to the poorest member countries in order to promote long-term development projects. The IFC promotes the development of private enterprises by making equity investments and providing loans. Operating as a catalyst, the IFC exits from the enterprise as it develops and matures. MIGA promotes overseas direct investment in developing countries by providing guarantees against noncommercial risks.

Other development banks, such as the IADB, the ADB, and the AfDB, have been formed to provide regional assistance in the Western Hemisphere, Asia, and Africa, respectively. The European Investment Bank and the European Bank for Reconstruction Development promote investments in the EEC and in Eastern Europe, while the OECF, established and funded by Japan, is expected to play a major role in financing Third World developing-country projects.

Discussion Questions

1. Discuss the GATT and its role in international trade.
2. What is the most-favored-nation clause?
3. What trading organization represents the international trade objectives of developing countries? How do the concerns of developing countries differ from those of the industrialized, developed countries?

4. What is a regional trade group? What are the advantages provided by these groups?
5. Describe the structure at the World Bank and the services of its four main agencies.
6. What types of loans does the World Bank provide? How are these different from loans provided by the IMF?
7. What will be the role of the World Bank in the future?
8. Identify three regional financial institutions and outline their financial services.

Bibliography

1989. "Schools Brief: That Trade Winds May Blow Fair." *The Economist* (October): 21.

BEN-AMI, DANIEL. 1989. "Industrial Bank of Japan: A Growing International Role." *Banking* (October): 21.

DUNKEL, ARTHUR. 1988. "At 40 Years, the GATT Examines Its Future." *Europe* (January/February): 49.

GAUNT, JEREMY. 1989. "GATT's Influence for Freer Trade." *Nation's Business* (December): 54–56.

LEAVY, JAMES. 1988. "Andean Pact Policy." *International Financial Law Review* (March): 36–39.

LOCSIN, RAUL. 1990. "ADB Prepares for a Reincarnation." *Asian Finance (Hong Kong)* (April 15): 14.

MORRISON, ANN V., and R. LAYTON. 1986. "GATT . . . A Look Back as the Ministerial Meeting Approaches." *Business America* (June 23): 2–5.

PART THREE

ENVIRONMENTAL CONSTRAINTS IN INTERNATIONAL BUSINESS

CHAPTER 7

Analyzing National Economies

CHAPTER OBJECTIVES

This chapter will:

- Describe the importance of national economic analysis and identify the major indicators used in this analysis.
- Describe the sources of data and research tools that can be incorporated in national economic analysis.
- Discuss the results of analysis as inputs to developing an international marketing strategy.

The Purpose and Methodology of Country Analysis

Targeting a new country either as a market or as a manufacturing location must be preceded by a detailed analysis of the past, present, and future economic situation of the country. This analysis is extremely important for a multinational corporation, because the nature and state of development of an economy are crucial factors in determining the suitability of a country. Emerging trends also must be analyzed to develop an estimate of how the corporation should respond.

Country analysis takes many forms, depending upon the type of information sought—the objectives, the required depth and detail, the time frame being considered, and so on. In general, four broad categories serve as starting points:

1. Leading economic indicators at a particular point in time.
2. Trends in different economic indicators.
3. Trends in various specific sectors.
4. Analysis of specific areas or sectors of the economy.

The methodology for analysis of the economic prospects of a country and its potential varies according to the purpose of the analysis and the situation of the MNC. If the MNC has a local subsidiary in the country and the object of the analysis is to plan for further expansion or diversification into new industries, a two-tier analysis is carried out. At the first tier, the local subsidiary gathers and processes all the available local data and passes on the resulting information, along with its own assessment of the situation and prospects to the home office overseas. The home office, which is the second tier, then examines the information and the recommendation of the subsidiary and makes its own assessment, keeping in mind its global corporate and strategic goals, as well as the opportunities and constraints available worldwide. The management of the local subsidiary is often closely consulted while the home office views are being formulated, because some strategic considerations may not be put on paper for security and confidentiality reasons. The home office usually has an independent economic research division or economic analysts to generate independent information that is compared with that supplied by the subsidiary and used to support or contest the latter.

If a country is totally new to an MNC, the methodology is different. Some corporations hire consultants who are experts on a particular country to do a comprehensive economic analysis. Information is also gleaned from the available materials, such as government publications, country studies, commercial publications, and so on. Local consultants are sometimes employed by MNCs because of their deeper understanding of the local environment and better access to relevant information. Another option is the use of international consultants who utilize local associates. The latter provides vital contacts and sources of information, while the former integrate and analyze the data and prepare the formal report on the country being studied.

Preliminary Economic Indicators

Regardless of the methodology employed by the MNC in its economic analysis of the potential of a country, potential either as a location for industrial production or as a market for its products or services, there are certain general economic criteria which are almost invariably considered. A discussion of the more important of these follows.

Size of the Economy

The size of the economy is a basic measure of a country's potential as a market for the products of an MNC. It is generally measured by the Gross National Product (GNP), which is the sum total of goods and services produced in an economy, including the net transactions it has with the external sector. The GNP is an important measure, because it shows the total level of economic activity in a country. An alternative measure is the gross domestic product, which indicates the gross amount of goods and services produced within the country. The GDP does not take into account the contribution of the external (foreign) sector to the economy.

Income Levels

Income levels of the citizens of a country are a very important economic indicator for an MNC. To a significant extent, the prevailing income levels influence the nature of the potential a country offers as a market for different types of goods. The broadest measure of the income levels enjoyed by a population is per capita GNP. Per capita GNP is determined by dividing the total GNP by the total population.

Per capita GNP varies greatly from country to country. Industrialized countries that have a high gross national product and relatively small populations tend to have high per capita GNP. On the other hand, the less-developed countries have a low GNP but relatively larger populations, which results in a very low per capita GNP.

The World Bank has formulated three categories of countries based on their per capita GNP:

1. Low-income countries with a per capita GNP of $545 or less.
2. Middle-income developing countries with a per capita GNP between $545 to $5,999.
3. Developed countries with per capita income levels exceeding $5,999.

Countries with a low per capita GNP would not have a very large potential as a market for such goods as automobiles and air conditioners, which are considered necessities in developed countries, but are luxuries in developing countries. On the other hand, countries with a low per-capita income are likely to have lower labor costs and could prove attractive to MNCs as sites for manufacturing facilities.

Income Distribution

Although the per capita GNP statistics provide a broad indication of the income levels of different countries of the world, this information is by no means adequate for assessment of a country as a potential market. GNP per capita is actually a very broad measure that does not take into account the distribution of income within a country. Moreover, it provides no information on the size of market segments that would be potential targets for an MNC marketing effort. For example, a small country such as Kuwait has a very large GNP because of a high per capita GNP and a very small population, but it is not a very large market for automobiles because of the limited number of people who would purchase autos. On the other hand, a very low per capita GNP of a country might mask the significant purchasing power of a particular segment of its citizens.

In most developing countries there are sharp inequalities of wealth, and a large percentage of the total wealth of the country is concentrated in the hands of a fairly small percentage of the population. This segment has significant purchasing power and offers considerable potential for different types of goods and services marketed by MNCs. This situation is particularly true in countries where the low level per capita GNP occurs because of a very large low-income population. Thus, a country may have a large GNP, but its per capita GNP comes down because of the large population dividing factor.

In countries where there is substantial purchasing power in the hands of a small percentage of the population, it should be kept in mind that the absolute size of this wealthy segment is considerable because it is a percentage of a very large absolute number. Thus, if a country has a population of 400 million and only 5 percent of its citizens are

wealthy enough to qualify as a potential market segment for an MNC, the total market would still be 20 million people, which is the size of the entire population of some industrialized countries.

The degree of income distribution also provides other important clues to the economy in general and different market segments within it in particular. A more even income distribution would generally be found in the developed or industrialized countries, which would offer large potential for standardized mass consumption products. The size of the very high-income group in the total population would reveal the potential of the country as a market for luxury goods, such as designer clothes and accessories, luxury automobiles, and so on.

Less-developed countries would show a very large percentage of very low-income groups that usually would not offer an immediate market for most products promoted by MNCs. The size of the wealth segments, on the other hand, would be a factor in determining the market size.

Another important indicator of market potential is the size of the middle-income groups within the overall income distribution. In the developed countries, the middle-income groups are usually the largest proportion of the population, which implies the existence of big markets for a wide range of mass-produced consumer products. The middle class is relatively small in most less-developed economies, which limits their potential as a market for a wide variety of consumer goods.

Trends and income distributions tend to move relatively slowly because they reflect basic socioeconomic structures and patterns that are fairly resistant to change. In less-developed countries, however, these patterns have been changing at a relatively rapid pace over the past four or five decades. The important trend has been the emergence of a large middle class with substantial purchasing power and a positive attitude toward utilizing that power for the purchase of consumer goods.

Personal Consumption

In addition to the income distribution patterns prevalent in a country, the prevailing consumption patterns influence its potential as a market. While income distribution statistics provide information on how and to whom income accrues, data on personal consumption indicates how this income is spent on goods and services. Personal consumption data indicates the buying habits of the citizens of a particular country—what they buy, in what quantities, in which parts of a country, and so on. This information is vital for an MNC because it indicates patterns of consumer behavior and thus sets parameters for marketing efforts. Thus, a country where the consumers spend a large proportion of their income on food and shelter offers no potential for luxury goods, such as VCRs. On the other hand, it may provide markets for inexpensive goods that meet the basic necessities of life. Although characterized by low consumption levels, a country may have substantial market segments comprised of persons with considerable discretionary income. Many MNCs develop market strategies on the basis of tapping consumption patterns. Thus, the pattern of consumption gives important clues to an MNC on the possibilities for marketing different types of goods in a particular country.

Growth and Stability Patterns

The size of the economy, income levels and distribution, and personal consumption are static indicators, in as much as they represent the position of a country at a particular point of time. An MNC contemplating long-term involvement in a country either as an exporter to that country or as a direct investor must also concern itself with the prior, current, and projected economic trends of a country.

The growth rate of a country's economy, for example, must be watched carefully. Past growth trends show how the economy has been moving and the rate at which it is contracting or expanding. Projected growth rates indicate how it may do in the future. The growth trends generally have a direct relation to the market size of different product and services markets in a country. A faster growth rate would indicate more rapid industrial development.

Countries that seek rapid rates of growth seek to achieve this largely through an increase in the level of their industrialization and modernization of existing industries by the introduction of modern technologies and new industries. Such countries are likely to welcome MNCs as direct investors in production facilities. Moreover, countries that have achieved a rapid growth rate over the past few years are usually the ones who have opened up their economies to external technologies, have pushed their export efforts, and have increased competitiveness and efficiency of their domestic economies. Such countries are likely to prove to be potential winners as markets for MNCs because they would have increased levels of income.

Rapidly growing economies are also characterized by the development of a professional middle class, which evens out the distribution of income relative to the past and provides a market base for MNC consumer products.

Growing economies also offer enhanced markets for capital goods, technology, and related services. MNCs, therefore, closely monitor future growth trends to identify potential countries for export marketing and direct investment activities. The absolute growth rate, as well as the growth rate per capita, are matched in this context. The absolute growth rate would indicate the overall level of economic activity and give the broadest indication of the enhancement to the market potential of a country. Growth rate per capita would indicate achievement not only on the economic front, but also, indirectly, on the population front. If the growth per capita is rapid, the country can be considered to have surmounted one of the most important economic problems that afflict most developing countries—overpopulation.

Actually, per capita GNP is also an important indicator because of its future implications. A higher per capita GNP would imply an increased availability of resources to invest that could be further deployed for accelerating economic growth and improving the living standards of the population, which would represent a real change in the economic profile of the country as a market for goods and services and as a location of overseas production. If the growth rate is matched or exceeded by the population growth, the economic benefits of progress would be lost.

Population

The population of a country represents an important economic statistic. It is an important factor in influencing the size of market potential for a large number of goods and services, especially goods for personal consumption.

Population density (the number of persons living per square mile) is a particularly relevant factor. A high population density could have both negative and positive implications. On the one hand, it may imply overcrowding, overpopulation, and pressure on the resource base of a country. On the other hand, it may also imply reduced transportation costs in marketing products, availability of large numbers of consumers, and an easily accessible pool of labor.

Geographical distribution of the population is also important. Areas of high population concentration within a country generally offer wider market potential and greater possibilities of servicing the labor requirements for an overseas manufacturing facility.

The educational level of the population is also extremely important. Consumption patterns, living standards, and so on vary considerably with the levels of literacy. A country with a high level of literacy is likely to offer greater potential for an MNC's products, because individuals are likely to have a broader outlook on the types of products they consume and would, in general, be willing to accept new products and services that might be offered by the MNC. For some types of products (books and other intellectual media, software, and so on), literacy levels are critical factors. Moreover, they also determine what sort of advertising strategy should be pursued to promote products locally. Literacy levels also indicate the potential of finding skilled labor and local managers for the operations of a company.

In general, literacy levels have a direct correlation with the level of per capita income. While developed countries have high literacy levels ranging from 95 percent to 100 percent, less-developed countries have levels that range from 5 percent to 40 percent.

The rate of population growth is another trend worth watching. A growing population indicates an expanding market in countries where the density of population is low and per capita incomes are rising. A high population rate in countries already overpopulated indicates growing economic difficulties that could be manifested in severe shortages of available resources, heavy pressures on the infrastructure and services system of a country, fiscal difficulties for the government, shortages of capital for investments, increasing levels of people living in poverty, and ever-increasing prices.

The age structure of a population should also be considered. In developed countries, larger proportions of the population tend to be over the age of eighteen, and there are a sizable number of people in the over-sixty age group. Less-developed countries, however, are characterized by fairly young populations, where persons below eighteen are the dominant segment. Relatively young populations imply possibilities for higher population growth over the next few years, particularly in countries where birth control is not practiced widely. Moreover, such countries are also characterized by high dependency burdens, where the income-earning members of the population have to support a large number of nonearning members on a per capita basis. Dependency burdens have important economic implications, in as much as they affect the amount of discretionary income a person may or may not have after taking care of the essential needs of dependents and himself. Most countries with high dependency burdens have lower levels of discretionary income, which limits their potential as markets for products to be promoted by the MNCs.

Sector Analysis

It is also important to analyze different sectors of the country's economy, to identify the particular areas that could offer business opportunities. The state of development of a particular sector of the economy would provide clues to its product needs and the possibilities of providing necessary imports and support for the establishment of a manufacturing operation by an overseas corporation. For example, an MNC looking to set up an automobile plant in a developing country would have to assess the engineering sector in general and the automotive industry in particular, to determine the degree and availability of local support by way of ancillary and spare parts manufactures, skilled labor, and locally trained production personnel.

On a broader level, sector analysis suggests the state of the overall economic development of a country. From a macroeconomic standpoint, economic activity is divided into three broad categories—the primary, secondary, and tertiary sectors.

The primary sector incorporates traditional economic activities, such as agriculture. The secondary sector comprises primarily manufacturing and industrial activity. The tertiary sector refers to services and related industries.

Industrialized and developed countries are characterized by a high proportion of their economic activity in the secondary and tertiary sectors. For example, in 1980 agriculture contributed only 2 percent of the GNP of the United States and Great Britain, and only 5 percent of Switzerland, Canada, and Sweden. On the other hand, the contribution of agriculture to the GNP of developing countries was extremely high, for example, 93 percent for Nepal, 82 percent for Upper Volta, and 80 percent for Malawi. A high concentration of economic activity in agriculture implies that the country is overdependent on one type of economic activity, has little industrial development, and is likely to have low levels of per capita income, relatively high rates of unemployment, and an unsteady economic performance. For an MNC such data suggests that these countries do not offer good potential for expensive products, but may prove reasonably good locations for setting up processing plants for raw materials and agricultural produce, because costs of material inputs and labor would be quite low. On the other hand, they

may lack the infrastructural facilities required for large-scale industrial plants.

A highly developed country would have its economy dominated by the industrial and services sector. For an MNC this economy would provide opportunities to market a wide range of industrial products and allow the establishment of almost any type of manufacturing operation. At the same time, such economies are likely to be characterized by strong competition both from domestic and international corporations.

Inflationary Trends

Local inflationary trends must also be closely watched. Inflation is the increase in prices over time measured against a certain bench mark, usually known as the base year. Different indices, consisting of different commodities at different market levels, are constructed to gauge the overall degree of price increases in a country. High inflation can have severe economic consequences. Generally, income levels do not keep pace with inflation, which reduces the purchasing power of consumers and erodes their potential as a market segment, especially for products that have relatively high income elasticities, such as nonessential goods and services. High inflation would also have severe implications for local manufacturing operations, because prices of inputs would increase and pressures would rise to increase wage levels.

Increased inflation in a particular overseas manufacturing location would also have serious effects on the competitiveness of the products produced in that location if they were to be exported to overseas markets. Moreover, in real terms, local inflation would devalue the local currency against the home currency of an MNC (if the local rate of inflation exceeds that prevailing in the home country of the MNC). As a result, the value of the profits to be repatriated to the home country would go down in home currency terms. High inflation in overseas locations also could prompt restrictive measures by the government, which could result in hampered operations of the MNC or erosion of their profitability.

In recent years, especially the 1980s, many countries have experienced hyperinflation—a situation where inflation occurs in hundreds of percent or even thousands of percent per year, which has been true in a number of Latin American countries, such as Brazil, Argentina, and Bolivia. In such situations, MNCs have to be extremely cautious in initiating new ventures and managing existing ones in order to avoid losing their profits.

External Financial Position: Extent of Debt

The external financial sector of a country is another extremely important variable that has to be considered very carefully by MNCs while evaluating the country as a site for potential investment or marketing efforts.

The primary indicator of the strength of a country's external sector is its balance of payments position. The balance of payments (BOP) is an annual record of all the external transactions of a country. A strong BOP position implies that a country can meet its external obligations. Such countries are ideally suited for investment by MNCs. They are not likely to have substantial import controls, because they are in a position to pay for imports with their current earnings of foreign exchange. A strong BOP position is also likely to foster a lenient policy toward foreign direct investment, because the country is able to generate the necessary foreign currency resources to permit conversion of local currencies into foreign currencies for repatriation of MNC profits.

A country facing BOP difficulties, in contrast, is likely to impose restrictions on imports in order to conserve foreign exchange resources. In such countries the changes of greater restrictions on repatriation of profits by MNCs are also high. As a result, an MNC may find it more difficult to do business.

Analysis of current and future trends is perhaps more important in this area than any other, as the balance of payments scenario changes quite rapidly. All too often a country that had an excellent BOP position and was encouraging foreign investment and imports had its external position deteriorate within a few years to such an extent that it was compelled to clamp down on imports and restrict foreign investment. Obviously, plans of many MNCs involved in such countries would be completely upset by such a policy reversal. It is, therefore, extremely important that an MNC keep an ongoing watch on the emerging trends in the BOP and make timely adjustments if the MNC foresees major changes in this area.

The volatility of the balance of payments of a country is generally higher if the composition of its exports is not diversified. It is imperative that the composition of exports of the potential investee country be analyzed closely. Countries that depend upon the exports of one commodity are generally prone to greater instability in their export revenues, because a decline in the prices and demand for that commodity in the international markets could jeopardize the whole BOP. This situation occurred in oil-exporting countries, such as Mexico and Venezuela, when oil prices dropped steeply in the early 1980s.

Exchange Rate Levels and Policies

Exchange rate trends are another vital consideration for MNCs contemplating overseas direct investment. An appreciation of the exchange rates in the potential country would increase the home currency value of the revenues generated in that country by the MNC. On the other hand, a depreciation of the currency of the investee country would have the opposite effect. The direction of the future movements of exchange rates has to be carefully monitored by the MNC, but, forecasting exchange rates is an extremely difficult proposition because there are a large number of factors that are involved. For many countries, however, an estimate of the future trends can be attempted on the basis of such economic fundamentals as balance of payments prospects, import and export trends, levels of overseas borrowings, debt service burden, local trends, and trends in inflation.

In many countries, especially LDCs, exchange rates are controlled and administered by authorities under various types of official arrangements. While some countries allow free conversion of their currency to other international currencies, others have their rates determined on the basis of a currency basket (see Chapter 5). Many countries also have dual or multiple exchange rates that are prescribed according to the type of transaction. Some countries also have different rates for repatriating profits out of the country. MNCs must be very careful in evaluating the exchange rate arrangements and regulations of the potential investee country and assess how they are likely to impact the translation of the revenues from the local currency to their home currency.

Many countries also follow preset exchange rate policies that are aimed to bring the rate, by administrative actions, to the levels desired by the monetary authorities. On other occasions, the policy could maintain the exchange rates within a certain band-width. Policies to attain exchange rate objectives may or may not be announced. When they are not announced, they must be estimated and appropriate action taken. The MNC must seek the assistance of its own or external experts to gauge the policy direction from the prevailing trends over a certain time period.

Banking and Financial Markets

Finance is a crucial resource to any business operation, and MNCs must carefully evaluate the banking and financial market structure of the target country. The banking sector must be well-developed and able to provide the needed working capital and term financing for meeting the operational requirements within the investee country. Moreover, the financial market structure must provide opportunities for raising funds to meet the cost of operations. The MNC must also evaluate the costs of funds in local markets and assess whether it would be cheaper to raise funds locally or to bring them in from abroad. The host country, however, may have regulations that either prohibit, restrict, or require the sourcing of funds from abroad or the local market.

Comparison of Similar Economies

Typically, an MNC has a global perspective and will analyze several countries as potential sites of direct investment or export marketing. Choosing the best option involves many considerations including a comparison of the economic structure and performance of different countries. There are several difficulties, however, in comparing economic data across different countries. For one, each country publishes data in its own currency, which must be translated into a standard international currency to permit any sort of comparison, and straight translation into an international currency may not yield accurate figures. Exchange rates of one country could be officially fixed at a value much higher than the actual market rate, which could artificially inflate certain crucial country data and provide misleading information.

Moreover, data standards vary greatly across countries in breadth and coverage. Some countries, especially the industrialized ones, have sophisticated data collection and processing systems at their disposal, while many developing countries may not be able to gather even the basic data. The data also vary considerably in their timing. At a particular point in time, data for the same period may not be available for a set of countries to be compared. The reliability of data is also not always certain. Political leaders in certain countries sometimes manipulate official data to present a better picture of the economy than is actually the case, in order to preserve their own support at home and abroad. Some data often are not comparable at all. If the basis of the computation of personal income or the definition of the level of incomes differ across two countries, for example, then the numbers for these two indicators cannot be compared accurately. Because the computational basis does differ, any comparative analysis has to make the necessary adjustments in the nominal figures published by the sources of each country.

Tax Systems

A very important constituent of the analysis is the prevailing tax system. Taxation levels have a crucial effect on MNC operations, because high tax rates can take a substantial proportion of MNC earnings in overseas locations. Complicated and cumbersome tax procedures and systems also can make it extremely difficult for an MNC to organize and manage its international accounting system.

Tax systems and tax rates vary considerably across the world. Some countries have taxes on production levels, which are based on the quantity of goods produced by the company, and such taxes are known as excise duties and are collected at the production site of goods. In other countries industries are taxed by the system of value addition.

Countries often indicate their attitudes toward foreign investment and economic activity by the design of tax provisions that concern foreign business entities. Some countries eager to attract foreign investments have liberal tax requirements and often provide incentives for foreign investors that lower their tax rates below domestic industries, but many other countries tax overseas business entities at differential rates that are higher than those levied on domestic business entities. Additional taxes often are levied in some countries on the repatriation of profits by overseas investors.

The tax consideration, therefore, weighs quite heavily in any economic analysis by an MNC on a targeted country. Some countries may have a double taxation avoidance treaty with the home country of an MNC, which is a treaty whereby the revenues of an MNC would not be taxed in the overseas location in return for the same tax treatment for the overseas country's companies in the home country of the MNC. Such countries would obviously provide the best tax environment for the operations of an MNC.

Fiscal and Monetary Policies Situations

The fiscal and monetary situation of any country is a key indicator of its economic health and the direction of future economic trends. The fiscal situation generally refers to the position of the finances of a government, whether it is able to match its expenditure with the revenues it generates, how those revenues are generated, and the effects of the fiscal policy on the general economic situation of the country. The monetary situation, on the other hand, refers to the picture of the economy as seen from the perspective of the money supply and other monetary aggregates and their influence on the general economic situation.

There is considerable debate on what constitutes a good local situation and what is an appropriate fiscal policy. Generally, the debate revolves around the size of the budget deficit or surplus and how a deficit is financed. It can be safely argued, however, that a stable fiscal policy and situation would imply a scenario where the government is able to incur enough expenditures to maintain a desirable rate of growth in the economy without building up too much public debt or by fueling inflationary expectations. Countries with large budget deficits that are financed by the creation of more money tend to be inflationary and could disrupt the real rate of economic growth. A country with large fiscal deficits financed by government borrowings could be a dangerous place to invest. The size of the deficit and the level of the government borrowing has to be examined in the context of the total size of the GNP. A large absolute deficit may be disastrous for one country, but may be manageable for another.

Any analysis has to bear in mind the current and indicative future effects of the continued deficits of a country. The economies of some countries may already be stretched, and a slight increase in the fiscal deficit may trigger immediate inflationary trends. On the other hand, there could be larger economies where deficits would not make such a large, immediate difference. Large deficits may also signal higher taxes, lower subsidies, and lower government expenditures, which could slow down the economy, depress prices, and possibly shrink the market for the MNC. Not only is it important for an MNC to watch the level of the fiscal deficit, but it is also important to consider how the government has been handling the situation and what economic consequences have emerged out of the effort.

The monetary situation is reflected to a large extent in the level of different measures of money supply in relation to the total size of the economy. An excessive money supply in theory, and to some economists in practice, pushes up prices, as too much money chases too few goods. Inflation, therefore, is often attributed to an excess money supply.

Central banks generally take this view and often try to control the levels of inflation in a country by adjusting the level of money supply through a series of monetary measures, some of which have a direct bearing on the profitability of an MNC. For example, if a central bank fears that there is excess liquidity in the economy, it may decide to raise the level of interest rates in the banking system, making it more expensive to borrow money from banks and thus eliminating the incentive for loans. Central banks in some countries even place restrictions on the volume and purposes for which credit can be extended by banks to their customers. In a situation where the authorities choose to follow a tight monetary policy, the MNC may find itself squeezed for liquidity to finance its operations. Interest rate hikes also tend to slow down economic activity, which could adversely affect export sales or those of local manufacturers being contemplated by an MNC.

Fiscal and monetary policies also interact in a number of ways with the external payments situation and the exchange rates. Trends in fiscal and monetary policies also provide clues, although no definitive answers, to the future movements of exchange rates between countries. Thus, the fiscal and monetary situations and the policy stances taken in this context by the authorities must also be carefully analyzed by an MNC.

Economic Planning: Ideology and Practices

In many countries the economy is expected to be directed by the government through a central planning authority, which formulates broad plans for the entire economy over the medium to long term. Typically, the length of an economic plan is five years. In most countries where economic planning is used, the entire economic development is strongly influenced by what is decided by the planners. For example, plans dictate which areas of industry, agriculture, or services will be emphasized or what will be the level of government expenditures on each of these sectors. Some plans even spell out specific projects in the public or government sectors that will begin during a particular plan period.

The development expenditures to be incurred are laid out for in different areas or provinces of a country. Thus, the plans provide a blueprint of the overall economy. Although in several instances plans are not adhered to fully, there is no doubt that they provide excellent insights into the direction an economy is likely to take, the activities that are likely to be encouraged, and what the economic priorities are of the host government.

The MNC considering investment in a planned economy has to place some importance on the plan in order to be able to position itself at the best strategic point, where it maximizes its own objectives and fits in best with the economic priorities of the host country. Thus, if a country is targeting to double the production of steel in a particular plan period, and it does not have the capability or the know how to do so on its own, it will present an excellent opportunity for MNCs who are in the business of setting up steel plants or other activities that are spinoffs of such projects.

Competition

The element of competition is ever-present in most countries, and if they are open to one multinational, they are open to others. The strengths of the competition; their marketing, production, and management strategies; their shares of the market; and the history of their emergence in the local markets must be analyzed, both to draw lessons and prepare a competitive strategy to enter and penetrate the overseas market. Competition can also arise from local manufacturers as well as state-owned entities. In fact, local competitors often have considerable influence with the host governments and are able to carve out privileges for themselves to secure their own market position. This is particularly true where the local competition happen to be government-owned enterprises.

Market Demand Forecasting

Purposes

Market demand forecasting is usually a secondary stage in the analysis of a country as a potential market and is attempted after the overall macroeconomic environment and business climate is found conducive to a marketing effort. The basic objective is to obtain reliable, current information to fashion a successful marketing program. This data can also be used to weigh the costs of exporting products to foreign countries against the prospective benefits of manufacturing these goods in those markets.

The methodology in gathering data is to first estimate the demand for potential sales of a type of product it wants to sell in the country in its entirety, then make an estimate of its potential share of that market. Through such a process, the firm will be better able to predict the costs, sales, and profits associated with marketing the product in the new area.

Gathering and processing data is done in several stages. At the first level, there can be causal surveys of existing information regarding market size and historic demand within an individual country market. Next, the company might expand its research to in-depth study, in order to identify specific demand, supply, and consumer character-

istics within the market. Third, the company must evaluate this data, in order to develop the most appropriate match of its resources within the network of existing opportunities. It can also use this information in its ongoing operations to change strategies in existing markets to develop, design, package, and promote products in future markets, and to control operations by giving the company a measure of potential market share.

Data Collection and Sources

The market researcher will first attempt to gather information or data from existing published sources, which is the least expensive method of gathering demand data. Sources of such information are numerous. In the United States, the Department of Commerce and the International Trade Administration provide a great deal of information regarding markets in other countries. The Department of Commerce also provides a series of marketing publications. One of these, *Foreign Economic Trends and Their Implications for the U.S.*, is prepared by U.S. embassies abroad and identifies key economic indicators within each country, describes the country's current economic situation, including inflation, consumption, investment trends, and debt levels. It also discusses attitudes in each country toward U.S. investments and the implications these trends and attitudes have for U.S. investors.

Another series is *Overseas Business Reports*, which provides information on marketing in individual countries. These pamphlets provide marketers with key information on all aspects of the marketing environment within a country, such as population, consumer and demographic trends, and information on the logistics of doing business in the country, such as specific regulations or procedures for marketing within its borders.

Organizations such as the World Bank, the U.S. Export-Import Bank, and the International Monetary Fund provide other sources of data. The Organization for Economic Cooperation and Development (OECD) publishes information on a full range of economic trends, providing data on production and productivity by industry classification, the structure and composition of the labor force, market consumption patterns, economic divisions within the country according to industrial sectors, relative profit shares and price structures in industries, costs of wages and labor, and financial indicators, inflation, and interest rates. In addition, the OECD provides a full range of information regarding each country's level and composition of foreign trade and official levels of reserves. The range and depth of these statistics are impressive, and they provide a great deal of valuable information for the market analyst. They are limited, however, to the OECD countries, which generally have highly developed statistical bases. Additional information regarding market behavior can be obtained from international trade associations, business groups, service organizations, chambers of commerce of individual countries, foreign groups, and the governments of other countries.

Many governments publish such data in annual statistical yearbooks, and some private firms make a business of providing such information services to companies or individuals requesting information about specific countries. These companies provide information on a large number of indicators, such as population, GNP, export composition, basic goods and energy production, balance of payments information, media availability and usage, plus information on history, problems, and the nuts and bolts of doing business in these countries.

Other firms develop and publish indices of market potential by identifying possible markets in three forms—according to size as a percentage of world consumption, according to intensity or degree to which consumers hold purchasing power, and according to historic growth patterns with a concentration on the past five years to identify past and potential trends. The objective is for the marketer to be able to see recent patterns in growth and make predictions about future growth areas by correlating the market characteristics and factors with detailed data on consumer and buying behavior. Thus, the next level of involvement in

marketing research is a detailed country investigation of existing data gathered by others.

Primary Research

A firm may decide to conduct its own primary research either through its own resources or through the services of an agent, consultant, or specialty firm. While collecting detailed data on consumer demand levels is arduous, this process is even more difficult in overseas markets for a number of reasons.

First, the physical distance between countries makes it difficult to conduct research on site. Second, collecting takes more time abroad than it does at home, thus creating time lags and reducing the currency of the information.

Gathering information from consumers in foreign locales is also fraught with problems based on cultural differences. For example, U.S. consumers think nothing of responding to surveys regarding buying behavior, habits, preferences, and use of goods. There may be cultural barriers in other countries to participating in such personal question-and-answer sessions, especially with interviewers of a different sex.

In addition, barriers frequently arise in the form of language and comprehension problems, where translations are either inaccurate or inappropriate or literacy levels are low. Similarly, researchers may encounter difficulty in developing a sample that is significantly representative of the population. For example, in many less-developed countries, the telephone is not as ubiquitous as it is in industrialized countries; fewer families own phones, and telephone books, when published, are often inaccurate. For this reason, researchers cannot use random samples gleaned from phone directories, as they do in the United States.

Consequently, when researchers evaluate primary data, they must be sure to regard those results with a healthy amount of skepticism and within a cultural framework or perspective similar to the country. They must also have an open mind in analyzing the results of such research and consider all possible explanations for buyer behavior.

Areas of Research

In order to evaluate total market potential, international marketers use a number of forecasting methods, which fall into four categories, depending on their types and treatment of data. Some methods analyze existing consumption patterns within the country under scrutiny; others look at historical market data regarding past market activities; others use data from other or comparable countries; and some attempt to find correlations between a number of descriptive factors and market demand.

All of these methods suffer from some basic shortcomings in many potential market areas, generally the less-industrialized countries of the world. Difficulties arise because:

- Sales data are often sparse, therefore the forecaster has no actual data upon which to base his projections of potential market share and must use other arbitrary determinations of demand, such as apparent consumption, which is a measure of local production plus imports adjusted for exports and domestic inventory variations.
- Data may be available for some but not all variables being used in market demand analysis models, so the researcher may not have information on enough variables to construct or use a viable computer model.
- Data availability may vary among countries, that is, some or all data may not be available for each country under consideration.
- Existing data may be out of date.

Given these caveats, marketers still find that the tools they have developed to estimate market demand are effective in assisting firms in the decision-making process.

Trade Activities

Market analysts look at existing patterns of consumption of goods and services in order to get a feel for prospective sales of their goods within that market, as well as its basic need levels. Some of this information can be gleaned from a look at the composition of the home country's exports to the target market. In the United States, for example, information regarding estimated U.S. market shares in foreign markets according to product types is published by the Department of Commerce. Alternately, or in addition to looking at export competition within its own sphere, the firm also examines the total composition of imports for the foreign market from all world competitors. This international information, organized according to standard industrial product codes, is available from supranational organizations, such as the United Nations or the OECD.

These kinds of import-export analyses are not, however, definitive, because they present a static historical perspective. The company has no assurance that the country:

- will continue to import the same levels or types of goods.
- will not mount efforts to increase its own local or nationalized production and displace imports or foreign subsidiary production.
- will not have political, economic, social, or legal problems in its future that lead to the imposition of trade barriers or limits on imports.

Input-Output Tables

Another method of looking at current consumption of goods and products in foreign markets is through the construction of input-output tables, which systematically organize usage flows of input and output goods in countries. These complex tables are constructed so that all industrial sectors are displayed along the vertical and horizontal axes. In these tables output or production for one industry becomes input or demand for another. For example, in the manufacturing of cars or trucks, the vehicles are outputs for the automobile manufacturer, but require inputs from such basic sectors as steel or aluminum. Similarly, construction output of houses, roads, and buildings require inputs of concrete, lumber, hardware, and other basic building materials. These tables show the relationship between volumes of goods sold among sectors and their interdependence or their independence from each other. If this information is analyzed in light of expectations regarding future economic trends in the nation, the forecaster can make some judgments regarding potential changes in demand for goods in that country. Input-output tables are particularly helpful if the analyst predicts a period of economic growth for the nation, in which case the analyst can attempt to predict in which sectors that growth will translate into market demand.

Most developed, industrial countries publish input-output tables as a matter of course. Increasing numbers of developing countries are publishing such tables, as an aid to promoting growth in their economies through accurate prediction of demand in appropriate sectors. While they are useful tools, these tables suffer from several limitations. One problem has to do with the reliability, breadth, and comparability of data among countries. Not every country has a complete and accurate set of data about production inputs and outputs. Another problem is that of dated information.

Input-output tables also suffer from their assumption of fixed relationships between two industries. Thus, they give a static picture of interactions between industries and use fixed coefficients to account for increases in demand for inputs from increases in production. They also do not take into account increases in production efficiencies, the use of new production processes, or other possible dynamics, such as new technological developments.

Historical Trends

Another basic method of examining and predicting market trends in a potential market is based on an analysis of past activity within the country. It is crucial in methods based on past usage that the data used are complete, broad, and reliable. The data set should include accurate figures from local production and inventory levels and for the country's imports and exports. Thus, an analyst can determine the country's apparent consumption or market demand, which is figured from lo-

cal production plus imports, total goods adjusted for exports, and fluctuations in inventory levels.

The analyst then determines the historical trends revealed by this information and extrapolates through a time series analysis to determine future trends. The crucial assumption made in this analysis is that past trends will continue to be in effect in the future and that consumer behavior, values, and buying activity will continue as it has in the past. This method is sometimes used in conjunction with a comparison of historical trends experienced by other, comparable nations in tandem with growth predictions for the target market country's GNP or levels of production.

Country Comparisons: Analysis by Analogy

The use of data from another country to predict market demand patterns for another country is referred to as analysis by analogy. This process makes a crucial assumption that products in new markets move along a universal path according to the level of development of a country. Using this method, comparable countries are identified as those that are reasonably similar in market, economic, political, and developmental structures and stages. The market researcher then looks at the consumption patterns for the product in relation to changes in the growth of the country. For example, the researcher might plot consumption with changes in personal income and increasing development in one country and then ascribe this predicted relationship to the fortunes of another country and make predictions about product use based on expectations of increases in personal income.

Analysis by analogy must also be used with caution. The use of blind, absolute analogy is dangerous because no two countries are exactly similar. They differ according to nonquantifiable but significant factors, such as cultural traditions, values, and tastes. They may also differ in levels of technology, the path their developmental growth takes, and the pricing of goods. Another key problem is the assumption that demand relates to a specific variable, such as personal income or aggregate GNP within a nation. In fact, other variables, such as pricing, may have as much or even more of an effect on market demand for the product. This method also explains a static, not dynamic relationship between demand behavior and the economic situation and cannot account for changes to be expected in the countries under comparison.

Regression Analysis

To deal with the need to account for the potential effects of a number of variables upon market demand, some analysts use a statistical technique called regression analysis to identify significant relationships between market demand and other variables, such as economic or population indicators. This method uses data collected from several countries on a historical basis for market demand levels and one or several other economic indicators, such as growth or price levels. One of the most widely used indicators is that of economic growth as calculated by gross national product (GNP). In regression analysis the relationship between the variables is characterized as a formula, $Y = a + bx$, where Y represents total market potential, a is equal to actual use, and bx is a function of consumer use of the product times the selected indicator. For example, statisticians may find a correlation between increases in GNP or country wealth (b) and purchases (a) of luxury or nonnecessities, such as appliances, designer clothing, automobiles, or leisure items.

While this linear method is helpful and can examine the relationship of several variables at once through expansion of the formula (for example, $Y = a + bx1 + bx2 \ldots zxn$), it is not also without its limitations. For example, while it uses specific indicators as variables, these do not account for consumer differences in tastes or for product changes. This is also a situation that uses static information to provide a snapshot of the existing situation. The regression model also does not account for the achievement of a saturation level where demand increases to a point, then levels out.

Income Elasticity

The most common and most frequently used variable affecting market demand is (not surprisingly) personal income levels. Thus, the forecasting method that uses income elasticities looks at the relationship between the two crucial variables of demand for a specific product and individual income levels. It analyzes the relationship between changes in the levels of both demand and income, which is accomplished by dividing the percentage change in product demand by the percentage change in income. If there is an increase or decrease in demand, the demand is considered to be elastic, and the ratio of the two is equal to or greater than one.

If a change in income yields less than an equal change in demand for a product, it is said to be inelastic and the value of the ratio is less than one. Frequently, elasticities follow the dictates of common sense. Food, for example, is a basic necessity and therefore demand is generally inelastic for food products, that is, regardless of changes in income, consumers maintain an even level of demand for food products. On the other hand, items that are considered luxuries are often highly elastic, and a correlation would be found between increases in demand for items such as televisions or radios and increases in income levels.

For example, sales of a luxury item such as a compact disc player is likely to be highly elastic, perhaps reaching 2.5. Such an elasticity would mean that for every unit of increase in average individual income, demand for CD players would rise two and one-half times. This demand elasticity will eventually level out, however, once a certain income level is reached and the market for CD players becomes saturated.

In order for a market researcher to use income elasticity analysis in forecasting foreign market demand, it is necessary that the researcher be able to accurately determine current demand levels for a given product in a country and develop reasonable expectations of forecasts of average per capita income changes in that country. Then, using elasticities found for the same items in similar countries, the researcher can make an estimate of foreign demand as a function of the foreign increase in income plus the elasticity for the product as seen previously. Thus, an expectation of a foreign increase in income of one quarter (.25) multiplied times a high elasticity given for a product (such as 2), will yield an expectation of an increase in demand of .5 or 50 percent in the foreign market.

Income elasticities, as with other market estimation procedures, raise warnings. Again, the method holds the relationship out as being static; elasticity is represented as a constant value and does not allow for the dynamics of the market.

The methodology also does not account for the importance of prices in the demand equation, even though they can have a direct effect upon demand, in that lowered prices often lead to increased demand or higher prices to lowered demand because of shifts of consumer purchases to lower-priced substitutes. The formula also does not account for differences in individual tastes for products and the proportion of demand generated by these preferences. Those using income elasticity analysis should keep in mind that high elasticity does not equal high-demand volumes. It merely signifies the relationship between income and demand for goods. Generally speaking, goods with high elasticities would be more likely to be low-volume, high-priced goods where high-sales-volume products are often those that are income inelastic.

Methods of Estimating Market Size and Share

Once the market researcher develops suitable market data, there are a number of methods available to estimate market size and probable share of that market. Three of these methods are the market buildup, chain ratio, and analogy methods.

Market Buildup

In the market buildup method, the marketing firm gathers data from a number of small separate segments within the overall market and estimates their potential market sales in each segment. These estimates are added to develop an aggregate market total. In evaluating market potential, the marketer must take into consideration differences between segments in consumer tastes, demographics, and competition and must be careful not to assume that similar market segment sizes provide similar market opportunities.

Chain Ratios

The chain ratio method is used for consumer products. It consists of a string of estimates regarding target market size and attributes. It is rough and varies according to the accuracy of the assumptions, data, and variables used. Still, if a firm knows its markets well and has high-quality data, this method can be useful in predicting sales levels.

As an example, assume that a U.S. brewing company, such as Rolling Rock, decides to market its beer, brewed in glass-lined tanks in Latrobe, Pennsylvania, to a particular target market in Canada. Rolling Rock would use the chain ratio method of estimating sales as follows. First, it would multiply the number of people in the target market times the estimated percentage of people who drink beer. This number would then be multiplied by the number of beer drinkers who drink imported beer times the estimated number of bottles of beer drunk per week by the average Canadian beer drinker. This number, multiplied by fifty-two weeks per year, divided by twenty-four bottles per case to yield a case volume times the price per case of beer yields a total dollar volume of imported beer sales in the Canadian target market. In this way, Rolling Rock would have an estimate of the total imported beer market in Canada and the challenge that faces it in penetrating that market.

Analogy with Known Data

Another method is used to estimate market size and share and works through analogy with known data from existing markets. The analogy method relates hard data about market size and penetration in one country to unknown information in another. Assume, for example, that Rolling Rock believes that its market share in the United States would correlate to possible market share in Canada according to the variable of total population. (It could also use another market indicator, such as per capita income.) Given these assumptions: If MUS = market demand in the United States, MC = Market demand in Canada, VUS = population of the United States, and VC = population of Canada, the formula that would yield an estimate of Rolling Rock's market share in Canada would be:

If:
$$\frac{MUS}{VUS} = \frac{MC}{VC}$$
Then:
$$MC = \frac{MUSVC}{VUS}$$

If the countries are dissimilar but the marketer has a fair estimation of relative proportion of the total population fitting the buying criteria, the marketer can adjust the formula to reflect that proportion by multiplying the ratio against his total.

Designing Initial Market Strategy

The tools and procedures for identifying economic trends and market demand are used by firms for developing an overall marketing plan, which incorporates the objectives of the firm into a strategy for approaching new markets successfully or for evaluating existing operations in foreign markets. One method of viewing the existing situation in foreign markets is to compare estimates of market demand and company share with actual company performance. Through such a comparison, the firm can identify competitive gaps in the market between its potential and actual shares of markets, which it can actively attempt to narrow through increases in sales and expanded market coverage.

If sales are lower than estimated potentials, the company may be missing competitive opportunities because of underuse of its products by con-

sumers, limitations in the product line, or gaps in the coverages of the entire market, either by being too thinly spread across the market and not focusing intensively enough on the most lucrative market segments or geographic areas. The company also may be missing an opportunity to increase market share at the expense of its competitors. By aggressively targeting the portion of the market covered by weak competitors, it may be able to increase its market share to its full potential.

In sum, through judicious use of these forecasting techniques, the company should be able to develop, hone, and coordinate its overall marketing plan in order to maximize opportunities that exist in new markets, develop and implement effective operating strategies, penetrate new markets, and gain market share. Market researchers must be sure, however, to not use such techniques blindly or alone. Instead, they must be tempered with common sense and be utilized in concert with other sources of information or analysis, such as expert opinions, field visits, and in-depth research to verify initial findings.

If the company is absolutely intent upon marketing in the new country and expects to reap large benefits in terms of increased sales and profits, it might be wise to spend resources to conduct primary research in that market area, to be more certain of consumer tastes, preferences, and buying behavior. Conducting this research, however, is difficult and expensive. Thus, its costs must be balanced against expectations of high demand and growth of markets and market share.

All of this market information must be integrated into the overall strategic marketing plan for all markets in all countries. At this stage, the company must decide upon the level of standardization that it will find most appropriate among the marketing programs. Through standardization, the company can realize economies of scale in using similar strategies for penetrating geographically diverse markets. In other situations or with other aspects of the marketing mix, the company may prefer to adapt its marketing program to the cultural and market differences to the separate marketing environments.

Similarly, the company must make sure that its collection process for market data be placed on an ongoing basis and coordinated in a systematic, timely, and centralized way. For this reason, many international marketing firms develop and maintain extensive marketing information systems, which contain the economic models used by market planners in the company and different levels of available market data obtained from a variety of sources, especially the field level offices in different countries. The key to the effectiveness of the system lies in continuous updating of all market information, so that the information is accurate, relevant, cost-effective, and convenient to use. An effective marketing information system provides the marketing firm with the tools to develop a comprehensive strategic global marketing plan that identifies not only which markets hold the greatest potential for the firm, but also give the firm a perspective on the best methods of entering the new markets.

The information provided by the marketing information system of a company and the strategic plans devised on that basis are essential not only to the continued growth and expansion of MNCs but also to their very survival. International markets are becoming increasingly competitive, and often the quality of information a particular company has is likely to make the difference between the winners and losers.

Summary

Country analysis must be viewed as a prerequisite for making decisions about expanding operations internationally, regardless of whether the planned venture is simply exporting or establishing a new manufacturing location. In order to assess the suitability of a new target country, analysis of general economic data is needed, such as country size, current stage of development, income distribution levels, personal consumption patterns, economic growth, and country stability. Understanding the target country's composition and mix of primary (agriculture), secondary (manufacturing), and ter-

tiary (services) sectors is important in determining whether the country has sufficient skills and resources to support the new venture. Inflation trends, balance of payments, and foreign exchange rates and policies are also important factors for determining the suitability of a country. Special consideration also must be given to the tax structure of the targeted country. After performing this type of analysis on numerous countries, the MNC can then select the location that best serves its project.

The fiscal and monetary policies of a country provide key information on the general health of the national economy. Also, economic plans developed by the central government help to identify the future growth directions of the country. The presence of multinationals and the current level of competition provide further information about the target country's suitability for expansion.

Market demand forecasts must be prepared using secondary data, such as from the Department of Commerce, world organizations such as the World Bank and the International Monetary Fund, or the target country itself. Primary data, such as consumer surveys, gathered by the MNC itself may also be considered when developing market demand forecasts. Four general methods are used to develop total market potential: analysis of existing consumption methods; use of historical data from past market activities; use of data from comparable countries, and development of correlations between a number of descriptive factors and market demand. Market size and share can be estimated by using market buildup, chain ratio, and analogy methods.

The quality of information and the strategic decisions developed from that information are critical to the survival and expansion of the MNC.

Discussion Questions

1. Why is country analysis important to the international businessperson?
2. If you are a manufacturer of toys looking to begin export operations, which economic in-

dicators would you choose to analyze country opportunities? How would these indicators change if you were considering building a computer manufacturing and assembly plant overseas?

3. What information results from a market demand forecast? Describe the general process of forecasting market demand.

4. What data problems occur when conducting a forecast?

5. Discuss alternative analysis techniques that can be used to estimate market demand.

Bibliography

CATEORA, PHILLIP R. 1987. *International Marketing.* Homewood, IL: Irwin.

INTERNATIONAL MONETARY FUND. 1988. *International Financial Statistics* (July).

———. 1988. *World Economic Outlook* (April).

ORGANIZATION FOR ECONOMIC COOPERATION AND DEVELOPMENT. *Historical Statistics, 1960–1986.* Washington, D.C.

WORLD BANK. 1990. *The World Development Report, 1990.* New York: Oxford University Press.

APPENDIX 7–1
A Step-by-Step Approach to Market Research

The U.S. company may find the following approach useful:

SCREEN POTENTIAL MARKETS

Step 1. Obtain export statistics that indicate product exports to various countries. *Export Statistics Profiles (ESP)* from the Department of Commerce can assist. If *ESP*'s are not available for a certain product, the firm should consult the *Custom Statistical Service* (Commerce), *Foreign Trade Report, FT 410* (Census), *Export Information System Data Reports* (Small Business Administration), or *Annual Worldwide Industry Reviews* (Commerce).

Step 2. Identify 5–10 large and fast-growing markets for the firm's product. Look at these over time (the past 3–5 years). Has market growth been consistent year to year? Did import growth occur even during periods of economic recession? If not, did growth resume with economic recovery?

Step 3. Identify some smaller but fast-emerging markets that may provide ground floor opportunities. If the market is just beginning to open up, there may be fewer competitors than in established markets. Growth rates should be substantially higher in these countries to qualify as up-and-coming markets, given the lower starting point.

Step 4. Target 3–5 of the most statistically promising markets for further assessment. Consult with U.S. and Foreign Commercial Service (FCS) District Offices, business associates, freight forwarders, and others to help refine targeted markets.

ASSESS TARGETED MARKETS

Step 1. Examine trends for company products, as well as trends regarding related products that could influence demand. Calculate overall consumption of the product and the amount accounted for by imports. *International Market Research (IMR)*, *Country Market Surveys (CMS)*, *Country Trade Statistics (CTS)*, *Export Statistics Profiles (ESP)*, *Annual Worldwide Industry Reviews (AWIR)*, all from Commerce, give economic backgrounds and market trends for each country. Demographic information (population, age, etc.) can be obtained from *World Population* (Census) and *Statistical Yearbook* (United Nations).

Step 2. Ascertain the sources of competition, including the extent of domestic industry production and the major foreign countries the firm is competing against in each targeted market. *IMR Studies* and *CMS*'s (both from Commerce) can be helpful. Look at U.S. market share.

Step 3. Analyze factors affecting marketing and use of the product in each market, such as end-user sectors, channels of distribution, cultural idiosyncrasies, and business practices. Again, *IMR Studies* and *CMS*'s are useful.

Step 4. Identify any foreign barriers (tariff or nontariff) for the product being imported into the country. Identify any U.S. barriers (such as export controls) affecting exports to the country. *IMR Studies* and *CMS*'s are useful.

Step 5. Identify any U.S. or foreign government incentives to promote exporting the product or service. Once again, *IMR Studies* and *CMS*'s are helpful.

DRAW CONCLUSIONS

After analyzing the data, the company may conclude that its marketing resources would be better used if applied to a few countries. In general, company efforts should be directed to fewer than 10 markets if the firm is new to exporting; one or two countries may be enough to start with. The company's internal resources should help determine its level of effort.

SOURCE: U.S. Department of Commerce, *A Basic Guide to Exporting* (September 1986), page 12.

APPENDIX 7–2
Sources of Market Research

Trade statistics indicate total exports or imports by country and by product and allow an exporter to compare the size of the market for a product among various countries. Some statistics also reflect the U.S. share of the total country market in order to gauge the overall competitiveness of U.S. producers. By looking at statistics over several years, an exporter can determine which markets are growing and which are shrinking.

Market surveys provide a narrative description and assessment of particular markets along with relevant statistics. The reports are often based on original research conducted in the countries studied and may include specific information on both buyers and competitors.

The potential exporter may find many of the reports referred to below at a U.S. and Foreign Commercial Service (FCS) District Office or at a business or university library. In addition, the Foreign Trade Reference Room in the U.S. Department of Commerce in Washington, DC (Room 2233), offers extensive trade statistics.

The sources that follow are listed in three groups. The first group, product/industry data resources, is useful when a U.S. firm wants to compare and select foreign markets for a specific product or industry. The second group, country data resources, is useful when a company has tentatively selected one or more countries for its exports and wants more detailed information on its product's market or on economic and political conditions in the area. Actual trade leads and contacts may also be provided, as well as special market conditions, such as trade barriers. The third group, worldwide background data, provides information on all countries concerning demographics, production, GNP, trade policy, political climate, consumer profiles, and trends.

PRODUCT/INDUSTRY DATA RESOURCES

Export Statistics Profiles (ESP). This publication analyzes exports for a single industry—product-by-product, country-by-country—over each of the last 5 years to date. Data are often rank-ordered by dollar value to identify quickly the leading products and industries. The basic element of the *ESP* consists of tables showing the sales of each product in the industry to each country, as well as competitive information, growth, and future trends. Each *ESP* also includes an Export Market Brief—a narrative analysis highlighting the industry's prospects, performance, and leading products. *ESP's* are currently available for 35 industries; the cost for each is $70. Contact the local US&FCS District Office or call (202) 377-2432.

Custom Statistical Service. This service offers data on products not covered in one of the standard *ESP* industries. In addition, this service allows the exporter to tailor data to meet his or her specific needs. Data are available in formats different from those contained in the standard *ESP,* such as quantity and unit value and percentages, as well as for imports of products. The cost ranges from $50 to over $1,000. Contact the local US&FCS District Office or call (202) 377-2432.

Foreign Trade Report, FT 410. The monthly *FT 410* provides a statistical record of shipments of all merchandise from the United States to foreign countries, including both the quantity and dollar value of exports to each country during the month covered by the report. It also contains cumulative export statistics from the first of the calendar year. *Report FT 410* (monthly and cumulative for U.S. Exports, Schedule E Commodity by Country) is available by subscription from the Superintendent of Documents, U.S. Government Printing Office, Washington, DC 20402, (202) 783-3238. The cost is $9.50 per single issue, $100 for a year's subscription. The reports may also be available at US&FCS District Offices and many large libraries.

International Market Research (IMR). These reports are in-depth analyses for those who want a more complete picture for one industry in one country. A report includes information such as market size and outlook, end-user analysis, distribution channels, cultural characteristics, business customs and practices, competitive situation, trade barriers, and trade contacts. *IMR's* cost $50 to $200. Contact the local US&FCS District Office or call (202) 377-2432.

Country Market Surveys (CMS). These surveys are 8- to 12-page summaries of *IMR* reports on industry themes. They highlight market size, trends, and prospects in an easy-to-read format. The CMS cost $10 for each country. Contact the local US&FCS District Office or call (202) 377-2432.

Competitive Assessments. The U.S. Department of Commerce has published over 20 industry studies that examine the present and future international competitiveness of each industry. Industries examined range from solid wood products to fiber optics. Topics usually include industry performance, recent foreign competition (and foreign government assistance), U.S. Government assistance, trends, and an assessment of future international competitiveness. Prices for the reports are usually $4–$6. Contact the local US&FCS District Office or the Office of Trade Information and Analysis, Industrial Analysis Division, Room 4881, U.S. Department of Commerce, Washington, DC 20230. Telephone: (202) 377-4944.

Annual Worldwide Industry Reviews (AWIR). This product is a combination of country-by-country market assessments, export trends, and 5-year statistical tables of U.S. exports for a single industry integrated into a report of one to three volumes. They show an industry's performance for the most recent year in many countries. Each volume covers 9–20 countries. A single volume costs $200, two volumes within the same industry cost $350, and three volumes within the same industry, $500. Contact the local US&FCS District Office or call (202) 377-2432.

Product Market Profiles (PMP). A PMP is a single product, multicountry report that includes trade contacts, specific trade leads, and statistical analysis. The cost is $300 to $500. Contact the local US&FCS District Office or call (202) 377-2432.

Comparison Shopping Service. This service provides a custom-tailored export market research survey on a U.S. client firm's specific product in a single country. The survey covers key marketing factors in the target country, including overall marketability, names of competitors, comparative prices, entry and distribution channels, and names of potential sales representatives or licensees. The survey is conducted on-site by U.S. commercial officers. The service is available for standard off-the-shelf products (no custom or specialty items) in selected countries. The cost is $500 per country involved.

Market Share Reports. This product provides basic data to evaluate overall trends in the size of markets for exporters. Also measures changes in the import demand for specific products and compares the competitive position of U.S. and foreign exporters. Commodity reports cost $6.50 each. Contact the National Technical Information Service, U.S. Department of Commerce, Box 1553, Springfield, VA 22161. Telephone: (202) 487-4630.

Export Information System (XIS) Data Reports. Available from the U.S. Small Business Administration (SBA) for approximately 1,700 product categories, the *XIS Data Reports* provide to a small business a list of the 25 largest importing markets for its product, the 10 best markets for U.S. exporters of that product, the trends within those markets and the major sources of foreign competition, based on Department of Commerce and United Nations data. There is no charge to small businesses for this service. For more information, the local SBA Field Office should be contacted.

FINDEX: The Directory of Market Research Reports, Studies and Surveys. This publication contains over 10,000 listings of market research reports, studies, and surveys and costs $245. Contact FIND/SVP The Information Clearinghouse, 500 Fifth Avenue, New York, NY 10036. Telephone: (212) 354-2424.

COUNTRY DATA RESOURCES

Country Market Profiles (CMP). These are single country, multi-industry reports that include relevant trade statistics, economic and market analysis, and trade contacts in a single report. The cost is $300 per country report. Contact the local US&FCS District Office or call (202) 377-2432.

Country Trade Statistics (CTS). Each CTS gives details of all U.S. exports to a single country over the most recent 5 year period. They show the exporter which U.S. industries look best for export to a particular country. Each country report contains four key statistical tables showing the leading and fastest growing U.S. exports of about 200 product categories to the country. The cost is $25 for each country with discounts for multi-country orders. Contact the local US&FCS District Office or call (202) 377-2432.

Foreign Economic Trends (FET). FET's present current business and economic developments and the lastest economic indicators for more than 100 countries. FET's are prepared either annually or semiannually depending on the country. The price for an annual subscription is $66, single copies are $1.75 each. Contact the local US&FCS District Office or call (202) 377-2432.

International Market Information (IMI). These special bulletins point out unique market situations and new opportunities to U.S. exporters in specific markets. IMI's cost $15 to $100. Contact the local US&FCS District Office or call (202) 377-2432.

Overseas Business Reports (OBR's). The reports provide background statistics and information on specific countries useful to exporters. They present economic and commercial profiles, issue semiannual outlooks for U.S. trade, and publish selected statistical reports on the direction, volume, and nature of U.S. foreign trade with the country. An annual subscription is $44 and can be ordered by contacting the Superintendent of Documents, U.S. Government Printing Office, Washington, DC 20402. Telephone: (202) 783-3238.

Background Notes. This series surveys a country's people, geography, economy, government, and foreign policy. Prepared by the Department of State, it includes important national economic and trade information, including major trading partners. Annual subscription is $34 and can be ordered by contacting the Superintendent of Documents, U.S Government Printing Office, Washington, DC 20402. Telephone: (202) 783-3238.

U.S. Agency for International Development's Congressional Presentations. These publications provide country-by-country data on nations to which the agency will provide funds in the coming year.

The publications also provide detailed information on past funding activities in each individual country. In addition, the publications list projects and their locations that the agency desires to fund in the upcoming year (i.e., a hydroelectrical project in Egypt). Since these projects require U.S. goods and services, the *Congressional Presentations* can give U.S. exporters an opportunity to plan ahead by allowing an early look at potential projects. For ordering information, contact the U.S. Agency for International Development (AID), Department of State, Washington, DC 20523. Telephone: (703) 235-1840.

Trade and Development Program's Congressional Presentation. This publication reports the dollar amount spent by the agency by industry in specific countries around the world for the past several years. For ordering information about Trade and Development's *Congressional Presentation,* contact Trade and Development Program, U.S. Department of State, Washington, DC 20523. Telephone: (703) 235-3663.

Exporters Encyclopedia. An extensive handbook on exporting, this publication contains market information on over 220 world markets, which are individually covered. The cost is $365. Contact Dun's Marketing Services, Three Century Drive, Parsippany, NJ 07054. Telephone: (800) 526-0651 (toll free).

Doing Business in Foreign Countries. A series on doing business in most foreign countries, these individual guides are often provided to clients or interested parties by some large or international accounting firms, banks, or other service firms. These publications provide information on specific countries and include demographic and cultural backgrounds, economic climates, restrictions and incentives to trade, duties, documentation requirements, tax structure, and other useful information.

WORLDWIDE BACKGROUND DATA

Statistical Yearbook. This international trade information on products is provided by the United Nations. Information on importing countries and, to help assess competition, exports by country are included. Paperback version costs $55, cloth-bound costs $65. Order by calling 800-521-8110 (toll free).

World Population. The U.S. Bureau of the Census collects and analyzes worldwide demographic data that can assist exporters in identifying potential markets for their products. Information on each country—total population, fertility, mortality, urban population, growth rate, and life expectancy—is updated every 2 years. Also published are detailed demographic profiles (including analysis of labor force structure, infant mortality, etc.) of individual countries (price and availability varies). *World Population* is free. Contact the Center for International Research, Room 407, Scuderi Building, U.S. Bureau of the Census, Washington, DC 20233.

International Economic Indicators. These are quarterly reports providing basic data (for years and quarters) on the economies of the United States and seven principal industrial countries. They include statistics on gross national product, industrial production, trade, prices, finance, and labor; they also measure changes in key competitive indicators. The reports can provide an overall view of international trends or a basis for more detailed analyses of the economic situation. Annual subscription is available for $13 through ITA Publications Sales Branch, Room 1617D, U.S. Department of Commerce, Washington, DC 20230. A single issue costs $4.

International Financial Statistics. This is a monthly publication produced by the International Monetary Fund. It presents statistics on exchange rates, money and banking, production, government finance, interest rates, and other subjects. The subscription rate for 12 monthly issues, including a yearbook issue and two supplemental series with expanded coverage is $100. The single issue cost is $10. Available from the International Monetary Fund, Publications Unit, 700 19th Street, NW., Washington, DC 20431. Telephone: (202) 473-7430.

World Bank Atlas. Published by the World Bank, this publication presents population, gross domestic product, and average growth rates for every country. The price is $2.50 and is available from

World Bank Publications, P.O. Box 37525, Washington, DC 20013.

DEPARTMENT OF COMMERCE

The U.S. Department of Commerce provides information on markets through seminars and personal counseling in local U.S. and Foreign Commercial Service (US&FCS) District Offices. In addition, several offices of the Department of Commerce in Washington, DC, offer specific market information to the U.S. company.

US&FCS FOREIGN OPERATIONS

The US&FCS Foreign Operations staff supports and represents U.S. trade interests abroad, particularly in export expansion. Approximately 175 US&FCS officers currently maintain offices in 66 countries. US&FCS officers develop country marketing strategies and can readily assist a business in its market research efforts. Regional Coordinators for the US&FCS can be contacted by calling:

- Africa, Near East and South Asia: (202) 377-1599.
- East Asia and Pacific: (202) 377-3922.
- Europe: (202) 377-2736.
- Western Hemisphere: (202) 377-2736.

EXPORT COUNSELING CENTER AND MARKET RESEARCH DIVISION

These US&FCS offices provide U.S. firms with assistance in market research efforts. The Export Counseling Center provides counseling on market research (among many other services) for a company's products and services overseas. The Export Counseling Center can be reached at (202) 377-3181. Many of the research reports described in this chapter are planned and prepared by the Office of Product Development and Distribution, Market Research Division, (202) 377-5037.

PRODUCT/SERVICE SECTOR COUNSELING

Trade and industry specialists within the Department of Commerce specialize in particular products or services and can provide information on potential markets, as well as other assistance. Specialists in the following areas are available:

- Aerospace: (202) 377-8228.
- Automotive and consumer goods: (202) 377-5783.
- Basic industries: (202) 377-0614.
- Capital goods and international construction: (202) 377-5455.
- Science and electronics: (202) 377-4466.
- Services: (202) 377-3575.
- Textiles and apparel: (202) 377-2043.

Each of these sectors has within it specialists for particular industries.

COUNTRY COUNSELING

Specific country counseling is available to a U.S. company through the Country Desk Officers within the Department of Commerce. There is at least one individual assigned to each country in the world, available to give advice on markets and related topics for that country.

SMALL BUSINESS ADMINISTRATION

Although known primarily for financial assistance, the Small Business Administration (SBA) also provides market related information to the U.S. business community. For more information on SBA counseling, the firm should contact its local SBA field office.

DEPARTMENT OF AGRICULTURE

The Department of Agriculture's Foreign Agricultural Service (FAS) administers several programs to assist the U.S. firm in its research efforts. Agricultural Attaches, Agricultural Overseas Trade Offices, and Commodity and Marketing Specialists can all assist the exporter in researching markets for agricultural products. Contact FAS Media and Public Affairs Branch, U.S. Department of Agriculture, Room 5918-South, Washington, DC 20250, (202) 447-7937.

ASSOCIATIONS AND CONSULTANTS

Many associations can provide advice on markets for the company's research efforts through publications or through direct advice by an international expert. Some consulting firms also provide market research assistance. Consultants may have expertise in a specific market (Japan, for example), or in specific industries (e.g., computer marketing). Before the U.S. company selects a consultant to perform research, it should examine samples of the consultant's work, and if possible, obtain specific recommendations from previous clients.

SOURCE: U.S. Department of Commerce, *A Basic Guide to Exporting* (September 1986), pages 13–16.

APPENDIX 7–3
Macroeconomic Information on World Markets

The World Bank's *World Development Report, 1990*, includes several tables of macroeconomic information on 121 nations, broken down by low-, middle-, and high-income economies. This Appendix includes five of these tables:

1. Basic indicators.
2. Growth of population.
3. Structure of production.
4. Structure of manufacturing.
5. Growth of merchandise trade.

SOURCE: World Bank, *World Development Reports, 1990*, pages 178–183, 188–189, 204–205.

TABLE 1
Basic Indicators

	Population (millions) mid-1988	Area (thousands of square kilometers)	GNP per capita[a] Dollars 1988	GNP per capita[a] Average annual growth rate (percent) 1965-88	Average annual rate of inflation[a] (percent) 1965-80	Average annual rate of inflation[a] (percent) 1980-88	Life expectancy at birth (years) 1988	Adult illiteracy (percent) Female 1985	Adult illiteracy (percent) Total 1985
Low-income economies	**2,884.0 t**	**36,997 t**	**320 w**	**3.1 w**	**8.8 w**	**8.9 w**	**60 w**	**58 w**	**44 w**
China and India	**1,904.0 t**	**12,849 t**	**340 w**	**4.0 w**	**2.8 w**	**5.8 w**	**63 w**	**56 w**	**42 w**
Other low-income	**980.0 t**	**24,149 t**	**280 w**	**1.5 w**	**18.2 w**	**13.8 w**	**54 w**	**62 w**	**51 w**
1 Mozambique	14.9	802	100	..	..	33.6	48	78	62
2 Ethiopia	47.4	1,222	120	−0.1	3.4	2.1	47	..	*38*
3 Chad	5.4	1,284	160	−2.0	6.2	3.2	46	89	75
4 Tanzania	24.7	945	160	−0.5	9.9	25.7	53	..	..
5 Bangladesh	108.9	144	170	0.4	14.9	11.1	51	78	67
6 Malawi	8.0	118	170	1.1	7.2	12.6	47	69	59
7 Somalia	5.9	638	170	0.5	10.3	38.4	47	94	88
8 Zaire	33.4	2,345	170	−2.1	24.5	56.1	52	55	39
9 Bhutan	1.4	47	180	..	..	8.9	48	..	..
10 Lao PDR	3.9	237	180	..	..	..	49	24	16
11 Nepal	18.0	141	180	..	7.8	8.7	51	88	74
12 Madagascar	10.9	587	190	−1.8	7.7	17.3	50	38	33
13 Burkina Faso	8.5	274	210	1.2	6.5	3.2	47	94	87
14 Mali	8.0	1,240	230	1.6	9.3	3.7	47	89	83
15 Burundi	5.1	28	240	3.0	6.4	4.0	49	74	66
16 Uganda	16.2	236	280	−3.1	21.2	100.7	48	55	43
17 Nigeria	110.1	924	290	0.9	13.7	11.6	51	69	58
18 Zambia	7.6	753	290	−2.1	6.4	33.5	53	33	24
19 Niger	7.3	1,267	300	−2.3	7.5	3.6	45	91	86
20 Rwanda	6.7	26	320	1.5	12.5	4.1	49	67	53
21 China	1,088.4	9,561	330	5.4	0.1	4.9	70	45	31
22 India	815.6	3,288	340	1.8	7.5	7.4	58	71	57
23 Pakistan	106.3	796	350	2.5	10.3	6.5	55	81	70
24 Kenya	22.4	580	370	1.9	7.3	9.6	59	51	41
25 Togo	3.4	57	370	0.0	6.9	6.1	53	72	59
26 Central African Rep.	2.9	623	380	−0.5	8.5	6.7	50	71	60
27 Haiti	6.3	28	380	0.4	7.3	7.9	55	65	62
28 Benin	4.4	113	390	0.1	7.5	8.0	51	84	74
29 Ghana	14.0	239	400	−1.6	22.8	46.1	54	57	47
30 Lesotho	1.7	30	420	5.2	8.0	12.2	56	16	26
31 Sri Lanka	16.6	66	420	3.0	9.4	11.0	71	17	13
32 Guinea	5.4	246	430	..	..	..	43	83	72
33 Yemen, PDR	2.4	333	430	..	..	4.5	51	75	59
34 Indonesia	174.8	1,905	440	4.3	34.2	8.5	61	35	26
35 Mauritania	1.9	1,026	480	−0.4	7.7	9.4	46	..	..
36 Sudan	23.8	2,506	480	0.0	11.5	33.5	50	..	..
37 *Afghanistan*	..	652	..	..	4.9	..	..	..	..
38 *Myanmar*	40.0	677	..	..	..	..	60	..	..
39 *Kampuchea, Dem.*	..	181	..	..	..	..	..	..	..
40 *Liberia*	2.4	111	..	..	6.3	..	50	77	65
41 *Sierra Leone*	3.9	72	..	..	7.8	..	42	79	71
42 *Viet Nam*	64.2	330	..	..	..	..	66	..	..
Middle-income economies	**1,068.0 t**	**37,352 t**	**1,930 w**	**2.3 w**	**20.4 w**	**66.7 w**	**66 w**	**31 w**	**26 w**
Lower-middle-income	**741.7 t**	**24,451 t**	**1,380 w**	**2.6 w**	**21.7 w**	**80.8 w**	**65 w**	**32 w**	**27 w**
43 Bolivia	6.9	1,099	570	−0.6	15.7	482.8	53	35	26
44 Philippines	59.9	300	630	1.6	11.7	15.6	64	15	14
45 Yemen Arab Rep.	8.5	195	640	..	..	11.6	47	97	86
46 Senegal	7.0	197	650	−0.8	6.5	8.1	48	81	72
47 Zimbabwe	9.3	391	650	1.0	5.8	12.1	63	33	26
48 Egypt, Arab Rep.	50.2	1,001	660	3.6	7.3	10.6	63	70	56
49 Dominican Rep.	6.9	49	720	2.7	6.8	16.8	66	23	23
50 Côte d'Ivoire	11.2	322	770	0.9	9.5	3.8	53	69	57
51 Papua New Guinea	3.7	463	810	0.5	8.1	4.7	54	65	55
52 Morocco	24.0	447	830	2.3	6.0	7.7	61	78	67
53 Honduras	4.8	112	860	0.6	5.6	4.7	64	42	41
54 Guatemala	8.7	109	900	1.0	7.1	13.3	62	53	45
55 Congo, People's Rep.	2.1	342	910	3.5	6.7	0.8	53	45	37
56 El Salvador	5.0	21	940	−0.5	7.0	16.8	63	31	28
57 Thailand	54.5	513	1,000	4.0	6.3	3.1	65	12	9
58 Botswana	1.2	582	1,010	8.6	8.1	10.0	67	31	29
59 Cameroon	11.2	475	1,010	3.7	8.9	7.0	56	55	44
60 Jamaica	2.4	11	1,070	−1.5	12.8	18.7	73	..	..
61 Ecuador	10.1	284	1,120	3.1	10.9	31.2	66	20	18
62 Colombia	31.7	1,139	1,180	2.4	17.4	24.1	68	13	12
63 Paraguay	4.0	407	1,180	3.1	9.4	22.1	67	15	12
64 Tunisia	7.8	164	1,230	3.4	6.7	7.7	66	59	46
65 Turkey	53.8	779	1,280	2.6	20.7	39.3	64	38	26
66 Peru	20.7	1,285	1,300	0.1	20.5	119.1	62	22	15
67 Jordan	3.9	89	1,500	..	..	2.2	66	37	25

Note: For data comparability and coverage, see the technical notes. Figures in italics are for years other than those specified.

			GNP per capita[a]		Average annual rate of inflation[a] (percent)		Life expectancy at birth (years)	Adult illiteracy (percent)	
	Population (millions) mid-1988	Area (thousands of square kilometers)	Dollars 1988	Average annual growth rate (percent) 1965–88	1965–80	1980–88	1988	Female 1985	Male 1985
68 Chile	12.8	757	1,510	0.1	129.9	20.8	72	..	6
69 Syrian Arab Rep.	11.6	185	1,680	2.9	8.3	12.9	65	57	40
70 Costa Rica	2.7	51	1,690	1.4	11.3	26.9	75	7	6
71 Mexico	83.7	1,958	1,760	2.3	13.0	73.8	69	12	10
72 Mauritius	1.1	2	1,800	2.9	11.8	7.8	67	23	17
73 Poland	37.9	313	1,860	..	..	30.5	72	..	..
74 Malaysia	16.9	330	1,940	4.0	4.9	1.3	70	34	27
75 Panama	2.3	77	2,120	2.2	5.4	3.3	72	12	12
76 Brazil	144.4	8,512	2,160	3.6	31.5	188.7	65	24	22
77 Angola	9.4	1,247	..	..	..	..	45	..	59
78 Lebanon	..	10	..	..	9.3	..	..	..	..
79 Nicaragua	3.6	130	..	−2.5	8.9	86.6	64	..	..
Upper-middle-income	**326.3 t**	**12,901 t**	**3,240 w**	**2.3 w**	**18.9 w**	**45.0 w**	**68 w**	**31 w**	**24 w**
80 South Africa	34.0	1,221	2,290	0.8	10.1	13.9	61	..	..
81 Algeria	23.8	2,382	2,360	2.7	10.5	4.4	64	63	50
82 Hungary	10.6	93	2,460	5.1	2.6	6.4	70	c	c
83 Uruguay	3.1	177	2,470	1.3	57.8	57.0	72	4	5
84 Argentina	31.5	2,767	2,520	0.0	78.2	290.5	71	5	5
85 Yugoslavia	23.6	256	2,520	3.4	15.3	66.9	72	14	9
86 Gabon	1.1	268	2,970	0.9	12.7	0.9	53	47	38
87 Venezuela	18.8	912	3,250	−0.9	10.4	13.0	70	15	13
88 Trinidad and Tobago	1.2	5	3,350	0.9	14.0	5.3	71	5	4
89 Korea, Rep. of	42.0	99	3,600	6.8	18.7	5.0	70	..	..
90 Portugal	10.3	92	3,650	3.1	11.7	20.1	74	20	16
91 Greece	10.0	132	4,800	2.9	10.5	18.9	77	12	8
92 Oman	1.4	212	5,000	6.4	19.9	−6.5	64	..	..
93 Libya	4.2	1,760	5,420	−2.7	15.4	0.1	61	50	33
94 Iran, Islamic Rep.	48.6	1,648	..	..	15.6	..	63	61	49
95 Iraq	17.6	438	..	..	..	..	64	13	11
96 Romania	23.0	238	..	..	..	..	70	c	c
Low- and middle-income	**3,952.0 t**	**74,349 t**	**750 w**	**2.7 w**	**16.5 w**	**46.8 w**	**62 w**	**51 w**	**40 w**
Sub-Saharan Africa	**463.9 t**	**22,240 t**	**330 w**	**0.2 w**	**12.5 w**	**15.5 w**	**51 w**	**65 w**	**52 w**
East Asia	**1,538.0 t**	**14,017 t**	**540 w**	**5.2 w**	**8.7 w**	**5.6 w**	**66 w**	**41 w**	**29 w**
South Asia	**1,106.8 t**	**5,158 t**	**320 w**	**1.8 w**	**8.3 w**	**7.5 w**	**57 w**	**72 w**	**59 w**
Europe, M.East, & N.Africa	**395.6 t**	**11,420 t**	**2,000 w**	**2.4 w**	**13.2 w**	**25.8 w**	**64 w**	**53 w**	**41 w**
Latin America & Caribbean	**413.6 t**	**20,293 t**	**1,840 w**	**1.9 w**	**29.4 w**	**117.4 w**	**67 w**	**19 w**	**17 w**
Severely indebted	**495.5 t**	**20,057 t**	**1,730 w**	**2.0 w**	**28.3 w**	**107.9 w**	**66 w**	**23 w**	**20 w**
High-income economies	**784.2 t**	**33,739 t**	**17,080 w**	**2.3 w**	**7.9 w**	**4.9 w**	**76 w**	**..**	**..**
OECD members	**751.1 t**	**31,057 t**	**17,470 w**	**2.3 w**	**7.7 w**	**4.7 w**	**76 w**	**..**	**..**
†Other	**33.1 t**	**2,682 t**	**8,380 w**	**3.1 w**	**15.9 w**	**10.8 w**	**71 w**	**..**	**..**
97 †Saudi Arabia	14.0	2,150	6,200	3.8	17.2	−4.2	64	..	..
98 Spain	39.0	505	7,740	2.3	12.3	10.1	77	8	6
99 Ireland	3.5	70	7,750	2.0	12.0	8.0	74	..	..
100 †Israel	4.4	21	8,650	2.7	25.2	136.6	76	7	5
101 †Singapore	2.6	1	9,070	7.2	4.9	1.2	74	21	14
102 †Hong Kong	5.7	1	9,220[b]	6.3	8.1	6.7	77	19	12
103 New Zealand	3.3	269	10,000	0.8	10.2	11.4	75	c	c
104 Australia	16.5	7,687	12,340	1.7	9.3	7.8	76	c	c
105 United Kingdom	57.1	245	12,810	1.8	11.1	5.7	75	c	c
106 Italy	57.4	301	13,330	3.0	11.4	11.0	77	4	c
107 †Kuwait	2.0	18	13,400	−4.3	16.4	−3.9	73	37	30
108 Belgium	9.9	31	14,490	2.5	6.7	4.8	75	c	c
109 Netherlands	14.8	37	14,520	1.9	7.5	2.0	77	c	c
110 Austria	7.6	84	15,470	2.9	6.0	4.0	75	c	c
111 †United Arab Emirates	1.5	84	15,770	..	..	0.1	71	..	..
112 France	55.9	552	16,090	2.5	8.4	7.1	76	c	c
113 Canada	26.0	9,976	16,960	2.7	7.1	4.6	77	c	c
114 Denmark	5.1	43	18,450	1.8	9.3	6.3	75	c	c
115 Germany, Fed. Rep.	61.3	249	18,480	2.5	5.2	2.8	75	c	c
116 Finland	5.0	338	18,590	3.2	10.5	7.1	75	c	c
117 Sweden	8.4	450	19,300	1.8	8.0	7.5	77	c	c
118 United States	246.3	9,373	19,840	1.6	6.5	4.0	76	c	c
119 Norway	4.2	324	19,990	3.5	7.7	5.6	77	c	c
120 Japan	122.6	378	21,020	4.3	7.7	1.3	78	c	c
121 Switzerland	6.6	41	27,500	1.5	5.3	3.8	77	c	c
Total reporting economies	**4,736.2 t**	**108,088 t**	**3,470 w**	**1.5 w**	**9.8 w**	**14.1 w**	**64 w**	**50 w**	**39 w**
Oil exporters	**593.3 t**	**17,292 t**	**1,500 w**	**2.0 w**	**15.1 w**	**21.4 w**	**61 w**	**43 w**	**35 w**
Nonreporting nonmembers	**364.5 t**	**25,399 t**	**..**	**..**	**..**	**..**	**70 w**	**..**	**..**

Note: For economies with populations of less than 1 million, see Box A.1. For nonreporting nonmember economies, see Box A.2. † Economies classified by United Nations or otherwise regarded by their authorities as developing. a. See the technical notes. b. GNP data refer to GDP. c. According to Unesco, illiteracy is less than 5 percent.

TABLE 2
Growth of Production

	GDP		Agriculture		Industry		(Manufacturing)[a]		Services, etc.	
Average annual growth rate (percent)	1965–80	1980–88	1965–80	1980–88	1965–80	1980–88	1965–80	1980–88	1965–80	1980–88
Low-income economies	**5.4 w**	**6.4 w**	**2.6 w**	**4.4 w**	**8.8 w**	**8.7 w**	**8.2 w**	**9.7 w**	**6.0 w**	**6.0 w**
China and India	5.3 w	8.7 w	2.7 w	5.4 w	8.2 w	11.4 w	8.0 w	10.5 w	6.3 w	8.6 w
Other low-income	5.5 w	2.0 w	2.3 w	2.3 w	10.0 w	1.7 w	9.1 w	5.9 w	5.7 w	3.4 w
1 Mozambique	..	-2.8	..	-0.8	..	-7.1	..	..	..	-3.1
2 Ethiopia	2.7	1.4	1.2	-1.1	3.5	3.5	5.1	3.7	5.2	3.6
3 Chad [b]	0.1	3.9	-0.3	2.6	-0.6	7.7	..	..	0.2	4.2
4 Tanzania	3.7	2.0	1.6	4.0	4.2	-2.0	5.6	-2.5	6.7	1.0
5 Bangladesh [b]	2.4	3.7	1.5	2.1	3.8	4.9	6.8	2.4	3.4	5.2
6 Malawi	5.6	2.6	4.1	2.7	6.3	3.0	..	..	6.7	2.4
7 Somalia	3.4	3.2	..	3.9	..	2.3	..	-0.1	..	1.2
8 Zaire [b]	1.4	1.9	..	3.2	..	2.5	..	1.7	..	0.3
9 Bhutan	..	..	..	..	..	..	..	..	..	..
10 Lao PDR	..	..	..	..	..	..	..	..	..	..
11 Nepal	1.9	4.7	1.1	4.4	..	..	..	..	..	..
12 Madagascar [b]	1.8	0.6	..	2.2	..	-1.0	..	..	..	-0.1
13 Burkina Faso	..	5.5	..	6.4	..	3.7	..	..	..	5.5
14 Mali [b]	3.9	3.2	2.8	0.3	1.8	8.1	..	..	7.6	5.8
15 Burundi	5.6	4.3	6.7	3.1	17.4	5.8	6.0	6.1	1.4	6.3
16 Uganda	0.8	1.4	1.2	0.3	-4.1	6.4	-3.7	2.3	1.1	3.4
17 Nigeria	6.9	-1.1	1.7	1.0	13.1	-3.2	14.6	-2.9	7.6	-0.4
18 Zambia [b]	1.9	0.7	2.2	4.1	2.1	0.3	5.3	2.5	1.5	0.0
19 Niger [b]	0.3	-1.2	-3.4	2.8	11.4	-4.3	..	..	3.4	-8.0
20 Rwanda [b]	4.9	2.1	..	0.3	..	3.6	..	3.4	..	3.4
21 China [b]	6.4	10.3	2.8	6.8	10.0	12.4	9.5 [c]	11.0 [c]	10.3	11.3
22 India	3.6	5.2	2.5	2.3	4.2	7.6	4.5	8.3	4.4	6.1
23 Pakistan	5.1	6.5	3.3	4.3	6.4	7.2	5.7	8.1	5.9	7.4
24 Kenya	6.4	4.2	4.9	3.3	9.8	2.8	10.5	4.6	6.4	5.5
25 Togo [b]	4.5	0.5	1.9	4.2	6.8	0.0	..	-0.5	5.4	-1.7
26 Central African Rep.	2.6	2.1	2.1	2.6	5.3	2.0	..	0.2	2.0	1.7
27 Haiti [b]	2.9	-0.2	..	..	..	..	..	..	..	..
28 Benin	2.1	2.4	..	4.2	..	5.8	..	7.4	..	-1.0
29 Ghana [b]	1.4	2.1	1.6	0.5	1.4	1.9	2.5	3.1	·1.1	4.9
30 Lesotho	5.7	2.9	..	1.8	..	1.6	..	12.4	..	4.1
31 Sri Lanka	4.0	4.3	2.7	2.7	4.7	4.4	3.2	6.2	4.6	5.3
32 Guinea [b]	..	..	..	..	..	..	..	..	..	..
33 Yemen, PDR	..	..	..	..	..	..	..	..	..	..
34 Indonesia [b]	8.0	5.1	4.3	3.1	11.9	5.1	12.0	13.1	7.3	6.4
35 Mauritania	2.0	1.6	-2.0	1.5	2.2	4.9	..	..	6.5	-0.5
36 Sudan	3.8	2.5	2.9	2.7	3.1	3.6	..	5.0	4.9	2.0
37 *Afghanistan*	2.9	..	..	..	..	..	..	..	..	..
38 *Myanmar*	..	..	..	..	..	..	..	..	..	..
39 *Kampuchea, Dem.*	..	..	..	..	..	..	..	..	..	..
40 *Liberia*	3.3	-1.3	5.5	1.2	2.2	-6.0	10.0	-5.0	2.4	-0.8
41 *Sierra Leone*	2.8	0.2	3.9	2.2	-0.8	-4.9	0.7	-2.0	4.3	0.7
42 *Viet Nam*	..	..	..	..	..	..	..	..	..	..
Middle-income economies	**6.1 w**	**2.9 w**	**3.2 w**	**2.7 w**	**5.9 w**	**3.2 w**	**8.2 w**	**3.8 w**	**7.2 w**	**3.1 w**
Lower-middle-income	6.5 w	2.6 w	3.3 w	2.8 w	7.8 w	2.5 w	7.9 w	2.4 w	7.0 w	2.6 w
43 Bolivia [b]	4.5	-1.6	3.8	2.1	3.9	-5.7	5.9	-5.6	5.4	-0.2
44 Philippines [b]	5.9	0.1	4.6	1.8	8.0	-1.8	7.5	-0.3	5.2	0.7
45 Yemen Arab Rep. [b]	..	6.5	..	2.9	..	11.5	..	12.8	..	6.2
46 Senegal [b]	2.0	3.3	1.3	3.2	4.8	3.8	3.5	3.4	1.3	3.2
47 Zimbabwe	5.0	2.7	..	2.5	..	1.7	..	2.1	..	3.4
48 Egypt, Arab Rep.	6.8	5.7	2.7	2.6	6.9	5.1	..	5.6	9.4	7.3
49 Dominican Rep. [b]	7.9	2.2	6.3	0.8	10.9	2.5	8.9	1.0	7.3	2.5
50 Côte d'Ivoire [b]	6.8	2.2	3.3	1.6	10.4	-2.4	9.1	8.2	8.6	4.2
51 Papua New Guinea [b]	4.1	3.2	3.2	2.7	..	5.6	..	1.0	..	2.0
52 Morocco [b]	5.6	4.2	2.4	6.6	6.1	2.8	..	4.2	6.8	4.2
53 Honduras	5.0	1.7	2.0	1.1	6.8	0.8	7.5	1.9	6.2	2.4
54 Guatemala [b]	5.9	-0.2	..	..	..	..	..	..	..	..
55 Congo, People's Rep. [b]	6.3	4.0	3.1	2.0	9.9	5.1	..	7.1	4.7	3.5
56 El Salvador [b]	4.3	0.0	3.6	-1.4	5.3	0.4	4.6	0.3	4.3	0.7
57 Thailand [b]	7.2	6.0	4.6	3.7	9.5	6.6	11.2	6.8	7.6	6.8
58 Botswana [b]	14.2	11.4	9.7	-5.9	24.0	15.1	13.5	5.0	11.5	10.3
59 Cameroon [b]	5.1	5.4	4.2	2.4	7.8	7.8	7.0	6.2	4.8	5.5
60 Jamaica [b]	1.3	0.6	0.5	0.9	-0.1	0.0	0.4	1.6	2.7	0.9
61 Ecuador [b]	8.7	2.0	3.4	4.3	13.7	2.2	11.5	0.6	7.6	1.1
62 Colombia	5.8	3.4	4.5	2.4	5.7	5.1	6.4	2.9	6.4	2.7
63 Paraguay [b]	6.9	1.7	4.9	2.7	9.1	0.1	7.0	1.3	7.5	2.0
64 Tunisia	6.6	3.4	5.5	2.4	7.4	2.4	9.9	6.0	6.5	4.4
65 Turkey	6.3	5.3	3.2	3.6	7.2	6.7	7.5	7.9	7.6	5.1
66 Peru [b]	3.9	1.1	1.0	3.6	4.4	0.4	3.8	1.6	4.3	1.2
67 Jordan	..	4.2	..	6.0	..	3.6	..	3.4	..	4.4

Note: For data comparability and coverage, see the technical notes. Figures in italics are for years other than those specified.

	GDP		Agriculture		Industry		(Manufacturing)[a]		Services, etc.	
	1965–80	1980–88	1965–80	1980–88	1965–80	1980–88	1965–80	1980–88	1965–80	1980–88
68 Chile[b]	1.9	1.9	1.6	3.8	0.8	2.2	0.6	2.0	2.7	1.3
69 Syrian Arab Rep.[b]	8.7	0.5	4.8	0.5	11.8	1.4	..	..	9.0	0.2
70 Costa Rica[b]	6.2	2.4	4.2	2.5	8.7	2.3	..	..	6.0	2.5
71 Mexico[b]	6.5	0.5	3.2	1.2	7.6	−0.1	7.4	0.2	6.6	0.7
72 Mauritius	5.2	5.7	..	4.0	..	9.0	..	11.4	..	4.6
73 Poland[b]	..	..	..	..	..	..	..	7.3	..	..
74 Malaysia[b]	7.3	4.6	..	3.7	..	6.1	4.7	0.7	..	3.6
75 Panama[b]	5.5	2.6	2.4	2.5	5.9	−0.8	..	..	6.0	3.5
76 Brazil	8.8	2.9	3.8	3.5	10.1	2.6	9.8	2.2	9.5	3.1
77 Angola	..	..	..	..	..	..	..	..	..	..
78 Lebanon[b]	−1.2									
79 Nicaragua[b]	2.6	−0.3	3.3	−0.2	4.2	0.4	5.2	0.6	1.4	−0.9
Upper-middle-income	5.6 w	3.3 w	3.2 w	2.5 w	4.7 w	3.7 w	..	..	7.5 w	3.7 w
80 South Africa	3.8	1.3	..	1.7	..	0.2	..	0.2	..	2.6
81 Algeria[b]	6.8	3.5	5.7	5.6	7.1	3.8	9.5	6.1	6.7	2.7
82 Hungary[b]	5.6	1.6	2.7	2.4	6.4	1.0	..	..	6.2	1.9
83 Uruguay	2.4	−0.4	1.0	0.3	3.1	−1.8	..	−0.5	2.3	0.2
84 Argentina[b]	3.5	−0.2	1.4	1.4	3.3	−0.8	2.7	−0.2	4.0	−0.2
85 Yugoslavia	6.0	1.4	3.1	1.2	7.8	1.3	..	..	5.5	1.4
86 Gabon[b]	9.5	−0.2	..	..	..	..	..	..	..	..
87 Venezuela[b]	3.7	0.9	3.9	3.8	1.5	−0.1	5.8	3.3	6.3	1.4
88 Trinidad and Tobago	5.1	−6.1	0.0	4.5	5.0	−8.6	2.6	−9.5	5.8	−3.4
89 Korea, Rep. of [b]	9.6	9.9	3.0	3.7	16.4	12.6	18.7	13.5	9.6	8.9
90 Portugal[b]	5.3	0.8	..	−0.9	..	1.0	..	..	..	1.3
91 Greece	5.6	1.4	2.3	−0.1	7.1	0.4	8.4	0.0	6.2	2.5
92 Oman[b]	13.0	12.7	..	9.4	..	15.1	..	37.9	..	12.2
93 Libya	4.2	..	10.7	..	1.2	..	13.7	..	15.5	..
94 Iran, Islamic Rep.	6.2	..	4.5	..	2.4	..	10.0	..	13.6	..
95 Iraq	..	..	..	..	..	..	..	..	..	..
96 Romania	..	..	..	..	..	..	..	..	..	..
Low- and middle-income	5.8 w	4.3 w	2.8 w	3.7 w	6.8 w	5.3 w	8.2 w	5.9 w	6.9 w	3.9 w
Sub-Saharan Africa	4.8 w	0.8 w	1.3 w	1.8 w	9.4 w	−0.8 w	8.7 w	0.2 w	5.0 w	1.4 w
East Asia	7.2 w	8.5 w	3.2 w	5.7 w	10.8 w	10.3 w	10.6 w	10.2 w	8.6 w	8.0 w
South Asia	3.7 w	5.1 w	2.5 w	2.5 w	4.4 w	7.3 w	4.6 w	7.9 w	4.5 w	6.1 w
Europe, M.East, & N.Africa	6.1 w	..	3.5 w	..	4.9 w	..	..	..	8.6 w	..
Latin America & Caribbean	6.0 w	1.5 w	3.3 w	2.5 w	6.0 w	1.1 w	7.0 w	1.3 w	6.6 w	1.6 w
Severely indebted	6.0 w	1.5 w	3.2 w	2.7 w	6.2 w	1.0 w	7.1 w	1.3 w	6.6 w	1.6 w
High-income economies	3.7 w	2.8 w	0.8 w	2.3 w	3.2 w	1.9 w	3.6 w	3.2 w	3.7 w	3.0 w
OECD members	3.6 w	2.9 w	0.8 w	2.2 w	3.1 w	2.2 w	3.6 w	3.2 w	3.7 w	3.0 w
†Other	8.0 w	−1.3 w	..	12.7 w	..	−7.0 w	..	6.0 w	..	4.6 w
97 †Saudi Arabia[b]	11.3	−3.3	4.1	15.2	11.6	−6.0	8.1	7.9	10.5	2.6
98 Spain[b]	4.6	2.5	2.6	0.9	5.1	0.4	5.9	0.4	4.1	2.1
99 Ireland	5.0	1.7	..	2.2	..	1.7	..	..	..	0.6
100 †Israel[b]	6.8	3.2	..	..	..	..	..	..	..	..
101 †Singapore[b]	10.1	5.7	2.8	−5.1	11.9	4.5	13.2	4.8	9.4	6.6
102 †Hong Kong	8.6	7.3	..	..	..	..	..	3.5	..	2.0
103 New Zealand[b]	2.4	2.2	..	3.3	..	4.2	..	3.5	..	3.7
104 Australia[b]	4.0	3.3	2.7	4.4	3.0	2.2	1.3	1.1	5.7	3.7
105 United Kingdom	2.4	2.8	−1.6[d]	3.4	−0.5[d]	1.9	−1.2[d]	1.5	2.2[d]	2.5
106 Italy[b]	4.3	2.2	0.8	1.0	4.0	1.1	5.1	1.9	4.1	2.7
107 †Kuwait[b]	1.2	−1.1	..	23.6	..	−2.3	..	1.4	..	−0.9
108 Belgium[b]	3.8	1.4	0.4	2.5	4.4	1.1	4.6	2.3	3.7	1.2
109 Netherlands[b]	3.8	1.6	4.7	4.1	4.0	0.8	4.8	..	4.4	1.6
110 Austria[b]	4.1	1.7	2.1	0.7	4.3	1.1	4.5	1.6	4.2	1.9
111 †United Arab Emirates	..	−4.5	..	9.3	..	−8.7	..	2.7	..	3.7
112 France[b]	4.0	1.8	1.0	2.3	4.3	0.1	5.2	−0.4	4.6	2.4
113 Canada	5.1	3.3	0.8	2.7	3.5	3.0	3.9	3.6	6.9	3.2
114 Denmark	2.7	2.2	0.9	3.3	1.9	3.4	3.2	2.4	3.2	2.0
115 Germany, Fed. Rep.[b]	3.3	1.8	1.4	1.9	2.8	0.4	3.3	1.0	3.7	2.1
116 Finland	4.0	2.8	0.0	−1.1	4.2	2.7	4.9	3.0	4.8	3.3
117 Sweden	2.9	1.7	−0.2	1.8	2.3	2.9	2.4	2.9	3.4	0.8
118 United States[b]	2.7	3.3	1.0	3.2	1.7	2.9	2.5	3.9	3.4	3.3
119 Norway	4.4	3.8	−0.4	1.3	5.7	4.7	2.6	1.8	4.1	3.4
120 Japan[b]	6.5	3.9	0.8	0.8	8.5	4.9	9.4	6.7	5.2	3.1
121 Switzerland[b]	2.0	1.9	..	..	..	..	..	..	..	..
Total reporting economies	4.1 w	3.1 w	2.0 w	3.2 w	3.9 w	2.5 w	4.3 w	3.8 w	4.2 w	3.2 w
Oil exporters	6.4 w	1.0 w	3.1 w	2.7 w	6.3 w	−0.1 w	7.7 w	3.7 w	7.6 w	2.4 w
Nonreporting nonmembers	..	..								

Average annual growth rate (percent)

a. Because manufacturing is generally the most dynamic part of the industrial sector, its growth rate is shown separately.   b. GDP and its components are at purchaser values.   c. World Bank estimate.   d. Data refer to the period 1973–80.

TABLE 3
Structure of Production

	GDP[a] (millions of dollars)		Agriculture		Industry		(Manufacturing)[b]		Services, etc.	
	1965	1988	1965	1988	1965	1988	1965	1988	1965	1988
Low-income economies	161,340 t	886,620 t	44 w	33 w	28 w	36 w	21 w	..	28 w	32 w
China and India	117,730 t	610,250 t	44 w	32 w	32 w	40 w	24 w	..	24 w	28 w
Other low-income	42,660 t	273,080 t	45 w	33 w	17 w	27 w	9 w	..	38 w	40 w
1 Mozambique	..	1,100	..	62	..	20	..	..	..	18
2 Ethiopia	1,180	4,950	58	42	14	17	7	12	28	40
3 Chad[c]	290	920	42	47	15	18	12	15	43	35
4 Tanzania	790	2,740	46	66	14	7	8	4	40	27
5 Bangladesh[c]	4,380	19,320	53	46	11	14	5	7	36	40
6 Malawi	220	1,080	50	37	13	18	..	..	37	44
7 Somalia	220	970	71	65	6	9	3	5	24	25
8 Zaire[c]	3,140	6,470	21	31	26	34	16	7	53	35
9 Bhutan[c]	..	300	..	44	..	28	..	6	..	28
10 Lao PDR	..	500	..	59	..	20	..	7	..	21
11 Nepal	730	2,860	65	56	11	17	3	6	23	27
12 Madagascar [c]	670	1,880	*31*	41	*16*	16	*11*	..	*53*	43
13 Burkina Faso	260	1,750	53	39	20	23	..	13	27	38
14 Mali[c]	260	1,940	65	49	9	12	5	5	25	39
15 Burundi	150	960	..	56	..	15	..	10	..	29
16 Uganda	1,100	3,950	52	72	13	7	8	6	35	20
17 Nigeria	5,850	29,370	54	34	13	36	6	*18*	33	29
18 Zambia[c]	1,060	4,000	14	14	54	43	6	25	32	43
19 Niger [c]	670	2,400	68	36	3	23	2	9	29	41
20 Rwanda[c]	150	2,310	75	38	7	22	2	15	18	40
21 China[c]	67,200	372,320	44	32	39	46	31[d]	33[d]	17	21
22 India	50,530	237,930	44	32	22	30	16	19	34	38
23 Pakistan	5,450	34,050	40	26	20	24	14	17	40	49
24 Kenya	920	7,380	35	31	18	20	11	12	47	49
25 Togo[c]	190	1,360	45	34	21	21	10	8	34	45
26 Central African Rep.	140	1,080	46	44	16	12	4	8	38	44
27 Haiti[c]	350	2,500	..	31	..	38	..	15	..	31
28 Benin	220	1,710	59	40	8	13	..	6	33	47
29 Ghana[c]	2,050	5,230	44	49	19	16	10	10	38	34
30 Lesotho	50	330	65	21	5	28	1	13	30	52
31 Sri Lanka	1,770	6,400	28	26	21	27	17	15	51	47
32 *Guinea*[c]	..	2,540	..	30	..	32	..	5	..	38
33 *Yemen, PDR*	..	*840*	..	*16*	..	*23*	..	..	..	*61*
34 Indonesia[c]	3,840	83,220	56	24	13	36	8	19	31	40
35 Mauritania	160	900	32	38	36	21	4	..	32	41
36 Sudan	1,330	11,240	54	33	9	15	4	8	37	52
37 *Afghanistan*	600	..	..	..	..	..	..	..	..	..
38 *Myanmar*	..	..	..	..	..	..	..	..	..	..
39 *Kampuchea, Dem.*	..	..	..	..	..	..	..	..	..	..
40 *Liberia*	270	*990*	27	*37*	40	*28*	*3*	*5*	34	*35*
41 *Sierra Leone*	320	1,270	34	46	28	12	6	3	38	42
42 *Viet Nam*	..	..	..	..	..	..	..	..	..	..
Middle-income economies	199,900 t	2,200,750 t	20 w	12 w	33 w	40 w	19 w	24 w	46 w	50 w
Lower-middle-income	111,840 t	1,061,910 t	22 w	14 w	28 w	38 w	19 w	25 w	50 w	50 w
43 Bolivia[c]	710	4,310	23	24	31	27	15	17	46	49
44 Philippines[c]	6,010	39,210	26	23	28	34	20	25	46	44
45 Yemen Arab Rep.[c]	..	5,910	..	23	..	26	..	12	..	50
46 Senegal[c]	810	4,980	25	22	18	29	14	19	56	49
47 Zimbabwe	960	5,650	18	11	35	43	20	31	47	46
48 Egypt, Arab Rep.	4,550	34,330	29	21	27	25	..	14	45	54
49 Dominican Rep.[c]	890	4,630	23	23	22	34	16	16	55	43
50 Côte d'Ivoire	760	*7,650*	47	*36*	19	25	11	*16*	33	*39*
51 Papua New Guinea[c]	340	3,520	42	34	18	31	..	9	41	36
52 Morocco[c]	2,950	21,990	23	17	28	34	16	18	49	49
53 Honduras	460	3,860	40	25	19	21	12	*13*	41	54
54 Guatemala[c]	1,330	8,100	..	..	..	..	..	..	..	..
55 Congo, People's Rep.[c]	200	2,150	19	15	19	30	..	8	62	54
56 El Salvador[c]	800	5,470	29	14	22	22	18	18	49	65
57 Thailand[c]	4,390	57,950	32	17	23	35	14	24	45	48
58 Botswana[c]	50	1,940	34	3	19	55	12	5	47	42
59 Cameroon[c]	810	12,900	33	26	20	30	10	13	47	44
60 Jamaica[c]	970	3,220	10	6	37	42	17	21	53	52
61 Ecuador [c]	1,150	10,320	27	15	22	36	18	21	50	49
62 Colombia	5,910	39,070	27	19	27	34	19	20	47	47
63 Paraguay[c]	440	6,040	37	30	19	25	16	17	45	46
64 Tunisia	880	8,750	22	14	24	32	9	16	54	54
65 Turkey	7,660	64,360	34	17	25	36	16	26	41	46
66 Peru[c]	5,020	25,670	18	12	30	*36*	17	*24*	53	*51*
67 Jordan	..	3,900	..	10	..	25	..	12	..	65

Note: For data comparability and coverage, see the technical notes. Figures in italics are for years other than those specified.

	GDP[a] (millions of dollars)		Agriculture		Industry		(Manufacturing)[b]		Services, etc.	
	1965	1988	1965	1988	1965	1988	1965	1988	1965	1988
68 Chile[c]	5,940	22,080	9	..	40	..	24	..	52	..
69 Syrian Arab Rep.[c]	1,470	14,950	29	38	22	16	..	..	49	46
70 Costa Rica[c]	590	4,650	24	18	23	28	..	..	53	54
71 Mexico[c]	21,640	176,700	14	9	27	35	20	26	59	56
72 Mauritius	190	1,600	16	13	23	33	14	25	61	54
73 Poland[c]	..	..	..	..	..	..	..	..	..	..
74 Malaysia[c]	3,130	34,680	28	..	25	..	9	..	47	..
75 Panama[c]	660	5,490	18	9	19	18	12	8	63	73
76 Brazil	19,450	323,610	19	9	33	43	26	29	48	49
77 Angola	..	..	..	..	..	..	..	..	..	..
78 Lebanon[c]	1,150	..	12	..	21	..	..	..	67	..
79 Nicaragua[c]	570	3,200	25	21	24	34	18	24	51	46
Upper-middle-income	88,200 t	1,138,840 t	18 w	..	39 w	..	..	..	42 w	..
80 South Africa	10,540	78,970	10	6	42	45	23	25	48	49
81 Algeria[c]	3,170	51,900	15	13	34	43	11	12	51	44
82 Hungary[c,e]	..	28,000	..	14	..	37	..	..	..	49
83 Uruguay	930	6,680	15	11	32	29	..	24	53	60
84 Argentina[c]	16,500	79,440	17	13	42	44	33	31	42	44
85 Yugoslavia	11,190	61,710	23	14	42	49	..	..	35	37
86 Gabon[c]	230	3,320	26	11	34	51	..	..	40	38
87 Venezuela[c]	9,820	63,750	6	6	40	36	..	22	55	58
88 Trinidad and Tobago	690	4,400	8	5	48	31	..	9	44	64
89 Korea, Rep. of [c]	3,000	171,310	38	11	25	43	18	32	37	46
90 Portugal[c]	3,740	41,700	..	9	..	37	..	..	..	54
91 Greece	5,270	40,900	24	16	26	29	16	18	49	56
92 Oman[c]	60	8,150	61	3	23	43	0	6	16	54
93 Libya	1,500	..	5	..	63	..	3	..	33	..
94 Iran, Islamic Rep.	6,170	..	26	..	36	..	12	..	38	..
95 Iraq	2,430	..	18	..	46	..	8	..	36	..
96 Romania	..	..	..	..	..	..	..	..	..	..
Low- and middle-income	363,680 t	3,060,950 t	31 w	18 w	31 w	39 w	20 w	..	38 w	44 w
Sub-Saharan Africa	27,490 t	149,550 t	43 w	34 w	18 w	27 w	9 w	..	39 w	39 w
East Asia	92,420 t	893,410 t	41 w	22 w	35 w	43 w	27 w	..	24 w	36 w
South Asia	64,510 t	312,070 t	44 w	33 w	21 w	27 w	15 w	17 w	35 w	39 w
Europe, M.East, & N.Africa	69,200 t	..	24 w	..	34 w	..	..	..	40 w	..
Latin America & Caribbean	95,330 t	808,340 t	16 w	10 w	33 w	39 w	23 w	27 w	51 w	52 w
Severely indebted	105,150 t	897,390 t	17 w	10 w	34 w	39 w	23 w	27 w	50 w	52 w
High-income economies	1,391,700 t	13,867,530 t	5 w	..	41 w	..	30 w	..	55 w	..
OECD members	1,373,380 t	13,603,060 t	5 w	..	41 w	..	30 w	..	55 w	..
†Other	11,020 t	234,370 t	6 w	..	54 w	..	11 w	..	41 w	..
97 †Saudi Arabia[c]	2,300	72,620	8	8	60	43	9	8	31	50
98 Spain[c]	23,750	340,320	15	6	36	37	..	27	49	57
99 Ireland	2,340	27,820	..	10	..	38	..	..	..	52
100 †Israel[c]	3,590	44,960	..	..	..	..	..	..	..	..
101 †Singapore[c]	970	23,880	3	0	24	38	15	30	74	61
102 †Hong Kong	2,150	44,830	2	0	40	29	24	22	58	70
103 New Zealand[c]	5,410	39,800	..	10	..	33	..	23	..	57
104 Australia[c]	22,920	245,950	9	4	39	34	26	18	51	61
105 United Kingdom	89,100	702,370	3	2	46	42	34	27	51	56
106 Italy[c]	72,150	828,850	10	4	37	40	25	27	53	56
107 †Kuwait[c]	2,100	19,970	0	1	70	51	3	10	29	48
108 Belgium[c]	16,840	153,810	5	2	42	34	31	24	53	64
109 Netherlands[c]	19,640	228,280	..	5	..	37	..	24	..	58
110 Austria[c]	9,480	127,200	9	4	46	45	33	32	45	51
111 †United Arab Emirates	..	23,850	..	2	..	55	..	9	..	44
112 France[c]	99,660	949,440	8	4	38	37	27	27	54	59
113 Canada	46,730	435,860	6	4	41	40	26	23	53	56
114 Denmark	8,940	90,530	9	5	36	37	23	25	55	58
115 Germany, Fed. Rep.[c]	114,790	1,201,820	4	2	53	51	40	44	43	47
116 Finland	7,540	91,690	16	7	37	43	23	29	47	50
117 Sweden	19,880	159,880	6	4	40	43	28	30	53	54
118 United States[c]	700,970	4,847,310	3	2	38	33	28	22	59	65
119 Norway[c]	7,080	91,050	8	4	33	45	21	21	59	51
120 Japan[c]	91,110	2,843,710	9	3	43	41	32	29	48	57
121 Switzerland[c]	13,920	184,830	..	..	..	..	..	..	..	..
Total reporting economies	1,755,990 t	17,018,400 t	10 w	..	39 w	..	28 w	..	52 w	..
Oil exporters	77,910 t	921,070 t	19 w	12 w	32 w	35 w	14 w	16 w	48 w	51 w
Nonreporting nonmembers	..	..	..	..	..	..	..	..	..	..

a. See the technical notes.   b. Because manufacturing is generally the most dynamic part of the industrial sector, its share of GDP is shown separately.   c. GDP and its components are shown at purchaser values.   d. World Bank estimate.   e. Services, etc. include the unallocated share of GDP.

TABLE 4
Structure of Manufacturing

	Value added in manufacturing (millions of current dollars)		Distribution of manufacturing value added (percent; current prices)									
			Food, beverages, and tobacco		Textiles and clothing		Machinery and transport equipment		Chemicals		Other[a]	
	1970	1987	1970	1987	1970	1987	1970	1987	1970	1987	1970	1987
Low-income economies	45,816 t	..										
China and India	38,394 t	..										
Other low-income	6,285 t	..										
1 Mozambique	..	..	51	..	13	..	5	..	3	..	28	..
2 Ethiopia	149	564	46	49	31	19	0	2	2	4	21	27
3 Chad[b]	51	106	..	..	..	..	..	..	..	..	..	..
4 Tanzania	116	146	36	32	28	23	5	9	4	6	26	30
5 Bangladesh[b]	387	1,313	30	26	47	32	3	5	11	16	10	21
6 Malawi	..	..	51	33	17	21	3	3	10	17	20	26
7 Somalia	26	51	88	59	6	13	0	2	1	13	6	13
8 Zaire[b]	286	374	38	..	16	..	7	..	10	..	29	..
9 Bhutan	..	16	..	..	..	..	..	..	..	..	..	..
10 Lao PDR	..	47	..	..	..	..	..	..	..	..	..	..
11 Nepal	32	165	..	..	..	..	..	..	..	..	..	..
12 Madagascar[b]	118	..	36	49	28	25	6	5	7	9	23	12
13 Burkina Faso	..	220	69	..	9	..	2	..	1	..	19	..
14 Mali[b]	25	100	36	..	40	..	4	..	5	..	14	..
15 Burundi	16	96	53	..	25	..	0	..	6	..	16	..
16 Uganda	158	162	40	..	20	..	2	..	4	..	34	..
17 Nigeria	543	5,196	36	..	26	..	1	..	6	..	31	..
18 Zambia[b]	181	568	49	46	9	11	5	14	10	6	27	23
19 Niger[b]	30	189	..	..	..	..	..	..	..	..	..	..
20 Rwanda[b]	8	314	86	65	0	3	3	0	2	5	8	28
21 China[b]	30,466 c	92,800 c	..	12	..	14	..	25	..	11	..	38
22 India	7,928	43,331	13	12	21	15	20	26	14	15	32	32
23 Pakistan	1,462	5,001	24	34	38	19	6	9	9	14	23	24
24 Kenya	174	839	31	38	9	11	18	13	7	11	35	27
25 Togo[b]	25	94	..	..	..	..	..	..	..	..	..	..
26 Central African Rep.	12	79	..	..	..	..	..	..	..	..	..	..
27 Haiti[b]	..	..	..	..	..	..	..	..	..	..	..	..
28 Benin	19	83	..	..	..	..	..	..	..	..	..	..
29 Ghana[b]	252	501	34	..	16	..	4	..	4	..	41	..
30 Lesotho	3	37	..	..	..	..	..	..	..	..	..	..
31 Sri Lanka	321	967	26	..	19	..	10	..	11	..	33	..
32 Guinea[b]	..	117	..	..	..	..	..	..	..	..	..	..
33 Yemen, PDR			..	..	..	..	..	..	..	..	..	..
34 Indonesia[b]	994	12,876	..	22	..	13	..	8	..	9	..	48
35 Mauritania	10	..	..	..	..	..	..	..	..	..	..	..
36 Sudan	140	1,111	39	..	34	..	3	..	5	..	19	..
37 *Afghanistan*	..	..	..	..	..	..	..	..	..	..	..	..
38 *Myanmar*	..	..	..	..	..	..	..	..	..	..	..	..
39 *Kampuchea, Dem.*	..	..	..	..	..	..	..	..	..	..	..	..
40 *Liberia*	15	47	..	..	..	..	..	..	..	..	..	..
41 *Sierra Leone*	22	24	..	65	..	1	..	0	..	4	..	30
42 *Viet Nam*	..	..	..	..	..	..	..	..	..	..	..	..
Middle-income economies	63,448 t	451,574 t										
Lower-middle-income	36,839 t	225,539 t										
43 Bolivia[b]	135	675	33	30	34	7	1	1	6	4	26	58
44 Philippines[b]	1,622	8,424	39	43	8	8	8	8	13	10	32	30
45 Yemen Arab Rep.[b]	10	578	20	..	50	..	..	..	1	..	28	..
46 Senegal[b]	141	868	51	48	19	15	2	6	6	7	22	24
47 Zimbabwe	293	1,637	24	34	16	16	9	9	11	9	40	32
48 Egypt, Arab Rep.	..	4,244	17	..	35	..	9	..	12	..	27	..
49 Dominican Rep.[b]	275	843	74	..	5	..	1	..	6	..	14	..
50 Côte d'Ivoire	149	1,191	27	..	16	..	10	..	5	..	42	..
51 Papua New Guinea[b]	35	227	25	..	1	..	37	..	5	..	33	..
52 Morocco[b]	641	3,398	..	..	..	..	..	..	..	..	..	..
53 Honduras	91	515	58	..	10	..	1	..	4	..	28	..
54 Guatemala[b]	..	..	42	45	14	9	4	3	12	13	27	30
55 Congo, People's Rep.[b]	..	147	65	42	4	10	1	4	8	8	22	35
56 El Salvador[b]	194	809	40	37	30	14	3	5	8	16	18	28
57 Thailand[b]	1,130	11,543	43	29	13	18	9	13	6	7	29	33
58 Botswana[b]	5	82	..	52	..	7	..	0	..	6	..	36
59 Cameroon[b]	119	1,632	47	..	16	..	5	..	4	..	28	..
60 Jamaica[b]	221	639	46	..	7	..	..	..	10	..	36	..
61 Ecuador[b]	305	2,073	43	32	14	13	3	6	8	8	32	41
62 Colombia	1,487	7,244	31	36	20	14	8	8	11	13	29	30
63 Paraguay[b]	99	735	56	..	16	..	1	..	5	..	21	..
64 Tunisia	121	1,265	29	20	18	19	4	4	13	9	36	47
65 Turkey	1,930	15,863	26	17	15	15	8	15	7	11	45	43
66 Peru[b]	1,430	6,232	25	25	14	12	7	8	7	11	47	43
67 Jordan	32	552	21	22	14	3	7	1	6	7	52	67

Note: For data comparability and coverage, see the technical notes. Figures in italics are for years other than those specified.

		Value added in manufacturing (millions of current dollars)		Distribution of manufacturing value added (percent; current prices)									
				Food, beverages, and tobacco		Textiles and clothing		Machinery and transport equipment		Chemicals		Other[a]	
		1970	1987	1970	1987	1970	1987	1970	1987	1970	1987	1970	1987
68	Chile[b]	2,092	..	17	26	12	7	11	4	5	8	55	56
69	Syrian Arab Rep.[b]	..	..	37	24	40	10	3	3	2	15	20	48
70	Costa Rica[b]	..	..	48	..	12	..	6	..	7	..	28	..
71	Mexico[b]	8,449	36,381	28	24	15	12	13	14	11	12	34	39
72	Mauritius	26	358	75	27	6	52	5	2	3	4	12	15
73	Poland[b]	..	..	20	14	19	16	24	31	8	6	28	34
74	Malaysia[b]	500	..	26	21	3	6	8	22	9	15	54	37
75	Panama[b]	127	422	41	47	9	7	1	3	5	8	44	34
76	Brazil	10,429	78,995	16	15	13	10	22	21	10	12	39	42
77	Angola	..	..	..	..	..	..	..	..	..	..	..	..
78	Lebanon[b]	..	..	27	..	19	..	1	..	3	..	49	..
79	Nicaragua[b]	159	759	53	54	14	12	2	2	8	10	23	22
	Upper-middle-income	26,419 t	..										
80	South Africa	3,914	17,790	15	14	13	9	17	19	10	12	45	47
81	Algeria[b]	682	7,196	32	20	20	17	9	13	4	3	35	47
82	Hungary[b]	..	..	12	7	13	10	28	35	8	12	39	37
83	Uruguay	..	1,690	34	29	21	19	7	11	6	9	32	32
84	Argentina[b]	5,750	22,024	20	21	18	12	17	15	7	11	38	41
85	Yugoslavia	..	..	10	14	15	17	23	25	7	7	45	37
86	Gabon[b]	..	..	37	..	7	..	6	..	6	..	44	..
87	Venezuela[b]	2,140	10,779	30	18	13	7	9	8	8	8	39	59
88	Trinidad and Tobago	198	416	18	43	3	6	7	6	2	4	70	42
89	Korea, Rep. of [b]	1,880	42,286	26	12	17	17	11	28	11	8	36	35
90	Portugal[b]	..	..	18	17	19	25	13	13	10	10	39	34
91	Greece	1,642	7,170	20	20	20	25	13	10	7	8	40	36
92	Oman[b]	..	464	..	..	..	..	..	..	..	..	..	..
93	Libya	81	..	64	..	5	..	0	..	12	..	20	..
94	Iran, Islamic Rep.	1,501	..	30	..	20	..	18	..	6	..	26	..
95	Iraq	325	..	26	14	14	9	7	10	3	16	50	50
96	Romania	..	..	..	..	..	..	..	..	..	..	..	..
	Low- and middle-income	110,929 t	..										
	Sub-Saharan Africa	3,376 t	..										
	East Asia	38,947 t	..										
	South Asia	10,359 t	51,621 t										
	Europe, M.East, & N.Africa	..	..										
	Latin America & Caribbean	34,698 t	180,987 t										
	Severely indebted	38,028 t	202,164 t										
	High-income economies	608,635 t	2,895,002 t										
	OECD members	604,270 t	2,855,538 t										
	†Other	2,387 t	32,313 t										
97	†Saudi Arabia[b]	372	6,085	..	..	..	..	..	..	..	..	..	..
98	Spain[b]	..	66,408	13	18	15	9	16	21	11	11	45	40
99	Ireland	785	..	31	27	19	6	13	26	7	17	30	25
100	†Israel[b]	..	..	15	12	14	8	23	32	7	8	41	39
101	†Singapore[b]	379	5,741	12	5	5	4	28	52	4	12	51	27
102	†Hong Kong	1,013	9,825	4	6	41	40	16	19	2	2	36	33
103	New Zealand[b]	1,777	7,101	24	26	13	10	15	16	4	6	43	43
104	Australia[b]	9,051	31,547	16	18	9	7	24	21	7	8	43	45
105	United Kingdom	36,044	116,553	13	14	9	6	31	32	10	11	37	36
106	Italy[b]	30,942	175,443	10	8	13	14	24	32	13	10	40	36
107	†Kuwait[b]	120	1,902	5	10	4	7	1	4	4	6	86	73
108	Belgium[b]	8,226	32,303	17	19	12	8	22	23	9	13	40	36
109	Netherlands[b]	8,545	39,759	17	19	8	4	27	27	13	13	36	37
110	Austria[b]	4,873	30,879	17	17	12	8	19	25	6	6	45	43
111	†United Arab Emirates	..	2,155	..	14	..	1	..	..	..	..	..	84
112	France[b]	38,861	191,692	12	13	10	8	26	30	8	9	44	41
113	Canada	17,001	..	16	15	8	6	23	26	7	9	46	45
114	Denmark	2,929	17,230	20	22	8	5	24	23	8	10	40	40
115	Germany, Fed. Rep.[b]	70,888	359,754	13	10	8	4	32	40	9	13	38	33
116	Finland	2,588	19,132	13	12	10	6	20	25	6	7	51	50
117	Sweden	8,477	33,282	10	10	6	2	30	34	5	9	49	45
118	United States[b]	253,863	868,233	12	12	8	5	31	35	10	10	39	38
119	Norway	2,416	12,337	15	21	7	2	23	25	7	8	49	44
120	Japan[b]	73,339	689,295	8	10	8	5	34	37	11	10	40	38
121	Switzerland[b]	..	..	10	..	7	..	31	..	9	..	42	..
	Total reporting economies	722,228 t	3,551,267 t										
	Oil exporters	19,643 t	128,122 t										
	Nonreporting nonmembers	..	..										

a. Includes unallocable data; see the technical notes.   b. Value added in manufacturing data are at purchaser values.   c. World Bank estimate.

TABLE 5
Growth of Merchandise Trade

	Merchandise trade (millions of dollars)		Average annual growth rate[a] (percent)				Terms of trade (1980 = 100)	
	Exports 1988	Imports 1988	Exports 1965-80	1980-88	Imports 1965-80	1980-88	1985	1988
Low-income economies	107,355 t	131,444 t	5.6 w	4.1 w	4.5 w	2.6 w	92 m	93 m
China and India	62,140 t	77,751 t	4.8 w	10.0 w	4.5 w	10.2 w	104 m	101 m
Other low-income	45,215 t	53,693 t	5.9 w	0.5 w	4.5 w	-3.2 w	91 m	93 m
1 Mozambique	104	706	..	..	..	..	..	..
2 Ethiopia	374	1,099	-0.5	-0.7	-0.9	7.2	99	104
3 Chad	148	366	..	..	..	..	..	..
4 Tanzania	373	1,185	-4.0	-5.4	1.6	0.5	90	94
5 Bangladesh	1,231	2,987	..	6.1	..	3.3	124	111
6 Malawi	301	412	4.1	3.3	3.3	-3.4	69	72
7 Somalia	58	354	3.8	-9.7	5.8	-4.1	91	91
8 Zaire	2,207	1,954	4.7	-2.9	-2.9	0.2	82	96
9 Bhutan	..	..	..	..	..	..	..	..
10 Lao PDR	58	188	..	..	..	..	..	..
11 Nepal	186	628	-2.3	5.5	3.0	7.0	91	93
12 Madagascar	282	382	0.7	-3.5	-0.4	-1.8	104	95
13 Burkina Faso	249	697	6.8	6.5	5.8	2.2	80	69
14 Mali	255	513	11.0	7.0	6.2	3.7	82	88
15 Burundi	123	165	3.0	8.4	2.0	1.1	100	81
16 Uganda	298	518	-3.9	2.6	-5.3	4.6	96	78
17 Nigeria	7,390	6,324	11.4	-3.6	15.2	-13.7	90	40
18 Zambia	1,073	889	1.7	-3.7	-5.5	-4.8	71	107
19 Niger	369	430	12.8	-4.9	6.6	-4.2	109	83
20 Rwanda	113	370	7.7	1.3	8.7	5.8	102	108
21 China*	47,540	55,251	5.5	11.9	7.9	13.1	95	84
22 India	14,600	22,500	3.7	4.7	1.6	5.4	114	119
23 Pakistan	4,362	7,521	4.3	8.4	0.4	3.8	88	106
24 Kenya	1,034	1,989	0.3	0.1	1.7	-0.6	92	91
25 Togo	334	411	4.6	-0.3	8.6	-3.8	91	80
26 Central African Rep.	132	236	-0.4	0.1	-1.1	3.5	87	94
27 Haiti	207	300	7.0	-2.6	8.4	-2.4	97	101
28 Benin	225	413	5.2	2.4	6.7	2.7	90	94
29 Ghana	882	1,091	-1.8	1.1	-1.4	-1.4	91	78
30 Lesotho	55	534	.. [b]	.. [b]	.. [b]	.. [b]	.. [b]	.. [b]
31 Sri Lanka	1,472	2,241	0.5	5.8	-1.2	3.4	99	102
32 Guinea	584	468	..	..	..	..	..	..
33 Yemen, PDR	80	598	-13.7	1.9	-7.5	4.4	99	76
34 Indonesia	19,677	15,732	9.6	2.9	14.2	-2.1	94	70
35 Mauritania	433	353	2.7	9.7	5.4	2.4	112	104
36 Sudan	486	1,223	-0.3	2.7	2.3	-7.9	90	86
37 Afghanistan	..	..	..	..	..	..	..	..
38 Myanmar	299	611	-2.1	-7.0	-1.7	-8.0	70	72
39 Kampuchea, Dem.	..	..	..	..	..	..	..	..
40 Liberia	382	308	4.5	-3.2	1.5	-9.8	91	103
41 Sierra Leone	106	156	-3.8	-3.2	-2.7	-13.1	100	94
42 Viet Nam	..	..	..	..	..	..	..	..
Middle-income economies	341,143 t	338,711 t	2.4 w	5.8 w	5.9 w	0.6 w	92 m	86 m
Lower-middle-income	172,809 t	163,123 t	5.8 w	6.0 w	5.2 w	-0.2 w	92 m	87 m
43 Bolivia	541	700	2.8	-0.5	5.0	-2.6	84	57
44 Philippines	7,074	8,159	4.7	0.4	2.9	-1.7	92	110
45 Yemen Arab Rep.	853	1,310	2.8	35.6	23.3	-10.0	93	40
46 Senegal	761	1,147	2.4	7.0	4.1	2.8	100	96
47 Zimbabwe	1,589	1,325	3.4	1.5	-1.8	-6.0	84	83
48 Egypt, Arab Rep.	4,499	10,771	2.7	6.2	6.0	1.5	84	62
49 Dominican Rep.	893	1,608	1.7	0.0	5.5	2.3	66	76
50 Côte d'Ivoire	2,359	1,542	5.6	1.5	8.0	-2.2	96	92
51 Papua New Guinea	1,464	1,589	12.8	6.4	1.3	1.1	95	89
52 Morocco	3,624	4,818	3.7	5.0	6.5	1.8	89	103
53 Honduras	919	940	3.1	2.8	2.5	-0.3	93	102
54 Guatemala	1,074	1,548	4.8	-2.0	4.6	-3.0	87	87
55 Congo, People's Rep.	912	611	12.5	4.6	1.0	-2.1	94	49
56 El Salvador	573	975	2.4	-4.4	2.7	-0.6	96	86
57 Thailand	15,806	17,876	8.5	11.3	4.1	6.2	74	82
58 Botswana	1,418	1,031	.. [b]	.. [b]	.. [b]	.. [b]	.. [b]	.. [b]
59 Cameroon	1,639	1,484	5.2	6.8	5.6	2.5	92	64
60 Jamaica	832	1,428	-0.3	-4.5	-1.9	-0.5	95	97
61 Ecuador	2,203	1,714	15.1	5.7	6.8	-2.8	94	50
62 Colombia	5,339	4,515	1.4	8.2	5.3	-3.5	98	68
63 Paraguay	919	878	7.9	15.7	4.6	4.9	82	102
64 Tunisia	2,397	3,692	10.8	3.0	10.4	-1.6	83	77
65 Turkey	11,662	14,340	5.5	15.3	7.7	10.3	91	115
66 Peru	2,694	2,750	2.3	-2.5	-0.2	-3.2	81	80
67 Jordan	875	2,751	13.7	6.5	9.7	0.3	93	102
* Data for Taiwan, China, are:	60,382	44,584	19.0	13.9	15.1	8.5	104	105

Note: For data comparability and coverage, see the technical notes. Figures in italics are for years other than those specified.

		Merchandise trade (millions of dollars)		Average annual growth rate[a] (percent)				Terms of trade (1980 = 100)	
		Exports 1988	Imports 1988	Exports 1965-80	Exports 1980-88	Imports 1965-80	Imports 1980-88	1985	1988
68	Chile	7,052	4,833	7.9	4.5	2.6	−6.0	79	94
69	Syrian Arab Rep.	1,345	2,223	11.4	−0.5	8.5	−8.2	97	56
70	Costa Rica	1,270	1,409	7.0	2.9	5.7	−0.3	95	98
71	Mexico	20,658	18,903	7.6	5.5	5.7	−4.9	98	67
72	Mauritius	1,110	1,115	3.1	12.1	6.4	8.7	90	117
73	Poland	13,211	12,064	..	4.7	..	2.3	106	116
74	Malaysia	20,848	16,584	4.4	9.4	2.9	0.4	87	74
75	Panama	2,352	2,815	..	1.2	..	−5.6	94	104
76	Brazil	33,689	14,691	9.3	6.0	8.2	−2.9	89	117
77	Angola	..	..	..	..	..	..	..	..
78	*Lebanon*	..	..	..	..	..	..	..	..
79	*Nicaragua*	236	791	2.3	−6.3	1.3	0.4	85	84
	Upper-middle-income	**168,333 t**	**175,588 t**	**0.9 w**	**4.4 w**	**6.8 w**	**1.4 w**	**91 m**	**75 m**
80	South Africa	19,714	16,664	6.1[b]	0.2[b]	0.1[b]	−6.6[b]	75[b]	73[b]
81	Algeria	7,674	7,432	1.5	3.4	13.0	−5.9	97	41
82	Hungary	9,922	9,326	..	5.4	..	1.7	92	75
83	Uruguay	1,402	1,177	4.6	2.1	1.2	−4.2	87	99
84	Argentina	9,134	5,324	4.7	0.1	1.8	−8.0	90	86
85	Yugoslavia	12,779	13,329	5.6	0.9	6.6	−1.3	111	120
86	Gabon	1,204	998	8.1	−2.2	10.5	0.8	90	54
87	Venezuela	10,234	11,581	−9.5	0.4	8.7	−3.9	93	41
88	Trinidad and Tobago	1,160	1,247	−5.5	−6.0	−5.8	−15.0	96	55
89	Korea, Rep. of	60,696	51,811	27.2	14.7	15.2	9.9	106	108
90	Portugal	10,218	16,038	3.4	11.6	3.7	6.3	85	107
91	Greece	5,400	11,978	11.9	4.6	5.2	3.4	88	89
92	Oman	*3,941*	*1,822*	..	..	..	..	..	..
93	Libya	5,640	6,386	3.3	−5.4	15.8	−14.8	91	47
94	*Iran, Islamic Rep.*	..	9,454	..	..	..	..	..	..
95	*Iraq*	*9,014*	10,268	..	..	..	..	..	..
96	*Romania*	..	..	..	..	..	..	..	..
	Low- and middle-income	**448,498 t**	**470,155 t**	**3.2 w**	**5.4 w**	**5.6 w**	**1.1 w**	**92 m**	**89 m**
	Sub-Saharan Africa	**28,871 t**	**32,738 t**	**6.6 w**	**−0.7 w**	**4.9 w**	**−5.0 w**	**91 m**	**92 m**
	East Asia	**173,653 t**	**167,930 t**	**9.7 w**	**10.4 w**	**8.6 w**	**6.9 w**	**94 m**	**84 m**
	South Asia	**21,712 t**	**35,950 t**	**1.7 w**	**5.4 w**	**0.6 w**	**4.4 w**	**95 m**	**104 m**
	Europe, M.East, & N.Africa	**102,798 t**	**138,333 t**	**..**	**..**	**..**	**0.3 w**	**92 m**	**83 m**
	Latin America & Caribbean	**101,750 t**	**78,540 t**	**−2.0 w**	**3.2 w**	**4.4 w**	**−4.1 w**	**90 m**	**86 m**
	Severely indebted	**127,659 t**	**101,688 t**	**−1.0 w**	**3.6 w**	**5.6 w**	**−2.3 w**	**92 m**	**92 m**
	High-income economies	**2,178,528 t**	**2,265,978 t**	**7.0 w**	**3.4 w**	**4.4 w**	**4.9 w**	**95 m**	**98 m**
	OECD members	**2,024,259 t**	**2,110,250 t**	**7.2 w**	**4.1 w**	**4.2 w**	**5.1 w**	**94 m**	**103 m**
	†Other	**154,269 t**	**155,728 t**	**6.0 w**	**−4.2 w**	**10.4 w**	**0.6 w**	**96 m**	**64 m**
97	†Saudi Arabia	23,138	20,465	8.8	−16.3	25.9	−9.3	95	54
98	Spain	40,458	60,434	12.4	7.7	4.4	7.2	90	103
99	Ireland	18,736	15,558	9.8	7.8	4.8	3.2	107	112
100	†Israel	9,605	15,030	8.9	7.6	6.3	4.4	94	92
101	†Singapore	39,205	43,765	4.7	7.3	7.0	4.9	101	101
102	†Hong Kong	63,161	63,894	9.5	12.3	8.3	10.4	103	105
103	New Zealand	8,785	7,304	4.2	3.9	1.1	3.5	97	110
104	Australia	*25,283*	*29,318*	5.5	*5.8*	0.9	*3.0*	89	74
105	United Kingdom	145,076	189,466	4.8	3.1	1.4	4.9	96	93
106	Italy	128,534	135,514	7.7	3.8	3.5	4.3	95	108
107	†Kuwait	7,160	5,348	−1.9	−2.9	11.8	−5.5	95	54
108	Belgium[c]	88,953	91,098	7.8	4.7	5.2	2.8	87	89
109	Netherlands	103,206	99,743	8.0	4.7	4.4	3.4	91	91
110	Austria	28,111	36,579	8.2	4.3	6.1	4.0	90	98
111	†United Arab Emirates	*12,000*	*7,226*	10.9	*0.1*	20.5	*−7.1*	91	54
112	France	161,702	176,745	8.5	3.4	4.3	2.6	94	101
113	Canada	111,364	112,180	5.4	6.4	2.6	8.4	122	119
114	Denmark	27,816	26,458	5.4	5.8	1.7	5.2	96	107
115	Germany, Fed. Rep.	322,555	248,999	7.2	4.6	5.3	3.3	88	106
116	Finland	21,639	20,911	5.9	3.5	3.1	4.2	96	114
117	Sweden	49,867	45,793	4.9	5.5	1.8	3.3	89	95
118	United States	315,313	458,682	6.4	1.2	5.5	8.9	114	118
119	Norway	22,503	23,212	8.2	6.3	3.0	3.5	97	67
120	Japan	264,772	183,252	11.4	5.3	4.9	5.0	112	157
121	Switzerland	50,633	56,325	6.2	4.3	4.5	4.5	88	103
	Total reporting economies	**2,627,026 t**	**2,736,133 t**	**6.1 w**	**3.8 w**	**4.6 w**	**4.1 w**	**93 m**	**92 m**
	Oil exporters	**161,995 t**	**163,458 t**	**3.0 w**	**−3.6 w**	**9.3 w**	**−5.5 w**	**94 m**	**54 m**
	Nonreporting nonmembers	**..**	**..**	**..**	**..**	**..**	**..**	**..**	**..**

a. See the technical notes. b. Figures for the South African Customs Union, comprising South Africa, Namibia, Lesotho, Botswana, and Swaziland, are included in South African data. Trade among the component territories is excluded. c. Includes Luxembourg.

221

Chapter Case Study

The Republic of Mazuwa

It was only 8:00 A.M., but nearly all of the top managers were already in at McBride and Mackers corporate headquarters in Minneapolis, Minnesota. The company was a leading consulting organization specializing in market research, especially in the area of international marketing. Founded in 1965, the company had established an enviable track record in international marketing research and counted a number of top corporate names among its clients.

The company was founded by Walter McBride, a graduate of Columbia University, where he received an MBA with a major in marketing. Three years after establishing his firm, McBride was joined by Jim Mackers, a practicing management consultant with one of the large accounting firms. The firm grew steadily over the years, and by 1990 total billings were approximately $4 million.

In the 1960s and most of the 1970s, much of the company's business was doing marketing research for companies looking for business opportunities in Latin America, especially Brazil, Chile, and Argentina. In the 1970s, as the focus shifted to the Middle East, the company earned substantial revenue from undertaking consulting contracts for business opportunities in that region.

They have just won a contract for doing a market study for a large diversified manufacturer of consumer goods that was looking at the Republic of Mazuwa as a potential export market. McBride and Mackers had little experience with Africa, and its only connections were some minor research projects done for North African countries in conjunction with studies on Middle Eastern markets. It had won the contract primarily on the basis of its excellent record in other markets and its competitive bids.

Having received the contract, the company had to come up with a strategy to analyze the Mazuwan economy. As a first step, a preliminary study team was sent to Mazuwa to get a sense of the situation there and to report back to headquarters with its recommendations on the best possible way to look at the economy of Mazuwa and study it as a possible market for export of the client's products. In the meanwhile, back at the head office, a preliminary fact sheet had been put together by other members of the project team, on the essential features of Mazuwa (see Figure 7–1).

The study mission returned after a four-day stay in Silvata, the main business center and port of Mazuwa. They also visited the capital city of Kilbanga and met with government officials in the ministries of finance and trade and the Bureau of Statistics. Shortly after their return, they prepared a brief but well-documented summary of their findings, which was circulated to the members of the policy committee, which comprised all the top managers of the company. McBride called an urgent meeting to discuss the findings and to make a decision on the best strategy to adopt in this connection.

Five top managers attended the meeting— McBride, as president of the company, is in charge of corporate policy and overall management of the company; Mackers is executive president and in charge of day-to-day operations, with personal responsibility for the management consulting division; John Waters, an MBA from Stanford and head of the marketing research division, with the title of senior vice-president; Gilbert Harris, head of financial advisory services, a CPA by profession and a senior vice-president; and Robert Ponsford, senior vice-president and head of the management information systems consulting division.

Jacob Peters, vice-president of the marketing research division, and Charles Seldman, assistant vice-president in the division who had done the preliminary study, have also been invited to attend. The meeting began at 8:30 A.M.

FIGURE 7–1
The essential features of the Republic of Mazuwa.

Country Data Sheet

1.	Country	Republic of Mazuwa
2.	Population	38 million
3.	Area	267,000 square miles
4.	Per capita GNP (annual)	US$450
5.	Ratio of Urban/ Rural Population	60% rural–40% urban
6.	Foreign Debt (commercial credits)	US$ 3 billion
7.	Debt Service Rate (Debt Service/Exports)	42%
8.	Main Exports	Copper, coffee, unfinished leather
9.	Main Imports	Petroleum & petroleum products, fertilizers, arms
10.	Main Industries	Agro-processing, mineral extraction, small industrial goods
11.	Balance of Payments	Average debt of US $410 million over the past three years
12.	Total Export Volume	US$740 million (1989)
13.	Total Import Volume	US$1,190 million (1989)
14.	Form of Government	Military dictatorship with provincial councils headed by presidential appointees

and McBride called it to order and began the discussion.

McBride: Good morning and welcome to the meeting. It's nice to see all of us together at once. Most of you are usually several thousand miles apart for most of the time. You have already had a look at the preliminary report by Jacob and Charles. It is a good job—thanks to both of you. We will do this as quickly and smoothly as possible. I'll shoot off any comments to begin with and then everyone can make his own comments in turn. We'll give Jacob and Charles time to respond to the comments and answer any questions. I'll conclude by summarizing the issues, and we'll make a decision once Charles and Jacob have given their responses to our questions.

As you have read in the summary, Mazuwa is, by any standards, a difficult country to do research in, in the best of circumstances. Most of the data is available only through government sources, and most of the official figures are fairly unreliable. Further, whatever data we get is dated, and by the time we do the numbers at our end, I am not sure we'll be able to make much of a contribution to the client's marketing plans. I am therefore forced to rethink the whole project and am inclined to tell our clients quite clearly that there is little we can do for them in Mazuwa, at least at this stage. I am being pessimistic, but the picture drawn by Charlie and Jacob does not appear to be too encouraging.

Mackers: Walter, I think you are really being overcautious. We have done new countries in the past and made a success of it. In the Middle East we had all kinds of cultural and language problems, not to mention dealing with the arbitrary system of administration. I know Mazuwa's data are dated, it is extremely difficult to gather, and some of it could be pretty much unreliable. However, I think we should make a go of it and tell our client that this analysis is based on this type of data and must therefore be treated with that amount of caution. Anyway, if we don't go ahead with this project, I am sure someone else will, since Peitra is interested quite seriously in expanding into Africa. I know there is a risk of us spending a lot of time and effort on this and not being able to come up with any useful information at all, but then we are in this business, and having gone international, there are some risks we have to take.

Waters: I have been rolling this over in my head ever since Peitra, our clients, approached us the first time around. The more I think about it, the more convinced I get of the feasibility of this project. All we really have to do is to put in enough effort and commitment into the exercise. What I propose is that we send three of our best analysts down to Silvata and Kilbanga and have them pick up this data firsthand from the government and the chamber of commerce. Their presence will allow for a thorough recording, analysis, cross-referencing, and verification of the data. Being present there, any doubts and discrepancies can be discussed with local officials, who, on the first visits, were quite helpful and open, much to our surprise. I am aware that nearly all the records are maintained manually and that computers are few and far between, but with our analysts on the spot, we can overcome these problems and come out with a good information set that we can use to put together what I would call a pioneering marketing research effort for our client.

Harris: I agree with John that the project is doable and that we can come out with a fairly decent report on the business possibilities for Pietra in Mazuwa, but I think we need to take a different approach to doing this. Putting a team of three of our best analysts in this area is really going to add up to enormous costs, and we will have a hard time justifying the expense to our clients. Moreover, our people are needed in other, much higher-value contracts, and taking them away for an extended period of time could

hurt business at that end. My thought in this matter would be to get hold of a local research firm. I know there are a couple of good business consulting groups in neighboring Dolawi, who could gather the data and send it to us for less than half the cost. Obviously, we will not have the quality and reliability of the data that our own analysts would generate, but then, that's the tradeoff we will have to make.

Peters: As the person who has been down at the field level, I can only testify that the difficulties are real and challenging but are not insurmountable. What will be critical is the strategy we adopt. Perhaps we can look at a few country studies done on other, similarly placed African countries and see how such situations have been approached before. There must be some information available from secondary services. There have been a number of World Bank loans to Mazuwa, and I am sure there must be considerable economic data available at the major international development institutions. Our preliminary findings would certainly benefit from access to this type of information.

McBride: Thanks, Peter. There have been a number of different views on this and I am of the opinion that most of us really want to do this. The only question, and a very important one, is how. I believe, that this is in principle worth taking a crack at. However, while devising a strategy on how to do this project, I want the following to be kept in mind. First, we don't want to be seen giving wrong information to our clients. Second, the project shouldn't cost us more to do than we are being paid—loss leaders are okay but not at this point of the company's financial situation. Third, I do not want this project delayed. We have built a reputation for timely delivery after years of sustained efforts—let's keep it that way.

Questions

1. If you were present at the meeting, what would be your position?
2. Prepare a strategy for doing a study for the client, keeping in mind the considerations established by Mr. McBride.

CHAPTER 8

International Law

This chapter will:

- Briefly describe how legal systems differ between countries.
- Discuss the legal concepts that are important in the international business environment.
- Identify current U.S. laws that specifically affect international trade and multinational corporations.
- Examine the importance of intellectual and industrial property rights.
- Define the methods for resolving international business conflicts and the legal organizations that are available in the international arena.

Public and Private Law

International transactions are complex and tend to be risky. Consequently, disputes often arise between business partners. To the international businessman, however, the normal recourse to national law is not always available, because host-country laws often discriminate in favor of their citizens. Moreover, there is no international body of law that governs international transactions. Thus, when people refer to the study of or the conducting of international law, they are merely referring to the laws that govern the activity of nations in their relationships with each other. This is referred to as the public law of nations, which reflects individual methods of each country in dealing with other nations of the world. Public law is based not only on written law, but also on unwritten customs and conventions.

Public law, that is, the manner in which nations interact according to a legal framework, differs from private law. Private law applies not to nation-states, but to individuals within those nation states. These parties enter into agreements called contracts, in order to establish a set of rules and regulations regarding their mutual interests and interactions. Their contract stipulates the terms of their agreement regarding what is to be exchanged, when, where, and for what price in what currency. This private law is still affected, however, by the rules and regulations emanating from public law—overall stipulations regarding permissible behavior between the contracting parties. For example, despite having contracts to the contrary, private citizens may be prohibited by the laws of their countries from buying goods that a nation has barred for importation, because of public policy or national economic goals.

Civil, Common, and Religious Law

The legal systems of different countries are based in one of three legal traditions or foundations—civil, common, and religious law. Civil law traces its origins from ancient Roman law and, more recently, the Napoleonic Code and is practiced in most European nations and the former colonies of those countries. Civil law is a body of law that is written essentially in the form of statutes and is constructed and administered by judicial experts in government. A hybrid of civil law is practiced, for example, in Japan and the USSR. Under the hybrid systems, government experts are involved in the development of new statutes, but before even being proposed, these potential laws generally achieve political consensus. Law is seldom modified or amended in civil law systems.

Common law, which is practiced in Great Britain and its former colonies, such as the United States, is more susceptible to challenge, change, and amendment. The common law system is based not on federal administration but on judicial interpretation of the law as well as customs or usages existing within the nation. Under common law, decisions made by the court are based on preceding judicial judgments rendered by prior courts.

The countries that adhere to religious law are primarily Muslim. In these nations, religious law is generally mixed to an extent with other forms of law, such as civil or common systems. In some countries, such as Saudi Arabia, religious precepts referred to as the Shari'a (one translation of which is "way to follow") govern all behavior and are administered by the government and Islamic judges.

International Treaties Framework

These legal traditions and systems provide each nation with its own public law and a framework for conducting its relationships with other countries and the relations of its citizens with private citizens from other nations. This framework, a law of nations, is formalized for individual countries through their agreements either developed individually or within a block with other nations. These agreements outline rules and regulations to be observed by the parties with regard to economic or commercial matters. The more important of such accords are treaties, and those that are considered less important are called protocols, acts, agreements, or conventions.

These agreements are binding on the parties that enter into them. If there are only two nations involved, the treaty is termed bilateral; if there are more than two nations entering into agreement, the treaty is termed multilateral. Treaties are entered into primarily to facilitate the conduct of commerce between nations. They determine the rules to be followed, define the rights and obligations of each party, and provide for the enforcement of judgments when the terms of the treaties are violated.

There are many different kinds of treaties entered into by nation-states. The most fundamental provide the basis for conducting business between nations by allowing the citizens of the counterpart country to participate in business activity in the home country through trading, investing, or operating or owning a business. Such treaties are known as treaties of friendship, commerce, and navigation and stipulate fundamental parameters to be observed by citizens within each nation while interacting with those from the other and establish guidelines for doing business across borders. Thus, they address such issues as the entry of people, goods, ships, cargoes, and capital into countries. They also establish guidelines regarding the acquisition of property by foreign nationals, as well as the protection of their own citizens and their property abroad. Similarly, they address flows of resources between countries in the transfer of funds or currencies between the two nations.

Tax treaties allow for countries to establish criteria for determining who has jurisdiction over income earned, how double taxation is to be avoided, and how the countries can cooperate to reduce the evasion of taxes by each other's citizenry.

Legal Concepts Relating to International Relations

Sovereignty

Even casual examination of international law requires the definition of the concept of sovereignty, which is the principle that individual nations have absolute power over the governing of their populace and the activities that occur within their borders. In order to be considered a sovereign entity, a nation must be independent, have a permanent population and well-defined boundaries, possess a working economy and government, and have the capacity to conduct foreign relations. In order to be sovereign and conduct relations with other nations, the country must be recognized as such by those other nations. Recognition is the official political action taken by the countries of the world to accept the status of a country as a legal entity and a full-fledged member of the political and economic system of the world.

Sovereign Immunity

Sovereignty implies the nation can impose laws and restrictions, levy taxes, and circumscribe business activities. A manifestation of this sovereign power is the doctrine of sovereign immunity, which is the principle that a sovereign state enjoys immunity from being held under the jurisdiction of local courts when it is the party of a suit unless the state itself consents to be a party in that suit. Therefore, courts have no jurisdiction to hear claims against a sovereign nation.

In order to deal with this problem, the United States passed the Foreign Sovereign Immunity Act (FSIA) in 1977 in an attempt to clarify the situation. This law stipulated that, in the eyes of the United States, a foreign nation waives its right to sovereign immunity when it or its agency engages in a commercial activity. The FSIA focused on the nature and the purpose of commercial activity undertaken and covers business activities that take place in the United States, are performed in the United States but involve activities elsewhere, or that have a direct effect on the United States, even if performed outside the borders of the country.

Act of State

The Act of State Doctrine is a legal principle that refers to claims made by foreign parties whose assets or belongings have been taken by the state in public actions. This doctrine holds that sovereign nations can act within their proper scope in confiscating these assets. To be an act of state, however, the activity must satisfy several conditions. It should be an exercise of foreign power, conducted within a country's own territory, with a degree of consequence calculated to affect a foreign investor or party, and it must be an action that is taken by the state in the public interest.

Because acts of state are considered to be within the rights of sovereign entities, judicial bodies in other countries have no standing to consider the legality of such actions. The biggest issue in these actions arises in regard to foreign owners being compensated adequately for the loss of these assets. Although international law and convention requires that owners be paid appropriately for their confiscated or nationalized assets, the definition of appropriate varies according to each party's opinion and judgement. This problem is a major concern when investments are expropriated by developing nations, especially because some of these countries have repudiated the classical principles of compensation for expropriation, citing overriding development goals of the country.

Extraterritoriality

Extraterritoriality refers to the application of one country's laws to activities outside its borders. Such a transnational reach across borders comes into play when a government seeks to restrict, limit, or direct business activities, such as monopolistic practices, the collection of taxes, or allowable payments for corrupt practices. The United States, in particular, attempts to extend its regulatory and legal reach across national borders in all of these areas, although it is not always successful (see Perspective 8–1). One such attempt by the United States began in the early 1980s, when President Ronald Reagan decided to impose economic sanctions on the Soviet Union to protest Soviet pressure on Polish officials to impose martial law and crack down on leaders of the Solidarity trade union.

PERSPECTIVE 8–1   **Panel Says SEC Fails to Pursue Cases Abroad Lack of Foreign Cooperation Said to Hinder Insider Trading Probes**

If a Seattle stockbroker suddenly urges his clients to sell hundreds of thousands of shares of a Canadian stock just before its price soars, that would normally attract hungry investigators at the Securities and Exchange Commission.

But maybe not.

In this case, the shares in question were sold suspiciously through the broker to a pair of foreign accounts based in Liechtenstein. The owners of the accounts made more than $23.6 million on the purchases.

According to a House subcommittee report released today, substantial trading in foreign accounts like those in Liechtenstein often is so far beyond the SEC's reach that the agency just doesn't go after the culprits.

The Liechtenstein trades and other tales of foreign insider trading are contained in a report released yesterday by the House commerce, consumer and monetary affairs subcommittee. The report said the SEC regularly fails to pursue suspicious foreign trading.

According to the report, which cited several examples, the SEC is struggling to investigate suspicious foreign trading originating in Liechtenstein, Panama, France and elsewhere at a time when cross-border trading has been increasing dramatically. Lack of cooperation from foreign governments and insufficient resources at the SEC were the key reasons cited in the report for the SEC's difficulties.

The report said the SEC failed to pursue 73 percent of the suspicious foreign trades referred to it by the stock exchanges during the two-year study period. However, some of these may have been rejected for reasons other than those cited in the report. (Some of the trading may be legitimate, for example.)

Meanwhile, foreign activity in U.S. stocks increased last year to $481.9 billion, from $277.5 billion the year before and $25.6 billion a decade earlier.

"We believe there is no question this is a difficult area," said attorney Michael Mann, who spearheads the SEC's international enforcement efforts.

"But we don't think the results of this investigation by the committee reflect the progress which we have made in this area. We don't think it reflects the decision-making with respect to the individual cases. We don't think it tells the whole story."

SOURCE: David A. Vise, *Washington Post*, October 11, 1988.

While it may not tell the whole story, the subcommittee report does offer its own version of several SEC investigations that appear to have been thwarted or not initiated at all due to difficulties in obtaining cooperation from abroad.

"The subcommittee's investigation discovered that once an SEC investigation is initiated, the commission rarely pursues trading originating from certain countries such as Panama, Luxembourg, Liechtenstein and Monaco, with which the United States does not have a bilateral information-sharing agreement," the report said.

After the Chicago Board Options Exchange referred suspicious trading in Sperry Corp. stock options prior to Burroughs Corp.'s 1986 takeover bid for the company, the SEC identified the trades as originating from accounts in Switzerland, Luxembourg, Monaco and the Netherland Antilles. Although there were gross trading profits of $1 million, the SEC initially pursued only those trades originating from Switzerland, later dropping that line of inquiry as well when it turned out the traders may have already been under investigation in a separate matter.

In another case, the SEC requested French assistance in July 1987 to detect suspicious trading in International Business Machines Corp. stock options through accounts at three French banks. According to trading records, the banks bought 2,505 IBM put options—options to sell thousands of shares—just before the company announced bad news about foreign orders and shipments.

While the traders apparently realized profits of about $338,839 after the bad news depressed IBM's stock price, the French government has not provided the SEC with any information because "the banks have refused to cooperate," the report said.

The SEC's longest running and potentially biggest insider trading investigation ever in terms of dollars—the Ellis AG case—has dragged on for more than seven years as Swiss authorities have cooperated slowly. The case involves trading in scores of stocks by Americans through Swiss financial institutions, with profits running into tens of millions of dollars. The report said that because of the delay "serious doubts have been raised as to whether this investigation will result in any enforcement action."

In another case cited in the report, that involving trading in Sheller-Globe stock in 1986 prior to its acquisition by General Felt Industries, the SEC did not ask the Swiss government for information because it did not want "to wear out its welcome," the report said.

The SEC said in a letter to the committee that the reason it did not ask the Swiss for help was that the information would not help identify how the inside information was passed on, an assertion that the committee's investigators said was not substantiated by their probe.

"With respect to the Swiss, we believe we have gotten excellent cooperation when we have sought cooperation," the SEC's Mann said.

"Insider trading is one of the most difficult things to prove and the development of evidence for it requires an enormous amount of work," Mann continued. "You don't always succeed. However, we think we are substantially better than we were five years ago."

Both the committee and the SEC support legislation that would give the SEC greater law enforcement powers designed to boost its clout in international probes.

The sanctions prohibited American companies or their foreign subsidiaries and affiliates using U.S. licenses from selling equipment or technology to the Soviet Union for the transmission or refining of oil and gas. The sanctions were targeted at the Soviet Union's construction of a 2,600-mile natural gas pipeline from Siberia to Western Europe and raised a storm of controversy in the United States and Europe. At the center of the controversy were technological licenses issued by

General Electric to foreign affiliates in Scotland, France, Italy, and Germany, which the U.S. government forced GE to cancel. Protests by the licensees were made on the grounds that the sanctions violated international legal principles of the sanctity of valid contracts between parties and on the impropriety of the U.S. attempt to use extraterritoriality. Licensees appealed to their national governments, and European leaders rejected the sanctions out of hand, arguing that President Reagan had no right to extend U.S. laws beyond U.S. territory and instructed the licensees to continue their operation.[1]

Areas of Concern to Multinational Corporations

U.S. Trade Laws

One area in which nations use their legal systems to affect international commerce is trade law. One aspect of this legal jurisdiction is the granting of licenses allowing U.S. concerns to export goods. Through the issuing of such licenses, the governments of nations control how and to what degree national resources will be allocated to foreign users through the export of commodities, services, and technology. Other methods of controlling trade are the imposition of tariffs in the form of custom duties on imports and exports, and nontariff barriers that slow exchanges of goods and services by increasing the complexities of international commerce.

In addition to these controls on trade and international trading agreement participation under the General Agreement on Tariffs and Trade (GATT), the United States also has specific trade laws designed to protect U.S. citizens from the unfair trade practices of other nations, which include subsidies and pricing practices with countervailing and antidumping laws.

---

[1] Felton 1982.

Countervailing Duty

Countervailing duty (CVD) law is designed to provide for the imposition of tariffs to equalize prices of imports that are low because of subsidies provided by home governments to encourage trade. These subsidies can include financial help from a government, such as loans with special interest rates; providing input goods, raw materials or services at preferential rates; forgiveness of debt; or assuming costs of industry manufacturing, production, or distribution costs.

Before countervailing duties are levied, many legal steps must be taken. The legal proceedings follow two paths—determination of injury to an industry or firm and findings that imported goods have been subsidized. In the first situation, the U.S. government, through the efforts of the International Trade Commission (ITC), must decide that the existing or potential domestic industry has been injured by the practices of foreign exporters. Proceedings can be initiated by the government itself or through the petition of private parties (usually the injured industry).

After an action is initiated and a case is brought before the ITC, efforts are mounted along the second path to determine whether or not the goods being imported into the United States are subsidized. If it is found that prima facie subsidization exists, sales of those goods by the foreign interest are suspended in the United States, and the party must post a bond for the amount of the estimated subsidy. Within seventy-five days after a determination is made, the administering authority makes a final decision regarding the existence and the amount of the subsidy.

Following the finding of a subsidy, the ITC makes its final determination of injury. If both authorities rule affirmatively regarding subsidies and injury, then a countervailing duty is levied upon goods brought into the United States in the amount of the subsidization. The conduct of such cases is a lengthy, arduous, and expensive process that involves many teams of lawyers representing the domestic industry and the countries in question.

Antidumping Laws

U.S. antidumping laws also protect American industries and companies against the unfair practices of parties in other nations as they relate to pricing practices, specifically, predatory pricing. Through such a practice, a foreign competitor attempts to capture a large share of a target market by cutting prices below those charged locally. Once such a share is attained and domestic competition is eliminated, the exporter can freely raise prices to prior or even higher levels. This practice is considered predatory if the seller is charging a price that does not reflect the fair value of the goods and is counterbalanced by higher prices charged in domestic or other markets.

The legal process of imposing duties upon such dumped goods is similar to that in countervailing duty cases. The initiation of the case is the same, and the ITC is charged with determining both preliminary and final findings of injury to the domestic industry. Meanwhile, the administrative agency attempts to determine whether or not the goods are being sold for less than their fair market value. If the final findings of both determinations are affirmative, dumping duties equal to the amount of actual fair market value above the price charged in the U.S. market are assessed on the foreign goods in question. The duty remains in effect only as long and to the extent that the dumping practice continues.

Antitrust Laws

One special area of legal concern for practitioners of international business is the application of antitrust laws by the United States upon the activities of those engaging in international commerce. U.S. antitrust laws are based on free-market economic principles of competition. Thus, antitrust laws in the U.S. were enacted in order to prevent businesses from engaging in anticompetitive activities and to challenge the growth of monopoly power in industries.

The United States is noted in the international legal community for strict enforcement of these laws and for transnational application of these restrictions. The U.S. attempts to enforce antitrust statutes through the use of extraterritoriality and the imposition of its laws on the activities of U.S. business concerns in other nations. U.S. justification for such activity is that the United States rightly has extraterritorial reach if the action being disputed or acted against has the effect of materially affecting commerce in the United States.

The two main U.S. laws covering the antitrust area are the Sherman Act and the Clayton Act. The Sherman Act was instituted in 1890 with the goal of preserving competition in both U.S. domestic and export markets. It prohibits anticompetitive or monopolistic activities by business entities. Some such anticompetitive practices are trust-building, agreements to fix prices or allocate markets by industry participants or to engage in monopolistic activities in the United States or with foreign nations.

The antitrust purview was extended by the adoption of the Clayton Act, which prohibits the acquisition of the stock or assets of another firm if the effect of that acquisition is the reduction of competition within the industry or the creation of a monopoly. This law has been interpreted by U.S. courts to affect activity in international markets, because it requires only that the effect of the acquisition or merger be felt in the U.S. market; there are no geographic constraints as to the physical locale where these acquisitions were made. Thus, the statute would cover horizontal mergers between industry competitors, vertical mergers between producers and suppliers or distributors, and mergers that have the effect of eliminating potential competition in markets.

The Webb-Pomerene Act of 1918 allows some American firms to seek exemptions from the application of these antitrust laws, if they join together in order to gain access to foreign markets by exporting their goods. Under the Webb-Pomerene Act, firms are given specific exemptions from antitrust law and are allowed to join together to agree upon prices and market allocations if such activity does not have the effect of reducing competition within the United States. Similarly, in 1982 Congress passed the Export Trading Company Act, which provided some guidance for these companies to facilitate international trade by acting as middlemen between potential buyers and sellers of export goods. Frequently, these export trading companies (ETCs) trade simultaneously in products that compete against each other and represent competing firms. The purpose of the 1982 law was to provide an exemption from antitrust law so that U.S. firms could combine resources in pursuing these export activities, as long as competitiveness in domestic U.S. trade remained unaffected.

Foreign Corrupt Practices

In the 1970s questions about and interest in unethical behavior mushroomed as the events of Watergate unfolded. This interest was magnified with revelations that the Lockheed aerospace firm had made enormous payoffs to Japanese Premier Kakui Tanaka for his help in security contracts. It appeared also that other firms in such industries as construction, arms, aerospace, and pharmaceuticals routinely made payments to facilitate contract awards, sales orders, or project clearance by foreign regulatory agencies. In response to these revelations, the Foreign Corrupt Practices Act (FCPA) was enacted in 1977 to deal with payments abroad.

The FCPA contains three major provisions regarding the payment of bribes and payoffs. First, it sets standards for accounting for all businesses, so that enterprises keep accurate books and records and maintain internal controls on their accounting procedures and systems. Second, it prohibits the use of corrupt business practices, such as making gifts, payments, or even offers of payments to foreign officials, political parties, or political candidates, if the purpose of the payments is to get the recipient to act (or not act) in the interests of the firm and its business dealings. Third, it establishes sanctions or punishments for such behavior. Violation of the accounting standards of the law could lead to fines of up to $10,000, imprisonment

up to five years, or both. Violation of the corrupt practices sections of the act could result in fines of up to $1 million.

Under the terms of the act, the word "corrupt" is used to denote activity where it is clear that the payment or offer is being made with the purpose of inducing a public official to use his or her power wrongly in providing business for a firm or in obtaining special legislative or regulatory treatment for a company. The act also differentiates between bribes and payments made to facilitate international business by exempting payments made to minor officials in foreign bureaucracies. These payments, often called "grease," are routinely paid to smooth the path of business for international firms. For example, a payment may provide for faster service or red-tape clearance. These payments are considered a legitimate cost of doing business, but must be accounted for appropriately. There are those who oppose making such payments illegal and defend them as being a reasonable cost of doing business, especially in foreign environments with different cultural patterns, values, and mores. They criticize the law for being expensive in its compliance and reporting requirements and cite difficulties in making the necessary distinctions between facilitative payments and customary business expenses, such as entertainment of potential customers. These critics also believe that the law has worked to the detriment of American business by causing the loss of enormous volumes of business, especially to firms from other countries in which such payments are considered routine and ordinary operational costs.

The position of the United States and its laws regarding these payments differ from many other countries of the world, where such practices as making payoffs and paying bribes are considered ordinary costs of doing business in international settings. In Germany, such payments are considered customary and are accounted for as tax-deductible special expenses, just as they are in the United Kingdom. Similarly, France and Japan have no restrictions on making such payments to facilitate the development of business. The question still remains, however, as to whether or not these allowances for such payments put French, Japanese, German, and British firms at competitive advantage over American firms.

Tax Treaties

An area of particular interest for sovereign nations that affects international firms and their operations is that of taxation. Tax procedures and policies can have significant effects upon the well-being and health of firms. They can discourage growth, investment, and the pursuit of profits by being onerous, or they can stimulate economic development and growth by providing incentives for firms and individuals. Taxation policies and laws differ around the world; rates vary considerably as do types of taxes. Some countries, for example, allow for a lower tax on capital gains than regular gains, in order to provide incentives for long-term savings and investment, while others tax all gains at the same rate.

In general, income taxes are assessed in a progressive manner, that is, the larger one's income, the higher the tax rate. European countries levy a value-added (VAT) tax only upon the value that is added to products as they progress from raw materials to consumer goods. The VAT has the benefits of being relatively easy to collect and administer as well as being easily raised or lowered according to the economic needs of the country, but it has the disadvantage of not being progressive. Consequently, both low- and high-income members of society are taxed at the same rate, because their total tax obligations may differ only according to their purchases, not according to their levels of income.

Taxes are not only levied to produce income or revenues for nations. They are also put in place to effect public policy. For example, some taxes are intended to discourage the consumption of certain items. These so-called sin taxes are often levied on such goods as alcoholic beverages and tobacco products. Other tax policies provide incentives for firms to engage in particular activities. One such incentive in the United States encourages export activities by providing tax breaks for companies exporting as foreign sales corporations.

Countries differ greatly in the focus, provisions, regulations, levels of compliance, and enforcement of their tax policies. These differences can lead to significant problems for the multinational firm conducting business across the boundaries of different taxing authorities that vary in their determination of who is taxed on what property, what income, and at what rate. The question then becomes to which taxing authority must a multinational firm or an employee of that multinational firm remit taxes. The solution is one that recognizes both the concept that all sovereign nations have the authority to tax and that corporations or individuals should be spared from having undue or double tax liabilities.

In consequence, nations around the world enter into tax treaties that generally provide for credits in the home country for taxes paid in the host country by corporations or individuals. Thus, the entity is not taxed twice upon the same income or property. For example, the United States taxes personal income not according to the residence or site where the income was earned, but taxes according to the nationality of the taxpayer. Therefore, expatriates working abroad are liable for taxes on income earned in those foreign settings. Tax law, however, provides a break for these individuals by allowing them exemptions from taxes for housing allowances for foreign residences and income tax relief on a portion of their income earned abroad. The Tax Reform Act of 1986 set this exemption at $85,000 of foreign-earned income per year.

Tax conventions or treaties between nations define the basis for taxation, such as the site of the official residence of a firm or person or location of operations for that firm. The agreements also define what constitutes taxable income and provide for the mutual exchange of information and assistance to increase compliance with and enforcement of tax laws in order to decrease tax evasion.

Intellectual and Industrial Property Rights

Another crucial area of concern for multinational firms involved in research and development and advanced technology is the protection of such intangible assets as know-how, processes, trademarks, trade names, and trade secrets. These assets generally find protection under legal systems that provide for the creation of patents and copyrights. The dangers involved with such assets is that they will be stolen, used, copied, and sold without proper authority or compensation.

Patents are rights granted by governments to the inventors of products or processes for the exclusive manufacturing, production, sale, and use of those products or processes. Patents are the equivalent of the legal ceding of monopolistic power over the subject matter of the patent. They are intended to stimulate the creation of new technology and inventions by providing creators with assurances of gain from the potential benefit from their endeavors. Patents protect the subject from infringement of rights only in the country in which they are registered. Consequently, a multinational firm marketing its products or processes in a number of countries must make sure that its patents are protected in all existing as well as potential market areas.

Trademarks and Tradenames

Trademarks and tradenames are designs or logos and names used by manufacturers to differentiate and identify their goods with customers. They are considered an integral part of the total product, which is the entire image and package surrounding the actual product being marketed. Trademarks and names have an indefinite life and can be licensed to others, as long as they retain their brand distinction and do not pass into generic descriptive use, as happened with aspirin. Goods that use false trademarks are counterfeit products, and producers and sellers of such goods are subject to prosecution under trademark laws of individual countries. Trademarks are generally not considered infringed upon when they are imitated ("knocked-off"), as long as they are not characterized as the original merchandise.

The inappropriate use of tradenames and trademarks provides for legal conflicts around the world. Recently, the banking giant Citicorp filed a lawsuit against a small bank in New York City's Chinatown. The case revolved around the translation of the name, Golden City Bank into Chinese. Citicorp's lawyers claim that the translated name is "confusingly similar" to the conglomerate's main bank, Citibank. Citicorp requested that the small bank be stopped from using its name, that it remit to Citibank any profits it might have earned from such use, and that it destroy all documents carrying this name. Lawyers for the owners of Golden City Bank, most of whom are Taiwanese, maintained that their clients would fight the suit, because changing the bank's name would lead to a "loss of face."[2]

Patent Laws and Accords

Different countries around the world have different criteria for the proper registration and granting of patents. A multinational firm must take care to comply with the different requirements of each country. For example, the lifetime of a patent may vary from country to country; nations may have different requirements about products or processes having published descriptions, whether they were used or worked prior to patent application, and whether a product is substantially different from previously patented goods. The countries may also differ in the procedures used to resolve conflicts when more than one inventor claims the rights to the same patent. Consequently, ensuring protection of patents can be a complex, lengthy, involved, and expensive process for firms engaged in commerce in a multitude of markets.

These complexities and intricacies have led to the emergence of international agreements regarding the mutual recognition of patents upon goods

[2] Harlan 1988.

and processes of member countries. The largest of these is the Paris Convention, which provides for the protection of patents and trademarks. This convention, also called the Paris Union, was established in 1883. Under its terms, members agree to recognize and protect the patents and trademarks of member countries and allow for expedited (that is, a six-month priority period) registration for enterprises having filed in home countries that are members of the union. Similar patent agreements exist between the United States and Latin American countries in the Pan American Convention of 1929 and in subregional groups, such as the European Community and Sweden and Switzerland. In these nations, filing for patents in one of the member countries automatically confers protection in all member countries.

Trademarks are generally used without consent when a product with a worldwide reputation is not registered in all potential markets. Thus, with its reputation at stake, a multinational firm is faced in such situations with either having to litigate to regain use of its mark or name or to buying back that identifying symbol or name. While registration of all trademarks and names prevents these problems, such action becomes very expensive, especially if the firm markets extensive product lines in many markets where registration requirements differ substantially. For example, in some countries trademarks are registered only after they have been used, while in others, they cannot be used until they are registered.

To deal with these problems, attempts have been made to synchronize registration processes by cooperating international entities in recent years. The Madrid Agreement of 1991 provides for the protection of trademarks in a centralized bureau in Geneva, the International Bureau for the Protection of Industrial Patents, which is a part of the World Intellectual Property Organization. Registrations under this agreement have the benefit of being effective in several nations and potentially all members of the Madrid Agreement. Once the trademark is properly registered in its home country, an application may be made for international registration, at which point the mark is published by the international bureau and communicated to the member countries where a firm is seeking patent protection. It is then up to the member countries to decide within twelve months whether or not they wish to refuse acceptance of the mark, and, in that case, they must outline the grounds for such refusal.

Copyrights

Copyrights give exclusive rights to authors, composers, singers, musicians, and artists to publish, dispose of, or release their work as they see fit. The people in the music business face problems with the illegal use of their material ("piracy"), which is the unlawful duplication of sound recordings to make bootleg tapes and records. A major new area where copyrights are routinely infringed is in computer software.

Copyright protection is sought by creators of works of art, literature, and music to ensure that no one wrongly reaps the benefit of their creative efforts through the sale, use, or licensing of those works. Copyright protection falls in two categories—that which protects the right of a creator to economic benefits or returns from his work and a moral right to claim title to the work and to prevent its being altered without consent or published without permission.

International copyright protection is covered under the Berne Convention of 1886 for the Protection of Literary and Artistic Works, which has seventy-two signatory countries. In order to be covered under the Berne Convention, material must be published or generally made available in a member country. The author or artist need not be a citizen of that member country to be afforded copyright protection. Thus, artists from nonmember countries, such as the United States, gain coverage by publishing simultaneously at home and abroad.

A similar agreement that also provides for international copyright protection is the Universal Copyright Convention (UCC) of 1952, sponsored and administered by the United Nations Educational, Scientific, and Cultural Organization

(UNESCO). Members of the UCC are accorded national status within each other's borders, that is, citizens holding copyrights are entitled to the same protection against copyright infringement as national citizens. Many members of the Berne convention are also signatories of the UCC.

Operational Concerns of Multinational Corporations

Which Nationality?

In the world of international commerce, there is no such entity as an international corporation, rather, the multinational firm consists of connected groups of individual operating units organized to operate within a variety of nations. The nationality of each corporation depends not on its own choice or determination, but upon the laws within the nation of operation. In some countries, a corporation need only be incorporated within the national boundaries; in others, it must have a registered office on domestic soil; and in still others, it must be managed and operated within the country. Some nations allow for corporate dual citizenship.

The determination of nationality is a crucial matter, because it has the potential of affecting all business operations. For example, multi-national corporations may seek protection or assistance from their national governments or domestic courts of law in disputes with host countries. Nationality also determines tax liability and entitlement to government-sponsored incentive programs or tax breaks, as well as the degree of liability carried by the directors of a corporation. The determination of what constitutes a corporation also tends to differ among countries. All these factors imply that the multinational concern must seriously consider the form of organization it wishes to adopt in a particular country. The choice of form will depend upon the strategic objectives of the corporation in a particular country and the form that best serves these objectives.

Local Laws

Local laws affect the welfare and day-to-day operations of a firm (see Perspective 8–2). The labor laws of a nation, for example, will affect the multinational corporation's use of labor. Some of these laws stipulate minimum wages to be paid for labor, standards for working conditions, requirements for levels and types of fringe benefits, and the timing and the duration of holidays and vacations. In some countries management is considered fully liable for worker safety and faces possible criminal prosecution for worker injuries or deaths suffered on the job.

PERSPECTIVE 8–2   **Foreign Lawyers in Japan Chafe Under Restrictions**

TOKYO—Foreign law firms in Japan have to play a name game: Their local offices must identify themselves first by the names of the resident partners, second by a Japanese phrase meaning foreign business lawyer—and only then by the "trademark" names that the rest of the world knows them by.

So on office doors, business cards and letterheads and even in the membership directory of the American Chamber of Commerce, the Tokyo office of a well-known U.S. firm such as Coudert Brothers is called Stevens *gaikokuho-jimu-bengoshi* Coudert Brothers. Milbank, Tweed, Hadley & McCoy becomes a mouthful: Dickson, Green,

SOURCE: Damon Darlin, *Wall Street Journal*, February 7, 1989.

Benson *gaikokuho-jimu-bengoshi* Milbank Tweed, Hadley & McCoy.

A MINOR IRRITATION

Foreign lawyers in Japan, or "gai-ben" for short, say the rules on names are only a minor irritation. But they symbolize how almost two years after the U.S. forced Japan to open its door to foreign lawyers, the welcome mat still isn't out.

Under the trade agreement that gave foreign lawyers access, their practice is limited to foreign law: they can't give advice on Japanese law, even if they are qualified. A foreign lawyer's office can't hire a Japanese lawyer who is qualified to give such advice, nor can it forge a formal link with a Japanese law firm. Also, foreign lawyers are, in effect, barred from arbitration proceedings because of uncertainty over whether they have standing to participate. That's no small matter, since companies often use arbitration to avoid Japan's slow-moving courts, where cases can take 10 years or more to go to trial.

The Japanese bar, which opposed opening the nation's legal market, likes things this way. It still fears competition from abroad, even though fewer than 50 foreign lawyers, mostly Americans, have registered as gai-ben. By comparison, Japan has about 124,000 registered legal professionals, including tax attorneys and "scriveners," or preparers of legal documents.

"The hordes of lawyers the Japanese worried about didn't materialize," says Charles Stevens, the Coudert Brothers gai-ben.

Those foreign lawyers who have come are often frustrated by the restrictions. Carl J. Green, a partner with Milbank Tweed, says, "We'd like to see greater freedom." Among other changes, Mr. Green and many lawyers would like to see foreign firms able to merge with Japanese firms and hire Japanese lawyers, as well as hire foreign lawyers with less than the five years of experience in their home country that is now required. They also would like American lawyers recognized as having standing to take part in arbitration cases. Such changes would enable foreign firms to expand operations here and to handle more cases in their entirety.

That's important, U.S. lawyers say, in part because their Japanese counterparts sometimes don't represent foreign clients well, worrying more about preserving social harmony and business relationships than the interests of their clients. In one case, a big Japanese brokerage house got tipped off in advance of a company's bankruptcy filing and took possession of assets that belonged to a consortium of foreign banks that ranked higher on the list of creditors. The Japanese lawyers representing the banks never told them what had happened for fear that doing so would offend the brokerage house.

Also, Japanese lawyers often are unskilled in or afraid of pursuing fraud cases, particularly when they involve the *yakuza,* Japan's gangsters, U.S. lawyers say. "Japan is a paradise for the white-collar criminal," says Mr. Stevens. So Japanese companies often rely on American lawyers for informal guidance, because Japanese securities law is patterned on U.S. law.

A spokesman for the Japanese bar association says a growing number of lawyers are defending companies against yakuzas. But he adds: "Compared to other countries, you might say that Japan doesn't want to make a big deal of things." A member of the bar association's staff adds that Japanese lawyers are making moves to begin revising their ethics code, which was written 33 years ago.

PAYING TWO FIRMS

Some users of legal services agree with U.S. lawyers that the restriction on foreigners should be lifted. Many American companies complain that when they go to their U.S. law firm in Tokyo with a problem, it often involves Japanese law, so the American lawyers have to turn the matter over to a Japanese law firm for help—though they frequently monitor the case to make sure their client's interests aren't neglected. "That costs us twice as much," says an executive with a multinational manufacturer here. Still, he adds, "it is worth it to have the American firm watch the Japanese firm."

The American chamber's subcommittee for legal services hopes to press the Bush administration to take up the legal restrictions as a trade issue. But chances appear slim. By choice, no Japanese law firms have offices in the U.S., so Washington has little leverage. "Unless there is a loud cry from American clients, I don't see it happening," says

Edward F. Greene, a partner in the Tokyo office of Cleary, Gottlieb, Steen & Hamilton.

Even with the restrictions, gai-ben get a wide range of work. Foreign firms handle contracts, licensing arrangements, trade consulting, plant location in the U.S. and a range of matters pertaining to U.S. law. "A lot more of what was being done in New York is being done here," Mr. Stevens says.

Some nations have requirements that multinational firms employ certain percentages of local labor within their operating and managerial classes of employees and stipulate hiring and firing procedures and levels of severance pay when employees are terminated. All nations have national policies in place regarding contributions to the labor pool through immigration. They regulate or place limits on the number of foreigners or guest workers and the length of employment and sometimes types of jobs or positions they are allowed to hold.

Individual nations also impose standards on product safety and put into place testing requirements and compulsory regulatory processes for gaining product approval. In the United States, the Consumer Product Safety Commission evaluates the safety of various products and sometimes recommends that unsafe products be taken off the market. Similarly, the Federal Drug Administration tests and evaluates new pharmaceutical products, in order to determine whether or not they are safe to be used by the public. Internationally, more and more attention is being paid to the development, enforcement, and standardization of product safety laws.

Local laws also affect the operations of multinational firms when they involve controls upon wages, prices, or currency transactions. Wage and price controls are generally imposed as part of efforts to encourage and stimulate economic development by keeping the incomes of workers up through minimum wages or their costs down through limits on prices. Such controls are also used to bring down inflation, lower import vol-

umes, and raise exports in order to bring the balance of payments into equilibrium.

Similarly, some countries put limits upon currency exchanges because they wish to increase their store of hard currency. These nations often set limits upon the amounts of local currency that can be exchanged for hard currency and upon amounts paid for goods or profits that can be repatriated by multinational firms.

Resolving Business Conflicts

The problem of business conflicts is particularly complex in the arena of international business, primarily for three reasons. First, the contracting parties are generally not as familiar with each other as are parties from the same country, and they are subject to the jurisdiction of their own countries and laws. Thus, an injured party cannot claim redress in his domestic courts against the defaulting party if the latter is based in a foreign country.

Second, international transactions operate in a relatively uncertain environment and face the risks of fluctuations in prices and exchange rates, changes in laws and regulations, transit risks, and so on. The possibilities of transactions not being completed to the satisfaction of both parties are higher than in a domestic environment.

Third, business ethics, practices, and cultures vary considerably across countries. Language is often a barrier, and there is always a distinct possibility of a misunderstanding because of a communications gap between the two parties. Communications are also hampered by the fact that the parties can be at a great distance from each other during the life of the transaction.

Contracts

It is essential that conflicts in international business be avoided to the extent possible. One of the best ways to avoid conflicts in international business is to have a clearly drafted contract, with all terms and conditions well-understood by both parties. An international contract spells out details of the transactions, the obligations of the two parties, the consideration involved, and so on. A contract is defined as a promise or set of promises, for the breach of which the law gives a remedy, or the performance of which the law in some way recognizes as a duty. A commercial contract spells out such items as the details of the transaction, the obligations of the parties, and the consideration involved.

The international businessperson has to recognize the possibility of conflict. Thus, five specific steps should be taken when signing contracts with overseas parties:

1. The contract provisions must be unambiguous and clear and cover every relevant aspect of the transaction.
2. The applicable law used in the contract should be understood by the company.
3. The contract should stipulate the relevant jurisdiction where the potential disputes will be settled. This is known as the choice of forum.
4. Risk transfer must be clearly outlined in the contracts especially where the contract involves sale and purchase of goods. The contract should state clearly the stage at which the risk of loss of the goods passes over from the seller to the buyer.
5. The contract should contain some provisions for dispute resolution without resorting to arbitration or litigation.

Resolving Disputes

Despite the insertion of all precautionary clauses, disputes may emerge. Usually, the method adopted to deal with such situations is either arbitration or litigation, but, there are some interim dispute resolution methods that are quicker and less expensive—adaptation, renegotiation, and mediation.

ADAPTATION

Provisions can be inserted into a contract to enable the agreement to be adapted to changing circumstances over the life of the transaction, which is particularly important when the contract involves a long-term commitment by both parties. There are several issues on which the adaptability of a contract is desirable so that both parties enjoy some flexibility in the performance of their respective obligations. Typically, in long-term contracts, flexibility is sought in such issues as prices and delivery schedules. Most contracts contain a force majeure clause, which absolves the parties of their obligations under the contract if they are prevented from carrying them out by circumstances beyond their control.

RENEGOTIATION

If a dispute arises during the life of the contract over some provisions, the contract can be renegotiated between the two parties. In certain instances, the contract itself contains a proviso to the effect that under certain circumstances, if the parties differ, they will renegotiate certain parts of the contract. Renegotiation has obvious advantages. Apart from saving court fees and other charges involved in formal dispute resolution procedures, renegotiation can be an ongoing process that need not disrupt the continued progress of business under the contract.

MEDIATION

Mediation is a method of dispute resolution using the offices of a third party known as the mediator. The actual mediation proceedings are generally less formal and rigid than arbitration, but the nature of individual mediation proceedings does vary. Mediation, if carried out in a nonconfrontational and relatively cooperative manner, can be an effective way to resolve commercial disputes without resorting to the long and relatively difficult methods of arbitration and litigation. What is important is the cooperation of the two parties in the mediation proceedings, because they are not bound by the verdict of the mediator, whose role is essentially to moderate and balance the discussion and suggest ways to reach a common ground on a mutually agreeable basis. Of course, mediation can become a long and tedious process, if both parties adopt a confrontational approach and especially if the issues involved are complex and the mediator is relatively unfamiliar with them at the outset.

In summary, the international businessperson operating in overseas environments is faced with a multitude of complex, differing, and sometimes conflicting bodies of law regarding allowable forms and activities. Thus, it is crucial that the firm ensure adequate coverage by its own legal staff or by retaining effective local counsel. In doing so, the company can take the greatest amount of precaution to avoid problems that can arise in international legal disputes.

Local Courts, Local Remedies

If disputes are not resolved by the informal methods, parties to the contracts have at least two possible paths of dispute resolution to pursue—commercial litigation and international arbitration—which assume that other methods of dispute resolution have been ineffective. Before these methods can be used, another established rule of international law holds that recourse to international legal forms is only pursued once the parties have exhausted local possibilities for achieving relief. These local remedies include the use of local courts or action by national governmental and administrative bodies. This rule applies, however, only to actions between private

parties and not to those between states and individuals, because a state cannot be said to have local remedies to exhaust. The exhaustion rule protects the interests of both the foreign national and a host state. By respecting the sovereignty of states and the primacy of national jurisdiction in international disputes, the rule gives the states the necessary flexibility to regulate their internal affairs. At the same time, the rule requires states to recognize their international responsibility to offer justice to foreign nationals. Thus, the rule protects the interest of the multinational by promising either effective local remedies or a remedy in an international form.

The Principle of Comity

The principle of sovereignty provides for international etiquette in the form of reciprocal respect by countries for each other's laws and powers with respect to the acts of citizens abroad. This is the principle of comity, under which each nation defers to another's sovereignty in the protection of the rights of foreign citizens under their own legislative, executive, and judicial systems. The provision of comity is discretionary for each government and stems not from law, but from tradition and good faith. It accounts for the international convention of governments that provides immunity from the laws of the visited country for another nation's diplomats. The expectation is that in reciprocity the governments of foreign nations will similarly provide for diplomatic corps members working abroad.

Litigation

The litigation of international disputes involves the use of courts to apply both domestic and international law in order to resolve the stated conflicts between parties. In the event that litigation is necessary, parties look to the courts of the host country, the home country, or even the courts of a third country for a resolution of their legal differences.

Litigation through court systems has the disadvantage of being a lengthy and involved process that can use a vast amount of resources in the form of time and expenses for the firm. For example, obtaining evidence from one country while in another is an intricate process involving letters rogatory, which provide the means for courts of different countries to communicate with each other. Domestic lawyers obtain letters rogatory by petitioning the district court where the action is pending to issue letters to the appropriate judicial counterpart in the foreign country. The letters, couched in standard polite language, request the provision of certain evidence necessary to try the case in home courts. Generally, under the principle of comity, courts will grant such requests. Obstacles and refusals do arise in foreign environments when national interests or principles are involved, as is the case when U.S. courts seek evidence in antitrust suits intended to extend judicial extraterritoriality.

Another problem with litigation is that even if a party receives a judgment in its favor, it may have difficulty enforcing that judgment, particularly if the court used for settlement of the dispute does not have jurisdiction over the losing party. Jurisdiction is the capacity of a nation to prescribe a course of conduct for its citizens and to enforce a rule of law on its citizens. In order to enforce any legal rule, both jurisdiction to prescribe and jurisdiction to enforce that rule must be present. Because of all of these complexities and in the interest of expediency, those involved in disputes of an international nature often turn to arbitration, a quicker and easier method of resolving such disputes.

An example of the problems of jurisdiction is evident in the case of a major U.S. international bank, Banker's Trust Company, and Libya. In January 1986, in an effort to deter Libya from supporting the activities of terrorists in the Middle East and Europe, President Ronald Reagan instructed all Americans to leave Libya and placed a total ban on the conduct of trade between the two countries. In conjunction with the trade ban, and in order to protect U.S. companies with as-

sets in Libya against retaliation, Reagan ordered a freeze on all Libyan assets located in the United States or held by U.S. banks. Officials estimated that the freeze involved several hundred million dollars, primarily in cash and other liquid assets.[3]

At the time of the freeze, the Libyan government had deposits with Banker's Trust of nearly $300 million, with $161 million on deposit in the London branch and $131 million in New York—all of which was frozen. Subsequently, the Libyan Arab Foreign Bank sued in British courts for the return of its funds on the grounds that a freeze of assets by the United States was not enforceable overseas. The lawyer for the Libyan bank asserted that British law governed deposits in that country and that the policies and actions of other nations should not interfere. The "writ of the United States does not run in this country," he said.[4]

Banker's Trust argued the other side of the question, asserting that it could only repay foreign currency deposits in the currency concerned. Thus, to repay Libya it would have to use dollars in London and would therefore be breaking U.S. sanction law by releasing the funds denominated in dollars.

The British court ruled in favor of Libya on the grounds that U.S. law had no jurisdiction over English banking activities.

International Arbitration

In arbitration, parties to a dispute agree to take their case to a third party in the form of an agency of independent arbitration. They submit whatever documents of evidence they feel are relevant and agree to accept the judgment of the arbitrators, waiving their rights to appeal through court systems.

Arbitration has several advantages over litigation. It is a speedier process than court procedures; parties have a say in the choice of expert arbitrators, as compared to arbitrary judicial assignments;

---

[3] Felton 1986.
[4] Duffy 1987.

and the parties can have private adjudication. Results are achieved faster and less expensively in arbitration, because the proceedings are less complex and less formal than in litigation. The main drawback of international arbitration is that its use forecloses further appeals, because there is no parallel in arbitration to appellate courts within judicial systems.

The use of arbitration by international parties is backed by laws and governmental treaties that allow for the recognition and enforcement of awards made through arbitration. The United States is a signatory to many treaties providing for the recognition of arbitration, including the multinational treaties on arbitration in the New York Convention of 1958, the Inter-American Arbitration Convention of 1975, and the New York Convention on the Recognition and Enforcement of Foreign Arbitral Awards of 1970. This last treaty was signed by more than sixty countries, and it lends uniformity and credibility to the practice of international arbitration and provides for each country's recognition of arbitration awards and agreements. It also prevents the parties from appealing to the courts in each country from adjudicating disputes that they agreed to arbitrate.

In order to provide for arbitration rather than litigation of potential disputes between parties to an international contract, the terms of the contract must include a clause regarding the arbitration of potential disagreements. Arbitration clauses in international contracts must cover several important points of agreement between the parties, such as determination of the scope of the arbitration, the nature of potential disputes to be covered, and whether the arbitration findings are protected by national treaties. These clauses may even stipulate what language is to be used in the conduct of the arbitration.

More important, arbitration clauses in contracts between international parties include a choice of law under which to conduct the arbitration. Because each party usually prefers the procedural and substantive law of its own country to govern the proceedings, frequently the law of a third country is chosen as a compromise. Similarly, the contract clause often includes a choice of forum for the arbitration, which might be stipulated as an existing institutional framework, such as a major international arbitration center. One such center is the London Court of Arbitration, which has dealt with disputes regarding private international commercial transactions since 1982.

Other alternatives in the choice of arbitration forums are available. The parties can designate the use of a specific private and commercial arbitration firm or the creation of a commission to arbitrate the dispute. Many public entities choose the latter course because the commissions are composed of an equal number of arbitrators chosen by each side, to ensure proper airing of each party's position. Stipulating the choice of forum often has the advantage of simultaneously ensuring a choice of law under which there are minimal amounts of judicial interference prior to, during, and after the proceedings or of complex procedural requirements for conducting the arbitration. In England and France for example, statutes covering arbitration laws allow for judicial intervention in the process. The laws also allow for very narrow scopes of discovery and limited powers ceded to the arbitrator to force the production of evidence.

International Center for the Settlement of Investment Disputes

When the contract being disputed involves investments in foreign countries, the parties can seek adjudication through the International Center for the Settlement of Investment Disputes (ICSID), which is affiliated with the World Bank. This forum was established in 1967 through an international convention to settle disagreements arising between states and foreign investors, especially in cases of acts of state that result in the nationalization or expropriation of the assets of investors.

The role of the ICSID is not to develop rules and regulations regarding host country-investor relationships, but to establish a methodology and forum for disputing parties to resolve their differences. In order to use the ICSID, all parties must agree to refer their dispute to it and accept the ruling of that forum as final and binding. In addition, all signatory countries to the convention must accept the decision as binding. Signatories to the ICSID convention include most industrialized countries and many less-developed nations.

Most Latin American countries, however, do not subscribe to the ICSID, believing that its provisions infringe upon their sovereign rights. These nations subscribe to the Calvo Doctrine, which is the belief that when foreign interests choose to enter a nation and conduct business within that country, they are implicitly agreeing to be treated as if they were nationals and, thus, are subject to the laws and decisions of the sovereign nation and have no legal recourse outside that nation.

Disputes between states can be submitted for adjudication to the international court associated with the United Nations, the International Court of Justice at the Hague. All members of the United Nations by definition have access to this international court. The purpose of the court is to make judgments about disputes between nations that have chosen to submit to its jurisdiction. Problems or disagreements experienced by private individuals or corporate entities can only be brought before the court if they are sponsored or put forward by one of the court's member states. As with arbitration, the parties in the action must agree to submit to the jurisdiction of the court, but once a judgment is reached, there is no overriding international method of providing for the enforcement of that decision, saving through sanctions imposed by individual nations or other international pressures brought to bear on the transgressing party.

In the European Economic Community, members can seek redress of disputes through the Court of Justice, which not only rules on the constitutionality of EEC administrative activities, but also provides recourse for legal questions referred to it by any court in a member country. The judg-ments of the Court of Justice have the force of law in the EEC and are binding upon individuals, corporations, and governments. The purpose of the court is to provide for uniformity in the development of a legal process within the entire community.

Dispute settlement under trade agreements is generally achieved through consultations and negotiations between the parties. If terms cannot be reached they are sometimes taken to councils for consideration. Under the General Agreement on Tariffs and Trade (GATT), such a council can be appointed to hear such disputes and render an advisory opinion. Should one of the parties choose to ignore that advice, the complaining country is allowed to suspend its trade obligations with the other party of the suit.

Summary

The operations, profit, and welfare of the modern multinational corporation can be profoundly affected by differences in international legal systems or even the imposition of domestic laws upon the operations of a firm in foreign environments. These laws can be in the areas of antitrust activity, protection of intangible property rights, taxation, corrupt practices, and in all aspects of ongoing business operations for the multinational firm.

While the provision of treaties, trade agreements, and conventions among countries provide some international framework for a legal system, disputes continue to arise between parties in commerce. Some of these disputes can be avoided through the judicious writing of clear, unambiguous contracts that provide for these potential pitfalls. Some conflicts will still occur between private parties, between nations, or between nations and individual interests. The resolution of these conflicts involves the answering of questions regarding legal jurisdiction, statutory interpretation, and the enforcement of judgments by judiciaries or third-party arbitrators in either national or international forums.

Discussion Questions

1. Is there a single body of international law that governs all countries in the world?
2. What are the differences between civil law, common law, and religious law?
3. Why are international treaties important to conducting international business?
4. What is the doctrine of sovereign immunity?
5. What is extraterritoriality?
6. What is predatory pricing?
7. How do antidumping laws protect domestic manufacturers?
8. What are antitrust laws?
9. What U.S. law was enacted to control bribery and payoffs in international business? Why were bribes being paid? How do other countries view the practice of bribery?
10. What techniques can be used to resolve business disputes rather than resorting to litigation?
11. How is arbitration similar or different to litigation?
12. What is the International Court of Justice?

Bibliography

BRAND, RONALD A. 1990. "Private Parties and GATT Dispute Resolution: Implications of the Panel Report on Section 337 of the U.S. Tariff Act of 1930." *Journal of World Trade* (June): 5–30.

BROWN, JEFFREY A. 1986. "Extraterritoriality: Current Policy of the United States." *Syracuse Journal of International Law & Commerce* (Spring): 493–519.

CARROLL, EILEEN P. 1989. "Are We Ready for ADR in Europe?" *International Financial Law Review* (December): 11–14.

CHARD, J. S., and C. J. MELLOR. 1989. "Intellectual Property Rights and Parallel Imports." *World Economy* (March): 69–83.

DAVID, R., and J. BRIERLEY. 1978. *Major Legal Systems in the World Today,* 3rd ed. New York: Macmillan.

DUFFY, JOHN. 1987. "Libyan Bank Sues Bankers Trust." *American Banker* (June 10): 2.

FELTON, JOHN. 1982. "Congress May Weigh Limits on President's Authority to Impose Trade Restrictions." *Congressional Quarterly* (November 20): 2882–2884.

FELTON, JOHN. 1986. "Reagan Tightens Economic Sanctions on Libya." *Congressional Quarterly* (January 11): 59–60.

FOX, W. F. 1988. *International Commercial Agreements.* The Netherlands: Kluwer Law and Taxation Publishers.

GETZ, KATHLEEN A. 1990. "International Codes of Conduct: An Analysis of Ethical Reasoning." *Journal of Business Ethics* (July): 567–577.

GREER, THOMAS V. 1989. "Product Liability in the European Economic Community: The New Situation." *Journal of International Business Studies* (Summer): 337–348.

HARLAN, CHRISTI. 1988. "Citicorp Finds Name in Chinese Spells L-A-W-S-U-I-T." *Wall Street Journal* (September 7): 4.

KRUCKENBERG, DEAN. 1989. "The Need for an International Code of Ethics." *Public Relations Review* (Summer): 6–18.

LITKA, MICHAEL. 1988. *International Dimensions of the Legal Environment of Business.* Boston: PWS-Kent Publishing Company.

McGRAW, THOMAS K. 1986. *America versus Japan.* Boston: Harvard Business School Press.

Chapter Case Study _____

CompuSoft Systems, Inc.

It was a fairly thorough and well-drafted international sales and service agreement that CompuSoft Systems, Inc., of Palo Alto, California, had entered into with Los Santos Services, a large computer software reseller in the Latin American country of Cartunja. As Ken Rossi, marketing director of CompuSoft, read the fax message from Senõr Dom Simoes, executive vice-president of Los Santos, he regretted the decision to sell to Cartunja, even though the agreement had been hailed three years ago, upon its signing, as a major step forward in international market expansion in Latin America. "It's time to call in the attorneys," thought Rossi, as he reread the fax to let the implications of its contents sink in fully.

CompuSoft Systems began in 1981 as a small venture-capital enterprise, put together by a group of four young, technically qualified professionals. Mitch Holland had a Ph.D. in electrical engineering and had worked for four years with a large software development company in California's Silicon Valley. Tom Heilbroner held an M.S. degree in electronics and systems development from the University of Stanford and had been with the MIS division of a New York City-based multinational corporation for three years, where he developed specialized software and networking systems for the internal use of the company. Peter Daniels was a CPA and had worked in the consulting division of one of the Big 8 accounting firms for three years and had specialized in the development of computer-based accounting systems. Ken Rossi had an M.B.A. in accounting from Yale and also held an electrical engineering degree from Virginia Tech.

Like many Silicon Valley firms, CompuSoft had done extremely well. It had grown rapidly, and by 1987 sales had reached $640 million. The company was able to carve a small but significant niche in the accounting software market, and its wide range of accounting software applications packages had gained acceptance with a large number of U.S. companies. CompuSoft's products were known for their reliability and quality but further market expansion seemed difficult, given the growing intensity of competition especially from the larger and financially stronger software companies who offer aggressively priced products. Further, the market for accounting software in the United States appeared limited and overall market growth was leveling off.

In the face of these circumstances, CompuSoft concluded that the time was ripe for a shift in its strategy, and in 1988 the company decided to go international. None of the senior management had any international business experience, and initially there were some doubts about the wisdom of this move. It was felt, however, that the company need not take on the responsibility of marketing its products overseas itself and that this could be easily done through a local agent in a foreign country with whom the company would enter into a comprehensive agreement that would include all promises necessary to protect it from difficulties in the future.

Latin America was chosen as the first region for the international marketing effort of CompuSoft, and agreements were signed with three local software retailing companies in three countries, including Cartunja. The company hired a top San Francisco law firm specializing in such agreements to draft and negotiate the contracts with the local selling agents.

Under these contracts the local selling agents were to market CompuSoft's software packages in sealed covers, supplied in a fully finished form by the company. The agents were not permitted to make any alterations, modifications, or changes in either the contents of the software or in the external packaging. Another important provision of these agreements was that the reseller would advise each buyer in writing of the copyright to the software, and a statement of the restrictions on the use of the software was printed on the external cover of the software package. In addition, another leaflet defining the rights and obligations of the holder of the copyright (CompuSoft) was included in the package. The local agents also agreed to make all efforts to ensure that the copyrights of CompuSoft Systems were not violated in their respective countries.

For the first two years, things appeared to go well. The company had made considerable effort to adapt its accounting software to the needs of Latin American corporate customers, and the programs were an immediate success with local companies. The local agents also pushed the products because they were keen to maximize the attractive benefits of the graduated commission system put together by Rossi.

The first hint of problems came up in January 1990, when Senõr Simoes called Rossi to say that they would be lowering the estimates of sales to Peseta National Bank, a leading state-owned bank in Cartunja, which had 274 branches in 13 cities and townships all over Cartunja. Similarly, the estimated sales to eleven other state-owned banks were down by 60 percent. No reasons for the declines were given, except that the bank officials had informed Los Santos that their original interest in this software was only of a preliminary nature, and, on closer examination, they found that they were not ready to computerize their accounting systems using such sophisticated programs. The news came as a setback to CompuSoft, and, on closer analysis, it was felt that the reason given by the banks was not the real one. There was no competing product in Cartunja, and the banks badly needed to computerize their sys-

tems, having come under considerable criticism from the finance ministry and external auditors for having large arrears in the reconciliation of accounts between different branches and the corporate head offices. Further, Peseta National had already acquired the package from Los Santos, and it had been installed and running smoothly for the past four months. CompuSoft had also conducted a six-week training program, free of cost, for the accounting and systems personnel of Peseta National. The personnel were quite comfortable with the software and reported no problems. Therefore, in February 1990, Rossi called Simoes and asked him to dig further and find out what was really happening.

In the first week of March, Simoes came back with a startling answer—it appeared that the MIS division of Peseta National had copied the software and was busy installing it at seventy of its other branches. Further, he learned that Peseta was likely to pass the program on, along with installation services, to eleven state-owned banks. It was a clear violation of the copyright. CompuSoft's top management was, expectedly, disturbed. They called Simoes and asked him to take every possible step to stop Peseta National Bank from further infringing the copyright.

The fax on Rossi's desk was a reply from Senõr Simoes. In effect, it said that Peseta National Bank and the eleven other banks in question are 100 percent state-owned institutions, and any legal action against them would be tantamount to legal action against the government. Further, if Los Santos instituted a suit against Peseta National, it might lose substantial orders that it was negotiating with other state-owned enterprises. Given the power of the government, a suit would hurt Los Santos in its other lines of business and build an adversarial relationship with the government. It would therefore be better if CompuSoft would initiate action against the Peseta National Bank directly.

"This is a real big one," thought Rossi. "If we do go ahead and fight it out, the government may ban our products from official purchases. If we don't, everybody in Cartunja and everywhere else in Latin America will merely copy our software, and our entire international expansion effort there would come to naught."

Questions

1. What should CompuSoft Systems, Inc., do in this situation and why?
2. Suggest a strategy to deal with the situation, keeping in mind the possible international legal issues.

CHAPTER 9

Sociocultural Factors

CHAPTER OBJECTIVES

This chapter will:

- Define the term "sociocultural" as a combination of societal, political, and cultural norms and responses and discuss its influence in international business.
- Discuss how attitudes and beliefs influence human behavior, especially in attitudes toward time, achievement, work, change, and occupational status.
- Present the influence of aesthetics and material culture within different societies.
- Examine how language and communication, both verbal and nonverbal, may serve as barriers to international business operations.
- Investigate the importance of social status and the family within different cultures and their effect on the business environment.
- Identify the role of multinational corporations as agents of change in the international community.

Sociocultural Factors and International Business

Multinational corporations operate in different host countries around the world, and in doing so have to deal with a wide variety of political, economic, geographical, technological, and business situations. Moreover, each host country has its own society and culture, which is different in many important ways from almost every other society or culture, although there are some commonalities. Although society and culture do not appear to be a part of business situations, they are actually key elements in shaping how business will be conducted, from what goods will be produced, and how and through what means they will be sold, to establishing industrial and management patterns and determining the success or failure of a local subsidiary or affiliate.

Society and culture influence every aspect of overseas business of an MNC, and a successful MNC operation—whether it is marketing, finance, production, or personnel—has to be acutely aware of the predominant attitudes, feelings, and opinions in the local environment. Differences in values and attitudes between the management at the parent offices and expatriate managers at the subsidiary or affiliate level and local managers and employees can lead to serious operational and functional problems, which arise not because there are individual problems, but because of the important differences between the societies and cultures. Society and culture often mold general attitudes toward fundamental aspects of life, such as time, money, productivity, and achievement, all of which can differ widely across countries and lead to situations of differing expectations between the management in the home office and local employees of subsidiaries and affiliates.

While some sociocultural differences are obvious, others are relatively subtle, although equally important. It is often difficult for an international manager to catch on to these subtle differences if he or she has not lived or worked in cultures other than that of the home country (see Perspective 9–1).

PERSPECTIVE 9–1   Timely Tips: Some Friendly Advice for Our New Capitalist Friends

Welcome, Horst and Vlad and Todor and Piotr and, yes, even you, Boris! The era of international opportunity is thundering down upon us, and the borders that distinguished the old global order are fast becoming history. The world is opening like a giant bazaar, and in the not-too-distant future it is possible to see one giant market speaking one common language: capitalism. Bravo!

Many who ply their trade on an international scale will find it necessary to conduct some business right here in the U.S.A., even if we aren't the big shots we used to be. We want to do our share to help you. So here's our contribution: some all-American rules for non-U.S. business people as they wend their way around our halls of commerce.

TIP 1: JUST SAY YO!

At the start of any good American business relationship is a lusty American greeting. A crusty end-of-the-paw squeeze from a knobby cluster of British digits leaves a lot of us understandably cold. So get in there right off the bat and let us know you're darned happy to see us. Who knows? It just might be great to know us!

TIP 2: SISTERHOOD IS INEXORABLE

Cut out that sexism! Honestly. A female executive I know visited Japan a couple of years ago. She was one of about six people who could talk about her highly technological subject intelligently. She appeared in the board room of the corporation primed for a serious meeting. She wore her best suit. Within 15 minutes every senior Japanese official in the room had politely asked where her husband was. She replied that her husband was at home in New York, taking care of their three-year-old daughter. At last it dawned on them: *She was a secretary.* They brusquely asked to see her boss. She made it clear that *she was IT.* The meeting

SOURCE: Gil Schwartz, *Wall Street Journal*, September 21, 1990.

proceeded. The only other thing to report is that about halfway through the morning, my friend asked for directions to the Ladies' Room. There wasn't one.

Come on, guys. American women aren't going to go away even if you want them to. They're fit. They're rested. And they came to play. Get with the program.

TIP 3: EAT, DRINK AND BE MERRY

Americans love lunch. We also love breakfast and dinner. We'll even take a short snack, if we must. And in this era of contracting budgets, we do esteem those who feed and water us, whether the plastic is indigenous or imported from some outlandish location.

Remember, however, that most sane Americans still view such digestive events as essentially *social.* And watch that menu, OK? This is dinner, not a round of *quien es muy macho.* A pal of mine was over in Japan to close a deal not long ago. In the midst of negotiations, the group repaired to dinner. While eating his lobster, my friend was jolted when the creature turned its eye stalks around and gazed directly at him. It was... *alive.*

Don't forget: We like to kill our food before we eat it. You know that. Be nice.

TIP 4: THE CUSTOMER IS ALWAYS STRANGE

We're Americans! You may think you know us from Radio Free Europe or the Voice of America. But there are some things that may still surprise you. We don't take naps after lunch or drink tea unless we're sick, and we eat our salad *before* the main course. We're proud of the way we do things over here, even when we don't do them very well. And we have needs, see? Are you listening? Do you really and truly care? We'll love you for it!

TIP 5: NO GLOATING

The Germans have the World Cup. The Poles have the Pope. The Japanese have their entire perception of their perfect culture. We had adver-

tising. Now the British have it. That's fine. All's fair. But as you proceed to buy our businesses and mesmerize our consumers, try not to be so gosh-darned *jolly* about it. Just do it.

TIP 6: SPEAK SOFTLY BUT CARRY A BIG BERLITZ

Last month I tried to assemble a Korean-manufactured product. It was intended to be a bicycle when completed. About halfway through, I read something like: "Inserting pivot A axle and carefully into B groove not intended until sprocket assembly remaining when open (see Fig. 32¿B)."

We expect this from instruction manuals. We actually relish it. But not in person. When it comes to face-to-face conversation, we turn hopelessly xenophobic. Please to not it forget.

TIP 7: BROWN SHOES DON'T MAKE IT

Tune into the culture, babe. In most places except Los Angeles, the heavy business uniform is still dark blue or gray in winter and khaki on the most informal days of summer. A sport coat? Grow up.

This is as it should be. People are doing serious business here, or like to think they are. We don't, on the other hand, like to look like a bunch of FBI guys. Take my advice. Leaf through a couple of recent Esquires or GQs. Then go shopping.

TIP 8: CHARITY BEGINS WITH CONSULTING

So OK. Our products aren't necessarily the best. Our management style needs honing. Our workers are expensive and sometimes unproductive. We messed ourselves up! We admit it!

But we are the only ones who truly understand how we broke things well enough to fix them. And pretty soon, thanks to our performance in the '80s, a lot of us will be out there in the street, offering our wisdom. So hire us. Be forewarned: We don't come cheap. The going rate is $1,000 a day, minimum. Rest assured, though. We'll be forever grateful, and you'll get a full two-page report at the end of every month.

TIP 9: AS LONG AS YOU HAVE YOUR
HEALTH
Chill out, dudes. Wake up and smell the coffee.
Stop and smell the roses. The bird that's too early

can end up with nothing but worms. The 1990s
will be all about the reduction of international
stress. You first.

MNCs have realized, sometimes through costly blunders, that sociocultural factors are vital ingredients that make up the overall business environment and that it is essential to appreciate these differences and how they influence business before an attempt is made to set up an operation in a host country.

Society, Culture, and Sociocultural Forces

There are many definitions of culture. In general, culture can be defined as the entire set of social norms and responses that dominates the behavior of a population, which makes each social environment different and gives each a shape of its own. Culture is the conglomeration of beliefs, rules, techniques, institutions, and artifacts that characterize human population. It consists of the learned patterns of behavior common to members of a given society—the unique lifestyle of a particular group of people.

The various aspects of culture are interrelated; culture influences individual and group behavior and determines how things will be done. Features of culture include religion, education, caste structure, politics, language differences, and the process of production.

Society refers to a political and social entity that is defined geographically. In order to understand society and culture we must relate one to the other, hence the term "sociocultural." To be successful in their relationships with people in other countries, international managers must study and understand the various aspects of culture.

How should one begin? With as broad a concept as culture, it is necessary to utilize some type

of classification scheme as a guide to studying or comparing cultures. Figure 9–1 outlines Murdock's list of seventy cultural universals that occur in all cultures.* While this schematic is limited by its one-dimensional approach, it provides an initial guide and checklist to the international firm and manager. For example, the international firm selling contraceptives must be aware that it is dealing with the family customs, population policy, and sexual restrictions of different cultures. Since many individuals base their decisions regarding contraception on religious beliefs, the seller must also consider this aspect of various cultures in the plan.

Elements of Culture

There are too many human variables and different types of business functions for an exhaustive discussion about culture. Instead, we have broken down the broad area of culture into some major topics to facilitate study.

Attitudes and Beliefs

In every society there are norms of behavior based on attitudes, values, and beliefs that constitute a part of its culture. These vary from country to country. The set of attitudes and beliefs of a culture will influence nearly all aspects of human behavior, providing guidelines and organization to

---

* In George P. Murdock, "The Common Denominator of Cultures," in Ralph Linton, ed., *The Science of Man in the World Crises* (New York: Columbia University Press, 1945), pp. 123–142.

Cultural Universals

Age grading	Food taboos	Music
Athletic sports	Funeral rites	Mythology
Bodily adornment	Games	Numerals
Calendar	Gestures	Obstetrics
Cleanliness training	Gift giving	Penal sanctions
Community organization	Government	Personal names
Cooking	Greetings	Population policy
Cooperative labor	Hairstyles	Postnatal care
Cosmology	Hospitality	Pregnancy usages
Courtship	Housing hygiene	Property rights
Dancing	Incest taboos	Propitiation of sins
Decorative art	Inheritance rules	Supernatural beings
Divination	Joking	Puberty customs
Division of labor	Kin groups	Religious rituals
Dream interpretation	Kinship nomenclature	Residence rules
Education	Language	Sexual restrictions
Eschatology	Law	Soul concepts
Ethics	Luck/superstitions	Status differentiation
Ethnobotany	Magic	Surgery
Etiquette	Marriage	Tool-making
Faith healing	Mealtimes	Trade
Family	Medicine	Visiting
Feasting	Modesty concerning natural functions	Weaning
Fire-making	Mourning	Weather control
Folklore		

FIGURE 9–1   Murdock's List of Seventy Cultural Universals.

a society and its individuals. Identifying the attitudes and beliefs of a society, and how or if they differ from one's own culture, will help the businessperson more easily understand the behavior of people.

Attitudes toward Time

Everywhere in the world people use time to communicate with each other. In international business, attitudes toward time are displayed in behavior regarding punctuality, responses to business communications, responses to deadlines, and the amounts of time that are spent waiting in an outer office for an appointment. For example, while Americans are known to be punctual, few other cultures give the same importance to being on

time as Americans. In terms of business communications, Japanese companies may not respond immediately to an offer from a foreign company. What a foreign company may see as rejection of an offer or disinterest may simply be the lengthy time the Japanese company takes to review the details of a deal. In fact, the American emphasis on speed and deadlines is often used against them in foreign business dealings where local business managers have their own schedule.

Attitudes toward Work and Leisure

Most people in industrial societies work many more hours than is necessary to satisfy their basic needs for food, clothing, and shelter. Their attitudes toward work and achievement are indicative of their view toward wealth and material gain. These attitudes affect the types, qualities, and numbers of individuals who pursue entrepreneurial and management careers as well as the way workers respond to material incentives.

Many industrial psychologists have conducted research in this area to determine what motivates people to work more than is necessary to provide for their basic needs. One explanation is the Protestant ethic, which has its basis in the Reformation, when work was viewed as a means of salvation, and people preferred to transform productivity gains into additional output rather than additional leisure. Europeans and Americans are typically considered to adhere to this work ethic because they generally view work as a moral virtue and look unfavorably on the idle. In comparison, in places where work is only considered necessary to obtain the essentials for survival, people may stop working once they obtain the essentials.

Today, few other societies hold to this strict basic concept of work for work's sake, and leisure is viewed more highly in some societies than in others. It has been argued that many Asian economies are characterized by limited economic needs that reflect their culture. Therefore, it is expected that if incomes start to rise, workers would tend to reduce their efforts so that personal income remains unchanged. The promise of overtime may fail to keep workers on the job, and raising employee salaries could result in their working less, a phenomenon economists have called the backward bending labor supply curve. In contrast, the pursuit of leisure activities may have to be a learned process. After a long period of sustained work activity with little time for leisure, people may have problems in deciding what to do with additional free time.

These attitudes, however, can change. The demonstration effect of seeing others with higher incomes and better standards of living has motivated workers in such cultures to put in longer hours in order to improve their own financial status and material well-being. Additionally, attitudes toward work are shaped by the perceived rewards and punishments of the amount of work. In cultures where both rewards and punishments from greater or lesser amounts of work are low, there is little incentive for people to work harder than absolutely necessary. Moreover, when the outcome of a particular work cycle is certain, there is little enthusiasm for the work itself. Where high uncertainty of success is combined with some probability of a very positive reward for success, one finds greatest enthusiasm for work.

Attitudes toward Achievement

Cultural differences in the general attitude toward work are also accompanied by significant national differences in achievement motivation. In some cultures, particularly those with highly stratified and hierarchical societies, there is a tendency to avoid personal responsibility and to work according to precise instructions received from supervisors that are followed to the letter. In many societies, especially where social security is low and jobs are prized, there is a tendency to avoid taking risk and little innovation in work or production processes. In such cultures, the prospect of higher achievement is not considered attractive enough to warrant taking avoidable risks. In many industrial societies, however, attitudes toward personal achievement are quite different. Personal responsibility and the ability to take risk for potential gain are considered valuable instruments in achieving higher goals. In fact, in many cultures the societal pressure on achievement is so intense that individuals are automatically driven toward attempting ambitious goals.

The types of attitudes among workers and managers often influence the types of management that has to be utilized to achieve corporate goals. In a culture that emphasizes risk-taking, greater responsibility, and individual decision, a decentralized management system would be more appropriate. In a culture where there is a tendency to put in only adequate amounts of work and where achievement is not a valued attribute in a person, the company will follow a more centralized management system, with only limited delegation of decision-making authority.

Attitudes toward Change

The international manager must understand what aspects of a culture will resist change and how those areas of resistance differ among cultures, how the process of change takes place in different cultures, and how long it will take to implement change. There are two conflicting forces within a culture regarding change. People attempt to protect and preserve their culture with an elaborate set of sanctions and laws invoked against those who deviate from their norms. When differences are seen, they are perceived as, "My method is right and thus, the other method must be wrong."

The contradictory force is one in which the public is aware that the cultural environment is continually changing and that a culture must change in order to ensure its own continuity. In other words, in order to balance these attitudes, the manager must remember that the closer a new idea can be related to a traditional one when illustrating its relative advantage, the greater the acceptance of that new concept. Usually cultures with centuries-old traditions that have remained closed to outside influences are more resistant to change than other cultures. The level of education in a society and the exposure of its people to knowledge and the experience of other cultures is an extremely important determinant of its attitude toward change. The influence and nature of religious beliefs in a society also influences attitudes toward change.

Attitudes toward Jobs

The type of job that is considered most desirable or prestigious varies greatly across different cultures. Thus, while the medical and legal professions are considered extremely prestigious in the United States, civil service is considered the most prestigious occupation in several developing countries. The importance of a particular profession in a culture is an important determinant of the num-

ber and quality of people who will seek to join that profession. Thus, in a country where business is regarded as a prestigious occupation, the MNC will be able to tap a large, well-qualified pool of local managers. On the other hand, if business is not considered an important profession, much of the talent of the country will be focused elsewhere.

There is great emphasis in some countries on being one's own boss, and the idea of working for someone, even if that happens to be a prestigious organization, tends to be frowned upon. In many countries, however, MNCs are able to counter the lower prestige of business as a profession by offering high salaries and other forms of compensation. Some, in fact, succeeded in luring some of the best local talent away from jobs that are traditionally considered the most prestigious in those countries. In most cultures, there are some types of work that are considered more prestigious than others, and certain occupations carry a perception of greater rewards than others, which may be because of economic, social, or traditional factors.

Does Religion Affect Commerce?

International business is affected by religious beliefs in many ways, because religion can provide the spiritual foundation of a culture. Business can bring about modernization that disrupts religious traditions, and international business can conflict with holy days and religious holidays. Cultural conflicts in the area of religion can be quite serious. For example, a MNC would have problems with a subsidiary where employees traditionally enjoy a month-long religious holiday.

Religion can also impose moral norms on culture. It may insist on limits, particularly the subordination of impulse to moral conduct. Another example of business conflicting with religion is the development of a promotional campaign for contraceptives in any of the predominantly Roman Catholic countries.

In certain countries, religion may require its followers to dress in a particular manner or maintain a certain type of physical appearance, which may conflict with the appearance and presentation norms of the MNC. Certain products manufactured by the MNC or some ingredients used in manufacturing may be taboo in some religions. For example, beef and tallow are taboo in the Hindu religion and cannot be used as ingredients in soap manufacturing in India. Similarly, pork products cannot be sold or used in manufacture in Moslem countries because pork is religiously impure according to the tenets of Islam.

In many religions, the ideas of reality are completely different from the Western world. Within some Asian religions, for example, the notion exists that nothing is permanent and therefore the world is an illusion. To followers of such beliefs, time is cyclical—from birth to death to reincarnation and the goal of salvation is to escape the cycle and move into a state of eternal bliss (nirvana). These religious beliefs directly affect how and why people work, as in the Buddhist and Hindu religions, where people are supposed to eliminate all desires and, therefore, may have little motivation for achievement and the acquisition of material goods.

Aesthetics

Aesthetics pertains to the sense of beauty and good taste of a culture and includes myths, tales, dramatization of legends, and more modern expressions of the arts—drama, music, painting, sculpture, architecture, and so on. Like language, art serves as a means of communication. Color and form are of particular interest to international business because in most cultures these are used as symbols that convey specific meanings. Green is a popular color in many Moslem countries, but it is often associated with disease in countries with dense, green jungles. In France, the Netherlands, and Sweden, green is associated with cosmetics. Similarly, different colors represent death in different cultures. In the United States and many European countries, black represents death, while in Japan and many other Asian countries, white signifies death.

In many countries physical contact in public by persons of opposite sexes is not considered proper and exposure of the human body is treated as obscene. MNCs must be exceptionally careful in designing their advertising programs, the packaging of their products, and the content of their verbal messages to ensure that they do not hurt the aesthetic sensibilities of the country they are operating in.

Material Culture

Material culture refers to the objects and things used and enjoyed by people and includes all human-made objects. Its study is concerned with technology and economics. Material cultures differ very significantly, because of tradition, climate, economic status, and a host of other factors. Material culture is an extremely important issue to be considered by an MNC. Almost everything a society consumes, or, in other words, whatever the MNC sells or hopes to sell, will be determined by the material culture of the population. For example, selling humidifiers in a tropical country would be a failure, because they are not needed by the local people and are simply not a part of the material culture. Alternatively, selling American-style barbecues would be a failure in parts of the world where outdoor cookery is not a part of popular material culture.

Technology is an important factor that affects the material culture of a society. As more and more new products and processes are made available by technology, and if they are used by the people, they ultimately become a part of the material culture. A recent example is the personal computer, which has become an integral part of the material culture of most industrialized societies. Therefore, a U.S. multinational might target France or Australia as a major market for selling computer peripherals. There would not, however, be a market for this product in sub-Saharan Africa, at least at present, because computers are not a part of the material culture in these countries.

Tradition also determines material culture to a considerable extent. The French, for example, prefer drinking wine, while Germans prefer drinking beer, the distinction being largely traditional, but critical for a company aiming to establish a market for alcoholic beverages in these countries.

The particular physical and geographic circumstances of a country will also play an important part in influencing the material culture of a country. Space limitations in Japan prevent the development of large domestic appliances, such as big-capacity deep freezers or refrigerators, or for a real estate market featuring rambling suburban homes, even though the economy may be prosperous enough to pay for these luxuries. Thus, suburban home-owner living is not a part of the material culture of Japan, and this affects the type of products the Japanese middle class will or will not buy. For example, sales of lawn mowers, backyard pools, and home security systems are likely to be extremely low in Japan, while those of compact, sophisticated appliances and luxuries that can be accommodated in small apartments are likely to be very high.

Literacy Rate

The literacy rate is used by many areas of the international business firm. The marketer uses it to determine the types and sophistication of advertising. The personnel manager uses it as a guide in estimating the types of people available for staffing the operation. Literacy rate numbers, however, rarely provide any information about the quality of education.

Countries with low literacy rates are less likely to provide the MNC with all the qualified personnel it needs to staff its local operation and will necessitate the transfer of a large number of expatriate managers. Literacy rates have to be used with caution, however, because they often hide the fact that a country with a low literacy rate but a very large population may have a large number of qualified professionals who, as a percentage of the population may be very small, but form a fairly large absolute number by themselves. Lit-eracy rates generally have a more direct bearing on the general level of education and abilities of the workers at the lower levels, because much of the population that suffers from illiteracy is at the lowest economic level in society.

Education Mix

When considering education as an aspect of culture, an MNC should look not only at literacy rates and levels of education, but also try to understand the education mix of a certain society, that is, which areas are considered important for concentrated education? For example, a combination of factors caused a proliferation of European business schools patterned on American models. First, increased competition in the European Economic Community resulted in a demand for better-trained managers. Second, Europeans began establishing their own business schools after they were educated at American business schools and returned home. Third, the establishment of American-type schools with faculty from the United States was frequently accomplished with the assistance of American universities.

This trend toward specialized business education is slower in lesser-developed countries. Historically, higher education in LDCs has focused on the humanities, law, and medicine; engineering has not been popular, with the exception of architectural and civil engineering, because there were few job opportunities, and business careers have lacked prestige.

Brain Drain

Brain drain is a phenomenon experienced by many developing nations. Because governments over-invested in higher education in relation to the demand, developing nations have seen rising unemployment among the educated. These unemployed professionals must emigrate to industrialized nations, which effectively represents a loss to the country that has spent substantial amounts of scarce public resources to finance professional education.

Communication and Language

Communication and language are closely related to culture because each culture reflects what the society values in its language. Culture determines to a large extent the use of spoken language—specific words, phrases, intonations by people to communicate their thoughts and needs. These verbal patterns are reinforced by unspoken language—gestures, body positions, and symbolic aids.

Speaking becomes a cultural barrier between different countries and regions. In one country, verbal language can consist of many dialects and different colloquialisms and may be totally different from the written language. There is no way to learn a language so that the nuances, double meanings of words, and slang are immediately understood, unless one also learns other aspects of the culture.

Languages delineate culture. In some European countries there is more than one language and, hence, more than one culture. Belgium and Switzerland are two such examples, with French and Dutch spoken in the former, and German and French spoken in the latter. Different cultures exist within each country. One cannot conclude, however, that where only one language exists, there will be only one culture. Both the people of the United States and Great Britain speak English, but both countries have their own cultures. An example of the problems facing an international firm that must respond to the language aspects of a culture, is the sort of the computer hardware marketed in Canada.

Canada's heated debate about its official language may affect both typists and computer users. After several years of study, a joint government-industry committee has come up with Canada's first national standard for typewriter and computer keyboards with both English and accented-French letters.

Although the Canadian government is officially bilingual, English remains the dominant language.

Many English speakers resent the government's move to promote French, which is dominant only in Quebec. Hence, selling keyboards with both English and accented-French letters could prove to be an obstacle in the English-speaking provinces of Canada.

Where many spoken languages exist in a single country, one language usually serves as the principal vehicle for communication across cultures. This is true for many countries that were once colonies, such as India, which uses English. Although they serve as national languages, these foreign substitutes are not the first language of the populace and are, therefore, less effective than native tongues for reaching mass markets or for day-to-day conversations between managers and workers. In many situations, managements try to ease difficulties by separating the work force according to origin. The preferred solution is to teach managers the language of their workers.

When communication involves translation from one language to another, the problems of ascertaining meaning that arise within one culture are multiplied many times. Translation is not just matching of words with identical meanings. It involves interpretation of the cultural patterns and concepts of one country into the terms of those of another. It is often difficult to translate directly from one language to another. Many international managers have been unpleasantly surprised to learn that the noddings and yes responses of their Japanese counterparts did not mean that the deal was closed or that they agreed, because the word for yes, "hai", can also simply mean "it is understood" or "I hear you." In fact, it is typical of the Japanese to avoid saying anything disagreeable to a listener.

Many international business consultants advise the manager in a foreign country to use two translations by two different translators. The manager's words are first translated by a non-native speaker, then a native speaker will translate the first translator's words back into the original language. Unless translators have a special knowledge of the industry, they will often go to a dictionary for a literal translation that frequently makes no sense or is erroneous.

Nonverbal language is another form of communication. Silent communication can take several forms, such as body language, space, and language of things. Body talk is a universal form of language that may have different meanings from country to country. Usually, it involves facial expressions, postures, gestures, handshakes, eye contact, color or symbols, and time (punctuality). The language of space includes such things as conversational distance between people, closed office doors, or office size. Each of these has a different connotation and appropriateness in different cultures. The language of things includes money and possessions.

Groups: Families and Friends

All populations—men, women, and children—are commonly divided into groups, and individuals are members of more than one group. Affiliations determined by birth, known as ascribed group memberships, are based on sex, family, age, caste, and ethnic, racial, or national origin. Those affiliations not determined by birth are called acquired group memberships and are based on religious, political, and other associations. Acquired group membership often reflects one's place in the social structure. Employment, manners, dress, and expectations are often dictated by each culture to its members. Group rituals, such as marriage, funerals, and graduations, also form a part of the societal organization.

In some societies, acceptance of people for jobs and promotion is based primarily on their performance capabilities. In others, competence is of secondary importance. Whatever factor is given primary importance (seniority, sex, and so on) will determine to a great extent who is eligible to fill certain positions and their compensation. The more egalitarian or open a society, the less difference ascribed group membership will make.

Three types of international contrasts indicate how widespread are the differences in group memberships and how important they are as business considerations. These are sex, age, and family. Differences in attitudes toward males and females are especially apparent from country to country. The level of rigidity of expected behavior because of one's gender is indicative of cultural differences. Often, these differences are clearly reflected in education statistics, although many countries have instituted or have plans to institute additional educational opportunities for females.

In many countries age and wisdom are correlated. Where this is so, advancement has usually been based on seniority. In the past, this has been a common practice in Japan. Contrary to this, in many countries retirement at a particular age is mandatory and relative youthfulness may be an advantage in moving ahead. Barriers to employment on the basis of age or sex are undergoing substantial changes around the world and data that are even only a few years old are not considered reliable.

Kinship, or family associations, may play a more active role as an element of culture in some societies than in others. An individual may be accepted or rejected based on the social status of his or her family. Because family ties are so strong, there is a compulsion to cooperate closely within the family but to be distrustful of links involving others outside the family.

In some countries, the word "family" may have very different connotations. In the United States, we have come to depend on the nuclear family—mother, father, and children—as the definition of family. In other societies, the extended family may be the norm. A vertically extended family includes grandparents and possibly great grandparents as part of a single family, while horizontally extended families include aunts, uncles, and cousins.

The impact of the extended family on the foreign firm derives from the fact that it is a source of employees and business connections. Responsibility to a family is often a cause of high absenteeism in developing countries where workers are called to help with the harvest. Motivation to work also may be affected where workers are responsible for the welfare of their extended families. When additional income means additional mouths to feed and further responsibility, workers may reduce output if they are given an increase in salary.

The international firm may be directly affected by the cultural aspect of group and social organizations. Even if individuals have qualifications for certain positions, and there are no legal barriers for hiring them, social obstacles still may make the international firm think twice about employing them. Class structures can also be so rigid within one type of group that they are difficult to overcome in other contexts. For example, in a society where caste structures are deeply ingrained, serious problems could arise if these caste levels are not considered in determining work groups, supervisor roles, and managerial promotions; if individuals in a lower caste are placed higher within the corporate hierarchy than members of higher caste groups, internal tensions may arise.

Gift Giving and Bribery

Gift giving is a custom that has great value within a business environment. It is important not only to remember to bring a gift, but also to make certain that the gift you have chosen is appropriate. In some cultures, gift giving is not expected or encouraged, and the international business person must be familiar with the appropriate behavior in each environment.

Gift giving is viewed as a different and separate activity from bribery, at least in the United States. During the 1970s many large international companies were faced with serious problems after they were caught paying bribes to government officials to obtain large contracts from foreign business firms. While much of the criticism has been vented against multinational companies, especially those from the United States, it is important to note that the practice was widespread. In

1977, however, the United States passed the Foreign Corrupt Practices Act, making illegal certain payments by U.S. executives of publicly traded firms to foreign officials. The legislation has been controversial and often called inconsistent. One such inconsistency is that it is clearly legal to make payments to people to expedite their compliance with the law, but illegal to make payments to other government officials who are not directly responsible for carrying out the law. It is important for the international business executive to identify the thin line between complying with foreign expectations and bribery and corruption.

Management of Cultural Change

Managers must understand what aspects of a culture will resist change, how those aspects will differ among cultures, how the process of change takes place in different cultures, and how long it will take to implement changes. They must also consider that change may occur in different ways—their organization may act as an agent of change, influencing the foreign culture; it may be somewhat changed itself; or both create change and may be changed at the same time (see Perspective 9–2).

In deciding how much change an organization will assume and how an organization may attempt to influence the host environment, a manager must consider the value system of the organization and its strategic mission, goals, and objectives. In addition, the costs and benefits of change need to be outlined, because the costs of change may far outweigh the benefits reaped from change.

PERSPECTIVE 9–2   Culturing Change

The face a company presents to the world is determined by its corporate culture—the set of basic values, assumptions, goals and beliefs which

guides the way it operates. Culture gives firms their character: West Germany's Siemens and America's General Motors are conservative, reluctant

SOURCE: *The Economist*, July 7, 1990, page 65.

to change; Honda and SMH, a Swiss group that makes the Swatch watch, are mould-breaking innovators.

By their nature, corporate cultures evolve over a long period of time. They also tend to reflect the values of a company's founders: the service ethic of Ray Kroc has never left McDonald's, even though he died in 1984. But because old corporate cultures die hard, they can cause problems when firms try to change or merge with rivals. So how can companies, in a world of megamergers, shortening product cycles and fragmenting markets, turn corporate culture into a competitive tool, rather than a liability?

For part of the answer, look to Japan. Japanese firms appear to be steeped in corporate culture. The imposition of a "Japanese" management culture is often credited with vast improvements in productivity, labour relations and absenteeism in Japan's overseas ventures.

The car-assembly plant in Fremont, California, closed by GM in 1982 and reopened as a joint venture with Toyota the following year with 85% of the original, unionised workforce, is a good example. Called NUMMI, the firm now regularly achieves double the productivity of GM's other plants. Absenteeism, 18% per day before the joint venture, is negligible these days; quality is GM's highest. Mr. Charles O'Reilly, of the University of California at Berkeley, reckons a revitalised corporate culture is the key.

In one important respect Japanese firms are "thin-cultured." At the company level culture is expressed as a series of general principles: to strive for quality, to trade ethically, to be market leader, and so on. Honda's corporate credo trumpets its dedication to "supplying products of the highest quality yet at a reasonable price for worldwide customer service."

This thin, company-level culture imbues a common mission but is vague enough to survive the most rapidly changing business environment. Cynics may condemn such creeds as platitudes which are ignored by employees, but Japanese companies reckon they help workers to know

what their firm stands for, and to identify their aims with those of the firm. Honda believes that its culture breaks down traditional hierarchical relations between managers and managed. At NUMMI that is what happened. Before Toyota turned up, workers at the Fremont plant viewed GM as the enemy.

Honda goes further than bland, company-level mission statements, however. Each of its three main divisions has spawned an individual culture tailored to its own aims. Honda's R&D division, for instance, is an independent company with its own president and a deep culture of innovation and eagerness for change. "Idea contests" ingrain that culture in employees by rewarding promising, but still-uncommercial, projects with seed funding.

Honda reckons that encouraging the emergence of competing cultures within each of a firm's business units helps them (and thus the entire company) to be more responsive to fast-changing markets. It also creates "role-models": a firm's other business units can learn from the culture of the most successful division.

Western companies are beginning to learn from this. BP, the world's third-biggest oil company, is in the throes of overhauling its corporate culture. BP completed a takeover of America's Standard Oil in 1987; a year later it snared Britoil, another British oil company. Bringing together three diverse cultures was difficult. BP probably had an ingrained "civil-service" mentality (it was once state-owned), but its business outlook was solidly international. BP thought Standard's inward-looking, provincial culture had led it to make a string of bad business decisions (like squandering billions of dollars looking for non-existent giant American oilfields, rather than pursuing better opportunities abroad). Standard Oil's attitude to its new owner was not helped by the swift sacking of Mr. Al Whitehouse, its chief executive, to be replaced by BP's Mr. Robert Horton (now its chairman).

Backed up by an ambitious programme of restructuring—a third of BP's headquarters team has been scrapped and 70 of the group's central committees disbanded—Mr. Horton is implementing a long-term programme to create a new, tiered corporate culture, guided by an internal "culture change group". The end result will look distinctly Honda-ish.

At group level, BP's corporate culture will be barely visible—just the usual commitments to quality of service and environmental responsibility. Instead, each of BP's four operating divisions is supposed to be developing its own culture.

So far only BP Exploration, which has been advised by Mr. Richard Pascale, a lecturer at California's Stanford University, has made significant headway. It has come up with six culture "guidelines": people, openness, teamwork, simplicity, trust and empowerment. Consultants' platitudes? BP thinks not. It reckons that by concentrating people's minds (and actions) on those six words it will produce a workforce that is freer from bureaucracy, more flexible and more innovative. BP Exploration has already whittled down seven layers of management to four. Decision-making and responsibility are being pushed further down the firm.

The danger is that fragmented cultures can cause corporate civil war. A firm with several competing cultures can end up pulling in many directions at once. Stanford's Mr. Pascale believes that this generates "constructive tension", and that, to quote from the subtitle of his new book, "Managing on the Edge", "the smartest companies use conflict to stay ahead". Internal conflict, says Mr. Pascale, can sharpen competitive instincts. That may work for Japanese companies like Honda, whose natural commitment to teamwork is deeply enough ingrained to withstand and even benefit from such competitive conflict; western companies may find it harder to adopt. BP could end up either becoming an honorary Japanese oil company—or tearing itself apart.

If it is determined that some change is necessary in the foreign locale, the international manager should remember that resistance to change is low if the number of changes is not too great. If too much change is perceived by individuals within a certain culture at the outset, resistance will be stronger. In the same vein, individuals will be more apt to allow and accept change, if they are involved in the decision and participate in the change process. Also, people are more likely to support change when they see personal or reference group rewards.

In order to ease the problems with change, the international manager must find opinion leaders and try to convince those who can influence others. The international firm should also time the implementation of change wisely. Change should be planned for a time when there is the least likelihood of resistance. When considering timing, all elements should be considered to avoid conflict, such as political disturbances or religious holidays. Moreover, the international manager needs to look toward the home office for possible areas for change that will improve the potential for acceptance and success within the foreign environment.

Summary

When businesses cross national borders, they face a diversity of societies and cultures quite different from their own. Society refers to a political and social entity that is geographically defined and is composed of people and their culture. Culture is a set of social norms and responses that conditions the behavior of a population. The term "sociocultural" describes how society and culture relate to each other.

When studying culture, the major topics are attitudes, beliefs, religion, aesthetics, material culture, education, language, and society organizations. Attitudes and beliefs influence human behavior by providing a set of rules and guidelines including attitudes on time, achievement and work, change, and the importance of occupation. Religion provides the spiritual basis for a society by imposing moral norms and appropriate behavior. Aesthetics include various forms of artistic expression. Material culture refers to objects and possession by others and focuses on technology, while nonmaterial culture covers a set of intangibles. Communication and language can be silent, as well as spoken or written, and may be a barrier to an international organization. Silent language includes body language, gestures, color, and symbols.

Societal organizations may take a number of different forms and indicate the level of social stratification within a society. Social groups may be either ascribed (determined by birth) or acquired.

Business customers may differ from one country to another and must be understood before beginning any negotiations or business dealings outside one's own culture. Understanding the importance of gifts and how they differ from bribes can be critical to international business relations.

The international organization must understand cultural differences when attempting to initiate change in a foreign location. Change must be carefully planned and the costs and benefits of change must be clearly identified.

Discussion Questions

1. Define the term "sociocultural." Why should international business managers be aware of this term when making their everyday decisions?
2. What are the elements of culture?
3. What is the typical American and European attitude toward work? Do you personally hold this attitude toward work?
4. How can religious beliefs affect international business decisions in the Middle East?

5. You have found out that your competitor is paying bribes to generate new business. Should you also pay them? Explain.
6. How can nonverbal communication affect a business relationship?
7. How might family groups and extended families affect the decisions of an international manager?
8. Why might multinational corporations act as agents of change? Provide some examples.
9. How can managers of a multinational firm get their local employees to accept new ideas?

Bibliography

1983. "Some Guidelines on Dealing with Graft in Korean Operations." *Business International* (February 25): 62.

1984. "All in Favor of Bribery, Please Stand Up." *Across the Board* (June): 3–5.

1988. "A People Problem." *The Economist* (November 26): 49–50.

1989. "Islam for Beginners." *The Economist* (March 18): 95–96.

COMMISSION OF THE EUROPEAN COMMUNITY. 1985. *The European Community and Education.* Brussels: Commission of the European Community.

FATEMI, KHOSROW. 1985. "Multinational Corporations, Developing Countries, and Transfer of Technology: A Cultural Perspective." *Issues in International Business* (Summer/Fall): 1–6.

JACOBY, N. H., P. NEHEMKIS, and RICHARD EELLS. 1977. *Bribery and Extortion in World Business.* New York: Macmillan.

KIM, W. CHAN, and R. A. MAUBORGNE. 1987. "Cross-Cultural Strategies." *The Journal of Business Strategy* (Spring): 28–35.

REARDON, KATHLEEN. 1981. *International Business and Gift-Giving Customs.* Janesville, WI: Parker Pen.

TERPSTRA, VERN, and K. DAVID. 1985. *The Cultural Environment of International Business,* 2nd ed. Cincinnati: South-Western Publishing.

Chapter Case Study

Delis Foods Corporation

The year 1989 was a very good one for Delis Foods Corporation, a San Francisco-based food conglomerate. Its domestic sales were $24 billion and its international sales were $7 billion, making it one of the largest companies in the processed foods business. Innovative product development and strong marketing strategies were two of the main reasons for its success. Its international operations were directed out of San Francisco by William Shaefers, an executive with almost eighteen years of experience in international marketing, the last ten of which had been in the marketing of food products. Shaefers was proud of the 1989 performance, in which his division had registered a worldwide sales increase of 12 percent over the previous year. Despite the overall results, however, there were two areas that continued to trouble him. Both were in the Asian country of Dikorma.

Dikorma, a small country in Southeast Asia with a population of about 60 million, is a nation that is fast industrializing, and the per capita GNP has risen to $6,600 per annum from a level of only $2,400 per annum twelve years ago. It was viewed by Delis foods as an important target market that presents excellent opportunities. There is a large middle class that was fairly cosmopolitan and sophisticated. The country has a relatively free export-import market and the balance of trade was maintained comfortably. Retail distribution is well-developed and necessary ancillary services—transportation, banking, and commercial codes—are also not a problem. The initial experience of Delis Foods with its large-scale marketing of instant noodles in Dikorma had been a great success. Delis soon became a household brand name, and it was able to penetrate the market quite successfully with other

products, such as ketchup, instant coffee, and nondairy creamers.

Following up on its success, Delis Foods decided to make a bid for a segment of the huge cold-drink market. Dikorma is a tropical country and temperatures remain above 90 degrees for the entire year except for one month. There is a large urban middle class, which provides a steady market for cold drinks. Delis Foods decided to introduce instant iced tea into this market. The product idea was fairly simple. The company would market iced tea in concentrate liquid form, and the consumer would only have to add water and ice to get a cool drink. There was no other iced tea brand available and Delis Foods would have a monopoly. Moreover, Dikorma's middle class had proven receptive to new ideas in the past—the case of instant noodles was clear evidence.

The company decided on a hard-sell campaign across the country, utilizing all major media, including television, radio, newspapers, magazines, and roadside signs. The main theme was simple: "Beat the heat with Velima Iced Tea." A number of promotions were carried out, and the distributors and retailers were given attractive discounts to push the product.

Despite the initial effort, sales did not take off, and three months after the product launch, it began to become increasingly clear that the company had a loser on its hands. Shaefer was extremely annoyed and placed the blame on the marketing staff who designed and implemented the campaign. He asked them to find the reasons why the product had not taken off and to modify the campaign accordingly.

The marketing group in Dikorma analyzed the entire project quite intensively, but it came up with little that could be called a mistake in the campaign. Moreover, there was apparently no dissatisfaction with the quality of the product. True, the coverage of the product had been limited to the urban centers, but that was because it was relatively highly priced and the rural market could not afford a sophisticated product like instant iced tea. The product was retested but it was found to conform to all standard requirements and there were no quality problems.

Confident that they had corrected the few errors in the campaign and assured that the product had no quality problems, the local marketing group of Delis Foods launched another, bigger campaign, promoting the product much more aggressively than in the previous campaign. This time attractive consumer incentives were offered, such as a free crystal glass with the purchase of every bottle of iced tea. The results were somewhat better. Attracted by the offer of free glasses and by the glittering campaign, consumers reacted positively and sales started to improve. The marketing group heaved a sigh of relief, but not for long.

Within the next six months, for what appeared to completely inexplicable reasons, sales began to drop off again. The company had not increased the price, nor were the initial incentives withdrawn, although it was proving quite expensive to the company to maintain these incentives. The drop in sales continued and began to become more accentuated each month. The marketing group and Shaefer were perplexed. They seemed to have done everything right, but all of a sudden, everything seemed to go wrong.

After eight months of the second promotion, sales were so low that the company started to lose money on the product. The retailers also became nervous and stopped ordering. Some then complained that they were having trouble disposing of their inventories. Schaefer had to make a painful decision—to admit that the product had failed and to withdraw it from the market. He did so in July 1989 and Velima Iced Tea was taken off the shelves in Dikorma. The chairman of Delis Foods, Peter Sanderson, was

quite philosophical about the issue and told Schaefer not to be too hard on himself. "We all learn from our mistakes," he told Schaefer and asked him to find out why the product had failed.

Thinking over this issue, Schaefer realized that it might be a good idea to get an external view of the problem. After all, in-company analysis, however sharp and intense, still has its limitations. Moreover, in this case the limitations were exposed beyond doubt. Delis Foods had tried to think of all the reasons why its iced tea failed, but did not come up with any that would explain in concrete form, why an excellent product failed in an excellent market despite a great campaign and all other positive circumstances. He called MacArthur & Associates in Jakarta and asked for Gayle Johnston. Johnston was the chief marketing consultant at MacArthur & Associates and was an expert on Southeast Asia markets. "He should be able to tell us what really went wrong," thought Schaefer, as he noted his appointment with Johnston for next Thursday in San Francisco.

The meeting with Johnston was quite illuminating. Johnston brought to bear a whole new line of thinking. According to him, it was a sociocultural asymmetry that caused problems for Delis Foods in Dikorma. According to Johnston, there was no way an iced tea product could have succeeded in Dikorma because it clashed very strongly with ingrained sociocultural values. People in Dikorma, Johnston pointed out, do not drink tea without milk. In Dikorma iced tea by definition is drunk with milk and the entire campaign showed the beverage as being essentially sweetened black tea with ice. The other cultural barrier, Johnston continued, was that tea in Dikorma was viewed as a hot drink, not a cold one. Dikormans have been drinking hot tea for hundreds of years and were not likely to see it as a cold drink. Cold milk, yes, even perhaps cold coffee, but certainly not iced tea.

Schaefer protested that Dikormans had reacted positively to instant noodles, and they had never had those before. They also had adopted several other new products—ready-baked cakes, frozen pizzas, and so on. Why this hostility for iced tea? "That is simple," replied Johnston. He explained that they did not have pizza or cake ingrained in them as a part of their traditional culture. These were new products and they accepted them as such. What was not new and was ingrained in their culture was tea. It is general experience that ingrained dietary habits are quite difficult to change, especially if the change is dramatically opposite of the existing culture.

"Perhaps you are right," Schaefer said. "At least the market has proved that you are. In the future we should do better. How about doing a study of the sociocultural traits of Dikorma and of our products to suggest which products we should try to keep out of this market?"

"That will be no problem. Only please make sure that you tie in the recommendations of my study with those of your marketing group," concluded Johnston.

Questions

1. What kind of strategy would you advise Delis Foods Corporation to adopt to avoid this kind of situation in the future? Analyze the sociocultural traits of a select country and devise a food product strategy that suits the cultural environment.

2. Suggest a list of typical processed food items that would in your opinion not be successful in a country with a tropical climate and explain why.

CHAPTER 10

Comparative Management

CHAPTER OBJECTIVES

CHAPTER OBJECTIVES

This chapter will:

- Present the commonly held management philosophies of Theory X and Theory Y as they are practiced globally.
- Compare the variety of decision-making and managerial methods in current international use.
- Discuss how different management styles result in different multinational corporate performance objectives.
- Describe how legal and political systems in different regions influence management practices.

Theory X versus Theory Y

Multinational corporations operating in different countries are faced with a wide variety of differing management styles in individual host countries. Differences in management style arise from a variety of factors—the history, culture, and traditions of the local society; the state of economic development; the corporate philosophy of other firms in the country; labor and corporate law structures; and the degrees of foreign influence. Each MNC also has its own corporate culture and management styles, which, in general, varies significantly from the style prevalent in the host country.

The two most commonly held streams of management philosophy, are known as Theory X and Theory Y, which were developed by Douglas McGregor. Theory X holds that workers are generally irresponsible, unwilling to work, and must be persuaded to perform their obligations to their employers. On the other hand, Theory Y holds that given an appropriate work environment and in the absence of exceptional disincentives, workers are dedicated to their tasks, are generally self-motivated, and will carry out their tasks with minimal direction from their superiors. The two basic styles are reflected in management policies on job design, training, employee security, reward structure, organizational structure, and industrial relations.

Comparative Management Philosophies: Who's Who

In North America, management philosophy is predominantly based on Theory X, although in some companies there are more participative management practices. Job security is limited and information is disseminated to the workers only to the extent of what they need to know to perform their specific jobs. The orientation of the managers is generally toward short-term profitability, and layoffs are common to improve the bottom line for a particular accounting period. Workers feel no particular loyalty to the company, and, in fact, adversarial relationships between the company and its employees are common in many industries.

In contrast, Japanese management philosophy centers on Theory Y. Because workers are deemed to be loyal and devoted, they are treated as valuable assets of the company and are invited not only to run their own jobs but also to contribute to the overall decision-making process within the company. The management philosophy is expressed in unique personnel policies followed by many Japanese corporations—lifetime employment, seniority-based wage increases and promotions, and in-house unions. Layoffs are rare, even when the company suffers from financial difficulties.

At the same time, workers tend to stay with the company for long periods, and employee turnover rates are much lower than the United States. The philosophy of rewarding workers based on seniority generally promotes more harmonious group relationships and adds to the incentive of staying with the company. Management respects senior members as key elements in maintaining good management-labor relationships and as repositories of valuable experience gained over the years.

Companies in Europe generally follow Theory X philosophies. Workers generally operate under close supervision with clear-cut operational guidelines. Job security is relatively low and employee turnover is high. Union management relations are generally adversarial, especially in Great Britain, Italy, and, more recently, in countries of the Eastern bloc. Management styles tend to be relatively more participative in Europe than in the United States, Latin America, and Asia, although less so than in Japan.

Latin American companies believe in Theory X and adversarial relations between workers and management are common, especially in Argentina and Brazil, which have extremely powerful and militant trade unions. There is considerable emphasis on maximizing management control over all aspects of corporate organization. The general philosophy and approach are clearly authoritarian, with superiors exercising close control over their subordinates across different levels in the organization.

Because many Latin American enterprises are family-owned or family-controlled, there is little professionalization of management, particularly at the senior- and middle-management levels. Given the innate authority of controlling family members, the workers and other low-level employees generally prefer to work within their prescribed parameters and are not overly ambitious in their efforts or contributions to the organization. The judgments of superiors are generally followed without question, even though the outcome may not be in the best interests of the company. Superiors often inspire awe and fear among subordinates.

Decision-Making

North America: Authoritarian

The authoritarian decision-making process is clearly hierarchical, and decision-making authority is given to managers according to their levels of responsibility in the organization. The emphasis is on practical, realistic, and rational decision-making, using hard data and, more recently, computerized decision support systems. Important decisions, however, are made only by a certain level of executive, and the lower-level employees do not participate in the decision-making process except to the extent of supplying information required by the top management. Although employee suggestions and input are welcomed, they are usually not actively encouraged, especially for day-to-day business decisions.

Western Europe: Limited Codetermination

European decision-making patterns are generally quite different among the various countries, ranging from limited codetermination in some Western countries to greater worker participation in the socialist countries. In Germany, for example, decision-making involves workers and management, acting together on many important issues, especially because of the legally mandated system of codetermination. Collective decision-making is facilitated by a common belief in high productivity and adherence to strict quality control among both the managers and workers. Also, the decision-making process tends to be built around low-risk conservative approaches.

In the United Kingdom, decision-making is usually split into two major levels. While the higher-level managers, usually from generalist backgrounds, make all the policy, strategic, and major organizational decisions, the technical and day-to-day operational decisions are left to middle management, people who are technically qualified for the purpose. The lack of persons with technical backgrounds at the top levels in several British firms often results in an avoidance of risky and aggressive decisions, because top managers feel uncertain about acting on technical information supplied by their subordinates, which they themselves are not in a position to evaluate with the requisite level of detail and thoroughness.

Decision-making in France tends to be highly centralized, and there is only limited delegation of authority, even to the middle managers. Strong and comprehensive direction and control from the French government and the relative lack of market competition lead to a general avoidance of risky decisions and reliance on conservative and standard policies in many large French corporations. Some studies have also found that the relatively hierarchical nature of French organizations acts against the middle managers exercising their decision-making capacity to the full, thereby resulting in lower performance levels than expected or achieved.

In Scandinavia, however, there is a relatively greater degree of codetermination, given the significance placed on the role of the individual within the organization. The management tries to tap the creative and thinking capacity of employees down the line to arrive at decisions that best suit corporate interests. The decision-making process is markedly less hierarchical than in the United States or France, and there is substantial bottom-up flow of suggestions and other input. Delegation of decision-making authority also covers larger spheres and levels of responsibility.

Japan: Consensual

Decision-making in Japan employs a unique process of consensus among different levels within the organization, known as the ringi seido (see Perspective 10–1). The ringi seido process involves a bottom-up approach to decision-making, where the initiative is taken by the person who is going to be directly affected by the decision. Decision proposals move up from the initiating individual to the section head, the departmental head, and then to top management. The proposal is circulated laterally across different divisions of the company to solicit the views and expertise of other persons in the company. The proposals are finally approved by management after obtaining the consent of all the departments affected by the decision. Although the decision process may be slow under this system, implementation is rapid, because all parties concerned have agreed in advance.

PERSPECTIVE 10–1 Can Japan's Giants Cut the Apron Strings? Top-to-Bottom Control from Tokyo Frustrates Overseas Managers

Japan's leading manufacturers, which once clung to domestic production strategies, have become zealous converts to the new creed of globalization. Scarcely a week goes by without a Japanese company announcing a U.S. acquisition, a design center in Europe, or a factory in Southeast Asia.

But Japan's international managers have a long way to go to catch up with their U.S. and European counterparts. Only a handful of Japanese companies—mainly in autos, electronics, tires, and steel—have put full-fledged research and production bases abroad. Most of Japan's overseas investment has been in assembly plants, with more sophisticated design and manufacturing work kept at home. Ricoh Corp.'s copier plant in Irvine, Calif., for example, triggered European protests of quota violations when it began exporting to Europe because its copiers' U.S. content was so low.

The Japanese management structure is also still mainly home-based. Even low-level decisions must come out of face-to-face meetings in Tokyo. U.S.-based managers make grueling 13-hour trips for one-day meetings so often that they call them "kamikaze flights." This consensus-building, involving thousands of trips a year, has made Japanese companies especially effective in carrying out decisions, but critics argue that it's self-defeating as the manufacturing giants expand. "It's their Achilles' heel," says Harvard business school management professor Christopher A. Bartlett.

Heavy-handed control also plays havoc with efforts to retain foreign executives. Two top American managers of Mazda Motor Corp.'s Flat Rock (Mich.) plant quit last October because they were shut out of key decisions. Since it was the second round of defections, Mazda replaced them with Japanese. And just months after Bridgestone Corp. named an American as chief of its re-

cently acquired Firestone Tire & Rubber Co., it sent Chairman Teiji Eguchi directly to Akron to help oversee the integration.

SUING

At dozens of other Japanese subsidiaries, U.S. executives have quit, and some are suing their employers for failing to live up to agreements. In a study of American managers at 31 Japanese-owned companies in the U.S., the University of Michigan's Vladimir Pucik found that even the most gung-ho Americans felt they had too little responsibility and too few chances for promotion.

Japanese executives acknowledge that their overseas units are far less autonomous than foreign subsidiaries of Western-style world companies. "We're 10 to 20 years behind in internationalization," says Shoichiro Irimajiri, senior managing director at Honda Motor Co. But Irimajiri and other corporate leaders insist that the gap will largely disappear.

To catch up, the Japanese are beginning to design and engineer more products in the U.S. and Europe, they're buying more parts locally, and they're donating millions to charity and civic causes. Keizai Doyukai, an association of top executives, is also calling on Japanese companies to promote more foreigners to senior posts. "To be truly localized, a Japanese company in West Germany should be regarded as totally West German, and in America as totally American," says Akio Tanii, president of Matsushita Electric Industrial Co., which manufactures in 28 countries.

FIRST ON BOARD

The Japanese manufacturers that come closest to being stateless are Sony Corp. and Honda. Sony

SOURCE: Amy Borrus with Wendy Zellner and William J. Holstein, *Business Week*, May 14, 1990, pages 105–106.

earned 66% of its $16.3 billion in revenues abroad in the year that ended in March, 1989, and it keeps a loose rein on its far-flung operations. Chairman Akio Morita is cultivating a corps of international managers so that Sony can better understand foreign markets. Last year, Sony became the first large Japanese manufacturer to name foreigners, one American and one Swiss, to its board.

Honda, which sells more cars in the U.S. than in Japan, has set up largely independent design, production, and sales operations in North America. The company's new Accord station wagon, which hits American showrooms this year, was designed at Honda's California studio and will be engineered and built in Marysville, Ohio. But the technology came from Honda's research and development center in Tochigi.

Although Honda's North American operations are still managed by a Japanese executive based in Tokyo, Honda's U.S. executives appear to have more power than their counterparts at many other Japanese companies. "I've never felt that my hands were tied," says Scott N. Whitlock, senior vice-president and plant manager for Honda of America Manufacturing Inc. in Marysville.

But even Sony and Honda occasionally betray a startling lack of savvy. The book *A Japan That Can Say No*, co-authored by Sony's Morita, enraged members of Congress by calling the U.S. a declining power, and Honda's American management got caught up in a racial-discrimination lawsuit over hiring practices in Ohio.

Other Japanese companies have been slower to put Americans or other foreigners in top positions. When Matsushita Electric Corp. of America named an American, Richard A. Kraft, as president and chief operating officer in April, 1989, it was a first in the U.S. subsidiary's 30-year

history. It took Kraft, a former Motorola executive, 16 years to reach the No. 2 spot in Matsushita's North American operations. "I look at myself, even after 16 years, as one of the early experiments in the internationalization of [Matsushita's] management," says Kraft. He still reports to Matsushita's U.S. chief, Akiya Imura.

American companies in Japan have been much quicker to localize their managements. A Japanese has headed IBM Japan since 1941, just two years after Big Blue opened its first factory in that country. And many American companies operate in Japan through Japanese-managed subsidiaries or joint ventures.

PLAN IN PLACE

The language barrier is partly to blame for Japanese companies' slowness to delegate responsibility. A deep-seated preference for centralized planning also plays a role. "When the plan is in place, you don't mess with it," says David M. Merchant, an ex-vice-president at Mazda USA who quit in 1988.

Yoshihiro Tsurumi, a specialist in Japanese corporate strategy at New York's Baruch College, says Japanese companies will continue to keep tight reins by sending Japanese executives abroad for longer assignments and by relying on "hardware" solutions, such as videoconferencing and faxes. "This is really occupation-force style," says Tsurumi. "You just send all your managers in."

Other management experts argue that Japanese companies are trying to "go global" without "becoming local" as U.S. and European companies have attempted to do. Right now, that's the case. But with most Western obstacles, Japan's corporations are likely to find their way out of this one with distinctively Japanese solutions.

Latin America: Paternalistic

Latin American corporations also have a highly centralized system of decision-making that vests nearly all this responsibility in the senior level of the organization. Like many other parts of the

developing world, Latin America's tradition of family-owned or family-controlled enterprises results in a greater emphasis on control over nearly all aspects or organizational activity, which results in limited decision-making powers to top management. Wherever delegation is permitted, it is limited to a particular functional responsibility and the delegatees are expected to stay within that framework. Most decisions are made on the basis of individual opinions and considerations, and internal consultation across different levels in the company or laterally across the organization is limited. Given the hierarchical nature of the decision-making process, subordinates usually do not contribute to the process and focus their attention on the routine performance of their assigned tasks.

Corporate Emphasis

North America: Short-Term Profit

Corporate emphasis varies widely, too. In North America managers tend to favor a rational approach that derives its primary justification from the ends it is likely to achieve, namely to improve the bottom line or some other practical, preset, clear corporate objective. Thus, policies are guided by an overriding concern for the interest of the company or their effect on its shareholders. Since most corporations are subject to relatively close scrutiny by their outside stockholders, on the basis of financial statements, managerial emphasis stresses improving financial indicators, such as profitability, leverage ratios, and net worth. There is, therefore, a tendency to overlook the long-term view. This short-term emphasis is also strengthened by pressure from boards of directors and the shareholders' representatives in top management, who fear being displaced if the company does not show continuously improving financial performance.

Western Europe: Employee and Corporate Interests

In Europe, there is considerable variance in corporate emphasis from country to country. Generally, Western European corporations rely on a rational approach with a bottom line orientation, much like their North American counterparts. The emphasis is also primarily on the corporate interest, and the interests of employees are clearly subordinate to those goals. A typical example of this approach is the practice of laying off large numbers of longtime employees simply to improve the financial results for a particular year. In other instances, companies have routinely compelled employees to take voluntary pay cuts so that overall corporate performance looks better.

Japan: Long-Term Market Share

Japanese corporate emphasis is totally different because managers tend to take a long-term view and are not as concerned with the immediate short-term performance as long as the corporation is moving satisfactorily toward its long-term objectives. Thus, even if a company temporarily has losses, Japanese companies do not routinely lay off longtime employees. In return they receive the loyalty of their employees. Substantial emphasis is also placed on employee welfare. Thus, significant fringe benefits are provided to employees of Japanese companies in addition to monetary benefits, unlike Europe and North America (especially the latter), where monetary compensation forms the dominant part of the total benefits package. Another important feature of Japanese management is the emphasis on personal relations between managers themselves as well as between managers and their subordinates at different levels of the organization.

Latin America: Continuous Adaptation

Social pressures are important in shaping the corporate emphasis in Latin America, where the higher echelons enjoy a clear status advantage, which translates into a corporate emphasis that relies on top management for all policies and decisions. There are wide disparities in compensation between the higher and lower level employees. There is great emphasis on controlling all operational aspects of corporate activity by top management, and this attitude often leads to decisions that may actually be counter to achieving maximum efficiency of activities. The emphasis on control and strict hierarchical divisions within the corporation is also largely because of family control of many corporations in this region.

As in many other areas of the world, Latin American family-controlled enterprises are usually interested in maximizing current revenues and realizing gains as opposed to investing in long-term growth and development. A part of the reason for this short-term approach to business strategy is the economic uncertainty in these countries, which stems, to a large extent, from the tradition of political instability that has characterized most countries of the region since they attained their independence or emerged as nation-states. The economic crisis of the 1980s, with hyperinflation, external debt, stagnant economic growth, and falling investment levels, has generated an increasing emphasis on risk management as a way of life for most corporations in the region. Given the prevailing economic uncertainty and fluctuation in various important economic variables, in practice it becomes almost impossible to take a long-term view. Many corporations, however, especially in Brazil, Mexico, and Chile, have shown a remarkable resilience in adapting to the rapidly changing and difficult economic situation.

Legal and Political Systems

Legal and political systems of a country are important determinants of the general business environment and affect the nature of management practices and philosophies adopted by business enterprises in different countries.

North America: Minimum Regulation

North America is characterized by a democratic political framework, with only a few political parties and no major ideological divisions between the mainstream political forces. Capitalism and free enterprise are the major economic ideologies at both ends of the political spectrum. Business is, therefore, to a large extent, free from government intervention, although the government has far-reaching powers that can and do influence business interests. Most intervention, however, is intended for the protection of national security, the conduct of external relations, preservation of the environment, and safeguarding the interests of the consumer. As long as businesses do not violate the laws in these areas and do not overstep the broad guidelines, they are free to conduct their affairs as they like. Individual intervention by way of nationalization or directives to a particular enterprise are rare, although there have been some major instances of nationalization of privately owned enterprises in Canada, including some held by foreigners. Intervention, thus, is in the form of legislated regulatory codes that are applicable uniformly to all businesses in a particular part of the country (state regulations) or a particular industry throughout the country (federal regulations). Informal business relationships with legislators and other officials are common and are channeled usually through lobby groups and liaison services that represent business interests either on the basis of a state, an industry, or even a single corporation. The private sector is predominant and is encouraged by the government, which awards important and large business contracts, research and development grants, and other types of support to private industry. The role of the public sector, on the other hand, is fairly limited, and the government lays down no economic directives that could be termed centralized planning.

The legal system relies on the courts, and recourse to litigation is frequent. The business environment is highly competitive, which is reflected in the intensity of litigation that takes place between business associates, competitors, and other parties. Litigation in business is also important because North American corporations operate under strict and comprehensive antitrust, patent, and environmental laws.

Management is, therefore, oriented toward an aggressive, outward-looking style and is used to operating with a fair degree of independence. Given the considerable economic and operational freedom, the management attitude is one of innovation, competition, and growth. Legal aspects of business management are considered critical, and legal departments are vital components of most large North American corporations.

Western Europe: Intermittent Regulation

Western Europe has a democratic political system, but in most countries there are more than two political parties, and there are major ideological differences between the two ends of the political spectrum. As a result, the attitude of the government toward business can change with a change in the government in office. In France, for example, the socialist government of Mitterand, in the early 1980's, started a major program of nationalization of a large number of key industries, but this program was stopped and later reversed by a more capitalist minded government that followed it into office. Similarly, the Tory government under Margaret Thatcher in the United Kingdom led to a major program of privatization of large sections of industry previously owned by the government, which would not have been possible under a Labor party government. Government involvement in industrial Western Europe is limited, although it is greater than in North America. There are greater limitations placed on business in Western Europe by the governments, primarily in the areas of social and public responsibility, industrial relations, and employee welfare. The legal systems in most Western European countries are well-established and some such as Great Britain, have a tradition going back many centuries. Business relations, however, are not as competitive or antagonistic as between corporations in North America, and recourse to the courts is limited. Settlement of business disputes through other methods, such as mediation, conciliation, and arbitration is more common in Western Europe than in North America, where litigation is favored over these alternatives.

Business legislation is comprehensive in most Western European countries, although in Germany antitrust laws are weak and interlocking ownerships and directorships are the rule. Patent laws are strong and well-established in most countries. After 1992 much regulation of business will be the responsibility of the European Economic Community as far as its members states are concerned, and business in these countries will operate under similar laws for many types of activities. In the socialist bloc countries, business law will have to be framed to suit the new, independent status of previously state-owned and state-run enterprises.

Japan

The Japanese political system, although a democracy, is dominated by one political party, the Liberal Democratic party (the LDP), which has been in power almost uninterrupted since the post–World War II period. The predominance of the LDP has been established, however, through a free election process, and there is vocal opposition and a free press. The continuance of LDP as the only political party to rule Japan can be ascribed to a number of factors, not the least being the Japanese concern for continued stability in its quest for rapid and consistent economic progress. The government plays a unique role in Japanese business life, because it works in close partnership with the business sector to achieve national economic goals. Government contact with business is conducted through the Ministry of International Trade and Industry (MITI), which provides funding for research and development, international market development, raw material sourcing, and so on, the benefits of which are shared across the industry. Although this process is not actually centralized planning, it does provide for significant coordination between different corporations within an industry. The government also influences the direction of the economy by regulating the flow of incentives, research and development, and promotion assistance. For example, in the 1980s significant government assistance was provided to industry for the development of technologies for high-definition television, supercomputers, and digital audio tapes. Through this government support, there is a great degree of collaboration between competitors. Businesses are usually closely aligned to recruit political parties, given their heavy dependence on official assistance in different ways. The recruit company scandal of the late 1980s revealed how closely business people were involved with political affairs in general and the electoral process in particular. The interconnection between the government and business is also evidenced by the common practice of the exchange of positions between senior executives of business corporations and high officials of the civil service. Another important feature of the Japanese business environment is the presence of trading companies (sogo soshas), which represent a large number, sometimes hundreds, of smaller Japanese companies in different parts of the world. This permits substantial economies of scale and provides access to international markets which the smaller Japanese companies would otherwise be unable to tap.

Given this highly unified and integrated political and business climate, it is not surprising that the legal system of Japan, especially for business disputes, relies more on consensus than on litigation. Most business disputes are settled out of court and the driving philosophy is to achieve a sense of common interest for all parties concerned. Corporate legislation allows for substantial vertical and horizontal integration, which is reflected in the presence of such large conglomerates as Mitsubishi, which comprises more than a hundred individual companies in a wide range of fields. Such conglomerates are generally known by the generic name "keiretsu." Although there are certain laws against monopolistic control, enforcement is not seriously undertaken, primarily because of the belief that the corporations enjoying the monopoly would use it to improve their efficiency of operation by utilizing scale economies provided by their privileged position and not utilize their advantages

to exploit customers or prevent competitors from coming into the field. Much of the business discipline exercised by Japanese corporations is purely voluntary or mandated by traditional and sociocultural considerations. In the area of environmental protection, Japanese laws have been found by the international community to be seriously lacking, and Japan has been criticized for endangering the environment in pursuit of economic gains.

Latin America

Much of Latin America has been under military rule, either by single dictators or Juntas, for a significant part of the twentieth century, although some countries have seen periods of functioning democracy. Latin America has long been a site of overseas direct investment, especially by U.S. multinational corporations, and both private and public sector companies exist in the region. Government control over the economy is pervasive, and the private sector has to operate within a highly regulated framework, made more difficult by the rapid and far-reaching changes in regulation brought about either by rapidly changing governments or the demand for new or different approaches to recurring crises.

There is some degree of economic planning in most Latin American countries, although it has generally featured a role for the overseas investors, given the local presence of powerful MNCs. Business law is relatively better developed in Latin America than in either Asia or Africa, and many legal systems of Latin America have specific and elaborate provisions for dealing with disputes arising out of overseas investment. Many of the governments also support business in their countries by providing incentives, subsidies, and tax relief, in order to promote production, especially for exports.

Beware of Managerial Diversity

As MNCs operate throughout the world, managers will encounter a diversity of cultures, economic systems, labor policies, legal structures, and government regulations. Because of this diversity, one single management style, while wholly appropriate in one particular environment, may not necessarily be appropriate in other environments. Therefore, managers must be responsive to this diversity by tailoring management styles to meet specific situations. Managers must be aware of the types of techniques and management methods that may be successfully transferred cross-culturally and internationally, and the types that may not be, by understanding the environments and cultural dimensions in which they are operating (see Perspective 10–2).

PERSPECTIVE 10–2   **Factors of a National Nature**

Scotland is one of the main European centres for semiconductor production, although the UK does not have a high-volume chip manufacturer. The bulk of British production of commodity ball bearings is in the hands of foreign-owned companies. Yamazaki, the Japanese company, produces about 20 per cent of all British-made computer numerically controlled machine tools in a UK market for general purpose machines dominated by foreign producers.

The UK Government's support for Japanese car producers in negotiations over the European Community's policy on imports shows Britain's national champions are likely to be foreign owned. So how can nationality be defined?

Take Unitech, a leading worldwide producer of power supplies for the electronics industry, which is always described as British. Its headquarters are in Reading, Berkshire, and most of its top management is British.

One criterion of nationality is ownership. The main shareholders in Unitech are Swiss. Yet few would describe Unitech as Swiss. Ownership can only be a partial definition of a company's nationality.

Where a company makes its money is another criterion. On this Unitech would certainly fail to be British. About 40 per cent of its sales are in Europe, with 25 per cent in the Far East and 35 per cent in North America. But what matters more is where the goods are made. If all the foreign sales were exported from a UK base, Unitech should be described as a British company.

Its workforce is liberally spread around the world. It has a total of 6,000 employees, with 1,000 in the Far East, 2,000 in North America and 3,000 in Europe, with a large share in France. Yet it would be inappropriate to call it an Anglo-French company or even a European company.

It might be objected that the distribution of manufacturing and assembly activities matters less than where research, development and design are located. Again Unitech would not count as purely British. It has research and development facilities in Britain, the Far East and the United States.

Finally, the location of top management matters. The company's headquarters in Reading is the main source of power within the group as a whole. It is to Britain that subsidiaries will turn for discussions on important decisions.

But that is no reason for the management of a British international company to favour the UK any more than the management of any other international company. There will be many sources of power within an international company. Moreover the nationality of top management cannot be a decisive criterion, for the chief executives of Glaxo and SmithKline Beecham, Britain's two leading pharmaceuticals groups, are both American.

One conclusion is that there is no single factor which can decide nationality. A profile has to be built up from several characteristics. Unitech has

SOURCE: Charles Leadbeater, *Financial Times*, May 21, 1990, page 34.

a predominantly British culture but that is not something which can be pinned down in figures. Perhaps it should be called a British international company or a predominantly British company.

More important, simple nationality tests are misleading. What matters are patterns of dependence and commitment. An important distinction is whether a company operates in international markets or whether it is dependent upon a single national market. These two types of companies will behave very differently.

Another distinction is whether a company is committed to the economy in which it operates, by contributing to its long-run capacity for innovation. People in South Wales joke that they are happier to have Japanese rather than English companies investing in the area because they are likely to survive longer and invest more.

Religious, political or social attachments, such as judaism, catholicism or environmentalism which span national borders, might be a better way of categorising companies' motives, culture and characteristics than outmoded notions of nationality.

Summary

Management styles differ between countries as a result of the diversity of historical, cultural, traditional, economic, and legal factors. Despite such diversity, two common management styles, or philosophies, are Theory X, which assumes workers are unwilling to work and management must persuade them to perform their obligations, and Theory Y, which assumes that workers are self-motivated and require little management. North American and European management styles are based on Theory X, while Japanese management style is based on Theory Y. Latin America is also based on Theory X.

North American decision-making is authoritarian and lower-level employees generally do not participate in the process. European decision-making involves lower-level employees to a greater degree and is codeterministic. Japanese decision-making, however, seeks consensus and begins with a bottom-up approach, while Latin America is highly centralized and paternalistic.

North American and European management generally focus on short-term profitability objectives, while Japanese managements have long-term perspectives. Because of hyperinflation and economic uncertainty, Latin American manage-ment is unable to take a long-term view and is constantly forced to adapt its style to meet current economic and political environments.

North America is subject to relatively little regulation and government intervention, but litigation risks are high. North American management, therefore, is competitive, seeks innovation, and relies heavily on legal counsel to identify risks. Europe is more highly regulated, and business disputes are settled using mediation, conciliation, and arbitration. The highly regulated political and business environments of Japan support a sense of common interest for all interested parties. Latin America is highly regulated, which is made even more difficult by rapidly changing governments, but governments are supportive, in the form of incentives and subsidies to promote production and exports.

Discussion Questions

1. Compare and contrast Theory X and Theory Y.
2. How does decision-making occur in the United States? In Japan?
3. What roles do workers in Sweden have in making decisions?

4. Discuss the differences in corporate emphasis and objectives between North America, Europe, Japan, and Latin America.
5. Discuss the government-business relation and how it affects management behavior in North America and in Japan.

Bibliography

CROSSON, CYNTHIA. 1990. "The Mundane Realities of Going Global." *National Underwriter* (May 7): 3, 5.

DERR, C. 1987. "Managing High Potentials in Europe." *European Management Journal* 5:72–80.

DLUGOS, G., W. DOROW, AND K. WEIERMAIR, eds. 1988. *Management Under Differing Labour Market and Employment Systems.* Berlin: W. de Gruyter.

EDGE, AL, AND B. KEYS. 1990. "Cross-Cultural Learning in a Multinational Business Environment." *Journal of Management Development* 9:43–49.

FARMER, R. N., AND B. M. RICHMAN. 1965. *Comparative Management and Economic Progress.* Homewood, IL: Irwin.

FUKUDA, K. JOHN. 1988. *Japanese-Style Management Transferred: The Experience of East Asia.* London: Routledge.

HARBISON, F., AND C. A. MYERS. 1959. *Management in the Industrial World.* New York: McGraw-Hill.

HOBERMAN, SOLOMON. 1990. "Organizational Variable and Management Development." *Public Personnel Management* (Summer) 135–145.

HOFSTEDE, GEERT. 1980. *Cultures Consequences: National Differences in Work Related Values.* Beverly Hills: Sage.

IMAI, MASAAKI. 1986. *Kaizen, The Key to Japan's Competitive Success.* New York: Random House.

LAURENT, A. 1986. "The Cross-Cultural Puzzle of International Human Resource Management." *Human Resource Management* 25: 153–162.

MARUYAMA, M. 1984. "Alternative Concepts of Management: Insights from Asia and Africa." *Asia Pacific Journal of Management* 1:100–111.

McGREGOR, DOUGLAS. 1960. *The Human Side of Enterprise.* New York: McGraw-Hill.

MENDENHALL, M., AND G. ODDOU. 1987. "The Cognitive, Psychological and Social Context of Japanese Management." *Journal of Management* (Fall) 169.

NATH, RAGHU, ed. 1988. *Comparative Management: A Regional View.* New York: Ballinger Publishing.

NEGANDHI, ANANT R. 1987. *International Management.* Boston: Allyn & Bacon.

OHMAE, KENICHI. 1982. "Japanese Companies Are Run from the Top." *Wall Street Journal* (April 26): 26.

OUCHI, W. C., AND A. M. JAEGER. 1981. *Theory Z: How American Business Can Meet the Japanese Challenge.* Reading, MA: Addison-Wesley.

PASCALE, R. T. 1978. "Zen and the Art of Management." *Harvard Business Review* 56:153–162.

PETERS, T. J., AND R. H. WATERMAN. 1982. *In Search of Excellence: Lessons from America's Best Run Companies.* New York: Harper & Row.

REDDING, S. G., AND G. WONG. 1986. "The Psychology of Chinese Organizational Behavior." In M. H. Bond, ed., *The Psychology of Chinese People.* Hong Kong: Oxford University Press.

RENSHAW, JEAN. 1987. "Cultural Savvy—The Essential Factor." *Multinational Business* (Summer): 33–36.

SHAEFFER, RUTH G. 1989. "Matching International Business Growth and International Management Development." *Human Resource Planning* 66:29–35.

SHANI, A. B., AND M. T. BASURAY. 1988. "Organizational Development and Comparative Management: Action Research as an Interpretive Framework." *Leadership & Organization Development Journal* 9:3–10.

WILSON, LAURIE J. 1990. "Corporate Issues Management: An International View." *Public Relations Review* (Spring):40–51.

Chapter Case Study _____

Sterling Securities International

Sterling Securities International is a large, highly specialized financial services firm based in London. Formed in 1964, it has grown to become a major force in the London securities markets and offers a wide range of services, including stock brokerage, underwritings, placements, mergers, and acquisitions advice. With the growing internationalization of securities markets in the 1980s and the lifting of regulations on international trading in equities, Sterling Securities International made a conscious decision to expand their operations across at least three different centers. New York City and Frankfurt were the first new overseas operations and were followed by a branch in Tokyo.

Tokyo was both a great opportunity and an enormous challenge. It is the largest securities market in the world and has a tradition of high volume and an almost continuous upward movement. There were very few non-Japanese firms that were members of the Tokyo Stock Exchange, and those who were had a great opportunity to cover a major share of the business emanating from Western and other non-Japanese investors eager to participate in the booming Japanese stock market, which opened to foreign investors, relatively recently in the mid 1980s. Moreover, by the 1980s, there were few restrictions on overseas investments and the size of potential business volumes was great. Further, the Japanese yen was likely to continue to remain strong, given the trade surpluses Japan continued to enjoy and the pressure from Japan's major trading partners, especially the United States, to not let the value of the yen drop, in order to sustain the relative competitiveness of U.S. exports. A strong yen meant that, in addition to the business profits, an overseas firm could make additional profits by way of repatriation of earnings into a home currency.

Despite these advantages, Sterling faced several challenges. The company had to master the trading practices and informal rules associated with doing business on the Tokyo stock exchange. Start-up costs were also quite high, especially in view of the high cost of real estate in Tokyo and the general cost of living that was reflected in the compensation paid to attract and retain top quality staff. Sterling's management felt that if they played their cards right and were able to hire local managers of the right caliber, Tokyo would become a major source of corporate revenues very soon. The company had been able to hire several excellent experienced professionals from other local securities firms and those operations ended in a neat profit in the first financial year.

Norman Woods, head of the Tokyo branch of Sterling Securities, was very pleased with the branch's results and decided to suggest an expansion of the company's operation by moving into hybrid securities. The rationale was simple. Sterling Securities had already made an impact on the local markets and had won the accounts of several major corporate clients active in the Tokyo market. For obvious reasons of prudence and initial caution, however, the company had provided only a limited range of services with which it felt comfortable in the new environment. Now that it was relatively well established, it could reasonably venture into new lines of more specialized activity. Further, in view of the growing availability of different types of instruments on the markets and the increasing sophistication of client needs, it is important that the company offer as wide a range of services as possible to its customers, if it wants to retain their business in a highly competitive environment. Hybrid securities (warrants, convertibles) are an important market that many participants want to tap.

The easiest way to enter that market, reasoned Wood, would be to acquire a small but well-established company in that business. The head office in London agreed with his plan and gave him the go-ahead signal, with the message to move quickly on the whole issue, in order to capitalize on advantages of early entry into the market.

Woods acted fast. He called two of his key managers, Fujito Nakamura and Takahide Takahashi to his office, gave them a detailed briefing on what had transpired with the head office, and asked them to do a rapid but comprehensive survey on firms that could be targeted for acquisition by Sterling Securities as a part of their strategy to expand into the hybrid securities market.

The response from the local managers was true to their traditional style of work. Within a week, Woods was looking at a comprehensive, well-prepared report that outlined three companies as possibilities for acquisition. The report contained all the relevant data on their operations, management, shareholding, and so on. Woods called Nakamura to his office and asked him to suggest which firm to target. Woods also advised him that once he had his suggestion, Sterling would develop an acquisition strategy that would be implemented as soon as possible. Nakamura was asked to make his suggestion within the next three days. At the end of the meeting, Woods left the office to play a round of tennis at the rooftop court in the downtown office building where their company had rented space. Despite a reasonably good game and a general sense of well-being, there was an element of discomfort in his mind that did not leave him even as he drove home through rush-hour traffic. It was the attitude of Nakamura in the late evening meeting. He seemed extremely ill at ease, and although he said that he would hand in his suggestion, his voice had lacked its normal conviction. It was obvious that he had something on his mind.

The next morning, Woods called Nakamura to ask how he was getting along with his appraisal of the difference choices. Again, there was a hesitant, almost nervous response. Woods was puzzled—after all, the strategy had been discussed in quite some detail with Nakamura and he had been one of the main sources for putting together the different options. So what was Nakamura's problem in coming up with a concrete suggestion that would form the basis for actions? Woods decided to go to the heart of the matter. He called Nakamura for another meeting and asked him point blank if there was a problem. At first, Nakamura hesitated and tried to evade the issue, but, when it became clear to him that Woods would not be satisfied with anything less than a firm and convincing answer, he opened up, although in an extremely indirect manner. He felt that he was making a major decision for the company and other managers should also be consulted, especially Mr. Takahashi. Woods protested that the matter related to Nakamura's division and that Takahashi was a subordinate. He also argued that Takahashi was put on the study to assist him. He said, "In any case, if we start involving the entire set of senior managers, there would be far too many opinions and the whole process would get delayed." Nakamura did not contest Woods' arguments, but he made it evident that making such a major decision without consulting other managers would have damaging effects. Woods brought the meeting to a close, telling Nakamura that he would think about involving other managers. He was still pondering the whole issue when his secretary brought him a fax from the head office that asked him to move quickly, because other companies in the Tokyo market had already made their first moves toward entry into the hybrid securities market.

Questions

1. What are the "damaging effects" that Nakamura referred to?
2. What approach would you recommend to Woods in this situation?

PART FOUR

REGIONAL ISSUES IN INTERNATIONAL BUSINESS AND THE NATION-STATE

CHAPTER 11

Foreign Investment: Researching Risk

CHAPTER OBJECTIVES

This chapter will:

- Look at the forces and opportunities that support foreign investment by multinational corporations.
- Discuss the role political risk plays in counterbalancing the benefits or opportunities of investing abroad.
- Describe the various ways host governments control foreign investment.
- Present management techniques that can be used to reduce political risk when investing abroad.

Why Invest Abroad?

Every firm that considers investing abroad must weigh the potential advantages against the potential risks. To do that, in-house analysis must identify and evaluate key factors on both sides. There are several reasons to consider initially as to why firms should invest abroad.

Bigger Markets

Many international firms decide to invest overseas to tap larger foreign markets. To keep growing, a firm must increase its sales, which may not always be possible in the domestic market. Domestic markets, however large, are limited to a particular size and rate of growth and are the target of competition from other domestic firms with similar products and marketing capabilities. In such situations, a move overseas is a logical step for a company wanting to tap a larger market. Apart from the fact that the existence of a new, larger customer base would help boost sales, overseas markets often confer additional advantages to the firm. For example, these markets may not have products that are similar or of the same quality as the firm going overseas, and the competition from overseas markets may not be as strong.

Host-Nation Demands

Occasionally firms must invest overseas to tap international markets because government restrictions require that the firm's products be manufactured locally. Such restrictions are generally imposed to boost the local economy and general domestic production and employment. Thus, the MNC that wants to tap an additional overseas market has to invest in overseas plants that are either run by domestic managers, local subordinates, or through some other arrangement.

Economies of Scale

A firm accessing an overseas market might want to invest there, if it finds that it is cheaper to manufacture goods locally, rather than at home and exporting them. When the local market is large and the demand is consistent enough to justify investment in the plant and equipment needed to set up a manufacturing operation, production economies can occur through other factors. For example, the labor costs may be lower in the overseas location, the sources of raw materials may be closer to the plant in the overseas location, and the costs of shipping and marketing the products may be lower than those of home-based operations. Another important factor is the location of the firm. An overseas plant location may also be better suited to serve a third-country market.

Competitive Motives

Often firms operate in head-on competition with other domestic and international firms. This type of competition is particularly severe in oligopolistic industries, where only a few large firms dominate the market. In such an environment, the moves of one firm are quickly duplicated and challenged by the others. Thus, if one firm moves abroad, its competitors make similar moves. One obvious motive for the move is to keep pace with the first firm in new markets and overall level of sales. The other motive is the need to match the overseas strategy of competitors, because if that

is not done, the competition could acquire additional strength from its overseas operation, which could be leveraged in the domestic market, too. Competition often occurs between firms of different countries who dominate parts of the same industry (for example, Caterpillar Company of the United States and Komatsu of Japan dominate the earth-moving machinery industry). If one company invades the home country market of another, it is very likely that the competitor will be motivated to retaliate by accessing the domestic market of the other.

Technology and Quality Control

Many firms feel that by licensing their technology to a company in the overseas location, their technology might be leaked to competitors. In fact, many companies, especially in the high-technology area, hold on to their know-how so closely that they do not license it as a matter of policy. The practice of retaining information within the company is often referred to as internalization. Some companies feel that licensing their technology may result in the licensee producing a product of inferior quality, which may be damaging to the product image. To obviate such possibilities, companies prefer to set up their own overseas manufacturing operations. Having their own operations also provides some companies with greater assurance of regular supply, better maintenance, and after-sales services for their products, which are crucial to retain customer loyalty in a highly competitive international environment.

Raw Materials

Many firms rely on raw materials imported from abroad, a reliance that can stem from both availability and cost considerations. The raw materials may not be available in the home country, or, alternatively, it may be economical to access raw materials from overseas if the price differences exceed the additional transportation costs. If a firm decides to rely on overseas raw materials, it often becomes dependent on a regular supply at predictable and relatively stable prices. Long-term contracts with the overseas suppliers are one way of achieving this objective. In some cases, however, companies are not willing to take the risk of the counterparty reneging on their contract and decide to invest in extractive mining and other such raw materials sourcing operations overseas. Sometimes such investments are motivated by the consideration that the necessary technology is not available in the source country and, therefore, must be provided by the corporation interested in extracting the materials. Often permissions from the governments of the countries where raw materials are available are centered on the type of technology that the overseas corporation is able to bring to use in the extractive processes.

Forward Integration

Many companies wish to eliminate middlemen from their operations and forward integrate the different stages involved in the manufacture of their products and their sale to the consumer. For example, a firm may be producing soft-drink concentrate and selling it to a local bottler overseas that would bottle and sell it in the foreign markets. The profits from the revenues generated from the sales of the soft drink would thus be shared by the company producing the soft drink concentrate and the local bottler. If the company selling the concentrate had its own bottling plant in the foreign country, it would be able to control the entire operation and eliminate profits that must be shared with the middlemen. This motivation may prompt the company manufacturing the concentrate to set up its own bottling operation overseas.

Technology Acquisiton

Multinational corporations often invest in other countries to gain access to new technologies that are not developed in the home country. Access to new technology is often sought by the outright acquisition of new firms possessing such knowl-

edge. These new technologies are generally intended to be integrated with the entire global corporate strategy of the MNC that acquires them. Often, the company that acquires a new technology through an overseas acquisition would normally set up an overseas facility, which enhances the existing operations by adding the managerial, financial, and technological strengths of the parent company.

Assessing Political Risk

Political risk for multinational corporations means adverse actions that may be taken by host country governments against the firms. These actions can include changes in the operating conditions of foreign enterprises that arise out of the political process, either directly through war, insurrection, or political violence, or through changes in government that affect the behavior, ownership, physical assets, personnel, or operations of the firm.

Political risk does not necessarily arise out of a upheaval in the political climate of the host country. Perceptions often change within the same government, and, as a result, decisions detrimental to the interests of the firm can be made. Moreover, because policies can and do change, some degree of political risk is present in nearly all countries.

Factors responsible for political risk can be grouped into two categories—inherent and circumstantial. Inherent factors are conditions that are present constantly around the world that generate a certain danger of adverse action by the host governments from the point of view of the multinational corporation. The circumstantial factors are those conditions that can arise out of particular events in different countries.

Inherent Causes of Political Risk

DIFFERENT ECONOMIC OBJECTIVES
The motivations and goals of a U.S. MNC are often at variance with those of the host govern-

TABLE 11-1
Conflicting Objectives between Developing Countries and International Multinational Corporations

Developing Countries	Multinational Corporations
Promote local ownership	Maintain global controls and efficiency
Increase local ownership and control	Minimize costs of technology and capital
Reduce duration of contracts and change payment characteristics	Receive reasonable returns for risk
Separate technology from private investment	Provide technology as part of long-term production and market development
Eliminate restrictive business clauses in technology and investment agreements	Maintain ability to affect the use of capital, technology and associated products
Minimize proprietary rights of suppliers	Protect rights for profit from private investments
Reduce contract security	Use contracts to create stable business environment; to develop trust
Encourage technology and R&D transfer to host country	Maintain control of technology and R&D paid for by company
Develop suitable products for host country	Gain global economies of scale to lower costs of products

SOURCE: Adapted for the President's Task Force on International Private Enterprise. 1984. *The Private Enterprise Guidebook.* Washington, DC: Government Printing Office.

ment (see Table 11–1). A primary example is in the area of balance of payments considerations. A host country may be facing difficulties with its balance of payments and would, therefore, seek to conserve its resources by maximizing the inflows and minimizing the outflows. It may also try to optimize the use of the available foreign exchange resources, which could lead to restrictions on repatriation of profits, dividends, or royalties by the multinational corporation to its home country. It may also result in government restrictions on the time lag permitted for import and export payments, which could interfere with the internal leading and lagging strategy of a company, which is devised to manage its finances and avoid exchange and interest rate risks.

MONETARY AND FISCAL POLICIES
The monetary and fiscal policies of a host government may be at variance with the desires of an MNC. For example, a host country that is faced with

impending inflationary conditions might want to raise the interest rates on bank lending, which may be detrimental to the interest of the MNC whose costs of funds, and therefore of production, would go up correspondingly. The banks may also be directed to maintain quantitative ceilings on lending to prevent excessive increases in the money supply of the host country. The MNC, on the other hand, would be keen to retain its financing sources according to its own requirements and attempt to circumvent these ceilings, which may further incur the displeasure of the host government and bear the risk of further punitive action.

Similarly, fiscal policies followed by host governments may not be in the interest of the MNC. The interest of the host government is invariably to maximize revenues, while that of the MNC would be to minimize its tax liability. Increasing taxes is a major inherent risk that an MNC faces while operating overseas. Moreover, most countries levy a heavier tax on the repatriable portions of an MNC's profits, which are often in addition to the normal corporate taxes paid by a local company. Sometimes under these regimes, separate exchange rates are specified for different transactions. The goal of the host country might be to defend a particular level of the exchange rate that it deems appropriate in the pursuit of its best economic interest. For the MNC, however, this might mean that there is an artificial distortion in the amount of funds it is able to repatriate, which adversely affects its overall profitability.

ECONOMIC DEVELOPMENT AND INDUSTRIAL POLICIES

The industrial and economic development policies of a host country can often pose a risk for an MNC. For example, countries may want to promote certain backward geographical regions where infrastructural facilities are low, and might require the expansion of MNCs to such regions even though investment there may not be economically feasible. Many host countries want to promote domestic industry and, particularly, small- and medium-size enterprises. To do so, host countries tend to provide subsidies or other fiscal incentives or reserve the production of certain goods for such industries. Another promotion mechanism is the purchase policy of the government.

In many host countries, especially less-developed countries, the government is the largest buyer of goods and services. Exclusion from government contracts, therefore, affects the sales of the products of MNCs significantly. Also, in many of the core and sensitive industries (for example, defense and infrastructure-oriented industries), MNC participation is simply prohibited. The risk arises from the possibility that some industries might be declared core or sensitive industries, and MNC operations may be expropriated or forcibly sold to local parties. The rationale behind the exclusion of MNCs from key industries is apparently apprehension in the minds of host governments that controls on key industries might hold dangers for national security and hamper the ability of the government to conduct an independent foreign policy.

COLONIAL HERITAGE

Many host countries are former colonies who have only recently gained their independence. The colonial era was marked by complete political domination by foreign powers and economic domination by foreign companies. Most of the foreign companies in that era used their privileged, often monopolistic, positions to exploit local resources, markets, and labor to maximize their profits. As a result, they were seen to be a drain on the economies of the colonies, which left a sense of distrust of MNCs in the minds of host-country governments, who fear that MNCs may still exploit their economies. As a result, they are extra careful in scrutinizing proposals for foreign direct investment by multinationals and monitor their activities closely. These concerns also explain to some extent why such stringent controls are placed on MNC activities. Thus, this fundamental apprehension does not permit MNCs to operate freely and creates a constant risk of adverse action by the host governments.

SOCIO-CULTURAL DIFFERENCES

To a degree, political risk arises out of the sociocultural differences between a host country and MNCs. Social codes of conduct in certain countries contrast sharply with those of the MNCs. While in a host country, the executives of an MNC face a risk of offending local sensibilities over crucial sociocultural issues. Moreover, some basic behavioral trends and norms followed by an MNC as a part of its usual way of functioning may prove offensive to the government or the clientele. For example, western companies often have female executives representing them in meetings and negotiations in Middle Eastern countries, which might offend host officials or clients because women are not expected to play such roles. Even relatively simple things, such as greetings, gift giving, and hospitality can become serious issues if they offend a key government official or a client in a host country. An MNC must always do its homework and adapt itself to local culture if it wants to avoid political risk.

Circumstantial Causes of Political Risk

CHANGE OF GOVERNMENTS

A change of government is a major political risk faced by MNCs. In many countries political opponents usually have differing positions on the economic policies of the government in office, and a new government is often keen to reverse the policies of its predecessors. Thus, an MNC that might have excellent relations with a host government may find its assets under the threat of expropriation because of a change in government. In addition to having a different economic policy, a new host government may be hostile toward an MNC, if the company is perceived as a supporter of its political opponents.

Political risk is particularly high in countries that are in the midst of a transition from one type of political system to another, such as from a capitalist to a socialist society. In many countries that have shifted from capitalist to socialist systems, entire assets of MNCs were expropriated, some with compensation, but some without.

POLITICAL DIFFICULTIES OF HOST GOVERNMENTS

In many countries where economic and social conditions are fairly unstable, it is often difficult for a government to manage the resulting public discontent. Many governments, in an attempt to shift blame for economic ills, will target MNCs as the cause of those problems. The politicians in power often play on the inherent mistrust that the general public has of these foreign, wealthy, and powerful firms.

POLITICAL ACTION BROUGHT ON BY OTHER GROUPS

MNCs also face the risk of adverse political activity from opposition parties seeking an issue to criticize the government. The support of a host government for an MNC provides an ideal issue to be used to manipulate nationalist feelings, by propagating the line that the country is exploited by the MNC and that this exploitation is supported by the party in power. Sociopolitical activists and environmental groups are another source of political risk. Many MNCs have large investments in factories and extractive industries, which easily attract attention. Therefore, many consumer, labor, and environmental groups can attack the safety and pollution standards of MNCs, even though those standards may be better than those of domestic corporations in the same industry. Moreover, such attacks are likely to evoke a more active response from the host governments, such as penalizing the MNC more heavily than a domestic industry for similar offenses.

BILATERAL RELATIONS BETWEEN THE HOST AND HOME GOVERNMENTS

The attitude of a host government to an MNC is dependent on the bilateral relations between the host government and the MNC's home government. If the home government of the MNC comes into conflict with the host government, it is likely that the latter will take direct or indirect action against the MNC. There have been several historical instances when hostilities have broken out between two countries, and the assets of MNCs have been confiscated without compensation. Even short of outright war, adverse action against MNCs can result. For example, if one country faces a ban on some of its exports to the home country of an MNC, it may retaliate by blocking the repatriation of the MNC's profits. Occasionally, action has been taken against MNCs to settle political scores. For example, if the home country of an MNC takes an opposite stance at international forums or supports indirectly enemy countries of the host country, the host can retaliate by taking action against the MNC within its jurisdiction.

LOCAL VESTED INTEREST

MNCs also face the possibility of adverse action from the lobbying efforts made by local vested interests. As a rule, MNCs have considerable competitive power because they enjoy many advantages. They introduce a dynamic competitive force into local economies that upsets the entrenched positions of local business people in the markets by capturing market share and reducing the ability to skim off the market by charging higher prices for their products. Moreover, by introducing new products of superior quality at relatively competitive prices, an MNC is often able to expose the weaknesses of local businesses and force them to improve their own economic and operating efficiencies in order to regain their competitiveness in the marketplace.

While some local businesses respond to the

MNC challenge in this way, there are many who do not. These businesses try to fight the MNC intrusion by pressuring the government to impose restrictions on the MNCs, in order to increase their costs and reduce their ability to compete. In some cases, local vested interests lobby the government to prohibit the entry of the MNCs into the country or attempt to have regulations introduced that prohibit MNCs from doing certain kinds of business (see Perspective 11–1). The local vested-interest groups are thus a serious political risk in many countries.

PERSPECTIVE 11–1 PepsiCo Accepts Tough Conditions For the Right to Sell Cola in India

In a race to expand its world market share, PepsiCo Inc. accepted tough conditions from the Indian government to make and sell Pepsi-Cola in a country that booted out Coca-Cola in 1977.

The large Indian market for soft drinks has been supplied by local bottlers selling local products with such brand names as Thumbs Up and Campa Cola.

PepsiCo said the joint venture will make an initial investment of $17 million in an industrial facility to make soft-drink concentrate, along with fruit juice concentrates and snack foods from locally acquired produce, in the state of Punjab. The locally made soft drinks will be distributed through franchised bottlers.

In return for the entry into the country, PepsiCo agreed that the venture would export from the venture five times the value of its imported components. If that condition isn't met, PepsiCo won't be able to repatriate royalties and profits.

PepsiCo, based in Purchase, N.Y., also won't hold a majority stake; it will own 39.9% of the venture and a corporation owned by Punjab state and the Indian central government will have a

36.1% stake. The Tata Group, India's largest industrial corporation, will own 24%.

PepsiCo officials acknowledge the agreement's terms are harsh in comparison with similar accords PepsiCo signed to gain entry into the Soviet Union and China. "We're willing to go so far with India because we wanted to make sure we get an early entry while the market is developing," said Robert H. Beeby, president and chief executive officer of the company's Pepsi-Cola International. "The Indian middle class is beginning to emerge, and we see that as a big growth market."

India has a population of 800 million people, and Indians drink about 2.4 billion bottles of name-brand soft drinks a year. Although that's a small number on a per-capita basis, industry analysts estimate the market is growing at 20% annually.

Pepsi's plant will make enough concentrate for 1.2 billion bottles of Pepsi a year. PepsiCo said it hasn't set a date when it would start selling the soft drink there.

Another reason for PepsiCo's move clearly was competition from its big rival, Coca-Cola Co., which is aggressively pursuing markets in China

SOURCE: Anthony Spaeth and Amal Kumar Naj, *Wall Street Journal*, September 20, 1988, page 44.

and the Soviet Union. "We found that it is better to [enter] a market with or ahead of Coca-Cola," said Mr. Beeby. He said Pepsi entered China a couple of years after Coke, and about 10 years ahead in the Soviet Union. "Viewing them [Coca-Cola] as our lead competitor, if we get into a big market ahead of them we are that much better," he said. "That was another reason for making such an attractive agreement with India."

Officials at Coca-Cola, based in Atlanta, had no comment on PepsiCo's move.

Coca-Cola left India after the government demanded that the company turn over its secret soft-drink formula to an Indian company and transfer other technical know-how to local management. The Indian government also announced that the soft-drink giant, along with other foreign compa-nies, couldn't own more than 40% of their Indian subsidiaries, a ruling that was tantamount to diminishing the companies' control over their Indian operations.

PepsiCo also operated in India for about two years in the mid-1950s. A company spokesman said the company left the country because "we were unable to build a viable business there."

Mr. Beeby said the company doesn't see any problem meeting the condition that PepsiCo must generate exports five times the value of imports to the joint venture. PepsiCo will have to import some parts of the concentrate to preserve the secrecy of its soft-drink formula. But by agreeing to this ratio, PepsiCo has voluntarily agreed to a limit on its soft-drink sales in India, if it doesn't meet that condition.

SOCIAL UNREST AND DISORDER

There are fundamental and deep-rooted tensions in some countries that fragment the local social order. Often, either on their own or at the manipulation of political interests, these tensions occasionally erupt into riots and other acts of public violence. In such situations, the law enforcement machinery of local governments is often inadequate to protect public property against destruction and looting. MNC assets have sometimes become the targets of arsonists and looters, especially if they are instigated by vested interests.

Types of Host National Control

The fact that host governments impose different types of controls on the activities of MNCs is self-evident, ranging from limits on the repatriation of profits to labor controls.

Limits on Repatriation of Profits

Many host governments place limits and conditions in different ways on the repatriation of profits, dividends, royalties, technical know-how fees, and other such revenues. Some governments impose an absolute ceiling on the amount of dividends that can be repatriated each year, and in some cases, these ceilings are subject to additional conditions that stipulate a maximum percentage of profits that can be repatriated. Moreover, corporations could also be asked to meet certain financial standards, such as debt-equity ratios, before permitting any repatriation of profits or dividends. In other countries there is a hierarchal approval process. Remittances of small amounts of profits are allowed freely, but higher amounts need the approval of the authorities, which could be the central bank or the government itself.

Certain countries facing severe balance of payments problems, place time restrictions on the repatriation of dividends and profits, which means that regulations are introduced whereby corporations have to retain their entire earnings in the host country for a certain time period, which can vary from a few months to several years. In countries faced with a shortage of foreign exchange, a time constrain can appear without a specific regulation to this effect. This constraint occurs when each request for repatriation must be approved by the central bank and only a limited number of requests can be approved each year. As a result, requests are rated sequentially, and repatriation must wait, which can take several years in countries that are in the midst of a serious and prolonged balance of payments crisis.

Curbing Transfer Pricing

Many host governments are alert to the practice of transfer pricing by MNCs. To eliminate the outflow of profits through this mechanism, they establish regulations that reduce the ability of the MNC to move funds by manipulating the intracompany pricing structure. Normally such regulations enable host-country authorities to disregard the internal prices charged by the parent to the subsidiary and to assess the company using an independent calculation that is based on standard international prices for that commodity instead of that shown on the books of the company. These regulations enable the host government to assess the tax and tariff liabilities of an MNC independently and reduce the advantages that an MNC tries to achieve through transfer pricing.

Price Controls

Many host governments have highly controlled economies. One of the important features of such an economy is the presence of price controls. An MNC entering such a country may be forced to sell its goods at the controlled prices, even though they may be well below the planned prices. In some instances, specific margins over costs are specified by host governments. Additional controls may also be imposed, usually in situations of shortages, impending inflation, or potential or active social discontent over prices.

Ownership Restrictions

Many governments restrict foreign ownership of MNCs to a certain percentage, which means that the remaining portion must be owned by local partners or offered as a public issue in the local stock market. For example, in India, most foreign companies can own only 40 percent of the shares; the remaining shares must be held by local residents. In such situations, the company often cannot exercise total control over operations, and limits are placed on the amount of profits it can repatriate. When total ownership is in the hands of the company, a very high dividend can be declared to transfer profits and capital out of the country. If the company is party owned by local nationals, this manipulation is not possible because local shareholders can question company policies. Moreover, the company cannot declare an unduly high dividend because the same level of dividend would have to be paid to local shareholders. In addition, once ownership is diluted, an MNC faces a takeover threat, because local interests can hold enough shares to acquire the local subsidiary and oust the management.

Joint Ventures

Some countries require that MNCs come into their country only as a partner in a joint venture with a local company. The motive of the host government is to secure monitoring and control leverage over the MNC through its local joint-venture partner and to promote domestic industrial capabilities by associating local companies with international corporations. These joint ventures can sometimes work to the detriment of an MNC, because a suitable joint venture partner may not be available or the one chosen may not perform its share of obligations. Moreover, some MNCs fear joint ventures with local companies because they fear the leakage of closely held advanced technical knowledge.

Personnel Restrictions

Some host governments require that local nationals be placed on the board of directors of an MNC's local subsidiary. In many instances conditions of an MNC's entry into a foreign country stipulate that a certain number of top positions be filled by local nationals. Quite often this regulation is implemented by making a reverse condition, such as limiting the number of expatriate employees or managers that a company can bring into its operations in the host country. These restrictions are made even more severe by stringent approval procedures for the issue of expatriate visas by home governments, and very often maximum salaries payable to overseas executives are subject to ceilings and higher tax rates.

Import Content

One of the primary concerns of many host governments is that MNCs are a drain on the foreign exchange resources of the country because they generate profits in local currencies and repatriate them in foreign currencies. To ensure that this foreign exchange drain is minimized, many host countries place restrictions on the amount of imports used for manufacturing products locally. The same objective is often achieved by specifying that a certain percentage of local inputs are used in the MNC's product. Some MNCs who rely largely on imported inputs for the domestic market and, therefore, cannot meet the import content requirements, must make up the foreign exchange loss by exporting either a certain percentage or a certain amount of their production. In other words, some sort of balance sheet of the foreign exchange inflows and outflows is often drawn up and the size of the export obligation is decided on the basis of projected foreign exchange outflows of an MNC's operations. Such restrictions can pose difficult problems for MNCs whose strategy is to basically produce and sell in the domestic market of the host country and whose products are designed for this purpose.

Discrimination in Government Business

Industrial policies followed by host governments are a major source of risk for MNCs. Discrimination in allocating government business is a major restriction on the scope and potential of MNC business opportunities in countries where the government plays a powerful economic role. Government purchases usually are made from domestic corporations. If such corporations happen to be the competitors of the MNC, then the former gains a major competitive edge through its access to an exclusive market. Moreover, government purchases are generally high in volume and result in substantial profits for companies who get that business.

Labor Controls

Some countries impose fairly comprehensive labor and social controls on MNCs. The stipulation can be targeted at ensuring that the labor for the firm will be recruited only through a government agency that screens all potential employees, which enables the government to influence the production of the company by controlling the supply of labor. The compensation paid to employees is also often regulated by host governments. Some host governments stipulate that the wage rates of local employees be higher than the rates paid by domestic corporations to workers performing comparable tasks. The host governments also sometimes require additional benefits for local employees, such as health insurance, various allowances, and arbitrary levels of bonuses.

Assessing the Risk

Assessing political risk is a two-stage process. In the first stage an assessment is made of the riskiness of the host country as a place to do business. In the second stage consideration is made of the risks involved in making a particular investment by an MNC. An investment should be made only if both are found to be acceptable.

Assessing Country Risk

Country risk is a very broad measure that focuses on the riskiness of the country as a whole for MNCs to conduct business. One prime consideration is the level of current and future political stability of the country. A stable country obviously provides a better investment climate. An assessment of political conditions is made by gathering relevant information from several sources—national and international media, diplomatic assessments, or professional agencies that specialize in monitoring developments in certain countries.

Some of these professionals develop their own ratings for the different degrees of risk in various countries with regard to foreign direct investment by MNCs. These ratings are developed by assigning weights to different political, social, and economic factors that could lead to political instability and disorder. These weights are then added and averaged according to a particular formula to arrive at a final rating of the level of risk for a country. Because different factors are included and the exercise of assigning risk weights is arbitrary, there is a strong element of subjectivity in this analysis. In general, Western industrialized countries carry low levels of risk for MNCs. Risks seem to increase in inverse proportion to the income of the countries, with the low-income countries posing higher risk. There are, however, important exceptions, because some middle-income countries prone to socio-political turmoil carry an even greater risk than some of the lower-income countries.

There are a few general factors that can be linked to the overall level of risk a particular host country holds for an MNC making a foreign direct investment. These are the attitude of the government, the political system in place, the level of public discontent or satisfaction, the unification or fragmentation of the local society on cultural and religious lines, the kind of internal and external pressures faced by the government, and the history of the country in the past few decades.

Assessing Investment Risk

One starting point in assessing the risk attached to making investments is to investigate the attitude and actions of the host government with regard to similar investments made by other MNCs. The existence of local lobbies and the influence they exert on the government is also a useful indicator of investment-specific risk. Powerful local lobbies in a particular industry imply higher risk.

Tax structures, industry standards, government discrimination, ownership and management requirements, repatriation conditions, export obligations, and location constrains should also be considered.

Managing Risk
Rejecting Investment

Many MNCs find that the risks in potential countries are too great in comparison to the expected returns. Therefore, they reject the potential investment. Rejection may also occur when the initial negotiation of terms between the host country and the MNC do not reach an agreement. Because the host country is eager to attract overseas investment, the MNC rejection may sometimes prompt the host government to relax some of the conditions.

Long-Term Agreements

Many MNCs find that one way to reduce political risk is to negotiate long-term commitments from the host government on the regulation of the firm. Negotiating these safeguards requires skill and foresight. A balance must be struck between achieving the safest possible terms for the company and the current national policies of the host government. The limitation of these safeguards, however, is that there is no practical way to enforce them in the event that the host government reneges on its part of the contractual obligations. A government is less likely to take any adverse actions if it is bound by a written agreement not to do so, as compared to a situation where it has not given any such assurances.

Lobbying

Many MNCs resort to lobbying politicians and officials of host governments to influence the direction of policies and decisions that affect them, because much political risk arises from the potential actions that can be taken by host governments. Direct lobbying is done by establishing a liaison or representative office in the capital city of the host country. The representative of the company establishes direct contacts with local officials and politicians and lobbies them to maintain favorable policies for the MNC. At other times, a local liaison agent is used to lobby local officials, especially in those countries where the domestic political and official structure is complex and not easily understood by outsiders.

Indirect lobbying is favored by many MNCs in countries where local officials are averse to dealing directly with foreigners. Lobbying can also take the form of influence-buying, by bribing the officials and politicians who are important players in the shaping of official policy and attitudes of the home government toward MNCs. Although many multinationals do not admit officially the taking of bribes, for obvious reasons, it is a common practice in many countries.

Legal Action

If threatened, MNCs can resort to legal action, but this approach is useful only in countries where there is an efficient legal system and independent judiciary. Recourse to the law would be warranted when a MNC is of the opinion that a new decision or regulation of the host government is illegal under the laws of the country or is in violation of any initial agreements made with the host government. Legal action, however, is a last resort, taken only when there is no other option. Moreover, such actions are usually taken only by those companies that have decided to divest their in-

vestments in the host countries, because bringing a legal suit against the host government is likely to bring forth retaliation.

Home-Country Pressure

Many MNCs, when faced with an adverse position taken by the host government, seek the intervention of their home governments, generally through diplomatic channels. The foreign office of the home country generally exerts informal pressure on the government of the host country to alter its attitude toward the MNCs. If the issue is important, this intervention can take place even at very high levels, such as heads of state. Apart from the general threat of deterioration of bilateral relations, home governments also occasionally hold out thinly veiled threats of retaliation against the corporations of the host country in the jurisdiction of the home country or threaten to erect trade or other barriers. This channel is effective when relations with the home country of the MNC are particularly important to the host country.

Joint Ventures: Increase Shareholding

Many MNCs decide to invest in host countries as joint-venture partners with local corporations; such ventures reduce the political risk. Once a local company is partnered with an MNC, any adverse government decision against the MNC also affects the local partner. A local partner would clearly exert a restraining influence on a government contemplating any such action. Moreover, the local partner, in all likelihood, would have significant contacts in the appropriate quarters of the host government that could be used for intensive lobbying on behalf of the MNC. Moreover, many host governments would take a more indulgent approach to the MNC operating as a joint venture because it would be perceived as sharing its profits and technical know-how with a local company and the traditional exploitative image of MNCs would be mitigated.

Many companies achieve similar objectives by using a slightly different route. Instead of taking on a local company as a joint-venture partner, they increase the level of local shareholding. In many instances the increase in local shareholding is effected at the behest of the host government, which imposes the increase as a condition for the continued operation of the MNC in its jurisdiction.

Increased local shareholding increases the benefits for the host country in many ways. The amount of profits to be repatriated abroad is immediately reduced when the local shareholders receive their dividends and other revenue in local currency. The foreign exchange liability arising out of share appreciation is also reduced because the basic foreign shareholding is replaced to some extent by domestic shareholding. With a large amount of local shareholding, the policies and operations of the corporation are more open to public and government scrutiny, and, therefore, to control. The possibility is also reduced that the MNC can indulge in financial and business transactions detrimental to the country.

Promoting Host Goals

In order to gain the acceptance of the host country to its operations, an MNC may, as a strategic move, attempt to promote host-country objectives, for example, maximizing foreign exchange earnings. MNCs try to contribute to this objective by either promoting exports of their own products or the products of other local manufacturers. The action is strategic in that it is taken to prevent future problems and does not form a part of the normal business operations and objectives of the company. Once export earnings have been generated by the MNC for the host country, it becomes fairly difficult for the host government to justify adverse action, because the drain on foreign exchange resources is removed.

Risk Insurance

Many countries have agencies that offer insurance coverage against the political risks faced by MNCs based in their countries. In the United States, the Overseas Private Investment Corporation (OPIC) guarantees risks faced by MNCs in developing countries. OPIC provides coverage against various eventualities that can adversely affect the MNC in a host country, such as expropriation, blocking of repatriation of funds by a host government, and problems created by the breakdown of law and order.

The World Bank, in an effort to promote private investment in developing countries, has created a new agency to protect corporations who invest in such countries from different forms of political risk. This agency, which completed one full year of its operation in 1989, is the Multilateral Investment Guarantee Agency (MIGA). The existence of risk coverage through MIGA is intended to allay fears of political risk that prevent many MNCs from investing in developing countries, even if the latter are open to overseas investment.

Contingency Planning

Despite whatever measures a company may adopt and however good its relations with a host government might be, there always remains a definite element of political risk of either nationalization, expropriation, or some other unacceptable form of regulatory imposition or control. To guard against such an eventuality, most MNCs have a contingency plan, which may or may not be in the form of a formal document. Some contingency planning is done when the investment is first made in the host country. If a country is considered risky in terms of possible expropriation, companies try to reduce the value of their physical investment and rely more on the supply of expertise and know-how that is paid for on a short-term basis. A country also may be considered dangerous because of technology leakage. In such a situation, the MNC would probably retain the know-how at its headquarters and supply intermediate products to its subsidiary for the final stages of processing or manufacturing.

Summary

Investment in international business requires a cost-benefits analysis of the benefits gained versus the risks encountered by the investing firm. Influencing the decision to expand internationally are the opportunities to tap larger markets, host-country regulations requiring local production, achieving economies of scale, competition, implementing quality controls, raw materials sourcing, forward integration to eliminate middlemen, and the acquisition of new types of technologies.

Counterbalancing these factors, MNCs face political risks from unilateral actions or expropriation by host-country governments. Political risks increase when the MNC and the host country have different economic objectives or conflicting fiscal and industrial policies. Circumstantial political risks may occur when the host government changes and the policies of the preceding government are reversed, or when the current government facing political difficulties or social unrest must amend its prior policies to the detriment of the MNC.

Host governments may also impose a variety of national controls on the activities on MNCs, including limitation on the repatriation of profits and dividends, efforts to curb transfer pricing, implementation of price controls, restrictions on foreign ownership, local staffing and management requirements, import content rules, and labor and social controls.

Assessing political risk involves first assessing the riskiness of the host country as a place to conduct operations and then identifying the level of risk assumed by the MNC for making a particular investment. Political risk cannot be eliminated totally, but management techniques can help **reduce** the level of political risk. Such techniques include avoidance or not investing in particular countries, establishing long-term agreements with host country governments, lobbying, legal action where a well-developed legal system exists within the host government, obtaining political pressure and assistance from the MNC's home country government, providing for local ownership or joint venturing, promoting host government objectives, developing contingency plans, and purchasing insurance coverage for political risk.

Discussion Questions

1. Discuss the various factors that cause multinational firms to invest abroad.
2. What role does political risk assessment have in shaping an MNC's foreign-investment decisions?
3. Is political risk assessment an exact science? Explain.
4. How do host governments try to control the activities of MNCs within their own countries?
5. Which at the following businesses are most and least vulnerable to expropriation?
   - Agriculture
   - Automobile manufacturers
   - Mining
   - Accounting
   - Heavy equipment manufacturers
   - Hotels
   - Restaurants
   - Oil fields
   - Personal electronic goods manufacturer
   - Banks
6. Identify techniques that MNCs use to manage country risk.

Bibliography

AUSTIN, J. E., AND D. B. YOFFIE. 1984. "Political Forecasting as a Management Too." *Journal of Forecasting* 3:395–408.

BLANDEN, MICHAEL. 1988. "Of Tin Hats and Crystal Balls." *Banker* (July): 44, 46.

DE LA TORRE, J., AND D. H. NECKAR. 1987. "Forecasting Political Risk." In Sypors Makridakis and Steven C. Wheelwright, eds., *The Handbook of Forecasting: A Manager's Guide,* 2nd ed. New York: John Wiley.

ENCARNATION, D. J., AND S. VACHIM. 1985. "Foreign Ownership: When Hosts Change the Rules," *Harvard Business Review* (September/October):152–160.

EROL, CENGIZ. 1985. "An Exploratory Model of Political Risk Assessment and the Decision Process of Foreign Direct Investment," *International Studies of Management and Organization* (Summer): 75–79.

FATEHI-SEDAH, K., AND M. H. SAFIZADEH. 1989. "The Association Between Political Instability and Flow of Foreign Direct Investment." *Management International Review* (Fourth Quarter):244

FRIEDMANN, ROBERTO, AND J. KIM. 1988. "Political Risk and International Marketing." *Columbia Journal of World Business* (Winter): 63–74.

GHADAR, F., AND T. H. MORAN, eds. 1984. *International Political Risk Management: New Dimensions.* Washington, DC: Ghadar & Associates.

GLOBERMAN, STEVEN. 1988. "Government Policies Toward Foreign Direct Investment: Has a New Era Dawned?" *Columbia Journal of World Business* (Fall): 41–49.

GODDARD, SCOTT. 1990. "Political Risk in International Capital Budgeting." *Managerial Finance* 16:7–12.

LICHFIELD, JOHN. 1989. "Trans-Atlantic Company Acquisitions Gain Momentum." *Europe* (April)24–25.

MILLER, VAN V. 1988. "Managing in Volatile Environments." *Baylor Business Review* (Fall):12–15.

PERLITZ, MANFRED. 1985. "Country-Portfolio Analysis: Assessing Country Risk and Opportunity." *Long Range Planning* (August):11–26.

RICE, GILLIAN, AND MAHMOUD, ESSAM. 1986. "A Managerial Procedure for Political Risk Forecasting." *Management International Review* (Fourth Quarter):12–21.

SCHMIDT, DAVID A. 1986. "Analyzing Political Risk." *Business Horizons* (July/August):43-50.

SETHI, S. P., AND K. A. N. LUTHER. 1986. "Political Risk Analysis and Direct Foreign Investment: Some Problems of Definition and Measurement." *California Management Review* (Winter):57–68.

STANLEY, MARJORIE T. 1990. "Ethical Perspectives on the Foregin Direct Investment Decision." *Journal of Business Ethics* (January):1–10.

TERPSTRA, V., AND K. DAVID. 1991. *The Cultural Environment of International Business,* 3rd ed. Cincinnati: South-Western.

Chapter Case Study _____

Amalgamated Polymers, Inc.

Martha Sanders was quite relaxed as she went on a round of the executive offices, distributing copies of the briefing papers for Monday's investment committee meeting. She would have a nice weekend, after all the hectic preparation and redrafting that had taken place during the week and at times had threatened to spill over into Saturday. Now with her work done, she could go home on time.

While Martha Sanders was looking forward to the weekend, James Hyman was growing increasingly tense. Martha was his secretary and had typed the briefs, several times, and now they were perfect documents and she could go home. The briefs contained a proposal for his company to take an equity stake in Hindorra Plastics, a medium-size company producing a wide variety of plastics in Mazirban, a small but wealthy Arab country in the Persian Gulf. The proposal had been prepared by Hyman after almost six months of preliminary groundwork, and on Monday the investment committee, which comprised the entire senior management of the company, was going to take their first look at it.

There were a number of reasons why the proposal made sense. Hyman's company, Amalgamated Polymers, Inc., was a leader in the production of plastics and similar petrochemical by-products. It was based in Edinburgh, Scotland, and had plants in Great Britain, the Netherlands, and Turkey. The company had its own in-house research and development facility, which had helped Amalgamated become one of the important forces in plastics technology during the past fifteen years. Its patented product, Amalite, was in great demand by household goods manufacturers for making such kitchen items as storage jars and plastic cutlery. Much of the company's sales

of Amalite were concentrated in Europe and North America, but competition in these markets was growing, and there was a need to expand sales in other areas. While Amalgamated Polymers had considerable international marketing skills and sales contacts, they were essentially handicapped by a limited production capacity. To export to other markets, especially in developing countries, would mean an expansion of production capacity in the existing plants or establishment of new plants. Expanding capacity in the existing plants would have been difficult and expensive. The Netherlands and Edinburgh plants faced severe environmental constraints and had come under pressure from local authorities, and particularly from environmental groups, because of their pollution-creating effects. The company had been forced to install very expensive equipment to reduce the harmful content of the emissions from its plants. Expanding capacity would no doubt give rise to pressures from local governments and other groups to install even stricter emission-control equipment. Further, given the high labor and production costs in Great Britain and the Netherlands, it did not make sense for the company to increase production at these plants in order to make sales in new markets where prices had to be extremely competitive. Similar problems were confronting the company in connection with opening new plants in Great Britain and the Netherlands. High costs, environmental concerns, and high wages ruled out a move to invest in new plants. Further, the company was already highly leveraged and did not want to take on additional debt to finance new operations. There were other problems in Turkey. They had received a license to establish and open one plant under a liberal foreign investment policy adopted by the government then in power, but another government had taken over and reversed that policy, and the chances of getting a license for a second plant were almost zero.

The scenario had prompted Amalgamated Polymers to look for other options. One option was to establish a new plant in a low-cost location that would be closer to potential markets. There were several countries that offered themselves as potential sites for this option. The company actively considered the opening of a new plant in a developing country because some of the constraints they faced in the developed countries were not present. The issue of over-leveraging the firm, however, by taking on excessive debt to finance an entirely new operation continued to dog this option. Further, setting up a new plant in a developing country would require a time lag that was incompatible with the need of the company to penetrate quickly into new markets and take advantage of its technological edge in certain areas. The issue of timing was particularly important, because other companies also had major technological research plans and could catch up very soon, eliminating the advantage enjoyed by Amalgamated.

These considerations had led to the idea of taking an equity participation in an ongoing company in a middle-income or low-income country. The strategy was to infuse new technical and management capability into the company and make it internationally competitive. Once this was achieved, its products could be exported to other, new markets. The option of a joint venture with an ongoing company in plastics manufacturing seemed to address all the fundamental concerns, at least in principle. To acquire an equity stake significant enough for the company to be able to influence the management of the joint venture, Amalgamated would not be pressed too hard financially. Further, since it was supplying technology and management know-how, its contribution could be capitalized to offset a significant part of the total equity contribution it had to make under the proposed joint venture. Because the existing company already had the basic infrastructure set up and would be sharing other costs, the total costs of capacity expansion would not be too high. There also would be no difficulty in directing some of the company's existing production capacity to the targeted markets, because the government of the company with which the joint venture was being contemplated was keen to earn foreign exchange. The costs would be further reduced because it would not be necessary, at least in the initial stages, to expand production capacity by too much.

Mazirban had offered an ideal opportunity to implement the joint-venture approach. The country was a large producer and exporter of crude oil and natural gas, which were its main sources of revenue, but, like many other states in the Persian Gulf, the government was eager to diversify the economy and invest the surplus oil revenues in new industries employing high technology. Petrochemicals were a natural choice, because the raw materials, crude oil and natural gas, were plentiful and available at a minimal cost. With the collaboration of major multinational firms, the government had established several petrochemical and oil refining complexes. To attract additional foreign investments, it had established a liberal investment policy that placed virtually no constraints on overseas parties to joint ventures in Mazirban. The only important conditions were that any overseas venture in Mazirban had to be established jointly with a local party and that the terms of this venture had to be approved by the government.

Amalgamated Polymer found a potentially ideal partner in Gulf Plastics Ltd, a major plastics company owned by members of the ruling family and based in Ochran, the main Port of Mazirban. Gulf Plastics was established in 1981 and for the past nine years had concentrated on the manufacture of basic plastic products, which it marketed primarily within the country. Gulf Plastics had been established with the help of a Japanese petrochemical company that also helped to run the company for the first five years. A few Japanese technicians still held key positions in the manufacturing operations division of the company. Gulf Plastics had been looking for a technical and management partner to upgrade its technology and help it move overseas. Amalgamated Polymers, which had compatible interests and strategies, appeared to be an ideal partner. The terms of the collaboration would also not present a problem, because these were fairly standard in the petrochemical industry and the details could be taken care of easily.

Despite all these positives, there were a number of questions that Hyman felt the executive committee would raise on Monday. He would have to spend the weekend in virtual self-isolation and think of what questions were likely to be raised and what responses should be present to justify this investment. After all, it was very important to him. If the project was approved, he would be placed in charge of his company's side of the venture, and eventually it would mean a senior position at the plant in Mazirban, boosting his career prospects. On the other hand, if the proposal was rejected by the committee, six months of work would come to nought, and he would face the additional embarrassment of giving the news to the Mazirban government and to Gulf Plastics, who were not likely to hide their feelings.

Question

Assume you are in James Hyman's position and prepare a list of possible questions that the investment committee might raise about the proposal and your responses to them.

CHAPTER 12

Doing Business with the Pacific Rim

CHAPTER OBJECTIVES

This chapter will:

- Present the economic emergence of the Pacific Rim nations in the current international business environment.
- Look at Japan's rise as an economic power and the collaborative relationship between Japanese business, government, and society.
- Discuss the four tigers of Southeast Asia and the economic successes of the past decade.
- Identify the industrial growth and economic potential of other Southeast Asia nations.
- Offer strategies for competing with the Pacific Rim challenge.

Pacific Rim Economies

One of the most important developments on the international business scene in the past three decades has been the rapid emergence of the Pacific Rim economies as industrial powers. These economies offer a head-on challenge to the United States and Europe for economic dominance around the world. The economic resurgence witnessed in the region in the post–World War II era was spearheaded by Japan and followed more recently by Korea, Taiwan, Singapore, and Hong Kong, the four tigers or the newly industri-

alizing countries (NICs). Other countries in the Pacific Rim that have made steady, if not spectacular, progress include Thailand, Malaysia, Indonesia, the Philippines, and the People's Republic of China. The region also has its share of less-developed countries that have not prospered economically. For example, North Korea, Vietnam, Cambodia, and Laos fall into this category.

Although significant progress in the region has been largely limited to Japan and the four tigers, the region's importance in the world economy has grown remarkably. It is estimated that by the year 2000, the region may account for about 25 percent of the world's GNP, up from 20 percent share it holds today. In comparison, North America is projected to account for approximately 30 percent of the world's GNP at the turn of the century. Growth rates for the region have been consistently higher than in most other parts of the world. Between 1989 and 1993, economies of the region are projected to grow at an annual rate of 6 percent, as compared to 3.5 percent per annum for growth in industrialized countries.

The increasing economic importance of the region is reflected in the changing patterns of international trade and foreign direct investment. In the 1960s, for example, U.S. trade with Asia was less than half its trade with Europe. According to projections developed by the U.S. President's Council on Competitiveness, however, the pattern could be reversed by 1995, and U.S. trade with Asia could be twice as large as with Europe. Patterns of foreign direct investment (FDI) into developing countries also reflect the increasingly important economic roles played by the region. For example, prior to 1982 Latin America was the most important regional recipient among developing countries of overseas direct investment, attracting 43 percent of all FDI flows to developing countries. After 1982, however, this position was taken by Asia, whose shares of FDI to developing countries rose from 22 percent between 1970 and 1982 to 37 percent between 1983 and 1987. The region has attracted substantial investments, not only from Japan, but also from the United States and major industrialized countries of Europe.

It is abundantly clear that this shift in the global economic scenario will be further accentuated by the continuing and rapid progress not only of the NICs but also of other countries in the region with similar growth potential. This progress will mean an increasingly multipolar world, where economic power will not be the sole monopoly of the industrialized nations of the West. With greater economic clout, countries of the region are expected to play a greater role in international economic decision-making and are already beginning to exert pressure for a greater say in such major supranational organizations as the International Monetary Fund and the World Bank.

The Example of Japan

The biggest success story in Asia and a prime model for countries looking to improve their own economic lot is Japan. In 1952 the U.S. occupation of Japan following World War II ended, and Japanese business and government leaders began to develop and implement policies aimed at promoting national economic growth. These policies centered on providing for increasing investment in the infrastructure and manufacturing capacity of the country and generating resources internally by personal consumption and government expenditures. Investment incentives were specifically targeted in special areas of the economy that utilized the relative advantages of the country.

Japan is severely limited in its physical attributes and has few resources in the form of land, energy sources, or minerals. Thus, development was directed away from agricultural production, which was relatively inefficient and of low value, and toward creating manufacturing capacity. This type of realistic focus led to an increase in Japan's GNP by five times in the period from 1954 to 1971.

Initially, in the 1950s Japan focused on export-led growth as a policy and looked to market opportunities in the U.S. market, which had the advantages of size, depth, and openness. In addition to these factors, the cold war between the United States and the Soviet Union served to promote close ties between the United States and Japan, an important ally country close to the Soviet Union's Pacific borders.

After identifying markets with the greatest long-term potential, Japanese policymakers looked closely at developing an appropriate group of products to promote for export to new markets and implemented policies to support and promote those specific industries in a timed sequence. At first the nation relied on areas where it already had some expertise and could use its labor advantages. These areas were textile manufacturing and toy production, and although the goods produced were relatively inexpensive, substantial profits were earned from the high sales volumes.

This growth in sales and markets allowed the Japanese focus to shift to higher value-added products, such as cameras, videotape players, watches, computers, printers, and word processors; vehicles, such as cars, trucks, motorcycles, and construction equipment; and capital-intensive goods, such as steel and ocean-going ships.

Japanese Methodology

In order to implement these plans and achieve success, it was necessary for Japan to embody these plans in effective and flexible national policies. The initial need was to generate money to be invested and channeled into the designated growth areas. Japan, therefore, chose a policy of encouraging private savings and investment, avoiding government borrowing from other countries or commercial lenders. The policy obviated the need to attract foreign direct investment and avoided state involvement in industry.

In order to yield sufficient savings to finance such rapid growth, Japan implemented a number of incentives for savings and investment by private citizens. These policies included penalizing consumer borrowing through taxes and promoting savings with tax exemptions for interest income on investments. In addition, the country established a national savings system and placed limits on capital transfers out of the country. The country's citizens also were provided with incentives to save for their future, because the government provided only a rudimentary public welfare system. Thus, taxation and other policies made it only reasonable for the Japanese to invest their funds where they would have the greatest tax-free returns to provide for retirement income. The result was a private savings rate of 28 percent in 1971, which was more than triple the average annual rate of citizens in most developed countries.

The savings system provided industry in Japan with an enormous pool of investment funds and allowed companies to operate and grow without incurring vast amounts of debt. The flow of these funds to appropriate industries and sectors of the economy was facilitated by the operation of the nation's banks and special purpose organizations designed to promote industrial development in the country. Overseeing the operation of these en-

tities were government ministries, primarily the Ministry of Finance and the Bank of Japan. This investment became the driving force in spurring economic development in the 1960s.

These government arms acted in concert with another powerful entity in Japanese economic circles—the Ministry of International Trade and Industry (MITI). This and other government agencies next looked toward developing a base of technological expertise that could move the economy from being labor intensive to being more capital intensive and make it less volatile and vulnerable. Thus, Japan began acquiring technological skills through a variety of methods, including buying and leasing technology from foreign suppliers; developing its own technological base through research and development; importing technology, by allowing foreign companies to work within the nation in joint ventures; and using reverse engineering to learn about technological developments, that is, buying products that use new technologies and closely observing and analyzing their operation in order to replicate them in home manufacturing facilities.

Japan's industrial base shifted from a reliance on textile and steel production to the export of sophisticated higher-priced and value-added goods, such as cars, ships, televisions, and tape recorders. Textiles, for example, had made up nearly half of Japan's exports in 1950 but comprised only 5 percent by 1985. Exports soared as Japan made the shift from cheap goods to high-quality, sophisticated, and technologically developed product classes.

At the same time, national policies were designed to emphasize production and exports while limiting imports into the country. The objective of these policies was to maintain a favorable balance of trade, with exports far outbalancing imports. Imports were kept low through the imposition of stiff tariffs and nontariff barriers. Although in recent years Japan has slowly opened its borders to foreign goods, under the pressure of its trading partners, these barriers to imports are still significant, especially for consumer goods. A U.S. journalist based in Japan, describing problems in the consumer economy of Japan, noted his 1988 attempt to buy slippers from a mail-order company in the United States for $27 that resulted in his paying import duties of $39 per pair. Such duties effectively prohibit the importation of many consumer goods into Japanese markets, and imports are composed mostly of luxury goods, entertainment items, and raw materials.

These policies were implemented as part of a comprehensive national industrial policy. As U.S. journalist Janus Fallows pointed out, "All parts of this strategy were supported by a pervasive, well-coordinated management of Japanese economic affairs by the elite bureaucracies. Seldom in the modern world, at least in peacetime, had the government of an advanced democratic country instituted such a thoroughgoing system of business incentives within a national economy, and never had such an effort under such conditions proved so phenomenally successful." These policies included not only a framework for the creation of economic growth through the promotion of investment in certain industries, but also provided for divestment in areas in which the country no longer held competitive advantage or preeminence. For these "sunset" industries, the government imposed a method of orderly shutdowns so that declines in specific industries did not lead to vast and extensive disruption in the economy.

The Japanese Way

One notable aspect of the business environment in Japan that differs greatly from most Western or industrialized countries, but which greatly facilitates the efficacy of industrial plans is the strong association between business and government in working toward mutual goals. This collaboration differs greatly from the United States, where the relationship between business interests and government is often more adversarial than collaborative. In Japan, goals are achieved through harmony, cooperation, and individual sacrifice. The structure of the business world is also more oriented toward collaborative efforts between government and with other businesses than in other nations. For example, in Japan much business is conducted by large groups of companies and banks called keiretsu. Within these groups, manufacturing is coordinated among the member companies, from the provision of raw materials to the production of intermediate goods, including parts of the overall financing of operations. This is accomplished through communication and coordinated decision-making throughout the network of affiliated businesses, corporations, and banks. It is common in Japan for banks to own stock in individual companies and for directors on their boards to sit on the boards of manufacturing companies. Such relationships and business activities would quickly run afoul of antitrust laws in countries such as the United States.

In addition to a healthy and productive relationship between government and business in Japan, economic progress and development has been achieved through systematic efforts to provide extensive education for the populace and by thorough training of corporate employees. In addition to sending many students abroad to study at universities that are strong in basic research, the government also sponsors study missions to learn from other countries. It also coordinates extensive research and development efforts at home by organizing collaborative efforts or consortia of scientists who work to develop technology for commercial product applications.

Japanese Economic Growth

Growth in the Japanese GNP has far outstripped growth in the U.S. GNP and in the countries of the European Economic Community (EEC). From 1961 to 1965, Japan's growth rate averaged 10 percent compared to levels closer to 5 percent for both the United States and the EEC. This spread widened to an average 11 percent from 1966 to 1970 for Japan, compared to only 3 percent for the United States and 4.4 percent for the EEC. Even in subsequent years, growth rates in Japan almost always exceeded those of other industrialized nations.

Japan's growth slowed in the 1970s, primarily because of the shocks experienced around the world because of rapid and severe increases in the prices of oil. These increases had a profound effect upon Japan, because the country had to import large amounts of fuel, particularly oil, which accounted for 90 percent of all its energy imports in 1973. The price jump led to serious problems in Japan in the 1970s—high inflation, a large balance-of-payments deficit, and the most severe recession since World War II. In addition, the country was also experiencing inflation because of continued stimulation of the economy by the government to maintain high levels of growth. In response to the economic problems existing in the country in 1974, the government tightened the money supply considerably to eliminate inflation and allowed higher prices for energy to flow through to consumer pocketbooks in the form of higher prices for consumer goods.

These increased costs created a major impetus to conserve energy in Japan and, consequently, spurred the development of new fuel-efficient technologies and more productive manufacturing practices to reduce Japanese dependence on expensive foreign oil and to cut labor and other production costs. Efforts toward developing greater efficiencies were conducted in tandem with organized industry reductions of excess capacity. In order to achieve capacity reductions, representatives of industry and government officials joined together to decide how to equitably reduce capacity within industry. The objective of these actions and policies was to raise productivity, lower labor costs, and reallocate labor to more productive areas, so that the efficient use of labor and energy would yield advantages to producers in the form of lower product costs and result in increased competitiveness for Japanese goods. Consequently, Japanese labor productivity increased by one-fifth between 1974 and 1980.

This movement was accompanied by the continuing shift in production emphasis from low-value to high-value products, such as electronic equipment and automobiles. In addition, production techniques began to rely more heavily on the use of industrial robots for repetitive processes. In the late 1970s, service industries expanded

rapidly, while there were continued reductions in oil use and increases in exports. In 1984 exports comprised 17 percent of the Japanese GNP, as compared to 9 percent of its GNP in the 1960s (see Figure 12–1).

Present-Day Japan

Throughout the 1980s, Japan has continued its shift to higher-value products and out of industries where it no longer holds a competitive edge in world markets, such as in shipbuilding and textile manufacturing. The current emphasis is on industries driven by high technology, such as consumer electronics, computers, and sophisticated technical equipment. After the recession of 1985, the country once again began a program of adjustment, which includes the contracting of extra production and labor capacity and the redirection of investment to new plants to reduce costs of production and maintain product competitiveness. The biggest difference between this adjustment and those of prior years is that Japan is now using a great deal of offshore production, where it formerly relied solely on efficiencies to be gained in domestic manufacturing. Thus, Japanese companies are expanding horizontally, but into other nations of east Asia, where labor costs are cheaper than at home.

Years of continued economic progress and trade surpluses have enabled Japan to build important competitive strengths. Partly because of its drive for production efficiency and conservation and partly because of the structural shift in Japanese industry, its dependence on raw material imports has fallen dramatically. In fact, Japan is less dependent on imported raw materials than Great Britain, France, West Germany, or Italy.

Substantial overseas investments during the years of consistent trade surpluses have begun to yield dividends. Income from "invisibles" (such as services) is beginning to exceed expenditures, which will add another major strength to Japan's balance of payments position and would serve as a stabilizer even in the unlikely situation that Japan faces a trade deficit in a particular year.

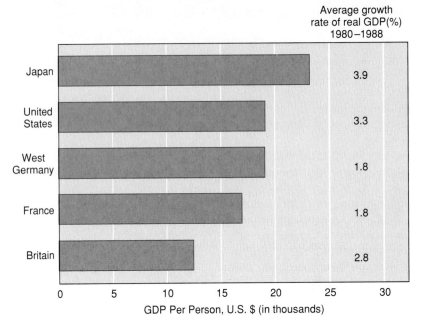

FIGURE 12-1   Japan's GDP per Person Ranks Number One.
SOURCE: World Bank and International Monetary Fund.

Given its lengthy period of domination in overseas markets in a wide range of products, Japan has established clear competitive advantages over other potential competitors, which offsets its relatively high labor costs and the adverse impact of a strong currency. Japan is particularly strong in application and development, and it is quickly moving into areas of emerging technology with the prime motive of developing commercial applications more quickly and efficiently than anyone else. Typical examples of Japanese dominance are likely to be commercial applications of superconductivity, high-definition television, digital electronics and high-speed mainframe computers. Vertical integration of major Japanese companies— Fujitsu, Toshiba, Hitachi, and Matsushita, for example—enable them to produce more efficiently and economically than their overseas competitors, who depend on external suppliers for key components of the manufacturing process. Another important strength of Japanese firms in international markets is their ability and willingness to diversify their product range to take advantage of

new markets that open up as existing ones mature and reach their full potential. A unique advantage enjoyed by Japan is the government support provided to selective companies regardless of their size. The view taken by the government is apparently to support a company that is likely to be best able to utilize the support and win in the international markets. Instead of allowing concerns of industrywide equity to become overriding and result in support being spent on smaller relatively uncompetitive companies, the Japanese government follows a pragmatic approach, which so far has yielded excellent results.

Another important recent development in Japan's industrial and manufacturing scenario is the emergence of the Japanese multinational. Until the 1960s most of Japan's exports were made at home and the only overseas presence of Japanese export-oriented companies was in the form of foreign sales promotion offices or representatives. The expansion overseas began with a move into Southeast Asia, notably Taiwan and Singapore, where Japanese companies set up plants oriented toward exports to industrialized countries. In the 1980s, however, forced by protectionist sentiments, a strong yen, and the availability of substantial resources for investments, Japanese companies established manufacturing facilities not only in Asia, but also in the United States and Western Europe. According to their Ministry of Finance, direct investment by Japan in the manufacturing industry in North America amounted to $9.9 billion by March 1987—Toyota made substantial investments in an automotive plant in Kentucky, and Sony acquired CBS Records. As more and more Japanese companies establish manufacturing operations in Western countries, it is expected that they will develop a truly multinational presence.

Simultaneously, Japan is increasing its direct investment in industries around the globe and is also focusing on tertiary industries such as finance and insurance companies and in real estate holdings abroad. The bulk of Japanese investments is in North America, where Japan has its largest markets and where the post-1985 fall of the U.S. dollar reduced acquisition costs. These investments, estimated at $58 billion at the end of 1986 by the Japan External Trade Organization (JETRO), are not always warmly received abroad, because many Western investors claim that reciprocal markets and opportunities are limited in Japan. As of March 1987, the total value of foreign investment in Japan was about $7 billion, with about half of that coming from U.S. investors in manufacturing concerns. Under pressure from industrialized trading partners and from the exigencies of a truly global economy, Japan has begun, and is likely to continue, to open its markets to foreign investment, rather than face further protectionist action by its major trading partners. Whether or not Western investors can or will avail themselves of these opportunities remains to be seen.

Another recent change in the Japanese economy is that the focus upon higher value-added products and the emphasis upon tertiary industries has put pressure on the labor force to change in Japan. As the nation moves from a manufacturing, production-based system to one which is focused primarily on knowledge-based industries, a concurrent need is arising for a greater number of educated white-collar workers than for blue-collar laborers. The reorientation also requires a change in focus on types of skills held by Japanese workers. Most recently this has been evidenced by the increased emphasis on gaining expertise in the service industries and zealous efforts to learn about new projects or business methods. Increasingly, Japanese visit the United States to study American techniques for success in the service industries.

Japanese research teams in the United States examine such American methodologies in the service industries as developing more creative flair and better retailing pizzazz, developing and marketing new financial instruments, and so on. Toward the end of the 1980s, subjects of interest to Japanese delegations included techniques used in arranging mannequin displays in Bloomingdale's department stores, operation of gasoline service stations, and trading techniques on Wall Street. Another focus of recent Japanese concern is on methods of developing better relationships between corporations and local communities. Japanese businessmen are also trying to emulate the American example of greater social and community responsibility.

Not only is Japan being challenged to develop greater capacity for high valued-added tertiary products, it must also face increasing challenges from growing competition from its neighbors in Asia. Many of these nations in the Pacific Rim have assumed production in areas forsaken by Japan, such as in the basic manufacturing industries of shipbuilding and textiles. Japan is finding more and more, however, that the newly industrializing countries are making forays into its market share in other product areas, such as low-end televisions and videocassette recorders. These nations are also targeting Japanese markets to sell low-priced imports, such as textiles and knitwear. The threat emerged in earnest in 1985 when the era of the cheap yen ended, and Japan began to look for offshore production sites that could make its products at lower costs. Thus, its investment in other countries of East Asia went from $1.4 billion in 1986 to $2.3 billion in 1987. The challenge for Japan is to determine the proper path for the future. As one Japanese businessman put it, "We used to aim to catch up. Now we must learn where to go next and how to be caught up with." In order to stay ahead of its neighbors, Japan will have to move quickly and increasingly toward the production of high-profit, high-technology consumer goods, such as video recorders and industrial goods, for example, computerized robots and complex software.

Japan is likely to weather these difficulties on the road ahead because the hallmark of its economic policy and industrial planning is the incorporation of flexibility and adaptability into the planning process and the ability to productively plan for the future and for change. Japan's position is enviable, because productivity is higher than for its peers, as are real earnings in manufacturing. Government spending is lower than the Group of Five peers, and GNP industry classifications show that the largest sectors of the Japanese economy at present are in high-profit services, manufacturing, and other industrial areas.

The Newest Success Stories in Asia: The Four Tigers

Close upon Japan's heels are the newer economic players and challengers in the Pacific Rim. There are four nations, nicknamed the four tigers, that have had a ferocious rate of economic growth in the past decade. These nations, South Korea, Singapore, Taiwan, and Hong Kong, are referred to collectively, but they are actually four very different places with very different problems. Hong Kong and Singapore are city-states that thrive as centers of international manufacturing and banking activity based on genuine free-trade principles. In contrast, South Korea and Taiwan have focused their energies on increasing national industrial development at the expense of allowing consumer expenditures to rise or funds to flow toward the improvement of social welfare conditions.

South Korea

Since the end of the Korean War, South Korea has moved from being a relatively underdeveloped country to a nation boasting a robust economy with an enormous amount of exports and double-digit rates of growth in its gross national product (GNP) (see Figure 12-2). When the war ended in 1953, per capita income (in current dollars) was a miniscule $450, and agriculture accounted for one-fifth of the GNP. By 1987 the per capita income level had reached $2,900 per person and was generated primarily from manufacturing in heavy industry.

The foundation of South Korea's success comes primarily from its imitating Japan's path to economic development and success. In the mid-1960s, South Korea began to focus in earnest upon industrialization. Rather than depend on the limited potential of domestic demand to fuel growth in that decade, the government focused on concentrating efforts and resources for developing export industries (see Figure 12–3). This concentration was fueled not only by borrowed funds, but also by social conditions in South Korea similar to those in Japan. Foremost of these is a social attitude that elevates personal sacrifice to communal goals and an ethic of hard work. South Korea now has a young, growing work force that is well-educated and willing to work hard. The South Korean worker puts in an average of more than fifty hours a week for comparatively low wages, 40 percent more hours than the average American and 25 percent more than most Japanese workers.

Like the Japanese of the 1960s, South Koreans are committed to the growth of their country. The savings rate in Korea is amazingly high, one-third of the GNP, and represents a fourfold increase from the early 1950s, when it was only 8 percent. Clearly, the country plows back much of the surplus revenue earned from increased exports. Radio commentators urge South Koreans to work hard to improve the nation's economic welfare. The saying "minjok chajon," which means "we can do it by ourselves," is practically a national slogan.

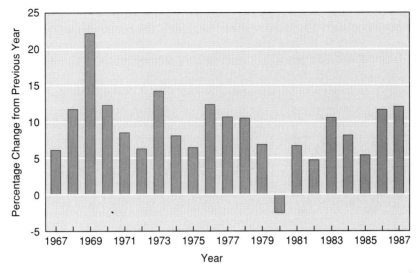

FIGURE 12–2   South Korea's Annual Change in Real GDP.
SOURCE: World Bank and International Monetary Fund.

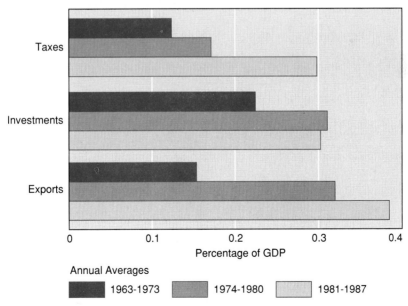

FIGURE 12–3   South Korea's Taxes, Investments and Exports (as a percentage of GDP).
SOURCE: Brookings Institute.

This dedication to national improvement in South Korea has been evidenced in growth rates that averaged more than 10 percent between 1982 and 1987. In 1987 the GNP of the country rose to $120 billion, generated primarily from manufacturing, especially heavy industries, such as automobiles and steel. This concentration of growth has helped to create monolithic corporate businesses much like the Japanese zaibatsu. These family-owned businesses, called chaebol, dominate South Korean industry; the ten largest chaebol account for a third of all manufacturing sales in South Korea. The largest conglomerate, Samsung, started in 1938 as a general store with forty employees. By 1987 it had sales of nearly $22 billion. South Korean conglomerates have a decidedly international orientation. All of its giants, such as Lucky Goldstar, Daewoo, Samsung, and Hyundai, build and operate plants all around the world. South Korean corporations are expanding rapidly and investing billions in attempts to expand and launch new industries such as aircraft and robotics production (Figure 12–4).

Although South Korea's success is remarkable, it does not come without problems and social dis-locations occasioned by rapid change. Thus, the country that is traditionally known as the Land of Morning Calm is becoming increasingly turbulent.

SOUTH KOREA'S PROBLEMS

One problem in South Korea comes from a work force and consumer class that is chafing increasingly against the self-discipline necessary to continue fueling such enormous growth rates. Workers believe that they should be realizing a greater share of the rewards of development in the form of increases in wages. Discord on this topic led to a series of strikes by South Korean workers and resulted in 40 percent increases in wage rates over the 1987-to-1988 period. These increases in wages raise problems in economic development efforts because they reduce the competitive advantages manufacturers gained from low labor costs. Thus, chaebols facing increasing costs in wages and decreased profits look more and more to moving their manufacturing facilities offshore in an effort to rationalize production. Government leaders seem to accept the fact that increases in wages will reduce the international competitiveness of

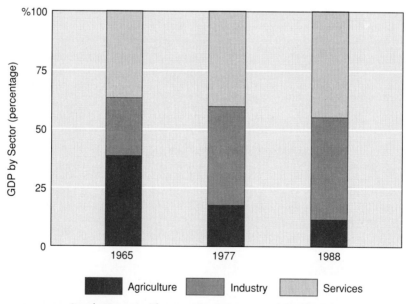

FIGURE 12–4   South Korea's Changes in Structure of Production.
SOURCE: World Bank and International Monetary Fund.

its exported products, but consider the tradeoff of improved social welfare important. Business interests in response are also turning efforts toward the production of higher-priced goods designed to compete in the upper end of markets.

In order to approach, compete, and succeed in new markets, however, South Korea will need to have access to technology to move it past a labor-cost orientation toward a proactive product-development orientation. This presents a problem because South Korea is finding it increasingly difficult to import technology from other countries, such as the United States. U.S. companies are increasingly charging South Korean partners more for the use of their technology and are pursuing cases of patent infringement. In one case, Samsung was sued by Texas Instruments for violating memory-chip patents and was required to pay penalties rumored to be about $90 million.

Thus, in order to develop better technological expertise and the facility to develop applications of that technology, South Korean companies are making increasing investments in research and development. In 1971 R&D levels in South Korea were less than a single percent of the national GNP, representing one-eighth of the percentage of U.S. investment R&D and one-sixth of the commitment by Japan to research efforts. By 1986 the percentage of the South Korean GNP committed to R&D had risen to 2 percent, and all the major conglomerates forecast R&D spending increases of between 50 percent and 100 percent in subsequent years.

In addition to problems in planning for further economic development, the government of South Korea also faces problems from fast rates of growth, including inflation, increasing polarization of economic activity and its concentration in Seoul (the capital city), and continued trade friction with trading partners, such as the United States. A solution for these problems would be for South Korea to focus on increasing domestic demand, rather than continuing emphasis on export trade. Such an increase would have the advantage of fueling continued growth through internal means, of potentially opening South Korean markets to foreign

suppliers, and of diverting production from export goods to Korean consumer goods.

Many believe, however, that growth in the economy overall may have to be slowed so that more attention can be paid to social demands in South Korea. Although income is considered to be relatively evenly distributed in South Korea, which has better-than-average standards of living, as compared to most other developing countries, there is considerable social discord within the egalitarian population. Many South Koreans believe that they have not benefited from the enormous economic success of the country as have the elite. In 1985, for example, the top 10 percent of the population accounted for slightly more than 28 percent of the national income, while the bottom 10 percent earned only 2.1 percent. As the nation increases its overall wealth, average South Koreans feel that there continues to be a gap between the wealthy and themselves.

These differences are also seen in regional differences in development progress. Seventy percent of the South Korean wealth, for example, is located in the northern part of the country and is concentrated in Seoul, which has only one-quarter of the population. Other regions of the country fall far behind the level of development in Seoul, which includes well-built highway systems and high-rise office buildings. Income in the countryside falls behind the rest of the country by an estimated 18 percent and development is uneven. Many South Koreans complain that the orientation of the government is toward business and not the betterment of the local population. They cite income gaps, concentrated development, and the lack of social support systems as being severe problems in the nation.

The government has responded to these complaints by proposing to spend some of its earnings on housing and rural infrastructure projects. It also proposes to launch a national pension fund and national medical insurance to provide a measure of security for members of society. In addition, the government is increasingly privatizing its interest in industries by making stock shares available to all citizens (especially middle-income people) and by forcing some of the large corporations in the nation to offer shares to individuals.

Dissatisfaction with the government of South Korea has created a great deal of political conflict in recent years. Students and workers routinely demonstrate and strike (see Perspective 12–1) and scandals are commonplace and often involve top officials. This situation may change, however, as South Korea enters what appears to be a period of political stability, which began with the election by democratic process of a new president to replace a military dictatorship. This democratization and the expansion of the middle class in South Korea is expected to moderate political extremes in the country and to soften political differences between opposing parties.

PERSPECTIVE 12–1   Rocky Labor Relations in South Korea Raise Concern About Impact on Economy

SEOUL, South Korea—Labor relations in South Korea have gotten off to a rocky start this year, raising concerns that the country's economic performance may be damaged if the pattern continues.

Many South Korean and foreign companies have been hit by strikes this month, and last week a senior Hyundai Group executive was arrested on charges of instigating an attack on labor organizers. Press reports said 19 past and present employees of Hyundai Group companies were injured and at least four hospitalized last week after they were attacked with baseball bats and steel rods.

The early rise of this year's labor disputes, well in advance of the traditional spring wage-negotiation season, caught many observers by surprise. "I had expected that the experience gained by both management and labor in extended disputes last year would help smooth relations in 1989, but then we get this kind of violence," said Park Young Bum, an analyst at the semigovernmental Korea Labor Research Institute. "I'm sure this [Hyundai incident] will add to this spring's labor disputes."

Last year, South Korea's manufacturing output was set back three trillion won, or $4.39 billion at current exchange rates, and exports were set back $696 million because of labor disputes, according to press reports citing Ministry of Trade and Industry figures.

STILL STRUGGLING WITH CHANGE

Analysts say South Korean corporations are still struggling to deal with a labor climate that was radically changed by the development of the country's first independent labor unions in 1987, following nationwide protests that also forced the government to broaden political freedoms.

With the rising won reducing South Korean export competitiveness, analysts say manufacturers this year may be more resistant to the kind of labor demands that in the past two years have boosted wages more than 13% annually on average and up to 20% or more a year at many large export-oriented companies.

Meanwhile, President Roh Tae Woo has promised to crack down on violations of labor laws by both management and labor. The government has taken a hands-off approach to previous labor disputes, in part, analysts say, to avoid political criticism.

TROUBLE AT HYUNDAI

"Last year the government refrained from taking legal action whenever possible. This year we will take a more active role in preventing violence by

SOURCE: Susan Moffat, Wall Street Journal, January 17, 1989.

both labor and management," said a Ministry of Labor official who asked not to be identified.

Hyundai was one of the groups hit hardest by labor disputes last year, largely because the conglomerate has chosen to take a hard line against unions, analysts say. A 23-day strike at Hyundai Motor Co. in June delayed production of 80,000 vehicles, and 70 days of strikes reduced sales markedly at Hyundai Heavy Industries Co., a company spokesman said.

Since Jan. 13 of this year, about 22,000 workers have been locked out of the Hyundai Heavy Industries shipyard in Ulsan, the largest in South Korea, following a strike that began Dec. 12 over a dispute centering on bonuses. Hyundai Engine & Machinery Co. has locked out about 2,300 workers, a company spokesman said.

Last Wednesday, Han Yu Dong, managing director of Hyundai Engine & Machinery, was arrested in Ulsan and admitted to police that he planned an assault on union organizers, according to a company spokesman. The Hyundai Group's honorary chairman, Chung Ju Yung, issued a public apology for last week's violence against labor organizers upon his return from a trip to Moscow Friday.

Last Thursday, 10,000 Hyundai workers held a rally in Ulsan to protest the attack, according to press reports, while about 20,000 workers and political dissidents gathered in Ulsan on Sunday, according to the Korean Federation of Metalworkers Trade Union.

WIDESPREAD DISPUTES

Besides Hyundai companies, the Samsung Group's Samsung Shipbuilding & Heavy Industries Co., several government research institutes and a number of foreign firms have been among those hit by labor disputes this month. Motorola Korea Ltd., a unit of Motorola Inc., and IBM Korea Inc., an arm of International Business Machines Corp., are among the units of foreign firms hit by labor disputes.

Some Samsung Shipbuilding workers who struck for three weeks in November and December are continuing to demonstrate, demanding the dissolution of what they call a pro-management union. Samsung so far has effectively prevented the formation of independent unions at most of its companies by granting pre-emptive wage increases and encouraging what is described as an environment of paternalism and strict discipline.

South Korea's political challenges are not only internal. One issue that is constantly on the back burner is that of long-term international relations, especially the long-term relationship between South Korea and the United States. At issue are continued trade disputes and pressure from the United States for South Korea to open its markets to U.S. goods and to allow the won, the South Korean currency, to strengthen against the dollar. In order to pressure South Korea to open its markets, the United States suspended preferential tariff treatment and threatened to initiate trade actions against unfair trading practices. The United States also has been applying pressure upon South Korea to share more of the military expenses incurred in maintaining a U.S. military

presence in South Korea as protection against the resumption of a conflict with North Korea.

The relationship between South Korea and North Korea will certainly be a prominent concern and may have a major effect upon the future of South Korea. Since the end of the Korean War in 1953, the two countries have been decisively separated and there is continuing hostility. North Korea has 800,000 troops and the support of the People's Republic of China and the Soviet Union. South Korea is allied with the United States and Japan and has 600,000 troops. This situation provides great potential for renewed conflict and fuels ongoing debate in South Korea, where opinion is divided regarding the future relationship between the two countries. Some believe that North Korea and South Korea should be reunified and that coordination of the resources of both could make for an unbeatable economic entity in the Far East. Others hold the political hard line and resist the unification idea. Talks between representatives of North Korea and South Korea have begun and will continue to be conducted in the truce village of Panmunjom. It is likely, however, that the process of reducing hostilities will take a long time and will engender continuing debate.

The Future of South Korea

Although the problems South Korea faces are formidable, it may be able to promote and benefit from the changes necessary to become a full-fledged member of the world economy. The goal for the nation, as envisioned by President Roh Tae Woo, is that South Korea will have an income of at least $5,000 per person by the year 1993 and that it will join other developed nations as a member of the Organization for Economic Cooperation and Development. Given the vast accomplishments and phenomenal ability to adapt to and benefit from change, South Korea is likely to achieve this goal.

Taiwan

Taiwan is also a formidable economic force in the Pacific Rim. This nation, as has South Korea, has seen drastic changes in its political composition but has also experienced phenomenal growth in recent decades. Taiwan, officially known as the Republic of China, is an island off the shore of the mainland of the People's Republic of China and is densely populated with 20 million people and has few natural resource endowments. Nevertheless, it has pursued a single-minded goal of regaining economic and political strength, toward which it has channeled its strong national work ethic. After four decades of effort, it has emerged as an economy with a per capita GNP that is more than ten times the GNP of the People's Republic of China.

Taiwan's economic statistics are impressive. In 1952, its GNP per capita was a mere $48; by 1988 it reached $5,000. In 1952 there was only one car

and one telephone for every one thousand people; by 1988 this level had reached forty cars and 400 telephones for every thousand people. Aggregate GNP reached $95 billion in 1987, while foreign exchange reserves touched $75 billion and foreign debt was scant at only $2.9 billion. Taiwan enjoys a large balance-of-trade surplus; in 1987 exports exceeded imports by more than $19 billion. Exported goods range from yachts and sophisticated computers to furniture, teapots, and toys. By 1987 Taiwan was the thirteenth largest trading nation in the world, with its primary market being the United States, which received 44.5 percent of Taiwanese exports in that year.

Taiwan's success came about through the success of directed efforts promulgated within a number of economic plans that were implemented within the structure of a highly disciplined society with stability enforced by a military regime. In 1953 the government began implementing a series of four-year economic plans that have brought the country from abject poverty to the brink of economic prosperity. This series of plans redeveloped the economy from its agricultural orientation to one that was composed primarily of manufacturing and industrial output. The success of this policy is evident from the fact that the Taiwanese economy has grown at an annual average rate of 8 percent for the past thirty years. In addition, major structural changes have occurred in the past forty years.

In 1952 agriculture in Taiwan comprised 32 percent of the GNP, while industry contributed 22 percent; by 1988 the share of agricultural production had fallen to 6 percent of the GNP, while that of industry had risen to about half of all the GNP. The original key to success in Taiwan was the institution of a land reform program, which gave local farmers a greater stake in production and freed landowners to reallocate their investment toward higher-profit manufacturing and urban opportunities. The result was greater agricultural output, declines in reliance on foreign exchange, and the creation of jobs that came about with the emergence of factories designed to produce such items as textiles, toys, paper, and canned pineapple.

By the 1960s economic development had progressed so far that additional factories were producing higher-value-added goods, such as more complex electrical appliances, televisions, refrigerators, and bicycles, many of which were targeted for export markets. This development was taken a step further in the 1970s, when an infrastructure was developed for international communication, intermediate-goods production and capital-intensive industries.

At present, manufacturing production in Taiwan is dispersed and not controlled by monolithic entities, such as the Japanese zaibatsu and South Korean chaebol. Production is expected to continue to move toward high-technology products, and the industry is moving toward greater energy efficiency, using automated methods of production. This growth, however, is not without its problems.

Industrial pollution, for example, has become a major environmental threat. Between 1950 and 1980, the number of factories in the country rose from slightly more than 5,500 to more than 60,000. Minimal controls of polluting practices, miniscule sewage treatment, and general neglect of safety measures have led to an environmental situation that is a cause for serious concern for Taiwanese authorities, especially as popular protests grow in frequency and intensity. The challenge for Taiwan is enforcement of antipollution standards in thousands of small factories, which is economically and politically very difficult.

Another problem has surfaced with the growth of the economy in Taiwan. Workers in Taiwan are in such high demand that each can choose from nearly three jobs. Employee bonuses are paid by some companies for the enlistment of a new worker. As with other nations in the Pacific Rim, Taiwanese employers are also finding that increasing wages are forcing them to either shift from labor-intensive industries to more sophisticated industries, such as computer production or to move their businesses to less expensive manufacturing sites in other countries, such as Thailand and the Philippines.

As in South Korea, Taiwan is also facing pressure from major trading partners, such as the United States, to allow its currency, the New Taiwan dollar, to rise against the U.S. dollar and to eliminate its protective tariff barriers in order to bring trade imbalances into alignment. Since 1987 Taiwan has made progress in lowering tariffs to realize a reduction in average ad valorem tariffs for 4,383 items, down to 16 percent from 20 percent. Nevertheless, Taiwan continues to enjoy massive trade surpluses and income from the balance of foreign exchange.

THE FUTURE OF TAIWAN

The future for Taiwan will depend on how the country builds on its successes. With huge levels of foreign reserves, strong export markets, extensive entrepreneurial strength and savings rates of 40 percent of the GNP, the nation clearly is in a position of strength to plan for the future. The crucial question is which goal Taiwan should focus upon. The plan promulgated by the Taiwanese government to keep the economy going into the next century is to upscale production to high-technology and value-added goods, such as computer chips, information technology, and biotechnology products, and to increase the focus on service industries, such as consulting. The goal is to diversify the export base to include high-technology goods, which are marketable in more than just U.S. markets and to provide the means to improve the quality of life in the country by reducing pollution, providing better health care, expanding labor rights, and improving the capacity of the population to enjoy a higher quality of life.

These goals must also be reconciled with the political situation which is overshadowed by the antipathy between the Taiwanese government and mainland China, both of which see their borders as rightly including all lands termed "China." Changes in political leadership in Taiwan after the death of President Chiang Chinkuo, the son of Chiang Kai-Shek, have apparently created an easing of martial law, which has been replaced by a national security law. The shift in power has also led to increasing liberalization of political freedoms in Taiwan. This momentum is expected to continue, at least as long as the country continues to enjoy increased prosperity.

Hong Kong

Hong Kong is a small territory ceded to Great Britain by a Chinese emperor in the nineteenth century. Under the recent agreement between Great Britain and the government of the People's Republic of China, control over Hong Kong is to be returned to China in 1997. Considerable anxiety has arisen about the shape of things in the post-1997 period, despite assurances from the Chinese government that no major changes will be made in Hong Kong, at least for the next fifty years. There are obvious reasons for the anxiety and concern in the minds of the people of Hong Kong.

During the period between 1900 and the 1980s, Hong Kong has become an economic power in its own right, growing at a spectacular pace in many different directions. Its key location amidst the major ocean trading routes and the policy of the British administration to promote the territory as a free port, enabled it to become an important entrepôt for Asia's trade with the rest of the world. Considerable impetus for growth was provided by large trading houses owned primarily by British interests that diversified into a wide range of businesses, bringing with them their business techniques, practices, and contacts. Although much of the growth of Hong Kong in the post-World War II era was based on its status as a trade entrepôt, since the 1950s the territory has emerged as an important manufacturing center with a diversified and dynamic industrial base. The industries were powered not so much by huge capital inputs or revolutionary innovation, but by the hard work of low-paid migrant labor from mainland China who accepted the harsh working conditions without protest, because they were still much better off than they would be in their homeland. Hong Kong specialized in light, labor intensive industries, because labor was the main competitive advantage and spatial resources were limited. The emphasis again was on exports, because the local economy was far too small to absorb the booming output levels.

As 1997 draws closer, the anxiety in Hong Kong is growing, primarily because Hong Kong represents the antithesis of Chinese official philosophy. There are virtually no controls on business, tax laws are lax, and the emphasis on free-market activity is pervasive. Many businesses and professionals, fearing a reversal of official policy with Chinese control, are leaving Hong Kong for other locations in different parts of the world, which puts a question mark on the future of Hong Kong, which could be of greater concern than actual control of the territory by the Chinese government after 1997.

By 1990 Hong Kong had reached a per capita GNP level of $9,673, and growth had averaged 7.3 percent per annum over the past five years. Over the past few years, however, as anxieties have grown, other types of problems have cropped up. Labor shortages and increasing local costs are affecting production, and many businesses are relocating to other Southeast Asian countries. Recognizing this trend, the official authorities predict a slowdown of the growth rate in the early years of the 1990s.

The greatest short-term challenge for Hong Kong is dealing with a severe shortage of labor. This shortage has led to requests that the nation relax its immigration laws to allow for the entry of more foreign workers. It is similarly suffering from increases in local costs, which are raising the prices of its export goods. The result is that many manufacturers in Hong Kong are moving to mainland China for production, and goods are then brought back to Hong Kong for reexportation. In 1988, for the first time ever, the ports and airports of Hong Kong handled more exports of reexported goods than of locally produced products.

Singapore

Singapore, a small city-state off the Malaysian peninsula, has also made rapid economic strides to emerge as an important newly industrialized country of the region. Its rapid ascent to economic preeminence began after it attained independence in 1964. The nation has averaged a growth rate of approximately 8 percent a year since independence and has become the world's leading exporter after the major industrialized countries. Per annual per capita income reached $7,600 at the end of the 1980s, which was among the highest in developing countries.

The rapid industrialization and expansion of Singapore was stimulated and overseen by its founder and former prime minister, Lee Kwan Yew. Active support of key industries, a closely controlled industrial relations climate, and continued emphasis on high productivity and lower production costs enabled Singapore to build a strong industrial base that relied on such industries as shipbuilding and electronics, in which Singapore enjoyed a distinct competitive advantage. The ideal location of Singapore also enabled it to act as a major transit point for international trade, which provided numerous opportunities for local businesspersons. The excellent industrial structures in the virtual absence of labor militancy and the positive attitude of the government enhanced the attractiveness of Singapore as a site for foreign direct investment by major multinational corporations, which brought with them the advantages of new technology and access to new markets for products made in Singapore.

Singapore's stock market and futures markets are among the best developed in Asia, as is its foreign exchange market. Singapore is host to almost every major international financial institution, especially banks and securities markets. The importance of Singapore as an international financial center is evident from the fact that the most funds in the region are raised in its markets, and the Singapore interbank offered rate is used as a major benchmark for setting interest rates and costs in large international financial transactions. The Singapore Mercantile Exchange, SIMEX, is also the only futures exchange in the region.

Singapore does face a number of challenges. Economic growth slowed for the first time in 1987 as overinvestment in certain industrial sectors, competition from other NICs of the region, and reduced domestic competitiveness because of higher wages contributed to a local recession. The pace of industrial development has outstripped the supply of skilled personnel, and the shortage of employable professionals has caused increasing anxiety to industry and government alike. Several large U.S. corporations, such as Apple Computers and Black & Decker, have major manufacturing establishments in Singapore. Like many other small NICs, Singapore is heavily export-dependent because of its limited internal market. Protectionism and recession in the industrial countries constitute an ever-present danger to economic growth, although the nation has survived major external shocks very well in the past.

In the last quarter of a century, however, Singapore has built considerable strength and resilience into its economy. The setback in 1987 was quickly rolled back as the economy recovered to continue on a growth path, albeit at a lower rate. The finances of the country are sound, debt-service obligations are small, and there is an educated work force that is capable of meeting the challenges of the structural changes needed to move the industrial sector into new areas of high-technology and sophisticated industries. There are, of course, uncertainties about the political future of Singapore, especially in view of the multiethnic character of the population, which always opens opportunities for political manipulation toward disorder and conflict. These uncertainties, however, are not likely to cause serious concern, because it has been shown by the people of Singapore that they are too concerned with economic progress to be led away from their economic path in pursuit of the uncertain gains of factional politics.

Potential Newly Industrialized Countries

The four tigers of Asia are not the only potential stars in the firmament of the Pacific Rim. Other nations in the region are poised to take advantage of their labor capabilities and markets in Japan and in the East in order to emulate the example of newly industrialized nations. The most likely nation in the area to become a new tiger is Thailand. Other nations with a great deal of potential are Malaysia, Indonesia, and the Philippines.

Thailand

Of all the developing nations in the Pacific Rim, Thailand is most likely to become another "tiger." It is a stable country politically that has never been colonized. The government, controlled by a prime minister, has a popular monarch and does not suffer from conflicts between ethnic groups. The nation also has the advantages of plentiful labor plus labor laws that allow for production in shifts around the clock. The labor force is young and inexpensive, and unskilled workers can be hired for as little as $3 a day.

The export earnings of Thailand come from the production of shirts, running shoes, semiconductors, and toys. Tourism is another major foreign exchange earner, bringing in more than $1.7 billion in 1987. The growth prospects of Thailand are constrained by the limitations imposed by lack of adequate industrial infrastructure and continuing inflation.

The Philippines

The Philippines has yet to recover from its serious political problems, beginning with the overthrow of President Ferdinand Marcos. President Corazon Aquino continues to battle communist insurgents, assassination and coup attempts, as well as a legacy of bureaucratic inefficiencies and corruption. These characteristics are not enticements for badly needed investment in the Philippines. In 1988 government officials predicted that the Philippines would realize annual growth levels of about 6 percent in gross domestic product, but as exports rose, imports rose faster, creating a trade deficit. The coup attempt in 1989 further shook confidence in a nation that needs sustained political stability for continued growth in the future.

Malaysia

Malaysia has traditionally relied upon the export of commodities, such as rubber, palm oil, and tin, as a leading part of its growth and development efforts. While the government has attempted to expand development into heavy industries, these efforts have been relatively ineffective, especially for state-owned industries. The greatest difficulty in Malaysia, and a barrier to the enticement of foreign investment, is the potential for discord between ethnic groups in the country, primarily between ethnic Malays, who make up the major part of the population, and Indians and Chinese, who make up the balance.

In the late 1980s the economic prospects of Malaysia were buoyed up by firm prices for its export commodities. For the nation to make any real headway, however, it will have to make far-reaching structural changes in its economy to reduce its overreliance on the export of nonrenewable natural resources and build up an economy based on efficient and productive manufacturing activity.

Indonesia

Indonesia has traditionally relied upon exports of oil from its state-owned industry to support its population, but it suffers from corruption and overreliance on oil. Monopolies and high prices for the importation of commodities needed for development—cement, steel, plastics, and other basic materials—also hinder progress.

By the end of the 1980s, petroleum prices, unlike other commodity prices, were weak, which hurt Indonesia even though the nation had been attempting to diversify its exports. Greater incentives for the private sector, increasing foreign direct investment, and development of financial markets are needed for Indonesia to emerge as an NIC. By the end of the 1980s, the country was making significant efforts toward this end, and the prospects look brighter than before, provided that Indonesia maintains the current emphasis.

Future Strategies

The Pacific Rim will continue to arouse increasing interest in its activities and markets and witness substantial and continued change and growth.

Many see increased economic development in the Pacific Rim as a threat to the economic power and preeminence of Western nations. Others, however, take the opposing view and maintain that growth in Asia will provide industrialized countries with more opportunities than threats. The key will be the interest of Westerners in recognizing and being in a position to take advantage of these opportunities.

The latter view holds that by identifying and targeting new opportunities in the Far East, Western industries, notably U.S. industries, can benefit greatly. The overall potential for trade in Asia is enormous, given the vast trade flows between East and West. In 1978, for example, trade between the United States and Asia accounted for less than one-quarter of all U.S. trade. A decade later this proportion had risen to more than one-third of total U.S. international commerce. This trade is largely composed of imports into U.S. markets from Asian nations, but it nonetheless includes increases in the sale of U.S. goods to its Asian trading partners. From 1983 to 1990, for example, four of the fastest-growing export markets for the United States were the Pacific Rim nations of Taiwan, China, Hong Kong, and South Korea. From 1980 to 1990 overall exports from the United States to Asia jumped by 20 percent. During the same period, exports to traditional U.S. trading partners in industrialized Europe remained almost the same.

This trend of expansion in Pacific Rim export markets is only expected to continue, because of

- The relative decline of the U.S. dollar versus the yen, which is reducing the cost competitiveness of products from Japan and increasing relative competitiveness of U.S. goods.
- Expectations of continued growth in the economies, population, and demand in Eastern export markets, causing them to outstrip the size of European trading partners.
- Close political and economic ties to Eastern nations, creating efforts on their parts to increase imports of U.S. products to allay political criticism and to minimize their own reliance on Japanese products.

In fact, American firms have been increasingly criticized for missing vast opportunities in world markets, primarily in the East, by being unwilling to change products and by not being aggressive enough in pursuit of business.

Lack of success in Eastern markets and dangerous attitudes regarding competitors in the East lead many in the West to promote the imposition of protectionist trade policies, evidenced by barriers to imports. This reaction often backfires in the long run. Imports may be restricted for a time, but the long-term effect is an increase of foreign direct investment in the protectionistic market. The result is that protectionism ultimately expands the market share of competitors at home and concedes their preeminence in newly emerging potential markets in the East.

Savvy Western firms can make use of Eastern manufacturing expertise while maintaining control over their technology, retaining domestic manufacturing capacity and keeping an edge of efficiency development. These firms can put themselves in a position of strength to be ready to take advantage of developing opportunities in Eastern markets.

Summary

The industrial development of the Pacific Rim since World War II has been one of the most important international business developments and is reflected in shifting international trade and foreign direct investment patterns. Continued economic growth will give Pacific Rim countries a larger decision-making role in international economics and a voice in supranational organizations.

The growth of Japan after World War II has been fueled by a collaborative business and government relationship and policies that promoted national economic growth. These policies included incentives to increase personal savings and invest in infrastructure and manufacturing capacity and to rely on internally generated funds, rather than acquire debt from other countries or institutions. Investment incentives have been targeted toward areas where national advantages exist and toward markets that offer the greatest long-term potential. Japanese manufacturing through the influence of the Ministry of Finance and MITI shifted from textile and steel production in the 1950s and 1960s to high-priced value-added goods in the 1970s and 1980s. In the 1990s, keiretsus, production efficiency, conservation, and an emphasis on high technology to replace high labor costs continue to fuel Japanese economic growth.

South Korea, Taiwan, Hong Kong, and Singapore are known collectively as the four tigers because of tremendous economic growth, yet each has achieved its growth through highly individual methods. The major assets of South Korea include a large, highly skilled work force and a self-disciplined dedication to national improvement. Problems exist in the areas of labor unrest, uneven distribution of income, and political instability. Taiwan has focused on producing higher-priced, high technology goods, which has fueled tremendous growth, but also has resulted in industrial pollution and a severe labor shortage. Hong Kong has long specialized in light, labor-intensive industries, but a severe labor shortage and uncertainty over its future after 1997 are generating considerable anxiety. Singapore stimulated rapid industrialization and built strong shipbuilding and electronics industries and has developed into an international financial center. Overinvestment and higher wages have slowed growth in Singapore, and its multiethnic population may cause future political uncertainty.

Thailand is most likely to become the next tiger, while Malaysia, Indonesia, and the Philippines are other potential economic stars.

U.S. firms must compete with the Pacific Rim by being willing to adapt products, aggressively pursuing business, and by making use of Pacific Rim manufacturing expertise while controlling their technology and efficiency of operations.

Discussion Questions

1. Describe the economic shifts that have occurred since World War II between North America, Europe, and the Pacific Rim.

2. What business policies did Japan implement after World War II that set the stage for its future growth?
3. How did personal savings contribute to Japanese growth?
4. What is a sunset industry?
5. What is MITI? What role does it play in setting the business direction of Japan?
6. What is a keiretsu? Name some of them. What businesses are they involved with?
7. How would you describe the relationship between the Japanese government and Japanese businesses? Compare your answer to government business relationships in the United States.
8. What advantages do Japanese multinationals have over U.S. and European multinationals?
9. How is the Korean business environment similar to or different from Japan?
10. What is a chaebol? Name some of them.
11. What problems are affecting economic growth in Taiwan?
12. What will occur in Hong Kong in 1997? How is this affecting current business activities?
13. What strategies would you use to compete against Pacific Rim competitors?

Bibliography

1990. "America and Japan: The Unhappy Alliance." *The Economist* (February 17): 21–24.

1990. "Japan in the 1990s." *Tokyo Business Today* (January):14–18.

AGGARWAL, RAJ, AND T. AGMON. 1990. "The International Success of Developing Country Firms: Role of Government-Directed Comparative Advantage." *Management International Review* (Second Quarter): 163–180.

CAPLEN, BRIAN. 1990. "Dawn of the Asian Millenium." *Asian Business* (January):22–27.

GRUB, P. D., T. C. HUNT, K. KUEN-CHOR, AND G. H. ROTT. 1982. *East Asia: Dimensions of International Business,* Sydney: Prentice-Hall International.

GUPTE, PRANAY. 1989. "Lee Kuan Yew's Recipe for an Ideal Leader." *Asian Finance* (December 15):18–19.

HO, JOSEPH M. L. 1990. "Investment Flows: The Third Wave in Asia." *Benefits and Compensation International* (July/August):23–28.

Holloway, Nigel. 1989. "An Idea Before its Time: Japan May Put More Emphasis on Regional Integration." *Far Eastern Economic Review* (June 15):58–59.

Koch, James V. 1989. "An Economic Profile of the Pacific Rim." *Business Horizons* (March/April):18–25.

Koretz, Gene. 1988. "Why Asia Looms Larger in the U.S. Trade Picture." *Business Week,* (July 18):16–17.

Lutz, James M., and Young W. Kihl. 1990. "The NICs, Shifting Comparative Advantage, and the Product Life Cycle." *Journal of World Trade* (February):113–134.

Montagu-Pollock, Matthew. 1990. "Asia 2000—Finance: Overtaking the West." *Asian Business* (January):48–51.

Saghafi, Massoud M., and C. S. Davidson. 1989. "The New Age of Global Competition in the Semiconductor Industry: Enter the Dragon." *Columbia Journal of World Business* (Winter):60–70.

Weiss, Julian. 1989. *The Asian Century: The Economic Ascent of the Pacific Rim and What It Means for the West.* New York: Facts on File.

West, Phillip, and Frans A. M. Alting von Geusau, eds. 1987. *The Pacific Rim and the Western World: Strategic, Economic, and Cultural Perspectives.* Boulder, CO.: Westview Press.

Chapter Case Study

Mercury Textiles Corporation

Mercury Textiles Corporation was one of the largest exporters of polyester and mixed content textiles from the United States until the early 1980s. In fact, it could be counted among the top fifteen textile exporters in the world. Its primary markets were Latin America, Africa, and, to a limited extent, in Europe. Latin America and Africa absorbed the bulk of the company's total exports of nearly $3 billion annually. In several countries Mercury was the dominant supplier and faced little or no competition from either domestic or overseas textile manufacturers. One important reason for Mercury's sustained dominance was the sheer size of its operations and marketing strength which made it extremely difficult for any potential competitor to wrest even a small amount of market share away from the giant company. The economies of scale it enjoyed, allowed Mercury to outprice all competition. Moreover, it was among the very few suppliers in Africa and Latin America who were able to assure ready and timely deliveries.

In the early 1980s, however, significant new forces had begun to emerge on the international textile market. These forces were the rapidly industrializing nations of Southeast Asia—Korea, Taiwan, Singapore, and Hong Kong. In addition, a number of other Asian countries had developed international competitive capabilities in textiles and were beginning to give the established manufacturers a run for their money.

The management of Mercury Textiles was aware of the rising threat, but it was not overly concerned. The U.S. Department of Commerce had taken a fairly protectionist stance against textile imports, and there was little that the overseas suppliers could do to penetrate the U.S. market under these circumstances. The threat on the export front also did not seem too great.

It seemed that most of these Southeast Asian countries targeted Europe and North America and did not want to market to Africa and Latin America. They could not really hope to match Mercury even in Europe, because the company controlled a small percentage of the high-end market, selling its premium brands at very expensive prices. Most of the newly industrializing countries did not produce textiles of that quality and grade and could not, therefore, pose a significant threat.

In the middle and late 1980s, things began to change in the African and Latin American textile markets. The debt crisis continued to dampen the interest of Western bankers in adding to their exposures in Latin America, and as export finance began to tighten, Mercury found that it could no longer continue to pursue the aggressive sales policies that had been its main weapon in the previous two decades. Moreover, the currencies of the Latin American countries continued to depreciate sharply against the U.S. dollar, making Mercury's U.S.-made products increasingly expensive in the local markets. Africa was in an almost identical state. Continued depression in commodity prices and rampant political instability plunged many of Mercury's main country markets into a deep economic recession, which was reflected in a dramatically reduced purchasing power of the locals.

Added to these disadvantages was a new and disturbing phenomenon from the standpoint of Mercury. As the 1980s wore on, it became increasingly clear that the Southeast Asian countries would not remain content with attempting to sell their products just to the Western world. They were going to seek the world market and that included Africa and Latin America. Taiwan began to take a particular interest in these regions as it looked for ways to sell its huge production of textiles and other clothing items to new markets. The Taiwanese exporters had several advantages. Their currency was definitely undervalued by the government in order to boost exports, which gave them an automatic price advantage over several other competitors. The government of Taiwan also had provided several incentives to its textile exporters, especially those who were engaged in efforts to penetrate new markets. Most such exporters had been provided with interest-free financing to meet their working capital needs. Other critical inputs, such as yarn and electricity, had been made available to exporters at subsidized rates. Over and above all these production incentives the government had declared a five-year tax holiday for all exporters earning at least 50 percent of their income from exports to new markets. Apart from the government-provided incentives, the Taiwanese textile exporters enjoyed certain inherent advantages. Given the work ethic of Taiwan and the extremely low wage rate, the Taiwanese textile manufacturers were able to move way ahead of others, especially U.S. exporters, in terms of productivity. In addition, there were virtually no environmental regulations or other industrial safety regulations. All this translated into cost savings that were reflected in the final price charged by the exporters.

With all these advantages, it was not long before the Taiwanese had begun to eat away at the long-established market shares of Mercury Textiles. Since most of these countries were in the low-income bracket, much of the textile demand was for low-price goods and quality, and material grade was not that important a concern, which worked to favor the Taiwanese, whose technology and comparative advantage was geared to making high-volume, mediocre quality, low-cost goods.

Within three years Mercury saw its market share drop by 30 percent in Latin America and by as much as 42 percent in Africa. It was not as though the company had given up without a fight. They had tried cutting production costs, improving sales commissions, and more aggressive advertising, but nothing seemed to work against the tidal wave of Taiwanese textile exports that repeatedly flooded the Latin American and African markets.

In December 1989 Mercury's executives came to the inevitable conclusion that, try as they could, they had no chance against the Taiwanese in these markets, at least under the present conditions. The Taiwanese had far too many advantages, which they were pressing home relentlessly. It was time, therefore, to take a fresh look at the whole situation and come up with options that went beyond the simple in-company strategies that had been tried without much success over the past three years.

Several strategies suggested themselves. Some were relatively standard and had been utilized by other companies in similar situations but with varying degrees of success. There were others that called for an untried approach.

One of the suggestions was that the company should buy a textile manufacturing plant in Singapore or Thailand, transfer some of its managerial know-how and technology, and thereby create a highly efficient and low-cost offshore production facility. In a similar vein and for similar reasons, it was suggested that Mercury enter into a joint venture with some company in Southeast Asia and target that company's production to the Latin American and African markets. Sponsors of this suggestion argued that a joint venture would allow the company to use low-cost resources for production, which could be marketed in the Latin American and African countries using the traditionally strong marketing skills of Mercury in these markets. A variant of this suggestion was that Mercury, instead of going through the painful process of establishing a new plant or attempting a potentially difficult joint venture, should simply acquire a functioning textile plant and use its production for sales to these markets.

A different line of thinking was adopted by some executives of the company. They suggested that it might be a good idea to seek out joint ventures with the Taiwanese themselves and, in the process, do some sort of market-splitting. Mercury could help the Taiwanese in Europe and North America with its existing marketing connections and other resources.

Some of the top management felt that the company should not be forced to fend off a competitor on its own, especially when the competitor had all the backing and support of its government. Proponents of this view held that the U.S. government should step in and actively support the U.S. textile companies, who were rapidly losing market share to an onslaught of government-backed exporters from Southeast Asia. After all, loss of market share meant loss of overall business, which in turn meant loss of jobs in the United States—reason enough, many at Mercury thought—for the U.S. government to actively aid the company and confer on it at least some of the privileges its overseas competition was enjoying from its own government.

Others in the top management felt the company should take a consortium approach. In effect, they suggested that U.S. textile manufacturers should map out a joint strategy to deal with the situation. A consortium, they pointed out, would result in important economies of scale that in turn would lead to improved pricing, in order to match the Taiwanese products. A joint effort would also mean a sharing of marketing and other resources both at home and abroad. The Taiwanese exporters were already doing this and were reaping considerable benefits from this approach. There was no apparent reason why the U.S. should not use the same approach to draw level with the Taiwanese in these markets.

The economists of the company, in the meanwhile, added a word of caution. There was only so much corporate strategy could do. The ultimate capability of the company to achieve its goals in the African and Latin American markets would depend to a great extent on the U.S. macroeconomic climate, which did not look too good at the moment, but at least there was no cause for despair, only for caution.

Questions

1. What strategy would you recommend to the CEO of Mercury to regain the market share in Africa and Latin America?
2. What economic developments would help or hurt this strategy?

CHAPTER 13

Doing Business with the European Economic Community (EEC)

CHAPTER OBJECTIVES

This chapter will:

- Analyze the nature of the EEC and the influence it has on trade, financing, and capital flows throughout the world.
- Discuss the process of economic integration and the resulting theoretical benefits.
- Review the origins and structure of the EEC as it moved toward economic integration.
- Identify the problems and opportunities associated with European unification in 1992.
- Present the concerns and responses of multinational corporations faced with both larger market opportunities and potential barriers.

International Business and the EEC

The EEC (also sometimes known simply as the EC) occupies a unique position in the international business world, because it is the most successful example of cross-national economic integration. The continued willingness of member states to promote international economic coordination has enabled this regional arrangement to emerge as one of the most influential economic forces. Together member states account for 28 percent of the world gross national product, 40 percent of exports, and 39 percent of imports.[1] Clearly no major participant in international business can afford to ignore its influence on trade, financing, and capital flow (see Figure 13–1).

[1] World Bank. 1990. *The World Development Report, 1990*. New York: Oxford University Press.

325

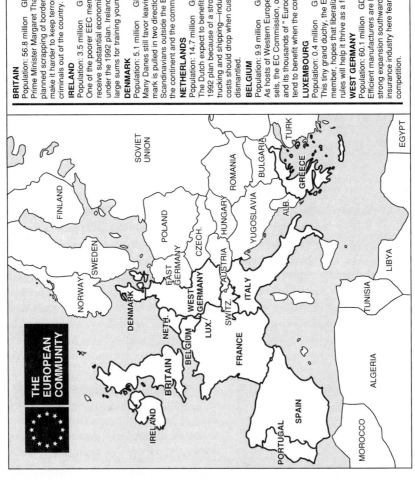

BRITAIN
Population: 56.8 million   GDP: $662.2 billion
Prime Minister Margaret Thatcher fears that planned scrapping of border controls may make it harder to keep terrorists and other criminals out of the country.

IRELAND
Population: 3.5 million   GDP: $29.1 billion
One of the poorer EEC members, Dublin is to receive substantial economic adjustment aid under the 1992 plan. Ireland already gets large sums for training young workers.

DENMARK
Population: 5.1 million   GDP: $101.4 billion
Many Danes still favor leaving the EEC. Denmark is pulled in two directions: toward fellow Scandinavians outside the EEC and toward the continent and the community.

NETHERLANDS
Population: 14.7 million   GDP: $214.6 billion
The Dutch expect to benefit greatly from the 1992 plan because of a strong presence in trucking and shipping—industries where costs should drop when customs controls are dismantled.

BELGIUM
Population: 9.9 million   GDP: $138.5 billion
As hosts of Western Europe's "capital" in Brussels, the EC Commission, or executive body, and its thousands of "Eurocrats." Belgians tend to benefit when the community prospers.

LUXEMBOURG
Population: 0.4 million   GDP: $6.2 billion
This tiny grand duchy, the EEC's smallest member, hopes that liberalization of banking rules will help it thrive as a financial center.

WEST GERMANY
Population: 60.1 million   GDP: $1,118.8 billion
Efficient manufacturers are looking forward to strong expansion southward. Highly regulated insurance industry here fears British and other competition.

FRANCE
Population: 55.6 million   GDP: $879.9 billion
Of the major capitals, Paris is most enthusiastic about Western European integration. Outsiders see the French as too sympathetic to creation of a protectionist "Fortress Europe".

PORTUGAL
Population: 10.2 million   GDP: $26.1 billion
Lisbon hopes a combination of fresh competition and EEC adjustment aid will give its economy a needed injection of dynamism.

SPAIN
Population: 38.7 million   GDP: $288.0 billion
Iberia expects to get a major influx of northern European manufacturing companies, banks, and other firms that will take advantage of relatively low wages and underexploited markets.

ITALY
Population: 57.3 million   GDP: $751.5 billion
Some high-powered Italian entrepreneurs see great opportunity to move north after 1992. Others fear added competition will hurt Italy, already saddled with a staggering budget deficit and cumbersome bureaucracy.

GREECE
Population: 10.0 million   GDP: $47.0 billion
A backward administrative structure and less-developed economy are expected to make it difficult for Greeks to adjust to the post-1992 world.

EEC TOTALS
Population: 322.3 million
GDP: $4,263.7 billion

UNITED STATES (for comparison)
Population: 241.6 million
GDP: $4,435.8 billion

FIGURE 13–1 Population (1986) and Gross Domestic Product (1987) Figures for the European Community.
SOURCE: Map by Larry Fogel; data compiled by James Schwartz, *Washington Post*, March 19, 1989.

Economic Integration

Economic integration is defined in different ways. One useful definition is:

> Economic integration can be considered as a process and as a state of affairs. Regarded as a process it encompasses measures designed to abolish discrimination between economic units belonging to different national states; viewed as a state of affairs, it can be represented by the absence of various forms of discrimination between national economies.[2]

Economic integration provides several benefits to countries that can establish workable arrangements to lower tariff rates, achieve mobility of labor and capital, reduce fluctuations in exchange rates, and ease movement of goods and services across borders. These benefits translate into a better allocation of the productive resources of a region, increased levels of international trade, and mutually beneficial utilization of competitive advantages.

To achieve economic integration, however, nations must sacrifice some of their domestic autonomy, because domestic policies must coincide with those of other states, if collective goals are to be achieved. Many countries find this politically difficult, especially when they are facing severe economic problems and domestic concerns are pressing and immediate. Control over domestic policy remains a key issue in the integration of the EEC. Certain countries, especially Great Britain, are taking a cautious approach in this regard.

Levels of Integration

There are six different phases of economic integration. Placed along a continuum from least integration to complete integration, these phases are the nation-state, free-trade association, customs union, common market, economic union, and complete economic integration or political union. Some people identify an additional stage, the inte-

[2] Balarsa, Bela. 1961. *The Theory of Economic Integration.* Homewood, IL: Richard D. Irwin.

grated supranational system, which includes political union and harmonized sociocultural systems.

THE NATION-STATE

The nation-state is the foundation for a single source of laws and regulation of business and social interactions with other nations. There is no organized integration between countries through the elimination of trade barriers or other such arrangements at the nation-state level.

FREE-TRADE AREA

The free-trade area (FTA) is the least restrictive form of economic integration. Under agreements designating an FTA, all barriers to trade are eliminated among member countries, including elimination of all tariffs and nontariff restrictions. Goods and services are freely traded within the FTA. No discriminating taxes, quotas, tariffs, or other trade barriers are allowed. One of the most important characteristics of an FTA is that each country sets its own policy regarding trade with nonmember countries. An FTA may also be formed for a particular class of goods. For example, an agricultural FTA would remove restrictions only on the trade of agricultural products of member countries.

The European Free Trade Association (EFTA) is probably the best-known FTA. Other FTAs, such as the Latin American Integration Association, have been formed but with less success.

CUSTOMS UNION

Members of customs union, as with those of an FTA, remove barriers to trade for the goods and services of member countries. In addition to abolishing internal tariffs, the customs union establishes a common external tariff system among members. Under the common-trade policy, imports from nonmember countries are subject to the same tariffs regardless of the importing member country. Tariff revenues are shared among members according to a specified formula.

Most experts agree that this was the first stage of development for the EEC. Customs unions have also been organized in other parts of the world, including the Andean Pact, the Central American Common Market, and the Caribbean Community and Common Market.

THE COMMON MARKET

A common market entails completely free movement of goods, capital, resources, and people among member countries; common external tariffs; harmonization of domestic policies; and coordination of international economic policies. Further along the continuum of economic integration, the common market maintains the basic elements of the customs union, but adds an additional dimension that provides for mobility of the factors of production among members. Restrictions on the factors of production—labor, capital, and technology—are abolished, such as immigration and emigration and cross-border investment. The purpose of removing these restrictions is to employ the factors of production in their most productive uses by making them freely mobile.

As a common market, member countries must coordinate their monetary, fiscal, and labor policies. While it is expected that common-market policies enhance the productivity of the common market as a whole, they do not guarantee that individual member countries will benefit uniformly.

ECONOMIC UNION

In addition to the characteristics found in a common market, an economic union includes establishment of a common currency, integrated domestic policies, and a common international economic policy. Under the economic union, member countries harmonize monetary policies, taxation, and government spending. All member countries use a common currency, which would be achieved by an internally fixed system of exchange rates.

COMPLETE ECONOMIC INTEGRATION (POLITICAL UNION)

The current trade situation among the individual states of the United States is characteristic of a complete economic integration or political union. The elements of the political union that complete the integration are unification of monetary, fiscal, social, and foreign policies and a supranational system that replaces the nation-state as the source of sovereignty and security.

Effects of Integration

In theory, one country purchases a product from another because it does not produce it itself or because comparable imported products from the other country are either cheaper or of better quality. If tariffs or nontariff barriers were imposed, the free flow of products and resources would be disrupted. With the imposition of such barriers, production of some products is shifted from the lower-cost foreign producers to the protected, higher-cost local producers, and consumer demand for foreign products is shifted to domestic goods because of the price changes that result from such tariffs or barriers.

For example, some trade analysts argue that the imposition of quotas on Japanese auto imports into the United States has resulted in the continuation of certain types of automobile manufacturing in the United States, despite the fact that it is less expensive to produce automobiles in Japan.

Although establishing a customs union increases or at least maintains a level of discrimination with nonmember countries, it reduces discrimination among member countries. The formation of the European Economic Community, for example, resulted in the lowering of tariffs and thus increased the mobility of goods among members. Nonmembers, such as the United States, on the other hand, still have tariff barriers to overcome in order to conduct business in the EEC.

The static effects of customs unions affect the efficiency of resource allocation. Production shifts toward the more efficient industries, while consumption shifts toward cheaper substitute products in member countries. The dynamic effects explain changes in total consumption and changes in internal and external efficiencies caused by growth. As the market size increases, firms are able to spread fixed costs of business over a greater number of units and can therefore produce goods at a cheaper price.

There are also arguments regarding the advantages and disadvantages of economic integration for firms both within and outside of the alliance. For example, trade creation is a major benefit derived from the elimination of trade barriers between two countries, allowing for redeployment of productive resources in each country according to comparative advantage. A firm in country A produces a product for $1.00, while a firm in country B produces the same product for $.95. If A imposed a tariff of $.15 on the import of the product from B, however, the firm in country B could not compete because it would no longer have the cost advantage in production of the product. Trade creation would result, however, from the institution of a customs union between countries A and B.

This solution does not appear to be the best, however, when a wider view is taken. If another firm manufactured the same product in country C outside the alliance for $.80, the result of such a customs union would in fact be trade diversion. The producer with a higher cost (B) would replace a producer with lower costs (C) and decreased trade would occur between A and C. From this standpoint, formation of a customs union benefits all members only if trade creation is greater than trade diversion.

Increased competition and economies of scale also result from economic integration. The basic effect of integration is to increase market size, and the larger market tends to increase the number of competing firms, resulting in greater efficiency and lower prices for consumers. In addition, integration leads to internal economies of scale, which are achieved through the lower production costs that result from large-scale production. External economies of scale in a common market may also be present because a common market allows factors of production to flow freely across borders. A firm may have access to cheaper capital, more highly skilled labor, and superior technology. For example, it is easier for the United States to achieve scale economies of a larger market than it is for the EEC because of common language, common currency, and a common set of laws.

Economic integration also influences factor productivity. When factors of production are freely mobile, there will be an increase in the wealth of common-market countries in the aggregate. The basic theory behind this assertion assumes that factor mobility will lead to the movement of labor and capital from areas of low productivity to areas of high productivity. In addition, a higher level of communication across cultures will result from the free movement of labor, which, in turn, will presumably lead to a greater level of cross-cultural understanding. There are drawbacks to such factor mobility. One example is brain drain, which occurs when the most talented individuals of a less-developed country move to areas with greater opportunities, thereby draining the first country of its skills and intelligence.

The European Economic Community (EEC)

Table 13-1 shows the original members and the current membership of the EEC since the Treaty of Rome was signed in 1957.

TABLE 13-1
The European Economic Community Membership

1957	1987
Belgium	Belgium
France	France
Italy	Italy
Luxembourg	Luxembourg
Netherlands	Netherlands
West Germany	West Germany
	Great Britain (1973)
	Ireland (1973)
	Denmark (1973)
	Greece (1981)
	Spain (1986)
	Portugal (1986)

The key to the success of the EEC is the balance between the common and national interests. There are four EEC organizations that enable such a balance—the European Commission, the Council of Ministers, the Court of Justice, and the European Parliament.

The European Commission is the executive body of the EEC. Similar to the cabinet of the executive branch of the U.S. government, the commission is the watchdog of the EEC. Its primary responsibilities are to draw up supranational policies, implement them when approved by the Council of Ministers, and ascertain that treaties and laws are adhered to by member countries. The commission is also responsible for all financial and budgetary matters of the community. Commissioners are appointed to serve as heads of various departments; the commission chief serves as the president of the EEC. The Treaty of Rome specifies that the allegiance of the commissioners be to the community rather than to their home countries.

Final authority to pass or reject legislation sponsored by the commission rests with the Council of Ministers. The council comprises one representative from each member government and is similar in structure to the U.S. Senate. The delegates have different voting powers relative to their country's population.

The European Parliament is an advisory body that is elected directly in each member country. Similar to the U.S. House of Representatives, each member country elects a certain number of delegates to the parliament, which is determined by country size. The parliament is only a consultative body whose representatives usually adhere to a particular philosophical persuasion rather than the wishes of their individual governments. Representatives of different countries with similar political leanings may in fact form coalitions in order to increase their power base. In the first five years of its existence, the parliament exercised little political influence, primarily because individual EEC member governments were hesitant to give too much political leverage to the body.

The Court of Justice of the EEC is analogous to the judicial branch of the U.S. government.

As the appeals court for EEC law, the Court of Justice adjudicates any disagreements over interpretation or enforcement of the Treaty of Rome. In fact, litigation concerning the treaty cannot be adjudicated in the national courts. Any member country, firm, or individual can bring the commission or council to court with charges of not acting according to the treaty. One member from each country in the EEC sits on the court.

Recent History of the EEC: Harmonizing Differences

By 1968 the EEC had become a full customs union. During the 1970s, formal barriers to the free flow of labor and capital were gradually removed, but difficulties still remain in practice, regardless of the theoretical progress of the EEC. For example, although labor is considered mobile, individuals often are confronted with regulations regarding certifications. Certain academic degrees or professional certificates from other member countries are not accepted in some member countries. In addition, there are still many instances of nontariff barriers to trade. Many border restrictions remain in place for health or security reasons, and it is believed that these restrictions are thinly veiled efforts to continue protectionist practices.

Free flow of capital and trade in financial services has also met with obstacles. In 1966 the Luxembourg Compromise gave member countries the right to veto any EEC decision that they felt threatened their "vital interests." This veto power has been accused of paralyzing the EEC since it is invoked when the slightest social or economic advantage is perceived.

In 1971 the Council of Ministers agreed to full economic and monetary union within ten years, but because of the upheaval in the global financial system during the 1970s, full economic union was not completed.

In 1987 the Single Europe Act was passed by the EEC as the latest move towards unity. The main provision of the act is the restriction of the ability of a single country to veto a proposal. A total of seventy-six votes were allocated among the twelve council members according to individual country populations; passage of a proposal requires fifty-four votes. Although a single country may still veto a proposal, it now has the burden of proof to show that its vital national interests are threatened.

In order to achieve a complete economic union, however, member countries must coordinate and harmonize other national policies.

Common Agriculture Policy

In most industrialized countries, such as the United States, Canada, or Japan there is large-scale government intervention in the agricultural sector. In the EEC, however, agricultural policies are implemented on a community-wide basis. The four main points of the common agricultural policy are:

1. Free trade in agricultural products, although to some extent the trade is still impeded by non-tariff barriers.
2. A price-support system, whereby EEC agricultural officials intervene in the market to keep farm product prices within a specific range. This was of special concern to Great Britain prior to joining the EEC, because of fears that higher continental farm prices would have damaging inflationary effects.
3. Variable duties or levies on farm imports to ensure that competitive foreign products would not be sold at less than prevailing continental prices.
4. Agricultural modernization projects designed to make farming in the EEC more efficient.

Regional Imbalance

Problems within the EEC center on the resentment of the richer, more industrialized countries toward more agrarian economies. The wealthier nations feel that they are subsidizing the poorer countries. Outside the EEC, especially in the United States, there have been charges against the EEC of unfair trade practices in the agricultural sector.

Agricultural Subsidies

During recent GATT talks held in Uruguay, representatives of more than one hundred countries met to draft a global policy on free trade. The U.S. government has been credited with making efforts to reduce the farm subsidies that have been blamed for creating worldwide overproduction and, in fact, has made a proposal to end all subsidies. Officials of the twelve EEC nations, however, argued that more than two-thirds of the 11 million Common Market farmers would be adversely affected by such a program and as an alternative, suggested short-term measures to ease subsidies.

Free Flow of Labor

A policy of relatively free labor mobility was followed after World War II in the effort to rebuild Europe. Since that time, the EEC has opened its doors to immigrants from other European countries, including Yugoslavia, Turkey, and Greece, to provide unskilled workers for production assembly lines and manual service industries and to relieve the tight labor supply. Originally the plan was for immigrant workers to come to the EEC for a period of one to three years without their families and eventually return to their home countries. Most itinerant workers, however, brought their families with them and became permanent residents, creating problems of integration, citizenship, housing, education, and welfare.

Free Flow of Capital

There are two important aspects regarding the flow of capital—information and currency convertibility. First, investors require high quality comparable financial information in order to make sound decisions. This is not always feasible, because of the differences in accounting principles and practices. As a result, the EEC passed the Fourth Directive, which required standardization of the presentation of financial statements. Along the same lines, other directives have been passed concerning consolidated financial statements and qualifications standards for auditors.

Currency convertibility also poses a problem for the EEC and its policy of free flowing capital. In 1971 countries were required to keep currency values within 2.25 percent of par value according to the Smithsonian Agreement of 1971. This spread of 2.25 percent is called the tunnel.

Although the European currency unit (ECU) is not a medium of exchange, it is used to settle all public and private debts. Financial instruments, such as bonds, may be denominated in ECUs. Additionally, the European Monetary Fund (EMF) holds part of each country's ECU reserves and is responsible for providing credit to countries in order to help keep currency value maintenance at specified levels. One of the current controversies within the EEC concerns the debate over a powerful European central bank and a common currency (see Perspective 13–1).

PERSPECTIVE 13–1   Europe—The Quest for Monetary Integration

Over the past 20 years, the European Community (EC) has tried several times to move in the direction of economic and monetary union. But these attempts have always fallen far short of their goals. Recent developments, however, have significantly altered the picture, for the first time giving rise to beliefs that over the next few years, a solid groundwork will be laid for such a union. These include:

■ The success of the European Monetary System (EMS). Following the comprehensive realignment of March 1983, the countries then participating in the exchange rate mechanism pursued policies that resulted in a greater convergence of costs and prices. Realignments occurred less frequently and the deutsche mark emerged as the anchor currency of the system. Thoughts turned to how the stability of the EMS could be enhanced and a more efficient framework provided for future cooperation in exchange rate and monetary policies.

■ The formation of a single internal market by the end of 1992. This promises the realization of still unattained objectives set by the founding fathers of the EC in the 1950s—notably, the establishment of a truly common market as the basis for full economic integration, closer po-

litical cooperation, greater social cohesion, and higher living standards.

In light of these developments, the debate over exactly what type of economic and monetary union (EMU) would be desirable, and how and at what pace this should be achieved, has intensified. Fundamentally, the debate is about the questions of whether, when, and to what extent, countries will be ready to surrender sovereignty in the economic, and in the last analysis, the political, field, Intergovernmental conferences on economic and monetary union, and political union—which are scheduled to begin on December 14, 1990, and may last well into 1991—must grapple with the many philosophical, as well as institutional and technical, issues.

BACKGROUND TO THE DEBATE

The debate about the form and objectives of future EC monetary cooperation and integration began in the mid-1980s with discussions on more technical issues, such as intervention practices, use of the very short-term financing facility of the EMS, and the role of the ECU (European currency unit)—a composite of a basket of the EC currencies that serves as the unit of account for the EMS. Initially, the key players were senior of-

SOURCE: Horst Ungerer, *Finance & Development*, December 1990, pages 14–17.

ficials of governments, central banks, and the EC Commission. But in early 1988, the debate gained significant momentum and a political dimension when politicians from various EC countries expressed support for EMU, although with differing degrees of urgency. Soon, EMU became a prominent subject at the regular meetings of the European Council (consisting of the heads of state and government of the EC countries), and in June 1988, the Council set up a special committee—chaired by EC Commission President Jacques Delors, and including the governors of the EC central banks—to outline concrete stages that would eventually lead to EMU.

The following April, the Delors Report was unveiled. It proposed the realization of EMU in three stages of undefined duration, with parallel progress envisioned in both the economic and monetary fields, reflecting a broadly held consensus that the building of institutions and the strengthening of policy coordination influence each other in a mutual and dynamic fashion. Monetary union was defined as total and irreversible convertibility of currencies; complete freedom of capital movements in fully integrated financial markets; and irrevocably fixed exchange rates, with no fluctuation margins between member currencies. Economic union was defined as a single market within which persons, goods, services, and capital could move freely; common competition, structural, and regional policies; and sufficient coordination of macroeconomic policies, including binding rules on budgetary policies regarding the size and financing of national budget deficits.

At the heart of the Delors Report was the proposal to set up a European System of Central Banks (ESCB) as the vehicle for creating a monetary union and a single currency. The ESCB would be organized in a federal form, consisting of a central institution and national central banks, with a Council composed of the governors of the central banks and the members of the Board (the latter to be appointed by the European Council). It would be committed to the objective of price stability, and, subject to this commitment, it would support the general economic policy set at the Community level. It would formulate and implement monetary policy, manage exchange rates and reserves, and maintain a properly functioning payments system. It would be independent of instructions from national governments and Community authorities and would not be allowed to lend to public sector authorities.

Stage one would aim at a greater convergence of economic performance through the strengthening of policy coordination within the existing institutional framework. All EC currencies still freely floating would have to be brought into the EMS exchange rate mechanism.

Stage two would be a period of transition, further promoting convergence and centering on institutional reforms—most importantly, the setting up of the ESCB, whose key task would be to begin the transition from the coordination of independent monetary policies to the implementation of a common monetary policy.

The *final stage* would start with a move to irrevocably locked exchange rates. Common structural and regional policies would be further strengthened, and rules in the macroeconomic and budgetary field would become binding. The transition to a common monetary policy would be made, and the ESCB would assume all its responsibilities. Decisions on exchange market interventions in third currencies would become the sole responsibility of the ESCB Council, and official reserves would be pooled and managed by the ESCB. The introduction of a single, common currency would also take place.

DEBATE OVER THE DELORS REPORT

Not surprisingly, the Delors Report met with a wide range of responses. There were those countries (mainly France and Italy) who, based on what they perceived to be the great challenges of European integration, argued for speedy moves toward common institutions and policies. There were others (mainly Germany and the Netherlands) who felt that an extended period of closer cooperation and greater economic convergence—

more or less circumscribed by the proposed first stage of the Delors Report—was required before more far-reaching institutional arrangements could be put in place.

In the United Kingdom, official reactions, particularly at the highest level of government, were less forthcoming. Nonetheless, at the European Council's June 1989 meeting in Madrid, it was agreed to launch stage one on July 1 of the following year. In November 1989, the UK authorities presented their own concept of EC monetary integration, advocating an "evolutionary" approach, as an alternative to the "institutional" approach of the Delors Report. They suggested that national currencies (and thus, national monetary policies) be allowed to compete with each other in a multicurrency system centered on national monetary authorities, thereby minimizing problems of political accountability. The EMS could evolve into a system of more or less fixed exchange rates, and a "practical monetary union" would be achieved. But although the proposal sparked some interest, there were serious doubts as to whether a "competition of currencies" would result in a stable and desirable monetary order for the EC. As long as national currencies were not irrevocably linked to each other, one could not speak of a monetary union, nor could one expect its full benefits—in terms of reducing transaction costs and eliminating exchange rate risks—to materialize.

In June 1990, the UK Chancellor of the Exchequer John Major presented another proposal, stressing the need to strive for more convergence in economic performance. It envisaged an important role for the ECU by having it exist alongside and compete with national currencies. First, a European Monetary Fund would be established that would issue ECUs on demand against EC currencies. Second, a "hard ECU" would be created as a genuine currency, which would never devalue against other EC currencies. In time, the ECU would be more widely used; it could become a common currency and, in the very long run, the single currency for the EC. But the UK proposal left open a number of questions, such as the insti-

tutional features of the European Monetary Fund. One of the main perceived shortcomings was that it provided little guidance on when the conditions would be right for moving to the final stage of full monetary union.

Among the many questions under discussion, there are two of particular importance.

How much power should be exercised at the Community level over macroeconomic policies? The Delors Report emphasized the need for action in the field of macroeconomic coordination, including binding rules in the budgetary field. It argued that uncoordinated and divergent national budget policies would undermine monetary stability and generate imbalances in the real and financial sectors of the Community. Since the Community's own budget was too small to play any significant role, the task of setting a Community-wide fiscal policy stance would have to be performed through the coordination of national budgetary policies. The report, therefore, advocated binding rules that would impose upper limits on budget deficits of individual member countries, exclude public sector access to direct central banking credit and other forms of monetary financing, and limit recourse to external borrowing in non-Community currencies.

There is general agreement that monetary and budgetary policies need to be compatible and that no—or only limited—recourse to monetary financing should be available. Also, undisciplined governments should not be bailed out. The question is whether the compatibility of policies can best be achieved by market forces, intensified coordination between individual countries, or a centralization at the Community level.

Some argue that without central bank financing—but with freedom of capital movements—financial markets would penalize undisciplined budgetary behavior with higher interest rates, thus creating pressure for convergence toward sound fiscal policies. Others stress that in view of the limited size of the Community budget, it is at the national budget level that coordinating action would be required. On the basis of experience, however, there is skepticism about placing too much faith in effective voluntary coordination. At the same time, financial markets are not seen by these skeptics as effectively improving budgetary discipline of divergent countries. Furthermore, in this view, should a country run into serious budgetary problems, political pressure on other member countries is likely to develop and a bailout could not be excluded.

How much independence should the future European central bank have? At issue is whether it should be independent of instructions from national governments and Community authorities. The background to this debate is a basic conceptual difference regarding the framework and objectives of economic policy. One concept holds that all aspects of economic policy, including monetary management, should be subject to a unified approach and be formulated, implemented, and made consistent by the government, which through parliament is answerable to the electorate. Price stability is only one—albeit often an important one—of several economic policy objectives, such as economic growth, high employment, balance of payments equilibrium, and exchange rate stability.

The other concept considers price stability to be an essential, quasi-constitutional part of the basic framework within which economic and social policy is conducted. This stability is regarded as a complement—as well as being equal to—other essential elements of a country's economic order, such as market economy principles, private property, and freedom to engage in domestic and international economic activity; hence the rationale for a high degree of independence for some central banks, such as in Germany, Switzerland, and the United States. While these central banks are independent in the pursuit of their tasks and their policies, they are not independent in the sense of being free of democratic control and outside the general process of opinion formation. Democratic control is exercised not by day-to-day government intervention in policy formation but in the setting of the determinants of monetary policy: the laws governing central bank responsibilities and activi-

ties; appointment procedures for top officials; and regular reporting to parliament and to the public at large.

Nigel Lawson, UK Chancellor of the Exchequer when the Delors Report was issued, emphasized the aspect of democratic accountability and found it wanting in the Delors proposals. Others, such as Deutsche Bundesbank President Karl Otto Pöhl, saw democratic control as ensured if a European central bank came about by an agreement between democratic governments and was provided with a clearly defined mandate. Top officials could be appointed by European political bodies, such as the European Council or the EC Council of Ministers.

INITIAL STEPS TOWARD EMU

On July 1, 1990, stage one of a process leading to EMU, as envisaged in the Delors Report, began. One of the immediate goals was to prepare the groundwork for an intergovernmental conference on EMU to draft amendments to the treaty that established the European Economic Community. The conference had been called for at the European Council's December 1989 meeting. Then in April 1990, the Council pronounced itself "satisfied with progress achieved so far towards establishing the single market without frontiers" and asked that the intergovernmental conference "conclude its work rapidly with the objective of ratification [of the Treaty amendment] by member states before the end of 1992." so as to coincide with the envisaged completion of the internal market. In June, the Council decided to open the conferences on EMU and political union in mid-December; both were to take place in Rome. At the European Council meeting in late October, the EC countries, with the exception of the United Kingdom, agreed to begin stage two on January 1, 1994, subject to further progress in economic and monetary integration. They also agreed that a new monetary institution for the EC should be established at the beginning of this stage.

During these months, a number of important events took place in the fields of financial and monetary integration. France and Italy abolished remaining capital restrictions (January 1 and May 14, 1990, respectively), ahead of the July 1 deadline stipulated in the 1988 EC directive on the liberalization of capital movements. Belgium-Luxembourg ended the dual-exchange market regime for current and capital transactions in March 1990. Spain joined the exchange rate mechanism (ERM) in June 1989, availing itself of the wider fluctuation margins, and Italy adopted the narrower margins in January 1990. Also of interest was Belgium's decision in June to tie the franc firmly to the deutsche mark. On October 8, the United Kingdom finally joined the ERM, a move expected to reduce sterling's fluctuations against ERM currencies and assist in lowering inflation.

The preparations for stage one started soon after the June 1989 European Council meeting. In March 1990, the EC Council of Ministers adopted amendments to decisions on economic convergence and central bank cooperation. The decision on convergence now refers explicitly to the achievement of "sustained non-inflationary growth, together with a high level of employment" and asks the Council of Ministers to survey member countries' economies, and together with the Commission, report the results to the European Council and the European Parliament.

The amendment to the decision on central bank cooperation expands and defines more precisely the mandate of the Committee of Central Bank Governors. This includes intensified coordination of monetary policies, with the aim of achieving price stability as a necessary condition for the proper functioning of the EMS and the realization of the objective of monetary stability. The Committee can express opinions to individual governments and the Council of Ministers on policies that might affect the Community's internal and external monetary situation, in particular, the functioning of the EMS. Further, the Committee is to prepare annual reports; its chairman may be invited to appear before the European Parliament and may be authorized by the Committee

to make the outcome of its deliberations public. In the meantime, the Committee has drafted statutes for the ESCB, and begun studying the compatibility of monetary targets for the major EC currencies.

Other EC bodies have also begun to prepare for the EMU conference. The Monetary Committee, consisting of senior officials of the finance ministries and central banks of EC countries and the EC Commission, has been discussing questions such as the extent to which central and binding coordination rules would be needed for budgetary policies to be consistent with a common monetary policy, and whether the final responsibility for exchange rate and exchange market intervention policy should rest with the political authorities or the ESCB.

The EC Commission in March 1990 endorsed the general approach of the Delors Committee to EMU, although it deviated by not calling for uniform binding rules on budgetary policy, arguing instead for binding procedures. The convergence of budgetary policies should mainly be sought by incorporating budgetary rules into national law and enforcing such strategies through regular mutual surveillance at the Community level. In October, the Commission published a report that examines in detail the likely economic effects—costs as well as benefits—of the move to EMU.

An issue that has created some controversy is whether EC countries (such as Belgium, Denmark, France, Germany, Ireland, Luxembourg, and the Netherlands) that have achieved a high degree of price and cost convergence, should move ahead in forming the EMU. Other countries would join as soon as they were ready, in particular in terms of inflation and budget performance. It was pointed out, however, that such a two-speed procedure would be damaging to the coherence and further development of the EC.

It will be up to the intergovernmental conference on EMU to resolve, or at least identify possible solutions to, numerous issues. They encompass institutional and technical problems: how a

European central bank should be organized and operate, the scope of of its responsibilities, and the degree of its independence from political interference. There are problems with economic and political significance: they relate to the speed of the process of monetary integration and the contentious issue of a possible "two-speed" process. Also, the question of the extent to which monetary and economic union should be developed simultaneously and at a similar pace is at the heart of the dispute about binding coordination procedures for budgetary policies. Ultimately, the underlying question is one of a willingness to surrender sovereignty to common European institutions and to share in a common decision-making process.

Foreign Banks

Another issue concerning capital markets in the EEC is the activities of overseas financial institutions vis-à-vis the community. By October 1988 the commission's proposal on the treatment of foreign banks was drafted for inclusion in the industry regulations. The rule would prevent foreign banks from establishing operations in Europe unless reciprocal opportunities for European banks were available in their home countries. Not only would this have repercussions for the Japanese, who are continually accused of protectionism within their banking markets, but it may also affect the United States.

The Impact of EEC Integration on U.S. Firms

Whether or not EEC integration is a threat or an opportunity for U.S. firms depends largely on whether they are inside or outside of the alliance. For the company operating within the EEC, there are clear opportunities available when trade barriers are dismantled. Their elimination means creating a larger market for the firm's goods and services, which, in turn, means the firm has opportunities to increase production and achieve scale economies in both production and marketing.

To the firm within the EEC, factor mobility also will provide opportunities, because although the firm is a seller of goods and services, it is a buyer of the factors of production. Capital and labor may in fact be cheaper to the firm because of increased competition for the sellers of such factor elements.

The situation is not paralleled outside of the EEC. For example, firms exporting to the EEC are likely to see their positions threatened. Their competitive edge will dull as they begin to operate at a competitive disadvantage relative to firms from member nations. In fact, in the case of a customs union, the entire market may be closed to some exporting firms.

1992: Current Issues

Since 1985, when the deadline for abolishing trade barriers within the EEC was set for 1992, tension has mounted both within the EEC and with their trading partners, because there are a number of unresolved concerns.

Euromergers

Mergers and acquisitions in the EEC are threatening to wipe out thousands of small firms in Europe. The advancement of plans to form a single market by 1992 has "accelerated Euromergers by the hundreds."[3] For small retailers in France, for example, the threat of huge conglomerates is enormous. One example of merger activity in the EEC is the joining of the German electronics company Siemens with General Electric Company, Britain's top electronics firm (see Perspective 13–2).

---

[3] Sullivan, Scott. 1988. "Who's Afraid of 1992?" *Newsweek* (October 31): 32.

PERSPECTIVE 13-2   American Takeovers Soaring in Europe As Firms Position Themselves for 1992

LONDON—The U.S. takeover wave is rolling into Europe.

Growing numbers of cash-rich U.S. corporations are scrambling to expand their presence in Europe's food and consumer-goods industries. Others hope to gain footholds in long-protected industries that are undergoing shakeups, such as telecommunications, financial services and heavy engineering.

Like their European rivals, American businesses seek to exploit the planned 1992 creation of a unified market of 320 million European consumers.

During 1989, there should be "some very large U.S. deals in Europe, possibly involving hostile takeovers," says Martin Waldenstrom, president of Booz Allen Acquisition Services, the Paris-based division of the U.S. management-consulting firm. "Both would be essentially unprecedented."

EUROPEANS BUYING MORE

Resistance to foreign bidders and a shortage of hefty targets means U.S. executives won't be drowning Europe with a flood of trans-Atlantic jumbo deals. And no one expects the accelerating Yankee invasion to match the foreign buying spree in the U.S., where European firms made 280 acquisitions worth $32.9 billion last year, compared to 221 valued at $38 billion in 1987, according to Mergers & Acquisitions, a U.S. magazine.

But U.S. acquisitions in Europe are definitely shifting into higher gear. Despite a weaker dollar, they nearly tripled to $3.6 billion last year from $1.3 billion in 1987, reports Acquisitions Monthly, a British publication. Americans may buy $5 billion worth of European businesses this year, predicts Colin Keer, who runs Bankers Trust Co.'s mergers and acquisitions activities in Eu-

rope. "People are realizing there's good value on the Continent."

In the latest example, General Electric Co. of the U.S. and unrelated British competitor General Electric Co., or GEC, announced plans Friday to merge their European consumer products, medical equipment and some electrical-equipment divisions. And American Telephone & Telegraph Co. still wants pieces of GEC, possibly as part of an international consortium that may make a wholesale assault worth up to £8 billion ($14.14 billion).

Other signs of increasing U.S. interest in buying European: American takeover specialists, such as investment bankers Wasserstein, Perella & Co. and Wall Street law firm Skadden, Arps, Slate, Meagher & Flom have opened London offices in the past year. Kohlberg, Kravis & Roberts, a U.S. leveraged buy-out firm, is looking into its first European foray.

ON THE PROWL

Major U.S. investors also are on the prowl in Europe. New York arbitrager Asher B. Edelman has said he plans to make most of his "concentrated investments" in Europe's undervalued companies. Last month, he disclosed a 5.1% stake in United Kingdom retailer Storehouse PLC, seen as a takeover candidate because of lagging profits. Ronald O. Perelman, linked to many U.S. takeover candidates in recent months, last fall said he wanted to do a deal in Britain because "the values over there really don't reflect what will happen when the Common Market opens up in 1992."

Entrepreneur Jeffrey Steiner, who heads Cleveland's Banner Industries Inc., made a hostile $179 million offer last fall for Avdel PLC, a British in-

SOURCE: Joann Lublin, Wall Street Journal, January 17, 1989, page A44.

dustrial fasteners maker. But Textron Inc. came to Avdel's rescue with a higher offer. This month, Banner let its bid lapse.

"I don't think we will see an electrifying increase in hostile bids from the U.S.," says John Marley, Avdel's chief executive, who bitterly opposed Banner's offer. But many U.S. concerns "are looking to strengthen their international operations by acquiring European companies on a friendly basis," Mr. Marley says.

European businesses are coming up for sale as diversified conglomerates shed chunks to become more competitive for the post-1992 era. Whirlpool Corp. of the U.S., for instance, last year agreed to pay N. V. Philips one billion Dutch guilders (at that time worth about $470 million) for a 53% stake in a joint venture that will make major appliances under the Dutch company's Philips brand.

But U.S. companies on the acquisition prowl in Europe often must settle for much smaller prey. Unlike the U.S., where foreign bids of more than $1 billion have become routine, Europe has yet to see its first successful $1 billion-plus takeover by an American. The largest one last year was St. Paul Cos.' $704.8 million bid for Minet Holdings PLC, a British insurance broker. One reason for the paucity of megabids is that laws still guard many of Europe's relatively few corporate giants. It isn't clear such protections will ease after 1992.

Acquisitions Limited

Political hostility to foreign takeovers also tends to limit the size of U.S. acquisitions in Europe. GE's accord last week with GEC—and AT&T's possible participation in a rival bid—could trigger resistance because of fears the U.S. might dominate Britain's electronics industry. In 1986, the Tory government unleashed a xenophobic furor when it proposed breaking up state-owned car maker Rover Group PLC and selling pieces of it to Ford Motor Co. and General Motors Corp.

With such barriers reducing the number of European targets, the result is soaring prices for those in play. Like many American concerns, "we are very much caught up in the spirit of 1992," says John Bryan, chairman of Sara Lee Corp. "But the prices are getting pretty high." The Chicago maker of food, household items and personal-care products has made two major European acquisitions since the autumn of 1987.

In a move that more U.S. companies may imitate as a test of Europe's waters, Sara Lee has acquired a stake in a third company. It has built about a 61% interest in Bic S.A.'s Dean Hosiery, Europe's biggest hosiery maker, over the past 18 months, after winning the French government's blessing for the purchases. Mr. Bryan declined to speculate if Bic will sell the remainder.

Such partial holdings or joint ventures may prove the only way American businesses can gain access, especially in Europe's politically sensitive telecommunications, financial services and defense industries. Trans-Atlantic acquisitions are tough enough to manage anyhow, says Morris Kramer, who directs Skadden Arps's European mergers and acquisitions practice in London. "I would advise U.S. companies looking at a takeover in the U.K. or the Continent to look at partnerships with European companies."

Rising Taxes

Another issue that has concerned members of the EEC commission is taxes. Value-added (VAT) and excise taxes vary significantly among the twelve EEC members. Such taxes range from 9 percent to 33 percent.

Local Content

For foreign manufacturers operating within the EEC, the question of local parts content of products also needs to be addressed. If each country within the EEC has distinct restrictions for local content percentage, the controversy will continue. Disputes involving local content practices have used 60 percent as the general determinant of European-made status. There are, however, no community-wide rules that encompass imported components and parts.

Labor Migrations

In addition to labor relations legislation, unions are also troubled by the free movement of capital policy. While economists view job redistribution as positive because of its advantages (availability and costs of factors of production), labor unions see diminishing bargaining power as a result of shifts in unemployment. For example, in a comparison of labor in Spain and Germany, it is easy to understand the surge of investment in Spain in 1987. In addition to lower wages and benefits, Spanish employment rules are more flexible and are not as susceptible to union influence as the rules in West Germany.

Such recommendations are in-line with most approaches to corporate strategic planning. Actions at the national level, however, whether they are reactive or proactive in nature, are needed to improve or to at least maintain the trade position of the United States with Europe, that is, increasing integration in North American trade. Although the idea of a North American common market is seen as a remote and unlikely possibility to most experts, there have been suggestions to that end. In 1989 legislation was passed creating the U.S.-Canada Free Trade Area. Discussions have slowed on the development of a free-trade agreement with Mexico, probably because the benefits to Mexico would be far greater than the advantages to the United States.

Integrating Financial Services

There is considerable progress in the removal of barriers to intracommunity trade in financial services. Eight members of the community agreed to do away with all controls on capital movements by July 1, 1990, and the remaining four (Greece, Portugal, Spain, and Ireland) have committed to do so later. Selling financial services is likely to become completely unrestricted, and financial firms will be allowed to set up their establishments in any member country.

Members of the EEC have also reached agreement on bank licensing. Beginning on January 1, 1993, EEC country banks will be permitted to operate in other countries of the community without requiring separate approvals from individual countries. Further regulations will have to be established on soundness and supervisory standards common to all EEC banks and applicable on a community-wide basis. EEC banks will, however, not face any limitations on securities transactions (such as those imposed on U.S. banks by the Glass-Steagall Act), and universal banking will be the norm in the European community.

Specification of Standards

Agreements have been reached between member countries on uniform technical specifications and standards to be adhered to by producers in the EEC for a wide variety of industrial and consumer goods. Acceptance of standards is likely to reduce delays at border points of transit and assist in community-wide marketing of products. The use of uniform standards also holds substantial potential for enabling specialization of production of different types of goods in different countries with the resulting advantages of scale economies and production efficiency.

Public Procurement

Public procurement is a relatively thorny issue. Although, in theory, government bidders from all member countries are allowed to bid on government contracts, in practice bidders from outside the host country are unlikely to win a tender. On average only 2 percent of all public contracts are awarded to companies of other members of the community. Certain measures have been agreed to, such as better tender procedures and the opening up of new areas of government contracts to community-wide bidding. Greater privatization of government enterprises may improve the scenario, because the private enterprises are likely to award their contracts on the basis of competitiveness instead of nationality considerations.

Tax Issues

Different systems and rates of taxation of manufacturing and trading activity inside member country borders are likely to continue to pose problems for the EEC. Most countries have different tax objectives and priorities, which they are not likely to change, and many have different systems of tax collection.

Relations with Nonmembers

The attitude of major members of the community vis-à-vis their relationships with nonmembers differs considerably. Although uniform tariffs are levied against nonmember country imports, there are wide variations in the types and degrees of nontariff barriers imposed by EEC countries. For example, many member countries have special trading arrangements with other countries outside of the community. Others have differing arrangements for enforcing voluntary export restraints by non-EC members on their exports to their countries. The clash of national interests with the objectives of total economic integration is likely to continue in this area (see Perspective 13–3).

PERSPECTIVE 13–3 Fortress Europe Feared by Tokyo and Washington

EUROPE'S plan for a single market by 1992 has been watched with a degree of both fascination and alarm in the capitals of the world's other two large trading powers, the U.S. and Japan.

While both Washington and Tokyo acknowledge the potential world economic benefits from a more dynamic Europe, they are also worried that the rapid pace of adjustment that 1992 will force on European industry will lead the Community to become more inward looking. In short, the danger is that, in trade terms at least, it could become a fortress.

Although the EC Commission in Brussels has now, belatedly, begun to grapple with the trade issues involved in its 1992 project, officials from both countries say they still find it hard to obtain clear answers on a number of key questions. Their fear is that, particularly in the service sectors which are not covered by the General Agreement on Tariffs and Trade, the EC might try to write its own rules in such a way as to keep foreign competitors out.

Such is the rhetoric of international trade politics that some at least of these fears are almost certainly overstated. But a quick glance at the trade issues facing the EC in the run-up to 1992 shows that they could have some profound implications for the trading system as a whole.

From the very outset Mr. Willy de Clercq, EC Commissioner responsible for external trade, has made it clear that, where trade in goods is concerned, the EC intends to abide by the rules of the Gatt. So far, so good, but the rules of the Gatt are frequently ambiguous and open to interpretation. What has also alarmed trading partners has been the EC's intentions in the new service areas that are outside the Gatt, like banking, insurance and some parts of government procurement. Here the

SOURCE: Peter Montagnon, *Financial Times*, November 17, 1988.

EC has insisted that it will not give away to outsiders the advantage of its newly-liberalised market without seeking something in return.

In recent months the debate has thus turned on the nature of the reciprocity that the EC will apply to trading partners which seek access to its markets. Under the worst case scenario the fear was that it would seek to apply reciprocity retrospectively to foreign firms already operating inside the EC, that it would demand opportunities for its firms in foreign markets identical to those available in Europe, and that such demands would be automatic and based on a case-by-case assessment.

Were this the case the EC would run the risk of bitter disputes with its trading partners and a slide into bilateralism that could ultimately undermine the multilateral world trading system.

Partly as a result of international pressure, the EC seems now to be backing away from such a determined stand. The Commission has recently ruled that reciprocity in financial services will not be retroactively applied. Nor will it in general be automatic. Nor will the EC use identical treatment as a yardstick; it will simply seek to ensure that there is no discrimination against its firms in foreign markets.

Its announcement came as something of a relief to the international banking community, but the Commission's rather general statement has not entirely dispelled worries about how it will operate in practice. Moreover there are several other areas besides banking where Washington and Tokyo have worries.

Among these are standards and certification of industrial products, an area where the U.S. fears that the EC could yet introduce procedures designed to keep foreign products out. For its part, Japan is particularly worried about cars.

Japanese car sales in Europe are basically free in Benelux and West Germany but restricted, sometimes heavily, in other markets such as France, Italy, Spain, Portugal and the UK. The Community has been toying with a Europe-wide quota to replace these national restrains after 1992. But this raises questions of whether it should simultaneously demand specific assurance for its own producers in the Japanese market and whether Europe should arbitrarily impose local content requirements on Japanese producers.

It will take some time before all these questions can be answered. Unlike the US whose room for manoeuvre in trade policy is set out in its omnibus trade legislation, the EC is expected to build up a policy piece-by-piece through a series of decisions on quite specific issues.

Officials like Mr. de Clercq are fond of reminding the public that with a 20 percent share in total world trade the EC cannot afford to espouse protectionism. Indeed, he says the EC intends to use the negotiating leverage it has obtained as a result of the 1992 project to foster a more general liberalisation of world trade by encouraging other countries to open up their markets, too.

Yet the tighter dumping rules adopted by the EC over the past couple of years underlines the protectionist pressures that Europe is facing from within. So does the fierce internal argument that raged in Brussels before the Commission ruling on the nature of reciprocity.

Though the current signs are that Europe would prefer to adopt a liberal approach to the outside world, these arguments have not yet played their course. With the pace of industrial adjustment set to quicken as 1992 draws nearer, they could even intensify. It would still be a bold person who would forecast that Europe after 1992 will not be defended by any fortress walls.

Recognition of Professionals

Community-wide recognition of professional degrees and other qualifications earned by doctors, lawyers, and other professionals has been agreed to by many EEC members, which will enable greater mobility of professionals among different countries within the community and create a more evenly balanced dispersal of qualified professionals, based on the relative attractiveness and suitability of opportunities offered for them by member states.

Mass Media

It is likely that television programming and broadcasting may become universal across member countries of the EEC. Local television, however, will continue to play a small but significant role. Although agreement on this issue has not yet been reached, it is likely that some compromise arrangement incorporating some proportion of universal and local broadcasting may be agreed to and implemented.

Other Problem Areas

Uniform standards for labor, elimination of controls on borders, total deregulation of continental transport (across land, sea, and air), health, hygiene, and standards for plant and animal exports and imports are some other areas where the member states seek an agreement, but are unable to reach it, because of a variety of complex considerations. Although there are a number of remaining issues and internal problems, the progress made so far is remarkable, especially in light of the constraints. Each proposal is minutely examined by twelve member states, many of whom have differing perceptions and come up with suggestions of formal or substantial significance. Negotiations are therefore tortuous, and the fact that each document has to be translated into the language of each member state does not help. Further, negotiators have to act under the direction of their political superiors, who in turn have to be sensitive to their own constituencies, that often reflect conflicting opinions. Post-1992 Europe is clearly going to consolidate its position as the world's most successful example of regional economic cooperation, even though it may still be far away from achieving total economic integration (see Perspective 13–4).

PERSPECTIVE 13–4   The Macroeconomic Effects of German Unification*

Germany is united again. Beyond the certainty of this union lie many questions about its economic effects, domestic and foreign. In order to obtain a clearer understanding of these effects, it is useful to examine them within a detailed quantitative framework. A study done within the International Monetary Fund recently and whose results are summarized here, concludes that the path taken by East Germany will have major implications for the economy of the united Germany but that the international effects of unification may be relatively moderate.

TRANSFORMING THE EASTERN ECONOMY

Will the evolution of the East German economy over the next decade reveal a new *Wirtschaftswun-der* (economic miracle) or the emergence of another regional problem within the European Community (EC)? In many respects, the prognosis is favorable. For example, the saving surplus in West Germany represents a ready source of financing for the investment needs of the east. Moreover, it may be possible to revive quickly the pre-World War II tradition of enterprise in the eastern part of the country, despite its long suppression by central planning. But capital is scarce in East Germany, and it will be some time before West German wage levels can be supported in the east. This creates obvious tensions. A slow closing of the earnings gap between the east and the west might result in a migration of the most skilled workers to the west, while a premature narrowing of the gap could well discourage investment; either situation might en-

SOURCE: Paul Masson and Donogh McDonald, *Finance & Development*, March 1991, pages 6–9.

danger the process of economic recovery in the east.

To analyze these issues, IMF staff developed a detailed macroeconomic model of east Germany's economy (see footnote* on model). Major uncertainties shroud the initial conditions in the east, the likely response of foreign investors, prospective migration patterns, the ability of east Germany to absorb large-scale investment (particularly in the initial years after unification), and the policy and institutional framework. The scenarios constructed with the model, therefore, are not predictions; rather they illustrate possible developments under carefully selected assumptions. They take as their starting point a profile of the economic situation in East Germany in the second half of 1990, assuming that, immediately prior to unification, underlying labor productivity in the east was about 30 percent of the level in west Germany. The growth rates required in the east to narrow the productivity gap over the next decade depend not only on the size of the initial gap but also on the increase in labor productivity in west Germany. The scenarios assume that labor productivity in west Germany will grow at about $2\frac{1}{2}$ percent a year, or cumulatively by close to one-third, between 1990 and 2001.

For productivity in east Germany to rise to west German levels by 2001, output in the east would have to increase at a rate of 13 percent a year, assuming that the labor force in east Germany declines by 10 percent (as a result of migration and lower labor force participation rates). Elimination of inefficiencies in the use of capital and labor would make a significant contribution to growth. However, even making some allowance for the benefits that might be associated with the relatively newer capital stock in east Germany, a cumulative net investment of some DM 1,800 billion (in 1990 prices) would also be needed over the period 1991–2000, an amount almost as large as the net national product of west Germany in 1990. A less ambitious target might be to achieve a productivity level in east Germany by 2001 that

is 80 percent of the level in west Germany. This would produce a productivity gap similar to that currently existing between the three poorest states of west Germany and the eight more prosperous ones. It would entail a cumulative net investment of DM 1,100 billion and an average output growth rate of $10\frac{1}{2}$ percent, still a rather formidable goal.

Scenario A, the more optimistic of the two scenarios discussed here, is consistent with this latter target (see chart). While unemployment is initially high—one-fourth of the labor force in 1991—it falls rapidly and by the end of the scenario is at about the same level (6 percent) as is assumed for west Germany. Gross investment averages a very large 43 percent of GDP in east Germany in 1991–92. This is financed entirely by external resources (including fiscal transfers from west Germany); indeed, external resources amount to about 150 percent of net investment as consumption in east Germany substantially exceeds net output. Over the period 1991–2001 as a whole, three-fourths of net investment is financed from outside east Germany (including fiscal transfers from west Germany). This estimate of external resource needs is, however, sensitive to the balance between fiscal transfers and other forms of external financing. The calculations here assume that government current account deficits in east Germany are wholly financed by transfers from west Germany.

Under Scenario A, imports into east Germany of goods and nonfactor services are initially of the order of DM 120–130 billion per year, or 5 percent of GNP in west Germany. Over time, these net imports decline and are close to zero by 2001. This happens partly because investment requirements fall in relation to output, but, more important, because the saving rate rises. Though private saving increases, the principal source of the stronger external position is the improvement in the government accounts. The general government deficit in the east is, in the early years, very large (almost one half of GDP in the east in 1991), but drops steadily with a primary budget surplus emerging in 2000.

Scenario B (also plotted in the chart) is less optimistic, with productivity in east Germany in 2001 at only 60 percent of that in west Germany and large-scale migration from east to west. Lower investment than in Scenario A and a slower reduction of inefficiencies in the use of labor and capital produce this less robust economic performance. Net investment in 1991–92 is only 60 percent of that in Scenario A, and this relative weakness persists throughout the scenario as the initial hesitancy of investors is reinforced by aggressive wage demands and by structural weaknesses in the economy. The fiscal imbalance starts out worse than in Scenario A and remains stubbornly high as low growth restrains revenue and boosts social expenditure relative to GDP; in the year 2001, the primary fiscal deficit in east Germany is around 9 percent of GDP. Larger accumulated deficits also increase interest payments, but given the assumption on transfers from west Germany, those interest costs are recorded in the government accounts of the western part of the country. Reflecting these fiscal developments, the imbalance in the external accounts is much larger than in Scenario A.

WORLD SAVING

In a world of high capital mobility, investment can tap an international pool of saving, rather than being restricted to a local capital market. A useful starting point in gauging the effects of unification beyond east Germany is to consider the extent to which increased investment and higher social spending in east Germany would draw upon global saving. Scenarios A and B produce broadly similar figures for east Germany's average net import demand over 1990–94 (averaging $60 billion a year)—lower output in Scenario B is offset by lower demand over this period. These net imports compare with world saving of $4 trillion. Clearly, the external resource needs of east Germany are relatively small—less than 2 percent of total world saving. An important issue is the extent to which those needs can be satisfied by higher saving in west Germany, and, in particular, by higher out-

put there. This will depend on supply capacity in west Germany, which, in turn, is influenced by the growth of the labor force there.

Unification has reestablished free mobility between east and west Germany. The resulting migration from the east can be expected to lead to increases in both aggregate demand and supply in west Germany. In Scenario A, net migration from east to west Germany is assumed to be 320,000 in 1990, falling to 70,000 in 1992, and 20,000 per year after 1993. As a result, potential output is projected to be $1\frac{1}{4}$ percent higher in west Germany by the year 2001 than it would have been in the absence of migration, assuming that investment increases sufficiently to maintain the capital to labor ratio. In Scenario B, net migration is assumed to be the same in 1990–91, but to be considerably higher from 1992 onward: 270,000 in that year, and declining to 90,000 in the year 2001. This boosts potential output in 2001 by $3\frac{1}{2}$ percent in the west. However, in the early years, the increase in potential output less increased consumption of the migrants and the higher investment mentioned above will, under both scenarios, be small relative to the external resource needs of east Germany.

EFFECTS IN GERMANY AND ABROAD

To quantify the impact of unification outside east Germany, various paths for net import demand, fiscal imbalances, and migration in east Germany were used as inputs to the IMF's global, macroeconomic model, MULTIMOD (see footnote explaining model), and scenarios were calculated relative to a baseline that excludes the effects of unification. Some of the main channels for the transmission of those effects can be sketched. With a rise in global investment relative to saving, real interest rates rise worldwide, though the size of the increase varies from country to country. Increased demand from east Germany is directed partly toward west German goods, which boosts output in west Germany, raises the price of German goods relative to foreign goods (appreciates the real ex-

	Optimistic Scenario (A)	Less optimistic Scenario (B)	Indirect tax increase	EMS realignment[1]
German variables[2]				
GDP (in percent)				
1990	0.6	0.6	0.6	0.6
1991	2.4	1.6	2.2	2.4
1992–4	4.2	2.2	3.9	4.2
2001	14.5	8.1	14.5	14.5
Rate of change of GDP deflator (in percent)				
1990	0.2	0.2	0.2	0.2
1991	0.7	0.8	1.7	0.5
1992–4	0.2	0.4	0.3	0.3
2001	−0.2	−0.1	−0.2	−0.2
General government balance (in percent of GDP)				
1990	−2.2	−2.2	−2.2	−2.2
1991	−4.4	−4.8	−3.7	−4.4
1992–4	−2.7	−3.8	−2.0	−2.6
2001	−0.6	−3.3	0.3	−0.7
Current account balance (in percent of GDP)				
1990	−1.3	−1.3	−1.3	−1.3
1991	−2.7	−2.6	−2.6	−2.6
1992–4	−2.3	−2.6	−2.1	−2.3
2001	−0.9	−2.3	−0.5	−0.6
Variables for other European countries[3]				
GDP (in percent)				
1990	−0.2	−0.2	−0.2	−0.2
1991	−0.1	—	−0.1	0.6
1992–4	−0.4	−0.3	−0.3	−0.1
2001	0.2	0.1	0.3	0.2
Rate of change of GDP deflator (in percent)				
1990	—	−0.1	−0.1	−0.1
1991	—	0.1	−0.1	1.3
1992–4	−0.1	0.1	−0.1	1.0
2001	0.3	0.3	0.3	0.4

SOURCE: International Monetary Fund, Occasional Paper No. 75, German Unification: Economic Issues. Chapter VI

[1] With a loss of credibility of "hard currency" policies by those countries in the Exchange Rate Mechanism (ERM) of the European Monetary System.

[2] Results for unified Germany.

[3] Members of the ERM.

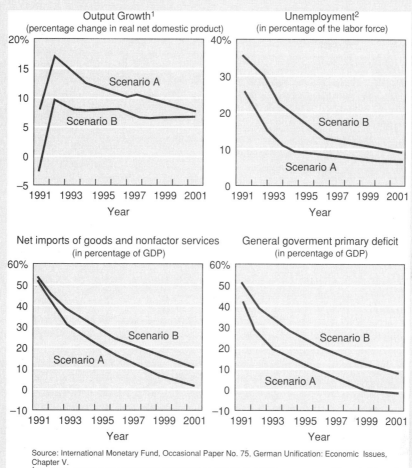

Output Growth[1]
(percentage change in real net domestic product)

Unemployment[2]
(in percentage of the labor force)

Net imports of goods and nonfactor services
(in percentage of GDP)

General goverment primary deficit
(in percentage of GDP)

Source: International Monetary Fund, Occasional Paper No. 75, German Unification: Economic Issues, Chapter V.
[1] For 1991, growth is measured using output in the second half of 1990 as a measure of the underlying value of output for all of 1990. Because of the sharp drop in output in the second half of 1990, official data will show negative growth in 1991.
[2] Including the effective period of unemployment for those on short-time work.

change rate of the deutsche mark, through both higher prices in Germany and a stronger currency), and lowers combined German net exports.

The extent of these effects depends on a number of factors. For example, how will unification affect the conduct of macroeconomic policy in Germany? Here, it is assumed that the Bundesbank continues to resist excess demand pressures in the same way as it has in the past, tax rates are unchanged, and increased budget deficits are financed by government debt.

The influence of the level of capacity utilization on inflation is also important. In MULTIMOD, productive capacity is not an absolute constraint on output. Instead, the higher the rate of capacity utilization, the greater are the upward pressures on inflation that result from an increase in demand. In the simulations presented below, the starting point for capacity utilization is high, but it is still below historical peaks reached in 1972–73 and 1979–80. Moreover, as discussed above, further migration from the east tends to increase output capacity. The pressures initially put on capacity in west Germany will also depend on the geographical distribution of east Germany's import demand. Here, two-thirds of the increase in demand is assumed to show up, in the first instance, in increased exports by west Germany, and the remainder in other countries' exports (allocated on the basis of historical shares in imports of the Federal Republic of Germany).

The assumed path for net imports into east Germany is illustrated in the chart. Under Scenario A, this stimulus to demand leads to an increase in the rate of growth in west Germany of 0.6 percentage points in 1990 and 1.3 percentage points in 1991. In subsequent years, output growth is lower than it would otherwise have been because the rate of change of net imports from east Germany is negative and because of lagged effects of increased interest rates and currency appreciation. Nevertheless, the *level* of output in the west is higher because of favorable supply effects, and output growth of Germany as a whole is persistently stronger (see table). Inflation pressures, however, are also larger: output prices rise by about one half of a percentage point faster on average over 1990–92 than in the baseline.

Output effects on other countries in the Exchange Rate Mechanism (ERM) of the European Monetary System are negative, but small, while they are slightly positive on non-ERM countries. Both sets of countries are affected to some extent by higher interest rates. The ERM countries, because of the assumed fixity of their central parities, also experience a real effective appreciation (as their currencies increase in value against the dollar and the yen along with the deutsche mark), which combined with the interest rate increase, offsets the stimulus from stronger exports from Germany. On balance, Scenario A suggests that the international effects of unification are not very large and that increased demand does not put unmanageable strains on German productive capacity. However, higher government spending in Germany leads to an increase of 16 percentage points, the combined government debt/GNP ratio for 1999,

which thereafter tends to decline back toward its baseline path.

Scenario B presents a less favorable picture for Germany as a whole, though not for west Germany alone, where output growth boosted by greater migration from the east. There is a larger deterioration in the combined fiscal balance as a ratio to GNP, due to increased unemployment benefits, slower revenue growth, less rapid output growth in the east, and higher interest payments on larger cumulated indebtedness. As a result, government debt reached 19 percent of combined GNP above baseline by 1995, and 30 percent by 2001. Despite this, effects on financial markets and on other countries differ little from Scenario A, and inflation effects are also similar.

POLICY ISSUES AND UNCERTAINTIES

The effects of German unification on government deficits and debt in Germany have been a central feature of the recent policy debate. In particular, the possibility of persistently high government deficits (see, for instance, the less optimistic scenario described above) has caused concern in many quarters. There is a consensus that expenditure reductions in west Germany, particularly of subsidies, are the preferred way of limiting these deficits. However, if sufficient budgetary savings cannot be achieved through expenditure measures, a tax increase may need to be considered. Because of the recent reform of income taxation, raising direct taxes might be counterproductive. Increasing value-added tax rates would appear to be a more attractive alternative; it would be consistent with the government's objective of improving the efficiency of the tax system and would help to bring German VAT rates closer to the EC average.

Scenario A was, therefore, simulated in MULTIMOD with a rise in indirect tax receipts of DM 20 billion in 1991, corresponding to an increase in VAT rates by a little under 2 points in west Germany (additional revenue from a similar VAT increase in east Germany would be some DM 3 billion). The Bundesbank is assumed to raise its monetary target to take into account the initial effect on prices of higher indirect taxes. The additional revenue helps to limit the medium-run budgetary impact of unification: instead of an increase relative to baseline in the combined government debt ratio of 16 percent of GNP in this year 1999 in Scenario A, it increases by only 10 percent in this simulation. The simulated tax increase leads to higher inflation for a while: relative to the baseline, the GNP deflator rises 1.7 percentage points faster in 1991 (one percentage point more than in Scenario A). Since such price rises might kindle fears that inflation would continue, an increase in indirect taxes would have to be weighed carefully.

Scenario A, which assumes that central exchange rate parities within the ERM are unchanged, leads to slightly lower output in other ERM countries. This might be avoided by a realignment of their currencies vis-à-vis the deutsche mark. However, negative effects on the credibility of the "hard currency" policies of ERM countries—that is, the commitment of monetary policy to price stability—would also have to be taken into account. In particular, through tight monetary policies and by avoiding realignment of their exchange rates against the deutsche mark, other ERM countries have, in many cases, succeeded in lowering their inflation rates in recent years close to the German level. Devaluation of their currencies against the deutsche mark might give rise to doubts concerning their anti-inflationary commitment.

The table shows the results of a scenario in which a depreciation of the other ERM currencies against the deutsche mark (by 4 percent) in 1991 induces expectations of further realignments (assumed to equal $1\frac{1}{2}$ percent a year) and consequently of higher inflation in future years. Other ERM countries experience greater inflation than in Scenario A, but also somewhat larger output. The effects on Germany are only slightly different.

CONCLUSION

Given the uncertainties involved in the transition from a centrally planned to a market econ-

omy in the former German Democratic Republic, the model simulations presented above must be seen as only rough quantifications of possible effects of German unification on other countries. In addition to uncertainties concerning economic policies and the behavior of individuals and firms in united Germany, there are other structural changes underway that may modify these results, including moves to greater integration of economies associated with the Single Market Program for the EC.

The general picture that emerges from the scenarios is that the international effects of German unification are relatively moderate. Moreover, these effects are not particularly sensitive to the success of the process of economic transformation in east Germany. This is hardly surprising given the small size of the resources needed in east Germany relative to global saving. But the path the east German economy takes over the coming years will have substantial implications for the now united Germany and may provide important lessons for other Eastern European countries.

---

* The modeling exercise described in this perspective is based on information available in October 1990 and does not incorporate subsequent economy developments and policy announcements. East Germany is treated as a separate economy; there is, for example, a completely separate fiscal sector. While this approach is clearly not consistent with the institutional features of the united Germany, it facilitates the analysis of the effects of unification without causing any fundamental distortions. The scenarios for East Germany are based on a detailed model that integrates the demand, supply, and income sides of the economy. The model is described in Occasional Paper No. 75.

To assess the effects of unification outside East Germany, the results of the scenarios for East Germany have been fed, as an external influence, into the Fund's MULTIMOD model. MULTIMOD constitutes an integrated framework with separate submodels for each of the seven largest industrial countries (of which the model for Germany is, however, based on data for the Federal Republic before unification), for the remaining industrial countries as a group, and for developing countries (divided into capital-exporting and capital-importing countries). It is described in *MULTIMOD MARK II; A Revised and Extended Model*, by Paul Masson, Steven Symansky, and Guy Meredith, Occasional Paper No. 71, International Monetary Fund, July 1990.

Summary

Economic integration is a process whereby independent nations agree to coordinate economic policies and sacrifice self-autonomy to achieve mutually beneficial economic goals. Economic integration moves through six different phases, from the independent nation-state, free-trade areas, customs unions, common markets, economic unions, and complete economic integration, as demonstrated by political union. The EEC is the most current and best example of economic integration and is a major economic force in the business environment. The forerunners of the EEC were the Organization for European Economic Co-operation (OEEC), established to promote reconstruction following World War II, and the European Coal and Steel Community, which created a common market for coal, steel, and iron ore. In 1957 Belgium, France, Italy, Luxembourg, the Netherlands, and West Germany signed the Treaty of Rome, its main provisions being a liberalization of trade by the formation of a free-trade association, unification of external relations, promotion of mobility of the factors of production and business enterprise through a common market, harmonization of internal conditions, including agricultural policy, and an increased movement of capital to promote develop underdeveloped areas of the community. Currently, the EEC has twelve members, the original six plus Great Britain, Ireland, Denmark, Greece, Spain, and Portugal.

The EEC has four structural organizations. The European Commission is the executive body of the EEC; it draws up and implements supranational policies after approval by the Council of Ministers. The Council of Ministers has final authority to pass or reject legislation sponsored by the commission. The Court of Justice acts as the supreme appeals court for the EEC. The European Parliament is an advisory body of elected member-country representatives, which until now has had little political influence.

The Single Europe Act of 1987 furthered economic integration by requiring that member countries who veto proposals must prove that the proposal threatens its vital national interests. A continuing conflict exists between richer and poorer member countries on the timing of the abolishment of internal trade barriers. Efforts to harmonize national policies include the Common Agriculture Policy and the European Monetary System which created the European currency unit. Debates continue over the creation of a European central bank and a single common currency.

Firms operating within the EEC will gain from the larger market, reduced trade barriers, and greater labor and capital mobility, resulting in significant advantages over firms operating outside the EEC. Non-EEC firms have been adjusting their corporate strategies to compete more effectively, which includes increased investment inside the EEC. Some progress, however, has been made in reducing trade barriers in financial services, standardizing product specifications, leveling public procurement policies on government contracts, improving relations with non-EEC nations, formalizing professional degrees and qualifications within member countries, and coordinating EEC-wide mass media with local broadcasting needs.

Discussion Questions

1. What is economic integration? Discuss the six different phases.
2. What are the advantages and disadvantages that result form economic integration?
3. Discuss the structure of the EEC.
4. How many votes are required to pass EEC legislation? What criteria must an EEC member country exhibit to veto proposed EEC legislation?
5. What purpose does the EMF have within the EEC?
6. How might U.S. banks be adversely affected by the EEC?
7. What are the issues that require resolution before full EEC integration occurs?

Bibliography

1986. "Evolution of the European Community." *Finance & Development* (September): 30–31.

1988. "Europe's Internal Market." *The Economist* (July 9): 11.

1988. "Panel's Proposal for European Unity May Be More General than Specific." *Wall Street Journal* (December 9): B7A.

1988. "Take Advantage of the EC Market Now." *Business America* (August 1): 1–6.

1988 "When 'Made-in-Europe' Isn't." *The Economist* (October 8): 63.

1990. "France Restricts Non-European Community Programming." *Video-News International* (February): 1.

AUERBACH, STUART. 1988. "Farmers Protest GATT Talks on Subsidies." *Washington Post* (December 6): B1.

BACON, KENNETH. 1988. "Will North America Follow Europe's Lead." *Wall Street Journal* (September 26): 1.

BALARSA, BELA. 1961. *Theory of Economic Integration.* Homewood, IL: Richard D. Irwin.

BARTHOLOMEW, MICHAEL. 1988. "Profit Now from Europe's 1992 Opening." *Wall Street Journal* (December 5): 16.

CHACE, JAMES. 1990. "Auf Wiedersehen USA." *International Management* (June): 28–36.

COMES, HENRY, ET AL. 1988. "Reshaping Europe: 1992 and Beyond." *Business Week* (December 12): 49.

DREW, J. 1979. *Doing Business in the European Community.* London: Butterworth.

EMERSON, MICHAEL. 1989. "The Emergence of the New European Economy of 1992." *Business Economics* (October): 5–9.

GREENHOUSE, STEVEN. 1988. "The Growing Fear of Fortress Europe." *New York Times* (October 23): 7.

GROSS, THOMAS F. 1989. "Europe 1992." *Management Review* (September): 24–29.

KHAMBATA, DARA. 1986. *The Practice of Multinational Banking.* Bridgeport, CT: Greenwood Press.

POEHL, KARL OTTO. 1988. "A Vision of a European Central Bank." *Wall Street Journal* (July 15): 14.

PRICE WATERHOUSE. 1988. "Europe 1992 and Beyond." *Price Waterhouse Review* 32: 2–5.

QUELCH, J. A., R. D. BUZZELL, AND E. R. SALANA. 1991. *The Marketing Challenge of Europe 1992.* Reading, MA: Addison-Wesley.

READING, BRIAN. 1989. "A Greater European Century?" *Across the Board* (December): 17–20.

RIVERS, R. R., AND G. S. VEST. 1989. "Making Deals in Post-1992 Europe." *Europe* (October): 18–20, 46.

SCHISSEL, HOWARD. 1988. "European Savings Banks: A Step Ahead of 1992." *Euromoney* (September): 16–19.

SULLIVAN, SCOTT. 1988. "Who's Afraid of 1992." *Newsweek* (October 31): 33.

THIMM, ALFRED L. 1989. "Europe 1992—Opportunity or Threat for U.S. Business: The Case of Telecommunications." *California Management Review* (Winter): 54–75.

WEIHRICH, HEINZ. 1990. "Europe 1992: What the Future May Hold." *Academy of Management Executive* (May): 7–18.

CHAPTER 14

Doing Business with Eastern Europe

CHAPTER OBJECTIVES

This chapter will:

- Review the rapid political and economic changes occurring in Eastern Europe.
- Identify the main areas that need economic reform.
- Present areas of opportunity for the growth of international business.
- Discuss the challenges and difficulties facing Eastern Europe as it moves toward free-market economies.

Political and Economic Changes in Eastern Europe

The year 1989 was a euphoric one for Eastern Europe, as totalitarian regimes crumbled in quick succession in the face of widespread popular protest. The regimes were replaced by democratic governments committed to the ideals of freedom and liberty. U.S. President George Bush's concept of a "Europe whole and free" aptly summarizes the euphoria of those times. Each country decided to adopt the three pillars of liberty, namely political, economic, and social reform. The countries individually agreed to adopt a multiparty democratic system of government, all countries decided to opt

for a market economy, and, in the social sphere, they all decided to go in for a civil society.

Much of the initial elation has faded in the face of harsh political and economic realities, as it became evident that it was significantly more difficult than originally envisaged to change systems. Political reform is relatively simple if it is limited to organizing an election. According to political pundits, a country can only be deemed a stable democracy if it has changed its ruling political party at least twice in a peaceful manner. It took Germany thirty-five years to qualify as a stable democracy under this definition. On the economic front, the countries need to change ownership from "nobody's property" (the people's property) to "somebody's property." This requires a clear definition of property rights. The situation is further complicated in such countries as Czechoslovakia, which has adopted restitution laws. Another major decision was whether economic reform should be undertaken in a highly compressed time period using "shock therapy" or over a longer period using a more gradual approach. Here, the countries have differed. Poland has gone in for the shock therapy approach, while Hungary has adopted a more gradual system. The shock approach necessitates a three-pronged program:

1. Stabilization policies aimed at controlling inflation and government spending through tight monetary and fiscal policies.
2. Decentralization through price liberalization and demonopolization of state-owned enterprises.
3. Trade liberalization and currency stability and convertibility.

Economic adjustment under these conditions inescapably led to difficulties, as unemployment soared and prices rose without a corresponding increase in wages. If the level of unemployment were left totally to market forces, it could easily reach 30 to 50 percent of the labor force, which occurred in the eastern part of Germany.

The principal objective of social reform is the creation of a civil society where living spaces are free from state influence. A civil society is the ultimate requirement of democracy and requires separate independent economic agents, such as small and medium-sized enterprises and independent universities. Creating a civil society in Eastern Europe entails the large-scale dismantling of existing institutions and a major reallocation of social rights and privileges across different segments of the population.

These broad tasks are common to all Eastern European countries in transition and form the backdrop to the challenge of privatization and securities market development. The unique circumstances of Eastern Europe deeply influence these processes and call for innovative and unorthodox solutions that may not have been applied elsewhere.

The Privatization Process

The methodology to adopt for privatization is a major dilemma faced by all Eastern European countries. All countries have huge multifaceted state-owned enterprises that were built as monuments to socialism, rather than production units aimed at maximizing efficiency; inadequate savings in the hands of the local populations to buy privatized enterprises; and the concern of foreign domination of industries and accusations of selling the family silver to foreigners. The process is further complicated by the need to achieve privatization within a politically acceptable time frame, which governments have set at between three to five years. The enormity of the task can be realized by recalling that former British Prime Minister Margaret Thatcher needed ten years to denationalize about ten companies that accounted for less than 1 percent of gross domestic product, while the countries of Eastern Europe are trying to privatize on average 90 percent of their productive units. Within this common constraint, each country has developed its own approach to the problem. A brief survey of the Soviet Union, Hungary, Poland, and Czechoslovakia is presented as follows. The other countries of Eastern Europe, such as Bulgaria, Romania, and Yugoslavia, are in such disarray that any semblance of order and economic stability will take several years.

The Soviet Union

The anti-Communist revolution that swept through most of Eastern Europe in 1989 reached the Soviet Union in August 1991. Creating a stable and prosperous economy after the old totalitarian order will prove to be considerably more difficult in the original homeland of socialism than in its Eastern European satellites. The transition from a one-party state to a multiparty democracy after more than seven decades will cause tremendous upheaval.

Covering almost 20 percent of the earth's surface, the Soviet Union is the last multinational empire in the world, with over a hundred nationalities, many of which are clamoring for independence. Many democratic politicians believe that the Soviet Union will disintegrate as a geopolitical entity. More than half of the 15 republics in the Soviet Union have declared independence and many have been recognized by the West as separate countries.

The country faces severe problems, such as a slump in industrial production, acute shortages in the supply of food, ethnic conflicts, and, in the worst-case scenario, a full-blown civil war.

The dissolution of the Communist Party will remove some of the major obstacles to political and economic reform, but it will also deprive the country of much of its administrative structure as well as law and order. Establishing new structures of power will prove to be easy, however, compared to putting the economy back on its feet after seventy years of mismanagement. In the short run the new democratic rulers will be forced to impose severe sacrifices on the population to make the transition to a market economy. The economy will have to cope with rampant inflation and unemployment along with falling living standards and quality of life. The scale of economic disruption is likely to be much greater than in Eastern Europe, where some agriculture and business was in private hands.

In the long run, MNCs will have tremendous opportunities for expansion and profits in the new countries that emerge from the Soviet Union.

Hungary

Hungary has been flirting with capitalism for far longer than is commonly realized (see Perspective 14–1). The Communist government had permitted the establishment of privatized small and medium industries as early as 1982. Strictly speaking, privatization started in 1989 with the introduction of the Companies Act and the Foreign Investment Act, which was the first legislation of this kind in Eastern Europe. The Foreign Investment Act guaranteed foreigners the right to repatriate their original capital, dividends, and capital gains in foreign exchange. The State Property Agency (SPA) was established in April 1990 to speed up the process of privatization and to halt some of the more obvious abuses of the so-called spontaneous privatization. At present, enterprises can be privatized in three different ways:

1. Spontaneous privatization, where management, either on its own or with another entity, comes up with a privatization plan and takes it to the SPA for approval.
2. Investor-initiated privatization, where either friendly or hostile outside bids are made.
3. Active privatization, where companies are chosen by the SPA and actively privatized with the help of investment advisers working on behalf of the SPA (twenty enterprises so far have been privatized in this manner).

PERSPECTIVE 14–1   Hungary's Reforms: Past and Present

The first steps toward policy reforms in Hungary can be traced back to the 1950s. Following two waves of political thaw in 1953 and 1956, Hungarian economists tried to implement their ideas on the transformation of the Soviet-type centrally planned economy. But they succeeded only in mitigating the effects of the most striking distortions. No comprehensive changes could be made because

SOURCE: Imre Tarafas, *Finance & Development*, March 1991, pages 12–14.

of the subsequent deterioration of the political climate in the Union of Soviet Socialist Republics and, as a result, in Hungary.

The first radical reform was introduced on January 1, 1968, after several years of political, academic, and organizational preparation. The reform package included an attempt to combine central planning and market mechanisms, abolition of mandatory plan commands, moves toward enterprise autonomy, and gradual introduction of market prices and profit incentives. But ideological barriers and an unchanged political and institutional framework stood in the way of this effort. The situation was aggravated by attacks by conservative forces within the communist party leadership. As a result, the economic reform process came to a halt by 1972–74.

Despite that, the idea of the 1968 reform could not be totally banished from Hungarian public thought. Gradually, Hungary moved away from the rigid Soviet economic model. This relative freedom allowed Hungarians to enjoy better living conditions and to have a healthier domestic economy than most of their neighbors in Eastern Europe for nearly two decades. But many economic problems remained.

The oil price shock of 1973–74 should have led to further, drastic reordering of economic priorities, but this did not take place. Instead, the government chose to cushion the population against the rise in oil prices and the deterioration of the terms of trade with budgetary subsidies sustained by increased borrowing, without changing the production structure or dampening demand. The country's standard of living rose in this period, but so did its external debt. By 1978, the leadership realized that the accumulation of debt could not be sustained. But instead of restarting the reform process to revitalize the economy, it cut back on imports from convertible currency areas and encouraged export-led growth mostly by administrative measures. The deterioration of the external balance slowed down, but without the necessary improvement in efficiency and profitability.

A new wave of reform gained momentum by the 1980s, including price reforms (linking domestic prices to those in the world market), a new bankruptcy law for all types of enterprises, a two-tier banking system (i.e., a central bank and commercial banks), and a new company law. But by the second half of the 1980s, the leadership realized that the old system could not be simply improved; it needed to be changed radically. Today, we do not speak of a combination of a planned and a market economy, nor even about a socialist market economy, but about a social market economy, with a high degree of social sensitivity, along the lines of systems prevalent in Western Europe.

PREVIOUS REFORMS

Earlier reforms were partial and half-hearted. For a variety of reasons, including political compromises and lack of synchronization between different elements of a reform package, earlier reform efforts failed to improve radically the functioning of the Hungarian economy. For example, the 1980 reform concentrated on building up a market for goods and services, but not for capital, because capital ownership and income from speculation were seen as concepts opposed to the nature of a socialist social and economic order. The central command system—though in a somewhat indirect form—remained predominant for many investments and therefore affected structural development, as did the over-centralized, monopolistic system of enterprise organization. Individual reform measures were not part of a coherent and unified system. All these reforms were never allowed to cross political and ideological boundaries, so that they were often reversed.

The question of ownership—the central element of the market economy—was missing. In the state-owned sector, both the branch ministries and the self-governing bodies of the enterprises proved to be extremely incapable representatives of the state as the owner. In the cooperative sector, the ownership rights of the members were severely restricted by the interference of the political institutions. Earlier reforms did not tackle the issue of ownership directly. They made certain concessions for small-scale private industrial and trading activities and private agricultural production, mostly on the household plots of the cooperative farmers. Of course, many realized that the economic ills of the socialist society stemmed from the weakness of the interest of individuals. But because of the ideological barriers, no solution was found, until very recently, to the question of how to create and foster individual interest at all levels of the economy.

The root of the problem is that egalitarian tendencies have always been extremely strong in socialist countries. Generations grew up on the belief that this approach showed the moral superiority of socialist society over the capitalist one.

Radical reforms could have led to the predominance of private ownership; this, however, would have threatened political power as well. For these reasons, in the past the efficiency and incentives emerging from the creation of self-interest were always sacrificed on the altar of political power.

Another fundamental problem was the selection and behavior of managers of state enterprises in a socialist economic system. Although the executive was, in principle, selected on the basis of his managerial talents, his interests lay more in implementing the directives of his superiors than in following the imperatives of the market. Such a manager—unlike a private owner—is not sufficiently sensitive to demand, or to the future. He is less likely to have an interest in technical development or market research, and more interested in raising wages for the sake of good worker-manager relations, instead of accumulating wealth for the enterprise, or for the economy at large.

The predominance of Comecon trade. The huge captive market of the Comecon countries (also known as the Council for Mutual Economic Assistance) was not as demanding in terms of quality and speed of delivery as Western markets. This made it all very comfortable for the supplier enterprises. As a result, the structure of production in Hungary remained unchanged and the

technical gap between Comecon and the Western economic system widened.

Trade with the Comecon countries grew rapidly, and this, for a long time, indirectly impaired the competitiveness and thwarted the export efforts of the Hungarian industry in the Western markets. In the Comecon trade system most of the deals were struck between governments. Once agreements had been reached between governments companies found that they could bargain for favors from the government. They argued for subsidies, preferential credits, and other types of assistance as preconditions for the fulfillment of obligations made by the governments. This practice essentially removed the possibility of the emergence of market forces in the operation of these enterprises.

The lack of a change in the political system. Perhaps the most important reason behind the failures of the previous reforms was the fact that economic reforms were not linked to political ones. The abolition of the centrally directed system of the command economy put an end to the links with the centralized political system. But the declaration of enterprise autonomy could not produce a breakthrough in economic thinking and productivity because executive appointments continued to be influenced by political factors. Most of the economic policy decisions were based on short-term political considerations, laced with reverence for socialist values.

Political, economic, and social processes have their own logic, their own dynamics, and necessities. Thus, reforms were often viewed by the authorities as an admission of weakness; hence they tried to restrict such efforts to a minimum. It became clear that so long as decisions on economic matters and the appointment of executives remained a political issue, economic efficiency could not fully become a reality. This state of affairs concentrated substantial informal powers in the hands of the state and party bureaucrats, many of whom were unfamiliar with particular economic issues or industries.

Along with "true values" of socialism, such as free health care and education, security of being, and full employment, socialism also produced pseudo-values, such as artificially low prices of certain basic foodstuffs and services, and cheap rents. These led to shortages of commodities and of housing, and to the neglect and deterioration of the existing housing facilities. The transition to a true market economy requires overcoming the ideological taboos—for instance, that only physical and intellectual work is ethical, trade or entrepreneurship is dubious at best, and income from capital is immoral—that have taken such deep roots in public thinking in the course of the past 40 years.

WILL THIS REFORM SUCCEED?

What factors make it likely that the current transformation will continue and be successful?

The change toward a market economy is so major an undertaking that it could not be accomplished without accompanying political changes. The most important domestic political changes have already taken place. By mutual consent of those in power and those in opposition, multiparty parliamentary elections were held this spring, similar to those of the Western democracies. These changes occurred not through a coup, but as a matter of political evolution. Although Hungarian political life is characterized by keen debates, these have been contained within the parliamentary framework.

Following change in the political system of the country and as a result of the changes taking place in the Comecon countries, the international environment has also become supportive of reforms. Thus, the opportunity is now there for the establishment of the institutional system necessary for a market economy and for the introduction of privatization.

Further, the Hungarian reforms are not isolated this time. All of Eastern Europe and, what is of particular importance, even the Soviet Union, is undergoing an enormous change. Each of these countries is seeking to find the political and economic solutions best suited to its own situation.

The rearrangement of relations between them is also in progress. This implies the development of frameworks within which standardized political and economic solutions associated with Comecon are not needed any more. Moreover, it will be possible to build up economic ties, closer than before, with various organizations in the advanced market economies. The other important factor in this rearrangement of relations is that the former Comecon countries will, from January 1, 1991, settle their trade accounts without obligatory interstate agreements, based on world market prices, and with payments in convertible currencies. Although this shift will put a major financial burden on Hungary, in addition to a number of other problems, it is also expected to do away with the undesirable effects of the earlier transferable rouble trade that hindered technical development, competition, and renewal in the past.

As a result of successive reform efforts over the past two decades, and particularly in the past two years, the basis for the establishment of a market economy has emerged in Hungary. With the command plan abolished more than 20 years ago, and the other forms of centralized direction of enterprises gradually reduced, the autonomy of the enterprises is, by now, virtually complete. Most managers have obtained the skills needed to operate in a market economy; partnerships and joint ventures are sprouting; various forms of modern financial instruments have appeared; and a taxation system, in line with those in Western Europe, has been established. Foreign trade, prices, and wages have been greatly liberalized; good progress has been attained in making the national currency convertible.

The settlement of ownership issues is important. The decision on the sale of state-owned assets has already been made. The parliament adopted the necessary legal framework and the process of large-scale privatization unfolded in the last two years. Many state-owned enterprises have established joint ventures with foreign firms and the government has launched a massive privatization program. Privatization is partly led, partly controlled by the State Property Agency. Privatization can be initiated by this Agency, by the enterprises concerned, or by prospective buyers. Privatization is a market-based process and is helped by favorable credits.

One of the most important tasks ahead is to improve the performance of state enterprises. A part of the solution is to privatize as many enterprises as possible. This, however, will take time and has certain limits. Therefore, the reform of the state enterprise sector is unavoidable and cannot be bypassed by privatization. The reform may have different forms but some basic principles should be observed: the state-owned enterprises should be run by autonomous and accountable managers like private firms and conglomerates; they should be subjected to real market forces and should be supervised by professional, business-oriented bodies, whose sole responsibility is to assure high profitability within the framework of legal regulations and business ethics.

The establishment of new private enterprises, including from the beginning of 1991 foreign trade activities and joint ventures, is completely free and requires no specific license. At the same time more than 90 percent of imports and domestic prices will be liberalized, Special laws and a broad range of measures will ensure fair trade practices and counter monopolistic tendencies.

The state will decrease its participation in the economy: it will decrease subsidies radically and will not make any investment in the competitive segment of the economy. The financing of health, education, and housing sectors will be reformed radically.

The prospects of the political and economic changes in Hungary have been improved by the strengthening of links to Western market economies. Hungary's exports to these markets have already reached $7 billion per annum, or about a quarter of its GDP. The barriers in the way of the movement of capital and commodities are being demolished on both sides, while the transfer of technology has become easier. Hungary is seeking an early association agreement with the European Community, as a prelude to full membership. It will continue to count on the support of the international financial community and multilateral organizations in its move toward a fully functioning and successful market economy.

In 1991 there were two thousand state-owned enterprises with a book value of U.S.$25 billion, comprising 90 percent of productive assets. Of these, about two hundred, which account for 7 to 8 percent of the GDP, have been or are in the process of being privatized. In addition, several hundred joint ventures have been established, and overseas direct and portfolio investments have amounted to $1.5 billion. To encourage overseas investment, enterprises with foreign ownership of 30 percent or more qualify for special tax advantages. Unlike its neighbors, Hungary has concluded that little surplus and profit were likely to remain at the end of the privatization process, after one considers the high value of public domestic debt and that several state-owned enterprises have negative net worth. As a result, the country deliberately decided not to go in for a free distribution of assets to the public by means of a voucher scheme.

Among the East European countries, securities market development has advanced most in Hungary. It is interesting to note that preparations for a stock and bond market began as early as 1985 under the Communist party. A stock exchange was established in Budapest in 1989.

Poland

On January 1, 1990, Poland decided to adopt an aggressive plan for economic reform based on the principles of shock therapy. The reform package resulted in the liberalization of prices, enactment of comprehensive privatization measures, and the formation of the Ministry of Ownership Changes, which is charged with overseeing the privatization process. Further, a legal basis for a stock exchange was established and bankruptcy laws were amended. In early 1990, Poland took the courageous decision to make its currency convertible.

The privatization process in Poland has been structured according to the size of the enterprises. There are eight thousand large state-owned enterprises that will come up for privatization. Privatization of these companies will be done on a case-by-case basis, with foreign investment banks and accounting firms acting as advisers.

Simultaneously, about sixty thousand small enterprises, such as restaurants and shops have been privatized, principally by means of an auction system. A voucher scheme is being contemplated for the two hundred or so large state-owned enterprises that account for 40 percent of sales in the enterprise sector. The modalities of the voucher scheme are being studied. The current thinking is to distribute a portion of the enterprise shares through the voucher scheme to the general public. Employees are likely to be given a certain percentage of shares in their enterprises, and some shares are likely to be used to fund the social security system. In addition, the treasury may retain a minority shareholding in the enterprises as a purely passive investor.

As currently envisaged, the stock market will play a vital role in the privatization process. The Securities Market Law has been passed in the lower house of Parliament and trading on the Warsaw Stock Exchange commenced on April 16, 1991. The exchange is modeled on the Lyon Bourse and is initially operating on the basis of one quotation per day and a five-day settlement period. It is also expected that vouchers will be traded on the exchange. Consequently, the stock exchange will be a vital and integral part of the privatization process in Poland.

Czechoslovakia

The Czechoslovakian privatization program began to take shape in April 1990, when the government assembly enacted legislation to dismantle state ownership and encourage private ownership. Citizens were permitted to own privatized enterprises with no limit on the amount of property or employees. The government was given the right to break up monopolies, and some state-owned enterprises were permitted to make economic decisions.

The government has developed a four-pronged approach to privatization:

1. Restitution, through which the government has agreed to return property to those who owned it as of February 25, 1948. It is expected that about 30 percent of commercial property will be handled on this basis.

2. Privatization through the auction system is envisaged for small enterprises and service units. In these instances, the shops and restaurants will be bought or leased by the new owners. Seventy thousand such enterprises have been identified and some have been sold. The process was started in 1991 and is expected to last two years. Foreigners are not permitted to participate unless the minimum price threshold is not reached.

3. Privatization through foreign investment is actively encouraged. A joint-venture law has been enacted, permitting 100 percent foreign ownership in most industries. Four thousand joint ventures have been signed, of which 75 percent are very small, although a few very large deals, such as Skoda and Volkswagen, have also been concluded.

4. Three thousand larger stated-owned enterprises are targeted to be privatized via the voucher scheme. The vouchers will be distributed to all nationals over the age of eighteen, the first privatization to take place in early 1992.

At present, financial markets are virtually nonexistent in Czechoslovakia. Ad hoc financial legislation is being passed, such as a bond law and a mutual fund law. A more comprehensive securities market law is likely to be drafted. Czechoslovakians hope to have a functioning securities market by January 1992 and expect to trade vouchers.

While stock markets clearly have a role in the privatization process, authorities should realize that capital markets have a role to play in and of themselves, and their successful future development will, to a great extent, be determined by the real and perceived integrity of the process. Inadequate legislative and regulatory frameworks will invariably result in fraud or market manipulation and could impede the process of financial market development, which might hurt the privatization program.

Main Areas of Economic Reform in Eastern Europe

The years 1989 to 1990 saw enormous changes in the political structure of Eastern Europe as one-party rule perpetuated by Communist governments crumbled in one country after another. Change has been so swift and far-reaching that within eleven months of the opening of the Berlin Wall, East Germany and West Germany were united as one country. The speed of such change surprised even the most knowledgeable observers. The transformation, however, led to considerable disarray, as old institutions stood discredited and no new ones had been established as replacements. It is apparent that reorienting the political, legal, and economic structures of these countries will be a long and difficult task, and much confusion is likely to reign in the intervening period.

These historic changes hold promising opportunities for international business managers. Although it is not clear how the changes will unfold, certain trends are becoming increasingly apparent. To transform their mismanaged economies, governments in Eastern Europe are likely to institute reforms in several significant areas.

Price Controls

Prices in Easter European countries are determined not by costs of production or demand-and-supply conditions, but by official policy, which leads to considerable distortions and misallocation of re-

sources. The elimination of price controls would reduce to a great extent the intervention of the state in resource allocation and improve the efficiency and competitiveness of the production process.

Free Trade and Currency Convertibility

International trade in Eastern Europe is controlled by the government through a vast array of import and export regulations, licensing requirements, and so on. Foreign exchange for imports is allocated by the bureaucracy on the basis of a plethora of complex rules, and different exchange rates are used to convert local currency into foreign exchange for different types of transactions. By permitting a sharp devaluation of the home currency and tight monetary, fiscal, and credit policies, Eastern European governments can eliminate these problems and open their economies to free trade.

Development of Private Economic Activity

Development of private economic activity is a key reform measure in the restructuring process for the economies of Eastern Europe. Governments are likely to follow two routes to this end. One would be to permit and actually encourage the setting up of private industrial enterprises by removing the bureaucratic barriers and controls, high marginal tax rates, and restrictions on collaboration with overseas partners. The other is likely to come from large-scale privatization of state-owned enterprises in a phased manner, especially those continuously making losses.

Elimination of Other Distortions

Eastern European economies suffer from serious distortions, massive state subsidies, below-market rates of finance and unconditional financial guarantees to state enterprises, and control over retail trade. It is likely that most of these distortions will be gradually eliminated as countries move toward increasing the market orientation of their economies.

Opportunities for Western Multinationals

These far-reaching developments in Eastern Europe open up vast new opportunities for Western businessmen, including industrial investment, export of services and managerial expertise, new industrial products, and financial cooperation.

New Industrial Investment

Industries in Eastern Europe are by and large characterized by old outmoded machinery that badly needs modernization and the infusion of new Western technology. Clearly, Eastern European governments are going to be looking at joint ventures and other participative arrangements with Western companies to attract new technology to upgrade their smoke-stack industries and improve productivity levels. Currency convertibility and the opening of the economies to free trade can be expected to facilitate the large-scale entry of Western business firms into this new environment.

Export of Services

Service industries in Eastern Europe are even less developed than the manufacturing sector and do not even approach Western standards. The emphasis of many Eastern European governments is likely to shift sharply from an overreliance on large and heavy industrial projects to more efficient and productive service industries. Given the advanced service technology available to companies of industrialized countries, there will be considerable opportunity for service exports.

Managerial Expertise

In addition, Western companies are likely to receive significant business for exporting managerial expertise, which is singularly lacking in most East European countries. Reorganization and restructuring of industries from a state-owned, subsidized, protected, and virtually unaccountable environment to a highly competitive, bottom-line-oriented setup will need a complete restructuring of managerial attitudes, techniques, and procedures.

New Industrial Products

The cold war era was one of mutual distrust and hostility between the United States and Western Europe on one hand and countries of the Soviet bloc on the other. The events of 1989 and 1990, however, changed this attitude substantially, and prospects for improved political relations between the West and the Eastern bloc countries have improved sharply. The easing of political tensions is likely to result in the lifting of restrictions on exports of sensitive technologies and products to Eastern bloc countries. Companies involved in such technologies, especially computer firms, stand to gain enormous business opportunities, because most Eastern bloc countries use primitive and outmoded computer hardware and software.

Another opportunity for international business in this area is the possibility of the joint development of computer programs. Many Eastern bloc countries, and especially the Soviet Union, have vast pools of skilled computer programmers, but lack the hardware and software technology needed to utilize their full potential. The latter can be supplied by U.S. and Western European companies that, in turn, need substantial human resources to complete their program development projects.

Financial Cooperation

Most Eastern European countries have virtually no institutional arrangements for handling a privately owned and run financial system. This infrastructure is critical to the successful implementation of the reforms sought by most governments. The export of financial expertise, the establishment of financial institutions, and the opening of joint ventures in the financial area offer a number of opportunities, particularly for the commercial banks, investment houses, and securities firms of the Western countries (see Perspective 14–2).

PERSPECTIVE 14–2   Wall Street Wizards Give Soviets a Crash Course on Capitalism

MOSCOW—The cream of Wall Street is in Moscow this week to explain to Soviets how the New York Stock Exchange works. But they are finding that sophisticated talk about zero-coupon bonds and credit ratings doesn't mean much in a nation where there is no private property and no corporations, and where buying low and selling high is still a criminal offense.

"It is difficult for many to understand what you are talking about," complained Yuri Chetverikov, an aspiring Soviet banker, after listening to the first day of American lectures. "Please give us practical recommendations. What do we have to do to get started?"

"We may be experts in our business, but we aren't experts in creating a stock exchange from scratch," shot back James L. Massey, chief executive of Salomon Brothers International Ltd. "The first step is that some form of private ownership has to be created before an exchange can have a reason to function."

'LANDMARK' SEMINAR

Even though the participants may at times be talking at cross purposes, Soviet officials are hailing a three-day seminar being held here by the New York Stock Exchange as a landmark. The seminar, which grew out of President Bush's pledge at the 1989 Malta Summit of U.S. economic cooperation, is sponsored on the Soviet side by the State Bank and the Finance Ministry. Topics include how a market works, what brokers do, and what rights shareholders have.

The timing couldn't be better: Moscow is currently preparing a drastic overhaul of its economy and is eager to learn about, and perhaps copy, many of capitalism's basic institutions. Financial markets are considered a priority. Blueprints for reforming the economy include plans for everything from simple auctions to a full-fledged stock market.

LINGERING OBJECTIONS

The most radical plan, drafted by Stanislav Shatalin, President Gorbachev's economic adviser, even foresees a Moscow bourse opening next month—a timetable the government deems unrealistic. Nonetheless, it is backing a committee that has started work on detailed plans for a Moscow exchange sometime in the future. Similar proposals are being considered in some of the nation's 15 republics.

For all their obvious enthusiasm, the Soviets have a long way to catch up with Hungary's recently created small stock market, let alone the New York Stock Exchange. "A whole body of laws is needed" before any Soviet exchange can start to function, says John J. Phelan Jr., the NYSE's chairman and leader of the U.S. delegation. But if the required laws are passed, "in reasonable time there could be the small beginnings of an exchange,' Mr. Phelan said. Such modest progress

SOURCE: Andrea Rutherford, Wall Street Journal, October 9, 1990, page A18.

has already been made by China, where the NYSE held a similar seminar in 1986.

The Soviets have yet to pass unambiguous laws allowing private property, to which ideological objections still linger. Legislation on securities and bankruptcy doesn't exist and Soviet accounting practices are opaque. Moreover, "speculation"—the official euphemism for profit-making—is illegal and punishable by a jail term.

Soviet officials say they are starting to address these issues. Laws on enterprise and investment are being drafted as part of the economic reform plans. Only yesterday, the national parliament considered legislation to create a new-style banking system loosely modeled on the U.S. Federal Reserve. But some concede that deeply rooted popular antagonism to financial markets may be even harder to overcome than legislative hurdles.

Soviet citizens recall with bitterness their post-war experience with government-issued bonds. Under leaders Josef Stalin and Nikita Kruschchev, the population was compelled to buy bonds, even though the bonds didn't pay interest. Holders of one issue were paid back at par value only this year, 36 years after they bought the bonds. "We have a prejudice against them," said Mr. Chetverikov, the Soviet banker.

INVESTOR CONFIDENCE

Others worry about a public backlash against capital gains. Oleg Churbanov, a bank economist from the provincial town of Ryazan, said ordinary people would lose faith in a market economy if brokers "manipulate stock values to earn money without doing good for society."

American speakers struck a chord with their audience when they emphasized the importance of investor confidence in the workings of the market. "Our psychology is accustomed to everything being run by the government," said Valery Nikolayev, a foreign trade official, echoing fears that any bourse here would quickly be regulated to death. One questioner even raised the possibility that the government might set up its own competing stock exchange, forcing a private market out of business.

The U.S. speakers seemed bewildered by such notions. But the feeling of incomprehension was mutual, with many of the Soviet participants unable to understand the financial jargon occasionally thrown around. The Americans said they tried to keep their language simple: one said he was "embarrassed" when he showed his nuts-and-bolts talk to his sophisticated Wall Street boss.

Even so, references to "yield curves" and "underwriting syndicates" crept into the talks, and seemed to go over the heads of many of the Soviet participants. Ending his presentation on the workings of a secondary market, Robert E. Diamond Jr., managing director of Morgan Stanley International, told the seminar: "Hopefully, this topic has confused the audience and I look forward to questions."

The audience responded with a quiet murmur of *vsyo pravl'no*, Russian for "quite right."

Challenges and Difficulties

Although a number of important opportunities are likely to arise for corporations in the industrialized world, there are a number of factors that suggest that this optimism should be mixed with a certain degree of caution. Although political change has come rapidly and relatively smoothly (except in the case of the USSR and Romania), economic change is a different matter. Restructuring an economy implies the simultaneous implementation of a wide range of sharp policy reversals, many of which are likely to cause economic hardship in the initial stages of their implementation. Consumers in most East European countries, for example, are accustomed to subsidies, thus paying extremely low prices for many products. Workers are accustomed to wage increases that accrue routinely, without any relationship to their own performance or that of their enterprises. Imposing economic rationalization would involve reducing subsidies, closing loss-making industries, eliminating price controls, decontrolling state monopolies, realistic assessment of wage rates (see Figure 14–1), and tighter fiscal and monetary policies.

In combination, these policies are likely to raise prices sharply and reduce real wages, at least at first. Moreover, as an economy transforms itself into a modern, market-oriented form, there may be temporary increases in unemployment, as inefficient plants close and workers have to be retrained to operate high-technology equipment. In consequence, reform measures are likely to face substantial popular opposition, which may be exploited by populist politicians in the now-pluralistic political setup of these countries. Many governments may thus hesitate to implement the needed reform measures, which may in turn delay or reduce opportunities for international businessmen to participate in the restructuring process and expand their presence in these countries.

Overdependence on the West

Many East European governments feel that the basic underlying antagonisms with the West will continue. This underlying philosophy prompts concerns of becoming overdependent on Western products and services.

Residual Fear of USSR

Although Western countries have welcomed and supported the process of change and reforms in Eastern Europe, the Western view of the Soviet Union has shifted more slowly. The USSR is undergoing considerable internal strife, generated by shortages in essential commodities, such as food and gasoline, as the old centralized form of government is restructured and distributes greater independence and authority to the Soviet republics (see Perspective 14–3). Some hard-line policymakers in the West even suggest that a reformed and more efficient Eastern Europe would present an even greater threat than it did under the com-

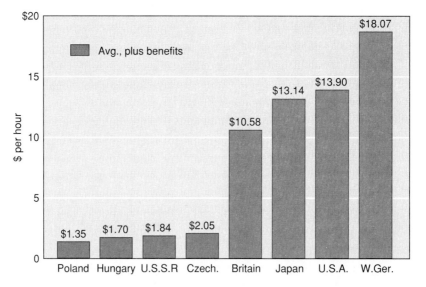

FIGURE

14–1   East versus West–Labor Cost Comparison Hourly Industrial Wage, 1988.
SOURCE: Planecon; DRI/McGraw-Hill and PlanEcon, Inc.

munist system. Although there is some reduction in military expenditures and preparedness in both blocs, the basic posture remains much the same. Combining this with the instability of the USSR, Western controls over export of computers and other advanced technology to Eastern Europe may continue to limit the possibility of increased exports and technology transfer to Eastern Europe.

PERSPECTIVE 14–3 The State of the Soviet Economy

As the Union of Soviet Socialist Republics (USSR) struggles to craft and implement far-reaching economic and political reforms, global attention has focused on the state of the Soviet economy. At the July 1990 "Houston Summit," the heads of state and government of the seven principal industrial democracies and the President of the Commission of European Communities requested the International Monetary Fund, the World Bank, the Organization for Economic Cooperation and Development (OECD), and the designated president of the European Bank for Reconstruction and Development to undertake a joint study of the Soviet economy. The team undertaking this study was also requested to make recommendations for reform of the Soviet economy and establish the criteria under which Western economic assistance could effectively support such reforms.

The Soviet authorities cooperated with this study and provided an unprecedented amount of information to the team. The study was completed in December 1990. The accompanying tables and charts, which try to recapture briefly the main recent economic trends in the USSR, are based on the summary report of the study. This report is now available from the World Bank.

SOURCE: *Finance and Development*, March 1991, page 10–11.

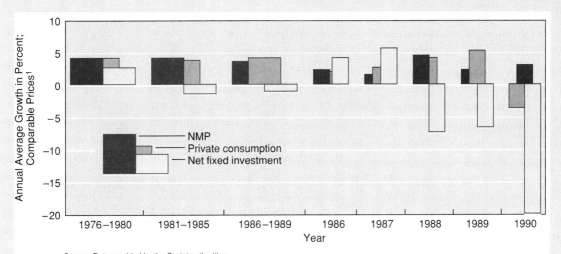

Source: Data provided by the Soviet authorities.
[1] This is similar, though not identical, to the Western concept of constant prices. It is widely believed that official Soviet statistics underrecord inflation and, hence, overestimate real growth in both output and expenditures.

	1985	1986	1987	1988	1989	1990[1]
External debt[2]	28.9	31.4	39.2	43.0	54.0	52.2[1]
of which:						
Short-term	6.9	7.4	8.6	11.2	17.7	10.0[1]
External debt						
service[3]	—	7.8	8.8	8.2	9.4	13.4
(In percent of goods						
and services)[4]	(—)	(27.7)	(26.5)	(23.1)	(24.2)	(33.0)
Foreign exchange						
reserves[5]	12.9	14.7	14.1	15.3	14.7	5.1

SOURCE: Data provided by the Soviet authorities, the Bank for International Settlements
(BIS), and staff projections.
[1] Staff projections, June 1990.
[2] External debt contracted or guaranteed by the Vneshekonombank.
[3] Total debt service on debt contracted or guaranteed by the Vneshekonombank, excluding
repayments of short-term debt.
[4] In convertible currencies.
[5] BIS data.

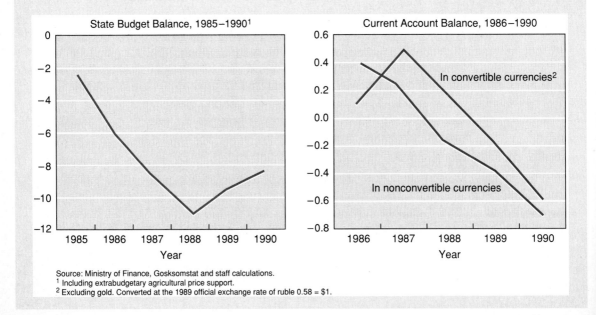

Source: Ministry of Finance, Gosksomstat and staff calculations.
[1] Including extrabudgetary agricultural price support.
[2] Excluding gold. Converted at the 1989 official exchange rate of ruble 0.58 = $1.

	Population	NMP	Deliveries to other republics	Exports abroad
	(Percent of total in 1989)	(Current prices, percent of total in 1988)	(Percent of republican NMP in current domestic prices in 1988)	
Armenia	1.1	0.9	64	1.4
Azerbaidzan[1]	2.5	1.7	59	3.7
Belorussia	3.6	4.2	70	6.5
Estonia	0.5	0.6	67	7.4
Georgia[2]	1.9	1.6	54	3.9
Kazakhstan	5.8	4.3	31	3.0
Kirgizia	1.5	0.8	50	1.2
Latvia	0.9	1.1	64	5.7
Lithuania	1.3	1.4	61	5.9
Moldavia	1.5	1.2	62	3.4
RSFSR[3]	51.3	61.1	18	8.6
Tadzhikstan	1.8	0.8	42	6.9
Turkmenistan	1.3	0.7	51	4.2
Ukraine	18.0	16.3	39	6.7
Uzbekistan[4]	7.0	3.3	43	7.4
Total	100.0	100.0	...	...

SOURCE: Data provided by the Soviet authorities.

[1]Includes 1 autonomous republic.

[2]Includes 2 autonomous republics.

[3]Russian Soviet Federated Socialist Republic, includes 16 autonomous republics.

[4]Includes 1 autonomous republic.

* Note: Net material product differs from GDP largely due to the exclusion from the former of depreciation and the value-added of services provided by the so-called non-material sector that do not contribute directly to material production.

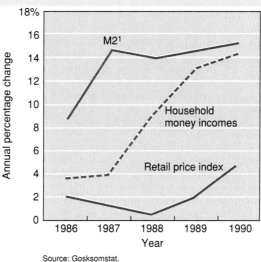

Source: Gosksomstat.

[1]M2 is composed of currency, demand deposits, time deposits, and lottery bonds.

Eastern Bloc Financial Problems

Trans-bloc trade may also be limited by the inability of East European countries to pay for their imports. Nearly all European countries face severe shortages of hard currencies, with their balance of payments under considerable strain. Many East European countries, especially Poland, Hungary, and Yugoslavia, are reeling under enormous levels of external debt, with Poland and Yugoslavia having problems in meeting the scheduled amortization.

Much of the debt in these countries was contracted by inefficient state-owned enterprises and was invested without any concern for achieving an economic rate of return that would generate income streams to service the obligation. As a result, most of these countries are saddled with a burden that they cannot shake off, at least in the near future.

One solution is for Western creditors to agree to write off significant portions of the debt, so that the scarce resources are rechanneled into badly needed modernization. Given the experience with the Latin America debt crisis, however, commercial banks are not likely to be cooperative and can be expected to stall any move toward outright cancellation of their loans. At best, they may agree to rescheduling agreements with some new money and piecemeal debt writeoffs, using such compromise mechanisms as debt-equity conversions.

The real issue at stake for the economies of the Eastern bloc countries is their ability to import substantial quantities of machinery, equipment, managerial expertise, and technology. Until they have acquired the financial wherewithal to do so, little progress in expansion of business opportunities with the Eastern bloc can be expected.

Entrenched Bureaucracies

The massive transition to a market-oriented free-enterprise economy will inevitably face a number of problems as the economies and individuals adjust to change. A major problem that may slow down opportunities for Western businessmen is the attitude of the entrenched bureaucracy, which has hitherto controlled and monopolized foreign trade in most of these countries.

There is no doubt that despite the reforms at the political level, vested business interests will attempt to retain their privileges in this area and thus hamper Western businessmen. Moreover, the straitjacket system of foreign trade that existed in the past did not permit businesspeople in the East European countries to carry out foreign-trade transactions on a purely commercial and free basis. Foreign trade was conducted under bilateral agreements with state officials, who did all the negotiating. As a result, Eastern block businesspeople have little actual exposure to international trade, while Western businessmen have little information on the location of potential markets and customers.

Managerial Inexperience

Another problem is the inexperience of East European managers, suddenly bereft of the detailed government guidelines. The greater autonomy provided by the reform measures also implies that managers must make all decisions themselves and be responsible for any failures. This autonomy has bred, at least initially, substantial insecurity in their minds, leading to a general reluctance to make important business decisions. Unfortunately, delays in decision-making could make things difficult for Western businessmen, who are used to working on tight schedules and making on-the-spot business decisions. Thus, deals may take longer to negotiate and slow the process of interbloc trade.

Government Regulation of Joint Ventures

Although most East European governments are actively promoting joint ventures with Western corporations, the latter must work under stringent conditions. Local equity content, control over joint-venture policy and operations, rates of taxation, and employee hiring and termination policies may become grounds for disputes.

The repatriation of profits is the primary concern of investors. Hence, the availability of hard currency and the restrictions on its transfer would have a significant impact on the decision-makers. Furthermore, restrictions on foreign ownership of domestic companies, as well as a judicial system for handling contract disputes, would be of paramount concern to investors considering entering Eastern Europe (see Perspective 14–4).

PERSPECTIVE 14–4 **Going East**

Eastern Europe has found democracy on its own, but it will have plenty of help in discovering capitalism.

A new survey shows that one-third of corporate chief executive officers in the U.S., Asia and Western Europe plan to build or buy factories in Eastern Europe over the next five years. The CEO's bullish investment plans reflect a belief that political liberalization in Eastern Europe is paving the way toward eventual profits for foreign investors.

Earlier this year, for example, General Electric Co. paid $150 million to buy a majority interest in Tungsram Co., a Hungarian lighting company. GE Chairman Jack Welch said when the investment was announced that he was making a "substantial bet" that moving into Hungary would pay off.

OPTIMISTIC, BUT NOT GIDDY

But while international executives are optimistic, they are also wary. They display, for instance, little of the giddy optimism that abounded five to 10 years ago when China appeared to be undergoing a similar opening to foreign trade. The reasons for the current caution? Executives cite concerns about Eastern Europe's bureaucracy, its political instability and its restrictions on foreign companies' ability to extract hard currency.

Those are some of the preliminary findings that emerge from a poll of chief executive officers in the U.S, Europe, Japan and Pacific Rim nations. The survey was conducted jointly by The Wall Street Journal, the management consulting firm of Booz-Allen & Hamilton Inc, and Nihon Keizai Shimbun, Japan's leading business newspaper.

Some 158 responses were tabulated at press time; subsequent calculations may slightly alter some of the exact percentage responses but won't change broad trends.

"Executives see opportunities in Eastern Europe because of the large consumer market and the educated labor force," explains Joseph Nemec, a senior vice president of Booz-Allen. Most of that interest is concentrated among manufacturing companies, Mr. Nemec observes; service and financial companies aren't yet convinced that Eastern Europe's business climate is suitable.

CAPITAL INVESTMENTS

The survey shows that interest in Eastern Europe has picked up decisively, compared with a similar 1989 survey of chief executives. Last year, a mere 5% of executives said they planned to make capital investments in either Eastern Europe or the Soviet Union in the next five years. This year, 34% of executives say they intend to make Eastern Europe part of their capital-investment mix by 1995. Meanwhile, 13% of executives say the U.S.S.R. will be part of their investment mix by 1995.

Don't expect foreign companies to start making toothpaste in Tirana or sofas in Sofia, though. The capital cities of Albania and Bulgaria—in

Source: George Anders, *The Wall Street Journal*, Friday, September 21, 1990.

fact, those entire nations—aren't likely to see much foreign investment.

Instead, U.S., Asian and West European chief executives cite a narrowly drawn list of East European countries that appeal to them. No. 1 on the list is East Germany, soon to become part of a unified Germany. Of executives planning to make an East European investment, 87% expect to do so in what is currently East Germany. Next on their list is Hungary, cited by 68%, followed by Poland, at 55%, and Czechoslovakia, at 47%.

Yugoslavia, Romania and Bulgaria appeal to only a few hardy (or naive) chief executives. And absolutely none of the executive surveyed say they plan to invest in Albania. That's little wonder: Albania is the only East European nation to have largely withstood the wave of political liberalization sweeping through the region. It also has the least developed local economy.

JAPANESE BULLS

The most optimistic outlook toward Eastern Europe and the Soviet Union comes from Japanese executives. Only 3% of Japanese executives, for instance, see serious trouble financing any East European or Soviet expansion. In contrast, 36% of U.S. executives and 27% of West European executives identified financing as a major barrier to entering those markets.

Similarly, just 30% of Japanese executives iden-tified East European government regulations as a major impediment to doing business in the region. That compares with 42% for both U.S. and West European executives.

Still, Japan isn't exactly putting its money where its mouth is. Eastern Europe accounts for just 0.7% of Japanese companies' world-wide capital-spending plans by 1995. That compares with 1.8% of U.S. companies' overall spending plans and 4.6% of Western European companies' spending plans.

The predominant areas for capital investment world-wide remain the U.S. and Canada, which get a 36% share, Western Europe, at 21%, and Japan, at 18%.

Although few executives plan to do much investing in the U.S.S.R., they have plenty of opinions about the Soviet Union. A remarkable 96% say they like Soviet leader Mikhail Gorbachev, though nearly one-third of executives have some doubts that he can keep his position until 1995.

Some 86% of respondents think there will be sustained economic liberalization in the Soviet Union in the next five years. Most of them, however, seem to believe that the Soviet economy is too backward to register much global clout in the next five years. Only 19% of respondents think it's likely that the U.S.S.R. will become a major economic power.

Trade Imbalances

One of the important factors in the development of significant trade relationships between Western countries and the Eastern bloc is the ability of the latter to export goods, at least in reasonable proportion to its imports. At the moment, most Eastern European countries are clearly in an uncompetitive position, given their inefficient production methods, lack of managerial expertise, and outmoded technologies. Moreover, since foreign trade had been the monopoly of official bodies, private businesspeople have little experience in international marketing. Moreover, they have little or no brand recognition in overseas markets be-cause they were not exporting on an individual basis. If they are unable to export, they can earn no hard currency, but without it, they cannot pay for Western imports. Without hard currency trade stops.

As things stand now, Eastern Europe remains in flux. Corporations interested in doing business with these countries must identify both the opportunities and risks in an environment where uncertainty and anxiety are endemic. Further, while opportunities are obvious, the risks are not, and they must be carefully assessed.

In the long run, it is apparent that the opportunities will outweigh the risks, as long as the path chosen by these countries is not reversed. There is no doubt, that if the nations of Eastern Europe become market economies, they will need substantial support from the West. In this process, there should be an ever-increasing scope for new business for corporations from the developed countries.

Summary

The political changes in Eastern Europe are reshaping the international business environment. Economic reform in this region is resulting in elimination of price controls, development of free trade and currency convertability, and development of private ownership. With the elimination of state subsidies and state controls over trade, new business opportunities are developing, including industrial investments, consulting and financial services, and the possibility of exporting formerly sensitive technologies. Western concerns over security and Eastern European fears over excessive dependence on Western industrialized countries may, however, inhibit the development of business relations with Eastern Europe.

Modernization of the Eastern European infrastructure will require massive sums of cash. Eastern European countries are generally in poor financial shape and must rely on Western loans to support the needed modernization effort. Questions remain as to when or if Eastern European countries will be integrated into the European Economic Community. The existence of an entrenched bureaucracy that previously controlled and monopolized foreign trade, and the inexperience of local managers may serve to delay important business decisions at the local level.

While an attractive form of entry, joint ventures in Eastern Europe remain under government regulation on issues such as local equity content, control over policy and operations, taxation, and employee hiring and termination policies. Repatriation of profits, conversion into hard currencies, and agreement on markets served by products of joint ventures are also areas of concern for Western corporations.

Discussion Questions

1. Eastern Europe is currently undergoing dramatic changes. How long do you think this process will take?
2. Discuss the economic reforms that are reshaping Eastern Europe. How will these reforms affect living standards in Eastern Europe in the short-term? In the long-term?
3. What risks does a corporation from the West face if it invests in Eastern Europe?
4. How can managerial inexperience and entrenched bureaucracies in Eastern Europe hamper the reform process?
5. If you were a businessperson who wished to expand operations internationally, would you consider Eastern Europe an attractive opportunity? Why or why not?

Bibliography

1987. "Soviet Joint Ventures: Some Answers Coming Slowly." *Business Eastern Europe* (October 12): 32.

1988. "Common Market Opens Round of Talks to Expand Economic Ties with Soviets." *Wall Street Journal* (November 4): B6B.

1988. "A Gold Rouble." *The Economist* (November 5): 14.

BAIR, FRANK E. 1985. *International Marketing Handbook.* Detroit: Gale Research Company.

BOUKAOURIS, G. N. 1989. "Joint Ventures in the USSR, Czechoslovakia and Poland." *Case Western Reserve Journal of International Law* (Winter): 1–53.

CIESLIK, J., AND B. SOSNOWSKI. 1985. "The Role of TNCs in Poland's East-West Trade." *Journal of International Business Studies* (Summer): 121–137.

DIEHLE, JACKSON. 1988. "Communist World Can't Jump Price Reform Hurdle." *Washington Post* (October 16): A1, A34.

DOBBS, MICHAEL. 1988. "Gorbachev Appeals for Political Reforms." *Washington Post* (November 30): A1, A34.

———. 1988. "Gorbachev Assails Collective Farms as Resounding Failure." *Washington Post* (October 14): A27.

———. 1988. "Reforms Brew Explosive Mix." *Washington Post* (November 27): A1, A30.

GUMBEL, PETER. 1988. "Funny Money." *Wall Street Journal* (September 23): 16R.

———. 1988. "German Banks Increase Loans to Soviets and Introduce Moscow to Bond Markets."*Wall Street Journal* (May 16): 1.

JOYNER AND ASSOCIATES. 1980. *Joyner's Guide to Official Washington for Doing Business Overseas.* New York: Pergamon Press.

KURTZMAN, JOEL. 1988. "Of Perestroika, Prices and Pessimism." *New York Times* (November 6): 1, 17.

MALTSEV, YURI N. 1990. "When Reform Collides with Ideology." *The American Enterprise* (March/April): 89.

NELSON-HORCHLER, JOANI. 1990. "Hungary: Bridge Between East & West." *Industry Week* (February 5): 40–42.

NELSON-HORCHLER, JOANI, AND N. E. BOUDETTE. 1990. "Poland: Chance of a Lifetime for the West; Czechoslovakia: The Absurd Powerhouse." *Industry Week* (February 5): 43–47.

NEWMAN, BARRY. 1988. "Protests Swell as Yugoslav Economy Stalls." *Wall Street Journal* (July 27): 23.

PORTES, RICHARD. 1989. "Economic Reforms, International Capital Flows and the Development of the Domestic Capital Markets in CPEs." *European Economic Review* (March): 466–471.

REMNICK, DAVID. 1988. "Soviet Official for First Time Acknowledges Existence of Inflation." *Washington Post* (November 2): A23.

SCHARES, GAIL E. 1990. "Hunting Pay Dirt in Eastern Europe." *Business Week* (June 18): 37, 68.

TULLIS, MELISSA, AND OLIVIER BOUIN. 1990. "Investment Prospects in Eastern Europe." *Multinational Business* (Spring): 17–23.

WEIDENBAUM, MURRAY. 1990. "Poland: The Bright Side to Waste and Featherbedding." *Across the Board* (March): 12–13.

WEINER, BENJAMIN. 1988. "U.S.-Soviet Trade: Lessons of Detente." *Wall Street Journal* (September 9): p. 19.

PART FIVE

FUNCTIONAL OPERATIONS IN INTERNATIONAL BUSINESS

CHAPTER 15

International Marketing

CHAPTER OBJECTIVES

This chapter will:

- Review the key elements in creating and maintaining a viable marketing mix in the international business arena.
- Contrast the views of product standardization and product differentiation, and which types of products best benefit from local adaptation.
- Discuss the issues surrounding the question of centralized versus decentralized marketing management in a world-wide market.
- Discuss the major marketing mix decision—product, promotion, pricing and distribution—within the international business context.

What Must Be Done: The International Marketer's Dilemma

Marketing is one of the most important areas of operation for multinational corporations. With the internationalization of business, MNCs face increased competition at home from both foreign and domestic competitors and internationally as the MNC seeks to enter new markets. In developing a competitive strategy, firms utilize the marketing process to identify, create and deliver products or services that are in demand and that customers are willing to buy. Performed successfully, the marketing process identifies profitable areas in which

resources should be focused, increases sales revenues, generates profits, and creates a long-term, sustainable, competitive advantage for the MNC. Performed inadequately, the results can be disastrous.

The basic marketing-mix decisions consist of four separate but interconnected functions. These are the four Ps of marketing—product, price, promotion, and placement. Companies satisfy consumer needs by developing and manufacturing the goods desired in that market; educating potential clientele regarding the existence and qualities of those products; assuring that product cost is balanced between quality and price; and ensuring that adequate volumes of products are distributed to sales outlets or customers in a timely fashion.

While these marketing subfunctions are complex enough on the domestic level, internationalization significantly increases their complexity. Foreign markets are not only physically removed but also differ culturally. Specific cost structures in the foreign market may dictate special pricing, distribution channels found in the domestic environment may be unavailable in the foreign market, portions of the product may need to be modified to meet local tastes, and promotional methods may need to be adjusted to local media. Thus, every single function of the marketing mix may require modification, or at least fine-tuning, in order to do business in the foreign locale.

International marketing entails operating simultaneously in different environments, coordinating these international activities, and learning from the experiences gained in one country to make marketing decisions in other countries. The international marketing firm must make important strategic global decisions about what to sell in which markets. Thus, the company requires huge amounts of accurate and timely information on the nature, economic condition, and consumer needs of the foreign market. The company must understand the conditions of the foreign market, and the competitive movements of other firms operating in that environment. As a result, the MNC must rely heavily on conducting appropriate and accurate assessments to determine whether these potential markets will prove profitable despite the added costs (see Perspective 15–1).

PERSPECTIVE 15–1   Anheuser-Busch's Strategy: Innocent Abroad

A flat American beer market is presenting Anheuser-Busch with its greatest challenge since Prohibition. The family-run company has flourished by dominating the American beer market under the leadership of four Busch generations. With American beer sales stagnant, and likely to stay that way, Anheuser-Busch must venture abroad to keep growing. Despite its marketing triumphs at home, executives are daunted by the challenge of pulling off the same coups in crowded and bruisingly competitive foreign markets.

On the back of such popular brands as Budweiser ("the king of beers") and Michelob, Anheuser-Busch's share of an increasingly concentrated American market for beer has grown relentlessly, form 6.5% in 1950 to 44.3% in 1989, with an especially remarkable spurt in the 1980s (see chart). Sales trebled from $3.2 billion in 1979 to $9.5 billion in 1989, while net profit rose from $144m to $762m.

This prosperity is threatened by stricter drink-driving laws and worries about health. The average American swallowed 7% less beer in 1988 than in 1980, according to Shanken Communications, a market-research firm. Total sales by volume have been flat for the past two years.

So Anheuser-Busch's bosses are looking abroad. So far, the St. Louis brewer has failed to benefit from the Europe-wide switch from dark and draught beers to lighter lagers. Agreements licensing European companies to brew and distribute Budweiser locally have produced more problems than profit. Anheuser-Busch somehow has to overcome European drinkers' view of American lagers as weak, gassy and tasteless.

Accustomed to beating the competition at home, Anheuser-Busch has sometimes been outgunned and outsmarted by rivals more adept at nurturing international brands. In Britain sales of Foster's Lager, promoted by television commer-

SOURCE: The Economist, March 17, 1990, page 72.

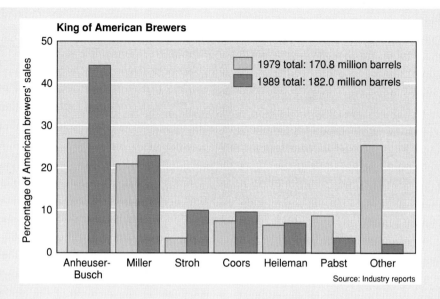

King of American Brewers

Percentage of American brewers' sales

1979 total: 170.8 million barrels
1989 total: 182.0 million barrels

Anheuser-Busch Miller Stroh Coors Heileman Pabst Other

Source: Industry reports

cials that feature Mr. Paul Hogan, the Australian star of the film "Crocodile Dundee", have dwarfed those of Budweiser. On March 8th Elders IXL, the debt-ridden Melbourne-based conglomerate that owns Foster's, announced plans to sell off many of its natural-resource, agricultural and financial-services businesses to concentrate on brewing. This could make it an even more formidable opponent. A complicated swap of British assets between Elders and Britain's Grand Metropolitan, announced on March 13th, will strengthen Elders's already powerful stake in British brewing even further.

Anheuser-Busch is thinking about buying brewers in Europe. Mr. Jerry Ritter, right-hand man of August Busch III, the chief executive and the founder's great-grandson, says the company could afford to spend $1 billion "if an outrageously attractive opportunity presented itself". He is not sure that it will. The price of European brewers, he says, is inflated by their property holdings: for example, tied pubs in Britain and city-centre brewers in West Germany.

Mr. Ritter says Anheuser-Busch is not interested in investing in property, nor in paying premium prices for breweries in northern European markets, where demand for beer is growing slowly, if at all. Southern Europe is more attractive. Beer consumption there is low, but growing at a good pace. In a fragmented market, though, it is hard to pick out a Mediterranean brewer worth buying. So Anheuser-Busch is also toying with the idea of building its own breweries in Europe.

Whatever happens, profits from abroad will not flow strongly this century. So at home the company is determined to increase its share of the American market to 50% by the mid-1990s, by grabbing sales from Stroh, G. Heileman and other struggling brewers whose long-term survival is in question. Sceptics are told to look at the 1980s, when the nation's beer sales rose by only 0.9% a year in volume, but Anheuser-Busch achieved a rise of 5.7% a year and increased its sales lead over its nearest competitor, Miller, to almost two to one.

That triumph emerged from a change in strategy after Philip Morris, Miller's owner and the tobacco industry's most brilliant marketing machine, threw Anheuser-Busch off balance with its aggressive promotion of Miller and Miller Lite. In reply, Anheuser-Busch expanded its range of beers from three to five by the start of the 1980s, and now markets 17 brands. It still relies most on three basic brands: Busch, a cheap beer aimed at the sort of people who go bowling; Budweiser, a mid-market product advertised heavily on television broadcasts of baseball, motor racing and football; and Michelob, a premium product aimed at the golfing and tennis set.

Natural Lite and Classic Dark brands have been added, along with light (low calories) versions of Budweiser and Michelob and a "dry" (little after-taste) version of Michelob. The company is importing three beers from Carlsberg, Denmark's largest brewer, to blunt the foreign challenge. It is also producing two losers in-house: a low-alcohol beer and an almost-no-alcohol one. Hardly anybody drinks them, but they are there to appease the neo-Prohibitionists, who want to make it as socially unacceptable to drink beer in America as it is to smoke—a campaign that has scared Anheuser-Busch into running advertisements to encourage people to drink less ("Know when to say when"). With most of its business in America, the company cannot afford to let American beer drinkers become stigmatised as anti-social.

To Centralize or Decentralize: The First Key Decisions

In developing a successful international marketing program, a firm must make several key decisions about its prospective strategy in world markets. Two crucial questions are:

1. Whether or not the marketing program can or should be standardized across all markets or adapted individually to each separate market.
2. Whether marketing should be centralized in company headquarters or decentralized to individual market locations or foreign manufacturing subsidiaries.

It may be human nature that prompts management to attempt to standardize the marketing function throughout the world, because it greatly simplifies the complexity of marketing and probably provides significant cost benefits to a firm. Selling the same product throughout the world achieves greater efficiencies and scale economies in many areas of operation. Production runs can be longer, thus lowering unit costs. Research and development expenses normally required to adapt the product to each foreign market can be eliminated. Specific creative work required to adapt advertising and promotional campaigns for the foreign market are not required, nor are specialized sales training programs. Pricing standardization obviates the need for calculating different prices in individual markets.

The major drawback of standardization involves the risk of market loss by not being attuned to individual differences in consumer tastes or local behavior. This cost is difficult to assess, and it is only through definitive, exhaustive market research that a firm can determine whether its standardized marketing program is losing customers.

In general, the question of standardization or adaptation is related to the nature of the product or service. Industrial products sold to other firms or businesses or to governments can be sold relatively unchanged throughout the world. Dynamic random access memory chips (DRAMs), for example, are an important part of the personal computer and are in standard use in the manufacture of computers in the United States, Europe, Japan, and Southeast Asia. In contrast, consumer goods, including such items as automobiles, furniture, and clothing, are tied intricately to personal taste preferences or fads and require more adaptation.

Deciding the degree of standardization also relates to the degree of comparative differences between the two environments in their cultures, physical attributes, institutional infrastructure, and political and economic composition. The greater the degree of difference between a foreign market and the domestic marketers, the more likely it is that the attributes or promotion of a product are inappropriate. For example, although there are distinctive differences between markets in the United States and Canada, products would be more likely to pass unchanged from one to the other, which would be far less true if the two cultures differed significantly, such as United States and Nigeria.

Similarly, firms must make decisions about the planning, implementation, and control processes involved in their world marketing programs. Should programs be created, developed, and implemented from headquarters, or from on-site subsidiary locations, where personnel are aware of and understand the differences between marketing environments? Proponents of decentralized marketing functions would argue that the advantages of subsidiary involvement in the process are that the local personnel are more familiar with the characteristics and problems of the local target markets and would be better suited to adjusting the marketing mix to suit those necessities and to solve problems. Detractors of this recommendation point out that the MNC, by having a decentralized program, would lose control of the program and that overall corporate costs would be increased through replication of activity in various subsidiary markets.

The pattern that generally emerges is somewhere between these two extremes. Most multinationals have a combination of marketing programs that are, to some degree, both centralized and decentralized, which ensures that the company has control over activities within the subsidiary and the ability to formulate a global marketing program where warranted. It can also pinpoint those areas where it is possible to standardize portions of its marketing program across markets. By the same token, however, input from subsidiaries is crucial if the firm is to develop effective marketing programs in individual foreign target markets.

The organizational structure that evolves finds the headquarters of a multinational enterprise taking responsibility for developing the company's philosophy and overall strategy, developing products and product strategies, name brands, and packaging. The foreign subsidiary, on the other hand, takes advantage of invaluable on-site experience and information to tailor the promotion, distribution, and pricing of the product so that it meets the needs or characteristics of the market. When such an intertwining of responsibilities between the headquarters and the subsidiary is created, it is crucial that there be ongoing communication between the two parties. In this way, the MNC can maintain control over its subsidiary's operations and institutionalize efficiencies between headquarters and subsidiaries as well as between the subsidiaries themselves.

Product Decisions

When most people think of products, they think of things or services for sale by companies. The physical product as we know it, however, is actually only part of the total product. The total product is the entire package of the physical product and includes its type and form, its brand name, instructions for use, accessories, and even the level of after-sales service. These attributes of the total product help determine the image that the product develops among consumers and the value it provides to purchasers.

Desired product attributes vary among users in different cultures or countries. For example, one study conducted on consumer attitudes regarding product attributes of soft drinks found that French, Brazilian, and Indian college students found it important that the drinks not contain any artificial ingredients, while students in the United States ranked taste and availability through vending machines as more important.[1]

There are two general classes of products marketed domestically and internationally—industrial products and consumer goods. Industrial products are goods sold to manufacturing firms, businesses, or governments and include such durables as steel, hardware, machinery, parts, electronic components, and other equipment. Industrial goods tend to be more universal in specifications and are consequently far more frequently standard-

[1] Green et al. 1975.

ized than consumer products. Consumer goods, on the other hand, are purchased by a large number of individuals who may vary drastically in their needs and tastes. These goods are frequently mass-merchandise items, including clothing, luxury goods, food products, appliances, and automobiles. Because of differences in taste, such goods far more often require adaptation to personal preferences, differences in culture, education levels, or even fads or fashions within countries than do industrial products.

Product-Positioning Decisions

The decisions regarding the positioning or development of a product in different markets depends on three crucial factors—the individual characteristics of each market and the environment in which the product will be sold; the functional need for the product (or the use to which it will be put) in the market; and a company's financial requirements and its competitive position in that foreign market.

The environment of each market can have a profound effect on the optimal product characteristics in that locale. The type of product marketed can be affected by the legal, economic, social, cultural, and physical forces of the targeted market. For example, types of products sold are definitely affected by the physical characteristics of a country, such as geography, terrain, and climate. Automobiles sold in tropical climates, for example, would be less likely to require rustproofing than those in snowy climates where roads are salted.

Economic forces similarly help determine which products are appropriately marketed in foreign markets, especially if they are tied to levels of economic development. For example, it would be foolish to attempt to market electric-powered products in countries that do not have sufficient or reliable sources of power. Relative income levels and standards of living in each market determine, to a very large extent, the nature of consumer needs in that country, as well as the consumers' definition of appropriate price and product quality. Thus, a marketer must be sure to correctly identify those needs so that the product is not overly sophisticated or is mismatched in other attributes. For example, products such as snack foods, which enjoy high-volume sales in industrialized countries, might be considered luxury goods in a less-developed country and would not find a ready market.

Cultural or sociological forces also have a profound effect on the appropriateness of products in different cultures. In a country with high illiteracy rates, it would, for example, be unwise to package products so that the goods could not be determined easily from photographs on the labels, but care must be taken not to confuse individuals with these illustrations. Take, for example, the experience of a baby food manufacturer that attempted to sell its product in an African nation by using the same label it used in other markets. The label showed a picture of a baby with the type of food spelled out on the jar. Sales were, of course, abysmal, because local consumers interpreted the labels to mean that the jars contained ground-up babies.[2]

Other products are affected by different traditions. For example, package sizes must be smaller in markets in which there is little refrigeration and shopping is done on a daily basis. Some products literally do not suit foreign tastes and must be made saltier or sweeter or offered with different condiments. French fries, for example, in the United States are served with ketchup; in Great Britain, "chips" are served with vinegar. Similarly, brand names may be affected. In Asian markets, such as Taiwan, a very popular brand of toothpaste is named "Darkie," but such a brand name would definitely find disfavor in American markets, where consumers are conscious of the use of any sort of racial stereotyping (see Figure 15–1).

Even colors hold different meanings in different cultures and must be considered for suitability in product designs. Red, for example, connotes richness or wealth in some countries, but may

---

[2] Ricks 1983.

Old Names and New Names

The best-known—and most highly regarded—brand names in the world, according to a survey of 3,000 consumers:	The following is a breakdown of the top 10 categories of trademark applications filed with the Patent and Trademark Office from January 1986 through October 21,1988.

<table>
<tr><td>

1 Coca-Cola
2 IBM
3 Sony
4 Porsche
5 McDonald's
6 Disney
7 Honda
8 Toyota
9 Seiko
10 BMW
11 Volkswagen
12 Mercedes
13 Pepsi-Cola
14 Kleenex
15 Nestle
16 Rolex
17 Jaguar
18 Xerox
19 Lipton
20 Hilton

</td><td>

	Applications Filed
Publications (includes books, magazines and computer software)	20,872
Advertising and Business Services (includes retail stores, consultative services, real-estate brokerage)	17,442
Clothing	16,402
Miscellaneous Services (includes restaurants, hospitals, hotels)	15,644
Foods	14,203
Measuring and Scientific Products (includes computer hardware, photography, calculators)	12,467
Games, Toys and Sporting Goods	10,555
Electrical Apparatus	9,983
Education and Entertainment	9,053
Cutlery, Machinery and Tools	8,520

</td></tr>
</table>

Source: Landor Associates | *Source: Thomson & Thomson*

FIGURE 15-1   Best-known brand names and the top ten categories of trademark applications
SOURCE: *Wall Street Journal,* November 29, 1988.

be considered blasphemous in some African countries. While black symbolizes death or mourning for Americans and Europeans, white has the same connotation in Japan and other Asian nations.[3]

Many products are evaluated by consumers in light of their country of origin. Indeed, a great deal of research has been conducted on this topic by a number of marketers. This research has shown that products from the Soviet Union, for example, are seldom rated as being stylish, whereas products from France or Germany are expected to be well-designed.

Different markets have different legal criteria and standards for products. Some of these are stan-

[3] Ibid.

dards for safety and content purity. Others have differing requirements regarding labeling. For example, in some countries all contents must be indicated on the package or the source of the contents must be delineated. Other countries may have limits on the types or sources of goods imported into the country, or restrictions regarding the use of brand names or the recognition of copyrights from other countries.

Through an exhaustive analysis of these attributes of foreign market environments, the marketing program can determine the appropriate mix of products for each foreign market. This mix is the variety or assortment of products offered in each quality and price. Thus, a firm might have several established lines that it markets in different locations according to the local needs and desires.

In determining the appropriate product line, a firm also takes into consideration the position of the product in its life cycle. For example, a consumer good in the stage of maturity for domestic home markets may be ripe for introduction into a new market that lags behind home markets in development, but would be expected to behave similarly over time.

Product Strategies

A multinational corporation has three different alternatives in targeting the foreign market. It can either extend its product line, or adapt or create an entirely new line of products for the market.

In product extension, a firm markets the same products abroad as it does at home, in the expectation that tastes and demands are similar enough to guarantee consumer acceptance. This product strategy is generally used when research determines that crucial characteristics of the domestic and international target markets are similar.

In product adaptation, a firm modifies its existing product line to take into account the cultural, legal, or economic differences between domestic and foreign markets. For example, product colors might be switched, electrical specifications might be modified to accommodate different voltages, or measurements might be changed to the metric

system. Automobiles sold in countries where motorists drive on the left side of the road such as England and Japan, must be adapted to a right-hand drive.

The third product strategy is to create a new product specifically for a targeted international market. The product might be within a firm's area of expertise, but is not included in its existing product line. For example, a form of transportation used in Barbados and other Caribbean nations and tropical locales is the moke, a vehicle that resembles a cross between a jeep and a golf cart. This gasoline-powered vehicle is open to the elements but is smaller than conventional vehicles, seats four, and is perfectly suited to the needs of tourists for transportation over short distances on narrow island roads.

Once a firm has made the crucial decisions regarding the appropriate product mix, it needs to decide what message should be communicated about that product and how it should be delivered in its new markets. A firm has many alternatives regarding the content of its promotion message. It can either extend its message from existing markets or adapt its message to the target market, which yields a scenario of five different overall product and promotion strategies for the international enterprise.[4] Their use depends on the features of the product, its expected benefits for buyers, its expected functional use, and its competitive position against other products. These five methods are product extension/message extension; product extension/message adaptation; product adaptation/message extension; product adaptation/message adaptation; and new product.

The easiest method is marketing the same product with the same message. This method of product extension/message extension works well when there are few differences between domestic and foreign markets and the product is used for the same purposes. It is also the most profitable, because no additional expenses are incurred for adaptations to individual market areas. Examples of this type of strategy are those used by soft-drink

---

[4] Keegan 1969.

manufacturers in world markets who are marketing the same product, a nonalcoholic beverage, which is used for the same purposes, quenching thirst (see Perspective 15–2).

In some instances, a firm might market the same product in a foreign target market, but that prod-uct may be used for a different function or purpose, and the message regarding its attributes must be adapted for the target market. In such a product extension/message adaptation strategy, a company merely changes the message communicated to its consumers. For example, goods that might be con-

---

PERSPECTIVE 15–2   Coca-Cola Plans a New Ad Campaign in Its International Marketing Effort

ATLANTA—Using its first new international advertising pitch in six years, Coca-Cola Co. plans to roll out a campaign to nearly 100 countries.

The theme, "You Can't Beat the Feeling," already in use in the U.S. for the past 15 months, will replace "Coke is it!" overseas.

In addition to new radio and print adds, the international campaign has more than 12 television commercials—the most Coke has ever produced for the overseas market in one year. McCann Erickson Inc., part of Interpublic Group of Cos., will shepherd the project for Coke through its branches world-wide, with help from some affiliated agencies.

"We don't change campaigns easily or quickly," says Ira C. Herbert, Coke's executive vice president. The "Can't Beat the Feeling" ad campaign helped raise awareness of the company's U.S. flagship Coca-Cola Classic 50% this year over 1987, Coke said. And it thinks the campaign will do much of the same the world over.

The people who push archrival Pepsi aren't so sure. "It may be tough to export the current campaign internationally," says Bill Katz, senior vice president, management representative, for Omnicom Group Inc's BBDO, the ad agency that handles the PepsiCo Inc. account. Mr. Katz says his agency's data shows "Can't Beat the Feeling" has neither done exceptionally well nor exceptionally poorly in the U.S. compared with some recent Coke campaigns.

Although such things are tough to quantify, Coke's advertising strategies lately have been overshadowed by those of Pepsi, industry executives and marketers have said. Pepsi has pursued what it calls "big event" marketing, using highly visible events such as boxing championships or the America's Cup race, and attention-getting people such as Michael Jackson and Mike Tyson.

While conceding that Coke outmuscles Pepsi overseas, outselling it in some markets nine to one, Mr. Katz believes Coke's current U.S. campaign has its shortcomings. " 'Can't Beat the Feeling' is an ethereal thought," the competing ad executive says. "What is the feeling? Why can't you beat it? It just doesn't express anything."

The positive results of Coke's research in eight countries abroad, though, have made Mr. Herbert confident the theme will last the five to seven years typical of successful Coke campaigns. By the middle of next year, Coke said the initial TV spot, featuring a variety of young and old people dancing to the upbeat "Can't Beat the Feeling" song, will be seen by two billion people world-wide. The company will alter the commercial for certain markets. One version of the ad, called "Dance," will be shown in the Caribbean, Africa and the South Pacific with the tune played in reggae style, and with more blacks appearing in the shot.

Not surprisingly, a pitch with a trendy phrase like "Can't Beat the Feeling" needs to be tailored here and there to work in foreign tongues. In

SOURCE: Michael J. McCarthy, *Wall Street Journal*, December 12, 1988.

Japan, for instance, the spots will say the equivalent of "I feel Coke." In Italy, "Unique sensation." In Chile, "The Feeling of Life."

West Germany proved a problem. No translation really worked, so the ad's lyrics will be in German, but because the country has a relatively large bilingual audience, the last line will be in English.

Despite the wide cultural differences a global market presents, Coke believes its core target consumers—12- to 24-year-olds—are becoming increasingly homogenous. Because of the widening availability of commercial television worldwide, says Mr. Herbert, "a German teenager is interested in the same kinds of things as the guy from Peoria."

So, says Jack Morrison, Coke's vice president, creative services, as Coke executives kick around ad themes these days, the big question is: "Will the idea travel?"

sidered luxury items used to pursue leisure activities in one market might be necessities in another. For example, bicycles, motor scooters, and cross-country skis might be touted for leisure use in one country, but as being vehicles of basic transportation in another.

In product adaptation/message extension, the product is changed but the message is extended. This strategy is effective in markets where the product serves the same functional use but under different environmental conditions, where products must be slightly adapted to suit local tastes. Examples are fast foods that require different menus or recipes, or vehicles with different tires designed to suit the physical conditions of road in different markets. This strategy has the advantage of establishing a consistent product image across markets and standardization of the communication message with its associated cost savings.

In product adaptation/message adaptation, both the product and the message are changed to meet conditions in foreign target markets where both the characteristics of the market and the use of the product differ from those in domestic spheres. Because the product is put to a different use in the foreign market, it follows that its message differs from that used at home. Under this strategy, however, the firm may still realize some cost benefit in using the same basic research and development or production costs if several of the product attributes are similar.

Developing a new product specifically for new markets generally requires communications designed specifically to suit the international market. Sometimes, however, the firm may be able to extend a message if the product developed is serving a slightly different function but one similar to its domestic product line. While this new product strategy is the most expensive to follow, it may ultimately yield success in the form of high sales because the firm has developed a product that meets the needs of customer in the target market.

Promotion Decisions

As with product decisions, the development of appropriate promotional efforts raises the question of standardization or adaptation. Promotion involves reaching potential consumers and providing them with information on the product's existence, attributes, and the needs it satisfies. The promotional mix, which includes advertising, personal selling, and sales promotions, must create a relationship between a firm and its customers, as well as enhance long-term sales potential and consumer confidence in the product and the firm (see Perspective 15–3). Naturally, the more this promotional program can be standardized, the greater the potential savings to the firm because of achieved efficiencies.

Once a firm has established its target market and defined its characteristics, it then decides on its communications message and which promotional tools and media will be most effective in

PERSPECTIVE 15-3   The Revenge of Big Yellow

Throughout the 1980s, Eastman Kodak looked like just one more fat-and-unhappy American company incapable of defending itself against a Japanese onslaught. Fuji Photo Film attacked the American and European markets, where for decades Kodak had enjoyed a lucrative dominance in colour film. It squeezed Kodak's margins, and forced it into a divisive and not always successful panic to slash costs. "Big Yellow," as Kodak is known on Wall Street because of its bright yellow boxes of film, received the thumbs down from investors. Its share price underperformed the market for years, prompting rumours of eventual break-up.

Then Kodak struck back. Its executives in Rochester, New York, admitted to themselves that their company faced a global challenge from Fuji that would only grow. They decided to invade their rival's home market. Since re-entering the Japanese market in 1984, Kodak's local operation has grown from a pokey office housing 15 people to a business with 4,500 employees, a fancy headquarters in Tokyo, a corporate laboratory in nearby Yokohama, manufacturing plants and dozens of affiliated companies. Meanwhile, Kodak's sales in Japan have soared sixfold, to an estimated $1.3 billion this year. All this has been achieved against fierce resistance from Fuji and Konica, the entrenched Japanese film suppliers.

Kodak's push into the Japanese market has not been cheap. Its Japanese operations are now making an operating profit, but it may be years before they pay back the $500m spent to build them up. But Kodak spotted that the Japanese market is the world's second largest. It judged that its invasion would put Fuji on the defensive, forcing it to divert resources from overseas in order to defend itself at home, where it had enjoyed a 70% share of the market in colour-film. Some of Fuji's best executives have now been pulled back to Tokyo. Fuji's domestic margins have been squeezed. Fuji has proved as vulnerable to attack in Japan as Kodak was in America.

Kodak has been selling photographic materials in Japan since 1889. But after the second world war the American occupation forces persuaded most American firms, including Kodak, to leave Japan to give war-torn local industry a chance to recover. Kodak handed over the marketing of its products to Japanese distributors. Over the next four decades Fuji gained its 70% share of the Japanese market, and then launched its export drive. Konica, a latecomer, grabbed 20% of domestic sales, leaving Kodak and a handful of European firms to share a miserable 10%.

By 1984 repeated rounds of trade negotiations had dismantled most of the postwar barriers protecting the Japanese film market. Kodak set out to make its yellow-packaged boxes as familiar and friendly to Japanese customers as any local product. Its strategy was to boost:

- **Distribution.** Kodak realised that it had to get control of its own distribution and marketing channels. "Using a trading company helps at the start," says Mr. Albert Seig, the president of Kodak's Japanese subsidiary, "but few trading companies take a strategic view." Rather than go it alone, Kodak established a joint venture with its distributor, Nagase Sangyo, an Osaka-based trading company specialising in chemicals. Kodak won the support of Nagase's 1,500 employees with two years of patient wooing.
- **Local investment.** To nurture relations with its suppliers, Kodak also took equity stakes in them. It now has 20% of Chinon Industries, a supplier of 35mm cameras, videocamera lenses, printers and other computer accessories which Kodak sells under its own label. Kodak has acquired a good deal of manufacturing know-how from Chinon, and is expected to increase its holding in

SOURCE: *The Economist*, November 10, 1990, page 77.

it still further. When Kodak needed to hire 100 systems engineers quickly, it invested in Nippon Systems House. Likewise, Kodak Imagica, a photo-finisher that provides developing facilities around Japan, is 51% owned by Kodak. Kodak Information Systems, formerly part of a microfilm and electronic-imaging equipment supplier called Kusuda, is now a wholly-owned subsidiary.

- **Promotion.** At a time when Fuji and Konica were committed to heavy spending on promotion abroad, Kodak spent three times more than both of them combined on advertising in Japan. It erected mammoth $1m neon signs as landmarks in many of Japan's big cities. Its sign in Sapporo, Hokkaido, is the highest in the country. It sponsored sumo wrestling, judo, tennis tournaments and even the Japanese team at the 1988 Seoul Olympics, a neat reversal of Fuji's 1984 coup when it won the race to become the official supplier to the Los Angeles Olympics.

Kodak's cheekiest ploy was to spend $1m on an airship emblazoned with its logo. It cruised over Japanese cities for three years, mischievously circling over Fuji's Tokyo headquarters form time to time. To Fuji's chagrin, Japanese newspapers gleefully picked up the story. The Japanese firm was forced to spend twice as much bringing its own airship back from Europe for just two months of face-saving promotion in Tokyo.

Half of all Japanese consumers can now recognise Kodak' goods instantly. This brand awareness has helped Kodak grow in Japan at about twice the pace of Fuji or Konica. Kodak's share of sales to amateur photographers has grown by a steady 1% each year for the past six years. Kodak now has a 15% slice of that market and is expected to overtake second-place Konica within the next few years. Kodak's success in Tokyo has been even more impressive. It now has 35% of the amateur market there, even though amateur photography is not Kodak's biggest business in Japan. Medical x-ray film and photographic supplies to the graphic arts and publishing industries are bigger. In these markets Kodak's share reaches 85%.

Kodak's counter-attack has been possible only because of an abrupt change in attitude back in Rochester. Kodak has shed the worst of its fabled parochialism, even though the parent company still has no foreigners on its main board. Technically brilliant, the company had become complacent and slipshod in marketing. It was not until 1984 that Kodak started printing in Japanese on its packaging in Japan—and not until 1988 that it launched a film (Kodacolor Gold) that offered the more garish colours which Japanese consumers prefer.

Today Kodak thinks just like a Japanese company—at least in Japan. Apart from a small unit headed by Mr. Seig which liaises with Kodak's headquarters, the rest of the local subsidiary is entirely Japanese, complete with a Japanese boss and Japanese management. There are only 30 foreigners among Kodak's 4,500 people in Japan. So thoroughly Japanese has Kodak become that it even has its own *keiretsu*—a family of firms with cross-holdings in one another. And so thoroughly has it been accepted that some of Kodak's largest business customers are asking that Kodak take a small equity stake in them too. That is a significant gesture of both market anticipation and good-will. The global battle with Fuji will continue, but it is now being waged on both sides of the world.

Snapshots

1989	Eastman Kodak	Fuji Photo Film
Sales, $bn	18.4	6.7
Net profit, $bn	0.5	0.6
Net profit, 1985–89 annual growth, %	−4.4	6.0
Return on assets, %	3.5	6.3
Number of employees	137,800	19,000

SOURCES: Morgan Stanley Capital International; Company reports

communicating that message. Great care must be taken to ensure that the content of the message is appropriate to different cultures. Mistakes in this area, such as inappropriate brand names or advertising copy, are very expensive, embarrassing, and unfortunately, all too frequent. For example, General Motors attempted to market its Nova (literally "star") automobile in Mexico without considering that the name when spoken could be interpreted as "nova", which means "no go" in Spanish. Similarly, Coca-Cola experienced difficulties in China in attempts to market its product under a brand name designed to be the equivalent of the English pronunciation of "Coca-Cola," but the Chinese characters translated literally into "bite the wax tadpole."[5]

Promotional Tools

The tools used in promotion include advertising, personal selling, sales promotions, publicity, and public relations.

Advertising methods are similar around the world, primarily because they are based on those developed in the advertising industry in the United States and focus on print, television, and radio advertising. The actual advertising programs may differ, however, because they are directly connected to reaching consumers by addressing their specific cultural values and needs. Where possible, international firms attempt to standardize their advertising in order to achieve savings. Some companies, for example, create a logo that is used internationally, such as McDonald's golden arches.

While companies may wish to develop an advertising program that can be carried across borders, they must be attuned to differences between cultures in order to reach the proper market and deliver the appropriate message. In Japan, for example, earthier advertisements are permitted than in the United States, and television and print advertisements include bathroom humor and sexual frankness, such as topless models. Similarly,

products banned from being advertised in the United States are advertised in Japan. Imagine the shock of a Westerner encountering explicit ads for such products as tampons, laxatives, hemorrhoid medicines, toilet bowl cleaners, and condoms.[6]

Similarly, an international promotion planner must be apprised of the availability of different types of media in each market. A television campaign suitable for markets in developed countries, where many people own sets, would not reach many potential consumers in poor, developing countries where TV sets are rare. Countries also vary in the availability of their print advertising sources and radio programming and the number of stations. Thus, advertising programs must be developed with the assistance of someone knowledgeable about the available advertising channels in the overseas market. This person helps to identify appropriate media for use in each country and avoid potential problems and mistakes because of cultural insensitivity to the meaning of colors, symbols, and nonverbal and verbal messages being delivered to the buying public or to the use of media. For example, in India owls do not connote wisdom as they do in the United States; they indicate bad luck. In land-poor and urban Hong Kong, consumers could not identify with the Marlboro man's riding the range on horseback. Adaptation of the copy showing him as a stylized urban cowboy with a pick-up truck was found to be far more relevant to consumers.

On-site resources can also prevent companies from choosing inappropriate media. For example, billboards cannot be used in parts of the Middle East, not because of cultural considerations, but merely because under local weather conditions an outdoor advertisement would last less than two weeks.[7]

Personal Selling

Another promotion tool used by international marketers is that of personal selling, where indi-

[5] Ricks 1983.

[6] Damon Darlin. 1980. "Japanese Ads Take Earthiness to Levels Out of This World." *Wall Street Journal* (August 30): 11.
[7] Ricks 1983.

vidual salespeople communicate the qualities and characteristics of the products to prospective customers. The use of personal selling by firms depends on a number of factors. One of these is product type. Generally personal selling is used more for industrial products, which are purchased by agents for companies or governmental concerns in larger numbers, than for consumer products which rely on mass merchandizing to stimulate high volumes of sales. An exception is Avon, which has successfully used its own version of personal selling to promote the sale of its lines of cosmetics, fragrances, jewelry, and gifts to customers around the world.

The use of personal selling also depends on the resource characteristics of the target country. In some nations where the costs of labor are low, firms might find it more cost-effective to employ hundreds of sales representatives than to buy expensive and limited air time on a federally controlled television station or attempt to reach a highly illiterate consumer population through media advertising. Still, the use of personal selling may be difficult or impossible in other countries, where street addresses or doorbells are not to be found or where such intrusive hard-sell methods are not welcome.

Even with personal selling, firms attempt to standardize their programs by using the same training programs and recruiting for their sales forces around the world. Indeed, some firms attempt to establish an international sales force in the hope of achieving strategic advantages over competitors. For example, Steelcase, Inc., a multinational firm and distributor of office furniture headquartered in Grand Rapids, Michigan, trains its global sales force using the same basic program with only slight modifications to accommodate differences between countries. The company believes that this training provides for a uniform sales culture and the generation of additional business opportunities, such as approaching sales prospects working for multinational firms at several locations at the same time. For example, if a sales representative for Steelcase meets with a multinational's purchasing officer for the domestic location, the represen-

tative's counterpart can be meeting simultaneously with equipment buyers for the firm's foreign subsidiaries in overseas locations. An added benefit to the firm is that a consistent training program allows Steelcase to integrate its sales approaches and strategies and coordinate sales activity around the globe.[8]

Sales Promotions

Sales promotions are those activities pursued by a firm in an attempt to generate interest in the company's products, greater levels of sales, and enhanced distributor effectiveness. Some of the most popular promotional efforts are those that involve contests or sweepstakes. Other promotions include company sponsorship of sporting or cultural events or participation in trade shows. Sales promotions also come in the form of cents-off coupons on company products, in-store samples and demonstrations of products, and point-of-purchase displays designed to catch the attention of shoppers.

As with the other tools of the promotional mix, these efforts may be constrained by foreign legal requirements, such as limitations on premium amounts and prior government approval of discounts. Some countries may not allow companies to give free gifts. Other constraints may come from the sociocultural aspects of the target market. For example, it may not be worth a company's effort to attempt to stage store demonstrations if the product is sold to consumers in small rural markets rather than in supermarkets. Still, sales promotions may be effective in those markets that have limited opportunities for utilization of the other promotion tools.

Publicity and Public Relations

Publicity and public relations refer to a firm's relationship with entities in its markets other than the buyers of its product, which include noncon-

---

[8] Flynn 1987.

suming members of society as well as agents from the various arms of government. Public relations programs are put in place to allow the company a method of communicating about itself, not merely about its products. Thus, public relations departments generally communicate with the press about the activities of the firm, including work with consumer groups and corporate charitable programs, such as scholarship programs or dollar contributions to local charities.

Pricing Decisions

Pricing is crucial to the success of any marketing program. An overpriced product may fail to attract customers, and an underpriced product may lower profitability. Pricing must therefore be carefully balanced to achieve the optimum level of sales and revenue. The optimum level can, of course, depend upon the corporate objective, which can vary from maximizing profit to maximizing market share.

Thus, a company may wish to lower prices in order to achieve maximum competitiveness or market share in individual markets, or it may wish to see high prices and, in turn, higher sales revenues figures on its balance sheet. In other situations, a company might be concerned about the relationship between prices charged and taxes payable in high-tax countries. Therefore, an international corporation must review and establish its pricing policies in light of overall short-term and long-term strategic objectives. Consequently, price-setting is customarily carried out as a function at corporate headquarters.

Pricing is a difficult part of the international marketing mix to administer because of its complexities. While a firm may prefer to charge the same price for its goods in all markets, the differences between these markets frequently indicate a need to set different prices in different locales. For example, a company determines an appropriate price for its goods as they are exported across borders. This price would not be appropriate, however, for goods produced by offshore subsidiaries

because of differences in relative costs of labor and resources, competitive forces, governmental regulations, and even market strategies. A firm, therefore, would pursue a course where goods are priced according to the exigencies of the local markets, not on an international basis.

Pricing Methods

An international marketer considers several crucial factors in determining the appropriate price structure. These factors fall into three general categories—the strategic objectives of the firm, the costs involved in the production of goods, and the competitive forces interacting in the market in relation to consumer demand. The goal of the multinational firm is to develop a competitive pricing structure that will provide for both short-term and long-term profitability, as well as for some flexibility to allow for individual differences between markets.

COST-BASED PRICING METHODS

Some pricing methods begin with production costs as a determination point. In cost-plus pricing, an additional amount is added to the cost of production to determining appropriate pricing at the next level of distribution. The cost-plus method has the advantages that it is simply administered once all related costs of production are identified. It does not, however, take into account the competitive environment in which the goods are to be sold.

Determination of costs is often also achieved through the use of average cost pricing, in which the firm identifies both the variable and fixed costs of production. Variable costs are those that vary with the levels of production. For example, labor or raw materials used in the manufacture of goods are variable costs, while fixed costs are those that do not change regardless of production levels. Some fixed costs are rent, plant and equipment, and basic overhead costs. Through an examination of its cost structure, a firm can determine its average variable costs and average fixed costs to determine a total cost figure upon which prices can be based according to expected levels of production.

Another easy method of price-setting is using target return levels in setting prices. In this method, a company wants to achieve a specific return level in relation to costs or to the original investment. Thus, a fixed percentage or level of monetary return is added to the total costs of the product to determine its ultimate price.

The pricing of goods produced for export must also take into account added costs from their being produced in one country and transported to another. Price escalation in the context of exports refers to the additional costs associated with the movement of the goods from the domestic manufacturer to the foreign consumer, which involves several intermediaries. The escalation occurs because at each level a percentage markup is taken against not only the original factory price, but the aggregate of all markups as well.

These cost-based pricing methods have the distinct drawback of being focused on short-term objectives and of being inflexible. They are often not integrated into a strategic plan and may or may not provide for a company's long-term benefit by providing for future expenses. For example, cost-based pricing may cover research and development prior to a product's introduction, but it may be insufficient to fund ongoing research essential to the future strength of the company. In addition, such a pricing program may not allow the firm or subsidiary the flexibility necessary to meet the demand or competition in the market.

Demand is, in fact, an important determinant of appropriate prices to be charged in various markets because in market economies, especially for interchangeable commodities, it is the market that ultimately sets the price or value of goods to consumers. Elasticities of demand in relation to income are an important characteristic of markets. Similarly, demand is affected by the prices charged for goods. Some products are highly sensitive to price, and an increase can result in an equal or larger decrease in demand. Other products are not price sensitive and experience no changes in demand regardless of price shifts. It is

important, therefore, for international marketers to have a feel for the competitive relationship between prices and demand in foreign marketing environments in order to determine appropriate price levels.

Many firms price their goods entirely in relation to the prices charged within the market by competitors, which is especially true for smaller companies that follow the moves of the market leaders in oligopolistic markets, where a few large firms hold the largest portion of the market for certain goods or products. Other firms meet competitive challenges by using factors other than prices, such as offering exemplary service or stressing other attributes of the total product package.

Some firms use pricing in order to achieve strategic or marketing objectives, deemphasizing the importance of production costs in setting prices. For example, some firms attempt to reap high profits from their markets; they set high prices for new products to cash in on their novelty value and the fact that competitive products are not yet available. Alternatively, the firm may use pricing to gain market penetration at the expense of profits. In this method, the firm intentionally keeps prices low in order to capture large portions of the market, allowing room for increasing prices once its position is firmly entrenched in the foreign market. Care must be taken in using this approach to avoid being charged by countries with trade actions based on accusations of dumping or predatory pricing.

Dumping, which is considered an unfair trade practice, occurs when exporting nations purposefully underprice their goods for foreign markets only to displace domestic competition and gain market share, with the ultimate objective of raising prices when that position is well established. Dumping pricing differs from market-penetration pricing in that it is lower than the price the exporter charges for the same goods in its own markets or is less than the costs of production.

TRANSFER PRICING

Transfer pricing is a specific concern of multinational firms with production facilities and subsidiaries in many different parts of the world, and is the determination of appropriate prices to be charged between different branches of the same firm that are conducting business between each other. This basic problem with these intracompany transfers is one of conflicting objectives by supplier subsidiaries and recipient subsidiary branches. The supplier wishes to charge the branch operations the same price it charges other purchasers in order to boost sales revenues and profit determinations on its balance sheet. By the same token, manufacturing subsidiaries receiving the goods also wish to put their balance sheet in the best light and look for the lowest possible cost for input resources or goods, and greater flexibility in using costs to determine competitive prices in local markets.

Four typical methods of assessing costs in transfer pricing are:

1. Charging the subsidiary buyer for the direct manufacturing costs in order to cover all production costs for the transferred goods.
2. Charging the subsidiary buyer cost-plus-expenses to adjust for production and fixed costs in the manufacture of the goods.
3. Charging prices in accordance with those the subsidiary buyer would pay for the same goods in local markets.
4. Charging the subsidiary buyer according to arm's length, that is, quoting the subsidiary buyer the same price as for all customers. This method has the advantage of dispelling any suspicions that a firm is using pricing policies for any other purposes than for accounting properly for the transfer of goods and materials between different operating units of the same enterprise.

The objectives of the individual operating units in transfer pricing must also be considered in light of overall multinational corporate objectives. For example, a firm might want to support operations in specific locales by holding costs down until a certain level of market coverage or penetration is reached. In this case, a firm would direct that the transfer prices to the subsidiary be held to a minimum. Transfer pricing may also be used to achieve other objectives, such as shifting revenues from countries with high taxes to those with low taxes. For example, if a parent company in a high-tax country charged low prices on input goods for a subsidiary in a low-tax country, it could realize higher income in the second country and pay less tax, while keeping expenses high in the country with high tax rates. This practice may be illegal in some countries, as in the United States, where suspicion of the use of transfer pricing for tax evasion can lead to the Internal Revenue Service challenging a company's tax returns and determining tax liability using arm's length pricing.

Transfer pricing also can be used to circumvent restrictions by foreign governments on the repatriation of profits to the multinational parent or on the convertibility of currencies into the currency of the home country. In these situations, the parent artificially hikes the prices of transferred goods for the subsidiaries and their payment of these "costs" are happily received by a third arm of the company in a different location. Similarly, transfer pricing can be used to lower profits to avoid government pressure to reduce prices. Profits can be lowered to avoid concessions to the demands of labor to share in company profits.

International pricing is also affected by other factors in world markets. One major force is that governmental power over pricing that is exercised in order to achieve national or economic objectives. To achieve goals such as economic or production growth, nations sometimes intervene in the pricing process by levying duties or tariffs on goods and services entering their country and, in turn, raising their cost to importers. For example, the Irish government imposes an excise duty of 24 percent and a 20 percent value-added tax on imported new cars. These taxes mean that car prices in Ireland are at least 40 percent more than those in neighboring Great Britain and that the supply for cars falls far short of the demand.

Producers of goods within countries also might face government intervention in pricing through the establishment of price freezes, price subsidies, floors or ceilings on prices, or artificial limits for goods considered as satisfying basic or fundamental needs of the populace.

A second problem encountered by firms that vary their pricing procedures according to prices set by differing markets is that of grey market exports, which are situations where individuals take advantage of a firm's pricing policies that account for market variations in demand and acceptable prices. With gray market exports, goods are legally imported from the producing country into another country, and then are reexported to a third country where higher prices are charged for the same goods. Thus, because of pricing differences by the original firm, the exporters of the second country can compete successfully with the MNC in selling its own goods in foreign markets. These gray markets exist in many industrialized countries where currencies are strong and markets for goods are large. In the United States, for example, gray markets flourish in foreign-made consumer goods, such as watches or cameras.

Setting prices can also be affected by legal constraints in individual countries. In the United States, under the terms of antitrust laws, price-fixing or the administration of prices is illegal, but legal restrictions in other nations may differ on prices administered nationally or internationally.

Placement Decisions: Distribution of Products

The Importance of Placement

The marketing function of distribution involves the critical process of ensuring that the products of a firm reach the proper location for sale at the proper time and in proper quantity. Breaks in the distribution flow can have critical ramifications, in the form of disgruntled customers, spoiled or damaged goods, excessive costs, and lost sales.

Thus, the type of product being transported determines the appropriate method of distribution and choice of channel. For example, one of the companies of United Technologies manufactures refrigerated transportation containers for fresh produce in which temperatures must remain constant, or importers are faced with receiving, say, instead of bananas, a shipment of imported brown mush.

Distribution decisions are also of critical importance because they are often long-term in nature, involving the signing of contracts with transporters or equipment leasers or the development of expensive capital equipment or infrastructures, such as rail lines, wharfs, ports, docks, and loading facilities.

This process, difficult in domestic markets, grows more complicated in international environments because it has two stages. First, the international exporter must transport goods from the domestic production site to the foreign market, then establish methods of distribution for the goods within the foreign country.

Numerous players within distribution systems are required to get goods to market. The distribution chain begins with the producer of the goods and then generally flows through an intermediary in the form of a wholesaler or distributor, who in turn provides the retailer with his goods for sale. Other services provided in the distribution of goods are storage facilities, transportation to markets via rail, truck, barge, or plane, and insurance services for those goods being carried between nations.

This relatively simple scenario becomes much more complicated with the addition of the international component, at which point other people enter the act to facilitate these exchanges. There are freight forwarders, who see to the details of international transportation, and exporters and importers, who conduct their international trading as either agents or brokers. Sometimes these individuals take title to the goods and trade them on their own behalf (merchant middlemen); alternatively, they represent the firm's interests and arrange for the distribution of goods for a fee (agent middlemen). Other players in the distribution game are resident buyers who work in foreign markets to acquire goods, and foreign sales agents who sell a product line in international markets. These classifications are augmented by such entrants in the process as export management companies, which provide distribution services for firms under contract; buyers for exports, who actively seek merchandise for purchase by the principals they represent; and selling groups, such as those established in the United States under the terms of the Webb-Pomerane Act to promote trade. Some agents specialize and focus primarily on barter or countertrade agreements with nonmarket economy countries. Further down the chain, key players are those who deal directly with customers, such as a sales force, door-to-door salespersons, individual merchants, and the customers themselves.

Factors Involved in Distribution Decisions

Distribution choices depend on several factors. One is the nature of the product. Is it perishable or fragile or a product that will require after-sales service? Might it be better distributed by an authorized company dealer? Another consideration is the degree of control over distribution. Greater control over the distribution process requires greater involvement by a firm in terms of time, money, and energy.

Another factor is costs. Whatever mix a firm wishes to employ may be constrained by the availability of middlemen or channels of distribution, by physical limitations imposed by the characteristics of the country, or by infrastructural deficiencies in the country, which limit types and methods of usable distribution modes. In some countries foreign firms do not have access to all distribution modes, as in Japan, where the distribution system is controlled predominantly by sogo shosha, enormous general trading companies that control much of the import and export trade.

The choice of a distribution program is also constrained or defined by the nature of the outlets for goods or services, and nations differ quite extensively in these frameworks. While some countries, such as the United States, have a variety of small and large retail outlets, other countries, such as Japan, have an enormous number of mom-and-pop retail outlets which provide Japanese customers with individualized service. In France, a U.S. cosmetics company made a strategic mistake by assuming that its products would be appropriately distributed through a chain store's sole rights to distributorship. Its assumption was wrong, because in France cosmetics are traditionally distributed by perfumers, small retailers who specialize in cosmetics and are considered the ultimate arbiters of fashion.

The developmental level of a nation also affects its distribution resources and networks. A lack of refrigerated methods of transportation will limit the marketing for frozen goods or fresh produce. Similarly, income levels might support the air-freight delivery of live lobsters in rich countries, while poorer countries rely on slow delivery by boat of less-exotic foodstuffs.

Distribution decisions can be even more complex in less-developed countries where distribution channels are dominated by specific ethnic groups within the country. This control, called ethnodomination, means that a multinational firm must be aware of and gain access to the members of the distribution channel in order to get its goods to retail outlets. Examples of ethnodomination are the Chinese ethnic groups who control the wholesale trade of vanilla and cloves in Madagascar, rice distribution and milling in Vietnam, retail trade in the Philippines and Kampuchea, and poultry and pineapple production in Malaya.

The standardization debate on international marketing strategies was raised in the 1960s among members of the marketing community who put forth that the world was developing into an enormous global market where few differences existed between consumers from various countries in their tastes, standards of living, and buying behavior. Others discovered, however, that crucial differences between countries militated against such

TABLE 15-1

Obstacles to Standardization in International Marketing Strategies

	Elements of Marketing Program	
Factors Limiting Standardization	Product Design	Pricing
Market characteristics Physical environment	Climate Product use conditions	
Stage of economic and industrial development	Income levels Labor costs in relation to capital costs	Income levels
Cultural factors	"Custom and tradition" Attitudes toward foreign goods	Attitudes toward bargaining
Industry conditions Stage of product life cycle in each market	Extent of product differentiation	Elasticity of demand
Competition	Quality levels	Local costs Prices of substitutes
Marketing institutions Distributive system	Availability of outlets	Prevailing margins
Advertising media and agencies		
Legal restrictions	Product standards Patent laws Tariffs and taxes	Tariffs and taxes Antitrust laws Resale price maintenance

globalization of markets and the standardization of the marketing function. Table 15–1 outlines obstacles to standardization in world markets.

Indeed, many have found that standardization efforts are foiled primarily by the vast diversities among consumers in world markets. Indeed, there may be a class of world consumers that con-

sists of well-traveled and sophisticated people who are receptive to universal advertising and global themes.[9] Still, this group of consumers is very small and the majority of consumers, internationally, varies enormously in their national identi-

[9] Ryans 1969.

TABLE 15-1 *(continued)*
Obstacles to Standardization in International Marketing Strategies

	Elements of Marketing Program	
Distribution	Sales Force	Advertising and promotion Branding and Packaging
Customer mobility	Dispersion of customers	Access to media
		Climate
Consumer shopping patterns	Wage levels, availability of manpower	Needs for convenience rather than economy
		Purchase quantities
Consumer shopping patterns	Attitudes toward selling	Language, literacy
		Symbolism
Availability of outlets Desirability of private brands	Need for missionary sales effort	Awareness, experience with products
Competitors' control of outlets	Competitors' sales forces	Competitive expenditures messages
Number and variety of outlets available	Number, size, dispersion of outlets	Extent of self-service
Ability to "force" distribution	Effectiveness of advertising, need for substitutes	Media availability, costs, overlaps
Restrictions on product lines	General employment restrictions	Specific restrictions on messages, costs
Resale price maintenance	Specific restrictions on selling	Trademark laws

ties, tastes and preferences, languages, and cultural environments. Thus, all facets of the marketing function are susceptible to failure because of improper attention to the differences between markets that are caused by differences between cultures.

Summary

The basic marketing functions of the four Ps—product, pricing, promotion, and place (distribution)—are similar for both domestic and international marketing. Because of the complexities and differences of cultural, legal, and political environments, international marketing becomes much more complex. Two crucial decisions facing the international marketer are the extent to which products are standardized or adapted to meet the needs and wants of the local consumer, and whether international marketing programs should be centralized or decentralized. Industrial products are more easily standardized, while consumer products generally require adaptation to meet local preferences. Management of international marketing programs tend to rely on corporate headquarters for overall strategy, research and development, brand names, and packaging, with the foreign subsidiary developing locally sensitive pricing, promotion, and distribution strategies. Extensive ongoing communication between headquarters and the foreign subsidiary, however, is crucial to effective coordination of the marketing program.

Five product-promotion strategies can be adopted to market the same product, an adapted product, or a totally new product using the same message or an adapted message specially designed for the foreign market.

While advertising methods are relatively similar throughout the world, actual promotional campaigns must be adapted to meet the product characteristics, cultural environment, and media availability in foreign markets. Personal-selling programs may be standardized, however, while other promotion tools, such as sales promotion and publicity, require adaptation to the local environment and must be responsive to legal constraints.

Various pricing methods, such as cost-plus and target-return, can be used, but consideration of long-term strategic objectives of MNCs and applicable governmental regulations should also be included in the development of an international pricing strategy. Distribution channels, their availability and limitations in different locations, and the extent to which the marketed product requires follow-up servicing and support can create a wide degree of variability when developing an international distribution policy.

Discussion Questions

1. What are the four Ps of marketing?
2. How does international marketing differ from solely domestic marketing?
3. What are the advantages of a standardized marketing strategy? What are the disadvantages?
4. What types of products are best suited to standardization?
5. How does the total product differ from the physical product?
6. Discuss the five basic strategies through which multinationals introduce and promote products in a foreign market.
7. Discuss the four major tools used in promotion. What are the types of concerns of an advertising manager in the MNC home office when developing a promotion strategy?
8. What is cost-plus pricing? Average cost-pricing?
9. How can transfer-pricing costs be assessed within a multinational corporation?
10. What factors should be considered when making distribution decisions?

Bibliography

Buzzell, Robert D. 1968. "Can You Standardize Multinational Marketing?" *Harvard Business Review* (November/December): p. 74.

Douglas, S. P., and Yoram Wind. 1987. "The Myth of Globalization." *Columbia Journal of World Business* (Winter): 19–29.

Flynn, Brian H. 1987. "The Challenges of Multinational Sales Training." *Training and Development Journal* (November): 54–5.

Foxman, Ellen R., Patriya S. Tansuhaj, and John K. Wong. 1988. "Evaluating Cross-National Sales Promotion Strategy: An Audit Approach." *International Marketing Review* (Winter): 7–15.

Green, Robert T., W. H. Cunningham, and Isabella C. Cunningham. 1975. "The Effectiveness of Standardized Global Advertising." *Journal of Advertising* 4: 25–30.

Jain, Subhash C. 1990. *International Marketing Management*, 3rd ed., Boston: Kent.

———. 1989. "Standardization of International Marketing Strategy: Some Research Hypotheses." *Journal of Marketing* (January): 70–79.

JAIN, SUBHASH C., AND LEWIS R. TUCKER, JR. 1986. *International Marketing: Managerial Perspectives,* 2nd ed. Boston: Kent.

KAHLER, RUEL. 1983. *International Marketing,* 5th ed. Cincinnati: South-Western.

KEEGAN, WARREN J. 1969. "Multinational Product Planning: Strategic Alternatives." *Journal of Marketing* (January): 58–62.

LEAVITT, THEODORE. 1983. "The Globalization of Markets." *Harvard Business Review* (May/June): 92–102.

MUSKIE, EDMUND S., AND DANIEL J. GREENWOOD III. 1988. "The Nestlé Infant Formula Audint Commission as a Model." *Journal of Business Strategy* (Spring): 19–23.

NAGASHIMA, AKIRA. 1970. "A Comparison of Japanese and U.S. Attitudes Toward Foreign Products." *Journal of Marketing* (January): 68–74.

———. "A Comparison 'Made-In' Product Image Survey Among Japanese Businessmen." *Journal of Marketing* (July): 95–100.

PEEBLES, D. M., AND J. K. RYANS. 1984. *Management of International Advertising: A Marketing Approach.* Newton, MA: Allyn & Bacon.

QUELCH, JOHN A., AND EDWARD J. HOFF. 1986. "Customizing Global Marketing." *Harvard Business Review* (May/June): 59–68.

REIERSON, CURTIS. 1967. "Attitude Changes Toward Foreign Products." *Journal of Marketing Research* (November): 385–387.

RICKS, DAVID A. 1983. *Big Business Blunders: Mistakes in Multinational Marketing.* Homewood, IL: Dow Jones-Irwin.

RYANS, JOHN K., JR. 1969. "Is It too Soon to Put a Tiger in Every Tank?" *Columbia Journal of World Business* (March/April): 69–75.

SAMIEE, SAEED. 1987. "Pricing in Market Strategies of U.S. and Foreign-Based Companies." *Journal of Business Research* (February): 17–30.

SIMMONDS, KENNETH. 1985. "Global Strategy: Achieving the Geocentric Ideal." *International Marketing Review* (Spring): 8–17.

SIMON-MILLER, FRANCOISE, ET AL. 1986. "World Marketing: Going Global or Acting Local? Five Expert Viewpoints." *Journal of Consumer Marketing* (Spring): 5–15.

TERPSTRA, VERN. 1985. *International Dimensions of Marketing,* 2nd. ed. Boston: Kent.

APPENDIX 15–1
A Checklist for Export Marketing

Market Potential

Segmentation	1. Are the ultimate consumers American tourists or foreign citizens?
	2. Are we tapping the burgeoning middle class in industrialized nations?
	3. Are our customers the wealthy elite in the underdeveloped countries?
	4. Are our buyers affiliates of our company?
Size of Market	1. How large is the sales potential?
	2. What volume could be sold at higher/lower prices?
	3. What sales potential do we estimate for the next few years?
Special Opportunities	1. Would differential pricing be noticed—and be objectionable?
	2. Do prices abroad fluctuate seasonally?
	3. Could some particular price policy foster trust and long-term relations?
	4. How does the delivered price relate to other elements of the marketing mix?

Marketing Mix

Individualizing and Adaptation	1. Should our product be modified (simplified or embellished) to increase its suitability for foreign markets?
	2. How should we position our product to gain for it the appropriate level of price perception?
	3. Could special packing or packaging enhance the value of our product?
	4. Would freight, customs duty, and so on be substantially lower for separate components to be assembled abroad?
	5. Is assembly abroad less expensive than in the United States?
Reducing the Buyer's Risk	1. Does our price include warranty service?
	2. How quickly and assuredly are spare parts available?
	3. Might feasibility studies cause our product to be specified?
	4. In the country of destination, at what stage of the product life cycle is our offering?
Buyer-Seller Relationship	1. How closely can we estimate what the buyer is willing to pay?
	2. What is our reputation for quality and commercial integrity?
	3. Have we avoided misunderstandings about measurement units such as "ton" and commercial terms such as "CIF"?
	4. Should our quotation include a cushion for later price concessions?

(continued)

Channel	1. At what point in the distribution process is our price compared with those of competitors?
	2. How many middle agents are in the distribution chain, and what functions do they perform?
	3. Can we reduce the cost of distribution?

Foreign Market Environment

Degree of Market Control	1. Is the price of our commodity determined through market institutions?
	2. How closely do we control the availabilities and prices of our line at the point of final sale?
Foreign Attitudes	1. How important is price in the purchasing decision?
	2. Is the prevalent business philosophy "low turnover–big markup"?
	3. Are high-priced goods subject to special tariff surcharges?
	4. What is the business culture with respect to haggling, price-fixing, and boycotting the price-cutters?
	5. Are price deals effective?
	6. In what ways are we affected by any foreign laws in margins, prices, price changes, intercompany pricing, and "most favored customer clause"?
Competition	1. In our line, how active is worldwide competition?
	2. Are the competitor's quotations valid?
	3. Is our price level encouraging foreign imitators?
Some Alternatives	1. What do we learn from foreign competitors' prices about manufacturing opportunities abroad?
	2. Have we considered licensing as an alternative to selling?
	3. Could multilateral transactions in foreign exchange of foreign merchandise make our product's final price more attractive?

Cost Considerations

Commercial Risks	1. What are the costs and risks of submitting a foreign quotation?
	2. Could our exported merchandise be shipped back to the United States and interfere with our domestic marketing?
Incremental Costs	1. Are foreign orders absorbing idle capacity?
	2. Are we disposing of excess inventory?
	3. Does potential foreign business warrant expansion that captures economics of scale?
	4. Are we pricing a product line, a single product, or a one-time opportunity?
	5. Have we separated our variable and fixed costs?
	6. Do foreign orders require special production changes, extra shifts, or other costly adjustments?

(continued)

7. What are the differential marketing and administrative costs of selling abroad?
8. What is the total impact of export sales on our costs?
9. How closely does the country of destination enforce its antidumping laws?

Special Risks and Opportunities

1. Have we costed out all possible modes of transportation?
2. Do our costs include insurance on our goods until we receive payment, even if the purchaser insists on insurance coverage?
3. Do our credit terms reflect various risks: (a) commercial, (b) inflation, (c) currency exchange rate, (d) blocking of remittances, (e) expropriation, (f) interest rate fluctuations?
4. Do export sales offer any tax advantages?
5. What is our profitability mix between original equipment and spare parts, initial order and reorders?

Administrative Considerations

Internal Organization

1. What are our objectives in international business?
2. What are our specific goals with respect to the present quotation?
3. Who (title and location) is authorized to quote a binding price?
4. What intrafirm conflicting interests regarding international marketing must be resolved?
5. Do our affiliates in different countries compete against each other?

Price Policy

1. What is our basic price policy (such as same FOB factory price to everybody)?
2. What is our stance toward competition—price higher, same, lower, ignored?
3. How flexible are we—to accommodate good customers, meet competition, offset new duties or changes in currency values?
4. How important is foreign business for us?
5. Could our foreign involvement harm our image domestically?

Procedures

1. Have we ensured compliance with applicable U.S. laws?
2. Do we use standard forms for preparing quotations?
3. Do our quotations have a time limit?
4. Do we formally review quotations accepted and rejected?

Intracompany Pricing

1. Is pricing a legal means of repatriating earnings?
2. Are we permitted to avoid foreign customs duties through high prices on raw materials and low prices on finished goods?
3. What is the influence of our intracountry pricing on income taxes in the United States and in the country of destination?
4. Are we quoting "arm's length" prices to our affiliates?

SOURCE: S.C. Jain, *International Marketing Management*, 3rd ed., Boston: Plus-Kent ©1990. Reprinted by permission.

APPENDIX 15–2
Do You Really Have a Global Strategy?

The threat of foreign competition preoccupies managers in industries from telecommunications to commercial banking and from machine tools to consumer electronics. Corporate response to the threat is often misdirected and ill-timed—in part because many executives don't fully understand what global competition is.

They haven't received much help from the latest analysis of this trend. One argument simply emphasizes the scale and learning effects that transcend national boundaries and provide cost advantages to companies selling to the world market. Another holds that world products offer customers the twin benefits of the low-cost and high-quality incentives for foreign customers to lay aside culture-bound product preferences.

According to both of these arguments, U.S. organizations should "go global" when they can no longer get the minimum volume needed for cost efficiency at home and when international markets permit standardized marketing approaches. If, on the other hand, they can fully exploit scale benefits at home and their international export markets are dissimilar, U.S. executives can safely adopt the traditional, country-by-country, multinational approach. So while Caterpillar views its battle with Komatsu in global terms, CPC International and Unilever may safely consider their foreign operations multidomestic.

After studying the experiences of some of the most successful global competitors, we have become convinced that the current perspective on global competition and the globalization of markets is incomplete and misleading. Analysts

are long on exhortation—"go international"—but short on practical guidance. Combine these shortcomings with the prevailing notion that global success demands a national industrial policy, a docile work force, debt-heavy financing, and forbearing investors, and you can easily understand why many executives feel they are only treading water in the rising tide of global competition.

World-scale manufacturing may provide the necessary armament, and government support may be a tactical advantage, but winning the war against global competition requires a broader view of global strategy. We will present a new framework for assessing the nature of the worldwide challenge, use it to analyze one particular industry, and offer our own practical guidelines for success.

THRUST & PARRY

As a starting point, let's take a look at what drives global competition. It begins with a sequence of competitive action and reaction:

- An aggressive competitor decides to use the cash flow generated in its home market to subsidize an attack on markets of domestically oriented foreign competitors.
- The defensive competitor then retaliates—not in its home market where that attack was staged—but in the foreign markets where the aggressor company is most vulnerable.[1]

As an example, consider the contest between Goodyear and Michelin. By today's definitions, the tire industry is not global. Most tire companies manufacture in and distribute for the local market. Yet Michelin, Goodyear, and Firestone are locked in a fiercely competitive—and very global—battle.

In the early 1970s, Michelin used its strong European profit base to attack Goodyear's American home market. Goodyear could fight back in the United States by reducing prices, increasing adver-

[1] See Craig M. Watson, "Counter-Competition Abroad to Protect Home Markets," *Harvard Business Review,* January-February 1982, page 40.

tising, or offering dealers better margins. But because Michelin would expose only a small amount of its worldwide business in the United States, it has little to lose and much to gain. Goodyear, on the other hand, would sacrifice margins in its largest market.

Goodyear ultimately struck back in Europe, throwing a wrench in Michelin's money machine. Goodyear was proposing a hostage trade. Michelin's long-term goals and resources allowed it to push ahead in the United States. But at least Goodyear slowed the pace of Michelin's attack and forced it to recalculate the cost of market share gains in the United States. Goodyear's strategy recognized the international scope of competition and parried Michelin's thrust.

Manufacturers have played out this pattern of cross-subsidization and international retaliation in the chemical, audio, aircraft engine, and computer industries. In each case international cash flows, rather than international product flows, scale economies, or homogeneous markets, finally determined whether competition was global or national. (For a detailed explanation, see the vignette on cross-subsidization.)

The Goodyear vs. Michelin case helps to distinguish among

- Global competition, which occurs when companies cross-subsidize national market share battles in pursuit of global brand and distribution positions.
- Global businesses, in which the minimum volume required for cost efficiency is not available in the company's home market.
- Global companies, which have distribution systems in key foreign markets that enable cross-subsidization, international retaliation, and world-scale volume.

Making a distinction between global competition and a global business is important. In traditionally global businesses, protectionism, and flexible manufacturing technologies are encouraging a shift back to local manufacturing. Yet competition remains global. Companies must distinguish

between the cost effectiveness based on off-shore sourcing and world-scale plants and the competitive effectiveness based on the ability to retaliate in competitors' key markets.

IDENTIFYING THE TARGET

Understanding how the global game is played is only the first step in challenging the foreign competitor. While the pattern of cross-subsidization and retaliation describes the battle, world brand dominance is what the global war is all about. And the Japanese have been winning it.

In less than 20 years, Canon, Hitachi, Seiko, and Honda have established world-wide reputations equal to those of Ford, Kodak, and Nestlé. In consumer electronics alone, the Japanese are present in or dominate most product categories.

Like the novice duck hunter who either aims at the wrong kind of bird or shoots behind his prey, many companies have failed to develop a well-targeted response to the new global competition. Those who define international competitiveness as no more than low-cost manufacturing are aiming at the wrong target. Those who fail to identify the strategic intentions of their global competitors cannot anticipate competitive moves and so often shoot behind the target.

To help managers respond more effectively to challenges by foreign companies, we have developed a framework that summarizes the various global competitive strategies (see Appendix Table 15-1). The competitive advantages to be gained from location, would-scale volume, or global brand distribution are arrayed against the three kinds of strategic intent we have found to be most prevalent among global competitors: (1) building a global presence, (2) defending a domestic position, and (3) overcoming national fragmentation.

Using this framework to analyze the world television industry, we find Japanese competitors building a global presence, RCA, GE, and Zenith of the United States defending domestic dominance, and Philips of the Netherlands and CSF Thomson of France overcoming national fragmentation. Each one uses a different complement of competitive weapons and pursues its own strate-

APPENDIX TABLE 15–1
A Global Competitive Framework

1965	Access volume		
		Response lag	Response lag
1970	Redefine cost-volume relationships		
		Match costs	
1975	Cross-subsidize to win the world		Reduce costs at national subsidiary
		Amortize world-scale investments	
1980	Contiguous segment expansion		Rationalize manufacturing
		Gain retaliatory capability	
1985			Shift locus of strategic responsibility
1990			

404 Functional Operations in International Business

gic objectives. As a result, each reaps a different harvest from its international activities.

By the late 1960s, Japanese television manufacturers had built up a large U.S. volume base by selling private-label TV sets. They had also established brand and distribution positions in small-screen and portable televisions—a market segment ignored by U.S. producers in favor of higher margin console sets.

In 1967, Japan became the largest producer of black-and-white TVs; by 1970, it had closed the gap in color sets. While the Japanese first used their cost advantages, primarily from low labor costs, they then moved quickly to invest in new process technologies, from which came the advantages of scale and quality.

Japanese companies recognized the vulnerability of competitive positions based solely on labor and scale advantages. Labor costs change as economies develop or as exchange rates fluctuate. The world's low-cost manufacturing location is constantly shifting: from Japan to Korea, then to Singapore and Taiwan. Scale-based cost advantages are also vulnerable, particularly to radical changes in manufacturing technology and creeping protectionism in export markets. Throughout the 1970s, Japanese TV makers invested heavily to create the strong distribution positions and brand franchises that would add another layer of competitive advantage.

Making a global distribution investment pay off demands a high level of channel utilization. Japanese companies force-fed distribution channels by rapidly accelerating product life cycles and expanding across contiguous product segments. Predictably, single-line competitors have often been blind-sided, and sleepy product-development departments have been caught short in the face of this onslaught. Global distribution is the new barrier to entry.

By the end of the decade, the Japanese competitive advantage had evolved from low-cost sourcing to world-scale volume and worldwide brand positions across the spectrum of consumer electronic products.

RCA AT HOME

Most American television producers believed the Japanese did well in their market simply because of their low-cost, high-quality manufacturing systems. When they finally responded, U.S. companies drove down costs, began catching up on the technology front, and lobbied heavily for government protection.[2] They thought that was all they had to do.

Some could not even do that; the massive investment needed to regain cost competitiveness proved too much for them and they left the television industry. Stronger foreign companies purchased others.

Those that remained transferred labor-intensive manufacturing offshore and rationalized manufacturing at home and abroad. Even with costs under control, these companies (RCA, GE, and Zenith) are still vulnerable because they do not understand the changing nature of Japanese competitive advantage. Even as American producers patted themselves on the back for closing the cost gap, the Japanese were cementing future profit foundations through investment in global brand positions. Having conceived of global competition on a product-by-product basis, U.S. companies could not justify a similar investment.

Having conceded non-U.S. markets, American TV manufacturers were powerless to dislodge the Japanese even from the United States.

While Zenith and RCA dominated the color TV business in the United States, neither had a strong presence elsewhere. With no choice of competitive venue, American companies had to fight every market share battle in the United States. When U.S. companies reduced prices at home, they subjected 100% of their sales volume to margin pressure. Matsushita could force this

---

[2] See John J. Nevin, "Can U.S. Business Survive Our Japanese Trade Policy?" *Harvard Business Review,* September-October 1978, p. 165.

price action, but only a fraction of it would be similarly exposed.

We do not argue that American TV manufacturers will inevitably succumb to global competition. Trade policy or public opinion may limit foreign penetration. Faced with the threat of more onerous trade sanctions or charges of predatory trade tactics, global competitors may forgo a fight to the finish, especially when the business in question is mature and no longer occupies center stage in the company's product plans. Likewise, domestic manufacturers, despite dwindling margins, may support the threatened business if it has important interdependencies with other businesses (as, for example, in the case of Zenith's TV and data systems business). Or senior management may consider the business important to the company's image (possible motivation for GE) for continuing television production.

The hope that foreign companies may never take over the U.S. market, however, should hardly console Western companies. TVs were no more than one loose brick in the American consumer electronics market. The Japanese wanted to knock down the whole wall. For example, with margins under pressure in the TV business, no American manufacturer had the stomach to develop its own videocassette recorder. Today, VCRs are the profitability mainstay for many Japanese companies. Companies defending domestic positions are often shortsighted about the strategic intentions of their competitors. They will never understand their own vulnerability until they understand the intentions of their rivals and then reason back to potential tactics. With no appreciation of strategic intent, defensive-minded competitors are doomed to a perpetual game of catch-up.

LOOSE BRICKS IN EUROPE, TOO

Philips of the Netherlands has become well known virtually everywhere in the world. Like other long-standing MNCs, Philips has always benefited from the kind of international distribution system that U.S. companies lack. Yet our evidence suggests that this advantage alone is not enough. Philips has its own set of problems in responding to the Japanese challenge.

Japanese color TV exports to Europe didn't begin until 1970. Under the terms of their licensing arrangements with European set makers, the Japanese could export only small-screen TVs. No such size limitation existed for Japanese companies willing to manufacture in Europe, but no more than half the output could be exported to the rest of Europe. Furthermore, because laws prohibited Japanese producers from supplying finished sets for private-label sale, they supplied picture tubes. So in 1979, although Europe ran a net trade deficit of only 2 million color televisions, the deficit in color tubes was 2.7 million units. By concentrating on such volume-sensitive manufacturing, Japanese manufacturers skirted protectionist sentiment while exploiting economies of scale gained from U.S. and Japanese experience.

Yet just as they had not been content to remain private-label suppliers in the United States, Japanese companies were not content to remain component suppliers in Europe. They wanted to establish their own brand positions. Sony, Matsushita, and Mitsubishi set up local manufacturing operations in the United Kingdom. When, in response, the British began to fear a Japanese takeover of the local industry, Toshiba and Hitachi simply found U.K. partners. In moving assembly from the Far East to Europe, Japanese manufacturers incurred cost and quality penalties. Yet they regarded such penalties as an acceptable price for establishing strong European distribution and brand positions.

If we contrast Japanese entry strategies in the United States and Europe, it is clear that the tactics and timetables differed. Yet the long-term strategic intentions were the same and the competitive advantage of Japanese producers evolved similarly in both markets. In both Europe and the United States, Japanese companies found a loose brick in the bottom half of the market structure—small-screen portables. And then two other loose bricks were found—the private-label business in the United States and picture tubes in Europe.

From these loose bricks, the Japanese built the sales volume necessary for investment in world-scale manufacturing and state-of-the-art product development; they gained access to local producers, who were an essential source of market knowledge. In Europe, as in the United States, Japanese manufactures captured a significant share of total industry profitability with a low-risk, low-profile supplier strategy; in so doing, they established a platform from which to launch their drive to global brand dominance.

REGAINING COST COMPETITIVENESS

Philips tried to compete on cost but had more difficulties than RCA and Zenith. First, the European TV industry was more fragmented than that of the United States. When the Japanese entered Europe, twice as many European as American TV makers fought for positions in national markets that were smaller than those in the United States.

Second, European governments frustrated the attempts of companies to use offshore sources or to rationalize production through plant closings, layoffs, and capacity reassignments. European TV makers turned to political solutions to solve competitive difficulties. In theory, the resulting protectionism gave them breathing space as they sought to redress the cost imbalance with Japanese producers. Because they were still confined to marginal, plant-level improvements, however, their cost and quality gap continued to widen. Protectionism reduced the incentive to invest in cost competitiveness; at the same time, the Japanese producers were merging with Europe's smaller manufacturers.

With nearly 3 million units of total European production in 1976, Philips was the only European manufacturer whose volume could fund the automation of manufacturing and the rationalization of product lines and components. Even though its volume was sufficient, however, Philip's tube manufacturing was spread across seven European countries. So it had to demonstrate (country by country, minister by minister, union by union) that the only alternative to protectionism, was to support the development of a Pan-European competi-

tor. Philips also had to wrestle with independent subsidiaries not eager to surrender their autonomy over manufacturing, product development, and capital investment. By 1982, it was the world's largest color TV maker and had almost closed the cost gap with Japanese producers. Even so—after more than ten years—rationalization plans are still incomplete.

Philips remains vulnerable to global competition because of the difficulties inherent in weaving disparate national subsidiaries into a coherent global competitive team. Low-cost manufacturing and international distribution give Philips two of the critical elements needed for global competition. Still needed is the coordination of national business strategies.

Philips' country managers are jealous of their autonomy in marketing and strategy. With their horizon of competition often limited to a single market, country managers are poorly placed to assess their global vulnerability. They can neither understand nor adequately analyze the strategic intentions and market entry tactics of global competitors. Nor can they estimate the total resources available to foreign competitors for local market share battles.

Under such management pressure, companies like Philips risk responding on a local basis to global competition. The Japanese can "cherry pick" attractive national markets with little fear that their multinational rival will retaliate.

WHAT IS CROSS-SUBSIDIZATION?

When a global company uses financial resources accumulated in one part of the world to fight a competitive battle in another, it is pursuing a strategy we call "cross-subsidization." Contrary to tried-and-true MNC policy, a subsidiary should not always be required to stand on its own two feet financially. When a company faces a large competitor in a key foreign market, it may make sense for it to funnel global resources into the local market share battle, especially when the competitor lacks the international reach to strike back.

Money does not always move across borders, though this may happen. For a number of reasons (taxation, foreign exchange risk, regulation) the subsidiary may choose to raise funds locally. Looking to the worldwide strength of the parent, local financial institutions may be willing to provide long-term financing in amounts and at rates that would not be justified on the basis of the subsidiary's short-term prospects. One note of caution: If competitors learn of your subsidiary's borrowing needs, you may reveal strategic intentions by raising local funds and lose an element of competitive surprise.

Cross-subsidization is not dumping. When a company cross-subsidizes it does not sell at less than the domestic market price. Rather than risk trade sanctions, the intelligent global company will squeeze its competitor's margins just enough to dry up its development spending and force corporate officers to reassess their commitment to the business.

With deteriorating margins and no way of retaliating internationally, the company will have little choice but to sell market share. If the competitor uses simple portfolio management techniques, you may even be able to predict how much market share you will have to buy to turn the business into a "dog" and precipitate a sell-off. In one such case a beleaguered business unit manager, facing an aggressive global competitor, lobbied hard for international retaliation. The corporate response: "If you can't make money at home, there's no way we're going to let you go international!" Eventually, the business was sold.

gic responsibility away from country organizations. That need conflicts with escalating demands by host governments for national responsiveness. The resulting organizational problems are complex.

Nevertheless, companies must move beyond simplistic organizational views that polarize alternatives between world-product divisions and country-based structures. Headquarters will have to take strategic responsibility in some decision areas; subsidiaries must dominate in others. Managers cannot resolve organizational ambiguity simply by rearranging lines and boxes on the organization chart. They must adopt fundamentally new roles.

National subsidiaries can provide headquarters with more competitive intelligence and learn about world competitors from the experiences of other subsidiaries. They must fight retaliatory battles on behalf of a larger strategy and develop information systems, decision protocols, and performance measurement systems to weave global and local perspectives into tactical decisions. Rather than surrender control over manufacturing, national subsidiaries must interact with the organization in new and complex ways.

Such a realignment of strategic responsibility takes three steps:

1. Analyze precisely the danger of national fragmentation.
2. Create systems to track global competitive developments and to support effective responses.
3. Educate national and headquarters executives in the results of analysis and chosen organization design.

This reorientation may take as long as five years. Managing it is the hardest challenge in the drive to compete successfully.

THE STRATEGIC IMPERATIVE

International companies like General Motors and Philips prospered in the fragmented and politicized European market by adopting the "local face" of a good multinational citizen. Today Philips and other MNCs need a global strategic perspective and a corresponding shift in the locus of strate-

A NEW ANALYSIS

Managers must cultivate a mind-set based on concepts and tools different from those normally used to assess competitors and competitive advantage.

For example, the television industry case makes clear that the competitive advantage from global distribution is distinct from that due to lower manufacturing costs. Even when they don't have a cost advantage, competitors with a global reach may have the means and motivation for an attack on nationally focused companies. If the global competitor enjoys a high price level at home and suffers to cost disadvantage, it has the means to cross-subsidize the battle for global market share.

Price level differences can exist because of explicit or implicit collusion that limits competitive rivalry, government restrictions barring the entry of new companies to the industry, or differences in the price sensitivity of customers.

The cash flow available to a global competitor is a function of both total costs and realized prices. Cost advantages alone do not indicate whether a company can sustain a global fight. Price level differences, for example, may provide not only the means but also the motivation for cross-subsidization.

If a global competitor sees a more favorable industry growth rate in a foreign market populated by contented and lazy competitors, who are unable or unwilling to fight back, and with customers that are less price sensitive than those at home, it will target that market on its global road. Domestic competitors will be caught unaware.

The implications for these strictly domestic companies are clear. First, they must fight for access to their competitors' market. If such access is unavailable, a fundamental asymmetry results. If no one challenges a global competitor in its home market, the competitor faces a reduced level of rivalry, its profitability rises, and the day when it can attack the home markets of its rivals is hastened. That IBM shares this view is evident from its pitched battle with Fujitsu and Hitachi in Japan.

Global competitors are not battling simply for world volume but also for the cash flow to support new product development, investment in core technologies, and world distribution. Companies that nestle safely in their home beds will be at an increasing resource (if not at a cost) disadvantage. They will be unable to marshal the forces required for a defense of the home market.

Not surprisingly, Japanese MNCs have invested massively in newly industrializing countries (NICs). Only there can European and American companies challenge Japanese rivals on a fairly equal footing without sacrificing domestic profitability or facing market entry restrictions. The failure of Western organizations to compete in the NICs will give the Japanese another uncontested profit source, leaving U.S. and European companies more vulnerable at home.

New Concepts

Usually, a company's decision whether to compete for a market depends on the potential profitability of a particular level of market share in that country. But the new global competition requires novel ways of valuing market share; for example:

- Worldwide cost competitiveness, which refers to the minimum world market share a company must capture to underwrite the appropriate manufacturing-scale and product-development effort.
- Retaliation, which refers to the minimum market share the company needs in a particular country to be able to influence the behavior of key global competitors. For example, with only a 2% or 3% share of the foreign market, a company may be too weak to influence the pricing behavior of its foreign rival.
- Home country vulnerability, which refers to the competitive risks of national market share leadership if not accompanied by international distribution. Market leadership at home can create a false sense of security. Instead of granting invincibility, high market share may have the opposite effect. To the extent that a company uses its market power to support high price levels, foreign competitors—confident that the local company has little freedom for retaliation—may be encouraged to come in under the price umbrella and compete away the organization's profitability.

CRITICAL NATIONAL MARKETS

Most MNCs look at foreign markets as strategically important only when they can yield profits in their own right. Yet different markets may offer very different competitive opportunities. As part of its global strategy, an organization must distinguish between objectives of (1) low-cost sourcing, (2) minimum scale, (3) a national profit base, (4) retaliation against a global competitor, and (5) benchmarking products and technology in a state-of-the-art market. At the same time, the company will need to vary the ways in which it measures subsidiary performance, rewards managers, and makes capital appropriations.

PRODUCT FAMILIES

Global competition requires a broader corporate concept of a product line. In redefining a relevant product family—one that is contiguous in distribution channels and shares a global brand franchise—an organization can, for example, scrutinize all products moving through distribution channels in which its products are sold.

In a corollary effort, all competitors in the channels can be mapped against their product offerings. This effort would include a calculation of the extent of a competitor's investment in the distribution channel, including investment in brand awareness, to understand its motivation to move across segments. Such an analysis would reveal the potential for segment expansion by competitors presently outside the company's strategic horizon.

SCOPE OF OPERATIONS

Where extranational-scale economies exist, the risks in establishing world-scale manufacturing will be very different for the company that sells abroad only under license or through private labels, compared with the company that controls its own worldwide distribution network. Cost advantages are less durable than brand and distribution advantages. An investment in world-scale manufacturing, when not linked to an investment in global distribution, presents untenable risks.

In turn, investments in worldwide distribution and global brand franchises are often economical only if the company has a wide range of products that can benefit from the same distribution and brand investment. Only a company that develops a continuous stream of new products can justify the distribution investment.

A company also needs a broad product portfolio to support investments in key technologies that cut across products and businesses. Competitors with global distribution coverage and wide product lines are best able to justify investments in new core technologies. Witness Honda's leadership in engine technology, a capability it exploits in automobiles, motorcycles, power tillers, snowmobiles, lawnmowers, power generators, and so forth.

Power over distribution channels may depend on a full line. In some cases, even access to a channel (other than on a private-label basis) depends on having a "complete" line of products. A full line may also allow the company to cross-subsidize products in order to displace competitors who are weak in some segments.

Investments in world-scale production and distribution, product-line width, new product development, and core technologies are interrelated. A company's ability to fully exploit an investment made in one area may require support of investments in others.

RESOURCE ALLOCATION

Perhaps the most difficult problem a company faces in global competition is how to allocate resources. Typically, large companies allocate capital to strategic business units (SBUs). In that view, an SBU is a self-contained entity encompassing product development, manufacturing, marketing, and technology. Companies as diverse as General Electric, 3M, and Hewlett-Packard embrace the concept. They point to clear channels of management accountability, visibility of business results, and innovation as the main benefits of SBU management. But an SBU does not provide an appropriate frame of reference to deal with the new competitive milieu.

In pursuing complex global strategies, a company will find different ways to evaluate the geographic scope of individual business subsystems—manufacturing, distribution, marketing, and so on. The authority for resource allocation, then, needs to reside at particular points in the organization for different subsystems, applying different criteria and time horizons to investments in those subsystems.

Global competition may threaten the integrity of the SBU organization for several reasons. A strong SBU-type organization may not facilitate investments in international distribution. To justify such investments, especially in country markets new to the company, it may have to gain the commitment of several businesses who may not share the same set of international priorities.

Even if individual SBUs have developed their own foreign distribution capability, the strategic independence of the various businesses at the country level may make it difficult to cross-subsidize business segments or undertake joint promotion. The company loses some of the benefits of a shared brand franchise.

Companies may have to separate manufacturing and marketing subsystems to rationalize manufacturing on a local-for-global or local-for-regional basis. Economic and political factors will determine which subsidiaries produce which components for the system. In such a case, a company may coordinate manufacturing globally even though marketing may still be based locally.

Companies might also separate the responsibility for global competitive strategy from that for local marketing strategy. While national organizations may be charged with developing some aspects of the marketing mix, headquarters will take the lead role in determining the strategic mission for the local operation, the timing of new product launches, the targeted level of market share, and the appropriate level of investment or expected cash flow.

GEOGRAPHY-BASED ORGANIZATIONS

For the company organized on a national subsidiary basis, there is a corollary problem. It may be difficult to gain commitment to global business initiatives when resource allocation authority lies with the local subsidiary. In this case, the company must ensure that it makes national investments in support of global competitive positions despite spending limits, strategic myopia, or the veto of individual subsidiaries.

MARRIAGE: AN ACCEPTABLE SOLUTION

... the White House ... should investigate a simpler supply side solution to the nation's monetary and fiscal problems—merger between the U.S. and Japan.

... an American-Nippon union would vastly increase the supply of savings in the U.S. financial markets.

Marriage has long been an acceptable solution to the micro-economic problems of individuals. . . .

Like all insecure nations, modern Japan has a great propensity to work and save. Like all imperial powers in transition to humbler status, the U.S. has a great compulsion to borrow and spend in order to maintain a lifestyle which it can no longer really afford. . . .

It was once fashionable to argue that capitalist countries had to pursue expansionary foreign policies in order to find new markets. But Japan and the U.S. have turned traditional theories about imperialism upside down.

The U.S. has solved the old problem of underconsumption by creating a welfare state and military industrial complex. It no longer needs a reserve army of consumers, but a reserve army of savers.

In Japan, by contrast, the financial system discourages consumption and the constitution prohibits rearmament. Japan has thus evolved into a natural saver of last resort for the U.S.

Why solemnise this relationship in a formal union when the current dalliance is so satisfactory? . . .

First, the U.S. economic boom is maturing. As inflationary wrinkles appear in 1985, even the Japanese will begin to wonder if they should recycle their dollars as freely as they have so far. . . .

Secondly, . . . If the U.S. would eliminate the fiction of having a financial system autonomous from Japan's, dollar interest rates could collapse and alleviate Latin American's [sic] debt servicing problem.

Third, union with Japan will permit the U.S. to continue looking after the defence needs of its older relatives in Europe. . . .

The final argument . . . is that the U.S. Treasury may accidentally destroy the unique trans-Pacific financial equilibrium now sustaining U.S. recovery and rearmament.

SOURCE: David Hale "A Modest Proposal for Marriage," *Financial Times* October 17, 1984. Reprinted by permission of the publisher.

Finally, the time limit for investments in global distribution and brand awareness may be quite different from that required for manufacturing-cost take-out investments. Distribution investments usually reflect a long-term commitment and are not susceptible to the same analysis used to justify "brick and mortar" investments.

NEW STRATEGIC THOUGHT

Global competitors must have the capacity to think and act in complex ways. In other words, they may slice the company in one way for distribution investments, in another for technology, and in still another for manufacturing. In addition, global competitors will develop varied criteria and analytical tools to justify these investments.

In our experience, few companies have distinguished between the intermediate tactics and long-run strategic intentions of global competitors. In a world of forward-thinking competitors that change the rules of the game in support of ultimate strategic goals, historical patterns of competition provide little guidance. Executives must anticipate competitive moves by starting from new strategic intentions rather than from precooked generic strategies.

It is more difficult to respond to the new global competition than we often assume. A company must be sensitive to the potential of global competitive interaction even when its manufacturing is not on a global scale. Executives need to understand the way in which competitors use cross-sub-sidization to undermine seemingly strong domestic market share positions. To build organizations capable of conceiving and executing complex global strategies, top managers must develop the new analytic approaches and organizational arrangements on which our competitive future rests.

Chapter Case Study

Euromanagé, Inc.

Euromanagé, Inc., was established in Lyons, France, in 1957 by the Picard brothers, Alain and Michel, as a manufacturer of high-quality baked products that were sold to gourmet shops throughout France, especially in the major cities. As the company grew in strength financially it expanded its product line to include soft drinks (both bottled and powdered), snack foods, and breakfast cereals. By 1989 the company was a leading processed-food and soft-drink manufacturer in France and had established its presence in Switzerland, West Germany, Austria, and the Netherlands.

Having gained considerable international experience in Europe, the company made the decision in 1988 to expand into Latin America, starting with Massilia, one of the largest countries in Latin America, with a per capita income of $6,800 a year, nearly the highest among all countries of the region. Although under considerable Spanish and Portuguese influence because of its heritage, Massilia had a large middle-class population that was increasingly open to international products of different categories. Premarketing research had shown that there was a substantial market for the high-quality, upper-end soft drinks and processed cheese products of Euromanagé. Estimated sales for the first year were $40 million.

Massilia had a mixed retail system for soft drinks and processed foods. Soft drinks were sold primarily through individually owned small stores that also sold other types of groceries. Large supermarkets in the major cities were also a major source of soft drink sales (about 15 percent). The balance was sold through a variety of outlets, including automatic vending machines (11 percent), restaurants and similar establishments (6 percent), and miscellaneous outlets (8 percent). The large international soft drink manufacturers dominated the

market and had established their own bottling plants in four key regions and set up a comprehensive distribution system operated through local distributors, who had signed agreements with the franchisees.

Euromanagé considered several strategies to break into the market and reached the conclusion that it could achieve maximum penetration by attacking the high end of the market and carving a niche in the mineral water, fruit juice, and fruit drink markets. Much of this market was concentrated in the urban areas, where the professional class was located. With a well-designed marketing plan, Euromanagé hoped to put forth an image of aesthetic social superiority of its products that would appeal instantly to the upwardly mobile and the ambitious sections of Massilia's middle class.

It was also evident that the initial marketing arrangement would be made with the large supermarkets, where most of the higher income middle-class customers in urban areas did their shopping. Although in some areas there were high-end individually owned stores, the supermarkets controlled as much as 70 percent of the middle-higher income retail market in the urban areas. Further, the supermarkets also stocked a wide variety of imported foods, and they could also carry Euromanagé processed cheese products. Further, at some point in the future, the supermarkets could carry more items from the Euromanagé product line. Initial surveys had shown that customers at the major supermarkets welcomed the availability of high-quality French soft drinks and cheeses. Although this issue was settled fairly quickly, the international marketing strategy for Massilia became bogged down in indecision on a choice of a distribution system. Massilia was located on a different continent, and the company's experience in establishing distribution networks in Europe could not be easily duplicated. Considerable effort, including on-the-spot studies of the distribution system in Massilia, enabled the company to narrow down the options to two. The first was to establish a distribution office of the company in Mardoe, the major port city and capital of Massilia. Under this arrangement an executive of Euromanagé would be placed in overall charge of the Massilia distribution operation and would be assisted by a small locally recruited staff. The office would maintain direct contact with all the supermarkets selling Euromanagé products and coordinate imports and local transportation to various supermarket locations. Letters of credit for imports would be opened by the distribution office on receipt of the supermarket purchase orders. The local office would also be in charge of collections and assist the supermarkets in efficient inventory control of Euromanagé products.

The proposal seemed to offer many advantages. Euromanagé was entering into a fairly competitive market with well-entrenched competition. Pricing was a key factor and the existence of an in-house distribution arrangement would save considerably on the middleman's commission. Further, the distribution office could keep in close touch with the supermarket and offer excellent feedback on the market response to Euromanagé products. Further, the executive in charge of the distribution center could actively follow up the promotion of Euromanagé in the new markets.

The second distribution option was to appoint a local agent in Mardoe as the company's sole distributor of soft drinks and processed cheese products. The distributor would import the products after receiving and consolidating orders from the supermarkets. All transportation, collection, and other arrangements would be made by the distributor, who would also provide periodic market feedback to Euromanagé. The latter would, at the same time, be free to talk directly to supermarkets on such issues as the market response to new products, needed changes in product quality and varieties, nature of store-level promotions, and so on. The dis-

tributor would charge a commission on a graduated scale, depending upon the level of sales achieved each year, over a given base. There would, however, be a minimum fixed amount of commission payable to the distributor to cover fixed costs.

There were considerable advantages in this proposal, too. The wholesaler would obviously have a better knowledge of the local market and arrive at arrangements with the local supermarkets more easily than would be possible for Euromanagé to accomplish directly. Further, with local experience, the wholesale distributor would be able to smooth out routine problems with the supermarkets more effectively. Because letters of credit would be opened for the account of the wholesaler, Euromanagé would be safe from the credit risk involved in collecting payments from the supermarket outlets. At the same time, the company would also be relieved of the difficult job of handling collections in a foreign country. The wholesaler already had an office and the necessary facilities in Massilia and would not need additional investments. Moreover, the distributor would have considerable experience and business contacts within the local distribution system and would easily be able to route Euromanagé products to the supermarkets.

Pierre Goulet, vice-president of international marketing for Euromanagé, was perplexed. Both options seemed to have great advantages, but each also had several disadvantages, and what might have worked in Europe might not work in Latin America. Goulet wrote an informal interoffice memo to his marketing manager of the Western Hemisphere, Guy Lassalles, asking him to evaluate the difficulties and risks in each alternative from the long-term perspectives of the company, before the executive committee had to make a decision the following week.

Question

1. Assume you are Guy Lassalles and draft an interoffice memo providing the analysis sought by Goulet.

CHAPTER 16

International Finance

This chapter will:

- Emphasize the importance of managing working capital within the multinational corporation.
- Outline the development of the international capital markets, Euromarkets, and the international equities markets.
- Describe techniques for dealing with inflation, taxes, and blocked funds.
- Present sources of capital for financing MNC operations.

Financing International Business

The financing of international business operations is a far more complex, tricky, and challenging task than managing the finances of a domestic business. Several additional considerations and factors that affect finances come into play when a business goes international. Many of these factors are positive ones, for example, newer, larger, and more flexible sources of financing and access to a greater variety of financial instruments for more efficient use of financial resources. On the other hand, financial operations become subject to a variety of new constraints and risks. The task of financial managers in international business, therefore, becomes a twofold operation—minimizing the risks to the finances of a company, maximizing the utilization of the new opportunities presented by the international environment.

Working Capital Management

In an international business, the management of working capital has several imperatives in addition to the traditional requirements. In domestic selling optimal working capital management requires the following: the availability of liquid resources in adequate amounts to meet due obligations; management of the timing of the flow of financial resources, accelerating the inflow of receivables and lagging the outflow of payables; and maintaining an optimum level of liquid cash in order to minimize the occurrence of idle balances.

In addition to these basic factors, several other considerations come into play when working capital requirements of an MNC spread across several countries. The first factor is the availability of the appropriate currency. Unlike a purely domestic business, an MNC can have short-term financial obligations falling due in several currencies at its different locations around the globe. The financial manager, therefore, must decide between maintaining liquid reserves of the needed foreign currencies or moving the currencies in the spot exchange market, or, if it is available, making necessary arrangements through the forward exchange market.

The requirements of financing in different currencies to meet short-term obligations can also be met by borrowing locally in the different money and financial markets. These options generate the consideration of whether the option of borrowing locally is better than taking a covered position in the forward exchange market. In other words, a choice has to be made between a money market hedge and an exchange market hedge. The decision will depend on several factors, primarily the expected rates of exchange fluctuation and the interest rate differentials and their expected reliability.

The presence of exchange risk and the policy of the international corporation are other crucial variables that impact on the management of working capital across national boundaries. Exchange risk will depend on the foreign currency liabilities created by a firm that are not matched by offsetting transactions. How a firm chooses to determine its level of tolerable exposure and how it deals with it depends largely on the internal policy of the firm. Attitudes vary considerably in this respect. Several firms will spend considerable time, effort, and money at minimizing their exposure to currency fluctuations. On the other hand, many firms prefer to take the risk exposure and hope to profit from favorable currency movements.

The necessity to manage working capital over a wide geographical base is another major challenge faced by international financial managers. In a multifaceted organization with financial centers located in different cities, there is a need to coordinate the financial position of different offices, which is vital to secure the optimum utilization of company funds and avoid unnecessary costs because of idle funds or short-term borrowing.

Management of working capital in different countries also implies the necessity of ensuring a relatively smooth transfer of funds, both within and outside the corporation. There are distinct possibilities that unexpected hurdles may arise because of government restrictions, exchange controls, or other political risk-related factors that may prevent funds from reaching their destination on time. Moreover, these considerations also influence fundamental financing decisions, such as whether to bring funds from the home country, a third country, or to raise resources locally. Although modern technology has made almost instantaneous transfer of funds around the world fairly easy, there are still the possibilities of snafus, because of inaccurate messages, incorrect codes, and transit system failures. It is clearly more difficult to ensure the reliability of international financial technology in a wide range of countries, many of which are not advanced technologically.

Another challenge that confronts international managers is taxation. Taxation laws vary between countries and are often fairly complex. Moreover, in several countries there are frequent major changes in tax laws that could adversely affect the management of working capital, which is run on a fairly tight basis and which has little room for maneuvering. Moreover, different tax laws often require that transactions be structured in such a way to minimize tax liability and achieve the lowest possible post-tax financing costs.

Intracompany Pooling

Intracompany pooling is a financing technique that seeks to optimize the total availability of resources on a worldwide or area-group basis. A multinational corporation is likely to have several offices, each of which generates income and incurs expenditures and, therefore, has either operational surpluses or shortages of financial resources at any given time. The advantages of this technique are obvious. The surplus funds held with one office or subsidiary of a company would essentially be idle, because they are not utilized products. If intracompany pooling is effective, the corporate financial headquarters or regional control centers will know the exact locations of surpluses and shortages. With this knowledge available at a centralized point, instructions can be sent to move funds from the surplus to the deficit locations, which evens out the imbalances. Considerable cost savings are achieved because the idling of funds is avoided and the need to borrow funds at high interest is obviated. Consider an example of a company with one branch in Manila, the Philippines, and other in Cairo, Egypt. The corporate headquarters of the company, located in Phoenix, Arizona, keeps a constant eye on the funds position of the overseas offices. In the course of business, it is possible that one of the branches, say Manila, is saddled with surplus funds of $300,000, while the Cairo branch finds itself confronted with a short-term deficit of $250,000. In the absence of intracompany pooling, the Manila funds would be idle for perhaps a month, while the Cairo branch would have to borrow $250,000 for a month, which could be at a rate of 10 percent per annum, or as much as $2,083 in interest charges. If, however, the Phoenix headquarters can monitor this situation, they can arrange for the Manila branch to remit $250,000 to the Cairo branch, reducing the former's idle funds and saving the interest charges of the Cairo branch.

Another strategy that corporate headquarters can devise, at their level or at that of a regional center especially designated for this purpose, is a policy that requires all surplus balances of the different branches and offices of a company to be maintained at a particular central place. Several benefits accrue from such a strategy. First, the different locations minimize the size of their resources and are in fact saved from the effort involved in utilizing them productively. Moreover, adequate opportunities for renumerative investments of short-term funds may not be available in many branch locations.

Centralized pooling of additional resources, therefore, can be located at centers where there are wide opportunities for short-term investments at competitive terms. Such centers would have the necessary liquidity for absorbing sizable investments without any significant effect on market conditions. Pooling of surplus balances at one location also creates personnel economies because this task is consolidated at one point and can be managed more efficiently with fewer staff than if it was managed at several locations. Further, expertise in funds management can be concentrated at one point and used effectively, and funds from many branches would contribute toward sizable volume at the central location, reducing transaction costs and increasing the possibility of securing better returns on short-term investments.

Centralizing the management of funds reduces to some extent the political risk associated with assets held in overseas locations. The MNC is able to move funds to a safe location before a restriction comes into effect. As a result, the total volume of funds exposed to an impending or even possible government restriction on repatriation is substantially reduced. The centralized management of funds makes it possible for the corporation to devise and implement a global financial strategy that ties into the overall strategy for achieving the global corporate objectives.

Global coordination and pooling of intracompany transactions is, however, not free from problems. Transferring funds out of certain countries is subject to exchange and capital controls and may, therefore, not be possible at all. Moreover, many countries have differing laws that could levy a tax on even the temporary repatriation of funds from the country. Also, devising and installing an efficient and versatile global electronic communication and funds transfer system, generally through a multinational financial institution, is quite expensive, both in terms of initial and recurring costs (service, rental, and maintenance). A corporation has to clearly weigh the expenses against the potential benefits of such an arrangement. Usually only large companies with locations in different parts of the world find it economically viable to establish intracompany funds transfer and management systems.

Even those companies that find the establishment of an intracompany funds transfer system viable must take several other measures to make the system cost effective. Costs involved in intracompany transactions can be considerable, and reducing them can add significantly to the company's bottom line. Minimizing transaction costs can be achieved by reducing the number of individual transactions through the consolidation of small transactions. Alternatively, offsetting arrangements can be made for different branches of the company, and only the residual balances need to be actually transferred through the system. Transaction costs can also be reduced by using more efficient and cost-effective means of funds transfer, such as on-line computerized transfers through major banks.

Hedging against Inflation

Dealing with inflation in different countries calls for active working capital management policies. High inflation tends to erode the value of receivables, but also lessens the burden of payables in real terms. When inflation is expected to rise, plans are made for local receivables to be delivered at the earliest possible date. Leading is the technical term for the early receipt of goods. Conversely, an MNC would tend to delay its payables. The policy of creating deliberate delays with respect of outflows or inflows is called lagging. Centralized cash management systems also help in the corporate efforts to minimize the inflationary erosion of liquid assets by permitting their transfer to locations where there are lower inflation rates and expectations.

Managing Blocked Funds

Blocked funds are generally those resources of overseas entities that are not allowed to be repatriated, at least temporarily, by national governments. Blocking of funds can take place for a number of reasons. A governments may face dif-

ficulties in its balance of payments, which would bring down the available resources of foreign exchange. In order to optimize the use of limited resources, a government may block repatriable funds of overseas entities and limit foreign exchange to financing essential imports and other payments. Occasionally a change of government can lead to an across-the-board blocking of funds usually repatriable by overseas entities, which could be motivated by political considerations of discrediting the former government or overturning its policies. In specific cases blocking may occur if a particular overseas corporation fails to comply with certain local regulations or requirements or is considered politically to be working against the best interests of the host nation.

Blocking can take various forms. At one end the host currency is deemed nonconvertible and repatriation of any funds is ruled out. Other forms of blocking would involve repatriation of only a portion of the funds, repatriation only after a certain time lag, a combination of restrictions on the percentage of assets to be repatriated and the time constraints, absolute ceilings on the total quantum of funds that can be repatriated over a certain time period, preapproval requirements for repatriation of funds, and special conditions placed on companies seeking repatriation.

TECHNIQUES FOR DEALING WITH BLOCKED FUNDS
Export Orientation for Multinationals

Because the basic rationale for nearly all decisions and regulations that block funds is the shortage of foreign exchange, many MNCs seek to address host country concerns by developing an export orientation that would create foreign exchange inflows that offset the outflows because of the repatriation of assets. Thus, many MNCs whose primary business is production, sales, or services for the domestic market tend to divert some of their production to other foreign markets, thereby earning foreign exchange for the host country. In some instances, MNCs who do not produce exportable goods in the host country use their international marketing prowess, through their branches and affiliates abroad, to market goods produced by other manufacturers in the host country. Some MNCs, in fact, go so far as to start new export-oriented product lines either through their existing company or through another local subsidiary. The export earnings achieved are surrendered to the national authorities, who, in turn, unblock MNC funds, which can be repatriated.

Substitution of Fresh Investments Many MNCs substitute blocked funds for fresh investments from abroad. If funds are not allowed to be repatriated, a company often uses them to meet local expenses connected with fresh investments, either in new projects or the expansion of existing ones. These funds are used in some instances to defray the ongoing expenses that arise in the course of day-to-day operations. This utilization is tantamount to repatriation, in as much as funds would not be required to be remitted from the head office. In some countries, such adjustments are prohibited and firms must bring in additional resources of foreign exchange from abroad if they wish to make new investments in startups or expansions. In the case of investments where the company is bringing advanced and new technology to the country, however, authorities tend to take a more lenient view and permit such arrangements. Such companies usually face fewer restrictions on repatriation of their funds.

Nonformal Techniques MNCs very often use informal means to secure repatriation of blocked funds. One important way is the exertion of pressure on the host government through diplomatic channels. At other times pressure is exerted through the home government of the parent company on the host government. Occasionally, MNCs seek to influence host governments through their own governments at a time of negotiations for aid programs or other economic agreements from which the host country is expected to benefit substantially.

Direct attempts to influence government decisions are not uncommon. The frequency of such attempts and the degree of their success varies from country to country. In some countries attempts to bribe government officials are taken as almost routine, and several instances have been reported in the international press where multinationals have sought to directly influence government officials in order to obtain repatriation approvals. In some situations, however, such attempts rebound. For example, an MNC may become extremely influential with a particular host government and secure favorable terms. In the event this particular government is removed from office, the ties with the ousted government can be held against the MNC, and it may face an extremely hostile attitude from the new government, including placing the repatriation of its funds in jeopardy.

Financial Techniques Blocked funds take the form of idle balances when they cannot be repatriated, invested in new projects or expansions, or be used to meet the operating expenses of the company. In this eventuality, MNCs attempt to seek direct answers in the local financial markets and indirectly in the international financial markets. In the local financial markets, corporations attempt to invest the blocked funds in instruments whose maturities are similar to the expected duration of blocking. Of course, an ideal match is not always available because of the relatively undeveloped financial markets of many countries and the fact that the exact duration the funds will remain blocked is rarely known.

Accessing the international markets for utilizing blocked funds is, however, not straightforward and involves, in most cases, either circumvention of host country regulations or, at a minimum, exploitation of certain loopholes. One way this is done is to place the blocked funds as security or collateral with multinational banks located in the host country for loans taken abroad by branches in other countries. It is extremely difficult for authorities in the host countries to monitor all such deals and prove the precise links between a particular deposit locally and a loan extended overseas.

Parallel or back-to-back loans are another technique employed by MNCs to use blocked funds productively through the international markets.

Under this arrangement, blocked funds are lent out to a local company, who arranges an equivalent loan to the parent company overseas.

Transfer Pricing

Transfer pricing is one of the most controversial issues surrounding the operation of MNCs in different countries. The term itself refers to the pricing arrangements made between different units of a multinational corporation. Transfer pricing is discussed in the context of international marketing in Chapter 15; the discussion in this chapter focuses on the financial implications of this technique. In any MNC, affiliates receive from one another a wide array of raw materials, intermediate products, semifinished goods, services, technical know-how, patents, and so on, which must be paid for. Because both parties in these transactions belong to the same organization, the main determinant of prices will be the policy of the headquarters. Actually, the pricing decision in this instance would not be derived so much economically as administratively or strategically. It is inherently difficult in this situation to ensure a fair price. First, the definition of what is fair will vary from the perspective of the host government, that of an MNC, and often even from the perspective of an MNC's home government. Second, given this leverage, an MNC is bound to use it to offset constraints in other areas of its operation. It is treated, in fact, more as a fund management technique by MNCs, because it offers considerable manueverability in moving funds from one subsidiary to another, avoiding taxes, dodging tariffs, and financing imbalances in different operational locations.

Capital Budgeting and Financial Structure of an MNC

The financial analysis needed to make decisions about investments in different countries must go beyond the exercise for domestic investments and incorporate several additional factors and variables that influence project performance and returns.

Exchange Control Restrictions on Remittances

A project may be financially stable in terms of the revenue it generates in the country where it is located, but government restrictions may not allow the profits to be either partially or fully repatriated or may place time constraints on the repatriation. From the point of view of the parent company, this would not be a financially viable project because the actual returns on investment would not meet acceptable standards.

Political Risks

Political risks are connected to the issue of government restrictions of remittances. Such risks arise from the possibility of new or more stringent regulations being imposed by the host government. Such regulations could be imposed not only on the remittance of profits, but also on the type of activities an MNC can perform or on the manner in which it conducts its business. Political risk also incorporates the possibility of expropriation of assets, and the risk becomes an important factor in new investment decisions, because it raises the kind of uncertainty that would affect future returns on investments. Although it is difficult to quantify political risk because of several subjective considerations, methods have been devised to provide a numerical grading of the different levels of political risk attached by overseas investors with respect to different countries. The basis of most of these methods is a relative weighting scale of comparative risks in different countries. There is some justification to this approach, because in many instances the investment decision for an MNC involves a choice of locating the investment in several countries.

Tax Considerations

Tax regimes vary greatly in different countries, both with respect to the statutes and implementation procedures and practices. A financial analyst of an MNC evaluating an investment decision in an overseas location must factor in the implications of the host country's tax regulations. In most countries income on investments by overseas entities is taxed at special or different rates, which may be higher in cases of repatriation of funds.

Sources of Funds

Sources of funds for financing investments overseas are important considerations that enter into any financial analysis preceding the investment decision. A corporation may have access to cheaper local financing or in greater volume because of its credit rating in the overseas market. It may be able to raise funds in third-country markets. At the same time, it may face funding constraints because local regulations prohibit overseas borrowings for projects located in a host country. Local financing may be accompanied by special disclosure, operating, and reporting requirements. There also may be certain local restrictions placed on overseas entities receiving funds from particular sources.

Currency of Borrowing Investments

In overseas investments the commitment of an MNC's own or borrowed resources has to be made in a particular foreign currency. The investment decision must be aware of the different options available with regard to the choice of currency. The wrong choice of currency for borrowing could lead to substantial financial losses because of adverse fluctuations in exchange rates over the life of the loan.

Different Inflation Rates

Different inflation rates are an extremely important consideration in evaluating investment deci-

sions because the entire profitability of a project could be eliminated by inflation losses. Inflation rates became particularly important in the 1980s because many developing countries where MNCs of industrialized countries have substantial investments experienced hyperinflationary rates. When making a decision to invest in a country where inflation rates are expected to be high, the financial manager has to realistically assess the impact of inflation on net returns to the parent company and devise inflation-adjusting mechanisms in the financing strategy, so that the returns can be made to the greatest extent possible, immune from inflationary conditions in the host country.

International Capital Markets

International capital markets have become increasingly important as a source for financing the operations of MNCs, not only because of the decline in bank financing, but also largely because of several developments that have increased the competitiveness, size, and sophistication of the financial markets themselves. International capital markets or international financial markets are terms used to describe the three basic types of markets where MNC's can raise money—national financial markets, Eurocurrency markets, and national stock markets.

It should be noted, however, that both national financial markets and national stock markets are international in the sense that, although they are located in a particular country and are subject to that country's laws and regulations, they are open to foreign borrowers and investors. The degree to which they are internationalized varies, of course, but in general the financial and equity markets of nearly all the industrialized countries are open to foreign borrowers.

An essential difference between borrowing funds from a bank and raising funds from a financial market is that when a corporation borrows from a bank, the bank takes on the risk, and the depositors who place funds with the bank are not in any way responsible. Because the bank is taking the risk and going through the effort of pooling the funds of depositors, it receives a certain remuneration, which can be quite high. On the other hand, borrowing in a financial market implies that a corporation is reaching the investing public directly, without using the intermediary services provided by the bank. The corporation has to make the necessary arrangements on its own to inform the investors that it is in the market to raise funds and to convince them of its credit worthiness. Some banks, especially investment banks, do play a role in such transactions, but it is marginal in the sense that they provide only certain types of services, which are paid for by fees. Generally, therefore, corporations find it cheaper to raise funds through the international capital markets because they are able to save the intermediation costs involved in bank financing.

Another important reason why MNCs would use this option is the sheer size of the resources that can be raised in these markets. There are limits on which banks can lend funds because they do not have such large resources at their disposal and are not willing to take excessive risks.

Financial markets provide a wide variety of financial instruments that can be combined and tailored to serve individual financing needs. Almost every aspect of a financing transaction can be custom designed to serve the purpose of an MNC—the maturity, currency, dates of transaction, repayment schedule, and types of interest rate arrangement.

The Emergence of International Capital Markets

Bank lending dominated the international financial arena through the 1970s, although signs of strains had become evident toward the end of the decade. The international debt crisis, which became publicly known in 1982, signaled a formal end to the domination of bank lending as the main source of international finance.

Through the 1970s and the 1980s, several developments had prepared the financial markets of the world to literally take off. One important step in this direction was financial deregulation in many industrialized countries. The United States, Great Britain, France, and Japan introduced, at different stages, legislation that eliminated to a significant extent restrictions on the free flow of funds across their countries. The deregulation measures also improved the access of borrowers from these and other countries to overseas markets.

Dramatic improvements in information and telecommunication technology enabled the transfer of funds and market information around the world almost instantaneously, which gave the financial community the power to deal in several markets simultaneously. Effectively, the communications and information revolution integrated the international markets to a much higher degree. The widespread use and application of computer technology enabled financial managers to create a wide array of highly complex financial instruments that could be fine-tuned to client requirements.

The distinction between domestic and international markets has become blurred with the rapid mobility of capital and almost instantaneous communication. What has emerged is a truly international market that offers a wide range of financing options to MNCs.

National Financial Markets

The major national financial markets that serve as international financial centers are New York City, Tokyo, and London. Other important national markets that are open to foreign borrowers as well as investors are Geneva, Hong Kong, Paris, Frankfurt, and Singapore.

These markets are generally free from government control as far as day-to-day operations are concerned. There are few, if any, restrictions on the inflow and outflow of funds from these markets to and from other financial centers. All of these markets have excellent communications and other infrastructural facilities necessary for the smooth operation and execution of a very large volume of transactions on a daily basis. As can be expected, most of the major international financial players— commercial banks, investment banks, and securities and brokerage houses—have a presence in nearly all of these markets.

Most of the borrowings in national markets by foreign borrowers is done in the form of bond issues and commercial paper. Bonds are fixed-term promissory notes, usually issued at a discount from face value, which is equal to the rate of interest received by the investor of the bond until maturity. A corporation that wants to raise funds through a bond issue usually hires an investment bank or securities brokerage house to underwrite and actually make the transaction. The lead underwriter or lead manager generally organizes a syndicate of other similar financial institutions that agree to underwrite some part of the issue for a share in the fees. The actual arrangements can vary considerably, depending upon the kind of services to be performed by the underwriter or lead manager. Often the underwriter or lead manager, along with the syndicate, buys the entire issue of bonds from the borrowers and then sells or places them with investors. The difference between the price at which the lead manager and syndicate buy the bonds and the price at which they sell them constitutes their spread or profit margin. In addition, the lead manager gets a separate fee for bringing together the syndicate and arranging the various services required for a bond issue. Alternatively, the bonds can be sold directly to investors with the underwriters agreeing, for a certain fee, to buy on their own account any bonds that are not sold.

Bonds issued by a foreign party in a national market requires the services of a local underwriter or lead manager familiar with local regulations and market conditions and with the necessary connections in the financial and investment community who can successfully launch and sell the bonds. Because the bonds represent an unsecured loan to a particular company that is not located within the sovereign jurisdiction of the country, investors have to be absolutely certain of the credit-worthiness of the foreign issuer. Moreover,

the regulatory authorities of certain countries, especially the United States, impose stringent disclosure requirements on foreign issuers before they can float their bonds. In addition to disclosure, in most instances a foreign issuer must obtain a report on its credit-worthiness from a leading rating agency. The two leading agencies are Moody's Investor Service and Standard & Poors, both located in New York City. The rating given a particular corporation or other borrower not only determines whether it will be able to issue bonds in a particular market, but also the rate of interest it will have to pay on the bonds. A company that receives a better credit rating will be able to borrow at a lower interest rate because investors will be willing to accept a lower return in exchange for a better risk.

Despite their openness, national bond markets are somewhat restricted for overseas borrowers with respect to taxes and the amounts that can be issued.

Foreign bond issues in different markets are known by individual market names. Those issued in the United States are known as yankee bonds, in Japan as samurai bonds, in Great Britain as bulldog bonds.

The Euromarkets

Euromarkets refer to three main types of financial markets that emerged in the 1970s and 1980s and how they dominate the financial arena. They are Eurocurrency markets, Eurobond markets, and Euroequities markets. The prefix *Euro-* does not imply that the currency, bond, or a particular equity is that of a European country. A Eurocurrency, in effect, is any freely convertible currency (including the U.S dollar) that is held in a bank outside the country of its origin. For example, if U.S. dollars are deposited with Natwest Bank London, these dollars would be termed Eurodollars. It is not necessary that the bank may be a foreign one. The important factor here is that it be located outside the country of the relevant currency. If U.S. dollars were held in the Paris branch of Citibank, they would still be Eurodollars. The crucial feature in the creation of Eurocurrency is the shifting of their ownership outside the country of their origin. The dollars deposited with Citibank Paris or Natwest London will be credited to the bank's account in dollars, which will be maintained in the United States. Thus, there would be no outflow of actual dollars from the United States, but from the U.S. standpoint, these funds would become deposits held by overseas entities. Eurodollar deposits can be created in a number of ways. For example, an Austrian company sells chemicals to a U.S. importer and receives payments in U.S. dollars and wants to reclaim its earnings in dollars. It can either deposit these dollars with a bank in the U.S. or a bank elsewhere. If it takes the latter option and deposits the dollars with a bank in, say Frankfurt, it would create a Eurodollar deposit. The Frankfurt bank, which now holds the funds, can lend them to another bank or borrower, and then lend the funds to additional banks. Borrowers using the funds to finance purchases can lead to the creation of further Eurodollar deposits, because their suppliers could again redeposit the funds with a bank outside the United States. Thus, the Eurodollar volume can increase in multiples of the original through this sequence of deposits and loans. In fact, the Euromarkets have grown tremendously over the years, especially during the 1970s and 1980s. This growth was not only because of the process of multiple deposit-loan creations. Several additional factors were responsible for its explosive increase in size, activity and depth.

ORIGINS AND DEVELOPMENT OF THE EUROMARKETS

Although as far back as the 1920s, European banks took deposits in the currencies of countries other than the ones in which they were located, Euromarkets as they exist today began to emerge only after World War II.

Postwar tension between the United States and the Soviet bloc countries generated the fear of a general freeze on the latter's dollar assets held in the United States. To preempt such an eventuality, these countries moved their dollar assets from banks in the United States to banks in Europe. A large proportion of these dollar funds were deposited with two Western Europe branches of two Russian-owned banks—the Banque Commerciale pour l'Europe du Nord in Paris and the London branch of Moscow Nardony Bank. The funds were channeled into other European-based banks, primarily in London.

This initial impetus to holding U.S. dollars outside the United States was encouraged by a series of U.S. government regulations that made holding Eurodollars a profitable proposition. Interest rate ceilings were imposed by the U.S. government under Regulation Q in 1966, which led U.S. depositors to place their funds with European banks in order to take advantage of the prevailing higher interest rates. The demand for U.S. dollars based outside the country also arose simultaneously, because heavy taxes were levied on foreign borrowers raising funds in U.S. markets. Dollar funds could be raised at lower costs in Europe, where the European banks could lend their dollar assets without borrowers having to pay high U.S. taxes. The difficulties of the U.S. dollar in the Bretton Woods system had become quite apparent by the late 1960s. In 1968 the U.S. government, keen to slow down the building up of external obligations in U.S. dollars, restricted U.S. corporations from exporting domestic capital (that is, dollars) to finance their overseas expansion. This move created an enormous demand for non-U.S.-based dollar funding, which was met to a great extent by the Euromarkets.

Apart from U.S. government restrictions, the international monetary developments under the Bretton Woods arrangements also helped create the Eurodollar market. Under the Bretton Woods arrangements, the U.S. dollar became, in addition to gold, one of the major forms of holding international reserves by the world's central banks, which led to an accumulation of dollar assets held outside the United States, in effect creating a huge supply of Eurodollars. Added to this basic accumulation were the commercial banks and other financial institutions in Europe who had dollar balances to their credit. They found that holding dollars outside the United States gave them greater operational flexibility and, for the most part, offered a better return than dollars held in the United States.

The increase in supply of U.S. dollars was matched by an increase in demand for non-U.S.-based dollar loans. The imposition of exchange controls on the lending of pound sterling funds to nonresidents of the United Kingdom also stimulated the demand for the lending of U.S. dollars by London banks, who now could not make loans in their own currency.

Apart from these historical factors, there are some general factors that attracted both borrowers and investors to the Euromarket. For one, the markets are decidedly more efficient than the traditional banking markets. This efficiency translates into a lower spread or interest differential between the borrowing and lending rates. The lower spread implies that intermediation costs are lower, and both the borrowers and investors benefit. The borrowers can raise funds at a lower interest rate, while the investors get a higher rate of return.

There are several reasons why interest rate spreads are lower in the Euromarkets. For one, the banks do not have to maintain any specified reserves of Eurocurrencies and are not subject to central bank regulatory requirements, which lowers the costs for the bankers because a greater proportion of the funds can be now utilized for lending and do not have to be blocked up as required reserves.

Funds held by banks outside the country of their origin are also cheaper to hold, because they are not covered under any federal deposit insurance scheme and no premium has to be paid for the purpose. The savings can be passed on, in part, to the depositors by allowing them a higher rate of interest on deposits of the same maturity in the domestic market.

Transactions in the Euromarket are usually for very large amounts. Moreover, there is acute competition for business among major international banks. The huge size of the transactions brings in economies of scale, thereby reducing costs. Costs are pared still further by competition, because

banks try to underprice competitive offers in an effort to obtain huge volumes of business, which is very profitable because of the overall turnover. Transactions in the international capital markets generally involve a direct deal between a corporation (issuer) and the investing public, and therefore only companies with excellent credit ratings can expect to access these markets for any sizable amounts. Therefore, nearly all participants in the Euromarkets are entities with high credit ratings and are generally known internationally. Such companies usually demand and receive the best rates for their transactions, which reduces the overall average cost of funds raised in the Euromarkets.

The Euromarket, in effect, is a wholesale market where transactions generally range in multiples of millions of dollars and the smallest deals are about $500,000. The large size of transactions introduces economies of scale because the overhead costs incurred by financial institutions (which are primarily fixed costs) can be spread over the transaction.

There are, however, certain risks attached to Euromarket operations. Deposits and investments are not guaranteed by any central bank, and if one party reneges on a contract, there is no recourse available with the monetary authorities of the reneging party's country. Also, because the market consists of funds held in countries other than those from which they originate, there is no lender of last resort, which means that in the event of a financial panic, such as a market crash, there is no safety net that can prevent the bottom of the market from falling out. Thus, if a crash occurs, instability and chaos can be expected, because there is no authority, such as a central bank, in charge of restoring orderly conditions.

Another danger that has emerged from the rapid development of Euromarkets is the possibility of taking high and unwarranted risks. These markets are free from regulatory controls, which leaves the participants free to determine their own degree of risk exposure. In the absence of regulatory control and in the face of the possibility of extremely high profits, it is quite possible that many participants might be tempted to take unwarranted risks and destabilize the entire market, or at least parts of it if they find their gambles failing. The lack of disclosure requirements in the markets, as well as the fact that many Euromarket accounts do not show up on the balance sheets of financial institutions, increases the possibility of a buildup of hidden risks that could overwhelm participating institutions without a warning. The absence of such activities from balance sheets also prevents regulators in the home countries of Euromarket participants to effectively monitor and supervise their activities.

International Equities Markets

Raising funds by listing and selling corporate stocks on exchanges outside a home country has become an important source of financing for corporations involved in international business. During the 1980s many stock markets of the world showed impressive performances and registered substantial gains. Many investors and multinational corporations realized that listing in different stock exchanges of the world could lead to a better diversification of risks because many stock markets do not move in tandem. Thus, losing in one market can be offset by gains in another, which would add to the financial stability of an overall portfolio.

Many of the world's stock markets also grew considerably in size and depth over this period, as more and more companies listed their shares and there was an increase in trading volume. An important factor that encouraged this trend was the deregulation of some of the major stock exchanges, which widened the scope for international participation. The major stock markets of the world are located in Tokyo, New York, London, Taiwan, Hong Kong, Frankfurt, and Paris.

Many companies are finding overseas listings attractive because it increases the overall demand for their shares, which pushes up their values. The international character of a company is also firmly established with an internationally listed equity.

In addition, a company is able to lower the cost of the capital, because it is able to raise equity instead of going in for high-cost debt financing. In addition, the option of listing internationally opens up a whole new avenue of raising capital.

Listing on an international stock exchanges can be done by either a Euroequity issue or a dual equity issue. In a Euroequity issue, shares are sold solely outside the country of the issuer. On the other hand, a dual equity issue is split up into two parts, one sold domestically and the other overseas.

Usually, the markets of the industrialized countries permit the listing of foreign stocks and their purchase and that of local stocks by foreign investors. Some newly industrialized countries permit overseas listings, while others permit limited investment by overseas investors.

TOKYO

The Tokyo stock exchange is the largest in the world in terms of market capitalization (the value of total stocks outstanding at a particular point of time). The market is extremely active and has generally been characterized by upward movements, so that is has an extremely high price-earnings ratio—the ratio of the prices of shares of listed companies to their earnings. Nominal prices are kept extremely low and tradable amounts are denominated in units of 1,000 shares. There are still some restrictions on foreign ownership of shares in Japanese companies and foreign membership in the Tokyo stock exchange, but these are gradually being liberalized. Tokyo handles more than 80 percent of all transactions conducted in the stock exchanges of Japan, and the market is dominated by four major securities houses—Nomura, Nikko, Daiwa, and Yaimaichi. Market capitalization of the Tokyo stock exchange as of December 31, 1989, stood at $4,392 billion.

NEW YORK

New York is the world's second largest securities market. Generally, the shares of larger and well-established companies are listed on the New York exchange. There are various types of memberships in the stock exchange, which provide the right to perform different types of stock market activities. For example, commission brokers execute orders on behalf of customers and convey them to floor brokers who do the actual trading on the floor of the exchange. The New York Stock Exchange, like all other exchanges in the United States, is controlled by a federal authority, the Securities and Exchange Commission. The SEC guidelines and supervisory activities are intended to ensure smooth operation of stock market activities and prevent any fraudulent or unethical trading practices or transactions. The main indicator of the overall price movements on the New York Stock Exchange is the Dow Jones Industrial Average. The Standard & Poor's 500 Index is another widely published and accepted index. As of December 31, 1989, the total market capitalization of the NYSE stood at $3,505.7 billion.

LONDON

London is a truly international stock exchange, with more than five hundred overseas companies listed, representing more than 20 percent of the total exchange. Two main types of stocks are available—ordinary and preferred. Ordinary shares confer voting rights, while preferred shares give the first right to holders on the assets of the company. The most commonly quoted index is the Financial Times (FT) Index. After 1986, many regulations that limited activity on the London Stock Exchange were removed, and banks were permitted to undertake securities transactions by acquiring securities houses. This reform also removed the distinction between different types of stock market functionaries—brokers and jobbers. Since the 1986 reforms, which were known as the "big bang", London has grown to be a major center for the listing and trading of international stocks. As of December 31, 1989, the total market capitalization of the London Stock Exchange stood at $827 billion.

PARIS

The Paris stock market has been liberalized considerably in recent years and a large number of international stocks are listed there. Although in absolute size the Paris market is considerable, it is relatively small in relation to the industrial size of France because of several historical reasons, chiefly the tendency of French companies to rely on debt rather than equity financing to meet their needs. The market is organized in two sections—spot and forward. Special procedures apply in the Paris market for the trading of stocks. Prices are set at periodic fixings, usually twice a day. The price established at the fixing is the official price, although other market-determined prices can prevail with respect to the orders executed in between the fixings. The forward market operates on the basis of a call-over method, where stocks are traded as they are called up. Securities of small companies are traded on an over-the-counter market located within the exchange and operated by stockbrokers who are members of the exchange. The total capitalization of the Paris Stock Exchange as of December 31, 1989, stood at $365 billion.

FRANKFURT

Frankfurt is another major European stock market, which had a market capitalization of $365.2 billion as of December 31, 1989. Regulation of the Frankfurt Stock Exchange is somewhat more stringent than the exchanges of other industrialized countries. Independent stockbrokers are not permitted, and brokerage services are provided by commercial banks. Trading is limited on the Frankfurt exchange because many Germany companies are closely held. In addition, German shareholders tend to take a long-term view of their equity investments and to hold on to shares even if the companies are not performing up to the expected level at a particular point in time. Moreover, high listing costs and availability of other financing services have discouraged several German companies from using the stock exchange to mobilize resources. Shares are usually not registered and there are no limits placed on foreign ownership of equity in German companies. The Frankfurt Stock Exchange uses the trading post system, where transactions in specified securities are conducted at a particular place on the trading floor. Frankfurt is the main stock exchange of West Germany. Open-market operations of the German central bank are also conducted through Frankfurt.

HONG KONG

Hong Kong is one of the most important stock exchanges in the Far East. It has extremely active primary and secondary markets. The uncertainties about Hong Kong's status after 1997 have prompted considerable volatility in the market through the 1980s, although on the whole it has continued to grow in size and rise in value. A large percentage of companies on the Hong Kong exchange are real estate firms, reflecting the importance of this business for Hong Kong. The Hong Kong exchange is under the supervision of the Securities Commission for general regulatory purposes. Day-to-day transactions are, however, unfettered by government regulations. Trading volume generally tends to be very high and the market offers excellent liquidity. The total market capitalization as of December 31, 1989 was U.S. $77 billion.

Emerging Markets

In the late 1970s and 1980s, several newly industrialized countries (NICs) and the stock markets of developing countries have been opened to foreign investors to varying degrees (see Figure 16–1). The most important of these are Taiwan, Malaysia, and South Korea. The Taiwanese market is one of the very large ones, with a market capitalization of $237 billion as of December 31, 1989. The market is dominated by a few very large companies whose individual market capitalizations are in excess of $1 billion. Taiwanese stocks, however, tend to be extremely volatile and regulatory and auditing standards are comparatively lax. The Malaysian stock markets are also considerably well-developed, especially by developing-country standards. As of December 31, 1989, the market capitalization of the Kuala Lumpur market was

$39.8 billion. A number of Singapore and British stocks are listed on the Kuala Lumpur exchange, which has had considerable activity ever since its inauguration in 1973, which is attributed largely to greater demand from the investing public. Several public brokerage firms perform brokerage services. Stocks on the Kuala Lumpur exchange also can be bought through the Singapore exchange. To list its shares on the Kuala Lumpur stock exchange, a company has to meet certain requirements set by the Malaysian authorities.

The South Korean equity market grew rapidly in the late 1970s and the 1980s. As of December 31, 1989, its market capitalization was $140.9 billion. There are certain restrictions on foreign ownership of Korean stocks, but there are special channels, such as country funds, through which overseas investors can participate in the Korean stock market.

It is expected that along with the general economic development, newly industrializing countries and other more advanced developing countries will witness an increase in the size, sophistication, and activity of their capital markets. These markets are expected to open up in a phased manner, first to overseas investors and then to borrowers. Once this occurs, it will be possible for multinational corporations to raise equity capital in local markets and diversify the composition of their international asset holdings by including in them stocks listed on the exchanges of various developing countries.

Summary

In addition to the needs of maintaining liquid resources, managing the timing of cash flows, and minimizing idle cash balances required by domestic finance operations, international finance requires the management of currency exchange risks, the transfer of funds between countries, and international tax issues. Intracompany pooling optimizes the total availability of capital resources on a global basis; surplus funds from operations in one location are used to offset shortages in an-

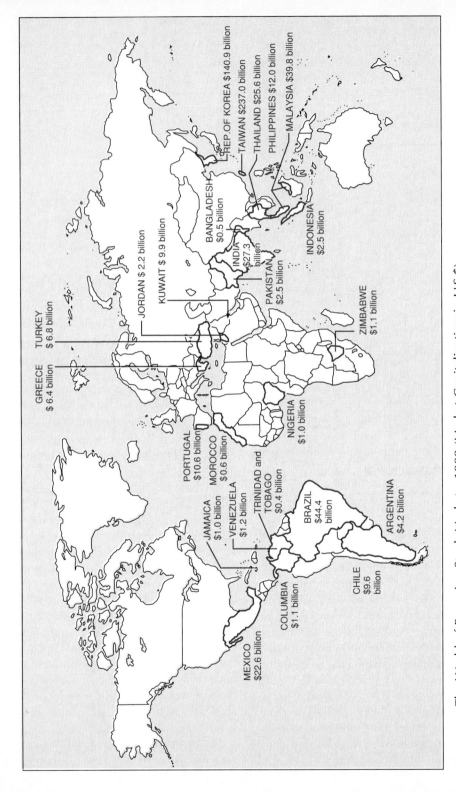

FIGURE 16–1   The World of Emerging Stock Markets, 1989 (Market Capitalization in U.S.$).
SOURCE: International Finance Corporation.

REP. OF KOREA $140.9 billion
TAIWAN $237.0 billion
THAILAND $25.6 billion
PHILIPPINES $12.0 billion
MALAYSIA $39.8 billion
BANGLADESH $0.5 billion
INDIA $27.3 billion
INDONESIA $2.5 billion
JORDAN $ 2.2 billion
KUWAIT $ 9.9 billion
PAKISTAN $2.5 billion
ZIMBABWE $1.1 billion
TURKEY $ 6.8 billion
GREECE $ 6.4 billion
NIGERIA $1.0 billion
PORTUGAL $10.6 billion
MOROCCO $0.6 billion
TRINIDAD and TOBAGO $0.4 billion
VENEZUELA $1.2 billion
JAMAICA $1.0 billion
BRAZIL $44.4 billion
ARGENTINA $4.2 billion
CHILE $9.6 billion
COLUMBIA $1.1 billion
MEXICO $22.6 billion

other location. International financial managers must consider host country foreign exchange and capital repatriation controls, as well as taxation laws, in determining whether to centralize or decentralize working capital funds.

Leading and lagging techniques in receivables and payables serve to offset the effects of high inflation in the host country. To deal with blocked funds, MNCs may develop various strategies—develop an export orientation, use the blocked funds for investments in the host country, exert pressure on the host government through diplomatic channels, or invest in financial instruments in the local financial market. Transfer pricing is a technique that MNCs use to avoid taxation and tariffs and improve their competitive positions.

MNCs must constantly manage foreign exchange and transaction exposure. Parallel loans, timing of funds transfers, centers for fund transfers, and credit and currency swaps are useful techniques. Debt-equity decisions, local ownership laws, and host government attitudes affect the financial structure of MNC subsidiaries and affiliates. External sources of funds for investments are the large commercial banks and international capital markets, such as the Eurocurrency markets and national capital and stock markets. Eurocurrency markets offer a variety of financial instruments in hard currencies held outside the national borders of the currency, including Eurocredits, certificates of deposit, Eurobonds, swaps, note issuance facilities, and Eurocommercial paper. In addition, to the Tokyo, New York, and London stock exchanges, other stock markets, such as Paris, Frankfurt, Hong Kong, Taiwan, Malaysia, and South Korea, are playing increasingly important roles as external sources of capital (see Table 16–1).

Discussion Questions

1. What are the two major tasks of the international financial manager?
2. What is intracompany pooling?
3. What is leading and lagging? How can these techniques benefit the MNC?
4. How can a multinational utilize funds in a foreign subsidiary that have been blocked by the host government?
5. What are some of the additional factors that must be included in a financial analysis when making an international rather than a domestic investment decision?
6. What are the advantages of raising capital in the financial markets rather than through a bank? What are the disadvantages?
7. Discuss the services investment banks provide. What is a lead underwriter? What is a syndicate?
8. What are Euromarkets? Where are they located?
9. Where are the international equity markets located? What are their current capitalizations?

Bibliography

Argy, Victor E. 1982. *Exchange Rate Management in Theory and Practice,* Princeton, NJ: International Finance Section, Department of Economics, Princeton University.

Babbel, David F. 1983. "Determining the Optimum Strategy for Hedging Currency Exposure." *Journal of International Business Studies* (Spring/Summer): 133–139.

Griffith, V., and H. Southworth. 1990. "Chaos Theory." *Banker* (January): 51, 54.

Herring, Richard J., ed. 1983. *Managing Foreign Exchange Risk: Essays Commissioned in Honor of the Centenary of the Wharton School, University of Pennsylvania,* New York: Cambridge University Press.

Kenyon, Alfred. 1981. *Currency Risk Management.* New York: John Wiley & Sons.

Kettell, Brian. 1981. *The Finance of International Business.* Westport, CT: Quorum Books.

Madura, Jeff. 1989. *International Financial Management,* 2nd. ed., St Paul, MN: West Publishing Co.

———. 1985. "Development and Evaluation of International Financing Models." *Management International Review* (Fourth Quarter): 17–27.

Meek, G. K., and S. J. Gray. 1989. "Globalization of Stock Markets and Foreign Listing Requirements: Voluntary Disclosures by Continental European Companies Listed on the London

TABLE 16-1
Market Capitalization, 1980–1989
(Millions of U.S.$)

Market	1980	1981	1982	1983	1984	1985	1986	1987	1988	1989
Developed markets										
Australia	59,700	54,400	41,500	59,600	49,900	59,877	94,035	171,035	183,483	136,626
Austria	2,000	1,600	1,500	1,500	1,500	4,602	6,656	7,411	8,862	22,261
Belgium	10,000	8,400	8,500	10,800	12,200	20,871	37,337	41,377	58,920	74,596
Canada	118,300	105,500	103,500	140,600	134,700	147,000	166,300	218,817	241,880	291,328
Denmark	5,400	6,200	5,500	10,600	7,600	15,096	16,284	20,181	30,178	40,152
Finland	—	—	2,759	4,134	4,167	5,855	11,692	19,698	30,179	30,652
France	54,600	38,100	28,000	38,100	41,100	79,000	149,500	172,048	244,833	364,841
Germany	71,700	62,600	68,900	82,600	78,400	183,765	257,677	213,166	251,777	365,176
Hong Kong	39,104	38,912	18,784	17,095	23,602	34,504	53,789	54,088	74,377	77,496
Israel	4,828	6,972	15,894	5,083	6,120	7,626	9,884	12,001	5,458	8,227
Italy	25,300	24,000	19,900	20,900	25,700	58,502	140,249	119,559	135,428	169,417
Japan	379,679	417,943	417,405	545,848	644,412	948,263	1,842,916	2,802,956	3,906,681	4,392,597
Luxembourg	4,017	4,457	4,686	5,799	6,648	12,658	26,163	38,277	44,808	79,979
Netherlands	29,300	23,000	25,700	33,700	31,100	59,363	83,714	86,240	113,565	157,789
New Zealand	—	—	—	—	6,161	8,761	22,215	15,713	13,163	13,487
Norway	3,190	3,334	2,396	4,597	5,793	10,063	10,122	11,818	14,332	25,285
South Africa	100,000	74,900	77,800	82,800	53,400	55,439	102,652	128,663	126,094	131,059
Singapore	24,418	34,808	31,235	15,525	12,247	1,069	16,620	17,931	24,049	35,925
Spain	16,600	16,700	11,100	10,900	13,200	19,000	48,922	71,188	174,869	122,652
Sweden	12,900	17,200	18,600	30,200	25,700	37,296	63,354	70,564	100,083	119,285
Switzerland	37,600	35,200	36,800	42,500	38,700	90,000	132,400	128,527	140,527	104,239
United Kingdom	205,200	180,600	196,200	225,800	242,700	328,000	439,500	680,721	771,206	826,598
United States	1,448,120	1,333,385	1,520,167	1,898,063	1,862,945	2,324,646	2,636,598	2,588,890	2,793,816	3,505,686
Developed markets	2,651,956	2,488,211	2,656,826	3,286,744	3,327,995	4,521,256	6,368,579	7,691,617	9,488,568	11,095,353
Emerging markets										
Argentina*	3,864	2,056	974	1,386	1,171	2,037	1,591	1,519	2,025	4,225
Bangladesh	27	30	34	48	87	113	186	405	430	476
Brazil (Sao Paulo)*	9,160	12,598	10,249	15,102	28,995	42,768	42,096	16,900	32,149	44,368

Market	1980	1981	1982	1983	1984	1985	1986	1987	1988	1989
Chile*	9,400	7,050	4,395	2,599	2,106	2,012	4,062	5,341	6,849	9,587
Côte d'Ivoire	344	274	321	248	237	302	332	458	437	–
Colombia*	1,605	1,399	1,322	857	762	416	822	1,255	1,145	1,136
Costa Rica	–	–	–	118	156	195	246	–	–	–
Egypt (Cairo)	246	216	654	1,106	1,691	1,382	1,716	1,826	1,760	–
Greece*	3,016	2,266	1,923	964	766	765	1,129	4,464	4,285	6,376
India (Bombay)*	7,585	11,802	11,497	8,510	8,018	14,364	13,588	14,480	23,845	27,316
Indonesia	63	74	144	101	85	117	81	68	253	2,514
Jamaica	54	127	177	113	142	266	536	631	796	957
Jordon*	1,605	2,457	2,845	2,713	2,188	2,454	2,839	2,643	2,233	2,162
Kenya	–	–	–	–	–	–	–	–	474	–
Korea*	3,829	4,224	4,408	4,387	6,223	7,381	13,924	32,905	94,238	140,946
Kuwait	–	–	–	–	–	–	10,108	14,196	11,836	9,932
Malaysia*	12,395	15,300	13,903	22,798	19,401	16,229	15,065	18,531	23,318	39,842
Mexico*	12,994	10,100	1,719	3,004	2,197	3,815	5,952	8,371	13,784	22,550
Morocco	441	377	292	253	236	255	279	357	446	621
Nigeria*	3,118	3,010	1,458	2,970	3,191	2,743	1,112	974	960	1,005
Pakistan*	643	864	877	1,126	1,226	1,370	1,710	1,960	2,460	2,457
Peru	–	1,371	685	546	397	760	2,322	831	–	–
Philippines*	3,478	1,738	1,981	1,389	834	669	2,008	2,948	4,280	11,965
Portugal*	191	156	92	84	73	192	1,530	8,857	7,172	10,618
Sri Lanka	–	–	–	–	–	365	421	608	471	–
Taiwan, China*	6,082	5,312	5,086	7,599	9,889	10,432	15,367	48,634	120,017	237,012
Thailand*	1,206	1,003	1,260	1,488	1,720	1,856	2,878	5,485	8,811	25,648
Trinidad and Tobago	–	1,175	1,357	1,011	843	463	374	388	268	411
Turkey*	477	511	952	968	956	–	935	3,221	1,135	6,783
Uruguay	189	60	24	9	9	15	34	40	24	–
Venezuela*	2,657	2,441	2,415	2,792	–	1,128	1,510	2,278	1,816	1,156
Zimbabwe*	1,456	–	355	265	176	360	410	718	774	1,067
IFC composite markets*	84,761	84,287	67,711	81,001	89,892	110,991	128,528	181,484	351,296	596,219
All emerging markets	86,125	87,991	71,399	84,554	93,775	115,224	145,164	201,292	368,491	611,130
World	2,738,081	2,576,202	2,728,225	3,371,298	3,421,1770	4,636,480	6,513,743	7,892,909	9,857,059	11,706,483

*Emerging markets included in IFC Composite Index
–Not available
SOURCE: IFC: "Emerging stock markets factbook"; 1990

431

Stock Exchange." *Journal of International Business Studies* (Summer): 315–336.

PARROTT, M., S. KANJI, D. LANE, AND E. COHEN. 1988. "European Stock Markets: A Bad Hangover." *Banker* (January): 25–32.

RODRIQUEZ, RITA M. 1980. *Foreign Exchange Management in U.S. Multinationals.* Lexington, MA: Lexington Books.

VINSON, JOSEPH D. 1982. "Financial Planning for the Multinational Corporation with Multiple Goals." *Journal of International Business Studies* (Winter): 43–58.

WARREN, GEOFFREY. 1987. "Latest in Currency Hedging Methods." *Euromoney* (May): 245–264.

Chapter Case Study

Scrinton Technologies

The party at the banquet hall of Grosvenor House Hotel in London was a glittering affair. A large number of top bankers, CEOs of industrial companies, and important government officials were attending the formal celebration marking the commissioning of Scrinton Technologies new plant in Southampton, England, that would be manufacturing a small range of state-of-the-art medical diagnostic equipment, including computer-enhanced imagery and hi-tech scanning systems. Scrinton was a world leader in diagnostic equipment, and the new plant represented the most advanced manufacturing facility of its type in the world. Only Scrinton's own plant in Sacramento, California, was anywhere near this facility in terms of technical sophistication and advancement of production equipment and processes.

The Southampton plant was a major commitment for Scrinton, involving an outlay of $110 million. Scrinton's top management had viewed this project as a strategic move, in order to have a manufacturing facility in Europe before 1992. At the same time, it was considered essential that only the highest technology and processes be used in the plant to ensure products of futuristic sophistication and unquestioned quality and reliability. The European market was large and growing, but at the same time was itself highly sophisticated and competitive. Competition was particularly strong from German and Swiss companies, many of whom had been supplying hospital equipment to medical centers all over Europe for several decades. Although it lacked the long-standing relationships of its competitors, Scrinton was confident that, with its edge in technology, it would be able to catch up with the competition and successfully wrest market share. Some European hospitals and clinics were already using Scrinton's equipment and were appreciative of the quality and reliability of its products. The need to keep a distinct technological edge over the competition, now and in the future, meant that the company had to find considerable resources to finance an ambitious and extremely expensive venture.

Scrinton had decided to go ahead with the Southampton plant. The financing was raised from five sources:

1. Syndicated Euromarket loan: £40 million.
2. Bond issue in the U.S. market repayable in seven years: $38 million.
3. Long-term loan from a consortium of major main commercial banks: $16 million.
4. Equity issue on Wall Street: $12 million.
5. Internal resources: $4 million.

The project took three years to complete, and the debt service schedule of Scrinton U.K., a wholly owned subsidiary that had taken the loans and made the equity and bond issues, was repayment of the bank loan in five years, repayment of the syndicated loan in seven years, and redemption of the bond issue in seven years.

Revenues of the company were going to be principally in three currencies: pounds sterling, deutsche marks, and French francs. It was decided not to invoice products in other European currencies, and all attempts would, as a matter of policy, be made to invoice only in these currencies. Exceptions would be made only in rare cases, generally where a particular sale was of strategic or critical importance to the company.

The Amortization schedule of the company appears at the bottom of page 434.

The company expected to make substantial sales and generate adequate revenue to cover the entire amortization schedule without any need to draw on the resources of the parent company, but a major issue was the possible fluctuation of interest and exchange rates over the life of the repayment plan. The company was exposed, because its syndicated loan in the Euromarket was at variable rates, and its liability could increase substantially if interest rates went up. Further, although its revenues were going to be denominated in three European currencies, it had substantial liabilities in U.S. dollars, and any major appreciation of the dollar against the European currencies would place the entire debt-servicing of the project in serious jeopardy.

Bill Smythe, finance director of Scrinton U.K., was concerned about these issues as he made small talk with a London investment banker at the party. "I'll deal with this in the morning," he thought, forcing the problem away and beginning to pay more attention to his companion, who had moved away from the subject of a possible minicrash on the stock market in the next three months to the more timely subject of the latest rumors on the activities of the younger members of the British royal family.

The next morning, Bill Smyth looked over the projection of estimated revenues for each year. The pound liability was apparently no problem from an exchange risk point of view, because the pound revenues of the company were sufficient to cover the liability. The syndicated loan, however was at a variable rate of .25 percent over the London interbank offer rate. If LIBOR moved up, the value of the pound liability could increase considerably and significantly increase the company's debt service costs.

The dollar borrowings presented a bigger problem. Both exchange and interest rate exposure was present because the repayment obligations were denominated in dollars. Further, the long-term loan from the consortium of banks was at a variable rate of .5 percent over the prime rate.

"There are so many options available to hedge these risks," thought Smythe, "but should we? After all, there is going to be a substantial hedging cost and I wonder if it will be worth it?"

Amortization Schedules

Syndicated Euromaket Loan

	Principal	Interest	Total
	(in millions of pounds sterling)		
Year 1	5	.6	5.6
Year 2	5	.6	5.6
Year 3	5	.5	5.5
Year 4	5	.5	5.5
Year 5	5	.4	5.4
Year 6	5	.3	5.3
Year 7	10	.3	10.2

Long-term Consortium Loan

	Principal	Interest	Total
	(in millions of U.S. dollars)		
Year 1	2	.25	2.25
Year 2	2	.25	2.25
Year 3	3	.25	3.25
Year 4	3	.25	3.25
Year 5	6	.25	6.25

Bond Issue

Year	Interest	Principal	Total
		(in millions of U.S. dollars)	
1	.4		.4
2	.4		.4
3	.4		.4
4	.4		.4
5	.4		.4
6	.4		.4
7	.4	38	38.4

	Total Dollar Liability	
Year		Amount (in millions)
1		2.65
2		2.65
3		3.65
4		3.65
5		6.65
6		.4
7		38.4

Year	DM	French Franc	Pound
4	46.5	42.1	22.80
5	51.0	47.0	26.22
6	56.1	52.6	30.15
7	61.71	58.9	34.67

	Estimated Revenues		
Year	DM	French Franc (in millions)	Pound
1	35	30	15
2	38.5	33.6	17.25
3	42.5	37.6	19.83

Questions

1. What could be the main options for dealing with the company's exposure?
2. Under what circumstances would the company suffer the greatest loss if its exposure were left completely uncovered?

CHAPTER 17

International Accounting

CHAPTER OBJECTIVES

This chapter will:

- Present the role and importance of accounting information to internal and external users.
- Describe the differences in accounting conventions and disclosure requirements as practiced around the world.
- Discuss the current efforts toward harmonization of accounting standards in the United States and the rest of the world.
- Identify special accounting problems affecting multinational corporations.
- Examine the accounting functions of planning, control, and auditing within a multinational context.

What Is Accounting?

Accounting is essentially the recording and interpretation of financial information related to the functioning of a business. Accounting systems provide valuable information about the financial activity and position of a firm, which is interpreted for different users. Information users can be divided into two categories—external and internal. Information users in each category require different types of accounting information, and their needs are met by two different types of accounting functions—managerial and financial accounting.

Managerial accounting is concerned with the information needs of the internal users of an enterprise who require detailed information on all of its business activities. Financial accounting is oriented toward external users and is concerned with providing relevant information about the activities of the enterprise.

External users can be classified according to their use of financial information. Potential investors want detailed information on past sales, earnings performance, and present strength. With such information, they can formulate expectations of future performance and potential returns of a firm and make appropriate decisions.

Creditors are also interested in the future performance of a firm but more so in relation to evaluating its credit-worthiness. Thus, banks making loans or suppliers providing credit need to determine the ability of a business to meet its obligations.

Government representatives also use financial information, not only as potential creditors or customers of the firm, but also as regulators that monitor the activities of an enterprise to ensure that they are within the bounds of law. Customers and employees require information about a firm in order to make decisions about what products to buy, who to do business with, and where to seek employment.

In order to meet the financial information needs of all interested parties, business enterprises must maintain and provide data on its activities from a number of perspectives and in a number of forms.

The task of meeting the financial information needs of internal and external users becomes extremely complex when an enterprise takes its business activities across borders. Additional problems arise not only from transactions between countries, such as the buying and selling of goods, but also because multinational operations are conducted in the sovereign jurisdiction of other countries. A firm must first recognize and respond to the accounting practices, conventions, reporting requirements, and currencies of different nations. Then it faces the problem of integrating the accounts of subsidiaries prepared in accordance with local conventions and regulations with the consolidated accounts of the entire corporation.

Differences in Accounting Practices among Countries

Factors Affecting Accounting Systems

Differences in accounting practices, standards, and conventions among different countries exist because of diverse economic, legal, political, and sociocultural environments. The level of develop-

ment in each country is directly related to the degree of sophistication required by the system. For example, nations with highly developed manufacturing and service sectors and a great deal of international trading activity will require more-detailed accounting and recording systems than countries with limited economic activity.

The nature of business activities in each nation also contributes to the molding of accounting systems. Systems are developed to cater to particular types of business activities. For example, countries with a concentration of large corporations and complex business structures are likely to have more advanced accounting systems than countries with simple business organizations.

Accounting systems in different countries are also directly affected by **legal** considerations. In some countries accounting practices are determined almost entirely by legal constraints.[1] In other countries, such as the United States, accounting practices develop through a mixture of law and standards set by members of the accounting profession.

The accounting system of a nation is also determined, in part, by its political orientation and the level of government involvement in business activity. For example, in a market-based economic system, the financial reporting function is geared toward information disclosure for several interested parties—investors, creditors, regulators, employees, and customers. Thus, the reports are varied in their form and content. In contrast, in a nonmarket economy, where the government owns and runs large portions of business operations, accounting systems are oriented not to external users but to the internal users, that is, the government. Thus, the emphasis of such systems would be on standardization and uniformity of information in order to facilitate centralized, state control. Between these two extremes exist nations that have mixed political systems and correspondingly hybrid accounting systems.

The development and nature of accounting systems in different countries are also affected by

[1] Arpan and Radebaugh 1985.

sociocultural factors. For example, in a country where the virtues of trust and honor are highly prized, such as Japan, it would be considered offensive to ask for proof or documentation of business activities in an audit. Similarly, other attributes, such as conservatism and fatalism, affect the nature and development of accounting conventions. Conservatism might evidence itself in larger estimates of bad debt reserves or smaller projections for sales estimates. Planning and budgeting for the future are likely to hold little importance or credence among members of a fatalistic society.

Notions of time affect not only the frequency of reporting, but also the long-term and short-term views. What might be considered short-term or current in one accounting system might be considered long-term in another.

The educational, training, and learning characteristics of a nation also affect the type and level of accounting systems used, because relative levels of literacy and sophistication of the work force affect the applicability or utility of information.

An accounting system is also affected by attitudes commonly held within a country regarding business operations and the nature of the accounting profession. If business is considered as a force that is to be mistrusted, then pressure would be expected upon an enterprise to have larger and fuller disclosure of operations. Similarly, if business is esteemed and trusted, one would expect to see less public scrutiny of operations. In countries where the accounting system is not well-developed, there is less interest and credence placed in accounting practices.

Table 17–1 shows the results of a study regarding differences in the accounting standards of ten countries, delineating differences in thirty-two complex accounting standards for recordkeeping and reporting.

What Type of Differences Emerge?

The practice of holding reserves is one of the most important differences encountered in the account-

ing practices of different countries. In general, reserves are held by firms to protect against special situations, such as expectations that all the debts of a firm will not be repaid. In some countries, however, reserves are used much more extensively for situations that some consider the normal ups and downs of business operations. In these cases, reserves are used to smooth incomes and taxes from year to year. In profitable years, funds are moved to reserve accounts and thus escape taxation; in less profitable years, the firm can draw upon this cushion to boost flagging income. Reserves are used to stabilize income by a majority of firms in Switzerland, about half of Italian companies, and in at least a dozen other countries.[2] This practice, however, has the effect of reducing the significance of a firm's income statements to such users as investors or creditors.

Other differences are found in definitions, terminology, and formats. For example, in the United States, long-term investments, assets, and liabilities are defined as those held for more than one year. In other countries, this definition may provide for longer holding periods, such as three years or more. The meaning of turnover varies even in English-speaking countries. In the United Kingdom turnover is another term for sales, while in the United States, it refers to the renewal or replenishment of inventory stock.

Differences in Valuation

Differences also emerge in the way firms measure the value of assets and the way they determine income. These differences become apparent in a number of procedural areas, such as accounting for leases, carrying long-term debt, assigning value to shares held of a company's own stock, research and development expenses, depreciation, and inventory valuing techniques.[3] For example, in the United States depreciation is calculated according to the normal life of an asset. The value of the asset, however, is adjusted for the amount of money

---

[2] Ibid.
[3] Arpan and Al-Hashim 1984.

expected to be gained when that asset is ultimately sold. This eventual sales price is referred to as the salvage value. While U.S. firms are only allowed to depreciate assets minus salvage value, in other countries the final asset is depreciated according to its full purchase price.

Other valuation and income differences emerge when countries do not agree on the use of the matching concept of accounting, a term that refers to the cash method of accounting, in which a business attempts to match expenses to the revenues associated with the incurring of those expenses, despite any differences in timing. Still more differences occur when it is accepted practice to keep certain business items off the balance sheet and out of the public or regulatory eye.

Occasionally off-the-balance-sheet items derive from the pursuit of illegal activities (for example, illegal payments or bribery) by businesses in countries with little regulatory supervision. The United States, for example, imposes strict requirements on accounting for legal facilitative payments made to low-level foreign officials to smooth the progress of business in foreign countries. Payments or gifts made to high-level government officials are outlawed. In other countries, these practices are considered to be ordinary expenses of doing business abroad and are deductible for tax purposes.

The Impact of Accounting Differences

The existence of accounting differences create difficulties for financial analysts to compare the financial information of companies around the world. For example, ratios customarily used to evaluate performance, such as return on income or equity, are not comparable. Thus, statements from foreign firms and the financial data they contain must be evaluated in light of relevant differences, and the analyst of an international firm must be aware of likely differences and make necessary adjustments.

The main differences in accounting practices and conventions can be summarized as follows:

- The availability and the reliability of financial information varies from country to country.
- Financial statements and reports differ in language and terminology.
- Financial statements from different countries may include the same information but present it in different formats.
- Currencies used in the statements will generally differ.
- The amounts and types of information disclosed on financial statements are different from country to country.

All of these differences must be considered by any financial analyst before making judgments about the strength or prospects of a firm. Foreign firms should be evaluated in the perspective of their own country and industry, not according to a home-country reference point.

Differences in Disclosure

Information disclosure varies considerably across different countries. Disclosure requirements are a measure of public scrutiny of business enterprises within a country. Greater disclosure implies that the internal strengths and weaknesses of a company are made known to the general public. The differences lie not only in the level of detail, but in the types of disclosed business activities. The amounts and types of disclosure required are determined by several factors—social pressures, legal requirements, and the forces of industry competitors and external users of accounting information.

In the United States, for example, all firms that issue securities (publicly held companies) must file regular, detailed, and extensive reports with the Securities and Exchange Commission (SEC) regarding their business activities. Access to these reports is available to anyone who visits the SEC's public information office in Washington, D.C., or subscribes to an information service that, for a fee, will provide copies of corporate filings.

Pressure for extensive disclosure is sometimes encouraged by private interests, such as consumer groups. Corporations, on the other hand, tend

TABLE 17-1
Choi-Bavishi Synthesis of World Diversity in Financial Accounting Principles

Accounting Principles	Australia	Canada	France
1. Marketable securities recorded at the lower cost or market?	Yes	Yes	Yes
2. Provision for uncollectible accounts made?	Yes	Yes	No
3. Inventory costed using FIFO?	Yes	Mixed	Mixed
4. Manufacturing overhead allocated to year-end inventory?	Yes	Yes	Yes
5. Inventory valued at the lower of cost or market?	Yes	Yes	Yes
6. Accounting for long-term investments: less than 20 percent ownership; cost method.	Yes	Yes	Yes*
7. Accounting for long-term investments: 21–50 percent ownership; equity method.	No(G)	Yes	Yes*
8. Accounting for long-term investments more than 50 percent ownership; full consolidation.	Yes	Yes	Yes*
9. Both domestic and foreign subsidiaries consolidated?	Yes	Yes	Yes
10. Acquisitions accounted for under the pooling of interest method?	No(C)	No(C)	No(C)
11. Intangible assets: goodwill amortized?	Yes	Yes	Yes
12. Intangible assets: other than goodwill amortized?	Yes	Yes	Yes
13. Long-term debt includes maturities longer than one year?	Yes	Yes	Yes
14. Discount/premium on long-term debt amortized?	Yes	Yes	No
15. Deferred taxes recorded when accounting income is not equal to taxable income?	Yes	Yes	Yes
16. Financial leases (long-term) capitalized?	No	Yes	No
17. Company pension fund contribution provided regularly?	Yes	Yes	Yes
18. Total pension fund assets and liabilities excluded from company's financial statement?	Yes	Yes	Yes
19. Research & development expensed?	Yes	Yes	Yes
20. Treasury stock deducted from owner's equity?	NF	Yes	Yes
21. Gains or losses on treasury stock taken to owner's equity?	NF	Yes	Yes
22. No general purpose (purely discretionary) reserves allowed?	Yes	Yes	No
23. Dismissal indemnities accounted for on a pay-as-you-go basis?	Yes	Yes	Yes
24. Minority interest excluded from consolidated income?	Yes	Yes	Yes
25. Minority interest excluded from consolidated owner's equity?	Yes	Yes	Yes
26. Are intercompany sales/profits eliminated upon consolidation?	Yes	Yes	Yes
27. Basic financial statements reflect a historical cost valuation (no price level adjustment)?	No	Yes	No
28. Supplementary inflation-adjusted financial statements provided?	No**	No**	No
29. Straight-line depreciation adhered to?	Yes	Yes	Mixed
30. No excess depreciation permitted?	No	Yes	No
31. Temporal method of foreign currency translation employed?	Mixed	Yes	No(E)
32. Currency translation gains or losses reflected in current income?	Mixed	Yes	Mixed

Yes—Predominant practice.
Yes*—Minor modifications, but still predominant practice.
No**—Minority practice.
SOURCE: Frederick D. S. Choi and Vinoci B. Bavishi, "Diversity in Multinational Accounting," *Financial Executive*, August 1982, pages 46–49.

Germany	Japan	Neth.	Sweden	Switz.	U.K.	U.S.
Yes	Yes	Yes	Yes	Yes	Yes	Yes
Yes	Yes	Yes	Yes	Yes	Yes	Yes
Yes	Mixed	Mixed	Yes	Yes	Yes	Mixed
Yes	Yes	Yes	Yes	No	Yes	Yes
Yes	Yes	Yes	Yes	Yes	Yes	Yes
Yes	Yes	No(K)	Yes	Yes	Yes	Yes
No(B)	No(B)	Yes	No(B)	No(B)	Yes	Yes
Yes	Yes	Yes	Yes	Yes	Yes	Yes
No**	Yes	Yes	Yes	Yes	Yes	Yes
No(C)	No(C)	No(C)	No(C)	No(C)	No(C)	Yes
No	Yes	Mixed	Yes	No**	No**	Yes
Yes	Yes	Yes	Yes	No**	No**	Yes
No(D)	Yes	Yes	Yes	Yes	Yes	Yes
No	Yes	Yes	No	No	No	Yes
Yes	Yes	Yes	No	No	Yes	Yes
No	No	No	No	No	No	Yes
Yes	Yes	Yes	Yes	Yes	Yes	Yes
No	Yes	Yes	Yes	Yes	Yes	Yes
Yes	Yes	Yes	Yes	Yes	Yes	Yes
No	Yes	Mixed	NF	NF	NF	Yes
No	No**	Mixed	NF	NF	NF	Yes
No	No	No	No	No	Yes	Yes
Yes	Yes	NF	Yes	NF	Yes	NF
No	Yes	Yes	Yes	Yes	Yes	Yes
No	Yes	Yes	Yes	Yes	Yes	Yes
Yes	Yes	Yes	Yes	Yes	Yes	Yes
Yes	Yes	No**	No	No	No	Yes
No	No	No**	No	No**	Yes	Yes
Mixed	Mixed	Yes	Yes	Yes	Yes	Yes
Yes	Yes	No	No	No	No	Yes
No(E)	Mixed	No(E)	No(L)	No(E)	No(E)	Yes
Mixed	Mixed	No(J)	Mixed	No(H)	No	Yes

No—Accounting principle in question not adhered to.
NF—Not found.
Mixed—Alternative practices followed with no majority.
B—Cost methods is used.
C—Purchase method is used.
D—Long-term debt includes maturities longer than four years.
E—Current rate method of foreign currency translation.

F—Weighted average is used.
G—Cost or equity.
H—Translation gains and losses are deferred.
I—Market is sued.
J—Owners' equity.
K—Equity.
L—Monetary/Nonmonetary.

to minimize the extent of information they must distribute. The reluctance of corporations to part with information can be attributed to a desire to protect their strategic advantages over competitors.

The type of disclosure required in the United States contrasts with other countries, such as Switzerland, where secrecy is the norm. In Switzerland, which is known for supremely confidential bank accounts, little if any financial information is provided in annual reports, and no information is provided on the derivation of that information. Patterns of disclosure therefore vary around the nations of the world, with some countries requiring greater disclosure than the United States and others requiring very little.

Segmentation of Accounting

In the United States, firms are required to report their results according to segments of business activities,[4] that is, they are required to disclose in their public reports where large percentages of their business are concentrated (for example, in industry lines, foreign operations, export sales, or to single customers, such as governments). Segments that comprise more than 10 percent of world revenues, total profits or losses, or total assets of a company must be reported separately.

Once these individual segments are identified, the firm must disclose revenues, operating results, and identifiable assets associated with each segment. The company, however, does have discretion in its segmentation criteria for sales abroad. While many companies segment foreign sales separately as a whole, others segment according to geographic operating areas, such as Europe and North America. The choice of definitional criteria can disguise critical information from the eyes of competitors. For example, a firm might hide its enormous sales in a central African country

by treating sales for the entire continent as one segment.

The latest annual reports of Sony Corporation segment sales by area and product group. The areas used are Japan, the United States, Europe, and "other areas", even though sales to other areas in 1988 represented more than 14 percent of the firm's total sales. Product groups were divided into four areas—video equipment, audio equipment, televisions, and other products (see Table 17–2).

The segmentation at Nestlé is more extensive. The company's annual report for 1987 shows sales in millions of Swiss francs and as percentages for Europe, North America, Asia, Latin America, the Caribbean, Africa, and Oceania, as well as sales in main country markets for that year. The report does not provide prior-year information regarding sales in those segment areas. The Swiss firm also segments sales according to all main product groups, from drinks, comprising 30.1 percent, to hotel and restaurants providing 0.8 percent of sales for the year (see Figure 17–1).

Research conducted by Frederick D. S. Choi and V. B. Bavishi on comparative requirements across countries of geographic disclosure by multinational firms in Europe, North America, and Japan show that nearly all firms report foreign sales in general and by geographic area (see Table 17–3). Disclosure falls off, however, in reporting more sensitive data, such as that on income generated by foreign operations, assets held in foreign geographic areas and exports and capital expenditures by foreign sources and geographic areas.

Social Reporting

One area in which reporting requirements for firms operating in different environments differ substantially is in the area of social reporting in financial reports, which goes far beyond the disclosure of such items on a balance sheet and income statement as assets, sales, earnings per share, and taxes. Social reports answer questions raised about the socioeconomic effects of a firm's operations on the quality of life or economic status of a nation. Ac-

---

[4] Financial Accounting Standards Board. 1977. Statement 14, "Financial Reporting for Segments of a Business Enterprise."

TABLE 17-2
Sony and Subsidiaries Composition of Net Sales by Area and Product Group

| | Millions of yen | | | | | | | Thousands of U.S. dollars |
| | Year ended October 31 | | | | | Year ended March 31 | | Year ended March 31 |
	1983	1984	1985	1986	1987	1987	1988 (Unaudited)	1988
Sales by Area								
Japan	¥ 321,556 / 28.9%	¥ 345,059 / 27.4%	¥ 366,511 / 25.8%	¥ 391,319 / 29.5%	¥177,472 / 32.4%	¥ 395,428 / 30.5%	¥ 479,422 / 33.5%	$ 3,835,376
United States	317,315 / 28.6	428,207 / 33.9	477,559 / 33.6	426,676 / 32.2	160,865 / 29.4	405,322 / 31.3	426,132 / 29.8	3,409,056
Europe	232,372 / 20.9	220,788 / 17.5	249,123 / 17.5	278,258 / 21.0	132,086 / 24.1	291,702 / 22.5	316,766 / 22.1	2,534,128
Other areas	239,778 / 21.6	267,492 / 21.2	327,592 / 23.1	228,905 / 17.3	77,326 / 14.1	202,592 / 15.7	208,592 / 14.6	1,671,216
Net sales	¥1,111,021	¥1,261,546	¥1,420,785	¥1,325,158	¥547,749	¥1,295,044	¥1,431,222	$11,449,776
Sales by Product Group								
Video equipment	¥ 457,051 / 41.1	¥ 512,041 / 40.6	¥ 515,531 / 36.3	¥ 462,264 / 34.9	¥182,219 / 33.3	¥ 431,428 / 33.3	¥ 437,190 / 30.6	$ 3,497,520
Audio equipment	245,887 / 22.1	271,517 / 21.5	338,356 / 23.8	345,520 / 26.1	151,241 / 27.6	355,448 / 27.5	394,150 / 27.5	3,153,200
Televisions	267,176 / 24.1	297,172 / 23.6	364,827 / 25.7	319,414 / 24.1	127,888 / 23.3	307,502 / 23.7	310,120 / 21.7	2,480,960
Other products	140,907 / 12.7	180,816 / 14.3	202,071 / 14.2	197,960 / 14.9	86,401 / 15.8	200,666 / 15.5	289,762 / 20.2	2,318,096
Net sales	¥1,111,021	¥1,261,546	¥1,420,785	¥1,325,158	¥547,749	¥1,295,044	¥1,431,222	$11,449,776

SOURCE: Sony, *Annual Report, 1988.*

FIGURE 17–1   Nestlé 1987 Sales by Geographical Subdivision, in Main Markets; and by Main Product Groups.
SOURCE: Nestlé, *Annual Report, 1987.*

Geographical subdivision of 1987 sales
(in millions of Swiss francs)

Europe	**15,194**	(43.1%)
North America	**10,058**	(28.5%)
Asia	**4,577**	(13.0%)
Latin America and Caribbean	**3,509**	(10.0%)
Africa	**1,043**	(3.0%)
Oceania	**860**	(2.4%)

1987 Sales by Main Products Groups

Drinks	30.1%
Dairy products	17.9%
Culinary products	11.7%
Frozen foods and ice-cream	10.5%
Chocolate and confectionery	7.9%
Refrigerated products	7.9%
Infant foods and dietetic products	5.7%
Petfoods	4.3%
Pharmaceutical and cosmetic products	2.2%
Subsidiary products/activities	1.0%
Hotels and restaurants	0.8%

Sales in Main Markets

	1987 Sales in millions of francs	Differences in francs	1987/1986 in local currency
United States	**9,298**	−15.7%	+ 1.5%
France	**4,160**	+ 5.3%	+ 10.1%
Federal Rep. of Germany	**3,837**	+ 1.8%	+ 1.7%
Japan	**2,266**	−12.1%	− 9.4%
United Kingdom	**1,852**	− 6.1%	+ 1.6%
Brazil	**1,628**	− 3.0%	+231.4%
Spain	**1,522**	− 4.1%	+ 1.8%
Italy	**939**	+ 1.5%	+ 5.9%
Switzerland	**872**	+ 3.1%	+ 3.1%
Canada	**760**	− 9.7%	+ 3.5%

TABLE 17-3
Foreign Operations Disclosures by Multinational Corporations—Geographic Area Disclosures

Disclosure Item	By Selected Countries								
	European						North American		Japan (N=34)
	United Kingdom (N=58)	West Germany (N=28)	France (N=13)	Netherlands (N=9)	Sweden (N=13)	Switzerland (N=11)	United States (N=94)	Canada (N=11)	
Foreign sales	93%	90%	87%	89%	100%	91%	100%	100%	65%
Sales by geographic areas	93	71	87	67	100	91	86	91	29
Foreign income	74	7	87	33	23	0	98	73	12
Income by geographic areas	67	0	40	22	23	0	84	64	0
Foreign assets	19	10	40	22	31	18	92	91	15
Assets by geographic areas	17	0	13	22	15	18	85	46	3
Exports from home country	78	61	13	11	62	10	25	27	53
Exports by geographic areas	14	10	0	0	8	0	5	18	21
Capital expenditures: foreign	19	36	20	33	39	46	15	9	15
Capital expenditures by geo. areas	19	23	20	33	15	46	11	9	3
Avg. no. of geo. areas reported	6.3	3.5	4.1	4.6	10.6	5.8	3.2	4.0	3.9

SOURCE: F. D. S. Choi and V. Bavishi, "A Cross-National Assessment of Management's Geographic Disclosures," paper presented at the Fourth Annual Meeting of the European Accounting Association, Barcelona, Spain, March 1981.

cording to one classification, these special impact reports take three forms: environmental quality, the effect a company has on its employees and the community, and national income accounting.[5]

The topics covered by special reports include controlling or correcting environmental pollution and ensuring product safety; assuring employee welfare in terms of equal opportunity, safe working conditions, and personnel practices; community involvement and contributions; and corporate morals, as embodied in codes of conduct and ethical guidelines. In some countries firms must attempt to identify the extent of their contribution to the national economic situation, both directly, as a result of investment and operations, and indirectly, by way of its contribution to increased employment. In France any firm with three hundred or more employees must prepare a *bilan social,* or social balance sheet. A similar kind of report, the *Social Jaareslag,* is required in the Netherlands and *social bilanz* in Germany.

The trend toward requiring firms to be accountable for the social effects of their operations is growing worldwide. A MNC must take this aspect into consideration when devising accounting procedures and practices for an overseas subsidiary. Necessary expertise must be created to generate such reports, and the company's operations must be sensitive to these concerns. The result is that accountants in these nations and those responsible for reporting from a multinational perspective must enlarge their views and take these reporting requirements into consideration and develop expertise in new areas.

Policy Formation and Harmonization

Determining Policy

The determination of accounting policy—the setting of objectives, standards, and practices used by accounting professionals in each nation of the

[5] Arpan and Radebaugh 1985.

world—derives from two sources. Policy emanates either from national laws and the codification of practices, or it is developed by members of the accounting profession itself, who represent their entire national membership and agree upon standards to be observed by practitioners.

The legal requirements of, or restrictions upon, accounting practices come either from regulations imposed by government users of accounting information, such as tax authorities, or from planning agencies or national legislators. The relative importance of the roles played by these entities in the determination of accounting policy depends on two major determinants—the status and size of the accounting profession in each nation and the degree to which each government seeks to control or monitor business activity. Thus, it is not surprising that government forces are exceedingly strong in setting accounting policy in nations with planned economic systems, and that they are far weaker and less intrusive in market economies.

Policymaking in the United States

Accounting policy in the United States is determined primarily by members of its highly sophisticated and well-regulated accounting profession. These members create policy by working together to develop a set of generally accepted accounting principles. The main policy-setting body in the United States is the Financial Accounting Standards Board (FASB), which determines accounting policy and promulgates such determinations through its publication of statements on issues of concern. The policies and statements are accepted by the American Institute of Certified Public Accountants (AICPA), another independent body of professionals, which sets auditing standards for external accounting requirements. Accounting practices are also delineated by law in the United States and are primarily requirements established by the SEC for all companies that issue securities to the public and by federal tax law, as set forth in the federal tax code.

Policymaking in Other Countries

Policymaking in other countries varies along a continuum, because all countries include some combination of accounting policy set by legislation and by professional practice. The differences in policy come from differences in political orientation, levels of professionalism, the development of the accounting profession in each country, and from the nature and depth of business within each country.

Some countries that rely more on legislation than on practice are those with strong governmental intervention in economic activity, such as France, Germany, Egypt, and Brazil. Other nations, such as England, have a greater combination of law and professional involvement in standard-setting, while others, such as the Netherlands and Switzerland, experience minimal influence from legislative efforts.

Some nations, such as Japan, have only recently developed accounting standards and have patterned their systems on those of other nations—in Japan's case, the United States and Germany. Some countries, particularly less-developed nations, have adopted the principles of their former colonial governments and rely on legislation to set standards, because the membership of the accounting profession is small and not well-regarded.

Harmonization

Divergences have always existed among accounting systems around the world. These differences lead to complications that are intensified with the increase in international business activity. To combat these problems, efforts have been mounted to standardize accounting functions to some degree on a regional and international basis. Such efforts are generally known as harmonization among accounting executives, practices, and standards.

Three different methods of attempting to establish harmony among accounting methods that differ according to the requirements of users or circumstances have been identified—absolute uniformity, circumstantial uniformity, and purposive uniformity models.[6] Absolute uniformity proposes that accounting methods be standardized regardless of the different circumstances of different users. This model has been criticized as being too inflexible and too radical, although it would, theoretically, be easier to administer than other models.

Circumstantial uniformity would use different practices according to the variations in the circumstances of economic facts and conditions. Once these circumstances are identified, accounting practices can be put into place to deal with them on a consistent basis. Purposive uniformity would vary the determination of accounting practices and standards according to both diversity of users and circumstances. This model has the advantage of providing flexibility for differing environmental situations and purposes and is embodied in U.S. regulatory practices.

The greatest effort to bring the postulates and practices of accounting into harmony in the international accounting arena is the International Accounting Standards Committee (IASC), which was formed in June 1983 and in 1991 consisted of accounting professionals representing sixty-two countries and eighty-eight accounting organizations. The purpose of the IASC is to provide a forum through which members of professional accounting groups can attempt to develop international standards that can be used in domestic operations. The representatives of the IASC are hampered, however, in that they have no authority to enforce any decisions and can only promise to promote such standards in the publication of financial statements, with policy-setting organizations, and with government or regulatory officials. The hope is that each nation will adopt their standards and resolutions, either as professional standards or as national law.

Another international organization is the International Federation of Accountants (IFAC), which was formed in 1977 to succeed the International Coordination Committee for the Account-

[6] Ibid.

ing Profession. The objective of the IFAC is to provide a forum through which members of the world's accounting profession can meet to establish international standards and principles for auditing practices, as well as standards for the training, education, and codes of ethics of accountants. The IFAC consists of members from sixty-two countries and represent more than eighty professional accounting groups.[7]

Regional Harmonization Efforts

Regional efforts at harmonization often fall in line with historical economic or political groupings of nations. Some of the regional national accounting associations are the Inter-American Accounting Association (IAA), the Union of European Accountants (UEC), and the Confederation of Asian and Pacific Accountants (CAPA). The problem with these groups is that although they can meet and attempt to harmonize standards, they are generally comprised of practitioners who have no authority behind their decision-making to promote standardization. They can, however, use their influence to affect policy-setting in individual countries and among their own national professional associations.

One regional grouping where the force of law is brought to bear on the practice of accounting, however, is the European Economic Community (EEC), which will be fully integrated by 1992. In the EEC accounting standards are developed through the issuance of directives developed by its Council of Ministers. The EEC's progress toward harmonization of accounting practices has led to mandates for member countries to bring their laws into harmonization on selected topics. In 1978, for example, the council issued its Fourth Directive, which covered the presentation of financial statements and established minimum disclosure requirements, with the underlying principle that presentations be made in a manner that is

a true and fair representation of the operating results and financial position of companies and that the interests of third parties are protected.

Special Accounting Problems

Despite efforts to harmonize accounting practices and standards around the world, the managers of enterprises with operations in multiple foreign settings face formidable difficulties. Four specific problems faced by multinational firms are accounting for differences in gains and losses because of differences in currency exchange rates, the question of consolidating returns, accounting under conditions of inflation, and the problems faced in attempting to establish appropriate prices and costs for a multinational's products around the world and between units.

Differences in Currency Exchange Rates

One of the most crucial problems that international firms face is accounting for a transaction that is conducted in a different currency. How is such a transaction to be recorded on the books or reported to management in a consistent manner?

Differences in exchange rates between currencies cause two separate problems for the international business firm. The first is that of accounting for business **transactions** and gains and losses from currency rate differentials that arise during such business activity. The second problem is interpreting financial results of transactions conducted in different currencies or devising **translations** of currencies to yield comparable and measurable results.

Accounting procedures designed to treat these transactions follow either the one-step transaction or the two-step transaction approaches, both of which provide methods for recording business transactions in a home currency.

[7] Ibid.

The one-step method records the transaction using the spot rate for the foreign currency in effect on that day. Assume, for example, that Bob of Bob's Lawn and Garden Store wants to acquire lawn ornaments from a German supplier to round out his inventory in anticipation of heavy summer sales. Thus, on January 1, Bob buys 10,000 gross of pink flamingos for 60,000 DM payable by February 1. On the first of January the deutsche mark is trading for $.50 (that is, each dollar is worth 2 DM). Consequently, under the one-step method Bob's ledger entries would be as follows:

Purchases: Pink Flamingos $30,000
Accounts Payable $30,000
DM @ $.50

If, however, exchange rates change between the time Bob places his order, records it in his books, and pays his account with the German flamingo maker, he will need to change his records to record the facts and the rate of exchange when the transaction is completed or actually settled. For example, if the value of the dollar falls and it takes $.75 to buy a DM, Bob's costs for his pink flamingos will rise and must be accounted for as an adjustment to the original cost of the flamingos. The entries he must make will be:

Purchases $30,000
Accounts Payable $15,000
    Cash $45,000
    DM @ $.75

The two-step method of accounting for gains or losses in transactions separates the activities of business activity and currency exchanges. The key difference from the one-step method is that gains or losses from the transaction do not affect the value of the asset acquired but are treated separately, as a result of assuming risk in engaging in the activity and opening the firm to fluctuations in exchange rates. Consequently, under this method our transaction above would be noted as follows:

Accounts Payable $30,000
Exchange Adjustment: Loss $15,000
    Cash $45,000
    DM @ $.75

In this method, the pink flamingos retain their value of $30,000 on Bob's books, and the difference between the agreed-upon price or costs and the actual amount paid is noted in an exchange adjustment account that is eventually netted and applied as an adjustment to shareholder equity.

Some countries require the use of the one-step method, others employ the two-step method. The United States employs the two-step method and requires the immediate recognition of gains or losses from foreign currency transactions. In other countries it is common accounting practice to defer gains and losses from accounts payable and receivable until the transactions are completed, and these results are not taken to the income statement.

These accounting steps become far more involved when firms engage in hedging to protect themselves from fluctuations in rates of exchanges between countries. It must be remembered, however, that such complications arise only when the transaction is denominated in a foreign currency. Bob could have asked to pay his bill in dollars, in which case, he would have no risk because of changes in the rate of exchange between deutsche marks and dollars. Instead, the German manufacturer would take the currency risk and account for any changes in the dollar's value.

Problems arise for multinational firms with business operations that are carried out in different locales and reported in different currencies. When MNCs are required to translate local currency accounts into home currency at the close of the financial year, what criteria does a MNC use to report and compare its operations in different environments? These problems are not ones of valuation (determining appropriate values for assets in terms of other currencies) or of converting currencies from foreign to a uniform home currency, but are those involved in restating operational results. The objective is that such results can be integrated so that they can be analyzed by management and reported to regulatory authorities. The process of restating financial statements into a uniform currency is called **translation.** When the financial statements from all operating units of a MNC are combined, they are said to be **consolidated.**

Foreign statement translation is a two-step process for the controller of a MNC. First, the accounts must be brought into consistency by being restated according to the same accounting principles, such as those for valuing inventories and assets and determining depreciation. After the basis of the accounts has been adjusted to provide for consistency, the foreign currency amounts represented in the results can be translated into the reporting or home currency. Translation must not be confused with conversion. Translating is merely the restating of currencies, while conversion refers to the actual physical trade or exchange of units of one currency for another.

Accountants use four different methods of translating statements from local currencies to the reporting or home currency—the current rate method, the temporal method, the monetary-nonmonetary method, and the current-noncurrent method (see Table 17–4).

Statement number 52 of the Financial Accounting Standards Board (FASB) introduced some new definitional concepts to the translation of foreign exchange accounts. The first is the use of a **functional currency,** which is defined as the "currency of the primary economic environment in which the entity operates".[8] It is differentiated from the **reporting** currency, which is the reporting currency of the parent. The determination of a functional currency is tricky for some subsidiaries. It could be the local currency if most of the subsidiary's business of buying, selling, or manufacturing is conducted using the local currency. The parent company's reporting currency could also be the functional currency, if the subsidiary's operations consist mostly of selling goods to the parent, or even be the currency of a third country, if the bulk of the entity's business is conducted in a third country.

The responsibility for choosing the functional currency rests with each firm, based on operational criteria regarding currencies involved in cash

[8] Financial Accounting Standards Board 1981.

TABLE 17-4
Exchange Rates Employed in Different Translation Methods for Specific Balance Sheet Items

	Current	Current-Noncurrent	Monetary-Nonmonetary	Temporal
Cash	C	C	C	C
Accounts receivable	C	C	C	C
Inventories				
Cost	C	C	H	H
Market	C	C	H	C
Investments				
Cost	C	H	H	H
Market	C	H	H	C
Fixed assets	C	H	H	H
Other assets	C	H	H	H
Accounts payable	C	C	C	C
Long-term debt	C	H	C	C
Common stock	H	H	H	H
Retaining earnings	*	*	*	*

NOTE: C = current rate; H = historical rate; and * = residual, balancing figure representing a composite of successive current rates.

flows, prices, sales market, expenses, financing, and intercompany indicators. Functional currencies can change, but only if there is a change in the initial underlying operational criteria, a stipulation imposed by the FASB to prevent arbitrary changes in functional currencies that aggressive accountants might make to put financial statements in the best possible light.

Once the functional currency is determined, a firm can begin its process of translating statements under FASB #52 and consolidating, or combining, the results of disparate operations. The use of either the current or the temporal rate is determined by the location of operations and resulting functional currency. If the books and records are kept in the currency of the parent, no restatement is necessary. If, however, the books and records are kept in a local currency, the subsidiary has three different translation routes, depending on the functional currency.

If the functional currency is the local currency of the subsidiary, the parent merely translates the statements into U.S. dollars using the current-rate method. This situation holds unless the functional currency is a local currency in a high-inflation country, in which case the firm must use the temporal method of translation. High-inflation countries are defined as those as with inflation rates greater than 100 percent for three consecutive years.

If the functional currency is the parents' home currency, even if the books are kept in the local currency, the firm uses the temporal method to remeasure results. If the functional currency is a third currency, the firm remeasures from the local to the functional currency using the temporal method and then translates the result into the home currency using the current rate method. Figure 17–2 provides a clearer description of this process.

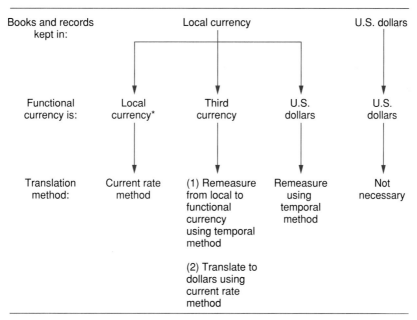

*In the case of a highly inflationary economy, the local currency may be the functional currency from an operating standpoint, but the dollar is considered the functional currency from a translation standpoint.

FIGURE 17–2　Translating a Firm's Functional Currency into a Reporting Currency.

Consolidation Problems

The results of these financial machinations are then integrated into a firm's comprehensive reckoning of operations and results. This consolidation process raises some special considerations for a MNC and questions about a firm's organizational and investment decisions. For example, what operations should be consolidated into the firms overall operations? Some countries require only that the parent report the results of its operations and do not require the integration of the results of subsidiary or affiliated arms. In the United States, for example, tax laws require that firms consolidate their operations globally, because firms are taxed on worldwide income (although they are given credit for taxes paid to other governments). Some other issues raised are: What if a parent corporation owns only part interest in a subsidiary? What level of investment determines ownership or determines control? What distinction is made between having an investment in another concern or that concern's being an integral part of the parent corporation's network?

CONSOLIDATION RULES IN THE UNITED STATES

In the United States the questions about whether or not a parent consolidates the results of subsidiary operations into its own depends on the level and type of involvement of the parent in the activities of the subsidiary. There are three different ways an investment in another enterprise can be handled under accounting rules—the **cost method,** the **equity method,** or **consolidation.** The cost method is employed when the parent firm holds an unsubstantial investment in the subsidiary. Under this method, the parent carries the investment as such and only reports income from the subsidiary when the subsidiary declares a dividend to the parent. The cost method can only be used in the United States when the parent owns less than 20 percent of the voting stock of the affiliate and was acquired initially through purchasing. Monies flowing back to the parent are

treated as dividends and do not change the level of the investment account of the parent.

If the parent owns a substantial portion of the stock of the subsidiary, from 20 percent to 50 percent, it reports income from the subsidiary as it is earned, not as it is received. The investment is carried on the parent's books at original cost and is adjusted according to earnings or dividends received from the subsidiary. Income from the foreign subsidiary increases the value of the parent's investment (whether it is received or not), and thus the value of the holding is adjusted upward to reflect an increase in the share of profits. Any dividends received by the parent from its holdings in the subsidiary have the effect of reducing the investment's book value, because it is considered to have the effect of lowering the profits of the subsidiary.

If the parent owns more than 50 percent of the subsidiary, it has a controlling interest in the foreign affiliate and must consolidate the results of the affiliate into its own reports. The consolidation process is carried out line by line to agree with the financial statements of the parent. Thus, before the two sets of figures are aggregated, they must be adjusted to agree according to the accounting principles used, and foreign currencies must be translated into the reporting currency. The parent and the affiliate must also adjust their books to correct for their intercorporate transactions and profits that have resulted from business dealings between the two entities.

Inflation

Companies doing business in high-inflation countries must develop special procedures for dealing with the effects of inflation on the valuation of assets. Inflation also raises problems for MNCs in their attempts to evaluate and predict purchasing power for foreign operations and in evaluating their financial reports. As long as there are few changes in prices in a country, MNCs attempting to value their assets can use historical costs for those assets as appropriate measures. When inflation is significant, however, the value of those assets stated in historical terms inaccurately represents the wealth of the firm.

There are basically two responses when dealing with inflation. One can either reestablish a new basis for historical values that reflects the effects of inflation, or one can put into place a system that constantly corrects for changes in prices. In practice, under the first model, all financial statements are adjusted at a single point in time, and these adjusted costs become the new historical basis; under the second model, values are indexed on a continual basis according to changes in prices.

In accounting practice the use of models depends on the objectives of the financial reports. The two methods of handling inflation in terms of accounting methods are constant dollar (or general purchasing power) accounting and current cost accounting.

The goal of **constant dollar accounting** is to report assets, liabilities, expenses, and revenues in terms of the same purchasing power. The original basis of the valuations, the historical costs, does not change under this accounting method. Instead, nonfinancial items are restated to reflect the purchasing power in effect on the date of the balance sheet. Financial items on the statements, such as cash, receivables, and payables, would not be restated because their monetary valuation would already reflect the purchasing power of the currency on the date of the report.

In **current cost accounting,** the emphasis is not on the loss of purchasing power associated with a specific currency, but the amount of money it would take to replace assets because of price increases. Thus, under current cost accounting, historical costs are supplanted by new, adjusted costs, such as replacement costs. Its objective is to account for the effects of inflation as it relates to the increases in the costs of specific assets and not overall prices.

The treatment of inflation in the presentation of accounting records differs around the world. In the United States, firms are required to continue to use the historical cost standard as their basis for reporting financial results, but they are also required to disclose supplementary information re-

garding both price level and current cost accounting. Other countries have different requirements. In Great Britain, current cost balance sheets and income statements must be presented, and such financial statements may be presented as supplements to or in place of historical costs financial statements.[9] Some high-inflation countries, such as Brazil and Chile, require that firms adjust their statements to reflect the enormous rates of inflation, and require the use of an inflation index and a monetary correction systems, respectively.

The result of these different methods of accounting for inflation is that the MNC operating in a multitude of foreign environments must often keep multiple sets of books in order to adhere to the reporting requirements of each jurisdiction and the parent firm's home authorities.

Transfer Pricing and Costing

The international nature of the business of MNCs introduces a number of factors that have to be accounted for in determining the costs of their products around the world. Although multinational firms use the same methods for determining costs as domestic enterprises, their efforts are greatly complicated by the nature of operations in a global environment. For example, products and raw materials are not only affected by domestic forces, such as inflation and availability, but are also affected by such international forces as changes in exchange rates, transportation fees, insurance costs, customs duties, and facilitating payments. Similarly, costs involved in conducting international trade are often influenced by government subsidies that are intended to promote exports sales.

Such costing and pricing problems are significant for exported products manufactured domestically; they are even worse for firms that have raw material and parts sources in several parts of the world. The complications become enormous, as costs accountants attempt to allocate costs to

---

[9] Arpan and Radebaugh. 1985.

different products and operating units within different countries.

Transfers within the various affiliated arms of an MNC, especially for transfer pricing for goods and services between different parts of the company, create complex accounting issues. MNCs can use transfer pricing to achieve a variety of corporate objectives, such as reducing overall tax burden, avoiding restrictions on repatriation of earnings, or the exchange of local for home country currencies. Thus, transfer prices set by MNCs not only concern the strategic decision-makers in the company, but they also often come under scrutiny of external government officials. A MNC can deal with this problem to some extent by adjusting its performance measures for the subsidiary to focus on different criteria, such as achieving production efficiencies and maintaining low costs.

Companies have three ways of valuing goods and services that pass between arms or branches of the same corporation. They can use a cost-plus method, where they take actual costs of production and add a fixed monetary amount or percentage. Alternately, they can use the market price, less a certain percentage discount. Under arm's-length pricing they can charge the same price for affiliates or parents as they do for third-party buyers. While cost-based transfer pricing has the advantage of providing the firm with flexibility, most governments prefer the easily determined and monitored use of market-based pricing systems by MNCs. The United States requires that firms use arm's-length prices, unless they can justify why different prices based on costs are more reasonable than those based on market prices.

Other International Accounting Issues

Accounting for Expropriation

One potential problem for any firm conducting business in a foreign environment is the politi-

cal risk that its assets will be taken over by the government through expropriation or nationalization. When a firm is remunerated by a country for expropriated assets, many questions arise about determining the appropriate value of those assets in relation to the monies received. Book or historical values are not usually representative of true, current value, because they may not reflect what it would cost to replace the assets or what monies would actually be received if those assets were sold on the open market. The determination of value is generally arbitrary, not market-oriented, because expropriation usually results from political action. Similarly, there are seldom comparable sales of similar assets or replacement assets in the country on which to base an estimation of value for the expropriated assets.

Consequently, in order to determine its position regarding gain or loss on the disposition of the assets, MNCs in such situations must use an adjusted asset book value that accounts for increases in economic value over time. Thus, values placed on expropriated property are highly subjective. Once these values are estimated and compared to payments made by the expropriating government, the firm must deal with its gain or loss on the property. Such gains and losses shown as operating items do not affect the financial results of the firm in the United States, where losses because of expropriation are reported net of tax effects and are classified as extraordinary items. Most other countries allow such losses to be taken as direct write-offs against owners' equity or equity reserve accounts.[10]

Planning and Control

One of the biggest problems faced by MNCs in the implementation of international accounting methods and systems is the sheer multitude and variety of players, reporting sites, requirements, and forms. Thus, it is crucial that the international firm have a well-organized and comprehensive system of financial reporting and control in

[10] Frederick D. S. Choi and Gerhard G. Mueller. 1984. *International Accounting*. Englewood Cliffs, NJ: Prentice-Hall.

place to generate accurate, timely, and usable information. Many firms often take their existing domestic systems abroad, but these systems may need to be adjusted for local needs and different accounting requirements and conventions. For example, employees at a foreign site may find systems designed for the home environment too sophisticated for their levels of expertise, training, or abilities.

Ideally, MNCs should develop reporting functions and formats that can be used by all members of the network. Information supplied by all parts of the operating system must be uniform. Therefore, a MNC must decide beforehand on common formats, language, and currencies, as well as a set of procedures to be followed. Similarly, care must be taken in the development of budgets, goals, and objectives for MNC subsidiaries and affiliates. A MNC must take into account different operating environments in setting goals and in evaluating relative performance.

Auditing

Once an accounting system is in place and operational, its **efficiency** must be continually monitored by auditing. There are two types of auditing in a corporation. Internal audits assess whether or not the firm has proper operational and financial controls to assure the security of its assets and the compliance of individual employees in the operation of the system. External audits look objectively at the ledgers of a firm and provide an opinion as to whether or not the information recorded is valid, reliable, and accurate. This is the attest function of accounting. External auditors base their judgments on standards developed by the accounting profession; they are accounting professionals who have no affiliation with the corporation. Conducting external, independent audits provides a large portion of the business of the major accounting firms in the United States.

For internal audits conducted at a foreign subsidiary level, a firm has the choice of using local auditors or bringing in personnel from headquarters. The use of both types of auditors presents

problems. Local auditors might facilitate the auditing process in keeping expenses down and avoiding language and cultural differences. Problems might arise, however, in terms of the rigorousness of corporate standards applied by local personnel because of their potential lack of familiarity with corporate requirements. Whereas auditors from headquarters could better examine subsidiary procedural lapses, they would run up against problems of their being unfamiliar with the language, the people, and the business practices accepted in the foreign environment.

Summary

International business transactions present several accounting problems and raise many accounting issues because they encompass different environments, currencies, reporting requirements, and forms. The challenge of satisfying these financial and managerial accounting information needs must be met with an eye to developing uniform systems of reporting information in a manner that provides for its efficient integration and utilization by all users. Effective and accurate reporting of business transactions is required in order to present an accurate picture of the economic situation of the firm to both internal and external users.

Discussion Questions

1. Who are the users of accounting information?
2. What factors influence the development of international accounting systems?
3. What is financial disclosure? Can this vary between countries? Explain.
4. What are the main differences in accounting conventions?
5. What is social reporting?
6. What role does the FASB have in setting accounting policy? Explain in terms of its domestic and international roles.

7. What regional international accounting organizations are trying to harmonize accounting practices? Discuss.

8. What is the difference between functional currency and reporting currency?

9. What are the four main accounting problems faced by multinationals?

10. How do multinationals account for losses due to expropriation?

11. Why are planning, control, and auditing important accounting functions?

Bibliography

ARPAN, JEFFREY S., AND DHIA D. AL-HASHIM. 1984. *International Dimensions of Accounting* Boston: Kent Publishing.

ARPAN, J. S., AND L. H. RADEBAUGH. 1985. *International Accounting and Multinational Enterprises,* 2nd ed. New York: John Wiley & Sons.

BUCKLEY, ADRIAN. 1987. "Does FX Exposure Matter?" *Accountancy* (March): 116–118.

CAIRNS, DAVID. 1989. "IASC's Blueprint for the Future." *Accountancy* (December): 80–82.

CARSBERG, B. 1983. "FASB #52—Measuring the Performance of Foreign Operations," *Midland Corporate Finance Journal* 1: 47-55.

CHOI, FREDERICK D. S. 1975. "Multinational Challenges for Managerial Accountants." *Journal of Contemporary Business* (Autumn): 51–68.

CHOI, FREDERICK D. S., AND VINOD B. BAVISHI. 1981. "A Cross-National Assessment of Management's Geographic Disclosure," paper presented at the Fourth Annual Meeting of the European Accounting Association, Barcelona.

———. 1982. "Diversity in Multinational Accounting." *Financial Executive* (August): 45–49.

———, AND G. G. MUELLER. 1987. *An Introduction to Multinational Accounting.* Englewood Cliffs, NJ: Prentice-Hall.

FINANCIAL ACCOUNTING STANDARDS BOARD. 1981. *Statement of Financial Accounting Standards. No. 52: Foreign Currency Translation,* Stamford, CT: Financial Accounting Standards Board.

CHAPTER 18

International Taxation

CHAPTER OBJECTIVES

This chapter will:

- Present a rationale for the role and purpose of tax policy in modern society.
- Discuss the major forms of taxation employed by governments, including income, transaction, excise, severance, and tariff taxes, and the differences in compliance and enforcement of tax laws between countries.
- Describe special tax problems, treaties, and credits that may influence site selection for multinational operations.
- Review the advantages offered by international tax havens.
- Examine the types of incentives governments offer to corporations and to foreign nationals to promote international business.

Taxes are what we pay for a civilized society.
Oliver Wendell Holmes

Why Taxes?

Taxes paid to governing bodies represent the contributions that all individual citizens and businesses make to public coffers. These funds finance most public services, including public education, state and federal government systems, local police and national defense forces, highway and waterway systems, protection of the environment, maintenance of state and federal parks and wilderness areas, and social programs that provide for the less fortunate by establishing housing, education, health care, and nutritional services.

The societal expectation underlying the principle that all wage earners should make a contribution to society is that it be a fair or equitable share. Every corporation or citizen in the same economic or business situation should thus be required to pay the same level of taxes. While the notion of equity underlies most national tax sys-

457

tems, it is not "fair" because every citizen does not pay the same proportion of wages in taxes. Therefore, most tax systems are progressive, and the more a person or corporation earns, the higher their tax bill because they are considered to be better able to pay a larger share.

In addition to the fairness or equity principle, tax systems are frequently based on the notion of neutrality, which means that business decisions and economic activities should not be prejudiced or directed by the consequences of tax policy. The rationale is that economic efficiency dictates that funds or capital should flow to the most efficient use. In practice, however, nations use tax policy to achieve other objectives, often at the expense of reducing economic efficiency of capital resources.

Governments may, for example, assess taxes to discourage consumption of scarce or unhealthy goods, such as alcohol and tobacco. Taxes may be applied to imports to raise their prices, discourage their purchase, and increase the relative attractiveness of domestic goods. Similarly, tax breaks may be instituted to encourage investment in specific industries, such as developing new sources of energy.

Policy objectives differ around the world, as do systems of taxation. These differences create problems for MNCs, which seek to minimize their multinational tax burden while optimizing the use of their financial and other resources in several countries.

Unfortunately, taxes often have a major impact on operational decisions. What international activities should be pursued? In what countries? How should activities be financed? Tax considerations are also involved in decisions concerning the form taken by different subsidiaries of an MNC and how prices will be determined between various segments and corporate headquarters.

Tax law is generally complex. U.S. federal tax law, for example, was simplified (theoretically) in 1986. In published form, however, Public Law 99-499 alone covers more than 6,500 pages of text. Further explanations of the law and accompanying regulations constitute many thousands more pages of text. In 1988 the Internal Revenue Ser-

vice found that the tasks of recordkeeping, learning about the law, and filing the basic 1040 tax return took longer than an average day's work (nine hours and five minutes). The addition of other schedules, such as Schedule A for itemized deductions or Schedule B for interest and dividend income, were estimated to require an additional 4.5 and 1.5 hours, respectively.

Multiply such complexity by the addition of business technicalities and information, as well as by the number of international environments in which modern MNCs operate, and you have an idea of the difficulties involved in managing the tax function of a multinational enterprise. These complications also increase the difficulty for managers to factor all relevant tax consequences into business decision-making.

Types of Taxes

Income Taxes

There are many different types of taxes levied throughout the world. **Income taxes** are those levied by nation-states on the earnings or other inflows of money of individuals and businesses. Such taxes are generally levied in a progressive manner; the more one earns, the higher a person is taxed. Income taxes are determined according to a person or firm's taxable income, that is, income that has been adjusted or reduced by deductions allowed by law.

Tax deductions account for expenses incurred by businesses or individuals and are subtracted from the taxpayer's total income. Tax deductions for individuals may be itemized or a standardized allowable sum The standard deduction may be subtracted from income. For individuals, such items as medical expenses, charitable contributions, mortgage interest, and losses from disaster or theft can be itemized and deducted from income before taxes are levied. Alternatively, individuals can take standard deductions, which, under 1986 U.S. law, range from $3,000 for individuals to $5,000 for married couples filing together or spouses surviving widowhood. In addition, income is adjusted for family size and special circumstances through the allowance of exemptions, each worth $1,080 in deductions from income. Deductions from income yield savings in taxes at the applicable tax rate, not in a dollar-for-dollar manner, because they reduce the income upon which taxes are levied. Thus, if the tax rate applied to one's income is 33 percent, each dollar's worth of tax deductions yields a savings of $.33.

Once taxable income is determined, taxes are calculated according to that amount. Adjustments to (reductions in) the amount of taxes due are characterized as tax credits. Because these credits reduce the actual tax liability, they yield tax savings on a dollar-per-dollar basis. Credits are allowed for individuals in the United States for such items as care for children, dependents, or disabled people; for contributions to political parties; taxes paid to foreign governments; and general business credits.

Companies are allowed such credits against their tax bills as expenses for general business; taxes paid to U.S. possessions or foreign governments; and the production of orphan drugs or energy from nonconventional sources. These credits show some of the social considerations taken into account in the development of tax policy. Orphan drugs for example, are those produced in very small quantities and are used by very small groups of consumers. Consequently, they may be economically inefficient to produce by large drug manufacturing concerns. To compensate drug companies for providing this service, a tax credit gives companies an incentive to provide for the medical needs of these citizens. Similarly, a credit for the production of energy from nonconventional sources (such as grain, wind, or solar power) provides incentives for citizens to look to new energy sources and to reduce reliance on fossil fuels.

Transaction Taxes

Another method of assessing taxes is that applied to transactions. **Transaction taxes** are levied at the time a transaction occurs or an exchange takes place. The most common transaction tax encountered by citizens of the United States are state and local sales taxes, which are paid when items are purchased. Sales or transaction taxes are not progressive and do not discriminate in their application. All people are taxed at the same rate on their purchases, regardless of their individual wealth.

Value-Added Taxes

One variation of the transaction tax that is widely used in European countries is the **value-added tax** or **VAT**. The VAT was first put into effect in France in 1954 and takes the place of income taxes in some countries. It is a tax that is assessed only upon the value added to products at each level of production. Take for example, a French boutique that sells high-fashion clothing on the retail level. The VAT tax in France is assumed to be 10 percent. The first stage in the process of producing these items comes with the purchase of material to make the garments; thus, F200 million worth of fabric is bought from suppliers. The VAT tax on the purchase is 20 million francs (10% × F200 million).

At the next stage, the garment pieces are cut and assembled. This production work doubles their value, thus they sell at the wholesale level for F400 million and the VAT connected with the sale is F20 million (10% × (F400 − F200 million)). Finally, the suits sell to the boutique owner for F500 million, and the VAT generated at this stage is F10 million (10% × the value added of F100 million). Thus, the total VAT collected is F50 million on the total value of F500 (see Table 18–1).

In practice, at each stage the buyer pays the VAT on the entire amount, and the seller forwards the tax to the country's treasury department. In our example, the first buyer is the manufacturer (M) who buys fabric for F200 million plus F20 million in VAT. The manufacturer's supplier (S) remits the tax to the appropriate tax authorities. M then sells the fabric as garments to the retailer

TABLE 18-1
Example of the Application of a VAT (in millions of French francs)

Production Value Stage of Product	Value Added		VAT Generated
Raw Material	200		20
Manufacturing	400	200	20
Retail	500	100	10
TOTAL VAT			50

(R) for F400 million plus F40 million in VAT. M sends the VAT to the government, but applies for a refund of the VAT withheld by the original supplier (S). In this way M is assessed only on the value it added to the raw materials through production efforts of cutting and assembly (400 − 200 × 10% = 20 million).

The VAT is generally passed through to the consumers as an indirect tax; it can, however, be absorbed by the producer. If the product is taken out of the country as an export the VAT is not applied and is rebated entirely to the exporter. Such rebates create incentives to export because prices for export goods are cheaper than for domestic goods. These rebates on goods exported from European countries have created controversy among members of the international community, who claim that rebating VAT for exports yields incentives that are unfair under the terms of the General Agreement on Tariffs and Trade (GATT).

In general, VAT taxes have the advantage of being easily administered; they can be raised or lowered easily. They have the disadvantage of not being progressive in that rich and poor people alike make the same contribution to taxes by the purchase of goods, regardless of the type of goods.

Excise Taxes

Another type of taxes, **excise taxes** are imposed upon the manufacture, sale, or use of goods or on an activity or occupation. They are frequently levied on luxury commodities, such as tobacco or liquor products (in which case they are often referred to as sin taxes); on such basic commodities as gasoline, or on services, such as entertainment. Excise taxes have the advantage of being applicable in specific situations for specific products in order to achieve policy objectives. Some of these objectives may be to limit the use of unhealthy or socially undesirable products, to ration scarce resources, or to regulate the use of specific products.

Extraction Taxes

Another type of selective and special tax is a **severance** or extraction tax. This type of tax is levied upon producers of mined, extracted, or harvested resources, such as minerals, ores, timber, and fuel products. The severance tax serves to reimburse the local or national community for the depletion of its natural resources. It may be assessed on a per-ton basis for ores or as a stumpage fee for timber depletion.

Tariffs (Border Taxes)

Taxes imposed at the borders of a country are generally characterized as tariffs. These border taxes not only allow governments to derive revenue from the entry of goods into the country, but serve to discourage the sale of imports by raising prices in the home market. Tariffs, therefore, encourage or support internal domestic production and the entry of foreign producers to build production facilities in the host country. Thus, tariffs are used by countries to achieve economic objectives of growth and domestic production.

Tax Compliance and Tax Enforcement

In addition to this formidable array of tax types, national governments impose many other types of taxes. Some are taxes upon personal property, gifts received by individuals, estates of those who die, and employment taxes to fund various types of social programs. The relative frequency of use of these taxes in different nations is determined by the objectives of the government. In less-developed countries, for example, it is difficult to impose an income tax because income levels are low, and it is difficult to enforce tax compliance. Therefore, in LDCs it would make sense to impose excise taxes upon luxury goods (paid by those who can most afford them) and severance taxes upon extraction activities to fund the operation of government and government programs.

If the types of taxes imposed vary among countries, so does the level of compliance by corporate and individual citizens and the level of enforcement by national officials. Some nations, such as Italy, are considered lax; others, such as Germany and the United States are considered strict. U.S. tax law makes extensive provisions for the assessment of penalties, fines, and interest payments for failure to file, for a substantial understatement of tax liability and income, for failure to pay taxes due, and for failure to pay estimated taxes. Nevertheless, many Americans continue to engage in tax evasion by attempting to hide income or by conducting business covertly and using cash transactions. Failure to comply with tax laws, however, may include criminal penalties, if the taxpayer intends to defraud the government. Thus, tax laws have been successfully used to prosecute criminals who profit from illegal activities, such as selling drugs or illegal gambling.

Some believe that the level of tax compliance in a country depends not as much on enforcement as on whether or not the public perceives the tax system to be fair. These perceptions explain the foundations of the massive reform effort mounted in the mid-1980s to change U.S. tax law. The belief among some policymakers was that making the law more equitable would induce Americans to pay their fair share. Thus, the 1986 law tightened a number of loopholes and reduced many tax benefits (especially those regarding tax shelters). Still, the United States is actually at the low end of the tax scale. Countries that levy much higher taxes include Sweden and France, which have extensive social welfare systems. In comparison, tax rates are lower in countries that are more oriented toward free-market capitalism, such as Japan and the United States, which also do not have as extensive a net of social welfare programs to support the populace.

International Taxation

Taxes: MNCs

Multinational corporations begin to encounter serious tax problems when they establish operations overseas because they must operate under a new tax code, with its own provisions and compliance procedures. Sales of goods through exports do not affect significantly the tax management of an MNC. Sales made from domestic shores are simply included in total domestic sales. Thus, the source of taxable income is unchanged as is the taxation jurisdiction of the company. Once an MNC establishes operations abroad, however, issues arise over the tax treatment of earnings made overseas by the tax authorities of the parent country. In its tax treatment of arms of parent corporations, the United States differentiates tax treatment by the form of the overseas affiliate, that is, between a **branch** and a **subsidiary**.

Foreign branches are integral parts of MNCs and treated as if they were merely domestic branches. Thus, income from overseas branches is added to the parent's domestic income, and taxes are assessed on that amount. As with domestic branches of a parent corporation, income from a foreign branch is taxed as it is earned, not as it is received. The advantage to an MNC of forming a branch overseas is that any losses in operations from that branch can immediately be offset against domestic earnings. The disadvantage is that taxes are immediately payable and cannot be deferred (postponed) because they are applied to income earned by the branch, not as profits are received.

Foreign affiliates of parent corporations formed as subsidiaries receive different tax treatment because they are incorporated within the borders of a different nation, and thus operate under the principle of *juridic domicile* of the country where they are located and which has taxing jurisdiction. Subsidiaries are liable for taxes paid to the foreign (host) government. Income sent to the parent is considered taxable when actually remitted as dividends, not when earned. Thus, through the reinvestment of profits or holding off on declared dividends, the parent is able to defer home country taxes on certain portions of the income from the subsidiary.

Besides deferral of taxes, subsidiaries have other advantages, such as avoiding border taxes or import duties by manufacturing or producing within the country. They sometimes enjoy lower tax rates in the country of incorporation (host country) than in their home country. From a tax perspective, the drawbacks of using a subsidiary form of organization are that losses cannot be used against parental income and the foreign government may impose withholding taxes on the remittance of dividend income to the parent. In some overseas locations, local taxes may be higher than the home country, and the tax procedures could be more cumbersome.

Taxes: U.S. Controlled Foreign Corporations

Because income generated from the operation of subsidiaries can enjoy deferral of taxes by being reinvested, U.S. tax authorities were faced with the problems created by the establishment of paper corporations abroad by U.S. taxpayers to shelter earnings from taxation. Thus, tax law was amended to provide for taxation of income earned overseas but not remitted to owners.

Under amendments to tax law enacted in 1975, limits were set upon the deferral of income for U.S. controlled foreign corporations (CFCs). Controlled foreign corporations are defined as those in which more than 50 percent of the voting stock of the foreign corporation is owned by U.S. shareholders of any type—individual citizens, partnerships, trusts, or corporations. Therefore, a foreign corporation would be a CFC if five

or more entities hold at least 10 percent ownership each, but not if twenty shareholders each own a 3 percent interest.

If the corporation is defined as a CFC, the owners cannot defer taxes on income, which is defined as Subpart F. Subpart F is a section of the 1962 Revenue Act that contains provisions for taxation of income accruing to U.S. shareholders in foreign incorporated affiliates of U.S. companies, provided such affiliates are deemed to be controlled foreign corporations. Specifically, income arising out of intracorporate deals, known as Subpart F income, is subject to tax under this provision.

Classification of Subpart F income of a U.S. affiliate that is also a CFC is a complex process because there are several exceptions and connected regulations that must be considered. Once, income is classified as belonging to Subpart F, however, it becomes taxable by U.S. authorities at the time it is earned, regardless of whether it is remitted or not from the overseas affiliate to the U.S. shareholders. Typically, income that is taxable under Subpart F arises out of investment returns by way of dividends, royalties, interest, and so on.

Double Taxation

A major problem that occurs for an MNC with overseas operations is that its existence in a multitude of environments subjects it to the jurisdiction of different taxing authorities and to double taxation on the same income. Thus, income earned by an MNC may be taxed when it is earned in the foreign location and again when it is remitted to and realized by the parent corporation. This situation also exists for individuals who earn income abroad. They are taxed on the income earned within the foreign country and by the U.S. government on their worldwide income.

Such double taxation is a clear violation of the U.S. tax principles of equity and fairness. Thus, in order to provide fair treatment of such income, U.S. law provides for a credit against U.S. tax liabilities that can be taken by both corporations and individuals for taxes paid on income to a foreign taxing authority.

Tax Treaties

Bilateral and multilateral tax treaties provide a basis for reciprocal recognition of taxes paid to other nations and the allowance of credits for taxes paid in each other's jurisdiction. These treaties also often include provisions for reciprocal reductions in foreign withholding taxes on income earned on licenses, stocks, interest, royalties, and copyrights. They also establish the allocation of certain types of income to certain countries and allow tax audits to take place between countries. Tax treaties frequently also provide for the reciprocal exchange of tax information between nations, which is very important for enforcement of tax laws.

At present, the U.S. is signatory to more than thirty tax treaties with foreign nations, many of which are intricate and complicated. For example, the tax treaty with Canada is more than 11,000 pages long.

Foreign Tax Credits for U.S. Corporations

Foreign tax credits accorded to U.S. taxpayers are based on income taxes paid by a U.S. taxpaying entity to another country's treasury department or revenue service, which means that U.S. taxpayers are not given credits for the payment of value-added, sales, excise, or any other taxes paid to foreign concerns.

The purpose of foreign tax credits is to ensure that taxpayers are not penalized for engaging in foreign operations and that their tax bills abroad do not exceed domestic liabilities. Thus, if the rate paid on income abroad is less than the home or U.S. rate, taxpayers will be liable to the U.S. Treasury Department for the difference. In this way, they take care of their liability and pay their due share, but they are not unduly taxed on the same income.

For example, assume that a U.S. firm has a majority ownership in a subsidiary in Botswana, where the tax rate is appreciably higher at 60 percent than the U.S. tax rate of 34 percent. If the subsidiary declares earnings of $100 million in Botswana, it is assessed, and must pay (in pula, the local currency) $60 million in taxes. If that income is also declared in the United States, the parent is liable for $34 million. The payment of $60 million to Botswana, however, not only satisfies that liability but generates an additional foreign tax credit of $26 million ($60 million minus $34 million), which the firm can apply against its total U.S. income tax bill.

If Botswana's tax rate is lower than that of the United States, say 20 percent, the parent corporation is given credit for $20 million paid to tax authorities in Botswana, but must pay $14 million to satisfy the domestic tax bill of $34 million on the same $100 million of income taxed at a rate of 34 percent.

The key to determining whether or not U.S. firms can use foreign tax credits on taxes paid to foreign governments depends on whether or not an MNC declares the same income that was taxed abroad on its U.S. tax return. Thus, in order to take the credit for taxes paid abroad, the firm must recognize the income at home.

Foreign tax credits for corporations can be either direct or indirect, depending on the tax imposed by the foreign government. Direct taxes are those that are charged directly to the taxpayer, and, in this instance, would consist of foreign taxes on an MNC's branch income or foreign withholding taxes on remittances to a parent or U.S. investors. Under U.S. tax law, credits against U.S. tax liability may be taken in the amount of these paid taxes.

The code also provides a tax credit for indirect taxes paid by different segments of an MNC. These taxes come about when a subsidiary is taxed on its income earned in the foreign site and then the parent is taxed again on dividends it receives from the subsidiary. Thus, the code provides for an indirect foreign tax credit that can be taken in addition to the direct foreign tax credit. Parent corporations are allowed to make use of the indirect foreign tax credit when they own 10 percent or more of the voting stock of the foreign subsidiary. This credit is called a deemed paid credit and is based on the dividends paid by the subsidiary and the amount of foreign income taxes paid. The formula for determining the deemed paid credit is:

$$\frac{\text{dividend (including withholding tax)}}{\text{earnings net of (minus) foreign income taxes}}$$

$$\times \text{ foreign tax } = \text{ deemed paid credit}$$

Thus, many international corporations are not penalized for doing business in different international operating environments because they receive credit for direct and indirect income taxes paid to foreign governments. The use of foreign tax credits is, however, subject to limits and does raise some issues in taxation.

LIMITS AND ISSUES IN ALLOCATION OF FOREIGN TAX CREDIT

The use of the foreign tax credit is subject to two major limitations. The first is that credit can only be taken against income taxes paid to foreign tax authorities, not on sales, value-added, or excise taxes. This limitation is a special concern for subsidiaries operating in countries where the government relies more on the use of a VAT or other transaction than on income tax.

The second major limitation is that foreign tax credits can only be used to offset taxes to the full extent of a person's or a company's U.S. tax liability. (Exceeding such liability would give the taxpayer a negative tax bill and entitle him to a rebate from the government.) Thus, a situation can arise for multinational firms where they develop credits for foreign taxes paid in excess of domestic liabilities. U.S. law provides relief for these individuals and allows tax credits to be carried back and forward by the taxpayer. The carryback is allowed for two years and is utilized by filing amended tax returns for prior years. Excess tax credits can be carried forward for five years. If the taxpayer does not have enough tax liability to use these credits within the carry-back and carry-forward periods, they are lost.

Beyond these limitations, concerns also arise in relation to issues regarding the administration and determination of foreign tax credits used against U.S. liabilities. Two such issues are the determination of taxable income and the allocation of deductions according to foreign-based and home-based income. Because taxable income (not gross income or sales) determines the amount of foreign taxes paid and resultant foreign tax credits, differences in accounting and tax practices between countries can lead to controversy in the determination of taxes and tax credits. Remember, gross income figures are reduced by deductions for the costs and expenses of doing business to arrive at an adjusted figure representing taxable income.

What may be considered an expensible deduction under the accounting practices of one country may not suffice under the tax law of another. Such differences often lead to disputes between MNCs and the tax authorities of the countries involved over what expenses are allowable in the conduct of business. Frequently, even if the corporations and the tax authorities agree about the method used to determine the firm's expenses and income, they may disagree on the allocation of that income to the expenses incurred in its generation among worldwide locations.

U.S. accounting conventions hold that expenses are matched to income for appropriate characterization of financial flows. In the operation of a global company, the question arises as to how to allocate deductible expenses. For example, what if a multinational firm is organized so that all international functions and operations are coordinated from a central headquarters? What portion of the company's general and administrative expenses for operating their headquarters should be applied to foreign income earned? The same problem arises in the allocation of research and development expenses for products marketed in a multitude of locations. To satisfy these questions, the Internal Revenue Service issued stricter regulations in 1977 regarding the allocation of administrative and research expenses of multinationals to foreign-source income.

A problem remained, however, in that the resultant allocation of expenses is not always reciprocally recognized by foreign tax officials and does not always lead to a reduction of the related foreign source taxable income. The foreign government taxes them on the amount that the U.S. government considers expenses (and, therefore, nontaxable). Thus, they pay more in foreign taxes than they are allowed by U.S. authorities as a foreign tax credit. The solution pursued by multinationals is to create additional Subpart F income, from which they can generate and use more foreign tax credits.

Special Issues and Problems in International Taxation

Tax Havens

Despite extensive nets cast by U.S. tax authorities to capture taxes owed, many individuals and corporations attempt to avoid being taxed on their income earned abroad. Although this activity has been limited by the imposition of regulations and taxes on unremitted earnings, crafty financiers continue to attempt to shelter income. One method of accomplishing that objective is to keep income overseas (and, thus, off domestic books) in countries without tax treaties with the MNC's home government. These countries provide sanctuary for foreign-earned income and impose few or no taxes at all and are termed **tax havens**. Monies deposited in these nations are safe from taxation until the subsidiary declares a dividend to the parent, at which time the remittance becomes taxable by the home tax authority.

In order to be efficient sanctuaries for a corporation's worldwide income, tax havens must satisfy several criteria:

- They must not have a tax treaty with the corporation's domestic government that allows for the reciprocal tax treatment of income. Such a treaty would entail the sharing of earnings information and data.

- These nations must have low or no taxes on foreign-source funds. (Some tax haven countries do not provide equivalent tax amnesty for earnings within their own countries.)
- The countries must provide stable political and economic environments, so that funds deposited there will remain safe.
- The nations must allow for the free convertibility of currencies and have few if any restrictions on the inflow and outflow of currencies.
- The policies of the nations must be centered on a positive attitude toward businesses and their activities and, thus, have liberal incorporation laws.
- To accommodate financial flows, the countries must have well-developed banking systems with some degree of banking secrecy.
- The countries must also have infrastructures that support and facilitate general business operations, including such amenities as dependable telecommunications and transportation systems. A tax haven's close physical proximity to the home country makes it easier for depositors, who may then use the same lines or systems of communication and be in the same time zones.

Tax havens vary in their structure. Some countries, such as Caribbean tax havens, have very low or zero taxes on foreign or domestic income. These tax haven countries include the Bahamas, the Cayman Islands, Bermuda, the British Virgin Islands, and the Netherlands Antilles and are often used by U.S. nationals and corporations.

Other nations provide sanctuary for foreign sources of funds, but tax domestically produced income. Some such countries are Panama, Hong Kong, and Liechtenstein. Still other countries provide havens from taxation only for specific purposes or industries. These countries are primarily those that encourage investment within their boundaries by providing for tax exemptions for certain periods of time to promote industrial development. One such country that provides tax holidays is Ireland, which provides tax incentives or lowered rates for the establishment of facilities in specific regions or zones.

Transfer Pricing

Multinational firms use the pricing of goods and services between their different operating arms to achieve a number of objectives, such as increasing rates of return in specific operating locations, lowering product prices in specific markets, circumventing restrictions regarding repatriation of parent company profits, and getting around inconvertibility of host country currencies. In addition, the uses of transfer pricing in intracompany transactions can also provide a method for MNCs to manage their international tax liability.

By shifting costs to countries with high tax rates, an MNC can enjoy savings on its tax bills, because by raising the costs of goods sold, a company can lower its taxable income, shifting profits to countries where tax rates on corporate profits are lower. U.S. companies usually attempt to shift deductible costs to themselves or to a parent corporation's accounts from the books of the affiliates. Thus, the costs of such items as intracompany loans, the sale of inventory and machinery, and the transfer of intangible property and their associated deductibility are transferred to high-tax-rate environments.

Such practices have come under intense scrutiny both by host governments and the U.S. Internal Revenue Service, and the IRS can now challenge prices set by MNCs. Under certain circumstances, the IRS has the authority to recalculate those prices and assess tax liabilities according to prices set at arm's length, those prices that would have been reached if two independent parties engaged in the same transaction.

Unitary Taxes

A special problem that has emerged in international taxation is the issue of applying unitary taxes, taxes imposed by a specific state on the basis of an MNC's multistate or worldwide profits, not merely those profits generated by operations in that state. This practice, originally developed in California, includes the assessment of a tax upon the firm's total domestic or worldwide earnings based on a specific percentage figure. This percentage is derived from the proportion of the company's in-state sales, property, and personnel payroll in relation to its total national or global figures for sales, property held, and payroll. A rationale for the levying of such taxes by states is that doing so keeps corporations from using transfer pricing within different branches to shift income and tax bills to states that impose lower tax rates.

The use of unitary taxation has come under a great deal of criticism from all sides. U.S. multinational firms and the Treasury Department and foreign MNCs and their governments have protested loudly against the practice of levying unitary taxes and the method of income allocation. Severe criticisms have emerged from U.S. trading partners, such as Great Britain and Japan.

This pressure from foreign multinational corporations is giving impetus to a proposed solution of water's edge taxation, which would limit states to taxing only income from operations within the United States, not from global sales. It is more likely that changes in unitary taxation policy by individual states will come from opposition by MNCs and their decisions to disinvest in such states and move to states that do not apply the unitary tax concept.

Tax Incentives for International Business

Governments are not only concerned with garnering tax income from the operations of international firms, but they also use taxation policy as a tool to promote international trade. Countries that impose value-added taxes frequently rebate those taxes on exported goods in order to encourage exports. Similarly, the United States promotes exports of U.S. goods through tax policy. At one time, the United States had six different incentive programs to encourage international trade by U.S. companies. Each involved the formation of special corporate entities for conducting such trade to keep it segregated from normal operations to receive special treatment.

Foreign Sales Corporations

At present, the only existing incentive programs are foreign sales corporations (FSCs) and possessions corporations, which operate within possessions of the United States.

Foreign sales corporations were established to encourage and support the sale of U.S. goods and services abroad. These corporations must be established outside the United States in a possession or country that has a tax treaty (and that exchanges financial information) with the United States. FSCs (pronounced "fisks") act as sales agents for U.S. goods in foreign markets. The products sold are then exported from U.S. suppliers to foreign buyers. The advantages to forming a FSC is that a U.S. business receives favorable tax treatment of qualified foreign-source income, and its member companies receive full deductibility of qualified dividend distribution from the FSC. This tax treatment is, however, subject to many rules and stipulations.

The FSC, for example, must generate foreign gross sales receipts to qualify for special tax treatment. It must have no more than twenty-five members, a board of directors that includes at least one non-U.S. resident, no affiliation with an established domestic industrial sales corporation, and no preferred stock. It must also meet specific requirements regarding foreign management and foreign economic process requirements in order to generate its foreign receipts. Income from sales generated by the FSC is segregated according to IRS rules into exempt and nonexempt portions. The exempt portions receive favorable tax treatment, while nonexempt portions are not accorded such privileges.

Tax law includes provisions for slightly less involved legal requirements for the establishment of a small FSC, which does not have to meet the foreign management or economic process requirements of a larger FSC and enjoys the same tax benefits, but only up to $5 million per year of for-

eign gross trading receipts. Small U.S. businesses are also taking advantage of FSC law by joining together in a net tax-saving vehicle called a shared foreign sales corporation.

Small businesses can profit by using these vehicles to generate reductions on tax bills through FSC exempted income. They can afford to comply with the regulations by using management firms to coordinate much of the recordkeeping and managerial work of the corporations. These management firms are beginning to set up shared FSCs to allow small businesses access to the tax incentive program, while eliminating the need to deal with the complicated workings of the law. Small business owners must, however, maintain some records to ensure that only products produced in the United States (not imports from other countries, such as Canada) are shipped overseas. They must also be sure to calculate profits according to special FSC rules regarding marginal costing and transfer pricing of products.

Domestic International Sales Corporations

FSCs were established in 1984 to replace export promotion programs called DISCs—domestic international sales corporations—which were similarly organized in the interest of promoting U.S. export trade. If a firm organized as a DISC met the requirements set by law that 95 percent of the assets and 95 percent of the corporation's sales were export-related, it was allowed to defer 50 percent of its tax liability from such activity either permanently or until it no longer met the 95 percent requirements. At such a time, all the deferred taxes were due. The DISC program was eliminated after major U.S. trading partners, particularly Japan and Canada, complained that DISCs constituted an unfair export subsidy in terms of the General Agreement on Tariffs and Trade (GATT). Consequently, FSCs were established, and DISCs were given five years in which to establish FSCs outside of the United States. The law did provide, however, an escape clause for DISCs, which qualified tax-free income as $10 million worth of export receipts.

The escape clause exempted small DISCs, which could continue to operate if they met the stipulations of the law. They differ, however, from original DISCs in that even through they can permanently defer taxes on eligible income, they must pay interest to the IRS on the amount of deferred tax. Thus, the primary benefit accorded small DISCs is the financing of export sales. Thus, such DISCs are properly referred to as interest-charge DISCs.

U.S. Possessions Corporations

If a domestic operation derives at least 80 percent of its income from a U.S. possession (excluding the Virgin Islands) and generates at least 50 percent of its gross income from active trade, it may be able to take advantage of tax benefits established for **U.S. possessions corporations**. If these conditions are met for three years prior to the establishment of the corporation, it has the advantage of limitations on taxation of income from outside the United States, tax-free repatriation of earnings to the United States, liberal interpretation of transfer prices, and possible exemption from Puerto Rican taxation if it operates manufacturing facilities in certain areas of Puerto Rico.

Influence of U.S. Tax Law on Corporate Operations

Clearly, managing the international tax function for a major MNC corporation involves many different facets that relate directly to managerial decision-making. The effects of taxation upon the future and operations of a corporation play a large role in determining where activities are carried out and in what type of legal form (branch, subsidiary, or export arm). Taxes must be factored into prices set for external and internal intracompany purchases, and must be considered in determining appropriate cash levels, flows, and locations among

worldwide operations. The international taxation situation is so complex that many MNCs use complex computer programs that can determine the tax effects of various managerial decisions regarding international financing, cash flows, and operations.

Taxation of Individual Foreign Source Income

The existence of business operations in a multitude of environments and of a far-flung management staff involves the compensation of employees in foreign tax jurisdictions and subsequent taxation complications. In some countries, the principle of *juridic domicile* is strictly applied, that is, the citizen's income is not taxed by his or her home country if it is not earned or received within that country. The United States, however, differs greatly in this approach. Under the Sixteenth Amendment to the U.S. Constitution, U.S. citizens are taxed on all of their income regardless of where it is sourced or earned in the world.

Naturally, the application of this principle could result in problems for U.S. citizens working in and being taxed by a host government, especially the problem of double taxation of the same income. Consequently, tax law provides relief for the U.S. expatriate who is earning income abroad and for the U.S investor receiving income from foreign sources. These situations provide for a distinction in foreign income determination between that which is earned and that which is unearned.

Foreign earned income consists of all monies employees receive as payment for services rendered and includes wages, salaries, and commissions. Earned income does not include wages or salaries received in return for services rendered by employees of the U.S. government. Foreign unearned income is that which is derived from an individual's overseas investments. These sources of income include interest on investments, dividends, pensions, annuities, and even gambling winnings.

In order to provide for equity or fairness in the

tax treatment of U.S. expatriates and to encourage citizens to work abroad, tax law provides for alternate forms of relief from taxes on foreign earned income and double taxation by both home and host governments. A U.S. citizen qualifies for special treatment if he or she satisfies the requirements of overseas employment by being either a bona fide resident of the foreign country or by being away at least 330 days during any twelve consecutive months.

An employee on foreign soil has two ways to treat foreign earned income. First, a portion of foreign earned income can be excluded up to a limit of $70,000 per year. If the minimum 330-day residency requirement is met, but was less than a year, the allowance is prorated proportionately to provide for a new maximum exclusion. Married employees may each use the exclusion if they satisfy the other requirements of the relief provision.

Prior to the 1986 changes in tax law, the exclusion for foreign earned income was $80,000 and was scheduled to increase to $95,000 over subsequent years. This provision was just one of many that were reduced or tightened up in the tax reform activity of 1986. The law also applied new rules to taxpayers who violated U.S. restrictions on travel. Under the changes, no exclusion for earnings or housing expenses is allowed if and while the taxpayer is present in countries restricted to travel by U.S. citizens. In 1987, the U.S. government limited travel for political reasons by its citizens to Cambodia, Cuba, Libya, North Korea, and Vietnam.

The second alternative open to expatriate employees in handling foreign earned income is to include it in their income bases but claim foreign tax credits on their returns for taxes paid abroad on those earnings or wages. Generally, most expatriates, especially those in low-tax foreign countries, use the income exclusion provisions of tax law. Thus, if the tax abroad is lower than at home, employees pay less tax because they do not have to make up the difference.

Alternatively, individuals use the foreign tax credit when their earnings or wages far exceed the amount of the exclusion and their foreign taxes paid far exceed comparable U.S. tax on the excluded amount. Expatriates also might chose to use the foreign tax credit rather than the exclusions, if the tax rate in the host country is much higher than that of the United States. In such a case, the international employee would use a credit to eliminate U.S. taxes for the existing year and in years ahead under carry-forward provisions. Once, however, an expatriate elects to use the foreign tax credit, it must be applied to all subsequent years unless it is actively revoked. A revocation is then effective not only for the year of change, but for four subsequent years.

As for corporations, the foreign tax credit of individuals is subject to limitations. For example it can only be calculated according to foreign taxes paid on income and the United States uses its own criteria in determining whether or not the tax paid is an income tax. Consequently, sales, value-added, property, severance, and excise taxes are not included in determining the credit. Some of these, however, may be deductible as a state, local, or personal property tax under Section 164 of the Internal Revenue Code. Also, according to the alternative minimum tax provisions of U.S. tax law, foreign tax credits cannot be used to reduce tax liability by more than 90 percent.

Expenses of U.S. Expatriates

U.S. tax law also takes into account the rigors and additional costs involved in overseas assignments and provides relief for expenses incurred abroad in securing scarce housing or paying a higher cost of living in a more expensive economy. Thus, the law provides relief for the expatriate who receives reimbursement for housing costs, which are deemed to include rent, insurance, and utilities. They do not include interest or taxes paid on housing, because these costs are deductible under other provisions of law. Under the provisions, the employee may exclude from income an amount in addition to basic exclusion to compensate for these additional costs. The excludable amount is the excess of such costs above 16 percent of the salary of a government employee at grade level GS-14.

Summary

The management of the international tax function for a multinational enterprise is very involved and complicated and can have a profound effect upon the welfare and profitability of a firm. The effects of taxation policies in home and foreign operating environments frequently determine managerial decisions regarding choice of international operations, the legal forms of such operations, price-setting between branches of the enterprise and with the public, and the financing and cash flows of international operations around the world.

Individual nations vary in the types of taxes they levy and in assessment rates. All countries provide relief for taxpayers from being doubly taxed on the same income, and in order to facilitate international trade and investment flows, nations join in agreements regarding taxation of their citizens and reciprocal recognition of taxes paid within their jurisdictions. These tax treaties also frequently provide for the mutual exchange of information regarding business operations of multinational firms and facilitate enforcement of tax laws. Some countries purposefully avoid entering into such agreements in order to provide sanctuaries for foreign earned income so that it can find a safe haven from the long arms of domestic tax authorities.

Nations of the world use taxation as an arm of policymaking to achieve social, economic, and political objectives, as well as to raise revenues. Most countries have as one such objective the increase of export trade from their borders. Consequently, they use tax incentive programs to promote such trade. Nevertheless, objectives, policies, and tax structures differ widely around the world. Thus, the tax manager of an international concern is faced with the formidable task of managing the multinational tax function in order to provide for the minimization of taxes in the pursuit of maximization of operational efficiencies and worldwide profitability.

Discussion Questions

1. Why do governments levy taxes? What services do they fund?
2. What is tax equity?
3. How can taxes encourage or discourage certain activities? Explain.
4. What types of taxes may be levied other than income taxes?
5. What is a VAT?
6. What is double taxation? How can individuals or corporations avoid double taxation?
7. What is a tax haven? Identify at least five countries that qualify as tax havens?
8. What are FSCs, and DISCs?
9. Why must MNCs concern themselves with taxes?
10. Does U.S. tax policy provide any incentives to U.S. citizens to work overseas?

Bibliography

1986. "Tax Reform Update." *International Tax Journal* (Fall): 327–361.

BISCHE, JON E. 1985. *Fundamentals of International Taxation,* 2nd ed. New York: Practicing Law Institute.

BOND, ERIC W., AND L. SAMUELSON. 1989. "Strategic Behavior and the Rules for International Taxation of Capital." *Economic Journal,* (December): 1099–1111.

BORSACK, SCOTT P. 1987. "Choosing to Do Business Through a Foreign Branch or a Foreign Subsidiary. A Tax Analysis." *Case Western Reserve Journal of International Law* (Summer): 393–419.

CHAMBOST, E. 1983. *Bank Accounts: A World Guide to Confidentiality,* New York: John Wiley & Sons.

DOERNBERG, RICHARD L. 1989. *International Taxation in a Nutshell.* St. Paul, MN: West Publishing Company.

GRANELL, A. W., B. HIRSH, AND D. R. MILTON. 1986. "Worldwide Unitary Tax: Is It Invalid Under Treaties of Friendship, Commerce and Navigation?" *Tax & Policy in International Business* 18: 695–758.

GUTFELD, ROSE. 1988. "It Seems like Days, but IRS Estimates Tax Filing Takes only about Nine Hours." *Wall Street Journal* (September 1): 23.

HOFFMAN, WILLIAM H., JR., AND EUGENE WILLIS. 1988. *West's Federal Taxation: Comprehensive Volume.* St. Paul, MN: West Publishing Company.

COMMERCE CLEARING HOUSE. 1988. *Internal Revenue Code of 1986.* Chicago: Commerce Clearing House, Inc.

MILLER, RICHARD BRADFORD. 1988. *Tax Haven Investing: A Guide to Offshore Banking and Investment Opportunities.* Chicago: Probus Publishing Company.

ROTHSCHILD, LEONARD W., JR. 1986. "Worldwide Unitary Taxation: The End is in Sight." *Journal of Accountancy* (December): 178–185.

SHAPIRO, ALAN. 1986. *Multinational Financial Management.* Newton, MA: Allyn and Bacon.

SINN, HANS-WERNER, AND R. J. PATRICK, JR. 1988. "U.S. Tax Reform 1981 and 1986: Impact on International Capital Markets and Capital Flows." *National Tax Journal* (September): p. 71.

SINNING, KATHLEEN E., ed. 1986. *Comparative International Taxation,* Sarasota, FL: International Accounting Association of the American Accounting Association.

TANNENBAUM, JEFFREY A. 1988. "Exporters Can Share Tax-Shaving Vehicle" *Wall Street Journal* (November 7): B1.

U.S. DEPARTMENT OF THE TREASURY, INTERNAL REVENUE SERVICE. 1986. *Explanation of Tax Reform Act of 1986 for Individuals,* Publication 920.

Chapter Case Study _____

Skytrack Instrumentation

Jerry Turner and William McKensie were in good spirits. Having finished a round of golf at the Green Holes Country Club at Quintacera, a resort town north of Divotia, the main business center in the Latin America nation of Celida, they headed for the clubhouse for a couple of drinks before lunch and an afternoon meeting with Jose Cervantes, their main consultant on government regulations. Turner and McKensie were president and chief financial officer of Skytrack Instrumentation, a British-based multinational specializing in air traffic control instruments for civilian airports. Skytrack was also an important supplier of aircraft instrument panels and navigational aids used in civilian aircraft. Their annual sales were approximately $6 billion, spread over forty-five countries on four continents. Skytrack Instrumentation Celida was established as a wholly owned subsidiary in 1988. The company had set up a highly automated manufacturing facility in a small industrial park just outside Divotia that had been created by the government of Celida to attract investment from overseas. With considerable cooperation from the government and the availability of many infrastructural facilities in Celida, Skytrack was able to set up the plant within two years and production was expected to begin within the next three weeks. Turner and McKensie were taking a well-deserved vacation before the commencement of operations. Meanwhile, McKensie also had to start charting the tax strategy of the company, something he had not done earlier. A preliminary meeting with Cervantes, a leading expert on government regulations for multinational enterprises in Celida seemed to be a good first step.

Cervantes was well-prepared for the discussion. He pulled out two separate briefs, detailing comprehensive outlines for two approaches that Skytrack could take to minimize their tax liability in Celida.

One of the approaches was based on the technique of transfer pricing, which the brief euphemistically called the "price adjustment approach." There was considerable scope with this technique because the subsidiary was importing nearly every component of its products from Great Britain and assembling them in Celida. In fact, the cost of components was almost 50 percent of the total costs of goods to be sold in Celida, according to early projections made by the company's accountants. If the import price were raised, the profit margins would be lowered and so would the tax liability. The tax rates on overseas corporations in Celida were as follows:

35% Corporate income tax	Computed on earnings, including interest earnings, for the financial year.
15% Withholding tax	On the amount of profits sought to be repatriated by the company.

Projected sales of Skytrack Celida, for the first year were approximately £160 million (calculated at the day's exchange rate of one pound for 34 Celidan pesos). The estimated costs of goods sold, selling expenses, interest expenses, and other costs were in aggregate £130 million. Net profit before taxes was estimated to be £30 million of this 3 percent, that is, £10.5 million was to be paid as corporate income tax, which would leave the company with £19.5 million in profits. According to the local regulations, overseas companies were allowed to repatriate 75 percent of their post-tax profits each year. Under this provision, Skytrack could repatriate £14 million to Great Britain. There would be, however, a withholding tax of 15 percent on this amount, or £2.2 million. The total tax liability of Celida would be approximately £12.69 million on a profit of £30 million, or approximately 42.3 percent.

If, however, Skytrack U.K. could increase the price of components sold to Skytrack Celida by 15 percent (on a total annual sales of approximately 85 percent), the tax liability could be reduced substantially. Cervantes showed them the computation (in millions of pounds):

Original cost of sales	£130
Increase in equipment prices	12.75 (15% of £85)
New cost of sales	142.75
Profit	17.25
Corporate income tax	6.0375
Net profit	11.21
Repatriated amount (75%)	8.40
Tax on repatriated amount	1.26
Total tax	7.296
Tax savings	5.40
Increase in Headquarters tax liability on account of increase in income	3.2
Net tax savings	£2.2 million

The other approach suggested by Mr. Cervantes was to use a tax-haven, where the tax savings would be even greater. Skytrack could ship components, on paper, to Skytrack Cayman Islands, at the same price it would be shipping to Skytrack Celida. Thus, there would be no increase in Skytrack U.K. income because of higher prices, but Skytrack Cayman Islands would notionally resell these components to Skytrack Celida at a markup of 15 percent and in the process make a "profit" of £12.75 million, on which there would be no tax liability because the Cayman Islands is a tax haven. At the same time, Skytrack Celida would have a reduced tax liability of £5.4 million. The net savings would be £3.2 million over the direct approach.

The tax haven approach, however, was more complex. It required documentation to be routed through the Cayman Islands and increased the risk of making Celidan authorities suspicious. On the other hand, £3.2 million a year was a large sum, even for a company of Skytrack's size, and the use of tax havens was quite common.

Question

Which of the following options would you choose if you were McKensie. Explain your reasons for accepting or rejecting each option.

1. No transfer pricing
2. Transfer pricing
3. Transfer pricing and using a tax haven
4. Are there other alternatives and what are their advantages and disadvantages?

CHAPTER 19

International Staffing and Labor Issues

CHAPTER OBJECTIVES

This chapter will:

- Identify common organizational structures used by multinational corporations.
- Discuss how MNCs recruit, select, train, and motivate management staffs.
- Describe the cultural and economic forces that influence the international manager's performance.
- Consider the problems of repatriating international managers and other ethical issues.
- Identify the trade-offs between localized and centralized management of labor.
- Discuss the major labor issues of wages and benefits, job security, and productivity as they relate to MNC operations.
- Present how international labor movements and codetermination are influencing MNC operations.

Organizing a Multinational Corporation

International firms can organize their operations in a number of different ways. Four of these organizing strategies are the functional structure, the regional structure, the product structure, and the matrix structure.

Function Structure

Under this structure, responsibilities at headquarters are divided according to functions, such as marketing and finance, and the head of each division is responsible for the conduct of that function internationally. This strategy is efficient if there is a standardized product line. It permits coordination of the aspects of a function in one department, but this strategy also encourages a narrow viewpoint, is inflexible, and can be time-consuming. It is hard to adapt this centralized approach to changing local conditions, and the overall integration of the various functions internationally is very difficult to achieve.

Regional Structure

In the regional structure of an MNC, the headquarters retains responsibility for overall global strategy and control, but an area manager has responsibility for all the operations and functions of a certain region. The regions should be organized on the basis of similar characteristics with less emphasis on the basis of functional categories. This structure also integrates the separate functions very well throughout each region, but its drawback is that each function must be standardized in order to integrate across all the regions.

Product Structure

As with the regional structure, corporate headquarters has control of overall global strategy in a product structure. Within the guidelines set down by headquarters, a manager has international control over all the operations related to a single product. A major advantage of this structure is that all the functions relating to a single product are integrated and perform as a whole internationally. The major drawback is that it is difficult to coordinate policies and strategies across product lines.

Matrix Structure

The matrix structure involves dual lines of authority in which managers may report to two or more superiors. For example, they may have to report to the head of the product line and to the chief of a geographical region. This structure provides for coordination of the various departments, while still recognizing differences, and leads to standardization of functions and overall control, and imparts flexibility to respond to environmental differences.

International Staffing

International staffing involves the four basic stages of recruitment, selection, training, and motivation of the right person to fill a job available in a foreign setting.

Recruitment

Recruitment is the process of attracting people to apply for job vacancies within a firm. There are two main sources of recruitment for international positions—internal and external. Internal sources consist of promotion from within the company and employee referrals. Promotion from within is a very low-cost method for the firm. It has the added benefit of increasing employee morale because they see an opportunity for advancement. Uncertainty about an applicant and training costs are reduced because employees are already familiar with the objectives and procedures of the firm. Employee referrals involve the recommendation by a present employee of a family member or friend and encouraging them to apply. The benefits of an employee referral are the low cost to the firm and the fact that the referrals will probably be fairly well-informed about the various aspects of the firm.

External sources of recruitment include newspaper and radio advertising, trade schools, employment agencies, job fairs, and labor unions. There is a difference, however, between recruitment in industrialized countries and in the less-developed countries. In the less-developed countries, there is an overabundance of unskilled workers because of high unemployment and a shortage of skilled workers. Newspapers may not be effective in LDCs because much of the population may be illiterate, and there are usually very few employment agencies. In industrialized countries, the problems are reversed; there are too many skilled workers and too few unskilled workers.

Selection

Employee selection involves choosing from an available pool of applicants that the firm considers best able to meet the requirements of the position. In industrialized countries the firm considers people through standardized procedures, such as application forms, personal interviews, and possibly a physical or psychological exams. The selection process in LDCs is less formal and involves less testing. Such considerations as family ties, social status or caste, language, and common origin tend to influence the selection process.

Training

For an MNC training of its overseas employees is an extremely important issue. Employees in overseas locations come from a different society and culture, which means that they have varying attitudes toward work, conduct, and other behavioral aspects that may be quite different from the expectations and standards of an MNC. It is therefore critical for an MNC to train its overseas employees to orient them toward its work ethics, discipline, efficiency standards, operating procedures, and, of course, the necessary operational skills.

One major limitation in many countries is that adequate training resources by way of instructors, experienced personnel, and training facilities may not be available. Generally, MNCs fly in large numbers of key technical personnel to train newly hired employees in foreign locations, who lead training sessions for both theoretical and on-the-job training. Some personnel in charge of sensitive and complex industrial operations have to remain at the overseas locations before the local trainees are considered adequately trained and have enough experience to run the operations themselves.

For lower-level employees, typically factory workers, language is another important barrier to overcome. Companies take different approaches to this problem. Interpreters are used where language is an intractable problem. Often companies train bilingual local employees, who in turn pass on the training to those local employees who do not understand the foreign language. Because most workers at the plant floor level are not involved in significant amounts of theoretical work, this problem

is mitigated to a large extent as long as they are able to understand the operating instructions for their specific tasks.

Motivation

Motivating overseas employees also presents complex problems. Employees, especially at the lower levels, are relatively ethnocentric in their views, and their priorities and goals often differ from their counterparts in Western countries. While mobility, compensation, challenges in the work environment, and independence in functioning are important motivating factors for employees in Western industrialized countries, workers in LDCs tend to attach greater value to job security, number of holidays, working hours, social benefits, and so on. An MNC, therefore, must judge the local climate and expectations very carefully and come up with an appropriate mix of incentives that would motivate employees without being unduly expensive.

Compare, for example, workers in a developed country and a developing country. The worker in the developed country is consumption-oriented and wants compensation in terms of money. While vacation days are desirable, the employee tends to work more days of the year to increase the compensation package. The employee is interested in moving up the ladder to better jobs, but not necessarily in the same company.

A worker in a developing country, on the other hand, wants job security because industrial jobs are scarce, and if the worker loses his job, there may not be any other means of livelihood, especially because there would ordinarily be no social security or unemployment insurance.

There are a number of religious festivals in societies where the hold of traditional socioreligious practices is still strong, and workers in developing countries would like to be certain that they have those days off. Most workers in developing countries expect their employers to provide them with housing assistance or similar benefits because these are not readily available. Thus, an MNC may have to create a compensation package that relies less on salary and more on other benefits for its workers in developing countries. Salary levels, however, also must be a little higher than the local going rate to guard against allegations that the MNC is exploiting local workers.

Managerial Staffing
Value to Firm

Choosing a manager for an overseas operation is an important task because this choice can profoundly affect overseas growth and operations. The subsidiary manager will have a great deal of responsibility, more than a counterpart in a home production facility. The overseas manager must be bicultural and sensitive to business practices and customs of the host country, while being responsible for following the global objectives of the MNC and being able to put these objectives ahead of the local operation's well-being.

The success of its overseas managers is particularly important to MNCs for a number of reasons. A failure in the overseas assignment leads to large corporate costs in time and resources in replacing the expatriate, the lost productivity of the manager, and slowdowns in productivity at the overseas plant. Bereft of skillful management, the overseas operation is more likely to experience such problems as increases in labor strikes, employee problems, government relations problems, and legal suits, because backup management resources may not be easily forthcoming.

To motivate their overseas managers, MNCs provide huge employment incentives in the form of large increases in salary and benefits (see Perspective 19–1) and most assignments carry the glamour of widening horizons, enriching experiences, and an excitingly different lifestyle[1] (see

[1] Harris and Moran 1987.

PERSPECTIVE 19–1   A Checklist for Accepting a Job Abroad

When a New York marketing executive was sent to work in London four years ago, his company subsidized his housing costs abroad, handled the rental of his New York home, gave him a car and, as an added inducement, paid for course work that his wife needed to complete her graduate education.

For the most part, today's expatriates are still getting premium salaries and company-paid home leaves, but some of the other extras are being squeezed out under pressure from the weakening dollar and the rising cost of doing business abroad.

"Most large international companies want their career-track executives to have some experience overseas but they are equally interested in con-

trolling the cost," said John P. O'Hagan, an international consultant with Hewitt Associates, based in Lincolnshire, Ill. "The trend is that more and more companies are reducing or eliminating" as many perquisites as possible.

As a result, people who are considering international assignments should familiarize themselves with their company's transfer policies. And executives weighing offers from foreign employers may want to sit down with accountants familiar with international law. Otherwise, they run the risk that the seesawing dollar, the vagaries of foreign tax codes and a lack of planning will play havoc with their finances.

The first question is often whether to sell the

SOURCE: *New York Times*, July 17, 1988.

home in the United States or rent it for the duration of the overseas assignment. Executives who live in an area where real estate prices are rising should be aware that, if they sell, they may be closed out of the market when they return. In addition, they may be giving up a very favorable mortgage.

Furthermore, those who choose to sell may face a hefty capital gains tax on their profit if they take too long in buying another house. As a general rule, the tax on the gain from the sale of a residence is deferred when the money is reinvested in another home within two years; the two-year period is extended to four years for people living overseas. In addition, the exclusion is available only for personal residences. Thus people who rent their homes out immediately before selling may find that the entire profit is subject to tax.

Another consideration is whether to get paid by the employer in dollars or foreign currency. A combination of the two is best, said Alan J. Straus, a partner with Edward Isaacs & Company, a New York accounting firm. Generally, it is easier to convert dollars to foreign currency than it is to convert foreign currency to dollars. Moreover, some governments place restrictions on how much foreign currency can be taken out of the country, and commissions paid to convert the unused money to dollars can be expensive. The rule of thumb: figure out how much is needed to cover living expenses, take that in local currency and have the balance deposited in dollars in an American bank.

The method of payment can be important for other reasons as well. In Japan and certain other countries, money received offshore for services rendered outside the country is not taxed. Thus, an American manager responsible for the Southeast Asia region, who is based in Japan, may want to have part of his salary deposited directly into an American bank account to sidestep the Japanese tax, said Thomas M. Field, an international tax partner with Price Waterhouse.

All Americans working abroad should ask a lawyer to review their wills, to make certain the current will is valid under the foreign country's estate laws. Those who live in countries that have no tax treaties with the United States, or who plan to stay longer than permitted by the treaty, could be risking liability for foreign estate taxes. That risk could be lessened or eliminated by planning.

Employees recruited to go overseas should know exactly what is covered by their compensation packages. Major employers who regularly send people abroad generally have set policies. Employees of smaller companies and Americans considering overseas positions with foreign employers "will have to pay attention to the real cost of living in a foreign location," Mr. Strauss said. He suggested that executives ask for a paid house-hunting or fact-finding trip to the new location.

Most companies allow their expatriate employees to return home for visits once or twice a year. Some permit employees to travel coach rather than first class, and use the difference to pay for a second visit. Find out company policy governing special trips, say, to attend a funeral or a child's graduation.

International relocation of two-career couples is an "issue that's heating up right now," said Lisa L. Hicks, assistant director of advisory services for Catalyst, a nonprofit research group in New York. Because moving abroad may be a serious career setback for the spouse of the transferred executive, more companies are exploring the possibilities of hiring the spouse, negotiating to find a position for the spouse overseas or providing other job-hunting assistance, she said.

Before going overseas, employees should also determine how the time they spend abroad will affect participation in the company's benefits package, including pension and profit-sharing plans. Some companies provide separate medical insurance for expatriates, as one executive found out to his dismay. When he returned to the United States, he was refused coverage under the company plan—even though he had been working for an overseas subsidiary—because he had developed an illness abroad.

Americans living overseas may have to pay

income taxes in both jurisdictions. The Internal Revenue Service excludes $70,000 of income earned abroad from taxes, plus certain housing benefits, and credits a portion of foreign taxes paid against United States taxes. Any cost-of-living allowances or housing subsidies granted by the employer are included in taxable income, however.

To compensate, most companies have some form of "tax equalization" policy. Tax differences are neutralized by calculating a hypothetical tax and reimbursing executives for any difference between this and their actual tax bills. The key issue is how the company treats outside income like dividends, interest, capital gains and spouse's earnings, said Steven M. Kates, director of expatriate services for the accounting firm of Arthur Young in New York.

Executives should find out how the company will treat stock options, for example. Some foreign governments tax the grant or exercise of incentive stock options, even though there would be no comparable taxation in the United States.

Looking back on her experience in London, the wife of the marketing executive from New York said that the couple should have consulted an accountant before going overseas, even though the benefits were greater then. "We didn't think the finances were as complicated as they turned out to be," she said.

Perspective 19–2). Nevertheless, one out of every three expatriate workers from the United States finds that the assignment has gone wrong. A recent study by Rosalie Tung found that "incidences where expatriates had to be recalled to corporate headquarters or dismissed from the company because of their inability to perform effectively in a foreign country were numerous."[2] More than half of the eighty companies she surveyed reported failure rates of between 10 and 20 percent. Some es-

[2] Tung 1984.

PERSPECTIVE 19–2   Losing Innocence, Abroad

Richard W. Siebrasse, president of CPC International Inc.'s worldwide consumer foods division, has never worked overseas. Neither has Colby H. Chandler, chief executive of the Eastman Kodak Company. But there is a good chance that their successors—or their successors' successors—will have a foreign stint on their résumés.

"I intend to make international experience for our American managers a key issue," said Mr. Siebrasse, who was named head of the new CPC division in January. Mr. Chandler is already holding annual meetings with his senior managers at which they map out overseas assignments for junior people with potential. "These days, there's not a discussion or a decision that doesn't have an international dimension," he said. "We'd have to be blind not to see how critically important international experience is."

Slowly but surely, hands-on international experience is moving out of the "nice but not necessary" category and into the "must have" slot for those on the corporate fast track. Numerous companies are redesigning their management development programs to include international assignments. Many are cutting older people without such experience from succession plans, and asking executive recruiters to find high-level internationalists to fill the gaps.

SOURCE: Claudia H. Deutsch, *New York Times*, July 10, 1988.

The reason for the change: competition from foreign companies, both in overseas markets and at home. The rivalry has intensified in nearly every industry, and American companies are rolling out all competitive weapons in their arsenals. They are buying materials from all over the world to keep costs down. They are tailoring products to the tastes of different cultures. And they are encouraging geographically dispersed divisions to share ideas.

"In the past, multinational companies could get away with operating a loosely connected group of activities that happened to be located around the world," Mr. Chandler said. "Now those activities are truly integrated."

That means that few United States companies can afford the once-common luxury of employing permanent expatriates, or using overseas slots as temporary dumping grounds for managers not good enough to promote but too good to fire. Instead, they are sending their best and brightest, hoping to accomplish a great deal:

- Beef up the skills level in international divisions.
- Help managers shake off the assumption that products or methods that work at home will automatically work in foreign lands.
- Gain insights into how foreign competitors operate and form strategy.
- Give those on the fast track experience in running a good-sized operation without constant oversight from headquarters.

"There was a time, years back, when we had real career expatriates, guys who said, 'Send me any place except the United States,' " said Gerald Hornsby, the Dow Chemical Company's vice president of human resources. "They don't exist here any more. Today, we are identifying people willing to gain specific developmental experiences, sending them where their skills are needed, and bringing them back to jobs where they can use their new skills."

The trend is not yet overwhelming. Even within companies, it varies among divisions. Each

of the General Electric Company's 14 key businesses are in "various stages of globalization," said James P. Baughman, manager of corporate organization and management development. The company's plastics, aircraft engines and turbine businesses, for example, place a high premium on overseas experience. Many other businesses do not.

"We're trying to deal with it business by business, rather than through a top-down, company-wide undifferentiated push for global experience," Mr. Baughman said. "You have to develop role models, people who went overseas, came back and did well. And that takes a long time."

So far, such role models are few and far between. But many are in very visible jobs.

D. Wayne Calloway, Pepsico's chief executive, spent a year in Canada. Fredrick S. Meils, chief financial officer of Pepsico Worldwide Beverages, ran the company's Philippines operation in 1983. Frank Popoff, Dow's chief executive, was for years a marketing executive in Europe. C. Michael Armstrong, an I.B.M. executive regarded as a contender for the chairmanship, is the first American to run the company's Paris-based European operations. And Charles M. Berger spent several years in Italy and England for the H. J. Heinz Company before Anthony J. F. O'Reilly, Heinz's Dublin-born chief executive, chose him to run the company's Weight Watchers International subsidiary on Long Island.

"I had no experience running a service company, but that didn't bother Tony," Mr. Berger said. "He told me that the reason he wanted me to run Weight Watchers was that I had multinational experience."

Heinz and other companies want more than the corporate equivalent of a junior year abroad. They want executives who have immersed themselves in another culture and who can apply what they learned about that culture when they come home.

Jacques Sardas is a case in point. An Egyptian by birth who worked in Brazil and France before coming to the United States, Mr. Sardas is an executive vice president at the Goodyear Tire and Rubber Company and president of Goodyear International, which handles all of the company's business outside the United States and Canada. His background filled a critical need when Goodyear started facing heavy domestic competition from Michelin, the French tire giant, a few years ago.

"Knowing Michelin was a tremendous help to me, to be able to predict how they would market, how they would go about distributing, how they would go about contacting large fleet accounts," Mr. Sardas said. "We never did lose share to them.'

But rarely are the benefits of international experience easily quantifiable. And the lack of tangible results has skeptics questioning whether the costs of sending Americans overseas can be justified. The process is expensive, involving premium salaries, costs of annual home leaves and possible cost-of-living increases. These days, with the weakness of the dollar, the price tag is even higher.

What's more, the trend to ship Americans out is on a collision course with another, equally strong, corporate trend: that of placing foreign nationals in charge of American businesses in their countries. Many American multinational companies have decided that local people are the most likely to understand the cultures of workers and customers. And, because they are paid in local currency, they do not require cost-of-living increases when the dollar weakens.

"We don't have to bring people across borders, because now we bring technologies across borders," said Donald P. Jacobs, dean of Northwestern University's J. L. Kellogg Graduate School of Management. "Foreign nationals have ready-made connections, and come cheaper."

That view has plenty of adherents. The American Cyanamid Company has fewer American employees living outside the United States today than 10 years ago, even though the company's overseas business is increasing. "The trend for us in other countries is to have subsidiaries headed by local people," said W. Perry Brown, vice president of personnel.

That is true at the Allied Signal Corporation as well. "We have not concluded that an assignment overseas must be part of a normal career path progression," said Edwin M. Halkyard, senior vice president of human resources. The company conducts senior-level courses on what Mr. Halkyard calls "the unique requirements of dealing in a world economy." The classes, he maintains, give managers knowledge of a host of cultures, while overseas assignments only teach them about one.

But book knowledge cannot replace experience, other management experts say. "You are not an internationalist unless you've lived as a minority in another environment," said William Voris, president of the American Graduate School of International Management, in Glendale, Ariz.

"Decision making is slower overseas, the nuance of dealing with governments is different," said Carl W. Menk, president of Canny Bowen, a recruiting firm that has seen requests for executives with international experience triple in the last three years. "It is hard to understand this if you've never worked there."

What overseas experience provides generally, say human resource professionals, is the ability to recognize that things work differently elsewhere. "You gain a certain appreciation that there are other ways to do things than the American way, that other economies play a part in the world, that the sun does not rise and set in New York City," said John Borgia, director of human resources for the Bristol-Myers Company.

"It is not just language and culture; these people develop a broader set of problem-solving skills," said John R. Fulkerson, director of human resources for Pepsi-Cola International, a Pepsico division that handles the sale of beverages outside the United States. "If they've seen people delivering things on bicycles in China, they will be more willing to look at alternatives of how to get something from point A to point B here."

Few human resources people suggest that Americans should be sent overseas in place of local nationals. Instead, they are seeking ways to get the two groups to coexist.

At Kodak, Americans are often placed in the No. 2 or No. 3 spots overseas, leaving the top spot to a foreign national. Cyanamid has rotated about 30 people into the No. 2 spots at foreign-run subsidiaries over the last decade. "Anyone we think has the potential to be an operating division president goes off to a foreign assignment," Mr. Brown said.

Other companies are bringing foreign managers to the United States for a year or two to get a better feel for the company, while their American counterparts are shipped out to their jobs to learn more about their cultures. "Rotating people through other countries is a formal part of the career path for people with high potential, and that means putting people from our domestic operations overseas, and vice versa," said Mr. Sardas of Goodyear.

Absorbing the costs and finding the right slots may be the easy part of moving Americans overseas. The hard part is overcoming an ingrained—and long-justified—antipathy to overseas assignments.

Ambitious managers have traditionally had good reason to shy away from foreign assignments. "Out of sight, out of mind" was more than just a cliché at most multinational companies. People would go overseas for a few years, then be brought back—only to discover that there was no meaningful work to give them.

That is still the case at many businesses, management experts say. "Companies are only beginning to assault their own internal rewards system," said Mary Ann Devanna, associate dean of executive education at Columbia Business School. "Most are not past the lip-service stage. They have yet to promote a lot of people who've been overseas."

"An overseas assignment can actually delay a career," said David F. Smith, managing director of executive recruiters Korn/Ferry international.

"Companies bring people back from overseas and don't know what to do with them." Indeed, Mr. Smith talks of the high-level manager he knows who did an exemplary job running a foreign subsidiary, only to be dumped into his company's real estate department when he came home.

Human-resource executives concede that repatriation remains their most difficult problem. Many have started to comb other divisions and subsidiaries of their companies for jobs for Americans ready to return from overseas. Mr. Fulkerson of Pepsi-Cola International has been checking with his counterparts at Pepsico corporate headquarters and at various Pepsico subsidiaries like Kentucky Fried Chicken, Taco Bell or Pizza Hut to spot appropriate positions for people who will return from overseas in the next few years.

For now, the traffic flows primarily from his international group to the domestic subsidiaries, but Mr. Fulkerson predicts that will soon change. "Three years down the road, we'll see a lot more of our sister divisions saying, 'Hey, we've got someone who needs international experience,'" he said. "But you have to make sure you have a landing pad for them when they come back and that means planning in advance."

The repatriation process need not be confined to human resources departments. At Dow, for example, every executive who is sent overseas is assigned a "godfather" at home. The godfather, who is generally at least one level above the overseas executive's immediate boss, is responsible for keeping tabs on the temporary expatriate's performance and insuring that, after a few years, that person's name is automatically considered when an appropriate job opens up back in the states.

That sort of high-level participation can be the make-or-break factor in getting a program for international development to work. That is one reason that Kodak's Mr. Chandler gets personally involved in the process. "It's hard to get management to pay attention to it," he said. "But if you get the CEO sitting in, pretty soon you'll have full participation."

timates hold that failure rates for poorly trained expatriate managers and personnel, based on location, are more in the range of 33 to 66 percent.[3]

The answer to minimizing failures in deploying personnel abroad lies in planning the management of a global corporation and carefully selecting and training these global managers. Managers with aptitude, ability, and willingness for serving in international assignments must be identified by the corporation and trained extensively. Appropriate financial and career incentives have to be created to attract managers to international assignments and reward those who accept them.

Branch Manager versus Home Office: Who Is in Charge?

Overseas managers of MNCs face several challenges that arise from their unique position between not only two parts of a company (the parent corporation and the subsidiary), but also between two countries and two cultures. In addition, there is always a considerable physical distance between them and the corporate office. Consequently, overseas managers have a much greater degree of autonomy than their peers at the corporate office. As heads of local operations, they are fully responsible for their performance and must make a variety of executive decisions. Greater decision-making authority devolves both by design as well as circumstance. The costs and delays associated with overseas communication encourage the parent corporation to give substantial leeway to the local manager. Even in areas where the decision-making is reserved by the parent office, the local manager may have to exercise discretionary authority in emergency situations, when there is a breakdown in the communication channels, especially when decisions are needed immediately and cannot wait for a response from the head office.

Many parent offices delegate substantial authority to on-the-spot local managers in the belief that they will be able to make better-informed decisions. Generally, day-to-day operational decisions are vested with the local managers, while the overall global strategic decisions are made by the corporate office. Overseas managers have to adjust their decision-making to corporate policy and maintain the fine balance needed for exercising just the right degree of discretionary authority at the local level.

Overseas managers have the effective responsibilities, in many ways, of the CEOs of corporations. Therefore, they must have an overall perspective of their operations, the internal and external environments, the trends in the local political and economic situations, and a clear perception of the opportunities and threats to the local operations. As the head of a local operation, the overseas manager represents the MNC to the local government, other firms, customers, and suppliers. It is essential that the manager deal effectively with each of these entities, all of whom are important for the success of any business operation.

Adaptability is probably one of the most important qualities required of an overseas manager. Managers sent to different countries land in a completely different professional and cultural environment. In addition, there are the problems of adjustment by spouses and families which have to be addressed. A large number of expatriate managers have failed in their assignments because their families had difficulty adjusting to the changed environment. Thus, the adaptability of both manager and family is crucial to success in an overseas assignment.

Branch Managers: Who Should Firms Choose?

A major issue for an MNC in staffing overseas facilities is whether to use a home country national, a host country national, or a third-country national.

Home country nationals are citizens of the country where the headquarters are located. Home

[3] Harris and Moran 1987.

country nationals who live and work in foreign countries are called expatriates. Host country nationals are citizens of the country where the subsidiary exists. They are local employees. Third-country nationals are citizens of neither the country of the subsidiary or the headquarters. For example, a German working in Brazil for a U.S.-based company would be a third-country national.

Home country nationals as overseas managers offer several advantages for managing a foreign subsidiary. Home country managers are well-trained and familiar with the company's operating requirements and practices. Thus, they have a better perception of corporate goals, policies, and strategies and would design their local operations accordingly. Overseas assignments will broaden the perspectives of home country managers, and they will begin to factor in the worldwide implications of decision-making, which is essential for all top executives of the firm. The overseas assignment of home country executives thus provides valuable training for the company's future senior management. A home country national in an overseas location provides headquarters with a presence in the foreign environment and enables the firm to stay abreast of developments first hand. A home country national also can represent the firm's interests with the host government more easily than a host country national, who might encounter a conflict if asked to handle a confrontation with the host government.

Host country nationals also have several advantages as local managers. They know the local language, the culture, and the customs and may have valuable contacts in the local business world. Costs associated with hiring a local manager are usually lower because there are no relocation costs. Training costs can sometimes be higher, because the manager may need to be trained in the home country, but, in the long run, these costs generally are not significant. Hiring a host country national may ease tensions with the host government and may in fact serve to comply with local requirements. The local manager may also be able to deal better with local employees, especially unions.

There are also disadvantages in using host country nationals. These managers may be unfamiliar with home country cultures and the MNCs' policies and practices and may have different attitudes and values than those of the people at headquarters. Occasionally, these employees are hired away from the MNC by local competitors after the MNC has spent considerable time and money in training, and local mangers may experience conflicts in loyalty between their country and the MNC.

Third-country nationals may be hired for several reasons. They may possess skills lacking in both home and host country nationals. They may be more familiar with the language and culture of the host country than a home country national, and they may appease the host government by being a third-country national. Many times there is the natural progression from one post to another. For example, a French national in charge of a French subsidiary may be relocated to head the Mexican subsidiary.

Choosing Branch Managers: Selection Criteria
Labor Pool

The labor pool has a direct effect on the MNCs' choice of a manager. The availability, quality, and technical competence of managers in the host country is an important factor in deciding on the overseas assignment. If the local labor pool is unable to provide managers with the required qualifications, a home country national will have to be sent abroad.

Corporate Policies

The corporate objectives and policies of a firm will affect its choice of an overseas manager. If the firm wants to maintain a high level of control of the subsidiary operations and ensure that things are done strictly according to the policies of headquarters, it will choose to send home country nationals to overseas posts. Also, the MNC may want to promote management development of headquarters personnel by expanding their perspectives to include global considerations and exposing them to the overall corporate system.

Environmental constraints, the costs involved, and the legal and cultural environments of the host country will also affect the courses of action available to the firm. If the cost of relocating and compensating a headquarters employee is prohibitive, a host country national may be chosen. Similarly, there may be legal restrictions requiring the use of host country nationals or restricting the number of foreign personnel allowed into the country. If foreign personnel are allowed into the country, permission from the government may be slow and difficult to obtain.

Desired Local Image

The type of local image the firm portrays is very important. Most MNCs want to have a favorable local image in order to attract and retain employees and to smooth governmental relations. Choosing a host country national may reduce tensions with the host government and can result in considerable goodwill that may be of use later. In addition, the image of the firm with the local population may be enhanced and, thus, possibly increase sales and the morale of the employees.

Local Employee Incentives

If host country nationals are hired for management positions, it may give current local employees an incentive to remain with the firm and to work harder because they can see a possible future with the firm, because there is the possibility of advancement. Therefore, the multinational enterprise will tend to limit the management positions filled by expatriates.

Existing Methods of Selection

MNCs may find personnel for overseas assignments through a number of methods. If they ac-

quire a local, ongoing business, the personnel resources of that entity become available from which managers can be selected for the local operation. If the local operation is in the form of a joint venture, the partner in the venture may contribute the management expertise and personnel to the project. This may not always be the best alternative, however, because the partner's personnel may lack the necessary technical knowledge, be unfamiliar with the practices of the parent firm, and be difficult to control because of an allegiance to the MNC's partners and not the MNC itself.

Home country records can be used as a tool in selecting management personnel. Personnel records for each employee can include information on technical knowledge, language abilities, willingness to relocate, and the results of any adaptability tests. It is extremely important to consider the spouse of a potential candidate, because it is usually more stressful for the spouse to relocate to a foreign country.

Potential for Culture Shock

Culture shock can be identified as a pronounced reaction to the psychological disorientation caused by moving to a totally different environment. When a person is relocated to a different country, there is an initial phase of excitement and enchantment with the new culture, then a period of disillusionment and negative feelings sets in toward the culture. This disillusionment may be because of a lack of adaptability or, alternatively, a firm's lack of knowledge of a situation and not fully preparing a person for possible difficulties. Culture shock can result in extreme bitterness toward the foreign country and its culture, and even in physical illness. There may also be reverse culture shock when an expatriate is repatriated to the home culture.

Two factors may help to lessen the effects of culture shock—empathy and the avoidance of stereotypes. Empathy is the ability to understand what another person is feeling, in essence, to be able to see the world through their eyes. If the expatriate is able to expand this ability to encompass the whole culture, to achieve cultural empathy, that person will go a long way to understanding the views and actions of the members of the foreign culture.

Training Branch Managers

Alternative Models

Training is necessary to avoid problems in sending people to work abroad and to ensure project completion. In general, the depth of cross-cultural training for an overseas manager ranges from reading up on the assignment locale to ad hoc corporate training and in-depth immersion programs. A variety of resources are available for training. These vary from how-to books for conducting business abroad to videotapes and orientation programs. The effectiveness of this training correlates with the amount of preparation engaged in prior to a manager's departure for an overseas assignment. The highest degree of expatriate success is experienced by managers who have had individual training tailored to their assignment in a specific country.

One categorization of cross-cultural training programs lists four different training models.[4] The intellectual model consists of readings and lectures about the host culture and assumes that an exchange of information about another culture is effective preparation for living or working in that culture. The area simulation model is a culture-specific training program based on the belief that an individual must be prepared and trained to enter a specific culture. It involves the simulation of future experiences and practice functioning in the new culture.

The self-awareness model is based on the assumption that understanding and accepting oneself is critical to understanding a person from another culture. Sensitivity training is a main component of this method. The cultural awareness model, which is practiced in current progressive training programs, assumes that in order to function successfully in another culture, an individual must learn the principles of behavior that exist across cultures. Understanding intercultural communication from the perspective of recognizing that one's own culture influences personal values, behaviors, and cognitions is expected to result in an enhancement of a person's skill at diagnosing difficulties in intercultural communication.

Business Council for International Understanding

One example of a comprehensive cross-cultural training program for overseas managers and their families is the program given by the Business Council for International Understanding (BCIU) Institute. The objective of the BCIU Institute is not to brief managers and family members, but to provide them with the tools to ensure their ability to adapt to, or cope with, difficulties encountered abroad. The orientation strives to portray the situation as realistically as possible, which means discussing the negative as well as the positive aspects of overseas assignments.

The program at the institute includes five specific components—language studies, intercultural communications, area/country studies, practical training tailored to the specific country and the manager's functional area, and addressing spousal and family needs.

While the global manager learns some of the practicalities of doing business in the assignment country, family members receive concurrent training on problems to be expected and on alternatives to their current lifestyles. For example, spouses of managers going abroad may have to deal with the issue of trying to find employment in the foreign country or coping with a change from working outside to working inside the home. In some Middle Eastern countries, for example, female spouses are not allowed to work officially, but can find jobs through informal channels. Other issues dealt with include managing a domestic staff, raising a family abroad, and transferring activities and interests to another environment.

[4] Ibid.

Compensating Branch Managers

Wages

There are many problems associated with deciding on the amount of compensation to be given to an overseas manager. The local rate may be above or below the person's current salary, thus causing pay differentials between home and host country nationals performing the same job. An expatriate is usually paid an allowance and bonuses above the local rate. Problems arise when a person is transferred to another post or back to headquarters. What salary does the firm pay? Does the firm lower the salary to the old level or keep it elevated? There is also the problem of which currency to use to pay a salary because of fluctuating exchange rates. Compensation is usually paid in some combination of both currencies, thereby allowing tax breaks and an ability to save money in the home country.

Allowances are paid to cover the additional costs of living overseas. They are meant to keep the manager's standard of living approximately the same while in the foreign country

TABLE 19-1

A Price Comparison for Overseas Managers Incomes and Selected Expenses in Five Countries. Percentage of income in parentheses.

	Japan	U.S.	Argentina	Brazil	Mexico
Monthly pay for a manager	$5,000.00 (100%)	$4,170.00 (100%)	$1,530.00 (100%)	$837.60 (100%)	$1,000.00 (100%)
Ready-made men's suit	$460.00 (9.2%)	$400.00 (9.6%)	$306.00 (20%)	$91.11 (10.9%)	$135.14 (13.5%)
200 grams of sirloin steak (.44 lbs.)	$7.00 (0.14%)	$1.50 (0.04%)	$0.73 (0.05%)	$0.43 (0.05%)	$1.99 (0.2%)
One dozen eggs	$1.54 (0.03%)	$1.00 (0.02%)	$0.57 (0.04%)	$0.73 (0.09%)	$0.53 (0.05%)
One liter of gasoline	$1.54 (0.03%)	$0.30 (0.01%)	$0.49 (0.03%)	$0.60 (0.07%)	$0.22 (0.02%)
Base taxi fare	$3.62 (0.07%)	$1.15 (0.03%)	$0.37 (0.02%)	$2.89 (0.35%)	$0.20 (0.02%)
Square meter of land (1.2 sq. yards)	$7,692.00 (154%)	$100.00 (2.4%)	$459.00 (30%)	$232.67 (27.8%)	$75.32 (7.5%)
2-bedroom apartment (rent per month)	$1,150.00 (23%)	$1,600.00 (38.4%)	$995.00 (65%)	$186.32 (22.2%)	$177.23 (17.7%)

SOURCE: Data from Bank of Tokyo, *Wall Street Journal*, August 31, 1988.

(see Table 19–1). Allowances cover the differing costs of housing, food, utilities, transportation, clothing, personal and medical services, and education for any children. In addition, the firm will always cover the cost of additional taxes incurred in a foreign country.

Bonuses are usually paid to compensate an employee for any hardships, sacrifices, and inconveniences incurred as a result of the move. Bonuses are rare, however, and are usually given only if the manager is assigned to a particularly underdeveloped, violent, or dangerous country.

In addition to allowances and bonuses, a firm will usually provide home leaves for expatriates and their families and pay for periodic trips home. Home travel is considered essential for expatriate managers and their families to alleviate the pressures and tensions of overseas assignments.

Taxes

Tax laws vary greatly from country to country. In some countries, foreign workers are only taxed on the income they receive in the country. In the United States, the Tax Reform Act of 1986 allows a U.S. citizen to exempt the first $70,000 of income earned abroad from U.S. taxes. The rest is taxed at the regular rate. If the United States has a tax treaty with the foreign country in question, the amount of foreign taxes paid on unearned income (interest, dividends) can be credited against the amount of owed U.S. taxes. In order to get a foreign tax credit on the amount of earned income (salaries), expatriates must prove that they have been residents in a foreign country for at least a year and the assignment to a foreign location must be for at least two years.

Repatriating Branch Managers

Reverse Culture Shock

There are three problem areas associated with the repatriation of employees—personal finances,

readjustment to home country corporate structure, and reacclimatization to life in the home country. Upon reentry into the home country, an expatriate will lose all the allowances and bonuses that encourage foreign assignments. For many, this means a substantial decrease in salary. Also, they may find that consumer prices and housing costs have greatly increased during the time abroad.

Once back at headquarters, managers may find that peers have been promoted and that they have less autonomy in decision-making and fewer responsibilities. A manager also may feel left out of the corporate information loop. The corporation should make foreign assignments as prestigious and important as possible in the corporate framework in order to attract candidates, which will help to ease the transition back into the corporate scheme by increasing the esteem a manager is given at headquarters by peers.

The family of an expatriate may find that their comparative social status has dropped. In many countries subsidiary managers are thought of as corporate "big wheels" representing the entire company and, as such, receive club memberships and invitations to important government and social functions. Once at home, however, the situation changes and they are no longer the center of such attention. Children must adjust to new schools and lifestyles, and spouses who have grown accustomed to domestic help may find themselves on their own again.

To help with the problems associated with repatriation, there are several things that can be done while an employee is still at the overseas assignment. The earlier the notification of return, the longer the time for adjustment. Headquarters can give the maximum amount of information available about the new job to the expatriate to allay fears of a demotion. The firm also should bring the employee back to headquarters periodically so that the employee will not feel isolated and forgotten. A mentor might also be assigned to look out for the interests of the expatriate and to help with readjustment. The firm can also provide housing assistance and an orientation program once the family is back.

Ethical Issues

Female Managers Overseas

There is a definite lack of consideration of women as candidates for expatriate assignments. According to a 1983 study by Nancy Adler of McGill University, only 3 percent of expatriate managers from 686 North American firms were women.[5] Adler attributes this scarcity to three beliefs held by MNC executives:

1. Women do not want foreign assignments.
2. Corporations resist sending women abroad.
3. Women would not be effective because of the prejudices of foreigners.

Adler refutes the first point, having found that there is no difference between men and women MBAs in attitudes toward overseas assignments. Rather than differences, she found that males and females showed equal interest in pursuing international careers.

Adler found confirmation of the second belief that corporations are indeed hesitant to assign women overseas. The reasons cited by respondents in her study were the prejudices of foreigners, dual-career marriages, a scarcity of women willing to go abroad, and concerns regarding the possible dangers to personnel based overseas from isolation and hardship. In addressing the third point, that corporations assume that women will have reduced effectiveness overseas because of the prejudice of foreigners against women in the work world, Adler asserts that while there "are genuine barriers in many Middle Eastern nations, most countries make a distinction between American women professionals and local women."

Overseas Assignments as Dumping Grounds

One important issue that an MNC faces in making decisions on selecting personnel for overseas assignments is the possible use of these assignments to remove undesirable or inefficient executives. This is a dangerous trend, however, that could harm the interests of the corporation in the long run. For example, the demands of an overseas assignment are usually much more complex and intense than a domestic assignment, and an executive who is regarded as a failure in a home country could be an even bigger failure overseas. The failure of local operations in one country may not affect the overall bottom line of a large MNC significantly, but it could prove damaging to its global image. Another problem associated with this approach is that the company is not likely to find good personnel in the future willing to take overseas assignments, once it is known within the corporation that they have been used to ease out inefficient or difficult personnel.

International Labor Issues

International labor issues are important considerations for multinational corporations operating manufacturing or service facilities in different countries. Managing a labor force that comprises different nationalities, has different work ethics and cultures, is governed by a variety of local laws, and has different traditions of union activities is an extremely complex and often a very difficult proposition.

Managing an International Work Force

Given the differences in union-management relations around the world and the need to maintain a uniform industrial relations policy throughout a corporation, MNCs are invariably faced with the decision of whom to give the responsibility for handling overall industrial relations. The approach that an MNC takes generally depends on its world view, whether it is ethnocentric, polycentric, or geocentric. Although MNCs are found to be widely different in their overall manage-

[5] Adler 1984.

ment policies from these three standpoints, some do take an ethnocentric view, where the parent office exercises substantial control over the local subsidiaries. When it comes to dealing with industrial relations in different countries, however, most companies give substantial freedom to their local managers to deal with local industrial relations problems.

Different social and political structures, different local laws, varying labor psychology, and unique traditions that influence industrial relations are the primary factors that justify this policy, which places substantial responsibility on local managers to deal with industrial relations problems as they arise. Moreover, the active and continuous involvement of local managers in handling local issues provides them with the opportunity to develop an ongoing relationship with workers and union representatives, which is essential to the smooth functioning of any operation and for the building of a basic understanding between management and labor.

Most corporations, however, do insist on a certain level of control by the parent company over the industrial relations policies followed by subsidiaries. On most occasions, however, this control simply takes the form of coordination, where the overall policy is decided by the parent office and local issues are left to the subsidiary managers.

Some major corporations have a tendency to create an industrial relations arrangement where unions are not a part of the scene. While this could work in certain countries, it may not in others. It is clear that while coordination is workable, central control is not practical in organizing and managing industrial relations in a multinational corporation. Some multinationals use their multiple sourcing and labor transfer capabilities to exercise leverage against unions in particular countries. For example, if a plant in one country is closed by striking union members, an MNC can shift production to a plant in a different country and maintain its stance against the striking workers in the first country.

Wages and Benefits

Wages and benefits vary around the world. The differences in the levels of wages and benefits workers enjoy are particularly pronounced when compared between industrialized and developing countries. There are also substantial differences within the industrial countries and developing countries themselves.

There are several reasons why such important differences exist. First, wages are determined by the local cost of living, which may be determined by a comparative index. This general determination is influenced by the existing wages in some industries or comparative industry sectors for comparative jobs. Government legislation or intervention is also a determinant. Many countries have minimum wage legislation, and some have legislation on maximum wages that can be paid. Tax issues also influence wage levels, because in high-tax countries companies must pay higher wages or provide additional benefits to offset the impact of higher taxation levels. The level and militancy of union organizations in different countries and the capacity for collective bargaining is often an important determinant of wage levels.

Patterns of fringe benefits also differ widely. In countries with a strong welfare or socialist sociopolitical orientation, greater emphasis is placed on fringe benefits as a part of the overall compensation package, unlike some industrial nations where compensation is almost entirely in the form of monetary income. In many countries certain fringe benefits are required by government legislation to be paid by companies. Thus, the percentage of fringe benefits in the total compensation package varies considerably in different countries.

Country	Compensation as Benefits
U.S.	35%
Germany	45%
Belgium	55%
France	70%
Italy	92%

Workers in Europe receive additional compensation according to the number of family members they support, or if they work in unpleasant conditions. In Belgium and the Netherlands, commuting costs are reimbursed to workers. One of the most comprehensive fringe benefits systems is found in Japan, where Japanese workers receive a family allowance, housing subsidies, free lunches, free education for their children, and subsidized vacations.

Procedures for increasing levels of compensation also vary considerably. In the United States wages are governed usually by labor management contracts that have a particular life span, usually three years, after which they have to be renegotiated. Increases are often determined on the basis of a mutually agreed formula that links wage increases to some cost-of-living index. There is room within the general formula for individual wage increases on the basis of performance during a particular time period, typically a year. In Japan a certain group of unions, which are seen as role models for a particular industry, lead the way for wage negotiation, which, among other things, takes into account the increases in the cost of living since the last wage settlement.

Once agreements have been reached with the leading unions in a particular industry, other unions in the same industry come to an agreement with their managements, more or less on the same basis. Wage increases in Great Britain are somewhat less stable and can be demanded by individual groups of workers within a particular company, and the demands often may not be related to the compensation being paid to workers in different companies in the same industry, or, for that matter, other groups of workers within the same company. Industry-wide wages are generally standard in West Germany, however, and strikes that demand wage increases outside the scope of industry-wide agreements are not recognized. In most developing countries, collective bargaining by unions and intervention by the government are the main determinants of wage increases.

Usually MNCs have to pay a relatively higher wage to their employees in developing countries, in comparison to wages being paid for similar work in the industry by domestic companies. This differential wage policy is necessitated by the need for an MNC to counter and prevent criticism from the government, local politicians, the media, and trade union organizations that it is an agent of foreign exploitation of the country. Foreign exploitation is a particularly sensitive issue in most newly independent developing countries, given the colonial legacy in which these countries were subjected to substantial economic exploitation by their rulers and by companies from the ruling countries.

Job Security and Layoffs

Emphasis on job security varies widely from country to country, and MNCs must take into consideration local laws, practices, and socioeconomic conditions while formulating policies and procedures for layoffs, suspensions, and termination of employee services. The emphasis on job security is perhaps the highest in developing countries, where jobs are scarce and there is no system of social security to take care of employees who cannot find employment in other jobs. In such countries layoffs and retrenchments are difficult to implement, because both union and government pressures tend to be strongly against them. Moreover, industry practices in developing countries do not permit layoffs, especially of the type witnessed in the United States, where companies routinely lay off thousands of employees either to improve profitability, restructure the organization, or because demand for the products has fallen off. In fact, to prevent worker hardship, many governments have nationalized operations of MNCs who have decided to lay off large numbers of workers. In developed countries job security is important, although not quite to the same extent as developing countries. Among the industrialized countries, Japan and West Germany place a particularly strong emphasis on job security. Japanese industry has been long noted for its tradition of lifetime employment. Although this is no longer true of a large number of companies in Japan, substantial benefits are available to Japanese workers who lose their jobs, especially because of corporate policies. These benefits include salary payments, retraining, assistance in finding alternative employment, and relocation assistance. Similarly, in West Germany assistance is provided to workers who lose their jobs because of corporate decisions. In many instances companies must seek approval from the government and come to an understanding with unions before effecting any significant layoffs of employees.

Labor Productivity

Labor productivity is a critical issue for MNCs. It determines, to a significant degree, the level of competitiveness an enterprise can hope to achieve in the local and international markets. Labor productivity varies greatly in different countries, but this variance is not only because of differences in labor quality. In fact, eight factors can be identified, that are crucial to improvement of labor productivity:

1. Government must have an active role. Laissez-faire attitudes will tend to keep productivity at current levels rather than increasing it.
2. Worker quality and skills. The labor force must be constantly upgraded through training in the latest methods and technologies.
3. Research and development. A high level of R&D is needed to remain abreast of and preferably ahead of the competition. New products and information must continue in a steady stream.
4. Business savings and investment are a major source of capital, R&D, and training.
5. Personal savings and investment provide a pool of funds to be used for investments by commercial banks, which in turn stimulate the economy's growth.
6. Natural resource development and substitution. Obviously, there is a limit on the amount of natural resources that can be utilized. Thus,

new sources must be developed to provide for the needs of business.
7. Production techniques and systems must be constantly upgraded and changed because of the high rate of obsolescence. The personal computer industry is a good example.
8. Management techniques and philosophy. Management must take a long-term view of the future. Short-term goals have proved to be ineffective and costly, and productivity can only be increased over the long term.

Table 19–2 provides indices of manufacturing productivity and other measures for some of the industrialized countries.

Technology

Of the many issues that affect labor productivity, technology is one of the most important and presents major problems to MNCs seeking overseas locations for their plants. Many LDCs have major unemployment problems and are eager to develop industries that are labor intensive and provide maximum job opportunities. Modern technology is often capital intensive, however, and relies on reducing the role of human effort in accomplishing production goals with minimum costs and maximum efficiency. As a result, in many instances MNCs have to use technology that is relatively less advanced to meet host country requirements of providing greater job opportunities. Thus, a certain amount of productivity and efficiency have to be sacrificed to gain entry into a new market.

Labor Unions

The concept of collective bargaining is central to the functioning of labor unions (see Perspective 19–3). After a union is certified by workers and recognized by management, it is the sole representative of those workers. It represents all the workers collectively when negotiating with management for compensation and working conditions and signs agreements into legally

TABLE 19-2

Manufacturing Productivity, Compensation, and Unit Labor Costs (average annual rates of change)

	Productivity			Labor Compensation (U.S. dollar basis)		
	1973–87	1982–87	1987	1973–87	1982–87	1987
United States	2.5	4.5	3.3	7.4	3.5	2.1
Canada	2.1	4.3	1.7	7.2	3.3	9.5
Japan	5.3	4.8	4.1	12.9	15.2	18.1
France	3.9	3.0	3.7	10.5	9.2	19.1
West Germany	3.3	3.3	1.3	10.2	11.4	25.6
United Kingdom	3.2	5.5	6.9	10.8	6.0	20.9
Weighted average, 11 foreign countries	3.8	4.3	3.4	10.4	9.6	18.3

	Unit Labor Costs (national currency basis)			Unit Labor Costs (U.S. dollar basis)		
	1973–87	1982–87	1987	1973–87	1982–87	1987
United States	4.8	−1.0	−1.2	4.8	−1.0	−1.2
Canada	7.1	0.5	2.7	5.0	−1.0	7.7
Japan	2.6	−1.4	−2.5	7.3	10.0	13.5
France	8.7	4.2	−0.2	6.4	6.0	14.9
West Germany	3.8	1.5	2.7	6.7	7.8	23.9
United Kingdom	10.5	1.7	1.1	7.4	0.5	13.0
Weighted average, 11 foreign countries	5.0	1.1	0.8	6.4	5.1	14.4

NOTE: The 11 foreign countries are Belgiem, Canada, Denmark, France, Italy, Japan, the Netherlands, Norway, Sweden, the United Kingdom, and West Germany.
SOURCE: U.S. Department of Labor, Bureau of Labor Statistics.

binding labor contracts. The contracts cover such issues as wages, fringe benefits, holidays, vacations, promotion policies, layoff policies, job security provisions, stipulations regarding working conditions and safety, administration of the contract, and grievance and dispute settlement.

UNITED STATES

Labor-management relations in the United States are relatively nonpolitical, in that the govern-ment is not a part of the collective bargaining process, but legislation does establish and enforce rules regarding the framework of collective bargaining (for example, both parties must bargain in good faith). The labor contract is enforceable through the courts, and either side can be sued for any breach of the contract. For the most part, collective bargaining takes place at the company or plant level, that is, on a company-by-company basis. Some exceptions include the trucking and construction industries, which have regional con-

PERSPECTIVE 19–3   Workers of the World Disunite

Some 31% of American workers belonged to a trade union in 1970. By the late 1980s the figure was barely half that, at 17%. Union membership is now no higher as a share of the labour force than in the 1920s. The fall in the private sector has been sharper still, offset partly by some growth in public-sector unions.

According to conventional wisdom, the power of trade unions has faded throughout the industrial world. Highly unionised industries, such as shipbuilding and steel, have declined; the rise in unemployment in the 1980s, especially in Europe, has shifted the balance of power from workers to employers; and the political mood has swung against unions. Labour parties in Europe and the Antipodes have adopted "right-wing" poli-

cies, while President Reagan's sacking of America's air-traffic controllers in 1981, and Mrs. Margaret Thatcher's defeat of Britain's ministers in 1985, gave the nod to union-busting by firms.

In this hostile climate, trade unions might be expected to be in retreat everywhere. Though it is generally true that unions are flexing their muscles rather less than they used to, only a few countries have seen significant deunionisation. Union membership has fallen in Britain, Japan, Holland and Italy, though nowhere near as sharply as in America. In most countries membership remained firm in the 1980s, or even rose, as in Sweden and Denmark (see chart).

Outside America the average percentage of workers belonging to a trade union rose from

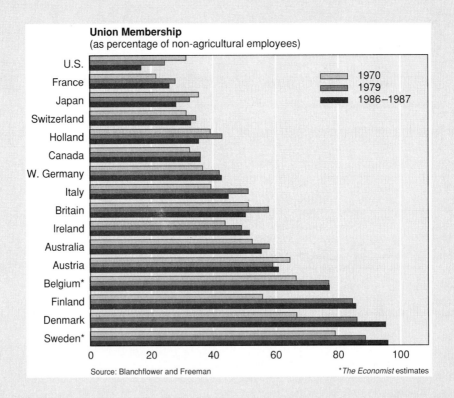

Union Membership
(as percentage of non-agricultural employees)

Countries (top to bottom): U.S., France, Japan, Switzerland, Holland, Canada, W. Germany, Italy, Britain, Ireland, Australia, Austria, Belgium*, Finland, Denmark, Sweden*

Legend: 1970, 1979, 1986–1987

Source: Blanchflower and Freeman   *The Economist estimates

SOURCE: *The Economist*, August 18, 1990, page 57.

48% in 1970 to 55% in 1979, and has since remained broadly unchanged. If anything, the increasing importance of trade and expanding production by multinational firms should have caused greater convergence in industrial-relations trends. It hasn't: so much, brothers, for all the talk of a world labour movement.

Why has America taken a different path than most? A recent paper by two economists, Messrs. David Blanchflower and Richard Freeman, suggests one possible explanation. They argue that the decline in American trade unions is not simply a consequence of the crushing of the air-traffic-controllers union, but is more deeply rooted: American trade unions have been too successful in winning wage increases for their members. Employers have therefore had a greater incentive to oppose unions.

American unions have indeed lifted their wages relative to non-union pay by more than in other countries. The gap between average union and non-union pay in America rose from 15% in the 1960s to 22% by the late 1970s—three times as big as the average union differential in other countries where such data are available. For example, in Britain workers in trade unions earn, on average, 10% more than non-union workers; in West Germany and Australia the gap is 8%; in Canada 15%; in Switzerland 4%; in Japan there is no differential for male workers.

The greater "success" of American trade unions might encourage more workers to join them. But this is outweighed by the fact that a wage premium of 22% puts unionised firms at a serious disadvantage when competing against imports or non-unionised domestic firms. Employers therefore have greater reason to declare war on unions and to keep them out of the workplace.

The union-pay premium increased in the 1970s at the very time when productivity growth slumped. This inevitably led to job losses and hastened deunionisation. Other American studies have found that industries with the biggest wage differentials had the most rapid declines in union membership.

To what extent can the gap between union and non-union pay account for the movements in union membership in different countries? Unfortunately, data on wage premiums are not available in most countries. Instead, the authors examine trends in union penetration in countries with different types of wage-bargaining systems.

Their assumption is that, in countries with centralised wage-setting systems, unions are likely to have a smaller differential impact on wages than under decentralised collective bargaining, so employers will have less incentive to resist trade unions. This is because national unions are more likely to take account of job prospects; they also often set wages for the whole economy, not just for their members.

This seems to fit the facts. In the 1970s and 1980s union membership fared better in countries with centralised industrial-relations systems—e.g., Sweden and West Germany—than in countries with decentralissed ones, such as Britain and Italy.

But surely Canada's experience contradicts the theory? It has the second biggest union-wage differential after America, and yet membership has stayed broadly constant. True, but it has fallen relative to the OECD average over the past two decades. More important, union membership in Canadian manufacturing—which is the sector most exposed to foreign competition—has slumped from 49% to around 40% since the late 1970s.

Looking ahead, the authors conclude that unless American trade unions change their tactics and develop a new brand of unionism which deals not just with wages, but with other interests of workers as well, they are doomed to extinction. This is precisely what the United Auto Workers is doing in its attempt to get America's big three carmakers to agree to job-guarantees during the current industry-wide contract negotiations. If other unions do not begin to look beyond their pay packets, predict the authors, union penetration in America will drop into single figures in the early 1990s, leaving "ghetto unionism" in just a few aging industries and the public sector.

tracts, and the steel industry, which has a national contract.

The contract agreed upon is usually very extensive and covers almost every contingency. Its terms apply to all workers in the bargaining units, and individual workers cannot negotiate individually with management to obtain better terms. During the life of a contract, strikes and lockouts are usually banned, but if an old contract expires and a new one is still being negotiated, strikes and lockouts are allowed. Strikes occur when the workers walk out and refuse to work. Lockouts occur when the employer closes or locks the plant and bars workers from entering. Strikes are generally more frequent than lockouts. A wildcat strike occurs when the workers strike during the life of an existing contract and give little or no notice. There are relatively few strikes in the United States, but they tend to last a long time. Figure 19–1 provides data on numbers of strikes and days of work lost in different countries. The emphasis in labor management relations in the United States is on keeping the firm going and profitable.

GREAT BRITAIN

Labor-management relations in Great Britain are much more political and contentious than in the United States. Unions see the negotiation process as more of a class struggle and going on strike as an exercisable right. The unions are guided by the principle of voluntarism, which states that workers alone will define and pursue their self-interest, which makes them militant and abrasive with authority, and they have very little regard for the welfare of the enterprise. They are also a powerful political force, in that a major political party the Labor party, espouses this class-struggle mentality, but the situation has been changing through the Tory party, which is trying to institute legal restraints on the unions, based on the belief that too many strikes are destroying the very jobs they are trying to protect by forcing firms into bankruptcy. Great Britain's unions have been subject to new legal constraints and have lost much of their erstwhile unity, while membership has dwindled (see Perspective 19–4). In fact, union membership declined by 20 percent between 1979 and 1986.

Strikes. Are workers getting less bolshy? The chart compares the average number of working days per 1,000 employees lost through strikes in 1986 with the number lost on average over the previous ten years. Of the twenty countries in the chart, thirteen had fewer strikes in 1986 than the ten-year average. The traditionally strike-bound trio of Britain, Spain, and Italy saw the biggest improvements. Finland had a rotten 1986 with 1,320 days lost, compared with its ten-year average of 530 days. For New Zealand (which lost 1,110 days) and Norway (560 days), 1986 was also a year of discontent. Unsurprisingly, Japan's ten-year average was just twenty days a year, against ten days in 1986. Switzerland and Austria did even better—during the ten years each lost fewer than five days per 1,000 employees.

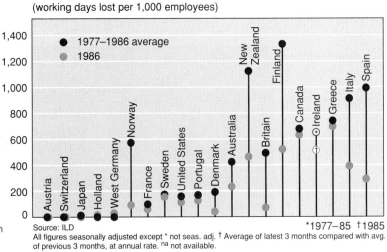

Strikes
(working days lost per 1,000 employees)

Source: ILD

All figures seasonally adjusted except * not seas. adj. † Average of latest 3 months compared with avg. of previous 3 months, at annual rate. na not available.

FIGURE 19–1   Working Days Lost Because of Strikes
SOURCE: Data from International Labor Organization, *The Economist*, June 25, 1988, page 105.

PERSPECTIVE 19–4   Britain's Unions, Cowed for a Decade, Demanding Big Wage Increases . . .

LONDON—It wasn't supposed to happen. Under Margaret Thatcher's program to transform Britons into hard-working, thrifty capitalists, the labor unions have lost clout and membership. Today, the days when a handful of labor bosses virtually ran Britain and crippled the economy are only a memory.

But after a decade of failed strikes and union-busting legislation, the unexpected has happened: The labor unions are back. Emboldened by the country's recent economic boom and shortage of skilled workers, labor is demanding big wage increases to cope with an annual inflation rate that is currently 7.5% and rising. Employers, fearful of losing workers, are finding it easier to capitulate.

As a result, "Inflation will become ingrained at a far higher level than (the government) forecasted," says Bill Martin, chief United Kingdom economist at London brokers Phillips & Drew. "One important reason is the tenacious influence of the wage-price spiral in which we've now become enlocked. All the major indicators relevant for national pay bargaining are flashing red."

Inflation, which the government hopes will cool to 5% by the end of the year, erupted at the worst time, amid Britain's annual winter round of wage talks. No fewer than 3.6 million workers, about 40% of total union membership, are negotiating. Among them are members of the biggest and most powerful unions. At the least, they insist on matching the current 7.5% inflation; some want much more.

"SOMETHING AROUND 10%"

"The lads'll demand a decent increase; they'll be looking for something around 10%," says a union steward involved in nationwide pay bargaining

for the 78,000 workers at Britain's state-owned electric-power stations. "I'm prepared to do anything this time to get it."

What's happening isn't another violent episode in Britain's labor relations. Unions aren't paralyzing the country with strikes or throwing rocks at police from picket lines. What they are doing is quieter, but more effective than the battles of the early Thatcher years. And this time, they have the cooperation of employers eager to avoid disruptive strikes and the loss of skilled workers.

Over the past two and half years, Britain's unemployment rate has plunged by almost half to 7%. That's far from full employment. But unemployed workers' lack of skills means employers in some parts of the country face shortages of suitable labor for the first time in years.

High wage settlements are "driven by employers; that's what the absolute paradox is," says David Metcalf, professor of industrial relations at the London School of Economics and Political Science.

Average earnings, which include wages plus overtime and bonuses, are rising at an annual rate of 8 3/4%. With employers' easy-going attitude and workers' demands, private economists expect the growth to reach 10% this year, and to remain above 8% through 1990. Earnings in Britain's major overseas competitors, the U.S., Japan, France and West Germany, are rising at half Britain's current rate.

Ironically, the Thatcher government itself has done the most to spark this latest threat from labor. About a year ago, strong consumer demand fed by generous tax cuts and low interest rates began pushing inflation sharply higher. Chancellor of the Exchequer Nigel Lawson lifted interest rates to choke consumer demand and cool infla-

SOURCE: Barbara Toman, *Wall Street Journal*, March 9, 1989, page A12.

tion. But because mortgage rates—up by a third since June—are folded into Britain's inflation index, higher interest rates also feed inflation.

STANDARD OF LIVING

In addition, workers anxious about rising interest rates and mortgage payments want to protect the higher standard of living they have come to enjoy under Mrs. Thatcher. They followed her advice to join the "property-owning democracy" and some 67% of British families now own their own homes, one of the highest percentages in Europe. House prices in southeast England have posted annual double-digit percentage increases for four years.

The government has been reduced to pleading with employers and workers to show restraint in pay bargaining. The pleas are ironic because government employees such as nurses and firefighters won some of the heftiest raises.

Workers aren't buying the government line. "For the last few years we've had this rosy picture painted," says Tony, a 30-year-old accounts clerk at a power-distribution station in north London. "We're told [by the government] we're all doing very well, thank you. But now I'm thinking I'm not. Where's my share?"

Tony wants a 15% raise on his £8,000 ($13,780) a year take-home pay, to cover rising food prices and enable him to buy a car. For Peter, married with two teenage sons, "the mortgage is the biggest worry." In the past year, he says, his monthly payments jumped 21% to £328 ($565).

In November, Ford Motor Co.'s U.K. workers received an 8.9 % pay increase after an earlier strike brought an inflation-linked settlement. Zurich Insurance Co. in January gave 11% to 1,500 workers; Royal Insurance U.K. Ltd. granted wage raises and bonuses that will increase payroll costs at least 16.5% over 15 months.

PRODUCTIVITY GAINS

The biggest surprise of the current pay round was the decision by Japan's Nissan Motor Co. to give workers at its new U.K. plant raises of 18% to 22.5% over two years. Nissan dismisses suggestions that the pact is inflationary. A spokeswoman says the wage costs will be offset by productivity gains, and so won't necessarily result in higher car prices. "We don't see it as inflationary in any way," she says.

The productivity argument, that workers who produce more can be paid more without raising total costs, is fashionable among companies who have given generous pay raises. But, says William Brown, professor of industrial relations at Cambridge University, "That's a very slippery slope, because [productivity improvement] is a very difficult thing to measure. People can fudge together all sorts of bogus figures saying they're being more productive than they actually are."

At any rate, British wages now are rising so fast that even last year's robust 7.7% increase in manufacturing productivity—higher than any major competitor's, except Japan—can't compensate.

Another problem in Great Britain is the dualism of labor representation. Generally, unions are organized on a geographic basis, but there are also councils of stewards that represent only workers at a single company or plant, which results in serious conflicts between the union for the area and the steward's council. For example, the union may reject an agreement that has already been reached between the stewards and the management of that company. The problems resulting from dual-

ism, coupled with the philosophy of voluntarism, lead to numerous strikes. Although unions and workers strike frequently, the strikes are usually not of very long duration and not too many days are lost.

WEST GERMANY

In West Germany union membership is purely voluntary. There is only one union for all workers in a single industry. Labor agreements cover only major issues such as wages. All the other issues, such as vacations and shifts, are negotiated at the plant level. Legally established work councils are able to codetermine issues involving safety and plant practices with management. Members of the work council are elected by the firm's workers. Strikes and lockouts during the life of an existing contract are illegal, regardless of the contract's provisions. They are legal when the existing contract has expired or is being renegotiated. A unique feature of West German labor relations is that an individual worker can negotiate individually with management to try to obtain better terms.

JAPAN

Japanese unions are usually company unions, organized by enterprise. A union is made up of employees within a single company or single operational unit, regardless of occupations or positions. There is legislation in Japan that determines minimum wages, hours per week, overtime, vacation, sick leave, sanitary conditions, and layoff policies and procedures, which leaves little for collective bargaining. Thus, negotiations are limited mostly to wages, but wages, positions, and promotions are usually determined through seniority. Every spring all the unions from every company embark upon *shunto*, or the spring wage offensive, when the few negotiations take place. Unions want companies to remain profitable for the good of the groups, so they will never ask for too much. This attitude is diametrically opposed to the attitude of the unions in Great Britain. *Shunto* is an effort by the unions to raise wages across the country, so that no single firm will become less competitive than another. There are very few strikes in Japan, and what strikes there are usually take place during *shunto*. The strikes are for very short periods of time, sometimes only half a day, and merely demonstrate worker support for the unions. Japanese workers in the unions also promote a company's well-being and profitability because its success benefits the whole group (see Perspective 19–5).

PERSPECTIVE 19–5   ... While Japan's Labor, as Usual, Curbs Demands for Sake of Corporations

TOKYO—With Japan's economy booming and corporate profits soaring, Japanese unions could be reaching for the sky in their annual spring wage offensive.

Yet despite an acute labor shortage, unions—as usual—are showing little inclination to push for raises in line with the kind of prosperity that corporate Japan is enjoying. Most observers expect labor to settle for increases of between 5% and 6% this year, up but slightly from last year's 4.4% average.

"There is nothing unfavorable for labor unions," declared Takeshi Kurokawa, chairman of the General Council of Trade Unions of Japan. This pronouncement aside, leaders of Japan's unions, which are organized along company lines, seem to be heeding management appeals that they consider the good of the corporation in their wage demands. Ryohei Magota, a labor consultant who specialized in wage issues, deplores what he sees as a lack of guts among union leaders, saying they

SOURCE: Masayoshi Kanabayashi, *Wall Street Journal*, March 9, 1989, page A12.

are "too compromising." He notes that as long as unions are obsessed with their companies' prosperity, it will be hard to realize a sharp wage increase. "Unions should try to take as much as they want, particularly when they can," says Hirohide Tanaka, a professor at Chukyo University.

The spring wage offensive, know as *shunto,* has been a fixture of Japanese labor relations since the mid-1950s. Under the system, almost all major company unions negotiate individually in early April; smaller unions follow the pattern set by the big unions. But the days of strong unions using nationwide solidarity to force double-digit wage increases are in the past. For a decade, management has had the upper hand in negotiations: Increases have averaged 5.4%, and only 3% to 4% in the past three years.

Labor has been handicapped by the decline of unions in the work force. In 1949, 56% of Japanese workers were unionized. Now only 27% are, and there is an almost complete absence of industrywide unions. Moreover, unions are less inclined to strike in support of demands. The Labor Ministry counted only 473 strikes in the fiscal year that ended last March 31, off from a recent peak of 5,197 in fiscal 1975.

"It is out of fashion now to resort to a strike," says one worker. Management has been able to take advantage of workers' strong loyalty to the company and their willingness to sacrifice, particularly at times of economic shocks like rising oil prices or an appreciating yen.

This year, the unions appear to be holding a strong hand, especially after the low wage settlements of recent years. Japan's economy is expected to grow more than 4%, and corporate profits are expected to post average increases above 20%, according to the Bank of Japan. Moreover, companies are having a hard time filling jobs; in January there were 114 jobs available for every 100 applicants.

Yet unions are approaching the wage talks with moderate demands. To be sure, some labor leaders have spoken out for big raises, calling for more than 8%. But this is viewed as posturing; they are prepared to settle for 5% to 6%, observers say.

The influential All Japan Federation of Electric Workers' Unions, which represents electronics companies, is expected to set the pace in this year's offensive by negotiating early. It is only asking for 0.5 percentage point above last year's 6% increase. "We have to think of the overall economy," says a federation spokesman. "If we escalate our demand too much, it would incur cost inflation," undermining the pay raise.

That view, mirrored by other union leaders, offers evidence of the persuasive powers of management in dealing with company unions. Despite the current economic boom, labor has some concern about the acceleration of Japanese plant investments in lower-wage countries, which has eliminated jobs at home. In dollar terms, Japanese wages are among the highest in the world.

In effect, employees are being pressed to ensure long-term prosperity by eschewing large increases. Afraid of being ostracized by fellow managers. Japanese companies give weight to this balance, even if they are willing to grant more.

The union moderation also represents a victory for Bank of Japan Gov. Satoshi Sumita, who has been warning of the inflationary dangers of wage increases. Japan's consumer price inflation is almost nonexistent by industrialized-nation standards, but the central bank governor is concerned about the impact of large raises and a 3% consumption tax to be imposed April 1.

Yet many analysts brush off such concerns. "Unless [wage increases] go beyond 6%, it would be within the range of an [expected] growth of labor productivity," says a Nomura Research Institute analyst.

Another factor behind the moderate pay demands is a move for shorter working hours in the spring negotiations. Encouraged by a government policy to reduce working hours to a nationwide average of 1,800 hours a year by 1993 from the current 2,111 hours, many unions are calling for more time off.

In 1988 *shunto* was expanded to include a demand for shorter working hours, primarily because of foreign pressure aimed at getting Japan to promote more leisure time and thus increase domestic demand for consumer goods and services. The government has led the way by closing some of its offices on Saturdays and is trying to reduce the work-week from forty-eight to forty hours within the next two years, and banks and post offices have switched to a five-day week.

MNC Tactics

Over the past several years, the AFL-CIO has maintained that MNCs have several detrimental effects on U.S. industry. First, MNCs use capital resources for foreign investment that are needed for domestic investment and expansion. Second, MNCs export U.S. technology to other countries in order to take advantage of low-cost foreign labor, which denies American workers from gaining the rewards of using the technology. Third, MNCs replace U.S. exports with foreign-produced goods, which worsens the trade balance and decreases domestic employment. Fourth, MNCs use imports from their subsidiaries in low-wage countries instead of using domestically produced goods.[6]

Unions feel threatened by the rising power of MNCs and the advantages they have because of multiple production locales. When a firm decides to locate operations abroad, it is no longer dependent on only domestic plants, and the domestic union will have no control over what happens half a world away. Most of the concerns of unions are in part because of the huge amount of resources at the command of MNCs. More important, an MNC's power and decision-making capabilities are outside every country in which they operate except headquarters.[7] Some of the specific concerns unions have regarding MNCs include:

- The ability of MNCs to relocate facilities if a contract is not agreeable to them.

[6] Levine 1987/1988.
[7] Ibid.

- Restricted access to data by unions, especially financial data, to combat MNCs. For example, if an MNC says it is losing money on overseas operations and thus needs to cut labor costs, the union cannot confirm or deny this statement.
- The ability of an MNC to pick and choose where to locate and thus take advantage of differences in the amount and level of benefits they are required to provide by law.
- The ability of an MNC to withstand strikes by threatening to close the facility and relocate, and because that factory is only one part of the corporation, the MNC will be able to obtain cash and production from other plants.

One example of MNC exploitation is the example of Kader Enterprises Ltd., a toy factory in Shokou, China. Its female workers, mostly aged seventeen to twenty-five, typically work fourteen hours a day, seven days a week. Recently, they were ordered to put in one or two twenty-four-hour shifts a month to help meet the Christmas demand. Most of the women come from Hong Kong, where the labor laws are stricter. The Chinese unions have complained about the harsh conditions, but continue to be disregarded. The Chinese government has added its complaints to those of the unions, but the company has resisted all attempts to shorten working hours and threatened to relocate its factories in Thailand.

Counter-Tactics by Labor

The only hope for unions to compete with MNCs lies in international rules and regulations and international cooperation. There are two main international labor organizations that make efforts in this direction.

THE INTERNATIONAL LABOR ORGANIZATION

The ILO was established in 1919 under the Treaty of Versailles. It is now affiliated with the United Nations and is composed of government, industry, and union representatives. Its premise is that the failure of any country to promote humane working conditions is an obstacle to nations that want to improve the conditions in their own countries. The ILO tries to define and promote international standards regarding safety, health, and other working conditions.

ORGANIZATION FOR ECONOMIC COOPERATION AND DEVELOPMENT

The OECD also consists of government, industry, and union representatives. It has developed a set of voluntary guidelines for MNCs and for host countries regarding labor conditions and fair practices. Figure 19–2 provides a summary of these guidelines.

THE EUROPEAN ECONOMIC COMMUNITY

The EEC also attempts to coordinate the evolution of industrial relations standards within the member countries by issuing directives on issues of common concern. These directives are approved by the council of ministers before they become effective. Existing directives cover such issues as employee participation on company boards and the safeguarding of employee interests and the right of employee representatives to information and consultation in the event of a change of ownership of a business. Some of the EEC directives, once accepted by the council of ministers, are incorporated into the national laws of member states. The impact of EEC directives on national labor laws of member states is increasing, especially as integration of the community draws nearer. After 1992 it is likely that MNCs outside the community are likely to have similar requirements for dealing with local unions and workers regardless of their location. In some instances, they are likely to be governed by uniform laws that apply in the same way to all member countries.

International Unions

The prospect of international unions sounds very promising for solving many problems. International unions could employ transnational bargaining, which would mean a centralized and coordinated collective-bargaining strategy between an employer and a union or group of unions for employees in facilities located in two or more nations.[8] In other words, one union could negotiate for all the plants that a single firm has around the world, thus guaranteeing equal treatment for all workers and restoring the power of the unions. In the real world, this is much easier said than done. The few international unions that exist are in similar countries, such as the United States and Canada. Table 19–3 is a list of international trade secretariats.

Codetermination

One final possibility of increasing the impact of workers on firms is the concept of codetermination. Codetermination means employee participation in management. An early example of codetermination was in the German coal and steel industries in 1951. By law, codetermination gave the representatives of workers and shareholders 50 percent each of the directorships, with one neutral director to break any ties. Codetermination has gained importance in many other countries as the emphasis of collective bargaining shifts, little by little, to agreements and counterbalancing of labor-management interests.

Summary

The four most common structures used by MNCs to organize and manage operations are functional, regional, product line, and matrix structures. Staffing is crucial for MNCs because of technological advances, worldwide competition for skilled labor, and the constant need to increase productivity, reduce costs, and increase intracompany communication and information flows. International staffing involves recruitment, selection, training, and motivation and requires a bi-

---

[8] Ibid.

Employment and Industrial Relations Guidelines—OECD

Enterprises should, within the framework of law, regulations and prevailing labour relations and employment practices, in each of the countries in which they operate:

1. respect the right of their employees to be represented by trade unions and other bona fide organisations of employees, and engage in constructive negotiations, either individually or through employers' associations, with such employee organisations with a view to reaching agreements on employment conditions, which should include provisions for dealing with disputes arising over the interpretation of such agreements, and for ensuring mutually respected rights and responsibilities;

2. a) provide such facilities to representatives of the employees as may be necessary to assist in the development of effective collective agreements,
   b) provide to representatives of employees information which is needed for meaningful negotiations on conditions of employment;

3. provide to representatives of employees where this accords with local law and practice, information which enables them to obtain a true and fair view of the performance of the entity or, where appropriate, the enterprise as a whole;

4. observe standards of employment and industrial relations not less favourable than those observed by comparable employers in the host country;

5. in their operations, to the greatest extent practicable, utilise, train and prepare for upgrading members of the local labour force in co-operation with representatives of their employees and, where appropriate, the relevant governmental authorities;

6. in considering changes in their operations which would have minor effects upon the livelihood of their employees, in particular in the case of the closure of an entity envolving collective lay-offs or dismissals, provide reasonable notice of such changes to representatives of their employees, and where appropriate to the relevant governmental authorities, and co-operate with the employee representatives and appropriate governmental authorities so as to mitigate to the maximum extent practicable adverse effects;

7. implement their employment policies including hiring, discharge, pay, promotion and training without discrimination unless selectivity in respect of employee characteristics is in furtherance of established governmental policies which specifically promote greater equality of employment opportunity;

8. in the context of bona fide negotiations* with representatives of employees on conditions of employment, or while employees are exercising a right to organise, not threaten to utilise a capacity to transfer the whole or part of an operating unit from the country concerned nor transfer employees from the enterprises' component entities in other countries in order to influence unfairly those negotiations or to hinder the exercise of a right to organise**;

9. enable authorised representatives of their employees to conduct negotiations on collective bargaining or labour management relations issues with representatives of management who are authorised to take decisions on the matters under negotiation.

---

* Bona fide negotiations may include labour disputes as part of the process of negotiation. Whether or not labour disputes are so included will be determined by the law and prevailing employment practices of particular countries.

** NOTE: This paragraph includes the additional provision adopted by OECD Governments at the meeting of the OECD Council at Ministerial level on 13th and 14th June, 1979.

FIGURE 19-2   OECD guidelines for multinational corporations.
SOURCE: Organization for Economic Cooperation and Development.

TABLE 19-3
International Trade Secretariats

	Head-quarters	Number of members	Number of Affiliates	Number of Countries	Year
International Federation of Building and Woodworkers(IFBWW)	Geneva, Switzerland	3,000,000	110	55	1979
International Federation of Chemical, Energy, and General Workers' Unions (ICEF)	Geneva, Switzerland	5,500,000	110	66	1978
International Federation of Commercial, Clerical, and Technical Employees (FIET)	Geneva, Switzerland	6,400,000	179	80	1979
Universal Alliance of Diamond Workers (UADW)	Antwerp, Belgium	11,000	4	4	1974
International Secretariat of Entertainment Trade Unions (ISETU)	Vienna, Austria	350,000	67	35	1978
International Union of Food and Allied Workers' Association (IUF)	Geneva, Switzerland	1,800,000	167	60	1979
International Graphical Federation (IGF)	Berne, Switzerland	650,000	35	26	1979
International Federation of Journalists (IFJ)	Brussels, Belgium	83,000	28	25	1978
International Metalworkers' Federation (IMF)	Geneva, Switzerland	13,700,000	168	70	1979
Miners' International Metalworkers' Federation (IMF)	London, England	1,200,000	35	32	1979

SOURCE: Organization for Economic Cooperation and Development.

cultural sensitivity toward the host country environment. High failure rates among expatriate managers have caused MNCs to carefully select and train global managers.

International staffing may involve filling the management position with expatriates, host country nationals, or third-country nationals; each selection offers different advantages and disadvantages. Staff selection is affected by the availability of trained candidates in the host country location, corporate policies regarding local versus corporate control, a candidate's knowledge of the local environment, the local image the MNC wants to project, and employment incentives. Also, the candidate's technical skills, language abilities, and adaptability must be evaluated. Adaptability assessment through an early identification program test is important in order to minimize the effects of management, culture shock, and ineffectiveness on local operations. Cross-cultural training techniques are useful in reducing candidate failure rates and help ensure their success.

Specialized compensation arrangements for international managers make these positions very attractive. Income taxes and repatriation, however, are additional problems for an international manager. Gender biases in many countries may slow foreign assignments for female managers. The dumping of inefficient personnel in international positions may occur, but can harm the long-term interests of an MNC.

International managers are faced with a diversity of nationalities, languages, cultures, and work ethics, which can complicate motivation and management of the local labor force. To develop management-labor relations essential for efficient operations, local managers must have sufficient authority and flexibility. Centralized corporate control, through industrial relations policy, however, is required to achieve MNC-wide cohesion. Host country laws and practices also may limit local management flexibility.

Wage and fringe benefit systems should reflect local costs of living and the extent of existing social welfare benefits. Further, MNCs must be careful not to exploit lesser-developed countries in terms of wages and benefits to prevent criticism from host governments, local media, and trade unions. Policies and procedures for employee layoffs, suspensions, and terminations must also reflect the traditions and practices of the host country.

Labor productivity can vary in different countries. Improvements in productivity are a function of government support, worker quality and skill, research and development, innovation, business savings and investment, personal savings and investment, natural resources, production systems, and management techniques and philosophies. Because modern technology is capital intensive and may be unavailable, MNCs can sacrifice productivity and efficiency for low labor costs when expanding production into new markets. Labor relations and the role of unions also differ between nations. International unions are seeking greater cooperation across national boundaries, but nationalistic attitudes, different goals, and physical distance may impede their growth. Codetermination is a recent development that attempts to increase worker influence and responsibilities in MNC operations.

1. When staffing an MNC for positions outside the home country, what are some advantages and disadvantages of hiring host country nationals? Expatriates?
2. Who is a global manager?
3. Why do expatriate managers frequently receive additional compensation over their colleagues at equivalent positions in the corporate office? Why are these packages more complicated than packages provided to domestic employees?
4. What problems do expatriates face at the completion of their foreign assignments?
5. What obstacles do women executives encounter when seeking international staff positions?
6. Before investing in a production plant in a foreign country, what are some of the questions concerning labor management should address?

7. What is collective bargaining? How does collective bargaining differ in the United States, Great Britain, Germany, and Japan?
8. How is productivity affected by a shortage of skilled labor?

Bibliography

ADLER, NANCY. 1982. "Expecting International Success: Female Managers Overseas." *Columbia Journal of World Business* (Fall): 82.

CAMPBELL, DUNCAN C. 1989. "Multinational Labor Relations in the European Community." *ILR Report* (Fall): 7–14.

CHARNOVITZ, STEVE. 1987. "The Influence of International Labor Standards on the World Trading Regime," *International Labor Review* (September/October): 9–17.

CLARKE, CHRISTOPHER J., AND K. BREENAN. 1990. "Building Synergy in the Diversified Business." *Long Range Planning* (April): 9–16.

DANIELS, J. D. 1986. "Approaches to European Regional Management by Large U.S. Multinational Firms." *Management International Review* (Second Quarter): 27–42.

DOWLING, PETER J. 1987. "Human Resource Issues in International Business." *Syracuse Journal of International Law & Commerce* (Winter): 255–271.

———. 1989. "Hot Issues Overseas." *Personnel Administrator* (January): 66–72.

DUFF, MIKE. 1985. "Hands Across the Water." *Supermarket Business* (February): 45, 47.

FANNING, W. R., AND A. F. ARVIN. 1986. "National or Global? Control versus Flexibility." *Long Range Planning* (October): 84–88.

GELLERMAN, SAUL W. 1990. "In Organizations, as in Architecture, Form Follows Function." *Organizational Dynamics* (Winter): 57–68.

HARRIS, PHILLIP R., AND ROBERT T. MORAN. 1987. *Managing Cultural Differences*, Houston: Gulf Publishing Company.

HOGAN, GARY W., AND JANE R. GOODSON. 1990. "The Key to Expatriate Success." *Training and Development* (January): 50–52.

LEONTIADES, JAMES. 1986. "Going Global—Global Strategies versus National Strategies." *Long Range Planning* (December): 96–104.

LEVINE, MARVIN. 1987/1988. "Labor Movements and the Multinational Corporation: A Future for Collective Bargaining?" *Employee Relations Law Journal* (Winter): p. 47–57.

MORGENSTERN, FELICE. 1985. "The Importance, in Practice, of Conflicts of Labour Law." *International Labour Review* (March/April): 119–131.

NARASIMHAN, R., AND J. R. CARTER. 1990. "Organization, Communication and Coordination of International Sourcing." *International Marketing Review* 7: 6–20.

RAY, GEORGE F. 1990. "International Labour Costs in Manufacturing, 1960–88." *National Institute Economic Review* (May): 67–70.

SAVICH, R. S., AND W. RODGERS. 1988. "Assignment Overseas: Easing the Transition Before and After." *Personnel* (August): 44–48.

SCHULTZ, T. PAUL. 1990. "Women's Changing Participation in the Labor Force: A World Perspective." *Economic Development & Cultural Change* (April): 457–488.

SERVAIS, J. M. 1989. "The Social Clause in Trade Agreements: Wishful Thinking or an Instrument of Social Progress?" *International Labour Review* 128: 423-432.

STAIGER, ROBERT W. 1988. "Organized Labor and the Scope of International Specialization." *Journal of Political Economy* (October): 1022–1047.

TUNG, ROSALIE. 1984. "Strategic Management of Human Resources in the Multinational Enterprise." *Human Resource Management* (Summer): 129.

WEISZ, MORRIS. 1988. "A View of Labor Ministries in Other Nations." *Monthly Labor Review* (July): 19–23.

Chapter Case Study 1

Remagen Brothers Ltd.

The protest meeting at the locked gates of Remagen Brothers Ltd. was getting increasingly turbulent. More than two thousand unionized workers of the Weranpura factory were demanding a 26 percent increase in wages and an increase in the number of paid holidays to twenty-one. The management's offer of a 9 percent pay increase led to a fairly quick breakdown in negotiations. The workers had gone on an indefinite strike that was now in its nineteenth day, with no chance of settlement.

Remagen's Weranpura plant had a history of troubled industrial relations from its outset. The plant was located in an industrial park set up by the government of Trivana, a small island country in South Asia. Remagen Brothers was a leading cosmetics, toiletries, and detergent manufacturer based in the Netherlands, with factories and other operations in eighty-two countries around the world. With sales revenues exceeding $2 billion annually, Remagen was a leading multinational in the industry, and its products had a well-differentiated brand image and enjoyed considerable brand loyalty worldwide. Remagen's decision to invest in Weranpura was motivated primarily by the attractive incentives offered by the Trivianian government in the special industrial zone. Remagen was allowed to import all its plant equipment as well as raw materials and intermediate products free of customs duties. The government provided excellent infrastructure facilities to the company, including banking and financial services within the industrial park zone. Remagen's income from its Weranpura factory also was free from Trivanian taxes for five years and, after that was to be taxed at a special rate. Profits and other remittances out of Trivana were freely allowed, although periodic reports had to be filed with the central bank.

Attracted by these incentives, Remagen's senior management had made the decision to establish a large plant to manufacture soaps and detergents to be marketed primarily in Southeast Asia. Trivana's labor costs were even lower than those of Southeast Asia, and Remagen's products were expected to have the edge needed to penetrate that highly competitive market.

Although Remagen's planners focused in on the economics provided by Trivana's labor, other aspects of the local labor force were not studied in detail. Weranpura was located in the Southeastern part of Trivana, which had a predominantly Marxist political orientation. All plants in the Weranpura industrial zone were unionized, and almost all the unions were affiliated with the People's Movement for Labor Rights (PMLR), an avowed Marxist labor federation that continually advocated militant action on the part of its affiliated unions to secure labor rights.

Remagen's managers began to sense the difficulties that lay ahead when the commissioning of the plant was delayed by a month because of a sudden strike by the workers of the plant's packaging unit. Top management, however, eager to start production, decided to lay off all the striking employees and hire new ones in their place. The view at that point was that the company should not be cowed by the union and should adopt a strong stance. This view was based on the face that Remagen was paying at least 10 percent higher wages than any other employer in the Weranpura industrial zone and it could hire new workers whenever it wanted.

This view did not prove to be an effective strategy in dealing with labor issues. Once the workers were fully unionized, it became difficult to terminate the services of employees.

The union provided excellent legal help for all its members, and an employee could involve the company in a long and fractious and expensive litigation process. Labor laws in Trivana heavily favored employees over employers, and Remagen had no financial advantage it could leverage in the litigation process.

Further, the workers were now governed more by the orders of union leaders than the edicts of the personnel department. The union's management was prone to ordering strikes even if a single employee was to be replaced.

During its first two years, the company had, therefore, adversarial industrial relations and eighty-seven work days had been lost because of strikes. The management's policy continued to be based on maintaining a strong posture against the militant trade unions and refusing to give in on their demands. In the early strikes, although the company did lose work days, the unions were not able to make much headway. The personnel department of Remagen's head office was pleased with the record of the Weranpura management, and the personnel manager had received two letters of commendation.

This strike, however, was different. The workers and their leaders were apparently bent upon getting the company to agree to their demands. Further, it was also clear that the PMLR federation was providing financial support to the striking employees and that with this support they could carry on the strike indefinitely.

The local manager of Remagen's personnel division, Mr. Ratnapure, was of the opinion that this time the company should negotiate with the striking workers and raise the level of compensation it was willing to offer in order to bring it nearer to union demands. He reasoned that the company's image in Weranpura was at stake, and the PMLR had successfully carried out a campaign against it by branding Remagen a "foreign exploiter." The government, although somewhat centrist in its political inclinations, was sensitive to the views of the PMLR, because the next provincial elections were in six months, and there was talk of an alliance between the ruling party and the Marxists in this region. Therefore, if matters came to a head, Remagen could, at best, expect the government to be a mute bystander, caught between its political priorities and eagerness to attract overseas investment in special industrial zones. Perhaps it would be better, argued Ratnapure, to involve the leaders of the PMLR in the talks, as the union leaders had been demanding, which would be viewed as a major concession and perhaps could lead to a moderation of the worker demands on the compensation package.

Johann Michuft, the general manager of the plant, was initially taken aback by Ratnapure's suggestion, which seemed to go almost directly against the company's global industrial relations management policy. The company had a standard policy to make a firm and final offer, in line with industry wages (or better) in terms of compensation. Further, the policy of the management was not to negotiate with any party other than the bonafide representatives of the plant's unions. Talking to PMLR's representatives would clearly violate this policy. The company was doing quite well, and it could afford to give a raise to the workers that would be in line with what they were demanding, but that amount would be way ahead of the industry average in Weranpura, (although much lower than wages paid to workers for similar jobs in the company's plants in Europe and North America). Further, dealing with the PMLR would be seen as a sign of weakness on the part of the company's management and could lead to another set of demands.

On the other hand, if the company did not negotiate with the unions and the representatives of the PMLR, it faced the possibility of a long drawn-out strike that could result in the closure of this highly profitable plant. Moreover, the company's image as an employer would suffer in many countries of the region, where it was planning to establish other manufacturing facilities.

As he pondered these issues, Michuft dictated a confidential telex on his dictaphone for his personal secretary to send to headquarters in the Netherlands, seeking instructions on whether company policy could be modified in Weranpura.

Question

What would be your instructions to Michuft if you were the director of international human resource management at Remagen's world headquarters in the Netherlands?

Chapter Case Study 2

Air America

Herbert Manning, general manager of Air America's Qamran office, had been with the company for twelve years. Manning had an undergraduate degree in economics and business and had worked for a leading travel agency in San Francisco, California, before joining Air America as a sales executive. With his earlier experience and his enthusiasm and energy on the job, Manning had made a favorable impression within the company very quickly. Within two years he had been promoted to the rank of area sales manager and had been elected as vice-president of Air America's worldwide sales club, having had the second highest amount of sales among all of Air America's sales executives worldwide. Manning continued to perform well as area sales manager, and three years later he was moved to the company's corporate headquarters in Dallas, Texas. His headquarters assignment was a major move upward; he was named vice-president of international marketing and sales with responsibility for planning and implementing the company's marketing and sales strategies in the Middle East, Africa, and Southern Asia. Air America, although a major international airline, was not very strong in these markets, which it perceived would become increasingly important in the future. Manning took up the challenge with his well-known drive and energy, and during the next three years, Air America succeeded in negotiating air route agreements with four countries in North Africa, three in the Middle East, and three in southern Asia. Qamran, a small sheikdom in the Middle East was designated as the regional base for this area and as a hub location for the airline. In three years, Manning's region had become an important source of revenue from international operations for Air America. Apart from an aggressive and well-

targeted sales policy, overall increase in passenger traffic arising out of the oil price boom helped to boost the ticket sales.

Toward the end of the third year, however, Air America, like many other airlines operating in the region, were suddenly hit with a sharp decline in demand as oil prices declined sharply and the economy of the region went into a deep recession. As the market shrank, competition intensified, and it became increasingly difficult to hold on to market share. By 1985 Air America's share of the Persian Gulf market had dropped by 7 percent and, combined with a sharp decline in overall market size, led to a steep reduction in total revenues.

Concerned with the difficult situation in the region, Air America's senior management decided that an aggressive strategy had to be adopted to recapture market share and rebuild the airline's image as a dominant force in the region. A key element of the strategy was to appoint Manning as the regional manager of the Middle East and north Africa.

It was a big promotion for Manning. Regional managers were considered to be senior management in the company and were responsible for participating in the formulation of global strategy. Moreover, Air America's corporate policy was one of considerable delegation and decentralization. Regional managers were, therefore almost completely independent in their local operations and were primarily responsible for their own results. Manning was elated when his boss told him the news. He had wanted to go back to the field for some time now, and the position apparently offered all what he was looking for. In addition, relocation as a regional manager in Qamran meant that he would have several liberal fringe benefits given to Air America's expatriate managers—a large, furnished company house, chauffeur-driven car, at least four servants, and additional allowances, including a large entertainment budget.

Manning's first year was extremely successful. He brought a new level of drive and enthusiasm to his job, which was infused throughout the local office, because he set a good example by his own untiring efforts. His years in the marketing division had provided him with considerable background knowledge of the operations, and he used that knowledge to seek and implement new ways to fight off Air America's competitors. Market share began to inch back upward and the revenue drop was reversed. Although the revenues were helped by a slight improvement in market conditions, there was no doubt that Manning's arrival had been a key factor in the reversal of Air America's fortunes in the region.

The second year was good, too, although not as good as the first. Market share increased, as did the revenues by smaller degrees. One significant explanation for the slowing of increases offered by Manning was that other airlines had initiated equally aggressive counterstrategies, and it was not possible to improve the rate of America's gains without seriously compromising profitability.

Things, however, started to decline in the third year. Market share gains slid back by 2 percent and revenues showed a slight decline. Manning seemed to have lost the drive and initiative that had characterized his work just a few months ago, and some of Manning's subordinates seemed unhappy with his behavior and left the company. Gilbert Wyles, Air America's senior vice-president of human resources, was quick to guess that the problem was Manning and decided that a meeting would be useful to discuss the whole issue. Manning was after all a star performer, and if he was facing any problems the company was fully prepared to help him.

The meeting lasted three hours. Manning was initially hesitant to state the real problem and hedged around the issue, in vague terms, calling the difficulties personal matters. When asked to be more specific, however, and realizing that he had a sympathetic audience, Manning came out with it. The real problem, he said, was his wife's difficulties in adjusting to life in Qamran. Back in the United States, she was a client relations executive in a small advertising company. It was not a very high position, but it was important to her. She liked the job, it enabled her to keep busy and do something everyday, and used her skills at dealing with people constructively. She had developed a fairly close network of good friends and a large circle of pleasant acquaintances through her job. Her decision to leave the job and accompany Manning to Qamran had not been easy, but she had been sporting about it and decided to make the best of a new lifestyle that awaited her in their new overseas home. She did make a sincere effort at adjustment, but Qamran's society was governed by strict Islamic tenets, which meant that social freedoms for women were severely restricted. Although the Mannings had a nice social life, with a number of social activities involving diplomats and other expatriates, there was nothing much she could do during the day. Women were not allowed to work in Qamran, and they were granted special work permits only in exceptional cases. Even then women had to dress in a particular fashion prescribed by the authorities.

After the first year, Mrs. Manning grew increasingly restless about her new situation. Her problems were accentuated by the long absences of her husband, who went on frequent business trips that were essential to the success of his assignment. Mrs. Manning thought of various solutions and different ways in which her life could be made more interesting, but nothing worked and the mental discomfort of Mrs. Manning continued to increase. In the past few months, Mrs. Manning had long periods of depression and was not responding very well to treatment, which caused Manning tremendous anxiety and had adversely affected his professional performance.

Gilbert Wyles suggested that Manning take a vacation quickly, at the place of his choice, and that by the time he returned the company would have an answer to his problem. Manning was somewhat relieved, but at the same time, he was skeptical of the company's intentions. As he walked out of the corporate headquarters to catch a cab for his hotel, he wondered whether he had done the right thing.

Meanwhile, Wyles, in his well-appointed office, got busy, putting together a confidential memo to the international human resources policy group, a small set of top Air America executives in charge of framing company policies in international human resources management. The memo explained the background and circumstances of the situation and placed three options before the members:

1. The option suggested by Manning, to give Mrs. Manning a job in his office in Qamran as a public relations officer. This was possible, if the group were to modify the company policy on employment of spouses and enough pressure was exerted on the Qamran government.
2. Replace Manning with another expatriate executive, which could be easily done, but there might be similar problems for the replacement.
3. Appoint a local national as regional manager or bring in a third-country national from its other overseas offices.

Questions

1. Which of the three options would you recommend to Air America and why? What would be the problems with the other options?
2. Is there a need for Air America to change its international staffing policies to avoid sending expatriate managers to overseas locations?

PART SIX

STRATEGIC ISSUES IN INTERNATIONAL BUSINESS

CHAPTER 20

International Planning, Control, and Management Information Systems

CHAPTER OBJECTIVES

This chapter will:

- Identify the key elements of international strategic planning.
- Discuss the question of centralized or decentralized control in the context of the multinational corporation.
- Describe the levels of control inherent within the organizational structure of the MNC.
- Examine the role and importance of management information systems within MNCs.
- Present a definition of global strategy and its importance to the long-term success of an MNC.

Why Plan? Why Control? Why MIS?

Given the complexity and size of the operations of MNCs and the rapidly changing business environments in which they operate around the world, MNCs must attach strong emphasis to the issues of planning, control, and management information systems (MIS). The three are both interlinked and global. Once an understanding of its current po-

sition is determined, an MNC must set the objectives to be attained over a specific time frame. The objectives could be a rate of growth, level of profit, volume of sales, share of markets, penetration into new markets, or entry into new business or product areas. Once these objectives are established, a MNC must decide on a strategy and detailed plan of action. The emphasis could be on utilizing strengths, remedying weaknesses, exploring new opportunities, exploiting existing opportunities to a greater degree, defending market share, or increasing the share in existing or new markets.

Control is especially critical for an MNC because of its global reach. In addition, most MNCs are usually diversified and have a wide range of products and services, some unrelated to each other, making control essential.

The same applies to management information systems (MIS), which are vital to achieving success in effective planning and control. MIS have been defined as a set of procedures that are used for collecting, processing, storing, retrieving, and disseminating information needed to support planning, control, and decision-making within an organization. The main task of MIS is to deal with the vast array of information that an MNC needs to achieve its planning and control objectives and to make decisions. It is especially critical because of the large amount of information, from a variety of sources, that is needed to keep track of many different activities in different countries and time zones. The telecommunications and computer revolution, however, has provided powerful tools to MNCs for designing appropriate MIS.

Planning Strategy

Justification

Through the strategic-planning process businesses attempt to position themselves in order to take the greatest advantage of opportunities through maximum allocation and use of resources. The strategic planning process provides a business or enterprise with a method through which it can answer key questions, such as what does the firm hope to accomplish, what magnitude of production does it foresee, when will this activity occur, where will it take place, how will goals be reached, and which methods must be considered.

This planning process varies in detail, depth, and scope. A single proprietor or self-employed businessperson may make these decisions on an ad hoc basis as needs arise. A large corporation or conglomerate, however, must use a rigorous, highly detailed, comprehensive, and long-term strategic planning process that coordinates activities around the world in order to provide for optimal operations and market servicing.

International Complications

The entire planning process is difficult enough in a domestic environment where the planners have a basic understanding of their own competitors and economic, political, and social systems. The process is further complicated by the addition of multiple international elements. The internationalization of business brings with it the necessity of considering environments that differ substantially from the company's home turf. Strategic planners in a multinational firm must deal with different geographic characteristics; social and cultural differences in markets; additional risks arising from political or economic variations between countries; and very real problems arising from the physical and cultural distance between operating environments.

Added to these difficulties of planning in an international environment are the extensive problems and complications that arise in firms attempting to implement plans and provide for control. Table 20–1 illustrates some sources of potential strategic management problems that could arise from the addition of a multinational component to a domestic enterprise.

The Planning Process

MISSION STATEMENT

The first step in the planning process is the identification by an enterprise of its corporate mission or objectives—the purpose for its existence. The identification of this purpose, as put forth in a corporate mission statement, provides all employees of a firm with an operating framework. It focuses the activities of an enterprise on a common goal and reinforces the values to be upheld within the corporate culture.

TABLE 20-1
Differences between U.S. and Multinational Organizations that Affect Strategic Management

Factor	U.S. Operations	International Operations
Language	English used almost universally	Local languages must be used in many situations
Culture	Relatively homogenous	Quite diverse, both between countries and within a country
Politics	Stable and relatively unimportant	Often volatile and of decisive importance
Economy	Relatively uniform	Wide variations among countries and between regions within countries
Government Interference	Minimal and reasonably predictable	Extensive and subject to rapid change
Labor	Skilled labor available	Skilled labor often scarce, requiring training or redesign of production methods
Financing	Well-developed financial markets	Poorly developed financial markets, capital flows subject to government control
Market Research	Data easy to collect	Data difficult and expensive to collect
Advertising	Many media available; few restrictions	Media limited; many restrictions; low literacy rates rule out print media in some countries
Money	U.S.$ used universally	Must change from one currency to another; changing exchange rates and government restrictions are problems
Transportation/ Commu- nication	Among the best in the world	Often inadequate
Control	Always a problem; centralized control works well	A worse problem, centralized control will not work, Must walk a tightrope between overcentralizing and losing control through too much decentralization
Contract	Once signed, is binding on both parties, even if one party makes a bad deal	Can be avoided and renegotiated if one party becomes dissatisfied
Labor Relations	Collective bargaining; can lay off workers easily	Often cannot lay off workers; may have mandatory worker participation in managmeent; workers may seek change through political process rather than collective bargaining
Trade Barriers	Non-existent	Extensive and very important

SOURCE: R. G. Murdick, R. C. Moor, R. H. Eckhouse, and T. W. Zimmerer. 1984 *Business Policy: A Framework for Analysis*, 4th ed. Columbus, Ohio: Grid.

The mission statement of an enterprise should reflect the philosophical underpinnings of the enterprise and identify the image it wants to project. It should define the company's view of itself; identify the products, markets, and customers the firm seeks to serve; and emphasize all this in a way that includes attention to the company's system of values.[1] Thus, mission statements identify the business of the company, its objectives and expected clientele, and the manner or the product that will be used to satisfy that purpose.

Company missions can vary considerably, depending on the nature of the business, the shareholders, decision-makers, and founding purpose. Some companies may have profitability or growth as a goal, while others, such as nonprofit service agencies, may wish to provide as much service as possible to those in need. A company formed as a cooperative by farmers, for example, may be more concerned about providing its members with an assured supply of products critical to their agricultural needs than with generating a large return.

INTERNAL ANALYSIS

The next step is the analysis of the firm's internal environment—its company profile or character. Through such an analysis the company can identify its crucial strengths and weaknesses, which can be determined by identifying the competitive advantages a firm enjoys in the marketplace and how these advantages position it against its competitors. This analysis takes into account the history of the firm and its operations. It includes an identification and quantification of the company's markets and market shares, personnel strengths, features of products and product lines, and forecasts of the expected future direction of the firm if policies should remain unchanged.

At this stage in the planning process, it is crucial that the company have an accurate, objective view of its relative strengths and weaknesses. The painting of an accurate picture of the company's strong points and weak areas allows results to be

[1] Pearce and Robinson 1988.

evaluated in terms of the external environment facing the operation of the firm. The forces that operate in the internal environment are sometimes called controllable forces, the assumption being that through strategic decision-making, a firm can effect changes in various characteristics of the firm through a reallocation or refocusing of resources and emphasis.

EXTERNAL ANALYSIS

The external environment, in contrast, includes forces that are uncontrollable from the vantage point of a corporation. These forces take a variety of shapes and arise from a number of sources. They can come from government in the form of legal, political, or regulatory actions, and they can derive from economic events, such as recessions or inflation. They can also spring from the opinions or actions of the client base, from actions taken by industry competitors, or from nature itself in the form of natural disasters. While we tend to think of these forces as being negative or as threats to the operation of a firm, external forces also provide a corporation with opportunities.

Even though these forces are uncontrollable, strategic analysts look closely at the external environment to attempt to identify trends and changes. In this way a company can prepare itself to react quickly. Thus, strategic planners attempt to assess the relative positions of their competitors and take as many other factors as possible into consideration to predict future trends for the industry, the company, and competitors in light of expected events in the external environment. This determination includes not only the use of quantifiable data, such as income figures, sales, economic growth in host economies, and so on, but also includes subjective feelings about the future.

Forecasting and planning are formidable tasks for MNCs operating in many locations. The effect of political factors alone on business both at home and abroad can be substantial. The impact can be minimal (small tax increases) or drastic (limits on raw materials or use of resources). Political developments can also jeopardize operations in foreign environments (expropriation of assets). For these reasons, it is absolutely crucial that MNCs engage in careful scanning of the external environment to identify potential threats and risks involved in foreign business operations.

These environments also provide opportunities. The alert international businessperson or firm can benefit greatly from early and accurate identification of foreign markets ripe for its goods, or of new sources of supplies or materials. Through an accurate view of the external environment, an MNC can identify where it faces threats or where it has opportunities.

Data used to assess the external environment comes from a variety of sources. External sources include the general business press, trade journals, business periodicals, government sources, and specialized services, such as those that provide information on political risks to be borne in specific international operating environments. Key information, especially information regarding the activities of competitors and the characteristics of foreign markets, also comes from internal sources. These sources are employees of an MNC—those in the sales field witnessing the activities of competitors, subsidiary managers who have an ear to the ground in foreign locales, trade association connections, and the usual information channels of all firms and industries that constitute the grapevine.

The key to a valid assessment of the external trends based on this information is to make proper assumptions regarding what is expected to happen and the consequent effect on a firm. For example, an analyst could determine that if the economy grows by 3 percent, sales for the firm should grow by half as much and rise by 1.5 percent.

THE LONG-RANGE OR GRAND PLAN

These forecasts of expectations and related effects on sales and production for companies allow them to take the next step in the strategic planning process, that of developing the strategy.

There are two levels of strategic planning for a firm. The first is the long-range plan or grand plan. Long-term objectives might include increases in productivity and profitability. Goals could also be related to relative performance within the industry, such as improved competitive position in the industry or leadership in technological developments. A company's aim could also be improved relationships with individual employees, or the public, or an improvement of a firm's use of human and other resources.

These long-term objectives are then used as the foundation for the firm to develop its grand plan for the future. Depending on a company's objectives, such a plan could include strategies for diversifying product lines or types of subsidiaries; it could also consist of retrenching and divesting itself of unprofitable affiliates or the liquidation of assets. Some grand strategies are based on reaching goals through horizontal or vertical integration.

IMPLEMENTATION PLANS: ANNUAL BUDGETS

The next step in the process involves translating the long-range objectives into feasible, understandable, and workable implementation plans, which are blueprints for action to help a firm coordinate all the functional activities within the company to achieve the ultimate goals. These functional strategies are much more detailed and shorter-term in nature. They involve the establishment of goals and aims for individual operating arms and the allocation of resources necessary to achieve these ends. Functional and operating strategies are implemented through developing annual objectives for each division and are supported by the establishment of overall corporate policies that link functional activity to overall enterprise goals.

The most widely used tool in developing annual objectives for the functional arms of a firm are annual budgets, which outline future expectations for every department and which provide a standard against which each can measure its progress. Budgets use assumptions regarding sales forecasts, related costs, and expected productivity.

As an example of a very simplified overall plan, imagine a firm that has as its long-term objective the doubling of its market share from 25 percent to 50 percent within five years. This plan can be broken down into an annual market-share increase of an additional 5 percent. To achieve this increase however, more capital and personnel resources must be allocated to the marketing function and, in turn, there must be increases in production, distribution and support functions.

Thus, the annual budget of the marketing department might include line items to provide for additional sales staff and funds for increased promotion efforts to fuel the move to market expansion. Simultaneously, the production arms of a firm have expectations of increases in productivity or capacity utilization built into their budgets. These functional strategies and budgets are generally framed on a very short-term (one-year) basis and must be flexible enough to provide cushioning against unexpected changes in the environment.

Three Planning Options

Corporate strategies are developed in a number of ways. From the top down, from the bottom up, and a combination of the two. Top-down planning begins in the upper echelons of management. It has the advantage of a wide vision and perspective regarding the overall activities of the firm, but has the disadvantage of being distanced from the operating environments and their realities.

In bottom-up planning the strategic plan is developed in an incremental fashion beginning with the functional managers, who set their own objectives that filter up to the top of the pyramid to aggregate into a firm's overall goals. This method has the very real disadvantage of lacking overall coordination of objectives into a focused enterprise goal. Individual managers are likely to set goals related to their own agendas or objectives, not in accordance with an overall plan or scheme for a firm. Bottom-up planning does, however, have the advantage of being realistic, because those setting the objectives are also responsible for implementing them. Thus, their stake in meeting goals is higher.

In practice, most firms use a combination of top-down and bottom-up planning. Individual unit managers may propose objectives for their di-

visions which are weighed and evaluated by senior staff and planners and revised in accordance with overall strategic objectives for a firm. Thus, an appropriate balance is achieved, where overarching objectives are established to provide a focus for operations of the enterprise, but includes individual and realistic inputs regarding the smaller objectives which must be met in order to reach the general corporate objectives.

Once the overall strategy and integral functional strategies are developed, a business reinforces the underlying notions by institutionalizing the strategy within the enterprise and making it an integral part of the culture of the firm. Thus, the strategy becomes an integral part of daily operations and decision-making, so that all activity is consistent with the goals of the firm. Thus, the enterprise establishes policies and procedures that support its strategy and develop lines of authority, which in turn provide for efficient management, operations, and the resolution of conflicts.

To assure compliance and an honest attempt by members of a corporation to put it into effect, a strategic plan must be continually monitored and its systems controlled in order to be effective. This control function ensures that all aspects of the plan and operations are coordinated. It is crucial to the successful implementation of a strategic plan and is especially crucial to the coordination of activity across multinational environments.

Controlling Strategically
Areas to Control

The control process involves continuous monitoring of the strategic plan to measure its effectiveness and to make corrections where necessary, in either the plan itself or in compliance.

Three major areas of importance to an MNC with regard to controlling international operations include controlling foreign exchange risk, adjustments needed in routine control systems because of differences in various branch operating environments, and control of risks arising out of foreign operations, including relations with host governments.

Establishing systems of internal control in an MNC is far more difficult than in a domestic enterprise. The communication of goals and objectives and corrections may be impeded by the distance between the parent company and its branch or subsidiary, as well as by differences in languages and operating procedures. The form of an operation may be such that a firm may have only partial ownership and not have full authority to impose control measures. Similarly, the operating environment may have such external characteristics that the control measures may be unachievable. For example, an attempt to bring sales profitability levels up to corporate objectives by raising prices might be stymied in a foreign environment because of controls on price levels set by governments.

Locating Decision Authority

The key factor in the control process for an MNC is the location of the decision-making authority between headquarters and subsidiaries. This problem is often referred to as centralization versus decentralization of control. Centralized decision-making vests all important decisions with the headquarters of the firm, while decentralized decision-making means that decisions are made entirely under the authority of subsidiary heads. These situations represent extreme ends of a continuum, but there is a middle ground, where some decisions come from headquarters and others remain within the subsidiary.

The structuring of the locus of authority for decision-making includes a tradeoff between the realization of different objectives. While centralized decision-making provides for the overall integration of objectives and potential efficiencies for a firm in worldwide operations, it also distances subsidiary management from making valuable inputs to the process and adding their own expertise to provide for local operating efficiencies. Total decentralization of decision-making may provide for local efficiencies, but it could also result in

a loss of control by headquarters and in overall systems-wide suboptimal operations.

The types of decisions involved include resource allocation, acquisition of capital equipment, employment of personnel, and use of liquid or capital assets. Other decisions involve the use of profits, determination of prices, reinvestment or repatriation of earnings, and determining the sources and prices to be paid for raw materials or inventory goods. Decision authority regarding marketing and production, such as adaptations to products and product lines, markets served and methods of serving those markets, types of promotion and distribution, and channels to be utilized must be allocated between the parent and the subsidiary or affiliate.

The degree of autonomy accorded to subsidiaries by MNCs depends on a number of factors, one of which is the mode of international operations. International activities, such as licensing and export functions, are usually carried out from corporate headquarters, but affiliates or subsidiaries based abroad require some degree of localized decision-making to keep operations efficient.

Another factor is the nature of the industry and its technology. If a company's advantage is based in product development and the marketing of these products using the same technology worldwide, the firm is likely to have centralized decision-making.

The size and maturity of an MNC also help place decision-making authority. An older, larger MNC might concentrate experienced personnel at headquarters and coordinate activities and decision-making from that centralized location, while a younger, smaller operation might be operating in an ad hoc manner and would continue to locate decision-making authority in the subsidiary because the company lacks experienced personnel to run those functions from the central location.

The competence of subsidiary managerial staff plays a large part in the determination of whether decision-making authority should be placed there or not. If local personnel are of high quality with good experience and business judgment, they will be given more authority.

Similarly, centralization of decision-making is affected by the local political environment and the sensitivity of an industry. An industry such as telecommunications is more sensitive to local political pressure because it is deemed essential to the welfare of the host country. Thus, local powers would impose pressure for more decentralized than centralized authority in the subsidiary.

In some countries the vesting of authority in local personnel may be an issue of political sensitivity with regard to the welfare of home country nationals. In many situations, the host government feels that centralized authority and decision-making by an MNC disenfranchises host country nationals from authority, retarding their educational and career growth and, in turn, the development process overall.

If a decision needs to be made quickly, it is more likely to be made locally. Similarly, the importance or magnitude of a decision also influences its reference to headquarters or not. Generally, a headquarters gets into the act of making decisions about large amounts of assets or strategic activities, such as the expansion of production capacity, the acquisition of capital assets, and the introduction or development of new products.

Branch Goals versus Headquarters Goals

In addition to the factors which are characteristic of an industry, a subsidiary, and the decisions themselves, the locus of decision-making is also affected by two potentially opposing forces—the objectives of the parent firm and the subsidiary. Subsidiary managers may, for example, be directed to set prices at certain levels or to allocate the results of production to other subsidiaries and not to high-profit markets. These decisions may benefit an MNC in the aggregate but reduce the performance of a subsidiary. Thus, any benefits to the overall firm through the centralization of decision-making may be negated by increasing frustration at the subsidiary level, which may lead to a lack of motivation or performance problems on the part of the subsidiary staff.

The result of opposing pressure is a balancing act between efficiencies to be achieved through centralization; the allocation of resources, assets, and profits among subsidiaries; the allocation of resources, assets, and profits between branches of a firm; and the operating integrity of the subsidiary. If an MNC truly operates from a global perspective, the overall coordination of the operations must also be integrated in a worldwide system.

Other Control Concerns

Other control concerns arise in situations where firms lack full ownership of a subsidiary and operate instead in a cooperative agreement or a joint venture. In these instances, an MNC may find its hands tied in efforts to centralize operations control of the affiliate.

An MNC must decide at the outset its minimum required level of control, but it must be realistic about limitations on its ability to control, and accept that it may not be able to make unfettered decisions regarding the allocation of production from the subsidiary or the repatriation or reinvestment of its resources.

Another control concern deals with the selection of managerial staff for a subsidiary. While an MNC can gain additional control from the use of expatriate corporate staff, it could lose access to the home country operating environment. Thus, some firms make it a practice to use host country nationals in subsidiaries, but also provide training and exposure to operations in corporate headquarters in order to familiarize them with the corporate culture, objectives, policies, and procedures. The goal is to provide subsidiary executives a common basis with headquarters staff.

Evaluation of branch managers is a final important aspect of international control. The optimal situation is one that balances the objectives of an enterprise and its subsidiary in determining performance criteria. Thus, a subsidiary manager's performance should not be judged according to profits from sales if the MNC objective (as determined centrally) is to gain market share through lowered prices in the market served by the subsidiary, or if the central authorities determine that production should be allocated to other arms of the company. Instead, the manager's performance should be evaluated according to relevant criteria which are both quantifiable and qualitative. In this way, performance appraisal is divorced from operational profitability results and is linked instead to criteria more relevant and appropriate to the situation.

Structuring the Organization

In general, methods and systems of control in an MNC are responses to an overall need by a firm to establish lines of authority and reporting methodologies. These systems emerge as part of corporate organization, which outlines the hierarchy of authority and decision-making. The way a corporation is structured determines the channeling of authority, the allocation of decision-making, and the adjudication of problems. These structural forms frequently change with the evolution of an enterprise from a domestic company to a full-fledged global corporation.

In the earliest stage, a company's international activity consists primarily of exports of goods to new markets overseas or across borders. The form this activity takes within the firm is the export department and the appointment of an export manager who handles the technicalities and the coordination of export sales. This manager generally reports to the director of a functional area, such as marketing (see Figure 20–1).

International Division

As the international segment of their businesses grow, many firms establish special operating arms to conduct this activity. The international division is responsible for the coordination of international strategy and operations and exists in conjunction with and parallel to other functional areas of a firm, but generally has less autonomy than those areas because an international division needs to rely upon the resources of other functional areas within the firm and to coordinate its actions with their operations (see Figure 20–2).

The advantages to MNCs of having an international division is that by allocating staff and resources to the international function, it is accorded importance, standing, and some budgetary resources in the firm. Therefore, international perspective and strategies can be clearly focused. International activity can be centralized in one area of the firm, and emphasis can be placed on in-

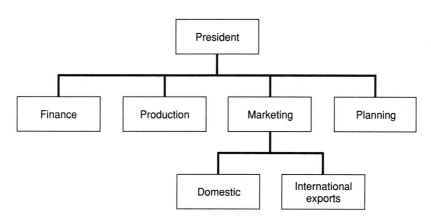

FIGURE 20–1   Export Sales Structure

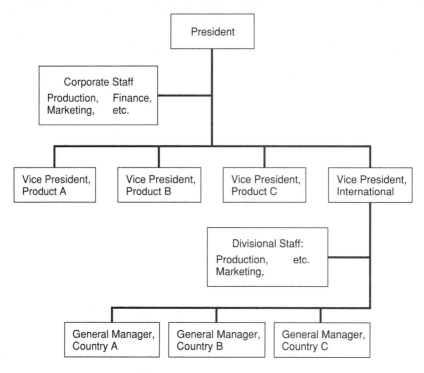

FIGURE 20–2   International Division Structure

ternational business and widening the perspective of the firm to a world view. The disadvantages of an international division structure are primarily in its interaction with other segments of the firm. In order to achieve its own objectives, the international division must rely upon the concurrence or coordination of the objectives of other functional divisions in those objectives. For example, a firm cannot plan to market a new product in a new market if the marketing, production, and distribution divisions of the company cannot provide support for the activity. Thus, the greatest drawback in a separate international division comes with the need for communication and coordination and, in the absence of such interaction, from the need to adjudicate disputes regarding the allocation of resources between the functional and international divisions of the firm.

Because of intrafirm conflicts and problems, many large corporations frequently replace the international division with a different kind of inter-

national structure that attempts to integrate international activity into other corporate activity through the establishment of a functional, geographic, or product organization.

Functional Structure

A functional organizational structure is a useful form for industries in which technology used by a firm and the products marketed around the world are basically the same. Under this type of organization, all functions, whether domestic or international, are centralized and include an international component (see Figure 20–3). Here, the division head vice presidents report to the president and are responsible for the worldwide activities of their divisions. A functional system is useful in providing for centralization of the control function and of protecting against subsidiary conflicts in small industries. It can, however, only work when the products and markets are homogenous

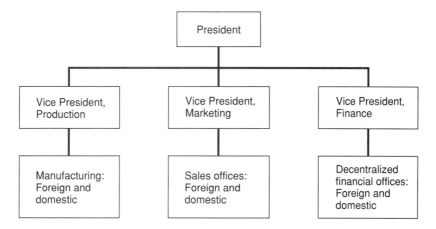

FIGURE 20–3   Functional Structure

around the world because it does not readily provide for coordination between divisions, which is necessary to implement product or market adaptation in a number of market areas.

The functional organizational structure is used primarily in extractive industries, such as petroleum development or mining. Its suitability decreases as a firm grows and communication between divisions becomes unwieldy. Such growth leads to inefficiency of operations and slowdowns in decision-making, and provides opportunities for clashes between divisions and their objectives, and results in power struggles between competing executives. The major disadvantage of using such a structure, therefore, is that it does not provide flexibility for a firm attempting to market a number of products in a number of markets. Another disadvantage with a functional structure is that it allows for a great deal of duplication of effort between divisions, especially with regard to the scanning and analysis of foreign operating environments.

Product Structure

An alternative that addresses the problem of coordination in the marketing of a variety of products in worldwide markets is the organizational structure, which is developed according to the products marketed by the firm. Under this structure (see Figure 20–4), responsibilities for all functions involved in marketing a specific product group or class throughout the world are delegated to a group within each product division. The product divisions have a great deal of autonomy, although they may be subject to some centralized authority on perhaps financial matters or overreaching functions, such as strategic planning and research and development.

The advantages of having a product structure are that the managers of these groups (often called strategic business units) develop a great deal of knowledge about their products, competitors, production intricacies, market, and customer characteristics. They understand the environmental constraints of products and how best to position these products in various markets for a variety of users. The product managers can also develop a worldwide perspective regarding sales and marketing for their groups.

The greatest disadvantage of a structure organized according to product groups is coordinating the efforts of various product line groups in overlapping market areas. How does a firm settle problems that arise in attempts to appropriately allocate company resources to different product lines? How does it adjust for product managers who have strong product knowledge but poor schooling in

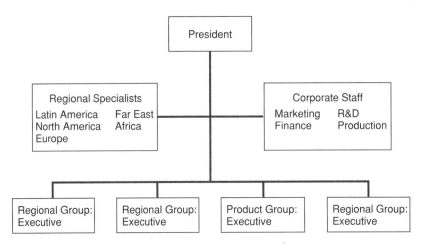

FIGURE 20-4   Product Division Structure

the conditions and requirements of local market environments? At the other extreme, how does a firm protect against creating too much expertise and the duplication of functions among different product groups? Such duplication of effort creates corporate inefficiencies and results in missed opportunities to achieve economies of scale in functional areas.

Area Structure

To avoid such duplication of efforts, some international corporations organize international functions according to various geographic areas of its international markets served (see Figure 20-5). The configuration of the geographic structure depends on the markets in which an MNC operates,

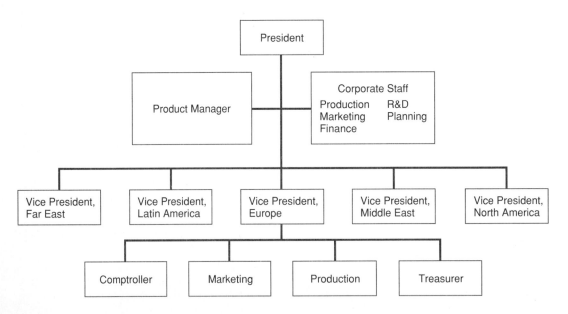

FIGURE 20-5   International Area Structure

but typical divisions occur according to major market areas, such as North America, South America, Europe, Asia, and Africa. Each group has its own vice president who reports to the president of the firm and who is responsible for all products, distribution, marketing, production, and operations within the geographic area of responsibility. This formation has the advantage of allowing a firm to place greater emphasis on the specific needs, market characteristics, and requirements of the individual market areas. This structure works well for stable firms that have very large, worldwide operations evenly spread across a number of diverse, strong market areas, and where operations would be enhanced through attention paid to product adaptation to suit the individual requirements of markets.

The major drawback to a geographic orientation of a firm is that by emphasizing regional operations it fails to facilitate the development of the coordination of functional or product line activity worldwide. Thus, a firm may miss opportunities to achieve economies of scale in production or in raw materials sourcing, and may be drawn away from a global strategic perspective to focus primarily on the regional groupings. Another drawback to this type of organization is that it requires the allocation of considerable resources to establish separate regional headquarters headed by area managers. Again, it may lead to the duplication of some activities and consequent inefficiencies throughout the corporation.

The Matrix Structure

To accommodate these problems and to increase the channels and flows of communication, some firms organize themselves according to a matrix or a grid in which authority for activities is shared by more than one individual. Under such a structure, a general manager of an international division might report to two different individuals—a chief for the marketing area and a director for the individual product group. These matrices may be organized according to two or more dimensions, such as according to a functional area and a prod-

uct group. They provide benefits to an international firm by giving it a form through which a balance can be struck between competing pressures emanating from different functional, regional, or product areas within an MNC.

The result of such a structure, however, is that there is no longer a straight, pyramid-shaped line of authority from a manager to superiors. Instead, authority for decision-making is shared between one or more persons. The major problem with this type of structure develops, not surprisingly, from the overlap of authority in the coordination of policy formation and operations and competition by various individuals for corporate resources. A firm thus has a diffused decision-making structure. Each major decision has to be cleared by more than one individual, and there is considerable scope for conflict, not only from genuine professional differences in points of view, but also from personal considerations that are a factor in every corporate organization around the world. In the matrix structure the role of the top manager as mediator and adjudicator of disputes is therefore critical because speedy reconciliation of opposing viewpoints is often needed to make timely decisions.

The greatest advantage of the matrix structure is that it reconciles the competing demands of regional or product-oriented managers and concerns about the retention of global competitiveness of the firm. At the same time, the emergence of contradictory but valid arguments about a particular issue from the product- or region-oriented manager and the globally oriented managers enables an MNC to make the best-informed decision that would be effective in serving overall corporate goals, rather than the narrower ends of a particular segment of a company. Thus, the structure allows an MNC to take a view from all angles simultaneously and make a decision that would consider the impact and implication for all relevant facets of the company's operations, instead of considering an impact only on limited sectors of operation.

Obviously, the greatest danger in a matrix organization is the possibility of mismanagement or ineffective handling of conflicts, which are bound to arise within the firm. This situation may become particularly problematic when there are managers who are either too gain-oriented and overly aggressive or are not really concerned and do not make the required effort to air their point of view. Another difficulty with the structure is its inherent complexity which multiplies with the increase in the number of products, markets, or other matrix elements that are used by any multinational organization. These difficulties could blur the lines of authority to such a degree that decisions could be significantly delayed, and international coordination rendered virtually impossible to achieve. Organizations have to take great care to avoid the matrix structure taking over the organization. Caution must be exercised to retain clarity of decision-making levels and procedures, as well as for dispute resolution and internal coordination.

Crucial Structural Considerations

The key consideration of a firm in determining the appropriate form it should take to provide for the efficient allocation of resources and appropriate decision-making is that it maintain a balance between centralization and decentralization of control. If the scales tip toward centralization, the firm forgoes local expertise and valuable input and becomes a rigid organization. At the other end of the spectrum, total decentralization of decision-making can lead to complete anarchy within a firm and a total misinterpretation or ignoring of corporate goals and objectives. Many believe that the best structure is one that includes decentralization to encourage inputs, flexibility, and responsiveness to local conditions with an overlay of centralization to provide structure and cohesiveness in the overall operation of a firm. To achieve such a balance, some firms centralize decision-making in some key functional areas, such as financial management, product design, and strategic planning, and allow much more decentralization of decision-

making in other areas, such as marketing and personnel.

Some firms attempt to adjust for coordination problems among various forms of organization by providing for special functions within MNCs. Some such functions might be the assignment of a global product manager to report on a product function in a firm organized according to geographic settings. Other firms assign personnel to act specifically as liaisons between various geographic, functional, and product groups. Still other firms make it a policy to give their senior executives a variety of assignments to familiarize them with all operational aspects of a firm and to help them open communication channels between segments on a less formal basis than through formal reporting channels to senior management.

The Organizational Choice

Multinational corporations more often evolve into different types and mutations of organizational forms, rather than actively choosing or deciding on their form of structure. The type of organizational structure employed depends on a number of factors, and there is no such thing as a proper structure for a multinational firm. Instead, the appropriate structure is the one that matches the goals, nature, and culture of a firm. Generally speaking, most international corporations have a mixed form of structure that slowly evolves over time. This structure is seldom permanent and changes as a firm changes and grows.

In general, the form a corporation takes is directly related to the philosophy of its leadership, the nature of the corporate mission, and the operational specialization of the firm. The more specialized these operations are, the more likely it is that a firm has a complex organizational structure to provide for the coordination of all aspects of operations. Thus, structure follows the determination of organizational needs and provides a method of establishing formal systems of control and lines of authority in the firm. The idea is that information regarding objectives and control over the system can flow downward through the system and result in changes or corrections in managerial and operational behavior to achieve corporate objectives. By the same token, the organizational structure should provide for both upward and lateral communications to encourage the sharing of information between units of an enterprise, as well as from the bottom up in the hierarchy.

Management Information Systems

MIS in an MNC

The appropriate transfer and analysis of information regarding markets, operations, customers, and enterprise activities can be a crucial factor in the success or failure of a firm and its international activities. In the best of circumstances, the use of relevant information can provide a multinational concern with competitive advantages over its competitors by allowing it to develop a strategic position of strength.

On a more routine level, an MNC must manage its information flows from subsidiaries about operations, markets, and potential just to maintain its existing operating strengths in current markets across the globe. This is a major challenge for an MNC, considering the distance involved, both physical and cultural, and the need to transfer data and information from a variety of environments. Moreover, information must be comparable and standardized, if it is to be aggregated for analysis by an MNC.

Corporate Reports

One method of control used by MNCs is the establishment of reporting requirements and procedures for staff and departments within the organization. These reports constitute a steady stream of information that flows to headquarters and is analyzed to provide input in strategic decision-making about overall corporate resource allocation by senior management. Because written reports often represent the only formal presentation of information from the subsidiaries or operating branches regarding their activities, and because these reports often provide the basis for performance evaluation, it is crucial that subsidiary managers understand the reporting requirements, format, and purposes.

In order to be effective tools of control and decision-making, it is imperative that reports from branches and arms of the firm be timely, so that an MNC is able to respond with adjustments and corrections. Similarly, reports must contain complete information that is relevant to the needs of an MNC in its evaluation of the subsidiary's performance. Information must be presented in an understandable, comparable format and include data that is usable by top management and strategic planners. Accuracy of data is critical because some mistakes in reports from one region may upset calculations for the entire corporation.

Corporations require a variety of reports on activities in their worldwide operations, which fall into four categories—financial reports, operating reports, in-country reports, and market-based reports. Financial reports provide an MNC with information regarding the flow of funds within the subsidiary and between its suppliers and customers. They quantify the results of operations and provide information on the status of the on-site currency. These reports must be presented in an established form, use standardized currency conversions, and use the same conventions to permit comparison with the results of other corporate segments. This presentation of financial data may not be in the same format as that required by the host government regulatory standards. In many instances, therefore, it is necessary for a subsidiary to maintain separate sets of books for official reporting requirements in the host country.

Reports on operations give management a view on the performance of subsidiaries and indicate such information as production volumes, inventory levels, supply contracts negotiated, and expended raw materials and energy. These reports frequently also note staffing changes, technological developments regarding operating procedures and compliance with local laws, such as environmental or social welfare reporting requirements. The reports comprise the core of the information sent to headquarters, and they chronicle the day-to-day achievements, problems, and status of the operating arms of an MNC and give it a basis of comparison from reporting period to reporting period. From formal operating reports and informal communications with branches, top management can keep its finger on the pulse of the enterprise and be aware of what resources are being utilized where, to what end, and how efficiently.

Subsidiaries also perform a valuable function by giving the managers at headquarters key information from the foreign operating environment. These in-country reports provide information on developments in the host country on economic, political, and social fronts. Such information provides a firm with timely data on which to base revisions of risk factors or to limit or increase operations in the host country. They can also provide the firm with an advantage in the event of potential crises, such as political or military upheavals, by providing top management with early warning signals, so that the loss of company assets and danger to company personnel can be minimized.

Subsidiaries also provide an MNC with information regarding activities in the market it serves. This information concerns the actions of a firm's competitors in existing market areas, consumer behavior, buying patterns, and demand and pricing structures. On-site personnel often also provide information to a firm about potential market development through the examination of new markets or the development of new products to satisfy different needs of consumers in existing markets.

The information provided by these reports assists a firm in its efforts to develop and fine tune its implementation of strategic and operating objectives. Consequently, to ensure that it is interpreted and used correctly, it is essential that the information provided in these reports be accurate, reliable, and consistent across all arms of a firm in terms of the use of the same standards of measurement, accounting principles, and definitions.

Formal written reports are also supplemented with informal reports made in face-to-face contacts with subsidiary managers and through frequent telephone conversations. These channels of informal reporting are also important because they provide a subsidiary manager with a method for reporting on smaller occurrences that might not warrant formal reporting, but which may be significant. They also keep communication lines open in the event that there is need for further information on more important issues. To encourage this interaction (and to provide nontraditional support for expatriate or subsidiary managers), some firms assign managers a corporate mentor, who is charged with staying in touch with the manager so that he is involved in the activities of the firm at headquarters.

Despite the care that is taken to ensure comparability and compatibility of reports from all arms of an MNC, problems nevertheless arise in the management of information systems across international borders. Some firms assume that they can use the same reporting systems abroad as they do at home. This is not always the case because of differences in the operating environments. For example, in some countries where computer skills are low, the use of computerized reports by overseas employees is not feasible. Similarly, if a system requires the use of computerized data collection or report transmittal, a myriad of compatibility problems arise.

International Data Processing: Integration Issues

There is a constant interchange of information between the parent office and subsidiaries in every MNC operation. Figure 20–6 illustrates the process of information interchange between a parent and a single subsidiary. The interchange pattern becomes vastly more complex when multiplied by a number of subsidiaries involved in the overall structure of an MNC.

The complexity of these networks and the involvement of the international component of information management raises several issues of con-

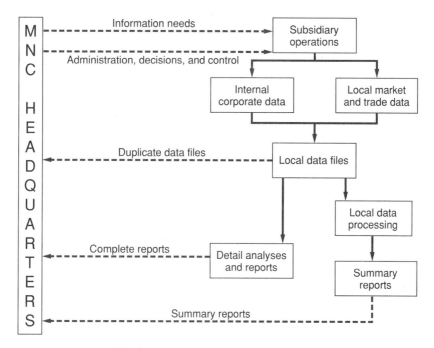

FIGURE 20-6   Typical Information Flow between an MNC and Its Subsidiaries

cern to MNCs. These issues stem mostly from problems regarding compatibility of data processing systems, the establishment of controls on data compilation and its transfer across national borders by host governments, and the risks involved in using multinational computer networks.

An MNC often has problems in sharing information with its subsidiaries because of differences in data processing capabilities and sophistication of systems. While an MNC may have highly sophisticated fast computer systems, its subsidiaries may be equipped with much less sophisticated equipment, either because a subsidiary's information management needs are less extensive or because the capabilities of the personnel in a subsidiary do not allow for the efficient use of such equipment. Alternatively, a subsidiary may have different software and hardware.

Another problem in integrating information systems of a parent and subsidiaries is the high costs of centralization of information systems. Moreover, an attempt by MNCs to impose tight controls upon their branches with respect to data processing and transmittal leads to additional administrative costs, delays in having information or data files transmitted, the need for extensive and expensive computer systems, and the need to protect against loss of data during transmittal by piracy.

Through decentralization of information management, an MNC can avoid these higher costs and allow subsidiaries to make their own decisions regarding computer systems. The tradeoff, however, is a lack of parental control over the management of the system. As with all aspects of the centralization versus decentralization debate, an MNC must balance these opposing outcomes in an effort to reach an appropriate level of managerial control over the information system for efficiency's sake without sacrificing subsidiary autonomy.

Another enormous problem for MNCs in the management of data and information is a result of forces in the external environment on the use of information systems. These are primarily the forces that emanate from political or governmental entities in host countries, which have concerns about national security in their country, protection of economic forces, and, to some degree, about cultural independence.

These concerns may lead to host country union requirements regarding the employment of local data processors and laws regarding privacy and the carrying of data across national borders. For example, some countries do not allow data to be transmitted for processing elsewhere across their borders. These restrictions are intended to retain employment in the country and to force firms to use local labor to satisfy the labor requirements of their data processing.

In some firms or businesses, this function can be a very large component of overall business activity. International banks are a prime example of a business that is based on the fast, reliable, and accurate use of computer systems to chronicle individual banking transactions. International banks frequently spend millions of dollars to establish data processing systems and computer networks to facilitate the flow of information and data processing from branches around the world.

In these instances, the speed of processing has a very real economic effect on business because the slow transfer of invested funds means losses in interest earned. In Canada, for example, a foreign bank's financial records must be initially processed in-country, can only be transferred to corporate headquarters abroad if prior approval is received from the inspector general of banks, and must be duplicated within the country. These laws were imposed to attempt to keep data processing capabilities in-country, but they result in additional processing costs and complexities for foreign subsidiary banks in that country.

International firms can also be affected by government controls imposed to deal with the treatment of the issue of privacy of personal information. Such treatment usually includes limits on the uses of computer systems by firms in order that individuals have control over the content of

personal information, can correct it when necessary, and must give consent for it to be used by other parties. Such information could include personal data regarding sex, religion, race, or political orientation, but could also include personal academic, criminal, and financial information.

Limits on the transmittal of such information affect an MNC in the area of transmitting personnel records to headquarters, and may result in additional expenses to insure compliance with local laws or act as barriers to having complete records at centralized locations. In Norway, for example, a centralized data inspectorate must be given notice each time personal information is sent abroad.

Governments use other methods to control transnational data flows. Some countries have attempted to limit the flows by considering the imposition of a tax on information leaving the country. Such taxation is difficult to implement because it is virtually impossible to objectively determine the value of economic information except on a case-by-case method. Other countries merely make it expensive to move data out of the country. In Japan, for example, Control Data Corporation was forced to pay for its own private telephone line between that country and the United States (at a cost of $33,000 per month) and, because of restrictions, can only use that line at 10 percent of its capacity.

Besides these additional costs and procedural problems involved in operating information systems in an international setting, MNCs also face a high level of risk in managing transnational information networks. The biggest problems a firm faces are maintaining the integrity of data through a control process that oversees data inputs to the system, and the management of the information at the local level to correspond to data needs at the corporate level. Other risks involved are the loss of data in transmittal because of unreliable channels or through the piracy (or theft) of the data. Developing protection against such risks is very expensive for a firm and involves such measures as the establishment of a company's own computer system or the purchase of private communication lines.

The goal of an MNC is to take advantage of its operation as an integrated system, of which the management of information is a major part. The aim of the firm is to minimize duplication of efforts and facilities and to maximize operating efficiencies by coordinating information concerning operations and business opportunities around the world. Issues raised in the control of transnational data flows have the potential of adversely affecting the ability of MNCs to pursue these objectives by placing limits on their ability to exchange and analyze this crucial information or by imposing additional operating costs through restrictions on the processing, location, and transmittal of data. These controls are a significant issue for the modern MNC that attempts to develop an information management system that strikes a balance between costs and benefits, and has the capability of synthesizing data from worldwide operations while maintaining the appropriate technology at the subsidiary level.

Should International Firms Go Global?

The process of controlling international operations is a formidable challenge for a firm attempting to make the best of its corporate strengths while simultaneously remaining aware of its limitations. Some analysts believe, however, that the progressive firm should not content itself with an international focus, but should adopt a global orientation toward operations and planning.

Some companies are merely multinational; they operate a variety of subsidiaries in a number of countries. In such a portfolio approach, individual operating arms or companies in a conglomerate are ranked according to criteria, such as their individual market strength and market growth, not as part of the global system, such as those within the Boston Consulting Group matrix of

business units, which are categorized as "cash cows," "stars," "dogs," and "question marks." This focus and orientation is limited and leads to suboptimization of operations and resources and to the company's missing opportunities to be exploited by integrating all operations worldwide. Rather than comparing individual units against each other in terms of a firm's entire portfolio of business activities, a firm would be better off if it looked at international factors from a global perspective to identify possibilities for operating synergies.

Similarly, a firm must consider worldwide competition in designing its strategy—the forces of global competition that may lead a firm toward the establishment of less profitable business units as a defensive posture, rather than an offensive move toward profitability. Such a defensive action could be costly in the short-term, but pays dividends from a long-term, global perspective.

By accurately assessing the forces of global competition and a firm's relative advantages and strengths, an enterprise can devise a global strategy to become effective in world markets. Such a strategy may hinge on competing in all product lines, or in a product area that is protected from competition, or on a global strategy area focusing on a specific market (global niche), or on a particular national or regional area market. Although the process of planning and subsequent implementation and control is highly complex because of the assimilation and analysis of information about a variety of operating and supply environments, it can provide incomparable strategic advantages for a corporation willing to take on such a global challenge.

Summary

MNCs commit significant time and resources in planning and controlling because of the size and complexity of their global operations. The key questions that MNCs plan for are what does the firm hope to accomplish, what is the magnitude of production, when will the activity occur, where will the activity take place, how will goals be reached, which resources will be used, and which methods must be considered. The strategic planning process involves identifying the mission statement, performing internal and external analysis of controllable and noncontrollable forces, forecasting the future, and developing a long-range (grand) plan. Implementation of the long-range objectives must be translated into annual objectives, generally by using an annual budgeting process. Planning can occur from the top down, the bottom up, or a combination of both. Institutionalizing the strategic plan is critical to its successful implementation.

Controlling multinational operations requires continuous monitoring and can be impeded by distance, language, and operating procedures. MNCs must determine whether to centralize or decentralize decision-making authority, which is influenced by the mode of international operations, the nature of the industry and technology, the size and maturity of the MNC, the competence of the branch managerial staff, the local political environment, and the required speed of decision-making and the magnitude of the decision. The level of ownership and investment affects whether an MNC has the authority to centralize decision-making for the branch. Thus, an MNC must decide at the outset its minimum level of necessary control. Control issues are also influenced by the decision to staff branches with host country nationals or corporate expatriates and the criteria used in evaluating management performance. Multinational organizations can be structured in a variety of ways, including the international division, the functional structure, the product structure, the area structure, and the matrix structure. MIS can be a crucial factor in the success or failure of an MNC by coordinating information flows and providing financial and operating reports for use in planning and controlling the global activities of an MNC. Information and data flows can be slowed by the incompatibility of hardware and software systems used in the corporate and branch offices as well as by political or governmental regulations.

Discussion Questions

1. How does planning for a multinational corporation differ from planning for a domestic organization? What additional problems does the MNC face?
2. Why have MNCs found it necessary to institute global strategic planning?
3. What is a mission statement?
4. Discuss a firm's internal and external environment. How do they differ?
5. You are the CEO of Proctor & Sons, Inc., a large U.S. firm manufacturing personal care and soap products in twenty-five countries around the world. You have recently purchased a small Swedish family-owned yet highly profitable kitchen appliance manufacturer. Ulpsala International, which has been in business for seventy-five years, employs five hundred workers, uses very advanced technology in manufacturing its products, and exports throughout Europe. What level of autonomy and decision-making authority would you delegate to this new subsidiary? What organization structure would you use? Explain.
6. What types of control concerns may occur when staffing a foreign subsidiary with host country nationals versus expatriates from corporate headquarters? What are the advantages of using host country nationals?
7. Compare the organizational illustrations in this chapter's text. You are president at Paxson Industrial Tools and you are interested in exporting your product line of drill presses and lathes to Japan and Latin America. What organizational structure should you use? Why?
8. How can MIS make or break a multinational corporation?
9. What data problems might occur between the parent office and its subsidiaries?

Bibliography

AGTHE, KLAUS E. 1990. "Managing the Mixed Marriage." *Business Horizons* (January/February): 37–43.

DICKIE, PAUL M., AND N. S. ARYA. 1970. "MIS and International Business." *Journal of Systems Management* (June): 8–12.

EARL, M., D. FEENY, M. LOCKETT, AND D. RUNGE. 1988. "Competitive Advantage Through Information Technology: Eight Maxims for Senior Managers." *Multinational Business* (Summer): 15–21.

FAUTL, IRVIN L. 1975. "Control and the Internal Audit in the Multinational Firm." *International Journal of Accounting* (Fall): 57–65.

GARLAND, JOHN, AND RICHARD N. FARMER 1986. *International Dimensions of Business Policy and Strategy.* Boston: PWS-Kent Publishing Company.

GRINDLEY, KIT. 1988. "MIS Spending Booms in Japan." *Datamation* (March 15): 106–107.

MALJERS, F. A. 1990. "Strategic Planning and Intuition in Unilever." *Long Range Planning* (April): 63–68.

OHMAE, KENICHI. 1985. *Triad Power.* New York: Free Press.

———. 1990. *The Borderless World.* New York: Harper Business.

PEARCE, JOHN A., AND RICHARD B. ROBINSON. 1988. *Strategic Management: Strategy Formulation and Implementation.* Homewood, IL: Irwin.

PORTER, MICHAEL. 1980. *Competitive Strategy: Techniques for Analyzing Industries and Competitors.* New York: Free Press.

———. 1985. *Competitive Advantage.* New York: Free Press.

———. 1986. *Competition in Global Industries.* Boston: Harvard Business School Press.

———. 1990. *The Competitive Advantage of Nations.* New York: Free Press.

SAMIEE, SAEED. 1984. "Transnational Data Flow Constraints: A New Challenge for Multinational Corporations." *Journal of International Business Studies,* (Spring/Summer): 141–150.

VALDERRABANO, J. L., AND V. VENKATAKRISHNAN. 1990. "Business Impact of Strategic Data Planning." *Journal of Information Systems Management* (Winter): 48–52.

VERNON-WORTZEL, H., AND L. H. WORTZEL. 1988. "Globalizing Strategies for Multinationals from Developing Countries." *Columbia Journal of World Business* (Spring): 27–35.

VERNON-WORTZEL, H., AND L. H. WORTZEL, eds. 1989. *Strategic Management of Multinational Corporations: The Essentials,* 2nd ed. New York: John Wiley.

Chapter Case Study _____

International Credit Bank

The annual performance review meeting at the headquarters of International Credit Bank had not turned out very well for Gregory Fuller, regional vice-president for Asia. He had expected trouble at the meeting, but he did not expect the kind of intensely negative feedback he received from Timothy Martin, Jr., the bank's president and chief executive officer. Fuller's area of responsibility included the bank's overall operation in Southern and Southeast Asia, and the bank had not done very well in the region during the past two years. Martin was extremely upset about this, because the entry of International Credit Bank into this region was his idea, and he had visualized spectacular growth for the bank in this region, which he felt was going to be the main growth area for the next two decades. In fact, Martin had felt that the only real chance for the bank to grow internationally was in this area and other options were almost nil. Africa had been doing so badly that even such international lending agencies as the World Bank were losing heart. On the other hand, Latin America continued to be mired in debt, which only seemed to grow larger each day. He, for one, was not going to commit the bank to that part of the world, at least for now and not until the crisis had passed, which meant that for the foreseeable future Latin America was forbidden territory for any international expansion plans for International Credit Bank.

International Credit Bank was a major commercial bank based in the United States. Founded in 1920, it had survived the depression years and become an important player in the international banking markets by the 1960s. The bank's international approach, exemplified by its strong presence in Europe and Australia, had enabled it to grow rapidly in the 1970s and the early 1980s. Commercial banks in general,

however, were hit by the growing securitization of international financial markets and International Credit Bank was no exception. Although it was a large bank, it was quite conservative in its approach and did not wish to set up overseas investment banking subsidiaries to take advantage of new opportunities that were becoming available in the financial markets. As a matter of policy, the bank had decided to expand its commercial banking operations into other countries, both to keep growing and to offset the decline in its European commercial banking business.

The bank, and especially Martin, had great expectations from its move into the Asian countries. The growth prospects were good, the infrastructure was in decent shape, and the Asian economies had been doing quite well. Most countries had proven to be good hosts for foreign direct investment and had done very well on the international front, especially in exports. Both the increasing domestic prosperity, led by industrialization, and rapid international trade growth signaled important opportunities for a commercial bank such as International Credit Bank, which had excellent facilities for financing both domestic and cross-border transactions.

The bank faced few problems in establishing a presence in most of these countries. Corresponding banking relationships were already there, and the bank's Southeast Asia representatives had maintained excellent contacts with the senior government officials in these countries. Approvals for establishment of branches were therefore fairly easy to come by, and within two years the bank had a network of seven branches in four countries of the region. In all four countries there were a number of international companies that were the bank's clients in Europe and North America and early business development was greatly facilitated. After the initial progress, however, the bank's business did not increase as rapidly as Martin had anticipated. His frustration grew as the bank witnessed only very slow growth for two years after three years of relatively rapid expansion. What was worrying Martin was that despite a 100 percent ownership of all the branches, productivity per employee was consistently lower than the branches in Europe and North America. In the performance review meeting he had let his concerns be known quite clearly to Fuller, who had come up with one major reason to explain this problem.

According to Fuller, the bank was growing slowly not because there was not enough business or because the local management was not expending enough effort to obtain new business, but because the local management did not want to take on new business until they were certain that they could handle it effectively and efficiently. At this point, all branches had portfolios that were up to their maximum capacity, and any abnormal expansion of business would have an adverse effect on the quality of work, which could severely damage the excellent reputation Credit Bank had built up over the years in the region. When Martin pointed out that they could expand business with the existing and available resources because the productivity was low, Fuller became quite upset. He said that it was unfair to measure productivity of branches in southern and Southeast Asia using the same criteria used for branches in Europe and North America. Fuller pointed out that there were a number of special constraints on the branches in the region, one of which was the almost total absence of computerization. Only the lending officers and the branch managers had personal computers and even they had problems in working with these. Martin knew that these branches had limited computerization and asked why they could not computerize now. He asked Fuller to go back to the central management information systems division of the bank and put together a plan for fully computerizing the seven branches in the region.

Fuller wasted no time in following up. Three days later he was flipping over a short but well-documented report from the MIS department on the issue of computerizing the seven branches in Southeast Asia. The report suggested that over the next six months nearly all operations of the branches could be fully computerized. Retail checking and savings, discounting of commercial bills of exchange, letters of credit, accounting and maintenance of ledgers, payroll and benefits, maintenance of credit records and profiles, and information and backup all could be put on a single integrated system. Moreover, if the system worked, they could hook up these branches with the bank's dedicated communication system with a satellite network channel that was going to be commercially available in the next three months. The initial costs would be comparatively high, because external consultants would be required to install, debug, and test the system and train the staff. System maintenance would also be an important cost factor, because the hardware supplier did not have a full-service office in two of the four countries to be covered by this project.

As he was reading the report, Fuller felt uneasy about the whole thing as one doubt after another rose in his mind. Is it really a good idea, he was thinking when the phone rang. It was Julia Peterson, Martin's executive assistant. It appeared that Martin had seen a copy of the report and was excited about it and wanted Fuller to stop by and discuss it right away. Oh no, thought Fuller, as he collected his ideas en route to Martin's plush office. This is going to be quite a difficult job if Martin has made up his mind on this. In any case, I have no choice but to say my bit, since there is no way I am going to take the blame for this thing if it goes awry, when I had opposed it in the first place.

Martin welcomed Fuller quite warmly, apparently quite pleased with the prospect of his branches in Asia being fully computerized and ready to make the productivity gains he had been seeking for so long. "This is going to really get us a jump start on the competition," he told Fuller. "It seems none of the foreign banks in that part of the world is fully computerized yet. So with one stroke not only will we improve our productivity and increase our business, but will also get ahead of the competition. And I am sure the local governments are going to love this, since we will be bringing in high technology. The costs do appear quite high, but then that is to be expected. You can't really get the returns unless you make the investment and I believe this is one investment that is really worth making. Maybe we should have done so earlier, but I guess bunching these costs along with startup costs would have killed us. Anyway, better late than never and in this case it is earlier than the competition. I am sure you agree, don't you, Gregory?"

Fuller spoke with some difficulty. It was obvious that there was a crisis in his mind. Here was the boss, upset with him over the performance of the bank in the region, now wanting to boost it through a means that Fuller did not think was correct. Nevertheless, he must be honest with himself and Martin and speak his mind. "Well,

sir," he began, "the project is technically sound as it is conceived, but there are a number of problems on the ground, in these countries that suggest that we do not commit ourselves so rapidly and fully to the type of computerization and automation that has been suggested by the MIS people. These guys are technically sound, but they really do not have an appreciation of the realities as they exist in the field. I know you are concerned about performance there and are of the view that the answer lies in rapid computerization and automation of the operations. Nevertheless, I feel very strongly that we should not ignore the problems that may arise and install a system that may cause more harm than good."

"Well," said Martin, sounding a bit dubious, "it's really your area. Why don't you specify the problems you feel are going to arise and let me have a small executive brief on this by Tuesday morning."

Question

Prepare a short brief on what problems might arise in computerizing the operations of branches in Southeast Asia.

CHAPTER 21

Managing Production and Technology

CHAPTER OBJECTIVES

This chapter will:

- Present the interrelated nature of the production process and technology.
- Identify efficiencies achieved through standardization of the international production process.
- Describe key inputs for designing and developing the local production system.
- Briefly discuss the advantages of the Japanese just-in-time production system.
- Examine the role technology holds in maintaining a competitive advantage.
- Discuss the methods multinationals use to acquire, transfer, and protect technology.

Production, Technology, and International Competition

With increasing worldwide competition, the strategic implications of decisions concerning the choices of an MNC for production and technology become even more important. These two elements influence where and how a company will operate. Decisions as to what and where it will produce to maintain a competitive edge are closely related to its technological and production resources. Al-

though some international business experts have chosen to treat technology and production in the international arena as separate factors, the two are interrelated issues because of the impact that technology has on international production decisions.

International Production

International management of production may be very similar to production in a home country. Common to both are considerations regarding the efficient use of all the factors of production,

539

productivity improvements, research and development, and the extent of horizontal and/or vertical integration. The international environment, however, includes other considerations. Before making production decisions, an MNC must consider such additional factors as different wage rates, industrial relations, sources of financing, foreign exchange risk, international tax laws, control, the appropriate mix of capital and labor, access to suppliers, and the production experience curve in each country. While many MNCs attempt to standardize their production systems on a worldwide basis by transferring production processes and procedures unchanged from the parent, these environmental influences often make such standardization unsuccessful or at best difficult.

Worldwide Standardization

On one hand, there is strong justification for worldwide standardization. First, the capacity of management to develop a successful organization is improved, primarily by making it easier to carry out the home office management functions. Organization and staffing are simpler when overseas production facilities are replications of existing facilities because future plants are reduced or enlarged versions of existing plants, and there are fewer labor hours and fewer costs involved with plant design. In addition, because technical assistance workers are familiar with the standard plant design, the overseas technical staff can be smaller, and home-based technical workers can assist the foreign operation on an as-needed basis. Furthermore, production specifications are more easily maintained and updated. If changes are necessary in production specifications, there is no need for a plant-by-plant evaluation to determine which operations are affected, which also implies cost savings in specifications maintenance for unified production processes.

Supply

The second area that experiences direct benefits from standardization is supply. Increased profits are realized when all production facilities can be organized into one logistics system for supplies. This single system would detail the activities between suppliers, facilities, consumers, and the corresponding requirements for raw materials and inventory (parts and finished products). In addition, with production processes standardized, machinery and parts necessary for the process would also be standardized, allowing for interchangeable parts and machinery.

The option of using a production rationalization strategy is available if a company chooses to standardize product offerings, even if only regionally. Under rationalization, a subsidiary changes its purpose for production from manufacturing for its own market to manufacturing a limited number of component parts for use by several or all subsidiaries. This strategy has the advantage of production and engineering economies of scale and allows for higher-volume production with lower production costs than if the subsidiary manufactured for only end-product sales in its local market.

Control

Control is also affected by worldwide standardization. When all manufacturing facilities are expected to adhere to the same standards, quality control is easier to monitor, with quicker response to variances in quality control reports. Similarly, while human and physical factors will affect production and maintenance standards, machinery will be expected to produce at the same rate of output and with the same frequency of maintenance service. It will be possible to schedule maintenance of equipment based upon historical records of similar equipment to avoid costly unexpected breakdowns.

Planning and design of production facilities under standardization strategies are also simpler and quicker to complete. Donald A. Ball and Wendell H. McCulloch, Jr. list five steps in the process for planning a new plant based on a standardized system[1]:

---

[1] Ball and McCulloch 1988.

1. Design engineers need only copy the drawings and lists of materials that they have in their files.
2. Vendors will be requested to furnish equipment that they have supplied previously.
3. The technical department can send the current manufacturing specifications without alteration.
4. Labor trainers experienced in the operation of machinery can be sent to the new location without undergoing specialized training on new equipment.
5. Reasonably accurate forecasts of plant erection time and output can be made based on the experience with existing facilities.

With all of the advantages, it would appear that MNCs would strive for standardization, but environmental forces affect host nation operations, resulting in a variety of sizes, equipment, and procedures for plant operations of the same company. In addition to the environmental forces, the plant designer must consider economic, cultural, and political forces that may limit or at least affect direct alternatives.

Designing the Local Production System

The local production system will be somewhat reflective of the parent organization. For example, a foreign subsidiary is usually a smaller version of the parent company and will have a similar organizational structure. If a parent company is structured according to functional divisions, for example, the foreign subsidiary will also be organized by functional departments. Furthermore, because the local production system is most likely to be smaller than the parent company, it will not be integrated vertically or horizontally. Because of the increased investment necessary for vertical integration, it is often only conducted to the extent necessary to obtain scarce raw materials. Also, countries such as Mexico require foreign manufacturers to purchase inputs from local suppliers and legally restricts vertical integration. As for horizontal in-

tegration, the subsidiary is unlikely to expand in such a way because it often becomes a conglomerate in its own right.

There are four elements in the design of a production system—plant location, plant layout, materials handling, and staffing. These elements, while directly applicable to the production of tangible goods, can also be applied to the design of a system for the production of services.

Plant Location

Factors affecting plant location include government incentives, land and labor costs, location of competition, employee preference, location of suppliers and infrastructure (such as ports), and conditions imposed by local authorities. Which particular factors will be most important will depend to a great extent on the type of investment, such as market-seeking, labor-efficiency, or extraction mining. Because production and distribution costs are often in conflict, a plant designer often must choose between locating away from a major city because of government incentives and lower land and labor costs or locating near an urban center because of the availability of skilled labor, access to consumer markets, and a better infrastructure to support transportation (see Perspective 21–1).

Table 21–1 shows the overall survey results by country of a study conducted by Kinnear Consulting Ltd. The purpose of the survey was to provide a guide for potential investors, by ranking the countries in the EEC as locations for new manufacturing industry according to political situation, economic situation, labor situation, and investment incentives. Ireland was found to be the most attractive site for new overseas investment, primarily because of attractive investment incentives, trouble-free industrial relations, and a promising economic outlook.

Plant Layout

Plant layout should be determined before the construction of buildings. The plant will not only need to accommodate current production needs

PERSPECTIVE 21–1   Japanese Manufacturers Step Up Moves to Locate Production Plants in Britain

LONDON—Japanese manufacturers' race to become European insiders is quickening their invasion of Britain.

Today, Fujitsu Ltd. will announce its choice of Britain for its first semiconductor production plant in Europe. Toyota Motor Corp., Japan's biggest car maker, yesterday confirmed it has picked a British site for its first European auto factory, a $1 billion facility that will be able to produce 200,000 cars a year starting in 1992.

Canon Inc., which already makes copiers in three European nations, is expected to announce plans soon for a facility in Britain. And Toshiba Corp., considering a semiconductor plant in Europe, favors Britain as a site, industry officials say.

Britain's low labor costs, booming economy and friendly political climate, plus Japanese executives' widespread familiarity with English, long have lured manufacturers from Japan. Now, Japanese companies consider the United Kingdom an important beachhead in their scramble to get inside Europe's walls and avoid a new wave of protectionism. The Japanese fear Europe will erect higher barriers against imports when the European Community lowers internal barriers by 1992.

SUPPLIERS FOLLOW CUSTOMERS

About 392 big Japanese producers have opened facilities or announced plans for plants in Europe, with 92, or about 23%, locating in Britain. The British share of Japanese plants, which was 16% in 1983, may reach 29% by 1992, says Toshiaki Kitamura, commercial counsellor for the Japanese Embassy in London.

Japanese manufacturers also are picking their British sites faster. In Scotland, where Japanese companies have put up 16 plants, some have

cut their typical search time to two years from three. The fastest decisions seem to be made by Japanese suppliers, who tend "to come right behind" their fellow manufacturers, said Howard Moody, marketing director for the Scottish Development Agency in Glasgow.

Silicon-wafer producer Shin-Etsu Handotai opened an £8 million plant in Livingston, Scotland this week that claims to be the first raw-silicon facility outside Japan. Shin-Etsu Handotai will supply semiconductor makers; the electronics industry has attracted the largest number of Japanese manufacturers to Britain.

Similarly, in an apparent effort to supply Britain's burgeoning Japanese auto makers, Mitsui & Co. struck a deal in late February that gave Japan its first toehold in the British steel industry. Mitsui, a big Japanese trading house, set up a joint venture with William King Ltd., a West Bromwich, England steel processor. The venture will operate a processing plant in Washington, England, near a Nissan Motor Co. factory where Europe's biggest Japanese auto maker began assembling cars in 1986.

OFFICIAL WELCOME

Nissan received £125 million in state aid to construct its £600 million facility. That is typical of the incentives Britain has used to court Japanese manufacturers and land new jobs. But increased EC resistance to such aid means Britain won't be able to dispense the largesse so readily. "That could remove the edge of some of Britain's current advantages," says George Bull, director of the Anglo-Japanese Economic Institute, a London promotional group funded by Japan's Foreign Office.

SOURCE: Joann S. Lublin, *Wall Street Journal*, April 12, 1989, page A11.

However, the strong yen and Japanese manufacturers' healthy profits mean they may not miss the loss of subsidies.

Britain's outspoken advocacy for current Japanese manufacturers also plays a significant role in wooing others. For example, the British government is embroiled in a flap with France over Bluebird cars made in Britain by Nissan. France threatened to count the cars against its 3% Japanese import ceiling until 80% of their content is European made. Britain, carrying the banner for Nissan, last month again demanded that the EC force France to treat the cars as British.

"From watching the Nissan affair," Japanese executives see "that the U.K. government can be

very credible and very supportive to Japanese manufacturers," says Mr. Kitamura of the Japanese Embassy. "That is very important."

But British manufacturers are increasingly unhappy about the competitive threat posed by the mounting invasion from Japan. Reflecting such worries, some are fighting to keep a half-dozen Japanese electronics makers from joining the Electronic Engineering Association, a British trade group.

Howard Pye, an association spokesman, expresses hope the dispute will end soon. "It's a double-edged sword," he says. "We want them [Japanese] in, don't we? But are they going to take over? That's the question."

for maximum utilization and return on investment, but also must include possibilities for future expansion. Accurate forecasts become crucial in terms of estimating future plant requirements, but plant layout may also be dictated occasionally by acquisition of an existing building.

TABLE 21-1
EEC Countries Ranked as Locations for Manufacturing

Country	Rank	Total Points
Ireland	1	118
Greece	2	92
Italy	3	77.5
France	4	75.5
W. Germany	5	71.5
Netherlands	6	66.5
Belgium	7	64
U.K.	8	58.5
Denmark	9	55.5
Luxemborg	10	36

SOURCE: Kinnear Consulting Ltd. 1988. "Where are the Best Manufacturing Locations in the European Community?," Grant Thornton International.

Materials Handling

Management may be able to achieve considerable production costs savings by careful planning for materials handling. Materials handling includes obtaining necessary inputs and maintaining appropriate inventories. If materials handling is inefficient, management may find surplus parts inventories at some sites, while other sites are shut down because of a lack of parts. The logistics of the production system, or coordination of the movements and storage of inputs and outputs, are an intricate part of the materials handling function. The objectives of the logistics system of MNCs is to minimize costs, secure supplies, and satisfy demand. For the ethnocentric MNC, logistics are confined to exporting with the least cost and in the least amount of time. Polycentric MNCs, on the other hand, have a tendency to deemphasize logistics. The foreign subsidiary of such an MNC may not have rapid response to the introduction of new products by competitors or to excess demand or production stockouts. The geocentric MNC will most likely maintain a separate logistics department that coordinates the activities between the markets, production location, and suppliers of its many subsidiaries (see Perspective 21–2).

PERSPECTIVE 21-2   Global Manufacturing Is an Intricate Game

Gerrit Jeelof, one of the ranking officers of Holland's Philips group, has some rueful words about wildly fluctuating currency-exchange rates.

Speaking at the University of Oregon Graduate School of Management last month, he said: "There is a joke about buying a huge ship, equipping it with CAD-CAM automated production capability and dropping anchor on the shore of whatever country at the moment offers the best currency-exchange opportunity."

For Philips, the joke isn't funny. When the company translated its world-wide sales to Dutch guilders last year, a nominal 7% rise became a 2% decline, mainly because of the U.S. dollar's sharp drop. The exchange conversion and the effects of the soft dollar on Philips's competitive position brought about a 19% slump in net income from 1986.

Given the modern marvels of CAD (computer aided design) and CAM (computer aided manufacturing) a floating factory is not as far-fetched as it might sound. Such equipment has made labor content a relatively small part—often well under 10%—of light manufacturing, particularly in electronics. Plant siting priorities now focus less on cheap labor and more on proximity to markets since many components buyers want deliveries to flow right into their own production streams. Keeping up with technology and getting maximum use of capital equipment are other priorities. As to anticipating exchange rates, that is next to impossible.

Philips's production already is "floating" in a sense as the company seeks more efficient logistics. Since 1985, it has moved output of 14-inch TV sets from the U.S. across the Pacific to Tai-

wan and then back again to Juarez, Mexico. It has found that it is once again cheaper to make some products for the European market in Bruges, Belgium, than in Singapore.

In other words, you have to be agile, as Mr. Jeelof's own recent experience attests. He is vice chairman of the board of management of the parent company, N.V. Philips Gloeilampenfabrieken of Eindhoven, the Netherlands. Two months ago, he also became chairman and chief executive of North American Philips Corp., which became a wholly owned subsidiary last year when Philips bought the 42% interest that had been publicly owned. Since then, he has divided his time about equally between New York and Eindhoven.

Mr. Jeelof believes that his having one foot on each continent furthers Philips's goal of making itself into a truly global company. "It's so useful sitting at the top of the organization in Holland to get this direct input from the U.S. market, the U.S. environment, the U.S. way of thinking."

In one sense, Philips has been "global" for many years. Its light bulbs, for example, are in stores throughout the world. But, says Mr. Jeelof, "we were a federation of national organizations. We had organizations in 60 countries. You have to take away some of the autonomy of the national organizations. We are now running the business much more based on the accountability of the product divisions.

"The minimum step is to go for three major regions, Europe, North America and the Far East. That's why we put a lot of emphasis in the U.S. because that is 40% of the world market in many products, plus the fact that I believe that the connection between the U.S. and Japan is very im-

SOURCE: George Melloan, *Wall Street Journal*, November 29, 1988, page A23.

portant. When the Japanese develop new products it is always with the U.S. market in mind. There is a great deal of pressure from the Japanese side for some kind of free-trade arrangement with the U.S. Whether it will ever happen I don't know, but if it does, the U.S. becomes even more important to us.

"I believe that you should try to get your resources in these three major blocs in the world very much in proportion to the activities you have there. You must become much more a part of the environment and behave as if you were a national company." The U.S. now accounts for 30% of Philips's $26 billion world-wide sales, up sharply from under 3% a decade ago. It employs more than 50,000 people in the U.S., which makes it one of the largest foreign-owned operations. Magnavox, Sylvania, Philco, Norelco and Selmer (musical instruments) are among Philips brands familiar to Americans.

Only with a global market can a company afford the large development costs necessary to keep up with advancing technology, Mr. Jeelof says. He notes, for example, that the old pre-1950s telecommunications switching systems cost about $10 million to develop and had a useful life of about 25 years. "In the 1980s, when the first digital systems were developed, costs had risen to $1 billion for a life expectancy of eight to 12 years. Calculations tell us that digital development costs of $1 billion require roughly 8% of the world market share just to recover costs." No single market in Europe, including West Germany, can deliver more than 6%. So either you sell globally or you don't play.

Two problems, exchange rates and product standards, confront the global company. Philips regards currency-exchange swings as a source of economic inefficiency, not unlike trade barriers. The company's chief executive, C.J. van der Klugt, has been a foremost advocate of European monetary integration as a start toward a more stable world monetary system. He, along with a good many other European CEOs, would welcome a European currency and a European central bank. Philips, to make a point, has a table in its 1987 annual report reporting results in European Currency Units (ECUs), even though ECUs at this stage are nothing more than a central bank unit of account.

Standardization has become highly important in electronics because so many electronics products today must "interface" with items made by other firms. "When we came out with our compact disk we decided right away we had to go for a world standard," says Mr. Jeelof. "The stand-alone character of many electronic products is disappearing. It is always interfaced with something, either with software, or the program, or the network. You can't just bring out something on its own. It always has to fit in somewhere, so the need for a standard is absolutely necessary. We've seen it in computers and of course consumer electronics."

One of the most promising global products for the years ahead is high definition TV (HDTV), which gives TV pictures movie quality. There's a large standardization effort, says Mr. Jeelof, but it is hard to standardize both the TV sets and broadcasting equipment. "In Japan and Europe that's fairly easy because broadcasting is government owned. But in the U.S. it's private, and they have big fights with the cable people. That makes it so difficult to come to one world standard. The Japanese are willing to go very far, to a standard that makes everything obsolete. That you can do that in Japan because in Japan consumerism is not that well developed. But you have to forget about the United States because if you came out with a standard that made everything obsolete you would have people screaming."

Global manufacturers scream, too, of course, about the obsolescence of factories brought about overnight by currency swings. Since the floating factory is probably some years away, maybe their best bet is to scream a little louder and hope that monetary policy makers of the major industrial nations will pay them heed.

Staffing

The labor element is often overlooked in the design of a production system. The human factor, however, can be the key to the success of a production plant. Because temperature, lighting, noise level, and aesthetics in a plant can affect the productivity of workers, an evaluation is needed of these aspects of the work environment and their respective impact on workers. Decisions made in this regard are typically a function of host country norms.

Production Management

There are two categories of activities inherent to production, productive activities and supportive activities. In terms of productive activities, given a period of introduction and orientation, managers of the productive activities expect the system to operate at a sufficient and prescribed level of output in order to meet demand (see Table 21–2). If the system fails to produce at such levels, managers, including the line organization, must determine where or what the impediment is and how to correct it. Potential obstacles with which management must work are low output, inferior product quality, and excessive manufacturing costs.

Productive Activities

First, management must verify supplies of raw materials. In addition to poor quality, the failure of vendors to meet delivery dates or to supply materials according to specifications may cause disruptions in the production process. Although this is a problem in both developing and industrialized countries, it is often more common in the developing countries, where the raw materials supply is a seller's market. When such a problem is identified, it is the responsibility of the purchasing department to educate suppliers, notifying them of exact standards and delivery date requirements and providing technical assistance when needed. It is necessary often to pay a higher price to obtain better service.

In addition to problems with outputs to the production system, management may find scheduling problems within the system itself. In a system of sequential steps, for example, poor scheduling will result in bottlenecks and excessive inventories in some areas and work stoppages because of a lack of work in others. If back orders are a problem, a company may be running many short runs to fill these orders, thereby perpetuating the problem. This situation has been found to be an even greater predicament in many cultures where long-term planning is frowned upon culturally or socially. To rectify the situation, management may incorporate additional training for the scheduling staff, which includes stressing the importance of their work, providing additional supervision, or encouraging more cooperation between the marketing and production departments to avoid a back-order problem.

High absenteeism also may contribute to a low-output problem. In many developing countries, production workers are often called away from work to assist in seasonal family business, such as helping with the harvest. Furthermore, where transportation systems are inadequate, it may be very difficult for workers to commute; management may need to organize its own transportation for workers. In addition, where absenteeism is caused by sickness, management may choose to provide in-house lunch programs to provide better nutrition, which, besides reducing the instances of absenteeism because of illness, also reduces the risk of work injuries. In a situation where absenteeism is a result of low morale, management must again evaluate cultural factors. While some international production managers accept high absenteeism and low productivity as problems inherent in the foreign environment, others have found solutions to these problems by utilizing the same techniques found at home with modifications for their local environment.

Another obstacle to maintaining production standards designed for the foreign production system is that of inferior product quality. Because quality is relative to the standards of a particular environment, it may be impossible to meet standards set up by home office managers. The marketing staff should evaluate the quality standards demanded by the market and then set the price-quality combination that reflects this demand, which would also include quality standards for inputs of raw materials. When a home office is concerned about global reputation for its name-brand quality standards, it may be possible for the foreign subsidiary to produce under a different name.

Excessive manufacturing costs will affect the ability of production management to meet the prescribed standards for the system. Anything that is of significant variance from the projected budget is of concern. Again, low output may be the culprit, perhaps the budget assumptions were completely out of line with the market, or poor inventory control of inputs and finished products may exist (imported supplies may be necessary because of the uncertainty or quality of supplies in the local market).

Supportive Activities

Supportive activities include quality control, inventory control, purchasing, maintenance, and technical functions.

Production depends on the purchasing department obtaining raw materials, component parts, supplies, and machinery to produce a finished product. If a firm is unable to obtain these things, the production facility may experience costly shutdowns and lost sales. If such inputs are obtained at a higher cost than that paid by a competitor, a company must either charge more for its finished products or price competitively and realize a smaller profit. Purchasing agents must search for suppliers that will provide quality inputs and reliable service at the lowest possible price. If the quality of raw materials is low, the quality of the finished product will also be low.

Purchasers must be able to locate vendors and, if necessary, be familiar with the process and players associated with importing. A company that is establishing a production facility in another country must decide between hiring purchasing staff from the home country or within the host country. While natives have knowledge and acquaintance advantages, they may be susceptible to cultural influences, such as favoring family or extended family members for sourcing supplies.

In order to prevent unexpected work stoppages caused by equipment failures, maintenance must be conducted on buildings and equipment. While preventive maintenance will help to avoid unexpected breakdowns, many less-developed countries are subject to the cultural influences that often cause the attitude, "Why fix it if it isn't broken?" In addition, the maintenance team is under pressure from marketing and production to keep the machinery running constantly, which perpetuates a short-term view of the maintenance role.

The local environment may necessitate more frequent maintenance than that mandated by headquarters. Temperature and climate and the handling of equipment by locals may cause unforseen wear and tear not experienced in the home production plant.

The last element of the supportive function is technical assistance. The technical assistance staff is responsible for providing production with manufacturing specifications and for checking the quality of the inputs and the finished products. Often, the technical staff must find substitutes for hard-to-find raw materials or may be required to visit suppliers to educate or train them so that they can meet requirements and delivery dates.

Just-in-Time System

While some have argued that the Japanese advantage exists because of culture (societal and corporate), quality circles, lifetime employment, or other sociocultural factors, more and more experts are identifying the abilities of Japanese companies to manage effectively as the key to their success. Some have stated that the Japanese advantage in production costs and product quality stems from the superior organization and administration of their production.[2]

[2] Rugman, Lecraw, and Booth 1985.

TABLE 21-2
The "Stateless" World of Manufacturing

This is a sampling of manufacturing companies with a minimum $3 billion in annual sales that derive at least 40% of those sales from countries other than their home country. It does not include state-owned companies or holding companies.

Company	Home country	1989 Total Sales in Billions	Sales outside home country	Assets outside home country	Shares held outside home country	Management approach
Nestlé	Switzerland	$32.9*	98.0%	95.0%	Few	CEO is German. Has 10 general managers, of whom five are not Swiss
Sandoz	Switzerland	8.6*	96.0	94.0	5.0%	All Swiss at top, more conservative in style than other Swiss companies
SKF	Sweden	4.1	96.0	90.0	20.0	Foreigners have cracked board and top management group
Hoffmann-La Roche	Switzerland	6.7*	96.0	60.0	0.0	All-Swiss board, but next level of managers mixed
Philips	Netherlands	30.0	94.0	85.0*	46.0	Solidly Dutch company, but number of senior foreign managers is increasing
SmithKline Beecham	Britain	7.0	89.0	75.0	46.0	Joint U.S.-British management at all levels
ABB	Sweden	20.6	85.0*	NA	50.0	Moved headquarters to Switzerland; managers are Swedish, Swiss, German
Electrolux	Sweden	13.8	83.0	80.0	20.0	Of 50 top managers outside Sweden, only five are Swedish
Volvo	Sweden	14.8	80.0	30.0	10.0	Solidly Swedish at all top management levels
ICI	Britain	22.1	78.0	50.0	16.0	40% of top 170 executives are not British; top ranks include four other nationalities
Michelin	France	9.4	78.0	NA	0.0	Secretive, centralized, with top management almost entirely French
Hoechst	W. Germany	27.3	77.0	NA	42.0	No foreigners on board, but most foreign operations are run by locals
Unilever	Britain/Neth.	35.3	75.0*	70.0*	27.0	Five nationalities on board, thoroughly stateless management
Air Liquide	France	5.0	70.0	66.0	6.0	English is official language, but it considers itself thoroughly French
Canon	Japan	9.4	69.0	32.0	14.0	Foreigners run many sales subsidiaries, but none in top ranks
Northern Telecom	Canada	6.1	67.1	70.5	16.0	Thoroughly Canadian, but has assumed U.S. identity
Sony	Japan	16.3	66.0	NA	13.6	Only major Japanese manufacturer with foreigners on board
Bayer	W. Germany	25.8	65.4	NA	48.0	No foreigners on board, but six of 25 business groups run by foreigners
BASF	W. Germany	13.3	65.0	NA	NA	Relies on local managers to run foreign operations, but none in top ranks
Gillette	U.S.	38	65.0	63.0	10.0*	Three foreigners among top 21 officers

Company	Country					Comments
Colgate	U.S.	5.0	47.0	64.0	10.0*	CEO, other top execs have had several foreign posts; many multilingual
Honda	Japan	26.4	35.7	63.0	6.9	Foreigners running offshore plants, but none at top levels at home
Daimler Benz	W. Germany	45.5	NA	61.0	25.0*	Similar to other German giants
IBM	U.S.	62.7	NA	59.0	NA	Relies on locals to manage non-U.S. operations; increasing number of foreigners in top ranks
NCR	U.S.	6.0	40.5	58.9	NA	Nationals run foreign operations, but none in top ranks
CPC International	U.S.	5.1	62.0	56.0	5.0*	One third of officers are foreign nationals
Coca-Cola	U.S.	9.0	45.0	54.0	0.0	Thoroughly multinational management group making big international push
Digital	U.S.	12.7	44.0	54.0	NA	Five of top 37 officers are foreign; most foreign operations run by locals
Dow Chemical	U.S.	17.6	45.0	54.0	5.0	Out of top 25 managers, 20 have experience outside U.S.
Saint-Gobain	France	11.6	50.0	54.0	13.0	Of 25 top managers, only two are not French
Xerox	U.S.	12.4	51.8	54.0	0.0	Major joint ventures with Rank, Fuji have shaped top management thinking
Caterpillar	U.S.	11.1	NA	53.0	NA	Of top five executives, four have foreign experience, including CEO-elect
Hewlett-Packard	U.S.	11.9	38.6	53.0	8.0	Five of top 25 officers not U.S. citizens; many units managed offshore
Siemens	W. Germany	36.3	NA	51.0	44.0	Some business groups managed from outside Germany by non-Germans but none on management board
Corning	U.S.	3.1*	45.0*	50.0*	NA	Company is leader in use of joint ventures to penetrate markets
Johnson & Johnson	U.S.	9.8	48.0	50.0	NA	First foreign national on board in 1989; senior managers include foreign-born
United Technologies	U.S.	19.8	26.7	49.7	NA	Because of U.S. defense business, few foreigners at top
UNISYS	U.S.	10.1	31.0	49.0	10.0	Aside from Japanese joint venture, management is largely American
MERCK	U.S.	6.0	NA	47.0	NA	Top management is American, but foreign nationals run overseas operations
Nissan	Japan	36.5	20.0	47.0	2.9	Foreign operations managed by locals; completely Japanese at headquarters
3M	U.S.	12.0	42.0	46.0	15.0	CEO pushing to raise foreign sales to 50% of total by 1992
Du Pont	U.S.	35.5	20.0	44.0	24.0	Has two foreign directors, both Canadians, but top management is heavily American
Matsushita	Japan	41.7	NA	42.0	7.0	American named No. 2 for North America, but no foreigners in top ranks
Heinz	U.S.	6.0	41.0	40.0	0.6	CEO is Irish citizen, management thoroughly mixed
P&G	U.S.	21.4	32.0	40.0	NA	International operations chief recently named CEO

SOURCE: *Business Week*, May 14, 1990, page 103.
NA = Not available
Data: Company reports
* BW Estimates

One such element of superior organization and administration that is now being implemented in many American and European companies' production systems is the *kanban* or just-in-time (JIT) inventory system. JIT requires that externally sourced inputs never arrive at the production plant before they are needed. Parts arrive exactly when they are needed, suppliers know the production schedule, and parts arrive from suppliers several times a day. Although JIT schedules are frozen for a certain period, the system is still fairly flexible.[3] There are many benefits to such a system when it is carefully implemented, primarily because many costs are reduced as the work-in-process inventory and warehousing space requirements are greatly reduced. JIT works toward zero inventories, reducing warehousing, handling, and financing costs and time for tracking stocks and movements. Companies using JIT perceive buffer stocks as a hidden inefficiency that only adds costs to production.[4]

International Technology

An integral part of any production system is the technology used in the manufacturing process. Technology also may be separate from the production system itself in the form of the end product or finished good. After World War II, government officials and experts believed that increasing capital inputs was the key to rapid economic growth, but the basis for this belief weakened, as capital became more accessible and developments were not always successful. The importance of technology for stimulating expansion then became more important, and technology transfer became an issue in world economies. As a result, developing, exploiting, and maintaining technological advantages became crucial issues for MNCs.

The question for an MNC and for a government official is "How will we obtain the desired technology?" Often the choice for a firm is either

through its own research and development efforts or by acquisition from another firm. For the government of a developing country, on the other hand, the choice is more limited. The technology usually must be transferred from sources other than those within the country. Within industrialized countries, the main focus is the protection of technology and the creation of new technologies. LDCs, however, must be concerned with the opposite—restrictions on transfers, royalty limitations, lack of patent protection, and other legal constraints. For LDCs international firms are responsible for a large share of technology transfers, but there are also noncommercial organizations that provide international transfers, such as development programs funded by other industrialized nations.

Definition of Technology

Technology has been defined as a perishable source comprising knowledge, skills, and means for using and controlling factors of production for the purpose of producing, delivering to users, and maintaining goods and services for which there is no economic and/or social demand.[5]

There are several elements of technology that can be used for classification purposes. First, there are three types of technology—product technology, which is knowledge used to make a product; process technology, which is knowledge used in the process of making a product, including the organizing of the inputs of machinery and equipment necessary for the production process; and management technology, which is knowledge used in running the business, including managerial skills that make the firm competitive.

A second level of classification within technology concerns the particular characteristics of the technology. These include hard/soft technology, proprietary/nonproprietary technology, front end/obsolete technology and bundled/unbundled technology. Hard technology includes the physical hardware, capital goods, blueprints and specifica-

---

[3] Hall 1983.
[4] Rugman 1985.

[5] Robock and Simmonds 1983.

tions, and knowledge necessary to use the hardware, while soft technology encompasses the management, marketing, financial organization, and administrative techniques that can be combined with the hard technology to serve the needs of the user. Technology that is owned or controlled by an individual or organization is proprietary and may be either controlled as a trade secret or patented. An example of proprietary technology that is controlled as a trade secret is the formula developed by the Coca-Cola Company for the production of its soft drink of the same name. Nonproprietary technology is knowledge found in technical literature, hardware, and services that may be copied without infringing on proprietary rights. This reproduction often is achievable through reverse engineering, where the technology is broken down to learn how it was created. State-of-the-art technology is considered front-end, while old technology is termed obsolete. Bundled technology is another aspect of controlled technology, where the owner is only willing to transfer it as part of a package or system. Unbundled technology is available separate from the total system of technology of the supplier.

Technology Development

There are three stages of technology development. Invention is the first stage. At this level, new knowledge is created that may be applied to business or industry. The next step is innovation, where the new knowledge is introduced into the marketplace. It is not uncommon for a technology to complete the first stage and not reach the second or third stages. In fact, most inventions never reach the innovation stage. If they do, the next step is diffusion, or the spread of the new knowledge throughout the marketplace. Computer technology is well into the diffusion phase, but with developments in superconductivity, this industry is experiencing new invention and innovation stages, and diffusion is well underway in some other high-tech industries.

A technology advantage is one held by a firm whose employees possess a superior business knowledge (product, process, or management) that is not held by other firms. In the interest of maintaining this advantage, a firm may seek to protect their proprietary possession of the technology, usually through patents. It is necessary for firms to continually develop new technology to perpetuate their advantages, because most patents are of limited duration.

Research and development is the prime source of a company's technology advantage. An MNC will find pressure from a host country to combine research and development facilities with production facilities. One motivation for establishing research and development in a foreign country is that such facilities can aid in the transfer of technology by making easier product and process modifications for local markets and by strengthening the competitive stance of a subsidiary by offering local technical assistance to purchasers. Foreign research and development sites also allow subsidiaries to develop products in accordance with local market needs and to identify those needs that differ from the perception of the home country. Local knowledge and skills can also be a benefit that is derived from locating the research and development abroad. Before a company can complete its decision to locate a research and development function in a host country, an evaluation must be made of host government controls and incentives. The ultimate question is whether or not such controls or incentives justify the economics of a research unit, in light of the availability of adequate universities, infrastructure, and local supply of technical skills.

Technology Transfer

Technology transfer is the process by which knowledge is diffused through learning from its place of origin and introduction to other world markets. Depending on the characteristics of the technology to be transferred, the time and expense involved will vary, and the choice of transfer method must incorporate such factors as the nature of the technology, the capabilities and objectives of the parties involved, and the elements of the sociocultural environment that enable the recipient country to assimilate and synthesize the technology. The transfer process also has distinct phases, from planning and product and facility design to personnel training, engineering for quality control, and technical support for local suppliers.

The transfer of technology may take place through market transactions, which creates issues for both governments and for international managers. Host governments are concerned with obtaining up-to-date technology at low cost from MNCs, while companies are interested in protecting and realizing benefits from their technology.

Noncommercial ways of transferring technology usually involve foreign study in university programs, which enable foreign nationals to acquire knowledge and then bring the knowledge back to their own country. There are also government-to-government agreements for technology transfers. Some examples are development aid programs for infrastructure, nuclear energy programs, and space research programs. Commercial methods for transferring technology are more varied, including foreign direct investment, turnkey projects, trade in goods and services, contracts and agreements, research and development programs located in foreign countries or through joint research efforts, migration of trained personnel or employment of local nationals by foreign firms, international tender offers, and industrial espionage.

In general, strategies for conducting technology transfers and exploiting technology advantages fall within two broad categories. Which strategy the firm chooses is determined by the type of business and the type of technology. The first type of strategy involves extending the firm's own operation, which is known as internalizing. Internalizing requires a company to utilize foreign subsidiaries and affiliates in different markets to sell its products or services in local markets. In smaller markets, a company trying to internalize will attempt to meet demand through exports. This approach is best when:

- The firm makes new products that are not easily copied by others.

- Outside firms also use the technology and serve part of the market, because economies of scale the firm achieves on products would be lost.
- The firm depends greatly on the sale of the product or service that uses the technology.
- The firm is so small that it does not have the personnel to both use the technology internally and sell it to outsiders, or the firm is so large that it can easily exploit the technology through its own affiliates.
- The technology is more important to the firm than to potential buyers of the technology.
- The technology is costly to transfer from one firm to another.[6]

This strategy is the same approach as for finding and exploiting other sources of competitive advantages, but another approach the firm might choose is that of externalizing. Using external markets has become increasingly important in light of the current wave of restrictions imposed by foreign governments on direct investment. Through this strategy, a company would contract with other firms to sell the technology itself, rather than sell the final product that results from such technology. Such contracts may be in the form of licensing agreements or management contracts.

There are two approaches, in particular, that have become more common external market strategies—turnkey projects and licensing. Turnkey projects are contracted projects that encompass all elements of the project, usually including training. When the project is completed, the contractor turns the entire system over to the purchaser. A popular strategy in such industries as chemicals, petrochemicals, and petroleum refining, this method often includes an equity position for the contractor, which enables the firm to reap the benefits of their technology over a longer period of time.

The other external market strategy that has increased in practice is licensing. Table 21–3 explains the appropriate situations in which licensing would be considered the best strategy. For

---

[6] Grosse and Kujawa 1988.

small companies that have inadequate capital or management expertise for international expansion via foreign direct investment, licensing is an advantageous option. There are, however, several arguments against using licensing. The strongest argument is that a licensor may lose its competitive advantage to a licensee over time and, in the process, be prohibited from future direct investment in the market served by the licensee. On the other hand, if the licensor is a participant in the foreign venture, there is an infusion of protection against such an event. Furthermore, trademarks can be utilized as part of the licensing agreement, because trademarks remain the property of the licensor in perpetuity despite the fact that the license is for a limited time only.

In general, externalizing is best when:

- The firm's products are not central to the ability to survive in competition.
- The firm's greater skill is in creating the technology than in producing and marketing the final products.
- The firm's financial and personnel capabilities make it desirable to let another firm use the technology.
- The firm cannot protect its technology with a patent, and it could lose the benefits of that technology unless it is compensated for the technology's use by rival firms.
- The firm's technology is not costly to transfer between firms.[7]

Choice of Production Technology

Once a company has decided to internalize, it often obtains its competitive advantage through overseas production facilities, and a company must determine the choice of technology to implement in such plants. This issue becomes particularly controversial in developing countries, where many government officials are concerned that technology transferred by foreign firms for local produc-

tion be appropriate to the resources of the country and not necessarily the same technology that is used in capital-rich countries with large markets or the home country of the foreign firm. In most instances, this results in pressure from host governments to establish smaller, more labor-intensive facilities. In other situations, however, host country policies may invite capital-intensive production technologies in order to obtain state-of-the-art systems.

Before the choice is made, a firm must consider the availability of production technology alternatives that are, in reality, commercially feasible for operation. In some industries, this may mean many more options than for others, depending on the nature of the product. Cost and availability of information concerning specific technologies also will impact the decision. It is much easier to obtain information regarding capital-intensive equipment because information and technology flows are more likely to be from industrialized countries to developing countries than between developing countries.

Market sizes, which vary from one country to the next, also influence the plant design choice. Capital-intensive technology incorporates automated, high-output machinery, but it is often severely limited in flexibility regarding the production and size range of products. A capital-intensive system can produce in a few days what may be a year's supply in some markets. For these smaller markets, the design choice may be to install only one machine. Unfortunately, in some cases, the capacity of one such machine would still greatly overproduce for the demand in a particular market. Labor-intensive technology, on the other hand, employs more people and incorporates semi-automated general-purpose equipment with lower productive capacity.[8]

Labor and capital intensity are not the only contributing factors to the technology decision. The decision must include quality control maintenance, waste minimization, response time to market demand fluctuations, training costs, labor rela-

---

[7] Grosse and Kujawa 1988.

[8] Wells 1974.

TABLE 21-3
Licensing as a Preferred Strategy under Following Circumstances

Strategic Concept	Conditions	Empirical Support/Studies
1. Product Cycle Standardization	—Obsolescing products considered for licensing —Imminent technology or model change —Increasing competition in product market	Stobaugh(1971), Telesio(1977), Contractor(1980)
2. Environmental Constraints on FDI or FDI income	—Government regulations restricting FDI to selected sectors only —High political risk in nation —Market uncertain or volatile, licensor lacking in requisite marketing abilities, or market too small for FDI.	UN(1978), Ozawa(1979), UN(1977), Hayden(1976), Sagasti(1979)
3. Constraints on imports into license nation	—A high ratio for transport cost to value for item —Tariff or non-tariff barriers	Dunning(1980), Contractor(1981)
4. Licensor firm size	—Licensor firm too small to have financial, managerial or marketing expertise for overseas investment —Licensor firm too big (see 12 below)	Telesio(1977)
5. Research intensity	—Licensor firm will remain technologically superior, so as to discount licensee competition in other markets	Hayden(1976), Telesio(1977), Baranson(1978)
6. High rate of technological turnover	—Change so rapid, and technologies so perishable (e.g., semi-conductors) that even with equally proficient licensees, a design or a patent may be transferred with little fear of significant competition.	Contractor(1981)

554

7. Perpetuation of licensee dependency	— Even without or beyond the licensing agreement, effective licensee dependency maintained by trademarks, required components or licensee hunger for technical improvements.	Davies(1977), UN(1975), Lall(1976)
8. Product vs Process Technologies	— Licensing opportunities is auxiliary processes (e.g., galvanizing in the steel industry, or anodizing aluminum) even if the basic product technologies not licensed.	Teece(1977), Contractor(1981)
9. Reciprocal exchanges of technology	— Licensing as a valuable tool for obtaining tehnology of market rights, in industries characterized by high R & D and market development costs and product diversity (e.g., Pharmaceuticals, Electricals, Chemicals).	Telesio(1977)
10. "Choosing" competition	— With a patent about to expire, licensing gives a head start to a licensee firm favored by present patent holder. (May be illegal in some countries.)	Contractor(1981)
11. Creation of auxiliary business	— Even if direct royalty income is inadequate, margins on components to or from licensee can be handsome (in the extreme, e.g., licensing automobile assemblers, licensing is tantamount in disguised imports). Other auxiliary business can be turnkey plants, joint bidding with licensee, etc.	Hayden(1976), Baranson(1978), Contractor(1981)
12. Diversification and product-line organization in licensor firm	— Especially in large diversified firms, with dimensional attention focused on the "product imperative", a centralized examination of the product/country matrix reveals neglected market penetration possibilities via licensing, (especially where considerable diversifcsation puts a constraint on the financial and managerial resources available for equity ventures overseas).	Contractor(1981), Telesio(1977)

SOURCE: F. Contractor, "The Role of Licensing," *Columbia Journal of World Business*, Winter 1981, page 76.

tions, and the image or prestige factor of front-end equipment.

Until recently it was thought that a choice between labor and capital intensity was the only available option. There is a third alternative that, because of its limited application, high costs, and high technological content, is only now becoming available in industrialized nations. Such technology would create a mix of labor and capital and is known as hybrid plant design. In addition, when faced with the need for a production design that incorporates both labor and capital requirements, there are the options of intermediate technology and appropriate technology. Hybrid designs also offer solutions to the problem of choosing between labor- and capital-intensive production technologies. These designs are geared toward obtaining a certain product quality, while ensuring a labor-intensive production method. In such a design, the production process includes both types of technology in distinct phases. Intermediate technology uses a combination throughout the process. It is not a question of using capital intensity in some steps of production and labor intensity in others, but it is the utilization of a less than fully automated process. In recent years, many LDCs have looked to intermediate technology as a means to create more jobs, use less capital, and still be able to produce the desired product quality. Although many governments are urging investors to implement intermediate technology, it is not easily accessed from industrial nations. Because this technology is currently being developed and created for developing nations, it is not available through transfers from MNCs in industrialized countries. Moreover, there may be higher start-up costs associated with intermediate technology implementation than can be justified by the savings in reduced capital costs.

Appropriate technology considers the optimum technological mix by matching a country's markets with its resources and ability to produce certain components. Unlike an approach that would use intermediate technology, the emphasis is on applying the technology that is most appropriate to the immediate economic, sociocultural, and political variables. This approach may range from the most primitive of production processes to high-tech systems and takes into consideration that with some products the superiority in productivity and quality of a modern process is so significant as to make labor-intensive methods completely inappropriate. It is often the government that must choose between the use of less capital-intensive technologies to save scarce capital resources and create new jobs and more capital-intensive methods that will provide less expensive products for its citizens.

Pricing Technology Transfers

Unlike most free-market transactions where market demand and supply determine price, there is relatively little information available regarding pricing of technology transfers. In most instances, negotiating parties do not have access to data regarding previous sales or transfers of technology for similar products or between similar parties. Furthermore, because technology transfers may include many different types of services and, therefore, payments, even if price information were available, it would be difficult to discern what products, services, and prices would be comparable to the technology transfer negotiations currently underway.

Pricing of technology in recent years has become a controversial issue, especially for developing countries. Host government intervention is common because it is commonly assumed that such transfers are overpriced to developing nations. Transfer pricing is also suspected when payments are made to parent companies by foreign affiliates.

Developing countries often see themselves in a vulnerable and weak negotiating position and assume that higher prices are set than for similar technology transfers between industrial countries. In addition, there is a common belief that technology is protected by a patent monopoly that enables a seller to set excessive monopoly prices. It is the opinion of the governments of these developing countries that the sunk costs of developing the technology have already been amortized over the home market sales, and international transfers do not need to compensate for much more than the incremental costs of the transfer.

To combat these fears of host governments, there has been an increasing exchange of information among national agencies that are trying to better prepare a host country for negotiations. In defense against the patent monopoly claim, it is argued that this point confuses the concept of a patent as a monopoly with monopoly power in the marketplace. Despite the fact that the technology is patented, it still faces competition in the market from substitute technology. Furthermore, the claim that development costs have already been amortized does not consider the fact that several industrialized countries, including the United States, have tax agencies that instruct that such costs should be shared by all users of a technology in order to avoid the loss of income tax revenues that would result if companies expended all sunk costs within the home country. Companies involved in research and development plan that the pricing of currently available technology will cover sunk costs plus future research and development.

Protecting Technology

There are different issues imbedded in the problem of protecting technology. Primarily, there is the question of how an MNC can implement control measures for proprietary technology. Obtaining patents is one way to protect one's technology. In most countries, if the knowledge possessed by a firm is a manufacturing process and it produces a new product, that process and the product can be protected with a patent (see Table 21-4). Patents are usually held for limited periods of time. Copyrights are another tool available

TABLE 21-4
Top 10 Corporations Receiving U.S. Patents

Japanese manufacturers grow more inventive than their U.S. rivals

Ten years ago, American companies took the top three places and five out of the top ten slots in the race for new patents issued by the U.S. patent office. Last year, Japanese companies swept the top three spots, while only four U.S. manufacturers placed in the top ten.

1987		1978		1978–1987	
Canon	847	GE	820	GE	7,504
Hitachi	845	Westinghouse Electric	488	Hitachi	5,333
Toshiba	823	IBM	450	IBM	4,952
GE	779*	Bayer	434	RCA	4,336
U.S. Philips	687	RCA	424	Toshiba	4,228
Westinghouse Electric	652	Xerox	418	AT&T	4,213
IBM	591	Siemens	412	U.S. Philips	4,127
Siemens	539	Hitachi	388	Siemens	4,099
Mitsubishi Denki	518	Du Pont	386	Westinghouse Electric	3,953
RCA	504*	AT&T	370	Bayer	3,878

SOURCE: *Wall Street Journal*, October 4, 1988.
* General Electric acquired RCA in 1986, but their patents are listed separately.

for protecting proprietary technology which covers knowledge which is embodied in text. Similarly, trademarks will protect knowledge which is embodied in a product which can be sold. Trademarks usually imply a high standard of quality or expertise in services. There are other methods available such as hiding the technology, e.g., the Coke secret "formula," requiring key technical or research and development employees to sign agreements whereby they are prohibited from using new technology which they acquired outside the firm, or rapid exploitation of the technology which would establish a large market share and discourage competitors from entering the market.

Despite these mechanisms for establishing and maintaining control, it is not uncommon for a firm to lose control. For example, companies in countries such as Korea have reputations for manufacturing branded copies of products that have been patented, copyrighted, or otherwise protected. Similarly, industrial espionage is almost considered merely a modern inconvenience, often depicted in television and screen productions as normal corporate behavior. Also, the mobility of employees makes it almost impossible to control one hundred percent of a company's proprietary technology. Even in the absence of malice, an employee may unwittingly incorporate some of the learned technology in future projects with other companies.

Protecting technology is not only an issue for an MNC, but also for national governments. The private interests of the parties involved in buying and selling technology may not be compatible with the national interests of a government. The home country or seller's country is concerned with the control of technology for national security reasons, while the host country becomes more active in monitoring international transfers as a guideline for future negotiations.

In reality, because of these issues, an international manager must constantly be aware that negotiations regarding technology transfer are between four players—the buyer, the seller, the home country, and the host country—without losing sight of the fact that this is not necessarily a win-lose situation. There may in fact be an arrangement that is mutually beneficial to all parties.

Summary

In the international business arena, production and technology can influence how and where a company will operate. International production management for an MNC may in fact be very similar to production in the home country. The international environment, however, includes other considerations. Before making production decisions, an MNC must consider such additional factors as different wage rates, industrial relations, sources of financing, foreign exchange risk, international tax laws, control, and the production experience curve in each country. While many MNCs attempt to standardize their production systems on a worldwide basis, local environmental influences often make such standardization unsuccessful or at best difficult. The benefits of standardization are ease and simplification, which result in cost savings in organization and staffing, supply systems, options for rationalization, control, and planning. There are four elements in designing a local production facility—plant location, plant layout, materials handling, and the human factor.

Production management encompasses two categories of activities—productive activities and supportive activities. Productive activities require that deviations from expected output are investigated and corrected. Low output, possibly caused by inadequate raw materials or poor scheduling, inferior product quality, or excessive manufacturing costs, is an indication that corrective actions are necessary in order to achieve planned output objectives. Supportive activities include quality control, inventory control, purchasing, maintenance, and technical functions. The Japanese production method is often evaluated to discover the secrets of Japanese business success, but there is no single element of Japanese business that determines this success. It is the ability of the Japanese to efficiently and effectively manage all elements of the production process that leads to their successful performance, which is best exemplified by the inventory control system used by many Japanese companies that is called the just-in-time system.

Technology is knowledge that can be applied in a business environment. It is an integral part of any production system, although it may be separate from the production system itself in the form of the end product or finished good. Technology can be created through research and development or acquired with experience in business operations and transactions. In addition, technology may be purchased from the individuals or firms that have developed the technology, and it is often transferred between parties and across national boundaries for a cost. In terms of production technology, the choice of technology that is implemented in a foreign country depends on the cost-benefit evaluation of capital-intensive versus labor-intensive methods. Such evaluation must also consider the environmental (economic, political, and cultural) influences that affect technology.

The competitive advantage of any MNC is considerably dependent on technology advantages, whether they be a process, product, or management technology. An MNC must constantly be concerned with maintaining and improving this advantage. The perishability of technology requires that an MNC continue to make gains in technology improvements. For an MNC, technological advances can be transferred between affiliates and subsidiaries in different countries.

Pricing of international technology transfers has become a major issue between the governments of developing countries and owners of technology in industrialized countries. In the future, it is expected that such governments will share information regarding technology transfers and pricing among themselves in order to become better equipped to negotiate for such transfers.

For an MNC, control over proprietary technology is a difficult management task. Although there are protection measures and tools available to assist in control, there are also many instances where protection has been inadequate and a firm has lost its proprietary advantage. Because technology is closely associated with national security, governmental controls also affect an MNC and its ability to transfer technology.

Discussion Questions

1. Why are production and technology so important to maintaining a multinational corporation's competitive edge?
2. Discuss the three key production issues as they relate to following types of firms:
   - Manufacturer of trucks
   - Manufacturer of welding equipment
   - Consumer electronics manufacturer (TVs, portable CDs)
   - Textiles manufacturers
3. You are the CEO of a U.S. automobile manufacturer who is interested in building a new production plant in Eastern Europe. What are the factors that you should review in order to make your decision?
4. Volkswagen acquired Traubant, an East German auto manufacturer. What decisions do you think Volkswagen made about the existing plant? Research your answer.
5. What advantages do manufacturers have when implementing a just-in-time system? How do you think suppliers respond to charges from their standard distribution approaches?

Bibliography

BADEN-FULLER, C., AND J. M. STOPFORD. 1988. "Why Global Manufacturing?" *Multinational Business* (Spring): 15–25.

BALL, DONALD A., AND W. H. MCCULLOCH, JR. 1988. *International Business*, Plano, TX: Business Publications.

CARNOY, MARTIN. 1985. "High Technology and International Labor Markets." *International Labour Review* (November/December): 643–659.

CONTRACTOR, F. 1981. "The Role of Licensing." *Columbia Journal of World Business* (Winter): 76.

DAVIDSON, W. H., AND D. G. McFETRIDGE. 1985. "Key Characteristics in the Choice of International Technology Transfer Mode." *Journal of International Business Studies* (Summer): 5–21.

DUNNING, J. H. 1981. *International Production and the Multinational Enterprise.* London: Allen & Unwin.

GOSHAL, S., AND C. A. BARTLETT. 1987. "Innovation Processes in Multinational Corporations: Proceedings of the Symposium on Managing Innovation in Large Complex Firms." INSEAD (September).

———. 1988. "Creation, Adoption, and Diffusion of Innovations by Subsidiaries of Multinational Corporations." *Journal of International Business Studies* (Fall): 365–388.

GROSSE, ROBERT, AND D. KUJAWA. 1988. *International Business,* Homewood, IL: Richard D. Irwin.

HAKANSON, L., AND U. ZANDER. 1986. *Managing International Research and Development.* Stockholm: Mekanforbund.

HALL, ROBERT. 1983. *Zero Inventories,* Homewood, IL: Dow Jones-Irwin.

JOHANSON, J., AND L. G. MATTISON. 1987. "Internationalization in Industrial Systems: A Network Approach." In V. Hood and J. E. Vahne, eds., *Strategies in Global Competition.* London: Croom Helm.

KELLER, R. T., AND R. R. CHINTA. 1990. "International Transfer: Strategies for Success." *Academy of Management Executives* (May): 33–43.

MUNKIRS, JOHN R. 1988. 'Technological Change: Disaggregation and Overseas Production." *Journal of Economic Issues* (June): 469–475.

PORTER, MICHAEL, ed. 1986. *Competition in Global Industries.* Boston: Harvard Business School Press.

RASTOGI, P. N. 1988. *Productivity, Innovation, Management, and Development: A Study in the Productivity Culture of Nations and System Renewal.* New Delhi: Sage Publications.

ROBOCK, STEFAN H., AND KENNETH SIMMONDS. 1983. *International Business and Multinational Enterprises.* Homewood, IL: Richard D. Irwin.

RUGMAN, ALAN H., D. J. LECRAW, AND L. D. BOOTH. 1985. *International Business.* New York: McGraw-Hill.

SMITH, CHARLES. 1990. "Two's Company: Mitsubishi and Benz Plan Wide Links." *Far Eastern Economic Review* (May 24): 67.

STOBAUGH, R., AND L. T. WELLS, JR., eds. 1984. *Technology Crossing Borders: The Choice, Transfer, and Management of International Technology Flows.* Boston: Harvard Business School Press.

WELLS, LOUIS T., JR. 1974. "Don't Overautomate Your Foreign Plant." *Harvard Business Review* (January/February): 84–97.

Chapter Case Study

Milford Processes, Inc.

Kenneth Briggs, general manager of the technical division of Milford Processes, finished reading a long, well-prepared brief written by a task force put together by him to report on the severe quality control problems of the wholly owned subsidiary's plant in Matumba, East Africa. Reports of problems with the chemical-producing plant had been coming in for the last six months, and they had become more serious in the last two months. Concerned with the future of the plant, Briggs put together a small task force of head office and subsidiary technicians to investigate the problems and recommend solutions.

The report was extremely direct. Quality at the plant was dropping and the productivity had fallen. The defective rate of chemical batches had risen from twelve per thousand to ninety eight per thousand over the past six months. Productivity had decreased by 16 percent in the past quarter.

The statistics troubled Briggs. The plant in Matumba had gone on line only a year ago and was equipped with the latest equipment and machinery and the most advanced processing technology. The entire technical side of the operation was run by Milford's engineers, who had several years of experience. The first six months, in fact, had been a great success, and Matumba's productivity had matched Milford's worldwide standards in nearly every way.

After the first two quarters, however, things began to go wrong. One of the most difficult problems was electricity. When the plant was set up, the Matumba government had guaranteed an uninterrupted electricity supply to the plant as a part of the package of incentives it had offered to attract Milford into setting up an advanced technology facility in the country. However, much of Matumba's electricity generating capacity was based on hydroelec-

tric projects, and these were dependent on the degree of rainfall that the country's catchment areas received during the rainy season, during the first four months of the year. This year the rains had failed to come, and water levels in the hydroelectric project reservoirs fell below operating levels. There was nothing the government or anyone else could do to generate power in adequate amounts to meet the needs of the country. Bound by its promise and eager to maintain a hospitable environment for overseas investment, Matumba authorities had given high priority to the Milford plant's power needs. Despite their best efforts, however, the plant had no power for one day a week in the past four months, and in the past six weeks, production had to be shut down for two days a week. In order to keep up production volume and minimize production losses because of the plant shutdown, the production managers had reduced the number of quality-control checks both at the point of raw-material feeding and final-production testing. The electricity shortage also resulted in the malfunctioning of the plant's temperature control systems at two stages of the production process, and this was also affecting quality.

The task force had come up with two options, both of which assumed that the electricity situation in Matumba was not likely to improve soon, and that over the long term, it could fluctuate considerably, depending upon the pattern of annual rainfall. Moreover, if Matumba's drive to attract other overseas companies to the country met with even moderate success, the demand for industrial consumption would go up sharply, and Milford would lose its most-favored status in this regard. The government was already under criticism from some quarters of the political opposition for bending over backward to please Milford. The opposition was actively calling for retracting Milford's privileged access to the country's generating capacity in times of scarcity.

The first option recommended that the company set up a captive power station, which, in effect, meant the building of a complete power-generating facility to supply electricity exclusively to Milford's plant. The plant would cost an estimated $16 million to build and could be completed in about a year and a half. The facility would ensure that the chemicals factory would receive an uninterrupted supply of electricity, which would lead to consistent production performance and progressively higher productivity standards.

The other option was to modify the subsidiary's technological processes to be less dependent on electricity and meet its energy needs from other sources, especially natural gas, which was readily available in Matumba at relatively inexpensive rates. Although using natural gas was relatively cheaper, even after taking into account the costs involved in modifying some of the plant's technological processes and equipment, the option did pose some difficulties. The processes using natural gas were not as advanced as those using electricity, and there could be a marginal decline in product quality, even though the production volume could be maintained at the same level. Another issue was safety. Although Milford's safety standards were quite strict and well-developed, it was possible that they could be compromised at the sub-

sidiary level. The main problem was the safety orientation of local employees. Most had little experience in working in such a plant. A comprehensive safety training program and continued emphasis on safety consciousness could reduce the risks significantly but not eliminate them.

Briggs looked at the report, which concisely put together the main pros and cons of each option and closed with a clear and strong emphasis on the need for early action. "We'll have to decide within the next few weeks," thought Briggs. "Before the Germans and Italians come in and set up their operations, we have to dig in and dominate; it will be impossible to do it later." The next morning the members of the technical operations committee received a notice of a policy meeting to be held Thursday in the main conference room to discuss the problems at the Matumba plant. Attached to the notice was a copy of the report with a request for each member to read it before the meeting.

Question

Assume that you were a member of the Milford technical operations committee. What questions would you raise at the meeting? Which of the options would you suggest? In your opinion, would there be other approaches that could be taken by Milford to resolve these issues?

PART SEVEN

SOCIAL AND ETHICAL ISSUES AND THE FUTURE OF INTERNATIONAL BUSINESS

CHAPTER 22

Ethical Questions: Multinationals and Earth's Environment

CHAPTER OBJECTIVES

This chapter will:

- Review the major environmental concerns affecting the global community and the implications they have on multinational corporations at home and abroad.
- Identify new challenges and opportunities that MNCs face as a result of growing environmental concerns.

Emerging Environmental Concerns

National and international concerns about the environment have increased dramatically over the past decade. Although damage to the earth's environment has been an issue in development and industrial policies in many countries for the past several years, it has not been in the forefront of international attention because other issues, such as economic growth, industrialization, population growth, and poverty, have occupied the center stage.

Concern for the environment has grown for several reasons. First, damage to the environment is becoming increasingly visible. A number of envi-

ronmental and ecological disasters, including several involving large MNCs, have served to attract world attention. Second, environmental action groups have become more powerful. The ability of these groups to influence public policy has increased greatly following sustained support, both political and financial, from different sections of society that are more concerned with the environmental future than ever before. Third, a number of international bodies, such as the United Nations, the World Bank, and national governments, have become responsive to the issue and have demonstrated it by establishing environmental guidelines and, in the case of governments, by passing laws aimed at protecting the environment.

Concerns for the environment have wide-ranging implications for MNCs both in their home and host countries because not only are MNCs affected by general environmental guidelines, but because they are viewed as one of the prime sources of danger for the world's environment. This view is valid to a significant extent, given the fact that MNCs influence nearly 25 percent of the world's assets by their actions and affect, in one way or another, nearly 70 percent of internationally traded products and 80 percent of the world's land devoted to the cultivation of export-oriented crops. In many developing countries, MNCs are usually the prime source of industrial activity. Even where their share in total industrial activity is not large, they are the most visible and, therefore, the first focus of attention of environmentalists and similar groups (see Perspective 22–1).

These developments present both challenges and opportunities for MNCs. The challenges arise in the form of new considerations that MNCs

PERSPECTIVE 22–1   Curbing Pollution in Developing Countries

Pollution of the air, land, and sea poses serious risks to present and future generations, but policies aimed at controlling pollution—especially in developing countries—are far from adequate and could be improved at a low cost. Those that are in place tend to be either poorly designed or not enforced. General economic policies often exacerbate the problems, failing to take into account possible effects on the environment.

As developing countries begin to redesign policies to control pollution more effectively, they will need to find ways to minimize possible adverse effects on other critical objectives—such as growth, revenue raising, and equity. They will also have to keep in mind important administrative, technological, and institutional constraints, drawing heavily on a wide array of fiscal tools to complement more traditional pollution control instruments.   •

THE NEED FOR REFORM

Government intervention is generally needed to prevent or alleviate pollution, because of a fundamental failure of the market to take into account the interests of those that are being hurt. Since pollution usually affects the well-being of many individuals who have not had any role in the activities causing it, government action should be aimed at making polluters behave as if they have the interests of the victims at heart. This can be accomplished either through regulatory or price intervention. Possibilities include a tax on emissions, a limit on the amount of pollution, subsidies to cleaner alternatives, and, at times, the assignment and enforcement of property rights (see box).

In some developing countries today, policies to control pollution levels do not even exist. For example, imports of heavily polluting used cars, although high in number, are often not subject to any emission constraints. For most, however, these policies are in place—in fact, the standards for individual polluters and environmental quality are frequently similar to those in Europe and the United States—but they have not been effective. One reason, as noted in the World Bank's *Annual Report on the Environment 1990*, is that monitoring, enforcement, and regulatory capacities have tended to be weak in these countries. In Mexico, for instance, the influence of regulations has been limited by the resources of the enforcement agency and the low level of fines. In Columbia,

SOURCE: Gunnar S. Eskeland and Emmanuel Jiminez, *Finance & Development*, March 1991, pages 15–18.

Environmental Property Rights

The environment could be effectively protected through a reassignment of property rights—giving the rights of clean air and water to consumers and letting them sell as few or as many pollution permits as they like. But one problem with this approach is that without monitoring, enforcement of rights to open access resources such as clean air and water is virtually impossible; polluters will have all rights *de facto*. Another problem is that since everyone can enjoy the general air quality, each individual will have excessive incentives to sell the rights to polluters. Thus, pollution rights must be sold collectively, not individually.

Under special conditions, polluters and victims can negotiate socially optimal pollution levels without government intervention. According to an argument attributed to economist Ronald Coase, as long as negotiations are not too costly and bargaining works, these levels can be achieved, regardless of the initial allocation of rights. For example, in the Philippines, soil sediments caused by a single logger threatened tourism development in a bay. In such a case, direct negotiation between polluter and victim would have been feasible. Similarly, transborder pollution issues between two sovereign nations, such as acid rain, are often resolved without the involvement of a supranational governing entity. But this solution tends not to be efficient when a large number of people are involved and information about their stakes is imperfect. In Mexico City, air pollution from 30,000 industrial firms and 2.6 million motor vehicles affects 20 million inhabitants.

laws have included formulas for calculating a tax on discharges to water, but no apparatus has been in place to monitor and bill polluters. In India, inefficient legal processes have reduced the disincentive effects of lawsuits against polluters. Even in developed countries, subsidized and mandated pollution control equipment has often been ineffective. For example, a recent study of monitoring and enforcement of pollution regulation in the United States found that during the 1970s and 1980s, much more public attention was focused on getting pollution equipment in place than ensuring its proper maintenance and use.

Another reason is that pollution control policies often are not well designed, meaning that they would have been both weak and unnecessarily costly even if they had been implemented vigorously. Emission regulations, the most popular form of intervention, frequently provide no incentives for polluters to choose least-cost abatement options. In Brazil, for example, studies show that some industrial polluters could reduce emissions at much lower costs than others. Incentives—as opposed to rigid regulations—would have been able to exploit these differences by allowing polluters flexibility in finding where and how pollution can be reduced at the lowest cost. Even in industrial countries, surprisingly little use has been made of incentives, despite many studies demonstrating that savings would often be in the range of 50 to 90 percent of the costs of existing controls.

Often exacerbating the deficiencies of environmental policies is the fact that general economic policies may have environmental effects, and these are not considered when the economic policies are formed. Subsidized charges for energy (particularly fossil fuels), water, pesticides, and fertilizers, as well as selective investment incentives to industries, may be costly ways of reaching other objectives if they contribute simultaneously to pollution problems. Economic interventions must take into account whether the stimulated activities are good or bad for the environment.

	Direct Instruments	Indirect Instruments
Market-based incentives:	Effluent charges, tradable permits, deposit refund systems	Input/output taxes and subsidies to substitutes and to abatement inputs
Command and control:	Emission regulations (source specific, non-transferable quotas)	Regulation of equipment, processes, input and output
Government production or expenditures:	Purification, cleanup, waste disposal, enforcement and agency expenditures	Technological development

NOTE: A direct instrument addresses the level of damages or emissions directly, whereas indirect instruments work via other variables.

POSSIBLE APPROACHES TO REFORM

What options are open to governments? Typically, there is a much wider range of policy instruments at their disposal than those now being systematically exploited (see table). Traditionally, analysts have proposed "direct" instruments, which attempt to correct directly for the imposition of pollution on others by, for example, levying charges, issuing permits, or setting standards based on emissions. When such constraints are source specific and nontradable, they are termed command and control, since they mandate where and how to abate. They contrast with market-based instruments, which provide abatement incentives to polluters, who can then choose among options. A long-standing theoretical result—which has also been confirmed by empirical analysis—is that taxes or tradable quotas on emissions will achieve a given emission reduction at the lowest possible cost. Abatement will be cheap if polluters face an emission tax, because only polluters with low abatement costs will choose to reduce emissions, while those with higher costs will prefer to pay the charge.

In addition, there are "indirect" instruments—those that are not directly related to emissions, but that nonetheless have important environmental effects, sometimes unintentionally. Public finance policies, through their impact on relative prices, will often have a strong impact on pollution. Other policies, such as those related to macro or trade balances, are also potentially important.

Minimizing trade-offs with other objectives. In assessing the relative merits and design of these policy instruments, developing countries should strive to avoid, or at least minimize, potential trade-offs with other objectives, such as economic growth, revenue mobilization, and equity. This will also facilitate adoption and implementation.

Some pollution control policies may actually complement efforts to meet growth and narrowly defined efficiency objectives. For example, reducing energy subsidies to industries may lower pollution and enhance efficiency by subjecting firms to fair competition and forcing them to economize in the use of energy. Subsidy reductions, in turn, may also contribute to net public revenue, and employment may be generated if energy and labor are substitutes. Trade-offs are more likely to be avoidable if resource allocation has been extensively distorted due to past policies—the situation in Eastern Europe and the Union of Soviet Socialist Republics. Heavily subsidized prices for certain key polluting commodities could have encouraged overutilization and waste. A first step may then be to remove subsidies and move to marginal cost pricing for such items as water supply, electricity, fossil fuels, pesticides, and fertilizers.

When public budgets are tight, the case is strengthened for environmental taxes (or auctioned tradable permits) rather than regulation. Developing countries often use tax instruments to a point where distortions are very costly—export taxes discourage cash crops, sales taxes distort consumption, and so on. For them, using pollution control instruments that generate revenue would be particularly useful, since this would enable governments to lower other tax rates. While pollution taxes are only a fairly recent innovation and not yet significant in terms of general revenue, a recent study by the Organization for Economic Cooperation and Development shows that environmental taxes have been a significant source of funding selected environmental expenditures in developed countries. The magnitude of the revenue potential of pollution-related taxes in developing countries still has to be seen in practice. But since fuel constitutes 10 to 20 percent of imports for many, there is no doubt that taxation of fuels—which could then be motivated by environmental, as well as fiscal objectives—holds substantial revenue potential. Some countries where intensive pesticide use is subsidized at a rate of 44 percent of retail cost could save hundreds of millions of dollars per year and reduce health risks as well.

The possible trade-offs with equity and efficiency also have to be assessed, especially when the major expenditure items and revenue sources of poor households are concerned. Often, these trade-offs can be avoided altogether. For example, on the production side, many studies of individual industries have estimated that energy and labor are substitutable, indicating that price-induced energy efficiency can increase employment and labor income. On the demand side, many studies indicate

that the use of petroleum fuels (except possibly kerosene) and electricity vary greatly with income levels in developing countries, making these potential tax bases for distributive reasons, too. If a policy has adverse consequences for the poor, it can still be attractive if there is scope for compensating measures, such as lowering the price for other essential items.

Adjusting to administrative and technological constraints. These constraints are likely to be different, at least in degree, from those confronted by developed countries. In particular, one must take into account the government's ability to monitor pollution damage and enforce regulations. For direct instruments to be effective, the regulator has to be both technologically capable and sufficiently accountable to withstand pressure from interested parties, since policy instruments based on environmental monitoring have monetary implications for the polluters.

The theoretical case for market-based instruments (such as effluent charges or tradable emission permits) is very strong, as these exploit information held by the polluters to seek out the cheapest way to reduce pollution. Under such a regime, polluters facing high costs of pollution abatement would prefer to pay the charges, while those facing lower costs would prefer to avoid the charges by reducing emissions. Command and control measures cost more because the regulator must decide where and how emission reductions should take place. The theoretical case for direct rather than indirect instruments is also strong. Actual monitoring of emissions allows perfect incentives for all actions that can reduce emissions, whereas indirect instruments can only imperfectly mimic such an incentive scheme. For example, a fuel tax can act as an effluent charge in the absence of continuous emission monitoring, but it will only imperfectly mimic a tax on actual individual emissions. In particular, it will fail to induce any actions that can reduce emissions per unit of fuel consumed (such as installation of filters and catalytic converters).

But in the real world, monitoring each polluting source (and enforcing taxes or regulations related to such monitoring) is often costly or impossible, and thus it might be more effective to use selective taxes or regulations to stimulate pollution control indirectly. Such policies could include subsidies to pollution control equipment and public transport, taxes on polluting inputs, and noneconomic regulatory approaches (e.g., fuel efficiency standards). These indirect instruments can often be implemented without reliance on technically and institutionally vulnerable monitoring and enforcement functions.

The problem, of course, is not only a question of technological feasibility but also of whether institutions are strong enough to cope with pressure from special interest groups and corruption. Indirect instruments may thus be more efficient even though, for instance, fuel consumption is only an imperfect indicator of emissions. Moreover, these measures—whether they be taxes on polluting inputs, or take the form of tax concessions and subsidies to low-polluting products and processes—can be administratively easy to carry out if they can be grafted onto existing systems of indirect taxation.

It may turn out that for some activities, emissions and damages are affected mostly by inherently unobservable actions, such as whether combustion machinery is adjusted and used carefully. Under such circumstances, there will often be no good substitute for monitoring emissions. In general, however, policymakers will be able to find appropriate indirect instruments, and the key in their use will be the identification of polluting sectors and instruments affecting their mode of operation. For instance, if household use of energy is found to be a major contributor to pollution (as in Ankara and Beijing), changing the availability or relative prices of alternative energy sources will probably be the major instrument. In addition, some improvement may come from reducing the consumer prices of selective appliances (e.g., improved ovens and stoves).

One weakness of indirect instruments such as fuel taxes or subsidies to less-polluting equipment may be undesired incentive effects and distortions in behavior. A fuel tax, for instance, treats all users of the fuel as if they pollute equally per unit of fuel. The cement industry, which retains practically all the sulfur content of its fuels, would then be taxed at too high a rate, and its use of high-sulfur fuels would be unnecessarily discouraged. The problem could be overcome, however, by instruments that differentiate according to user characteristic, if they are not too costly to administer. In the above example, sulfur taxes paid on fuels could be refunded when regulators are convinced that the shipment was used in cement production.

Taking the institutional dimension into account. A major issue here is jurisdictional— whether it arises because the desired tool for pollution control is national (possibly a gasoline tax) while the problem is strictly local, or because a municipality or state is polluted by activities outside its authority. A good example of the latter would be Paraiba, the river that runs through Rio de Janeiro from São Paulo. A solution would be to give responsibility for water quality to a higher federal authority that would monitor discharges and enforce regulations affecting them. The constitution, however, gives the states this authority, and it remains to be seen whether negotiations between the two states can induce abatement within São Paulo in order to benefit Rio.

Another concern is the ability and willingness of governments to take firm actions when the interests of strong and influential private groups are put in jeopardy. Many analysts argue that industrialized countries have chosen costly environmental regulation rather than more efficient instruments because established industries are favored, while costs are borne by unorganized consumers and potential competitors. In developed and developing countries alike, excessive depletion of resources, such as forests, is often explained by the fact that well-placed groups can take advantage of such exploitation, while the benefits from sustainable management would go to others.

CONCLUSION

In a country facing severe revenue constrains and a weak institutional framework, much of the pollution control work in the early phases should be done by taxing fixed inputs (e.g., combustion machinery) and variable inputs (e.g., fuels), according to the level of expected emissions. These instruments may be more effective than traditional regulatory approaches, which rely heavily on monitoring and enforcement. Moreover, they should contribute to—rather than burden—public budgets. Indeed, studies performed in developed countries clearly show that an extensive regulatory framework brings little relief if the combined effect of monitoring, enforcement, and the size of penalties does not support compliance. An indication that developing countries must deal with the same constraints comes from the mixed experience with efforts to enforce regulations on safety standards and overloading of motor vehicles. The stakes for the involved personnel are very high and the task is immense.

Although we have focused primarily on local or national pollution problems, the same principles apply to transnational issues. When several nations are involved, agreement about emission levels will have to come about in the context of negotiations, with international transfers playing a facilitating role—as is the case with the recently established global fund to help phase out the use of chlorofluorocarbons (CFCs) in developing countries. Each nation, in turn, will then have to find the most cost-effective way of dealing with the problem within its own borders.

Recommendations about how to intervene depend heavily on assumptions regarding behavioral responses, and a common one is the assumption of competitive behavior. This, of course, warrants some caution, especially since in many developing countries, the role of prices and competition is often not clear. For instance, when prices are controlled, or the firms involved are parastatals, this should be taken into account. Another cautionary note is that the benefits and costs of pollution abatement are often uncertain, and policy recommendations may hinge on which type of uncertainty is more important. Carefully thinking through how individuals and firms will respond to policy instruments holds the potential to greatly reduce the costs and enhance the efficiency of intervention, in turn determining the affordability of environmental protection.

must bear in mind while making investment and operating decisions and the additional costs they must incur to ensure that their operations are environmentally safe and comply with the regulations of the host countries. In some instances, MNCs may be required to close or completely modify the production of certain plants for environmental reasons. Along with these challenges are new opportunities. Concerns with the preservation of the environment call for new types of products and new lines of business and, consequently, create new markets.

Major Environmental Issues

Greenhouse Gases

Greenhouse gases is a general term used to denote gases that contribute to global warming by trapping heat in the earth's atmosphere. It is predicted that if such gases continue to accumulate at the present rate, they will lead to an increase in the atmospheric temperature by 1.5 to 4.5°C by the year 2050. This warming could have a disastrous impact on the world's ecological systems and lead to a rise of sea levels by as much as 1.5 meters and cause the flooding of low-lying coastal areas, many of which are industrial and urban centers with a high population concentration. The gases that contribute most to global warming and the greenhouse effect include carbon dioxide, methane, and nitrous oxide. The most significant contributors to global warming are carbon dioxide and methane, which will account for nearly 70 percent of the warming effects.

A major source of accumulation of carbon dioxide in the atmosphere is industrial combustion of fossil fuels. MNCs are major users of fossil fuels in a number of ways. They extract, refine, and transport much of the world's supply of fossil fuel and are significant consumers of such fuels, both as an intermediate and final source of energy. Table 22–1 illustrates the main economic activities that contribute to global warming. The production of greenhouse gases as a direct or indirect result of transnational corporations is shown in Table 22-2.

Depletion of the Ozone Layer

The earth's environment is protected by a layer of ozone gas in the stratosphere that shields the surface from potentially deadly ultraviolet radiation. In recent years the ozone layer has been seriously damaged by man-made chemicals, especially chlorofluorocarbons (CFCs). CFCs are used to lower temperatures in refrigerators and air conditioners and in making aerosol and foam propellants. Some chlorofluorocarbons also contribute to global warming, and these and similar chemicals are expected to account for 15 percent to 20 percent of global warming between 1991 and the middle of the next century. The depletion of the stratospheric ozone (which forms the shield against ultraviolet radiation) leads to the accumulation of tropospheric ozone, which is a contributor to global warming through the greenhouse effect.

TABLE 22-1
Economic Activities and Global Warming

Activity	Contribution to greenhouse warming (percentage)
Energy use and production of which:	57
Industrial	22
Transportation	20
Residential/commercial	15
Use of chlorofluorocarbons	17
Agricultural practices	14
Deforestation and other land use modifications	9
Other industrial	3
Total	100

SOURCE: U.S. Environmental Protection Agency, "Policy Options for Stabilizing Global Climates," draft report to Congress, 1989, page 55.

TABLE 22-2
Greenhouse Gas Production

Gas	Amount of gas generated by transnational corporations (approximate % of total amount generated)	Significant sources of greenhouse gases
CO_2	50	Emissions from automobiles. Three-quarters of oil and gas use in OECD countries. Half of coal use in OECD countries. Half of fossil fuel use in developing countries.
Methane	10–20	Half from oil and gas production and use. Half from emissions from coal mines.
CFSs[a]	66	Use of aerosol sprays, car air-conditioners, solvents, and refrigerators in OECD countries.
Other[b]	50	Emissions from automobiles. Three-quarters of oil and gas use in OECD countries. Half of coal use in OECD countries. Half of fossil fuel use in developing countries.

NOTE: A designation of transnational corporation involvement is not meant to exclude involvement by any others in the emissions of greenhouse gases—for instance, in the use of cars or other consumer goods. The estimates are designed to indicate an order of magnitude of emissions which could be affected by measures taken by transnational corporations, whether self-initiated or government-mandated.

[a] Chlorofluorocarbons
[b] Such as nitrogen oxides and ozone

SOURCE: United Nations Economic & Social Council, Commission of Transnational Corporations.

MNCs have been found responsible for a large part of this damage, because they are the main producers of products using and producing CFCs and other chemicals that damage the ozone layer. In fact, all major manufacturers of CFCs are multinational corporations, and the focus of world attention has been quite sharp on this aspect of their activity.

Deforestation

The disappearance of the world's forests has had and is likely to continue to have extremely dangerous ecological consequences. The scale of the problem has already assumed alarming proportions. According to one source, every year 6 million hectares of dryland turns into nonarable desert. More than 11 million hectares of forests are depleted every year, an area approximately the size of India.

Deforestation has a number of adverse effects for the global environment. The loss of forest cover on mountains and hillsides loosens the soil-retention capacity, which leads to rainwater washing away valuable topsoil into rivers, reducing their depth and making them prone to flooding. The lack of forest cover reduces the potential rainfall in a particular area and limits the supply of oxygen, which means that carbon dioxide increases in proportion and adds to global warming.

MNCs have been viewed as responsible for deforestation in many different countries for a variety of reasons. Many MNCs are large producers and transporters of timber and timber products. Others have been associated with large industrial and civil construction projects that have been established on former forest lands.

Hazardous Waste

The production, handling, transport, and disposal of hazardous industrial waste has become a serious concern in many countries, given the risks it carries both for the quality of the local environment and for general public health. According to the U.S. Environmental Protection Agency, "Uncontrolled hazardous [waste] sites may present some of the most serious environmental and human health problems the nation has ever faced." Concerns about hazardous industrial waste are now worldwide, the problem being equally serious in many less-developed countries where regulations relating to the disposal and treatment of hazardous waste are not as well established. Hazardous wastes are generated by a wide variety of industries, both in developed and developing countries. Table 22–3 illustrates some of the key industries

in industrializing nations that produce hazardous wastes.

Several ecological accidents and disasters involving hazardous industrial wastes have shown how serious this threat is becoming. For example, thirteen children died in 1981 from mercury poisoning in Indonesia after eating fish caught in a tributary of Jakarta Bay. Mercury levels in the water, polluted by chemical and heavy metal wastes from nearby factories, were found to be more than sixty times those deemed safe by international standards. Similarly, a company in Mexico was forced to close after it was discovered to have been pumping highly toxic chromium wastes directly into the aquifer in the Mexico Valley area, threatening the water supply of nearly 20 million people. Table 22–4 provides an estimate of the generation of hazardous waste in selected developed and developing countries.

A critical issue in hazardous waste disposal is the transport of the waste. Companies in countries with heavily regulated hazardous waste-disposal methods attempt to circumvent the regulations by transporting the wastes to other developing countries with little or no regulations.

The International Transport of Hazardous Wastes

A major concern among the newly industrializing nations is that the substantial tightening of requirements concerning hazardous wastes may be creating perverse incentives for private entrepreneurs to dispose of them in more surreptitious ways.

The new procedures for handling, transporting, treating, storing, and disposing of hazardous wastes have clearly increased costs to industrial producers. In the long term, these should stimulate recycling and cost-effective waste reduction production processes. But in the short term, many fear that these new regulations in the industrialized nations may lead to longer on-site storage, increased illegal transport, and midnight dumping of wastes and the shipping of wastes across international borders.

Thus, one aspect of the hazardous waste problem in industrializing countries that has received considerable media attention in recent years is "waste tourism"—the growing transport of hazardous substances from the industrialized nations with stringent regulations requiring expensive disposal and storage

TABLE 22-3
Industries Producing Hazardous Wastes

Key manufacturing industries for industrializing nations	Hazardous wastes produced
Metal finishing, electroplating, etc.	Heavy metals, fluorides, cyanides, acid and alkaline cleaners, abrasives, plating salts, oils, phenols
Leather tanning	Heavy metals, organic solvents
Textiles	Heavy metals, toxic organic dyes, organic chlorine compounds, salts, acids, caustics
Pesticides	Organic chlorine compounds, organic phosphate compounds, heavy metals
Pharmaceuticals	Organic solvents and residues, heavy metals (esp. mercury)
Plastics	Organic chlorine compounds
Paints	Organic solvents and residues, organic pigments, heavy metals (esp. lead, zinc)

SOURCE: H.J. Leonard, "Hazardous Waste: The Crisis Spreads," *National Development*, April 1986.

TABLE 22-4
Hazardous Waste Production by Country

Country	Estimated annual hazardous waste (metric tons)	Hazardous waste per capita (metric tons)	Hazardous waste per sq. km. (metric tons)
United States	300.0 million	1.3	32.0
Brazil	33.9 million	0.3	4.0
Mexico	21.9 million	0.3	11.1
Spain	17.3 million	0.5	34.3
India	13.6 million	0.02	4.1
South Korea	7.6 million	0.2	77.6
Yugoslavia	6.1 million	0.3	23.8
Turkey	5.0 million	0.1	6.4
Indonesia	4.4 million	0.03	2.3
Thailand	3.5 million	0.07	6.8
Egypt	3.5 million	0.08	3.5
Philippines	3.0 million	0.06	10.0

SOURCE: Data based on 1983 industrial production statistics from the World Bank.

to less industrialized countries with fewer restrictions.

In recent years a number of proposals have been made by waste disposal companies in the United States and Europe to export hazardous wastes to other countries in return for currency, technology, and services. For example, several years ago, China reportedly offered to accept hazardous wastes from the Federal Republic of Germany in return for heavy machinery—a deal that apparently did not materialize. In 1985, a U.S.-based firm, Gestion Chipano Marina Unida de Costa Rica, applied to the Costa Rican government for permission to burn American chemical wastes at the Port of Limon. This proposal was eventually refused by the Health Ministry of Costa Rica. A 1980 proposal by a U.S. firm, Nedlog Technology Group, to pay a $25 million annual licensing fee to Sierra Leone in exchange for dumping hazardous wastes, stirred protests from groups in the United States and Sierra Leone, as well as from the governments of neighboring Nigeria and Ghana, before it was dropped.

Nevertheless, the number of formal proposals for waste transport probably represents only a small portion of the total, particularly when heavily regulated nations share borders with countries where concerns about hazardous waste have not yet led to new disposal restrictions. It is likely that the illegal flow of waste is increasing. This is especially evident between the United States and Mexico, where officials on both sides of the border worry that the volume of hazardous waste flowing into Mexico may be on the rise. Already, there have been minor diplomatic incidents. In 1981, for instance, a U.S. businessman was arrested for illegally shipping and dumping 260 drums of toxic chemical wastes, including 42 drums of waste PCBs, in the vicinity of Zacatecas.

The situation is acute in the far west border region where a number of hazardous waste dump sites in southern California have closed or are less willing to take on certain wastes. A recent internal EPA document concluded, in fact, that "current U.S. and Mexican efforts have been inadequate to prevent the indiscriminate and uncontrolled transborder movement of hazardous materials."

A major contributing factor to the inability of officials on either side to keep abreast of the movement of hazardous materials is that U.S. laws covering the export of hazardous wastes, namely the Resource Conservation and Recovery Act and the Hazardous and Solid Waste Amendments of November 1984, leave several loopholes. First, although shippers are required to notify the EPA and the receiving country governments, the EPA has no authority to prohibit waste shipment. Moreover, the definition of hazardous waste excludes that which is a "product" or intended for reuse. This ambiguity leaves wide latitude in the materials that are brought to Mexico for land disposal.

This problem is likely to intensify because a recent report from the EPA contended that more than two-thirds of all toxic waste dumps in the United States are not complying with new requirements for permanent operating permits and must cease operations in the near future. In light of the anticipated efforts to ship wastes across the border to Mexico, some U.S. officials expect this subject to become an increasingly contentious one in U.S.-Mexican relations if Mexican officials press the matter.[1]

MNCs have been accused of not paying enough attention to the problems of hazardous waste in their host countries that do not have a well-developed regulatory framework for environmental control. This issue has been brought into the spotlight by several ecological problems and disasters in developing countries that have occurred because of MNC laxity in observing environmentally safe procedures for the disposal and treatment of hazardous wastes generated by their overseas plants. Perhaps the most tragic environmental disaster was the leak of lethal MIC (methyl, isoCynate) gas from Union Carbide's pesticide plant in Bhopal, India, in 1984, which caused more than 2,500 deaths and serious impairments to several thousand more people.

Air Pollution

The problems of industrial pollution became increasingly serious in the late 1980s as industrialization expanded and intensified. Air pollution

---

[1] H. Jeffrey Leonard, "Hazardous Waste: The Crisis Spreads," *National Development*, April 1986.

occurs primarily from emissions from factory chimneys, while water pollution occurs primarily because of the discharge of industrial effluents into local water bodies. In many countries the air has been so polluted at industrial centers that the local residents have increased incidence of respiratory and other diseases. In other countries, water pollution has ended the use of local rivers, lakes, and bays.

MNC Responses

Multinational corporations, for valid reasons, have been held responsible for their contribution to the increased environmental problems the world faces today and are called upon to adjust virtually every aspect of their activities.

Establishing In-House Environmental Ethics

The approach of MNCs to battling the problems of environmental pollution and ecological degradation is dependent to a large degree on the ethics of the corporation. The response of the corporation to this problem depends on what the MNC sees as its responsibility. MNCs have tremendous political leverage, particularly so in the smaller LDCs, which are in need of their technology, industrialization, and economic growth. Environmental laws are less developed in LDCs, while public awareness of environmental issues is limited, and there are few channels for the effective and voluble expression of public opinion. The ruling powers in LDCs generally tend to have almost universal authority and their decisions are difficult to challenge, which allows MNCs to establish environmentally unsound projects, should they decide to do so, as long as they have the confidence of the local authorities. Many studies have shown that MNCs have tended to locate their more polluting plants in developing countries to escape the strict environmental standards and regulations imposed by developed countries.

It is extremely important for MNCs to take a responsible approach to the environmental issue. Many corporations have adopted such an approach and have voluntarily restricted their environmentally unsound operations and even stopped production of environmentally unsafe products. Many others have not.

Relocation of Production

In the past, location decisions made by MNCs were principally dependent on techno-economic criteria—the raw material supply, infrastructural facilities, availability of a trained work force, proximity to markets, availability of transportation, and so on. Now decisions to establish plants must evaluate potential effects on the environment. Not only must the economic consequences (such as feasibility and rate of return) be forecast, but plans must be made to protect the local environment. Thus, while prior permission from a government had been sufficient to establish a factory in a host country, MNCs are now likely to be required to discuss their site plans with local representatives in order to take into consideration their concerns about the actual and potential impact of a plant on the local environment and ecological balance.

Modification of Technology

Traditionally, the main motivator of technological change was a search for more advanced and economically efficient technologies that would generate new and better products at lower costs. More recently, however, technology development has also focused on environmental safety. Technologies that are being developed must be monitored from the viewpoint of their environmental consequences.

Raw Material Use

Raw material use is an important focus of technological modification. The raw materials currently in use may not be available in the future, principally for two reasons—they may be nonrenewable, such as fossil fuels, and their use may result in consequences that are harmful to the earth's environment. As concerns with the environment grow, MNCs will be called on to look at raw materials not only in terms of their monetary price but their ecological consequences. Limitations imposed by these considerations will exert pressure on MNCs to use technologies that reduce industrial waste, maximize consumption efficiency of raw materials, promote recycling of waste and used products, and concentrate on more durable and lasting products.

Energy Use

Energy use is another important area of concern in the general technological modifications that MNCs will have to undertake as part of their response to environmental imperatives. Typical approaches in this area would be a gradual phasing out of energy-inefficient technologies and the introduction of technologies based on clean, renewable, and environmentally safe sources of energy (for example, solar power), as opposed to those based on polluting, nonrenewable sources, generally limited to fossil fuels. The problem has been complicated by nuclear accidents at Three Mile Island in the United States and Chernobyl in the Soviet Union, which have placed a major question mark over the future of nuclear energy as an alternative to conventional fossil fuels.

Energy sources are likely to be increasingly expensive and scarce, while patterns of energy use are likely to be under increasing scrutiny from a number of different quarters, including environmental groups and the media. MNCs will have to ensure that they use energy sources in an environmentally sound manner, which will require substantial investments in new or modified equipment, such as energy-efficient industrial furnaces, boilers, and exhausts, and new equipment to control atmospheric emissions, such as air filters and gas treatment chambers. Energy use will have to be modified not only in production but in all other facets of activity, including transportation.

Environmental Restoration

The response to the environmental challenge will not be limited to in-company modifications in production, technologies, energy, product mix, or location decisions. It will have to extend beyond the corporation because the environmental impact of the operations of industrial concerns extends to the local community and, in an aggregate sense, to its home or host country. Company responses will have to be designed to compensate for those aspects of environmental regeneration that are most directly and visibly linked to the areas of the corporation activities. For example, companies that use substantial quantities of wood would be called upon to support local and national reforestation and social forestry programs. Companies that have had a role in adding to atmospheric pollution would have to support programs that attempt to remedy the consequences of such pollution, such as the cleanup of lakes and other freshwater bodies damaged by acid rain. More generally, it is becoming a growing responsibility of corporations to foster environmentally responsible behavior both among their employees and in the communities in which they are located.

Pollution Disclosure

Environmental disclosure will be an important responsibility of MNCs in the future. MNCs will have to remain aware of and appropriately informed about the environmental impact of their activities through an efficient internal information system. This data would have to be shared with the outside world, both voluntarily and through mandatory reporting requirements and environmental audits. A touchy issue would be the environmental compliance by an MNC's joint-venture partners or partly owned subsidiaries in host countries. While an MNC may prescribe a certain environmental standard for itself and wish to have that replicated by its joint-venture partners or overseas subsidiaries, that may not be a reciprocal wish. Similarly, overseas partners may impose more stringent environmental constraints that an

MNC may not wish to be bound by. The issue of environmental safety has become an important one in many negotiations for international joint ventures, and environmental responsibilities are often incorporated as fundamental provisions in the terms of agreement between the negotiating parties. MNCs have become particularly sensitive to this issue because of the dangers of environmentally unsound acts that might be committed by their joint venture partners and for which they might have to take the blame in both their home and host countries, and which could damage their reputation for environmental responsibility in other countries.

It is extremely important that MNCs disseminate information on their own about the consequences, both favorable and unfavorable, of their operations on the environment. Proper disclosure of such information will be extremely important in maintaining the environmental image of a corporation and facilitating a feeling of confidence among different groups—local governments, creditors, consumers, suppliers, investors—in the environmental soundness of the firm. Proper disclosure of the environmental status of a firm's activities also has an important damage-control role, inasmuch as it informs the public about any possible dangers. Any harmful consequences for the environment emanating from MNC activity would be much more damaging to a firm if it becomes known that the MNC had prior information about such a possibility and that it had chosen to suppress it.

In-House Environmental Training

Environmental education will become critical for corporate success. As a part of overall corporate planning, the environmental consequences of all future company activities will have to be assessed well in advance. A serious commitment to this will enhance the corporate image.

One way of demonstrating this commitment is to include the environmental approach of the corporation in the mission statement of the company and in the listing of corporate objectives. Any business plan intended for external audiences would have to include the environmental goals defined by the company, as well as specific plans for implementation. Planning for environmental safety must be comprehensive, covering future investments in plants and other physical facilities, use of natural resources, treatment of industrial wastes, prevention of environmental damage, protection of water resources, and prevention of accidents.

No plan can be successfully implemented if the staff at the operating level is not actively educated. This is all the more true of plans for environmental soundness and safety because the plans are likely to be viewed by the operating level staff as peripheral to their central functions, not because of their antipathy to the environment, but simply because of their perception of its relative importance in the context of their work. MNCs must, therefore, engender a sense of commitment to environmental safety and responsibility among management and staff in order to elicit optimal cooperation in the achievement of the company's environmental objectives.

Personnel must also be informed about the nature of the environmental problems that confront the world in general, and environmental consequences of their activities as company workers in particular. One way to give meaning to this exercise would be to spell out ways in which employees could contribute to overall environmental safety in their own tasks. To ensure that these guidelines are taken seriously, firms must establish an incentive structure that would encourage employees to monitor environmental standards and provide practical suggestions on how the environmental performance of the company could be improved. A reward structure could also be established on a group or unit basis, where the group could be rewarded on the basis of the environmental safety or standards it is able to maintain over a given period of time. It is essential to involve employees, both at the management and staff levels, if any environmental safety program is to be successful.

MNC Opportunities

While the environmental challenges facing MNCs are daunting, a number of opportunities have also arisen. Many MNCs have been quick to anticipate the trends in the world's regulatory, economic, political, and social environments and have been positioned to derive the maximum advantage.

New Consumer Products

As the world grows more environmentally conscious, there will be an increasing need for products that are environmentally safe. This demand points to the opening of new markets, first in the developed and later in developing countries. Environmentally safe products have already made their appearance in many countries and embrace a wide range—from personal goods to consumer durables.

New Technologies

Firms specializing in technology development are already receiving large orders for new, environmentally safe technologies in a wide range of industries. Environmental-control technologies are in particular demand. Furnaces that burn cleaner, more efficient production processes, and technologies to treat toxic emissions and effluents are all in great demand.

New Industrial Products

A large number of mechanical modifications are required by today's plants to meet environmental standards. Water treatment plants, emission control filters, waste management systems, and the like represent new markets and opportunities that are going to expand across the world.

Substitute Products

A number of products that are in wide use but are considered dangerous to the environment are likely to be phased out and replaced. Certain types of plastic products that were found to be resis-

tant to biodegradation, for example, have been replaced with other polyurethane foam products, which are either biodegradable or can be recycled.

New Energy Sources

A number of companies are doing intensive research in the development of new sources of energy for the future. Along with developing energy sources, firms are attempting to develop new devices and products that run on such sources of energy. One of the most important examples of such an energy source is solar power, which is clean, environmentally safe, and virtually unlimited. Working models of solar-powered automobiles have been developed and other solar-powered products have been in use for several years.

Environmental Consulting

Corporations specializing in environmental technology, environmental design, and management, and similar areas are already flooded with contracts and offers to develop environmental safety programs in several different countries. This area is likely to grow rapidly as industrial concerns, local and national governments, and communities attempt to upgrade the environmental quality of industries, neighborhoods, and other aspects of everyday activities. The growing support from the developed countries for such concerns has enabled the collection of substantial funds from various charitable and other foundations to be used to finance such services across a broad spectrum of countries.

The Environment Is Center Stage

The environmental issue has clearly moved from the periphery of MNC concerns to center stage. The issue now has to be factored into almost every decision and top management can no longer simply delegate the responsibilities in this area. It is an issue for the headquarters of every MNC to consider when planning global and local strategies, whatever the internal organization structure of the business. MNCs that take an enlightened approach to this issue are quick to capitalize on opportunities while managing risks effectively and

are likely to end up the winners. Unlike other forms of corporate activity, however, it is not enough if one corporation wins and another loses. Everyone must win if the earth's fragile and currently endangered environment is to be nurtured and sustained (see Perspective 22–2).

PERSPECTIVE 22–2   Accounting for the Environment

Measuring the effects of the interaction between the environment and development recalls the conundrum: If a tree falls in the forest and no one hears it fall does it make a noise? Increasingly, economists have been attempting to include not only fallen trees but also other natural resources in their calculations of national products and incomes. The reason is that current national accounting systems do not capture the value of natural resources adequately and, therefore, development strategies that rely on standard income accounting techniques may not result in sustainable development.

With the rise in awareness of environmental issues in the 1980s, attention is now turning to the need to better understand the value of environmental resources and services and to improve the current United Nations System of National Accounts (SNA) to account for the environment in income estimation. Improved measurement of economic performance should in turn lead to better economic decisionmaking. National authorities and multilateral institutions, such as the United Nations, the International Monetary Fund, and the World Bank, among others, are seeking to address this need. This article traces the rise of this consciousness and the work being done by World Bank staff in this direction.

In conducting economic analyses, measuring economic performance, and directing public pol-

icy, the Bank as well as its member countries rely heavily on the major aggregates shown in the national income accounts, compiled in accordance with the United Nations' SNA. The current SNA, published in 1968, emphasizes GDP. The GDP is a useful measure, mainly of market activity (although it includes some estimates of nonmarketed goods and services), and is an important indicator for macromanagement of an economy. But it has increasingly met criticism, mainly because it takes no account of consumption of natural capital and, therefore, is seen to discourage the implementation of policies that result in sustained development. The SNA framework does not provide for measures such as a net domestic product (which takes account of depreciation of man-made capital). A few countries actually calculate an NDP, but this measure, too, does not capture the loss or depletion of national environmental resources.

DEFICIENCIES

The existing SNA is contained within a well-defined receipt and payment framework that generally relies on market prices. But some of the effects of degradation, pollution, and waste disposal, together with their repercussions on society, cannot be captured by market-based information and standard accounting techniques. Thus, the challenge is to capture these effects statistically and to link them to economic activities.

SOURCE: Ernst Lutz and Mohan Munasinghe, *Finance & Development*, March 1991, pages 19–21.

The deficiencies in the ability of the current national accounting framework to take natural resources and the environment into account arise, in part, out of an inconsistent treatment of man-made and natural capital. There are three specific shortcomings:

- Natural and environmental resources are not included in balance sheets; national accounts, therefore, represent limited indicators of national well-being, since they measure poorly—or even "perversely"—changes in environmental and resource conditions;
- Conventional national accounts fail to record the depreciation of natural capital, such as a nation's stock of water, soil, air, nonrenewable resources, and wildlands, which are essential for human existence.
- Cleanup costs (e.g., expenditures incurred to restore environmental assets) are often included in national income, while environmental damages are not considered. For private firms, defensive environmental expenditures (i.e., measures to reduce or avoid environmental damage) are netted out of final value added. In contrast, such cleanup costs are considered as productive contributions to national output if they are incurred by the public sector or by households. The calculation of GDP is distorted in two ways—undesirable outputs (e.g., pollution) are overlooked and beneficial environment-related inputs related to environmental needs are often implicitly valued at zero.

These deficiencies point to the need for an accounting framework that addresses the preceding concerns and permits the computation of measures such as an environmentally adjusted net domestic product (EDP) and an environmentally adjusted net income (ENI). Such measures would attempt to better account for the depreciation of both man-made and natural capital, exclude relevant categories of defensive environmental expenditures, and estimate damages to the environment as a result of economic activities.

Taking into account depreciation of natural capital and calculating an EDP would likely result in a lower level of measured income and perhaps also a lower growth rate. While other methodological approaches could be sued, the results of the World Resources Institute are illustrative of how adjusted national income figures might differ from traditional ones. They calculated depreciation for oil, timber, and topsoil for Indonesia and found that the growth rate of the adjusted NDP for the period 1971–84 was only 4 percent compared to GDP growth of 7.1 percent.

There are differing views on whether defensive expenditures should be deducted from GDP in order to come closer to a sustainable income as defined below. Generally, progress toward a new accounting framework has been slow. Reasons for this include conceptual and measurement difficulties, as well as uncertainties about the benefits of gathering additional data relative to its costs.

BACKGROUND TO SNA

The foundations of the current approach to national income accounting were laid about half a century ago, when the world's population and the size of the world economy, as measured by GDP, were much smaller. Consequently, the emphasis on natural resources and the environment was much less at the time, and it is understandable that better treatment of natural resources and the environment in the SNA was not a major concern. Yet, some of the early literature that provided the intellectual underpinning of the SNA anticipated the importance of natural capital and helped to define broad concepts of "true" income that were not limited to output derived from man-made capital.

Sir John Hicks defined the concept of income as follows: "The purpose of income calculation in practical affairs is to give people an indication of the amount which they can consume without impoverishing themselves" (John R. Hicks: "Value and Capital," Second edition, Oxford University Press, Oxford, UK, 1946, p. 172). The same basic idea holds at the national level. True income is a practical guide to the maximum amount a nation can consume without depleting its stock of assets in the future. This would be true to the extent that allowance is made for depreciation of capital (or productive assets), broadly defined. Clearly, GDP, or even NDP as computed under the existing SNA, is not consistent with the spirit of the above definition by Hicks, and hence the urgent need to re-evaluate the SNA.

THE BANK AND SNA

Based on its work since 1983, the Bank has actively encouraged the inclusion of environmental issues in the current revision of the SNA and proposed as an interim measure that a set of environmental "satellite" accounts be created to accompany the SNA framework. This proposal was accepted by the SNA expert group meeting in January 1989. The revised "Blue Book" of the SNA (expected to be issued in 1993) will include a discussion on this issue and justify the need for satellite accounts that permit income computations that take environmental concerns into account.

The Bank has surveyed the experience of industrial countries with various environmental and resource accounting approaches to see what lessons could be learned for developing countries to better deal with environmental issues in accounting.

Some of the Bank's current research in this area, carried out jointly with the United Nations Statistical Office (UNSO), is being conducted in two developing countries—Mexico and Papua New Guinea. The UNSO Framework being used in these studies is a system for environmentally adjusted economic accounts (SEEA), which derives EDP and ENI. It tries to integrate environmental data with existing national accounts information, while maintaining SNA concepts and principles as far as possible. The challenging empirical question is the extent to which it will be possible to actually value environmental assets and flows of services from them.

By expanding the SNA to SEEA, the total coverage of productive assets has been increased by adding environmental assets (such as soil, wildlands, and biodiversity) as stores of wealth, provided they are linked to economic activities. Similarly, additional costs related to the environment (e.g., cleanup expenditures by government), are also included in the system. These costs are directly related to productive activities and the generation of value added, and include:

- imputed charges for the depletion of minerals and other natural resources; and
- costs of degradation of land, water, air, and so on, as a result of productive activities.

Such costs, in addition to the depreciation of man-made capital, are deducted from GDP to arrive at the EDP. This EDP does not include damages that are unrelated to productive activities (e.g., natural disasters, naturally occurring erosion, and so on), but they, nevertheless, affect well-being through changes in assets (as a store of wealth). Further, as tentatively suggested in the UNSO Framework, these costs would be reflected in an environmentally adjusted net income (ENI). To arrive at ENI, the following five items would be subtracted from EDP:

- environmental protection expenditures of government and households, which are treated as final expenditures in the SNA;
- environmental effects on health and other aspects of human capital;
- environmental costs of household and government consumption activities;
- environmental damage from capital goods that are discarded; and
- negative environmental effects in the country caused by production activities in other countries (negative entry), and negative environmental effects transferred abroad (positive entry). In the case of beneficial effects transmitted across borders, the signs would be reversed.

Some National Approaches to Environmental Accounting

Norway   Norway probably has the longest-running interest in environmental and resource accounting. The intent of the Norwegian system is not to provide a better measure of true income and make possible adjustments to GDP, but to assist the government in making decisions on managing resources that are economically and politically most important.

The resource accounts include petroleum, minerals (iron, titanium, copper, zinc, and lead), forest products, fish, and hydropower. Accounts for mineral resources exist for only a few selected years, while forest statistics have been available since 1970, and those for fish, since 1974. The environmental resources accounts are confined to land-use statistics, the discharge of selected air pollutants, and two water pollutants. The coverage of the Norwegian resource accounts could be expanded to cover other resources, but cost-benefit considerations have so far not encouraged such a move.

United States   Environmental and resource accounting in the United States has so far been limited to the collection of data on pollution abatement expenditures. Before 1989, the Bureau of Census undertook a survey of about 20,000 establishments in the manufacturing sector, while the Bureau of Economic Analysis drew its data from a survey of about 9–14,000 firms in both the manufacturing and non-manufacturing sectors. Since 1989, only a sample of 600 firms has been surveyed.

Because of a strong lobbying effort by environmental groups, the calculation and publication of a measure called "gross sustainable productivity" was made a requirement for the Commerce Department (Public Law 101–45, June 30, 1989). Also, the bill requires the Secretary of State to instruct the United States representatives to the Organization for Economic Cooperation and Development, the United Nations, and the multilateral development banks to seek revisions to the current accounting systems to take into account the depletion or degradation of natural resources. One problem with the proposed measure is that it has not been clearly defined, and even if agreement on the definition were reached soon, sizable resources might be required for data gathering and estimation of the new measure.

France   For a considerable time, French experts have been trying to set up a system known as "patrimony accounting." The system is expected to be comprehensive, consisting of seven levels, starting from specific resource data at level one to aggregate welfare indicators at level seven. The intent is to analyze and describe the natural environment in its three basic functions: economic, ecological, and social.

While a lot of thought has gone into the development of patrimony accounting, very limited resources have been available for its implementation, which is why the process has been slow. So far, it appears that the empirical side of this approach has mainly concentrated on the establishment of resource accounts similar to those established in Norway.

Conceptually expanding the SNA to a SEEA as outlined above is relatively easy; the difficult part would be to produce actual estimates. Where the estimation work is undertaken, the satellite accounts will provide the countries with considerable flexibility in calculating EDP, ENI, or other selected aggregates. Aside from the explicit suggestions contained in the UNSO Framework (and the forthcoming UNSO handbook), countries may wish to adopt certain specific methods and compute their own indicators.

It should be noted that while flexibility at the

experimental stage is desirable, there is obviously a trade-off with comparability across nations, which is needed for cross-country analyses.

One of the options with which countries may experiment is the user cost approach. Under this approach, the revenue from the sale of a depletable resource (net of extraction cost) is split into a capital element, or user cost, and a value-added element, or "true" income. The capital element is considered asset erosion and is therefore not included in GDP. A formula for determining the size of the capital element has been proposed by the Bank's Salah El Serafy. According to this approach, the larger the current annual exploitation of the resource is in comparison with the known reserves, the larger the user cost and the smaller the income component. Complicating issues regarding this approach are the size of the discount rate to be used in the formula and the size of the proven reserves (which may actually increase over time, as in the case of oil during the last few decades).

In estimating the depreciation of capital in abroad sense, it is already clear from the initial work on Mexico that all kinds of assets could be considered, but with various degrees of difficulty. For example, capital that might be considered includes subsoil assets, forests, fisheries, soil, water, air, biodiversity, and historical monuments. However, data availability and reliability of estimates in such cases will clearly be very difficult and may not be consistent for the various categories.

The Bank is of the view that, at a conceptual level, there is a need to have a broad framework that can handle all kinds of capital (or productive assets). At the practical level, a pragmatic approach would be appropriate, which would suggest seeking initial agreement for appropriate treatment of certain expenditures (e.g., those incurred by governments) to protect the environment and marketable subsoil assets. One could leave other, more difficult areas to be incorporated after further research. In the meantime, while this work proceeds, and until firm conclusions have been reached, users of conventional national income aggregates, such as GDP, should keep the limitations in mind and use supplementary environmental information as far as possible to obtain a more balanced picture.

The World Bank has already published one compendium volume on environmental accounting. It is planning to prepare a second containing the UNSO framework, the results of the case studies, the survey of environmental accounting approaches in industrial countries, and other relevant papers. Based on the experience of the case studies, the UNSO plans to further develop its draft handbook into a useful guide for countries wishing to deal better with environmental and natural resource issues.

Summary

Environmental concerns over greenhouse gases, depletion of the ozone layer, deforestation, hazardous wastes, and industrial air pollution have moved to the forefront of international concern and attention. Because of the significant control and influence that MNCs have over world resources, they are being challenged to operate in more environmentally responsible ways. These challenges include conducting business ethically, conducting environmental impact studies before making plant location decisions, implementing technological modifications to reduce waste and increase environmental safety, developing environmentally safe energy sources, accepting social responsibilities for environmental regeneration, diversifying manufacturing, planning, educating, sharing information, and increasing investment in research and development.

New opportunities, however, are being created as new products and markets designed to meet environmental concerns become available.

Discussion Questions

1. Why should MNCs be concerned with global environmental issues?
2. What are greenhouse gases?
3. What has been causing the depletion of the ozone layer? What role have MNCs played in this process?
4. What are hazardous wastes? Find some recent examples (from the *Wall Street Journal* or other periodicals) where MNCs have been involved in either producing or cleaning up hazardous wastes.
5. How can MNCs be more responsible for the global environment? Explain your answer.
6. What new opportunities will MNCs enjoy as a result of increased attention to environmental problems?

Bibliography

BRUCE, LEIGH. 1989. "How Green Is Your Company?" *International Management* (January): 24–27.

JAY, LESLIE. 1990. "Green About the Tills: Markets Discover the Eco-Consumer." *Management Review* (June): 24–28.

JOHNSTONE, BOB. 1990. "A Throw-Away Answer." *Far Eastern Economic Review* (February): 62.

LEONARD, H. JEFFREY. 1986. "Hazardous Waste: The Crisis Spreads." *National Development* (April): 44.

LEONARD, RICHARD. 1986. "After Bhopal: Multinationals and the Management of Hazardous Waste." *Multinational Business* (Issue 2): 1–9.

MAHON, JOHN F., AND PATRICIA C. KELLEY. 1987. "Managing Toxic Wastes—After Bhopal and Sandoz." *Long Range Planning* (August): 50–59.

ROBERTS, GERALD. 1989. "World Energy Outlook: What Managers Should Expect." *Multinational Business* (Spring): 33–36.

SMITH, DOUGLAS N. 1990. "EC Toughen Pollution Regulations." *Business Insurance* (March 5): 21.

TERPSTRA, V., AND K. DAVID. 1991. *The Cultural Environment of International Business*, 3rd ed. Cincinnati: South-Western.

UNITED STATES ENVIRONMENTAL PROTECTION AGENCY. 1989. "Policy Options for Stabilizing Global Climates." Draft report to the U.S. Congress.

Chapter Case Study _____

Alapco Chemicals Ltd.

Wilbur Stevens looked in dismay at the mound of toxic waste piled high in a closed-off area near his factory as he was driven past the dumping ground on his way to another busy day at his office in the Los Helios factor of Alapco Chemicals, where he was general manager. Los Helios was a major industrial location in the southern part of Valdina, a small country in Central America that had close ties with the United States and was heavily dependent on U.S. aid for its continued survival. Alapco Chemicals had established its factory in Los Helios in 1934 and expanded operations considerably. The main products of the Los Helios factory were pesticides and insecticides that were in great demand in Valdina by farmers whose crops were always in danger from grave damage by weeds and pests that flourished in the hot and humid climate of Valdina. Alapco was the only important producer of these products in the country and enjoyed a monopoly over the market.

Although the company had shown consistent growth both in sales and profitability over the past decade, recently its environmental record had begun to be called into question by environmental groups, especially those based in the United States. Attention to the environmental problems of Valdina had been attractive for a number of reasons. The air pollution in the country, especially in the area near Los Helios, was among the highest in the world. The country's forests had almost been completely decimated by indiscriminate logging both for revenue and for clearing land for new communities and industry in the small country. The nine main beaches of the country were so polluted by industrial and municipal waste that they had been declared unfit for swimming. One beach had been totally closed to the general public for the past five years.

A group of environmental activists had focused the blame on the government of Valdina and on local and foreign industry. Until two years ago there was no systematic legislation or even regulation of the environmental aspects of industrial and other forms of economic and development activities. The only regulation was in the form of some weak and often outdated factory codes, which were rarely enforced. Further, the government did not have a separate agency for environmental control, and the issues, if any were raised, were handled by the ministry concerned with a particular industry.

Growing international attention and increasingly visible effects of the environmental deterioration in Valdina had ultimately goaded the government into action. In 1987 legislation was passed containing environmental guidelines to be observed both by industry and agriculture. Globe-Watch, an active environmental action group in Washington, D.C., helped the government draft the legislation, which in its final form turned out to be fairly streamlined and quite stringent.

Enforcement of the legislation, however, was another matter. The government of Valdina, strapped for cash and deep in debt, did not have the resources to establish a system of periodic inspections and follow-ups to ensure that the guidelines were actually being followed. Moreover, being dependent on industry to raise revenues, especially the multinationals, the government could hardly have the political will to take stern measures to enforce its decree. As a result, much of the legislation remained merely on paper and whatever was implemented was done on a voluntary basis. Voluntary action was also limited because following the safeguards meant substantial capital outlay toward the purchase and installation of pollution-control equipment in factories or toward modifying a plant or processes to ensure that they were less damaging environmentally.

Alapco was one of the main polluters, partly because of the sheer size of its operation (it had the largest single plant in Valdina), partly because of the nature of the manufacturing process of chemicals, and partly because some of the processes it was using were quite old and had not been modified to control their effect on environmental degradation. Again, because Alapco was the only producer of some of the chemicals needed by Valdina's farmers and because the company's top executives had extremely close connections with the government, no action was taken to enforce the new regulations, and things remained pretty much as they were for the next year, until Stevens arrived in Los Helios as the new general manager of the plant.

Stevens was a brilliant engineer who held a master's degree in chemical engineering from Carnegie-Mellon University and had an M.B.A. from the Massachusetts Institute of Technology. He had worked with a tire company in Great Britain and with a chemical firm in Germany before returning to the United States as operations manager for Alapco's plant in Peoria, Illinois. At Peoria, Stevens had made an excellent impression with the senior management and the workers. His management style and unique abilities had been a major factor in turning around the plant's performance from subpar productivity to one of the highest among Alapco's fifteen plants within a space of three years. As a result, Stevens had been identified by top management as a potential candidate for the highest levels of the company hierarchy. As a part of the plan to groom him for senior management positions by giving him greater responsibilities and exposing him to an international situation, Stevens was appointed general manager and chief executive officer of the company's plant at Los Helios in Valdina.

On reaching Los Helios, Stevens was struck by the dominance Alapco enjoyed in the country. He was regularly invited to receptions given by senior government officials, and nearly every request he made on behalf of the company was quickly processed with a positive response. The plant was also operating with a reasonable degree of efficiency, considering its rather outmoded technology. Alapco's senior management had, as a matter of policy, continued to use this technology, taking the view that it was adequate to meet the current needs of the market in Valdina and that the introduction of new technology would result in high costs that the company would not be able to recover under the present conditions and market structure in Valdina.

Stevens soon began to feel quite comfortable in his new position. Valdina had an excellent school for children of American expatriates, which were many, and his family had managed to adjust to the new conditions quite well. After a few months, he received a group of visitors from Washington, who left him feeling quite uneasy. They were members of a delegation from Global-Watch, and they informed Stevens that their group had helped the government of Valdina formulate the environmental policy and that they were, on their own, following up on that legislation. At first Stevens was quite annoyed and stated that this was a matter between his company and the government of Valdina and that if his plant was violating any of the regulations, it was for the government of Valdina to say so and not any third party. Further, he added, not a single letter or any other communication had been received from the government of Valdina on this issue, and he therefore believed that his plant was complying with all government requirements. The environmentalists were very direct. They brought out a list of environmental violations that the operations of Alapco's plant were actually committing every day and compared them to the operations of Alapco's plants in other areas, especially in the developed world. Their presentation made clear that Alapco was following two different environmental standards—one in developed countries and one in the developing countries. As far as Valdina was concerned, the reason for the double standards was the absence of the ability or willingness of the government to enforce the legislation.

Stevens saw the point. He had been aware of this problem but he had not seen it in the same light as the environmental group, that is, as an ethical and moral responsibility of his company to their host country. Yes, there were toxic waste dumps just outside the plant and barely three miles from a densely populated residential area. A tropical storm could blow off the waste and cause serious damage. The emissions from the factory's chimneys were far higher in pollutants than at any of the other plants. The Valdina plant had no effluent treatment facility and all the chemical waste was routinely dumped into the sea. The problem was that in Valdina, all this seemed natural. Everyone was doing it and no one said anything. Nevertheless, he realized that this was fundamentally wrong and that the company should do something about it.

He called the company's headquarters in Lansing, Michigan, and suggested that unilateral action be taken to improve the environmental standards of the Alapco plant and bring them in line with the other plants of the company. He also submitted a cost estimate and pointed out that while there would be a slight erosion in the profits of the company, the benefits to the host country would be great. The head office, however, did not appear very enthusiastic. Although they did not say so directly, the message seemed to be if we don't have to do it, why should we?

Stevens was quite disappointed by this reaction. Maybe there is another way out of this mess he thought as he drove past the waste dump outside the factory.

Question

What would you do in this situation if you were:
1. Wilbur Stevens?
2. Director of Globe-Watch?
3. Minister for industries, Government of Valdina?

CHAPTER 23

Future Issues in International Business

CHAPTER OBJECTIVES

This chapter will:

- Summarize the latest trends in international relations and trade.
- Identify the role that technological innovation will have in creating greater efficiency and productivity.
- Present a forecast of how multinational corporations will evolve in areas of staffing, management style, and the location of manufacturing facilities.
- Offer other issues that will influence the MNC of the future.

Why Study the Future?

International business managers must not only manage their operations in the present, they must also anticipate future changes. The need to assess future trends that are likely to impact business operations is obvious. If a business is able to accurately anticipate future trends, it has that much more time to adjust its own business practices and strategies, and when the expected changes actually occur, it will be in an excellent position.

It is difficult to predict how and where changes will occur, but it is useful to assess future trends. Many firms develop sophisticated internal forecasting methods to generate possible scenarios in

their areas of interest. Other firms use the services of specialized agencies or consulting firms that concentrate on future analysis.

There are, however, a few identifiable broad trends and resulting scenarios that are likely to have a major impact on the functioning and responses of international businesses.

Future Trends Affecting International Business

East-West Détente

It is evident that the international relations scenario is going to change dramatically, given the far-reaching changes in 1989 and 1990. The international division of the world into superpower blocs that occurred after World War II was changed as the Communist bloc unravelled rapidly. Most European Communist countries have rejected communism as a form of social and political organization and have installed governments that believe in Western-style liberal democracy. These developments should lead to a climate of improved international relations, not only between the two power blocs, but also among other countries of the world. It is too early, however, to predict what the new diplomatic equation will look like once the transitory phase in Eastern Europe is over, but as the Soviet Union focuses on solving its internal domestic problems, a new collaborative relationship between the United States and the Soviet Union appears to be developing,

despite differences on national and international issues.

Investment in China

Developments in the relationship between the United States and Western European countries with China and Latin America will also be an important area for MNCs. The United States and many European countries already have substantial investments in China and are eager to improve relations with Beijing, which suffered a major setback in 1989 following the official crackdown on student protestors. The leadership in China will seek to improve relations with the West once the events of 1989 are finally relegated to the background (see Perspective 23–1).

Some evidence of this possibility was provided

PERSPECTIVE 23–1   **Going Global in the New World**

Tiananmen Square. Eastern Europe. Kuwait.

Change has rarely been so swift, so widespread. For business, the new order clearly offers the potential for incalculable prosperity.

But it comes at a difficult juncture. For at a time when "going global" has become a competitive necessity, the international business landscape seems to change almost daily.

China, for instance, has suddenly regressed— its image transformed from one of stability to one of fragility and riskiness. Eastern Europe, which a year ago seemed a backward bulwark of socialism, is widely regarded as one of the great economic growth areas of the 1990s. And in the Mideast, after the Iraqi invasion of Kuwait, oil prices turned suddenly volatile, threatening to toss the world's economies into recession.

Who will survive—and thrive—in this new world?

It isn't easy to predict, but one thing is clear: Companies can't simply pretend that the rest of the world doesn't exist. Wherever a company is based, whatever a company makes, competition is pushing it to think globally. Even the executives of a small Oregon company that makes robotic-vision systems to cut french fries discovered recently that a Belgian company had developed a similar, competing device.

Such competitive pressures are growing in all the world's major markets. U.S. companies are intensifying their efforts in Europe and Asia. European companies are pushing hard into the U.S. and Asia. And Japanese companies, once focused heavily on exports to the U.S., are buying and building aggressively almost everywhere.

The result is that companies that were primarily domestic, or merely exporters, are becoming truly global at a furious rate. All of which leads

SOURCE: Bernard Wysocki, Jr., *Wall Street Journal*, September 21, 1990.

to far-flung operations and a much greater degree of complexity.

How will American companies fare in this new world? Many U.S. companies long ago staked out beachheads overseas, especially in Europe. They also did what few European companies could bring themselves to do: They considered Europe a single market. Today, as Europe hurtles toward economic unity by the end of 1992, many American companies are already well positioned.

Ford Motor Co., Merck & Co., Coca-Cola Co., International Business Machines Corp. and Hewlett-Packard Co. are just a few of the companies with strong, profitable operations in Europe.

In Asia, too, many U.S. companies have persevered and prospered. McDonald's Corp. and Walt Disney Co. are among them. Also successful are companies as diverse as Du Pont Co. and Amway, the latter having sold more than $500 million in housewares door-to-door in Japan last year.

Yet there are also signs of American companies in retreat from abroad. Some U.S. companies, including Chrysler Corp. and Honeywell Inc., have cashed out part of their stakes in Japan. Many U.S. banks, in particular, are withdrawing from overseas, even from some of the fast-growing markets of Asia.

Does this matter? It could matter greatly. Competing in the 1990s is likely to require large amounts of long-term investment overseas in many of the most important industries—in autos, in electronics, in pharmaceuticals. The necessity to be "insiders" rather than mere exporters is growing day by day.

The insider status becomes particularly important should the world economy tumble into protectionist regional trading "blocs." If trade were to be relatively free within North America, Europe or Asia, but relatively restricted between blocs, then a significant presence inside each block would be crucial.

For the U.S. such a trading-bloc world conjures up a nightmarish scenario: An American regional bloc could turn out to be the debt bloc—a collection of countries that import capital, run big budget deficits, and invest pathetically small amounts in new ventures.

Fortunately, no such thing is preordained. These days, in fact, it seems that no idea is too bold, too farfetched, to be taken seriously. At a recent meeting at the Japan Society in New York, management guru Peter Drucker, asked about the likelihood of an East Asian trade bloc, responded, "If China breaks up under regional warlords, then we'll see an East Asian bloc."

Two years ago, Mr. Drucker might have been laughed out of the room. The breakup of China? Impossible.

It no longer seems like such a radical idea.

by the secret diplomatic missions that the United States sent to China after the 1989 events in Beijing. The importance of China to Western European and U.S. corporations is likely to grow because China is projected to have the potential for attracting substantial foreign direct investment in the next decade and beyond.

Deregulation in the LDCs

There is no doubt that political leaders in most countries are increasingly under pressure to provide more market orientation to their economies in order to improve the levels of productivity and efficiency. Economic reforms toward lowering the share of state-owned enterprises, increasing the number of international business transactions, and eliminating official subsidies and administered prices are likely to take place in many less-developed countries as a result of prodding both by their bilateral aid donors, such as Western governments, and by multilateral institutions, such as the World Bank and the International Monetary Fund. These reforms should result in more open economies with fewer government controls on international business. Consequently, business opportunities for MNCs in LDCs could increase substantially.

Global Resource Depletion

The next few decades are likely to be marked by rapid and far-reaching changes in the world economy that will influence international business in a variety of ways. The world's natural resources are likely to be depleted rapidly, and substitutes will have to be found. The depletion of such natural resources as oil, metallic ores, and minerals will weaken the economic position of those countries that rely almost solely on the export of such commodities for their foreign exchange earnings. On the other hand, exclusive monopoly over the technology used to manufacture substitutes could be acquired by large MNCs, which would increase their international economic dominance.

Environmental Degradation

By the end of the 1980s, international concerns about the rapid and far-reaching deterioration of the world's environment had gained significant public attention, and environmental action groups had acquired considerable political influence in many countries, especially in the United States and Western Europe. Environmental groups were also active in many LDCs in Latin America, Asia, and Africa.

Much of the blame for the damage to the environment has been, and continues to be, placed on the MNCs. Concerns for the environment are particularly strong in certain areas of ecological damage—harm to the earth's ozone layer, atmospheric pollution, deforestation, pollution of inland freshwater resources and coastal waters, and damage to the marine environment.

There is no doubt that pressures are likely to grow, and they may have several important consequences for MNCs. There is likely to be more stringent official regulation of the pollution and environmental effects of the manufacturing activities of MNCs both at home and in the host countries. Greater awareness of the harmful effects of manufacturing activity on its local environment by a host country is likely to result in tougher environmental standards that MNCs would have to meet when setting up overseas operations. Further, MNCs may be required to reduce the environmentally adverse effects of their existing operations by installing more sophisticated pollution-control equipment or spending more in remedying the existing environmental damage.

MNCs must also consider the possibility that political action will be taken against them by environmental activists, who are increasingly influential in many developing countries. It is indeed possible that while an MNC may meet the environmental standards laid down by the host government and have approval for its manufacturing operation, it may still face strong opposition from environmental activists who could attempt to stall actual implementation in a variety of ways. Such instances have occurred in a number of places around the world and it is possible that this may be a precursor to a growing global trend.

For MNCs this scenario implies a need for greater investment in research and development for new environmentally safe production technologies and effective and economical pollution-control methods. Further, since public concern is so widespread, it is important for MNCs to increase their public relations efforts to convince governments and the general public that their operations are not harmful to the environment. Thus, in addition to product image, brand image, corporate image, and social image, the MNC of the future will have to be increasingly concerned with its environmental image.

The concerns with the environment will also open new business opportunities for MNCs of the future. The development of pollution-control technologies and equipment by MNCs would put them in a position to market those to other MNCs and companies in host countries. Further concerns with the environment will open up demands for new types of technologies aimed at solving some of the world's environmental problems and preventing further damage. Recycling, waste management, and reforestation are some of the things that would immediately be important. In addition, there is likely to be considerable demand for environmentally sound products, such as biodegradable or recyclable materials. Many major corporations are now developing new products that address these concerns and most of them are selling well.

European Integration

Another important issue for the international business community is the economic integration of Europe, slated for 1992. The newly integrated European Economic Community is likely to pose a formidable challenge to outside investors and competitors. European companies will gain significant competitive advantages because they will be able to source raw materials and other inputs from all over Europe without any government interference or payment of duties. Moreover, in intra-Europe trade, companies based in Europe will have a clear edge because their products will not be taxed when exported to other European countries. MNCs outside Europe, therefore, are likely to find it more difficult to penetrate European markets. Moreover, internal collaboration within Europe will provide new strengths to European companies, which will be able to share expertise and common resources of other companies in the community to improve their productivity and competitiveness (see Perspective 23–2).

Competition from Asia

Asian competition is also likely to increase. Apart from Europe, Japan and the Pacific Rim countries are going to offer stiff competition to all comers. In the 1960s, 1970s, and early 1980s, competition from Japan and the newly industrialized countries was limited, to the extent that these countries did not have large MNCs with major manufacturing locations spread all over the world. By the end of the 1980s, however, Japanese companies had several overseas manufacturing facilities, including some in the industrialized countries, such as the United States. As the other Pacific Rim economies expand and grow, they have also begun to create multinational corporations, whose large number of overseas production and operational locations offer the older MNCs head-on competition.

Latin America: Rising Debt-Equity Swaps

Another issue that causes great concern for the international business community, particularly with respect to its future implications, is international debt. Although the debt crisis first became public knowledge back in 1982, it has not gone away. The only consolation that can be derived in this context is that the world's economy and financial system have at least survived the initial impact and have not collapsed, as was feared in certain quarters.

The debt crisis holds, nevertheless, many serious portents for international business. Countries severely in debt have virtually no capacity to generate foreign exchange earnings. In other words, repatriation of income and dividends from these countries is extremely difficult, which not only discourages further investment in these countries by MNCs, but also places existing investments in considerable jeopardy.

There are, however, hopeful signs. For one, there is increasing agreement, at least among the official policymakers in the lender countries, that some part of the external debt of the poorest and most heavily indebted countries be written off. If this is achieved, the current burden will be substantially eased, and these countries would regain their access to international funding, which is badly needed to revive their domestic economies and meet essential import requirements. Many of the heavily indebted countries are experimenting with various types of debt conversion programs that are utilized to convert the existing debt of a creditor into an investment. The conversion of debt into equity through debt-equity swaps actually increases opportunities for international business because it offers many potential investors an easy and inexpensive medium of investment in a country. By swapping into the equity of an existing company, the investor becomes a partner in the

PERSPECTIVE 23–2   Blocking Trade?

Regional trading alliances. Slowly—and halt-ingly—nations seem to be embracing them. Which leads to a question: Are trading alliances a boon or a hindrance to international trade?

The answer is yes.

Free-trade agreements within regions are de-signed to expand trade and are roundly welcomed by most economists. The worry is that such agree-ments can easily lead to the dreaded protectionist trading blocs—defensive pacts that set up barriers around regions and prevent the flow of goods from one region to another.

What might a world of regional trading blocs look like? One possible scenario, based on today's conventional wisdom, divides the world into three major trading blocs—the Americas bloc, the Eu-ropean bloc, and the Asian bloc.

The Americas bloc consists of three countries. As the strongest nation economically and politi-cally, the United States is naturally at the center of the bloc. Canada and Mexico would be impor-tant secondary players in the Americas bloc, as would the rest of Latin America.

The U.S.-Canada free-trade agreement, which took effect last year, is widely regarded in the U.S. as an expansion of free trade. But it is viewed with alarm by some Japanese as the beginning of a regional, protectionist bloc. The same is true about the recently discussed possibility of a free-trade agreement between the U.S. and Mexico.

The same conflicting perspectives define the second bloc—the European bloc. The 1992 economic integration of Western Europe and the dramatic developments in Eastern Europe

suggest a potential for a large and strong economic alliance. But the question remains: Will European unity be primarily a trade-expanding measure by the EC countries? Or will it facilitate the erec-tion of protectionist walls, the so-called fortress Europe?

And in Asia, there is much talk these days about a "yen" bloc, linking Japan's economy more closely with the economies of other Asian coun-tries. The result, as in North America and Europe, would be a more self-sufficient region, better able to provide both raw materials and markets within the region—and perhaps more willing to reduce trade with America or Europe.

Japanese government officials loudly assail re-gional trading blocks that serve as protectionist trade umbrellas. But they also concede that blocs may be an unfortunate but emerging trend.

"There is a little bit of cohesiveness among the nations of the Pacific Rim," said Kazuo Nukazawa, managing director of Keidanren, the Japanese big-business organization, on a recent Public Broad-casting Service television program. "Largely, they are afraid of American protectionism or European protectionism."

Whether blocs emerge is impossible to say. Al-ready, however, many companies are hedging their bets by establishing a large presence in each re-gion. Hence the recent flurry of cross-border ac-quisitions and the rash of global alliances and joint ventures. Direct investment, as the U.S. discov-ered in the 1950s and 1960s in Europe, is the way to become an "insider" in foreign lands. In a world of blocs, mere exporters are the biggest losers.

SOURCE: Bernard Wysocki, Jr., *Wall Street Journal*, September 21, 1990, page R31.

management and, therefore, joins in the efforts of the investee company to improve profitability and efficiency of operations. Thus, the debt-equity swap programs make the interrelationship between two parties more intensive and comprehensive.

They become joint partners in the business, where hitherto there was only a debtor-creditor relation-ship.

Debt-equity conversion programs do have some negative effects on the economy of the investee countries. They actually imply a devaluation of the exchange rate, because debt is sold at a discount, which results in more units of the local currency being paid for the same amount of foreign currency. Furthermore, heavily indebted countries suffer from either serious inflation or hyperinflation. The increase in money supply that occurs because of conversion of existing debt at a discount fuels the inflationary expectations. Many countries also feel that by using the debt-equity swap programs, foreign enterprises are likely to take control of domestic business and that overinvestment in various industries by foreigners could lead to heavy foreign exchange liabilities in the future because of dividend and profit remittances. Several countries, for these and other reasons, suspended their debt conversion programs toward the end of the 1980s.

Expanding Protectionism

In the late 1980s, there appeared to be a hardening of the differences of opinion between the industrialized and developing countries. The former are likely to press for a greater opening of LDC economies, not only to international trade in commodities but also to services, such as communications and banking. LDCs are likely to oppose this move, because they feel that they will not be in a position to compete with the industrialized countries on a free-competition basis. It is also possible that if the developing countries do not open up their economies to the extent sought by the industrialized countries, the latter may take retaliatory action by hiking up tariffs and putting up nontariff barriers in their own countries. The threat of future protectionism is very real and it could disrupt the flow of international trade and business. In 1989, for example, legislation was introduced in the United States declaring, among others, Brazil and India unfair trading partners, as a precursor to comprehensive protectionist measures against these countries.

Issues of protectionism and relative tariffs are also likely to arise within the industrialized countries. For example, Japan is going to be under increasing U.S. pressure to open up its economy for U.S. exports, in order to reduce the massive trade deficit of the latter. Similarly, the issue of trade between the European Economic Community and the rest of the world will have to be negotiated after the integration is implemented.

Technology Explosion: The Information Era

Technology has been one of the most important driving forces behind internationalization of business in the twentieth century. In the last years of this century and the early years of the next, this is likely to be even more so. Many major industrial corporations that have made large investments in futuristic technologies—lasers, hi-tech computers, fiber optics, superconductivity, digital electronics—are likely to find themselves at a significant competitive advantage vis-à-vis their competitors in their own and other countries. The depletion of natural resources and the growing consciousness about the threats to the environment are likely to spur new technological advances into safe and regenerative products.

Technology is also likely to make the working of international business more efficient and more competitive. The revolution in information and communications technology has already made it possible for a large MNC to monitor simultaneously from a single location the operation of hundreds of its locations and offices spread across different countries and time zones. The coming changes in communications and computing power are likely to make this control even more efficient and economical and add significantly to the business capabilities of MNCs. In fact, the types of communication and internal and external information services and systems available to a globally oriented company are likely to be an increasingly important factor in the firm's overall competitiveness. The edge provided by the access to advanced information technology will also expand the scope of international business because it will enable corporations to search, locate, analyze, evaluate, and choose new business opportunities and possibilities in different parts of the world with a facility that had not been possible in the past.

Technology is also likely to change the way business is accomplished (see Perspective 23–3). Electronic transmission of funds and financial information is already here. By the turn of the century, there is likely to be a substantial increase in the number of international transactions where the documentation is exchanged electronically. Automation of financial and commercial transactions will, of course, require the agreement of the different parties involved and will be possible only if both parties have access to the necessary technology and equipment. It is therefore apparent that such a scenario will become a reality first in the dealings of industrialized countries between themselves and only later in the developing countries.

PERSPECTIVE 23–3   Day in the Life of Tomorrow's Manager

6:10 a.m. The year is 2010 and another Monday morning has begun for Peter Smith. The marketing vice-president for a home-appliance division of a major U.S. manufacturer is awakened by his computer alarm. He saunters to his terminal to check the weather outlook in Madrid, where he'll fly late tonight, and to send an electronic-voice message to a supplier in Thailand.

Meet the manager of the future.

A different breed from his contemporary counterpart, our fictitious Peter Smith inhabits an international business world shaped by competition, collaboration and corporate diversity. (For one thing, he's just as likely to be a woman as a man and—with the profound demographic changes ahead—will probably manage a work force made up mostly of women and minorities.)

Comfortable with technology, he's been logging on to computers since he was seven years old. A literature honors student with a joint M.B.A./advanced-communications degree, the 38-year-old joined his current employer four years ago after stints at two other corporations— one abroad—and a marketing consulting firm. Now he oversees offices in a score of countries on four continents.

Tomorrow's manager "will have to know how to operate in an any-time, any-place universe," says Stanley Davis, a management consultant and author of "Future Perfect," a look at the 21st-century business world.

Adds James Maxmin, chief executive of London-based Thorn EMI PLC's home-electronics division: "We've all come to accept that organizations and managers who aren't cost-conscious and productive won't survive. But in the future, we'll also have to be more flexible, responsive and smarter. Managers will have to be nurturers and teachers, instead of policemen and watchdogs."

7:20 a.m. Mr. Smith and his wife, who heads her own architecture firm, organize the home front before darting to the supertrain. They leave instructions for their personal computer to call the home-cleaning service as well as a gourmet-carryout service that will prepare dinner for eight guests Saturday. And they quickly go over the day's schedules for their three- and six-year-old daughters with their nanny.

On the train during a speedy 20-minute commute from suburb to Manhattan, Mr. Smith checks his electronic mailbox and also reads his favorite trade magazine via his laptop computer.

The jury is still out on how dual-career couples will juggle high-pressure work and personal lives. Some consultants and executives predict that the frenetic pace will only quicken. "I joke to managers now that we come in on London

SOURCE: Carol Hymowitz, *Wall Street Journal*, March 20, 1989.

time and leave on Tokyo time," says Anthony Terracciano, president of Mellon Bank Corp., Pittsburgh. He foresees an even more difficult work schedule ahead.

But others believe that more creative uses of flexible schedules as well as technological advances in communications and travel will allow more balance. "In the past, nobody cared if your staff had heart attacks, but in tomorrow's knowledge-based economy we'll be judged more on how well we take care of people," contends Robert Kelley, a professor at Carnegie Mellon University's business school.

8:15 a.m. In his high-tech office that doubles as a conference room, Mr. Smith reviews the day's schedule with his executive assistant (traditional secretaries vanished a decade earlier). Then it's on to his first meeting: a conference via video screen between his division's chief production manager in Cincinnati and a supplier near Munich.

The supplier tells them she can deliver a critical component for a new appliance at a 10% cost saving if they grab it within a week. Mr. Smith and the production manager quickly concur that it's a good deal. While they'll have to immediately change production schedules, they'll be able to snare a new customer who has been balking about price.

While today's manager spends most of his time conferring with bosses and subordinates within his own company, tomorrow's manager will be "intimately hooked to suppliers and customers" and well-versed in competitors' strategies, says Mr. Davis, the management consultant.

The marketplace will demand customized products and immediate delivery. This will force managers to make swift product-design and marketing decisions that now often take months and reams of reports. "Instant performance will be expected of them, and it's going to be harder to hide incompetence," says Ann Barry, vice president-research at Handy Associates, Inc., a New York consultant.

10:30 a.m. At a staff meeting, Mr. Smith finds himself refereeing between two subordinates who disagree vehemently on how to promote a new appliance. One, an Asian manager, suggests that a fresh cam-

paign begin much sooner than initially envisioned. The other, a European, wants to hold off until results of a test market are received later that week.

Mr. Smith quickly realizes this is a cultural, not strategic, clash pitting a let's-do-it-now, analyze-it-later approach against a more cautious style. He makes them aware they're not really far apart and the European manager agrees to move swiftly.

By 2010, managers will have to handle greater cultural diversity with subtle human-relations skills. Managers will have to understand that employees don't think alike about such basics as "handling confrontation or even what it means to do a good day's work," says Jeffrey Sonnenfeld, a Harvard Business School professor.

12:30 p.m. Lunch is in Mr. Smith's office today, giving him time to take a video lesson in conversational Chinese. He already speaks Spanish fluently, learned during a work stint in Argentina, and wants to master at least two more languages. After 20 minutes, though, he decides to go to his computer to check his company's latest political-risk assessment on Spain, where recent student unrest has erupted into riots. The report tells him that the disturbances aren't anti-American, but he decides to have a bodyguard meet him at the Madrid airport anyway.

Technology will provide managers with easy access to more data than they can possibly use. The challenge will be to "synthesize data to make effective decisions," says Mellon's Mr. Terracciano.

2:20 p.m. Two of Mr. Smith's top lieutenants complain that they and others on his staff feel a recent bonus payment for a successful project wasn't divided equitably. Bluntly, they note that while Mr. Smith received a hefty $20,000 bonus, his 15-member staff had to split $5,000, and they threaten to defect. He quickly calls his boss, who says he'll think about increasing the bonus for staff members.

With skilled technical and professional employees likely to be in short supply, tomorrow's managers will have to share more authority with subordinates and, in some cases, pay them as much as or more than the managers themselves earn.

While yielding more to their employees, managers in their 30s in 2010 may find their own climb up the corporate ladder stalled by superiors. After advancing rapidly in their 20s, this generation "will be locked in a heated fight with older baby boomers who won't want to retire," says Harvard's Mr. Sonnenfeld.

4 p.m. Mr. Smith learns from the field that a large retail customer has been approached by a foreign competitor promising to quickly supply him with a best-selling appliance. After conferring with his division's production managers, he phones the customer and suggests that his company could supply the same product but with three slightly different custom designs. They arrange a meeting later in the week.

Despite the globalization of companies and speed of overall change, some things will stay the same. Managers intent on rising to the top will still be judged largely on how well they articulate ideas and work with others.

In addition, different corporate cultures will still encourage and reward divergent qualities. Companies banking on new products, for example, will reward risk takers, while slow-growth industries will stress predictability and caution in their ranks.

6 p.m. Before heading to the airport, Mr. Smith uses his video phone to give his daughters a good-night kiss and to talk about the next day's schedule with his wife. Learning that she must take an unexpected trip herself the next evening, he promises to catch the SuperConcorde home in time to put the kids to sleep himself.

Impact of Trends on MNCs

The multinational corporation is likely to remain the dominant form of corporate organization in international business for several years to come. Its form and manner of operation, however, is likely to change substantially in response to the changes and trends in the business environment.

The Megacorporation

Developments in information, communications technologies, computers, and transportation are likely to shrink the world further and enable easier geographical expansion for major corporations. It is likely that today's corporations, seeking expansion, will utilize these opportunities to increase the size of their operations.

Although the developments in technology are going to be rapid and far-reaching, they are also likely to be extremely expensive. Only the very large corporations are going to be able to afford the expense of dedicated computer and communication networks, state-of-the-art manufacturing technologies, and the massive investments needed to build entirely new plants based on the new technologies. These firms will thus have a massive technological and competitive edge over their competitors.

Smaller companies may fall by the wayside, either going out of business or readjusting their operational focus. Mergers and acquisitions are likely to become increasingly common because major international corporations will attempt to either eliminate or join the competition. Strategic alliances may become more common because major corporations eye the same markets and work out relationships that share resources, strengths, and competitive advantages. Some of these trends are already beginning to surface. Sony Corporation's purchase of CBS and the Time-Warner merger are examples of the coming megacorporations.

Geocentric Staffing

The personnel of MNCs are likely to become more geocentric than today. As the number of locations of operations increases, the parent office is likely to find it increasingly difficult to secure executives from the home country to fill positions in all locations. Moreover, as overseas personnel join MNCs in increasing numbers, a large pool of well-qualified local and third-country nationals is likely to emerge and be available for deployment in different operational locations of the globally oriented enterprise. In many developing countries, standards of technical and managerial education are rising rapidly. MNCs are finding it useful to recruit personnel locally for manning overseas operations, even at relatively senior lev-

els. The geocentric corporation of the future is likely to have an internationally varied managerial executive cadre (see Perspective 23–4), which is extremely mobile, regardless of the nationality of the individual.

PERSPECTIVE 23–4   Going Global

THE CHIEF EXECUTIVES IN YEAR 2000 WILL BE EXPERIENCED ABROAD

Since World War II, the typical corporate chief executive officer has looked something like this:

He started out as a finance man with an undergraduate degree in accounting. He methodically worked his way up through the company from the controller's office in a division, to running that division, to the top job. His military background shows: He is used to giving orders—and to having them obeyed. As the head of the United Way drive, he is a big man in his community. However, the first time he traveled overseas on business was as chief executive: Computers make him nervous.

But peer into the executive suite of the year 2000 and see a completely different person.

His undergraduate degree is in French literature, but he also has a joint M.B.A./engineering degree. He started in research and was quickly picked out as a potential CEO. He zigzagged from research to marketing to finance. He proved himself in Brazil by turning around a flailing joint venture. He speaks Portuguese and French and is on a first-name basis with commerce ministers in half a dozen countries. Unlike his predecessor's predecessor, he isn't a drill sergeant. He is first among equals in a five-person Office of the Chief Executive.

As the 40-year postwar epoch of growing markets and domestic-only competition fades, so

too is vanishing the narrow one-company, one-industry chief executive. By the turn of the century, academicians, consultants and executives themselves predict, companies' choices of leaders will be governed by increasing international competition, the globalization of companies, the spread of technology, demographic shifts, and the speed of overall change.

"The world is going to be so significantly different it will require a completely different kind of CEO," says Ed Dunn, corporate vice president of Whirlpool Corp. The next century's corporate chief, Mr. Dunn adds, "must have a multienvironment, multicountry, multifunctional, maybe even multicompany, multi-industry experience."

The changing requirements bemuse some who hold, or once held, the top slot. "I'm glad I lived when I did," says William May, who was chief executive officer of American Can Co. between 1965 and 1980. "I'd have to really learn a whole lot of new tricks" to be a chief executive today.

LOOKING AHEAD

With the 21st century slightly over a decade away, many companies are already trying to figure out just who the chief executive of the future ought to be.

To study that question, Dow Chemical Co. is setting up a world-wide panel of senior executives. "We want to know what kind of skills

SOURCE: Amanda Bennett, *Wall Street Journal*, February 27, 1989.

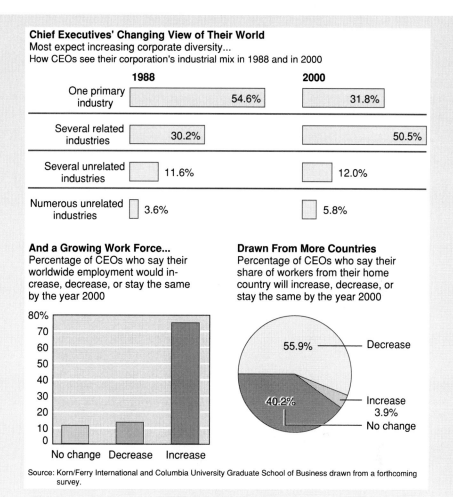

Chief Executives' Changing View of Their World
Most expect increasing corporate diversity...
How CEOs see their corporation's industrial mix in 1988 and in 2000

	1988	2000
One primary industry	54.6%	31.8%
Several related industries	30.2%	50.5%
Several unrelated industries	11.6%	12.0%
Numerous unrelated industries	3.6%	5.8%

And a Growing Work Force...
Percentage of CEOs who say their worldwide employment would increase, decrease, or stay the same by the year 2000

No change Decrease Increase

Drawn From More Countries
Percentage of CEOs who say their share of workers from their home country will increase, decrease, or stay the same by the year 2000

55.9% — Decrease
40.2%
Increase 3.9%
No change

Source: Korn/Ferry International and Columbia University Graduate School of Business drawn from a forthcoming survey.

and knowledge will be needed so we can give the heirs apparent that training in the next few years," says Willard B. Maxwell, a senior training consultant at Dow. Whirlpool, which until recently identified potential chief executives about five years in advance, now believes that the selection process may have to begin as early as 25 years ahead. "We're thinking more about development throughout someone's career," Mr. Dunn says.

Until recently, the road to the top in a big corporation has been fairly well marked. General Motors Corp., for example, has been run by a finance man for 28 of the past 32 years. More than

three-quarters of the chief executives surveyed in 1987 by search firm Heidrick & Struggles had finance, manufacturing or marketing backgrounds.

'CONVENTIONAL ROUTE'

Donald Frey, recently retired chairman of Bell & Howell Co., started in product engineering and product planning at Ford Motor Co. "It was a fairly conventional route for the sacred few in my generation. We became CEOs by virtue of being able to design and get products made."

In the future, however, specific functional backgrounds such as marketing or finance are becoming less important for chief executives. "Where they come from won't be at all relevant," says Jerry Wind of the University of Pennsylvania's Wharton School. With creative financing techniques that turn financial decisions into marketing questions, manufacturing processes that center on computer technology, and product designs that depend on rapid market feedback, the chief executive will, instead, need a varied background.

"It will be very difficult for a single-discipline individual to reach the top," predicts Douglas Danforth, former chairman of Westinghouse Electric Co.

Specific industry experience will also become less relevant because there will be fewer one-industry companies. More than two-thirds of chief executives in a survey to be released later this year by executive-search firm Korn/Ferry International and Columbia University Graduate School of Business said their companies would be involved in several different industries by the year 2000, compared with fewer than half who described their companies that way today.

Intensifying international competition will make the home-grown chief executive obsolete. "Global, global, global," is how Noel Tichy, a professor at University of Michigan's graduate school of business, describes the wider-ranging chief executive of the future. "Travel overseas," Mr. Danforth of Westinghouse advises future chief executives. "Meet with the prime minister, the ministers of trade and commerce. Meet with the king of Spain and the chancellor of West Germany. Get yourself known."

With over half of Arthur Andersen & Co.'s revenue generated outside the U.S., the company's next chief executive "will be a person with experience outside the borders of the U.S., which I have not," says Duane R. Kullberg, the head of the big accounting and consulting company. "If you go back 20 years, you could be pretty insular and still survive. Today, that's not possible."

TRAINING INTERNATIONALIZED

Dow Chemical figures that mere international exposure isn't enough. It wants chief executives who have run foreign businesses for a long time and foresees the day when may other companies will, too. "About five years of international experience" will do, says Dow Chemical Chairman Paul Orrefice, who worked for Dow in Switzerland, Italy, Brazil and Spain and was its first president of Latin American operations in 1966. "It should be long enough to really run it."

Others predict that by the next century, overseas executives will be equal contenders in the race for the top. This year, for the first time, Merck & Co. won't segregate its senior-executive training programs by country. "We have internationalized our training," says Art Strohmer, Merck's executive director of human resources. "We have high-level employees from Europe, Latin America, the U.S. and the rest of the world rubbing shoulders with each other." The model many cite for future chief executives is Coca-Cola Co.'s chairman, Roberto Golzueta, who started out with the company in Havana, Cuba, in 1954.

Computer-shy executives probably won't make it to the top of the company of 2000. Not that computer wizards or techies will be taking over—far from it. "The computer in the basement is a utility, not a source of competitive advantage," says Gerald R. Faulhaber, an associate professor at Wharton. Rather, chief executives will have to be comfortable exchanging information electronically and dealing with the ensuing organizational changes.

Five years ago, William McGowan, the chief executive of MCI Communications Corp., held a breakfast meeting every Monday morning at 7:30 with his 25 top executives to bring each other up to date. Today, that meeting is held electronically in the form of a memo—called "Breakfast"—that is compiled Friday afternoons from submissions by each former participant. Mr. McGowan says a chief executive has to get used to relinquishing some power. "The information has an immediacy to it. The person who receives the information can act on it right away," he says.

Mr. McGowan estimates that 15% of chief executives now get their information electronically. By 2000, he predicts, "you'll have a hard time finding one who isn't" computer-linked to the rest of his firm.

When Thomas A. Murphy was retiring as GM's chief executive in 1980, he spoke of how issues slowly percolated up through the company. By the time they reached him, he said most of the decisions had already been made, and all he had to do was give his imprimatur.

Future chief executives won't have that luxury. Decisions today are being made much faster than a decade ago, and corporate executives see the pace accelerating. In the 1960s, Westinghouse's Mr. Danforth says, the company "had plenty of time to plan a strategy for Latin America." He adds, "We could plan where we wanted to be, what we wanted to manufacture, we could align and train a work force and take six or seven years to do the whole thing." In the past decade, the process was shortened to two to three years in a Westinghouse venture in Korea. And in the future, "if Brazil is the hot place to be, you want to move much quicker than that," he says.

In fact, some say that, with the increasing complexity and speed of decision making, the lone chief executive will be gone. Richard Vancil, a professor at Harvard Business School, notes the increasing popularity of the "office of the chief executive officer." By 1984, he found 25% of American companies used this arrangement, which melds three to six top officers into a team led by the chairman; that's up from only 8% in the 1960s.

THE 'SIX-PACK'

Others predict that the trend will continue. "It's getting tougher to run a big organization," says Delta Consulting Group's David Nadler, who helps plan corporate successions. "There are fewer places where one brilliant or two brilliant people will have all the answers."

But obviously, such an arrangement requires a chief executive with "a more collegial working style," says Paul Regan, vice president and corporate director of executive personnel for Corning Glass Works. Corning has a six-person office of the chief executive—known as the "six-pack"—made up of the chairman, three group presidents

and the heads of research and finance. "It has a certain informality because they are all at the table together."

The transition to the new-style chief won't be easy, though; old habits die hard. Lester Korn, the chairman of Korn/Ferry, notes that most boards still stress conventional traits when seeking a new chief executive from the outside. "They want someone with successful general management experience, a strong profit-and-loss record, the capability of dealing with people, an orientation towards marketing and finance and towards communication."

What's more, he finds that although international executives tend to be well-paid and highly visible, the international track at most companies isn't, at the moment at least, the quick way to the top that many executives would like it to be. The international operative is "not usually the leading contender," Mr. Korn says. In a 1979 Korn/Ferry survey of lower-level executives, only 2% thought that the international route was a fast-track option. By 1985, that number had fallen to 0.5%. Only 4% in either survey predicted that the international arena would be important in 10 years, and only 14% had worked overseas, up from 11% in 1979.

Such attitudes will prevail unless companies radically alter promotion policies, says Robert W. Lundeen, former chairman of Dow Chemical. Today, as board chairman of Tektronix Inc., he is helping the Beaverton, Ore., electronics company grapple with the problem of getting good people to go overseas. "They say, 'What will there be for me when I get back?'" he observes.

Although organizations know they need some changes, they don't know how to get them. Merck, for example, sees a need for top officers who can work more skillfully with government. "We know we need to develop the skills, but we don't know the methodology," Mr. Strohmer says.

Frank Popoff, Dow Chemical's chief executive, professed himself at a loss when his 25-year-old son, an M.B.A. candidate, asked what career path to follow. "I said, 'Tom, it's not as simple as it used to be.'" recalls Mr. Popoff, who has a background in sales and marketing. Many now recommend as broad a background as possible, beginning with a liberal arts degree.

"The undergraduate ought to concentrate on the humanities and social sciences," says Jack Sparks, retired chairman of Whirlpool. The future chief executive "can't have had his head buried in his briefcase, his test tube or his computer." Graduate schools are struggling to figure out what they should teach.

But many say the disciplines that will be required of future corporate chiefs are too nebulous to be taught easily. Students often find courses in organizaitonal behavior, for example, too "touchy-feely," says Donald Jacobs, the dean of Northwestern University's Kellogg graduate school of management. He says he understands that: "I'm an old finance professor. I have a model, and the model gives me a solution. That's easy. The problem is, that's not the way the world works."

Multicultural Management

Management styles are likely to change considerably over the years, as global corporations respond to rapid changes. Corporations of the future are likely to incorporate management styles that will adapt to a host country sociocultural environment instead of imposing home country standards and practices. The experience gained managing in overseas locations, cultures, and environments is likely to generate a well-defined international management policy that will be based on a much better understanding of the different sociocultural environments of global corporation operations, which would definitely improve the interface with local governments, clients, and business associates and improve the efficiency and success rate of local operations.

Managerial Technocrats

Managers of the future must become technocrats, intimately familiar with the latest in communication and computer technologies, to be able to operate in their hi-tech office environments. There may be a lesser degree of physical effort required because improved communication facilities would cut down the need for the frequent traveling endured by today's international managers. Some indications of this scenario are already available in the form of videoconferencing facilities provided by specialized companies. In-house videoconferencing facilities may become standard office equipment for the MNC of the future. Increasing traffic

congestion and rising problems of inner-city living may prompt the development of the home office, which would enable a manager to work from home and be in constant touch with the office via advanced telecommunication facilities.

Overseas Manufacturing Facilities

Overseas manufacturing facilities are likely to become more common because the objectives of host countries and MNCs are likely to be better served by this arrangement. As host governments mature, politically as well as economically, they are likely to prefer direct investment in their countries by MNCs, instead of receiving finished products in the form of imports. Foreign direct investment generally stimulates the local economy and its benefits can be considerable if the local economy itself is well-managed and balanced.

As the trend toward greater openness and market orientation takes root, many host countries are likely to seek direct investment by foreign firms, either by participation in privatization programs of existing state-owned enterprises or by takeovers of loss-making units in the private sector. The benefits of the infusion of new technology and managerial skills and capital gained by the host countries will be recompensed by new business opportunities and a spread of the manufacturing base nearer the market for the MNCs.

Locating production overseas would give MNCs access to cheap labor and inexpensive inputs and reduce the transit costs. Moreover, a more open and market-oriented government would be less prone to expropriate or nationalize the assets of an MNC and, therefore, not constitute a great political risk—a much better climate for foreign direct investment.

The one constraint that might inhibit a rapid growth of foreign direct investment in many LDCs is the inability of the host countries to generate the foreign exchange resources necessary to enable a repatriation of profits by the foreign enterprises. One way out of this constraint is the linking of new investments by MNCs in foreign-exchange-strapped host countries to commensurate earnings by exports, either of its own products or those of other host country commodities or manufactures. Similarly, debt-equity swaps may result in additional investment, even in countries that are heavily burdened with external debt obligations.

Financial Integration

The 1980s saw several major changes in the fundamental relationships between the different international financial markets that were reflected in new levels of integration, modernization, and globalization. Financial markets of the future are likely to be even more integrated, as existing barriers crumble and the free flow of funds becomes still easier across national borders. While integration and deregulation are characteristic of today's markets only in the industrialized world, the future may see the further addition of new markets to the global financial network.

The markets of the newly industrialized countries, the more advanced developing countries, are likely to be the first to join in. At a later stage, markets of Eastern Europe that are currently in the process of being developed may be included. In this scenario MNCs would have an opportunity for a truly global sourcing of funds. The foreign exchange markets would, of course, become much more liquid and complex, because there would be a large number of freely convertible currencies trading on international exchanges.

Concerns with exchange risks and destabilizing capital movements are likely to bring greater emphasis on international cooperation in the supervision of activities, both domestic and international, of financial institutions. The major industrial countries have already agreed on standards of capital adequacy to be observed by banks in their countries. In the future, such standardized requirements are likely to be agreed to by an increasing number of countries who joined the global financial mainstream. Some evidence of a greater opening up of the financial sector to external participation in the developing countries was provided by the Uruguay Round of GATT talks, where many developing countries agreed to lower barriers to trade in financial services.

Rising Labor Unrest

MNCs are likely to meet with increasing demands for higher salaries and wages in most host country operations as expectations rise along with costs of living. The trends in trade unionism, however, are likely to vary. With the collapse of the Soviet bloc, one of the main sources of ideological and political support for trade union movements in many countries is gone. Trade unions have become stronger in many Third World countries, however, especially as worsening living conditions have led to increasing demands for higher compensation levels, while difficult operating conditions have reduced MNC profitability.

MNCs may nevertheless have increasing leverage in dealing with trade unions through their capacity to shift production to different overseas locations. Further, greater use of automated manufacturing processes, especially through the use of industrial robots, may lead to lesser dependence on human labor on the production floor, which would reduce the bargaining power of trade unions.

Summary

International business has changed dramatically in the past decade and will continue to change in the future (see Perspective 23–5). Responding to improving East-West relations, surging global

PERSPECTIVE 23–5   Nation-State: An Idea Under Siege

LONDON—At first glance the contrast could not seem more striking: While Western Europe's countries will open negotiations to surrender more of their state powers to the European Community, a host of small, nearly forgotten ethnic groups to the east—Serbs, Macedonians, Lithuanians, Armenians and others—are seeking to form new countries and gain some of those state powers.

The target of these seemingly conflicting movements is one of the world's most enduring institutions, the modern nation-state.

Pulled from above and torn from below, the nation-state is going through a period of stress and strain that analysts say could not only alter the political map of the world but also transform the notions of sovereignty and nationhood. . . .

The search for a new global order to replace the bipolar world of East versus West is leading to larger roles for supranational organizations such as the EC, the Conference on Security and Cooperation in Europe and even that old standby, the United Nations. All are moving into areas that were once the sole domain of individual countries: economics, defense and human rights. Issues such as the environment, terrorism and drug trafficking are demanding multinational action. . . .

Analysts say these centrifugal forces largely stem from the same sources: the thawing of the Cold War and the subsequent release of conflicting nationalisms after decades in the Soviet deep freeze, the "globalization" of the world economy and the search for ways to protect distinct cultures and human rights. . . .

All of this may seem like a major upheaval for a long established institution. But in fact, most of the nation-states we know today are jury-rigged contraptions that owe their existence to the 20th-century collapse of the Ottoman, Haps-

burg, British and French empires and derive most of their powers from distinctly 19th-century models. More than 90 of the U.N. General Assembly's 159 member states were born after World War II. Analysts say the problems of virtually every world trouble spot can be traced in part to defects in the nature of those states.

The borders for most of Africa's 50-odd states were drawn up by the great powers at the Berlin Conference in 1884 with maximum concern for the balance of power in Europe and little or none for the ethnic, linguistic or cultural affiliations of Africans. When the great empires withdrew from the continent four generations later, they left behind cardboard countries without the glue of nationhood. Many of the civil wars that ensued—in Nigeria, Sudan, Ethiopia, Angola and Mozambique, among others—were a direct result. . . .

In fact, historians say, the nation-state itself is often a contradiction in terms. States are legalistic, governmental entities that wield power; nations are vaguer: groups of substantial numbers of people who share a culture, language, religion, history, or all four. Some countries—the United States, Canada, Switzerland, Belgium, Sri Lanka—are not unitary nations at all but "multinational" states. And some nations—Kurds, Palestinians, Armenians, Basques, Crees—have no state.

There are few genuine "nation-states" where the two concepts come neatly together. Japan is one. Britain, with its unruly mixture of Scots, Welsh and English, and its twilight war zone in Northern Ireland, decidedly is not.

Lenin tacitly accepted these definitions when he called the czarist empire a "prison of nations." But the 15 supposedly voluntary members of the Union of Soviet Socialist Republics and their neighbors in Eastern Europe contend the Commu-

SOURCE: Glenn Frankel, *Washington Post*, November 11, 1990.

nists substituted one kind of prison for another. From their perspective, the collapse of the Soviet Union actually would represent a triumph of the nation-state, the long overdue death of the world's last empire. . . .

Margaret Thatcher sees further European economic and political union as a threat to state sovereignty.

Sovereignty means controlling one's own national destiny, Thatcher said. Practically put, most analysts define it as the right to print money and make war.

But many analysts contend national sovereignty in both areas—economics and defense—has long been eroded. The last time Germany's Bundesbank raised interest rates, the Bank of England followed suit within an hour. The nervous systems of the major national economies increasingly are linked like Siamese twins. If one country raises taxes or fails to provide adequate schools or infrastructure, firms are likely to pick up and move elsewhere. And when Washington or Tokyo gets a cold, London, Paris and Frankfurt increasingly feel the chill. . . .

Ultimately, the objections of Thatcher and her supporters are not only about sovereignty but about something even more elusive: national identity. Many Britons see themselves as different from other Europeans and fear their distinctiveness would be lost in a federal Europe that was somehow less democratic and more centrist. . . .

democracy, diminishing natural resources, diverging economic conditions, and regional economic integration will require development of new roles and business practices. Global competition and international debt problems will also force change. Increased protectionism may result as the dialogue between the industrialized and lesser developed countries becomes more acute. Technology improvements, offering the opportunity to create more efficient enterprises, will continue to be the driving force of internationalization.

Megacorporations will emerge. Multinational corporations will be staffed geocentrically, and management styles will adapted to incorporate host country sociocultural attitudes and beliefs. Managerial tasks will center around high technology communication and computer technologies and may promote the development of the home office. Overseas manufacturing facilities will become more common, and environmental issues will grow as ecological effects become visible. Greater international cooperation will develop as financial markets integrate and modernize their global networks. Automation may lead to lesser dependence on human labor in manufacturing facilities.

Discussion Questions

1. Why is anticipating future trends important to conducting business?
2. What are the major international political trends for the 1990s, and how might they affect business relationships? Decision-making?
3. How will depletion of raw materials affect international business structures?
4. How does technology affect a corporation's ability to survive and compete in the world of the future?
5. What is a megacorporation?
6. Discuss geocentric staffing as it relates to future recruiting and hiring practices within a multinational corporation.
7. How might you better prepare yourself for the challenges of doing international business in the future?

Bibliography

BERNUM, CYNTHIA F. 1989. "The Making of a Global Business Diplomat." *Management Review* (November): 59–60.

BEHRMAN, J. N. 1986. "The Future of International Business and the Distribution of Benefits." *Columbia Journal of World Business* 20: 15–22.

BLOCKLYN, PAUL L. 1989. "Developing the International Executive." *Personnel* (March): 2–5.

HAYDEN, SPENCER. 1989. "Execs Discuss Problems of International Business." *Management Review* (September): 35–38.

KNORR, ROBERT O. 1990. "Managing Resources for World-Class Performance." *Journal of Business Strategy* (January/February): 48–50.

LACZNIAK, G. R., AND J. NAOR. 1985. "Global Ethics: Wrestling with the Corporate Conscience." *Business* (July/September): 3–9.

SETHI, S. PRAKASH. 1987. "The Multinational Challenge." *New Management* (Spring): 53–55.

CASE STUDIES

Groupe Bull's Strategies in the Computer Industry

Jean-Baptiste Gabsi

George Washington University

Outlook of the Company

When Francis Lorentz became the chairman of La Compagnie des Machines Bull in the summer of 1989, the French state-owned manufacturer of computers was sailing in rough waters. Lorentz had taken over from the retiring Jacques Stern at a time when the computer industry worldwide was experiencing major market shifts. After three outstanding years, Groupe Bull reported a loss of F267 million in 1989 and its prospects looked very grim.

Lorentz attributed this loss to a combination of unfavorable conditions in the market, chief of which was a strong U.S. dollar, as well as the firm's substantial expenditures on research and development. In addition, competition in the European computer market had become very fierce, particularly after the West German firm Siemens decided to acquire its archrival, Nixdorf. With this acquisition, Siemens bolstered its position and emerged as the biggest challenger for Bull in the European market.

Although Lorentz felt that the European market was important for Groupe Bull, his main goal was to make the company a global computer manufacturer. Indeed, with the unprecedented internationalization of the world economy, one should not confine a company's scope to a small market niche, especially in the computer industry, where the stakes are high in trying to forge a worldwide competitive edge.

Groupe Bull was a founding member of the Grenoble-based Open Software Foundation (OSF), whose aim is to create industrywide software standards. Groupe Bull believes that the company's stature and visibility are likely to increase because of this type of involvement, and it could use the OSF platform to integrate its own proprietary machines with products based around the Unix operating system.

The Company's Goals

In his quest to make Groupe Bull one of the world's largest computer manufacturers, Lorentz has set six main goals for the company. His first goal is to focus on the European integrated systems market and by the mid-1990s become the continent's top supplier in this field.

The second goal pertains to developing a range of products that are compatible with the hardware of other suppliers. Bull's membership in OSF is in tune with this goal, which will enable it to mass produce high-quality software in the growing data-processing market.

The third goal is directly linked to the second. Groupe Bull's management believes that the integration of its activities can only be achieved by making inroads into large markets, such as the United States. In addition, the U.S. market will give Bull access to the type of technology that will increase the company's effectiveness and efficiency.

Groupe Bull also aims to be the flagship of France's computer industry. To achieve this goal, Bull intends to improve its productivity and profitability. Mainly, Chairman Lorentz feels that there is a need to synchronize the company's product line and exercise better control over its R&D expenditures.

Bolstering Bull's productivity and profitability, however, cannot be realized unless the company's management has the required skills to implement such a goal. Therefore, special attention is being devoted by Bull's CEO to this area, and he is personally involved in the hiring process of top management. Lorentz is also trying to secure the cooperation of the French government in carrying out Bull's objectives, given its status as a state-owned company. Such co-operation is crucial for the firm because it will help prevent the undermining of its strategies.

The sixth goal of Groupe Bull is to design an organizational structure that corresponds to the company's profile and increases its efficiency. Lorentz is convinced that Bull should move very quickly to become a pan-European company in order to take full advantage of the EEC 1992 program. In light of this program, the European computer industry is expected to grow quite substantially with a surging demand for computer hardware and software throughout all sectors of the EEC economy (see Exhibit 1–1).

Outlook of the Computer Industry

The computer industry is currently in the process of being substantially reshaped because market conditions are changing. In fact, Information Technology (IT) has become the cornerstone of today's world economy, and computer manufacturers are trying to take advantage of this emerging trend.

Although computer hardware still represents a major facet of competition in the computer

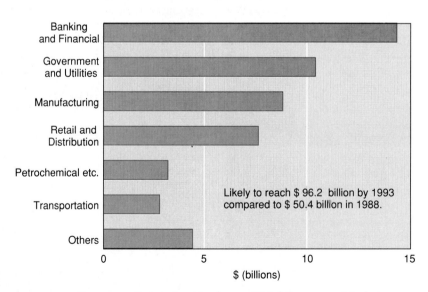

EXHIBIT 1–1   European Computer Hardware (Total European Market = $50.4 billion in 1988).
SOURCE:Frost & Sullivan.

industry, data processing has emerged as the most rapidly growing niche in the field. Indeed, software is now the driving force of any computer firm, and all innovation efforts are almost exclusively dedicated to improving its applications.

By the same token, as much as manufacturers are trying to bolster their technological capabilities and proprietary systems, a shift is taking place toward Open Systems. Attempts are currently being made to set industrywide standards and define rules that will allow computers to be connected and have a common applications interface.

The idea of open systems interconnection (OSI) is essentially centered around the two major operating systems that currently dominate the industry. The first is the Open Software Foundation (OSF), which includes IBM, Groupe Bull, and DEC among others. The other system is Unix International (UI), which includes among its members AT&T and Sun Microsystems. Firms that belong to these two systems are presently trying to agree on a common version of Unix, which will constitute the first step toward the creation of industrywide standards. Such standards are particularly important for mainframe computers and workstations because their usage is rising constantly.

The battle to increase market share in the area of mainframe computers is very intense. Recently, Japan's Hitachi Ltd. introduced a new line of IBM-compatible machines that are believed to be more powerful than those of IBM, Fujitsu, and Amdahl, companies that currently dominate the business. The Hitachi machines can operate at 124 million instructions per second (mips) when they are equipped with three central processors. With four central processors, the new Hitachi mainframe computers can run at 150 mips.

By contrast, IBM's most powerful machines run at 112 mips and Fujitsu/Amdahl's state-of-the-art mainframe computers have a maximum speed of 108 mips. Moreover, Hitachi will sell their new machines at a price which is 10 percent to 15 percent less than what IBM and Fujitsu/Amdahl charge for their units, which will

help the Japanese manufacturer play a major role in the high end of the mainframe market, where it has been a laggard until now.

As for personal computers, which revolutionized the industry in the 1980s, their growth is expected to continue in the 1990s and into the next century. Worldwide sales of PCs are approximately $45 billion in 1990 and may top the $100 billion mark in 1995, while new generations of PCs are on the rise, mainly in the areas of desktop and portable PCs.

The new portable PCs are smaller and lighter than ever before, thanks to the development of techniques to compress desktop computer functions onto as few as six computer chips. Similarly, desktop PCs have become very powerful with the availability of a new generation of 32-bit microprocessors, such as Intel's 486 and higher-density memory chips.

Software for PCs has also undergone a tremendous change, following the evolution of market demand and personal computer hardware. The inception of Microsoft's DOS operating system in the early 1980s provided a platform through which PC functions and features were standardized. Although DOS still remains a dominant force in the industry, other systems have emerged, such as IBM's OS/2 and AT&T's Unix.

The OS/2 system was designed to capitalize on the strong capabilities of the new high performance microprocessors. Its Presentation Manager (PM) provides a very sophisticated graphical user interface, as well as the possibility to perform several applications simultaneously. PM is also easy to use and represents, in this regard, a major challenge to Apple computers, whose market image centers around the simplicity of their system.

Microsoft is currently launching a new program called Windows, which is intended to upgrade DOS into a graphical multitask system and provide a set of Macintosh-like features on IBM PC compatibles. It is also instrumental in establishing a network through which PCs can be connected and have their applications increased quite substantially.

An emerging trend in the computer industry is to design personal computers that can run applications currently processed only by mainframes. PC versions for SAS, SPSS, Solomon, and other statistical and financial packages have been created after years of limiting the use of these programs to mainframes. Furthermore, PCs are expected to become even smaller yet more powerful. They will be able to have all of the functions of today's desktop machines, as well as the capacity to display video pictures, store voice messages, and interpret handwriting.

One should also notice that expenditures by corporations on data processing are growing quite vigorously (about 10.5 percent in Europe, according to Eurostat statistics). Thus, a major potential market in the area of data processing is on the rise. Such promising prospects are pushing many computer firms to form strategic alliances in order to forge a strong competitive edge.

These alliances are sometimes unusual, because they involve companies that are still competing against each other. For example, IBM and AT&T have recently agreed to join with other companies, as well as the government and university researchers, to develop new ways to transfer information from one computer to another at speeds substantially faster than now possible. IBM has also formed a joint venture with West Germany's Siemens called ROLM, and its mission is to pioneer high technology niches, such as phone mail, integrated automatic call distribution, and call path. The latter allows customers to link the power of their host computer data bases with the functionality of their voice processing system.

Many experts believe that such strategic alliances represent an emerging trend of the 1990s not just in the computer industry, but in other industries as well. Indeed, corporations are facing an environment that is producing a high degree of uncertainty and turbulence. They have chosen to pool their interests in order to bolster their strength and exert better control over this volatile environment.

The U.S. Computer Market

After enjoying a prolonged period of growth, the U.S. computer market is experiencing a sensible slowdown. Major firms, such as IBM and DEC, have reduced their work forces and are currently struggling to maintain their market share (see Table 1-1). In 1990 some 40,000 jobs were lost in the U.S. computer industry. In addition, U.S. computer companies are having problems financing their R&D expenditures, given the accelerating pace of technology change and sluggish economic conditions.

In a statement made in January 1990, IBM chairman John Akers declared that the U.S. computer market was characterized by "stress and turmoil." This prognosis applies particularly to desktop PCs, which sell for an average price of less than $5,000. In fact, 1990 sales of computers in the United States are expected to total about $80 billion, more than half of which will be generated through PCs (see Table 1-2). The growth rate of this niche over the 1989 sales will be less than 9 percent, compared to the PC market growth of 20 percent and more in previous years.

The market for powerful computer workstations, however, is expected to thrive, with a growth rate of 25 percent and total sales close

CASE STUDIES TABLE 1-1
U.S. Computer Manufacturers
with 1989 Revenues

	Billions of U.S.$	% Change 1988–1989
IBM	58.1	6
Digital Equipment	12.5	2
Hewlett-Packard	8.1	25
Unisys	7.6	1
NCR	5.3	0
Apple	5.3	21

SOURCE: Dataquest

CASE STUDIES TABLE 1-2

The U.S. Computer Market in 1989 with Forecasts for 1990 and 1993
(in millions of dollars)

	1989	1990	1993
Total computer systems	72.1	80.0	106.9
Corporate resource computers	15.0	15.7	18.8
Business unit computers	5.8	6.4	8.3
Large department computers	4.2	4.4	5.1
Small department computers	3.3	3.4	3.8
Work group computers	4.3	4.3	4.5
Workstations	2.9	3.6	6.3
Personal computers	36.9	42.1	60.3

SOURCE: Dataquest

to $4 billion in 1990. Competition in this area is becoming extremely fierce as prices are being slashed, making profit margins very slim. The battle revolves around performance and price, particularly through advances in microprocessor chip design.

With Sun Microsystems, Hewlett-Packard, and DEC leading this market, IBM is trying to reenter the workstation fray and outperform its competitors. The U.S. computer giant is about to launch a new range of highly sophisticated products in an attempt to gain at least a 10 percent share in this market. Similarly, DEC and Hewlett-Packard have designed new workstations aimed at both office and engineering applications, in order to compete with IBM's new offering. Hewlett-Packard has even accentuated its workstation offensive through its recent acquisition of Apollo Computer.

The unprecedented proliferation of desktop workstations and personal computers has created the need to link these machines and allow them to share data. Consequently, local area networks are emerging very rapidly across the United States. The scope of this networking is growing and currently encompasses all of the computer systems in corporation known as enterprise-wide networks. The major aim of such an endeavor is to move toward distributed computing based on the client-server model, in which "client" desktop computers share the resources of "servers," such as printers, database storage systems, and high-speed computing units.

In light of this development, U.S. computer manufacturers are working toward forging an open system, in order to implement industry-wide standards. Some manufacturers, however, are more active than others in this area. Chief among the active proponents of the open systems concept are Hewlett-Packard and Digital Equipment. The two companies have implemented this concept throughout their product range and aim to be the top suppliers of open systems in the 1990s.

Similarly, with the growth of distributed computing, mainframes are becoming more of a "server" than a "host" within the web of computer networks. The sales of these units in the U.S. market remain strong, and IBM is still enjoying the leading role in this field. Computer mainframes generate about one-fourth of the overall computer revenues in the U.S. market, and many compatible-plug makers, such

616   Case Studies

as Hitachi and Amdahl, have begun to seriously challenge IBM's supremacy.

Competition has never been more fierce in the U.S. computer market. Technology is changing rapidly and firms are moving toward making products that are powerful and easy to use. Furthermore, this market is no longer the privileged and exclusive turf of U.S. manufacturers. European and Asian firms are becoming very active in the United States by investing heavily in production plants, R&D, and distribution channels. Groupe Bull is among these corporations and plans to play a major role in the upcoming years.

The European Computer Market

Unlike the U.S. computer market, which is experiencing a period of stagnation, the European market is growing and is expected to be worth around $200 billion in 1993. The computer software and services segment totaling $42.9 billion in 1988 will reach $100.7 billion in 1993 (see Exhibit 1–2), while computer hardware is likely to increase from $50.4 billion in

1988 to $96.2 billion in 1993. These prospects are pushing European and other foreign firms to augment their presence in the EEC market in order to play a major role in it.

The creation of a single European internal market is scheduled to take effect by the end of 1992. This program calls for the harmonization of all technical and manufacturing standards, making the EEC the largest market in the world. Moreover, the European Commission intends to prohibit industrial and software piracy in an attempt to harmonize copyrights and patent rights. This provision of Jacques Delors's 1992 program applies directly to computer firms and represents a victory for those who are trying to protect their proprietary systems.

Likewise, the recent events in Eastern Europe have engendered a dramatic change in the continent's political and economic landscape. The two Germanies have already signed an economic and monetary treaty as a first step toward reunification. In addition, the European Development Bank has been launched in order to help Eastern European countries restructure

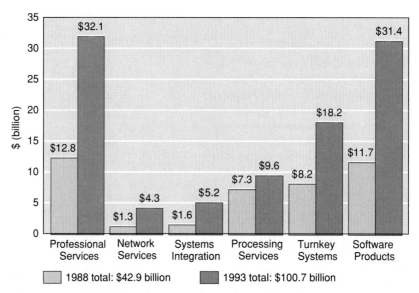

EXHIBIT 1–2   Computer Software and Services, Western European Market Sector Analysis.

their economies and implement a free-market system. The Western nations have also decided to ease their restrictions on the sales of high-technology products to the former Communist countries, and many computer companies have seized this opportunity to establish inroads in such a market.

The European computer market is still dominated by U.S. makers, such as IBM, DEC, Apple, and Compaq, but many European firms are emerging as strong competitors, thanks in part to their formation of strategic alliances. The bulk of the market share battle revolves around data processing, microchips, and enhanced information systems. Most of the European companies are currently trying to focus on putting together computer systems that are based on industry standards and on tailoring systems for specific industry applications.

Firms that have tried to promote their own proprietary operating systems and hardware technology have, by and large, gone under. West Germany's Nixdorf, which for years enjoyed a tremendous success in the area of mini-computers, was recently taken over by its rival Siemens. Nixdorf's management failed to recognize the need to adapt to market changes as the company continued to focus on very narrow market niches. Furthermore, by promoting its own technology, the company had to allocate huge resources to its R&D efforts, making its financial base very vulnerable.

Holland's N.V. Philips is experiencing the same problems. Its original goal was to become Europe's technology leader in minicomputers by engaging in the inception and production of all of its units' components. Because of the heavy losses that the company has compiled, its management team was changed drastically and a new CEO, Jan Timmer, was appointed to solve its woes. Timmer has already embarked on a series of measures to cut Philips's computer division losses, including a plan to retrench computer operations. Many observers believe that his strategy consists of repairing this division enough to make it an attractive candidate for sale or merger with a stronger rival.

By all accounts, Siemens is striving to become the computer industry's pan-European player. Indeed, since acquiring Nixdorf, the German firm has jointly purchased Plessey from GEC and Rolm Communications from IBM and signed joint-venture agreements with other companies, such as the one with Groupe Bull. The Siemens-Nixdorf fusion will enable them to topple IBM in the German market, although their revenues in Western Europe will still represent only 40 percent of those of the U.S. computer giant. The revenues of Siemens-Nixdorf, however, are nearly 75 percent higher than those of DEC, and the difference may increase in upcoming years.

In addition to Siemens, there are other European companies that are striving to become Europe's computer industry leaders. Britain's International Computer Ltd. (ICL), Italy's Ing. C. Olivetti, and France's Groupe Bull have all expressed their eagerness to strengthen their position and enlarge their scope in the European market. They understand that the stakes are very high and would like to have a piece of this multibillion-dollar market. Their U.S. and Asian counterparts have the same intentions and are reformulating their strategies to bolster their edge in such a market.

With the U.S. market stagnating and the Asian market being comparatively small and harder to enter, Europe is characterized by a high economic growth rate and the prospect of becoming the world's largest market in 1993. For example, U.S. computer firms are discovering that the European market can be a salvation for them, given the situation in their home country, where industry growth has been sluggish for the past three years. The market for data processing equipment, especially the smaller machines, is still very active in Europe, while it is close to saturation in the U.S.

It is within this framework that Groupe Bull is forging its European strategies, in order to achieve its objectives. These strategies are mainly oriented toward the long-run, which is in tune with the company's goal of becoming a truly pan-European computer manufacturer.

Groupe Bull's Strategies

Based on the company's goal to become a major player in both the U.S. and European computer markets, Groupe Bull has formulated a set of strategies to achieve such a goal. These strategies have taken into account the conditions that are inherent to its current markets. In fact, Chairman Lorentz believes that his firm must establish a match with its environment in order to ensure its success and that "the future presents as many opportunities as challenges for Bull."

Bull reported a loss of F276 million in 1989, the first time in three years it has fallen into the red. The production difficulties that the company had encountered at its printed circuit-board plant in Angers, France, are cited as the major reason for this loss. In addition, the stronger-than-expected exchange rate of the U.S. dollar in 1989 made the French manufacturer pay more for semiconductor chips and peripheral equipment. The company has also sustained heavy restructuring costs, following its decision to refocus its scope of endeavor.

Originally, Groupe Bull comprised two main organizational units—Bull S.A. and Bull H.N., the former U.S.-based Honeywell Bull. The latter is 69.4 percent owned by the French company, while 15 percent is held by Japan's NEC, and 15.6 percent is controlled by Honeywell. When Lorentz became Bull's CEO, he forged a plan to reorganize the company and implement a new structure in it. He did so in an attempt to create an organizational structure that will allow his firm to achieve its objectives as effectively as possible.

Mr. Lorentz's strategies to turn Bull around had three main dimensions. The first dimension was to establish strong inroads into the U.S. computer market and secure a consistent share. The second consisted of setting the grounds for his company to solidify its position in the European computer market and become its most active player. The third dimension of his plan was to envision an organizational structure that

corresponds to the firm's profile and long-term goals.

As soon as he assumed the chairmanship of Bull, Lorentz moved quickly to identify a strategy through which he could enter the U.S. market. He chose to do so via a takeover of Zenith Data Systems, a small but renowned U.S. microcomputer producer. He believed that this acquisition would enable his company to establish its image as a world player and gain access to state-of-the-art computer technology. In this regard, the takeover of Zenith lifted Bull from its rank as the world's tenth largest computer manufacturer to seventh. The firm now makes 70 percent of its sales, which totaled F32.7 billion in 1989, outside France and plans to move among the top five computer producers by the mid-1990s.

This acquisition was also motivated by Groupe Bull's eagerness to develop a complete microcomputer line, from low end to high end, for both desktops and laptops. Indeed, the company wants to assure itself substantial market positions in North America and Europe and "generate sufficient volume to compete effectively on a global scale," according to Lorentz. Although this transaction was marred by a disagreement over the price, it was in tune with Bull's strategy to realign its scope of endeavor.

The second facet of Groupe Bull's strategies was to forge a pan-European dimension and become one of Europe's major computer companies. Thus, the French firm started negotiations with some of its competitors to form strategic alliances and share technology. Bull has recently signed an agreement with West Germany's Siemens to cooperate in the area of R&D. When asked about the appropriateness of such a collaboration with the German company, Lorentz replied that "two businesses can be competitors and partners at the same time."

Furthermore, Bull is moving very swiftly to behave like a single European company. It has already embarked on a series of measures to reach this dimension, including hiring staff at a European level and setting up common training programs. The company has also increased its participation in the European joint R&D platforms, such as the Eureka Project and the EEC's Science Program. Eureka is mainly centered around financing projects designed to produce commercially viable results, while the EEC program is designed for more fundamental research. Bull's management believes that the European computer firms must be innovative and resourceful to counter the emergence of low-margin products, particularly from Asian suppliers. In turn, this will bring about price competition of the toughest type within the European computer market.

The final fold of Bull's set of strategies is to design an organizational structure that fits the company's needs and bolsters its effectiveness. Lorentz, a graduate from France's prestigious École Nationale d'Administration, started his career with Bull as president of Honeywell Bull in 1982. He stayed at the helm of this Franco-American venture until his nomination as CEO of Groupe Bull in June 1989. His tenure at Honeywell Bell allowed him to develop a full understanding of the peculiarities of the world's computer industry and exposed him to the type of competition that characterizes the industry.

Enlightened by this experience, Lorentz decided to reorganize Groupe Bull by giving it a more coherent structure. The aim of this newly designed structure was to help the French manufacturer cope more effectively with the fast changes taking place in the computer industry. Groupe Bull was divided into four operating units reporting to a central entity, Compagnie des Machines Bull. This central entity was to be responsible for formulating strategies, product line policy, and human resources, as well as the integration of R&D activities around the world.

The four operating units were based on market segmentation and geographic location. The units are Bull S.A. France, Bull International S.A., Bull HN, and Zenith Data Systems.

Bull S.A. France has a work force of 19,000 and engages in activities related to develop-ment, manufacturing, and sales in France. Bull International S.A. has a work force of 6,000 and supervises the group's operations in Europe, Africa, Latin America, and Southeast Asia.

Bull HN comprises a work force of 19,000 and oversees the activities that the company undertakes in North America, Mexico, Italy, Great Britain, and Australia. Zenith Data Systems, which is still in the process of being restructured following its takeover, focuses on technological development, manufacturing, and sales of Groupe Bull's worldwide microcomputer and workstation products. In 1989, sales generated through these products accounted for about one-third of the company's overall revenues.

This new organizational structure was implemented on January 1, 1990. It represents one of the items on Lorentz's ambitious agenda to make his company one of the world's top computer producers. Bull's chairman also aims, through his strategies, to put together different kinds of computers and software for a whole range of specific applications, which will enable Bull to add value to its basic hardware and have a solid base to compete against the industry's giants.

The French concern's management is convinced that, unlike the U.S. market, Europe's demand for computers is still booming. In a recent interview, Lorentz stated that "the European computer market is not fundamentally saturated," and that he is confident "that Bull will become Europe's top supplier of integrated systems by the mid-1990s." Indeed, there is a feeling that the pace of technological change is very fast and that such a change should be anticipated in order to ensure the company's long-run success.

Bull's strategies were conceived to clearly define the role that the company ought to play in the computer industry. They consisted essentially of reshaping the scope of endeavors, structure, and vision associated with the firm's future. Lorentz has also tried to encourage innovation within Groupe Bull and hire a work force dedicated toward meeting the company's expectations. Ambitious projects can only be realized if there is a commitment to excellence, as well as a corporate policy that is oriented toward the future. According to Lorentz, the challenge is to be innovative, to offer a range of products based on industry standards, and to tailor systems for specific industry applications.

The company, however, is not limiting its scope to certain markets or market segments. The world computer market has never been more internationalized and is expected to continue in this direction. The promising prospects embedded in Europe's single internal market represent an additional incentive for the French computer manufacturer to bolster its edge in the European market. Likewise, despite the slowdown that currently characterizes the U.S. market, America still represents an important arena for computer firms. Bull intends to strengthen its position in the United States and secure access to technology, particularly in the area of information systems.

The set of strategies that Groupe Bull has formulated are meant to give the firm a competitive advantage in carrying out its activities. These strategies not only provide a sense of direction for the company, but will also motivate its members to make extra efforts in achieving Bull's aims.

Guidelines for Analyzing the Groupe Bull Case

- Differentiate and define corporate and business strategies. For the purpose of this case study, use Hofer and Schendel's definitions. Corporate strategies identify the businesses in which a corporation should compete. Business strategies relate to the actions that a company should undertake to compete in a particular business.
- Analyze the situation in the world computer industry. Point out the emerging technological trends in the industry and the importance of strategic alliances. Discuss the efforts to forge industrywide standards, such as the OSF platform.
- Evaluate the prospects of economic growth in the United States and Western Europe. This evaluation should encompass the different dimensions of the environment in which Groupe Bull operates. Thus, the subsequent analysis of the company's strategies will be based on the evolution of its environment.
- Underscore the importance of Bull's status as a state-owned enterprise and how its policy must be in tune with that of the French government. Explain how Bull's management should go about resolving any conflicting relationship that might arise with the government.
- Depict the corporate and business facets of Bull's strategies and appraise the appropriateness of these strategies, given the company's goals and the characteristics of the environment.
- Some observers believe that Bull's acquisition of Zenith Data Systems was not the right strategy to enter the U.S. market, because Zenith was experiencing major financial and production problems when the takeover took place. Another way to enter the American market could have been through a joint-venture with a major computer firm operating in the U.S. Analyze this alternative and compare it to what Bull has actually done.
- Francis Lorentz believes that it is crucial for his company to become a pan-European computer firm, but he chose to concentrate his activities on enhanced services and integrated systems and purchase the hardware from external suppliers. Explain whether Bull is wasting an opportunity to tap a market where the demand is expected to rise quite substantially.
- In an attempt to bolster the effectiveness of its operations, Bull has espoused a new organizational structure, which revolves mainly around geographic considerations. For example, Bull International S.A. supervises activities in most of Europe, Africa, Latin America, and

Asia, whereas Bull HN monitors North America, Mexico, Italy, Great Britain, and Australia. This divisional structure seems to lack consistency. Discuss the pros and cons of Bull's new organizational structure.

Discussion Questions

1. Using Hofer and Schendel's definition of corporate and business strategies, identify and explain the main features of Groupe Bull's strategic plan. Were the actions taken by this company corporate-oriented or business-oriented?

2. Based on the U.S. computer market conditions, evaluate the appropriateness of the French firm's strategy to enter the U.S. market. Was there a better way to enter such a market?

3. In analyzing the characteristics of the European computer market, explain whether Bull has formulated the right strategies to bolster its competitive edge.

4. Appraise the new organizational structure that Bull has espoused as part of the implementation of its strategies. Does this structure fit the company's profile? Would you have recommended a different structure to its management?

PepsiCo, Inc.

Lynette Knowles Mathur

Southern Illinois University College of Business Administration

PepsiCo, Inc., the large U.S. food and beverage manufacturer based in Purchase, New York, markets Pepsi and 7-Up soft drinks, Frito-Lay snacks, and menu offerings from its Pizza Hut, Kentucky Fried Chicken, and Taco Bell franchises. The firm is highly successful in the United States and its overseas markets. In September 1988, PepsiCo received approval for foreign direct investment in India, an advantage that is still being denied its biggest competitor, the Coca-Cola Company. It was not until the approval was received that PepsiCo began to see itself changing from a U.S. firm with offshore interests to a global consumer products company.

Both PepsiCo and Coca-Cola have large shares of the U.S. market, holding 32 percent and 40 percent, respectively, in fall 1989. Each firm also has a significant presence in foreign markets, with the beverages of both available in more than 150 countries. In comparison, however, Coca-Cola receives considerably greater overseas income than PepsiCo. In Fall 1989, 50 percent of PepsiCo's sales and 15 percent of its operating earnings from soft drinks were foreign, while Coca-Cola's soft drink sales and operating earnings were much larger, at 66 percent and 80 percent, respectively.

The battle of PepsiCo and Coca-Cola over India is an excellent example of their continuing international rivalry. Interestingly, the firms have

histories of past investments in India, which may have played a part in the Indian government's decision to approve PepsiCo's entry while denying entry to Coca-Cola in 1990.

In the mid-1950s, PepsiCo had operations in India but withdrew after two years when it decided it could not develop a viable business venture. Coca-Cola, on the other hand, operated in India for twenty-seven years, but was essentially forced to divest by the Indian government in 1977. The government had demanded that Coca-Cola provide its soft drink formula and other technology to an Indian company, and it also had seriously altered its foreign direct investment policy, so that a foreign firm could hold only a 40 percent or less interest in an Indian subsidiary. Furthermore, the government purportedly was interested in punishing Coca-Cola's Indian bottler because the local firm had supported the opposing political party in the previous year's election. To protect its proprietary information and avoid the lessened control a reduced investment level would cause, Coca-Cola decided to fully divest its Indian operations. India was thus left with only domestic soft drink firms operating in its potentially large undeveloped market.

For several years since then, the two largest Indian soft drink makers enjoyed the lack of foreign competition. In the fall of 1989, the firms controlled 80 percent of the Indian market, while primarily limiting distribution to urban areas and charging consumers high prices. They also had no incentives to expand production or to develop the Indian soft drink market. Although this oligopolistic behavior was detrimental to the Indian consumer, it left the market virtually untouched and thus a prime target for a soft drink manufacturer capable of obtaining the Indian government's approval for direct investment.

Entry into India was particularly appealing to both PepsiCo and Coca-Cola because of the market's potential size. With a population of approximately 800 million in 1989, India had a middle-class of 150 million people with an annual estimated growth rate of 10 million. This large group of consumers forms the major potential customer base of the Indian soft drink market. In 1989 annual per capita soft drink consumption was only three bottles, compared to thirteen in Pakistan, where PepsiCo dominated the market.

India was also particularly important to both firms because it was the last large market either firm could conquer. Although PepsiCo and Coca-Cola were established in the USSR and China by the mid-1980s, the USSR was dominated by PepsiCo, and China was under Coca-Cola's control. Coca-Cola was even more concerned about India, however, because China's market had very limited potential because of the country's lack of a middle-class population.

Interestingly, considering each firm's level of international experience, PepsiCo and Coca-Cola chose very different strategies in applying to the Indian government for market entry. These strategies will result in different fates for the firms as global consumer products companies.

PepsiCo's form of market entry is a joint venture in Punjab State, in which it will own 39.9 percent of the venture, the maximum ownership it is allowed, for an initial $17 million. The other investments will be 36.1 percent by Punjab Agro Industries, a marketing firm owned by Punjab State and the Indian government, and 24 percent by Voltas, a unit of Tata Group, India's largest industrial firm. Soft drinks, fruit juice concentrates, and snack foods from local crops will be produced. Every year, local franchised bottlers will distribute 1.2 billion bottles of the soft drinks Pepsi Era, 7-Up Era, and Marinda Era.

Peripheral to the venture, but crucial to its acceptance, are the incentives PepsiCo is providing the Indian government. PepsiCo will export $5 of local goods for every $1 of materials it imports, a ratio much larger than its 1:1 ratios in the USSR and China. The imported materials are necessary for PepsiCo to preserve the secrecy of its soft drink formula. Most of the exports will be agricultural products, and the firm will use its own international distribution system. If the ratio is not met, PepsiCo will not be allowed to repatriate its royalties or profits. PepsiCo also will help shift the farming focus of India to more lucrative crops, establish a research center to develop better crops, and provide two food-processing plants for fruits and potatoes.

Several benefits to India should result from PepsiCo's plan, such as increased agricultural improvements, technology inflows, farming incomes, and export levels. Furthermore, the market should be more active for local bottlers and less oligopolistic, and consumers should have an increased selection of products at lower prices. The venture should also improve both the Indian government's positive signals to foreign firms about foreign direct investment and the image of Punjab State, which has had recent political unrest.

In contrast, Coca-Cola's rejected plan offered no incentives to the Indian government other than a $2 million plant it proposed to establish in an export-processing zone to produce the basic ingredients for Coke concentrate. Based on a loophole the firm had discovered in India's rules on export processing zones, it planned to sell 25 percent of its output in India while exporting 75 percent to nearby countries. Export-processing zones in lesser-developed countries such as India are intended to encourage exports by providing incentives to foreign firms to locate export manufacturing operations in the zones. Since sales of zone products in the domestic market are either denied or approved at very low levels, Coca-Cola's plan was probably an affront to that export intent.

Furthermore, Coca-Cola had apparently underestimated the impact of its history in India. Although consumers remember the soft drink Coke, Coca-Cola's divestment from India was not remembered favorably. The Indian government feared that reinvestment by the firm would be poorly received, especially considering its lack of peripheral incentives. To make the firm's proposal more appealing, the government asked it to reduce its intended domestic sales level by 15 percent, but the firm refused. Instead, in May 1989, Coca-Cola began laboring to modify its proposal for resubmission to include incentives similar to those provided by PepsiCo.

Although the Indian joint venture will not be profitable for PepsiCo until five years after its startup, entry into the Indian market was distinctly a significant win for PepsiCo. The firm was willing to forego immediate gain to enter a potentially huge developing market and recognized the need to respond to the concerns of the Indian government. In contrast, as of fall 1990, Coca-Cola had not yet been given permission to enter India.

Bibliography

BASILE, ANTOINE, and DIMITRI GERMIDIS. 1984. *Investing in Free Export Processing Zones.* Paris: OECD.

CHAKRAVARTY, SUBRATA N. 1989. "How Pepsi Broke into India." *Forbes* (November 27): 43–44.

SPAETH, ANTHONY. 1988. PepsiCo Accepts Tough Conditions for the Right to Sell Cola in India. *Wall Street Journal* (September 20): 42.

SPAETH, ANTHONY, and AJAY SINGH. 1989. "Coca-Cola and DuPont Test Attitude of India toward Foreign Investment." *Wall Street Journal* (May 26): A8.

———. 1990. "India Rejects Coca-Cola's Bid to Sell Soft Drinks, Giving Pepsi an Advantage." *Wall Street Journal* (March 16): B5.

WALDMAN, PETER. 1989. "Pepsi, Concerned about Market Share in France, Will Break with Local Bottler." *Wall Street Journal* (November 7): A4.

Plastech Chemicals, Inc.

J. T. Goode

Ohio State University College of Business

Company Overview

Plastech Chemicals, Inc. (PCI) is a wholly owned subsidiary of a diversified manufacturing company active in the production of a wide range of industrial goods. PCI has in recent years been a major source of profits for the parent company as a result of rapid growth in the demand for its major product line, ABS plastics.

ABS plastics has a number of desirable characteristics. They are durable, resistant to scratches, and structurally stable over a wide range of temperatures. In addition, by varying the formulation and processing recipe, they can be produced in an extremely wide range of colors and formulated to produce a variety of surface finishes and even a substantial amount of fire retardancy. They are marketed in the form of nodules, which can then be formed (e.g., by injection molding) by industrial users into an infinite variety of parts and components or into enclosures for other, nonplastic finished industrial and consumer goods.

PCI is believed to be the world's largest producer of ABS plastics, although there are many other large producers as well. PCI has the full benefit of available economies of scale in this product line and is therefore one of the lowest-cost producers. In addition, because of its volume, PCI is able to supply from inventory many unusual formulations of ABS plastics that smaller producers would have to produce to order when requested by a customer.

Entering the 1990s

Despite its strong position in a growth product, PCI management has come to feel that PCI faces major challenges in the 1990s, in large part because of the impact that environmental changes had had on international patterns of competition within downstream customer industries.

PCI had long been involved in international business and had direct or indirect involvement in all major national markets. It was structured as a multinational company and, except for exports from the United States to minor foreign markets, its involvement in any given national market was largely operationally independent of activities in other countries. While this facilitated considerable diversity in response to differences in national markets, recent changes suggested an increasing need for more international coordination of PCI's activities. This was particularly evident in the automotive industries.

Beginning with the energy crises of the 1970s and continuing throughout the 1980s, Japanese automobile manufacturers captured an increasingly significant share of the U.S. and world markets. Indeed, the Japanese share of the U.S.

625

auto market had risen to the point where suppliers to the U.S. industry were losing substantial volume to the Japanese auto firms' traditional suppliers based in Japan.

Moreover, spurred by protectionist sentiment (and "voluntary" auto quotas imposed on the Japanese industry as a result of U.S. pressure), a number of Japanese auto manufacturers decided to start up production in the United States. While much of Japanese production and almost all R&D remained based in Japan, the 1980s saw a rapid increase in U.S.-based production by Japanese firms.

This production meant that U.S. auto parts suppliers and their upstream suppliers, such as PCI, had the opportunity to develop new, local supply relationships with Japanese firms. On the other hand, many Japanese auto suppliers, following in the wake of their major customers, also began to establish U.S. production companies. How PCI could best respond to these changes was unclear, but it seemed evident that they had indications as to how to manage its global activities.

ABS Plastics in the Automotive Industries

While the use of plastics has been growing substantially in many fields, there has been a particularly rapid growth in their use within the automobile industry, probably because of two major factors.

First, there has been growing concern regarding the problem of rust damage to automobiles, which may reflect the increased concerns of consumers regarding the cost of repairing aesthetic damage to a car. It is certainly related, however, to the fact that the trend toward unibody or monocoque construction of automobiles makes the car body itself an integral part of the structure of the vehicle. Thus, unlike earlier platform construction techniques, wherein the structural integrity of the vehicle primarily rested on a heavy steel frame or skeleton, body rust can now seriously compromise the safety of the vehicle.

Second, the oil crises of the 1970s made the cost of fuel, and automotive fuel economy, a major consideration of consumers and of governments. Consumers increasingly showed an interest in fuel economy as one of the considerations in their purchase decisions. More important, the U.S. federal government mandated corporate average fuel economy (CAFE) requirements for domestic producers, which required U.S. manufacturers to rapidly improve the average fuel economy of their product mix. This also led to major efforts to reduce vehicle weight as a means of increasing fuel economy.

Plastics manufacturers benefited from both of these developments. For example, the CAFE requirements accelerated the trend toward monocoque construction techniques, which can save weight by having the body skin serve both as a surface cover and as a structural element to replace the frame. In addition, auto manufacturers looked for additional weight-saving through the use of thinner steel. Both of these changes, however, exacerbated the problem of rust-through. As a means of countering this problem more use was made of plastic shields to protect vulnerable areas of the automobile from direct exposure to road salt.

In addition, because plastic is rustproof and lighter than steel, there was a rapid trend toward the use of plastics to replace steel wherever possible. Thus, plastic has come to replace steel in a wide range of interior and exterior trim applications and in some major exterior body parts.

Marketing Plastics to the U.S. Automobile Industry

The marketing of ABS plastics compounds to auto manufacturers is a rather technology-intensive task that requires not only the efforts of a technically knowledgeable sales force to communicate product benefits to the auto manufacturers design and product planning groups, but also the efforts of production and applications specialists to work with the parts manufacturing units to achieve the specified results.

Within the U.S. industry many auto parts are produced within divisions or subsidiaries of the auto manufacturers. In plastics-related auto parts, however, there are a substantial number of independent precision molders that produce parts for the manufacturers. In these instances, there is some need to work with both design/product planning groups and with production/manufacturing groups, but they belong to separate corporate organizations and the primary focus is on the independent molders themselves.

U.S. manufacturers have traditionally provided specifications to their outside parts suppliers, and left the question of how the suppliers might meet those specifications in the hands of the suppliers themselves. The suppliers, for their part, have had to bid for supply contracts in open competition with their competitors, and then meet the required specifications at the bid price. Their ability to consistently do so at a profit depends in part on their ability to get the most out of the material they use. In the case of plastic parts this means that they will tend to use material supplied by plastics compounders who have consistently provided them with adequate technical support in the use of their compounds. Plastech has developed highly effective relationships with most U.S. molders and has captured a major share of the U.S. market.

Foreign Markets

THE IMPORTANCE OF JAPAN

The trend in plastics usage in all of the advanced industrialized countries parallels that in the United States. Plastech has been involved in most of these markets in a variety of forms. In some cases it has merely licensed technology to a strong foreign manufacturer, often in the form of cross-licensing agreements, whereby each party agrees to license new plastics-related technology to the other. In other cases, Plastech exports compounds to either an independent customer or to a joint venture or wholly owned subsidiary, which markets plastics compounds within the foreign market. In some of the major markets, PCI has utilized its technology to establish manufacturing joint ventures with local firms.

In the field of automotive plastics, however, Japan is far and away the most important market after the United States. The rapid increase in the Japanese share of global automobile production began in the late 1960s, and within fifteen years made the Japanese industry one of the most important factors in the global automotive industry.

MARKETING PLASTICS TO THE JAPANESE AUTO INDUSTRY

In its basics the marketing of plastics compounds to the Japanese auto industry is similar to the practice in the United States. The plastics compounds manufacturer has to interact effectively with both the auto manufacturer's design and product planning groups and with the parts production groups.

There is, however, a major difference in organizational structure within the industry. Traditionally, Japanese auto manufacturers have remained closer than U.S. manufacturers to being auto design, assembly and distribution specialists who rely greatly on outside suppliers for production of parts and components.

To a far greater degree than in the United States, therefore, upstream suppliers to the auto parts industry must interact with a large number of separate parts manufacturing firms, which are organizationally separate from the auto manufacturers themselves. Because the manufacturers depend so heavily on these parts suppliers, they are not indifferent to the relationship.

Indeed, Japanese auto manufacturers tend to nurture a longterm relationship with suppliers and are willing, when able, to provide equity or debt financing to preferred suppliers as required. While requiring suppliers to be cost competitive in the long-run, Japanese auto manufacturers, in sharp contrast to U.S. practice, have not typically thrown each new order for major parts open to competitive bidding. They have instead changed suppliers only after considerable cooperative efforts to rectify problems regarding price, delivery, or quality with existing suppliers.

This pattern has been strengthened in recent years as a result of Japanese innovations in production operations management in the 1970s. Beginning with Toyota, Japanese industry has implemented the concept of total quality control more thoroughly than has industry in any other country. The focus of this concept is on the elimination of waste costs in the production process through an ongoing organization-wide search for the root causes of problems and their solutions. An integral part of this process is the reduction of inventory levels and, a related issue, high-quality standards throughout the organization.

As a result, it has become even more important to interact with suppliers to ensure that quality and delivery standards are met, while maintaining competitive pricing, which has led to even closer cooperative interaction between auto manufacturers and their parts suppliers. In many cases, the auto manufacturer will work directly with suppliers to help bring their operations up to standards. As one part of this activity, manufacturers often test inputs used by parts suppliers and then provide not only parts performance specifications to the suppliers, but also indicate what specific grade and supplier of inputs must be used by the parts manufacturer.

The quality standards required are remarkably high. Indeed, PCI has directly experienced the difference between U.S. and Japanese quality standards in the marketing of plastics compounds. PCI, like other U.S. producers, has substantial expertise with the statistical process control techniques used to ensure quality standards. They are fully capable of meeting required average batch performance characteristics for any ABS plastics compound a customer might order. When asked to submit samples of a special formulation to a U.S.-based Japanese auto firm, the company was able to meet specific mean performance characteristics, but did not pass the required standards.

PCI subsequently learned that the standards of Japanese firms for within-batch variation were 3 percent, versus the U.S. standard of about 8 percent. While PCI is capable of meeting the Japanese standards for within-batch variation, it can do so only if it modifies its control techniques and incurs some additional costs. Unfortunately, these higher standards (and costs) will not fetch a higher price within the traditional U.S. industry, where almost all of its U.S. output is presently sold. The Japanese automobile manufacturers are also requesting more frequent delivery of smaller orders of ABS nodules, which implies higher overheads for PCI without any increase in price.

Plastech's Operations in Japan

Plastech has been involved in Japan for a very long time. In the late 1950s, when Japan began the development of new basic industries, such as petrochemicals and modern consumer goods, Plastech saw potential for its plastics, and in the early 1960s entered into a joint venture with a Japanese chemical company.

At this time, Plastech and other foreign firms in the chemical industry did not have an alternative to joint ventures. Foreign investment in Japan was rigorously controlled by the Ministry of International Trade and Industry (MITI) and 100 percent ownership of a Japanese subsidiary was not a possibility.

In any case, the joint-venture approach had a number of advantages. While their partner had little expertise in plastics, they did have an established and growing distribution network, within Japanese industry and were better able to deal with the distinctly different Japanese business and cultural environment.

In the early years, PCI enjoyed a rapid growth in exports to Japan via the joint ventures. As the market grew in importance, however, it became desirable to establish Japanese production facilities. Once Japanese production began, PCI export volume decreased, but joint-venture production rapidly increased and PCI continued to enjoy a rapid growth in revenues from activities in Japan.

Over the years Plastech contributed to the joint venture capital, technology licenses, and a continuing stream of technical expertise via PCI technical personnel, who were sent to Japan for both short troubleshooting missions and for longer sojourns (up to one year) to work with Japanese counterparts. In addition, a number of Japanese technical personnel spent time working and training in PCI's U.S. operations. Aside from the formal, contractual returns PCI received from the joint venture in the form of dividends and royalties (and occasional exports), there were other important, though less formal, benefits.

As the joint venture manufacturing experience matured, there were instances of PCI U.S. operations benefiting from problems and their solutions. As the Japanese chemical and plastics industry as a whole matured, it began to generate patentable technological innovations. Because of the continuous contact and involvement of PCI technical personnel with the Japanese, PCI was exposed to these developments in Japanese industry as they occurred. PCI was able to negotiate some important agreements to license Japanese technology as a result of this early awareness, and the assistance of its Japanese joint-venture partner.

In contrast to the benefits of organizational learning on the technology side, PCI gained relatively little knowledge in such areas as managing personnel, finance, and sales in Japan. This reflected the original strengths the partners had brought to the joint venture.

PCI direct exposure to Japan was determined by the PCI personnel sent to Japan. Practically all of these personnel were sent on technical missions. Managerial personnel were also sent to Japan, usually for much longer postings (up to five years). There were, however, seldom more than one or two such personnel at any one time,

and their role was primarily to act as caretakers for PCI's financial interests in the joint venture.

Thus, after almost twenty-five years of direct involvement in Japan, PCI had relatively limited experience at doing business in Japan. Of course, the company knew a great deal more about this than firms that had no involvement in Japan, but there were no PCI personnel who had other than second-hand anecdotal knowledge of such matters as managing the work force, dealing with Japanese suppliers, or front-line marketing of plastics to Japanese industry. Indeed, except for a retired Japanese executive (based in Tokyo) who acted as company adviser, Plastech had no personnel with the linguistic skills necessary to gain such experience.

Recent Developments

There have been a number of recent developments that have led Plastech to begin a major rethinking of its strategy in Japan. First, the growth of the auto industry in Japan has benefited PCI via its joint-venture operations, but less than PCI had hoped. The partner had many nonauto-related product lines that determined where it developed its major distribution and marketing strengths. Within the auto industry the partner, and therefore the joint venture, had been moderately successful with sales to some auto firms but much less so with others.

This probably reflected where the joint-venture partner enjoyed the most synergy between its existing nonauto business and the corporate relationships built in Japan. The patterns of intercorporate ties in Japan were complex and not always based on direct transactions or financial control relationships. Within the main corporate groups, or keiretsu, there were many relationships that, while neither formal or contractual, appeared to be valuable, as a basis for gaining the introductions and credibility necessary to develop new customers.

While pleased with the benefits the partner's network of intercorporate ties had brought to the joint venture, it was not clear that PCI's interests were best served by continuing to have its Japanese involvement constrained by the limits of the partner's effectiveness or willingness to build beyond these existing ties. The partner had, moreover, recently announced plans to independently build a plant in the southeastern United States, in order to take advantage of lower energy costs.

A second change was in the U.S. auto industry, which began to adopt total quality control techniques in the late 1970s and 1980s. The implications of this for suppliers to the U.S. auto industry were evolving from month-to-month, and no definitive conclusion had yet emerged. Nevertheless, it seemed clear that much could be learned by the industry from the earlier Japanese experience, even if that experience was not directly applicable in the U.S. environment.

Third, the exchange rate between the Japanese yen and U.S. dollar had dramatically changed in the mid-1980s, and by 1990 the Japanese yen had climbed to around 150 yen per U.S.$1, from the level of 360 yen per dollar in the 1960s. This had not only spurred Japanese interest in establishing U.S. production facilities to serve the U.S. market, it also greatly improved the international competitive position of U.S.-based producers. Honda, the first of the Japanese manufacturers to establish U.S. pro-

duction, exported an inaugural batch of special U.S.-produced Hondas to Japan in 1988, and by 1990 had plans to export some models from the United States into the European Economic Community.

Implications for PCI

The implications of these various changes for PCI were not all obvious. The specific example of Japanese growth in global market share in the automotive industries was both a pressing issue in its own right and a prominent example of larger issues. One thing that all PCI managers agreed upon was that PCI had to develop a much more systematic means of understanding the impact of present and future changes in the global environment on PCI and responding to them in a timely fashion.

To this end, a "Target: Japan" project team was formed to examine not only how PCI might now best respond to the specific changes that had occurred in its automotive-related business, but also how and when PCI might have responded earlier to these changes. It was hoped that this latter effort, to learn lessons from the immediate past, would be helpful in assessing the need for revising PCI's company-wide approach to managing in an increasingly global economy.

CASE STUDY *IV* [*]

Midnight Sun Meets Rising Sun

Thomas Singer

The American University, Kogod College of Business Administration

Stephen Passage, president and CEO of the Midnight Sun Brewing Company, sat in his office atop the Panhandle Building in downtown Juneau, Alaska, gazing out over the Gastineau Channel and the snow-capped mountains beyond. He was watching a lone humpback whale feeding in the cold March waters below. Glancing at his telephone, he muttered, "That whale has more guts than I do."

Passage was referring to the whale's annual migration to survive. Each year, as the winter's cold strips the ocean of food, whales have abandoned the coast of Alaska for the rich feeding grounds off the cost of Japan, and every spring they return to resume their interrupted feast. It was this act of evolutionary wisdom that Passage reflected on as he gazed out at the whale. For a cold dark winter appeared to be descending upon the U.S. microbrewery industry.

Ever since the August 2 invasion of Kuwait by Iraqi forces, U.S. consumers had seemed to have lost their taste for upscale products, including Midnight Sun Amber Beer, the best beer brewed in America. Sales of Midnight Sun had dropped off dramatically in the newly established Seattle market and were even softening in Alaska.

At the same time, Japanese beer connoisseurs continued to snap up every bottle of Midnight Sun that Passage could export. Exports had been running at about 2,400 cases per year, but any increase beyond this level was precluded by high transportation costs and Japanese tariffs on imported beer and by limited production capacity in Juneau.

With continued economic growth forecast for Japan, especially consumption of luxury foreign food items, his course of action was clear—follow the whales to richer feeding grounds. But what a long, risky journey. Passage wondered if he had as much courage as the whales.

The ringing of the telephone startled Passage from his reverie. "Hi Steve. This is Lynn. It's been over a week and I haven't heard from you, so I thought I'd call. You know, about the Japan deal. Everyone here at the bank is really excited about it. Have you made a decision yet to go ahead with the loan?" Passage swallowed hard as he prepared to answer.

Midnight Sun was one of the most successful of a new breed of American brewery. The U.S. microbrewery industry exploded onto the scene in the late 1970's as "real ale" enthusiasts discovered that a market existed for what had been, until then, essentially a basement hobby. Small breweries began to compete in local markets with imported European beers, and found

[*] This fictional case was prepared by Dr. Thomas Singer, Assistant Professor, The American University. Any resemblance to real individual, firms, or business conditions is unintentional.

a ready market for their colorful, flavorful local product. The "gourmet beer" industry was born.

Consumers were attracted by their evocative names and eye-catching labels, from Chesapeake Brewery's Tidewater Ale to Utah Brewing's Downhill Amber Beer. Many American beer drinkers had also become more health conscious and found the absence of preservatives, artificial colors, or other chemicals in microbrews a psychological antidote to its alcohol content. Its higher price also encouraged drinking in moderation. Perhaps most important, microbrews offered distinctive new tastes based on centuries-old German and English brewing traditions.

The microbrewery industry grew rapidly in the 1980s, providing "real ale" for purists and an alternative for beer-drinking yuppies to compete with wine enthusiasts. A beer industry trade association counted only seven commercial microbreweries in 1983, but by 1987 there were more than seventy such companies producting over 150,000 barrels of beer annually. Industry sales were estimated to have grown about 50 percent per year during this period. The market seemed so attractive that even major breweries in the United States, Canada, and Germany were launching joint-ventures to establish a presence in the gourmet beer market.

The number of microbreweries had been expected to double during the 1990s, that is, until major changes in the external environment—threats of war in the Middle East, higher oil prices, and recession in the U.S. economy—closed American wallets to luxury purchases and threatened the industry's continued domestic expansion.

Meanwhile, across the Pacific, the "Japanese miracle" continued unabated, despite financial instability and rising interest rates. To counter growing criticism of Japanese trading practices, the Japanese government had agreed to promote imports by encouraging its consumers to buy foreign goods. Luxury foreign food items were a prominent item in this strategy. Indeed, several American microbreweries had begun to export to Japan by the late 1980s. The Japanese had also promised to provide easier access for foreign firms seeking to make direct investments in Japan.

All of these recent world events had forced Midnight Sun to reconsider its expansion strategy. The company had been formed in the early 1980s after Passage spent several years doing research, planning, and experimenting with beer recipes. He had been able to convince about one hundred local residents—family, friends, and lovers of real ale—to each put up a small amount of capital, and he had Midnight Sun as a limited partnership with himself as managing partner.

Midnight Sun produced beer in commercial quantities for the first time in 1986. Since then, annual production had grown from 1,500 to 4,000 barrels, all at the Juneau brewery. Until recently, production had been unable to keep pace with demand, even at the premium price of $7 to $8 per six-pack.

The most successful product was Midnight Sun Amber Beer, winner of first prize in 1987, 1988, and 1990 at the premier industry event, the Great American Beer Festival. The regular product line also included Midnight Sun Pale Ale. The line was augmented periodically with seasonal ales, stouts, and porters, such as Gold Nugget Ale, Raven Porter, and King Salmon Stout. All of the beers included only yeast, malt, and hops brought up from the "lower 48" and water from the pure, glacier-fed streams of southeast Alaska. One internationally recognized beer critic said, "I rank Midnight Sun Amber Beer among the world's very best. There's a commitment to quality and consistency, and a local statement that's very important."

Once the company's basic objectives within Alaska had been met, Passage turned his attention to expansion. The first step was a relatively low-risk one—the Seattle area, where it was expected that strong demand during football season would help smooth out strong Alaskan sales during the spring and summer months. Fierce competition among regional microbreweries, however, and the industrywide slowdown in sales jeopardized this strategy. Still, Passage felt that expansion and diversification was essential to long-term success. Indeed, more than twenty microbreweries had failed even during the boom years, because of quality control, financing, and distribution problems.

Several months ago, Passage had received a luncheon invitation from a Japanese businessman, Mr. Oyama, whom he had met in Juneau several times before, where Oyama had bought a fish processing operation four years ago that shipped thousands of pounds of salmon, shrimp, and crab to Japan. He visited Juneau frequently, in truth, as much for the fishing and skiing as to inspect his operation.

At lunch, the conversation ranged from the upcoming fishing season to the state gubernatorial election and the prospects for Soviet tourism through northern Alaska and Japan. Over coffee, Oyama's expression became serious as he said "You know, I believe your Midnight Sun Amber Beer is the very best beer on the market. We Japanese prize quality, and I believe your product could be a huge success in my country. You will never reach your full potential with exports. I think you should brew Midnight Sun in Japan."

Passage was flattered, but only realized the extent of Oyama's seriousness as he unfolded a detailed proposal. Oyama wanted to form a fifty-fifty joint-venture with Midnight Sun to establish a brewery in Japan. Oyama believed that the operation, including a building, brewing and bottling equipment, and initial working capital, could be launched for about $2 million.

Oyama had investigated several major issues affecting the feasibility of the project. He assured Passage that the same quality ingredients were available in Japan. He had even located several sources of spring water that he believed would meet Midnight Sun's high standards. Oyama already possessed considerable expertise marketing Alaskan seafood, which was prized in Japan for its purity and freshness,

and felt that gourmet Alaska beer would also receive widespread market acceptance.

Oyama sold his seafood products though several large Japanese specialty supermarket chains that carried luxury foreign food and beverage items. One of these chains had declined to carry Midnight Sun in the past because of its small export volume. Oyama felt sure that they would welcome Midnight Sun once a larger, more reliable source of supply had been established, as would Japanese customers.

After reviewing a business plan prepared by Oyama and making a visit to the proposed site in Japan, Passage was convinced that the Japanese venture made sense for Midnight Sun. Oyama had been able to cover the Japanese end of the project, and all that remained for Passage was to finance his half of the project. He had decided to raise half of his share with equity from his enthusiastic limited partners. He planned to borrow the other $500,000 from his bank.

His banker, Lynn Canal, was skeptical at first. As manager of the Juneau branch of a major Seattle bank, Canal had never before approved a loan for an overseas project, but the head office was enthusiastic, and Canal was eager to close the deal. The bank was willing to provide the $500,000 for five years at a fixed interest rate of 1.5 percent over prime (which had been running at 10 percent). Passage had calculated

CASE STUDIES TABLE 4-1
Midnight Sun's U.S.$ Loan
($500,000 at 11.5% for 5 years discounted at 15%)

Year	Interest	Principal	Present Value
0			$441,337
1	$57,500		
2	$57,500		
3	$57,500		
4	$57,500		
5	$57,500	$500,000	

634   Case Studies

CASE STUDIES TABLE 4-2
Midnight Sun's Yen Loan
(Y64.5 million at 10% for 5 years discounted at 15%)

Year	Interest	Principal	Y/$	Interest	Principal	Present Value
0						$416,196
1	Y6,450,000		129	$50,000		
2	Y6,450,000		129	$50,000		
3	Y6,450,000		129	$50,000		
4	Y6,450,000		129	$50,000		
5	Y6,450,000	Y64,500,000	129	$50,000	$500,000	

the present value cost of the loan using Midnight Sun's cost of capital plus a premium for the additional risk, or 15 percent, as the discount rate. The dollar outflows for Midnight Sun and their present value are shown in Table 4-1.

Shortly after he had discussed the loan with Canal, Oyama called to inform Passage that Oyama's Tokyo-based bank was also interested in financing the debt portion of Midnight Sun's half of the project. Because interest rates in Japan were below those in the United States, the bank's terms were attractive. It would loan funds for five years at a fixed interest rate of prime (8 percent in Japan) plus 2 percent. The only catch was that what they were lending was yen. The $500,000 loan would be the equivalent of 64.5 million yen at the current spot rate during the period ($500,000 × Y129/$). The total dollar cost (outflow) of the yen financing for Midnight Sun is shown in Table 4-2.

Passage was attracted to the $25,141 savings promised by the yen loan, but was troubled by the prospect that changes in the yen/dollar exchange rate would change the dollar cost of his yen debt service in the future. Even though he was expecting to earn yen from beer sales in Japan, committing to a yen loan made him nervous. He knew that exchange rates had been somewhat volatile in recent years and decided to visit the local university library to investigate.

Checking in the IMF's International Financial Statistics, he found data for the yen/dollar ex-

change rate going back to the 1960s. Reasoning that more recent exchange rates were probably more relevant for the future, he focused on the exchange rate during the past ten years. These exchange rates are shown in Table 4-3.

Passage noted that the yen value of the dollar had varied substantially during this period, from Y249/$ in 1982 to Y128/$ in 1988, but he also noted that these figures were average exchange rates for each year. He decided to check with his banker to find out what the actual ten-year high and low exchange rates had

CASE STUDIES TABLE 4-3
Yen-Dollar Exchange Rates

Year	Average Annual Exchange Rate (Y/$)
1978	210
1979	219
1980	227
1981	221
1982	249
1983	238
1984	238
1985	239
1986	169
1987	145
1988	128

CASE STUDIES TABLE 4-4
Yen Loan Worst Case (Y114/$)
(Y64.5 million at 10% for 5 years discounted at 15%)

Year	Interest	Principal	Y/$	Interest	Principal	Present Value
0						$460,453
1	Y6,450,000		126	$51,190		
2	Y6,450,000		123	$52,439		
3	Y6,450,000		120	$53,750		
4	Y6,450,000		117	$55,128		
5	Y6,450,000	Y64,500,000	114	$56,579	$565,789	

CASE STUDIES TABLE 4-5
Yen Loan Best Case (Y251/$)
(Y64.5 million at 10% for 5 years discounted at 15%)

Year	Interest	Principal	Y/$	Interest	Principal	Present Value
0						$241,494
1	Y6,450,000		154	$41,883		
2	Y6,450,000		178	$36,236		
3	Y6,450,000		203	$31,773		
4	Y6,450,000		227	$28,414		
5	Y6,450,000	Y64,500,000	251	$25,697	$256,972	

been on any given day. Canal called back with the information—the yen had reached a ten-year low in 1984 at Y251/$, and a ten-year high of Y114/$ in recent months.

Passage decided to use these past extreme values as ranges for a best case-worst case sensitivity analysis of the impact of exchange rate changes on the dollar cost of the yen loan. In the worst case, he assumed that the yen would appreciate over the next five years from the current spot rate of Y129/$ to Y114/$, while in the best case the yen would depreciate over the term of the loan to Y251/$. The results of his analysis are shown in Tables 4-4 and 4-5.

Passage had been pondering these figures for the past week. It was more likely that the yen loan would be less costly than the dollar loan, with possible savings of from $25,141 to $199,843, but it was still possible that the yen would appreciate, raising the dollar cost of the loan by almost $20,000. It was time to make a decision. Clearing his throat and swallowing hard, he began. "Well Lynn,..."

Discussion Questions

1. How do interest rates affect the financing decision?

2. How does exchange rate variability affect the financing decision? Where could Passage have obtained forecasts of future Yen/dollar exchange rates?

3. Which currency would you borrow in and why?

4. Given that Midnight Sun's U.S. equity investors will expect their dividend payments in dollars, what can Passage do to protect against a drop in the dollar value of his yen earnings in Japan?

LUVS Disposable Diapers

Kamal Kurtulus

University of Istanbul, School of Business

Procter & Gamble of Cincinnati, Ohio, is one of the largest and most successful producers and marketers of household consumer goods in the United States and Europe. The prosperity achieved by Procter & Gamble in Europe has had a lot to do with the management styles that have been adopted in its European subsidiaries, each of which enjoys a great deal of autonomy and decentralized decision-making. Up until now, however, Procter & Gamble has had full ownership over these investments abroad, which stems from the company's evident superiority in production capabilities and marketing technologies, and which is why control is necessary. A Japanese joint venture has been the only exception to this policy, but because of disagreements, the joint venture soon failed. Thus, the general principal of P&G having full ownership was once again preserved.

In West Germany, the head of operations for Procter & Gamble is located in Frankfurt. Within the country, there are three large factories, and sales from these facilities reached 1.5 billion deutsche marks in 1982, predominantly from the production and sale of traditional P&G products, such as detergent, soap, supplementary cleaning materials, toothpaste, toilet paper, and Pampers, a disposable diaper. Pampers was introduced into the German market in the latter part of the 1970s and accounted for about half of the market sales.

A basic objective of P&G is aimed at supplying products to satisfy both consumer needs and market conditions in the quickest possible way. As a result, the company is continuously using all the major marketing tools and variables available to achieve these objectives. In turn, product development, variation, and differentiation became the key ways of further developing Pampers in the West German market. Pampers family-size packages were brought into the market and their introduction proved successful.

When Procter & Gamble was the leader in West Germany, they held a 50 percent market share. Molnex, a German firm, had a 20 percent share, and another German company, Born, held between 10 percent and 15 percent. The remaining market share was held by many other smaller firms.

The paper products manager of P&G believed that it was necessary to develop products continuously and to sell products that are superior to those of competitors with effective marketing programs. With this in mind, P&G set out to reexamine the diaper market and its opportunities. The idea was to come up with an idea or innovation that could increase P&G's share of the West German diaper market. Through formal research and studies came the idea of producing a new type of disposable diaper, one that had many new benefits and product features. This new diaper, which was to be introduced in the West German market in 1981, was to be of superior quality and design in comparison to the existing Pampers product. Elastic leg openings to prevent leakage, rubber sides for added comfort, and a more luxurious package were features to be included in their objective to produce a disposable diaper that was totally superior to the existing products of competitors. By improving the quality and design, it was to be targeted toward the upper end of the market. The average price of the product would be about 20 percent more than Pampers and its competitors. Roll-out of the new diaper to the market was not going to be on a wide scale or on a national basis. There also were plans to leave the final design of the diaper unfinished. In turn, this would reduce the amount of risk P&G would incur and provided a way for the company to see what product features the consumer desired most.

Knowing that it was difficult to estimate consumer reactions, this approach seemed to be the best path to success. Similar products had been successful in the past, but it was not easy to guarantee the same success, especially in West Germany. Procter & Gamble had run into this problem before in the European market and, therefore, decided to take extra steps in developing the German market on a limited scale with a lengthy two-year test period. The test period was set up to determine the consumer preferences toward the diaper and to establish the attributes or features that were to be incorporated into the final product. The product development managers decided to keep the LUVS brand name from P&G's existing brand available in the United States.

During the period of product development, the West German disposable diaper firm, Born, with the same goal, started to develop a similar product. Its new diaper was also geared toward

CASE STUDIES TABLE 5-1
Text Results for Two Alternative Products
(consumer preferences as percent)

	Single Rubbered	Double Rubbered
General evaluation	78	22
Important reason		
Cleaning power	29	22
Product fit	55	12
No irritation of skin	41	40

the upper consumer segments. After learning about Born's new product development, studies about LUVS were sped up, so that a full-scale introduction could take place. P&G's product development department emphasized two alternatives about the final design of LUVS. The first was that the diaper have two lines of rubber on each side to fit the baby's legs. The second alternative was having one line of rubber on each side of the diaper. The product group managers decided to test both alternatives in the market. Therefore, the decision was made to administer a blind test (without stating the brand name) on a sample that had national validity and reliability, based on past studies. The test was completed in a month, and its general results are shown in Table 5-1.

CASE STUDIES TABLE 5-2
Test Results for Two Brand Products
(consumer preferences as percent)

	LUVS		Born
General evaluation	71	×	29
Important reason			
Cleaning power	49	×	11
Safety against leakage	33	×	9
Product fit	56	×	31
Skin protection	2		9

NOTE: × indicates significant differences.

CASE STUDIES TABLE 5-3
Market Shares Results during 1981–82 Period (%)

	January–April 1981	May–September 1981	November–December 1981	January–February 1982	March–April 1982	May–July 1982
LUVS	4.6	7.4	8.2	8.7	8.5	8.6
Born	3.5	5.3	7.3	8.1	8.9	10.2
	+	+	+	+	−	−

Meanwhile, Born's new diapers were also to be introduced. Born's product was like LUVS, with one line of rubber on each side, and was at the same price level. In order to determine what consumers thought of both products, it was decided to make a second test and ask the consumers to evaluate (rank) the products by each of the various product characteristics, on a blind test basis. In this framework a market test was performed on a group that represented national characteristics. The basic results of the test are shown in Table 5-2.

The management group who evaluated these results believed that LUVS was superior to the Born product and would probably be more successful in the market. It was decided to supply LUVS in the West German market from the beginning of 1981 because of the firm's power and its preferred product characteristics. The market shares for LUVS and Born's product in West Germany by July 1982 are shown in Table 5-3.

The product group manager, after examining the declining market share results since March 1982, asked the product manager to prepare a report related to the subject.

Discussion Questions

1. Evaluate the marketing strategy that Procter & Gamble followed in the West German market.
2. Suppose that you were the product manager of LUVS. How would you prepare the report?

Toys 'R' Us

Lynette Knowles Mathur

Southern Illinois University College of Business Administration

The Japanese retailing industry had been considered impenetrable by most firms, but not by Toys 'R' Us, which announced in fall 1989 that it would expand into the Japanese market through company-owned stores. As this was the first market entry of this nature into Japan by a large U.S. retailer, it is regarded as a test case for future access to this growing retailing market.

Toys 'R' Us, a New Jersey chain, is the world's largest toy retailer, with 1989 annual sales at $4.75 billion, and control of almost one-fourth of the $13 billion U.S. toy market as of December 1988. While most of the 478 stores in operation in November 1989 were located in the United States, 9 percent of its sales were foreign, generated from outlets in Canada, Great Britain, France, West Germany, Singapore, and Hong Kong.

The success of Toys 'R' Us in the international toy market is based on several advantages it has developed over the years. First, the chain developed the supermarket form of toy retailing, offering complete product lines, not just a few items, and selling toys at low prices. This strategy has been a particularly strong contributor to the firm's rapid growth in the Canadian and European markets since the early 1980s, where the toy supermarket was almost nonexistent. Second, Toys 'R' Us often holds greater

power than its U.S. and foreign toy suppliers concerning pricing and production selection. In many cases, the firm's power base affects the ability of small toy manufacturers to enter the toy market. Third, the chain's competitive efforts over the years have created a year-round market for toys, resulting in greater income stability. Fourth, the firm has considerable financial strength with which to support and expand its U.S. and foreign operations.

Entry by Toys 'R' Us into Japan was encouraged by the country's great demand for toys, which is reflected in the $5.5 billion Japanese toy market. The complexity of the Japanese retailing distribution system, however, which is often viewed as a barrier to entry, made the firm realize that it would have to adjust its retailing strategy to ensure successful expansion.

Changes in the chain's strategy would have to address several differences between U.S. and Japanese retailing systems caused by cultural contrasts and higher real estate costs in Japan. First, U.S.-type shopping malls in Japan are rare, thus lessening the comparability of contemporary Japanese and U.S. toy retail locations. Second, the Japanese final consumers of toys and their parents have their own long-established buying behaviors that may be affected by differing retail forms and site locations. Third, the size and product offering of the average

Japanese toy store are much smaller than the average Toys 'R' Us store.

The typical Japanese store is a mom-and-pop operation that has 3,200 square feet of selling space and offers only Japanese goods. In fact, most of these outlets are manufacturer-owned stores that carry only that manufacturer's products, are managed by its retired employees, and very rarely offer discounted prices. This manufacturer-oriented relationship increases the difficulties in obtaining shelf space in the Japanese retailing system. The product selection thus offered by the average Japanese toy store is quite limited in both inventory volume and product mix compared to the average Toys 'R' Us outlet. Even the large Japanese food supermarket chains and department stores that account for half of Japan's imports of finished goods, yet form the minority of retailer numbers, would not be able to compete against the broader, more diverse, and more economical toy selection that Toys 'R' Us could offer Japanese consumers.

To continue use of the supermarket retailing form and avoid the product selection limitations of the Japanese retailing system, the toy chain decided to establish company-owned stores in Japan. To control real estate costs in finding optimal site locations, Toys 'R' Us decided to use an expert on Japanese real estate in its expansion. After a two-year search, Toys 'R' Us located Den Fujita, president of McDonald's Company of Japan.

McDonald's Japan is a 50 percent joint venture of McDonald's Corporation and Fujita and Company. As the real estate expert for Toys 'R' Us, the firm will own 20 percent of the toy chain's Japanese venture, but as a passive investor. Based in part on advice from McDonald's Japan, Toys 'R' Us plans to open from four to six stores in Japan by the end of 1991 and to eventually have 100 outlets in major metropolitan areas. The greatest benefit to McDonald's Japan from the venture, however, is its option to open its restaurants on the Toys 'R' Us sites. The combined-site location would increase bene-

fits for both firms. First, their customer bases are very similar and thus can be shared and optimized. Second, their combined-site locations replicate similar clusterings of retail outlets found in the United States, perhaps assuring the firms of some level of success, assuming similarities in consumer shopping patterns in Japan and the United States.

The store that Toys 'R' Us eventually designed for the Japanese market is basically the same as its average store in other countries. Its typical store is a large supermarket operation with 50,000 square feet of selling space and is stocked with 14,000 to 15,000 items from a product mix that is 80 percent American and 20 percent foreign. Each Toys 'R' Us store in Japan is expected to cost $2 million to establish, to show slow growth at first, and to have lower profit margins, primarily because of higher real estate costs. Volume sales should offset these setbacks, because they are forecasted to be double that of the chain's U.S. stores. The prospect of such high turnover would strongly benefit the U.S. and foreign suppliers to Toys 'R' Us because the chain would be their entry into the Japanese toy market.

The Toys 'R' Us stores would be able to compete heavily against local toy retailers, an aspect that has increased the concern of toy wholesalers and industry associations across Japan. The chain's first outlet, located in Niigata, with a population of nearly a half million, would be eighty times larger than the average toy store in that city, and its projected annual turnover, at $13.3 million, would be half the combined sales of local toy stores.

In reaction to this competitive threat by Toys 'R' Us, Japanese toy retailers pressured the Japanese government for increased protection under Japan's large-scale retail law. Under the law, enacted in 1973 and strengthened by the government in 1980, retailers wanting to open a store greater than 5,400 square feet had to obtain unanimous approval for the outlet from all local stores. The law increased the power of Japan's retailing industry, because only one dissenting shopkeeper could prevent a Japanese or foreign retailer from opening a large store.

The large-scale retail law created serious U.S.-Japan trade tensions and was discussed in negotiations between the two countries in February 1990. Subsequently, the Japanese government responded in May 1990 by ending its protection of Japanese stores through this law, thus opening Japan's retail market.

The Toys 'R' Us decision to expand its operations to Japan appears to be a natural extension of its successful foreign market activities. In terms of the timing of the decision, however, the chain has again demonstrated its unusual savvy and aggressiveness. First, the retailer appears to have considerable understanding of the predictable course of government policies since it announced its plans for the Japanese market just a few months before the scheduled U.S.-Japan negotiations. Undoubtedly, the large retailer accurately predicted the reactions of the Japanese retailing industry and the subsequent political decisions to open the Japanese retail market. Second, the Toys 'R' Us expansion into Japan resembles the firm's invasion of the Canadian and European toy markets, in that it will again conquer a large market with the benefits of the supermarket form of toy retailing.

Bibliography

1990. "Uncorking the Bottleneck." *The Economist* (June 16): 79–80.

DUNKIN, AMY. 1988. "How Toys 'R' Us Controls the Game Board." *Business Week* (December 19): 58–60.

GRAVEN, KATHRYN. 1990. "For Toys 'R' Us, Japan Isn't Child's Play." *Wall Street Journal* (February 7): B1, B4.

RESS, DAVID. 1989. " Toys 'R' Us Enters Japan through McDonald's Golden Arch." *American Shipper* (November): 10.

Neda International and the German Connection

M. Kavoossi

Howard University International School of Business

Multinational enterprises (MNEs) often run into conflicts with host governments, their parent country's government, or their local partners. Among the myriad sources of the conflict that affect the success or failure of international ventures, are differences in motives, objectives, and interests, both real differences and those perceived as such by foreign companies and the nation-state. Moreover, perceived national and corporate goals are not static, but evolve and change to reflect changing circumstances and environment.

Effective functioning of multinational ventures is affected both by aspects of the corporate culture and by the emerging patterns of interaction between the global enterprise and the institutions in the host country. Such hindrances to functioning can occur even when conflicts in objectives have been overcome to each other's satisfaction and benefit. In particular, it seems that more serious conflicts occur in businesses where the cross-cultural differences between the host country and the investing MNE are significant. Thus, a proper understanding of the nature of power relations, as well as the dynamics of the public-private sector interactions involved, will be helpful in managing conflict resolution.

Direct foreign investment is a relatively recent phenomenon for Germany. Throughout the 1960s, foreign capital inflows into West Germany were largely in the form of grants, and direct foreign investment.[1] The rapid economic growth, coupled with sustained political stability in West Germany, has attracted highly competitive loan capital from international financial markets. During the early stages of West Germany's export-oriented development, exports mainly consisted of labor-intensive manufacturing goods. Beginning in the late 1970s, the West Germany economy faced the need of another transition, from basic industries to more sophisticated high-technology endeavors. With rising wages in West Germany and competition from other European countries, sustained economic growth in West Germany required technology-intensive industries.[2] This transition would have to come through the inducements of MNEs. MNEs could offer technologies, foreign exchange, and access to international markets. Throughout the 1970s and 1980s, the

---

[1] 1990. "Germany." *World Economic and Business Review.*
[2] Marc Fisher. 1990. "West Germans Lose Euphoria." *Washington Post* (September 30).

West German government looked the other way while German companies or companies operating out of Germany supplied the world with chemicals. The West German government actively studied ways to strengthen the protection of industrial property rights of MNEs.

Neda International is a U.S. MNE involved in petrochemicals, and operating in West Germany, with German business entities acting as junior partners. Neda International is a major petrochemical manufacturer, currently under Iraqi government contract to complete a petrochemical project in Faw. The West German government's open attitude toward foreign investment enabled Neda International to invest and trade with Iraq in the development of their petrochemical industries. The ongoing liberalization of international business greatly enhanced the possibilities for Neda International to offer a wide range of services to Iraq. The German government displayed an unwillingness and inability to restrain export of chemicals, claiming they are for civilian purposes.

Neda International, however, is caught between Iraq and a hard place—Germany. Overreliance on foreign-based MNEs may not be considered in the best long-term interest of Germany. Given the government's power over the business community, it has begun to monitor whether Neda's operations are consistent with the national interest, given the fact that Neda has been instrumental in providing Iraq with the raw materials, facilities, and knowhow for producing chemical products, leading to the production of weapons. The German's stated long-term national interest being nonproliferation of chemical weapons has been one of the most important foreign policy objectives sought by West Germany.

One of the potent instruments used by the government for influencing business has been control of bank credit. Selective credit policies were used by the government to influence international business activities of MNEs. With access to low-cost capital in the 1960s and 1970s, the West German government was able

to play the role of arbiter, deciding which business groups could expand. Years of access to credit and bank-lending have made Neda International accustomed to heavy dependence on external financing through government intervention.

Neda should be aware of the three important factors in the West German government's dealings with the business community. First, German policymakers are, in general, goal-oriented. They have concentrated on what works. In order to achieve a desired goal, they are willing to experiment, without ideological prejudices, with any available policy instruments.

Another noteworthy aspect of government-business relations in West Germany is that the process of government decision-making is open to a wide range of opinions with virtually unlimited freedom of expression. Indeed, Neda International made use of this.

Third, the geopolitics of West Germany have promoted a kind of patriotic alliance between government and business, which have been supportive of each other's role in the pursuit of the common good. The influence of the business community, of which Neda International is a part, has been very much limited to providing opinions about the government and international business policies.

Unlike their local counterparts, Neda International is a legal alien standing in a special power relationship vis-à-vis the German government. To begin with, the bargaining leverage of the West German government derives from the value of business opportunities the German economy can offer Neda. Neda International is generally interested in establishing and maintaining a viable position in the German and Iraqi markets in order to assure for itself an adequate return on investment. The German government can, however, constrain Neda's position by its control of a number of factors affecting the performance of the firm—taxes, imports, and export licensings. In particular, for a country such as West Germany, which has extensive ties with the United States, it is accurate to characterize the German foreign business policy as sensitive to U.S. interests. The success of Neda's operation depends in large measure on the decisions of bureaucrats, considering the intricacies of German-U.S. interests. Therein lies an important source of conflict.

For example, while Neda may be constrained in its assertiveness by a need for caution in an unfamiliar setting, it can obtain assistance from the host government. Also, Neda can exercise bargaining leverage and show a significant power advantage through its significant market share in Iraqi petrochemical industries and the subsequent revenues brought back into Germany.

There is a particular reason for the West German stance on international business. German society is essentially xenophobic, an attitude stemming from a long history of foreign invasions and occupations. In comparison with other European community members with a less attentive government, and particularly when the issue deals with foreign business policy, Neda's influence on the West German government is one step further removed than the influence from domestic corporations.

Neda has two sources of support—West German geopolitics and the importance of the MNE's contribution to the local society. First, the government's bargaining position is limited by the country's geopolitical situation. West German defense depends on the security umbrella of the United States. A visitor to West Germany is immediately struck by the more than one hundred U.S. military bases in the country.[3]

Neda International also cites local German competition in the developing countries markets. Germany leads the world in producing and exporting chemical weapons, and no other country approaches the level of West German exports of chemicals useful for the production of chemical weapons. Neda's German competitors include Rotex Chemie, E.W.T. Company, Hempel, Degussa, and Imhausen, to name a few.

Moreover, MNEs, unlike their domestic counterparts, can enjoy special power because of the importance of the resources they bring to the host nation. For example, Neda's investments in Germany are associated with production for export markets promoting advanced technologies. These investment activities coincide with Germany's national interest as defined by the government. Beginning in the late 1970s, as West Germany needed to increase foreign capital and technology for intensive technological industrialization, the relative power shifted to some extent in favor of MNEs, in particular companies like Neda, which could offer new technological needs and could negotiate from a position of greater strength.

On the other hand, the foreign MNEs that make the investment mainly to supply the domestic market have been losing the bargaining leverage they previously enjoyed as the domestic market becomes saturated by local competition and the technologies they imparted to West Germany became obsolete.[4] The government will maintain its active role in managing industrial development, particularly in sectors regarded as saturated with domestic production. Petrochemical MNEs are a case in point. In the early 1970s, the West German government became involved in petrochemical industries and set the terms of their foreign activities. As the plan was being implemented, the government pushed for increased indigenous control of technology. The market conditions soon no longer justified the continued role of foreign capital. Foreign partners began to lose their power and were gradually bought out by domestic interests.

There is no clear-cut evidence, however, that the government could exercise a similar extent of dominance over majority-owned foreign

---

[3] There exist more than a hundred bases of operations by the U.S. forces.

[4] JUDITH PERERA. 1990. "Iraq's Chemical Weapons Capacity." *Middle East International* (August 31): 29.

MNEs. The state's interventions in multinationals have been ad hoc in nature, varying from one firm to another. They depended on the specific firm's leveraging power and characteristics.

As 1992 and unification of European markets approach, many MNEs are seeking to promote joint ventures with German firms,[5] primarily for two reasons. First, with the recent move toward German unification and relaxation of the highly centralized structure of the East German economy, foreign capital is sought for the private sector to spearhead sustained industrialization, in particular in technology-intensive industries. Second, joint operation seems an effective way to work in a cross-cultural environment.

As Iraq invaded Kuwait, and the UN Security Council imposed sanctions, the United States began to pressure the German government to identify companies such as Neda and punish them for providing the technology used by Iraq to build their arsenal of chemical weapons. The U.S. government cites international treaties against the use of chemical weapons, but there are no international treaties banning research and development of such weapons. The U.S. government amassed massive quantities of chemical weapons to deter the Soviets during the cold war era.

Neda International denies any wrongdoing in providing the technology to the Iraqi government. As one of the most important German manufacturers of petrochemicals, however, it has to explain the Iraqi acquisition of the technology. Neda's chief executive wants to prepare a policy for such future ventures. In the meantime the Iraqi government is demanding that Neda fulfill its contractual obligations inside Iraq. Neda is faced with layoffs and cuts in revenues.

To stop the illegal flow of chemical arms to developing countries, including Iraq, more than 170 German chemical companies are currently under investigation for selling weapons. As 1992 approaches, however, it appears that it may be much harder to stem the flow, partly because of the expansion of boundaries and the new unimarket. The European community is faced with a major task to stop leakages.

Discussion Questions

1. Is what Neda International did ethical?
2. Should Neda's behavior have been any different had this not been an Iraqi government contract?
3. What are the MNE interests in this problem?
4. Explain how this may be a good example of uncontrollable factors at work.
5. Do you think Neda International should stay and complete the contract in Iraq?
6. How can an overseas manager be prepared to face this problem?

---

[5] 1992 is the date set for the unification of the European markets into one united Europe.

International Pharmaceuticals, Inc.

Dara Khambata

American University, Kogod College of Business Administration

India no longer holds out a begging bowl to the rest of the world. In most years, it grows just about enough to feed its 800 million people, who represent one-sixth of the world's population. India is still mainly a farming country, with four out of five Indians working the land. This fact tends to limit the growth of the economy to agriculture, whose output has been expanding at about 2 percent annually.

Industry in India has only gradually increased in importance and accounted for approximately 20 percent of the gross domestic product in 1980. The country's economic development has involved a flawed marriage of convenience between the theory of socialism and the reality of India's feudal political culture. Although socialist by name, it is often suggested that the feudal political nature of Indian politics means that the politicians treat the state as their private property by lining their own pockets, providing jobs for friends and relatives, and setting up commercial ventures to suit their whims.

Mercantilist policies are aimed at encouraging the domestic manufacture of products in every industry. Thus, India produces virtually everything from needles and biscuits to steel-making equipment and supersonic aircraft. The obsession with self-sufficiency has made India a jack of many trades and a master of only a few. Moreover, these economic nationalistic policies have distorted the development of the economy and have partly dissipated India's comparative advantage in international economic competition. The basic elements of this advantage are an abundance of entrepreneurial talent, a first-rate civil service, masses of cheap labor, a wide range of raw materials, and extremely low wages. In practice, however, the effect of these advantages is reduced by low productivity and militant, strike-prone labor unions.

The large industries in which India could potentially realize competitive economies of scale are mainly in the public domain. It is these industries, unfortunately, that some people claim are dogged by inefficiencies, corruption, and political interference. To promote employment, blanket protection against imports has been given to almost all goods, even in cases where the size of the domestic enterprise was uneconomical and the technology third-rate. In general, management has tended to resist capital investment in plant and equipment modernization because there was little incentive to do so in India's sheltered markets.

The bureaucratic influence over the economy is epitomized by a pervasive system of controls and licenses. The pharmaceutical industry, for example, produces thousands of formulations, each of which is subject to government price control. It can take years to obtain approval for a requested price increase, and, when the increase is finally accepted by the government, it may be insufficient to cover the cost increase during the waiting period. Furthermore, it is alleged that politicians hold industry to ransom by demanding bribes for licenses and permits. It is rumored that where they used to ask for a lump sum, they now brazenly demand a percentage of the project costs.

The difficulty in accumulating capital in India is further mitigated by a corporate income tax of 60 percent, and a subsequent withholding tax is levied on distributed dividends at the rates of 22 percent for local owners and 34 percent for non-Indians.

The private sector in Indian industry is dominated by giant conglomerates. The two largest, by far, are those owned by the Tata and Birla families. The former is mainly involved in the manufacture of steel, trucks, power-generation equipment, and chemicals, and the latter has interests in the production of textiles, aluminum, cars, and paper.

The Indian government has lately put out a somewhat slippery welcome mat for multinational corporations. The essence of this policy change is that the requirement for Indian ownership of business operations has been reduced from a majority position to 35 percent in certain select situations. The establishment of free-trade zones is attracting some foreign investment, and the government is trying to reduce the bureaucratic inefficiencies for companies with significant exports. Most of the restrictive aspects of India's economic policies, however, remain in effect. As a result, several multinationals, including IBM, have decided that, because of the poor profits and rampant corruption, it makes sense to pull out of the country.

International Pharmaceuticals, Inc. (IPI) is a U.S. company that manufactures and markets medicines, cosmetics, pesticides, and fertilizers in its worldwide operations. The firm's international business is conducted in some sixty countries, mostly through sales agents and distributors, and manufacturing operations are based in eight countries—Australia, Brazil, Canada, Italy, Great Britain, Venezuela, West Germany, and India. The last facility is IPI's only manufacturing operation in Asia.

IPI sales in India represent roughly 8 percent of the company's total sales and have been approximately $100 million per year for the past three years. The lack of sales growth in this market has been because of the difficulties in the Indian economy and the recent worldwide recessions.

Ownership of IPI's Indian subsidiary is divided into two groups. The parent corporation owns 65 percent and a local Indian participant, Mr. Dinshaw, representing a wealthy family group, owns the remainder. The managing board is comprised of six members, with four appointed by the parent company and two members representing the Dinshaw family.

For the seventeen years of the subsidiary's existence, the managing director has been appointed by the parent company's corporate office in New Jersey. Mr. Anderson, the present managing director, assumed his position about six months ago. Prior to his posting in Bombay, he was in charge of the Venezuelan subsidiary.

IPI has about 2,000 employees in India, most of whom are members of the powerful and militant Congress Socialist Union. The average wage of the factory workers is $1.10 per hour, including fringe benefits.

Net worth and working capital amount to about $21 million and $12 million, respectively. IPI owns buildings, land, factories, equipment, and large inventories, all located in the vicinity of Bombay. Net profits in the past two years have hovered around $7.5 million per year, and dividends declared have been in the neighborhood of 12 percent to 13 percent of share capital. The product line is comprised of:

Medicines (prescription and over-the-counter drugs)	50%
Cosmetics	25%
Fertilizers (agrochemicals)	15%
Pesticides	10%

Since IPI has more than 2 percent of the pharmaceutical market in India, it must obtain clearance from the Monopoly Board, under the Monopoly Restrictions and Trade Practices Act, in order to acquire property, introduce new products, and increase prices. At present, the government drugs controller has authorized the marketing of twenty-four IPI prescription and over-the-counter drugs.

IPI sells its products to several large distributors in India, who subsequently sell the products to chemists, retailers, and other sales agents. Each distributor is required to keep a deposit of one month's purchases with the company, and, as a result, IPI has a remarkably low ratio of bad debts.

Subsidiary exports make up about 30 percent of its total output to the neighboring countries of Sri Lanka, Nepal, Malaysia, Bangladesh, and Thailand. These exports earn highly coveted hard currencies for the Indian government and facilitate the procurement of import licenses for IPI.

The company places a strong emphasis on the advertisement of over-the-counter drugs, cosmetics, and pesticides. The media used for the advertising are newspapers, television, radio, and billboards. It is against the law to advertise prescription drugs, and personal selling is the main promotion vehicle for the agrochemicals.

From the beginning, IPI has tried to tailor its local operations to the Indian environment. The subsidiary has engaged in some new product development, and it provides training and education facilities and housing for many of its employees. Housing is an enticing fringe benefit, because adequate housing is extremely scarce and expensive in the Bombay metropolitan area.

In recent months, Anderson has run into a series of difficult situations. The parent company in New Jersey has developed a revolutionary new prescription drug called Lotex, which is an extremely efficient pain-killer with no noticeable side effects. This new drug must be cleared by the drugs controller. Anderson has

been quietly informed that this approval will require a "donation" of $28,000, which is to be placed in a numbered bank account in Zurich, Switzerland. It has been made very clear that permission to manufacture and market the new drug in India will not be granted unless the payment is made.

To make matters worse, IPI had applied to the Ministry of Industries for permission to build a new plant in Poona, about 150 miles from Bombay. This new facility will cost $8 million, but would increase production efficiency and add at least 350 additional employees. Late one night, Anderson received a telephone call. The caller stated that the plant expansion plan would be stalled, and possibly grounded, if a small cash donation of $49,000 were not made to the local government's reelection campaign.

Anderson was accustomed to the general practice of "baksheesh" (i.e. gifts) for clearing products through customs or expediting income tax audits. He certainly had not been faced, however, with much larger demands, such as the ones being made now.

The executives in the corporate headquarters knew, of course, that some of the company's foreign subsidiaries made occasional payments, since many of its people had been in similar positions in the past. Nevertheless, they had not paid any attention to the overall problem and had more or less dismissed any mention of the subject by rationalizing that this was the way that business was conducted in these countries, and, thus, it was necessary for the survival of its foreign operations. Because of this implied understanding, the corporation had not formulated a clear, written policy on how foreign managing directors were to proceed in these situations. The executives were, of course, aware of the corruption scandals involving a number of large multinational corporations in the mid-1970s. To complicate matters, management was becoming increasingly concerned about investing additional capital in India because of the previously mentioned difficulties, even though the markets in India and surrounding countries still offered a potential opportunity.

Discussion Questions

1. How should Anderson handle these two situations? Explain the supporting arguments for your decision.

2. What should Anderson and the executive managers of IPI do about establishing a corporate policy for these situations?

3. After identifying the strengths and weaknesses of IPI's Indian subsidiary, evaluate the alternatives open to IPI in its business operations in India. What course of action do you recommend?

General Dynamics in Turkey

Gail Arch

University of Houston School of Business

No industry in the United States is more complex than the defense industry. Its environment is global, its institutions impacted by political as well as economic imperatives. Its technology includes the most sophisticated and sensitive in the world. Nationals security interests often impede the free-market flow of goods. Policymakers regulate the flow of all arms sales. From the government's indisputable role as a major actor comes the term "defense Keynesianism." Against this often chaotic background, a small number of giant corporations compete for both capital and human resources and for markets. The defense industry is seldom without critics and has often been treated harshly for its behavior. Charges of high-level impropriety by its corporate leaders and their government counterparts—scandals involving bribery, kickbacks, illegal transfers, and the like on a nearly inconceivable international scale—make this trillion dollar industry a fascinating if complicated study.

Among this handful of corporate giants, none is more representative of the industry's complex nature than General Dynamics. Weathering many a maelstrom in its long history, General Dynamics remains a global leader, parent

* This case was prepared for class discussion rather than to illustrate the effective or ineffective handling of an administrative situation.

to a long list of industrialized and developing nations' defense industries and defender of its own nation's national security.

General Dynamics negotiations and its activities in Turkey provide a clear picture of the problems and issues of global firms operating in developing nations, corporate/government or multinational/nation-state interactions, and issues in technology transfer.

In the 1980s intense global competition shifted arms sales to a buyers market. Developing nations in particular gained heretofore impossible bargaining power. Coupled with a political imperative that prodded the U.S. government to favor friendly nations, particularly strategically located ones, newly industrializing nations (NICs), such as Turkey, negotiated highly favorable offset programs that transferred advanced technology. In Turkey's case, General Dynamics agreed to provide the technology, including management know-how and hardware, for the F-16 fighter plane. In this offset plan, the majority of the sophisticated aircraft would be built in Turkey under a coproduction agreement with the Turkish government agency, TUSAS, while General Dynamics would provide its marketing expertise to a number of indigenous Turkish products on the world market. The Turkish government is the majority owner in the joint venture. It is a complex story of corporation/nation-state technology transfer.

The History of General Dynamics

Unlike many of its equally mammoth competitors—McDonnell Douglas, Northrup, Grumman and Rockwell, for example—General Dynamics is a highly diversified defense contractor with nearly a hundred-year-old history. At the turn of the century, the company's predecessor, and now one of its divisions, Electric Boat, began operations as a fledgling, undercapitalized producer of a new naval defense weapon, the submarine. Using foreign technology and much of the navy's money ($150,000 in 1900 alone), the captains of America's new defense dynasty saw markets for the undersea wonder at home and abroad. The company was virtually born a multinational.

The organization grew to its modern form during World War II and its cold war postscript. One of the original players in the war, Electric Boat received more than $20 million from the U.S. government in grants and subsidies and nearly $1 billion worth of contracts during the war years, its most profitable period until the defense-rich years of the Reagan administration. Expanding to meet the government's various defense needs, the company created new product areas and new divisions. In 1952 the complex corporate entity was renamed General Dynamics to more appropriately reflect its new character. The firm included Electric Boat, Canadair, and, the eventual prize, the huge aircraft company Convair. Its leaders hope to create a "General Motors of defense."

Today, General Dynamics operates in a number of business segments with nearly 95 percent of its business in defense-related products, a defense dependency figure consistently higher than its closest competitor, McDonnell Douglas. General Dynamics principal segments are government aerospace (including military aircraft, missiles, guns, space and defense electronic systems and products); submarines; land

systems (including tanks, land vehicles, and support systems); general aviation aircraft; material service and resources (including building products, lime and coal mining); and a number of lesser segments (including commercial space launch vehicles, ship management and maintenance, commercial aircraft subassemblies, and electric motors). In 1989 net sales, in millions of dollars, were $10,043, with net earnings of $293 (see Table 9-1). The company employs more than 100,000 workers. Dynamic marketing and a changing political scene since the 1960s steadily increased U.S. exports. The U.S. general aerospace industry accounts for nearly $19 billion in foreign trade.

Foreign Military Sales and General Dynamics

In the past decade, General Dynamics has become one of the world's major foreign military sales (FMS) contractors. A FMS program is a government-to-government military weapons sales program with particular emphasis on aircraft. The program assists strategic nations in buying for cash or credit arms they might otherwise be unable to purchase, thereby ensuring the defense needs of friendly nations as well as U.S. strategic interests. The U.S. government designed the FMS program specifically for aid to the governments of Turkey, Greece, Israel, Egypt, and Pakistan (see Exhibit 9–1).

As a total for all companies and for General Dynamics specifically, the FMS awards are significant—approximately 80 percent of all arms exports flow through the FMS channel. With support from the Department of Defense for its military program, General Dynamics received more defense dollars than any other U.S. contractor during the 1980s. In 1985 alone the corporation's FMS program contracts totaled over $1 billion (see Table 9-2).

General Dynamics aggressively pursues its international markets. The increased sales of the FMS program through foreign markets provide economies of scale for increased production

CASE STUDIES TABLE 9-1
General Dynamics 1989 Financial Highlights
(dollars in millions, except per share amounts)

	1989	1988	1987
SUMMARY OF OPERATIONS			
Net Sales	$10,043	$9,551	$9,412
Net Earnings	293	294	404
Net Earnings Per Share	7.01	7.00	9.47
Capital Expenditures	419	496	350
Company-sponsored			
Research & Development	465	463	352
AT YEAR END			
Total Backlog	$28,548	$24,456	$22,817
Shareholder's Equity	2,126	1,878	1,642
Total Assets	6,549	6,139	5,564
Outstanding Shares of			
Common Stock	41,579,300	41,688,996	41,924,750
Number of Employees	102,200	102,800	105,300
SUMMARY OF NET SALES AND OPERATING EARNINGS BY LINES OF BUSINESS			
NET SALES:			
Military Aircraft	$3,615	$3,417	$3,199
Missiles, Space and			
Electronic Systems	2,414	2,485	2,475
Total Government Aerospace	6,029	5,902	5,674
Submarines	1,679	1,548	1,603
Land Systems	989	1,001	1,043
General Aviation	601	454	457
Material Service and Resources	414	413	462
Other	331	233	173
	$10,043	$9,551	$9,412
OPERATING EARNINGS (LOSS):			
Military Aircraft	$237	$318	$322
Missiles, Space and			
Electronic Systems	149	143	160
Total Government Aerospace	386	461	480
Submarines	41	36	106
Land Systems	71	39	28
General Aviation	76	25	8
Material Services and Resources	27	(6)	21
Other	(17)	(33)	5
	$584	$522	$650

SOURCE: General Dynamics, *Annual Report, 1989.*

EXHIBIT 9–1   FOREIGN MILITARY SALES VERSUS DIRECT COMMERCIAL SALES

Once the U.S. government approves a weapons sale, the buyer must decide how to follow through. Whether a recipient nation should purchase U.S. military equipment through the government-to-government Foreign Military Sales program or through the company-to-government direct commercial sales avenue has become controversial. Before 1982, the choice was limited by a dollar value ceiling on commercial sales under the Arms Export Control Act of 1976, which decreed that equipment worth more than $25 million had to be sold through the FMS program. The ceiling—later raised to $100 million—was abolished early in 1981, thereby allowing U.S. defense contractors to sell "big ticket" items directly to foreign governments.

A recipient's decision on which of the vehicles best meets its needs depends on its estimate of the relative advantages and disadvantages of each, and the variables are numerous. Some customers find the FMS program desirable because the Department of Defense acts as the purchasing agent and negotiates with American companies on their behalf. Others, confident of their negotiating abilities, choose instead to deal directly with U.S. manufacturers. Each approach has potential benefits and drawbacks.

Critics of the FMS approach object that working through an additional layer of bureaucracy lengthens the period between the time an order is placed and the goods are delivered. They also complain that because the final prices and delivery schedules of FMS sales are estimates, buyers do not know exactly when the equipment will be delivered or how much it will cost. Companies selling directly to foreign countries, on the other hand, are able to offer fixed prices and delivery dates up front. Others,

however, find the Pentagon's presence helpful in the event of disputes with contractors and its established negotiating skills useful in securing the best deal possible.

Recently, the FMS program has come under attack from both U.S. companies involved in the arms trade and recipients of American arms. The director of foreign military procurement for Saudi Arabia—the largest FMS customer—and a vice president of Rockwell publicly criticized the program at an industry sponsored symposium late in 1986. The Saudi official complained that government-to-government sales allow for the intrusion of disruptive "political factors" into the transactions and introduce provisions that are "very one-sided to the United States." Industry officials, on their part, maintain that the total 4.5 percent of all sales' value assessed by the Pentagon as fees and surcharges to cover its administrative costs makes it difficult for U.S. firms to compete with foreign suppliers. Some in the industry claim that the DoD deliberately steers sales through the FMS program in order to secure the fees, which are used to fund the Defense Security Assistance Agency (DSAA). The DSAA budget is not appropriated by Congress, and the agency, therefore, relies on the fees from FMS sales for its livelihood. Industry representatives maintain that declining global arms sales are serving as an impetus for the DSAA to shunt arms sales through FMS channels in order to preserve its bureaucratic integrity and status.

A shift from FMS to commercial sales would make it more difficult for those interested in following corporate involvement in the arms trade. FMS sales are easier to track because the Pentagon keeps detailed records of contracts and awards. Commercial sales records are less comprehensive and harder to come by.

SOURCE: Ferrari et al. 1988.

CASE STUDIES TABLE 9-2
Foreign Military Sales (in millions of current dollars)

Company	1972	1973	1974	1975	1976	1977	1978
General Dynamics	$ 17	$ 14	$ 13	$ 73	$ 46	$303	$1476
Northrup	110	171	221	293	1293	853	267
McDonnell Douglas	802	224	120	419	480	446	274

Company	1979	1980	1981	1982	1983	1984	1985
General Dynamics	$518	$993	$377	$761	$450	$967	$1231
Northrup	472	859	164	894	181	162	296
McDonnell Douglas	639	471	1211	1032	501	993	1616

SOURCE: Ferrari et al. 1987, pages 302–303.

levels, which in turn enhance the firm's ability to market the plane in volume quantities. FMS program contract awards for the F-16 aircraft were $296 million in 1983, $801 million in 1984, and $836 million in 1985.

General Dynamics and the F-16

One of General Dynamics jewels is the fast, relatively cheap, enormously successful F-16 fighter jet. Originally designed in a prototype competition with little chance of getting off the drawing board and into service, the plane performed so well and could be built at so attractive a price that U.S. defense department policymakers reversed their position and issued an initial order for the aircraft to be built by General Dynamics. The firm first priced the jet at just over $6 million—low enough to encourage the volume contracts that General Dynamics hoped for. From this surprising start in 1974 the fighter plane has undergone numerous revisions, been blessed and burdened with some remarkable technological advances, and weath-

ered a number of high-tech snafus to remain one of the world's most popular military aircraft. Besides its price tag, the jet's success lies in its small size (one-seater or two-seater trainers), remarkable maneuverability at glaringly high speeds, and relative ease in flight operations. Today, in addition to the U.S. military, fifteen nations fly the F-16 as part of the their national defense program (see Table 9-3). Worldwide deliveries of the F-16 in 1989 were more than 2,500 planes, with a total ordered of nearly 4,000. Numerous F-16 variants are in simultaneous production at General Dynamics' Fort Worth, Texas, plant and several foreign sites. At a current cost of approximately $16 million per aircraft, the F-16 remains a mainstay for the firm, whose military aircraft division sales totaled $3.6 billion in 1989.

General Dynamics and Turkey

At first glance, General Dynamics operations in Turkey may seem an unlikely partnership. Turkey is a developing nation of 54 million

CASE STUDIES TABLE 9-3
F-16 Program Status

Country	Delivered in 1989	Delivered through 1989	Total Ordered as of 12/31/89
U.S. Air Force	158	1,583	2,459
U.S. Navy	–	26	26
Belgium	11	139	160
Denmark	5	70	70
Netherlands	13	188	214
Norway	2	74	74
Israel	–	150	210
Egypt	–	80	121
Pakistan	–	40	111
Venezuela	–	24	24
Korea	1	36	40
Turkey	21	43	160
Greece	34	39	40
Thailand	–	12	18
Singapore	–	8	8
Indonesia	4	4	12
Bahrain	–	–	12

SOURCE: General Dynamics, *Annual Report, 1989.*

people whose largely agrarian economy suffers from nearly three-digit inflation and a critical lack of capital reserves. It is a nation that, like its geography, spanning both the European and Asian continents, straddles East and West, being neither wholly European nor Middle Eastern in culture and mindset. Its geography is of great interest to the United States. Turkey is a southern neighbor of the Soviet Union and is that country's only conduit from the Black Sea to the Mediterranean. Soviet ships transit the Bosporus by the ancient city of Istanbul and out the Dardanelles, a critical passage during both peace and war. This same spot marks the northern and westernmost reaches of the Middle East. This strategic location made Turkey a powerful international player throughout history. Turkey is the closest ally of the United States against Russian operations in eastern and southern Europe as well as the Middle East.

In the 1980s Turkey reversed its industrial policy of state intervention in the nation's economic life and moved steadily toward free-market policies and trade liberalization. Given an extreme labor surplus, Turkey holds a comparative advantage in labor-intensive industries. Unlike similarly situated newly industrialized countries, such as South Korea and Taiwan, Turkey's export focus remains in textiles and clothing, and it has not attempted serious diversification into other profitable segments, such as electronics. The General Dynamics/TUSAS experiment is a method of capturing an advantage in the capital goods sector, a feature yet to be proved. Turkey's trade is primarily with Europe and the Middle East. OECD nations account for more than 64 percent of its exports—20 percent to the Middle East and Northern Africa.

It is critically important to U.S. defense policy that Turkey's military, including its stand-

CASE STUDIES TABLE 9-4
Top Ten Recipients of U.S. Economic and Military Aid, 1984–1988
(billions of U.S.$ for fiscal years)

	1984		1985		1986
Israel	2.61	Israel	3.35	Israel	3.62
Egypt	2.48	Egypt	2.48	Egypt	2.53
Turkey	.85	Turkey	.87	Turkey	.73
Pakistan	.57	Pakistan	.63	Pakistan	.67
Greece	.50	El Salvador	.56	Philippines	.48
Spain	.41	Greece	.50	El Salvador	.43
El Salvador	.40	Spain	.41	Greece	.43
Sudan	.23	Honduras	.28	Spain	.39
S. Korea	.23	Philippines	.26	Portugal	.18
India	.20	Sudan	.25	Honduras	.19
TOTAL AID	11.99		13.73		12.72

	1987		1988
Israel	3.00	Israel	3.00
Egypt	2.30	Egypt	2.29
Turkey	.71	Turkey	.91
Pakistan	.66	Pakistan	.68
El Salvador	.49	El Salvador	.43
Philippines	.38	Greece	.43
Greece	.34	Spain	.28
Honduras	.27	Honduras	.24
Guatemala	.16	Portugal	.21
TOTAL AID	14.80		15.24

SOURCE: O'Cleireacain 1990, page 183.

ing army, the largest in Europe, be properly equipped. U.S. economic and military aid to Turkey has been substantial (see Table 9-4). To increase Turkey's defense capabilities and to fulfill U.S. defense policy, the Turkish government and General Dynamics entered into the agreement to produce F-16s in a new plant at Murted, outside the nation's capital of Ankara. Turkey's political geography and its desire to rapidly industrialize brought the parties together. It is supposed that this high-tech exercise will help the nation "leapfrog into the twentieth century," as the Turkish president often reminds the nation.

In 1984 General Dynamics and TUSAS entered into the coproduction agreement to build F-16s over a period of ten years. The government's desire to create its own indigenous aircraft industry, TAI (Turkish Aerospace Industry) made the make-or-buy decision simple. Like a number of other NICs and a handful of industrialized nations, Turkey decided in favor of the more difficult and expensive manufacturing route (see Table 9-5).

As part of the FMS program, General Dynamics makes the planes, sells them to the U.S. government, who in turn sells them to the Turk-

CASE STUDIES TABLE 9-5
Nations with Aerospace Manufacturing
Operations—Airframe and/or Final Assembly

Industrialized Nations	NICs
France	China
West Germany	India
Italy	Brazil
Japan	Romania
Netherlands	Yugoslavia
Belgium	Israel
Sweden	South Korea
Switzerland	Taiwan
United Kingdom	Turkey
United States	

SOURCE: Todd 1988, page 101.

ish government, although the planes go directly from the General Dynamics/TUSAS plant into service. The negotiations resulted in a form of license agreement that provides that the planes be built directly from General Dynamics plans with no design requirements or modifications on the part of Turkey. This is the lowest level of technological complexity available in military production. General Dynamics is considered a prime or lead contractor, and therefore provides the technology in whole. The F-16 plant is built to General Dynamics design specifications, under their authority with Turkish personnel. From barren agricultural lands, the site now encompasses acres of the latest in aerospace production technology, and is scheduled to include a million square feet of space. Although the first jets contain many U.S. parts, the accord stipulates 100 percent Turkish content by the end of the agreement period. By 1994 the plane will be built completely with Turkish parts, except its weapon systems, which are still considered proprietary technology.

Turkey and Technology Offsets

General Dynamics agreement with Turkey was negotiated under the international trade form called countertrade. In this form, trade is not linear or one way from one nation to another, but encompasses a more complex form of reciprocal trade agreement. Simply put, the sale of one good into a nation is dependent upon the export of another good from that nation. There are a number of types of countertrade, including barter, switch trading, compensation deals, counterpurchase, and offsets.

General Dynamics and Turkey's agreement is in the countertrade form of technology offset, a form often used in the aerospace industry. There are two types of offset programs—direct and indirect offsets. Most agreements contain provisions for both forms. Direct offsets provide for trade or production favors that are directly related to the production of the good or service in question. In the General Dynamics case, direct offsets occur in the actual production of or are directly related to the F-16. The company agreed to provide $150 million in this form of offset. Direct offsets include provisions for local content (the making and buying of parts for the aircraft production in Turkey) and the development of the coproduction facility for the aircraft assembly.

Indirect offsets are export or trade agreements not specifically related to the particular industry. This type of trade agreement, only "indirectly" related to the aircraft manufacture, is usually a counterpurchase of goods or services. In the Turkish case, General Dynamics agreed to provide over $1 billion in indirect offsets. Under this plan, General Dynamics agreed to use its marketing strength to sell indigenous Turkish products on the world market. This portion is intended to increase foreign exchange in Turkey. The offset further stipulated that General Dynamics would help provide the technological capability to modernize Turkey's energy sector. General Dynamics is scheduled to help develop windmill, solar, and thermal energy plants. The package, both direct and indirect, constitutes a complex but typical technology offset agreement.

The direct offset is a success, given production benchmarks issued by General Dynamics and TUSAS. Deliveries of the aircraft are on schedule, and, remarkably, at least one aircraft has been delivered with zero defects, a superior achievement for any nation's production facility. The indirect offset has not enjoyed this success. General Dynamics is yet unable to realize its indirect obligations. In 1986, for example, the corporation received only half its offset credits for activities negotiated under this portion of the agreement.

The offset program, although far-reaching in its transfer of technology, has suffered serious criticism in Turkey. Fueled by pervasive economic problems, including near hyperinflation, volatile currency problems, and vast capital deficiencies, critics charge the $4.5 billion price tag for the program is a dangerous drain on an overburdened economy. Had the government's goal been primarily the delivery of the particular aircraft, the cost-effective decision would have been an off-the-shelf purchase. The planes can be purchased directly for far less than the multibillion dollar agreement. The cost penalty for the build decision caused widespread at-

tack. Other critics cite the technology transfer as inappropriate for a developing economy. Indeed, some analysts caution Third World nations about leapfrogging through any technological stages, as societies miss critical learning curves with the transfer of sophisticated technology. Analysts also argue against the policy decision that provided the large order. Critics charge that the planes are needed less for Turkey's own defense purposes than for U.S. and NATO military needs. If so, the United States or NATO should shoulder more of the huge financial burden, instead of capital-poor Turkey.

The capital needs of the nation were addressed in the offset agreement. Part of the accord stipulates that the Turkish plant build parts for the world export market. This portion of the plan intends to provide much-needed foreign exchange, thereby helping to ease the nation's capital burden (see Exhibit 9–2).

The development of an indigenous aerospace industry for this newly industrializing economy is purported to have widespread significance in subsidiary or tertiary markets, as well as pro-

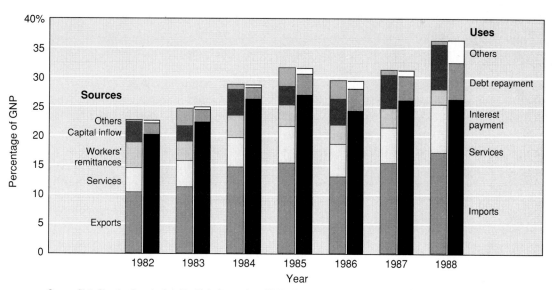

Source: State Planning Organization, *Monthly Indicators*; from OECD, *Turkey, OECD Economic Survey* (Paris: Organisation for Economic Cooperation and Development, 1990), p. 47.

EXHIBIT 9-2   Sources and Uses of Foreign Exchange Earnings in Turkey, 1982–1988.
SOURCE: Organization for Economic Cooperation and Development 1990, page 47.

viding technological competence in the primary industry, aerospace. The use of Turkish vendors and suppliers for parts and supplies provides the transfer of technological know-how for widespread use in numerous technologies. This form of transfer improves the rate and speed of industrialization throughout several sectors, particularly the machinery and capital equipment sector for electronics and heavy industry. This form of transfer further creates employment at all skill levels, a well-received benefit for Turkey, a labor exporter because of a lack of employment opportunities at all levels, including a serious brain drain of highly educated and skilled workers. A significant portion of the offset agreement's cost for both parties is the development of the sophisticated plant. With relative ease, the complex can be retooled to manufacture various products after completion of the scheduled order of F-16s.

General Dynamics venture in Turkey is a salient example of the problems associated with high-tech transfers from industrialized to developing nations. Government intervention from both nations complicate the economic transaction with varying and sometimes conflicting political imperatives. The stakeholders in the case are varied and, because it is a defense appropriation, include the nation's citizenry, as well as the obvious stockholders, employees, customers, vendors, and the like. The bargaining table is more evenly balanced between the multinational and the nation-state today than in earlier decades, when corporations made unilateral decisions devoid of host-nation political and economic needs. This is a story of powerful bargaining chips brought to the table by corporations and countries who cooperate for the prize—the high-tech transfer of technology.

Discussion Questions

1. What is meant by defense Keynesianism?
2. What is a technology offset? An offset program is not costless. With reference to the F-16 program offset, what are the pros and cons of an offset program for a newly industrializing nation? For the corporation? What are immediate, medium, and long-term benefits? What are the disadvantages?
3. Is Turkey in a position to create a free-standing military production capability or aerospace industry? What are its impediments?
4. Turkey's goal, besides acquiring the F-16 fighter plane, is to diversify its export base and to increase domestic industry in related sectors. Has this occurred? Have the apparent cost penalties associated with the F-16 purchase been outweighed by these related industrial policy objectives?
5. Discuss the merits of export-based growth versus import-substitution-led growth with reference to this case. What are the benefits and/or disadvantages?
6. General Dynamics has been criticized in Turkey for its role in the F-16 production. What are these criticisms? What should the corporation do to ameliorate the critics or resolve the issue?
7. Do a simple cost-benefit analysis for the role of General Dynamics in the program. Do the benefits outweigh the costs, including public perceptions, goodwill, stakeholder interests, as well as the obvious economic cost/benefits? How has the corporation benefited from the venture? What are the corporation's main costs associated with the program?
8. What is the role of the U.S. government in the transaction? To what extent is the corporation's economic environment impacted by U.S. political objectives? By Turkish political objectives?
9. What role should U.S. corporations play in the development of newly industrializing nations' defense industries? Is there a national or international organization that should monitor this interaction?
10. What is the FMS program? What benefit does U.S. industry derive from the program

and why? What do foreign nations derive and why?

11. Discuss General Dynamics' defense dependency figure. In a period of declining defense dollars within the United States, what does that figure mean for the company? What impact might foreign sales have in this type of environment? What is General Dynamics' strategy? What are the alternatives? What strategic position, vis-à-vis its international activities, should General Dynamics pursue? What position should it pursue vis-à-vis its competitors?

12. Turkey expects the program to help ease its foreign exchange problems. How might this occur? Is this a reasonable assumption? What other ways might the nation increase its capital reserves? Why is capital, particularly foreign capital, necessary for a country like Turkey?

Bibliography

FERRARI, PAUL, et al. 1987. *U.S. Arms Exports: Policies and Contractors.* Washington, D.C.: Investor Responsibility Research Center.

FRANKLIN, ROGER. 1989. *The Defender, The Story of General Dynamics.* New York: Harper and Row.

GENERAL DYNAMICS. 1989. *Annual Report.*

O'CLEIREACAIN, SEAMUS. 1990. *Third World Debt and Public Policy.* New York: Praeger.

ORGANIZATION FOR ECONOMIC COOPERATION AND DEVELOPMENT. 1990. *Turkey, OECD Economic Survey.* Paris: Organization for Economic Cooperation and Development.

TODD, DANIEL. 1988. *Defense Industries, A Global Perspective.* New York: Routledge.

Royal Jordanian Airlines

Muhsen Makhamrah

University of Jordan College of Business

On September 22, 1989, King Hussein of Jordan visited the headquarters of Royal Jordanian Airlines in Amman, Jordan, to chair the Board of Directors meeting. At the end of this meeting, he wrote the following in the visitors book:

> It is my pleasure and happiness to see Royal Jordanian, our national airlines, which emerged from our country's needs and aspirations to be our Ambassador to the world and the bridge for commercial and cultural exchange between Jordan and the friendly nations, and the carrier of our flag and message which extends the interaction, love and prosperity between our people and the people of the world.

These words by King Hussein are part of a persistent and continuous effort by Jordan, in general, and the king, in particular, to promote and develop the Jordanian national airline. These words also reflect the stated objectives of Royal Jordanian during the last three decades, which are:

1. To be a hard working airline, competing with other carriers, not simply an expensive display of national pride.
2. To be an ambassador of goodwill for Jordan both by performance, and by providing a closer link with other countries of the world.
3. To transport knowledge of the Arab world, its people, and culture, East and West.
4. To assist in the development of tourism in Jordan.
5. Eventually, to produce revenue for the country and be economically viable.

Civil Aviation in Jordan

Development of civil aviation in Jordan started as soon as the country gained independence in 1946. At that time, Arab Airways Jerusalem Ltd. was formed by British and Jordanian interests. It operated from Jerusalem to Beirut and Cairo using De Havilland Rapides. In 1950 Air Jordan was organized to operate the same routes using Air Speed Consuls. New capital was infused in both airlines in 1953.

Transocean Airline invested in Air Jordan, replacing the Air Speed Consuls with DC-3s. Air Jordan's weekly Cairo flight was extended to Benghazi and Tripoli, and a route to Dhahran was added. An unprofitable route to Afghanistan via Kuwait and Bahrain was discontinued after only six month's operation.

British Overseas Airline Corporation (BOAC) acquired a majority interest in Arab Airways. Arab Airway's De Havilland Rapides were replaced by DC-3s, its routes were extended to

Jeddah and Aden, and its route to Baghdad, recently shut down, was reopened.

Facing intense competition from other airlines, Arab Airways and Air Jordan joined to form Air Jordan of the Holy Land. Arab Airways received 25 percent of the new company's stock, and Air Jordan, 75 percent. While BOAC sold its interests, Transocean retained its proportionate share of the company and agreed to continue providing technical assistance. After the merger, Convair 240s were leased for Transocean, and the Cairo to Tripoli and Jeddah to Aden routes were suspended. In 1960 a DC-4 was added to the fleet and a direct Amman-Rome route was started.

In 1961 Air Jordan's license was canceled, as were the licenses of three inactive airlines. A new commercial airline, Jordan Airways, was founded, with shares held 25 percent by the Jordanian Government, 35 percent by Middle East Airlines (MEA), and the remaining 40 percent by Jordanian investors, including former Air Jordan stockholders. The new company operated with a fleet of three Viscounts and a crew leased from MEA. It discontinued service to Rome and Jeddah.

Royal Jordanian History

The Royal Jordanian Airlines (RJ) was founded on December 8, 1963, and commenced operations on December 15 with a fleet of one DC-7 and two Handy Page Heralds provided by the Royal Jordanian Air Force.

RJ reopened Jeddah service in 1964 and added service to Rome in 1965, after introducing the Caravelle 10-R to its fleet. Between 1963 and 1966, RJ's traffic increased threefold. Its share of traffic to and from Jordan grew, especially in the vital long-haul market, and this trend continued with a doubling in the frequency of flights to Europe.

However, the company's growth stopped abruptly because of the June war of 1967, when two DC-7s were destroyed by the Israelis, and operations to Jerusalem ended. The occupation

of the West Bank created untold hurdles in the airline's life.

There were many people at home and abroad who doubted the ability of RJ to overcome these problems. The Jordanian government came to the rescue when it bought all the stock in 1968. The airline started operations to Dhahran, Doha, Nicosia and Benghazi. In 1969, Munich, Istanbul, and Tehran were added to the route network.

Unfortunately, the situation was frequently aggravated by the continual uneasy political climate in the area, closures of airspace in 1971–1972, and another war in October 1973. The hard work and enthusiasm of the RJ staff and the change from a joint public-private venture to an entirely public corporation, helped the airline to progress and overcome the inability of the private sector to invest the capital required for a modern and efficient airline.

A major step was taken in 1971, with the introduction of two long range jets, Boeing 707-320Cs. Routes were extended to Karachi in the east and to Madrid, Casablanca, and Copenhagen in the west. At the same time, RJ cooperated with Pakistan International Airlines (PIA) under a three-year management and technical assistance program. RJ and PIA jointly operated a PIA route from Karachi to East Africa for a short period. With the addition of two Boeing 707s, two Boeing 720-Bs in 1972, and three Boeing 727s in 1974, RJ was able to cover points all over the world. Another major step taken by the airline was acquisition of two 747-200Bs in 1977.

In 1981, RJ acquired its first L-1011-500 Tristar aircraft to support its long- and medium-haul operations. Seven more were added to the fleet in subsequent years, elevating Tristar to the position of workhorse in the fleet: RJ expanded its U.S. network in 1984 to include Chicago and Los Angeles, catering to the traffic needs in the midwest and west coast regions of the United States. In 1988, RJ added two more destinations in North America, Miami and Montreal.

A strategy of economization was adopted and implemented by the management during the last quarter of 1989. High-cost long-routes were either suspended, such as Los Angeles and Miami, or reduced to a weekly service, such as New York, Kuala Lumpur, and Singapore.

RJ made extensive contributions to the promotion of air transport in the Arab world. It was the first Arab airline that operated nonstop to the United States, and the second Arab airline to operate to the Far East.

The opening of Queen Alia International Airport (QAIA), south of Amman, was one of the most important events in Jordan's aviation history. The airport, inaugurated on May 25, 1983, is a symbol of the country's solid past achievements and its unlimited future potential. The airport has two identical interlinked passenger terminals, each with six gates. Ten gates have boarding bridges. The modern passenger facilities can handle up to 5 million passengers per year, and could be expanded to cope with 8 to 10 million passengers annually by the year 2000. The airport has two runways in a parallel configuration.

The cargo facilities are designed to handle up to 430,000 tons of air cargo annually by the year 2000. Among other RJ facilities is a three-bay maintenance hangar which can accommodate one B-747 and two Tristar-sized aircraft, or up to five small aircraft, and can handle aircraft maintenance up to "D" check level.

RJ's catering building is capable of producing 10,000 meals per day for passengers and 2,000 meals per day for RJ staff. All buildings have been designed to allow future expansion as the airport develops.

RJ's engine overhaul facility is the only one in the region certified to handle Pratt & Whitney's JT 8D17 engines, Rolls Royce RB211-524B4s, General Electric's CF6-50E2s, Hamilton Standard ST6L73s, and Garrett Airesearch's GTCP 8598CKs and 660-4 units. RJ's engine test cell is rated to a 100,000 pounds thrust capability. The department can completely overhaul Boeing 707s, 727s, and Tristars, and can carry out most maintenance work on 747s. A new work-shop to support Airbus, which came into service in 1987, has also been constructed.

The 1,013-person department is composed of a maintenance unit, a technical planning section, quality control inspectorate, materials section, and engine overhaul section. A ground support equipment unit is responsible for all the airline's vehicles, including cars and its fleet of buses.

The U.S. Federal Aviation Administration has certified that RJ's engineering and maintenance department is authorized to work on and release any U.S. registered aircraft. Similar certification has been awarded by Bureau Veritas of France. The department is responsible for all RJ fleet maintenance and carries out engineering and maintenance for several foreign carriers.

In 1989, RJ's simulator facilities were increased by adding an A310 simulator to the existing 707, 727, and L15 simulators.

In 1988, RJ relocated its duty-free shop from the transit area to a more accessible location on the connecting bridge between the south and north terminals of QAIA and expanded the area from 950 square meters to 1,600. This move was aimed at better serving incoming and outgoing traffic, especially transit traffic.

In 1986, Landor Associates, the San Francisco-based design firm, was commissioned to produce an identity that conveyed the spirit of Jordan's heritage and positioned the airline as a prestigious international carrier. Moreover, the new identity highlighted the up-to-date technology of the fleet and reflected Jordan's traditional role as a gateway between East and West.

Aircraft exteriors were painted in medium grey and white, with a subtle dark grey motif of five tapered bands on the tail. Aircraft interiors were refurbished giving first-class passengers fully reclining sleeperette seats and providing business-class passengers more space and significantly improved seating. Flight cabin crews and ground staff were outfitted in new, distinctive uniforms, and several measures were taken to improve the quality of in-flight and ground services.

Organization

LEADERSHIP

In 1968, Ali Gandour, an aeronautical engineer at RJ, was appointed President and CEO. During his leadership, from 1968 until August of 1989, RJ expanded and developed significantly in terms of routes, aircraft, and manpower.

Mr. Gandour's strategy focused on growth and expansion of market share to achieve RJ's goals. He also worked continuously to modernize RJ's fleet and to improve services. During his tenure, route network increased more than ten times, covering forty-two cities in Asia, Africa, Europe and North America (see Exhibit 10–1). Its fleet increased more than four times to include seventeen modern aircraft (see Table 10-1).

In August 1989, Husam Abu-Ghazaleh, an engineer, took over as president and CEO. The strategy that has been adopted since then is for RJ to concentrate on operating the economically sound routes, using the most modern and technologically advanced aircraft.

STRUCTURE

RJ's recent organizational structure is shown in Exhibit 10–2. It consists of nine functional departments reporting to the president and CEO. They are: corporate planning, management control, corporate affairs, commercial and marketing, customer services, engineering and maintenance, flight operations, finance and investment, and administrative and personnel. All of the functional units are headed by executive vice-presidents, and all have been promoted from within. They have been with RJ from the beginning and have been responsible for its development and progress. Even the last two presidents and CEOs and been promoted from the RJ rank and file.

Marketing

During the period from 1970 to 1986, RJ's marketing strategy was based on price reduction to compete with other airlines for a market share.

RJ's local market is limited in its capacity. Thus, it sought to attract customers from other markets in order to better utilize its capacity. The only way to accomplish that was through price reduction. "As a regional airline for the Middle East and Europe," Ghassan Ali (marketing manager from 1987 to 1989) stated, "RJ was operating profitably. When RJ expanded to be an international airline, cost had increased and that reduced profit."

After 1987, RJ's marketing strategy shifted to one of increased price levels (ticket prices) combined with service improvement. This was coupled with the reduction of routes and flights to unprofitable destinations in North America and the Far East to meet the objective of serving the economically sound routes.

Finance

REVENUE

Tables 10-2 and 10-3 provide a basic summary of RJ income statements and balance sheets since 1979. Revenue increased steadily after 1979 and reached a record high in 1982. After that, revenue fluctuated and then fell, reaching a record low in 1986, which was because of the economic stagnation of the country and the area after 1982. Net losses started to appear on the company income statement after 1982, with the exception of 1985 and 1987.

Table 10-4 shows the sources of revenue to the company. During its years of existence, sources of revenue showed various trends. Passenger revenue is usually the prime source, but its proportion of total revenue has declined since 1980, while the proportion of all other revenue sources has increased. Other revenue, which includes services to other airlines, duty-free shop, catering, investment, and so on, shows the largest growth of any nonpassenger revenue source.

EXPENDITURES

RJ's expenditures have been increasing continuously because of increases in all cost items,

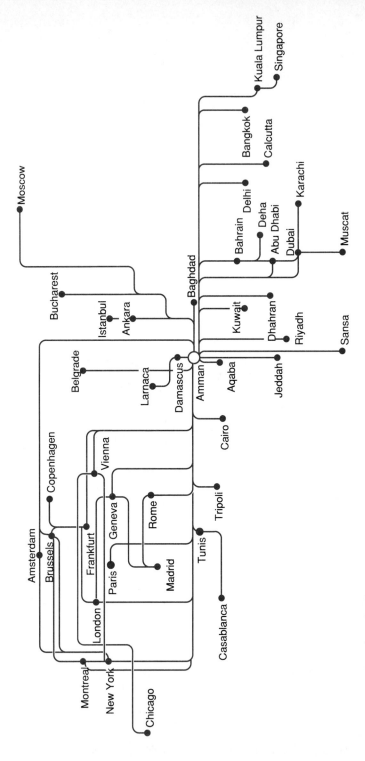

EXHIBIT 10–1   Royal Jordanian route map 1989.

CASE STUDIES TABLE 10-1
Royal Jordanian Routes and Number of Aircraft

Year	Unduplicated Route kms*	Number of Aircraft
1964	3,157	4
1965	5,523	4
1966	6,692	4
1967	11,796	3
1968	13,629	4
1969	17,888	4
1970	18,480	3
1971	20,465	5
1972	25,926	7
1973	30,538	5
1974	36,083	7
1975	40,710	9
1976	53,645	8
1977	57,325	10
1978	62,611	10
1979	63,897	12
1980	67,850	13
1981	70,754	18
1982	76,777	18
1983	76,090	17
1984	87,027	17
1985	101,769	17
1986	107,925	17
1987	102,029	18
1988	124,677	17
1989	139,613	17

* One mile = 1.6 km

especially aircraft handling and interest expenses. The increase in overall annual expenses is also because of the constant development and expansion of RJ operations over the years. Areas of expenditures are shown in Table 10-5.

Long-term liabilities have declined steadily since 1983. This reflects the sale and leaseback of some aircraft. On the other hand, current liabilities have steadily increased to reach a record high in 1987.

Operations

ROUTES AND AIRCRAFT

Royal Jordanian has shown continuous expansion throughout its years of existence. It expanded its services from the Middle East to destinations in Europe, North America, and the Far East.

In December 1989, RJ covered a total of forty-two cities located on four continents. RJ has also expanded significantly its route network and number of aircraft.

RJ entered its first jet age by buying three Caravelle 10-Rs, one each in 1965, 1966, and 1968. The second jet age started in 1971, with the addition of Boeing 707-320Cs. In 1977, RJ entered the wide-body era by adding the Boeing 747-200B, the Tristar, and the Airbus. At the end of 1989, RJ's fleet consisted of seventeen aircraft: three Boeing 707-320Cs, three Boeing 727-200As, six Lockheed L-1011-500s, and five Airbus 310-300s.

AIRCRAFT UTILIZATION

Utilization per aircraft per day for scheduled and nonscheduled hours flown has changed significantly since the company's inception. The general trend of utilization was a positive one. Every effort has been made to increase aircraft utilization within the scheduling constraints resulting from the geographical location of the company base in relation to the route network. It increased from a fleet average of 4.6 hours in 1964 to 8.3 hours in 1989. Average utilization rate achieved in 1987 represented a major improvement over that achieved in 1986. Seat and load factors (see Table 10-6) have fluctuated over time, but showed a constant increase from 1972 to 1982, an indication of better aircraft utilization. During the period from 1982 to 1986, seat and load factors started to decline because of the economic situation in Jordan.

TRAFFIC PERFORMANCE

Total traffic performance has grown steadily during the period 1973 to 1982. It reached its

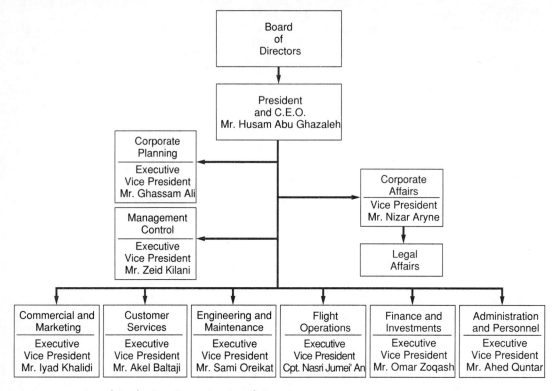

EXHIBIT 10–2   Royal Jordanian Organizational Structure.

peak in all traffic categories (passenger, cargo, mail, and excess baggage) in 1982 (see Table 10-7). After 1982 all traffic categories started to decline because of economic stagnation and the unstable political situation in the Middle East.

Discussion Question

Royal Jordanian has performed relatively well since its inception, despite the odds. It has passed through difficult periods, especially in 1967, 1970, 1971, and 1973. The support of the Jordanian government and, in particular, the support of King Hussein, was crucial to its survival. During the past three years, serious thought has been given to the idea of privatizing the company. In 1989, a change of management associated with a change of strategy, occurred, which should take RJ in a new direction. Given the economic and political uncertainties in the 1990s in the Middle East, what do you think would be the best possible strategy that should be undertaken?

CASE STUDIES TABLE 10-2
Consolidated Income Statement of Royal Jordanian Airlines
(in thousands of Jordanian dollars)

	1979	1980	1981	1982	1983	1984	1985	1986	1987
OPERATING REVENUE									
Scheduled Services:									
Passenger	41,779	59,964	77,332	92,421	87,419	82,793	89,140	73,401	73,601
Cargo	8,098	11,496	17,263	19,640	14,723	17,473	15,949	13,832	14,753
Excess baggage	1,142	1,882	3,174	4,180	2,848	1,981	2,342	1,870	1,673
Mail	140	204	328	400	276	302	364	417	462
Total Scheduled Services	51,159	73,546	98,097	116,641	105,266	102,549	107,795	89,520	90,489
Nonscheduled Services	1,755	1,407	3,136	5,480	2,168	3,002	2,732	4,730	8,206
Total Operating Revenue	52,914	74,953	101,233	122,121	107,434	105,551	110,527	94,250	98,695
OPERATING EXPENSES									
Flight operation	16,685	26,486	36,883	38,145	36,834	38,378	41,096	36,904	36,014
Maintenance & overhead	5,787	6,779	8,876	13,571	11,821	10,177	10,300	11,018	11,192
Aircraft lease payments	—	—	—	—	—	—	—	—	1,752
Depreciation of flight equipment	3,885	5,434	6,593	9,624	11,884	12,054	11,589	8,784	9,110
Station & ground	5,195	6,581	8,821	10,358	10,912	12,349	12,237	13,381	14,821
Passenger Services	5,127	7,225	8,979	9,922	10,401	10,226	11,086	11,487	12,288
Ticketing, sales & promotion	9,963	13,939	18,185	18,432	18,555	21,758	22,754	22,728	25,746
General & administrative	1,998	3,195	3,307	3,735	3,581	4,203	4,457	4,587	4,825
Total Operating Expenses	48,640	69,639	91,644	103,787	103,988	109,145	113,519	108,889	115,748
NET OPERATING INCOME	4,274	5,314	9,589	18,334	3,446	(3,594)	(2,992)	(14,639)	(17,053)
NONOPERATING REVENUE									
Other income	4,800	5,181	7,788	7,423	16,438	13,499	23,997	20,672	27,128
Interest & other expenses	(6,831)	(9,246)	(15,484)	(23,816)	(20,612)	(19,609)	(19,176)	(7,817)	(8,141)
Net nonoperating revenue	(2,031)	(4,065)	(7,696)	(16,393)	(4,174)	(6,110)	4,821	12,855	18,987
NET ANNUAL PROFIT	2,243	1,249	1,893	1,941	(728)	(9,704)	1,829	(1,784)	1,934

NOTE: Until 1988: 1 JD = 2.9 U.S.$; 1988–1990: 1 JD = 1.5 U.S.$

Consolidated Balance Sheet of Royal Jordanian Airlines (in thousands of Jordanian dollars)

ASSETS	1979	1980	1981	1982	1983	1984	1985	1986	1987
CURRENT ASSETS									
Cash on hand and at banks	1,798	2,045	7,241	21,205	18,253	18,965	17,097	16,167	17,635
Receivables less provision for doubtful accounts, spare parts, materials, and supplies at cost less	12,874	15,569	22,994	22,879	26,088	30,229	23,390	23,400	21,102
Provision for obsolescences	4,813	6,343	9,420	11,342	12,672	13,318	12,688	12,077	12,960
Total Current Assets	19,486	23,958	39,656	55,427	57,014	62,512	53,177	51,644	51,698
INVESTMENTS									
Shares in companies and subsidiaries	3,803	3,919	3,526	4,098	16,799	23,179	25,438	25,766	27,648
FIXED ASSETS									
Flight equipment	53,943	61,561	141,204	206,349	201,718	211,486	213,357	211,764	197,771
Ground equipment	3,439	4,567	5,684	7,726	10,398	11,522	12,253	13,277	14,189
Land and buildings	1,185	1,290	1,330	1,501	1,523	2,156	2,420	3,514	8,816
Total Fixed Assets at cost	58,568	67,418	148,219	215,577	213,639	225,165	228,032	228,556	220,777
Less: Accumulated depreciation	14,987	18,671	25,213	35,356	46,441	57,864	61,805	59,719	63,321
Net fixed assets	43,581	48,747	123,006	180,221	167,198	167,300	166,227	168,836	157,455
Deposits on account of new aircraft	1,770	24,160	18,117	—	1,361	4,671	—	23,010	11,135
Total Fixed Assets	45,351	72,907	141,123	180,221	168,559	171,972	166,227	191,846	168,591
OTHER ASSETS									
Shares in companies	—	—	—	—	—	—	—	—	—
Bills receivable within 2 years	—	—	—	—	—	—	—	—	—
Key money	—	—	—	—	—	—	—	—	—
Total Other Assets	—	—	—	—	—	—	—	—	—
Total Assets	68,641	100,785	184,306	239,747	242,374	257,664	244,843	269,259	247,938

LIABILITIES	1979	1980	1981	1982	1983	1984	1985	1986	1987
CURRENT LIABILITIES									
Due to banks	—	—	—	—	7,201	21,186	19,379	68,773	29,414
Current portion of long-term loans	4,250	5,857	14,926	18,400	14,790	20,938	22,891	23,328	75,059
Trade and sundry creditors in other accounts	3,209	4,129	6,907	7,548	6,235	8,181	13,992	24,177	32,106
Accrued charges	2,430	1,748	6,951	7,192	5,909	8,658	3,930	3,825	395
Unearned revenue	4,840	6,493	8,004	12,039	12,420	12,353	6,301	7,745	5,744
Total Current Liabilities	14,731	18,228	36,790	45,179	46,557	71,317	66,495	127,850	142,719
LONG-TERM LIABILITIES									
Foreign loans payable	25,464	45,755	104,839	133,788	128,172	132,870	132,425	104,304	71,727
Loan payable within Jordan	95,000	4,457	13,015	20,980	25,185	25,795	22,526	9,808	6,591
Bonds	—	—	10,000	16,000	16,000	16,000	15,008	—	—
Debentures	—	5,000	—	—	—	—	—	—	—
Less current portion of long-term loans	4,250	5,857	14,926	18,400	14,790	20,938	22,891	—	—
Net long-term loans	21,309	49,354	112,928	152,368	154,567	153,727	147,069	114,113	78,319
Provision for staff indemnities	2,120	2,099	2,571	4,742	2,720	2,812	2,780	2,836	2,893
Provision for fleet overhaul	3,710	3,083	2,104	6,104	8,011	8,993	5,856	3,601	1,213
Total Long-Term Liabilities	27,140	54,538	117,604	163,215	165,299	163,534	155,706	120,551	82,426
EQUITY									
Authorized capital	21,000	21,000	21,000	21,000	21,000	21,000	21,000	21,000	21,000
Paid-up capital	21,000	21,000	21,000	21,000	21,000	21,000	21,000	21,000	21,000
General reserve	3,529	5,769	7,019	8,912	10,244	9,517	(187,000)	1,641	(142,000)
Boeing 747 reserve	—	—	—	—	—	—	—	—	—
Net income for the year	2,240	1,250	1,892	1,439	(727,000)	(9,704)	1,828	(1,783)	1,934
Less payment ot Jordanian government	—	—	—	—	—	—	—	—	—
Net equity of Jordanian government	26,769	28,019	29,912	31,352	30,517	20,812	22,641	20,857	22,792
Total Liabilities & Equity	68,641	100,785	184,306	239,747	242,374	257,664	244,843	269,259	247,938

CASE STUDIES TABLE 10-4
Royal Jordanian Sources of Revenues

	Percentage of Total Revenue						
Year	PAX	Excess Baggage	Cargo	Mail	Charter	Other	Total
1965	80.8	1.0	2.5	0.5	11.9	3.3	100.0
1966	88.4	0.7	2.2	0.5	3.4	4.8	100.0
1967	85.1	1.2	2.6	0.9	7.1	3.1	100.0
1968	73.6	1.2	3.4	0.6	6.3	14.9	100.0
1969	77.0	1.3	3.9	0.7	1.1	16.0	100.0
1970	72.4	1.3	4.0	0.5	5.0	16.8	100.0
1971	61.4	1.4	4.5	0.4	6.9	25.4	100.0
1972	58.5	1.3	7.5	0.5	15.9	16.3	100.0
1973	61.3	1.2	7.2	0.4	12.1	17.8	100.0
1974	72.1	1.6	9.9	0.5	8.0	7.9	100.0
1975	72.8	1.4	11.1	0.4	9.1	5.2	100.0
1976	73.0	1.9	13.5	0.6	5.8	5.2	100.0
1977	68.0	2.0	15.8	0.4	8.5	5.3	100.0
1978	73.2	2.2	13.9	0.3	5.4	5.0	100.0
1979	72.4	2.0	14.0	0.3	3.0	8.3	100.0
1980	74.8	2.3	14.3	0.3	1.8	6.5	100.0
1981	70.9	2.9	15.8	0.3	2.9	7.2	100.0
1982	71.4	3.2	15.2	0.3	4.2	5.7	100.0
1983	70.6	2.3	11.9	0.2	1.7	13.3	100.0
1984	69.5	1.7	14.7	0.3	2.5	11.3	100.0
1985	66.3	1.7	11.9	0.3	2.0	17.8	100.0
1986	63.9	1.6	12.0	0.4	4.1	18.0	100.0
1987	58.5	1.3	11.7	0.4	6.5	21.6	100.0
1988	65.9	1.4	13.8	0.3	4.9	13.7	100.0
1989	55.9	0.9	12.0	0.2	5.1	25.8	100.0
E.90	51.5	1.0	13.6	0.2	11.6	22.1	100.0

CASE STUDIES TABLE 10-5
Royal Jordanian Areas of Expenditures (in thousands of Jordanian dollars)

Cost Item	1989	1988
Flight operations	53,790	40,117
Maintenance and overhaul	21,687	17,074
Aircraft rental expenses	6,698	10,748
Depreciation	18,150	4,387
Station and ground operations	23,673	18,758
Passenger services	18,369	14,950
Sales and promotion	45,578	31,681
General and administration	7,151	5,084
Interest and other expenses	52,573	79,404
TOTAL	247,669	222,203

NOTE: Until 1988: 1 JD = 2.9 U.S.$; 1990: 1 JD = 1.5 U.S.$

CASE STUDIES TABLE 10-6
Royal Jordanian Aircraft Utilization

Year	Revenue Hours Flown	Aircraft Utilization hours/day	Seat Factor %	Load Factor %
1964	5758	4.6	42.9	41.4
1965	5130	4.8	40.7	37.0
1966	5672	4.1	49.2	43.1
1967	4739	4.3	44.3	39.6
1968	5818	6.6	43.2	39.0
1969	7298	6.7	45.6	43.7
1970	8338	7.6	41.1	38.9
1971	10957	6.7	32.2	27.5
1972	12459	6.8	35.7	32.9
1973	11151	6.0	44.1	41.5
1974	12239	6.5	45.6	47.8
1975	17866	6.3	53.7	49.4
1976	23278	6.3	52.9	48.3
1977	23692	6.4	53.7	46.8
1978	27636	6.9	59.7	50.9
1979	31821	7.9	58.3	49.3
1980	37182	8.1	57.4	51.5
1981	47211	7.9	61.9	54.7
1982	47382	7.1	59.4	53.3
1983	41826	6.5	57.5	51.2
1984	42413	6.5	56.2	51.2
1985	42369	7.1	57.7	51.6
1986	42666	7.7	51.7	48.1
1987	45256	8.4	58.2	52.1
1988	50282	8.2	60.9	53.6
1989	51283	8.3	61.2	54.8

CASE STUDIES TABLE 10-7
Royal Jordanian Total Performance

Year	No. of Passengers	Cargo Tons	Mail Tons	Excess Baggage Tons
1964	86877	630	85	105
1965	111156	607	92	114
1966	151160	677	100	156
1967	108355	567	68	112
1968	106190	780	55	139
1969	120486	958	71	144
1970	118794	906	64	148
1971	124943	1401	101	129
1972	118794	1940	109	134
1973	162327	2110	85	156
1974	243355	3447	118	280
1975	379911	5770	144	360
1976	475470	9464	263	548
1977	546940	13768	232	709
1978	739335	17685	296	1103
1979	914483	25342	361	1451
1980	1112556	27090	454	2012
1981	1443281	33059	916	3671
1982	1667273	38223	1063	4047
1983	1457334	33866	704	2432
1984	1327592	35564	710	1607
1985	1290294	40620	711	1764
1986	1131967	42574	692	1353
1987	1177985	46451	942	1218
1988	1225934	49842	812	1124
1989	1204005	49717	782	885

Glossary

absolute advantage as stated by Adam Smith and David Ricardo, the specialization of each country in the goods that it can produce most efficiently

acceptance an agreement that specifies the price and other stated terms for the purchase of goods

ad valorem according to value

ad valorem duty determination of customs duties as a percentage of the value of the goods

advising bank a bank in the country of the exporter that informs the exporter that letters of credit have been made available by foreign banks. An advising bank has no responsibility of payment associated with the letters of credit

advisory capacity position of a shipper's agent that must obtain approval from the group or individual being represented before any decisions or adjustments can be made

agency office an office of a foreign bank located in the United States that solicits the business of U.S. firms operating internationally

air waybill a bill of lading accepted by the shipper, indicating that he has received the goods and agrees to deliver the goods to the specified airport

alongside upon delivery, placement of goods on a dock or a barge very close to the ship, so that the goods can be placed aboard the ship

American Depository Receipt (ADR) certificate issued by a U.S. bank to the owners of foreign stock certificates while the bank holds the actual stock certificates

arbitrage the process of buying goods in one market and selling them in another market. The profit is determined by the differential between the purchase price of the good and price at which the good is ultimately sold.

Asian dollars U.S. dollars held as deposits in Asia and the Pacific Basin

balance of payments an accounting system that reflects one country's financial transactions with the rest of the world

balance of trade the difference between a country's total exports and its total imports

banker's acceptance a draft drawn on a bank indicating that the bank agrees to pay according to the terms of the agreement

barter the exchange of goods or services for other goods or services without using money.

beneficiary the person in whose favor a letter of credit is issued or a draft is drawn

bill of exchange a written order requiring the party to which it is addressed to pay the bearer or another named party a particular sum of money at a future date

bill of lading a document that acts as both a receipt and a contract between a shipper and a carrier; acts as a receipt that goods have been received by the shipper and as a contract indicating the terms of the delivery

blocked account assets that cannot be exchanged for another currency or transferred out of the country without the consent of the government

bonded warehouse a warehouse in which customs duties are deferred until the goods are removed

brain drain a term describing the departure of a country's best-educated and most intelligent people

branch office   an office of a company at a location other than the headquarters

Bretton Woods   the location where 44 countries, including the United States, established the international monetary system that was introduced to stabilize the international flow of currencies

carnet   a document that allows the holder to bring goods into a country temporarily without having to pay the duties associated with the goods

cartel   a group of suppliers of a commodity who come together and agree to limit the supply of the commodity and charge an agreed-upon price

cash against documents (C.A.D.)   a payment method in which an intermediary processes the title documentation upon receipt of a cash payment

cash in advance (C.A.I.)   a payment method in which the full payment is made prior to the shipment of the goods

cash with order (C.W.O.)   a payment method in which the payment is made when the order is placed

caste system   an element of Hinduism in which the society is divided into four distinct classes in addition to outcasts

central banks   government institutions that control the growth of the money supply and regulate commercial banks

centrally planned economy   government-directed economic activity of a country through government ownership of the means of production

certificate of inspection   a document indicating the satisfactory condition of a good prior to shipping

certificate of manufacture   a document indicating that a product has been manufactured and is available for the purchaser

certificate of origin   a document that certifies the origin of a good

C&F (Cost and Freight)   a term indicating that the cost and freight expense are included in the quoted price of the good. This implies that the purchaser must secure insurance for the shipment of the goods.

channel of distribution   the means through which a firm markets a good to the consumer

C.I. (Cost, Insurance)   a term indicating that the cost and insurance are included in the quoted price of the good. This implies that the purchaser must secure shipment of the good.

C.I.F. (Cost, Insurance, Freight)   a term that indicates that the cost, the freight, and the insurance are included in the quoted price of a good

clean bill of lading   a receipt indicating the good condition of goods upon delivery to the shipper

clean draft   a draft that includes no other documents

Clearing House Interbank Payment System (CHIPS)   an international electronic system that transfers checks among major U.S. banks and foreign branches

COCOM   an alliance including most NATO countries. It has agreed to export controls concerning the export of certain advanced technology goods to the Soviet Union and China

codetermination   a management method that includes representatives of labor in the decision-making process and on the boards of the companies

collective bargaining   the process by which management and labor discuss wages and working conditions

collection papers   the documents presented to a purchaser in order to receive payment

commercial attache   embassy staff member considered an expert in commerce

commercial invoice   an itemized list of the goods shipped along with prices per unit

Common Agricultural Policy (CAP)   a policy of the European Community directed at price supports for existing agricultural programs

common carrier   a firm whose business is the transport of goods or people

common law   a law established through precedents resulting from the cultural traditions of a country

comparative advantage   the theory, first introduced by David Ricardo, that even when one country has an absolute advantage in the production of two goods it can still benefit from trade if it trades with a country that has a relative advantage in the production of one good

compensatory financing   programs that assist countries who experience significant reductions in export earnings resulting from natural causes, such as drought, or decreases in the price of an export good

confirmed letter of credit   a letter of credit confirmed by another bank that adds its guarantee

consignment   selling of goods by an agent representing the exporter; the agent delivers a payment, net of a commission, to the exporter

consular declaration   the formal statement intended for the consul detailing the goods to be shipped

convertible currency   currency that can be exchanged for another country's currency without the consent of the government

correspondent bank   a bank that conducts business with foreign banks located in its country

counterfeiting   illegally using a well-known name on copies of a firm's goods

countertrade   a means of exchange by which one government attempts to limit the outflow of hard currency from the country by providing payment in the form of other goods

countervailing duty   an added tariff applied to goods that have benefited from an export subsidy

country risk assessment   determination of the risk involved in lending or investing in a foreign country

credit risk insurance   a type of insurance that protects against nonpayment after the delivery of goods

credit swap   an agreement in which a foreign bank and a firm exchange currency at a particular rate only to reverse the transaction at a future date

cross rate   the exchange rate between two countries based on the exchange rate of each currency against a third currency, usually the U.S. dollar

cultural universals   similar elements that can be found in all cultures

culture   the learned beliefs and attitudes that characterize human populations, passed on from earlier generations

culture shock   the anxiety an individual experiences when introduced into a situation that is unfamiliar

currency area   countries that peg their currencies to a common trading partner's currency

currency exchange controls   a government's means of determining how much foreign currency citizens or visitors can have and the exchange rate they must pay for it

currency swap   an agreement in which currency is exchanged at a specified rate only to be reversed at a future date

current account   as part of the Balance of Payment account, this account measures the aggregate import and export of goods and services

customs   (1) the process of collecting the duties on exports and imports; (2) the officials who collect the duties

customs union   an agreement between two countries that eliminates import restrictions between the two countries and establishes a common tariff for all other countries

date draft   a draft that matures after a specified number of days following the date it is issued

deferred payment credit   a letter of credit that specifies payment at some time following review of the shipping documentation of the exporter

Delphi techniques   method of decision making in which the respondents maintain anonymity. The idea is to avoid the negative elements of group decision making while benefiting from the added perspectives of a group.

depreciation of a currency   a reduction in the worth of a currency when compared to another currency or gold

destination control statement   a government-required statement displayed on the export indicating the final destination of the export

devaluation a government's decision to reduce the value of its country's currency by increasing the amount of local currency needed to buy foreign currencies

developed countries the countries that are more advanced in GNP and living standards

developing countries the countries that are technologically less advanced

development banks banks that are established in developing countries to foster economic development through investment or loans

direct investment an operation that has sufficient foreign ownership such that the firm's management decisions are influenced by the foreign interest

dirty float a currency that periodically experiences governmental adjustments to ensure the desired exchange rate

discrepancy—letter of credit an inconsistency between the documentation and the letter of credit

disposable income the portion of an individual's income available for consumption after taxes

distributor an agent who maintains an inventory of the supplier's merchandise and sells directly to the consumer

documentary draft a draft that includes documents

documents against acceptance the draft that the buyer must agree to before the transfer of title of the delivered goods is made

Domestic International Sales Corporation (DISC) a subsidiary of a U.S. firm established solely for exporting goods. A DISC receives special tax incentives to operate.

draft (bill of exchange) the order given by the drawer for the drawee to pay the payee a specified amount at a future date

drawback the refund of duty on imported components used in the manufacture of goods that are exported upon completion

drawee the individual or firm responsible for payment of the indicated amount of a draft to the payee

drawer the individual or firm that issues a draft

dumping selling goods in a country at a price below the cost of production and freight or, in some circumstances, selling goods in a foreign country at prices lower than those charged for the same good in the home country

duty a tax one country must pay to sell its products in another country

Edge Act corporation subsidiaries of U.S. banks located in foreign countries with the consent of the U.S. government to perform any and all banking functions permitted by the local government

equity capital funds raised by selling ownership rights to the firm

ethnocentric pricing strategy a pricing policy in which a firm maintains the same prices in all the markets in which it operates

eurobonds bonds traded primarily in Europe and in a currency different from the currency of the country in which they are sold

eurocurrencies a currency in use in countries other than the nation of origin

eurodollars U.S. dollars on deposit in banks outside the United States

European Community formed in 1958 as a common market for its member nations. In 1991 there are 12 member countries: United Kingdom, Germany, France, Italy, Belgium, The Netherlands, Luxembourg, Denmark, Spain, Portugal, Greece, and Ireland.

European Currency Unit a basket of the currencies of the EC countries

European Free Trade Association (EFTA) a common market for some nations not in the EC, such as Norway, Iceland, Switzerland, and Austria

European Monetary Corporation Fund (EMCF) works with member nations to ensure that agreed-upon currency values are maintained

European Monetary System established in March 1979 in an effort to stabilize the currencies of European Community nations

exchange permit a permit, required by certain governments, that allows the importer to exchange his currencies into the necessary currency to pay the exporter

exchange rate a determination of value using only two currencies

exchange rate risk the risk that one currency will be lower in value than it was previously

Eximbank the Export-Import Bank of the United States, which assists U.S. exporting firms by issuing loans, guarantees, and insurance

export broker a firm or individual who locates and introduces buyers and sellers for a fee

export commission house an organization that acts as the buyer for a foreign firm

export license a permit that authorizes the export of specified goods to specified locations

export management company a firm that acts as the export department for other firms

export processing zones locations where import duties are not levied because the goods are re-exported

export trading company a firm that acts as the export department for other firms

exposure netting holding two currencies that are believed to be a hedge against each other

expropriation seizure of property by a foreign government

extraterritoriality government attempts to apply its laws outside its geographic boundaries

F.A.S. (free alongside) a term indicating that the quoted price includes the cost associated with delivering the goods to the desired vessel for shipment

F.I. (free in) a term indicating that the cost of loading and unloading the vessel is the responsibility of the firm or individual that has hired the vessel

Fisher effect the observation that in the long run, the real rates of return in countries that have no restrictions on the mobility of capital are the same, but the nominal rates will vary in proportion to the expected rate of inflation in a particular currency

floating exchange rates a process that allows for the valuation of currencies based upon the supply and demand of the currencies

floating-rate notes or bonds notes or bonds with interest rates that are adjustable periodically based on a particular interest rate, such as London Interbank Offered Rate (LIBOR)

F.O. (free out) a term indicating that the cost of loading the vessel is the responsibility of the firm or individual that has hired the vessel

F.O.B. (free on board) a term indicating that the quoted price includes loading the goods onto a vehicle at some particular location

force majeure a clause that excuses a party from fulfilling a contract because of conditions beyond its control

Foreign Corrupt Policies Act legislation directed toward the elimination of bribery between U.S. and foreign firms

foreign direct investment foreign investment in a firm that constitutes effective control of the firm

foreign direct investment deterrents and incentives legislation intended to limit or aid foreign direct investment

foreign exchange transactions involving the exchange of one currency for another

foreign sales agent an agent representing a firm abroad

Foreign Sales Corporation a firm provided for in the tax code that permits U.S. corporations to shelter income derived from exports

foreign tax credit an income tax credit available to citizens or corporations who paid tax abroad on the same income

foreign trade organization (FTO) an organization established in many ex-communist economies that is authorized to import and export goods of a particular industry

foreign trade zones locations determined by the government that do not need to pay tariffs or duties on imports, particularly goods that are assembled and re-exported.

forfaiting a means of selling the accounts receivable of a company

forward contract a contract that establishes an exchange for a particular currency to be delivered at a future date

forward rate same as forward contract

foul bill of lading a receipt issued by a shipping company indicating that the goods received were damaged

Fourth World the least economically developed nations of the world

fractional reserve   an amount of cash (as a percentage of the deposit taken) held by banks as a precaution; money that is not loaned by the bank

franchising   a licensing system in which a party is authorized to use the name and create the product of another firm for a fee

free port   a port that does not require the payment of duties for use

free trade zone   government-established zones that permit free entry and storage of goods. Duties do not need to be paid until the goods leave the zone.

freight forwarder   a firm that transports goods for export

functional currencies   the currency in which the case flow of the company is generated

GATT (General Agreement on Tariffs and Trade)   a treaty intended to limit trade barriers and promote trade through the reduction of tariffs among the signatory nations

general export license   a license required to export goods not needing special authorization

generalized systems of preference   the part of the GATT that permits goods of developing countries to enter the GATT countries duty-free

general trading companies   companies that have been successful in securing products for consumers and firms and in locating foreign firms for export. The Japanese version is the best known.

geocentric   hiring policy that disregards an employee's national origin or race

glasnost   a term used in the Soviet Union indicating an openness of information

GNP/capita   the amount of the nation's gross national product representing each individual of the total population

gold exchange standard   a system established at Bretton Woods in which the United States agreed to exchange gold for U.S. dollars at an agreed-upon rate

Gross Domestic Product   the aggregate value of a nation's output based upon factors of produc-

tion located within the country but excluding exports and imports

Gross National Product   the aggregate value of all goods and services produced by a country

gross weight   the entire weight of a shipment

Group of 5   a term used in reference to the meeting of the five heads of finance of the leading industrialized countries: United States, Japan, France, Germany, and United Kingdom

Group of 7   includes Italy and Canada along with the Group of 5

Group of 10   includes Belgium, The Netherlands, and Sweden along with the Group of 7

Group of 77   77 nations associated with the United Nations Conference on Trade and Development

guest workers   authorized foreign labor

hard currency   currency that can be exchanged for other currencies quickly and without government permission

hedging   using various instruments to protect against exchange rate risk

hit list, or super 301   a list of countries that prohibit U.S. access to their markets

home country nationals   citizens of the country in which the headquarters of a firm is located

import license   a license required by certain governments permitting goods to be imported into their country

import substitution   a policy of developing countries to promote the development of industries that are intended to replace the need for imports

indexing   a term that describes efforts to maintain a constant relationship among assets and liabilities that are affected by inflation

industrial targeting   government attempts to foster growth of particular industries

Inter-American Development Bank   a development bank located in Washington that is specifically geared toward the development of Latin America

interest arbitrage   earning profits on interest-bearing instruments through differences in the spot and forward exchange rates

interest rate swap   exchanging fixed interest rate instruments for those with floating interest rates

International Court of Justice   located in The Netherlands, the primary court of law for countries that have legal questions involving other countries

International Finance Corporation   a part of the World Bank that loans money for private development in developing countries

international law   rules that govern the activities and policies of nations with other countries. These are established between individual countries and apply only to countries that have entered into the agreements.

International Monetary System   the structures and policies needed for the international transfer and exchange of funds

international product life-cycle   the different phases in the manufacture, export, and, finally, import of a product

international trading companies   firms that supply most of the foreign goods to the markets in which they operate

intervention currency   a currency purchased by a government to affect the value of the government's currency

irrevocable letter of credit   a letter of credit that is payable if all the conditions of the letter of credit are met

J-curve effect   an effect associated with the devaluation of a currency in which the balance of payments actually worsens before it improves, thus the "J" shape of the curve

just-in-time   an inventory system in which deliveries are made as component parts are needed. This system is an effort to reduce the costs associated with carrying inventory.

key currencies   currencies held for no other purpose than as foreign exchange reserves

Leontief paradox   a discovery by Wassily Leontief that U.S. exports required less capital and more labor than U.S. imports

letter of credit   a credit instrument that guarantees the importer's bank will pay the exporter upon receipt of certain documents

licensing   a business arrangement that permits a firm or individual to use the patents, copyrights, and technology of another firm

lingua franca   a foreign language used as a common language in countries that have many languages

London Interbank Offered Rate (LIBOR)   the interest rate used among large banks on large, overnight eurocurrency loans

long position   a situation in which a firm makes a purchase of a currency or commodity in the expectation of a future appreciation in its value

managed float   a term indicating government involvement in maintaining the exchange rate of a particular currency

management contract   an agreement in which one firm supplies managerial assistance to another for a fee

maquiladoras   in-bond export industry in which components produced in the United States are exported duty-free to Mexico for assembly and then exported duty-free back to the United States for completion

marine insurance   insurance that covers losses at sea that are not covered by the insurance of the carrier

marketing management   the creation of a complete program that serves a particular market

marketing mix   addressing the marketing issues of price, promotion, distribution, and the product

marketing segmentation   the process of recognizing differences among consumers such that the firm can address those particular needs

marketing strategy   decisions made concerning the price, the product, the distribution channels, and the promotion of the product

marking   identification symbols used on cargo

Marshall Plan   program established by the U.S. government following World War II to aid European countries

matrix organization an organizational concept that superimposes one structure over another to gain both functional and creative expertise

nontariff barriers government policies that create restrictions on imports without the use of tariffs; for example, quotas, customs procedures, and safety and quality requirements

note issuance facility (NIF) a stand-by loan granted by a bank

official reserves the nation's holdings of monetary gold and internationally accepted currencies

on-board bill of lading a bill of lading indicating that the specified goods have been loaded onto the appropriate vessel

open account a method of trade in which the exporter ships without guarantee of payment from the buyer

open insurance policy an insurance policy that covers all shipments over a period of time

options the right to purchase or sell before or on a given date

Organization of Petroleum Exporting Countries (OPEC) a cartel of 13 oil-producing nations

Overseas Private Insurance Corporation a corporation of the U.S. government that insures U.S. business interests overseas against such things as expropriation and the inconvertibility of currency

packing list a list including quantities and identification of items being shipped

PEFCO (Private Export Funding Corporation) an organization that lends to foreign buyers in need of financing to purchase U.S. exports

pegged exchange rate a fixed relationship or parity of one currency with another currency

perils of the sea an insurance term used to denote marine occurrences such as stranding, lightning, collision, and sea water damage

political risk the risk associated with the political environment of a foreign country. This type of risk could include social unrest within the country or government actions that alter a firm's ability to operate in the foreign country.

premium (in forward exchange) a term indicating that the forward rate exceeds the spot rate

pro forma invoice a document sent to the buyer by the supplier indicating the quantity and description of the goods to be shipped

purchasing agent the agent who is responsible for the acquisition of goods for the government or a firm

purchasing power parity a method of determining exchange rates between two currencies based on the purchasing power of similar goods

quality circles a production method in which small groups meet periodically to discuss ways of improving the product or the production process

quota a specified amount of a product that a government will permit to be imported

quotation an offer stating the price and terms for the sale of goods

rationalized production a production method in which a firm takes advantage of cost savings around the world and varies production at locations accordingly

remitting bank the bank that initiates payment of money

revaluation of a currency an improvement of one currency in value in relation to another

revocable letter of credit a letter of credit that the opening bank has the right to modify or cancel without notifying the beneficiary

Schedule B assigns a seven-digit number to all commodities exported from the United States; full name is "Schedule B of The Statistical Classification of Domestic and Foreign Commodities Exported from the United States"

shipper's export declaration a document required by the U.S. Treasury Department declaring the basic information about the shipment

ship's manifest a list signed by the captain of the ship indicating the individual shipments of the cargo

sight draft   a draft that is payable upon presentation to the payee

Smithsonian Agreement   an agreement reached in December 1971 by the leading 10 industrialized nations that established a new international monetary system

snake   an effort by West European countries in the 1970s to maintain currency values within a specified range of each other by allowing the currencies to float in value in terms of the currency of another country such as the United States

soft currency   a currency that cannot be easily converted

soft loans   loans that can be repaid with a soft currency and which charge a low interest rate

Sogo sosha   a Japanese general trading company

sovereign debt   the debt of a national government

sovereign immunity   the immunity of a government from the courts of its own country

Special Drawing Rights   (also known as "paper gold")   created by the IMF and made up of a basket of five currencies: U.S. dollar, French franc, British pound, Japanese yen, and German mark

spot exchange   a situation in which a purchase or sale must be made immediately for delivery

spot rate   the exchange rate between two currencies used for immediate delivery

spread (in the forward market)   the difference between the spot rate and the forward rate

spread (in the spot market)   the difference between the quoted buy and sell rates of the foreign exchange trader

Standard Industrial Code (SIC)   a coding system used by the U.S. government to classify goods and services

Standard International Trade Classification   A United Nations coding system used to classify commodities involved in international trade

standardization of the marketing mix   maintaining equivalent pricing, product, distribution, and promotional strategies in all markets in which the firm operates

steamship conference   steamship operators who agree to charge the same freight rate

straight bonds   bonds issued with a fixed interest rate

subsidiaries   companies that are owned by a parent company

swap   an arrangement between two parties to make an exchange only to reverse the exchange at a later time

switch trading   a type of countertrade in which a country unable to pay in a hard currency locates goods for exchange from a third country to pay its debt

tare weight   the weight of the container and packaging containing a good

tariff   a tax assessed on goods that are imported or exported from a country

tariff quota   a tariff that requires a higher tax payment after a specified amount of the good has been imported or exported from the country

tax haven   a country with low or no required tax payments on income earned in other countries or on capital gains

tax haven subsidiary   a subsidiary of a company located in a tax haven

tax incentive   a tax holiday or reduction of taxes due granted to a company making an investment

tax treaty   an agreement between two countries concerning the taxation of citizens and corporations of each country operating in the other

tenor   the time period allowed in a draft

Third World   less developed countries (LDCs)

time draft   draft that allows a certain period of time to elapse before payment is made

trade creation   the resulting trading relationships once countries shift from a high-cost producer to a low-cost producer in the same customs union

tramp steamer   a vessel without a specified route or schedule

transaction exposure   the calculation of the loss or gain associated with transferring currencies over national borders; also known as the impact of foreign exchange rates on a company's accounts receivable and accounts payable

transaction statement   a document that specifies the terms between an importer and an exporter

transfer pricing   the price associated with the transfer or sale of goods between related companies or between a parent company and its subsidiaries

translation   the process in which financial statements are restated using a different currency

triangular arbitrage   taking profits from an imperfection in the exchange rates relating to three currencies; buying and selling the same currencies in different markets to make a profit from fractional differences in each market

turnkey operations   a contract in which one firm constructs a facility and prepares it for operation and then relinquishes it to its new owners

validated export license   a required license for certain exports

value added tax   a tax assessed based on an improvement made to the product that increases the value of the product

warehouse receipt   the receipt issued by a warehouse indicating what was received for storage

wharfage   the fee to use a pier or dock

without reserve   a term indicating that an agent or representative is authorized to make decisions without consulting the group that he represents

World Bank   established initially to assist the countries of Europe following WWII; now assists in the development of developing countries

Zaibatsu   large Japanese conglomerates that also have trading companies as integral components

zero coupon bonds   bonds, sold at a substantial discount from face value, that do not pay interest but mature at par value

Index of Subjects

Index of Companies

Index of Names